ALSO BY AMERICA'S TEST KITCHEN

More Mediterranean
The Complete Autumn and Winter Cookbook
Five-Ingredient Dinners
One-Hour Comfort
The Complete Plant-Based Cookbook
Cook for Your Gut Health
The Complete Salad Cookbook
Vegetables Illustrated
Bowls
The Ultimate Meal-Prep Cookbook
The Chicken Bible
Meat Illustrated
The Complete One Pot
Foolproof Fish
Cooking for One
How Can It Be Gluten-Free Cookbook Collection
The Complete Summer Cookbook
The Side Dish Bible
100 Techniques
Easy Everyday Keto
Everything Chocolate
The Perfect Pie
The Perfect Cake
The Perfect Cookie
How to Cocktail
Spiced
The Ultimate Burger
The New Essentials Cookbook
Dinner Illustrated
America's Test Kitchen Menu Cookbook
Cook's Illustrated Revolutionary Recipes
Tasting Italy: A Culinary Journey
Cooking at Home with Bridget and Julia
The Complete Mediterranean Cookbook
The Complete Vegetarian Cookbook
The Complete Cooking for Two Cookbook
The Complete Diabetes Cookbook
The Complete Slow Cooker
The Complete Make-Ahead Cookbook
Just Add Sauce
How to Braise Everything
How to Roast Everything
Nutritious Delicious
What Good Cooks Know
Cook's Science
The Science of Good Cooking
Bread Illustrated
Master of the Grill

Kitchen Smarts
Kitchen Hacks
100 Recipes: The Absolute Best Ways to Make the True Essentials
The New Family Cookbook
The Cook's Illustrated Baking Book
The Cook's Illustrated Cookbook
The America's Test Kitchen Family Baking Book
The Best of America's Test Kitchen (2007–2022 Editions)
America's Test Kitchen Twentieth Anniversary TV Show Cookbook
The Complete America's Test Kitchen TV Show Cookbook 2001–2022
Healthy and Delicious Instant Pot
Mediterranean Instant Pot
Cook It in Your Dutch Oven
Vegan for Everybody
Sous Vide for Everybody
Toaster Oven Perfection
Air Fryer Perfection
Multicooker Perfection
Food Processor Perfection
Pressure Cooker Perfection
Instant Pot Ace Blender Cookbook
Naturally Sweet
Foolproof Preserving
Paleo Perfected
The Best Mexican Recipes
Slow Cooker Revolution Volume 2: The Easy-Prep Edition
Slow Cooker Revolution
The America's Test Kitchen D.I.Y. Cookbook

THE COOK'S ILLUSTRATED ALL-TIME BEST SERIES

All-Time Best Brunch
All-Time Best Dinners for Two
All-Time Best Sunday Suppers
All-Time Best Holiday Entertaining
All-Time Best Soups

COOK'S COUNTRY TITLES

Big Flavors from Italian America
One-Pan Wonders
Cook It in Cast Iron
Cook's Country Eats Local
The Complete Cook's Country TV Show Cookbook

FOR A FULL LISTING OF ALL OUR BOOKS

CooksIllustrated.com
AmericasTestKitchen.com

PRAISE FOR AMERICA'S TEST KITCHEN TITLES

"The book's depth, breadth, and practicality makes it a must-have for seafood lovers."
PUBLISHERS WEEKLY (STARRED REVIEW) ON *FOOLPROOF FISH*

"Another flawless entry in the America's Test Kitchen canon, *Bowls* guides readers of all culinary skill levels in composing one-bowl meals from a variety of cuisines."
BUZZFEED BOOKS ON *BOWLS*

"*The Perfect Cookie* . . . is, in a word, perfect. This is an important and substantial cookbook. . . . If you love cookies, but have been a tad shy to bake on your own, all your fears will be dissipated. This is one book you can use for years with magnificently happy results."
THE HUFFINGTON POST ON *THE PERFECT COOKIE*

Selected as the Cookbook Award Winner of 2017 in the Baking category
INTERNATIONAL ASSOCIATION OF CULINARY PROFESSIONALS (IACP) ON *BREAD ILLUSTRATED*

"With 1,000 photos and the expertise of the America's Test Kitchen editors, this title might be the definitive book on bread baking."
PUBLISHERS WEEKLY ON *BREAD ILLUSTRATED*

"True to its name, this smart and endlessly enlightening cookbook is about as definitive as it's possible to get in the modern vegetarian realm."
MEN'S JOURNAL ON *THE COMPLETE VEGETARIAN COOKBOOK*

"Diabetics and all health-conscious home cooks will find great information on almost every page."
BOOKLIST (STARRED REVIEW) ON *THE COMPLETE DIABETES COOKBOOK*

"This book upgrades slow cooking for discriminating, 21st-century palates—that is indeed revolutionary."
THE DALLAS MORNING NEWS ON *SLOW COOKER REVOLUTION*

"Foolproof and high proof, this thoroughly researched and easy to follow volume will steady the hand of any home mixologist."
PUBLISHERS WEEKLY ON *HOW TO COCKTAIL*

"The book offers an impressive education for curious cake makers, new and experienced alike. A summation of 25 years of cake making at ATK, there are cakes for every taste."
THE WALL STREET JOURNAL ON *THE PERFECT CAKE*

"Offers a real option for a cook who just wants to learn some new ways to encourage family and friends to explore today's sometimes-daunting vegetable universe. This is one of the most valuable vegetable cooking resources for the home chef since Marian Morash's beloved classic *The Victory Garden Cookbook* (1982)."
BOOKLIST (STARRED REVIEW) ON *VEGETABLES ILLUSTRATED*

"This encyclopedia of meat cookery would feel completely overwhelming if it weren't so meticulously organized and artfully designed. This is *Cook's Illustrated* at its finest."
THE KITCHN ON *THE COOK'S ILLUSTRATED MEAT BOOK*

"Here are the words just about any vegan would be happy to read: 'Why This Recipe Works.' Fans of America's Test Kitchen are used to seeing the phrase and now it applies to the growing collection of plant-based creations in *Vegan for Everybody*."
THE WASHINGTON POST ON *VEGAN FOR EVERYBODY*

"Some books impress by the sheer audacity of their ambition. Backed up by the magazine's famed mission to test every recipe relentlessly until it is the best it can be, this nearly 900-page volume lands with an authoritative wallop."
CHICAGO TRIBUNE ON *THE COOK'S ILLUSTRATED COOKBOOK*

"The 21st-century *Fannie Farmer Cookbook* or *The Joy of Cooking*. If you had to have one cookbook and that's all you could have, this one would do it."
CBS SAN FRANCISCO ON *THE NEW FAMILY COOKBOOK*

"The go-to gift book for newlyweds, small families, or empty nesters."
ORLANDO SENTINEL ON *THE COMPLETE COOKING FOR TWO COOKBOOK*

"A one-volume kitchen seminar, addressing in one smart chapter after another the sometimes surprising whys behind a cook's best practices. . . . You get the myth, the theory, the science, and the proof, all rigorously interrogated as only America's Test Kitchen can do."
NPR ON *THE SCIENCE OF GOOD COOKING*

"An extensive guide to grilling and barbecueing with 692 recipes, ratings, tips and techniques for outdoor cooking. There is plenty of information for those new to grilling, those into serious barbecue and grilling or those who want new recipes."
DETROIT FREE PRESS ON *MASTER OF THE GRILL*

THE NEW COOKING SCHOOL COOKBOOK

FUNDAMENTALS

AMERICA'S TEST KITCHEN

Copyright © 2021 by America's Test Kitchen

All rights reserved. No part of this book may be reproduced or transmitted in any manner whatsoever without written permission from the publisher, except in the case of brief quotations embodied in critical articles or reviews.

Library of Congress Cataloging-in-Publication Data

Names: America's Test Kitchen (Firm), author.
Title: The new cooking school cookbook : fundamentals / America's Test Kitchen.
Description: Boston, MA : America's Test Kitchen, [2021] | Includes index.
Identifiers: LCCN 2021029057 (print) | LCCN 2021029058 (ebook) | ISBN 9781948703864 (hardcover) | ISBN 9781948703871 (ebook)
Subjects: LCSH: Cooking. | LCGFT: Cookbooks.
Classification: LCC TX714 .N47 2021 (print) | LCC TX714 (ebook) | DDC 641.5--dc23
LC record available at https://lccn.loc.gov/2021029057
LC ebook record available at https://lccn.loc.gov/2021029058

America's Test Kitchen
21 Drydock Avenue, Boston, MA 02210

Printed in Canada

10 9 8 7 6 5 4 3 2 1

Distributed by Penguin Random House Publisher Services
Tel: 800.733.3000

Editorial Director, Books **Adam Kowit**

Executive Food Editor **Dan Zuccarello**

Deputy Food Editor **Stephanie Pixley**

Executive Managing Editor **Debra Hudak**

Senior Editors **Valerie Cimino, Sacha Madadian, Kaumudi Marathé, and Sara Mayer**

Assistant Editors **Emily Rahravan and Sara Zatopek**

Contributing Editor **Elizabeth Wray Emery**

Design Director **Lindsey Timko Chandler**

Deputy Art Directors **Katie Barranger and Allison Boales**

Associate Art Director **Ashley Tenn**

Graphic Designer **Molly Gillespie**

Design Support **Courtney Lentz**

Photography Director **Julie Bozzo Cote**

Photography Producer **Meredith Mulcahy**

Senior Staff Photographers **Steve Klise and Daniel J. van Ackere**

Staff Photographer **Kevin White**

Additional Photography **Joseph Keller, Kate Kelley, and Carl Tremblay**

Food Styling **Tara Busa, Isabelle English, Joy Howard, Catrine Kelty, Chantal Lambeth, Kendra McKnight, Ashley Moore, Marie Piraino, Elle Simone Scott, Kendra Smith, and Sally Staub**

Photoshoot Kitchen Team

    Photo Team and Special Events Manager **Alli Berkey**

    Lead Test Cook **Eric Haessler**

    Test Cooks **Hannah Fenton, Jacqueline Gochenouer, and Gina McCreadie**

    Assistant Test Cooks **Hisham Hassam and Christa West**

Illustration **John Burgoyne; Jay Layman; MGMT.design, LLC; and Michael Newhouse**

Senior Manager, Publishing Operations **Taylor Argenzio**

Imaging Manager **Lauren Robbins**

Production and Imaging Specialists **Tricia Neumyer, Dennis Noble, and Amanda Yong**

Lead Copy Editor **Rachel Schowalter**

Copy Editors **Christine Campbell and Elizabeth Wray Emery**

Proofreader **Ann-Marie Imbornoni**

Indexer **Elizabeth Parson**

Chief Creative Officer **Jack Bishop**

Executive Editorial Directors **Julia Collin Davison and Bridget Lancaster**

CONTENTS

- ix   WELCOME TO AMERICA'S TEST KITCHEN
- x   INTRODUCTION
- xi   COURSE INSTRUCTORS
- xii   LIST OF RECIPES

- 1   COOKING BASICS
- 51   EGGS AND TOFU
- 91   VEGETABLES
- 147   SALADS
- 197   SOUPS
- 237   PASTA AND NOODLES
- 281   RICE, GRAINS, AND BEANS
- 339   MEAT
- 407   POULTRY
- 453   SEAFOOD
- 501   BREADS
- 557   DESSERTS

- 622   NUTRITIONAL INFORMATION FOR OUR RECIPES
- 638   CONVERSIONS AND EQUIVALENTS
- 640   INDEX

WELCOME TO AMERICA'S TEST KITCHEN

This book has been tested, written, and edited by the folks at America's Test Kitchen, where curious cooks become confident cooks. Located in Boston's Seaport District in the historic Innovation and Design Building, it features 15,000 square feet of kitchen space, including multiple photography and video studios. It is the home of *Cook's Illustrated* magazine and *Cook's Country* magazine and is the workday destination for more than 60 test cooks, editors, and cookware specialists. Our mission is to empower and inspire confidence, community, and creativity in the kitchen.

We start the process of testing a recipe with a complete lack of preconceptions, which means that we accept no claim, no technique, and no recipe at face value. We simply assemble as many variations as possible, test a half dozen of the most promising ones, and taste the results blind. We then construct our own recipe and continue to test it, varying ingredients, techniques, and cooking times until we reach a consensus. As we like to say in the test kitchen, "We make the mistakes so you don't have to." The result, we hope, is the best version of a particular recipe, but we realize that only you can be the final judge of our success (or failure). We use the same rigorous approach when we test equipment and taste ingredients.

None of this would be possible without a belief that good cooking, much like good music, is based on a foundation of objective technique. Some people like spicy foods and others don't, but there is a right way to sauté; there is a best way to cook a pot roast; and there are measurable scientific principles involved in producing perfectly beaten, stable egg whites. Our ultimate goal is to investigate the fundamental principles of cooking to give you the techniques, tools, and ingredients you need to become a better cook. It is as simple as that.

To see what goes on behind the scenes at America's Test Kitchen, check out our social media channels for kitchen snapshots, exclusive content, video tips, and much more. You can watch us work (in our actual test kitchen) by tuning in to *America's Test Kitchen* or *Cook's Country* on public television or on our websites. Listen to *Proof*, *Mystery Recipe*, and *The Walk-In* (AmericasTestKitchen.com/podcasts) to hear engaging, complex stories about people and food. Want to hone your cooking skills or finally learn how to bake—with an America's Test Kitchen test cook? Enroll in one of our online cooking classes. And you can engage the next generation of home cooks with kid-tested recipes from America's Test Kitchen Kids.

Our community of home recipe testers provides valuable feedback on recipes under development by ensuring that they are foolproof. You can help us investigate the how and why behind successful recipes from your home kitchen. (Sign up at AmericasTestKitchen.com/recipe_testing.)

However you choose to visit us, we welcome you into our kitchen, where you can stand by our side as we test our way to the best recipes in America.

facebook.com/AmericasTestKitchen
instagram.com/TestKitchen
youtube.com/AmericasTestKitchen
tiktok.com/@TestKitchen
twitter.com/TestKitchen
pinterest.com/TestKitchen

AmericasTestKitchen.com
CooksIllustrated.com
CooksCountry.com
OnlineCookingSchool.com
AmericasTestKitchen.com/kids

INTRODUCTION

Imagine being able to go to cooking school in your own kitchen. *The New Cooking School Cookbook* offers you that chance with a new exploration of the fundamentals of cooking. Pick out your favorite topics from this dynamic collection of 100 themed courses and learn by doing—it's that simple.

The kitchen experts at America's Test Kitchen are first and foremost educators, and they have taught millions of home cooks for more than 25 years. We make all the mistakes during recipe development so that you won't, and we pass on the insights we pick up along the way, allowing cooks of all skill levels to benefit from our recipes and instruction. Each course in this book is introduced by an ATK instructor and accompanied by their invaluable behind-the-recipe tips. The courses are arranged around a theme, such as Chicken Soups or Fried Rice, and the recipes within a course progress from basic (Skillet Pizza) to more involved (Thin-Crust Pizza) so that you'll build your skills and your confidence as you cook. Never even boiled water? Now you can boil water and also cook great carrots while doing so. You'll learn not only how to prep and boil the carrots but also why boiling them in very salty water seasons them to perfection—and how finishing touches of butter, lemon juice, and chives can make the simple side dish shine.

Every recipe has a brief overview of how the recipe works and a recap of the recipe's keys to success to reinforce the important takeaways. And we've woven core techniques, food science, and more into each course so that you'll pick up valuable supporting information as you cook. Learn everything from how to make an omelet to how olive oil is produced to why we prefer cottage cheese to ricotta in lasagna.

While we've designed the book so that you can dive into the courses in any order, we strongly encourage you to start by looking at the Cooking Basics chapter, where you'll find everything from what you need (and don't need) to set up a kitchen to how to stock your pantry and refrigerator to which knives and skillets we recommend as must-haves. It also contains a glossary of cooking terms, which will ensure that you're able to interpret any recipe, and a primer on how to season food.

Loaded with more than 400 recipes and tons of practical information designed to build your skills and confidence in the kitchen, *The New Cooking School Cookbook* will have you butchering a whole chicken into parts, salting and broiling eggplant, and making fresh pasta in no time. So put on an apron, turn to any page, pick up your knife, and start cooking.

COURSE INSTRUCTORS

JACK BISHOP
Chief Creative Officer
America's Test Kitchen

MORGAN BOLLING
Deputy Food Editor
Cook's Country Magazine

JULIA COLLIN DAVISON
Executive Editorial Director
America's Test Kitchen

KEITH DRESSER
Executive Food Editor
Cook's Illustrated Magazine

STEVE DUNN
Associate Editor
Cook's Illustrated Magazine

ANDREA GEARY
Deputy Food Editor
Cook's Illustrated Magazine

JOSEPH GITTER
Senior Editor
Books

LAWMAN JOHNSON
Senior Editor
Cook's Country Magazine

NICOLE KONSTANTINAKOS
Senior Editor
Books

LAN LAM
Senior Editor
Cook's Illustrated Magazine

BRIDGET LANCASTER
Executive Editorial Director
America's Test Kitchen

ASHLEY MOORE
Food Stylist
America's Test Kitchen

CHRISTIE MORRISON
Deputy Editor, Culinary Content and Curriculum
America's Test Kitchen

ANNIE PETITO
Senior Editor
Cook's Illustrated Magazine

STEPHANIE PIXLEY
Deputy Food Editor
Books

BRYAN ROOF
Executive Food Editor
Cook's Country Magazine

ELLE SIMONE SCOTT
Executive Editor and Food Stylist
America's Test Kitchen

DAN SOUZA
Editor in Chief
Cook's Illustrated Magazine

DAN ZUCCARELLO
Executive Food Editor
Books

LIST OF RECIPES

COOKING BASICS

28 Spice Blends and Pastes
Pistachio Dukkah
Ras el Hanout
Za'atar
Harissa
Garam Masala
Five-Spice Powder
Shichimi Togarashi

31 Back-Pocket Sauces
Cherry Tomato Salsa
Lemon-Yogurt Sauce
Chipotle Mayonnaise
Cilantro-Mint Chutney

EGGS AND TOFU

MODERN SCRAMBLED EGGS

54 Perfect Scrambled Eggs
56 Scrambled Eggs with Asparagus, Smoked Salmon, and Chives
56 Scrambled Eggs with Shiitake Mushrooms and Feta Cheese
57 Xīhóngshì Chao Jīdàn (Chinese Stir-Fried Tomatoes and Eggs)

FRY AN EGG

60 Perfect Fried Eggs
Eggs in a Hole
62 Avocado Toast with Fried Eggs
62 Fried Eggs over Garlicky Chard and Bell Pepper

HARD-COOKED AND SOFT-COOKED EGGS

65 Easy-Peel Hard-Cooked Eggs
Soft-Cooked Eggs
66 Curry Deviled Eggs
66 Bacon and Chive Deviled Eggs

POACHED EGGS

69 Perfect Poached Eggs
Make-Ahead Poached Eggs

EGG SANDWICHES

70 Ham, Egg, and Cheese Sandwiches
Bacon, Egg, and Cheese Sandwiches
71 Fried Egg Sandwiches
73 Egg Salad Sandwiches with Radishes and Watercress
73 Open-Faced Poached Egg Sandwiches

PUT AN EGG IN IT

74 Eggs in Purgatory
75 Green Shakshuka
76 Baked Eggs with Tomatoes, Feta, and Croutons
77 Sheet-Pan Huevos Rancheros

SIMPLE OMELETS AND FRITTATAS

78 Classic Cheese Omelet
Mushroom and Thyme Filling
Asparagus and Smoked Salmon Filling
80 Frittata with Parmesan and Herbs
Frittata with Broccoli Rabe, Sun-Dried Tomatoes, and Fontina
81 Frittata with Broccoli and Turmeric

LET'S MAKE TOFU

82 Tofu Scramble with Bell Pepper, Shallot, and Basil
Tofu Scramble with Tomato and Scallions
83 Sriracha-Lime Tofu Bowl
84 Tofu Banh Mi
85 Stir-Fried Tofu and Bok Choy
86 Teriyaki Tofu
86 Chilled Marinated Tofu
87 Marinated Tofu and Vegetable Salad

VEGETABLES

BASIC-NOT-BORING BOILED AND STEAMED VEGETABLES

- 95 Boiled Carrots with Lemon and Chives
  - *Boiled Carrots with Cumin, Lime, and Cilantro*
  - *Boiled Carrots with Fennel Seeds and Citrus*
  - *Boiled Carrots with Mint and Paprika*
- 96 Foolproof Boiled Corn
  - *Boiled Corn for a Crowd*
- 96 Green Beans with Toasted Almonds and Browned Butter
- 98 Steamed Broccoli with Lime-Cumin Dressing
  - *Steamed Broccoli with Spicy Balsamic Dressing and Black Olives*

SIMPLY SAUTÉED

- 101 Sautéed Carrots with Ginger, Maple, and Fennel Seeds
- 102 Sautéed Zucchini
- 103 Sautéed Mushrooms with Shallot and Thyme

DARK LEAFY GREENS

- 104 Spinach with Garlic and Lemon
- 105 Sautéed Swiss Chard with Sesame Sauce
- 105 Quick Collard Greens
- 106 Garlicky Braised Kale
  - *Garlicky Braised Kale with Bacon and Onion*
  - *Garlicky Braised Kale with Coconut and Curry*

PAN-ROASTING VEGETABLES

- 111 Pan-Roasted Brussels Sprouts with Lemon and Pecorino Romano
  - *Pan-Roasted Brussels Sprouts with Mustard and Brown Sugar*
  - *Pan-Roasted Brussels Sprouts with Gochujang and Sesame Seeds*
- 112 Pan-Roasted Cauliflower with Garlic and Lemon
  - *Pan-Roasted Cauliflower with Capers and Pine Nuts*
  - *Pan-Roasted Cauliflower with Cumin and Pistachios*
- 112 Pan-Roasted Asparagus

POTATOES 101

- 114 Smashed Potatoes
- 115 Easy Mashed Potatoes
- 115 Braised Red Potatoes with Lemon and Chives
- 116 Crisp Roasted Potatoes
- 117 Best Baked Potatoes
  - *Herbed Goat Cheese Topping*
  - *Creamy Egg Topping*

SWEET POTATOES

- 118 Mashed Sweet Potatoes
- 118 Roasted Sweet Potato Wedges
  - *Cumin and Chili Roasted Sweet Potato Wedges*
  - *Curry Roasted Sweet Potato Wedges*
  - *Spicy BBQ Roasted Sweet Potato Wedges*
- 120 Sweet Potato Crunch

EVERYDAY ROASTED VEGETABLES

- 124 Asparagus
- 125 Broccoli
- 125 Butternut Squash
- 125 Cremini Mushrooms
- 125 Green Beans
- 126 Brussels Sprouts
- 126 Carrots
- 126 Cauliflower
- 126 Fennel

SHAPE-SHIFTING CAULIFLOWER

- 128 Cauliflower Rice
  - *Curried Cauliflower Rice*
- 129 Cauliflower Cakes
- 131 Cauliflower Steaks with Salsa Verde

TURN ON THE BROILER

- 132 Broiled Asparagus with Garlic-Butter Sauce
- 133 Broiled Broccoli Rabe
- 134 Elote
- 134 Broiled Tomatoes with Goat Cheese and Bread Crumbs

WHAT TO DO WITH EGGPLANT

- 137 Broiled Eggplant with Basil
  - *Broiled Eggplant with Sesame-Miso Glaze*
- 137 Stir-Fried Japanese Eggplant
- 138 Braised Eggplant with Paprika, Coriander, and Yogurt

CONTINUES >

VEGETABLES (CONTINUED)

VEGETABLES ON THE GRILL

140 Grilled Fennel

141 Grilled Cabbage

142 Grilled Zucchini and Red Onion wth Lemon Vinaigrette

143 Husk-Grilled Corn

MORE TO EXPLORE: QUICK PICKLES

144 Quick Pickled Radishes

144 Quick Pickled Fennel

145 Quick Pickled Red Onions

145 Quick Pickle Chips

SALADS

CLASSIC VINAIGRETTES

152 Foolproof Vinaigrette

Foolproof Lemon Vinaigrette

Foolproof Balsamic-Mustard Vinaigrette

Foolproof Herb Vinaigrette

155 Make-Ahead Vinaigrette

Make-Ahead Sherry-Shallot Vinaigrette

Make-Ahead Balsamic-Fennel Vinaigrette

Make-Ahead Cider-Caraway Vinaigrette

GREEN SALADS

156 Simplest Salad

157 Bibb and Arugula Salad with Pear and Goat Cheese

158 Bistro Salad

159 Romaine and Watercress Salad with Asparagus and Prosciutto

159 Edamame Salad with Arugula and Radishes

161 Homemade Croutons for Salads

Parmesan Croutons

Herbed Croutons

161 Spiced Pepitas or Sunflower Seeds

161 Microwave-Fried Shallots

Microwave-Fried Garlic

VEGETABLE SALADS

162 Asparagus and Spinach Salad with Sherry Vinegar and Goat Cheese

163 Kale Cobb Salad Bowl

165 Beet Salad with Blue Cheese and Endive

165 Mediterranean Chopped Salad

166 Moroccan-Style Carrot Salad

166 Green Bean Salad with Cilantro Sauce

SIMPLY TOMATOES

168 Simple Tomato Salad

169 Tomato and Peach Salad

169 Tomato and Vidalia Onion Salad

170 Cherry Tomato Salad with Mango and Lime-Curry Dressing

POTATO SALADS

174 Classic Potato Salad

175 French Potato Salad with Dijon and Fines Herbes

177 Lemon and Herb Red Potato Salad

177 Sweet Potato Salad

SLAWS

179 Buttermilk Coleslaw

Lemony Buttermilk Coleslaw

Buttermilk Coleslaw with Scallions and Cilantro

180 Sweet and Tangy Coleslaw

180 Brussels Sprout Slaw with Pecorino and Pine Nuts

181 Brussels Sprout, Red Cabbage, and Pomegranate Slaw

SALADS WITH MEAT AND SEAFOOD

182 Creamy Chicken Salad with Fresh Herbs

Curried Chicken Salad with Dried Apricots

Creamy Chicken Salad with Grapes and Walnuts

183 Tuna Salad with Hard-Cooked Eggs, Radishes, and Capers

184 Arugula Salad with Steak Tips and Blue Cheese

185 Salmon, Avocado, Grapefruit, and Watercress Salad

SALADS (CONTINUED)

RESTAURANT FAVORITES

- 186 Caprese Salad
- 186 Wedge Salad
- 187 Panzanella
- 188 Horiatiki Salata
- 189 Caesar Salad
- 190 Kale Caesar Salad with Chicken

SAVORY FRUIT SALADS

- 192 Waldorf Salad
- 193 Watermelon Salad with Basil and Feta
- 194 Cantaloupe Salad with Olives and Red Onion
- 195 Citrus Salad with Orange-Ginger Vinaigrette

MORE TO EXPLORE: CREAMY AND CREAMLESS DRESSINGS

- 172 Blue Cheese Dressing
- 172 Ranch Dressing
    - Peppercorn Ranch Dressing
- 172 Vegan Ranch Dressing
- 173 Green Goddess Dressing
- 173 Creamy Avocado Dressing
- 173 Creamy Roasted Garlic Dressing

SOUPS

CHICKEN SOUPS

- 201 Chicken Noodle Soup
- 202 Caldo Tlalpeño
- 202 Tom Kha Gai
- 204 Chicken Soup with Parmesan Dumplings

RUSTIC VEGETABLE SOUPS

- 207 Gazpacho
- 208 Soup au Pistou
- 208 Hearty Cabbage Soup
- 210 Wild Rice and Mushroom Soup
- 210 Roasted Eggplant and Kale Soup

PUREED VEGETABLE SOUPS

- 214 Creamless Creamy Tomato Soup
- 215 Silky Butternut Squash Soup
- 216 Creamy Cauliflower Soup
- 217 Super Greens Soup with Lemon-Tarragon Cream

BEAN AND LENTIL SOUPS

- 220 Five-Ingredient Black Bean Soup
- 220 Creamy White Bean Soup with Herb Oil and Crispy Capers
- 222 Red Lentil Soup with North African Spices
- 222 Spicy Pinto Bean Soup
- 223 Chickpea and Escarole Soup

PANTRY NOODLE SOUPS

- 225 Pasta e Piselli
- 225 Chickpea Noodle Soup
- 226 Hot and Sour Soup with Vermicelli and Shrimp
- 227 Almost-Instant Ginger Beef Ramen or One

MEATY SOUPS

- 228 Caldo Verde
- 229 Old-Fashioned Beef and Barley Soup
- 230 Spicy Beef Soup with Scallions and Bean Sprouts
- 231 Sharba

BASIC BROTHS

- 232 Classic Chicken Broth
- 233 Beef Broth
- 234 Vegetable Broth Base

PASTA AND NOODLES

DRIED ITALIAN PASTA

- 240 Linguine with White Clam Sauce
- 241 Orecchiette with Broccoli Rabe and Sausage
- 243 Garlicky Spaghetti with Lemon and Pine Nuts
  - *Garlicky Spaghetti with Green Olives and Almonds*
  - *Spaghetti Aglio e Olio*
- 244 Orzo Salad with Broccoli and Radicchio
- 245 Warm Spiced Pearl Couscous Salad

FRESH ITALIAN PASTA

- 250 Fresh Pasta without a Machine
- 253 Fettuccine with Garlic Oil Sauce
- 253 Fettuccine with Browned Butter–Pine Nut Sauce

ONE-POT PASTA

- 257 One-Pot Penne Puttanesca
- 257 Skillet Ziti with Sausage and Peppers

BAKED PASTA

- 258 Baked Penne with Spinach, Artichokes, and Chicken
- 259 Baked Ziti with Ricotta and Eggplant
- 260 Macaroni and Cheese Casserole
- 261 Vegetable and Orzo Tian
- 261 Roasted Zucchini and Eggplant Lasagna
- 262 Sausage Lasagna

LO MEIN NOODLES

- 269 Sesame Noodles
- 269 Peppery Sesame Noodles with Bok Choy
- 270 Chicken Lo Mein with Broccoli and Bean Sprouts
- 271 Pork Lo Mein with Cabbage and Carrots

UDON AND SOBA NOODLES

- 272 Udon Noodles with Mustard Greens and Shiitake-Ginger Sauce
- 273 Vegetable Shabu-Shabu with Sesame Sauce
- 274 Soba Noodles with Pork, Scallions, and Shichimi Togarashi
- 275 Chilled Soba Noodles with Spring Vegetables

RICE NOODLES

- 276 Singapore Noodles with Shrimp
- 277 Spicy Peanut Rice Noodles
- 278 Pad Thai
- 279 Pad Kee Mao

MORE TO EXPLORE: TOMATO SAUCES

- 246 Classic Marinara Sauce
- 246 Fresh Tomato Sauce
- 247 Arrabbiata Sauce
- 248 Amatriciana Sauce
- 248 Simple Italian-Style Meat Sauce

MORE TO EXPLORE: PESTO

- 254 Basil Pesto
- 254 Spinach Pesto
- 255 Arugula-Almond Pesto
- 255 Kale–Sunflower Seed Pesto
- 255 Pesto Calabrese

RICE, GRAINS, AND BEANS

RICE 101

- 284 Everyday Long-Grain White Rice
  - *Everyday Short-Grain White Rice*
- 285 Everyday Brown Rice
- 286 Hung Kao Mun Gati
- 287 White Rice Salad with Oranges, Olives, and Almonds
- 287 Brown Rice Salad with Tomatoes, Avocado, and Jalapeño
- 288 Black Rice Salad with Snap Peas and Ginger-Sesame Vinaigrette
- 288 Foolproof Baked White Rice
- 288 Foolproof Baked Brown Rice
- 289 Baked Mexican Rice

RICE, GRAINS, AND BEANS (CONTINUED)

GRAINS 101

- 290 Easiest-Ever Quinoa
- 290 Tabbouleh
  - *Spiced Tabbouleh*
- 292 Millet Porridge with Maple Syrup
  - *Millet Porridge with Dried Cherries and Pecans*
  - *Millet Porridge with Coconut and Bananas*
- 292 Barley with Fennel, Dried Apricots, and Orange
- 293 Farro with Mushrooms and Thyme
  - *Farro with Lemon and Herbs*
- 294 Wheat Berry Salad with Endive, Blueberries, and Goat Cheese
  - *Wheat Berry Salad with Figs, Pine Nuts, and Goat Cheese*
- 295 Curried Baked Quinoa with Cauliflower
  - *Baked Quinoa with Scallions and Feta*
- 295 Baked Wild Rice with Cranberries and Almonds

RICE AND GRAIN PILAFS

- 296 Everyday Rice Pilaf
  - *Rice Pilaf with Apricots and Almonds*
  - *Spiced Rice Pilaf with Ginger, Dates, and Parsley*
- 297 Herbed Barley Pilaf
- 299 Bulgur Pilaf with Mushrooms
- 299 Freekeh Pilaf with Dates and Cauliflower

FRIED RICE

- 301 Hawaiian Fried Rice
- 302 Fried Rice with Gai Lan and Shiitake Mushrooms
- 302 Nasi Goreng
- 304 Kimchi Bokkeumbap
- 305 Fried Brown Rice with Pork and Shrimp

RISOTTO

- 307 Risotto with Parmesan and Herbs
  - *Risotto with Porcini*
  - *Risotto with Fennel and Saffron*
- 308 Spring Vegetable Risotto
- 309 Farrotto with Pancetta, Asparagus, and Peas

POLENTA AND GRITS

- 311 Creamy Parmesan Polenta
- 312 Fluffy Baked Polenta
  - *Sautéed Cherry Tomato and Fresh Mozzarella Topping*
  - *Broccoli Rabe, Sun-Dried Tomato, and Pine Nut Topping*
- 313 Creamy Cheese Grits
- 313 Baked Cheese Grits
- 315 Shrimp and Grits

DRESSING UP CANNED BEANS

- 319 Ultracreamy Hummus
- 320 Chickpea Salad with Carrots, Arugula, and Olives
  - *Chickpea Salad with Roasted Red Peppers and Feta*
- 320 Spiced Chickpea Gyros with Tahini Yogurt
- 321 Garlicky White Beans with Sage
- 321 Refried Pinto Beans
- 322 Black-Eyed Peas and Greens
- 322 Black Beans on Toast with Tomato and Avocado
- 323 Skillet Rice and Black Beans with Corn and Tomatoes

LENTILS

- 324 Lentils with Carrots and Parsley
  - *Curried Lentils with Golden Raisins*
- 325 Baked Lentils with Sausage
- 326 Lentil Salad with Pomegranate and Walnuts
  - *Lentil Salad with Hazelnuts and Goat Cheese*
- 327 Spiced Red Lentils
  - *Spiced Red Lentils with Cauliflower*

DRIED BEANS 101

- 328 White Beans with Tomatoes and Capers
- 329 Cowboy Beans
- 330 Baked Navy Beans
- 330 Falafel

TEMPEH

- 333 Crispy Tempeh
- 333 Pan-Seared Tempeh Steaks with Chimichurri Sauce
- 335 Tempeh with Sambal Sauce
- 335 Korean Barbecue Tempeh Wraps

MEAT

THE STEAKHOUSE
- 346 Pan-Seared Steak Tips with Roasted Potatoes and Horseradish Cream
- 347 Pan-Seared Sirloin Steaks with Mustard-Cream Pan Sauce
- 348 Bacon-Wrapped Filets Mignons
- 349 Pan-Seared Strip Steaks
- 349 Lamb Rib Chops with Mint-Rosemary Relish

PERFECT PORK CHOPS
- 356 Pan-Seared Thick-Cut Pork Chops
- 357 Citrus-and-Spice Pork Chops
- 358 Spiced Braised Pork Chops
- 359 Deviled Pork Chops

MEAT STIR-FRIES
- 361 Teriyaki Stir-Fried Beef with Green Beans and Shiitakes
- 363 Sichuan Stir-Fried Pork in Garlic Sauce

EVERYDAY ROASTS
- 367 Slow-Roast Beef
- 368 Roast Pork Loin with Sweet Potatoes and Cilantro Sauce
- 369 Broiled Pork Tenderloin with Sun-Dried Tomato and Basil Salsa

THE BRAISING POT
- 371 Classic Pot Roast
- 372 Red Wine–Braised Short Ribs with Bacon, Parsnips, and Pearl Onions
- 374 Braised Lamb Shanks with Lemon and Mint

MEAT STEWS OF THE WORLD
- 376 Best Beef Stew
- 378 Catalan-Style Beef Stew with Mushrooms
- 379 Chile Verde Con Cerdo
- 381 Goan Pork Vindaloo
- 382 Lamb Stew with Potatoes

GROUND MEAT MUST-KNOWS
- 384 Classic Beef Burgers
- 386 Spaghetti and Meatballs
- 387 Thai Pork Lettuce Wraps
- 388 Glazed Meatloaf
- 389 Spicy Lamb with Lentils and Yogurt

QUICK DINNER OFF THE GRILL
- 391 Grilled Steak Burgers
- 391 Grilled Flank Steak with Basil Dressing
- 393 Grilled Pork Tenderloin with Grilled Pineapple–Red Onion Salsa
- 394 Pinchos Morunos

EAT WITH YOUR HANDS
- 397 Steak Tacos
- 397 Pork Gyro
- 399 Philly Cheesesteaks

SPECIAL-OCCASION CENTERPIECES
- 401 Roast Beef Tenderloin
- 401 Pan-Seared Steaks with Brandy–Pink Peppercorn Sauce
- 403 Brisket Carbonnade
- 404 Roast Butterflied Leg of Lamb with Coriander, Cumin, and Mustard Seeds

MORE TO EXPLORE: SPICE RUBS, SAUCES, AND COMPOUND BUTTERS
- 352 Barbecue Rub
- 352 Classic Steak Rub
- 352 Herbes de Provence
- 352 Jerk Rub
- 353 Salsa Verde
- 353 Chermoula
- 353 Chimichurri
- 353 Mint Persillade

POULTRY

CHICKEN CUTLETS

- 410 Simple Sautéed Chicken Cutlets
- 411 Crispy Pan-Fried Chicken Cutlets
  - *Crispy Pan-Fried Chicken Milanese Cutlets*
  - *Crispy Pan-Fried Chicken Cutlets with Garlic and Oregano*
  - *Crispy Pan-Fried Deviled Chicken Cutlets*
- 412 Chicken Piccata
- 412 Best Chicken Parmesan

GREAT ROAST CHICKEN

- 414 Pan-Roasted Chicken Breasts
- 414 Chicken Leg Quarters with Cauliflower and Shallots
- 415 Weeknight Roast Chicken
- 416 Peruvian Roast Chicken with Garlic and Lime

LEARN YOUR WAY AROUND A CHICKEN

- 420 One-Hour Broiled Chicken and Pan Sauce
- 422 Barbecue Roast Chicken and Potatoes
  - *Herbes de Provence Chicken with Fennel*
  - *Five-Spice Roast Chicken with Turnips*
  - *Ras el Hanout Chicken with Carrots*
- 423 Chicken Cacciatore
- 423 Tandoori Chicken

STEWED AND BRAISED

- 426 Classic Chicken Stew
- 427 Lemon-Braised Chicken Thighs with Chickpeas and Fennel
- 429 Braised Chicken Thighs with Chard and Mustard

CHICKEN AND RICE

- 430 Chicken and Rice with Carrots and Peas
- 431 Curried Chicken with Coconut Rice and Lime-Yogurt Sauce
- 432 Arroz con Pollo
- 433 Khao Man Gai

CHICKEN STIR-FRIES

- 435 Stir-Fried Sesame Chicken with Broccoli and Red Pepper
- 436 Gai Pad Krapow
- 436 Kung Pao Chicken

SIMPLE FRIED CHICKEN

- 438 Karaage
- 439 Cast Iron Easier Fried Chicken
- 440 Fried Chicken Sandwiches

CHICKEN ON THE GRILL

- 442 Grilled Chicken Souvlaki
- 445 Grilled Bone-In Chicken
- 445 Grilled Wine-and-Herb Marinated Chicken

YOUR FIRST TURKEY

- 448 Easy Roast Turkey Breast
- 449 Easier Roast Turkey and Gravy
- 450 All-Purpose Gravy

MORE TO EXPLORE: PAN SAUCES

- 418 Tarragon-Lemon Pan Sauce
- 418 Thyme–Sherry Vinegar Pan Sauce
- 418 Sage-Vermouth Pan Sauce
- 419 Lemon-Caper Pan Sauce
- 419 Mustard and Cider Pan Sauce
- 419 Apricot-Orange Pan Sauce

SEAFOOD

CROWD FAVORITE: COD

- 458 Pan-Roasted Cod with Grapefruit-Basil Relish
- 459 Nut-Crusted Cod Fillets
- 460 Cod Baked in Foil with Leeks and Carrots

FIRM, MEATY WHITE FISH

- 462 Pan-Seared Swordfish Steaks with Caper-Currant Relish
- 463 Halibut en Cocotte with Garlic and Cherry Tomatoes
- 464 Roasted Snapper and Vegetables with Mustard Sauce
- 464 Grilled Swordfish Tacos

CONTINUES >

SEAFOOD (CONTINUED)

THIN WHITEFISH

- 469 Sautéed Tilapia with Cilantro Chimichurri
- 470 Pan-Fried Sole
  Sole Meunière
- 471 Cornmeal Catfish and Southwestern Corn
  Comeback Sauce
- 472 Baked Sole Fillets with Herbs and Bread Crumbs

SALMON SO MANY WAYS

- 475 Pomegranate Roasted Salmon with Lentils and Chard
- 477 Pan-Seared Salmon Steaks
- 478 Miso-Marinated Salmon
- 479 Grilled Salmon Fillets with Lemon-Garlic Sauce

POACHING FOR EVERY FISH

- 482 Perfect Poached Fish
- 483 Shrimp Cocktail

SERVING UP SHRIMP

- 485 Pan-Seared Shrimp with Pistachio, Cumin, and Parsley
- 486 Garlicky Roasted Shrimp with Parsley and Anise
- 488 Baked Shrimp and Orzo with Feta and Tomatoes

WORKING WITH BIVALVES

- 490 Pan-Seared Scallops
- 491 Fennel and Bibb Salad with Scallops and Hazelnuts
- 492 Brothy Rice with Clams and Salsa Verde
- 493 Oven-Steamed Mussels

THE FISH FRY

- 497 Crispy Fish Sandwiches
  Classic Tartar Sauce
- 499 Popcorn Shrimp

BREAD

SAVORY QUICK BREADS

- 510 Quick Cheese Bread
  Quick Cheese Bread with Bacon, Onion, and Gruyère
- 511 Brown Soda Bread
- 512 Southern-Style Skillet Cornbread

MORNING BREADS

- 515 Ultimate Banana Bread
- 516 Easiest-Ever Biscuits
- 518 Mixed Berry Scones
- 519 Whole-Wheat Blueberry Muffins

LOAVES FOR EVERY DAY

- 521 Easy Sandwich Bread
- 522 Anadama Bread
- 523 Oatmeal-Raisin Bread

CAN'T TOUCH THIS: NO-KNEAD BREADS

- 526 Almost No-Knead Bread
- 528 Almost No-Knead Brioche
- 530 Rosemary Focaccia

CLASSIC DINNER ROLLS

- 532 Fluffy Dinner Rolls
- 534 Rustic Dinner Rolls

WHOLE-WHEAT BREADS

- 536 Honey-Wheat Dinner Rolls
- 538 Whole-Wheat Quinoa Bread

FREE-FORM LOAVES

- 540 Classic Italian Bread
- 542 Cranberry-Walnut Bread

PIZZA, PIZZA

- 546 Skillet Pizza
  Skillet Pizza with Fontina, Arugula, and Prosciutto
- 548 Thin-Crust Pizza
  Thin-Crust Pizza with Sausage, Pepper, and Onion
- 549 Pizza al Taglio with Arugula and Fresh Mozzarella

FOUR FANTASTIC FLATBREADS

- 552 Flour Tortillas
- 553 Chapati
- 554 Pitas
- 555 Mana'eesh Za'atar

DESSERTS

CLASSIC DROP COOKIES

- 565 Perfect Chocolate Chip Cookies
- 567 Brown Sugar Cookies
- 568 Molasses Spice Cookies
  - *Molasses Spice Cookies with Dark Rum Glaze*
  - *Molasses Spice Cookies with Orange Essence*
- 568 Thin and Crispy Oatmeal Cookies
  - *Salty Thin and Crispy Oatmeal Cookies*
  - *Thin and Crispy Coconut Oatmeal Cookies*
  - *Thin and Crispy Orange-Almond Oatmeal Cookies*

SLICE-AND-BAKE COOKIES

- 571 Pecan Sandies
  - *Almond Sandies*
- 572 Chocolate-Toffee Butter Cookies

COOKIE CUTTER COOKIES

- 574 Foolproof Holiday Cookies
- 576 Nankhatai
- 577 Biscochitos

BROWNIES AND BLONDIES

- 578 Fudgy Brownies
- 579 Chewy Brownies
- 580 Rocky Road Brownies
- 580 Blondies
  - *Congo Bars*

EVERYDAY CAKES

- 585 Pound Cake
  - *Almond Pound Cake*
  - *Ginger Pound Cake*
  - *Orange Pound Cake*
- 586 Tahini-Banana Snack Cake
- 586 Simple Carrot Sheet Cake

BIRTHDAY CAKES

- 588 Chocolate Sheet Cake with Milk Chocolate Frosting
- 590 Buttery Yellow Layer Cake with Chocolate Frosting
- 592 Confetti Cake
- 592 Red Velvet Cupcakes

LEMON DESSERTS

- 596 Best Lemon Bars
- 598 Lemon Pudding Cake
- 601 Lemon Bundt Cake

SUMMER COBBLERS AND CRISPS

- 602 Skillet Cherry Crisp
- 603 Blueberry Cobbler with Biscuit Topping
  - *Blackberry Cobbler with Biscuit Topping*
  - *Peach or Nectarine Cobbler with Biscuit Topping*
  - *Strawberry Cobbler with Biscuit Topping*
- 604 Peach Crumble

APPLE PIES AND TARTS

- 606 Easy Apple Galettes
- 607 Skillet Apple Pie
- 608 Deep-Dish Apple Pie

THANKSGIVING FAVORITES

- 613 Pumpkin Pie
- 614 Pecan Pie
  - *Maple Pecan Pie*
- 616 Cranberry Oat Bars

COOL AND CREAMY DESSERTS

- 618 Coconut Rice Pudding
- 619 Pots de Crème
  - *Milk Chocolate Pots de Crème*
- 620 Chocolate Mousse
- 621 Vanilla No-Churn Ice Cream
  - *Mint-Cookie No-Churn Ice Cream*
  - *Strawberry-Buttermilk No-Churn Ice Cream*
  - *Peanut Butter Cup No-Churn Ice Cream*

MORE TO EXPLORE: FROSTINGS AND WHIPPED CREAM

- 594 Vanilla Frosting and Variations
- 594 Chocolate Frosting
- 595 Chocolate Ganache Frosting
- 595 Cream Cheese Frosting
- 595 Whipped Cream

MORE TO EXPLORE: FOOLPROOF ALL-BUTTER PIE DOUGH

- 610 Foolproof All-Butter Single-Crust Pie Dough
- 610 Foolproof All-Butter Double-Crust Pie Dough

CHAPTER 1

COOKING BASICS

2 **10 HABITS OF A GOOD COOK**

4 **COOKING TERMINOLOGY**

8 **A KITCHEN STARTER KIT**

10 **EQUIPPING YOUR KITCHEN**

16 **CLEANING AND CARING FOR YOUR COOKWARE**

18 **STOCKING YOUR PANTRY AND REFRIGERATOR**

22 **GETTING TO KNOW CHEESE**

24 **GETTING TO KNOW HERBS**

26 **GETTING TO KNOW SPICES**

30 **SAUCES 101**

32 **HOW TO SEASON FOOD**

34 **BASIC FOOD SAFETY**

36 **BASIC MEASURING SKILLS**

38 **BASIC KNIFE SKILLS**

40 **BASIC VEGETABLE AND FRUIT PREP**

10 HABITS OF A GOOD COOK

1 READ THE RECIPE CAREFULLY AND FOLLOW THE DIRECTIONS

Almost everyone has embarked upon preparing a recipe only to realize midway through that the dish needs hours of chilling before it can be served or that it calls for a special pan that you don't own. By reading the recipe through before you start to cook, you will avoid any surprises along the way. We also recommend making the recipe as directed the first time you cook it. Once you understand the recipe, you can improvise and make it your own, but first you have to give it a fair shot as written.

2 BE PREPARED

Set out and organize all of the equipment you will need for a recipe and prep all of the ingredients for it before you start to cook. (Be sure to prepare the ingredients as instructed—food that is uniformly and properly cut will cook more evenly and look better). A recipe is much easier to make when all the components and tools you need are at your fingertips. That way your pasta won't overcook when you can't find your colander at the last minute and you won't forget to add the baking soda to your cake.

3 START WITH GOOD INGREDIENTS

Don't expect to make a stunning salad from the wilting greens that have been in your fridge for two weeks. Freshness matters, and the components you use can make or break your dish. Low-quality ingredients will yield low-quality results.

4 KEEP SUBSTITUTIONS TO A MINIMUM

We've all done it—used brown sugar when there's no granulated sugar in the pantry, subbed in whatever cheese we have on hand for the Gruyère in the recipe, or poured the batter into a square pan when the round pan was nowhere to be found. In general, use the ingredients called for in the recipe to ensure your dish tastes the way it was intended to taste. This is especially true in baking, where even the slightest change can spell disaster.

5 USE THE APPROPRIATE SIZE COOKWARE

Make sure to use the cookware and bakeware noted in the recipe. If you pour cake batter into a 9-inch pan when the recipe says 8 inch, you will end up with thinner cake layers that cook more quickly. If you try to cook four chicken cutlets in a 10-inch skillet, rather than in the 12-inch skillet called for in the recipe, the chicken will steam rather than brown because the pan is too crowded.

6 ALWAYS PREHEAT

Most ovens need at least 15 minutes to preheat fully, so plan accordingly. If you don't preheat your oven correctly, your food will spend more time in the oven and, as a result, will likely be dry and overcooked (baked goods may suffer more dire consequences). Also, position the racks in the oven as directed—cookies that brown properly on the middle rack may overbrown when baked on a lower rack. The importance of preheating also applies to your pans on the stovetop. The temperature of the cooking surface will drop the minute food is added, so don't rush the preheating step. Wait for the oil to shimmer when cooking vegetables, and wait until you see the first wisps of smoke rise from the oil when you're cooking proteins.

8 TASTE THE DISH BEFORE SERVING

Most recipes end by instructing the cook to adjust the seasoning "to taste." This means you actually have to taste the food. We generally write our recipes so you're seasoning the food pretty lightly throughout the cooking process and then adding more as needed at the end. Foods that will be served chilled, such as gazpacho, should be tasted again when they are cold, since cold mutes the effect of seasonings. Don't forget that there are other ways to season besides salt and pepper—see page 32 for some guidelines.

9 LEARN FROM YOUR MISTAKES—YOUR KITCHEN EDUCATION IS LIFELONG

Even the experienced cooks in our test kitchen often turn out less-than-perfect food. (You have to work through the duds to get to the best possible recipes.) A good cook is able to analyze failure, pinpoint the cause, and then avoid that pitfall next time. A good cook also notices when something works particularly well, such as a combination of ingredients or a particular technique. Above all, a good cook is always learning. Don't make a new dish every night of the year; if you find something you like, prepare it again and again until you master it and add it to your regular repertoire.

7 MONITOR THE DISH AS IT COOKS

Ovens and stovetops can vary in intensity. And maybe you cut those carrots slightly larger than when we prepared the recipe. These little differences are why we often give a range when providing cooking times. You should treat cooking times as solid guidelines, but it is also important to follow the visual cues provided in the recipe. And don't wait until the prescribed time has elapsed to check the doneness of a particular dish: It is good practice to start checking 5 to 10 minutes before the recipe says the food will be done.

10 ENJOY YOURSELF

In the end, a successful cook is someone who enjoys cooking. Yes, sometimes you just need to feed yourself, but even the simplest cooking tasks can be enjoyable. Take pride in your accomplishments. If you enjoy cooking, you will get in the kitchen more often—and practice really does make perfect.

COOKING BASICS | 3

COOKING TERMINOLOGY

The first step to the successful completion of a recipe is understanding what the recipe is telling you to do. Some recipes are precise blueprints, specifying particular sizes, shapes, quantities, and cooking times. Other recipes are rough sketches that allow the cook to fill in the blanks. In addition to the level of detail supplied by the recipe writer, the level of knowledge the cook brings to the process varies. Unfamiliar language and terminology can be a challenge, especially for new cooks trying to work their way through a recipe. Here are some often-used recipe terms defined.

COOKING TERMS

BAKE
To cook by convective heat in a hot oven.

BLANCH
To quickly immerse food in boiling water, then transfer to an ice bath. For blanching vegetables, see page 99.

BLOOM
To cook ground spices or dried herbs in fat to intensify their flavor.

BOIL
To cook foods in boiling liquid in a pot set on a hot burner.

BRAISE
To cook foods by sautéing them and then adding liquid, covering the pan, and simmering.

BRINE
To soak food in a water and salt solution to season and tenderize it before cooking.

BROIL
To cook by direct exposure to a heating element in an oven. For broiling a pork tenderloin, see page 369.

CARAMELIZE
To set in motion the chemical reactions that take place when any sugar is heated to the point that its molecules begin to break apart and generate hundreds of new flavor, color, and aroma compounds.

DEEP-FRY
To cook in hot oil deep enough to fully surround the food.

DEGLAZE
To use liquid (usually wine or broth) to loosen the brown bits known as fond that develop and stick to a pan during sautéing or searing.

DREDGE
To coat food with flour, cornmeal, sugar, or some other dry ingredient.

EMULSION
A mixture of two liquids—such as oil and water—that would not ordinarily stay combined. In an emulsion, one liquid (often the fat) is broken into very small droplets that are suspended in the other liquid (often water). For how a vinaigrette emulsifies, see page 153.

EN PAPILLOTE
A cooking method of enclosing food in a parchment paper packet. The food steams in its own juices so that the flavors are pure and clean. Although parchment is the traditional choice in this classic French technique, aluminum foil can also be used. For cooking fish en papillote, see page 460.

BROIL
A broiler cooks food primarily with radiant heat, a form of invisible infrared light waves. Be sure your rack is properly spaced from the broiler's heat source.

BOIL VERSUS SIMMER
When a liquid boils, large bubbles energetically break the surface at a rapid and constant pace. It's simmering when small bubbles gently break the surface of the liquid at a variable and infrequent rate.

FOND
The caramelized browned bits that remain on the bottom of the pan after food has been sautéed or pan-seared.

GLAZE
To coat food with a glossy syrup or paste (frequently sugar-based).

GREASE
To coat the bottom and sides of a pan with vegetable oil spray or butter.

GRILL
To cook foods directly over an outdoor fire.

MARINATE
To let food sit in a seasoned mixture of oil, liquid, herbs, spices, and other flavorings before cooking to increase flavor and improve texture.

OFF HEAT
A recipe instruction that indicates a pot or dish should be removed from the heat source and placed on a trivet or cool, unused burner before continuing.

POACH
To cook foods in liquid that is well below boiling point in a covered pot.

PUREE
To grind ingredients to a fine, uniform consistency, often in a food processor or blender. The resulting mixture is also called a puree. For pureeing soups, see page 218.

REDUCE
To heat sauce or stock in order to partially evaporate the liquids and reduce the volume, concentrate the flavors, and thicken the consistency.

ROAST
To cook food in a pan in a high-temperature oven to promote browning.

SALT
To season with salt before cooking

SAUTÉ
To quickly cook food in a small amount of fat over moderately high heat while frequently moving the food around the pan.

SEAR
To cook food in a small amount of fat over high heat without moving the food in order to develop a flavorful, well-browned crust.

SHALLOW-FRY (PAN-FRY)
To cook in hot oil deep enough to partially surround the food; can be done in a skillet. For shallow-frying chicken cutlets, see page 411.

SHOCK
To move cooking food to an ice bath in order to quickly stop the cooking process. Often used for vegetables, see page 99.

SIMMER
To cook foods in liquid that is just below the boiling point.

SKIM
To remove the fat that rises to the surface of pan drippings or braising liquids after roasting or braising fatty cuts of beef, pork, or poultry.

STEAM
To cook foods suspended over simmering liquid in a covered pot.

STIR-FRY
To quickly cook thinly cut food in oil over high heat.

TOAST
To brown food by dry heat—without adding fat—using an oven or skillet. Frequently used to bring out the flavors of nuts, seeds, and whole spices.

CUTTING TERMS

(See page 38 for Basic Knife Skills.)

BUTTERFLY
To remove the backbone from a whole chicken or turkey (or other poultry) in order to flatten the bird for fast, even cooking. Also known as spatchcocking. You can also butterfly other large cuts such as pork roasts and shrimp.

CHOP
To cut food into small pieces.

CUT
To penetrate with an edged instrument.

DICE
To cut food into uniform cubes, which can be large or small.

GRATE
To shred a food into small, uniform pieces using a tool such as a box grater or rasp-style grater.

MINCE
To cut into ⅛-inch pieces or smaller.

SLICE
To cut food into pieces with two flat edges, the thickness of which depends on the recipe.

SMASH
To break or crush by force.

TEAR
To separate or pull apart into pieces with your hands.

ZEST
To remove a piece of the peel from a citrus fruit either with a knife or a grater. Also refers to the piece of peel itself.

KEEPING KNIVES SHARP

A sharp knife is a fast knife, and a dull knife is an accident waiting to happen. Dull knives are dangerous because they require more force to do the job and so there is a higher chance of the knife slipping and missing the mark. Even the best knives will dull over time with regular use.

A honing rod (also called a sharpening steel), the metal rod sold with most knife sets, doesn't really sharpen knives. Instead, it trues the edge of a slightly dulled blade. Over time, the sharp cutting edge of a knife blade can turn to the side, making the blade seem dull. A knife that feels dull may need only a few light strokes across a honing rod to correct its edge and restore sharpness without the need to run it through a sharpener. The honing process is also faster than sharpening a knife (about 1 minute to hone versus 5 minutes to sharpen) and doesn't remove metal from the blade.

The Paper Test

To determine if your knife is sharp, put it to the paper test: Holding a sheet of paper (basic printer/copy paper is best) firmly at the top with one hand, draw the blade down through the paper, heel to tip, with the other hand. The knife should glide through the paper and require only minimal pushing. If it snags, try realigning the blade's edge using a honing rod and then repeat the test. If the knife still doesn't cut the paper cleanly, use your sharpener.

How to Use a Honing Rod

1. Place the tip of the honing rod on the counter and place the heel of the blade against the other end of the rod, pointing the knife tip slightly upward. Hold the blade at a 15-degree angle to the rod.

2. Maintaining light, consistent pressure and a 15-degree angle between the knife blade and rod, slide the blade down the length of the rod in a sweeping motion, pulling the knife toward your body so that the entire edge of the blade makes contact.

3. Repeat this motion on the other side of the blade. Four or five strokes on each side of the blade (a total of eight to ten alternating passes) should realign the edge.

MIXING TERMS

BEAT
To stir into a froth or foam, usually with a whisk, fork, or electric mixer.

CREAM
To combine sugar and a fat into a homogeneous mixture.

FOLD
To mix delicate batters and incorporate fragile ingredients using a gentle under-and-over motion that minimizes deflation.

KNEAD
To work and press bread dough to develop gluten and create a strong network of cross-linked proteins.

SIFT
To put a powdered ingredient such as flour through a fine-mesh strainer or sieve to aerate and break up clumps.

STIR
To move parts by continuous circular movement.

WHIP
To quickly stir an ingredient, such as egg whites or cream, with a whisk or electric mixer in order to aerate and stabilize the ingredient and add volume.

WHISK
To beat food by hand with a light whipping motion. Also the name of the wire utensil used to do the whipping.

IS FOLDING THE SAME AS STIRRING?

Folding is gentler and more gradual than stirring, which makes it ideal for delicate mixtures.

The goal of folding is to incorporate delicate, airy ingredients such as whipped cream or beaten egg whites into heavy, dense ingredients such as egg yolks, custard, or chocolate without causing deflation. The tools required for folding are a balloon whisk and a large, flexible rubber spatula.

In the test kitchen, we like to start the process by lightening the heavier ingredients with one-quarter or one-third of the whipped mixture. A balloon whisk is ideal for the task: Its tines cut into and loosen the heavier mixture, allowing the whipped mixture to be integrated more readily. Next, the remaining whipped mixture can be easily incorporated into the lightened mixture. For this round of folding, we preserve the airiness of the dessert by using a rubber spatula, which is gentler than a whisk.

Don't cut corners when it comes to folding. Take your time and use a light hand to gradually incorporate beaten egg whites or whipped cream into heavier ingredients. To fold properly and avoid deflating your mixture, start with your spatula perpendicular to the batter and then cut through the center down to the bottom of the bowl. Holding the spatula blade flat against the bowl, scoop along the bottom and then up the side of the bowl. Fold over, lifting the spatula high so that the scooped mixture falls without the spatula pressing down on it.

WHISK
Use a balloon whisk to gently whisk together components until well combined.

COOKING BASICS | 7

A KITCHEN STARTER KIT

You don't need a lot of fancy equipment and gadgets in order to cook well and turn out great food. If you are just starting out and want to set up a solid base to work from in your kitchen, start with this list of what the test kitchen considers to be the real basics. With these essentials you will be able to tackle most recipes. The right tools definitely help, and the following pages give details about what's in this starter kit and more, including which brands we know are the best (because we tested all of them and use them every day).

1. **ALL-AROUND SPATULAS** (metal and plastic)
2. **BAKING DISH** (13 x 9)
3. **CAN OPENER**
4. **CUTTING BOARD** (wood, bamboo, or plastic)
5. **DUTCH OVEN**
6. **INSTANT-READ THERMOMETER**
7. **KNIVES** (chef's, paring, and serrated)
8. **MEASURING TOOLS** (cups and spoons)
9. **MIXING BOWLS**
10. **PEPPER MILL**
11. **RIMMED BAKING SHEETS AND WIRE RACK**
12. **SAUCEPANS** (traditional and nonstick)
13. **SILICONE SPATULA**
14. **SKILLETS** (traditional and nonstick)
15. **TONGS**
16. **WOODEN SPOON**

COOKING BASICS | 9

EQUIPPING YOUR KITCHEN

There are several categories of kitchen equipment and here we outline what is in each grouping and what each piece is for. We also include the test kitchen's buying recommendations (in bold) so that you know which brands we consider to be the best investment.

COOKWARE

SAUCEPANS

Every kitchen should be equipped with two saucepans: one with a capacity of 3 to 4 quarts, and a 2-quart nonstick saucepan. A larger saucepan is great for vegetables and sauces, while a smaller saucepan can be used for cooking foods that stick easily such as oatmeal. The test kitchen's favorite large saucepan is the **All-Clad 4-Quart Stainless Steel Sauce Pan with Loop Helper Handle** and our best buy is the Cuisinart MultiClad Unlimited 4-Quart Saucepan with Cover. Our favorite small saucepan is the **Calphalon Contemporary Nonstick 2½ Quart Shallow Saucepan with Cover**.

DUTCH OVEN

A Dutch oven is a kitchen workhorse that is useful for making soups and stews, braising, steaming, frying, and even baking bread. A good-quality heavy-bottomed Dutch oven conducts heat steadily and evenly. It should be easy to reach into and have a wide surface area for browning. The most useful size is 6 to 8 quarts. Our winning heavier Dutch oven is the **Le Creuset 7¼ Quart Round Dutch Oven** and our best buy is the Cuisinart Chef's Classic Enameled Cast Iron Covered Casserole.

RIMMED BAKING SHEETS AND WIRE RACKS

Rimmed baking sheets will be the busiest pans in your kitchen. The test kitchen uses them for everything from roasting vegetables and baking cookies to cooking meat and baking a sheet cake. Fitted with the right size wire cooling rack, a rimmed baking sheet can stand in for a roasting pan. We prefer baking sheets that are 18 x 13 inches and have a 1-inch rim all around. Buy at least two baking sheets. Our favorite rack—the **Checkered Chef Cooling Rack**—fits snugly in our winning baking sheet, the inexpensive **Nordic Ware Bakers Half Sheet**.

TRADITIONAL SKILLET

We prefer traditional skillets made of stainless steel sandwiched around an aluminum core. The finish (which is NOT nonstick) helps develop fond, the caramelized brown bits that stick to the bottom of the pan. Our winning traditional skillet, the **All-Clad D3 Stainless Steel 12" Fry Pan with Lid**, also comes in 10-inch and 8-inch versions.

NONSTICK SKILLET

The coating on nonstick pans helps delicate foods such as eggs and fish release easily. The nonstick coating will wear out over time and the skillet will need to be replaced, but our winning pan, the **OXO Good Grips Non-Stick Pro 12" Open Frypan**, is relatively inexpensive.

CAST-IRON SKILLET

A cast-iron skillet excels at searing and, if well seasoned, releases food as well as a nonstick surface. However, it does require extra effort to build and maintain its seasoning, so keep that in mind. Our roomy preseasoned favorite is the **Lodge Classic Cast Iron Skillet, 12"**.

CARBON STEEL SKILLET

Like cast iron, carbon steel also needs to be seasoned, but once it is, it offers the versatility of a traditional pan, the heat retention of cast iron at a lighter weight, and the slick release of a good nonstick skillet. Our winner is the **Matfer Bourgeat Black Steel Round Frying Pan, 11⅞"**.

FLAT-BOTTOMED WOK

This versatile pan is made of carbon steel so it transfers heat efficiently and sears foods effectively. It is suited to stir-frying, frying, and steaming. It offers a big, flat cooking surface and its flat bottom is stable on a flat stovetop. Our winning wok is the **Taylor and Ng Natural Nonstick Wok Set 12153 14" Carbon Steel**.

ROASTING PAN

This holiday staple is incredibly useful year-round. Besides roasting the Thanksgiving turkey, this pan shows up whenever we want to roast large cuts of meat. Its low sides and open design provide roasts with maximum exposure to the oven's hot air for even browning. Our winning roasting pan comes with a rack, the **Calphalon Contemporary Stainless Roasting Pan with Rack**.

BAKEWARE

BAKING DISHES

A 13 x 9 glass baking dish is functional, inexpensive, and great for baked ziti or a large fruit crisp but it can't go under the broiler to brown the top of a casserole. We found an alternative to our favorite **Pyrex Easy Grab 3-Quart Oblong Baking Dish** that was broiler safe and looked nice coming to the table for serving. **Mrs. Anderson's Baking Lasagna Pan with Handle (Rose)** has a large capacity and is easy to clean.

BAKING PANS

It's good to have two sizes of metal baking pans. An 8- or 9-inch square pan is good for snack cakes, brownies, and bar cookies. A 13 x 9-inch size is good for baking sheet cakes, bar cookies, and lasagna. And a loaf pan is perfect for quick breads and yeast breads (see right). Our winning pans are **Fat Daddio's Square Cake Pan** and **Williams Sonoma Gold Touch Nonstick Rectangular Cake Pan 9" x 13"**.

ROUND CAKE PANS

We primarily use 8-inch or 9-inch round cake pans to bake layer cakes but we also use them to bake rolls, pan pizza, and upside-down cakes. Solidly built, with a light gold nonstick coating, our winning **Nordic Ware Naturals Nonstick 8-Inch and 9-Inch Round Cake Pans** produce tall, fluffy, level cakes—and layers shape up perfectly, no matter how the pan is greased. Be sure to buy two.

PIE PLATE

The **Williams-Sonoma Goldtouch Nonstick Pie Dish** is a golden-hued metal plate that bakes crusts beautifully without overbrowning; even bottom crusts emerge crisp and flaky. Additionally, we like this plate's nonfluted lip, which allows for maximum crust-crimping flexibility.

LOAF PAN

Size matters with loaf pans. Our winning pan, **USA Pan Loaf Pan, 1 lb Volume**, produces professional-quality results and measures 8⅝ x 4½ inches. If your pan is 9 x 5 inches, you'll need to adjust the baking time as the recipe indicates. Many bread recipes yield two loaves so you will want two loaf pans.

BUNDT PAN

A bundt pan is a special tube pan with decorative ridges or fluting; it produces elegant-looking cakes that require little adornment. Our winning **Nordic Ware Anniversary Bundt Pan** is heavy and nonstick.

MUFFIN TIN

A standard 12-cup muffin tin with ½-cup wells is the most useful. Our favorite tin, the **OXO Good Grips Non-Stick Pro 12-Cup Muffin Pan**, perfectly releases muffins and cupcakes. It has an oversize rim running all the way around it, so there is a broad, secure place to grasp. Its gold finish creates the most appealing baked goods, too: evenly, lightly browned and elegantly shaped.

BAKING STONE AND STEEL

A baking stone or steel conducts heat and transfers it evenly and steadily to the bottom of the pizza or bread being baked on it. To see a stone in action, see page 554. Our co-winning steels are **The Original Baking Steel** and the **Nerd Chef Steel Stone, Standard ¼"**. Our best buy and best lightweight option is the Outset Pizza Grill Stone Tiles, Set of 4.

BAKING PEEL

A baking peel is used to move pizza, bread, and other baked goods into, out of, and within hot ovens. Our winning peel, the innovative **EXO Polymer Sealed Super Peel**, is made of wood and has a cloth conveyor belt with a polymer coating to make it more moisture-proof.

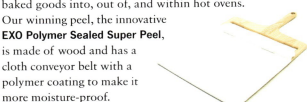

KNIVES

CHEF'S KNIFE

From chopping onions to mincing herbs to butchering a chicken, a chef's knife will handle 90 percent of your ingredient prep. If you buy only one knife, make it a reliable chef's knife like the test kitchen's longtime favorite, the **Victorinox Swiss Army Fibrox Pro 8" Chef's Knife**.

PARING KNIFE

A paring knife is key for tasks that require more dexterity than a chef's knife can provide: peeling and coring apples, deveining shrimp, cutting citrus segments, and more. Our winning paring knife is the **Victorinox Swiss Army 3¼" Spear Point Paring Knife**.

SERRATED KNIFE

The pointed serrations of a good serrated knife glide through crusty breads, bagels, and the tough skins of tomatoes to produce neat slices. We like the modestly priced **Mercer Culinary Millennia 10" Wide Bread Knife**.

HONING ROD

Our winning honing rod, the **Bob Kramer Double-Cut Sharpening Steel**, has a long and thick hone which makes it easy to use. The rod has two alternating textures, lightly ridged and smooth.

TOOLS

COLANDER

The test kitchen's longtime favorite colander, the **RSVP International Precision Pierced 5 Qt. Colander**, is stable and its bowl is covered with tiny, well-distributed perforations so liquids drain from it quickly.

CUTTING BOARDS

Wood and bamboo cutting boards take some work to clean and maintain but if properly cared for they can last a lifetime. Plastic boards are nearly as durable and less expensive to buy and replace. Our favorite large plastic cutting board is the **Winco Statik Board Cutting Board 15" x 20" x ½"** and our favorite wood cutting board is the **Teakhaus by Proteak Edge Grain Cutting Board**.

GARLIC PRESS

For most home cooks, a garlic press is a much easier way to get a fine, even mince or paste than using a knife. Our winning garlic press is the **Kuhn Rikon Epicurean Garlic Press**. Its comfortable stainless-steel handles open wide so loading cloves is easy.

GRATERS

A box grater with a variety of easy-to-use planes can handle almost any task from grating hard vegetables to shredding soft cheese. Our favorite is the **Cuisinart Box Grater**. We also love rasp-style graters which are ideal for finely grating hard cheeses, ginger, citrus zest, chocolate, and more. Our winning rasp grater is the **Microplane Premium Classic Zester/Grater**.

KITCHEN SHEARS

A pair of kitchen shears is one of the best all-around tools, useful for tasks such as butterflying chicken, trimming pie dough, shaping parchment paper, snipping herbs, and cutting kitchen twine. Our favorite shears are **Shun Multi-Purpose Shears**.

DRY MEASURING CUPS

Dry ingredients such as flour, sugar, grains, and other foods should always be measured in a dry measuring cup. These straight-sided cups typically have flat tops that make leveling dry ingredients easy. We prefer the **OXO Good Grips Stainless Steel Measuring Cups**.

LIQUID MEASURING CUP

For the utmost precision, use a liquid measuring cup for liquids. Our winning glass cup is the **Pyrex 1 Cup Measuring Cup** and winning plastic cup is the **OXO Good Grips 1 Cup Angled Measuring Cup**.

MEASURING SPOONS

We use these tiny tools to measure everything from baking soda to olive oil. We like the simple sturdy design of the **Cuisipro Stainless Steel 5-Piece Measuring Spoons**.

DIGITAL SCALE

When baking, weighing the ingredients is the most accurate method of measurement. But a scale is also useful for portioning out ground meat or weighing vegetables and fruits. We highly recommend the **OXO Good Grips 11 lb Food Scale with Pull Out Display** and our best buy is the Ozeri Pronto Digital Multifunction Kitchen and Food Scale.

MIXING BOWLS AND PREP BOWLS

Mixing bowls handle everything from mixing pancake batter to simply melting butter. Our winning stainless-steel bowls are the **Vollrath Economy Stainless Steel Mixing Bowls** and our favorite glass ones are the **Pyrex Smart Essentials Mixing Bowl Set with Colored Lids**. We also like to use small glass prep bowls to measure out the ingredients needed for a recipe. Our winning set is the **Anchor Hocking 6-Piece Nesting Prep Bowl Set**.

CLEANING YOUR CUTTING BOARDS

Routine cleaning is essential; scrub your board thoroughly in hot, soapy water (or put it through the dishwasher if it's dishwasher-safe) to kill harmful bacteria, then rinse it well and dry it completely. For stubborn odors, scrub the cutting board with a paste of 1 tablespoon of baking soda and 1 teaspoon of water, then wash with hot, soapy water. To remove stubborn stains from plastic boards, mix a solution of 1 tablespoon of bleach per quart of water in the sink and immerse the board, dirty side up. When the board rises to the surface, drape a kitchen towel or two over its surface and sprinkle the towel with about ¼ cup of the bleach solution. Let it sit overnight, then wash it with hot, soapy water.

If using a wood or bamboo board, maintain it by applying a food-grade mineral oil every few weeks when the board is new, and a few times a year thereafter. (Don't use olive or vegetable oil, which can become rancid.) The oil soaks into the fibers of the board, creating a barrier to excess moisture. Avoid leaving wood or bamboo boards resting in water, or they will eventually split.

PEPPER MILL

Preground pepper doesn't compare with freshly ground, which is what just about all of our savory recipes call for. The test kitchen's winning mill, the **Cole & Mason Derwent Pepper Mill**, is easy to load and grinds pepper from very fine to very coarse.

POTATO MASHER

A classic handheld masher is a good choice for making smooth mashes of all types. Our favorite masher is the **Zyliss Stainless Steel Potato Masher**.

ROLLING PIN

We prefer the classic French-style handle-free wood rolling pins; they easily turn and pivot and allow you to feel the thickness of the dough and apply pressure as needed. Look for a pin that's about 20 inches long like our winning pin, the **J.K. Adams Plain Maple Rolling Dowel**.

SALAD SPINNER
A salad spinner is the best way to get greens and other produce clean and dry. We like the **OXO Good Grips Salad Spinner** which has a large basket and a central pump mechanism.

SPATULAS
A good metal spatula is essential for flipping or transferring foods from metal cookware or bakeware. Our winner is the **Wüsthof Gourmet 7" Slotted Fish Spatula**. When cooking in nonstick pans, we prefer our winning all-purpose spatula, the **Di Oro Living Seamless Silicone Spatula—Large**.

FINE-MESH STRAINER
A fine-mesh strainer is great for rinsing rice, washing vegetables, sifting flour or confectioners' sugar, and straining sauces. The test kitchen's winner is the **Rösle Fine Mesh Strainer, 7.9 inches**.

INSTANT-READ THERMOMETER
An instant-read thermometer helps to ensure success in the kitchen since it takes the guesswork out of knowing when food is done. We love our longtime winning thermometer, the **Thermoworks Thermapen Mk4**. Our best inexpensive option is the Thermoworks ThermoPop.

TONGS
A good pair of tongs are a cook's best friend and should feel like a natural extension of your hands. The **OXO Good Grips 12-Inch Tongs** are our favorite; they grip food well and are comfortable to hold.

VEGETABLE AND FRUIT PEELER
A good peeler should be fast and smooth, shaving off enough skin to avoid repeat trips over the same section. Our winning Y-shaped peeler, the **Kuhn Rikon Original Swiss Peeler**, easily tackles every task thanks to its razor-sharp carbon-steel blade.

WHISK
A balloon-style whisk with wires that curve out just a bit is the best all-purpose tool; it can mix batters, beat eggs or cream, and make a pan sauce on the stove. Our winning all-purpose whisk is the **OXO Good Grips 11" Balloon Whisk**.

WOODEN SPOON
Wooden spoons are useful for a variety of stirring and scraping tasks, such as mixing stiff cookie dough and scraping up fond. Our co-winning wooden spoons are **Jonathan's Spoons Spootle** and **FAAY 13.5" Teak Cooking Spoon**.

SMALL APPLIANCES

BLENDERS
A blender is the only tool that can bring foods (hot or cold) to a uniformly smooth texture, whether you're pureeing soups and sauces or making smoothies and milkshakes. You might also consider an immersion blender (such as the Braun Multiquick 5 Hand Blender), which is useful for small jobs like blending salad dressings and pureeing soup right in the pot. We found a reliable blender at every price point.

Our high-end winner is the powerful **Vitamix 5200**. Our midpriced pick is the **Breville Fresh & Furious**. The inexpensive **NutriBullet Full Size Blender** has very basic controls but still gets every job done.

FOOD PROCESSOR
If you are investing in one big-ticket appliance, it should be a food processor. It can chop foods that blenders can't handle, as well as slice and shred and mix up batters and doughs. Our winning **Cuisinart Custom 14 Cup Food Processor** is powerful and easy to operate.

SPICE GRINDER
Freshly ground whole spices have a superior aroma and roundness of flavor versus preground spices. The test kitchen standard for grinding spices is a blade-type electric coffee grinder like our favorite **Krups Coffee and Spice Grinder**.

CLEANING YOUR BLENDER AND FOOD PROCESSOR

After you're done using your blender, clean it by "blending" a warm soapy water mixture until the blades and jar are mostly clean, and then rinse out the blender.

A similar technique works for your food processor. To quickly rinse the workbowl between tasks, add a few drops of dish soap and warm water to the liquid fill line, run the machine for a few seconds, and rinse the bowl well. To give a dirty processor bowl a good soak, put a wine or champagne cork in the center hole so you can fill the bowl all the way to the top.

HANDHELD MIXER
A handheld mixer is lightweight, easy to use, and great for most basic tasks, like whipping cream or egg whites, creaming butter and sugar, and making a batter; the only thing it can't handle is kneading dough (see the stand mixer for that). If you bake only occasionally, a handheld mixer is fine. The test kitchen favorite is the **KitchenAid 5-Speed Ultra Power Hand Mixer**.

STAND MIXER
A stand mixer usual comes with three attachments: a whisk, a paddle, and a dough hook for kneading dough. If you are a serious cook or baker, a stand mixer is simply something you need. Our winner is the **KitchenAid Pro Line Series 7 Quart Stand Mixer** and the best buy is the more reasonably priced KitchenAid Classic Plus Series 4.5 Quart Tilt-Head Stand Mixer.

CLEANUP

APRON
A good apron is the ideal kitchen companion; it protects your clothes and keeps essentials such as a thermometer, pen, or dish towel at hand. We highly recommend our winning apron, the **Bragard Travail Bib Apron**.

DISH TOWEL
A worthwhile dish towel must be absorbent, whether you are drying a dish or soaking up a spill. Our winning towel grows more absorbent the more it is used and washed. Look for **Williams-Sonoma Striped Towels, Set of 4**.

KITCHEN SPONGES
Doing dishes is a dirty job so use a kitchen sponge that makes it easier. The **O-Cedar Scrunge Multi-Use Scrubber Sponge** is our favorite.

FOOD STORAGE CONTAINERS
Our winning plastic food storage containers are well made and won't warp, stain, leak, or wear out too soon. Sizes of the **Rubbermaid Brilliance Food Storage Container** range from 1.3 cups to 9.6 cups to store everything from a small amount of leftovers to big batch cooking. Our top choice for glass storage is **OXO Good Grips 8 Cup Smart Seal Rectangle Container**.

CLEANING AND CARING FOR YOUR COOKWARE

We've created our share of messes in the test kitchen and have had a few cooking snafus that required tons of cleanup. Along the way, we've learned a few tricks to get those pans shining like new again.

CLEANING EVERYDAY MESSES

1. BOIL WATER
To clean a dirty traditional skillet (this usually isn't necessary for nonstick pans), fill it halfway with tap water. Bring to a boil, uncovered, and boil briskly for two or three minutes. Turn off the burner.

2. SCRAPE OFF RESIDUE
Scrape the pan with a wooden spatula, pour off the water, and let sit briefly. Residue will start to flake off as the pan dries. Wash the skillet with hot water and dishwashing liquid, and dry.

CLEANING STUBBORN MESSES

1. SPRINKLE ON CLEANSER
To clean stuck-on gunk, moisten the pan with water and shake on a powdered cleanser such as Cameo (for stainless steel, anodized aluminum, or nonstick surfaces) or Bar Keepers Friend (for stainless steel or nonstick surfaces).

2. SCRUB THE PAN
Using a copper scrubber for stainless-steel skillets and a nylon scrubber for nonstick or anodized aluminum skillets, scrub the pan with circular motions. Finish by washing the pan with hot water and dishwashing liquid, and dry.

CAST-IRON SKILLETS

A well-maintained cast-iron skillet will become more nonstick with time. While the skillet is still warm, wipe it clean with paper towels to remove excess food bits and oil. Rinse the skillet under hot running water, scrubbing with a brush or nonabrasive scrub pad to remove traces of food. Use a small amount of soap if you like, but make sure to rinse it all off. Dry the skillet thoroughly (do not let it drip-dry) and put it back on the burner over medium-low heat until all traces of moisture disappear (this keeps rusting at bay). Never put a wet cast-iron skillet away or stack anything on top of a skillet that hasn't been properly dried. Add ½ teaspoon of vegetable oil to the warm, dry skillet and wipe the interior with a wad of paper towels until it is lightly covered with oil. Continue to rub oil into the skillet, replacing the paper towels as needed, until the skillet looks dark and shiny and does not have any remaining oil residue. Turn off the heat and allow the skillet to cool completely before putting it away.

CARBON-STEEL WOKS AND SKILLETS

After you cook, rinse the pan with water, scrubbing gently with a soft-bristled brush or a sponge if necessary; avoid soap or abrasive scrubbers. Dry the pan thoroughly over a warm burner (but do not overheat, as that will weaken the seasoning and detach it from the expanding steel). Add ¼ teaspoon oil to the cleaned skillet or ½ teaspoon oil to the cleaned wok and, using a wad of paper towels held with tongs, spread evenly over the surface. Wipe away as much oil as possible with a paper towel (excess oil won't fully polymerize and will lead to tackiness). Continue to heat the pan, wiping away any beaded oil that forms, until the pan smokes (indicating oil breakdown). Let the pan smoke for 2 minutes, wiping away beaded oil with a paper towel. Turn off the heat and let the pan cool. (Note: If you are seasoning a wok, the sides will initially be less seasoned because they don't get as hot as the bottom. With use, the upper portion will become more seasoned.)

If the cooking surface feels bumpy or has tacky residue (caused by partially polymerized oil or food residue) or if the patina is chipped, scrub with a mixture of kosher salt and oil or a moderately abrasive sponge (it's also fine to use a little soap if the skillet or wok is tacky) until the patina feels even to the touch (the color does not need to be even). Repeat applying oil as directed above.

DUTCH OVENS

Enameled Dutch ovens are prone to staining, and while we're not concerned with keeping our cookware pristine, staining can be problematic if the bottom of the pot darkens so much that we can't monitor browning. We found that the best way to deep-clean a stained pot is to let it soak overnight in a solution of 1 part bleach to 3 parts water and then wash it thoroughly with soap and water.

A Dutch oven's enameled surface is very durable, but it's not completely impervious and can be subject to chipping. To help keep the enamel intact, don't subject your pot to dramatic temperature changes, especially near moisture. Don't clear food from utensils by whacking them on the pot's rim. And don't scrape metal utensils—specifically, sharp ones—along the bottom.

NONSTICK PANS

Nearly all nonstick pans rely on a top coat of polytetrafluoroethylene (PTFE) to keep the surface slick and prevent food from sticking. Cooking over high heat, using abrasive pads, or washing the pan in the dishwasher will all cause this polymer to wear away. To prolong the nonstick coating's life, wash nonstick pans gently with a nonabrasive pad, and once they are dry, we recommend storing them using one of the following two methods.

A. SEPARATE AND STACK
The surface of a nonstick skillet can chip or scratch easily, especially if you stack it with other pans. To protect the nonstick surface, place a double sheet of paper towels, bubble wrap, or a cheap paper plate between each pan as you stack them.

B. SEAL AND STACK
Alternatively, before stacking smaller nonstick pans, slide them into large zipper-lock bags (2-gallon size for 10-inch pans and 1-gallon size for 8-inch pans). The plastic will protect the nonstick surface. Note that a 12-inch skillet will not fit in a zipper-lock bag.

STOCKING YOUR PANTRY AND REFRIGERATOR

Your pantry is an ever-evolving collection of ingredients that reflects the kinds of food you enjoy cooking and eating. There are no hard-and-fast requirements, but this list presents many of the ingredients we most often call for in our recipes and which we think make the basis for a strong, adaptable home pantry.

IN THE PANTRY

ANCHOVIES
Even if you're not the type to eat these tiny fish right out of the tin, we recommend keeping some on hand. We use anchovies in a surprising number of recipes to build a strong umami (but not superfishy) base.

CANNED BEANS
Nine times out of ten, we rely on the convenience of canned beans. Our staples are black beans, cannellini beans, pinto beans, red kidney beans, and chickpeas.

DRIED BEANS AND LENTILS
When beans or lentils are the star of a dish, we prefer the superior flavor and texture of dried. We keep dried cannellini beans, pinto beans, and chickpeas on hand along with French or regular green and/or brown lentils.

BROTH
In the test kitchen we rarely go a day without using chicken broth, and not just in soup. We also recommend keeping vegetable broth and beef broth on hand (see page 199). Homemade is great (see our recipes starting on page 232), but store-bought works perfectly well in most applications.

CHILES
Dried chiles, chile flakes, and canned chipotle chiles in adobo sauce are all great shelf-stable standbys for when you need to turn up the heat a little.

FISH SAUCE
This salty liquid is made from fermented fish and is used as an ingredient and a condiment in Southeast Asian cuisines. In small amounts, it adds a well-rounded, salty flavor to sauces, soups, and marinades.

GARLIC
Everyday garlic is the base of an enormous number of recipes, in all kinds of cuisines.

GOCHUJANG
Gochujang is a Korean chile bean paste that has a smooth consistency and a rich, spicy flavor.

HOT SAUCE
Even cooks who don't crave spicy foods should keep a bottle of hot sauce on hand to give recipes a little kick. We like one with a little sugar in it to balance the heat with sweetness.

KETCHUP
We prefer ketchups made with sugar instead of high-fructose corn syrup; they have a cleaner, purer sweetness and fewer off-flavors.

MAYONNAISE
A good supermarket mayonnaise can rival homemade and certainly keeps for much longer. The best-tasting brands have the fewest ingredients.

MUSTARD
Mild yellow mustard is the most popular in American cupboards, but we use Dijon more frequently in recipes. You may also want spicy brown, whole-grain, or honey mustard.

OIL
Vegetable oil (we prefer canola) is a workhorse because of its neutral taste. Extra-virgin olive oil is great for cooking, as a condiment, or in a vinaigrette. Peanut oil works well for frying. Many other cooking and finishing oils are available, depending on your tastes and needs. See page 150 for more information.

OLIVES
As a pantry staple, we like jarred brine-cured black and green olives. For the best texture, buy unpitted olives and pit them yourself.

ONIONS
Yellow onions are our first choice for cooking for their rich flavor. Red onions are great grilled or raw in salad or salsa (sweet onions are also best raw). White onions are similar to yellow onions but lack their complexity.

PANKO BREAD CRUMBS
For a convenient store-bought option, Japanese-style panko bread crumbs have superior crunch.

PASTA AND NOODLES
There are many different shapes and sizes of dried pasta and Asian noodles. We recommend stocking a few favorites for quick, no-fuss dinners. See pages 239 and 267 for more information.

BLACK PEPPERCORNS
The scent and flavor of peppercorns start to fade as soon as they're ground, so buy whole peppercorns and grind them as you use them. See page 27 for more information.

DRIED PORCINI AND SHIITAKE MUSHROOMS
Dried mushrooms add potent savory flavor to dishes. Because the mushrooms are dried, their flavor is concentrated and they are conveniently shelf-stable. You can grind them into a fine powder using a spice grinder or mortar and pestle and then sprinkle it on pretty much anything you can think of for a meaty boost.

POTATOES
These fall into three categories (baking, boiling, and all-purpose) based on their starch levels and textures. Make sure you know which you have, since you can't always use any type and expect great results See page 122 for more information.

RICE AND GRAINS
White rice is a classic staple but we also love nutty whole-grain brown rice. We also suggest you stock at least one other grain; there's a world of options. See pages 282–283 for more information.

CANNED TOMATOES
Since canned tomatoes are processed at the height of freshness, they deliver more flavor than off-season fresh tomatoes. We rely on them in a variety of contexts. Canned whole tomatoes, diced tomatoes, crushed tomatoes, pureed tomatoes, and tomato paste all have their place. See page 249 for more information.

SALT
Table salt is our go-to for most applications, while kosher salt is great for seasoning meat. Flaky sea salt is best reserved for finishing dishes. See page 26 for more information.

SHALLOTS
With a complex, subtly sweet flavor, shallots are ideal in sauces, where they melt into the texture, and in vinaigrettes, where they add gentle heat.

SOY SAUCE
This dark, salty fermented liquid is a common ingredient and condiment that enhances umami flavor and contributes complexity.

SPICES
Most cooks typically rely on the convenience of preground spices but fresh-ground have a superior flavor. See pages 26–29 for more information.

TAHINI
This paste made from ground sesame seeds is most common in Middle Eastern dishes, but its nutty, buttery profile is a welcome addition in salads and grain dishes and on all types of meat and fish. We also love whole sesame seeds as a garnish.

TUNA
For a basic everyday canned tuna, look for wild albacore packed in water. If you like a fancier option (that actually tastes like fish), try fillets packed in olive oil.

VINEGAR
The types you should keep in your cupboard depend on what you like to use. We recommend having at least three: white wine vinegar, red wine vinegar, and balsamic vinegar. See page 130 for more information.

COOKING BASICS | 19

Baking and Dessert Ingredients

BAKING POWDER
Baking powder provides leavening for baked goods that have no natural acidity in the batter (it can also add extra lift alongside baking soda).

BAKING SODA
This leavener is used to provide lift to baked goods that also contain an acidic ingredient (such as sour cream, buttermilk, or brown sugar).

CHOCOLATE
Chocolate chips are probably the most convenient form, but we also like bars. We stock a dark chocolate with 60 percent cacao in addition to unsweetened baker's chocolate. See page 582 for more information.

COCOA POWDER
You will find cocoa powder in both Dutch-processed and natural versions. Dutch-processed cocoa has been treated with alkali to neutralize the powder's acidity and mellow its astringent notes (it also darkens the color). Both types will work in most recipes, although Dutch-processed cocoa will produce baked goods with a darker color and moister texture.

CORNMEAL
For a basic baking cornmeal, look for fine-ground whole-grain yellow cornmeal. We recommend stone ground over commercially processed.

FLOUR
There are many types of flour, and each has its place and uses. As its name suggests, all-purpose flour is the most versatile. We also call for whole-wheat flour, bread flour, and cake flour in certain recipes. See page 507 for more information.

DRIED FRUIT
Almost any fruit can be dried; the drying process concentrates flavor and sugar. Try dried fruit in baked goods, salads, or granola, or on cheese plates.

HONEY
Try different honeys to see what you like. Strongly flavored varieties such as buckwheat honey are too assertive for cooking—save them for your tea.

MAPLE SYRUP
Opt for 100 percent maple syrup rather than one blended with corn syrup.

NUTS
Keep a couple of your favorite nuts on hand for baking, granola, topping salads, and snacking. Store them in the freezer to prevent rancidity.

PEANUT BUTTER
Not just for sandwiches, peanut butter is useful in baking and in sauces. Texture matters most here, so we prefer creamy traditional peanut butter to grittier "natural" versions.

SUGAR
White granulated sugar, brown sugar (light and dark can pretty much be used interchangeably), and confectioners' sugar are the most common sugars for baking and beyond.

VANILLA EXTRACT
Get the real thing. Real vanilla extract has around 250 flavor compounds compared with imitation vanilla's one, giving it a unique complexity.

YEAST
We prefer instant (aka rapid-rise) yeast, which is the easiest to use; it can be added directly to the dry ingredients.

IN THE REFRIGERATOR AND FREEZER

BUTTER
We like unsalted butter for cooking and baking, but salted butter is great for spreading on toast or homemade bread and biscuits (see page 559).

CHEESE
The type depends on your taste, but we recommend at least having Parmesan, which is a common ingredient and also good as a topping. Buy the real thing and grate it yourself. Feta and cheddar are also versatile staples. See page 22 for more information.

CREAM
Heavy cream is good for whipping—better than whipping cream. Heavy cream or whipping cream works well in savory recipes, lending creaminess to soups and sauces.

EGGS
It's hard to overstate how many things you can do with eggs. They are one of the most versatile and valuable items in your pantry. We always call for large eggs in our recipes. See page 53 for more information.

HALF-AND-HALF
Half-and-half is a mixture of milk and cream and is used in baked goods, puddings, and more.

MILK
Low-fat milk is the most versatile. We often turn to whole milk and buttermilk when baking.

SOUR CREAM
Sour cream has a recognizable tangy flavor. It is used in cakes and other baked goods as well as in stews, sauces, and as a topping.

YOGURT
For eating plain and for recipes, we prefer whole-milk yogurt. We're also big fans of Greek yogurt, which has a smooth, thick, decadent texture.

BACON
From brunch to vegetable sides, bacon livens up pretty much any dish. Good bacon has balanced meaty, smoky, salty, and sweet flavors. We prefer cured, dry-smoked versions. See page 213 for more information.

FROZEN VEGETABLES
Many kinds of frozen vegetables make solid stand-ins for fresh. Frozen peas can even be sweeter than fresh ones, since they are frozen at the very peak of ripeness.

GINGER
Fresh ginger has a bite and pungency that you just can't get from powdered ginger.

FRESH HERBS
We frequently use a sprinkling of minced herbs to give dishes a fresh finish, or employ whole herb leaves to brighten salads and sandwiches. Parsley, cilantro, and basil are the ones we use most often. See page 24 for more information.

LEMONS AND LIMES
A squeeze of citrus can be just the thing to brighten up a dish. Keep lemons and limes in the refrigerator until you need them.

MISO
This incredibly versatile ingredient is a fermented paste of soybeans and rice, barley, or rye. It is salty and ranges in strength and color. Lighter misos are typically used in more delicate dishes such as soups and salads while darker misos are best in heavier recipes.

GETTING TO KNOW CHEESE

COOKING CHEESES

Whether crystalline or creamy, sharp or mild, blue or orange, cheese is used in countless recipes. Here are the kinds that we reach for often in the test kitchen.

MILD CHEDDAR
Whether British or American, all cheddars are made by a process called cheddaring, in which curds are cut into slabs, stacked, and pressed. American cheddar may be white or yellow, depending on the region it's from. The yellow (it's actually orange) is dyed with annatto seeds. Mild, young cheddar is moister and a better melter than its older siblings.

SHARP CHEDDAR
As cheddar ages, its texture firms and dries, and its flavor concentrates. While the U.S. Department of Agriculture (USDA) has no guidelines for aging and labeling, extra-sharp cheddar (at the far end of the cheddar spectrum) is usually nine to 18 months old. Older cheddar can curdle when melted. To prevent that, we shred it and toss it with cornstarch or combine it with better melters, such as Monterey Jack or American cheese.

MONTEREY JACK
When it comes to creamy melting and mild flavor, Monterey Jack sets the gold standard. A California native, it's also called Cali Jack, or just Jack cheese, and is rarely aged. Pepper Jack is its spicy cousin.

BLOCK-STYLE MOZZARELLA
Heat brings out the best in this low-moisture mozzarella which, though rubbery when raw, melts beautifully. You can use part skim and full fat interchangeably in recipes for lasagnas and pizza, but avoid pre-shredded. Don't confuse block-style with creamy fresh mozzarella, which is usually packed in whey or water, or shrink-wrapped.

PARMESAN
True Parmigiano-Reggiano is a cow's-milk cheese made in Northern Italy by strictly governed methods that have been around for 800 years. We love its buttery, nutty flavor and crystalline texture, a product of up to two years of aging. (American Parmesans are younger and use different rennet and pasteurized milk so may be sour, salty, and rubbery.)

RICOTTA
Fluffy, buttery, and slightly sweet, ricotta is versatile enough to use both in savory classics, like lasagna, and in desserts, such as cheesecake. Look for a brand of fresh ricotta that has no gums or stabilizers.

FETA
This salty, crumbly cheese often hails from Greece, where it must be made from at least 70 percent sheep's milk by law, but supermarket feta is often made elsewhere with cow's milk or goat's milk. To keep feta moist and fresh, store it in its brine.

BLUE CHEESE
Blue cheese is made by treating cow's-, goat's-, or sheep's-milk cheeses with a (harmless) mold. Bacteria grows in the ripening cheese, giving it a pungent, distinctive flavor and smell. Crumble and toss it in salads, stir it into dips, or mix it with softened butter and chives to melt over grilled steak or burgers. Blue cheese pairs well with grapes, apples, and pears.

FRESH GOAT CHEESE
Goat cheese is available fresh or aged, but fresh goat cheese is the soft cheese you often find in a log shape. Fresh goat cheese has a creamy, slightly grainy texture and an unmistakable tang. Avoid precrumbled cheeses; they tend to be chalky and dry.

SWISS CHEESE
Many Swiss cheeses you'll find in the supermarket are actually made in America. The real deal is Emmentaler Swiss cheese, which is nutty and complex when eaten out of hand and a classic for fondue. The holes, or "eyes," in Swiss cheese are formed when (good) bacteria release carbon dioxide as the cheeses age. Older cheeses have a stronger flavor—and larger eyes.

GRUYÈRE
Dense, creamy Gruyère, produced in France and Switzerland, is made from raw cow's milk and aged for about a year. Is has an assertively salty, nutty flavor. We like most every import; domestic Gruyères pale in comparison.

STORING CHEESES

The key to keeping cheese fresh for as long as possible is controlling moisture loss. If moisture evaporates too quickly, the cheese dries out; if it's trapped on the surface, it encourages mold. To find the best storage methods, we wrapped cheddar and Brie in a variety of materials and refrigerated them for one month, monitoring them for mold and dryness. We came away with the following recommendations.

In the Fridge: Allow Some Air

Wrapping cheese tightly in parchment (or waxed) paper and then loosely with aluminum foil mimics the two-ply construction of specialty cheese wraps. The paper allows the cheese to breathe, while the foil keeps out off-flavors from the refrigerator and prevents the cheese from drying out.

In the Freezer: Airtight Only

Conventional wisdom holds that cheese should never be frozen—but we found that almost any variety can be frozen for up to two months with no decline in quality. The trick is to wrap the cheese tightly in plastic wrap and then seal it in a zipper-lock bag (vacuum sealing is also a good option). Thaw it overnight in the fridge or for a few hours on the counter.

THE DIFFERENCE BETWEEN GRATING AND SHREDDING CHEESE

We consider grated cheese to be the delicate, tiny gratings of a hard cheese such as Parmesan or Pecorino Romano made with a rasp-style grater. The fluffy flecks easily incorporate into or disperse on top of foods. We consider shredded cheese to be the larger strands of semisoft block cheeses such as mozzarella, Monterey Jack, and cheddar made with the large holes of a box grater or a food processor. The large shreds are easy to sprinkle evenly, which promotes even melting.

A Shred of Advice

Because semisoft cheeses can often smear, break apart, and clog the holes of a grater when being shredded, we came up with this three-part fix:

1. Freeze the cheese for 30 minutes before grating to keep it firm while grating.
2. Use the large holes of a grater to prevent clumping.
3. Coat the face of the grater with vegetable oil spray to prevent sticking.

HOW CHEESE MELTS—OR DOESN'T

All cheeses can be categorized into two groups based on how they are coagulated: with acid (such as vinegar or lemon juice) or with an enzyme known as rennet (which can be either animal- or plant-derived).

Acid-coagulated cheeses (such as feta, ricotta, and fresh goat cheese) resist melting because the acid dissolves the calcium ions between the casein proteins and alters their electrical charge, both of which cause the proteins to link up tightly and clump. Heat then makes the proteins bond together even more tightly, which squeezes out the water and causes the cheese to dry out and stiffen.

Rennet-coagulated cheeses (such as cheddar, Monterey Jack, and mozzarella) melt in two stages: First, their fat globules change from solid to liquid, which makes the cheese more supple. Then, as the temperature continues to rise, the tightly bonded casein proteins loosen their grip on one another and the cheese flows like a thick liquid.

MEASURING CHEESE

We prefer to weigh cheese when cooking. You can use cup measures, but note that different graters will produce more or less volume from the same piece of cheese. To obtain the most accurate measure, cheese should be lightly packed into a measuring cup.

PARMESAN AND OTHER HARD CHEESES		
Fine holes of box grater	1 ounce =	½ cup
Rasp-style grater	1 ounce =	¾ cup
CHEDDAR, MOZZARELLA, AND OTHER SEMISOFT CHEESES		
Large holes of box grater	1 ounce =	¼ cup
BLUE CHEESE, FETA, AND GOAT CHEESE		
Crumbled by hand	1 ounce =	¼ cup

HOT TIP: GET SCRAPPY

Save the rinds of aged cheeses such as Parmesan, Pecorino Romano, or Gruyère and add them to a soup, stock, stew, or Sunday gravy to add body and flavor. Store them in a zipper-lock bag in the refrigerator or freezer.

BLOCK OR PRE-SHREDDED?

Most pre-shredded cheese contains anticaking agents such as cellulose powder (minuscule pieces of plant fiber) or cornstarch that can make the cheese stiff and dry, affecting its mouthfeel and meltability. For that reason, we usually like to buy a block or wedge of cheese and shred it ourselves. However, when cheese is used in smaller amounts or combined with other assertive ingredients, pre-shredded cheese can make a fine shortcut.

GETTING TO KNOW HERBS

Using fragrant, flavorful fresh herbs—whether delicate or hearty—can elevate your cooking. Here's what you need to know.

TWO BASIC CATEGORIES: HEARTY AND DELICATE

We classify most herbs as either hearty or delicate. These adjectives refer not only to their textural qualities (leaves that are sturdy and tough versus delicate and tender) but also to the strength or volatility of their flavor compounds; in general, volatile flavor compounds in hearty herbs are somewhat more heat-stable than those in delicate varieties. These categories also help clarify the best ways to prep, store, and cook most herbs.

HEARTY

Hearty herbs can be added to long-cooked foods at the beginning of cooking. We often add sprigs of rosemary or thyme to soups, stews, or braises and then remove them before serving.

HERB	DESCRIPTION
Marjoram	This potent, lightly spicy herb tastes like a mix of oregano (for which it is often mistaken) and juniper.
Oregano	Mediterranean oregano has a pleasantly perfume-y, musty, slightly spicy bite.
Rosemary	Piney and floral, a little goes a long way.
Thyme	Its distinct menthol flavor is slightly grassy.
Sage	These fuzzy leaves taste minty and musky.

DELICATE

Delicate herbs are most potent and fragrant with little to no cooking. Use them raw as a garnish or add them to dishes in the last moments on the heat.

HERB	DESCRIPTION
Basil	Genovese (or Italian) basil has a licorice flavor.
Chives	This tender herb is oniony and grassy.
Cilantro	It's aromatic and refreshing, with a peppery finish.
Dill	These feathery fronds have a bright, lemony flavor.
Mint	Both spearmint and peppermint, the two most common types of mint, feature a cooling, bright bite.
Parsley	These leaves are mildly astringent and pleasantly grassy-tasting.
Tarragon	It tastes of citrus and anise; a little goes a long way.

STORING FRESH HERBS

Short-Term
If you are lucky enough to obtain delicate herbs with the roots still attached, you can store them at room temperature in a glass with about an inch of water; change the water every day, and make sure the leaves are never submerged. Store all other herbs, both delicate and hearty, wrapped in damp paper towels in a plastic bag in the crisper drawer of the refrigerator. Using either method, the herbs should stay fresh for about a week (herbs with roots attached typically last a little longer).

Longer Storage
Freezing is an option, but delicate herbs will lose their bright color. That's why it's best to mix chopped delicate herbs with oil, which helps preserve their color, before freezing them. Pesto lovers, for instance, can puree fresh basil with oil and freeze the paste (portioning it in ice cube trays for freezing is a neat trick) for up to three months.

GUIDELINES FOR USING DRIED HERBS

Dried herbs are more convenient to use than fresh because they require no more prep than a twist of a lid. But they can add a dusty quality to recipes, especially when used to finish dishes. Here are some recommendations based on extensive testing in our kitchen.

1 Use in Long-Cooked Recipes
Only some dried herbs work well, mainly in recipes involving fairly long cooking times (20 minutes plus) and a good amount of moisture. Chili stands out as one dish that is better made with a dried herb (oregano) than with a fresh one. Dried rosemary, sage, and thyme also fare reasonably well in certain applications.

2 Avoid Some Dried Herbs
Those herbs that we consider delicate (basil, chives, and parsley) lose most of their flavor when dried; we prefer fresh forms of these herbs. Two herbs, tarragon and dill, fall into a middle category: They do add flavor in their dried form, but that flavor is more muted than that provided by other dried herbs.

3 Use Less than Fresh
Use one-third as much dried herbs as fresh, and add them early in the cooking process so they have time to soften.

4 Replace Frequently
Dried herbs lose their potency 6 to 12 months after opening; you can test dried herbs for freshness by rubbing them between your fingers—if they don't smell bright, throw them away and buy a new jar.

HOT TIP: MAKE FLAVORED VINEGAR

You can make flavorful herbed vinegars—and thus incredible vinaigrettes—by adding fresh herbs to distilled white vinegar, letting the mixture steep for two weeks, and then straining it.

DIY DRIED HERBS

The microwave, which quickly drives off water, is the fastest way to dry herbs.

Method Place hearty herbs in a single layer between two paper towels and microwave on high power for 1 to 3 minutes. When the leaves turn brittle and fall easily from the stems (a sure sign of dryness), they're done.

GETTING TO KNOW SPICES

When you hear "spice," you might immediately think of the earthy-toned ground spices sold in jars. Of course, those spices are ground from a particle bigger than themselves—whole spices, which are of different shapes and sizes as they come from various parts of plants. While there is no single definition for a spice and different resources categorize them in various ways, we're defining spices as anything from a plant that is dried and can flavor food.

SALT

Salt might not come from a plant, but we include this mineral because it's a primary—actually, the most essential—seasoning of food. It can come from salt mines or from evaporating sea water. While gourmet shops and supermarkets carry a staggering array of salts from all corners of the globe, there are really just three types of salt. What distinguishes one salt from another is texture, shape, and mineral content.

Salt Measure Conversions

We develop our recipes with Diamond Crystal kosher salt; if you're using Morton kosher salt, which is denser than Diamond Crystal, note that
3 teaspoons Diamond Crystal kosher salt =
2¼ teaspoons Morton kosher salt =
1½ teaspoons table salt.

What to Salt

We salt proteins knowing we'll let them sit so the moisture that's drawn out enters the meat again. We presalt vegetables, however, for a different reason. Sure, salting seasons them, but for ultrawatery vegetables such as cabbage, cucumbers, and tomatoes, we often want to get rid of that moisture for good so it doesn't lead to soggy salads and slaws or diluted dressings. Since it's so abundant, all that released water can just drain away or be blotted off. See page 102 for more information.

For eggplant, we often salt it before cooking (see page 137). Eggplant is chock-full of air pockets and water; when you cook it in oil without removing some of that water beforehand, the air sacs absorb the oil, which can turn the eggplant unpleasantly greasy. Tossing eggplant with salt pulls water out from inside the eggplant via osmosis, which in turn collapses some of the eggplant's cells, reducing the amount of air pockets so the eggplant absorbs less oil.

TABLE SALT
Fine-grain table salt, also known as common salt, can be used in most applications. It dissolves quickly and easily, making it especially great for baking or using in a brine.

KOSHER SALT
Kosher salt crystals are larger than those of table salt, making them easier to sprinkle over foods before cooking. Kosher salt is tops for seasoning meat in advance of cooking to promote tenderness.

SEA SALT
Sea salt can be purchased as fine grains, crystals, or flakes. There are tiny differences in flavor from brand to brand, and some have a welcome briny taste from the sea. Crystal size and "crunch" can also vary. For this reason, we suggest using sea salt for sprinkling as an at-table condiment.

PEPPER

We do not recommend buying ground pepper. The aroma and flavor of black peppercorns start to fade as soon as the shell of peppercorns is cracked open, so buy whole peppercorns and grind them as you use them for the freshest flavor. Replacing your pepper shaker with a good pepper mill is one of the simplest ways to enhance your cooking. Peppercorns come in different colors and have different effects and levels of spiciness.

BLACK PEPPERCORNS

Black pepper is the everyday pepper and is used in almost every dish. Black peppercorns have complexity and depth from sun-drying and add heat and sharp bite. Our favorite black peppercorns are Tone's Whole Black Peppercorns.

How to Crack Peppercorns

Cracked peppercorns should be about half the size of whole ones. In some elegant applications, when the texture of the pepper is of supreme importance, the inevitable dusty matter is sifted through a fine-mesh strainer and discarded.

To crack, rock bottom edge of skillet over 2 tablespoons peppercorns on cutting board until they crack; repeat as needed.

Pep Up—or Tone Down—Your Pepper

When exactly you apply black pepper to meat—before or after searing—will affect the strength of its bite. If you want assertive pepper flavor, season meat after searing since keeping the pepper away from the heat will preserve its volatile compounds. Alternatively, seasoning before cooking will tame pepper's punch.

5 SPICES TO LOVE

There are certain spices that are used over and over again in savory recipes. We recommend having these on hand, along with salt and pepper.

CAYENNE PEPPER

This spice usually contains not only fiery red cayenne pepper, but also a variety of other ground dried chiles. We use it to add kick to food or to enhance other flavors. The peppers are also sold fresh or dried.

CORIANDER

Coriander appears in a huge variety of recipes, from meat-heavy stews to spicy seafood dishes. The light brown spherical seeds are the dried fruits of the coriander plant, which cilantro also comes from. Coriander possesses a sweet, almost fruity flavor with just a hint of the soapy-metallic character of mature cilantro. Coriander seeds can be toasted to enhance their flavor.

CUMIN

Cumin's earthy, warm flavor pairs well with many ingredients, from fresh vegetables to roast chicken. When possible, buy whole seeds and grind them yourself; the flavor is more potent.

PAPRIKA

"Paprika" is a generic term for a spice made from ground dried red peppers. Whether paprika is labeled sweet, smoked, or hot is determined by the variety (or varieties) of pepper used and how the pepper is manipulated. Sweet paprika is the most common. Typically made from a combination of mild red peppers, it is prized for its deep scarlet hue.

RED PEPPER FLAKES

Red pepper flakes are just dried and crushed red chile peppers. Unlike cayenne pepper, red pepper flakes do not make every bite of a dish hot and spicy. They add another level of flavor to pasta sauces or roasted vegetables.

SPICE SMARTS

- Spices start losing flavor as soon as you grind them, so buy them whole, not preground, whenever possible, and grind them just before using, either with a small coffee grinder or a mortar and pestle.
- Label your dried herbs and spices with the purchase date and then regularly purge your pantry of jars that are more than 12 months old. Store in a cool, dark place to prolong freshness.
- Bulk spices aren't necessarily the freshest, but they can be useful if you need just a tiny amount of a very particular spice for one recipe.

SEASON FROM ON HIGH

Ever notice that some chefs season food by sprinkling it from a good foot above the counter? Is this just kitchen theatrics or is there a reason for the practice? We sprinkled chicken breasts with salt and pepper (so we could see the seasoning) from different heights—4 inches, 8 inches, and 12 inches—and found the higher the starting point, the more evenly distributed the salt and pepper, which means better-tasting food.

GETTING TO KNOW SPICES (CONTINUED)

SPICE BLENDS AND PASTES

Most cuisines around the world have characteristic spice mixes that serve as a great starting point or finishing touch to many flavorful recipes. They are easy to make yourself and taste much better than store-bought. Here are recipes for some of our favorite ones (and see page 352 for a few more), all of which are used in the book.

PISTACHIO DUKKAH

Makes: about ½ cup
Total Time: 10 minutes

Egyptian dukkah blends vary in ingredients and can provide different flavor profiles. This blend is warmly spiced and delightfully coarse and nutty from the finely chopped pistachios.

- 1½ teaspoons coriander seeds, toasted
- ¾ teaspoon cumin seeds, toasted
- ½ teaspoon fennel seeds, toasted
- 2 tablespoons sesame seeds, toasted
- 3 tablespoons shelled pistachios, toasted and chopped fine
- ½ teaspoon flake sea salt, such as Maldon
- ½ teaspoon pepper

Process coriander seeds, cumin seeds, and fennel seeds in spice grinder until finely ground, about 30 seconds. Add sesame seeds and pulse until coarsely ground, about 4 pulses; transfer to small bowl. Stir in pistachios, salt, and pepper. (Dukkah can be refrigerated for up to 3 months.)

RAS EL HANOUT

Makes: about ½ cup
Total Time: 15 minutes

This North African blend delivers complex flavor from a mix of warm spices. If you can't find Aleppo pepper, you can substitute ½ teaspoon paprika plus ½ teaspoon red pepper flakes.

- 16 cardamom pods
- 4 teaspoons coriander seeds
- 4 teaspoons cumin seeds
- 2 teaspoons anise seeds
- 2 teaspoons ground dried Aleppo pepper
- ½ teaspoon allspice berries
- ¼ teaspoon black peppercorns
- 4 teaspoons ground ginger
- 2 teaspoons ground nutmeg
- 2 teaspoons ground cinnamon

Process cardamom pods, coriander seeds, cumin seeds, anise seeds, Aleppo, allspice, and peppercorns in spice grinder until finely ground, about 30 seconds. Stir in ginger, nutmeg, and cinnamon. (Ras el hanout can be stored in airtight container for up to 1 month.)

ZA'ATAR

Makes: about ½ cup
Total Time: 10 minutes

Za'atar is an aromatic eastern Mediterranean spice blend that is used as both a seasoning and a condiment. The thyme gives it a round herbal flavor, the sumac lemony tartness, and the sesame seeds richness and subtle crunch.

- ½ cup dried thyme
- 2 tablespoons sesame seeds, toasted
- 1½ tablespoons ground sumac

Working in batches, process thyme in spice grinder until finely ground, about 30 seconds; transfer to small bowl. Stir in sesame seeds and sumac. (Za'atar can be stored in airtight container for up to 3 months.)

HARISSA

Makes: about 1 cup
Total Time: 15 minutes

Making harissa involves steeping spices in oil, but the product is more of a chile sauce or paste. If you can't find Aleppo pepper, you can substitute 1½ teaspoons paprika and 1½ teaspoons finely chopped red pepper flakes.

- ¾ cup extra-virgin olive oil
- 12 garlic cloves, minced
- ¼ cup paprika
- 2 tablespoons ground coriander
- 2 tablespoons ground dried Aleppo pepper
- 2 teaspoons ground cumin
- 1½ teaspoons caraway seeds
- 1 teaspoon table salt

Combine all ingredients in bowl and microwave until bubbling and very fragrant, about 1 minute, stirring halfway through microwaving. Let cool completely before serving. (Harissa can be refrigerated for up to 4 days. Bring to room temperature before serving.)

GARAM MASALA

Makes: about ½ cup
Total Time: 10 minutes

The warm, floral, and earthy flavor profile of garam masala ("warm spice blend") makes it a welcome addition to most curries or a great seasoning for meat.

- 3 tablespoons black peppercorns
- 8 teaspoons coriander seeds
- 4 teaspoons cardamom pods
- 2½ teaspoons cumin seeds
- 1½ (3-inch) cinnamon sticks

Process all ingredients in spice grinder until finely ground, about 30 seconds. (Garam masala can be stored in airtight container for up to 1 month.)

FIVE-SPICE POWDER

Makes: about ¼ cup
Total Time: 10 minutes

Five-spice powder has a kick that offsets richness in both sweet and savory recipes. In traditional Chinese cooking, the five elements of the cosmos—earth, fire, metal, water, and wood—are represented by five-spice powder.

- 5 teaspoons fennel seeds
- 4 teaspoons white peppercorns or 8 teaspoons Sichuan peppercorns
- 1 tablespoon whole cloves
- 8 star anise pods
- 1 (3-inch) cinnamon stick, broken into pieces

Process fennel seeds, peppercorns, and cloves in spice grinder until finely ground, about 30 seconds; transfer to small bowl. Process star anise and cinnamon in now-empty spice grinder until finely ground, about 30 seconds; transfer to bowl with other spices and stir to combine.

SHICHIMI TOGARASHI

Makes: about ½ cup
Total Time: 10 minutes

This Japanese seven-spice blend is pungent and spicy from chile heat, aromatic from additional spices, and fragrant from orange zest, which we microwave to dry. This complexity makes basic noodle dishes utterly intriguing and the spice really heats up a dish.

- 1½ teaspoons grated orange zest
- 4 teaspoons sesame seeds, toasted
- 1 tablespoon paprika
- 2 teaspoons pepper
- ½ teaspoon garlic powder
- ½ teaspoon ground ginger
- ¼ teaspoon cayenne pepper

Microwave orange zest in small bowl, stirring occasionally, until dry and no longer clumping together, about 2 minutes. Stir in sesame seeds, paprika, pepper, garlic powder, ginger, and cayenne. (Shichimi togarashi can be stored in airtight container for up to 1 week.)

SAUCES 101

Few things can transform a dish from simple to spectacular as quickly and as easily as a great sauce. But so many home cooks think of sauce as something to be feared or revered—something better left to the professionals. In this book, we help you bring simple, straightforward sauces to your table so you can add more flavor to your meals.

THE WHO'S WHO OF SAUCES

The definition of "sauce" can include not only classics such as hollandaise and pan sauces, but also things like vinaigrettes, pestos, and relishes. Here are some examples:

VINAIGRETTES
Oil meets vinegar—and with just a little coercion, they do mix. See pages 152–155.

DRESSINGS
Any sauce you put on salad. See pages 172–173.

RELISHES
Chunky sauces made with fruits, vegetables, and/or aromatics.

SALSAS
Relishes, in Mexican cuisine (they're not all spicy). See page 31.

HOLLANDAISE
The embodiment of indulgence: egg yolks, butter, and a squeeze of fresh lemon juice. See page 354.

YOGURT SAUCES
Cool, creamy, tangy sauces you'll want to put on everything. See pages 31 and 354.

HERB SAUCES
Sauces based on herbs add vibrant flavor and some color to just about anything. See page 353.

PESTOS
When it comes to these herb-based purees, basil is only the beginning. See pages 254–255.

TOMATO SAUCES
Pasta's perfect match can be made with fresh or canned tomatoes. See pages 246–248.

PAN SAUCES
Searing something? These put the flavorful browned bits in the pan to work. See pages 418–419.

MAKING THE MOST OF SAUCES

A sauce can instantly transform a dish from boring to best in show. Here are some of our favorite ways to use some of the sauces in the book.

1 Toss a pesto (see pages 254–255), Salsa Verde (page 353), or Harissa (page 29) with boiled sliced potatoes for an instant potato salad.

2 Drizzle a pesto (see pages 254–255) or Harissa (page 29) onto soups.

3 Spoon pretty much any sauce on top of roasted or grilled poultry, meat, or seafood, or brush onto roasted, grilled, or steamed vegetables.

4 Combine a pesto (see pages 254–255), Salsa Verde (page 353), or Harissa (page 29) with mayonnaise and sour cream to make a dip for crudités or potato chips. (Cherry Tomato Salsa, Lemon-Yogurt Sauce, Chipotle Mayonnaise, and Cilantro-Mint Chutney all make great dips as is.)

5 Spread a pesto (see pages 254–255) or Chipotle Mayonnaise onto sandwiches.

6 Toss any cooked vegetables—Roasted Carrots (page 126) and Crisp Roasted Potatoes (page 116) would both be great—with a pesto (see pages 254–255), Harissa (page 29), Salsa Verde (page 353), or Cilantro-Mint Chutney. Or dollop with Lemon-Yogurt Sauce or Chipotle Mayonnaise.

7 Use a pesto (see pages 254–255), Salsa Verde (page 353), or Cilantro-Mint Chutney to flavor fresh cheeses such as mozzarella or ricotta—or add to a cheese plate.

8 Top grilled or toasted bread with a pesto (see pages 254–255), Cherry Tomato Salsa, or Salsa Verde (page 353) for a quick bruschetta appetizer.

BACK-POCKET SAUCES

Here are four easy fresh and flavorful sauces that you can whip up anytime.

CHERRY TOMATO SALSA

Makes: about 1 cup
Total Time: 10 minutes

Combine 6 ounces quartered cherry tomatoes, 1 tablespoon extra-virgin olive oil, 1 tablespoon minced fresh cilantro, and 1½ teaspoons lime juice in bowl and season with salt and pepper to taste. (Salsa can be refrigerated for up to 24 hours.)

LEMON-YOGURT SAUCE

Makes: about 1 cup
Total Time: 40 minutes

Use whole-milk yogurt or low-fat yogurt in this recipe (not nonfat).

Whisk 1 cup plain yogurt, 1 tablespoon minced fresh mint, 1 teaspoon grated lemon zest, 2 tablespoons lemon juice, and 1 minced garlic clove together in bowl until combined. Season with salt and pepper to taste. Let sit until flavors meld, about 30 minutes. (Sauce can be refrigerated for up to 2 days.)

CHIPOTLE MAYONNAISE

Makes: about ½ cup
Total Time: 10 minutes, plus 1 hour chilling

You can vary the spiciness of this sauce by adjusting the amount of chipotle.

Whisk 3 tablespoons mayonnaise, 3 tablespoons sour cream, 2 tablespoons minced canned chipotle chile in adobo sauce, 1 minced garlic clove, and ⅛ teaspoon table salt together in small bowl. Cover and refrigerate for at least 1 hour. (Sauce can be refrigerated for up to 24 hours.)

CILANTRO-MINT CHUTNEY

Makes: about 1 cup
Total Time: 10 minutes

Combine 2 cups fresh cilantro leaves, 1 cup fresh mint leaves, ⅓ cup plain whole-milk yogurt, ¼ cup finely chopped onion, 1 tablespoon lime juice, 1½ teaspoons sugar, ½ teaspoon ground cumin, and ¼ teaspoon table salt in food processor. Process until smooth, about 20 seconds, scraping down sides of bowl as needed. (Chutney can be refrigerated for up to 2 days.)

HOW TO SEASON FOOD

You can follow a recipe to the letter and still end up with food that doesn't taste quite right to you; everyone's palate is different. We have tastebuds for salty, sweet, bitter, sour, and savory (or umami) distributed all over our tongues and the rest of our mouths. Thanks to genetic variation, different individuals taste things differently, so what the recipe developer thought was perfect may not be your cup of tea. It's important to understand how to make seasoning work for you.

While adding salt and pepper "to taste" is almost always the final step of a recipe, you can also use a whole range of other ingredients to bring a dish into balance. Just a small quantity of one of these finishing touches (from a pinch to ½ teaspoon) is a good starting place.

SALTINESS
Salt, soy sauce, fish sauce, feta cheese, Parmesan

WHAT IT DOES	SUGGESTED USES
Adds depth and offsets sweetness; tempers acidity and bitterness	Chocolate desserts, soups and stews, pasta, grains, fruit salads, dipping sauces

SWEETNESS
Granulated or brown sugar, honey, maple syrup, mirin, sweet wine or liqueur, jam or jelly

WHAT IT DOES	SUGGESTED USES
Rounds out sharp, bitter, or salty flavors	Salsas, sauces, bitter greens, vinaigrettes, relishes

SOURNESS
Vinegar, citrus juice, pickled vegetables (such as jalapeños)

WHAT IT DOES	SUGGESTED USES
Adds brightness to flat-tasting dishes, cuts through richness or sweetness	Meaty stews and soups, creamy sauces and condiments, braised or roasted meats

BITTERNESS
Dry or prepared mustard, beer, fresh ginger, chili powder, unsweetened cocoa powder, dark chocolate, horseradish, cayenne pepper, coffee, citrus zest

WHAT IT DOES	SUGGESTED USES
Cuts sweetness	Barbecued meats, slaws, chopped salads, chili

UMAMI
Worcestershire sauce, soy sauce, fish sauce, miso, Parmesan cheese, anchovies, tomato paste, mushrooms, sherry

WHAT IT DOES	SUGGESTED USES
Adds meatiness, depth, or earthiness; boosts dishes that taste a bit flat	Bolognese or other meaty sauces, hearty vegetarian sauces, soups, deli sandwich fillings such as tuna salad

RICHNESS
Heavy cream, butter, olive oil

WHAT IT DOES	SUGGESTED USES
Rounds out flavors, adds viscosity	Lean vegetable-based soups, sauces

HEAT
Dried chiles, fresh chiles

WHAT IT DOES	SUGGESTED USES
Adds heat and flavor	Chilis, enchiladas, sauces, stir-fries, tacos

5 EYE-OPENING PRINCIPLES OF HOW FLAVOR WORKS

1 Cold Dulls Flavor
The microscopic receptors in your tastebuds are extremely temperature-sensitive. They work much better at warmer temperatures than at cooler ones; when you eat cold food, they barely open, minimizing flavor perception. However, when food is hot, their sensitivity increases more than a hundredfold, making food taste way more flavorful. Cold food also has fewer aromas, which makes them taste less flavorful. So, dishes meant to be served hot should be reheated, and dishes served chilled must be aggressively seasoned to make up for the flavor-dulling effects of cold temperatures.

2 Fat Carries Flavor
Fat is not only an efficient carrier of flavor, it also dissolves flavor components, carrying them into sauce and other surrounding ingredients. Some meat scientists claim that if you removed all of the fat from meat you could not tell the difference between, say, pork and beef because so many of the flavor components reside in the fat. Fat also gives flavors roundness and, by coating your mouth, lets you savor them. This is why adding a fat (such as butter, sour cream, cheese, or oil) to an overly spicy dish can help counteract the offending ingredient and balance out the flavors.

3 Brown Is the Color of Flavor
Whether from the caramelization of sugars or the browning of proteins—a process known as the Maillard reaction—when a food turns brown during cooking, that indicates chemical changes that cause the development of tons of new flavor, color, and aroma compounds.

4 Flavor Changes over Time
Have you ever noticed how some soups and stews taste better the day after you make them? In addition to the changes that occur with temperature, there are many other chemical reactions that continue to take place after cooking ends. The sugars in dairy break down, the carbohydrates in onions develop into sugars, the starches in potatoes convert into flavorful compounds, and you end up with a deeper, more richly flavored dish. Flavors that may seem harsh at first, such as those of chile peppers, mellow with time. If a recipe specifically calls for you to let the dish sit so the flavors can meld, do it; it will result in a more balanced dish.

5 Salt Is Magic
Salt may well be the most important ingredient in cooking. It is one of our five basic tastes and it adds an essential depth of flavor to food. Salt also has the ability to change the molecular makeup of food and is used to preserve and to add moisture to meat. For more information, see pages 26 and 343.

---

5 NEVER-FAIL STRATEGIES FOR MAKING FOOD TASTE BETTER

1 Spice Up Spices
To intensify the flavor of preground spices, cook them briefly in a little butter or oil before adding liquid to the pan. If the recipe calls for sautéing aromatics, add the spices to the pan when the aromatics are nearly cooked.

2 Make Nuts Nuttier
Toasting nuts brings out their aromatic oils, contributing a stronger, more complex flavor and aroma. See page 614 for more information.

3 Be the Sauce Boss
Almost any dish can be improved with the addition of a sauce. Sauce is your secret weapon: Dollop it on vegetables, drizzle it on steak, or smear it on a sandwich. See some of our favorites on pages 30–31.

4 Add Just a Spoonful of Sugar
Browned food tastes better, and the best way to accelerate browning is with a pinch of sugar sprinkled on lean proteins (such as chicken and seafood) or over vegetables before sautéing.

5 Finish with Acid and Herbs
One of the easiest fixes for a dish that needs a little more life is a dash of brightness from something acidic, such as lemon juice or vinegar, and a sprinkle of freshness from minced herbs.

BASIC FOOD SAFETY

ANATOMY OF YOUR REFRIGERATOR

Your refrigerator is more than a box of cold air. There are actually different microenvironments inside a refrigerator, and understanding how they work can help you use the various zones to your advantage and keep your meat, dairy, and produce fresh and flavorful.

Ⓐ Cold Zone
BACK, TOP TO BOTTOM

The area of the shelves at the back of the fridge (and the bottom of the door) are normally the coldest areas (around 33 degrees). Meat, dairy, and produce that are not prone to chilling injury (apples, cherries, grapes) should be stored in these areas. This is also the best place for prepared foods and leftovers.

Ⓑ Moderate Zone
FRONT, TOP TO BOTTOM

The areas at the front of the refrigerator, from the top to the bottom shelves, are generally moderate, with temperatures above 37 degrees. Put eggs, butter, and fruits and vegetables that are sensitive to chilling injury (berries, citrus, corn on the cob, melons) in this area. This also includes the top shelves on the door, which can be warmer and should therefore be reserved for items such as beverages and condiments.

Ⓒ Humid Zone
CRISPER DRAWER

The crisper drawer provides a humid environment that helps keep produce with a high water content (artichokes, asparagus, beets, broccoli, cabbage, carrots, cauliflower, celery, chiles, cucumbers, eggplant, fresh herbs, green beans, leafy greens, leeks, lettuce, mushrooms, peppers, radishes, scallions, summer squash, turnips, zucchini) from shriveling and rotting. However, if the humidity is too high, water can accumulate and hasten spoilage. You can regulate the humidity by adjusting the vents; the more cold air that is let in, the less humid the environment will be. (If your crisper doesn't have a slide control, it is always at the highest humidity level of which it is capable.)

WHAT NOT TO STORE IN THE FRIDGE

Some produce is sensitive to chilling injury and should be stored **on the counter**.

Avocados*, Eggplant, Tomatoes*, Apricots, Bananas*, Kiwis*, Mangos, Nectarines, Papayas, Peaches, Pears, Pineapples, Plums

*Once ripe, these can be refrigerated to avoid overripening. Some discoloration may occur.

Some produce also needs to be kept **away from light and heat**. Store these at cool room temperature in a basket or other ventilated container.

Garlic, Onions, Potatoes, Shallots, Sweet Potatoes, Winter Squash

Storing bread in the refrigerator may seem like a good idea, but the cold speeds up the staling process. We store bread on the counter or in a bread box; otherwise we freeze it. The same is true for most baked goods.

FOOD SAFETY IN 10 EASY STEPS

Food safety may seem like a drag, but it can be a matter of life and death—or at least, life and extreme gastrointestinal discomfort. Luckily, it's actually pretty easy to keep your kitchen clean and safe. Most of our cleaning protocols are based on the judicious application of hot water, soap, and the occasional splash of bleach solution. Following basic sanitation practices can dramatically reduce the risk of foodborne illness for you and everyone else you're feeding.

1 Wash Your Hands

Washing your hands is one of the best (and easiest) ways to stop the spread of foodborne pathogens that can make you sick. Wash before and during cooking, especially after touching raw meat or poultry. The U.S. Food and Drug Administration (FDA) recommends washing for at least 20 seconds in warm, soapy water, i.e., for at least the length of the Happy Birthday song. So get scrubbing (and singing).

2 Sanitize Your Sink

Studies have found that the kitchen sink is crawling with even more bacteria than the garbage bin. The faucet handle, which can reintroduce bacteria to your hands after you've washed them, is a close second. Though we've found that hot, soapy water is amazingly effective at eliminating bacteria, for added insurance you should clean these areas frequently with a solution of 1 tablespoon bleach per quart of water.

3 Clean Your Gear

In terms of bacteria, your sponge is right up there with your sink. A wet sponge is an ideal host for bacteria, so whenever possible, use a paper towel or dishcloth instead. If you do use a sponge, disinfect it. Microwaving and boiling are effective ways to clean a sponge but since sponges have been known to catch fire in high-powered microwaves, we prefer to boil them for 5 minutes. Cutting boards are another key location for bacteria in the kitchen. We have found that cutting boards of all materials are best cleaned by a thorough scrub with hot, soapy water.

4 Season Safely

Though most bacteria can't live for more than a few minutes in direct contact with salt, it can live on the edges of a box or shaker. To avoid contamination, grind pepper into a clean small bowl and then mix it with salt. You can reach into the bowl for seasoning without washing your hands every time. At the end of meal prep, discard any leftover seasoning and wash the bowl.

5 Separate Raw and Cooked Foods

Keep raw and cooked foods separate to prevent the spread of bacteria. Never place cooked food on a plate or cutting board that came into contact with raw food (meat or not), and wash any utensil (including a thermometer) that comes in contact with raw food before reusing it.

6 Put Up Barriers

Items that come in contact with both raw and cooked food, such as scales and platters, should be covered with aluminum foil or plastic wrap to create a protective barrier. Once the item has been used, the protective layer should be discarded—taking any bacteria with it. Similarly, wrapping your cutting board with plastic wrap before pounding meat and poultry on it will limit the spread of bacteria.

7 Don't Rinse Raw Meat and Poultry

Avoid rinsing raw meat and poultry. Contrary to what some cookbooks might advise, rinsing is more likely to spread contaminants around your sink than send them down the drain. Cooking food to a safe internal temperature will kill surface bacteria more effectively than rinsing, and we've found no difference in flavor between rinsed and unrinsed meat.

8 Defrost in the Fridge

Always defrost meat and other proteins in the refrigerator. On the counter, the temperature is higher and bacteria multiply rapidly. Place food on a plate or in a bowl to collect any liquid it releases. Most food will take 24 hours to thaw. (Larger items, such as whole turkeys, can take far longer, about 6 hours per pound.)

9 Cool on the Counter

Don't put hot food in the fridge right away. This will cause the temperature in the refrigerator to rise, potentially making it hospitable to the spread of bacteria. The FDA recommends cooling foods to 70 degrees within the first 2 hours after cooking, and to 40 degrees within another 4 hours. We cool food on the counter for about an hour and then put it in the fridge.

10 Reheat Rapidly

When food is reheated, it should be brought through the danger zone (the temperature range from 40 to 140 degrees, where bacteria thrive) as rapidly as possible—don't let it come slowly to a simmer. Bring leftover sauces, soups, and gravies to a boil and make sure casseroles reach at least 165 degrees.

BASIC MEASURING SKILLS

HOW TO MEASURE

Accurate measuring is often the difference between success and failure in the kitchen. In an ideal world, everyone would measure all ingredients by weight at all times. But even though weight is a more accurate way to measure than volume, we know that most cooks rely on measuring cups and spoons, not scales, so here are some ways to increase your accuracy when using volume measures. Our biggest piece of advice: Don't use liquid and dry measuring cups interchangeably—if you do, your ingredient amounts may be significantly off.

MEASURING DRY INGREDIENTS

For absolute accuracy, always weigh flour and sugar when baking. Otherwise, for dry ingredients we recommend the "dip and sweep" method, which reliably yields a 5-ounce cup of all-purpose flour and a 7-ounce cup of granulated sugar. Dip the measuring cup into the container and scoop up the ingredient in a heaping mound. Use a straight edge, like the back of a knife, to sweep the excess back into the container. We also use dip and sweep with measuring spoons when meting out small amounts of dry ingredients such as baking powder.

MEASURING LIQUID INGREDIENTS

For liquid ingredients, use a liquid measuring cup set on the counter and lean down to read the measurement at eye level. Make sure the meniscus—the bottom of the curved surface line of the liquid—aligns with the measurement you're aiming for. When emptying the cup, use a rubber spatula to scrape it clean.

MEASURING IN-BETWEEN INGREDIENTS

For sticky and/or semisolid ingredients such as mayonnaise, peanut butter, sour cream, and honey, we prefer an adjustable measuring cup. An adjustable measuring cup has a clear cylinder with volume markings and a plunger insert. You withdraw the plunger to the desired measurement and then fill the cylinder, level it off, and plunge to empty it. This design makes it easy to push out every last bit of the ingredient. If you don't own an adjustable measuring cup, a dry measuring cup is the next most consistent tool.

MEASURING BROWN SUGAR

Brown sugar is clumpy, so it must be packed into a measuring cup to get an accurate reading. To do this, use your fingers or the bottom of a smaller cup to press the sugar into the measuring cup.

36 | The New Cooking School Cookbook: Fundamentals

WHEN TO MEASURE

In addition to how you measure, it matters when you measure. For instance, "1 cup walnuts, chopped" is not the same as "1 cup chopped walnuts." In the first example, the cook should measure out the whole walnuts and then chop them. In the second example, the cook should chop first, and then measure out a cup of the already-chopped walnuts. One cup of unchopped walnuts weighs 4 ounces, while one cup of chopped walnuts weighs 4.8 ounces—that's 20 percent more nuts. Apply this principle to other ingredients (such as "sifted flour" versus "flour, sifted") and you can see how this makes a significant difference in the final outcome of a recipe.

WHETHER TO WEIGH

A digital scale is critical for baking recipes, where measuring dry ingredients by weight is the only way to truly guarantee accuracy. Our testing has found that there can be up to a 20 percent variance in the weight between cups of flour measured by different cooks using a dry measuring cup—a range that can mean the difference between a cake that's squat and dense and one that's fluffy and tender. Scales have many applications in cooking, too. Using one to portion burgers, for example, means no more guessing if the patties are the same size and will thus cook at the same rate. Weighing ingredients may sound like a chore but is actually easier than measuring by volume, especially with a hyperprecise digital scale.

WHEN IS FOOD DONE?

There's nothing like a spectacular kitchen failure featuring leathery meat, disintegrated vegetables, or, worse yet, billowing smoke to drive home the importance of timing in cooking. Don't just glance at the clock or assume your internal timekeeping will be reliable enough; always set a timer. You can get a special timer specifically designed for use in the kitchen, but you can also use a microwave timer, oven timer, or the timer on your phone; just make sure you have some way of keeping time. All that being said, don't rely solely on timing to guide your cooking—other types of cues are also incredibly important. And if a recipe presents a range of time for a step, always start checking for doneness at the early end of the range. Trust your senses and your common sense alongside your reading of the recipe.

Use Your Eyes
Food changes color and appearance as it cooks; the difference between a crisp-tender, bright green piece of perfectly cooked broccoli and a dull gray-green piece of overcooked broccoli is easy to see. And if you want your chicken to have good flavor, don't take it out of the pan until it is golden brown all over.

Use Your Nose
Many foods have a distinct aroma when they're done, such as toasted nuts, baked goods, or caramelized onions. And unless you're making a recipe that's purposefully blackened or charred, if you can smell something burning, you should check on it, even if the timer says you still have 20 minutes left.

Use a Thermometer—Especially for Meat
When it comes to final doneness, numbers don't lie; the best and most foolproof way to determine when food is done is to use a thermometer, not only for proteins but also bread and custardy desserts. A good one is vital for ensuring success in the kitchen. See page 14 for our brand recommendations.

Use a Paring Knife

The texture of most foods changes during cooking. In order to gauge these changes, use a sharp paring knife to test foods for doneness cues; do the potatoes yield easily or does the blade meet resistance? When you nick a piece of fish or thin cut of meat, is it still raw inside?

Use Downtime
Don't forget about the magic of carryover cooking and the importance of resting meat (see page 343 for more information). Finished food often needs to rest after cooking in order for temperatures to equalize, juices to redistribute, and ingredients to cool enough that you won't burn your mouth. Your food isn't really done until this step is.

BASIC KNIFE SKILLS

HOLDING A KNIFE

Much like gripping a baseball bat, how you hold a knife makes a difference in terms of control and force. And don't forget about the other hand—the one that holds the food securely in place while you cut. How you hold the food steady makes a big difference in terms of the safety of your fingertips.

CONTROL GRIP

For more control, choke up on the handle and actually grip the blade of the knife between your thumb and forefinger. This will be the most common grip you use for ingredient prep.

FORCE GRIP

Holding the knife on the handle allows you to use more force and is helpful when cutting through hard foods or bone. Most ingredients don't require that much force, however.

PROTECT YOUR FINGERTIPS

Use the "bear claw" grip to hold food in place and minimize danger. Tuck your fingertips in, away from the knife, and rest your knuckles against the blade. During the upward motion of slicing, reposition your guiding hand for the next cut.

MOVING A KNIFE

FOR SMALL ITEMS, KEEP THE TIP DOWN

To cut small items, push the blade forward and down, using its curve to make smooth strokes. With each cut, move the knife (not the food). The blade should touch the board at all times when cutting small food.

FOR LARGE ITEMS, LIFT BLADE UP

To cut large items, such as an eggplant, lift the entire blade off the board to help make smooth strokes.

FOR TOUGH ITEMS, USE THE HEEL

To cut through tough foods, use one hand to grip the handle and place your flat palm on top of the blade. Cut straight down, pushing the blade gently. Make sure your hand and the knife are both dry to prevent slippage.

KNOW YOUR CUTS

The language of cutting—chopping, dicing, mincing—can seem mystifying. What exactly is the difference? It may not seem like it would matter that much, but because cooking times are calibrated for ingredients cut to a particular size, food that's cut incorrectly won't cook right. Here are some explanations for a few common and sometimes confusing prep terms that you should know.

CHOPPED FINE / CHOPPED / CHOPPED COARSE

Chopping is the most general word for cutting food into small pieces, but the size designations have pretty specific meanings. "Chopped fine" corresponds to food cut into ⅛- to ¼-inch pieces, "chopped" into ¼- to ½-inch pieces, and "chopped coarse" into ½- to ¾-inch pieces.

DICED

We don't call for dicing ("chopped" works for us) but the term refers to food cut into uniform cubes, which can be large or small. Since most ingredients don't have right angles, not every piece will be a perfect cube.

MINCED

Minced ingredients are cut into ⅛-inch pieces or smaller; this is likely the smallest cut most recipes will call for. Pungent ingredients such as garlic and herbs are often minced to make them easier to evenly distribute throughout a dish.

SLICED

In general, slicing calls for cutting food into pieces with two flat edges (the thickness will depend on the recipe. Orb-shaped foods such as onions are difficult to slice whole because they do not sit on a flat side. Unless whole sliced onion rings are the goal, halve an onion pole to pole, peel it, sit it on a cut side, and slice.

MATCHSTICKS

Also known as "julienne," this refers to cutting food into matchstick-size pieces, ¼ inch thick (or less) and 2 inches long, unless otherwise specified. Start by cutting the ingredient into 2-inch-long segments, then cut each segment into ¼-inch-thick planks. Working with a few planks at a time, stack the planks and cut them into ¼-inch-thick matchsticks.

ON THE BIAS OR DIAGONAL

Cutting on the bias or diagonal means to cut across the food with the knife held at a 45-degree angle to the food. This cut is usually used for longer, slender items.

COOKING BASICS | 39

BASIC VEGETABLE AND FRUIT PREP

Whether you are simply steaming a vegetable, preparing a fruit salad, or making a more involved recipe, usually some basic prep is required. After years of peeling, seeding, coring, and chopping in the test kitchen, we've found the following methods are the easiest and most efficient ways to prepare a number of vegetables and fruits for myriad uses.

VEGETABLES

ASPARAGUS: TRIMMING

1. Remove one stalk of asparagus from the bunch and bend it at the thicker end until it snaps.

2. With the broken asparagus as a guide, trim the tough ends from the remaining asparagus bunch using a chef's knife.

AVOCADOS: CUTTING UP

1. After slicing the avocado in half around the pit with a chef's knife, lodge the edge of the knife blade into the pit and twist to remove.

2. Use a dish towel to hold the avocado steady. Make ½-inch crosshatch incisions in the flesh of each avocado half with a knife, cutting down to, but not through, the skin.

3. Insert a soupspoon between the skin and the flesh and gently scoop out the avocado cubes.

BELL PEPPERS: PREPARING

1. Slice off the top and bottom of the pepper and remove the seeds and stem.

2. Slice down through the side of the pepper.

3. Lay the pepper flat, trim away the remaining ribs and seeds, then cut the pepper into pieces or strips as desired.

BOK CHOY: PREPARING

1. Trim the bottom 1 inch from the head of bok choy. Wash and pat the leaves and stalks dry. Cut the leafy green portion away from either side of the white stalk.

2. Cut each white stalk in half lengthwise, then crosswise into thin strips.

3. Stack the leafy greens and slice crosswise into thin strips. Keep the sliced stalks and leaves separate.

BROCCOLI: CUTTING UP

1. Place the head of broccoli upside down on the cutting board and use a chef's knife to trim off the florets very close to the head. Cut the florets into 1-inch pieces.

2. After cutting away the tough outer peel of the stalk, square off the stalk, then slice it into ¼-inch-thick pieces.

CABBAGE: SHREDDING

1. Cut the cabbage into quarters, then trim and discard the hard core.

2. Separate the cabbage into small stacks of leaves that flatten when pressed.

3. Use a chef's knife to cut each stack of leaves into thin shreds (you can also use the slicing disk of a food processor to do this).

CARROTS: CUTTING ON BIAS AND INTO MATCHSTICKS

1. Slice the carrot on the bias into 2-inch-long oval-shaped pieces.

2. For matchsticks, lay the ovals flat on a cutting board, then slice the ovals into 2-inch-long matchsticks, about ¼ inch thick.

CAULIFLOWER: CUTTING UP

1. Pull off any leaves, then cut out the core of the cauliflower using a paring knife.

2. Separate the florets from the inner stem using the tip of a paring knife.

3. Cut larger florets into smaller pieces by slicing through the stem.

CHILES: STEMMING AND SEEDING

1. Using a sharp knife, trim and discard the stem end. Slice the chile in half lengthwise.

2. Use a spoon to scrape out the seeds and ribs (reserve if desired). Prepare the seeded chile as directed.

CORN: STRIPPING

After removing the husk and silk, stand the ear upright in a large bowl and use a paring knife to slice the kernels off of the cob.

CUCUMBERS AND ZUCCHINI: SEEDING

Halve the cucumber lengthwise. Run a spoon inside each half to scoop out the seeds.

FENNEL: PREPARING

1. Cut off the stems and fronds. Trim a thin slice from the base. Remove any tough or blemished outer layers from the bulb.

2. Cut the bulb in half through the base, then use a paring knife to remove the core.

3. Slice each half into thin strips, cutting from the base to the stem end.

GARLIC: MINCING

1. Trim off the root end, then crush the clove between the side of the knife and the cutting board to loosen and remove the skin.

2. Resting your fingers on top of the knife blade, use a rocking motion to mince the garlic, pivoting the knife as you work.

MINCING TO A PASTE

Sprinkle the minced garlic with salt, then scrape the blade of the knife back and forth over the garlic until it forms a sticky paste.

GINGER: PREPARING

1. To peel ginger, hold it firmly against the cutting board and use the edge of a dinner spoon to scrape away the skin.

2A. To grate ginger, peel the small section and then grate the peeled portion with a rasp-style grater.

2B. To mince ginger, slice the peeled ginger into thin rounds, cut the rounds into thin strips, and mince the strips.

GREEN BEANS: TRIMMING

Line the beans up on a cutting board and trim the ends with one slice.

HEARTY GREENS (SWISS CHARD, KALE, COLLARD GREENS): PREPARING

1. Cut away the leafy portion from the stalk or stem using a chef's knife.

2. Stack several leaves and either slice them crosswise or chop them into pieces according to the recipe.

3. If using chard stems, cut them into pieces as directed. (Discard collard and kale stems.)

LEEKS: PREPARING

1. Trim and discard the root and dark green leaves.

2. Cut the trimmed leek in half lengthwise, then slice it crosswise.

3. Rinse the cut leeks thoroughly using a salad spinner or bowl of water.

MUSHROOMS: PREPARING

1. Rinse mushrooms just before cooking. Or, if the mushrooms will be eaten raw, simply brush the dirt away with a soft pastry brush or cloth.

2. Tender white button and cremini stems can simply be trimmed. Tough, woody shiitake and portobello stems should be removed.

OLIVES: PITTING

Place the olive on cutting board and hold the flat edge of a knife over the olive. Press the blade firmly with your hand to loosen the olive meat from the pit.

ONIONS: CHOPPING

1. Halve the onion through the root end, and then peel and trim the top. Make several horizontal cuts from one end of the onion to the other but don't cut through the root end.

2. Make several vertical cuts. Be sure to cut up to but not through the root end.

3. Rotate the onion so the root end is in the back; slice the onion thinly across the previous cuts. As you slice, the onion will fall apart into chopped pieces.

POTATOES: CUTTING

1. Cut a thin sliver from one side of the potato to create a stable base. Set the potato on the cut side and slice it crosswise into even planks.

2. Stack several planks and cut them crosswise, then rotate 90 degrees and cut them crosswise again to create even pieces as directed in the recipe.

SNOW PEAS: TRIMMING

Use a paring knife and your thumb to snip off the tip of the pod and pull along the flat side to remove the string at the same time.

SCALLIONS: PREPARING

1. Trim off the end of the scallion and cut to separate the white and light green part from the darker green leaves.

2. Slice the white and green parts thin, on the bias, or into pieces as directed in the recipe

SHALLOTS: MINCING

1. Make closely spaced horizontal cuts through the peeled shallot, leaving the root end intact.

2. Next, make several vertical cuts through the shallot.

3. Finally, thinly slice the shallot crosswise, creating a fine mince.

TOMATOES: CORING AND DICING

1. Remove the core of the tomato using a paring knife.

2. Slice the tomato crosswise with a sharp chef's knife or serrated knife.

3. Stack several slices of tomato and then cut them into pieces as desired.

COOKING BASICS | 45

WINTER SQUASH (BUTTERNUT SQUASH): CUTTING UP

1. After peeling the squash, use a chef's knife to trim off the top and bottom and then cut the squash in half where the narrow neck and wide curved bottom meet.

2. Cut a strip from the neck to create a stable base. Set the neck on the base and cut it into planks, then into pieces. (Or halve the neck lengthwise and slice each into half moons.)

3. Cut the bottom of the squash in half lengthwise, and scoop out and discard the seeds and fibers. Slice each half into even lengths and then into pieces according to the recipe.

FRUITS

APPLE: CORING

1A. If you don't have a corer, cut the sides of the apple squarely away from the core. Cut each piece of apple into slices according to the recipe.

1B. Or, for less waste, cut the apple in half. Make diagonal slices with a paring knife partway into the apple half on either side of the core and remove it.

2. Place each piece on its flat side. Cut straight down to make slices or at an angle toward the center for wedges.

BERRIES: WASHING

1. Place the berries in a colander and rinse them gently under running water.

2. To dry, line a salad spinner with layers of paper towels and carefully disperse the berries. Spin gently until dry, about 20 seconds.

CHERRIES: PITTING

Using a cherry pitter, punch the stone from the flesh of the cherry.

CITRUS: SECTIONING

1. Cut a thin slice from the top and bottom of the fruit.

2. Use a sharp knife to slice off the rind, including the white pith, following the contours of the fruit.

3. Insert the blade of a paring knife between the membrane and section, and then slice to the center of the fruit. Turn the blade outward and then slice along the membrane on the other side until the section falls out.

ZESTING

Rub the fruit against the holes of a rasp-style grater, grating over the same area of the fruit only once or twice to avoid grating the bitter white pith beneath the skin.

CUTTING STRIPS OF ZEST

Use a vegetable peeler to cut a wide swath of peel, avoiding the white pith.

JUICING

1. Roll the fruit vigorously on a hard surface to tear the juice sacs for maximum extraction of juice.

2. Slice the fruit in half, then use a reamer or citrus juicer to extract the juice.

KIWI: PEELING

1. Trim the ends of the kiwi, then insert a small spoon between the skin and the flesh. Gently slide the spoon around the fruit, separating the flesh from the skin.

2. Pull the loosened skin away from the flesh, then chop or slice according to the recipe.

MANGO: CUTTING UP

1. Cut a thin slice from one end of the mango so it sits flat on the counter. Resting the mango on the trimmed end, cut off the skin in thin strips from top to bottom.

2. Cut down along each side of the flat pit to remove the flesh.

3. Trim around the pit to remove any remaining flesh. Chop or slice according to the recipe.

MELON: CUTTING UP

1. Trim off a small slice from each end of the melon so it sits flat on the counter.

2. Resting the melon on one end, carefully cut off the rind in sections from top to bottom.

3. Once the rind is removed, cut the melon into thick slices and then cut the slices into cubes.

PEACH (FREESTONE): HALVING AND PITTING

1. Cut the peach in half, pole to pole around the pit, using the crease in the peach skin as a guide.

2. Grasp both halves of the fruit and twist apart. Remove the pit.

PEAR: CORING

1. Use a melon baller to cut around the central core of the halved pear with a circular motion and remove the core.

2. Draw the melon baller from the central core to the top of the pear, removing the interior stem. Remove the blossom end.

PINEAPPLE: CUTTING UP

1. Trim off the bottom and top of the pineapple so it sits flat on the counter.

2. Rest the pineapple on the trimmed bottom and cut off the skin in thin strips from top to bottom.

3. Quarter the pineapple lengthwise, then cut the tough core from each quarter. Slice the pineapple according to the recipe.

RHUBARB: PEELING

1. Trim both ends of the stalk. Partially slice a thin disk from the bottom end, being careful not to cut through the stalk entirely. Pull the partially attached disk away from the stalk to remove the outer peel.

2. Make a second cut partway through the other end. Pull back the peel and discard. Slice or chop according to the recipe.

STRAWBERRIES: HULLING

A. Use the serrated tip of a grapefruit spoon to cut around the leafy stem and remove the white core and stem.

B. Alternately, push a plastic straw into the bottom of the berry and up through the leafy stem end to remove the core as well as the leafy top.

CHAPTER 2

EGGS AND TOFU

COURSES

54 MODERN SCRAMBLED EGGS

60 FRY AN EGG

64 HARD-COOKED AND SOFT-COOKED EGGS

68 POACHED EGGS

70 EGG SANDWICHES

74 PUT AN EGG IN IT

78 SIMPLE OMELETS AND FRITTATAS

82 LET'S MAKE TOFU

EGG BASICS

BUYING EGGS

When eggs are the focal point of a dish, their quality and size make a big difference. We use large eggs in all our recipes. But even beyond size, there are numerous—and often confusing—options when buying eggs at the supermarket. Here's what we've learned.

Farm Fresh and Organic

In our taste tests, farm-fresh eggs were standouts. The large yolks were bright orange and sat very high above the comparatively small whites, and the flavor of these eggs was exceptionally rich and complex. Organic eggs followed in second place, eggs from hens raised on a vegetarian diet in came in third, and standard supermarket eggs finished last. Tasters easily detected differences in egg-based dishes such as an omelet or a frittata but not in cakes or cookies.

Eggs and Omega-3s

Many companies market eggs with a high level of omega-3 fatty acids, the healthful unsaturated fats also found in some fish. In our taste test, we found that eggs with more omega-3s had a richer egg flavor and a deeper yolk color. Why? Commercially raised chickens usually peck on corn and soy, while chickens on an omega-3-enriched diet also eat greens, flaxseeds, and algae, which add flavor, complexity, and color to their eggs. Look for products that guarantee at least 200 milligrams of omega-3s per egg.

How Old Are My Eggs?

Egg cartons are marked with a sell-by date and a pack date. The pack date is the day the eggs were packed, which is generally within a week of when they were laid but may be as much as 30 days later. The sell-by date is within 30 days of the pack date, which is the legal limit set by the U.S. Department of Agriculture. A carton of eggs may be up to two months old by the sell-by date. But eggs are still fit for consumption for an additional three to five weeks past the sell-by date.

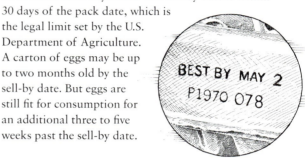

ANATOMY OF AN EGG

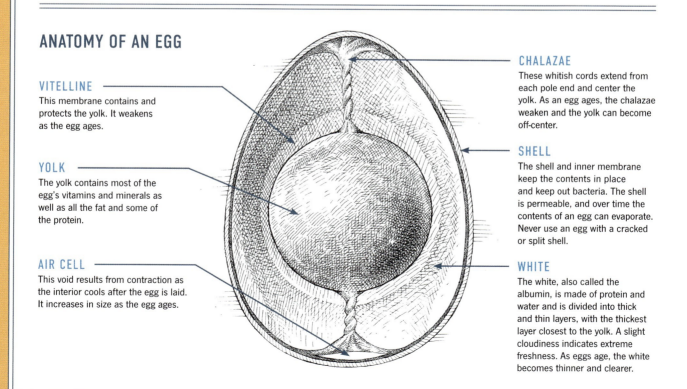

VITELLINE
This membrane contains and protects the yolk. It weakens as the egg ages.

YOLK
The yolk contains most of the egg's vitamins and minerals as well as all the fat and some of the protein.

AIR CELL
This void results from contraction as the interior cools after the egg is laid. It increases in size as the egg ages.

CHALAZAE
These whitish cords extend from each pole end and center the yolk. As an egg ages, the chalazae weaken and the yolk can become off-center.

SHELL
The shell and inner membrane keep the contents in place and keep out bacteria. The shell is permeable, and over time the contents of an egg can evaporate. Never use an egg with a cracked or split shell.

WHITE
The white, also called the albumin, is made of protein and water and is divided into thick and thin layers, with the thickest layer closest to the yolk. A slight cloudiness indicates extreme freshness. As eggs age, the white becomes thinner and clearer.

STORING EGGS

In the test kitchen, we've tasted two- and three-month-old eggs and found them perfectly palatable. However, at four months, the white was very loose and the yolk had off-flavors, though it was still edible. Our advice is to use your discretion; if eggs smell odd or are discolored, pitch them. Older eggs also lack the structure-lending properties of fresh eggs, so beware when baking.

In the Refrigerator

Eggs often suffer more from improper storage than from age. If your refrigerator has an egg tray in the door, don't use it—eggs should be stored on a shelf, where the temperature is below 40 degrees (the average refrigerator door temperature in our kitchen is closer to 45 degrees). Eggs are best stored in their cardboard or plastic carton, which protects them from absorbing flavors from other foods. The carton also helps maintain humidity, which slows down the evaporation of the eggs' moisture.

In the Freezer

Extra whites can be frozen for later use, but we have found their rising properties compromised. Frozen whites are best in recipes that call for small amounts (such as an egg wash) or don't depend on whipping (such as an omelet). Yolks can't be frozen as is, but adding sugar syrup (microwave 2 parts sugar to 1 part water, stirring occasionally, until the sugar is dissolved) to the yolks allows them to be frozen. Stir a scant ¼ teaspoon of sugar syrup per yolk into the yolks before freezing them. Defrosted yolks treated this way will behave just like fresh yolks in custards and other recipes.

Cold versus Room Temperature

Unless otherwise directed, you should keep eggs in the refrigerator until they are needed. However, some baking recipes call for room-temperature eggs. So when are room-temperature eggs essential?

In the test kitchen, we compared yellow cakes made with cold eggs against cakes made with room-temperature eggs and found both acceptable. Yes, the cake made with room-temperature eggs had a slightly finer, more even crumb, but the cake made with cold eggs was similar (although it did take an extra 5 minutes to bake). Cold eggs did cause a problem when we tested more-finicky recipes such as pound cake and chiffon cake. These recipes rely on air beaten into the eggs as a primary means of leavening. Cold eggs didn't whip as well as room-temperature eggs, and the resulting cakes baked up quite dense.

In sum, if a recipe says to use room-temperature eggs, there's probably a good reason. You can let eggs sit out on the counter for an hour, or you can speed up the process by placing the eggs in a bowl of warm water for about 5 minutes.

EGG SIZES

Eggs vary in size, and that variance can make a difference in recipes, especially those that call for several eggs. We call for large eggs in all our recipes, but you can substitute one size for another. For instance, four jumbo eggs is equivalent to five large eggs—each combination weighs a total of 10 ounces. This chart will help you make accurate calculations. For half an egg, whisk the yolk and white together, measure, and then divide the mixture in half.

LARGE		JUMBO	EXTRA-LARGE	MEDIUM
2 oz		2.5 oz	2.25 oz	1.75 oz
1	=	1	1	1
2	=	1½	2	2
3	=	2½	2½	3½
4	=	3	3½	4½
5	=	4	4	6
6	=	5	5	7

COURSE
MODERN SCRAMBLED EGGS

DAN SOUZA

Nothing cooks as quickly—and tastes so satisfying—as an egg. But sometimes the simplest things can be the hardest to get right. Scrambled eggs are a good example. A proper dish of tender, fluffy scrambled eggs requires attention to detail. That's why the right recipes and technique are so important. In this course you learn how to cook perfect scrambled eggs plain, made heartier with savory additions, and stir-fried with tomatoes.

DAN'S PRO TIP: *When it comes to scrambled eggs, everyone has their own definition of "perfect." Master the core tenets laid out here and you'll be able to adjust your technique with confidence to please even the pickiest eater.*

PERFECT SCRAMBLED EGGS

Serves: 4
Total Time: 10 minutes

RECIPE OVERVIEW Many people make the mistake of overcooking their scrambled eggs. To turn out rich and creamy—not dry and rubbery—scrambled eggs, we add a couple extra yolks and ¼ cup of half-and-half. This added fat prevents the eggs from overcooking, and seasoning the raw eggs with salt tenderizes them. To create large, even curds, we use a smaller (10-inch) nonstick skillet, which ensures a thicker layer of eggs. Stirring constantly (scraping along both the sides and bottom of the skillet) helps the eggs coagulate evenly, and dropping the heat partway through gives you more control over their doneness. To dress up the eggs, add 2 tablespoons of minced fresh parsley, chives, basil, or cilantro or 1 tablespoon of minced fresh dill or tarragon after reducing the heat to low.

- 8 large eggs plus 2 large yolks
- ¼ cup half-and-half
- ¼ teaspoon table salt
- ¼ teaspoon pepper
- 1 tablespoon unsalted butter, chilled

1. Adjust oven rack to middle position and heat oven to 200 degrees. Place 4 heatproof plates on rack.

2. Beat eggs and yolks, half-and-half, salt, and pepper with fork until thoroughly combined and mixture is pure yellow; do not overbeat.

3. Melt butter in 10-inch nonstick skillet over medium-high heat (butter should not brown), swirling skillet to coat. Add egg mixture and, using heat-resistant rubber spatula, constantly and firmly scrape along bottom and sides of skillet until eggs begin to clump and spatula leaves trail on bottom of skillet, 1½ to 2½ minutes. Reduce heat to low and gently but constantly fold eggs under and over until clumped and slightly wet, 30 to 60 seconds. Immediately transfer eggs to warmed plates and season with salt to taste. Serve immediately.

KEYS TO SUCCESS

- **Use a nonstick skillet:** Prevents eggs from sticking to pan
- **Use a fork:** Combines eggs more gently than a whisk or an egg beater
- **Add butter:** Contributes rich flavor
- **Scrape constantly:** Allows eggs to clump together
- **Start high, finish low:** Creates puffy curds and prevents overcooking

CORE TECHNIQUE Scrambling Eggs

BEAT LIGHTLY
Stop beating once large bubbles form.

LOWER HEAT
When your spatula just leaves a trail through the eggs, that's your cue to turn the heat to low.

COOK AND SCRAPE
Stir constantly to ensure that the eggs form large clumps and don't overbrown.

FORMULA FOR ONE TO FOUR SERVINGS OF SCRAMBLED EGGS

Half-and-half adds liquid that turns to steam when eggs are cooked, thus helping them cook into soft, fluffy mounds. You need 1 tablespoon of half-and-half for each serving of eggs. In addition to varying the amount of half-and-half to match the number of eggs, you will need to vary the amounts of seasonings and butter, the skillet size, and the cooking time. Here's how to do that.

SERVINGS	EGGS	HALF-AND-HALF	SEASONINGS	BUTTER	SKILLET SIZE	COOKING TIME
1	2 large, plus 1 yolk	1 tablespoon	pinch salt pinch pepper	¼ tablespoon	8 inches	30–60 seconds over medium-high, 30–60 seconds over low
2	4 large, plus 1 yolk	2 tablespoons	⅛ teaspoon salt ⅛ teaspoon pepper	½ tablespoon	8 inches	45–75 seconds over medium-high, 30–60 seconds over low
3	6 large, plus 1 yolk	3 tablespoons	¼ teaspoon salt ⅛ teaspoon pepper	¾ tablespoon	10 inches	1–2 minutes over medium-high, 30–60 seconds over low
4	8 large, plus 2 yolks	¼ cup	¼ teaspoon salt ¼ teaspoon pepper	1 tablespoon	10 inches	1½–2½ minutes over medium-high, 30–60 seconds over low

EGGS AND TOFU

SCRAMBLED EGGS WITH ASPARAGUS, SMOKED SALMON, AND CHIVES

Serves: 4
Total Time: 25 minutes

RECIPE OVERVIEW For hearty scrambled eggs, we have plenty of ideas for add-ins besides the usual ham and cheddar. To tenderize and lend richness to the eggs without adding moisture, skip dairy in favor of olive oil. Cooking the eggs quickly in more olive oil over medium-high heat and stirring constantly creates large curds. Folding in vegetables (previously cooked in the same skillet) once the curds are well established but still a little wet ensures that the eggs can set up around the vegetables and create a cohesive mixture. If you can't find thin asparagus spears, peel the bottom halves of thicker spears until the white flesh is exposed, and then halve each spear lengthwise before cutting it into ½-inch pieces. This recipe can easily be halved, if desired; use a 10-inch skillet.

- 8 large eggs
- 3 tablespoons extra-virgin olive oil, divided
- 2 tablespoons minced fresh chives, divided
- ¼ teaspoon table salt
- ¼ teaspoon pepper
- 1 garlic clove, minced
- 8 ounces thin asparagus, trimmed and cut into ½-inch pieces
- 2 tablespoons water
- 2 ounces smoked salmon, torn into ½-inch strips

1. In medium bowl, beat eggs, 2 tablespoons oil, 1 tablespoon chives, salt, and pepper with fork until no streaks of white remain. Heat 1 teaspoon oil and garlic in 12-inch nonstick skillet over medium heat until fragrant, about 1 minute. Add asparagus and water; cover; and cook, stirring occasionally, until asparagus is crisp-tender, 3 to 4 minutes. Uncover and continue to cook until moisture has evaporated, about 1 minute longer. Transfer asparagus mixture to small bowl and set aside. Wipe skillet clean with paper towels.

2. Heat remaining 2 teaspoons oil in now-empty skillet over medium-high heat until shimmering. Add egg mixture and, using rubber spatula, constantly and firmly scrape along bottom and sides of skillet until eggs begin to clump and spatula just leaves trail on bottom of skillet, 30 to 60 seconds. Reduce heat to low and gently but constantly fold eggs until clumped and just slightly wet, 30 to 60 seconds. Fold in asparagus mixture. Transfer to serving dish, top with salmon, sprinkle with remaining 1 tablespoon chives, and serve.

Variation
SCRAMBLED EGGS WITH SHIITAKE MUSHROOMS AND FETA CHEESE

Serves: 4
Total Time: 30 minutes

Oyster or cremini mushrooms can be substituted for the shiitake mushrooms, if desired; to prepare the oyster or cremini mushrooms, trim the stems but do not remove them. For the best results, buy a block of feta and crumble it yourself. This recipe can be easily halved, if desired; use a 10-inch skillet.

- 8 large eggs
- 3 tablespoons extra-virgin olive oil, divided
- ¼ teaspoon table salt, divided
- ¼ teaspoon pepper
- 1 shallot, minced
- 1 teaspoon minced fresh thyme
- 8 ounces shiitake mushrooms, stemmed and sliced thin
- ¼ cup water
- 1 ounce feta cheese, crumbled (¼ cup)

1. In medium bowl, beat eggs, 2 tablespoons oil, ⅛ teaspoon salt, and pepper with fork until no streaks of white remain. Heat 1 teaspoon oil, shallot, thyme, and remaining ⅛ teaspoon salt in 12-inch nonstick skillet over medium heat, stirring occasionally, until shallot is softened and beginning to brown, 2 to 3 minutes. Add mushrooms and water; cover; and cook, stirring frequently, until mushrooms are softened, 5 to 8 minutes. Uncover and continue to cook until moisture has evaporated, 2 to 3 minutes longer. Transfer mushroom mixture to small bowl and set aside. Wipe skillet clean with paper towels.

2. Heat remaining 2 teaspoons oil in now-empty skillet over medium-high heat until shimmering. Add egg mixture and, using rubber spatula, constantly and firmly scrape along bottom and sides of skillet until eggs begin to clump and spatula just leaves trail on bottom of skillet, 30 to 60 seconds. Reduce heat to low and gently but constantly fold eggs until clumped and just slightly wet, 30 to 60 seconds. Fold in mushroom mixture. Transfer to serving dish, sprinkle with feta, and serve.

KEYS TO SUCCESS
- **Cook in olive oil:** Doesn't add moisture that—with moist vegetables folded in—could otherwise make the eggs watery
- **Fold gently:** Produces large, tender curds
- **Cut small pieces of vegetables:** Easy to incorporate and won't break apart the curds; curds set up around the vegetables

XĪHÓNGSHÌ CHAO JĪDÀN (CHINESE STIR-FRIED TOMATOES AND EGGS)

Serves: 4
Total Time: 25 minutes

RECIPE OVERVIEW Stir-fried tomatoes and eggs is such a simple dish that it is often the first thing that Chinese children learn how to make. Sesame oil and Shaoxing wine add nutty flavor and help the eggs stay tender as well. The liquid and oil dilute the egg proteins and keep them from bonding too closely and turning tough. Quickly cooking the eggs promotes airier curds. For the sauce, garlic, ginger, and scallions provide savoriness to canned tomatoes, and simmering the tomatoes with some sugar makes the base concentrated and rich. You can serve the stir-fry with steamed white rice.

- 4 scallions, white parts sliced thin, green parts cut into 1-inch lengths
- 3 tablespoons vegetable oil, divided
- 3 garlic cloves, sliced thin
- 2 teaspoons grated fresh ginger
- 8 large eggs
- 2 tablespoons Shaoxing wine or dry sherry
- 1 teaspoon toasted sesame oil
- 1 teaspoon table salt, divided
- 1 (28-ounce) can whole peeled tomatoes, drained with juice reserved, cut into 1-inch pieces
- 2 teaspoons sugar

1. Combine scallion whites, 1 tablespoon vegetable oil, garlic, and ginger in small bowl; set aside. Whisk eggs, Shaoxing wine, sesame oil, and ½ teaspoon salt together in separate bowl.

2. Heat remaining 2 tablespoons vegetable oil in 12-inch nonstick skillet or 14-inch flat-bottomed wok over medium-high heat until shimmering. Add egg mixture. Using heat-resistant rubber spatula, slowly but constantly scrape along bottom and sides of pan until eggs just form cohesive mass, 1 to 2 minutes (eggs will not be completely dry); transfer to clean bowl.

3. Add reserved garlic mixture to now-empty pan and cook over medium heat, mashing mixture into pan, until fragrant, about 30 seconds. Add tomatoes and their juice, sugar, and remaining ½ teaspoon salt and simmer until almost completely dry, 5 to 7 minutes. Stir in egg mixture and scallion greens and cook, breaking up any large curds, until heated through, about 1 minute. Serve.

KEYS TO SUCCESS

- **A nonstick skillet or flat-bottomed wok:** For more information about using a wok, see page 17.
- **Shaoxing wine:** Dry sherry is a good substitute for this Chinese rice wine.
- **Cook eggs quickly:** Creates light and fluffy curds; warming eggs through before serving keeps them moist

RESOURCES FOR MODERN SCRAMBLED EGGS

ARE MY EGGS FRESH?

We've found that the age of eggs doesn't really matter when you're scrambling or frying them (but we prefer the freshest specimens possible for our Perfect Poached Eggs [page 69]). While some sources suggest that you can check freshness by putting eggs in a bowl of water—older eggs are more likely to float because the air sack expands over time—we found that this wasn't a reliable test since eggs didn't float until they were four to six months old. It's a safer bet to just check the sell-by date (see page 52); try to find eggs that are less than three weeks old.

HOT TIP: ELECTRIC STOVE? USE TWO BURNERS

Because electric stoves don't respond quickly to heat changes, it's best to heat one burner on low heat and a second on medium-high heat and then move the skillet between the burners when you need to adjust the temperature.

THE CLEANEST BREAK

There are best practices for even the simplest kitchen tasks. For example: cracking an egg. Do it thoughtlessly, and you'll end up with annoying bits of shell in the bowl. For the cleanest break, crack eggs against a flat surface rather than the edge of the counter or a mixing bowl.

Once you can crack eggs correctly, separating them is easy. We separate eggs if we need just the yolk or white (as we do for our Perfect Scrambled Eggs recipe [page 54], which calls for additional yolks) or if the two will be used in different ways. Separate eggs when they're cold: Cold yolks are less apt to break into the whites. To separate an egg, hold the halves of the cracked shell over a bowl and gently transfer the yolk back and forth between them, letting the white fall into the bowl; drop the yolk into a second bowl. (Alternatively, open the cracked egg into your cupped palm and slowly separate your fingers to allow the white to slide into the bowl, leaving the yolk intact in your palm.)

SCRAMBLED EGG EXTREMES

The best puffy scrambled eggs are neither hastily cooked over high heat nor gently cooked over low heat.

RUBBERY
Blasting the eggs over higher heat gets breakfast on the table in a hurry but produces dried-out, rubbery curds.

WET
Keeping the heat low might prevent the eggs from overcooking, but the result will be loose, tiny curds that look like lumpy custard.

WHAT KIND OF DAIRY?

We tested milk, half-and-half, and heavy cream while making scrambled eggs. Milk produced slightly fluffier, cleaner-tasting curds, but they were particularly prone to weeping. Heavy cream rendered the eggs very stable but dense, and some tasters found their flavor just too rich. Everyone agreed that ¼ cup of half-and-half fared best. The benefit of the dairy is threefold: First, the water it contains (half-and-half is 80 percent water) interrupts the protein network and dilutes the molecules, thereby raising the temperature at which the eggs coagulate and providing a greater safety net against overcooking. Second, as the water in the dairy vaporizes, it provides lift, which causes the eggs to puff up. And third, the fat in the dairy also raises the coagulation temperature by coating and insulating part of each protein molecule so that the molecules cannot stick together as tightly.

WHEN TO ADD THE MIX-INS

It's important to stir the mix-ins into the eggs when the curds are still a little wet; this way the eggs will set around the vegetables and form a cohesive dish. If the mix-ins are incorporated once the eggs are mostly dry, they won't fully integrate.

EGG SUBSTITUTES AND LIQUID EGG WHITES

Egg substitutes are made with egg whites along with a mixture of vegetable gums, dairy products, vitamins and other nutrients, water, and coloring agents. While we didn't like any of these products in savory egg-based recipes such as omelets, egg substitutes fared much better in baking tests: We couldn't distinguish between cakes, cookies, and brownies made with real eggs and those made with substitutes.

We tested liquid egg whites alongside hand-separated whites in egg white omelets, meringue cookies, and angel food cake. They made an acceptable substitute in omelets but not in baked goods. The U.S. Department of Agriculture requires that liquid egg whites be pasteurized; this process compromises the whites' structure such that they can't achieve the same volume, when whipped, as fresh whites. While we'd rather use the whites from whole eggs, liquid egg whites can be a good substitute for fresh whites in omelets, scrambles, and frittatas.

UNSCRAMBLING PERFECT SCRAMBLED EGGS

To get big, fluffy, tender, and rich-tasting curds, we experimented with every element of the process until we nailed the right formula.

8 EGGS PLUS 2 YOLKS

Adding yolks not only enriches the egg flavor but also provides extra fat and emulsifiers that raise the coagulation temperature to stave off overcooking.

HALF-AND-HALF

Half-and-half offers more rich-flavored fat than milk but also contains enough water to generate the steam necessary to make the eggs puff up.

10-INCH SKILLET

Trading the usual 12-inch pan for a smaller 10-inch one keeps the eggs in a thicker layer, thereby trapping more steam and producing heartier curds.

DUAL-HEAT METHOD

Starting the egg mixture over medium-high heat creates puffy curds; turning the heat to low once the eggs coagulate ensures that they won't overcook.

COURSE
FRY AN EGG

JULIA COLLIN DAVISON

You've probably made a fried egg or two before. But how many times did they come out perfect, with a tender, not-frazzled white and a creamy, unbroken yolk? Did they even come out of the pan? We believe that anyone can make a perfect fried egg, every single time, as long as they know the right method. This course is designed to teach you that method along with the essential tools and techniques for the job.

JULIA'S PRO TIP: *How you store fresh eggs matters! Don't store them in the refrigerator door or remove them from their original carton. The refrigerator door can be up to 15 degrees warmer than the interior shelves, and colder is better for egg storage. Also, egg cartons are designed to prevent the eggs from drying out and it protects them from picking up off-flavors in the fridge.*

PERFECT FRIED EGGS
Serves: 2
Total Time: 20 minutes

RECIPE OVERVIEW There are two common problems when it comes to fried eggs: undercooked whites and overcooked yolks. This method produces diner-style fried eggs with crisp edges and a runny yolk. The first thing you need is a nonstick skillet; there's no point in frying eggs in anything else. Next, don't skip preheating the pan: It ensures that the pan's surface will be evenly hot, which is extra-important for quick-cooking foods such as eggs. Once you raise the heat, don't dawdle; each step from here takes less than a minute. When checking the eggs for doneness, lift the lid just a crack to prevent loss of steam should they need further cooking. To fry just two eggs, use an 8- or 9-inch nonstick skillet and halve the amounts of oil and butter. You can use this method with extra-large or jumbo eggs without altering the timing.

- 2 teaspoons vegetable oil
- 4 large eggs, divided
- 2 teaspoons unsalted butter, cut into 4 pieces and chilled

1. Heat oil in 12- or 14-inch nonstick skillet over low heat for 5 minutes. Meanwhile, crack 2 eggs into small bowl and season with salt and pepper. Repeat with remaining 2 eggs and second small bowl.

2. Increase heat to medium-high and heat until oil is shimmering. Add butter to skillet and quickly swirl to coat skillet. Working quickly, pour 1 bowl of eggs in 1 side of skillet and second bowl of eggs in other side. Cover and cook for 1 minute. Let skillet stand off heat, covered, 15 to 45 seconds for runny yolks (white around edge of yolk will be barely opaque), 45 to 60 seconds for soft but set yolks, and about 2 minutes for medium-set yolks. Slide eggs onto plates and serve.

Variation
EGGS IN A HOLE

Use 6 eggs. Adjust oven racks to lowest and top positions, place rimmed baking sheet on lower rack, and heat oven to 500 degrees. Spread 2½ tablespoons softened unsalted butter evenly over 1 side of 6 slices hearty white sandwich bread. Using 2½-inch round cutter, cut out and remove circle from center of each piece of buttered bread. Remove hot sheet from oven, add 2½ tablespoons softened unsalted butter, and let melt, tilting sheet to let butter cover sheet evenly. Place bread circles down center of sheet and bread slices on either side of circles, buttered side up. Return sheet to lower rack and bake until bread is golden, 3 to 5 minutes, flipping bread and rotating sheet halfway through baking. Remove sheet from oven and set inside second (room-temperature) rimmed baking sheet. Crack 1 egg into each bread hole. Season eggs with salt and pepper. Bake on upper rack until whites are barely set, 4 to 6 minutes, rotating sheet halfway through baking. Transfer sheets to wire rack and let eggs sit until whites are completely set, about 2 minutes. Serve. Makes 6 toasts.

KEYS TO SUCCESS
- **Use a nonstick skillet with a lid**: Ensures that the eggs release easily
- **Preheat the skillet**: Prevents hot spots, helping the eggs cook evenly
- **Put eggs in small bowls (or tea cups)**: Allows you to add the eggs all at once
- **Cover the skillet**: Traps steam to cook the egg whites
- **Finish cooking off the heat**: Prevents the yolks from overcooking

CORE TECHNIQUE Frying Eggs

PREHEAT THE SKILLET
Low heat means the oil preheats without smoking.

PUT EGGS IN BOWLS
Eggs are easier to maneuver in small bowls. Plus, you can check for any pieces of shell.

ADD EGGS ALL AT ONCE
For even cooking, add eggs simultaneously.

COVER IT UP
The lid traps heat, so the eggs cook from above and below.

SCIENCE LESSON Egg Proteins

Eggs may seem simple but they are actually quite complex: The yolk and the white behave as two separate ingredients, combined. Not only do egg yolk and egg white proteins act inherently differently, they also solidify at different temperatures. The yolk begins to thicken at 150 degrees and is fully set at 158 degrees. The most abundant proteins in whites, called ovalbumins, set at 180 degrees.

Egg yolks solidify at 158 degrees, much lower than the 180 degrees at which egg whites are fully set.

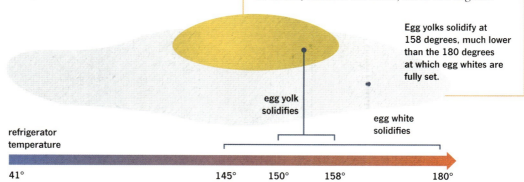

EGGS AND TOFU | 61

AVOCADO TOAST WITH FRIED EGGS

Serves: 4
Total Time: 40 minutes

RECIPE OVERVIEW Some dishes are so simple that they are not even worth talking about. But avocado toast definitely is, and it's here to stay: It's healthy and delicious, and it's one of the simplest things to make for a quick breakfast or lunch. We take ours up a notch by whisking together a lemony vinaigrette and mashing one of the avocados into it, giving our dish a distinct citrusy punch. With the vibrantly flavored spread smeared on toasted rustic country bread, topped with sliced avocado and a fried egg, and then sprinkled with a little coarse sea salt and red pepper flakes, our version of this dish is spectacularly tasty.

- 2 tablespoons extra-virgin olive oil
- 1 teaspoon grated lemon zest plus 1 tablespoon juice
- 1/8 teaspoon plus 1/4 teaspoon coarse sea salt or kosher salt, divided
- 1/8 teaspoon pepper
- 2 ripe avocados, divided
- 4 (1/2-inch-thick) slices crusty bread
- 1 recipe Perfect Fried Eggs (page 60)
- 1/4 teaspoon red pepper flakes (optional)

1. Adjust oven rack 4 inches from broiler element and heat broiler. Whisk oil, lemon zest and juice, 1/8 teaspoon salt, and pepper together in small bowl. Halve and pit 1 avocado. Carefully make 1/2-inch crosshatch incisions in flesh with butter knife, cutting down to but not through skin. Insert spoon between skin and flesh, gently scoop out avocado cubes, and add to bowl with oil mixture. Mash avocado into oil mixture with potato masher or fork. Halve remaining avocado, remove pit and peel, and slice thin; set aside.

2. Meanwhile, arrange bread in single layer on rimmed baking sheet and broil until bread is deep golden and toasted on both sides, 1 to 2 minutes per side.

3. Spread mashed avocado mixture evenly on toasts and arrange avocado slices evenly over top. Top avocado slices with fried eggs. Sprinkle with pepper flakes, if using, and remaining 1/4 teaspoon salt. Serve.

Put an Egg on It

Adding a fried egg is one of the easiest ways to add protein and richness to dishes and make them more meal-worthy. In addition to serving fried eggs over hearty vegetables, you can use them to turn salad greens (spinach is especially nice) into a light meal or top pasta with them. The silky, runny yolk acts as a luxurious sauce to moisten whatever it sits on.

FRIED EGGS OVER GARLICKY CHARD AND BELL PEPPER

Serves: 4
Total Time: 35 minutes

RECIPE OVERVIEW Hearty Swiss chard is an ideal partner for a fried egg, especially when the rich, drippy yolk breaks and mingles with the earthy greens. To keep this recipe quick, cook, or bloom, minced garlic in olive oil and then wilt handfuls of chard before adding red bell pepper and a pinch of red pepper flakes. The greens become tender in 5 minutes. Drain the vegetables and use the same skillet to quickly fry four eggs. A spritz of lemon adds brightness.

- 2 tablespoons extra-virgin olive oil, divided, plus extra for serving
- 5 garlic cloves, minced
- 2 pounds Swiss chard, stemmed, 1 cup stems chopped fine, leaves sliced into 1/2-inch-wide strips
- 1 small red bell pepper, stemmed, seeded, and cut into 1/4-inch pieces
- 1/4 teaspoon table salt
- 1/8 teaspoon red pepper flakes
- 4 large eggs, divided
- Lemon wedges

1. Heat 1 tablespoon oil and garlic in 12-inch nonstick skillet over medium-low heat, stirring occasionally, until garlic is light golden, 3 to 5 minutes. Increase heat to high; add chopped chard stems and then chard leaves, 1 handful at a time; and cook until wilted, about 2 minutes. Stir in bell pepper, salt, and pepper flakes and cook, stirring often, until chard is tender and bell pepper is softened, about 3 minutes. Off heat, season with salt and pepper to taste. Transfer to colander set in bowl.

2. Crack 2 eggs into small bowl and season with salt and pepper. Repeat with remaining 2 eggs in second bowl. Heat remaining 1 tablespoon oil in now-empty skillet over medium-high heat until shimmering; quickly swirl to coat skillet. Working quickly, pour 1 bowl of eggs in 1 side of skillet and second bowl of eggs in other side. Cover and cook for 1 minute.

3. Let skillet sit off heat, covered, 15 to 45 seconds for runny yolks (white around edge of yolk will be barely opaque), 45 to 60 seconds for soft but set yolks, or about 2 minutes for medium-set yolks.

4. Divide chard mixture evenly among serving plates, top each with 1 egg, and drizzle with extra oil. Serve immediately with lemon wedges.

KEYS TO SUCCESS

- **Use a 12-inch nonstick skillet with a tight-fitting lid:** Accommodates four eggs at once
- For how to stem and chop chard, see page 43.
- For how to stem and seed a bell pepper, see page 40.

COURSE

HARD-COOKED AND SOFT-COOKED EGGS

We've all tried to peel a hard-cooked egg only to have bits of the white pull away with the shell. Our foolproof method for easy-to-peel hard-cooked eggs finally solves that problem. Find out how a hot start produces eggs with shells that slip off easily, and then learn how to turn those flawless eggs into great deviled eggs. You'll also learn how the precise timing of our method for soft-cooked eggs delivers a set white and fluid yolk every time.

ANDREA'S PRO TIP: *These cooking times work for large eggs. Add 1 minute for extra large eggs and 2 minutes for jumbo eggs.*

ANDREA GEARY

EASY-PEEL HARD-COOKED EGGS

Makes: 6 eggs
Total Time: 40 minutes

RECIPE OVERVIEW Boiled eggs that start in cold water are hard to peel because the proteins in the egg white set slowly, giving them time to fuse to the surrounding membrane. When you try to remove the shell, parts of the white cling to the membrane, and the surface of the egg is then unattractively pockmarked. Instead of a cold-water start, we place cold eggs directly into hot steam, which causes the outermost egg white proteins to form a solid gel that shrinks and pulls away from the membrane. The shell slips off easily to reveal a smooth, unblemished surface. Be sure to use large eggs that have no cracks and are cold from the refrigerator. You can use this method for fewer than six eggs without altering the timing. You can also double this recipe as long as you use a pot and steamer basket large enough to hold the eggs in a single layer. There's no need to peel the eggs right away. They can be stored in their shells for up to 5 days and peeled when needed.

6 large eggs

1. Bring 1 inch water to rolling boil in medium saucepan over high heat. Place eggs in steamer basket. Transfer basket to saucepan. Cover, reduce heat to medium-low, and cook eggs for 13 minutes.

2. When eggs are almost finished cooking, combine 2 cups ice cubes and 2 cups cold water in medium bowl. Using tongs or spoon, transfer eggs to ice bath; let sit for 15 minutes. Peel before using.

Variation
SOFT-COOKED EGGS

With a set white and fluid yolk, soft-cooked eggs have the appeal of poached eggs but are less fussy and can be eaten out of the shell. Precise timing is critical, so use a digital timer. You can use this method for one to six large, extra-large, or jumbo eggs without altering the timing. We recommend serving these eggs in egg cups and with buttered toast sticks, or soldiers, for dipping, or simply use the dull side of a butter knife to crack the egg along the equator, break the egg in half, and scoop out the insides with a teaspoon and serve as you would a poached egg—over toast, salad, or cooked vegetables.

After adding steamer basket with eggs to saucepan of boiling water, reduce heat to medium-high and cook for 6½ minutes. Remove cover, transfer saucepan to sink, and place under cold running water for 30 seconds. Remove eggs from saucepan and serve, seasoning with salt and pepper to taste.

CORE TECHNIQUE
Hard- or Soft-Cooking Eggs

BOIL WATER
The starting temperature of the water is critical. Keep the water level below the bottom of the steamer basket.

LOWER EGGS
Since the eggs don't touch the water, they won't cause the water temperature to drop.

STOP THE COOKING
A bowl of ice and cold water is called an ice bath. It quickly stops the eggs from cooking.

SCIENCE LESSON
Blame the Membrane

Most cooks assume that when an egg is difficult to peel, it's because the shell is sticking to the egg white. But it's the membrane between the shell and the white that's really the problem. When an egg is very fresh or when it's cooked slowly, the proteins in the white bond to the membrane instead of to one another, and the membrane becomes cemented to the white and impossible to peel away. The solution? Plunging the eggs directly into hot steam, which causes the egg white proteins to denature and shrink, reducing their ability to bond with the membrane.

CURRY DEVILED EGGS

Makes: 12 eggs
Total Time: 25 minutes

RECIPE OVERVIEW Great deviled eggs start with smooth-surfaced hard-cooked eggs. In this version, we make a creamy, tangy filling by mixing the mashed yolks with fresh parsley and lemon juice, Dijon mustard, and curry powder. To slice the eggs, lay each egg on its side and sweep the blade cleanly down the center. Wipe the knife after slicing each egg. You can substitute reduced-fat mayonnaise in this recipe. If preferred, use a pastry bag fitted with a large plain or star tip to fill the egg halves.

- 1 recipe Easy-Peel Hard-Cooked Eggs (page 65)
- 3 tablespoons mayonnaise
- 1 tablespoon minced fresh parsley, plus 12 small parsley leaves for garnishing
- 1½ teaspoons lemon juice
- 1 teaspoon Dijon mustard
- 1 teaspoon curry powder
- Pinch cayenne pepper

1. Slice each egg in half lengthwise with paring knife. Transfer yolks to bowl; arrange whites on serving platter. Mash yolks with fork until no large lumps remain. Add mayonnaise and use rubber spatula to smear mixture against side of bowl until thick, smooth paste forms, 1 to 2 minutes. Add minced parsley, lemon juice, mustard, curry powder, and cayenne and mix until fully incorporated.

2. Transfer yolk mixture to small, heavy-duty plastic bag. Press mixture into 1 corner and twist top of bag. Using scissors, snip ½ inch off filled corner. Squeezing bag, distribute yolk mixture evenly among egg white halves. Garnish each egg half with 1 parsley leaf and serve.

BACON AND CHIVE DEVILED EGGS

Makes: 12 eggs
Total Time: 25 minutes

RECIPE OVERVIEW In these deviled eggs, bacon and fresh chives add savory flavor to the filling along with Dijon mustard and white vinegar. To slice the eggs, lay each egg on its side and sweep the blade cleanly down the center. Wipe the knife after slicing each egg. You can substitute reduced-fat mayonnaise in this recipe. If preferred, use a pastry bag fitted with a large plain or star tip to fill the egg halves.

- 2 slices bacon, chopped fine
- 1 recipe Easy-Peel Hard-Cooked Eggs (page 65)
- 2 tablespoons mayonnaise
- 1 teaspoon Dijon mustard
- 1 tablespoon minced fresh chives
- 2 teaspoons distilled white vinegar
- ⅛ teaspoon table salt
- Pinch cayenne pepper

1. Cook bacon in 10-inch skillet over medium heat until crispy, 5 to 7 minutes. Using slotted spoon, transfer bacon to paper towel–lined plate. Reserve 1 tablespoon fat.

2. Slice each egg in half lengthwise with paring knife. Transfer yolks to bowl; arrange whites on serving platter. Mash yolks with fork until no large lumps remain. Add mayonnaise and mustard and use rubber spatula to smear mixture against side of bowl until thick, smooth paste forms, 1 to 2 minutes. Add chives, vinegar, salt, cayenne, and reserved bacon fat and mix until fully incorporated. Stir in three-quarters of bacon.

3. Transfer yolk mixture to small, heavy-duty plastic bag. Press mixture into 1 corner and twist top of bag. Using scissors, snip ½ inch off filled corner. Squeezing bag, distribute yolk mixture evenly among egg white halves. Sprinkle each egg half with remaining bacon and serve.

KEYS TO SUCCESS

- **Make sure that the eggs are cold:** Use straight from the fridge with no cracks
- **Use a steamer basket:** Easily moves all the eggs into the saucepan; spoon or tongs also work
- **Start in steam:** Makes for easy peeling
- **Stop in ice bath:** Stops eggs from cooking

RESOURCES FOR HARD- AND SOFT-COOKED EGGS

THE EGG-DONENESS CONTINUUM

The fundamental challenge in egg cookery is that an egg is not really one ingredient but two—the white and the yolk—and each solidifies at a different temperature. Whites start to thicken at 145 degrees and are fully set at 180. Yolks begin to thicken at 150 degrees and are fully set at 158; this narrow range means that just a minute or two can completely change the consistency of your eggs from creamy to fully set to overdone, as the photos below show. Our steaming method ensures a consistent temperature, allowing us to nail down more precise timing than boiling would, since adding eggs to a pot of boiling water lowers the temperature of the water. Just make sure to set a timer!

SOFT-COOKED EGG

PERFECT HARD-COOKED EGG

OVERCOOKED EGG

YES, YOU CAN PEEL A SOFT-COOKED EGG

Though it seemed unlikely to us, soft-cooked eggs are actually easier to peel than are hard-cooked eggs. This is because the soft-cooked white is more yielding. Start by cracking the broad end of the egg against a hard surface and then peel away both the shell and the inner membrane. A quick rinse in warm water removes any remaining wisps of membrane and shards of eggshell. Split the egg in half and serve it over toast, or have it your usual way.

HOT TIP: SOFT-COOKED EGGS GONE COLD? REHEAT THEM

Bring ½ inch water to boil in medium saucepan over medium-high heat. Steam eggs, covered, for 3½ minutes. You can use a steamer basket but don't have to.

PEEL SIX EGGS IN 41 SECONDS!

Combined with our hot-start cooking method, this novel approach to peeling is so efficient that the shells slip right off. Instead of preparing the ice bath in a bowl, use a plastic container with a tight-fitting lid. Once the eggs are chilled, pour off half the water and, holding the lid in place, shake the container vigorously using a vertical motion (the eggs will hit the top of the container) until the shells are cracked all over, about 40 shakes. Peel, rinse, and use the eggs as desired. This is a great trick to use when you are making a lot of eggs for recipes such as egg salad (page 73).

COURSE
POACHED EGGS

CHRISTIE MORRISON

There are dozens of techniques claiming to produce perfectly poached eggs, and we've tried them all. It took a fair amount of experimentation to find the perfect formula for achieving fully cooked egg whites and a runny yolk. A raw egg white (albumen) has two consistencies: thick and thin. The thicker portion clings more tightly to the yolk, while the thinner portion is looser and will drain away through the holes of a colander. It is this thinner white that is most prone to spreading out into wispy tendrils in the water and cooking up ragged. Never again.

CHRISTIE'S PRO TIP: *For intact yolks, crack your eggs on a flat surface rather than the edge of a bowl. The shell is less likely to break inward and pierce the yolk.*

CORE TECHNIQUE — Poaching Eggs

DRAIN RAW EGGS
This gets rid of the loose, watery whites.

TIP INTO WATER
A liquid measuring cup makes it easy to gently tip the eggs into boiling water, one at a time.

COVER THE POT
Residual heat finishes cooking the eggs.

PERFECT POACHED EGGS

Serves: 2
Total Time: 20 minutes

RECIPE OVERVIEW Overcoming one of the biggest challenges to poaching eggs—producing a tender, tidy white—starts with draining the eggs in a colander. Why? This allows the thin, loose whites that would cook up ragged to slip away before cooking and results in perfectly shaped poached eggs. Transferring the eggs to a liquid measuring cup and depositing them into the water one by one prevents them from being jostled. Salted water with vinegar helps the whites set up quickly, ensuring that the faster-cooking yolks will still be liquid by the time the whites are cooked through. Poaching the eggs in a Dutch oven filled with just 6 cups of water leaves plenty of headspace above the eggs so that steam fully cooks the notoriously gooey portion of the white nearest the yolk. Finally, we gently poach the eggs by bringing the water to a boil, adding the eggs, covering the pot, and letting them cook off the heat for 3 minutes. Once the cover is removed, you can check the eggs individually, removing them once the white nearest to the yolk is just set. For the best results, be sure to use the freshest eggs possible. This recipe can be used to cook from one to four eggs. To make two batches of eggs to serve all at once, transfer four cooked eggs directly to a large pot of 150-degree water and cover them. This will keep them warm for 15 minutes or so while you return the poaching water to a boil and cook the next batch. We like to serve these eggs on buttered toast, in Open-Faced Poached Egg Sandwiches (page 73), or on salads made with assertively flavored greens.

- 4 large eggs
- 1 tablespoon distilled white vinegar
  Table salt for poaching eggs

1. Bring 6 cups water to boil in Dutch oven over high heat. Meanwhile, crack eggs, one at a time, into colander. Let stand until loose, watery whites drain away from eggs, 20 to 30 seconds. Gently transfer eggs to 2-cup liquid measuring cup.

2. Add vinegar and 1 teaspoon salt to boiling water. With lip of measuring cup just above surface of water, gently tip eggs into water, one at a time, leaving space between them. Cover pot; remove from heat; and let stand until whites closest to yolks are just set and opaque, about 3 minutes. If after 3 minutes whites are not set, let stand in water, checking every 30 seconds, until eggs reach desired doneness. (For medium-cooked yolks, let eggs sit in pot, covered, for 4 minutes, then begin checking for doneness.)

3. Using slotted spoon, carefully lift and drain each egg over Dutch oven. Season with salt and pepper to taste, and serve.

Variation
MAKE-AHEAD POACHED EGGS

For convenience, you can poach the eggs 15 minutes ahead—or even a few days in advance.

POACH 15 MINUTES AHEAD Transfer poached eggs to large pot of 150-degree water and let stand, covered, for up to 15 minutes.

POACH, REFRIGERATE, AND REHEAT Drop poached eggs into ice water to cool, then drain. Refrigerate for up to 3 days. When ready to reheat, bring 3 inches water to simmer in large saucepan, remove saucepan from heat, add eggs, and let stand for 1½ minutes.

KEYS TO SUCCESS

- **Use a colander:** Removes any loose egg whites
- **Use a liquid measuring cup:** Makes adding the eggs to boiling water easy
- **Poach in a Dutch oven:** Leaves room for steam that fully cooks the gooey portion of the white nearest the yolk
- **Salt and vinegar:** Help the whites set up quickly
- **Poach off heat:** Makes it possible to check the eggs' doneness and put them back in the water if they're not done

SCIENCE LESSON

Fresh Eggs = Thick Whites

A raw egg white (albumen) has two consistencies: thick and thin. The ratio of the two consistencies depends on the egg's age: In the freshest eggs, 60 percent of the white is thick, but as the egg ages, it drops to 50 percent and below. In most cooked egg applications, the albumen ratio won't be noticeable because the white is either scrambled, browned in a pan, or cooked in the confines of the shell. A poached egg is the exception since the thin white is able to freely flow away from the thick white and cooks up ragged and wispy, not plump and tidy. Our recipe gets around the issue of egg freshness by draining off the loose, watery white in a colander before poaching. But for the plumpest results, it's best to use the freshest eggs you can find.

FRESH

OLD

COURSE
EGG SANDWICHES

LAWMAN JOHNSON

No portable breakfast is as satisfying as a breakfast sandwich: It's hot, filling, and—when done properly—really, really good. The perfect egg sandwich starts with perfectly cooked eggs—but then it requires a bit of assembly know-how. The easy, tasty recipes for egg sandwiches in this course bring out their full potential. From ham and cheese to bacon and cheddar to goat cheese, tomato, and spinach to the best egg salad, you'll want to make them all—and not just for breakfast.

LAWMAN'S PRO TIP: *What a sandwich goes on is just as important as what goes into it. Choosing fresh, quality bread can elevate the ingredients, making a good sandwich into a great one!*

HAM, EGG, AND CHEESE SANDWICHES

Serves: 4
Total Time: 1 hour

RECIPE OVERVIEW A café breakfast sandwich is all about the eggs. Combining eggs, milk, and salt and baking the mixture in an 8-inch pan produces the perfect pillowy egg layer. Covering the pan with aluminum foil while baking delicately cooks the eggs. We cut the cooked egg sheet into four perfect squares that can be eaten right away or stored in the fridge for another morning. We add sliced ham and shredded Gruyère to the egg squares and pop them back in the oven to heat through and melt. Baby arugula provides freshness, while Dijon mayonnaise adds richness and a hint of spice. Potato, kaiser, and brioche buns measuring roughly 4 inches in diameter all work well here.

- 8 large eggs
- ½ cup milk
- ½ teaspoon table salt
- 3 tablespoons mayonnaise
- 1 tablespoon Dijon mustard
- 4 slices deli ham
- 4 ounces Gruyère cheese, shredded (1 cup)
- 4 hamburger buns, toasted
- 1 ounce (1 cup) baby arugula

1. Adjust oven rack to middle position and heat oven to 300 degrees. Generously spray bottom and sides of 8-inch square baking pan with vegetable oil spray. Whisk eggs, milk, and salt in bowl until well combined. Transfer egg mixture to prepared pan; cover tightly with aluminum foil; and bake until egg is set, 30 to 35 minutes, rotating pan halfway through baking.

2. Run thin knife between egg and side of pan. Invert egg onto cutting board and cut into four squares. Combine mayonnaise and mustard in small bowl. (Egg squares and mayonnaise-mustard mixture can be refrigerated separately for up to 3 days. To reheat egg squares, increase baking time in step 3 to 4 to 6 minutes.)

3. Arrange egg squares on greased rimmed baking sheet and top each square with 1 slice ham and ¼ cup Gruyère. Bake until ham is heated through and Gruyère is melted, 2 to 4 minutes.

4. Spread 1 tablespoon mayonnaise-mustard mixture on each bun top. Place egg squares on bun bottoms and top each with ¼ cup arugula and bun tops. Serve.

Variation
BACON, EGG, AND CHEESE SANDWICHES

Substitute 8 slices crisp bacon for ham, ¼ cup tomato chutney for mayonnaise-mustard mixture, sharp cheddar for Gruyère, and baby spinach for arugula.

KEYS TO SUCCESS
- **Bake in the oven:** Makes four servings hands-off
- **Cover with foil:** Steam gently cooks the eggs
- Can use glass or ceramic baking dish in place of metal. If using, increase baking time in step 1 to 40 to 50 minutes.

FRIED EGG SANDWICHES

Serves: 4
Total Time: 40 minutes

RECIPE OVERVIEW A classic fried egg sandwich is good 24-7, and with this recipe you can make four of them at once. Start by using the broiler to toast buttered English muffins. Next, cook bacon in a skillet, set it aside, and use the flavorful drippings to cook four eggs. After a minute over the heat, the eggs get topped with the crispy bacon and a handful of shredded cheddar cheese. Last, cover the pan and let it sit until the eggs are cooked through and the cheese is melted. Tomato and baby spinach add freshness, and a spicy mayonnaise adds richness and a kick of heat to these crispy, buttery sandwiches.

- 4 English muffins, split
- 3 tablespoons unsalted butter, softened
- ¼ cup mayonnaise
- 1 teaspoon hot sauce
- 4 large eggs, divided
- 6 slices bacon
- 4 ounces sharp cheddar cheese, shredded (1 cup)
- 1½ ounces (1½ cups) baby spinach
- 4 thin tomato slices

1. Adjust oven rack 5 inches from broiler element and heat broiler. Spread insides of muffins evenly with butter and arrange split side up on rimmed baking sheet. Combine mayonnaise and hot sauce in bowl; set aside. Crack 2 eggs into small bowl and season with salt and pepper. Repeat with remaining 2 eggs and second small bowl.

2. Cook bacon in 12-inch nonstick skillet over medium heat until crispy, 7 to 9 minutes; transfer to paper towel–lined plate. When cool enough to handle, break each slice in half.

3. Broil muffins until golden brown, 2 to 4 minutes, rotating sheet halfway through broiling. Flip muffins and broil until just crisp on second side, 1 to 2 minutes; set aside while cooking eggs.

4. Pour off all but 1 tablespoon fat from skillet and heat over medium-high heat until shimmering. Working quickly, pour 1 bowl of eggs in 1 side of skillet and second bowl of eggs in other side. Cover and cook for 1 minute.

5. Working quickly, top each egg with 3 pieces bacon and ¼ cup cheddar. Cover skillet; remove from heat; and let stand until cheddar is melted and egg whites are cooked through, about 2 minutes.

6. Spread mayonnaise mixture on muffin bottoms and place 1 bacon-and-cheese-topped egg on each. Divide spinach evenly among sandwiches, then top with tomato slices and muffin tops. Serve.

EGG SALAD SANDWICHES WITH RADISHES AND WATERCRESS

Serves: 6
Total Time: 55 minutes, plus 30 minutes chilling

RECIPE OVERVIEW The hallmark of egg salad—the creaminess—typically has to do with the amount of mayonnaise in the mix. This version lets the eggs take center stage instead. To achieve creaminess without relying solely on mayo, we take a cue from our method for deviled eggs and mash the yolks. Knocking a few minutes off the cooking time produces yolks that mash up perfectly creamy, with no hint of chalkiness. From there, add just 2½ tablespoons of mayonnaise and an equal amount of yogurt, plus lemon juice, mustard, salt, and pepper. This yields a velvety base into which you can fold the chopped egg whites and fresh scallions. A layer of vibrant radishes adds crunch, and watercress adds freshness. Be sure to use large eggs that have no cracks and are cold from the refrigerator. If you don't have a steamer basket, use a spoon or tongs to gently place the eggs in the water. It does not matter if the eggs are above the water or partially submerged.

- 10 large eggs
- 2½ tablespoons mayonnaise
- 2½ tablespoons plain yogurt
- 1½ tablespoons lemon juice
- 1 tablespoon Dijon mustard
- ½ teaspoon table salt
- ⅛ teaspoon pepper
- 3 scallions, sliced thin
- 12 slices hearty white or whole-wheat sandwich bread
- 6 radishes, trimmed and sliced thin
- 2 ounces (2 cups) watercress

1. Bring 1 inch water to rolling boil in large saucepan over high heat. Place eggs in steamer basket in single layer. Transfer basket to saucepan. Cover, reduce heat to medium-low, and cook eggs for 11 minutes.

2. When eggs are almost finished cooking, fill medium bowl halfway with ice and water. Using slotted spoon, transfer eggs to ice bath and let sit for 15 minutes to cool.

3. Peel eggs and halve lengthwise. Transfer egg yolks to large bowl. Using potato masher, mash yolks with mayonnaise, yogurt, lemon juice, mustard, salt, and pepper. Whisk mixture until smooth.

4. Chop egg whites into ¼-inch pieces. Fold whites and scallions into yolk mixture and refrigerate for 30 minutes. Season with salt and pepper to taste. Spread egg salad evenly over 6 bread slices. Arrange radishes evenly over egg salad, then top with watercress. Top with remaining 6 bread slices. Serve.

OPEN-FACED POACHED EGG SANDWICHES

Serves: 4
Total Time: 40 minutes

RECIPE OVERVIEW These poached egg sandwiches are a delicious fresh take featuring juicy tomatoes, greens, and cheese. They rely on soft egg yolks to provide richness. Tender baby spinach needs just a couple minutes to wilt in a skillet; sautéed garlic and mild shallot give the spinach great flavor. Next, to get perfect, tender poached eggs, we stick with our foolproof method (page 69). Then we simply spread toasted English muffins with creamy goat cheese brightened with lemon juice and top the goat cheese with fresh tomato slices, the spinach, and a perfectly poached egg.

- 4 ounces goat cheese, crumbled and softened (1 cup)
- 1 teaspoon lemon juice
- ¼ teaspoon pepper
- 4 English muffins, split in half, toasted, and still warm
- 2 small tomatoes, cored and sliced thin (16 slices)
- 4 teaspoons extra-virgin olive oil
- 2 shallots, minced
- 1 garlic clove, minced
- 8 ounces (8 cups) baby spinach
- ¼ teaspoon table salt
- 8 Perfect Poached Eggs (page 69)

1. Adjust oven rack to middle position and heat oven to 300 degrees. Stir goat cheese, lemon juice, and pepper together in bowl until smooth.

2. Spread goat cheese mixture evenly over warm English muffin halves and top with tomato slices. Arrange English muffins on baking sheet and keep warm in oven while preparing spinach and eggs.

3. Heat oil in 12-inch nonstick skillet over medium heat until shimmering. Add shallots and cook until softened, about 2 minutes. Stir in garlic and cook until fragrant, about 30 seconds. Stir in spinach and salt and cook until spinach is wilted, about 2 minutes. Using tongs, squeeze out any excess moisture from spinach, then divide evenly among English muffins. Return English muffins to oven.

4. Arrange 1 poached egg on top of each English muffin, season with salt and pepper to taste, and serve immediately.

COURSE
PUT AN EGG IN IT

JOSEPH GITTER

Iterations of eggs poached in a flavorful sauce stretch from Mexico across the Mediterranean to the Middle East. These easy and savory one-pan meals consist of eggs cooked directly in a saucy base of vegetables. Whether tomato- or greens-based, the savory sauce is the perfect medium in which to cook eggs. In this course you will learn an international array of baked egg recipes, all of which are richly flavored and feature perfectly oozy, creamy eggs.

JOE'S PRO TIP: *After cracking eggs into the indents of whatever sauce or stew I'm simmering or baking, I like to spoon a little of the sauce on top of the raw whites (but I avoid the yolks). It'll help set the whites fully while the yolks are still gloriously oozy.*

EGGS IN PURGATORY

Serves: 4
Total Time: 1¼ hours

RECIPE OVERVIEW This popular Italian American dish of quivering eggs poached directly in a spicy red sauce is equally as good for a meatless supper as it is for breakfast. We let the sauce thicken slightly on the stovetop and then take the skillet off the heat. Before adding each egg to the skillet, use a rubber spatula to clear a 2-inch-long well in the sauce (exposing the skillet bottom) to hold the egg. To evenly fit all eight eggs in the skillet, place seven eggs around the perimeter of the pan and one in the middle. Covering the skillet and cooking the eggs over medium heat helps start setting the whites; then, a flash of enveloping heat from the oven finishes the whites while leaving the yolks silky. This dish should be a little spicy, but if you're averse to heat, we've provided a range for the red pepper flakes.

- 8 (¾-inch-thick) slices rustic Italian bread
- 7 tablespoons extra-virgin olive oil, divided, plus extra for drizzling
- 4 garlic cloves, sliced thin
- ¼ cup grated onion
- 1 tablespoon tomato paste
- ¾–1¼ teaspoons red pepper flakes
- 1 teaspoon table salt
- ½ teaspoon dried oregano
- 1 cup fresh basil leaves plus 2 tablespoons chopped
- 1 (28-ounce) can crushed tomatoes
- 8 large eggs
- ¼ cup grated Parmesan cheese

1. Adjust oven rack to middle position and heat broiler. Arrange bread slices on baking sheet and drizzle first sides with 2 tablespoons oil; flip slices and drizzle with additional 2 tablespoons oil. Broil until deep golden brown, about 3 minutes per side. Set aside and heat oven to 400 degrees.

2. Heat remaining 3 tablespoons oil in 12-inch ovensafe skillet over medium heat until shimmering. Add garlic and cook until golden, about 2 minutes. Add onion, tomato paste, pepper flakes, salt, and oregano and cook, stirring occasionally, until rust-colored, about 4 minutes. Add basil leaves and cook until wilted, about 30 seconds. Stir in tomatoes and bring to gentle simmer. Reduce heat to medium-low and continue to simmer until slightly thickened, about 15 minutes longer, stirring occasionally.

3. Remove skillet from heat and let sit 2 minutes to cool slightly. Crack 1 egg into bowl. Use heat-resistant rubber spatula to clear 2-inch-diameter well in sauce, exposing skillet bottom. Using spatula to hold well open, immediately pour in egg. Repeat with remaining eggs, evenly spacing 7 eggs in total around perimeter of skillet and 1 in center.

4. Season each egg with salt and pepper. Cook over medium heat, covered, until egg whites are just beginning to set but are still translucent with some watery patches, about 3 minutes. Uncover skillet and transfer to oven. Bake until egg whites are set and no watery patches remain, 4 to 5 minutes for slightly runny yolks or about 6 minutes for soft-cooked yolks, rotating skillet halfway through baking.

5. Sprinkle with Parmesan and chopped basil and drizzle with extra oil. Serve with toasted bread.

> ### KEYS TO SUCCESS
> - **Use a box grater**: Large holes yield grated onion with the perfect texture
> - **Space eggs evenly**: Prevents whites from running together
> - **Go deep**: Really nestle the eggs into the sauce.

GREEN SHAKSHUKA
Serves: 4
Total Time: 1 hour

RECIPE OVERVIEW Shakshuka is a classic Tunisian dish featuring eggs poached in a spiced tomato sauce. This version goes green with a vibrant mix of Swiss chard and baby spinach. Cooking the sliced chard stems with onion creates an aromatic base, and we chose citrusy coriander and mild Aleppo pepper to flavor the greens. Cooking in a roomy Dutch oven allows us to wilt a large volume of raw greens easily. We blend some of the greens with broth to give the sauce a cohesive texture and add frozen peas for sweetness. To finish, we poach eight eggs directly in the sauce. If you can't find Aleppo pepper, you can substitute ⅛ teaspoon of paprika and ⅛ teaspoon of finely chopped red pepper flakes. The Dutch oven will seem crowded when you first add the greens, but the greens will quickly wilt down. Avoid removing the lid during the first 5 minutes of cooking in step 3; it will increase the total cooking time of the eggs.

- 2 pounds Swiss chard, stems removed and reserved, leaves chopped
- ¼ cup extra-virgin olive oil, divided
- 1 large onion, chopped fine
- ¾ teaspoon table salt
- 4 garlic cloves, minced
- 2 teaspoons ground coriander
- 11 ounces (11 cups) baby spinach, chopped
- ½ cup vegetable broth
- 1 cup frozen peas
- 1½ tablespoons lemon juice
- 8 large eggs
- ½ teaspoon ground dried Aleppo pepper
- 2 ounces feta cheese, crumbled (½ cup)
- 2 tablespoons chopped fresh dill
- 2 tablespoons chopped fresh mint

1. Slice chard stems thin to yield 1 cup; discard remaining stems or reserve for another use. Heat 2 tablespoons oil in Dutch oven over medium heat until shimmering. Add chard stems, onion, and salt and cook until vegetables are softened and lightly browned, 5 to 7 minutes. Stir in garlic and coriander and cook until fragrant, about 1 minute.

2. Add chard leaves and spinach. Increase heat to medium-high; cover; and cook, stirring occasionally, until wilted but still bright green, 3 to 5 minutes. Off heat, transfer 1 cup chard mixture to blender. Add broth and process until smooth, about 45 seconds, scraping down sides of blender jar as needed. Stir chard-broth mixture, peas, and lemon juice into pot.

3. Using back of spoon, make 4 shallow indentations (about 2 inches wide) in surface of greens. Crack 2 eggs into each indentation, sprinkle with Aleppo pepper, and season with salt. Cover and cook over medium-low heat until edges of egg whites are just set, 5 to 10 minutes. Off heat, let sit, covered, until whites are fully set and yolks are still runny, 2 to 4 minutes. Sprinkle with feta, dill, and mint and drizzle with remaining 2 tablespoons oil. Serve immediately.

BAKED EGGS WITH TOMATOES, FETA, AND CROUTONS

Serves: 6
Total Time: 45 minutes

RECIPE OVERVIEW The classic Greek dish called avga feta domata consists of eggs baked in a bed of savory tomato sauce and croutons and topped with tangy feta cheese. For our version, we use fresh cherry tomatoes and roast them to make the sauce. Tossing the tomatoes with a mixture of oil, garlic, oregano, tomato paste, and a bit of sugar and salt enhances the tomato flavor and encourages deep caramelization. To prevent the croutons from becoming mushy, we bake pieces of crusty bread in the oven while the tomatoes roast, and then we fold everything together and add the eggs. Letting the dish rest, covered, for just a few minutes before serving gives the eggs time to gently finish cooking. We simply sprinkle the feta on top just before serving. If you want your yolks fully cooked, bake until the whites are fully set before the resting period.

- 3 slices French or Italian bread, cut into ½-inch pieces (4 cups)
- ¼ cup extra-virgin olive oil, divided
- 6 garlic cloves, sliced thin
- 5 teaspoons minced fresh oregano, divided
- 2 teaspoons tomato paste
- 1½ teaspoons table salt
- 1 teaspoon sugar
- ¼ teaspoon pepper
- 2 pounds cherry tomatoes
- 6 large eggs
- 2 ounces feta cheese, crumbled (½ cup)

1. Adjust oven racks to upper-middle and lower-middle positions and heat oven to 450 degrees. Line rimmed baking sheet with parchment paper. Toss bread with 1 tablespoon oil in large bowl and season with salt and pepper. Spread bread into even layer in greased 13 by 9-inch baking dish; set aside.

2. Whisk garlic, 1 tablespoon oregano, tomato paste, salt, sugar, pepper, and 1 tablespoon oil together in large bowl. Add tomatoes and toss to combine. Transfer tomato mixture to prepared baking sheet and push tomatoes toward center of sheet. Scrape any remaining garlic and tomato paste from bowl into center of tomatoes.

3. Bake bread on upper rack and tomatoes on lower rack, stirring occasionally, until bread is golden and tomatoes begin to soften, about 10 minutes. Remove croutons from oven and let cool in dish. Continue to bake tomatoes until blistered and browned, about 10 minutes longer.

4. Add tomatoes and 1 tablespoon oil to croutons, gently fold to combine, and smooth into even layer. Make 6 shallow indentations (about 2 inches wide) in surface of bread-tomato mixture using back of spoon. Crack 1 egg into each indentation and season eggs with salt and pepper.

5. Bake until whites are just beginning to set but still have some movement when dish is shaken, 10 to 12 minutes. Transfer dish to wire rack, tent loosely with aluminum foil, and let sit for 5 minutes. Sprinkle with feta and remaining 2 teaspoons oregano and drizzle with remaining 1 tablespoon oil. Serve immediately.

SHEET-PAN HUEVOS RANCHEROS

Serves: 4
Total Time: 1¼ hours

RECIPE OVERVIEW To make huevos rancheros more manageable, we prepare them on a baking sheet. We build a strong tomato sauce by roasting diced tomatoes, onion, and chiles on the sheet for concentrated flavors and nice char. Stirring in tomato juice creates a saucy bed for our eggs. After sprinkling on pepper Jack cheese, we create eight wells with a spoon and then crack in the eggs. We discovered that the key to oven-poached eggs is to add a second baking sheet for insulation. We like our eggs slightly runny; if you prefer well-done eggs, cook them to the end of the time range in step 4. Use heavyweight rimmed baking sheets—flimsy sheets will warp. Serve with hot sauce.

- 2 (28-ounce) cans diced tomatoes
- 1 tablespoon packed brown sugar
- 1 tablespoon lime juice
- 1 onion, chopped
- ½ cup canned chopped green chiles
- ¼ cup extra-virgin olive oil
- 3 tablespoons chili powder
- 4 garlic cloves, sliced thin
- ½ teaspoon table salt
- 8 (6-inch) corn tortillas
- 4 ounces pepper Jack cheese, shredded (1 cup)
- 8 large eggs
- 1 avocado, halved, pitted, and diced
- 2 scallions, sliced thin
- ¼ cup minced fresh cilantro

1. Adjust oven racks to lowest and middle positions and heat oven to 500 degrees. Drain tomatoes in fine-mesh strainer set over bowl, pressing with rubber spatula to extract as much juice as possible. Combine 1¾ cups drained tomato juice, sugar, and lime juice in bowl and set aside; discard extra drained juice.

Poaching Eggs in Sauce

HOLLOW OUT WELLS
Use the back of a spoon to expose pan bottom and make indentations for the eggs.

ADD EGGS
Crack one egg into each well to cook.

2. Combine tomatoes, onion, chiles, oil, chili powder, garlic, and salt in bowl, then spread mixture out evenly on rimmed baking sheet. Wrap tortillas in aluminum foil and place on lower rack. Place sheet with tomato mixture on upper rack and roast until charred in spots, 35 to 40 minutes, stirring and redistributing into even layer halfway through roasting.

3. Remove sheet from oven and place inside second rimmed baking sheet. Carefully stir reserved tomato juice mixture into roasted vegetables, season with salt and pepper to taste, and spread into even layer. Sprinkle cheese over top and, using back of spoon, hollow out eight 3-inch-wide holes in mixture. Crack 1 egg into each hole and season with salt and pepper.

4. Bake until whites are just beginning to set but still have some movement when sheet is shaken, 7 to 8 minutes for slightly runny yolks or 9 to 10 minutes for soft-cooked yolks, rotating sheet halfway through baking.

5. Remove sheet from oven and top with avocado, scallions, and cilantro. To serve, slide spatula underneath eggs and sauce and gently transfer to warm tortillas.

KEYS TO SUCCESS

- **Space eggs evenly**: Keeps whites from running together
- **Hit bottom**: Expose the baking sheet to place the eggs.
- **Two baking sheets**: Second baking sheet provides insulation.

COURSE
SIMPLE OMELETS AND FRITTATAS

BRIDGET LANCASTER

A basic omelet should be creamy and tender, with perfectly melted cheese. But a hot pan and burner can quickly overcook the eggs. Our on-burner off-burner technique tempers the heat to turn out perfect omelets every time. (And satisfying fillings help turn an omelet into dinner.) A frittata cooks the add-ins into the eggs. Our stovetop-to-broiler technique ensures a moist and tender vegetable-packed frittata with a golden-brown exterior.

BRIDGET'S PRO TIP: *It's easy to turn out several omelets in a row to feed a crowd by prepping in advance. I'll have a tray with all the butter cut into 1½-teaspoon (½-tablespoon) pieces, and I'll measure different kinds of cheese into 3-tablespoon mounds. For a flourish, sprinkle the omelets with some finely chopped chives.*

CLASSIC CHEESE OMELET
Serves: 2
Total Time: 15 minutes

RECIPE OVERVIEW A quick and creamy cheese omelet makes the perfect breakfast (or easy dinner) for two, and once you master the basic technique of cooking the eggs and shaping the omelet, you can vary the filling to suit any taste. A good nonstick skillet is essential for perfectly stick-free omelets, since the eggs need to move freely so that the omelet can be folded over itself. To ensure that the cheese melts before the eggs overcook, finely shred it and remove the pan from the heat after adding the cheese to the eggs. The residual heat is enough to melt the cheese without overcooking the omelet. This technique results in moist and creamy eggs, with plenty of perfectly melted cheese. You can substitute cheddar, Monterey Jack, or any semi-soft cheese for the Gruyère. Making perfect omelets takes some practice, so don't be disappointed if your first effort fails to meet your expectations.

- 6 large eggs, divided
- 1 tablespoon unsalted butter, divided, plus 1 tablespoon melted, divided
- 6 tablespoons finely shredded Gruyère cheese, divided

1. Crack 3 eggs into small bowl, season with salt and pepper, and beat with fork until combined. Repeat with remaining 3 eggs in separate bowl.

2. Melt 1½ teaspoons butter in 10-inch nonstick skillet over medium-high heat. Add 1 bowl of egg mixture and cook until edges begin to set, 2 or 3 seconds. Using heat-resistant rubber spatula, stir eggs in circular motion until slightly thickened, about 10 seconds. Use spatula to pull cooked edges of eggs in toward center, then tilt skillet to 1 side so uncooked eggs run to edge of skillet. Repeat until omelet is just set but still moist on surface, 20 to 25 seconds. Sprinkle 3 tablespoons Gruyère across center of omelet.

3. Off heat, use spatula to fold lower third (portion nearest you) of omelet over filling; press gently with spatula to secure seams, maintaining fold.

4. Run spatula between outer edge of omelet and skillet to loosen. Pull skillet sharply toward you a few times so omelet slides up lip of far edge of skillet. Use spatula to fold far edge of omelet toward center. Press to secure the seam. Invert omelet onto warm plate. Tidy edges with spatula, brush with half of melted butter, and serve immediately.

5. Wipe out skillet and repeat with remaining 1½ teaspoons butter, remaining egg mixture, remaining 3 tablespoons Gruyère, and remaining melted butter.

KEYS TO SUCCESS
- **Have the correct size nonstick skillet:** Lets omelet move and won't brown the exterior
- **Use the skillet rim:** Helps in folding the omelet
- **Easy-melting cheese:** Doesn't add to the cooking time

Variations

MUSHROOM AND THYME FILLING

Melt 1 tablespoon unsalted butter in 10-inch skillet over medium heat. Add 1 minced small shallot and cook until softened, about 2 minutes. Add 2 ounces white mushrooms, trimmed and sliced ¼ inch thick, and cook until lightly browned, about 3 minutes. Transfer to bowl and stir in 1 teaspoon minced fresh thyme and season with salt and pepper to taste. Add half of filling with Gruyère in step 2 and remaining filling to second omelet with Gruyère in step 5.

ASPARAGUS AND SMOKED SALMON FILLING

Heat 1 teaspoon olive oil in skillet over medium-high heat until shimmering. Add 1 thinly sliced shallot and cook until softened and starting to brown, about 2 minutes. Add 5 ounces trimmed asparagus, cut on bias into ¼-inch lengths; pinch salt; and pepper to taste. Cook, stirring frequently, until asparagus is crisp-tender, 5 to 7 minutes. Transfer asparagus mixture to bowl and stir in 1 ounce chopped smoked salmon and ½ teaspoon lemon juice. Add half of filling with Gruyère in step 2 and remaining filling to second omelet with Gruyère in step 5.

CORE TECHNIQUE
Shaping a Filled Omelet

PULL EGGS IN
Pull the cooked eggs toward the center and tilt the skillet so that any uncooked eggs run to the edge of the skillet.

FILL AND FOLD
Use a spatula to fold the lower third of the omelet over the filling.

PULL SKILLET
Pull the skillet sharply toward you so that the unfolded edge of the omelet slides up the far side of the skillet.

FOLD AND PRESS
Fold the far edge of the omelet toward the center of the skillet and press to secure the seam.

FRITTATA WITH PARMESAN AND HERBS

Serves: 6 to 8
Total Time: 30 minutes

RECIPE OVERVIEW Perfecting the frittata, an Italian version of the filled omelet, can be an elusive task for home cooks due to the varying opinions on how best to cook it. Since few cookbooks agree on a method, we tested several to determine which would consistently yield the best results. Whereas an omelet should be soft, delicate, and slightly runny, a frittata should be tender but firm. And whereas an omelet usually encases its filling, a frittata incorporates it evenly throughout. It should also be easy to make. We found that starting the frittata on the stovetop and finishing it in the oven sets it evenly, so it doesn't burn or dry out. Once we perfected our method, we developed a more complex variation: one with broccoli rabe, fontina cheese, and sun-dried tomatoes. Conventional skillets require so much oil to prevent sticking that frittatas cooked in them are greasy, so we use an ovensafe nonstick skillet to ensure a clean release. Because broilers vary in intensity, watch the frittata carefully as it cooks. You will need a 12-inch ovensafe nonstick skillet for this recipe.

- 12 large eggs
- 3 tablespoons half-and-half
- ¾ teaspoon table salt, divided
- ¼ teaspoon pepper
- 2 teaspoons extra-virgin olive oil
- 1 onion, chopped fine
- 1 garlic clove, minced
- 2 ounces Parmesan cheese, grated (1 cup)
- ¼ cup minced fresh parsley, basil, dill, tarragon, and/or mint

1. Adjust oven rack 5 inches from broiler element and heat broiler. Whisk eggs, half-and-half, ½ teaspoon salt, and pepper in medium bowl until well combined, about 30 seconds.

2. Heat oil in 12-inch ovensafe nonstick skillet over medium heat until shimmering. Add onion and remaining ¼ teaspoon salt and cook until onion is softened and lightly browned, 5 to 7 minutes. Add garlic and cook until fragrant, about 30 seconds. Stir Parmesan and herbs into eggs; add egg mixture to skillet and cook, using heat-resistant rubber spatula to stir and scrape bottom of skillet, until large curds form and spatula begins to leave trail but eggs are still very wet, about 2 minutes. Shake skillet to distribute eggs evenly; cook without stirring for 30 seconds to let bottom set.

3. Transfer skillet to oven and broil until frittata has risen and surface is puffed and spotty brown, 3 to 4 minutes; when pierced with tip of paring knife, eggs should be slightly wet and runny. Remove skillet from oven and let sit for 5 minutes. Using spatula, loosen frittata from skillet and slide onto serving platter or cutting board. Cut into wedges and serve.

Variation
FRITTATA WITH BROCCOLI RABE, SUN-DRIED TOMATOES, AND FONTINA

Substitute 8 ounces broccoli rabe, cut into 1-inch pieces, for onion, and increase cooking time to 6 to 8 minutes, until broccoli rabe is beginning to brown and soften. Add ⅛ teaspoon red pepper flakes to skillet with garlic. Substitute 3 ounces Italian fontina cheese, cut into ¼-inch cubes, for Parmesan. Stir ¼ cup rinsed, patted dry, and coarsely chopped oil-packed sun-dried tomatoes into eggs with fontina and herbs in step 2.

Removing a Frittata from the Pan

GET UNDERNEATH
Run the spatula around the skillet edge to loosen the frittata and then carefully slide it out.

FRITTATA WITH BROCCOLI AND TURMERIC

Serves: 6
Total Time: 40 minutes

RECIPE OVERVIEW To make a substantial, veggie-packed frittata, we use a dozen eggs and a full 4 cups of broccoli, chopping the florets small so that they will be surrounded by the eggs, ensuring a cohesive whole. Adding healthful turmeric and black pepper gives the filling a bold, slightly spicy flavor. We opt for Parmesan cheese, since a little bit goes a long way in terms of cheesy flavor; just ¼ cup is all that's needed. To ensure that our frittata cooks fully and evenly, we start it on the stovetop, stirring until a spatula leaves a trail in the curds, and then we transfer it to the oven to gently finish. Adding milk and salt to the eggs ensures that they stay tender and fluffy, as the liquid makes it harder for the proteins to coagulate and turn rubbery and the salt weakens their interactions and produces a softer curd. This frittata can be served warm or at room temperature. When paired with a salad, it makes a nice meal.

- 12 large eggs
- ⅓ cup 1 percent low-fat milk or water
- ¼ cup grated Parmesan cheese
- 2 tablespoons extra-virgin olive oil, divided
- 1 tablespoon minced fresh tarragon
- ½ teaspoon table salt, divided
- 12 ounces broccoli florets, cut into ½-inch pieces (4 cups)
- 1 shallot, minced
- 1 teaspoon ground turmeric
- ¼ teaspoon pepper
- 3 tablespoons water
- ½ teaspoon grated lemon zest plus ½ teaspoon juice

1. Adjust oven rack to middle position and heat oven to 350 degrees. Whisk eggs, milk, Parmesan, 1 tablespoon oil, tarragon, and ¼ teaspoon salt in bowl until well combined.

2. Heat remaining 1 tablespoon oil in 12-inch ovensafe nonstick skillet over medium-high heat until shimmering. Add broccoli, shallot, turmeric, pepper, and remaining ¼ teaspoon salt and cook, stirring frequently, until broccoli is crisp-tender and spotty brown, 7 to 9 minutes. Stir in water and lemon zest and juice and continue to cook, stirring constantly, until broccoli is just tender and no water remains in skillet, about 1 minute longer.

3. Add egg mixture and cook, using rubber spatula to stir and scrape bottom of skillet until large curds form and spatula leaves trail through eggs but eggs are still very wet, about 30 seconds. Smooth curds into even layer and cook, without stirring, for 30 seconds. Transfer skillet to oven and bake until frittata is slightly puffy and surface bounces back when lightly pressed, 5 to 8 minutes. Using rubber spatula, loosen frittata from skillet and transfer to cutting board. Let sit for 5 minutes before slicing and serving.

KEYS TO SUCCESS

- **Use an ovensafe nonstick skillet:** Can take the heat of the oven or broiler
- **Stovetop start:** Sets the eggs quickly
- **Oven finish:** Cooks the eggs through gently

Traditional versus Nonstick Skillets: When to Use Which for What?

One of the big differences between types of skillets is whether the surface is traditional or nonstick. Traditional skillets are made from materials that allow food to adhere slightly, which is ideal for creating the browned bits of fond that are the foundation of a great seared steak or pan sauce. Nonstick skillets, on the other hand, have a coating that keeps food from sticking to minimize the need for lubricating fat. This makes it easier to cook delicate foods and also facilitates cleanup. A nonstick skillet is particularly useful in a recipe such as our Classic Cheese Omelet (page 78) since you need to be able to move the cooked omelet around in the pan to successfully fold it; however, we don't think you need a specially designed omelet pan for this task. We also use nonstick skillets for stir-fries. Other delicate ingredients that are well suited to nonstick are fish and seafood and lean meats such as chicken, turkey, and pork (as long as you're not making a pan sauce that requires a fond).

COURSE
LET'S MAKE TOFU

STEPHANIE PIXLEY

Tofu is a popular soy-based protein that can display a range of meaty textures. It tastes clean, nutty, and subtly sweet, making it an ideal canvas for other flavors. As an ingredient, it takes to a wide variety of preparations—from scrambling to sautéing to baking to broiling—and it even tastes great raw. It is high in protein and also rich in iron and calcium, making it a go-to for vegetarians, vegans, and anyone wanting to eat less meat. This course shows you how to make tofu shine in all its guises.

STEPH'S PRO TIP: *If you're new to tofu (or are serving it to picky eaters), start with a recipe that calls for coating the tofu in cornstarch and then pan-frying it. Stir-Fried Tofu and Bok Choy transforms tofu into a crispy and rich-tasting protein that everyone loves.*

TOFU SCRAMBLE WITH BELL PEPPER, SHALLOT, AND BASIL

Serves: 4
Total Time: 45 minutes

RECIPE OVERVIEW This satisfying scramble is as great for lunch or dinner as it is tucked into a portable breakfast burrito or soft taco. To achieve an egg-like texture, soft tofu proved the best choice for scrambling, yielding smooth and creamy pieces when crumbled. (Silken tofu produced a looser scramble, and firmer tofu varieties developed into hard curds.) We keep the vegetable additions simple with bell pepper and shallot, and basil stirred in at the end adds a fresh touch. A small amount of turmeric contributes subtle depth of flavor and a golden color. We also found that the tofu could be crumbled into smaller or larger pieces to resemble egg curds of different sizes. If you cannot find soft tofu, you can use silken tofu, but your scramble will be significantly wetter. Do not use firm tofu in this recipe.

- 14 ounces soft tofu, drained and patted dry
- 1½ teaspoons vegetable oil
- 1 small red bell pepper, stemmed, seeded, and chopped fine
- 1 shallot, minced
- ¾ teaspoon table salt
- ⅛ teaspoon ground turmeric
- ⅛ teaspoon pepper
- 2 tablespoons finely chopped fresh basil

1. Crumble tofu into ¼- to ½-inch pieces. Spread tofu on paper towel–lined baking sheet and let drain for 20 minutes, then gently press dry with paper towels. Heat oil in 10-inch nonstick skillet over medium heat until shimmering. Add bell pepper and shallot and cook until softened, about 5 minutes.

2. Stir in tofu, salt, turmeric, and pepper and cook until tofu is hot, about 2 minutes. Off heat, stir in basil and serve.

Variation
TOFU SCRAMBLE WITH TOMATO AND SCALLIONS
Omit red bell pepper. Add 1 seeded and finely chopped tomato and 1 minced garlic clove to skillet with shallot in step 1; cook until tomato is no longer wet, 3 to 5 minutes. Substitute 2 tablespoons minced scallions for basil.

> ### KEYS TO SUCCESS
> - **Use soft tofu:** Texture works best for scrambling
> - **Drain the tofu:** Means less moisture in the finished dish
> - **Use a nonstick skillet:** Makes it easy to move the scramble around
> - **Turmeric:** Adds depth of flavor and a nice color

SRIRACHA-LIME TOFU BOWL

Serves: 4
Total Time: 45 minutes

RECIPE OVERVIEW This slaw-like salad, sturdy enough to stand up to an overnight rest in the fridge, features tofu, napa cabbage, red bell pepper, and shredded carrots and delivers big flavor (and texture). And the dressing is a real stunner: a spicy-sweet-sour combo of lime juice, honey, fish sauce, fresh ginger, sriracha, and oil. Pressing the cubes of tofu to drain them before browning the tofu in a hot nonstick skillet ensures that each piece turns out creamy and custard-like, but with a slightly crispy exterior. A sprinkling of grassy cilantro and sweet, floral Thai basil provides herbaceous accents.

- 14 ounces firm or extra-firm tofu, cut into ¾-inch pieces
- ¼ teaspoon table salt
- ⅛ teaspoon pepper
- 2 teaspoons plus 2 tablespoons vegetable oil, divided
- 2 tablespoons lime juice, plus lime wedges for serving
- 5 teaspoons honey
- 5 teaspoons fish sauce
- 2 teaspoons grated fresh ginger
- 2 teaspoons sriracha, plus extra for drizzling
- 1 head napa cabbage, cored and shredded (12 cups)
- 2 carrots, peeled and shredded
- 1 red bell pepper, stemmed, seeded, and sliced thin
- ½ cup fresh cilantro leaves
- ½ cup chopped fresh Thai basil, basil, or mint

1. Spread tofu over paper towel–lined baking sheet, let drain for 20 minutes, then gently press dry with paper towels. Sprinkle with salt and pepper.

2. Heat 2 teaspoons oil in 12-inch nonstick skillet over medium-high heat until shimmering. Add tofu and cook, turning as needed, until lightly browned, 12 to 15 minutes; transfer to bowl.

3. Whisk lime juice, honey, fish sauce, ginger, and sriracha together in second bowl. While whisking constantly, slowly drizzle in remaining 2 tablespoons oil until combined. Toss cabbage with half of vinaigrette to coat, then season with salt and pepper to taste. Top with tofu, carrots, bell pepper, cilantro, and basil and drizzle with remaining vinaigrette. Drizzle with extra sriracha and serve with lime wedges. (Tofu, vinaigrette, and vegetables can be refrigerated separately for up to 2 days.)

KEYS TO SUCCESS

- **Use firm or extra-firm tofu:** Cubes hold their shape during high-heat cooking
- **Drain and dry tofu:** Cubes will brown better
- **Use any type of bell pepper:** In place of the red

CORE TECHNIQUE
Cutting and Drying Tofu

PLANKS
Slice the block of tofu crosswise into planks of the desired width.

FINGERS
Cut the tofu into planks, then slice each plank into fingers of the desired size.

CUBES
Cut the tofu into fingers, then cut each finger into cubes of the desired size.

DRAIN AND DRY
Spread the tofu on paper towels and let it drain. Gently press the tofu dry with paper towels.

TOFU BANH MI

Serves: 4
Total Time: 1 hour, plus 20 minutes draining

RECIPE OVERVIEW In Vietnamese, banh mi is the word for bread. However, it also refers to a sandwich featuring tofu, chicken, pork, or pâté and crunchy pickled vegetables. For our own version, we start by making crispy, flavorful tofu. We slice the tofu into sandwich-size slabs and drain them on paper towels to make it easier to get a crispy crust. Then we dredge the slabs in cornstarch and sear them in a hot skillet until they are nicely browned. For the vegetables, we quick-pickle cucumber slices and shredded carrot in lime juice and fish sauce (you can buy a vegetarian version, if desired). Sriracha-spiked mayonnaise gives the sandwich a spicy kick, while a sprinkling of fresh cilantro adds a flavorful green garnish.

- 14 ounces firm tofu, sliced crosswise into ½-inch-thick planks
- ¼ teaspoon table salt
- ⅛ teaspoon pepper
- 2 carrots, peeled and shredded
- ½ cucumber, peeled, halved lengthwise, seeded, and sliced thin
- 1 teaspoon grated lime zest plus 1 tablespoon juice
- 1 tablespoon fish sauce
- ¼ cup mayonnaise
- 1 tablespoon sriracha
- ⅓ cup cornstarch
- 3 tablespoons vegetable oil
- 4 (8-inch) sub rolls, split and toasted
- ⅓ cup fresh cilantro leaves

1. Spread tofu on paper towel–lined baking sheet and let drain for 20 minutes. Gently press dry with paper towels and sprinkle with salt and pepper.
2. Meanwhile, combine carrots, cucumber, lime juice, and fish sauce in bowl and let sit for 15 minutes. Whisk mayonnaise, sriracha, and lime zest together in second bowl.
3. Spread cornstarch in shallow dish. Dredge seasoned tofu in cornstarch and transfer to plate. Heat oil in 12-inch nonstick skillet over medium-high heat until just smoking. Add tofu and cook until crisp and browned, about 4 minutes per side; transfer to paper towel–lined plate.
4. Spread mayonnaise mixture evenly over cut sides of each roll. Layer tofu, pickled vegetables (leave liquid in bowl), and cilantro evenly in rolls. Press gently on sandwiches to set. Serve.

STIR-FRIED TOFU AND BOK CHOY

Serves: 4
Total Time: 45 minutes

RECIPE OVERVIEW It's easy to make a great tofu and vegetable stir-fry at home. Here are two keys to any great stir-fry: prepare all your ingredients in advance so that they are ready to use when the cooking starts, and add each one at the right time. For perfectly crispy tofu with a creamy interior, we use extra-firm tofu and cook it first, giving it plenty of room to brown in the hot pan, and then we set it aside until we're ready to finish the dish. Coating the tofu with a thin layer of cornstarch helps it develop a browned crust with a minimum of oil; the coating also helps the stir-fry sauce cling to the tofu cubes for lots of flavor in every bite. Sturdier bok choy stems and carrots are added before the quicker-cooking bok choy greens. The delicate aromatics, ginger and garlic, are added only near the end of cooking, followed by the flavorful sauce. Serve with white or brown rice.

Sauce
- ½ cup chicken or vegetable broth
- ¼ cup Shaoxing wine or dry sherry
- 3 tablespoons hoisin sauce or oyster sauce
- 1 tablespoon soy sauce
- 2 teaspoons cornstarch
- 1 teaspoon toasted sesame oil

Stir-Fry
- 14 ounces extra-firm tofu, cut into 1-inch cubes
- 1 small head bok choy (about 1 pound)
- 3 scallions, minced
- 3 garlic cloves, minced
- 1 tablespoon grated fresh ginger
- 2 tablespoons vegetable oil, divided
- ⅓ cup cornstarch
- 2 carrots, peeled and cut into matchsticks

1. FOR THE SAUCE Whisk all ingredients together in bowl.

2. FOR THE STIR-FRY Arrange tofu on rimmed baking sheet lined with several layers of paper towels and let sit for 20 minutes to drain.

3. While tofu drains, remove greens from stems of bok choy by cutting along either side of stems. Slice stalks thin on bias and slice greens thin. Combine scallions, garlic, ginger, and 1 teaspoon oil in bowl.

4. Gently pat tofu dry with paper towels. Place cornstarch in medium bowl. Working with a few pieces at a time, toss tofu gently in cornstarch to coat, then transfer to plate.

5. Heat 1 tablespoon oil in 12-inch nonstick skillet or 14-inch flat-bottomed wok over high heat until just smoking. Add tofu and cook, turning occasionally, until crisp and browned on all sides, about 8 minutes. Transfer to bowl (do not cover) and set aside.

Stir-Frying Tofu

PREP EVERYTHING
Stir-fries cook in a matter of minutes, so you want to be ready.

COAT TOFU
Tossing the tofu with cornstarch helps to create a light, crispy crust.

ADD AROMATICS
Clear a space then mash the aromatics quickly so that they don't burn.

FINISH WITH SAUCE
Add the sauce at the end to thicken.

6. Add remaining 2 teaspoons oil to skillet and return to high heat until shimmering. Add carrots and bok choy stalks and cook until vegetables are crisp-tender, about 4 minutes.

7. Clear center of skillet; add scallion mixture; and cook, mashing mixture into skillet, until fragrant, 15 to 30 seconds. Stir into vegetables.

8. Return tofu to skillet and stir in bok choy greens. Whisk sauce to recombine, then add to skillet. Simmer, tossing constantly, until tofu is heated through and sauce is thickened, 30 seconds to 2 minutes. Serve.

KEYS TO SUCCESS

- **Use extra-firm tofu:** Holds up to stir-frying
- **Coat with cornstarch:** Helps tofu develop a crispy crust
- For how to prepare the bok choy, see page 41.
- For how to cut carrots into matchsticks, see page 41.

TERIYAKI TOFU

Serves: 4 to 6
Total Time: 1 hour

RECIPE OVERVIEW Teriyaki sauce and tofu are a perfect match: Teriyaki sauce is easy to make from a few pantry ingredients, and the mild tofu readily soaks up the potent teriyaki flavors. First we make teriyaki sauce from scratch with soy sauce, sugar, mirin, garlic, ginger, and some cornstarch for thickening. To encourage the tofu to absorb as much flavor as possible, we use the slow, gentle heat of the oven and cut the tofu into slabs. The liquid released from the tofu during cooking can water down the sauce, even after draining the tofu for a full 20 minutes. Since it is impossible to drain the tofu of all its liquid, we account for the released liquid by overreducing the sauce to start. As the tofu bakes, it releases water into the concentrated sauce, diluting it to just the right flavor and thickness. You can substitute firm tofu for the extra-firm in this recipe. Serve over rice.

- ½ cup water
- ½ cup soy sauce
- ½ cup sugar
- 2 tablespoons mirin
- 1 garlic clove, minced
- 1 teaspoon cornstarch
- ½ teaspoon grated fresh ginger
- 28 ounces extra-firm tofu, sliced crosswise into ¾-inch-thick slabs
- 2 scallions, green parts only, sliced thin
  Lime wedges

1. Adjust oven rack to middle position and heat oven to 350 degrees. Whisk water, soy sauce, sugar, mirin, garlic, cornstarch, and ginger together in small saucepan until smooth. Bring sauce to boil over medium-high heat, whisking occasionally, then reduce heat to medium-low and simmer vigorously until sauce is thickened and reduced to ¾ cup, 12 to 15 minutes.

2. Arrange tofu in even layer in 13 by 9-inch baking dish and pour sauce evenly over top. Cover with aluminum foil and bake until flavors have melded and tofu is warmed through, about 30 minutes, flipping tofu halfway through baking.

3. Transfer tofu to platter. Season sauce with pepper to taste, pour over tofu, and sprinkle with scallions. Serve with lime wedges.

CHILLED MARINATED TOFU

Serves: 4 to 6
Total Time: 40 minutes, plus 20 minutes draining and 2 hours cooling

RECIPE OVERVIEW Marinated raw tofu, called hiyayakko or yakko-dofu, is served throughout Japan during the sticky summer months as a cool and refreshing appetizer or snack. In the best renditions, a flavorful marinade and a few choice garnishes amplify the tofu's delicate sweet-soy flavor. The marinade for this dish is typically a soy sauce–enhanced dashi, the ubiquitous Japanese broth prepared from kombu seaweed and bonito (skipjack tuna) flakes. We replace the bonito with a glutamate-rich combination of wakame seaweed, fish sauce, mirin, and sugar. This mixture produces a well-rounded marinade: sweet, salty, and robust—almost meaty in its intensity. A splash of rice vinegar, added off the heat after the broth steeps, provides a bit of balance. For the garnishes, we like a sprinkle of crumbled nori, sliced scallions, and a drizzle of toasted sesame oil. A sprinkling of Shichimi Togarishi (page 29) tastes good on this tofu. For an accurate measurement of boiling water, bring a kettle of water to a boil and then measure out the desired amount. For the fish sauce, you can use either Bragg's Amino Acids or a vegetarian fish sauce substitute, if desired.

- 14 ounces firm tofu, halved lengthwise, then cut crosswise into ½-inch-thick squares
- 2 cups boiling water
- ¼ cup fish sauce
- ¼ cup mirin
- 4 teaspoons sugar
- ¼ ounce wakame seaweed
- ¼ ounce kombu seaweed
- 4 teaspoons rice vinegar
- 2 sheets toasted nori seaweed, crumbled
- 2 scallions, sliced thin on bias
  Toasted sesame oil

1. Spread tofu over paper towel–lined baking sheet, let drain for 20 minutes, then gently press dry with paper towels. Season with salt and pepper.

2. Meanwhile, combine boiling water, fish sauce, mirin, sugar, wakame, and kombu in bowl. Cover and let sit for 15 minutes. Strain liquid through fine-mesh strainer, discarding solids, then return broth to now-empty bowl.

3. Add tofu and vinegar; cover; and refrigerate until cool, at least 2 hours or up to 2 days. To serve, use slotted spoon to transfer tofu to platter, top with nori and scallions, and drizzle with sesame oil to taste.

MARINATED TOFU AND VEGETABLE SALAD

Serves: 4
Total Time: 30 minutes

RECIPE OVERVIEW There's more to raw salads than leafy greens and basic vinaigrettes. This light and easy tofu salad boasts quick-marinated firm tofu and a bright and refreshing dressing over fresh, crunchy cabbage, snow peas, and bell pepper. Tofu takes particularly well to marinating, which is a great way to add flavor to recipes where the tofu is served raw. Firm tofu is tender and supple but still sturdy. A sriracha-based sauce does double duty in this recipe as both a marinade for the tofu and a dressing for the salad, adding a touch of heat and tons of flavor. Seasoned rice vinegar, which contains added sugar and salt, is one of our favorite shortcut ingredients and helps round out the marinade-dressing. Do not substitute other varieties of tofu in this recipe.

- 28 ounces firm tofu
- ¼ cup seasoned rice vinegar
- 3 tablespoons toasted sesame oil
- 2 tablespoons sriracha
- 2 teaspoons honey
- ¼ teaspoon table salt
- 2 tablespoons sesame seeds
- ½ small head napa cabbage, cored and sliced thin (4 cups)
- 6 ounces snow peas, strings removed
- 1 red bell pepper, stemmed, seeded, and cut into ½-inch pieces
- 2 scallions, sliced thin on bias

1. Cut tofu into ¾-inch cubes. Gently press tofu cubes dry with paper towels.

2. Whisk vinegar, oil, sriracha, honey, and salt together in large bowl. Gently toss tofu in dressing until evenly coated, then cover and refrigerate for 20 minutes.

3. While tofu marinates, toast sesame seeds in 10-inch skillet over medium heat, shaking skillet occasionally, until golden and fragrant, 3 to 5 minutes. Set aside to cool.

4. Add cabbage, snow peas, and bell pepper to bowl with tofu and gently toss to combine. Season with salt and pepper to taste and sprinkle with sesame seeds and scallions. Serve.

RESOURCES FOR TOFU

WHAT IS TOFU, EXACTLY?

Tofu is the result of a process that's similar to making cheese: Curds, made from coagulating soy milk, are set in a mold and pressed to extract as much (or as little) of the liquid whey as desired. Depending on how long the tofu is pressed and how much coagulant is used, the amount of whey released will vary, creating a range of textures from soft to firm.

CHOOSING THE RIGHT TOFU

Tofu is available in a variety of textures: extra-firm, firm, medium, soft, and silken. Reaching for the right variety is key to the success of any given recipe. In general, firmer varieties hold their shape when cooking, while softer varieties do not, so it follows that each type of tofu is best when used in specific ways. Regardless of type, tofu is highly perishable and is best used when it is fresh.

EXTRA-FIRM AND FIRM TOFU

We prefer extra-firm or firm tofu for stir-fries and noodle dishes, as they hold their shape in high-heat cooking applications and when tossed with pasta. These two varieties of tofu are also great marinated (they absorb marinade better than softer varieties do) or tossed raw into salads (page 87).

MEDIUM AND SOFT TOFU

Medium and soft tofu boast a creamy, custardy texture; we love to pan-fry these kinds of tofu, often coated with cornstarch, to achieve a crisp exterior, which makes a nice textural contrast to the silky interior. Soft tofu is also great scrambled like eggs (page 82).

SILKEN TOFU

Silken tofu has a very soft, ultracreamy texture and is often used as a base for smoothies and dips, in desserts such as puddings, or as an egg replacement in vegan baked goods.

HOW TO STORE TOFU

To store an opened package, cover the tofu with water and refrigerate it in a covered container, changing the water daily. Any hint of sourness means the tofu is past its prime.

We've always stored leftover tofu in water, unchanged. But we spoke to an artisanal tofu maker who recommended changing the water daily. We also read that storing it in lightly salted water is the best method. To find out which approach kept store-bought tofu tasting fresh the longest, we tried each using extra-firm, firm, and silken tofu, storing the samples in plastic containers. As a control, we also placed a sample of each style in zipper-lock bag with as much air pressed out as possible.

The samples without any liquid lasted only four to six days. We don't recommend storing leftover tofu in salted water: Although these samples stayed fresh for two weeks, they also picked up a noticeable salty flavor almost immediately. The samples stored in water that we changed daily were edible for 10 days, after which they began losing flavor. So, in the end, our preferred method is to submerge the tofu in plain tap water. This kept the tofu as fresh-tasting as straight-from-the-package tofu for 10 days and didn't require any maintenance. Just make sure that the water is clear; cloudy water can be a sign of bacterial growth, and the tofu should be discarded.

FREEZING TOFU

Freezing tofu will give it a spongy consistency and make it highly absorbent.

We've often wondered why some tofu in restaurants has a distinctive spongy texture that allows it to soak up more of the sauce in a dish. This texture is produced by freezing the tofu solid before thawing and cooking it—a method that was originally used in China (and Japan) to preserve tofu during the winter months. Tofu is about 88 percent water; as it freezes, the ice crystals expand, pushing apart the protein network. When thawed, the water drains away, leaving the tofu with a spongy consistency and highly absorbent. We experimented with freezing tofu in the test kitchen and quite liked the results. When stir-fried, the slabs did absorb sauce readily and had a resilient, slightly chewy texture that was far more meat-like than fresh tofu. And because the thawed tofu contained less water, it formed a nice crust when deep-fried. To freeze, slice extra-firm tofu into ½- to ¾-inch-thick slabs, spread the slabs in a single layer on a baking sheet or plate, and place them in the freezer overnight. (At this point, the tofu can be placed in zipper-lock bags and stored in the freezer for up to a month.) To use, thaw to room temperature and press each slab gently over a colander to expel any remaining water before cooking.

JOURNEY: FROM SOY BEAN TO TOFU

Tofu has been made by hand for 2,000 years. Today, the process of manufacturing the tofu that you find in the market has been turned into a science. Here are the steps that every package of tofu takes before making it to your fridge.

1 START WITH BEANS

Tofu starts with soybeans, soaked for 8 to 10 hours at 60 to 68 degrees. The soybeans are then ground, and new water is added during grinding to make a bean slurry—a rough version of soy milk. Both the amount of added water and the temperature at which the beans are ground are carefully controlled; they vary depending on which type of tofu is being made. Enough water is added so that the finished tofu will contain 88 to 90 percent water.

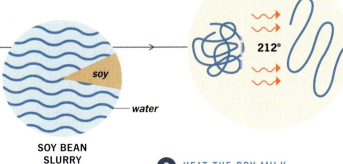

SOY BEAN SLURRY

2 HEAT THE SOY MILK

Next, this soy milk is heated for around 5 minutes at 212 degrees to inactivate enzymes. (One particular enzyme—lipoxygenase—is responsible for producing the undesirable "beany" flavor that can be present in soy milk.)

3 ADD A COAGULANT

The next step in the process is to coagulate the soy milk while it is hot. This is done by adding coagulants, which help link the soy proteins together to form a gel-like structure. There are four types: nigari, calcium and magnesium sulfate salts, GDL, and acids such as lemon juice. Each type of coagulant reacts at a different speed and is used to make a different type of tofu.

GOOD   **BAD**

4 FORM THE CURDS

With time and the proper amount of coagulant, the soy milk forms curds, which have a smooth and cohesive texture. When too much coagulant is used, the texture will become coarse and crumbly.

5 PRESS IT DOWN

Depending on the type of tofu, the curd may or may not be cut or broken before pressing to expel the whey. (It's necessary for soft, firm, and extra-firm tofu.) Longer pressing times and pressures are required for firmer tofus, and pressing is usually done in molds of various sizes. As a general guideline, tofu manufacturers apply light initial pressure for 5 to 10 minutes, followed by a stronger pressure for 10 to 15 minutes to make soft tofu. For firmer tofu, a higher pressure is applied for 20 to 30 minutes. Silken tofu is not pressed. All tofu is then packed in containers filled with water to keep it moist. It is then pasteurized and kept refrigerated for retail sale.

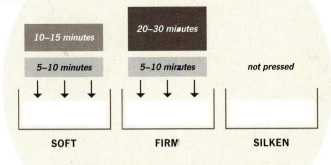

Most tofu is pressed to expel excess whey. (Silken tofu is not.) Soft and firm tofus are pressed lightly for 5 to 10 minutes. Soft tofu gets medium pressure for another 10 to 15 minutes, while firm tofu gets firm pressure for up to 30 minutes.

CHAPTER 3

VEGETABLES

COURSES

94 **BASIC-NOT-BORING BOILED AND STEAMED VEGETABLES**

100 **SIMPLY SAUTÉED**

104 **DARK LEAFY GREENS**

110 **PAN-ROASTING VEGETABLES**

114 **POTATOES 101**

118 **SWEET POTATOES**

124 **EVERYDAY ROASTED VEGETABLES**

128 **SHAPE-SHIFTING CAULIFLOWER**

132 **TURN ON THE BROILER**

136 **WHAT TO DO WITH EGGPLANT**

140 **VEGETABLES ON THE GRILL**

MORE TO EXPLORE

144 **QUICK PICKLES**

VEGETABLE BASICS

BUYING VEGETABLES

Search out the freshest vegetables possible at the market, since fresher vegetables mean fresher taste. It's a treat to shop for vegetables at a farmers' market if you have the opportunity because the vegetables will not have traveled far from the field or been stored for a long time. If you are lucky enough to grow your own vegetables, then you already know that the flavor of garden-fresh produce is amazing.

Should I Buy Organic or Conventional?

When it comes to produce, nutrition doesn't vary much between conventional and organic (local and seasonal are better markers of optimal nutrients). But there are pesticides to consider. The Environmental Working Group's "clean fifteen" and "dirty dozen" describe which conventional produce is safest to eat and which contains more pesticide residue, making organic a smart choice.

CLEAN FIFTEEN
Corn, avocados, pineapples, cabbage, onions, frozen sweet peas, papayas, asparagus, mangoes, eggplant, honeydew melon, kiwi, cantaloupe, cauliflower, grapefruit

DIRTY DOZEN
Strawberries, spinach, nectarines, apples, peaches, pears, cherries, grapes, celery, tomatoes, sweet bell peppers and hot peppers, potatoes

GET TO KNOW THESE TYPES OF VEGETABLES

Cruciferous
The large and diverse Brassica family (or cabbage family) of vegetables includes broccoli, broccolini, brussels sprouts, cabbage, cauliflower, kale, radishes, and more. They are all known for having strong flavors, brought out only when the cells are damaged by chopping, chewing, or massaging. It is key to prep and cook them properly in order to minimize their bitterness.

Root
Root vegetables grow underground and they have an earthy richness. This group includes carrots, beets, parsnips, and sweet potatoes as well as jicama and celery root.

Nightshade
The nightshade or potato family includes white potatoes, tomatoes, peppers, and eggplant. They are rich in antioxidants known to reduce inflammation and are also rich in fiber.

Allium
This family includes onions, garlic, shallots, leeks, and scallions. These bulbous, pungent vegetables are most frequently used to build flavor in a range of recipes.

STORING VEGETABLES

Store Most Vegetables in the Crisper Drawer

Virtually all vegetables do best in the relatively humid environment of the crisper drawer in your refrigerator; this includes artichokes, asparagus, beets, broccoli, cabbage, carrots, cauliflower, celery, chiles, cucumbers, eggplant, fresh herbs, green beans, leafy greens, leeks, lettuce, mushrooms, peppers, radishes, scallions, summer squash, sugar snap peas, turnips, and zucchini. We also put corn in the crisper drawer (see right). The sugar in corn begins to convert to starch from the moment the corn is picked; though this conversion is much slower in the supersweet varieties sold at most stores these days, storing corn in the refrigerator will slow the process even more.

Be sure to keep vegetables either in their original packaging or in partially open plastic produce bags (more specific tips below) to help prevent moisture loss.

Store Alliums, Potatoes, and Winter Squash in the Pantry

Garlic, onions, shallots, potatoes, sweet potatoes, delicata squash, and winter squash such as butternut, acorn, and hubbard should be kept at cool room temperature and away from light to prolong shelf life.

Why You Should Leave Produce in Its Original Packaging

In general, it's a good idea to store produce in the packaging in which it was sold. Sometimes ready-made packaging has a function beyond simple convenience and can actually help preserve the contents. For example, though they appear solid, the bags in which spinach and other greens are now sold are made of a polymer that allows ethylene to pass through freely, staving off spoilage. Other types of packaging often feature small perforations or other openings (such as the bags in which celery is sold); here, too, the intent is to allow ethylene to escape while also protecting the produce from the drying effects of air.

When to Wash Produce

It's best to wash most produce just before you use it. Moisture left on produce promotes the growth of mold and bacteria, which in turn causes spoilage. If you do wash produce ahead of time, make sure to dry it thoroughly before storing it. For information on washing salad greens, see page 149.

TIPS FOR EXTENDING THE LIFE OF YOUR PRODUCE

The following storage tips will help you make the most of the produce you buy.

Water Your Asparagus Spears

Asparagus stored in the refrigerator can quickly dry out and become tough. To keep the spears tender and flavorful, trim the ends, set the spears upright in an inch or two of water, and cover loosely with plastic wrap before placing them in the fridge. Limp broccoli, scallions, and celery benefit from the same treatment.

Keep Corn Moist

Our preferred way to store corn is to wrap the unhusked ears in damp paper towels (or place them in a wet paper bag), place the damp paper towel–wrapped ears in a plastic produce bag, and refrigerate them in the crisper drawer.

Store Whole Cucumbers, Zucchini, and Summer Squashes in Plastic Wrap

Following the lead of shrink-wrapped English cucumbers, we wrap American cucumbers as well as zucchini and summer squashes tightly in plastic wrap to help keep them crisp. Though it's not entirely airtight, plastic wrap forms an effective second skin that minimizes moisture loss in these vegetables. Tightly rewrapping these vegetables once they're cut will also help slow their deterioration.

Trim Carrots Before Storing

Carrots continue to feed their leafy tops in storage, which causes them to lose moisture far more quickly. We recommend first trimming the carrots of their tops (which can be used to make a sauce) and then placing them in an open zipper-lock bag. Stored this way, carrots should stay firm for at least a few weeks.

COURSE

BASIC-NOT-BORING BOILED AND STEAMED VEGETABLES

ANDREA GEARY

It's good to know how to prepare vegetables in the simplest (and quickest) way. Boiling and steaming both fit the bill with a minimum of work. Boiling allows you to season vegetables with salt as they cook but more flavor can be washed away. Steaming leaves vegetables more crisp than boiling but you can only steam in small batches. Whichever method you use, it is important to prep the vegetables properly and monitor the cooking time closely. This course shows you how.

ANDREA'S PRO TIP: *Boiling and steaming may not be the most glamorous cooking methods, but they produce consistent results, require minimal equipment, and the brief cook times are just long enough for you to prepare an elevating garnish.*

BOILED CARROTS WITH LEMON AND CHIVES

Serves: 4
Total Time: 30 minutes

RECIPE OVERVIEW Carrots are inexpensive and available year-round, making them a great go-to vegetable. Boiling them simply in very salty water is super-easy and beneficial: It seasons them as they cook so they become more flavorful, and it helps them cook faster. Seasoning the carrots as they cook makes them tastier than carrots that merely receive a sprinkle of salt after cooking. Finishing touches of fat (butter) for richness, acid (lemon juice) for brightness, and fresh herbs and spices (chives and black pepper) for flavor make this simple side dish a great complement to any meal.

- 1 pound carrots, peeled
- 2 teaspoons table salt
- 1 tablespoon unsalted butter, cut into 4 pieces
- 1 teaspoon lemon juice, plus extra for serving
- ⅛ teaspoon pepper
- 1 tablespoon chopped fresh chives

1. Cut carrots into 1½- to 2-inch lengths. Leave thin pieces whole, halve medium pieces lengthwise, and quarter thick pieces lengthwise.

2. Bring 2 cups water to boil in medium saucepan over high heat. Add carrots and salt, cover, and cook until tender throughout, about 6 minutes (start timer as soon as carrots go into water).

3. Drain carrots and return them to saucepan. Add butter, lemon juice, and pepper and stir until butter is melted. Stir in chives. Season with extra lemon juice to taste, and serve.

Variations

BOILED CARROTS WITH CUMIN, LIME, AND CILANTRO
Substitute extra-virgin olive oil for butter; ½ teaspoon grated lime zest plus 1 teaspoon lime juice for lemon juice; ½ teaspoon cumin seeds, crushed (use mortar and pestle or spice grinder to crush) for pepper; and cilantro for chives.

BOILED CARROTS WITH FENNEL SEEDS AND CITRUS
Substitute extra-virgin olive oil for butter; ½ teaspoon fennel seeds, crushed (use mortar and pestle or spice grinder to crush) for pepper; and parsley for chives. Add ½ teaspoon grated orange zest to carrots with lemon juice.

BOILED CARROTS WITH MINT AND PAPRIKA
Substitute sherry vinegar for lemon juice, ½ teaspoon paprika for pepper, and mint for chives.

SCIENCE LESSON — Make It Salty

Boiling the carrots in very salty water has a number of benefits: It seasons them, allows them to retain more of their own natural sugars and salt for even better flavor, and—most interesting—speeds up cooking. How? The sodium ions in salt displace some of the calcium ions that give strength to the carrots' pectin network, weakening it and allowing the carrots to soften more quickly.

CORE TECHNIQUES

Boiling, Blanching, and Steaming

BOILING
Bring water and salt to a boil. Cook the vegetable until tender and then drain well.

BLANCHING AND SHOCKING
Boil the vegetable until its color is bright and its texture is crisp-tender. Drain and plunge into an ice bath.

STEAMING
Lay the vegetables in a collapsible steamer basket, cover, and steam until tender.

KEYS TO SUCCESS

- **Buy carrots of the same diameter:** Between 1 and 1½ inches at the thick end
- **Cut same size pieces:** So carrots cook at the same rate
- **Start timing:** Begin as soon as the carrots go into the water
- **Black pepper:** Always use freshly ground

VEGETABLES | 95

FOOLPROOF BOILED CORN

Serves: 4 to 6
Total Time: 30 minutes

RECIPE OVERVIEW You might think that you don't need a recipe for boiled corn, but it's easy to overcook. To guarantee perfectly crisp, juicy corn every time, you want to cook it to its ideal doneness range of 150 to 170 degrees—this is when the starch granules in the corn have absorbed water and swelled but little of its pectin (the glue that holds the cell walls together) has dissolved. To consistently cook corn to the ideal temperature, you don't actually boil it. Instead, bring 4 quarts of water to a boil, shut off the heat, drop in 6 ears of corn, and let the corn stand for at least 10 minutes. Off heat, the temperature of the water drops as the corn temperature rises, until it hits its sweet spot after about 10 minutes (see page 99). And this method is flexible, accommodating 6 to 8 ears of different sizes, plus the corn can sit in the water for as long as 30 minutes without overcooking.

- 6 ears corn, husks and silk removed
- Unsalted butter, softened
- Table salt
- Pepper

1. Bring 4 quarts water to boil in large Dutch oven. Turn off heat, add corn to water, cover, and let stand for at least 10 minutes or up to 30 minutes.

2. Transfer corn to large platter and serve immediately, passing butter, salt, and pepper separately.

Variation
FOOLPROOF BOILED CORN FOR A CROWD

Our recipe for Foolproof Boiled Corn works best when cooking 6 to 8 ears. We adapted the method so you can cook as many as 24 ears at a time using a large cooler—which will also keep the corn hot for hours without continuing to cook it.

Place up to 24 husked ears in 50-quart cooler, pour enough boiling water over corn to cover by 1 inch, and close cooler lid for 45 minutes. Serve. (Corn can be held in water for up to 2 hours.)

> **KEYS TO SUCCESS**
> - **Pick good ears:** With packed, plump, firm kernels and green, pliable husks wrapped closely around the ears
> - **Add the corn to boiling water:** So its starch cooks through while leaving its pectin (which keeps kernels firm) mostly intact
> - **Shut off the heat:** To eliminate the risk of overcooking

GREEN BEANS WITH TOASTED ALMONDS AND BROWNED BUTTER

Serves: 4 to 6
Total Time: 45 minutes

RECIPE OVERVIEW Green beans are the simplest of green vegetables to cook. In this recipe you blanch and shock fresh green beans, meaning the beans cook in boiling water for just a few minutes and then get drained and immediately plunged into an ice bath to stop the cooking. Once blanched and shocked, the beans will keep for up to 3 days in the refrigerator. For serving, quickly reheat the beans in a skillet with a little water and then finish with browned butter and toasted almonds. This side dish is simple yet elegant enough for company.

- ½ cup slivered almonds (about 2½ ounces)
- 1 teaspoon table salt
- 1 pound green beans, trimmed
- 4 tablespoons unsalted butter

1. Finely chop slivered almonds. Toast in small skillet over medium heat until browned and fragrant, about 5 minutes. (Cooled, toasted almonds can be stored in airtight container for 3 days.)

2. Bring 2½ quarts water to boil in large saucepan over high heat. Add salt and green beans. Return to boil and cook until beans are bright green and crisp-tender, 3 to 4 minutes.

3. Meanwhile, fill large bowl with ice water. Drain beans in colander and transfer beans immediately to ice water. When beans no longer feel warm to touch, drain in colander again. Dry beans thoroughly with paper towels. (If desired, transfer beans to large zipper-lock bag and refrigerate for up to 3 days.)

4. Heat butter in small, heavy saucepan over medium heat and cook, swirling frequently, until butter turns chocolate brown and becomes fragrant, 4 to 5 minutes. Add almonds and cook, stirring constantly, until fragrant and combined, about 1 minute. Season with salt and pepper to taste.

5. Meanwhile, heat ¼ cup water and beans in 12-inch skillet over high heat. Cook, tossing frequently, until beans are warmed through, 1 to 2 minutes. Season with salt and pepper to taste.

6. Arrange beans on warm serving platter. Top beans with browned butter–almond mixture and serve immediately.

> **KEYS TO SUCCESS**
> - **Salt the water:** To season the beans
> - **Use an ice bath:** Stops the cooking of the beans (see page 95)
> - **Reheat with water:** Easy to cook the beans ahead
> - **Make browned butter:** See page 253 for how

STEAMED BROCCOLI WITH LIME-CUMIN DRESSING

Serves: 4
Total Time: 20 minutes

RECIPE OVERVIEW The tricky part about steaming broccoli is keeping the delicate florets from turning to mush while simultaneously cooking the dense stalks through until they are tender. Some recipes solve this by ignoring the stalks altogether, but we like the contrasting flavors and textures of the florets and stalks. You can steam both as long as you take the time to carefully prepare them. To guarantee even cooking, cut the florets into large 1-inch pieces and cut the stalks into small ¼-inch pieces. This results in tender, evenly cooked broccoli in about 5 minutes. To dress the broccoli simply, make a quick bright dressing flavored with lime and cumin. You will need a collapsible steamer basket for this recipe.

Dressing
- ¼ cup finely chopped red onion
- 3 tablespoons extra-virgin olive oil
- 1 teaspoon grated lime zest plus 1 tablespoon juice
- ½ teaspoon ground cumin
- ⅛ teaspoon hot sauce, plus extra for serving

Broccoli
- 1½ pounds broccoli, florets cut into 1-inch pieces, stalks peeled and sliced ¼ inch thick

1. FOR THE DRESSING Whisk all ingredients together in large bowl; set aside for serving.

2. FOR THE BROCCOLI Bring 1 inch water to boil in Dutch oven. Place broccoli in collapsible steamer basket, then transfer basket to pot. Cover and cook until broccoli is tender and bright green, about 5 minutes.

3. Transfer broccoli to bowl with dressing and gently toss to combine. Season with salt and extra hot sauce to taste. Serve warm or at room temperature.

Variation
STEAMED BROCCOLI WITH SPICY BALSAMIC DRESSING AND BLACK OLIVES
Whisk ¼ cup chopped pitted kalamata olives, ¼ cup extra-virgin olive oil, 2 teaspoons balsamic vinegar, 2 teaspoons red wine vinegar, 1 minced garlic clove, ½ teaspoon red pepper flakes, and ¼ teaspoon table salt together in bowl. Substitute for lime-cumin dressing.

KEYS TO SUCCESS
- **Cut the florets into pieces and peel and slice the stalks:** See page 41 for how to prep broccoli.
- **Use a steamer basket:** Perfect for holding vegetables and easily lifting them from the pot

HOW LONG SHOULD YOU COOK THAT VEGETABLE?

VEGETABLE	PREPARATION	BOILING TIME	STEAMING TIME
Asparagus	Tough ends trimmed and discarded	2 to 4 minutes	3 to 5 minutes
Broccoli	Florets cut into 1- to 1½-inch pieces, stalks peeled and cut into ¼-inch pieces	2 to 4 minutes	4 to 6 minutes
Brussels Sprouts	Stem ends trimmed, discolored leaves removed, and halved through stems	6 to 8 minutes	7 to 9 minutes
Green Beans	Ends trimmed	3 to 5 minutes	6 to 8 minutes
Snap Peas	Strings removed	2 to 4 minutes	4 to 6 minutes
Snow Peas	Strings removed	2 to 3 minutes	4 to 6 minutes

RESOURCES FOR BOILED AND STEAMED VEGETABLES

TWO STEPS FOR TENDER, BRIGHT VEGETABLES

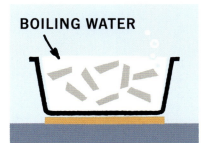

Blanch A quick blanch in boiling water cooks the vegetables until just tender, brightening their colors at the same time.

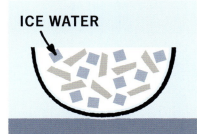

Shock Tossing the vegetables in ice water stops the cooking, preventing them from becoming mushy and drab.

SCIENCE LESSON: BOILING BASICS

At sea level, water boils at 212 degrees Fahrenheit. Large bubbles rise energetically and burst on the surface of the water, creating turbulence. Boiling is for hardy, sturdy foods of relatively small size that can withstand this turbulence and the churning action—there are, in fact, only a handful of foods that are cooked through via boiling: vegetables that are being blanched, dried pasta, and some grains are the most common. When bringing liquid to a boil, covering the pot will help speed heating because the lid will trap heat within the pot. It will also prevent moisture loss.

TRACKING HOW CORN COOKS

It's easy to overcook boiled corn, since the corn's temperature soon approaches that of the boiling water (212 degrees) and its pectin (the "glue" holding its cell walls together) rapidly dissolves. But if the heat is shut off right before the corn is added to the water, the temperatures of both will equalize somewhere between 150 and 170 degrees—the sweet spot where the corn's starches have absorbed water but little of its pectin has broken down—and the kernels still remain snappy.

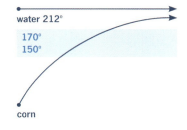

Corn temperature overshoots its ideal doneness range, and corn turns mushy.

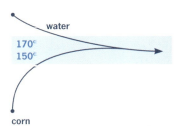

Corn and water meet at about 160°, ensuring perfect texture every time.

EASIEST-EVER WAY TO SHUCK CORN

Odd as it might sound, we've found that the easiest way to shuck corn is to briefly microwave it and then shake it, which makes the husk and silk slide right off. The cob will heat up a bit, but the kernels won't be cooked.

Cut off the stalk end of the cob just above the first row of kernels. Microwave 3 or 4 ears at a time on a plate for 30 to 60 seconds. Hold each ear by the uncut silk end; shake up and down until the cob slips free, leaving behind the husk and silk.

Don't Shuck in Advance Some markets and farm stands allow you to shuck the corn on site. Do this only if you plan to eat the corn that day, since the exposed kernels will be prone to drying out.

COURSE
SIMPLY SAUTÉED

LAN LAM

Sautéing is a simple and quick method of cooking food on the stovetop and it is a good technique for cooking vegetables. "Sauté" means to sear food in a small amount of hot fat so that it browns deeply and develops savory flavor. In this course you can practice this essential skill with recipes for sautéed carrots, zucchini, and mushrooms.

LAN'S PRO TIP: *I always make sure that my vegetables are uniformly cut because this ensures that they all finish cooking at the same time.*

SAUTÉED CARROTS WITH GINGER, MAPLE, AND FENNEL SEEDS

Serves: 4
Total Time: 20 minutes

RECIPE OVERVIEW This delicious and dead-easy carrot recipe is simple enough to serve any night of the week but is sophisticated enough for company. Cooking the carrots is a short project: Cutting them into uniform sticks, using a smoking-hot pan, and stirring minimally chars, caramelizes, and cooks them through in just minutes. The glaze features fennel seeds and ginger, and achieves the perfect sweet, salty, and tart balance using maple syrup, soy sauce, and balsamic vinegar. You can substitute anise seeds for fennel. Look for carrots with tops no larger than 1 inch in diameter for this recipe. If yours are larger, remove their fibrous cores before cooking.

- 2 tablespoons soy sauce
- 2 tablespoons balsamic vinegar
- 1 tablespoon maple syrup
- 1½ teaspoons fennel seeds
- 2 tablespoons minced fresh ginger
- 2 tablespoons plus 1 teaspoon vegetable oil, divided
- 1½ pounds carrots, peeled and cut into 2-inch-long by ½-inch-wide matchsticks

1. Stir soy sauce, vinegar, maple syrup, and fennel seeds together in bowl; set aside. Combine ginger and 1 teaspoon oil in separate bowl; set aside.
2. Heat remaining 2 tablespoons oil in 12-inch skillet over medium-high heat until just smoking. Add carrots and cook, stirring occasionally, until well charred and crisp-tender, 5 to 7 minutes.
3. Push carrots to sides of skillet. Add ginger mixture to center and cook, mashing mixture into pan, until fragrant, about 30 seconds. Stir ginger into carrots. Add soy mixture and toss to coat carrots; cook until liquid is reduced to syrupy glaze, about 15 seconds. Serve immediately.

KEYS TO SUCCESS

- **Mince the fresh ginger:** See page 43 for how
- **Cut the carrots into matchsticks:** See page 41 for how
- **Heat the oil until smoking:** Essential for getting good browning on the carrots
- **Cook the ginger mixture before stirring it into the carrots:** Heat blooms the flavor of the ginger.

CORE TECHNIQUE
Sautéing Vegetables

PREHEAT PAN
Wait for the oil to shimmer or start to smoke. Those are the visual cues that the pan is ready.

ADD VEGETABLES
Stir and shake the pan to make sure the vegetables are equally exposed to the heat.

SCIENCE LESSON
Stages of Doneness for Vegetables

Perfectly cooked vegetables can be a thing of beauty. Vibrant in color, full of fresh—even juicy—flavor, they can be an awakening for those accustomed to eating overcooked versions. But achieving the ideal doneness can be a challenge if you don't know what to look for.

When we expose vegetables to heat through various cooking methods, what we're really doing is breaking down and dissolving pectin (the glue that holds vegetable cell walls together). The more a vegetable is exposed to heat, the more pectin is dissolved, and the more limp, soft, and mushy a vegetable becomes. One way to know when that perfect crisp-tender texture has been achieved is to pay close attention to the vegetable's appearance. Green vegetables transform from brightly colored to drab and dull as they cook thanks to the way chlorophyll (the molecule that gives green vegetables their hue) reacts to heat. Once a vegetable brightens, it's a sign that heat has penetrated the cell walls and the vegetable is on its way to tenderizing. From there, it's a matter of taste. Like your vegetables on the tender side? Cook them a little longer. As long as you halt cooking before the color turns olive-green, the vegetables will be juicy and bright.

SAUTÉED ZUCCHINI

Serves: 4 to 6
Total Time: 20 minutes, plus 30 minutes salting

RECIPE OVERVIEW Vegetables, especially summer vegetables such as zucchini and yellow summer squash (and tomatoes) are made up of mostly water. When cooking, the biggest challenge is dealing with all this liquid so we often use salt to remove liquid from vegetables before using them in recipes. For sautéed zucchini and/or summer squash (a mix is nice) with concentrated flavor and an appealing texture, you must first eliminate excess water from the vegetable by salting and draining the squash for 30 minutes and then patting it dry. Sauté an onion first for some depth of flavor and then add the squash, along with some lemon zest, to a hot skillet, where the squash becomes tender and lightly browned with minimal stirring. Lemon juice and basil, stirred in off the heat, lend bright flavors. Do not add more salt when cooking or the dish will be too salty. Sprinkle with more basil before serving, if desired.

- 1½ pounds zucchini and/or yellow summer squash, trimmed and sliced ¼ inch thick
- 1 tablespoon kosher salt
- 3 tablespoons extra-virgin olive oil
- 1 small onion, chopped fine
- 1 teaspoon grated lemon zest plus 1 tablespoon juice
- 1 tablespoon minced fresh basil, mint, or parsley

1. Toss zucchini with salt in colander set over bowl and let drain until roughly ⅓ cup liquid drains from zucchini, about 30 minutes; discard liquid. Pat zucchini dry with paper towels and carefully wipe away any residual salt.

2. Heat oil in 12-inch nonstick skillet over medium heat until shimmering. Add onion and cook until almost softened, about 3 minutes. Increase heat to medium-high, add zucchini and lemon zest, and cook until zucchini is golden brown, about 10 minutes. Off heat, stir in lemon juice and basil and season with pepper to taste. Serve.

CORE TECHNIQUE
Salting Vegetables

TOSS
Add salt to the vegetable in a colander set in a bowl and toss.

DRAIN
Let stand for at least 30 minutes; discard liquid.

DRY
Pat vegetables dry with paper towels and carefully wipe away any visible salt.

SCIENCE LESSON
No More Watery, Bland Vegetables

Tossing watery vegetables such as zucchini, tomatoes, cucumbers, and eggplant with salt before cooking not only seasons them and rids them of excess moisture, but also draws out their flavor molecules. Many of these molecules are not only trapped within their cell walls; they are tightly bound to proteins that also make them inaccessible to our tastebuds. With time, the salt draws flavor compounds out of the cell walls while simultaneously forcing the proteins to separate from these molecules. The upshot? Produce with more intense flavor.

SAUTÉED MUSHROOMS WITH SHALLOT AND THYME

Serves: 4
Total Time: 35 minutes

RECIPE OVERVIEW Sautéing mushrooms the usual way means piling them in a skillet slicked with a couple of tablespoons of oil and waiting patiently for them to release their moisture, which then must evaporate before the mushrooms can brown. Instead, you can accelerate the process by adding a small amount of water to the pan and steaming the mushrooms, which allows them to release their moisture more quickly. The added benefit of steaming them is that the collapsed mushrooms won't absorb much oil; in fact, ½ teaspoon of oil is enough to prevent sticking and encourage browning. And because so little fat is used to sauté the mushrooms, the butter-based sauce doesn't make them overly rich. Adding broth to the sauce and simmering the mixture ensures that the butter emulsifies, creating a flavorful glaze that clings well to the mushrooms. Use one variety of mushroom or a combination. Stem and halve portobello mushrooms and cut each half crosswise into ½-inch pieces. Trim white or cremini mushrooms; quarter them if large or medium or halve them if small. Tear trimmed oyster mushrooms into 1- to 1½-inch pieces. Stem shiitake mushrooms; quarter large caps and halve small caps. Cut trimmed maitake (hen-of-the-woods) mushrooms into 1- to 1½-inch pieces. You can substitute vegetable broth for the chicken broth, if desired.

- 1¼ pounds mushrooms
- ¼ cup water
- ½ teaspoon vegetable oil
- 1 tablespoon unsalted butter
- 1 shallot, minced
- 1 tablespoon minced fresh thyme
- ¼ teaspoon table salt
- ¼ teaspoon pepper
- ¼ cup dry Marsala
- ½ cup chicken broth

1. Cook mushrooms and water in 12-inch nonstick skillet over high heat, stirring occasionally, until skillet is almost dry and mushrooms begin to sizzle, 4 to 8 minutes. Reduce heat to medium-high. Add oil and toss until mushrooms are evenly coated. Continue to cook, stirring occasionally, until mushrooms are well browned, 4 to 8 minutes longer. Reduce heat to medium.

2. Push mushrooms to sides of skillet. Add butter to center. When butter has melted, add shallot, thyme, salt, and pepper to center and cook, stirring constantly, until aromatic, about 30 seconds. Add Marsala and stir mixture into mushrooms. Cook, stirring occasionally, until liquid has evaporated, 2 to 3 minutes. Add broth and cook, stirring occasionally, until glaze is reduced by half, 2 to 3 minutes. Season with salt and pepper to taste, and serve.

Reinventing Sautéed Mushrooms: Add Lots of Liquid (Twice)

ADD WATER FIRST, OIL LATER
Steam cooks the mushrooms quickly so they collapse and release liquid. After the mushroom jus evaporates, add just ½ teaspoon of oil to brown the mushrooms.

ADD BROTH
Sauté aromatics in 1 tablespoon of butter, deglaze the pan, and then simmer the mushrooms in ½ cup of broth until it reduces to a silky, emulsified glaze.

KEYS TO SUCCESS

- **Steam briefly:** Causes mushrooms to collapse more rapidly
- **Minimal oil is absorbed:** Collapsed mushrooms can't absorb much oil.
- **Create a flavorful glaze:** When broth reduces

COURSE
DARK LEAFY GREENS

JACK BISHOP

Dark leafy greens, also known as hearty or sturdy greens, are robust green-leaved vegetables, mostly related to cabbage, that are at their best in the colder months. What's included in this category could be open to some debate, but here we've focused on mature spinach, Swiss chard, collard greens, and kale. They offer great earthy flavor and texture plus nutrients, but they do require some know-how to make them palatable. In this course you'll learn the proper prep and cooking steps to turn out tender and delicious results.

JACK'S PRO TIP: *Always start with WAY more leafy greens than you think you will need. They cook down WAY more than you think they will.*

SPINACH WITH GARLIC AND LEMON

Serves: 4
Total Time: 20 minutes

RECIPE OVERVIEW The pairing of tender sautéed spinach, savory garlic, and bright lemon is a classic favorite that still deserves attention to prepare it well. For the spinach, we prefer the hearty flavor and texture of curly-leaf spinach over baby spinach, which wilts into mush. Cook the spinach in extra-virgin olive oil and then use tongs to squeeze the cooked spinach in a colander to remove excess moisture. Lightly toasted minced garlic, cooked after the spinach, adds sweet nuttiness. As for seasoning, all the spinach needs is a sprinkling of salt and a squeeze of lemon juice. Leave some water clinging to the spinach leaves after rinsing to help encourage steam when cooking. Two pounds of flat-leaf spinach (about three bunches) can be substituted for curly-leaf, but do not use baby spinach because it is much too delicate.

- 3 tablespoons extra-virgin olive oil, divided
- 20 ounces curly-leaf spinach, stemmed
- 2 garlic cloves, minced
  Lemon juice

1. Heat 1 tablespoon oil in Dutch oven over high heat until shimmering. Add spinach 1 handful at a time, stirring and tossing each handful to wilt slightly before adding more. Cook spinach, stirring constantly, until uniformly wilted, about 1 minute. Transfer spinach to colander and squeeze between tongs to release excess liquid. Wipe pot dry with paper towels.

2. Add garlic and remaining 2 tablespoons oil to now-empty pot and cook over medium heat until fragrant, about 30 seconds. Add squeezed spinach and toss to coat. Off heat, season with salt and lemon juice to taste. Serve.

KEYS TO SUCCESS
- **Buy sturdy curly-leaf spinach:** For better texture and more flavor when wilted than more delicate varieties
- **Use a salad spinner:** To wash and dry the spinach; see page 149 for how
- **Preheat the pan:** Until the oil is shimmering
- **Thoroughly squeeze out moisture:** For spinach with a lighter and more distinct texture

SAUTÉED SWISS CHARD WITH SESAME SAUCE

Serves: 4
Total Time: 35 minutes

RECIPE OVERVIEW The key to mastering sautéed Swiss chard is to get the hearty stems to finish cooking at the same time as the tender leaves. Compared to spinach, which has stems that cook down as quickly as the leaves do, and kale, with ribs that are so tough that they are only good for the compost bin, Swiss chard stems fall somewhere in the middle. In this recipe, slice the stems thin on the bias so that they cook quickly and evenly. Giving the stems a head start over relatively high heat provides a desirable tender-crisp texture and lightly caramelized flavor that acts as a foil to the tender leaves, which are added later in two stages. An easy gingery sesame sauce stirred in at the end gives the simple chard a flavor boost. This recipe will work with any color of Swiss chard.

- ¼ cup plus 1 tablespoon sesame seeds, toasted, divided
- 2 teaspoons sugar
- 2 tablespoons water
- 1 teaspoon soy sauce
- 1½ teaspoons white miso
- ¼ teaspoon grated fresh ginger
- 1½ tablespoons vegetable oil
- ½ teaspoon toasted sesame oil
- 1½ pounds Swiss chard, stems sliced ¼ inch thick on bias (3 cups), leaves sliced into ½-inch-wide strips (10 cups)
- ¼ teaspoon kosher salt, divided

1. Process ¼ cup sesame seeds and sugar in food processor until it resembles coarse sand, about 15 seconds. Add water, soy sauce, miso, and ginger and pulse until combined, about 5 pulses. Transfer to bowl.

2. Heat vegetable oil and sesame oil in 12-inch nonstick skillet over medium-high heat until shimmering. Add chard stems and ⅛ teaspoon salt and cook, stirring occasionally, until spotty brown and crisp-tender, 5 to 6 minutes. Add two-thirds of chard leaves and cook, tossing with tongs, until just starting to wilt, 30 to 60 seconds. Add remaining chard leaves and remaining ⅛ teaspoon salt and continue to cook, stirring frequently, until leaves are tender, about 3 minutes longer. Remove pan from heat and stir in sesame sauce. Transfer to serving platter and sprinkle with remaining 1 tablespoon sesame seeds. Serve immediately.

KEYS TO SUCCESS

- **Prep the chard:** See page 43 for how to stem and slice stems and leaves.
- **Give the stems a head start:** Before wilting the faster-cooking leaves

QUICK COLLARD GREENS

Serves: 4 to 6
Total Time: 35 minutes

RECIPE OVERVIEW This quick blanch-and-sauté recipe for tough collard greens will give you the same tender results as long braising. Stemming the greens is a necessary first step, and blanching the leaves in salt water tenderizes them quickly and neutralizes their bitter qualities. To remove excess water left from blanching, use a spatula to press on the drained greens and then roll them up in a dish towel to dry them further. Chop the compressed collards into thin slices perfect for quickly sautéing with pungent, aromatic garlic and spicy red pepper flakes, which provide immediate potent seasoning. You can substitute mustard or turnip greens for the collards; reduce their boiling time to 2 minutes.

- Table salt for cooking greens
- 2½ pounds collard greens, stemmed and halved lengthwise
- 3 tablespoons extra-virgin olive oil
- 2 garlic cloves, minced
- ¼ teaspoon red pepper flakes

1. Bring 4 quarts water to boil in large pot over high heat. Stir in 1 tablespoon salt, then add collard greens, 1 handful at a time. Cook until tender, 4 to 5 minutes. Drain and rinse with cold water until greens are cool, about 1 minute. Press greens with rubber spatula to release excess liquid. Place greens on dish towel and compress into 10-inch log. Roll up towel tightly, then remove greens from towel. Cut greens crosswise into ¼-inch slices.

2. Heat oil in 12-inch nonstick skillet over medium-high heat until just smoking. Scatter greens in skillet and cook, stirring frequently, until just beginning to brown, 3 to 4 minutes. Stir in garlic and pepper flakes and cook until greens are spotty brown, 1 to 2 minutes. Season with salt and pepper to taste, and serve.

CORE TECHNIQUE
Prepping Collards

ROLL
Using a clean dish towel, roll the blanched greens into a tight log.

SLICE
Cut the log into ¼-inch slices. The greens are dry and ready to sauté.

GARLICKY BRAISED KALE
Serves: 4 to 6
Total Time: 55 minutes

RECIPE OVERVIEW A long cooking time helps to turn kale meltingly tender and tames its strong flavor. This straightforward one-pot approach will work equally well with any of the sturdy winter greens, such as collards or mustard greens. Adding the greens one handful at a time to the seasoned cooking liquid and letting them wilt briefly before adding more allows you to fit the large volume of leaves into the pot more easily. When the kale has almost the ideal finished tender texture, remove the lid to allow the liquid to cook off. Garlic, lemon, and red pepper is a classic flavor combo, but this cooking method also lends itself nicely to different flavors, as in the two variations that follow.

3 tablespoons extra-virgin olive oil, divided
1 onion, chopped fine
5 garlic cloves, minced
⅛ teaspoon red pepper flakes
1 cup chicken or vegetable broth
1 cup water
¼ teaspoon table salt
2 pounds kale, stemmed and cut into 2-inch pieces
2 teaspoons lemon juice, plus extra for seasoning

1. Heat 2 tablespoons oil in Dutch oven over medium heat until shimmering. Add onion and cook until softened and lightly browned, 5 to 7 minutes. Stir in garlic and pepper flakes and cook until fragrant, about 30 seconds. Stir in broth, water, and salt and bring to simmer.

2. Stir in kale, 1 handful at a time, and cook until beginning to wilt, about 5 minutes. Cover, reduce heat to medium-low, and simmer, stirring occasionally, until kale is tender, 25 to 35 minutes.

3. Uncover and increase heat to medium-high. Cook, stirring occasionally, until most of liquid has evaporated (bottom of pot will be almost dry and kale will begin to sizzle), 8 to 12 minutes. Off heat, stir in lemon juice and remaining 1 tablespoon oil. Season with salt, pepper, and extra lemon juice to taste. Serve.

Variations
GARLICKY BRAISED KALE WITH BACON AND ONION
Cook 6 slices bacon, cut into ¼-inch pieces, over medium heat until crisp, 5 to 7 minutes. Using slotted spoon, transfer bacon to paper towel–lined plate, then pour off all but 2 tablespoons fat. Substitute rendered fat for 2 tablespoons oil; 1 red onion, halved and sliced thin, for chopped onion; and cider vinegar for lemon juice. Stir reserved bacon into kale before serving.

GARLICKY BRAISED KALE WITH COCONUT AND CURRY
Substitute 2 teaspoons grated fresh ginger and 1 teaspoon curry powder for red pepper flakes and one 14-ounce can coconut milk for water. Substitute lime juice for lemon juice and sprinkle kale with ⅓ cup toasted chopped cashews before serving.

> **KEYS TO SUCCESS**
> - **Stem and cut up the kale:** See page 43 for how
> - **Wilt it down bit by bit:** That's how to fit 2 pounds of kale into the pan.
> - **Leave off the lid toward the end:** Lets the excess liquid cook off

RESOURCES FOR DARK LEAFY GREENS

DARK LEAFY GREENS BY ANY OTHER NAME

Curly-Leaf Spinach Curly-leaf spinach, also called savoy spinach, has sturdy, crinkly, dark green leaves with thick stems that need to be removed and lots of sandy grit that needs to be rinsed away. Semi-savoy spinach is a variety of curly leaf that has the same crinkly leaves and a similar crisp texture, but it's not as difficult to clean as regular savoy. Curly-leaf spinach has the most crisp texture of all the varieties and a stronger, slightly more bitter flavor than flat-leaf spinach. It is at its best in cooked preparations; even though it's getting harder to find these days, we often favor it in cooked dishes because of its good flavor and texture.

Curly Kale Curly kale (also called green kale) has broad, dark green, wonderfully curly and frilly leaves. It has an earthy, grassy flavor that takes on nutty notes when cooked. It's a true powerhouse of vitamin A, with double the amount typically found in other leafy greens.

Red Kale Red kale (also known as Red Russian kale or Winter Red kale) has tough, leathery leaves, even once braised. We prefer curly or Lacinato kales over red kale.

Lacinato Kale Lacinato kale (also called Tuscan kale, dinosaur kale, or black kale) has long, slender, very dark green leaves. It has a sweet, mineral-y flavor and a tender texture when eaten raw, and it becomes robust and rich when braised.

Collard Greens Collard greens have large, broad, flat, very stiff leaves—almost like fans—with firm veins running through them. They have a mild flavor and taste and feel a bit like cabbage, which won't be surprising once you know that this green is technically a cabbage.

Mustard Greens "Mustard greens" actually encompasses several varieties. Most commonly you'll see narrow, bright green frilly leaves with a leafier, less leathery texture than other hearty greens. Mustard greens can also have a purplish tinge, and the leaves can also be flat. They're peppery and pleasantly sharp-hot in flavor.

White Chard White chard, with its white stems and veins, was one of the only varieties of chard seen on the market for many years. Now you can find different varieties in brilliant colors in grocery stores and farmers' markets.

Red Chard For a long time, red chard—the variety of chard with red stems and red veins—was one of only two types of chard seen in markets. Red chard is slightly sweeter in flavor than white chard, although the difference is not great enough to impact any recipe you're cooking.

FOCUS ON: KALE

Kale comes in many forms: curly and smooth, green and purple and red, and one variety that grows so tall its stem can be turned into a walking stick. But all types have the same basic structure.

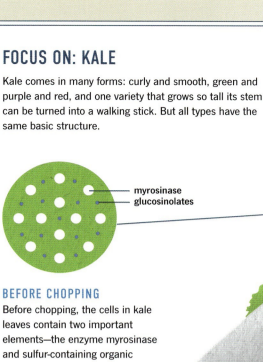

BEFORE CHOPPING
Before chopping, the cells in kale leaves contain two important elements—the enzyme myrosinase and sulfur-containing organic compounds called glucosinolates. In undisturbed leaves, they remain separate.

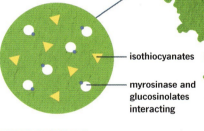

AFTER CHOPPING
When you start chopping up that kale leaf, the structure of the cells is disturbed. This means that the myrosinase and glucosinolates begin to interact. And when they interact the two come together to create isothiocyanates, or new sulfur-containing compounds that taste like the bitter, pungent kale you know.

STEM
Kale's thick stalk is tough, especially the bottom portion below the leafy green. In the test kitchen, we trim it before cooking, holding each leaf at the base of the stem and using a knife to slash the leafy portion from either side of the tough stem.

LEAF
After discarding the stem, we are left with the leaf, which is what we mainly cook with. Known for their health benefits, kale leaves are also packed with flavor—a flavor that doesn't come out until the leaf has been chopped, chewed, or massaged.

STORING
Store kale and other hearty greens in an open plastic produce bag or an open zipper-lock bag. In tests, we've found that trapped gases and too much constriction encourage rotting. This is because in sealed plastic bags the moisture and heat are retained, which encourages the growth of spoilage-promoting fungi and molds. Ripening enzymes in the vegetable do become more active, which leads to softening, but the fungi and molds are responsible for most of the damage.

COURSE
PAN-ROASTING VEGETABLES

ANNIE PETITO

Pan roasting is one of our favorite methods for speedily creating tons of flavorful browning on vegetables. This stovetop cooking technique usually involves covering a pan full of vegetables to trap in heat and steam and then, once the veggies have softened a bit, uncovering them to allow excess moisture to cook off. The natural sugars in the vegetables caramelize in the high heat for deeply browned, crisp-tender, sweet results. Here we'll apply the technique to brussels sprouts, cauliflower, and asparagus.

ANNIE'S PRO TIP: *Adding seasonings or flavorings near the end of or after cooking ensures they don't interfere with browning, and that the garnishes remain bright, fresh, and/or crisp for serving.*

PAN-ROASTED BRUSSELS SPROUTS WITH LEMON AND PECORINO ROMANO

Serves: 4
Total Time: 15 minutes

RECIPE OVERVIEW To create stovetop brussels sprouts that are deeply browned on the cut sides while still bright green on the uncut sides and crisp-tender within, start the sprouts in a cold skillet with plenty of oil and cook them covered. This gently heats the sprouts and creates a steamy environment that cooks them through without adding any extra moisture. Removing the lid and continuing to cook the sprouts cut sides down gives them time to develop a substantial, caramelized crust. Using enough oil to completely coat the skillet ensures that all the sprouts make full contact with the fat to brown evenly from edge to edge. Parmesan cheese can be substituted for the Pecorino, if desired. You will need a 12-inch nonstick skillet with a tight-fitting lid for this recipe.

- 1 pound brussels sprouts, trimmed and halved
- 5 tablespoons extra-virgin olive oil
- 1 tablespoon lemon juice
- ¼ teaspoon table salt
- ¼ cup shredded Pecorino Romano cheese

1. Arrange brussels sprouts in single layer, cut sides down, in 12-inch nonstick skillet. Drizzle oil evenly over sprouts. Cover skillet, place over medium-high heat, and cook until sprouts are bright green and cut sides have started to brown, about 5 minutes.

2. Uncover and continue to cook until cut sides of sprouts are deeply and evenly browned and paring knife meets little to no resistance, 2 to 3 minutes, adjusting heat and moving sprouts as needed to prevent them from overbrowning. While sprouts cook, combine lemon juice and salt in small bowl.

3. Off heat, add lemon juice mixture to skillet and stir to evenly coat sprouts. Season with salt and pepper to taste. Transfer to serving platter, sprinkle with Pecorino, and serve.

KEYS TO SUCCESS

- **Start in a cold skillet:** Allows the sprouts to heat slowly and release their moisture
- **Use plenty of oil:** Otherwise, sprouts will brown only at the center of the cut side
- **Use intense direct heat:** To achieve deep caramelization
- **Cook cut side down:** Cut sides brown and caramelize during contact with the skillet.

Variations

PAN-ROASTED BRUSSELS SPROUTS WITH MUSTARD AND BROWN SUGAR

Omit pepper and Pecorino. Substitute 1 tablespoon Dijon mustard, 1 tablespoon packed brown sugar, 2 teaspoons white wine vinegar, and ⅛ teaspoon cayenne pepper for lemon juice.

PAN-ROASTED BRUSSELS SPROUTS WITH GOCHUJANG AND SESAME SEEDS

Gochujang is a savory Korean red chili paste that can be found in Asian markets or large supermarkets.

Omit pepper. Substitute 1 tablespoon gochujang and 1 tablespoon rice vinegar for lemon juice and 2 teaspoons toasted sesame seeds for Pecorino.

CORE TECHNIQUE
Pan-Roasting Vegetables

HEAT OIL AND VEGETABLE TOGETHER
Combine the oil and vegetable in a skillet.

COVER SKILLET
Cover the skillet and parcook until the vegetable starts to brown.

UNCOVER SKILLET
Uncover the skillet and continue to cook until the vegetable is tender, moving as needed to prevent overbrowning.

PAN-ROASTED CAULIFLOWER WITH GARLIC AND LEMON

Serves: 4 to 6
Total Time: 40 minutes

RECIPE OVERVIEW Roasting cauliflower caramelizes its sugars and transforms it into something sweet and nutty-tasting. This stovetop method delivers oven results in a faster time frame. Cutting the cauliflower into planks and then florets provides lots of flat surfaces for browning. The oil and cauliflower start together in a covered skillet. The craggy exteriors brown before the interiors soften and then the cauliflower steams in its own moisture and accelerates the softening of the florets to tender-crisp. Garlic, lemon zest, and parsley perk up the flavors along with a sprinkle of crunchy toasted bread crumbs. You will need a 12-inch nonstick skillet with a tight-fitting lid for this recipe.

- 1 head cauliflower (2 pounds)
- 1 slice hearty white sandwich bread, torn into 1-inch pieces
- 5 tablespoons extra-virgin olive oil, divided
- 1 teaspoon plus pinch table salt, divided
- ½ teaspoon plus pinch pepper, divided
- 1 garlic clove, minced
- 1 teaspoon grated lemon zest, plus lemon wedges for serving
- ¼ cup chopped fresh parsley

1. Trim outer leaves of cauliflower and cut stem flush with bottom of head. Turn head so stem is facing down and cut head into ¾-inch-thick slices. Cut around core to remove florets; discard core. Cut large florets into 1½-inch pieces. Transfer florets to bowl, including any small pieces that may have been created during trimming, and set aside.

2. Pulse bread in food processor to coarse crumbs, about 10 pulses. Heat bread crumbs, 1 tablespoon oil, pinch salt, and pinch pepper in 12-inch nonstick skillet over medium heat, stirring frequently, until bread crumbs are golden brown, 3 to 5 minutes. Transfer crumbs to bowl and wipe out skillet.

3. Combine 2 tablespoons oil and cauliflower florets in now-empty skillet and sprinkle with remaining 1 teaspoon salt and remaining ½ teaspoon pepper. Cover skillet and cook over medium-high heat until florets start to brown and edges just start to become translucent (do not lift lid), about 5 minutes.

4. Uncover and continue to cook, stirring occasionally, until golden, about 12 minutes.

5. Push florets to edges of skillet. Add remaining 2 tablespoons oil, garlic, and lemon zest to center and cook, stirring with rubber spatula, until fragrant, about 30 seconds. Stir garlic mixture into florets and continue to cook, stirring occasionally, until florets are tender but still firm, about 3 minutes.

6. Remove skillet from heat and stir in parsley. Transfer florets to serving platter and sprinkle with bread crumbs. Serve, passing lemon wedges separately.

Variations

PAN-ROASTED CAULIFLOWER WITH CAPERS AND PINE NUTS

Omit bread and reduce oil to ¼ cup. Reduce salt in step 3 to ¾ teaspoon. Substitute 2 tablespoons capers, rinsed and minced, for garlic. Substitute 2 tablespoons minced fresh chives for parsley and stir in ¼ cup toasted pine nuts with chives in step 6.

PAN-ROASTED CAULIFLOWER WITH CUMIN AND PISTACHIOS

Omit bread and reduce oil to ¼ cup. Heat 1 teaspoon cumin seeds and 1 teaspoon coriander seeds in 12-inch nonstick skillet over medium heat, stirring frequently, until lightly toasted and fragrant, 2 to 3 minutes. Transfer to spice grinder or mortar and pestle and coarsely grind. Wipe out skillet. Substitute ground cumin-coriander mixture, ½ teaspoon paprika, and pinch cayenne pepper for garlic; lime zest for lemon zest; and 3 tablespoons chopped fresh mint for parsley. Sprinkle with ¼ cup pistachios, toasted and chopped, before serving and substitute lime wedges for lemon wedges.

PAN-ROASTED ASPARAGUS

Serves: 4 to 6
Total Time: 20 minutes

RECIPE OVERVIEW Pan roasting delivers crisp, well-browned asparagus spears without having to rotate each spear. Thicker spears are best because thin ones tend to overcook before they brown. To encourage caramelization, parcook the asparagus, covered, with oil and water. Then, remove the lid and crank up the heat until the spears are evenly browned on the bottom. Look for spears between ½ and ¾ inch in diameter. You can use white or green asparagus here; if using white, peel just the outermost layer of the bottom halves of the spears. You will need a 12-inch nonstick skillet with a tight-fitting lid for this recipe.

- 2 pounds thick asparagus
- 1 tablespoon extra-virgin olive oil
- 1 teaspoon water
- Lemon wedges

1. Trim bottom inch of asparagus spears and discard. Peel bottom halves of spears until white flesh is exposed. Heat oil in 12-inch nonstick skillet over medium-high heat until shimmering. Add half of asparagus with tips pointed in 1 direction and remaining asparagus with tips pointed in opposite direction. Shake skillet gently to help distribute spears evenly (they will not quite fit in single layer). Add water, cover, and cook until asparagus is bright green but still crisp, about 5 minutes.

2. Uncover, season with salt and pepper to taste, increase heat to high, and cook until asparagus is well browned on one side and tip of paring knife inserted at base of largest spear meets little resistance, 5 to 7 minutes. Transfer asparagus to serving dish and serve with lemon wedges.

COURSE
POTATOES 101

ASHLEY MOORE

Potatoes are usually one of the best parts of a meal, but they aren't always the most exciting. This course will change that. You'll learn not only the best ways to make a couple of classic potato dishes—mashed potatoes and baked potatoes—but also some interesting takes such as crisp roasted potatoes that are as good as french fries and braised potatoes. (If you've never braised potatoes before, our recipe will convince you to start.) You'll also learn about the vegetable itself: the different varieties and starch contents, and why those two things matter when choosing the right potato for your dish.

ASHLEY'S PRO TIP: *Have a thermometer handy for our Best Baked Potatoes. An interior temperature of 205 degrees will give you the best, fluffiest baked potato you have ever had!*

SMASHED POTATOES
Serves: 4 to 6
Total Time: 1 hour

RECIPE OVERVIEW Smashed potatoes have the rich, creamy puree of mashed potatoes accented by chunks of potato and skins. Low-starch, high-moisture red potatoes are the best choice for this dish. Their compact structure holds up well under pressure, maintaining its integrity. The thin skins are pleasantly tender and pair nicely with the chunky potatoes. Cooked whole in salted water with a bay leaf, the potatoes become lightly seasoned while also retaining their naturally creamy texture, as the skins protect the potato flesh from the water. For the best chunky texture, smash the potatoes with a rubber spatula or the back of a wooden spoon. Cream cheese and butter lend tang, richness, and body to the dish, and stirring in a little of the potato cooking water adds enough moisture to the smash to give it a unified and creamy consistency without diluting the potato flavor. Seasoned with salt, freshly ground black pepper, and a sprinkling of chopped chives for bright flavor and color, these potatoes are a no-fuss side dish to complement any casual dinner. Try to get potatoes of equal size; if that's not possible, test the larger potatoes for doneness (use a paring knife). If only large potatoes are available, increase the cooking time by about 10 minutes.

- 2 pounds small red potatoes, unpeeled
- ½ teaspoon table salt plus salt for cooking potatoes
- 1 bay leaf
- 4 tablespoons (½ stick) unsalted butter, melted
- 4 ounces cream cheese, at room temperature
- 3 tablespoons minced fresh chives (optional)
- ½ teaspoon pepper

1. Place potatoes in large saucepan and add cold water to cover by 1 inch; add 1 teaspoon salt and bay leaf. Bring to boil over high heat, then reduce heat to medium-low and simmer gently until paring knife can be inserted into potatoes with no resistance, 35 to 45 minutes. Reserve ½ cup cooking water, then drain potatoes. Return potatoes to the pot, discard bay leaf, and allow potatoes to stand in pot, uncovered, until surfaces are dry, about 5 minutes.

2. While potatoes dry, whisk melted butter and softened cream cheese in medium bowl until smooth and fully incorporated. Add ¼ cup reserved cooking water, chives (if using), pepper, and salt. Using rubber spatula or back of wooden spoon, smash potatoes just enough to break skins. Fold in butter–cream cheese mixture until most of liquid has been absorbed and chunks of potatoes remain. Add more cooking water as needed, 1 tablespoon at a time, until potatoes are slightly looser than desired (potatoes will thicken slightly with standing). Season with salt and pepper to taste, and serve.

KEYS TO SUCCESS

- **Use red potatoes:** Their low-starch, high-moisture, firm structure work best.
- **Leave the skins on:** Which are tender and add color and flavor
- **Cook the potatoes whole:** Intact skins prevent the potatoes from absorbing excess water.
- **Smash the potatoes gently:** With a rubber spatula or wooden spoon to break them up
- **Reserve some salty, starchy cooking water:** To adjust the consistency of the rustic mash

EASY MASHED POTATOES

Serves: 4
Total Time: 40 minutes

RECIPE OVERVIEW For easy, creamy mashed potatoes, start by cooking thick slices of Yukon Gold potatoes in well-seasoned water. Yukon Golds are less starchy and produce a creamier mash. Using half-and-half as the dairy and microwaving it with butter before combining the mixture with the mashed potatoes ensures a bowl of piping-hot potatoes on the dinner table. We prefer Yukon Gold potatoes here, but russet potatoes will work in a pinch.

- 2 pounds Yukon Gold potatoes, peeled and sliced ½ inch thick
- ¾ teaspoon table salt plus salt for cooking potatoes
- ¾ cup half-and-half
- 6 tablespoons unsalted butter
- ½ teaspoon pepper

1. Place potatoes and 1 tablespoon salt in large saucepan, add water to cover by 1 inch, and bring to boil over high heat. Reduce heat to medium and simmer until potatoes are tender and paring knife can be easily slipped in and out of potatoes, 18 to 22 minutes.

2. Meanwhile, combine half-and-half and butter in 2-cup liquid measuring cup and microwave, covered, until butter is melted and mixture is warm to touch, about 2 minutes.

3. Drain potatoes and return them to saucepan. Cook over low heat, stirring, until potatoes are thoroughly dried, about 30 seconds. Remove from heat and, using potato masher, mash potatoes until smooth and no lumps remain. Stir in half-and-half mixture, salt, and pepper until fully incorporated. Season with salt and pepper to taste. Serve.

BRAISED RED POTATOES WITH LEMON AND CHIVES

Serves: 4 to 6
Total Time: 50 minutes

RECIPE OVERVIEW You can get the creamy interiors produced by steaming red potatoes and the browned exteriors produced by roasting—without doing either of those things. Braising produces creamy-on-the-inside, crispy on the outside red potatoes. Simmer the potatoes in a covered skillet until tender, then remove the lid to evaporate the liquid. The butter eventually browns, coloring (and enriching the flavor of) the potatoes. Using butter rather than oil ensures that the potatoes really brown—the proteins in the milk solids amplify the process. And it's easy to add other flavors such as salt, pepper, garlic, and thyme. Simmering the whole garlic cloves mellows their bite, and the softened garlic is easy to mince into a paste and stir into the finished potatoes. A squeeze of lemon juice adds brightness and minced chives add fresh oniony flavor. Use small red potatoes measuring about 1½ inches in diameter.

- 1½ pounds small red potatoes, unpeeled, halved
- 2 cups water
- 3 tablespoons unsalted butter
- 3 garlic cloves, peeled
- 3 sprigs fresh thyme
- ¾ teaspoon table salt
- 1 teaspoon lemon juice
- ¼ teaspoon pepper
- 2 tablespoons minced fresh chives

1. Arrange potatoes in single layer, cut side down, in 12-inch nonstick skillet. Add water, butter, garlic, thyme, and salt and bring to simmer over medium-high heat. Reduce heat to medium, cover, and simmer until potatoes are just tender, about 15 minutes.

2. Remove lid and use slotted spoon to transfer garlic to cutting board; discard thyme. Increase heat to medium-high and vigorously simmer, swirling pan occasionally, until water evaporates and butter starts to sizzle, 15 to 20 minutes. When cool enough to handle, mince garlic to paste. Transfer paste to bowl and stir in lemon juice and pepper.

3. Continue to cook potatoes, swirling pan frequently, until butter browns and cut sides of potatoes turn spotty brown, 4 to 6 minutes longer. Off heat, add garlic mixture and chives and toss to thoroughly coat. Serve immediately.

CRISP ROASTED POTATOES

Serves: 4 to 6
Total Time: 55 minutes

RECIPE OVERVIEW When done right, roasted potatoes deliver the best of both worlds—creamy bites of potato surrounded by a crunchy crust. Parcooking is the key to ideal crisp roasted potatoes. Gently simmering sliced potato rounds draws starch and sugar to the surface. In the oven, the starch and sugar harden into a crisp shell. Tossing the parcooked rounds with olive oil and salt creates a rough surface, speeding evaporation and making the crusts even crispier. The medium starch and medium moisture content of Yukon Gold potatoes make them ideally suited to producing roasted potatoes that are crisp on the outside (from the starch) but still creamy in the middle (from the moisture).

- 2½ pounds Yukon Gold potatoes, unpeeled, cut into ½-inch-thick slices
- 1 teaspoon table salt, divided, plus salt for cooking potatoes
- 5 tablespoons extra-virgin olive oil, divided

1. Adjust oven rack to lowest position, place rimmed baking sheet on rack, and heat oven to 450 degrees. Place potatoes and 1 tablespoon salt in Dutch oven, then add cold water to cover by 1 inch. Bring to boil over high heat, then reduce heat and gently simmer until exteriors of potatoes have softened but centers offer resistance when poked with paring knife, about 5 minutes. Drain potatoes well and transfer to large bowl.

2. Drizzle potatoes with 2 tablespoons oil and sprinkle with ½ teaspoon salt; using rubber spatula, toss to combine. Repeat with 2 tablespoons oil and remaining ½ teaspoon salt and continue to toss until exteriors of potato slices are coated with starchy paste, 1 to 2 minutes.

3. Working quickly, remove sheet from oven and drizzle remaining 1 tablespoon oil over surface. Carefully transfer potatoes to sheet and spread into even layer (place end pieces skin side up). Bake until bottoms of potatoes are golden brown and crisp, 15 to 25 minutes, rotating sheet after 10 minutes.

4. Remove sheet from oven and, using metal spatula and tongs, loosen potatoes from sheet and carefully flip each slice. Continue to roast until second side is golden and crisp, 10 to 20 minutes longer, rotating sheet as needed to ensure potatoes brown evenly. Season with salt and pepper to taste, and serve.

KEYS TO SUCCESS

- **Get the pan hot:** Preheating an empty baking sheet jump-starts browning.
- **Cut thick rounds:** Ensures maximum contact with the baking sheet
- **Simmer gently:** Softens the potatoes without breaking them apart
- **Toss roughly to release starch:** Which leads to more browning and a crisp crust

Just Scratching the Surface

We discovered that parcooked potato slices browned faster in the oven than raw slices. When we subsequently "roughed up" the parcooked slices by tossing them vigorously with salt and oil, they browned faster still. The explanation? It's all a matter of surface area. Browning or crisping can't begin until the surface moisture evaporates. The parcooked, roughed-up slices—riddled with tiny dips and mounds—have more exposed surface area than the smooth raw slices and thus more escape routes for moisture. If you have trouble getting your head around two potato slices of identical width having vastly different surface areas, think of it this way: Five square miles of Colorado's mountain region will have far more exposed surface area than 5 square miles of the Kansas plains. (Just try walking them both.)

Roughed-Up Surface = Fast Evaporation

Smooth Surface = Slow Evaporation

BEST BAKED POTATOES
Serves: 4
Total Time: 1¼ hours

RECIPE OVERVIEW Baking a potato is about as basic as cooking gets—so basic, in fact, that it doesn't even seem to require a recipe. But following this precise roasting technique guarantees a perfect potato, one with a fluffy interior, deliciously crisp skin, and even seasoning. Our testing pointed us to an ideal doneness temperature: 205 degrees. Baking the potatoes on a wire rack prevents a leathery ring from forming beneath the peel, and using an instant-read thermometer allows you to determine the exact temperature. Coating the potatoes in salty water before baking seasons the skin; brushing on vegetable oil once the potatoes are cooked through and baking for 10 minutes more produces the crispiest exterior possible. It's crucial to cut the potatoes open immediately after baking to allow steam to escape; otherwise, even a perfectly baked potato will be gummy. Top them as desired, or with one of our toppings (recipes follow).

- 2 tablespoons table salt for brining
- 4 small russet potatoes (8 ounces each), unpeeled, each lightly pricked with fork in 6 places
- 1 tablespoon vegetable oil

1. Adjust oven rack to middle position and heat oven to 450 degrees. Dissolve salt in ½ cup water in large bowl. Place potatoes in bowl and toss so exteriors of potatoes are evenly moistened. Transfer potatoes to wire rack set in rimmed baking sheet and bake until center of largest potato registers 205 degrees, 45 minutes to 1 hour.

2. Remove potatoes from oven and brush tops and sides with oil. Return potatoes to oven and continue to bake for 10 minutes.

3. Remove potatoes from oven and, using paring knife, make 2 slits, forming X, in each potato. Using clean dish towel, hold ends and squeeze slightly to push flesh up and out. Season with salt and pepper to taste. Serve immediately.

HERBED GOAT CHEESE TOPPING
Makes: ¾ cup
Total Time: 15 minutes

- 4 ounces goat cheese, softened
- 2 tablespoons extra-virgin olive oil
- 2 tablespoons minced fresh parsley
- 1 tablespoon minced shallot
- ½ teaspoon grated lemon zest

Mash goat cheese with fork. Stir in oil, parsley, shallot, and lemon zest. Season with salt and pepper to taste.

CREAMY EGG TOPPING
Makes: 1 cup
Total Time: 10 minutes

- 3 hard-cooked large eggs, chopped
- ¼ cup sour cream
- 1½ tablespoons minced cornichons
- 1 tablespoon minced fresh parsley
- 1 tablespoon Dijon mustard
- 1 tablespoon capers, rinsed and minced
- 1 tablespoon minced shallot

Stir all ingredients together and season with salt and pepper to taste.

> ### KEYS TO SUCCESS
> - **Bake to the ideal doneness:** Which is 205 (or as high as 212) degrees for fluffy interiors
> - **Bake in a hot oven:** So potatoes cook evenly and don't develop a tough layer under the skin
> - **Season the exterior:** By dunking the potatoes in salty water
> - **Oil the skin:** The skin dehydrates during baking, then crisps in the oil.

COURSE
SWEET POTATOES

MORGAN BOLLING

Sweet potatoes are nearly as versatile as regular potatoes and can be cooked in many of the same preparations with a few adjustments to technique to account for their higher sugar and lower starch content. In this course you will learn how to cook these orange spuds into a creamy mash, give roasted wedges a variety of flavor profiles, and use the potatoes in a Thanksgiving-ready side dish full of contrasting textures.

MORGAN'S PRO TIP: *I know sweet potato casserole is often topped with marshmallows and I can get behind that occasionally. But I think it's fun to play around with different toppings that would give flavorful crunch: streusel (like in the Sweet Potato Crunch), crumbled oatmeal cookies, candied nuts, or cheesy bread crumbs.*

MASHED SWEET POTATOES

Serves: 4
Total Time: 45 minutes

RECIPE OVERVIEW With a deep, natural sweetness that doesn't require much assistance, the humble sweet potato tastes far better if prepared using only a modicum of ingredients. This straightforward recipe honors the sweet potato. We tried using whole milk and half-and-half, but a small amount of heavy cream, in combination with butter, steals the show. For seasonings, you need nothing more than a little sugar, salt, and pepper; the various baking spices often added to mashed sweet potatoes are simply distracting. This is a silky puree with enough body to hold its shape while sitting on a fork, and it pushes this root vegetable's deep, earthy flavor to the forefront, where it belongs.

- 2 pounds sweet potatoes, peeled, quartered lengthwise, and sliced crosswise ¼ inch thick
- 4 tablespoons unsalted butter, cut into 4 pieces
- 2 tablespoons heavy cream
- 1 teaspoon sugar
- ½ teaspoon table salt

1. Cook potatoes, butter, cream, sugar, and salt in large saucepan, covered, over low heat, stirring occasionally, until potatoes fall apart when poked with fork, 35 to 45 minutes.

2. Off heat, mash potatoes in saucepan with potato masher until smooth. Season with salt and pepper to taste, and serve.

KEYS TO SUCCESS
- **Cut thin slices:** So they cook evenly and faster
- **Season during cooking:** By simmering the potatoes with butter and a little cream for richer flavor
- **Skip draining:** Lift off the lid and mash the potatoes right in the pot

ROASTED SWEET POTATO WEDGES

Serves: 4 to 6
Total Time: 55 minutes

RECIPE OVERVIEW For roasted sweet potato wedges, it's important to cut the wedges wide enough so that they maintain their shape once they are cooked and to combat the sweet, almost syrup-like liquid the sweet potatoes exude as they cook. As this moisture tries to escape, the potatoes end up stewing in their own juice. After a quick toss with olive oil, salt, and pepper and a visit to a hot 450-degree oven, the wedges are nicely browned on their exteriors and have soft, tender interiors. We prefer to use small potatoes, about 8 ounces each, because they fit more uniformly on the baking sheet. They should be of similar size so they cook at the same rate. Be sure to scrub and dry the whole potatoes thoroughly before cutting them into wedges and tossing them with the oil and spices.

- 2 pounds small sweet potatoes, unpeeled, cut lengthwise into 1½-inch wedges
- 2 tablespoons extra-virgin olive oil
- ½ teaspoon table salt
- ½ teaspoon pepper

1. Adjust oven rack to middle position and heat oven to 450 degrees. Line rimmed baking sheet with parchment paper. Toss all ingredients together in bowl.

2. Arrange potatoes, skin side down, in single layer on prepared sheet. Roast until lightly browned and tender, about 30 minutes. Serve.

Variations

CUMIN AND CHILI ROASTED SWEET POTATO WEDGES
Add 2 teaspoons ground cumin, 2 teaspoons chili powder, and 1 teaspoon garlic powder to potato mixture in step 1.

CURRY ROASTED SWEET POTATO WEDGES
Add 4 teaspoons curry powder to potato mixture in step 1.

SPICY BBQ ROASTED SWEET POTATO WEDGES
Add 2 teaspoons smoked paprika, 2 teaspoons packed brown sugar, 1 teaspoon garlic powder, and ⅛ teaspoon cayenne pepper to potato mixture in step 1.

> ### KEYS TO SUCCESS
> - **Line baking sheet with parchment:** So wedges won't stick
> - **Bake in a hot oven:** Browns the exteriors and cooks the interiors at the same rate
> - **Place skin side down:** Produces crispy skins and browned exteriors

CORE TECHNIQUE
Cutting Sweet Potatoes into Wedges

HALVE LENGTHWISE
Halve the sweet potatoes, then cut the halves into 1½-inch-thick wedges.

CUT THICK INTO THIN
Cut thick wedges into thinner wedges, if the recipe directs.

SWEET POTATO CRUNCH

Serves: 8
Total Time: 2½ hours, plus 25 minutes cooling

RECIPE OVERVIEW This truly amazing sweet potato casserole features creamy sweet potatoes topped with a crunchy, salty-sweet topping. As the sweet potatoes roast, their flavor concentrates and they ooze a sort of natural sweet potato caramel. A splash of orange liqueur and a little brown sugar make them holiday-worthy. A simple stir-together streusel tastes great and provides a contrasting crunch on top of the creamy potatoes, while a pinch of cayenne carries a hint of heat. Buy potatoes of similar size and shape, no more than 1 pound each, so they cook at the same rate. Orange juice can be substituted for the Grand Marnier, if you prefer.

Sweet Potatoes
- 4 pounds sweet potatoes, unpeeled
- 4 tablespoons unsalted butter, melted
- 2 tablespoons Grand Marnier
- 1 tablespoon packed light brown sugar
- 1¼ teaspoons table salt
- 1 teaspoon grated orange zest

Topping
- ⅔ cup all-purpose flour
- ⅓ cup packed light brown sugar
- ¼ teaspoon table salt
- ⅛ teaspoon cayenne pepper
- 4 tablespoons unsalted butter, melted

1. FOR THE SWEET POTATOES Adjust oven rack to upper-middle position and heat oven to 400 degrees. Line rimmed baking sheet with aluminum foil. Poke potatoes several times with paring knife and space evenly on prepared sheet. Bake until potatoes are very tender and can be easily squeezed with tongs, 1¼ to 1½ hours. Let potatoes sit until cool enough to handle, at least 20 minutes.

2. Remove and discard potato peels. Transfer potato flesh to large bowl and mash with potato masher until smooth. Stir in melted butter, Grand Marnier, sugar, salt, and orange zest. Transfer potato mixture to 8-inch square baking dish and spread into even layer with rubber spatula.

3. FOR THE TOPPING Whisk flour, sugar, salt, and cayenne together in bowl until fully combined. Stir in melted butter until mixture forms clumps. Break into pea-size pieces and distribute evenly over sweet potato mixture.

4. Bake until topping is fragrant and darkened slightly in color and potatoes are hot, 25 to 30 minutes. Let cool for 25 minutes before serving.

KEYS TO SUCCESS
- **Roast, don't boil:** Concentrates flavor
- **Add flavor:** By stirring in butter, sugar, and orange zest and liqueur

Sweet Potato Varieties

Many varieties of sweet potatoes are available, and they can differ quite a bit in color, texture, and flavor. Often the conventional orange varieties found in supermarkets are not labeled as being particular varieties, which is usually fine since these sweet potatoes are fairly interchangeable in recipes. If we think a specific variety works best in a recipe, we'll make a note of that.

BEAUREGARD Beauregard (most often sold as the conventional sweet potato) has dusky red skin and is sweet, moist, and buttery. Its versatility makes it our favorite variety.

JEWEL Jewel, with copper skin and tender, moist orange flesh, is also frequently found in supermarkets and is another favorite of ours.

RED GARNET Red Garnet is named for its red-purple skin; it has orange flesh that is more savory and less dense than Beauregard or Jewel.

WHITE White sweet potatoes, such as Japanese White and White Sweet, tend to be less moist and are starchier than the orange-fleshed varieties.

PURPLE Purple sweet potatoes, such as the Stokes Purple, have a dry, dense texture and the highest level of antioxidants of all the sweet potato varieties.

Sweet Potatoes versus Yams

In the United States, sweet potatoes are often confused with yams. Although they are similar in shape, these two tubers are not closely related botanically. Yams, which are a staple food in parts of Asia, Africa, Central America, South America, and the West Indies, belong to the genus Dioscorea and typically have white flesh and sometimes a rough, shaggy exterior. Sweet potatoes, which are popular in the United States, belong to the genus Ipomoea and usually have smoother skins and orange flesh.

Sweet Potato

Yam

RESOURCES FOR POTATOES

CHOOSING THE RIGHT POTATO

Different varieties of potatoes can have wildly different textures depending on their starch level. This means you need to choose wisely based on your recipe.

BAKING POTATOES (RUSSET, IDAHO)

These dry, floury potatoes contain more total starch than other varieties, giving them a dry, mealy texture. They are the best choice when baking and frying. They work well when you want to thicken a stew or soup, but not when you want distinct chunks of potatoes.

BOILING POTATOES (RED BLISS, FRENCH FINGERLING)

These varieties contain a relatively low amount of total starch, which means they have a firm, smooth, and waxy texture. They are sometimes called new potatoes because they are less mature potatoes harvested in the late spring and summer. They also have thinner skins than other types of potatoes. Boiling potatoes are perfect when you want a variety that will hold its shape, as with potato salad. They are also a good choice when roasting or (unsurprisingly) boiling.

ALL-PURPOSE POTATOES (YUKON GOLD, YELLOW FINN)

These are considered "in between" potatoes. They contain less starch than baking potatoes but more than firm, waxy boiling potatoes. They also have a richer, more buttery flavor than other varieties. All-purpose potatoes can be used pretty successfully in most potato dishes, although sometimes there may be another variety that would be a better option.

CHILLING INJURIES FOR SWEET POTATOES

One potential chilling injury for sweet potatoes is hard-core formation. What does that mean? It means that the sweet potato forms a core of hard tissue in its center, which remains even after cooking. It can occur to some degree in all varieties of sweet potatoes that have been subjected to improper storage below 55 degrees followed by storage at room temperatures. Why? Normally, when vegetables are cooked they become soft due to the breakdown of pectin, which holds the cell walls together. However, when sweet potatoes are stored below 55 degrees, an enzyme called pectin methylesterase (PME) is activated. PME actually changes the pectin so that it combines with calcium ions in the cells, strengthening the pectin and keeping the cell walls, particularly in the center of the sweet potato, from softening, even during prolonged cooking. The solution? Keep your sweet potatoes in a cool (but not too cool), dry spot.

WE'RE NOT KIDDING ABOUT THE THERMOMETER!

It might sound fussy to take the temperature of a baked potato to see if the center has reached 205 degrees, but it's the only way to guarantee that you're getting a uniformly fluffy interior. The usual approach to checking for doneness, squeezing the potato, doesn't work because while the outer edge might feel soft, the center is likely dense and firm. This cross section shows how different the texture (and temperature) can be from the surface to the center.

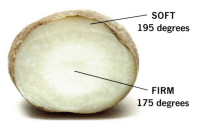

SOFT
195 degrees

FIRM
175 degrees

MUST YOU PRICK?

Everyone knows that you have to prick potatoes before baking them so steam doesn't build up inside and cause them to explode. Well, we baked 40 potatoes without doing this, and not one exploded. But since it takes so little effort, here's one time we'll err on the side of caution. It could be the 41st one that explodes.

WHY YOU SHOULDN'T MICROWAVE

Using a microwave might seem like a fast way to "bake" a potato, but we found two reasons why it's actually not a good idea. First, microwaves heat foods very unevenly, so some parts of the potato might rapidly reach 205 degrees while others get to only 180 degrees. Second, rapidly heating a potato causes pressure to build and cell walls to burst, releasing starch molecules that glue together the broken cell walls.

FAMILY TREE: POTATOES

Although all vegetables vary by size and freshness, most markets carry only a single variety. Broccoli is broccoli, carrots are carrots. Even when there are several varieties (as with heirloom tomatoes), most can be used interchangeably in recipes. Yes, one tomato might look a bit different or be a bit sweeter than another, but they all will taste fine in salads. With potatoes, this is not the case.

SWEET POTATOES

Like white potatoes, sweet potatoes contain a mix of starches and moisture. But there are many differences—white potato starch granules are larger than those of sweet potatoes, and white potato granules swell and gelatinize at a lower temperature. The biggest difference is the presence of enzymes, specifically amylase enzymes, which are found in all sweet potatoes and not found at all in white potatoes. They are important because amylase enzymes convert starches to sugars during the cooking process.

Beauregard, Jewel, Red Garnet, Hernandez, Centennial

Soft, moist fleshed
These sweet potatoes contain more amylase enzymes than firmer ones, meaning more of the starch in these sweet potatoes is broken down. With less starch these potatoes release more moisture and have a moist, soft texture.

O'Henry, Jersey, White Triumph, Southern Queen, Kotobuki, Okinawan

Firm, mealy-fleshed
These firm sweet potatoes have fewer amylase enzymes, meaning that less starch is turned into sugar, and they cook up less moist and more mealy. Many are white-fleshed and popular outside the U.S.

WHITE POTATOES

White potatoes are categorized into two major eating types: High-starch, low-moisture (which can be dry and mealy); and low-starch, high-moisture (also classified as smooth and waxy). These two types of potatoes differ in total starch content and the composition of the starch. But most importantly, the composition of the starch is quite different. Most starch in plants is made of two molecules: amylose and amylopectin. High-starch mealy potatoes contain about 25 percent amylose with the rest being amylopectin. But low-starch waxy potatoes contain almost no amylose.

High starch
These potatoes generally lose their shape when simmered. Because they have so little moisture, they soak up liquid as they cook and explode.

Medium starch
Medium-starch potatoes do a better job of holding their shape but share many traits in common with high-starch potatoes.

Low starch
Low-starch/high-moisture potatoes hold their shape better than other potatoes when simmered. They contain very little amylose.

YAMS
Yams are not potatoes. On a dry basis they contain about 90 percent starch, of which around 20 percent is amylose. So they do contain more starch than potatoes, and a little bit less moisture. The small number of varieties of edible yams are not toxic. But wild yams contain a toxic alkaloid called dioscorine.

SWEET POTATOES: HOW STARCH TURNS TO SUGAR
When sweet potatoes cook, a family of enzymes call amylases work to convert the starch present into a sugar called maltose. The amylase enzymes break down the starch, which is made up of chains of glucose molecules. The resulting maltose consists of two glucose molecules linked together, and is less sweet than glucose alone.

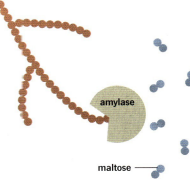

COURSE
EVERYDAY ROASTED VEGETABLES

KEITH DRESSER

Something magical happens when you roast vegetables. The oven's dry heat drives off water to concentrate flavor while the fat encourages browning, transforming raw vegetables into something entirely different. The trick is to use the right method for each vegetable. Roasting is a great way to breathe life into whatever produce is in your crisper drawer. Plus, it's mostly hands-free. This course provides a cheat sheet for doing it well.

KEITH'S PRO TIP: *Consistent size is key. When prepping vegetables for roasting it's important to keep everything the same size and create plenty of surface area. This will give you evenly cooked results with the best browning.*

CORE ROASTING TECHNIQUE 1

ROASTED ASPARAGUS
Serves: 4 to 6
Total Time: 25 minutes

RECIPE OVERVIEW To ready asparagus for roasting, trimming and peeling the spears is less wasteful than snapping off the ends. Preheating the sheet on the lowest rack helps the spears sear upon contact. Not moving the spears during roasting allows their undersides to brown deeply while the tops remain bright green. This recipe works best with thick asparagus spears that are between ½ and ¾ inch in diameter.

- 2 pounds thick asparagus spears, bottom inch of each trimmed, bottom half peeled down to white flesh
- 2 tablespoons oil
- ½ teaspoon table salt
- ¼ teaspoon pepper

Adjust oven rack to lowest position, place rimmed baking sheet on rack, and heat oven to 500 degrees. Toss asparagus with oil, salt, and pepper. Roast asparagus for 8 to 10 minutes (do not move spears during roasting).

KEYS TO SUCCESS
- **Trim the asparagus:** See page 40 for how
- **Do not move the spears:** Ensures a hard sear and intense, flavorful browning

ROASTED BROCCOLI

Serves: 4
Total Time: 25 minutes

RECIPE OVERVIEW This recipe produces evenly cooked roasted broccoli—both stalks and florets—and adds concentrated flavor and dappled browning. Cutting the broccoli crowns into wedges maximizes surface contact with the baking sheet to encourage browning. Adding a little sugar helps, too.

- 1 large head broccoli (about 1¾ pounds), stalks peeled and cut into 2- to 3-inch lengths and each length into ½-inch-thick pieces, each crown cut into 4 to 6 evenly thick wedges
- 3 tablespoons oil
- ½ teaspoon sugar
- ½ teaspoon table salt
- ¼ teaspoon pepper

Adjust oven rack to lowest position, place rimmed baking sheet on rack, and heat oven to 500 degrees. Toss broccoli with oil, sugar, salt, and pepper. Roast broccoli, flat sides down, 9 to 11 minutes.

> **KEYS TO SUCCESS**
> - **Cut the broccoli into wedges:** To create maximum surface area
> - **Don't skip the sugar:** It helps promote browning and tames any bitterness.

CORE ROASTING TECHNIQUE 2

ROASTED BUTTERNUT SQUASH

Serves: 4 to 6
Total Time: 45 minutes

RECIPE OVERVIEW This simplest of roasting methods achieves deep caramelization on slices of peeled butternut squash. Peeling the squash thoroughly, to remove not only the tough outer skin but also the fibrous layer of white flesh just beneath, ensures supremely tender results. For richer flavor, you can substitute melted unsalted butter for the oil.

- 1 large butternut squash (2½ to 3 pounds), peeled down to deep orange flesh, halved lengthwise, seeds removed, each half sliced crosswise ½ inch thick
- 3 tablespoons oil
- ½ teaspoon table salt
- ½ teaspoon pepper

Adjust oven rack to lowest position and heat oven to 425 degrees. Toss squash with oil, salt, and pepper. Roast squash on rimmed baking sheet for 25 to 30 minutes, then rotate sheet and roast 6 to 10 minutes longer. Flip squash and roast 10 to 15 minutes longer.

ROASTED CREMINI MUSHROOMS

Serves: 4 to 6
Total Time: 55 minutes

RECIPE OVERVIEW Roasting turns woodsy cremini mushrooms rich and deeply flavorful. Brining the mushrooms before roasting seasons them evenly and helps them stay moist during cooking. It takes almost an hour for them to become deeply browned.

- 1½ pounds cremini mushrooms, trimmed and left whole if small, halved if medium, or quartered if large
- 5 teaspoons table salt for brining
- 2 tablespoons oil

Adjust oven rack to lowest position and heat oven to 450 degrees. Dissolve salt in 2 quarts cold water and brine mushrooms for 10 minutes. Dry well. Roast mushrooms on rimmed baking sheet for 35 to 40 minutes, toss, then roast 5 to 10 minutes longer.

ROASTED GREEN BEANS

Serves: 4 to 6
Total Time: 35 minutes

RECIPE OVERVIEW Roasting quickly gives even tough supermarket green beans incomparable flavor and an appealing brown and blistered appearance. Lining the baking sheet prevents scorching and makes cleanup easy.

- 1 pound green beans, trimmed
- 1 tablespoon oil
- ½ teaspoon table salt
- ¼ teaspoon pepper

Adjust oven rack to middle position and heat oven to 450 degrees. Line baking sheet with aluminum foil or parchment paper. Toss beans with oil, salt, and pepper. Roast beans for 10 minutes, toss, then roast 10 to 12 minutes longer.

CORE ROASTING TECHNIQUE 3

ROASTED BRUSSELS SPROUTS

Serves: 4
Total Time: 35 minutes

RECIPE OVERVIEW Oven roasting is a simple way to produce brussels sprouts that are well caramelized on the outside and tender on the inside. Adding water to the oil helps the sprouts steam during the covered phase. Initially arranging the sprouts cut side down ensures that their flat surfaces brown deeply.

- 1¼ pounds brussels sprouts, trimmed and halved
- 2 tablespoons oil
- 1 tablespoon water
- ½ teaspoon table salt
- ¼ teaspoon pepper

Adjust oven rack to middle position and heat oven to 500 degrees. Line rimmed baking sheet with aluminum foil or parchment paper. Toss sprouts with oil, water, salt, and pepper. Roast sprouts, cut sides down and covered, for 10 minutes. Uncover and roast 10 to 12 minutes longer.

ROASTED CARROTS

Serves: 4 to 6
Total Time: 1 hour

RECIPE OVERVIEW Roasting carrots draws out their natural sugars and intensifies their flavor. Cutting the carrots into batons ensures that they cook evenly with the best browning. Lining the sheet prevents scorching and makes cleanup easy. For richer flavor, you can substitute melted unsalted butter for the oil.

- 1½ pounds carrots, peeled, halved crosswise, and cut lengthwise if necessary to create even pieces
- 2 tablespoons oil
- ½ teaspoon table salt
- ¼ teaspoon pepper

Adjust oven rack to middle position and heat oven to 425 degrees. Line rimmed baking sheet with aluminum foil or parchment paper. Toss carrots with oil, salt, and pepper. Roast carrots covered for 15 minutes. Uncover and roast 30 to 35 minutes longer, stirring twice.

ROASTED CAULIFLOWER

Serves: 4 to 6
Total Time: 1 hour

RECIPE OVERVIEW Roasted cauliflower is so sweet and rich in flavor that it needs little enhancement. Leaving the cauliflower core intact makes it easy to flip the pieces halfway through cooking. Rubbing the oil and seasonings into each piece ensures that the nooks and crannies are evenly coated.

- 1 head cauliflower (2 pounds), outer leaves trimmed, stem cut flush with bottom, and head cut into 8 equal wedges so that core and florets remain intact
- 2 tablespoons oil
- ½ teaspoon table salt
- ¼ teaspoon pepper

Adjust oven rack to lowest position and heat oven to 475 degrees. Rub oil, salt, and pepper into each wedge. Line rimmed baking sheet with aluminum foil or parchment paper. Roast cauliflower covered for 10 minutes. Uncover and roast for 15 minutes, flip, and roast 15 minutes longer.

KEYS TO SUCCESS

- **Cut into wedges:** Wedges provide great contact with the sheet, which means great browning.
- **Steam first:** Keeps the cauliflower from drying out
- **Flip halfway:** To ensure even cooking and color

ROASTED FENNEL

Serves: 4 to 6
Total Time: 45 minutes

RECIPE OVERVIEW Cutting the fennel bulbs lengthwise creates maximum surface area for browning. Leaving the core intact makes the halves easy to flip. Look for fennel bulbs that measure 3½ to 4 inches in diameter and weigh around 1 pound with the stalks (12 to 14 ounces without).

- 3 fennel bulbs, 3 to 3½ inches in diameter, stalks discarded, each bulb cut lengthwise through core (don't remove core) into 8 wedges
- 2 tablespoons oil
- ½ teaspoon table salt
- ¼ teaspoon pepper

Adjust oven rack to lower-middle position and heat oven to 425 degrees. Toss fennel with oil, salt, and pepper. Spray rimmed baking sheet with vegetable oil spray. Roast covered for 20 minutes. Uncover and roast 5 to 8 minutes, flip, and continue to roast until core is tender and fennel is browned, 3 to 5 minutes longer.

RESOURCES FOR EVERYDAY ROASTED VEGETABLES

THREE EASY ROASTING TECHNIQUES
CORE TECHNIQUE 1

1. PREHEAT BAKING SHEET
Preheating the baking sheet ensures that relatively quick-cooking vegetables will develop flavorful browning by the time they are tender.

2. ROAST UNCOVERED
Roasting the vegetables on the hot baking sheet without moving them sears and browns the undersides while the tops remain vibrant.

CORE TECHNIQUE 2

ROAST UNCOVERED
This simplest method works well for vegetables that will sufficiently soften by the time their exteriors develop flavorful browning.

CORE TECHNIQUE 3

1. ROAST COVERED
Initially covering the baking sheet with aluminum foil traps steam that helps dense vegetables soften and cook through.

2. ROAST UNCOVERED
Uncovering the sheet allows moisture to evaporate so that the vegetables can brown.

DRESSING UP VEGETABLES

A few flavorings can go a long way to prevent simply prepared vegetables from getting boring. A spoonful of this or that can enhance the dish. Use these easy flavor boosters with simple boiled, steamed, or roasted vegetables.

- A squeeze of citrus.
- Cook butter in a small skillet over medium heat until it browns, then drizzle over the vegetables and sprinkle with toasted nuts.
- Dot with a flavored butter (see page 355).
- Sprinkle with chopped fresh herbs.
- Sprinkle with fruity extra-virgin olive oil, grated Parmesan cheese, and a few red pepper flakes.
- Sprinkle with soy sauce or toasted sesame oil.
- Toss with a:
  - vinaigrette (see pages 152–155),
  - pesto (see pages 254–255), or
  - herb sauce (see page 353).
- Drizzle with a creamy sauce (see page 354) or yogurt-based sauce (see page 31).
- Sprinkle with a flavorful spice blend such as za'atar or dukkah (see page 28).

FIVE ROASTING RULES

These best practices apply to all vegetables and roasting methods.

1 Use a sturdy rimmed baking sheet
Flimsy sheets warp in a hot oven, causing oil to pool and food to brown unevenly.

2 Evenly coat the vegetables with oil and seasonings
Oil (use any neutral variety) encourages browning because it conducts heat efficiently from the metal sheet to the vegetable. Toss the pieces with oil, salt, and pepper in a bowl to ensure they are evenly coated.

3 Arrange the vegetables in a single layer
Doing so ensures even cooking and deep browning on each piece.

4 Don't crowd the sheet
Leaving space between the pieces prevents a buildup of steam that thwarts browning.

5 Don't flip too soon
The side touching the sheet should be brown.

COURSE
SHAPE-SHIFTING CAULIFLOWER

NICOLE KONSTANTINAKOS

Cauliflower's mild flavor makes it endlessly versatile and lends itself to all manner of preparation and flavorings. Earlier you learned how to pan-roast and oven-roast cauliflower florets. In a later chapter you will learn how to use cauliflower in several grain recipes. In this course you will learn how to magically turn cauliflower into "rice" to serve as a simple side or as a bed for other toppings, use it to create vegetable cakes, and place it center stage after cutting it into steaks and pairing it with a bright herby sauce.

NICOLE'S PRO TIP: *After breaking down a head of cauliflower for a recipe that calls for just florets, rather than discard the leaves and stem pieces, which are full of nutty, vegetal flavor, I find creative ways to cook with them—shredding them into slaws, simmering them into soups, or tossing them into stir-fry dishes.*

CAULIFLOWER RICE

Serves: 4 to 6
Total Time: 35 minutes

RECIPE OVERVIEW Cauliflower is a true shape-shifter of a vegetable. This method of preparing it results in a light, neutral-flavored side that works in any dish where you would use white rice. The key is to blitz the florets in a food processor until transformed into perfect rice-size granules. To make cauliflower rice foolproof, work in batches to make sure all the florets break down evenly. Shallot and a small amount of vegetable broth boost the flavor. To ensure that the cauliflower is tender but still maintains a rice-like chew, first steam it in a covered pot and then finish cooking it uncovered to evaporate any remaining moisture, for beautifully fluffy cauliflower rice.

- 1 head cauliflower (2 pounds), cut into 1-inch florets (6 cups)
- 1 tablespoon extra-virgin olive oil
- 1 shallot, minced
- ½ cup vegetable broth
- ¾ teaspoon table salt
- 2 tablespoons minced fresh parsley

1. Working in 2 batches, pulse cauliflower florets in food processor until finely ground into ¼- to ⅛-inch pieces, 6 to 8 pulses, scraping down sides of bowl as needed; transfer to bowl.

2. Heat oil in large saucepan over medium-low heat until shimmering. Add shallot and cook until softened, about 3 minutes. Stir in cauliflower, broth, and salt. Cover and cook, stirring occasionally, until cauliflower is tender, 12 to 15 minutes.

3. Uncover and continue to cook, stirring occasionally, until cauliflower rice is almost completely dry, about 3 minutes. Off heat, stir in parsley and season with salt and pepper to taste. Serve.

Variation
CURRIED CAULIFLOWER RICE

Add ¼ teaspoon ground cardamom, ¼ teaspoon ground cinnamon, and ¼ teaspoon ground turmeric to saucepan with shallot. Substitute 1 tablespoon minced fresh mint for parsley and stir ¼ cup toasted sliced almonds into cauliflower rice with mint.

KEYS TO SUCCESS

- **Cut the cauliflower into florets:** See page 42 for how
- **Use a food processor:** To get rice-size grains
- **Work in batches:** Breaks down the florets evenly
- **Finish cooking uncovered:** Evaporates any remaining moisture

CAULIFLOWER CAKES

Serves: 4
Total Time: 1½ hours, plus 30 minutes chilling

RECIPE OVERVIEW Vegetable cakes are a creative addition to the dinner table. These cauliflower cakes have creamy interiors, crunchy browned exteriors, and complex flavors. To ensure that the flavor of the cauliflower doesn't get lost and to drive off excess moisture that would make the cakes fall apart, cut the cauliflower into florets and roast them until they are well browned and tender. Tossing the florets with warm spices such as turmeric, coriander, and ground ginger gives the cakes an aromatic backbone. A binder is necessary to hold the shaped cakes together; egg and flour are standard additions, but adding some goat cheese provides extra binding, creaminess, and tangy flavor. Though these cakes hold together, they are very soft and tricky to flip in the pan. Refrigerating the cakes for 30 minutes before cooking them is the best solution. The chilled cakes transfer from baking sheet to skillet without a problem and are much sturdier when it comes time to flip them.

Yogurt-Herb Sauce
- 1   cup plain yogurt
- 2   tablespoons minced fresh cilantro
- 2   tablespoons minced fresh mint
- 1   garlic clove, minced

Cauliflower Cakes
- 1   head cauliflower (2 pounds), cut into 1-inch florets
- ¼   cup extra-virgin olive oil, divided
- 1   teaspoon ground turmeric
- 1   teaspoon ground coriander
- 1   teaspoon table salt
- ½   teaspoon ground ginger
- ¼   teaspoon pepper
- 4   ounces goat cheese, softened
- 2   scallions, sliced thin
- 1   large egg, lightly beaten
- 2   garlic cloves, minced
- 1   teaspoon grated lemon or lime zest, plus lemon or lime wedges for serving
- ¼   cup all-purpose flour

1. **FOR THE YOGURT-HERB SAUCE** Whisk yogurt, cilantro, mint, and garlic together in bowl until combined and season with salt and pepper to taste. Cover and refrigerate until ready to serve, at least 30 minutes.

2. **FOR THE CAULIFLOWER CAKES** Adjust oven rack to middle position and heat oven to 450 degrees. Toss cauliflower florets with 1 tablespoon oil, turmeric, coriander, salt, ginger, and pepper. Transfer to aluminum foil–lined rimmed baking sheet and spread into single layer. Roast until florets are well browned and tender, about 25 minutes. Let cool slightly, then transfer to large bowl.

3. Line clean rimmed baking sheet with parchment paper. Mash florets coarsely with potato masher. Stir in goat cheese, scallions, egg, garlic, and lemon zest until

Making Cauliflower Cakes

ROAST AND MASH
Roast cauliflower florets until they are browned and tender and then mash with a potato masher.

BIND AND CHILL
Mix the mashed cauliflower with goat cheese, egg, and flour and form into cakes. Refrigerate the cakes until firm.

well combined. Sprinkle flour over cauliflower mixture and stir to incorporate. Using wet hands, divide mixture into 4 equal portions, pack gently into ¾-inch-thick cakes about 3½ inches in diameter, and place on prepared sheet. Refrigerate cakes until chilled and firm, about 30 minutes.

4. Line large plate with paper towels. Heat remaining 3 tablespoons oil in 12-inch nonstick skillet over medium heat until shimmering. Gently lay cakes in skillet and cook until deep golden brown and crisp, 5 to 7 minutes per side. Drain cakes briefly on prepared plate. Serve with yogurt sauce and lemon wedges.

> **KEYS TO SUCCESS**
> - **Cut the cauliflower into florets:** See page 42 for how
> - **Roast the florets:** To drive off excess water
> - **Bind with goat cheese:** Adds tangy flavor

CAULIFLOWER STEAKS WITH SALSA VERDE

Serves: 4
Total Time: 45 minutes

RECIPE OVERVIEW When you cook thick slabs of cauliflower as vegetarian "steaks," they develop a substantial, meaty texture and become nutty, sweet, and caramelized. Recipes for cauliflower steaks abound, but many involve fussy transitions between stovetop and oven. For an easy way to produce four perfectly cooked cauliflower steaks simultaneously, simply use a rimmed baking sheet and a scorching oven. Steaming the cauliflower briefly by covering the baking sheet with foil, followed by high-heat uncovered roasting on the lowest oven rack, produces dramatic-looking, caramelized seared steaks with tender interiors. To elevate the cauliflower to centerpiece status, pair it with a vibrant Italian-style salsa verde—a blend of parsley, mint, capers, olive oil, and white wine vinegar. Brushing the hot steaks with the salsa verde ensures they soak up all of its robust flavor.

- 1½ cups fresh parsley leaves
- ½ cup fresh mint leaves
- ½ cup extra-virgin olive oil, divided
- 2 tablespoons water
- 1½ tablespoons white wine vinegar
- 1 tablespoon capers, rinsed
- 1 garlic clove, minced
- ⅛ teaspoon plus ½ teaspoon table salt, divided
- ¼ teaspoon pepper, divided
- 2 heads cauliflower (2 pounds each), outer leaves trimmed, stems cut flush with bottom, and heads halved, 1½-inch-thick slab cut from each half
  Lemon wedges

1. Adjust oven rack to lowest position and heat oven to 500 degrees. Pulse parsley, mint, ¼ cup oil, water, vinegar, capers, garlic, and ⅛ teaspoon salt in food processor until mixture is finely chopped but not smooth, about 10 pulses, scraping down sides of bowl as needed. Transfer salsa verde to small bowl and set aside until ready to serve.

2. Place cauliflower slabs on rimmed baking sheet and drizzle with 2 tablespoons oil. Sprinkle with ¼ teaspoon salt and ⅛ teaspoon pepper and rub to distribute. Flip slabs and repeat with remaining 2 tablespoons oil, remaining ¼ teaspoon salt, and remaining ⅛ teaspoon pepper.

3. Cover baking sheet tightly with aluminum foil and roast for 5 minutes. Remove foil and roast until bottoms of steaks are well browned, 8 to 10 minutes. Gently flip steaks and continue to roast until tender and second sides are well browned, 6 to 8 minutes.

4. Transfer steaks to platter and brush evenly with ¼ cup salsa verde. Serve with lemon wedges, passing remaining salsa verde separately.

CORE TECHNIQUE

Preparing Cauliflower Steaks

TRIM AND HALVE
Trim the leaves and cut the stem flush with the bottom florets. Halve the head lengthwise through the core.

CUT THICK SLABS
Cut one 1½-inch-thick slab from each half. Reserve the remaining cauliflower for another use.

ROAST COVERED THEN UNCOVERED
Steam the steaks covered in aluminum foil. Uncover and roast until the exteriors are caramelized and interiors are tender.

COURSE
TURN ON THE BROILER

LAWMAN JOHNSON

Broiling browns vegetables quickly and deeply. It is the indoor equivalent of cooking over an open flame and approximates the effects of grilling from above. Intense direct heat from the oven's broiler concentrates flavor while imparting charred caramelization to the vegetables. Broiling does require close attention but delivers fantastic results in mere minutes. It is a technique we'll show you how to use for buttery asparagus, garlicky broccoli rabe, cheesy corn on the cob, and easy stuffed tomatoes.

LAWMAN'S PRO TIP: *When broiling, always set a timer, don't walk away, and keep your eyes on the food.*

BROILED ASPARAGUS WITH GARLIC-BUTTER SAUCE

Serves: 4 to 6
Total Time: 30 minutes

RECIPE OVERVIEW Many people steam or roast asparagus, but broiling it is a great alternative. This simple recipe adorns tender, grassy-tasting asparagus with garlic butter. Browning larger stalks under the broiler deepens their flavor and draws out their sweetness, while a simple emulsion of garlic, butter, and water creates a thick, creamy sauce that clings luxuriously to the broiled spears. This sauce seems fancy, but it's deceptively easy to make. This recipe works best with asparagus spears that are ¾ inch thick at the base; do not use pencil-thin asparagus here.

- 2 pounds (¾-inch-thick) asparagus, trimmed
- 1 tablespoon extra-virgin olive oil
- 1 teaspoon chopped fresh thyme
- ¾ teaspoon table salt, divided
- 4 tablespoons unsalted butter, cut into 1-tablespoon pieces and softened, divided
- ¼ teaspoon pepper
- 4 garlic cloves, minced
- 1 tablespoon water

1. Adjust oven rack 6 inches from broiler element and heat broiler. Toss asparagus, oil, thyme, and ½ teaspoon salt together on rimmed baking sheet. Arrange asparagus in single layer.

2. Broil until asparagus is spotty brown and tender, 7 to 9 minutes, rotating sheet halfway through broiling. Transfer asparagus to serving platter.

3. Combine 3 tablespoons butter, pepper, and remaining ¼ teaspoon salt in bowl. Melt remaining 1 tablespoon butter in small skillet or saucepan over medium heat. Add garlic and cook, stirring constantly, until fragrant and just starting to turn golden, 1 to 2 minutes. Off heat, stir in water (mixture will sizzle).

4. Immediately whisk garlic mixture into butter mixture in bowl until emulsified (sauce should be creamy). Spoon butter sauce over asparagus and toss gently to coat with sauce. Serve.

KEYS TO SUCCESS
- **Trim the asparagus:** See page 40 for how
- **Keep an eye on browning:** Broiler heat varies from oven to oven.
- **Make a garlic-butter emulsion:** Which clings to the asparagus

BROILED BROCCOLI RABE

Serves: 4
Total Time: 20 minutes

RECIPE OVERVIEW Broccoli rabe is broccoli's spicy cousin and many recipes tend to wash out its distinctive flavor. Broiling broccoli rabe is a simple, superfast way to create deep caramelization, adding just a touch of contrasting sweetness to this bitter green vegetable. It takes mere minutes and requires nothing more than a rimmed baking sheet. To keep things streamlined, we skip the usual blanching step and simply cut the tops (the leaves and florets) from the stalks, but do no further chopping. Toss the pieces with the garlicky oil and they're ready for the oven.

- 3 tablespoons extra-virgin olive oil, divided
- 1 pound broccoli rabe, trimmed
- 1 garlic clove, minced
- ¾ teaspoon kosher salt
- ¼ teaspoon red pepper flakes
  Lemon wedges

1. Adjust oven rack 4 inches from broiler element and heat broiler. Brush rimmed baking sheet with 1 tablespoon oil.

2. Cut tops (leaves and florets) of broccoli rabe from stalks, keeping tops whole, then cut stalks into 1-inch pieces. Transfer to prepared sheet.

3. Combine remaining 2 tablespoons oil, garlic, salt, and pepper flakes in small bowl. Pour oil mixture over broccoli rabe and toss to combine.

4. Broil until exposed half of leaves are well browned, 2 to 2½ minutes. Using tongs, toss to expose unbrowned leaves. Return sheet to oven and continue to broil until most leaves are lightly charred and stalks are crisp-tender, 2 to 2½ minutes. Serve with lemon wedges.

KEYS TO SUCCESS

- **Use a salad spinner:** To easily dry the broccoli rabe after washing
- **Reduce bitterness:** By leaving leafy parts and florets intact during cooking
- **Broil:** To develop complex flavor and nutty-sweet caramelization

SCIENCE LESSON

Nipping Bitterness in the Bud

Cutting and chewing broccoli rabe releases compounds that are bitter. Since more of these compounds are in the florets, we leave the leafy part whole. Broiling the rabe also reduces bitterness, as heat exposure deactivates the enzyme (myrosinase) that causes the bitterness.

CORE TECHNIQUE
Broiling Vegetables

POSITION RACK
Make sure the oven rack is the proper distance from the broiler's heat source. An inch or two can mean the difference between perfectly charred and burnt.

TOSS WITH OIL
Oil encourages deeper browning under the broiler's heat. Use your hands or kitchen tongs to evenly coat the vegetables in oil.

CORE TECHNIQUE
Prepping Broccoli Rabe

TRIM ENDS
Trim and discard bottom 1 inch of stalk ends.

WASH AND DRY
Wash broccoli rabe in cold water and dry.

SEPARATE LEAVES
Cut the leaves and florets from the top and separate them from the stems.

ELOTE

Serves: 6
Total Time: 45 minutes

RECIPE OVERVIEW In Mexico, street vendors add kick to grilled corn by slathering it with a creamy, spicy, cheesy sauce. For this interpretation of traditional elote, we broil corn on the cob instead of heading out to the grill, first brushing the raw ears with olive oil to keep them from drying out. For the creamy coating we use mayonnaise dressed up with cilantro, garlic, lime, and chili powder instead of Mexican crema. We also substitute salty, crumbly feta for the cotija cheese traditionally sprinkled over elote. To keep it from crumbling right off the corn, we mix the feta in with the mayonnaise before brushing the mixture all over the charred corn and broiling it for another few minutes.

- 6 ears corn, husks and silk removed, stalks left intact
- 1 tablespoon extra-virgin olive oil
- ½ cup mayonnaise
- 1 ounce feta cheese, crumbled (¼ cup)
- 2 tablespoons minced fresh cilantro
- 1 tablespoon lime juice, plus lime wedges for serving
- 1 garlic clove, minced
- 1 teaspoon chili powder
- ¼ teaspoon table salt

1. Adjust oven rack 5 inches from broiler element and heat broiler. Line rimmed baking sheet with aluminum foil. Brush corn all over with oil and transfer to prepared sheet. Broil corn until well browned on 1 side, about 10 minutes. Flip corn and broil until browned on opposite side, about 10 minutes longer.

2. Meanwhile, whisk mayonnaise, feta, cilantro, lime juice, garlic, chili powder, and salt together in bowl until incorporated.

3. Remove corn from oven and brush evenly on all sides with mayonnaise mixture. (Reserve any extra mayonnaise mixture for serving.) Return corn to oven and broil, rotating frequently, until coating is lightly browned, about 2 minutes. Season with salt and pepper to taste. Serve corn with lime wedges and any extra reserved mayonnaise mixture.

> ### KEYS TO SUCCESS
> - **Husk the corn:** See page 99 for how
> - **Brush the corn with oil:** Keeps it from drying out
> - **Combine the feta with mayo:** To prevent the cheese from falling off of the cob

BROILED TOMATOES WITH GOAT CHEESE AND BREAD CRUMBS

Serves: 4 to 6
Total Time: 25 minutes

RECIPE OVERVIEW Broiled tomatoes make for an impressive side dish and come together quickly. We slice ripe tomatoes into planks (instead of halves) to create more surface area and to allow for a more substantial topping. Goat cheese is sprinkled over the planks, followed by a mixture of bread crumbs, Parmesan, and fresh basil. The success of this dish depends on using ripe, flavorful tomatoes. If you can't get your hands on in-season field-grown tomatoes, buy vine-ripened tomatoes; they are juicier and more flavorful than other varieties.

- 1 cup panko bread crumbs
- 2 tablespoons extra-virgin olive oil
- 1 ounce Parmesan cheese, grated (½ cup)
- 1 tablespoon chopped fresh basil
- ½ teaspoon table salt, divided
- ¼ teaspoon pepper, divided
- 2 pounds very ripe, in-season tomatoes, cored and sliced ¾ inch thick
- 1 ounce goat cheese, crumbled (¼ cup)

1. Adjust oven rack 6 inches from broiler element and heat broiler. Toss panko with oil in bowl, spread over rimmed baking sheet, and broil until golden, about 1 minute. Transfer to separate bowl and stir in Parmesan, basil, ¼ teaspoon salt, and ⅛ teaspoon pepper.

2. Lay tomato slices on rimmed baking sheet and sprinkle with remaining ¼ teaspooon salt and remaining ⅛ teaspoon pepper. Broil until heated through, about 3 minutes.

3. Remove tomatoes from broiler. Sprinkle with goat cheese and top with panko mixture. Continue to broil tomatoes until everything is heated through, about 2 minutes. Serve.

> ### KEYS TO SUCCESS
> - **Core and slice tomatoes:** See page 45 for how
> - **Pretoast the panko:** Turns the bread crumbs golden and prevents a soggy topping
> - **Secure the bread crumbs:** With a sprinkling of goat cheese over the top which melts and "glues" the bread crumbs in place

COURSE
WHAT TO DO WITH EGGPLANT

STEVE DUNN

The beauty of eggplants is that they can be prepared in so many ways. Their flesh turns creamy and silky when roasted and appealingly tender when sautéed and browned. But they are full of moisture, so the key to cooking eggplants is knowing when and how to salt them to draw out the excess water before cooking to avoid insipid flavors and a mushy texture. Oftentimes salting is necessary, but sometimes it is not—for example, there is no need to do so when braising or stir-frying. In this course you will learn three different ways to treat and cook eggplant.

STEVE'S PRO TIP: *Don't skimp on the oil when cooking eggplant. Many eggplant recipes call for more oil than you may be used to cooking with, but I urge you to follow the recipe and not cut the amount. Eggplant acts like a sponge when it cooks and cutting the oil will compromise its flavor and texture.*

BROILED EGGPLANT WITH BASIL

Serves: 4 to 6
Total Time: 40 minutes

RECIPE OVERVIEW Broiling is a great way to enjoy eggplant; that said, if you try to simply slice and broil eggplant, it will steam in its own juices rather than brown. So to get broiled eggplant with great color and texture, you need to salt it to draw out its moisture. After 30 minutes, pat the slices dry, move them to a baking sheet (lined with aluminum foil for easy cleanup), and brush them with oil. With the excess moisture taken care of, all the eggplant requires is a few minutes per side under the blazing-hot broiler to turn a beautiful mahogany color. With its concentrated roasted flavor, the only accent needed is a sprinkling of fresh basil (although a simple glaze is another great way to jazz it up). Make sure to slice the eggplant thin so that the slices will cook through by the time the exterior is browned.

- 1½ pounds eggplant, sliced into ¼-inch-thick rounds
- 1½ teaspoons table salt
- 3 tablespoons extra-virgin olive oil
- 2 tablespoons chopped fresh basil

1. Spread eggplant over rimmed baking sheet lined with paper towels, sprinkle both sides with salt (¾ teaspoon per side), and let sit for 30 minutes.

2. Adjust oven rack 4 inches from broiler element and heat broiler. Thoroughly pat eggplant dry, arrange in single layer on aluminum foil–lined baking sheet, and brush both sides with oil. Broil eggplant until tops are mahogany brown, 3 to 4 minutes. Flip eggplant and broil until second side is brown, 3 to 4 minutes.

3. Transfer eggplant to serving platter, season with pepper to taste, and sprinkle with basil. Serve.

Variation
BROILED EGGPLANT WITH SESAME-MISO GLAZE

Any type of miso will work well here. Mirin is a sweet Japanese cooking wine; sherry can be substituted for the mirin if necessary.

Substitute vegetable oil for olive oil and 1 sliced scallion for basil. Whisk 1 tablespoon miso, 3 tablespoons mirin, and 1 tablespoon tahini together in bowl. After browning second side, brush with miso mixture, sprinkle with 1 tablespoon sesame seeds, and continue to broil until miso and seeds are browned, about 2 minutes.

> ### KEYS TO SUCCESS
> - **Salt the eggplant:** To draw moisture to its surface where it can be wiped away
> - **Slice the eggplant thin:** To allow the pieces to cook through in less time

STIR-FRIED JAPANESE EGGPLANT

Serves: 4 to 6
Total Time: 25 minutes

RECIPE OVERVIEW Eggplant soaks up whatever flavors you cook it with, making it ideal for stir-fries with deeply savory sauces. We particularly like Japanese eggplant here for its very creamy flesh and relative lack of seeds. Cooking the eggplant over high heat in a shallow skillet allows its excess moisture to evaporate quickly, without presalting. A combination of soy sauce, Shaoxing wine, and hoisin sauce (for umami depth) makes a complex, flavorful stir-fry sauce. Scallions and fresh cilantro lend the dish some herbaceous notes. This recipe works equally well with Italian or globe eggplants. You can substitute dry sherry for the Chinese rice wine. You can serve over udon noodles or rice.

Sauce
- ½ cup chicken or vegetable broth
- ¼ cup Shaoxing wine or dry sherry
- 3 tablespoons hoisin sauce
- 1 tablespoon soy sauce
- 1 teaspoon cornstarch
- 1 teaspoon toasted sesame oil

Eggplant
- 6 garlic cloves, minced
- 2 tablespoons plus 1 teaspoon vegetable oil, divided
- 1 tablespoon grated fresh ginger
- 1½ pounds Japanese eggplant, cut into ¾-inch pieces
- 2 scallions, sliced thin on bias
- ½ cup fresh cilantro sprigs, cut into 2-inch pieces
- 1 tablespoon sesame seeds, toasted

1. FOR THE SAUCE Whisk all ingredients together in bowl; set aside.

2. FOR THE EGGPLANT Combine garlic, 1 teaspoon oil, and ginger in small bowl. Heat 1 tablespoon oil in 12-inch nonstick skillet over high heat until just smoking. Add half of eggplant and cook, stirring frequently, until browned and tender, 4 to 5 minutes; transfer to bowl. Repeat with remaining 1 tablespoon oil and eggplant.

3. Return first batch of eggplant and any accumulated juices to skillet and push to sides. Add garlic mixture to center and cook, mashing mixture into skillet, until fragrant, about 30 seconds. Stir garlic mixture into eggplant. Whisk sauce to recombine, then add to skillet and cook until eggplant is well coated and sauce is thickened, about 30 seconds. Off heat, stir in scallions and cilantro and sprinkle with sesame seeds. Serve.

> ### KEYS TO SUCCESS
> - **Skip presalting:** Moisture from the eggplant evaporates quickly over high heat.
> - **Use only a little cornstarch:** Thickens the sauce without turning it gloppy

BRAISED EGGPLANT WITH PAPRIKA, CORIANDER, AND YOGURT

Serves: 4 to 6
Total Time: 50 minutes

RECIPE OVERVIEW Braising eggplant turns it meltingly tender with a creamy texture. Start by cutting the eggplant into slim wedges, making sure that each piece has some skin attached to keep it from falling apart during cooking. Once the eggplant is tender, reduce the braising liquid to create a sauce. The eggplant is seasoned with warm spices and garnished with fresh cilantro and a drizzle of tangy yogurt. Serve braised eggplant as a robust side dish or pair it with rice for a vegetarian main course. Large globe and Italian eggplants disintegrate when braised, so do not substitute a single 1- to 1¼-pound eggplant here. You can substitute 1 to 1¼ pounds of long, slim Chinese or Japanese eggplants if they are available; cut them as directed.

- 2 (8- to 10-ounce) globe or Italian eggplants
- 3 tablespoons vegetable oil
- 2 garlic cloves, minced
- 1 tablespoon tomato paste
- 2 teaspoons paprika
- 1 teaspoon table salt
- 1 teaspoon ground coriander
- ½ teaspoon sugar
- ½ teaspoon ground cumin
- ½ teaspoon ground cinnamon
- ½ teaspoon ground nutmeg
- ½ teaspoon ground ginger
- 2¾ cups water
- ⅓ cup plain whole-milk yogurt
- 2 tablespoons minced fresh cilantro

1. Trim ½ inch from top and bottom of 1 eggplant. Halve eggplant crosswise. Cut each half lengthwise into 2 pieces. Cut each piece into ¾-inch-thick wedges. Repeat with remaining eggplant.

2. Heat oil in 12-inch nonstick skillet over medium heat until shimmering. Add garlic and cook, stirring constantly, until fragrant, about 30 seconds. Add tomato paste, paprika, salt, coriander, sugar, cumin, cinnamon, nutmeg, and ginger and cook, stirring constantly, until mixture starts to darken, 1 to 2 minutes. Spread eggplant evenly in skillet (pieces will not form single layer). Pour water over eggplant. Increase heat to high and bring to boil. Reduce heat to maintain gentle boil. Cover and cook until eggplant is soft and has decreased in volume enough to form single layer on bottom of skillet, about 15 minutes, gently shaking skillet to settle eggplant halfway through cooking (some pieces will remain opaque).

3. Uncover and continue to cook, swirling skillet occasionally, until liquid is thickened and reduced to just a few tablespoons, 12 to 14 minutes longer. Off heat, season with salt and pepper to taste. Transfer to platter, drizzle with yogurt, sprinkle with cilantro, and serve.

KEYS TO SUCCESS

- **Cut the eggplant into wedges**: And keep some skin so it stays intact after the flesh turns tender
- **Braise**: Traps steam that helps quickly tenderize the eggplant

SCIENCE LESSON   What Makes Braised Eggplant So Silky?

We've long been enamored by the almost custardy silkiness that eggplant develops in moist-heat preparations such as braising. But what gives it that unusual texture? As eggplant cooks, its uniquely air-filled flesh (which is technically called the aerenchyma) collapses, becoming denser and firmer. Meanwhile, the cell walls release pectin and hemicellulose, long branching molecules that dissolve into the water within the eggplant to create a smooth, soft texture.

RESOURCES FOR EGGPLANT

HOT TIP: STORING EGGPLANT

Always store eggplants at room temperature, rather than in the refrigerator, as the cold temperature can cause chilling injury.

PREPPING EGGPLANT FOR BRAISING

Peeled pieces of eggplant, as well as pieces that are too large, will disintegrate as they simmer. For intact pieces, it's important to choose a medium-size eggplant (if using a globe or Italian variety) and cut it so that each piece has some skin attached.

1. Cut eggplant in half crosswise.

2. Cut each half lengthwise to form two pieces.

3. Cut each piece into ¾-inch-thick wedges.

EGGPLANT VARIETIES

There are countless eggplant varieties, ranging from 2 to 12 inches long, from round to oblong, and from dark purple to striped to white. Here are some of the most common varieties you'll find in the market.

Globe The most common type in the United States, the bulbous globe eggplant has a mild flavor and tender texture that work well in most cooked applications. It not only contains far fewer seeds than smaller varieties such as Italian and Chinese, but its firm flesh also retains its shape even after cooking. It is a true multitasker and can be sautéed, broiled, grilled, and pureed. Because of its high water content, it's often best to salt and drain it before cooking.

Italian Also called baby eggplant, Italian eggplant looks like a smaller version of a globe eggplant. It is a bit more tender than the globe eggplant, with moderately moist flesh, lots of seeds, and a distinct spicy flavor. It can be sautéed, broiled, grilled, and more.

Japanese and Chinese Both of these types are long and slender, with Japanese having a deep purple hue and Chinese being lighter in color, sometimes almost lavender. Both are thin skinned and have few seeds and creamy flesh. They are perfect for use in grilling or stir-frying.

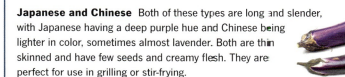

Thai These eggplants are small and apple shaped and usually have a greenish-white hue. They are becoming increasingly easier to find in large supermarkets. They are notable for tasting bright and grassy, and are appealing even when eaten raw. They are terrific roasted with pungent spices or used in Thai curries.

Indian Also sometimes called baby eggplant, these are smaller and more squat than Italian eggplants, with a dark reddish-purple color. They make a pretty presentation halved and stuffed, and they are great cooked and mashed into dips.

TAMING EGGPLANT'S BITTER BITE

Ever wonder why eggplant sometimes makes your mouth tingle? So did we. Eggplants are members of the botanical genus Solanum, a group commonly referred to as nightshades. (Tomatoes and peppers are also in this genus.) Plants in this group often have chemical defenses such as bitter-tasting alkaloids or even, in some cases, poisons. A common example of such a chemical defense is capsaicin, which gives hot peppers their burn. Selective breeding has reduced or eliminated most of these chemicals in many cultivated members of the genus, but bitter alkaloids, which can cause a tingling sensation, are often found in mature eggplants. The bitter alkaloids in eggplant are concentrated in the seeds.

The Bottom Line To avoid tingling, select eggplants that are medium-size or smaller. If you're stuck with a large eggplant, slice or cube it, place the pieces in a colander, toss them with salt, and let them sit for 30 minutes to drain. Quickly rinse and thoroughly dry the eggplant before cooking. The salt masks some of the bitterness.

COURSE
VEGETABLES ON THE GRILL

DAN ZUCCARELLO

Grilling can bring out the best in vegetables, imparting smoky char and leaving their flesh tender and sweet and their exteriors beautifully caramelized. Prepping and heating the grill ensures that your vegetables will cook and release with ease. Slicing vegetables properly ensures there is plenty of surface area for browning. So fire up the grill to learn how to turn fennel, cabbage, zucchini, and corn on the cob into something special.

DAN'S PRO TIP: *While most fennel recipes don't utilize the stalks, I never throw mine away. Their minced fronds make an excellent garnish for soups and a flavorful addition to salads. I also like to chop the stalks and add them with other aromatics to recipes and to the pot when making chicken or fish broth.*

GRILLED FENNEL

Serves: 4
Total Time: 40 minutes

RECIPE OVERVIEW Grilling caramelizes the sugars in fennel and brings out its anise flavor. The high heat softens its fibrous texture to just shy of creamy. But the fennel bulb's awkward shape and dense texture meant we had to find the right way to cut it to prevent it from falling through the cooking grate. Plank-like cross sections with the core left intact work best, and ¼-inch-thick slices cook through in just about the time the slices brown. You can serve the fennel dressed with a vinaigrette (see pages 152–155), if desired.

- 2 fennel bulbs, stalks discarded, base trimmed, tough or blemished outer layers removed, bulb sliced vertically through core into ¼-inch-thick slices
- 3 tablespoons extra-virgin olive oil
- ¼ teaspoon table salt
- ⅛ teaspoon pepper

1A. FOR A CHARCOAL GRILL Open bottom vent completely. Light large chimney starter filled with charcoal briquettes (6 quarts). When top coals are partially covered with ash, pour evenly over half of grill. Set cooking grate in place, cover, and open lid vent completely. Heat grill until hot, about 5 minutes.

1B. FOR A GAS GRILL Turn all burners to high, cover, and heat grill until hot, about 15 minutes. Leave all burners on high.

2. Clean and oil cooking grate. Toss fennel slices, oil, salt, and pepper together in large bowl. Grill fennel slices (on hotter side if using charcoal), turning once, until tender and streaked with dark grill marks, 7 to 9 minutes. Season with salt and pepper to taste. Serve hot, warm, or at room temperature.

> **KEYS TO SUCCESS**
> - **Set up a half-grill fire:** See page 447 for how
> - **Make the right cut:** Slice the fennel to maximize surface area for browning.
> - **Toss with oil:** Encourages even browning and helps prevent slices from sticking to the cooking grate

CORE TECHNIQUE — Slicing Fennel

CUT SLICES
After trimming, cut the fennel bulb into slices leaving the core intact.

GRILLED CABBAGE

Serves: 6 to 8
Total Time: 1¼ hours

RECIPE OVERVIEW The fire of a hot grill tames cabbage's crunch, turning the cabbage tender, sweet, and deliciously smoky. Slicing the head into thick wedges keeps it intact on the grill. To make sure the interior softens before the exterior overcooks, salt the wedges to draw out moisture so the moisture then turns to steam on the grill. Brushing a simple lemon vinaigrette on the cabbage both before and after grilling adds bright flavor.

- 1 teaspoon table salt
- 1 head green cabbage (2 pounds), cut into 8 wedges through core
- 6 tablespoons extra-virgin olive oil
- 1 tablespoon minced fresh thyme
- 2 teaspoons minced shallot
- 2 teaspoons honey
- 1 teaspoon Dijon mustard
- ½ teaspoon grated lemon zest plus 2 tablespoons juice
- ¼ teaspoon pepper

1. Sprinkle salt evenly over cabbage wedges and let sit for 45 minutes. Whisk oil, thyme, shallot, honey, mustard, lemon zest and juice, and pepper together in bowl. Measure out and reserve ¼ cup vinaigrette for serving.

2A. FOR A CHARCOAL GRILL Open bottom vent completely. Light large chimney starter half filled with charcoal briquettes (3 quarts). When top coals are partially covered with ash, pour evenly over grill. Set cooking grate in place, cover, and open lid vent completely. Heat grill until hot, about 5 minutes.

2B. FOR A GAS GRILL Turn all burners to high, cover, and heat grill until hot, about 15 minutes. Turn all burners to medium.

3. Clean and oil cooking grate. Pat cabbage wedges dry, then brush 1 cut side of wedges with half of remaining vinaigrette. Place cabbage on grill, vinaigrette side down, and cook (covered if using gas) until well browned, 7 to 10 minutes. Brush top cut side of wedges with remaining vinaigrette. Flip and cook (covered if using gas) until second side is well browned and fork-tender, 7 to 10 minutes. Transfer cabbage to serving platter and drizzle with reserved vinaigrette. Season with salt and pepper to taste. Serve.

KEYS TO SUCCESS

- **Salt the cabbage:** Draws out moisture so the interior cooks through properly
- **Keep the core intact:** Keeps the wedges together on the grill
- **Set up a single-level fire:** See page 447 for how

GRILLED ZUCCHINI AND RED ONION WITH LEMON VINAIGRETTE

Serves: 4 to 6
Total Time: 1 hour

RECIPE OVERVIEW For this summery side dish, we pair thick slices of zucchini with thick slices of sweet red onion, cutting the vegetables into similar-size pieces so that they can grill in sync over a medium-hot fire. After about 5 minutes, faint grill marks begin to appear on the undersides of the vegetables; adjust their position on the grill or the heat level as needed to brown both sides. The zucchini and onions are perfectly tender and full of smoky flavor in about 20 minutes. To bump up their flavor, whisk together a quick lemony vinaigrette with a touch of Dijon mustard to drizzle over the vegetables after they come off the grill. Finish with a sprinkle of chopped fresh basil. The vegetables can be served hot, warm, or at room temperature.

- 1 red onion, sliced into ½-inch-thick rounds
- 1 pound zucchini, trimmed and sliced lengthwise into ¾-inch-thick planks
- 6 tablespoons extra-virgin olive oil, divided
- 1¼ teaspoons table salt, divided
- ½ teaspoon pepper
- 1 teaspoon grated lemon zest plus 1 tablespoon juice
- 1 garlic clove, minced
- ¼ teaspoon Dijon mustard
- 1 tablespoon chopped fresh basil

1. Thread onion rounds, from side to side, onto 2 metal skewers. Brush onion and zucchini with ¼ cup oil and sprinkle with 1 teaspoon salt and pepper. Whisk lemon zest and juice, garlic, mustard, remaining 2 tablespoons oil, and remaining ¼ teaspoon salt together in bowl.

2A. FOR A CHARCOAL GRILL Open bottom vent completely. Light large chimney starter half filled with charcoal briquettes (3 quarts). When top coals are partially covered with ash, pour evenly over grill. Set cooking grate in place, cover, and open lid vent completely. Heat grill until hot, about 5 minutes.

2B. FOR A GAS GRILL Turn all burners to high, cover, and heat grill until hot, about 15 minutes. Turn all burners to medium.

3. Clean and oil cooking grate. Place onion and zucchini on grill. Cook (covered if using gas), turning as needed, until tender and caramelized, 18 to 22 minutes. Transfer vegetables to serving platter as they finish cooking. Remove onion from skewers and discard any charred outer rings. Whisk dressing to recombine and drizzle over vegetables. Sprinkle with basil and serve.

KEYS TO SUCCESS

- **Set up a single-level fire:** See page 447 for how
- **Use 2 skewers:** Keeps the onion rings together and makes them easier to flip over
- **Slice thick planks:** So the zucchini holds up on the grill

Skewering Onion for Grilling

USE 2 SKEWERS
Thread the onion rounds onto 2 skewers.

HUSK-GRILLED CORN

Serves: 6
Total Time: 50 minutes

RECIPE OVERVIEW Grilled corn on the cob is a summer classic. The husk prevents the kernels from drying out, but if you leave the husk on the whole time the corn doesn't pick up the grill's signature smoky flavor. Shucking the corn, rolling the ears in butter, and then returning them to the grill caramelizes the kernels perfectly and maximizes the grill flavor. One last roll in the butter and the corn is ready. Substitute a flavored butter (see page 355) for the plain, if desired. Set up a cutting board and knife next to your grill to avoid traveling back and forth between kitchen and grill.

- 6 ears corn (unshucked)
- 6 tablespoons unsalted butter, softened
- ½ teaspoon table salt
- ½ teaspoon pepper

1. Cut and remove silk protruding from top of each ear of corn. Combine butter, salt, and pepper in bowl. Fold one 14 by 12-inch piece heavy-duty aluminum foil in half to create 7 by 12-inch rectangle, then crimp into boat shape long and wide enough to accommodate 1 ear of corn. Transfer butter mixture to prepared foil boat.

2A. **FOR A CHARCOAL GRILL** Open bottom vent completely. Light large chimney starter mounded with charcoal briquettes (7 quarts). When top coals are partially covered with ash, pour evenly over half of grill. Set cooking grate in place, cover, and open lid vent completely. Heat grill until hot, about 5 minutes.

2B. **FOR A GAS GRILL** Turn all burners to high, cover, and heat grill until hot, about 15 minutes. Leave all burners on high.

3. Clean and oil cooking grate. Place corn on grill (over coals, with stem ends facing cooler side of grill, for charcoal). Cover and cook, turning corn every 3 minutes, until husks have blackened all over, 12 to 15 minutes. (To check for doneness, carefully peel down small portion of husk. If corn is steaming and bright yellow, it is ready.) Transfer corn to cutting board. Using chef's knife, cut base from corn. Using dish towel to hold corn, peel away and discard husk and silk with tongs.

4. Roll each ear of corn in butter mixture to coat lightly and return to grill (over coals for charcoal). Cook, turning as needed to char corn lightly on each side, about 5 minutes total. Remove corn from grill and roll each ear again in butter mixture. Transfer corn to platter. Serve, passing any remaining butter mixture.

KEYS TO SUCCESS

- **Set up a half-grill fire:** See page 447 for how
- **Start with the husk on:** To trap moisture and lightly steam the corn
- **Return husked corn to the grill:** To get good char

HOW TO GRILL VEGETABLES

To easily grill a simple vegetable to serve with dinner, use this chart as a guide. Brush or toss the vegetables with oil and sprinkle with salt and pepper before grilling. Grill vegetables over a moderate fire (you can comfortably hold your hand 5 inches above the cooking grate for 3 to 4 seconds).

VEGETABLE	PREPARATION	GRILLING DIRECTIONS
Asparagus	Snap off tough ends.	Grill, turning once, until streaked with light grill marks, 5 to 7 minutes.
Bell Pepper	Core, seed, and cut into large wedges.	Grill, turning often, until streaked with dark grill marks, 8 to 10 minutes.
Eggplant	Remove ends. Cut into ¾-inch-thick rounds or strips.	Grill, turning once, until flesh is darkly colored, 8 to 10 minutes.
Endive	Halve lengthwise through stem end.	Grill, flat side down, until streaked with dark grill marks, 5 to 7 minutes.
Portobello Mushrooms	Discard stems and wipe caps clean.	Grill, turning once, until streaked with dark grill marks and quite soft, 7 to 9 minutes.
White or Cremini Mushrooms	Trim thin slice from stems, then thread onto skewers.	Grill, turning several times, until golden brown, 6 to 7 minutes.
Cherry Tomatoes	Remove stems, then thread onto skewers.	Grill, turning often, until streaked with dark grill marks, 3 to 6 minutes.
Plum Tomatoes	Halve lengthwise and seed if desired.	Grill, turning once, until streaked with dark grill marks, about 6 minutes.
Zucchini or Yellow Summer Squash	Remove ends. Slice lengthwise into ½-inch-thick strips.	Grill, turning once, until streaked with dark grill marks, 8 to 10 minutes.

MORE TO EXPLORE

QUICK PICKLES

To make tangy, crisp, flavor-packed pickles without having to turn to special canning equipment, work with bushels of produce, or wait weeks to enjoy the fruits of your labor, look to quick pickling, which provides (nearly) instant gratification. Quick pickles are super simple to make and transform vegetables with salt and acidity—usually in the form of a vinegar brine soak—into a tangy, crunchy topping for salads, sandwiches and burgers, and grain bowls.

QUICK PICKLED RADISHES

Makes: 1 cup
Total Time: 25 minutes

With their distinctive lime aroma and clean, fresh bite, quick-pickled radishes add a layer of crunch and liveliness to countless dishes. Cutting radishes into thin slices creates delicate, elegant pickles and exposes a generous amount of surface area to absorb the flavorful brine. Some sugar and a touch of salt are all that's needed to balance the bright, aromatic acidity of the lime juice. Thin slices of shallot add a touch of sweetness and character. After draining, the radishes can be served immediately or held in the refrigerator for up to 1 hour. Avoid pickling the radishes for longer than 1 hour; they will begin to turn limp, gray, and bitter. Choose radishes that are firm and heavy for their size.

- ¼ cup lime juice (2 limes)
- 1 teaspoon sugar
- ½ teaspoon kosher salt
- 6 large radishes, trimmed and sliced thin
- 1 shallot, sliced thin

Whisk lime juice, sugar, and salt in medium bowl until sugar and salt have dissolved. Stir in radishes and shallot and let sit for 15 minutes for flavors to blend (or refrigerate for up to 1 hour). Drain vegetables before serving.

QUICK PICKLED FENNEL

Makes: one 1-pint jar
Total Time: 20 minutes, plus 3 hours cooling

You will need a 1-pint Mason jar with a tight-fitting lid for this recipe. Heating the jar with hot water and then draining it before adding the hot brine ensures that the jar won't crack from the abrupt temperature change. You can easily double this recipe.

- ¾ cup seasoned rice vinegar
- ¼ cup water
- 1 garlic clove, peeled and halved
- 1 (1-inch) strip orange zest
- ¼ teaspoon fennel seeds
- ⅛ teaspoon black peppercorns
- ⅛ teaspoon yellow mustard seeds
- 1 fennel bulb, stalks discarded, bulb halved, cored, and sliced ¼ inch thick

1. Bring vinegar, water, garlic, orange zest, fennel seeds, peppercorns, and mustard seeds to boil in medium saucepan.

2. Fill one 1-pint jar with hot water to warm. Drain jar, then pack fennel into jar. Using funnel and ladle, pour hot brine over fennel to cover. Let jar cool completely, cover with lid, and refrigerate for at least 2½ hours before serving. (Fennel can be refrigerated for up to 6 weeks; it will soften significantly after that.)

QUICK PICKLED RED ONIONS

Makes: about 1 cup
Total Time: 10 minutes, plus 1 hour cooling

Pickled onions are an absolute breeze to make—just a few minutes of hands-on preparation plus a 30-minute brine bath transform simple slices of red onion into a vibrant topping for tacos, burgers, bowls, and more. Look for a firm, dry onion with thin, shiny skin and a deep purple color.

- 1 cup red wine vinegar
- ⅓ cup sugar
- ¼ teaspoon table salt
- 1 red onion, halved and sliced thin through root end

Bring vinegar, sugar, and salt to simmer in small saucepan over medium-high heat, stirring occasionally, until sugar has dissolved. Off heat, stir in onion, cover, and let cool to room temperature, about 1 hour. (Pickled onions can be refrigerated in airtight container for up to 1 week.)

QUICK PICKLE CHIPS

Makes: about 2 cups
Total Time: 20 minutes, plus 30 minutes cooling and 3 hours chilling

For guaranteed crunch, choose the freshest, firmest pickling cucumbers available; we like Kirby cucumbers. You will need a 1-pint Mason jar with a tight-fitting lid for this recipe. Heating the jar with hot water and then draining it before adding the hot brine ensures that the jar won't crack from the abrupt temperature change. You must refrigerate the pickles for 3 hours before serving.

- ¾ cup seasoned rice vinegar
- 1 garlic clove, peeled and halved
- ¼ teaspoon ground turmeric
- ⅛ teaspoon black peppercorns
- ⅛ teaspoon yellow mustard seeds
- 8 ounces pickling cucumbers, trimmed, sliced ¼ inch thick crosswise
- 2 sprigs fresh dill

1. Bring vinegar, ¼ cup water, garlic, turmeric, peppercorns, and mustard seeds to boil in medium saucepan over medium-high heat.

2. Fill one 1-pint jar with hot tap water to warm. Drain jar, then pack with cucumbers and dill sprigs. Using funnel and ladle, pour hot brine over cucumbers to cover. Let cool to room temperature, about 30 minutes. Cover and refrigerate until chilled and flavors meld, about 3 hours. Serve. (Pickles can be refrigerated for up to 6 weeks.)

How to Quick-Pickle Anything

Recipes are great when you're aiming for a particular flavor profile, but the beauty of quick pickling is flexibility. With the following basic brine formula and method, you can turn just about any produce—in any amount—into a punchy condiment. Feel free to tweak the ratios and add seasonings as you like.

1 Prep produce
Trim and cut 1 pound of vegetables or fruit into evenly thick pieces for uniform pickling. Depending on the porosity of the produce and the length of pickling, thicker slices might retain a sturdy crunch, while thinner pieces will likely wilt.

2 Mix and boil brine
Combine 1½ cups vinegar, 1½ cups water, 3 tablespoons sugar, 2½ tablespoons kosher salt, and seasonings (i.e., citrus zest, spices, aromatics, herbs), if using, in a medium saucepan. Bring the mixture to a boil over medium-high heat. If using seasonings, cover the mixture and let it steep off heat for 10 minutes.

3 Temper jars
Rinse your jars under hot running water until heated through, 1 to 2 minutes; shake dry. Tempering the glass helps prevent it from cracking when the hot brine is added. You can use any heatproof container with a tight-fitting lid.

4 Marry brine with prepared produce
Tightly pack the produce into jars. Return the brine to a brief boil and ladle over the produce to cover (a funnel will help contain the brine but is not essential), distributing any aromatics and spices evenly among the jars.

5 Cool, cover, and wait
Let the jars cool completely, cover with their lids, and refrigerate until pickles are evenly flavorful. Pickling times will depend on the thickness and porosity of the produce pieces: Thin-sliced produce is likely ready to eat when cool; denser root vegetables such as carrots might take days. The easiest way to judge? Taste a piece.

CHAPTER 4

SALADS

COURSES

152 CLASSIC VINAIGRETTES

156 GREEN SALADS

162 VEGETABLE SALADS

168 SIMPLY TOMATOES

174 POTATO SALADS

178 SLAWS

182 SALADS WITH MEAT AND SEAFOOD

186 RESTAURANT FAVORITES

192 SAVORY FRUIT SALADS

MORE TO EXPLORE

172 CREAMY AND CREAMLESS DRESSINGS

SALAD GREENS

HEADS OF LETTUCE

Crisp Heads
Iceberg and Romaine

Profile: Crunchy, mild; romaine has slightly bitter spine

Tip: The sturdy leaves make a good base for chopped salad and can work as handheld cups for chicken salad, grain salad, or other components.

Pair with: Stronger greens, creamy dressings, avocado, bacon, steak, mushrooms

Leafy Heads
Green Leaf, Oak Leaf, Red Leaf

Profile: Earthy; tender edges, crisp spine

Tip: The leaves' uneven surfaces are great at capturing mix-ins and flaky salt; use as a bed for deli-style salads.

Pair with: Romaine, arugula, watercress, any dressing, crunchy ingredients, nuts, fruit, shrimp

Tender Heads
Bibb, Boston, Butter, Mâche

Profile: Tender, smooth, grassy

Tip: For a longer shelf life, leave the root intact until ready to use.

Pair with: Assertive or crunchy greens, fresh herbs (dill, chives, parsley leaves), citrusy dressing, creamy cheese

OTHER SALAD GREENS

Baby Greens
Baby Arugula, Baby Kale, Mesclun, Mustard Greens, Baby Spinach

Profile: Tender; mild or slightly peppery/spicy

Tip: Use baby arugula or baby kale in cooking; add during the last couple minutes to soups, stews, or pasta.

Pair with: Lemon vinaigrette, asparagus, goat cheese, fish, scallops (mesclun). Creamy or bold dressings, roasted vegetables, grains, potatoes, chicken, steak (baby arugula, baby spinach, or baby kale)

Bitter Greens
Endive, Escarole, Frisée, Radicchio

Profile: Bitter, crisp

Tip: Trim any wilted leaves, but don't bother washing endive or radicchio; it's rare for dirt to get into the tightly packed heads.

Pair with: Milder greens, bold dressings (mustard, balsamic), fruits (apples, citrus), poached/fried eggs, cheese, rich proteins (salmon, bacon)

Spicy Greens
Arugula, Mizuna, Watercress

Profile: Peppery, tender, juicy

Tips: Bunched arugula and watercress can be very sandy, so wash them in several changes of water. Watercress stems are edible; trim only the tougher lower parts.

Pair with: Milder greens, any dressing, fruits, nuts, proteins

BUYING GREENS

Prewashed bags of arugula and mesclun mix offer great convenience. Be sure to turn over the bags and inspect the greens as closely as you can, though; the sell-by date alone doesn't ensure quality, so if you see moisture in the bag or hints of blackened leaf edges, move on.

Don't buy bags of already cut lettuce that you can otherwise buy as whole heads, such as romaine, Bibb, or red leaf; leaves begin to spoil once they are cut (bagged hearts of romaine are fine). Endive and radicchio are always sold in heads.

WASHING AND DRYING GREENS

SWISH Fill salad spinner bowl with cool water, add greens, and gently swish them around. Let grit settle to bottom of bowl, then lift greens out, leaving sediment behind, and drain water. Repeat until greens no longer release any dirt.

SPIN Rinse bowl before using spinner to spin greens dry. Spin greens dry, stopping several times to dump out excess water.

TOWEL-DRY Blot greens dry with paper towels.

THE BEST WAY TO STORE GREENS

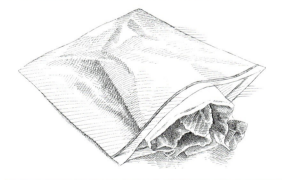

Store washed and dried leaves as well as intact heads of lettuce lightly rolled in moist paper towels in a partially open plastic produce bag or zipper-lock bag for up to one week. Never store lettuce in the refrigerator without any protection, as it will rapidly go limp.

Heads: Core crisp heads such as iceberg and romaine before storing, but leave the root ends of more tender lettuces intact.

Leaves: Store in their original container if prewashed. If not prewashed, store the washed and dried greens wrapped as above. You can also store greens directly in a salad spinner between layers of paper towels for up to two days.

DRY BEFORE YOU DRESS

Excess moisture that's left on greens will dilute your dressing. That's why we highly recommend double-drying your greens, first in a salad spinner and then with paper towels. If you don't have a salad spinner, rinse your salad greens in a bowl of water, shake them dry in a colander, and then place the greens on a clean dish towel or paper towels to wick up any remaining moisture.

HOT TIP: WILTED LETTUCE? ICE IT

Revive slightly wilted lettuce in ice water to restore its crispness. Fill a large bowl three-quarters full with ice water and soak the wilted leaves for 30 minutes.

OIL AND VINEGAR

OIL

Extra-Virgin Olive Oil
A good extra-virgin olive oil is a must when making vinaigrettes or other dressings. Avoid "pure" and "light" olive oils, both of which are lower-grade products akin to vegetable oil in flavor, and seek out the "extra-virgin" option. This is the first oil expressed and extracted from fresh olives. Extra-virgin olive oil can have fruity, grassy, buttery, and even spicy notes. We like to keep one moderately priced, good-quality extra-virgin olive oil for everyday cooking and a higher-quality extra-virgin olive oil for uncooked uses where its flavor and aroma will be noticeable—in salads and as a finishing drizzle for all kinds of dishes.

Neutral Oil
You will also need a neutral oil for salads when the flavor of extra-virgin olive oil would be out of place or overpowering. You can use all-purpose vegetable oil, but the quality can be inconsistent. To be sure that you're getting a higher-quality oil, look for one made from a single ingredient; canola oil and grapeseed oil are both good choices. You can also opt for expeller-pressed oil, which, like extra-virgin olive oil, is minimally refined and retains more flavor and nutrients. Note that it is also more expensive and heat sensitive and has a shorter shelf life.

BUYING AND STORING OILS

When buying high-end olive oil, check the harvest date printed on the label to ensure the freshest bottle possible. Don't buy olive oil in bulk if you can't use it quickly. Once you have invested in some good-quality oil, make sure that you store it properly. It doesn't belong on your counter or windowsill because strong sunlight will oxidize the chlorophyll in the oil, producing stale, harsh flavors. Keep all your oils in a dark pantry or cupboard. Use a sticker to write the purchase date on bottles because oils have a very short shelf life once opened. Unopened oil will be good for one year. Once a bottle of any oil has been opened, its shelf life reduces to three months.

Store all oils in the pantry (toasted sesame oil belongs in the fridge). For optimal flavor, replace all oils three months after opening them. To check if an oil is fresh, heat a little in a skillet. If it smells rancid once heated, throw out the bottle.

VINEGAR
Bright and acidic, vinegar is essential to making many salad dressings. Because different vinegars have distinctly different flavors and acidity, which affects tartness, we suggest stocking several. A lower-acid vinegar requires less oil to make a smooth-tasting dressing.

Sherry Vinegar (6–8% Acidity)
Spanish sherry vinegar, made from sherry, tastes like a mix of balsamic and cider vinegars. It has complex savory flavors and a sweetness that adds fruity depth to vegetable salads.

Balsamic Vinegar (6% Acidity)
The best Italian balsamic vinegars are aged for years to have complex flavor, sweetness, and color. The expensive ones are stunning simply drizzled on fresh strawberries. Moderately priced ones are best in vinaigrettes or drizzled with olive oil on fresh greens.

Red Wine Vinegar (5–7.5% Acidity)
Slightly sweet, sharp red wine vinegar is delicious in bold vinaigrettes.

White Wine Vinegar (5–7% Acidity)
Milder, more delicate white wine vinegar works for subtle dressings and in potato salad, where the color of red wine vinegar would detract from the presentation.

Cider Vinegar (5–6% Acidity)
Made from fermented apple juice, this vinegar is fruity, sweet, and slightly tart. Its round flavor and rich color evoke ripe apples, so it works well in salads tossed with apple, other fresh fruits, or even dried fruits.

Rice Vinegar (4% Acidity)
Made from fermented rice, this vinegar is light-colored and sweet, perfect for salads where mild acidity is called for.

Lemon Juice (4% Acidity)
You can also use fresh lemon or lime juice and zest instead of vinegar in your salad dressings to add bright, sweet-tart flavor to your salads.

JOURNEY: EXTRA-VIRGIN OLIVE OIL PRODUCTION

Every stage of the process of making olive oil affects the quality of the oil. Let's take a closer look.

1 START WITH OLIVES

Producers must start with good fruit—that is, ripe olives that have been harvested carefully and aren't bruised or fermented—and get it to the mill as quickly as possible before spoilage sets in. To produce extra-virgin olive oil, the olives are harvested when they are midway between semiblack and completely black. At this stage, both the volatile aroma compounds and oil (23 to 27 percent by weight) are at their highest levels. In Italy the olives must be delivered to the processing facility within 24 hours of harvesting to ensure freshness.

TYPES OF OLIVES

There are several thousand varieties of olives grown around the world, but 22 are most often used to produce olive oil. The most common olive varieties for producing extra-virgin olive oil are Arbequina and Picual from Spain, Koroneiki from Greece, and Coratina from Italy. Arbequina is noted for its ripe fruitiness, low bitterness, and pungency. Coratina is strongly green, herbaceous, bitter, and pungent. Koroneiki is strongly fruity and herbaceous, with mild bitterness and pungency. Picual is very fruity, with medium bitterness and pungency.

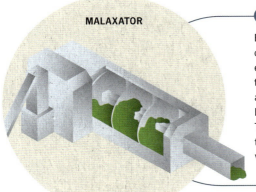

MALAXATOR

2 PRESS THEM

Extra-virgin olive oil must be pressed—and spun out by a centrifuge to separate the water from the oil—with clean equipment and without using high heat or chemicals. For this, whole olives are crushed into a paste and pumped into a machine called a malaxator where they are mixed and tumbled for 15 to 30 minutes to agglomerate the droplets of oil. Then the paste moves to a horizontal centrifuge to separate the oil, water, and solids. The crude oil is then pumped to a vertical separator to remove the last of the water.

3 DO NOT USE HEAT

While heat and chemicals extract more oil from the olives, it's at the cost of losing important aromatics and antioxidants that help keep the oil fresh-tasting.

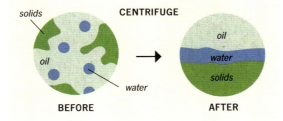

5 SENSORY TESTING

To meet sensory criteria, an oil must not just taste flawless—or have what experts call "zero defects"—but also possess good fruity flavor.

OTHER TYPES OF OILS
The lower grades of olive oils range in acidity from 1 percent to 2 percent (as opposed to 0.8 percent in extra-virgin) and exhibit a less distinctive flavor and several identifiable defects. Regular olive oils are blends of chemically refined (neutralized) high-acid oil and higher-quality or extra-virgin oils. "Light" olive oil means that the amount of extra-virgin oil in the blend is low rather than light in calories. It's light only in flavor.

4 TRANSPORT AND STORE

Producing high-quality oil is only half the challenge. Because olive oil begins to degrade as soon as it's exposed to air, heat, and light, producers must transport and store it carefully to preserve its freshness. In large operations the oil may be allowed to rest in big containers for up to several months before bottling. The oil may be bottled unfiltered, or it may be filtered to produce clear, transparent oil. Extra-virgin olive oil is produced by purely mechanical means, with no refining other than optional filtration, and therefore contains all the natural constituents. Olive oil has a short shelf life—it's best consumed within 12 months of the harvest date. Look for olive oils that are sold in dark-colored bottles. Those sold in clear glass or even plastic bottles expose the oil to more damaging light.

SALADS | 151

COURSE
CLASSIC VINAIGRETTES

JACK BISHOP

Vinaigrettes and dressings bring salad ingredients together cohesively, binding them with flavor, richness, and aroma and showing them off with gloss. They can also add brightness, acidity, and richness to other savory dishes when used as a marinade or sauce. In this course, we show you how to emulsify oil and vinegar into vinaigrettes the classic way—whisking—and with a quick, easy method—shaking. You will also learn about the ingredients that help bring oil and vinegar together into a smooth vinaigrette that does not easily separate.

JACK'S PRO TIP: *The better your oil, the better your dressing. Give your salads the respect they deserve and invest in a high-quality extra-virgin olive oil just for dressings.*

FOOLPROOF VINAIGRETTE
Makes: about ¼ cup (enough for 8 cups greens)
Total Time: 10 minutes

RECIPE OVERVIEW The smoothest-tasting, creamiest vinaigrettes depend on oil and vinegar coming together—and staying together—as an emulsion. That word refers to a cohesive combination of two liquids that don't ordinarily mix (such as oil and water or vinegar). To make an emulsion of oil and vinegar, we combine them so strenuously that the oil breaks down into such tiny droplets that they remain separated and surrounded by the vinegar droplets and the two liquids become one. This sort of emulsified vinaigrette works best for keeping your salad greens crisp and unwilted and clings more effectively to greens, guaranteeing balanced flavor in every bite. Mustard and mayo are emulsifiers that help bring and hold the oil and vinegar together and add creaminess and flavor. This master recipe works to dress nearly any type of green. Our variations offer different flavors with the same technique.

- 1 tablespoon red wine, white wine, or champagne vinegar
- 1½ teaspoons very finely minced shallot
- ½ teaspoon regular or light mayonnaise
- ½ teaspoon Dijon mustard
- ⅛ teaspoon table salt
- 3 tablespoons extra-virgin olive oil

1. Whisk vinegar, shallot, mayonnaise, mustard, and salt together in small bowl. Whisk until mixture is milky in appearance and no lumps of mayonnaise remain.

2. Whisking constantly, slowly drizzle in oil until emulsified. If pools of oil gather on surface as you whisk, stop adding oil and whisk mixture well to combine, then resume whisking in oil in slow stream. Vinaigrette should be glossy and lightly thickened, with no pools of oil on surface. Season with pepper to taste.

Variations

FOOLPROOF LEMON VINAIGRETTE

This vinaigrette is best for dressing mild greens.

Substitute lemon juice for vinegar. Omit shallot. Add ¼ teaspoon grated lemon zest and pinch sugar along with salt.

FOOLPROOF BALSAMIC-MUSTARD VINAIGRETTE

This vinaigrette is best for dressing assertive greens.

Substitute balsamic vinegar for wine vinegar, increase mustard to 2 teaspoons, and add ½ teaspoon chopped fresh thyme along with salt.

FOOLPROOF HERB VINAIGRETTE

Add 1 tablespoon minced fresh parsley or chives and ½ teaspoon minced fresh thyme, tarragon, marjoram, or oregano to vinaigrette just before using.

KEYS TO SUCCESS

- **Use a 3-to-1 ratio:** The classic oil-to-vinegar ratio for making a vinaigrette
- **Use two emulsifiers:** Mayonnaise and mustard help the vinaigrette hold for up to 90 minutes
- **Add the salt with the acid:** Helps it dissolve before oil is whisked in (salt won't dissolve in oil)
- **Remember to taste:** Your whisked vinaigrette and add more pepper as needed

---

SCIENCE LESSON

The Three *M*'s of Emulsification

In our Foolproof Vinaigrette, we use mustard and mayonnaise as emulsifiers to bind oil and vinegar together. Mustard contains a polysaccharide, and the egg yolks in mayonnaise contain lecithin; both of these agents attract oil and are compatible with water, so they hold the two disparate components together. For our Make-Ahead Vinaigrette (page 155), we add mustard; mayo; and molasses, a stabilizer, for long-term holding power. Molasses contains large compounds called melanoidins that increase the viscosity of the emulsion and make it difficult for the oil droplets to coalesce and separate from the water.

CORE TECHNIQUE

Whisking a Vinaigrette

SLOWLY ADD OIL
Whisking constantly, slowly drizzle in the oil. If pools of oil gather on the surface as you whisk, stop adding the oil, whisk the mixture well to combine, and then resume whisking in the oil in a slow stream.

WHISK SIDE TO SIDE
Use a side to side whisking motion for quicker emulsification. The vinaigrette is ready when it is glossy and lightly thickened, with no pools of oil on the surface.

SCIENCE LESSON

Emulsified or Broken

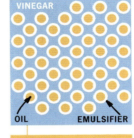

EMULSIFIED
When oil and vinegar are emulsified, tiny droplets of oil are surrounded by an added emulsifier and dispersed in vinegar.

BREAKING
With time, however, the droplets of oil begin to find each other and coalesce.

BROKEN
Eventually the oil and vinegar separate into distinct liquids, resulting in a broken vinaigrette.

MAKE-AHEAD VINAIGRETTE

Makes: about 1 cup
Total Time: 15 minutes

RECIPE OVERVIEW This vinaigrette can be stored in your fridge, so you never need to buy bottled dressing again. To make it longer-lasting, we use two emulsifiers, mustard and mayonnaise, and add molasses, which acts as a stabilizer. We also cut the olive oil, which congeals in the cold, with vegetable oil to produce a dressing that's always pourable and pairs well with nearly any green. Using two emulsifiers and a stabilizer means that there's no need to whisk this vinaigrette: Simply shaking the jar periodically after a few additions of oil is sufficient, and the jar can then be stored right in the fridge. After a few days, a very thin layer of vinegar will settle to the bottom of the jar but is easily reincorporated with a quick shake before serving.

1	tablespoon regular or light mayonnaise
1	tablespoon molasses
1	tablespoon Dijon mustard
½	teaspoon table salt
¼	cup white wine vinegar
½	cup extra-virgin olive oil, divided
¼	cup vegetable oil

1. Combine mayonnaise, molasses, mustard, and salt in 2-cup jar with tight-fitting lid. Stir with fork until mixture is milky in appearance and no lumps of mayonnaise or molasses remain. Add vinegar; seal jar; and shake until smooth, about 10 seconds.

2. Add ¼ cup olive oil; seal jar; and shake vigorously until combined, about 10 seconds. Repeat with remaining ¼ cup olive oil and vegetable oil in separate additions, shaking vigorously until combined after each addition. Vinaigrette should be glossy and lightly thickened after all oil has been added, with no pools of oil on surface. Season with salt and pepper to taste. (Vinaigrette can be refrigerated for up to 1 week; shake to recombine before using.)

Variations
MAKE-AHEAD SHERRY-SHALLOT VINAIGRETTE
Add 2 teaspoons minced shallot and 2 teaspoons minced fresh thyme to jar with mayonnaise. Substitute sherry vinegar for white wine vinegar.

MAKE-AHEAD BALSAMIC-FENNEL VINAIGRETTE
Toast the fennel seeds in a skillet and crack them in a mortar and pestle or on the counter using the bottom of a heavy skillet. Press firmly to crack them.

Add 2 teaspoons toasted and cracked fennel seeds to jar with mayonnaise. Substitute balsamic vinegar for white wine vinegar.

MAKE-AHEAD CIDER-CARAWAY VINAIGRETTE
Toast the caraway seeds in a skillet and crack them in a mortar and pestle or on the counter using the bottom of a heavy skillet. Press firmly to crack them.

Add 2 teaspoons toasted and cracked caraway seeds to jar with mayonnaise. Substitute cider vinegar for white wine vinegar.

> **More Ways to Use Make-Ahead Vinaigrette**
> - Toss with roasted or steamed vegetables
> - Stir into rice, grains, and beans
> - Drizzle on grilled or roasted poultry and fish
> - Use in a sandwich

BACON AND BROWNED BUTTER VINAIGRETTE

Makes: about 1 cup
Total Time: 25 minutes

RECIPE OVERVIEW Browned butter is butter that has been heated until its water evaporates and its milk solids undergo the Maillard reaction (see page 33), creating hundreds of new, complex-tasting flavor compounds. The nuttiness of browned butter pairs well with bacon and maple syrup. Though it is an unusual addition to a vinaigrette, we like using it in this easy, rich dressing for hearty salads.

8	tablespoons unsalted butter, divided
1	slice bacon, chopped fine
3	tablespoons sherry vinegar
3	tablespoons vegetable oil
1	shallot, minced
1	tablespoon maple syrup
2	teaspoons Dijon mustard

1. Melt 6 tablespoons butter in 10-inch skillet over medium-high heat. Cook, swirling skillet constantly, until butter is dark golden brown and has nutty aroma, 1 to 3 minutes. Remove skillet from heat and transfer browned butter to large heatproof bowl. Stir remaining 2 tablespoons butter into hot butter to melt. Wipe skillet clean with paper towel.

2. Cook bacon in now-empty skillet over medium heat until crispy, 5 to 7 minutes. Using slotted spoon, transfer bacon to paper towel–lined plate. Pour off any bacon fat into browned butter. Add vinegar, oil, shallot, maple syrup, and mustard to browned butter mixture; whisk until emulsified, about 30 seconds. Stir in bacon.

COURSE
GREEN SALADS

KEITH DRESSER

When people think of salads, greens immediately come to mind. In this course, we showcase the versatility of a simple green salad; share how to make salad with more than one kind of green; and show you how to incorporate vegetables, fruits, and other add-ins. You'll learn how to toss greens to great effect and find a template for mixing and matching ingredients to ensure that even the simplest of salads are interesting and well-made.

KEITH'S PRO TIP: *Season your salad. Even though dressings contain salt, I like to sprinkle a salad with some coarse sea salt before serving. This allows you to adjust the seasoning without adding dressing and it adds pops of salt throughout.*

Tossing a Simple Green Salad

ADD FLAVOR
Rub a clove of garlic across the inside of a wooden salad bowl.

ADD OIL
Drizzle oil over washed and dried greens, tossing gently to coat.

ADD VINEGAR
Season the greens with vinegar, salt, and pepper.

SIMPLEST SALAD
Serves: 4
Total Time: 15 minutes

RECIPE OVERVIEW The simplest of all salads requires no measuring, no whisking, and (virtually) no thought. You need only four ingredients: greens, extra-virgin olive oil, vinegar, and half a garlic clove (for rubbing the bowl). It is important to use high-quality ingredients, as there are no bells or whistles here to camouflage old lettuce, flavorless oil, or harsh vinegar. Since we do not suggest measured amounts of oil and vinegar here, this is when you can start thinking about the 3:1 oil-to-vinegar ratio typically used for dressings. Be sure to use interesting leafy greens, such as mesclun, arugula, or Bibb lettuce, rather than those with a more neutral flavor, like iceberg, and remember that you can add croutons, spiced nuts, sliced fruit, or cheese if you wish.

- ½ garlic clove, peeled
- 8 ounces (8 cups) lettuce or other greens, torn into bite-size pieces if necessary
- Extra-virgin olive oil
- Vinegar

Rub inside of salad bowl with garlic; discard garlic. Add lettuce to bowl. Slowly drizzle oil over lettuce, tossing lettuce very gently, until lettuce is lightly coated and just glistening. Sprinkle with small amounts of vinegar, salt, and pepper to taste and toss gently to coat. Serve.

> ### KEYS TO SUCCESS
> - **Dress the salad just before serving:** To prevent the salad greens from wilting
> - **Toss lightly:** By hand or with tongs to avoid bruising the leaves
> - **Season to taste:** Add acid, salt, and pepper to suite your preferences

BIBB AND ARUGULA SALAD WITH PEAR AND GOAT CHEESE

Serves: 4
Total Time: 25 minutes

RECIPE OVERVIEW You rarely go wrong when adding fruit, nuts or seeds, and cheese to salad for a combination of sweet, salty, and rich flavors. We choose pear, tangy goat cheese, and toasted pepitas. For a base, one green is nice, but two are even better (see page 148); here peppery arugula balances buttery Bibb. We use lemon juice instead of vinegar for our creamy dressing because it pairs well with the pear. Toast the pepitas in a dry skillet over medium heat until they're fragrant (about 1 minute), and then remove from the heat so that the pepitas won't scorch.

Dressing
- 1 tablespoon lemon juice
- 1½ teaspoons very finely minced shallot
- ½ teaspoon mayonnaise
- ½ teaspoon Dijon mustard
- ⅛ teaspoon table salt
- 3 tablespoons extra-virgin olive oil

Salad
- 1 head Bibb lettuce (8 ounces), torn into bite-size pieces (8 cups)
- 3 ounces (3 cups) arugula, torn into bite-size pieces
- 1 Bosc pear, halved, cored, and sliced thin
- 3 ounces goat cheese, crumbled (¾ cup), divided
- ¼ cup raw pepitas, toasted, divided

1. FOR THE DRESSING Combine lemon juice, shallot, mayonnaise, mustard, and salt in medium bowl and season with pepper to taste. Whisk until mixture is milky in appearance and no lumps of mayonnaise remain. Whisking constantly, very slowly drizzle oil into lemon juice mixture until glossy and lightly thickened, with no pools of oil visible. (If pools of oil are visible on surface as you whisk, stop addition of oil and whisk until mixture is well combined, then resume whisking in oil in slow stream.)

2. FOR THE SALAD Place lettuce, arugula, pear, half of goat cheese, and half of pepitas in large bowl. Toss to combine. Drizzle with dressing and toss until greens are evenly coated. Season with salt to taste. Sprinkle with remaining goat cheese and remaining pepitas. Serve immediately.

Mix and Match Greens

Sure, you can make a salad with one kind of lettuce or greens, but pairing two creates a visually appealing salad with varied colors, textures, and flavors. Try combining greens of different colors, such as red and green lettuce, or Boston lettuce with multicolored mesclun. Mixing baby greens left whole with torn mature greens also layers different shapes. For an interplay of textures, mix a crispy green such as romaine or frisée with delicate Bibb. And for varied but balanced flavor, bring spicy or bitter greens such as watercress or radicchio together with mild lettuces such as romaine.

BISTRO SALAD

Serves: 4
Total Time: 20 minutes

RECIPE OVERVIEW In this decadent green salad inspired by the French classic frisée aux lardons, the bitterness of the wildly curly chicory green is mellowed by a fried egg cooked in rendered bacon fat and crispy bits of thick-cut bacon. Think of the runny egg yolk as part of the dressing—it's going to mingle with the dressing and greens as soon as you dig in, adding rich flavor and substance. Romaine gives crunch and added body to the salad. Frisée is sturdy, so it holds up nicely to warm ingredients without wilting.

- 8 slices thick-cut bacon, cut into 1-inch pieces
- 4 large eggs
- ⅜ teaspoon table salt, divided
- ¼ teaspoon pepper, divided
- 1 tablespoon red wine vinegar
- 1½ teaspoons minced shallot
- ½ teaspoon mayonnaise
- ½ teaspoon Dijon mustard
- 3 tablespoons extra-virgin olive oil
- 1 head frisée (6 ounces), trimmed and cut into 1-inch pieces
- 1 romaine lettuce heart (6 ounces), trimmed and cut into 1-inch pieces

1. Cook bacon in 12-inch nonstick skillet over medium heat until crispy, 5 to 7 minutes. Using slotted spoon, transfer bacon to paper towel–lined plate.

2. Crack eggs into 2 small bowls (2 eggs per bowl) and sprinkle with ⅛ teaspoon salt and ⅛ teaspoon pepper. Heat fat left in skillet over medium-high heat until shimmering. Pour 1 bowl of eggs into 1 side of skillet and second bowl into other side. Cover and cook for 1 minute. Remove skillet from heat and let sit, covered, for 15 to 45 seconds for runny yolks (white around edge of yolk will be barely opaque) or 45 to 60 seconds for soft but set yolks.

3. Meanwhile, whisk vinegar, shallot, mayonnaise, mustard, remaining ¼ teaspoon salt, and remaining ⅛ teaspoon pepper together in bowl. Whisking constantly, slowly drizzle in oil until emulsified. Add frisée and lettuce and toss to coat. Divide salad among 4 serving bowls, sprinkle with bacon, and top each serving with 1 fried egg. Season with salt and pepper to taste. Serve.

KEYS TO SUCCESS

- **Double-dry your greens:** So that they can hold on to the vinaigrette
- **Whisk the vinaigrette in the salad bowl:** To make building your salad in layers easy
- For more information on frying eggs, see page 61.

ROMAINE AND WATERCRESS SALAD WITH ASPARAGUS AND PROSCIUTTO

Serves: 4
Total Time: 25 minutes

RECIPE OVERVIEW Great salads are all about contrasts. Here we pair two greens, earthy, crunchy romaine lettuce and spicy, tender watercress, to balance neutral and spicy flavors and crunchy and soft textures. We also add raw asparagus, using a vegetable peeler to shave thin strips that combine cohesively with the greens and also add crunch. To balance the vegetal elements, we include salty prosciutto and rich toasted pine nuts. The choice of vinegar matters, too: Aromatic sherry vinegar gives our dressing a rounded, nutty flavor to complement the peppery watercress and salty pork.

Vinaigrette
- 1 tablespoon sherry vinegar
- 1½ teaspoons very finely minced shallot
- ½ teaspoon mayonnaise
- ½ teaspoon Dijon mustard
- ⅛ teaspoon table salt
- 3 tablespoons extra-virgin olive oil

Salad
- 1 small head romaine lettuce, torn into bite-size pieces
- 3 ounces (3 cups) watercress, torn into bite-size pieces
- 8 ounces asparagus, trimmed and shaved lengthwise
- 1½ ounces thinly sliced prosciutto, cut into ½-inch pieces
- 3 tablespoons pine nuts, toasted, divided

1. **FOR THE VINAIGRETTE** Combine vinegar, shallot, mayonnaise, mustard, and salt in medium bowl and season with pepper to taste. Whisk until mixture is milky in appearance and no lumps of mayonnaise remain. Whisking constantly, very slowly drizzle oil into vinegar mixture until glossy and lightly thickened, with no pools of oil visible. (If pools of oil are visible on surface as you whisk, stop addition of oil and whisk until mixture is well combined, then resume whisking in oil in slow stream.)

2. **FOR THE SALAD** Place lettuce, watercress, asparagus, prosciutto, and half of pine nuts in large bowl. Toss to combine. Drizzle with vinaigrette and toss until greens are evenly coated. Season with salt to taste. Sprinkle with remaining pine nuts. Serve immediately.

EDAMAME SALAD WITH ARUGULA AND RADISHES

Serves: 6
Total Time: 15 minutes

RECIPE OVERVIEW Instead of snacking on edamame steamed in their shells, you can make a filling salad pairing the hearty, mild beans with spicy arugula, basil, and mint. The sweetness of the basil and mint complement the peppery arugula, and the edamame's neutral flavor and satisfying pop of texture pair well with them, too. Though fresh herbs are often used in minimal amounts for seasoning, here we treat them like salad greens and use a handful of each, ensuring both deep flavor and extra vitamins and minerals. Thinly sliced shallot gives mild onion flavor, and just a couple radishes bring crunch and color. For the vinaigrette, rice vinegar gives mild acidity that complements, not overpowers, the edamame, while honey adds sweetness and helps emulsify the dressing. The finishing touch is a sprinkling of roasted sunflower seeds for nuttiness and crunch.

- 2 tablespoons unseasoned rice vinegar
- 1 tablespoon honey
- 1 small garlic clove, minced
- ¾ teaspoon table salt
- 3 tablespoons extra-virgin olive oil
- 20 ounces frozen shelled edamame beans, thawed and patted dry
- 2 ounces (2 cups) baby arugula
- ½ cup shredded fresh basil
- ½ cup chopped fresh mint
- 2 radishes, trimmed, halved, and sliced thin
- 1 shallot, halved and sliced thin
- ¼ cup roasted sunflower seeds

1. Whisk vinegar, honey, garlic, and salt together in large bowl. Whisking constantly, slowly drizzle in oil until emulsified.

2. Add edamame, arugula, basil, mint, radishes, and shallot to bowl and toss to combine. Sprinkle with sunflower seeds and season with salt and pepper to taste. Serve.

CORE TECHNIQUE
Shaving Asparagus

USE PEELER
For crunchy asparagus ribbons that don't require cooking, trim the spears with a knife. Then use a Y-shaped peeler to shave each spear away from you. Gather the ribbons for use as desired.

HOW TO MAKE A GREAT SALAD

Base
Head lettuces provide bulk in the salad bowl, and their mild flavors make them extremely versatile. Think of them as a functional base you can accessorize with more-assertive accent greens, herbs, and vegetables.

Add Strong Accents
A generous handful of spicy, bitter, crunchy, or frilly greens will make your salad pop.

Herbal Essences
Herbs are greens, too, and they pack intense flavor. Add whole leaves of tender fresh herbs (parsley, cilantro, basil, chervil, tarragon, mint, or dill) or 1-inch pieces of fennel fronds to the salad bowl. (Save woodier herbs such as rosemary, thyme, and sage for cooking.)

Make the Dressing in the Bowl
Whisk your dressing in your serving bowl, layer greens and add-ins over it, and toss the salad just before you are ready to serve.

Season the Salad, Too
We like to season the salad itself with kosher or flake sea salt to taste after dressing it. This also creates appealing pops of salty crunch.

Leave Some Add-Ins for the Top
Reserve half of heavier nuts and cheeses to sprinkle over the dressed salad as garnishes.

HOW TO MEASURE SALAD GREENS

We like to measure greens for a salad using a very large glass measuring cup. For a side salad we usually call for 2 cups of lightly packed greens per person. To lightly pack greens, simply drop them by the handful into a measuring cup and then gently pat them down, using your fingertips rather than the palm of your hand.

TEAR, DON'T CUT

Gently tear greens into bite-size pieces with your hands. Don't use a knife to cut them, as it will cause bruising and discoloration. (Sturdy romaine and iceberg are exceptions.)

SALAD BY THE NUMBERS

3:1	2–3	3:1	¼
RATIO OF HEAD LETTUCE TO ACCENT GREENS (APPROX.)	ADD-INS	RATIO OF OIL TO VINEGAR	CUP DRESSING PER 10 CUPS GREENS

SALAD TOPPERS

Croutons, nuts, seeds, Parmesan or other cheeses, minced herbs, and citrus zest add color, aroma, crunch, and flavor to salads. Here is how to make some of these toppings.

HOMEMADE CROUTONS

Makes: 4 cups
Total Time: 50 minutes

Homemade croutons are easy to make and taste far better than those you can buy. You can make good croutons using nearly any type of bread, from stale pieces of baguette to the end slices of a sandwich loaf. The variations offer different flavors.

- 3 tablespoons extra-virgin olive oil
- 2 garlic cloves, minced
- ¼ teaspoon table salt
- 4 cups (½-inch) bread cubes

Adjust oven rack to middle position and heat oven to 350 degrees. Whisk oil, garlic, and salt together in large bowl; add bread; and toss to coat. Spread bread onto rimmed baking sheet and bake until golden, 20 to 25 minutes. Let croutons cool before serving. (Croutons can be stored in airtight container at room temperature for up to 1 week.)

Variations
PARMESAN CROUTONS
Increase oil to 6 tablespoons and stir 1 cup grated Parmesan into oil.

HERBED CROUTONS
Whisk 2 teaspoons minced fresh rosemary (or ½ teaspoon dried); 2 teaspoons minced fresh thyme, sage, or dill (or ½ teaspoon dried); and ¼ teaspoon pepper with oil.

SPICED PEPITAS OR SUNFLOWER SEEDS

Makes: ½ cup
Total Time: 20 minutes

- 2 teaspoons extra-virgin olive oil
- ½ cup raw pepitas or sunflower seeds
- ½ teaspoon paprika
- ½ teaspoon ground coriander
- ¼ teaspoon table salt

Heat oil in 12-inch skillet over medium heat until shimmering. Add pepitas, paprika, coriander, and salt. Cook, stirring constantly, until pepitas are toasted, about 2 minutes; transfer to bowl and let cool. Serve. (Pepitas can be stored in airtight container at room temperature for up to 5 days.)

MICROWAVE-FRIED SHALLOTS

Makes: ½ cup
Total Time: 20 minutes

Fried shallots deliver bursts of crunch and savory flavor, but they're easy to overcook. The microwave makes the method foolproof and hands-off.

- 3 shallots, sliced thin
- ½ cup vegetable oil for frying

1. Combine shallots and oil in medium bowl. Microwave for 5 minutes. Stir and continue to microwave for 2 minutes. Repeat stirring and microwaving in 2-minute increments until beginning to brown (4 to 6 minutes).

2. Repeat stirring and microwaving in 30-second increments until deep golden brown (30 seconds to 2 minutes). Using slotted spoon, transfer shallots to paper towel–lined plate; season with salt to taste. Let drain and crisp for about 5 minutes. Serve.

Variation
MICROWAVE-FRIED GARLIC
Substitute ½ cup sliced or minced garlic cloves for shallots. After frying, sprinkle garlic with 1 teaspoon confectioners' sugar (to offset any bitterness) before seasoning with salt.

TOASTED NUTS

Toasted nuts make a great topping for salads, adding crunch as well as some protein. See page 614 for how to toast a small batch of nuts or seeds.

COURSE
VEGETABLE SALADS

ELLE SIMONE SCOTT

Since salads can be more than just tossed greens, in this course you'll learn some of the vegetables that work well for salads and explore how to combine them. From kale and spinach to asparagus, beets, and carrots, you'll find out how to prepare vegetables to draw out the most flavor (cutting, salting and draining, marinating, or cooking), how to use them on their own, and how to pair them with greens for a satisfying salad.

ELLE'S PRO TIP: *Salad is a complete sentence! Having salad for dinner is a great way to make vegetables a priority. I like to add a protein like chicken or white beans to a vegetable salad to take it from side dish to main course.*

ASPARAGUS AND SPINACH SALAD WITH SHERRY VINEGAR AND GOAT CHEESE

Serves: 4 to 6
Total Time: 30 minutes

RECIPE OVERVIEW Salads are often associated with raw vegetables, but they can be a great vehicle for cooked vegetables, too. In this case, we choose bright, in-season asparagus. We sauté it briefly over high heat to develop deep flavor and tender texture and contrast the green color of the asparagus and spinach with strips of red pepper, which also add sweetness. A zesty sherry vinegar dressing gives the asparagus bold flavor, and the addition of creamy, delicate goat cheese makes this salad richer and more substantial.

- 6 tablespoons extra-virgin olive oil, divided
- 1 red bell pepper, stemmed, seeded, and cut into 1 by ¼-inch strips
- 1 pound asparagus, trimmed and cut on bias into 1-inch lengths
- ½ teaspoon table salt, divided
- ¼ teaspoon pepper, divided
- 1 shallot, sliced thin
- 4 teaspoons sherry vinegar
- 1 garlic clove, minced
- 6 ounces (6 cups) baby spinach
- 4 ounces goat cheese, cut into small chunks

1. Heat 2 tablespoons oil in 12-inch nonstick skillet over high heat until just smoking. Add bell pepper and cook until lightly browned, about 2 minutes. Stir in asparagus, ¼ teaspoon salt, and ⅛ teaspoon pepper and cook until asparagus is browned and almost tender, about 2 minutes. Stir in shallot and cook until softened and asparagus is crisp-tender, about 1 minute. Transfer to large plate and let cool for 5 minutes.

2. Meanwhile, whisk vinegar, garlic, remaining ¼ teaspoon salt, and remaining ⅛ teaspoon pepper together in bowl. Whisking constantly, drizzle in remaining ¼ cup oil.

3. Toss spinach with 2 tablespoons dressing in bowl, then divide among individual plates. Toss asparagus mixture with remaining dressing in now-empty bowl and arrange over spinach. Sprinkle with goat cheese and serve.

KEYS TO SUCCESS

- **Sauté asparagus briefly:** To soften and flavor it and help it retain its color
- **Toss greens and vegetables with dressing separately:** To ensure both are well-flavored
- **Cut cheese into chunks:** Instead of crumbling so it makes a bigger impact

KALE COBB SALAD

Serves: 4
Total Time: 25 minutes

RECIPE OVERVIEW With an array of components, including eggs, avocado, tomato, chicken, and smoky bacon, Cobb salad is colorful and satisfying for lunch or dinner. Romaine is the classic choice for Cobb, but we find that the subtle flavor and light texture fall flat when we pile on so many toppings. Instead we turn to sturdier kale. The trick to using kale in salads is to wilt it slightly, making it more pliable and easy to eat raw. We tenderize it in a hot-water soak. It's important to use very hot tap water (110 to 115 degrees) when soaking the kale or the leaves will stay tough. We also use heat to crisp up some bacon and sauté chicken in the rendered fat for added flavor. Our homemade Blue Cheese Dressing (page 172) is made lighter with yogurt, garlic, and lemon juice.

- 4 slices bacon, chopped fine
- 1 pound boneless, skinless chicken breasts, trimmed and cut into ½-inch pieces
- ¼ teaspoon table salt
- ¼ teaspoon pepper
- 8 ounces kale, stemmed and sliced crosswise into ½-inch-wide strips (8 cups)
- ¾ cup Blue Cheese Dressing (page 172), divided
- 8 ounces cherry tomatoes, quartered
- 1 avocado, halved, pitted, and cut into ½-inch pieces
- 2 Easy-Peel Hard-Cooked Eggs, quartered (page 65)

1. Cook bacon in 12-inch nonstick skillet over medium heat until crispy, 5 to 7 minutes. Using slotted spoon, transfer bacon to paper towel–lined plate to cool. Pat chicken dry with paper towels and sprinkle with salt and pepper. Add chicken to bacon fat in skillet and cook over medium-high heat, stirring occasionally, until cooked through, 4 to 6 minutes. Let sit off heat until ready to serve.

2. Meanwhile, place kale in bowl, cover with very hot tap water, and let sit for 10 minutes. Swish kale around to remove grit, then drain and spin dry in salad spinner. Pat kale dry with paper towels if still wet.

3. Thin dressing with water as needed, then toss kale with half of dressing in bowl to coat and season with salt and pepper to taste. Divide among individual serving bowls, then top with chicken, tomatoes, avocado, and egg. Drizzle with remaining dressing and sprinkle with bacon. Serve.

KEYS TO SUCCESS

- **Wilt the kale:** To make sure that it is soft and easily digestible
- **Thin out your dressing:** In case it's too thick; makes it easier to toss with the kale
- **Taste the dressing:** After thinning to make sure that it still has enough salt; reseason if needed

BEET SALAD WITH BLUE CHEESE AND ENDIVE

Serves: 6
Total Time: 50 minutes

RECIPE OVERVIEW Vibrant beets make a sweet, substantial base for a vegetable salad that's especially good when paired with salty and bitter components—here, endive and tangy blue cheese. Although beets are delicious, they are dense and take a long time to cook. For ease and speed, we microwave beets in a covered bowl with a small amount of water; the microwave causes the water molecules inside the beets to boil rapidly and intensely, so they cook through in about 30 minutes. Peeling them before cooking eliminates the time spent waiting for them to cool before peeling. Instead of just tossing the salad components together, which causes the beets' color to bleed, we use the cheese as an anchor for the other ingredients. We thin out the blue cheese with sour cream, lemon juice, and water; spread it on a platter; and top it with lightly dressed beets and endive and toasted hazelnuts for crunch. You can substitute 5 ounces of baby arugula for the endive, if desired. For the best presentation, use red beets here, not golden or Chioggia beets.

- 2 pounds beets, trimmed, peeled, and cut into ¾-inch pieces
- ½ teaspoon plus 2 pinches table salt, divided
- 4 ounces blue cheese, crumbled (1 cup)
- ¾ cup sour cream
- 3 tablespoons minced fresh chives, divided
- 5 teaspoons lemon juice, divided, plus extra for seasoning
- ¼ teaspoon pepper
- 2 heads Belgian endive (8 ounces), bases trimmed, sliced crosswise into ½-inch-wide pieces
- ¼ cup hazelnuts, toasted, skinned, and chopped, divided
- 1 tablespoon extra-virgin olive oil, divided

1. In largest bowl your microwave will accommodate, stir together beets, ⅓ cup water, and ½ teaspoon salt. Cover with plate and microwave until beets can be easily pierced with paring knife, 25 to 30 minutes, stirring halfway through microwaving. Drain beets in colander and let cool.

2. In medium bowl, use rubber spatula to mash together blue cheese, sour cream, 2 tablespoons chives, 2 teaspoons lemon juice, and pepper. Slowly stir in up to 5 tablespoons water until mixture has consistency of regular yogurt. Season with salt, pepper, and extra lemon juice to taste. Spread blue cheese mixture over serving platter.

3. In large bowl, combine endive, 2 tablespoons hazelnuts, 2 teaspoons oil, 1 teaspoon lemon juice, and pinch salt and toss to coat. Arrange endive mixture on top of blue cheese mixture, leaving 1-inch border of blue cheese mixture. Add beets to now-empty bowl and toss with remaining 2 teaspoons lemon juice, remaining 1 teaspoon oil, and remaining pinch salt. Place beet mixture on top of endive mixture. Sprinkle salad with remaining 2 tablespoons hazelnuts and remaining 1 tablespoon chives and serve.

KEYS TO SUCCESS

- **Layer, don't toss, the beets:** Keeps their color from bleeding into the salad
- **Add water to the dressing slowly:** To ensure the proper consistency; the moisture content of blue cheese varies
- **Taste before seasoning:** To avoid a salty dressing; the salt content of blue cheese varies

CORE TECHNIQUE Prepping Beets

PEELING RAW BEETS
Use a vegetable peeler to peel the raw beets. You can wear gloves when peeling and dicing the beets to prevent your hands from becoming stained.

MEDITERRANEAN CHOPPED SALAD

Serves: 4
Total Time: 30 minutes

RECIPE OVERVIEW The best chopped salad is a lively, thoughtfully chosen composition of lettuce, vegetables, and sometimes fruit, cut into bite-size pieces, allowing you to taste some of everything in each bite. We scoop the seeds out of our cucumber, and salt it and the tomatoes to pull out and drain away excess water that would dilute our dressing. While we often use a 3:1 ratio of oil to vinegar for our dressings, here an assertive blend of equal parts oil and vinegar delivers a bright acidic kick. Letting some of our ingredients marinate in the dressing for 5 minutes blends flavors and mellows the raw onion. Then we toss in the lettuce and feta for a fresh and assertive chopped salad.

- 1 cucumber, peeled, halved lengthwise, seeded, and cut into ½-inch pieces
- 10 ounces grape tomatoes, quartered
- 1 teaspoon table salt
- 1 romaine lettuce heart (6 ounces)
- 3 tablespoons extra-virgin olive oil
- 3 tablespoons red wine vinegar
- 1 garlic clove, minced
- 1 (15-ounce) can chickpeas, rinsed
- ½ cup pitted kalamata olives, chopped
- ½ small red onion, chopped fine
- ½ cup chopped fresh parsley
- 4 ounces feta cheese, crumbled (1 cup)

1. Combine cucumber, tomatoes, and salt in colander set in sink and let drain for 15 minutes.

2. Cut lettuce in half lengthwise, then cut each half lengthwise to make quarters. Finally, cut each quarter crosswise into ½-inch pieces.

3. Whisk oil, vinegar, and garlic together in large bowl. Add chickpeas, olives, onion, parsley, and cucumber-tomato mixture. Toss, then let stand for 5 minutes at room temperature to meld flavors. Add lettuce and feta and toss to combine. Season with salt and pepper to taste, and serve.

KEYS TO SUCCESS

- For more on cutting orange segments, see page 47.
- **Use a box grater**: To create larger and more-appealing carrot shreds than a food processor
- **Set the strainer over a bowl**: To capture the drained-off orange juice for use in the dressing
- **Marinate, and then drain**: Seasons the salad and avoids pools of watery dressing

MOROCCAN-STYLE CARROT SALAD

Serves: 4 to 6
Total Time: 35 minutes

RECIPE OVERVIEW Salads do not have to use greens as a base. You can use other vegetables instead or even pair those vegetables with greens. For this salad, we choose shredded carrots and flavor them with olive oil, citrus, and warm spices. To complement the earthy carrots, we add juicy orange segments, reserving some of the orange juice to add to the salad dressing. We balance the sweet orange juice with a squeeze of lemon juice and small amounts of cumin, cayenne, and cinnamon. A touch of honey provides a pleasing floral note. For color and freshness, we stir in some minced cilantro before serving. Use the large holes of a box grater to shred the carrots.

- 2 oranges
- 1 tablespoon lemon juice
- 1 teaspoon honey
- ¾ teaspoon ground cumin
- ½ teaspoon table salt
- ⅛ teaspoon cayenne pepper
- ⅛ teaspoon ground cinnamon
- 1 pound carrots, peeled and shredded
- 3 tablespoons minced fresh cilantro
- 3 tablespoons extra-virgin olive oil

1. Cut away peel and pith from oranges. Holding fruit over bowl, use paring knife to slice between membranes to release segments. Cut segments in half crosswise and let drain in fine-mesh strainer set over large bowl, reserving juice.

2. Whisk lemon juice, honey, cumin, salt, cayenne, and cinnamon into reserved orange juice. Add drained oranges and carrots and toss gently to coat. Let sit until liquid starts to pool in bottom of bowl, 3 to 5 minutes.

3. Drain salad in fine-mesh strainer and return to bowl. Stir in cilantro and oil and season with salt and pepper to taste. Serve.

GREEN BEAN SALAD WITH CILANTRO SAUCE

Serves: 6 to 8
Total Time: 35 minutes

RECIPE OVERVIEW Green beans are often steamed or sautéed until they're soft, but they're also delicious when left barely cooked and crunchy and used in a simple salad. This one is especially bright, thanks to a pesto-like cilantro dressing. The trick is to not overcook the beans so that you maintain their vibrant color. We blanch the beans in salted water and quickly shock them in ice water to halt the cooking and set their color. Don't worry about drying the beans before tossing them with the sauce; any water that clings to the beans will help thin out the dressing.

- ¼ cup walnuts
- 2 garlic cloves, unpeeled
- 2½ cups fresh cilantro leaves and stems, tough stem ends trimmed (about 2 bunches)
- ½ cup extra-virgin olive oil
- 4 teaspoons lemon juice
- 1 scallion, sliced thin
- ½ teaspoon table salt, plus salt for cooking green beans
- ⅛ teaspoon pepper
- 2 pounds green beans, trimmed

1. Cook walnuts and garlic in 8-inch skillet over medium heat, stirring often, until toasted and fragrant, 5 to 7 minutes; transfer to bowl. Let garlic cool slightly, then peel and roughly chop.

2. Process walnuts, garlic, cilantro, oil, lemon juice, scallion, salt, and pepper in food processor until smooth, about 1 minute, scraping down sides of bowl as needed; transfer to large bowl.

3. Bring 2 quarts water to boil in large pot over high heat. Meanwhile, fill large bowl halfway with ice and water. Add ¼ cup salt and green beans to boiling water and cook until crisp-tender, 3 to 5 minutes. Drain green beans; transfer to ice bath; and let sit until chilled, about 2 minutes. Transfer green beans to bowl with cilantro sauce and toss gently until coated. Season with salt and pepper to taste. Serve. (Salad can be refrigerated for up to 4 hours.)

KEYS TO SUCCESS

- For more on blanching and shocking green beans, see page 95.
- **Save the stems:** They're full of flavor and tender enough to eat

Prepping Vegetables, Cheese, Fruit, and Herbs for Salads

Cut vegetables, cheese, fruit, and herbs in a way that maximizes their flavor and appearance. Different cutting methods can give you more surface area for ingredients to be coated with dressing.

CUT ON BIAS
Cut long vegetables, scallions, and chives on the bias to increase their surface area and make them larger and more pleasing to the eye in a salad where small pieces would not be clearly visible.

SHAVE INSTEAD OF GRATE
Try shaving shards of hard cheese with a vegetable peeler for a restaurant-style garnish.

KEEP FLAVORS INTACT
Coarsely chop fruit such as peaches or nectarines and cut apples or pears into slices to keep the juiciness or crispness intact.

CHOP OR TEAR
Both chopping and tearing herbs help release their natural oils and accentuate their flavors. Tear basil so that you don't bruise the leaves. Chop other herbs so that the pieces disperse throughout the salad; wait until the last minute so the leaves don't turn black.

COURSE
SIMPLY TOMATOES

MORGAN BOLLING

Tomatoes add welcome sweetness, acidity, and color to salads and in this course you learn how to make tomatoes the centerpiece of the dish. You also learn how to core them, salt and drain them to remove excess moisture and use the drained juice in salad dressings, and how to macerate them to deepen their flavor. You'll also discover the variety of tomatoes you can pick from and which ingredients pair well with ripe tomatoes, such as good-quality olive oil, fresh basil, pine nuts, onions, and even peaches.

MORGAN'S PRO TIP: *Using a mix of different colored and sized tomatoes is an easy way to take a simple salad up a notch.*

SIMPLE TOMATO SALAD
Serves: 4
Total Time: 15 minutes

RECIPE OVERVIEW This is the salad to make at the peak of tomato season. Use the ripest tomatoes you can find, and feel free to experiment with heirloom or other varieties. Because tomatoes are already fairly acidic, we find that a dressing made with the typical 3:1 ratio of oil to acid is too sharp here. We use more oil and less acid, adjusting the amount of lemon juice to perfectly balance the salad. Great tomatoes don't need much else, but a minced shallot adds a bit of sweetness while toasted pine nuts give a buttery nuttiness and some textural diversity. Serve this salad with crusty bread to sop up the juices.

- 1½ pounds mixed ripe tomatoes
- 3 tablespoons extra-virgin olive oil
- 1 tablespoon minced shallot
- 1 teaspoon lemon juice
- ½ teaspoon table salt
- ¼ teaspoon pepper
- 2 tablespoons pine nuts, toasted
- 1 tablespoon torn fresh basil

Slice tomatoes ¼ inch thick using sharp knife or serrated knife. Arrange tomatoes on large, shallow platter. Whisk oil, shallot, lemon juice, salt, and pepper together in bowl. Spoon dressing over tomatoes. Sprinkle with pine nuts and basil. Serve immediately.

KEYS TO SUCCESS

- **Refrigerated tomatoes:** Should come to room temperature before being prepped for a salad
- **Tear (don't cut) the basil:** To prevent the cut edges from becoming bruised
- For more on toasting pine nuts, see page 614.

CORE TECHNIQUE: Coring Tomatoes

PLACE TOMATO ON ITS SIDE
Rest the tomato sideways on the cutting board and insert the tip of a sharp paring knife at an angle along the outside of the core, 1 inch into the fruit.

USE SAWING MOTION
Using a slight sawing motion, cut into the fruit around the outside of the core, rotating the tomato toward you till the core pops out.

FOR PLUM TOMATOES
Simply cut the tomato in half and cut out the core by cutting around it on either side.

TOMATO AND PEACH SALAD

Serves: 4 to 6
Total Time: 20 minutes, plus 30 minutes salting

RECIPE OVERVIEW Tomatoes and peaches share an acidic juiciness (and overlapping growing seasons) and complement each other in a savory-sweet summer salad. Here we go a step further than in our previous salad and salt the tomatoes to remove excess liquid that would have watered down the salad, concentrating their flavor. Their acidity balances the natural sweetness of the peaches, as does cider vinegar, lemon juice, and lemon zest in the dressing. Thinly sliced shallot keeps the salad on the savory side, and torn mint leaves add a refreshing note. For the best results, use the ripest in-season peaches and tomatoes you can find.

- 1 pound ripe tomatoes, cored
- 1 teaspoon table salt, divided
- 3 tablespoons extra-virgin olive oil, plus extra for drizzling
- 2 tablespoons cider vinegar
- ½ teaspoon grated lemon zest plus 1 tablespoon juice
- ½ teaspoon pepper
- 1 pound ripe peaches, halved, pitted, cut into ½-inch-thick wedges, and wedges halved crosswise
- 1 shallot, sliced into thin rings
- ⅓ cup fresh mint leaves, torn

1. Halve tomatoes through core, cut into ½-inch wedges, then cut wedges in half crosswise. Combine tomatoes and ½ teaspoon salt in bowl and toss to coat; transfer to colander and let drain in sink for 30 minutes.

2. Whisk oil, vinegar, lemon zest and juice, pepper, and remaining ½ teaspoon salt together in large bowl. Add peaches, shallot, and tomatoes to dressing and toss gently to coat. Season with salt and pepper to taste. Transfer to serving platter and sprinkle with mint. Drizzle with extra oil. Serve.

TOMATO AND VIDALIA ONION SALAD

Serves: 4 to 6
Total Time: 15 minutes, plus 1 hour resting

RECIPE OVERVIEW Sometimes we add sliced onion to our salads featuring summer tomatoes; the onion's pungency accents the tomatoes' sweetness and tartness. A sweet Vidalia onion also balances the tart cider vinegar in the vinaigrette. Letting the dressed salad rest for an hour allows the flavors to meld and draws liquid out of the tomatoes. Instead of diluting the vinaigrette, the liquid adds sweetness. If you cannot find Vidalia or other sweet onions, use a white or yellow onion; place the sliced onion in a colander and rinse it under cold running water for about 20 seconds to reduce its pungency. Pat the slices dry with paper towels and combine them with the tomatoes. Use the ripest, most colorful tomatoes you can find for this salad.

- ¼ cup extra-virgin olive oil
- 3 tablespoons cider vinegar
- 1 teaspoon table salt
- 1 garlic clove, minced
- ¼ teaspoon pepper
- 2 pounds ripe tomatoes, cored
- 1 small Vidalia onion, quartered through root end and sliced thin crosswise

1. Whisk oil, vinegar, salt, garlic, and pepper together in large bowl. Halve tomatoes through core, cut into 1-inch wedges, then cut wedges in half crosswise.

2. Add tomatoes and onion to vinaigrette and fold gently with rubber spatula to combine. Let salad sit for 1 hour at room temperature, stirring halfway through. Serve. (Salad can be refrigerated for up to 2 days.)

CHERRY TOMATO SALAD WITH MANGO AND LIME-CURRY DRESSING

Serves: 4
Total Time: 30 minutes, plus 30 minutes salting

RECIPE OVERVIEW Unlike beefsteak tomatoes, cherry tomatoes are of relatively high quality year-round. They make a lovely salad but can exude too much juice. To remove some liquid without draining away flavor, we salt them and use a salad spinner to separate the liquid from the flesh. Instead of wasting the juice, we cook it down to a flavorful concentrate with shallot, lime juice, and curry powder and reunite it with the tomatoes as a dressing. If you don't have a salad spinner, wrap the bowl tightly with plastic wrap after the salted tomatoes have sat for 30 minutes and gently shake to remove excess liquid. Strain the liquid and proceed with the recipe. If you have less than ½ cup of liquid after spinning, proceed with the recipe using the entire amount of liquid you do have and reduce it to 3 tablespoons as directed (the cooking time will be shorter).

1½	pounds cherry or grape tomatoes, quartered
½	teaspoon sugar
¼	teaspoon table salt
1	mango, peeled, pitted, and cut into ½-inch pieces
½	cup slivered almonds or chopped shelled pistachios, toasted
3	tablespoons chopped fresh cilantro or mint
1	shallot, minced
4	teaspoons lime juice
¼	teaspoon curry powder
2	tablespoons extra-virgin olive oil

1. Toss tomatoes with sugar and salt in bowl and let sit for 30 minutes. Transfer tomatoes to salad spinner and spin until seeds and excess liquid have been removed, 45 to 60 seconds, stopping to redistribute tomatoes several times during spinning; reserve liquid left in spinner. Add tomatoes, mango, almonds, and cilantro to large bowl; set aside.

2. Strain ½ cup tomato liquid through fine-mesh strainer into liquid measuring cup; discard remaining liquid. Bring tomato liquid, shallot, lime juice, and curry powder to simmer in small saucepan over medium heat and cook until reduced to 3 tablespoons, 6 to 8 minutes. Transfer to small bowl and let cool completely, about 5 minutes. Whisking constantly, slowly drizzle in oil. Drizzle dressing over salad and toss gently to coat. Season with salt and pepper to taste. Serve.

KEYS TO SUCCESS

- **Buy vine-ripened cherry tomatoes:** If you can find them; they'll have more flavor
- **Add a little sugar:** Like salt, sugar helps draw out moisture and adds flavor
- See page 48 for how to cut up a mango.

CORE TECHNIQUE
Salting and Draining Tomatoes

REGULAR TOMATOES
Chop them or cut them into wedges, toss them with salt, and let them drain in a colander or salad spinner for 30 minutes. If using a colander, place it in a bowl if you want to reserve the liquid.

CHERRY OR GRAPE TOMATOES
Let the salted tomatoes drain in a salad spinner, and then spin to remove (and reserve) the liquid.

RESOURCES FOR TOMATOES

ANATOMY OF A FLAVORFUL TOMATO

The best-tasting tomatoes tend to have thin walls, which leave more room for the most flavorful part of the tomato: the jelly that surrounds the seeds, which is three times richer in savory glutamates than the flesh.

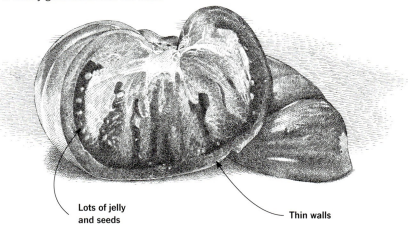

Lots of jelly and seeds

Thin walls

HOW TO PICK A TOMATO

Buying tomatoes at the height of summer is the first step toward getting juicy, flavorful fruit. Here are a few other shopping guidelines.

GO FOR LOCAL

The best way to ensure that you get a flavorful tomato is to buy a locally grown one. Why? First, the shorter the distance the tomato has to travel, the riper it can be when it's picked. Second, commercial high-yield production can strain the tomato plant, resulting in tomatoes without enough sugars and other flavor compounds to make them tasty. Third, to withstand the rigors of machine harvesting and long-distance transport, commercial varieties are bred to be sturdier, with thicker walls and less of the jelly and seeds that give a tomato most of its flavor.

LOOKS AREN'T EVERYTHING

Oddly shaped tomatoes are fine (only commercial tomatoes have been bred to be perfectly symmetrical). Even cracked skin, which you see often on heirloom varieties, is OK. Just avoid tomatoes that are bruised, overly soft, or leaking juice. Choose tomatoes that smell fruity and feel heavy for their size.

GO AHEAD AND REFRIGERATE RIPE TOMATOES

Standard wisdom dictates that ripe tomatoes shouldn't be refrigerated because cold kills their flavor-producing enzymes and ruins their texture by causing cells to rupture. But recently, numerous cooking blogs have challenged this thinking, so we decided to conduct our own tests. We found that the flavor of whole tomatoes was unaffected by refrigeration. Plus, refrigerating them prolonged their shelf life by five days. Cut tomatoes didn't last more than a day at room temperature but held fine for up to two days in the refrigerator. So, to prolong their shelf life, store both cut and whole ripe tomatoes in the refrigerator. To keep them from picking up off-flavors, store the cut tomatoes in an airtight container, which works better than plastic wrap to keep out odors.

A FEW TOMATO TYPES

VINE-RIPENED

"Vine-ripened" tomatoes are left on the plant until at least 10 percent of their skin has turned red. They are sweeter and juicier than regular supermarket tomatoes.

HEIRLOOM

Any variety that is not associated with large-scale commercial production may be labeled "heirloom." Because heirloom varieties generally can't withstand the rigors of long-distance shipping, most are locally grown and can be readily found at farmers' markets. Grown for decades from naturally pollinated plants and seeds that haven't been hybridized (unlike commercial varieties), heirlooms are some of the best local tomatoes you'll find.

ROMA

The firm texture of these plum tomatoes makes them great for cooked sauce. But when eaten fresh, most supermarket Roma tomatoes underdeliver on flavor.

CAMPARI

Often sold with a portion of the vine attached, these deep-red, relatively compact tomatoes are prized for their sweet, juicy flesh.

KUMATO

These green-brown beauties have more fructose than most conventional tomatoes, so they taste sweeter and have a hefty, meaty texture.

WORTHY TOMATO TOOL

A knife works well to core a tomato, but so does a corer, and it cuts prep time in half—handy when you're working with large quantities of tomatoes for stuffing, canning, or sauce.

SALADS | 171

MORE TO EXPLORE

CREAMY AND CREAMLESS DRESSINGS

A creamy dressing offers a lusciousness that tart vinegar- or citrus juice–based dressings do not. And it needn't include dairy. Here are several creamy dressings along with plant-based options that draw creaminess from ingredients such as avocado and roasted garlic.

BLUE CHEESE DRESSING

Makes: ¾ cup
Total Time: 10 minutes

Pair this dressing with sturdy greens or serve it with buffalo wings. Use a mild blue cheese such as Gorgonzola. If you don't have buttermilk, substitute milk and increase the vinegar to 2½ teaspoons. You will need about 2 tablespoons of dressing per 2 cups of greens.

- 2½ ounces mild blue cheese, crumbled (⅔ cup)
- 3 tablespoons buttermilk
- 3 tablespoons sour cream
- 2 tablespoons mayonnaise
- 2 teaspoons white wine vinegar
- ¼ teaspoon sugar
- ⅛ teaspoon garlic powder

Mash blue cheese and buttermilk in bowl with fork until mixture resembles cottage cheese with small curds. Stir in sour cream, mayonnaise, vinegar, sugar, and garlic powder until combined. Season with salt and pepper to taste. (Dressing can be refrigerated for up to 1 week; whisk to recombine before using.)

RANCH DRESSING

Makes: 1½ cups
Total Time: 10 minutes

Bright and bold, ranch dressing is an American classic, used both as a salad dressing and as a dip for chips, vegetables, and fried chicken. The defining flavors of ranch are dill, garlic, onion, and parsley in a base of tangy mayonnaise, sour cream, buttermilk, or yogurt. The dressing should be rich but not heavy, flavorful but not cloying. We developed a quick and easy homemade version without preservatives that just bursts with flavor and creaminess. Once you learn how easy it is to replicate the flavors you love, you'll be making it all the time.

- ⅔ cup plain yogurt
- ½ cup buttermilk
- ¼ cup sour cream
- 1 tablespoon finely chopped shallot or red onion
- 1 tablespoon minced fresh parsley
- 1 tablespoon minced fresh dill
- 1 garlic clove, minced
- 1 teaspoon lemon juice
- ½ teaspoon table salt
- ¼ teaspoon coarsely ground pepper
  Pinch sugar

Whisk all ingredients together in bowl. Season with salt and pepper to taste. (Dressing can be refrigerated for up to 4 days; whisk to recombine before using.)

Variation
PEPPERCORN RANCH DRESSING

Increase pepper to 2 teaspoons.

VEGAN RANCH DRESSING

Makes: about ½ cup
Total Time: 10 minutes

If you don't use dairy, this supereasy vegan recipe is for you. Plant-based mayonnaise and yogurt give creaminess, white wine vinegar adds tartness, and chives give us that classic onion flavor.

- ½ cup plant-based mayonnaise
- 2 tablespoons plain plant-based yogurt
- 1½ teaspoons minced fresh chives
- 1½ teaspoons minced fresh dill
- 1 teaspoon white wine vinegar
- ¼ teaspoon garlic powder
- ⅛ teaspoon table salt
- ⅛ teaspoon pepper

Whisk all ingredients in bowl until smooth. (Dressing can be refrigerated for up to 4 days.)

GREEN GODDESS DRESSING

Makes: about 1¼ cups
Total Time: 25 minutes, plus 1 hour chilling

This classic herbaceous, creamy dressing is said to have been created in California by chef Philip Roemer. The dressing's green tint comes from a variety of fresh herbs such as chervil and tarragon and its savory quality from an anchovy. Instead of chervil, use readily available parsley and chives and dried tarragon since it is not always available fresh. To refresh the dried tarragon, soak it briefly in lemon juice and water before using the liquids to process the ingredients till smooth in the blender. This dressing is great to pour on crisp romaine or toss with potatoes or cubed cooked chicken for a vibrant salad.

- 1 tablespoon lemon juice
- 1 tablespoon water
- 2 teaspoons dried tarragon
- ¾ cup mayonnaise
- ¼ cup sour cream
- ¼ cup minced fresh parsley
- 1 garlic clove, minced
- 1 anchovy fillet, rinsed
- ¼ cup minced fresh chives

Combine lemon juice, water, and tarragon in small bowl and let sit for 15 minutes. Process tarragon mixture, mayonnaise, sour cream, parsley, garlic, and anchovy in blender until smooth, scraping down sides of blender jar as needed; transfer dressing to clean bowl. Stir in chives and season with salt and pepper to taste. Refrigerate until flavors meld, about 1 hour. (Dressing can be refrigerated for up to 4 days; whisk to recombine before using.)

CREAMY AVOCADO DRESSING

Makes: about 1 cup
Total Time: 10 minutes

An avocado provides the creaminess for this dressing that's full of fresh, California-inspired flavor. Pair it with sturdy greens or drizzle it over tacos. You will need about 2 tablespoons of dressing per 2 cups of greens.

- 1 avocado, halved, pitted, and cut into ½-inch pieces
- 2 tablespoons extra-virgin olive oil
- 1 teaspoon grated lemon zest plus 3 tablespoons juice
- 1 garlic clove, minced
- ¾ teaspoon table salt
- ¼ teaspoon pepper

Process all ingredients in food processor until smooth, about 30 seconds, scraping down sides of bowl as needed. Season with salt and pepper to taste. Use immediately.

CREAMY ROASTED GARLIC DRESSING

Makes: about 1 cup
Total Time: 1¾ hours

This dressing relies on three heads of roasted garlic for creamy texture and sweet-savory flavor. Pair it with sturdy greens or use it as a sauce for roast chicken or potatoes. You will need about 2 tablespoons of dressing per 2 cups of greens.

- 3 large garlic heads (3 ounces each), outer papery skins removed and top third of heads cut off and discarded
- ¼ cup white wine vinegar
- 3 tablespoons water
- 2 teaspoons honey
- 1 teaspoon Dijon mustard
- 1 teaspoon minced fresh thyme
- ¼ teaspoon table salt
- ¼ teaspoon pepper
- ⅓ cup extra-virgin olive oil

1. Adjust oven rack to middle position and heat oven to 350 degrees. Wrap each garlic head in aluminum foil and roast until golden brown and very tender, 1 to 1¼ hours. Remove garlic from oven and carefully open foil packets. When garlic is cool enough to handle, squeeze cloves from skins (you should have about 6 tablespoons); discard skins.

2. Process garlic, vinegar, water, honey, mustard, thyme, salt, and pepper in blender until smooth, about 45 seconds, scraping down sides of blender jar as needed. With blender running, slowly add oil until incorporated, about 1 minute. Season with salt and pepper to taste. (Dressing can be refrigerated for up to 1 week; whisk to recombine before using.)

SALADS | 173

COURSE
POTATO SALADS

CHRISTIE MORRISON

Everyone loves potatoes. There are so many ways to serve it, but potato salad is evocative of summer picnics and cookouts. In this course, make salad with a variety of potatoes—Yukon Gold, red, even sweet—and learn which potatoes keep their shape and which give you the most flavor. You'll also acquire tips for how to avoid overcooking potatoes, discover which ingredients enhance them (beyond bacon and eggs, use fresh herbs, vinegar, and celery seeds), and learn how to make delicious potato salads with and without mayonnaise.

CHRISTIE'S PRO TIP: *It may be best to dress your potato salad while the potatoes are warm, but don't forget to check the seasoning again after the salad has chilled. Chilling will dull the salad's flavor, so you may need to add more salt and pepper before serving.*

CLASSIC POTATO SALAD

Serves: 4 to 6
Total Time: 45 minutes, plus 45 minutes chilling

RECIPE OVERVIEW For our rich, flavorful version of an all-American potato salad, we use Yukon Gold potatoes because they are not as starchy as russets but soften when boiled and don't fall apart. Since potatoes absorb moisture right after they cook, adding mayonnaise too early can lead to a dry, dull salad. We wait to add the mayonnaise, but in the meantime we drizzle our just-cooked potatoes with a tangy, briny mixture of pickle juice and mustard. After the potatoes have cooled, we add our creamy dressing, onion, celery, and pickles. Make sure not to overcook the potatoes: Keep the water at a simmer. This recipe can be easily doubled; use a Dutch oven to cook the potatoes in step 1.

- 2 pounds Yukon Gold potatoes, unpeeled, cut into ¾-inch pieces
- ½ teaspoon table salt, plus salt for cooking potatoes
- ¼ cup finely chopped dill pickles, plus 3 tablespoons brine, divided
- 1 tablespoon yellow mustard
- ¾ cup mayonnaise
- ½ cup finely chopped red onion
- 1 celery rib, minced
- 2 tablespoons distilled white vinegar, plus extra for seasoning

- ½ teaspoon celery seeds
- ¼ teaspoon pepper
- 2 Easy-Peel Hard-Cooked Eggs (page 65), chopped (optional)

1. Place potatoes and 1 teaspoon salt in large saucepan and cover with cold water by 1 inch. Bring to simmer over medium-high heat and cook until potatoes are tender, 10 to 15 minutes.

2. Drain potatoes thoroughly in colander, then spread out on rimmed baking sheet. Mix 2 tablespoons pickle brine and mustard together in bowl, then drizzle over potatoes, tossing gently until evenly coated. Refrigerate potato mixture until cooled slightly, about 15 minutes.

3. Combine mayonnaise, onion, celery, vinegar, celery seeds, pepper, salt, pickles, and remaining 1 tablespoon pickle brine in large bowl. Add potato mixture and toss to combine. Cover and refrigerate until well chilled, about 30 minutes. (Salad can be refrigerated for up to 2 days.) Gently fold in eggs, if using. Season with extra vinegar, salt, and pepper to taste before serving.

> **KEYS TO SUCCESS**
> - **Use a knife to tell doneness:** A paring knife should slip easily into the potatoes and meet no resistance.
> - **Sprinkle the hot potatoes with brine:** To absorb flavor immediately after cooking
> - **Cook your eggs first:** So that they are ready when you want to add them to your salad

FRENCH POTATO SALAD WITH DIJON AND FINES HERBES

Serves: 4 to 6
Total Time: 45 minutes

RECIPE OVERVIEW Fresh green herbs and a vinaigrette are the hallmarks of a French potato salad, making the dish pleasing not only to the eye but also to the palate. Small red potatoes are the traditional choice, and they should be tender but not mushy, with the flavor of the vinaigrette fully permeating the mild potatoes. To eliminate torn skins and broken slices, a common side effect of boiling skin-on red potatoes, we slice the spuds before boiling. To evenly infuse the potatoes with the garlicky mustard vinaigrette, we spread the warm potatoes on a baking sheet and pour the vinaigrette over the top. Gently folding in the minced fresh herbs just before serving helps keep the potatoes intact. If fresh chervil isn't available, substitute an additional 1½ teaspoons of minced parsley and an additional ½ teaspoon of tarragon. Use small red potatoes measuring 1 to 2 inches in diameter.

- 2 pounds small red potatoes, unpeeled, sliced ¼ inch thick
- Table salt for cooking potatoes
- 1 garlic clove, peeled and threaded on skewer
- ¼ cup extra-virgin olive oil
- 1½ tablespoons champagne vinegar or white wine vinegar
- 2 teaspoons Dijon mustard
- ½ teaspoon pepper
- 1 small shallot, minced
- 1 tablespoon minced fresh chervil
- 1 tablespoon minced fresh parsley
- 1 tablespoon minced fresh chives
- 1 teaspoon minced fresh tarragon

1. Place potatoes and 2 tablespoons salt in large saucepan and add water to cover by 1 inch. Bring to boil over high heat; reduce heat to medium-low; and simmer until potatoes are just tender and paring knife can be slipped in and out of potatoes with little resistance, 5 to 6 minutes.

2. While potatoes cook, lower skewered garlic into simmering water and blanch for 45 seconds. Run garlic under cold running water, then remove from skewer and mince.

3. Drain potatoes, reserving ¼ cup cooking water. Arrange hot potatoes close together in single layer on rimmed baking sheet. Whisk oil, garlic, vinegar, mustard, pepper, and reserved potato cooking water together in bowl, then drizzle evenly over potatoes. Let potatoes sit at room temperature until flavors meld, about 10 minutes.

4. Transfer potatoes to large bowl. Combine shallot, chervil, parsley, chives, and tarragon in small bowl, then sprinkle over potatoes and gently combine. Serve.

Making French Potato Salad

SLICE RAW POTATOES
This eliminates torn skins and broken slices.

DRESS POTATOES
Spreading them out before dressing them ensures that you evenly cover the potatoes, which soak up more flavor when warm.

LEMON AND HERB RED POTATO SALAD

Serves: 8
Total Time: 45 minutes, plus 30 minutes cooling

RECIPE OVERVIEW Mayonnaise-based potato salad needs to be served cold, but for a potato salad you can serve warm or at room temperature, try this one with a light vinegar-based dressing paired with bright herbs. We boil chunks of red potatoes, adding a little vinegar to the cooking water to help them keep their shape. The acid minimizes their breakdown. A mixture of briny capers and tart lemon juice complements the earthiness of the potatoes while tarragon, parsley, and chives give the salad freshness and color. Adding some of the dressing while the potatoes are still hot lets them absorb all its flavor. To remove some of the onion's harshness after chopping, place it in a fine-mesh strainer and run it under cold water. Drain, but do not rinse, the capers.

- 3 pounds red potatoes, unpeeled, cut into 1-inch pieces
- 2 tablespoons distilled white vinegar
- 1 teaspoon table salt, plus salt for cooking potatoes
- 2 teaspoons grated lemon zest plus 3 tablespoons juice
- ½ teaspoon pepper
- ⅓ cup extra-virgin olive oil
- ½ cup finely chopped onion, rinsed
- 3 tablespoons minced fresh tarragon
- 3 tablespoons minced fresh parsley
- 3 tablespoons minced fresh chives
- 2 tablespoons capers, minced

1. Combine potatoes, 8 cups water, vinegar, and 2 tablespoons salt in Dutch oven and bring to boil over high heat. Reduce heat to medium and cook at strong simmer until potatoes are just tender, 10 to 15 minutes.

2. Meanwhile, whisk lemon zest and juice, pepper, and salt together in large bowl. Slowly whisk in oil until emulsified; set aside.

3. Drain potatoes thoroughly, then transfer to rimmed baking sheet. Drizzle 2 tablespoons dressing over hot potatoes and toss gently until evenly coated. Let potatoes cool, about 30 minutes, stirring halfway through cooling.

4. Whisk dressing to recombine and stir in onion, tarragon, parsley, chives, and capers. Add potatoes to dressing and gently stir to combine. Season with salt and pepper to taste. Serve warm or at room temperature.

SWEET POTATO SALAD

Serves: 4 to 6
Total Time: 45 minutes, plus 45 minutes chilling

RECIPE OVERVIEW Unlike their starchy white counterparts, sweet potatoes quickly become waterlogged and mushy when they are boiled. Steaming, however, is a relatively gentle process, which avoids any waterlogging, giving the sweet potatoes the moist, tender texture we love. We contrast their sweetness and color with a crunchy red bell pepper and a tangy, peppery dressing. This dressing gets a hint of heat from cayenne, which balances the soft sweetness of the vegetables, too.

- 2 pounds sweet potatoes, peeled and cut into ¾-inch pieces
- 1 red bell pepper, stemmed, seeded, and chopped fine
- 2½ tablespoons cider vinegar
- 1½ tablespoons Dijon mustard
- ½ teaspoon table salt
- ¼ teaspoon pepper
- Pinch cayenne pepper
- ¼ cup extra-virgin olive oil
- 2 scallions, sliced thin
- 2 tablespoons minced fresh parsley

1. Fill Dutch oven with 1 inch water and bring to boil over high heat. Reduce heat to medium-low and carefully lower steamer basket into pot. Add potatoes to basket; cover; and cook until potatoes are nearly tender, about 15 minutes.

2. Add bell pepper to basket; cover; and cook until potatoes and bell pepper are tender, 2 to 4 minutes. Transfer vegetables to large bowl.

3. Whisk vinegar, mustard, salt, pepper, and cayenne together in small bowl. Drizzle half of vinegar mixture over vegetables; toss gently to combine; and refrigerate until vegetables are cool, about 45 minutes.

4. Whisking constantly, drizzle oil into remaining vinegar mixture, then gently stir into vegetables. Stir in scallions and parsley, season with salt and pepper to taste, and serve.

KEYS TO SUCCESS

- **Steam the sweet potatoes:** Rather than boiling them so that they don't get waterlogged
- **Chill the cooked sweet potatoes:** Before dressing to prevent them from getting mushy

SCIENCE LESSON Sweet Potatoes

Sweet potatoes are only distantly related to white russet potatoes, but they have a very similar starch content to most white potatoes, making them great for use in potato salads. However, more starch is broken down during the cooking process of a sweet potato than of a white potato. So while sweet potatoes get soft and moist after cooking rather than fluffy like white potatoes, they can also get overly mushy and watery if boiled. For this reason, we prefer to steam these tubers when using them in salads. Chilling them before dressing helps, too.

COURSE
SLAWS

JULIA COLLIN DAVISON

Discover the secrets to great cabbage salads. Typically tangy with a hint of sweetness, coleslaw is frequently made with green cabbage. This salad can also include other ingredients, such as red cabbage or brussels sprouts. Coleslaws and slaws can be dressed with or without mayonnaise, and you'll learn both versions in this course. You'll also learn techniques to get maximum flavor out of the vegetables, such as cutting and rinsing, salting and draining, and chilling.

JULIA'S PRO TIP: *Freezing extra buttermilk is a great way to store it long-term. Simply use ice cube trays to freeze it into manageable pieces (standard ice cubes are 2 tablespoons), then just thaw what you need, when you need it. You can thaw it in the fridge or the microwave, and you may need to whisk the whey and solids together before using. (Buttermilk can be frozen for up to a month.)*

BUTTERMILK COLESLAW

Serves: 4 to 6
Total Time: 20 minutes, plus 1 hour salting and 30 minutes chilling

RECIPE OVERVIEW Crisp coleslaw with a light but flavorful dressing is the quintessential picnic side dish, but it's also often one of the most disappointing because homemade coleslaw is prone to turning watery and wilted. For a crisp coleslaw where the buttermilk dressing clings to the cabbage instead of collecting in the bottom of the bowl, you need to salt and drain the cabbage first. This process removes excess water and softens the cabbage to a pickle-crisp texture. For a hefty and tangy dressing, we combine buttermilk, mayonnaise, and sour cream.

- ½ head red or green cabbage, quartered, cored, and shredded (6 cups)
- ¼ teaspoon table salt, plus salt for salting cabbage
- 1 carrot, peeled and shredded
- ½ cup buttermilk
- 2 tablespoons mayonnaise
- 2 tablespoons sour cream
- 2 tablespoons minced fresh parsley
- 1 small shallot, minced
- ½ teaspoon cider vinegar
- ½ teaspoon sugar
- ¼ teaspoon Dijon mustard
- ⅛ teaspoon pepper

1. Toss cabbage and 1 teaspoon salt in colander set over large bowl and let sit until wilted, at least 1 hour or up to 4 hours. Rinse cabbage under cold running water. Press, but do not squeeze, to drain, and blot dry with paper towels.

2. Combine cabbage and carrot in large bowl. In separate bowl, whisk buttermilk, mayonnaise, sour cream, parsley, shallot, vinegar, sugar, mustard, pepper, and salt together. Pour dressing over vegetables and toss to combine. Refrigerate until chilled, about 30 minutes. Serve. (Coleslaw can be refrigerated for up to 3 days.)

Variations

LEMONY BUTTERMILK COLESLAW
Substitute 1 teaspoon lemon juice for vinegar. Add 1 tablespoon minced fresh chives and 1 teaspoon minced fresh thyme to dressing in step 2.

BUTTERMILK COLESLAW WITH SCALLIONS AND CILANTRO
Omit mustard. Substitute 1 tablespoon minced fresh cilantro for parsley and 1 teaspoon lime juice for vinegar. Add 2 thinly sliced scallions to dressing in step 2.

KEYS TO SUCCESS

- **Salt the cabbage:** To extract excess liquid from the leaves
- **Blot the cabbage dry:** After rinsing to ensure that the dressing will cling
- **Chill the slaw:** To allow the flavors to permeate

CORE TECHNIQUE
Prepping Vegetables for Slaw

CORE CABBAGE
Remove the tough center with a sharp knife before cutting or shredding.

SHRED OR CUT VEGETABLE
Use a grater, knife, or food processor to cut cabbage or brussels sprouts fine.

DRAIN VEGETABLE WELL
Remove excess liquid from the vegetable and flavor it at the same time by tossing the shredded vegetable and 1 teaspoon salt in a colander set over a large bowl.

RINSE VEGETABLE
Rinse the vegetable under cold running water. Press, but do not squeeze, to drain, and blot the vegetable dry with paper towels.

SWEET AND TANGY COLESLAW

Serves: 4
Total Time: 45 minutes

RECIPE OVERVIEW The great thing about coleslaw is its blend of crunchy and soft textures with tangy and sweet flavors. Whether you are dressing the vegetables with mayo or with vinegar, as in this recipe, the key is to get the balance right. We toss the cabbage with salt and sugar, both of which draw out liquid and season the vegetable; the sweetness helps balance the vinaigrette. Instead of letting the treated cabbage sit and waiting for moisture to be released, we speed things up by using the microwave and then spin-dry the partially wilted greens in a salad spinner. Since the microwave warms the shredded cabbage, we chill the dressing in the freezer; a quick toss and our slaw is rapidly cooled. If you don't have a salad spinner, use a colander to drain the cabbage, pressing out the excess moisture with a rubber spatula. This recipe can be easily doubled.

- ¼ cup cider vinegar, plus extra for seasoning
- 2 tablespoons vegetable oil
- ¼ teaspoon celery seeds
- ¼ teaspoon pepper
- ½ head green or red cabbage, halved, cored, and shredded (6 cups)
- ¼ cup sugar, plus extra for seasoning
- 1 teaspoon table salt
- 1 large carrot, peeled and shredded
- 2 tablespoons chopped fresh parsley

1. Whisk vinegar, oil, celery seeds, and pepper together in medium bowl. Place bowl in freezer and chill until dressing is cold, at least 15 minutes or up to 30 minutes.

2. Meanwhile, in large bowl, toss cabbage with sugar and salt. Cover and microwave until cabbage is just beginning to wilt, about 1 minute. Stir briefly; cover; and continue to microwave until cabbage is partially wilted and has reduced in volume by one-third, 30 to 60 seconds.

3. Transfer cabbage mixture to salad spinner and spin until excess water is removed, 10 to 20 seconds. Remove bowl from freezer; add cabbage mixture, carrot, and parsley to cold dressing; and toss to coat. Season with salt, pepper, extra vinegar, and extra sugar to taste. Refrigerate until chilled, about 15 minutes. Toss coleslaw again before serving.

> ### KEYS TO SUCCESS
> - **Microwave the salted cabbage:** To wilt it and reduce its volume
> - **Spin the wilted cabbage:** In a salad spinner to drain it of excess moisture
> - **Chill the slaw:** After dressing it, to allow the flavors to meld

BRUSSELS SPROUT SLAW WITH PECORINO AND PINE NUTS

Serves: 8
Total Time: 25 minutes, plus 30 minutes resting

RECIPE OVERVIEW Cabbage isn't the only vegetable that benefits from the slaw treatment. Brussels sprouts are especially good candidates; making them into a slaw is a way to get rid of some of their vegetal rawness while still enjoying their crunchy texture. To avoid a chewy slaw you need to slice the sprouts very thin and then marinate them in an acidic dressing; we make ours with lemon juice, Dijon mustard, shallot, and garlic. The 30-minute soak in the dressing softens and seasons the sprouts, bringing out and balancing their flavor. Stirring in toasted pine nuts and shredded Pecorino Romano just before serving adds a layer of crunch and creamy, nutty richness. Slice the sprouts as thin as possible. Shred the Pecorino Romano on the large holes of a box grater.

- 3 tablespoons lemon juice
- 2 tablespoons Dijon mustard
- 1 small shallot, minced
- 1 garlic clove, minced
- ½ teaspoon table salt
- 6 tablespoons extra-virgin olive oil
- 2 pounds brussels sprouts, trimmed, halved, and sliced very thin
- 3 ounces Pecorino Romano cheese, shredded (1 cup)
- ½ cup pine nuts, toasted

1. Whisk lemon juice, mustard, shallot, garlic, and salt together in large bowl. Whisking constantly, slowly drizzle in oil.

2. Add brussels sprouts, toss to combine, and let sit for 30 minutes.

3. Stir in Pecorino and pine nuts and season with salt and pepper to taste. Serve.

> ### KEYS TO SUCCESS
> - **Halve the brussels sprouts:** Creates a flat base to make slicing easier
> - For more on toasting pine nuts, see page 614.

BRUSSELS SPROUT, RED CABBAGE, AND POMEGRANATE SLAW

Serves: 4
Total Time: 20 minutes

RECIPE OVERVIEW Green cabbage is a coleslaw standard, but here we combine red cabbage and thinly sliced brussels sprouts to create a vibrant color contrast. Pomegranate seeds provide bright sweetness, and toasted sliced almonds add crunch. Instead of a traditional mayonnaise dressing, we use a vinaigrette of cider vinegar, pomegranate molasses, and olive oil, so the salad tastes lighter but still has sweet-tart notes. You can substitute 2 teaspoons of lemon juice plus 2 teaspoons of molasses for the pomegranate molasses. The brussels sprouts and cabbage can be sliced with a knife or the slicing disk of a food processor. Either way, slice them as thin as possible.

- 2 tablespoons cider vinegar
- 1½ teaspoons pomegranate molasses
- ¼ teaspoon plus ⅛ teaspoon table salt
- ⅛ teaspoon pepper
- 1½ tablespoons extra-virgin olive oil
- 8 ounces brussels sprouts, trimmed, halved, and sliced very thin
- 1½ cups thinly sliced red cabbage
- ¾ cup pomegranate seeds
- ¼ cup sliced almonds, toasted
- 1 tablespoon minced fresh mint

1. Whisk vinegar, pomegranate molasses, salt, and pepper in large bowl until well combined. Whisking constantly, slowly drizzle in oil until combined.

2. Add brussels sprouts, cabbage, pomegranate seeds, almonds, and mint and toss well to coat. Season with salt and pepper to taste. Serve.

> ## KEYS TO SUCCESS
> - **Use red cabbage:** Provides great texture and bright color
> - **Double dose of pomegranate:** Tangy pomegranate molasses in the vinaigrette and crunchy seeds in the salad
> - **Toast sliced almonds:** They provide a nutty foil to the fruit.

COURSE
SALADS WITH MEAT AND SEAFOOD

Adding meat or seafood helps turn salad into a satisfying meal. The protein might be pan-seared steak or a creamy, mayonnaise-dressed chicken or fish that you can eat wrapped in lettuce or spread between slices of bread. This course focuses on how to get the most flavor out of the protein of your choice and what to pair it with for a satisfying main course.

ASHLEY'S PRO TIP: *For the ideal picture-perfect tuna salad, blot away as much water as possible after draining. This will ensure that you have the best texture and flavor—no sogginess at all!*

ASHLEY MOORE

CREAMY CHICKEN SALAD WITH FRESH HERBS

Serves: 4
Total Time: 1 hour, plus 2 hours chilling

RECIPE OVERVIEW To ensure silky, juicy, and flavorful chicken for this easy salad, we use tender poached chicken breasts. We cube the breasts rather than shred them, which gives us satisfying bites of chicken that hold on to fresh herbs and a creamy dressing, perfect for a picnic or a summer supper. For the homemade dressing, we combine mayonnaise with bright, fragrant lemon juice. Finely chopped celery provides crunch, and fresh chives, tarragon, and dill make the salad ultrarefreshing. We like poaching our own chicken for this recipe, but any cooked chicken works, too.

Poached Chicken
- 4 (6- to 8-ounce) boneless, skinless chicken breasts, trimmed
- Table salt for poaching chicken

Salad
- ⅔ cup mayonnaise
- ¼ cup finely chopped celery
- 3 tablespoons chopped fresh chives or scallions
- 4 teaspoons chopped fresh tarragon or mint
- 1 tablespoon chopped fresh dill
- 1 tablespoon lemon juice
- ½ teaspoon table salt
- ¼ teaspoon pepper
- 10 ounces (10 cups) mesclun or 1 head Boston or Bibb lettuce (8 ounces), leaves separated

1. FOR THE POACHED CHICKEN Pound thick ends of chicken breasts to uniform thickness. Whisk 4 quarts cool water with 2 tablespoons salt in Dutch oven. Arrange chicken in steamer basket without overlapping. Submerge basket in pot. Heat over medium heat, stirring occasionally, until water registers 175 degrees, 15 to 20 minutes. Turn off heat; cover pot; remove from burner; and let sit until chicken registers 160 degrees, 17 to 22 minutes.

2. Transfer chicken to cutting board and let cool for 10 to 15 minutes. Cut into ½-inch pieces. (Chicken can be refrigerated for up to 2 days. Let come to room temperature before using.)

3. FOR THE SALAD Combine chicken, mayonnaise, celery, chives, tarragon, dill, lemon juice, salt, and pepper in large bowl. Cover with plastic and refrigerate for at least 2 hours to allow flavors to meld. (Salad can be refrigerated for up to 2 days.) Serve with mesclun, spooning chicken mixture into leaves.

Variations
CURRIED CHICKEN SALAD WITH DRIED APRICOTS
Omit chives, tarragon, and dill. Add ½ cup finely chopped dried apricots, 6 tablespoons toasted slivered almonds, 4 thinly sliced scallions, and 2 teaspoons curry powder to bowl with chicken and mayonnaise.

CREAMY CHICKEN SALAD WITH GRAPES AND WALNUTS

Omit tarragon and dill. Add 1 cup halved seedless grapes; 6 tablespoons walnuts or pecans, toasted and chopped; and 3 tablespoons chopped fresh parsley to bowl with chicken and mayonnaise. Substitute Dijon mustard for lemon juice.

> ## KEYS TO SUCCESS
> - **Pound the breasts to the same thickness using a meat pounder or small skillet**: Ensures that the breasts cook evenly
> - **Cut the chicken into cubes**: For hearty texture and to allow just enough dressing to cling

---

CORE TECHNIQUE
Poaching Chicken

START WITH COLD WATER
Ensures that the chicken cooks through gently as the water temperature increases.

MONITOR WATER TEMPERATURE
Heating the water to 175 degrees ensures that the chicken will cook to 160 degrees off the heat.

POACH CHICKEN OFF HEAT
Covering the pot and letting the chicken cook in the residual heat ensures gentle, even poaching.

TUNA SALAD WITH HARD-COOKED EGGS, RADISHES, AND CAPERS

Makes: 2 cups
Total Time: 25 minutes

RECIPE OVERVIEW Tuna salad, so familiar, simple, and beloved, can often be bland, chalky, and watery. This recipe gives you a tuna salad to love. After tasting every variety of canned tuna sold in supermarkets—both packed in oil and packed in water—we decided on solid white tuna packed in water for the best flavor. We blot the tuna dry

with paper towels to avoid a watery salad. We then use the microwave to quickly cook some onion in oil and add that along with lemon juice for flavor and tang. Hard-cooked eggs, radishes, and capers transform this everyday tuna salad into a rich, peppery, briny dish. For a slightly milder dish, substitute shallot for the onion.

- ¼ cup finely chopped onion
- ½ cup extra-virgin olive oil, divided
- 3 (5-ounce) cans solid white tuna in water
- 2 Easy-Peel Hard-Cooked Eggs (page 65), sliced thin
- 1 celery rib, minced
- 2 radishes, trimmed, halved, and sliced thin
- ¼ cup capers, minced
- 2 teaspoons lemon juice
- ½ teaspoon sugar
- ½ teaspoon table salt
- ½ teaspoon pepper
- 10 ounces (10 cups) mesclun

1. Combine onion and 2 tablespoons oil in small bowl and microwave until onion begins to soften, about 2 minutes. Let onion mixture cool for 5 minutes. Drain tuna in fine-mesh strainer and press dry with paper towels. Transfer tuna to medium bowl and mash with fork until finely flaked.

2. Stir eggs, celery, radishes, capers, lemon juice, sugar, salt, pepper, onion mixture, and remaining 6 tablespoons oil into tuna until well combined. Season with salt and pepper to taste. (Salad can be refrigerated for up to 24 hours.) Serve with mesclun, spooning tuna mixture into leaves.

> ### KEYS TO SUCCESS
> - **Blot the tuna dry**: To prevent a watery salad
> - **Microwave the onion and oil**: To infuse the dressing with flavor and tame the onion's bite

ARUGULA SALAD WITH STEAK TIPS AND BLUE CHEESE

Serves: 4
Total Time: 40 minutes

RECIPE OVERVIEW For the allure of a steakhouse at home, make this quick salad of juicy steak, peppery arugula, and blue cheese. You'll get a salad course and a steak course combined. The freshness of greens gets richness from blue cheese, hearty medium-rare steak brings satisfaction, and Dijon mustard in the vinaigrette complements the arugula's spiciness. Sirloin steak tips,

also known as flap meat, can be sold as whole steaks, cubes, and strips. To ensure uniform pieces, we prefer to purchase whole steaks and cut them ourselves. For optimal tenderness, make sure to slice the cooked steak against the grain (perpendicular to the fibers).

- 1 pound sirloin steak tips, trimmed
- ¾ teaspoon table salt, divided
- ½ teaspoon pepper, divided
- 6 tablespoons extra-virgin olive oil, divided
- 1 shallot, minced
- 2 tablespoons cider vinegar
- 2 garlic cloves, minced
- 1 teaspoon Dijon mustard
- 1 teaspoon honey
- 12 ounces (12 cups) baby arugula
- 6 ounces blue cheese, crumbled (1½ cups)

1. Pat steak dry with paper towels and sprinkle with ½ teaspoon salt and ¼ teaspoon pepper. Heat 2 tablespoons oil in 12-inch nonstick skillet over medium-high heat until just smoking. Add steak and cook until well browned all over and meat registers 125 degrees (for medium-rare), 8 to 10 minutes. Transfer to plate, tent with aluminum foil, and let rest for 5 minutes.

2. Whisk shallot, vinegar, garlic, mustard, honey, remaining ¼ teaspoon salt, and remaining ¼ teaspoon pepper together in large bowl. Whisking constantly, slowly drizzle in remaining ¼ cup oil until emulsified. Add arugula and blue cheese to vinaigrette and toss to combine. Season with salt and pepper to taste. Slice steak against grain ¼ inch thick. Divide salad among individual plates. Serve, topping individual portions with steak.

SALMON, AVOCADO, GRAPEFRUIT, AND WATERCRESS SALAD

Serves: 4
Total Time: 55 minutes

RECIPE OVERVIEW Seafood is a great ingredient to mix into a main dish–worthy salad without weighing it down. This simple salad showcases ingredients that brighten up lunch or dinner. Salmon and avocado both bring richness and make the meal filling and satisfying. For a sweet-tart contrast and vibrant color, segment two red grapefruits and reserve some of the juice to whisk up a simple citrus vinaigrette brought into focus with a little white wine vinegar and Dijon mustard. For greens, watercress balances the sweetness and richness with its peppery punch. Finally, add a sprinkle of crunchy toasted hazelnuts and torn mint leaves for complexity.

- 2 (6- to 8-ounce) skin-on salmon fillets, 1 inch thick
- 1 teaspoon plus 3 tablespoons extra-virgin olive oil, divided
- ¾ teaspoon table salt, divided
- ⅛ teaspoon pepper
- 2 red grapefruits
- 1 small shallot, minced
- 1 teaspoon white wine vinegar
- 1 teaspoon Dijon mustard
- 4 ounces (4 cups) watercress, torn into bite-size pieces
- 1 ripe avocado, halved, pitted, and sliced ¼ inch thick
- ¼ cup fresh mint leaves, torn
- ¼ cup hazelnuts, toasted, skinned, and chopped

1. Adjust oven rack to lowest position, place aluminum foil–lined rimmed baking sheet on rack, and heat oven to 500 degrees. Make 4 or 5 shallow slashes, about 1 inch apart, on skin side of each fillet, being careful not to cut into flesh. Pat salmon dry with paper towels, rub with 1 teaspoon oil, and sprinkle with ¼ teaspoon salt and pepper.

2. Reduce oven temperature to 275 degrees and remove sheet from oven. Carefully place salmon skin side down on prepared sheet. Roast until center is still translucent when checked with tip of paring knife and registers 125 degrees (for medium-rare), 8 to 12 minutes. Transfer salmon to plate. Let cool completely, about 20 minutes. Using 2 forks, flake salmon into rough 2-inch pieces, discarding skin.

3. Meanwhile, cut away peel and pith from grapefruits. Holding fruit over bowl, use paring knife to slice between membranes to release segments. Measure out 2 tablespoons grapefruit juice and transfer to separate bowl.

4. Whisk shallot, vinegar, mustard, and remaining ½ teaspoon salt into bowl with grapefruit juice. Whisking constantly, slowly drizzle in remaining 3 tablespoons oil until combined. Arrange watercress in even layer on serving platter. Top with salmon, grapefruit, and avocado. Drizzle dressing over top, then sprinkle with mint and hazelnuts. Serve.

KEYS TO SUCCESS

- **Cut slashes in the salmon skin:** So that the fat is rendered during cooking
- **Preheat the baking sheet:** To jump-start the cooking before gently finishing the salmon
- **Flake the salmon into big pieces:** For an attractive presentation
- For more on cutting citrus segments, see page 47.

COURSE
RESTAURANT FAVORITES

STEVE DUNN

You don't have to go to a restaurant to eat your favorite Caesar or caprese salad. You can make these favorites and more at home. Whether it is fresh horiatiki salata (the real Greek salad), a rich steakhouse wedge salad, or a simple panzanella, you can make them any time you like. These salads come together using easily learned techniques.

STEVE'S PRO TIP: *For the best salads, keep all prepped greens and vegetables (except tomatoes) in the fridge until just before composing your salad and serving. Dressing chilled vegetables at the very last minute ensures a refreshing salad with maximum crispness.*

CAPRESE SALAD

Serves: 4 to 6
Total Time: 15 minutes

RECIPE OVERVIEW Italy's simplest salad might well be the caprese, which highlights fresh ingredients: soft mozzarella, ripe tomatoes, and fragrant basil. In a salad where the ingredients are barely seasoned and shine on their own, it is important to use fully ripened tomatoes and a good-quality fresh mozzarella packed in water. The other thing to remember is a ratio of 3 parts tomato to 2 parts mozzarella. Some recipes call for finely chopped red onion and red wine vinegar, too; however, we like the salad simply drizzled with oil, seasoned with salt and pepper, and sprinkled with basil, so the acidity of the tomatoes and the delicate flavor of the mozzarella stay at the fore. Make sure to use a good extra-virgin olive oil and coarse salt. Table salt will be too harsh for this light, aromatic salad. Serve with crusty bread to sop up the tasty tomato liquid.

- 1½ pounds very ripe tomatoes, cored and sliced ¼ inch thick
- 1 pound fresh mozzarella cheese, sliced ¼ inch thick
- 2 tablespoons coarsely chopped fresh basil
- ¼ teaspoon kosher salt or coarse sea salt
- ⅛ teaspoon pepper
- ¼ cup extra-virgin olive oil

Alternately shingle tomatoes and mozzarella in concentric circles over platter. Sprinkle with basil, salt, and pepper, then drizzle with oil. Let salad sit until flavors meld, 5 to 10 minutes. Serve.

KEYS TO SUCCESS

- **Choose high-quality ingredients:** Nothing hides their flavors in this salad
- **Top with coarse salt:** Adds pops of contrast to the sweet tomatoes

WEDGE SALAD

Serves: 6
Total Time: 25 minutes

RECIPE OVERVIEW A crisp, chilled wedge salad—cool, crunchy iceberg lettuce; rings of red onion; a slice or two of beefsteak tomato; and creamy blue cheese dressing—is an ideal accompaniment to a steakhouse-style dinner. A sprinkling of diced bacon is the pièce de résistance. To replicate the wedge salad at home, we use lots of crumbled Stilton—there's a reason the British call it the "king of cheeses." For balanced creaminess and tang, we include both mayonnaise and sour cream in the dressing, thinned with a little milk, so it clings to the edges of the cut lettuce. We use shallot rather than red onion, soaking it briefly in vinegar to tame its bite (and we use that vinegar in the dressing). Cherry tomatoes are a more flavorful year-round choice than beefsteak tomatoes.

- 1 large shallot, sliced into thin rings
- ¼ cup red wine vinegar
- 4 slices bacon
- 4 ounces Stilton blue cheese, crumbled (1 cup), divided

186 | The New Cooking School Cookbook: Fundamentals

- ⅓ cup mayonnaise
- ¼ cup sour cream
- 3 tablespoons milk
- 1 garlic clove, minced
- ¼ teaspoon table salt
- ¼ teaspoon pepper
- 1 head iceberg lettuce (2 pounds), cored and cut into 6 wedges
- 12 ounces cherry tomatoes, halved

1. Combine shallot and vinegar in bowl and let sit for 20 minutes. Meanwhile, cook bacon in 10-inch nonstick skillet over medium heat until crispy, 5 to 7 minutes. Using slotted spoon, transfer bacon to paper towel–lined plate; set aside.

2. Using fork, remove shallot from vinegar and set aside. Measure out and reserve 2 tablespoons vinegar. Whisk reserved vinegar, ¾ cup Stilton, mayonnaise, sour cream, milk, garlic, salt, and pepper in bowl until combined.

3. Arrange lettuce wedges on platter, drizzle with dressing, and top with shallot and tomatoes. Crumble bacon over top and sprinkle with remaining ¼ cup Stilton. Serve.

PANZANELLA

Serves: 4
Total Time: 1 hour

RECIPE OVERVIEW Panzanella is an Italian bread and tomato salad in which the sweet juice of tomatoes and a bright-tasting vinaigrette moisten chunks of thick-crusted bread until they're softened but still just a little chewy. Panzanella is traditionally made with leftover stale bread as a way to use it up. We use fresh bread here and toast it in the oven, which adds flavor from browning and causes it to lose enough moisture so that it absorbs the dressing without getting waterlogged. A 10-minute soak in the dressing yields perfectly moistened bread ready to be tossed with the tomatoes, which we salt to intensify their flavor. A thinly sliced cucumber and shallot give crunch and bite, and chopped fresh basil brings the elements of the salad aromatically together. As with other minimalistic salads, the success of this recipe depends on high-quality ingredients, including ripe, in-season tomatoes; good olive oil; and fresh basil.

- 6 cups rustic Italian or French bread cut or torn into 1-inch pieces (8 to 16 ounces)
- ½ cup extra-virgin olive oil, divided
- ¾ teaspoon table salt, divided
- 1½ pounds tomatoes, cored, seeded, and cut into 1-inch pieces
- 3 tablespoons red wine vinegar
- ¼ teaspoon pepper
- 1 cucumber, peeled, halved lengthwise, seeded, and sliced thin
- ¼ cup chopped fresh basil
- 1 shallot, sliced thin

1. Adjust oven rack to middle position and heat oven to 400 degrees. Toss bread with 2 tablespoons oil and ¼ teaspoon salt in bowl; arrange bread in single layer on rimmed baking sheet. Toast bread until just starting to turn light golden brown, 15 to 20 minutes, stirring halfway through toasting. Set aside and let cool completely.

2. Gently toss tomatoes with remaining ½ teaspoon salt in large bowl. Transfer to colander set over bowl and let drain for 15 minutes, tossing occasionally.

3. Whisk vinegar, pepper, and remaining 6 tablespoons oil into drained tomato juice. Add bread; toss to coat; and let stand for 10 minutes, tossing occasionally.

4. Add tomatoes, cucumber, basil, and shallot to bowl with bread and toss to coat. Season with salt and pepper to taste, and serve immediately.

> **SCIENCE LESSON**
>
> **Is Dried Bread and Stale Bread the Same?**
>
> In a word, no. Stale bread may feel firm and dry like dried bread, but it has hidden reserves of water. The firmness of stale bread is the result of a process known as retrogradation, whereby cooked starch molecules slowly rearrange themselves into a brittle, crystalline structure that traps moisture already in the bread and limits its ability to absorb more. And that's a problem, because absorption is needed when you're making a salad such as panzanella and you want the bread to take on the flavor of the tomatoes and dressing. You can still use your stale bread, though. Just dry it out in the oven first so that it can trap lots of flavorful liquid.

HORIATIKI SALATA

Serves: 4 to 6
Total Time: 55 minutes

RECIPE OVERVIEW Greek salad in the United States often means tomatoes, cucumbers, and feta on lettuce. But the real Greek salad, or horiatiki salata, is made up of sweet tomatoes, briny olives, savory onion, crunchy cucumber, and tangy feta, without any lettuce filler. Since ripe tomatoes are loaded with juice that can flood the salad, we salt and drain halved wedges first. Soaking onion slices in ice water lessens their bite by washing away the thiosulfinates alliin and allicin (also present in garlic) while maintaining a fresh, crisp texture. A creamy feta brings richness to the lean vegetables. Vinaigrette is never used to dress horiatiki salata, but we tweaked the custom of drizzling different components of the salad separately with oil and vinegar, ensuring that the mixture was lightly

but evenly dressed. Use only large, round tomatoes here, and choose the ripest in-season ones you can find. A fresh, fruity, peppery olive oil works well if you have it.

- 1¾ pounds tomatoes, cored
- 1¼ teaspoons table salt, divided
- ½ red onion, sliced thin
- 2 tablespoons red wine vinegar
- 1 teaspoon dried oregano, plus extra for seasoning
- ½ teaspoon pepper
- 1 English cucumber, quartered lengthwise and cut into ¾-inch pieces
- 1 green bell pepper, stemmed, seeded, and cut into 2 by ½-inch strips
- 1 cup pitted olives
- 2 tablespoons capers, rinsed
- 5 tablespoons extra-virgin olive oil, divided
- 1 (8-ounce) block feta cheese, sliced into ½-inch-thick triangles

1. Cut tomatoes into ½-inch-thick wedges. Cut wedges in half crosswise. Toss tomatoes and ½ teaspoon salt together in colander set in large bowl. Let drain for 30 minutes. Place onion in small bowl, cover with ice water, and let sit for 15 minutes. Whisk vinegar, oregano, pepper, and remaining ¾ teaspoon salt together in second small bowl.

2. Discard tomato juice and transfer tomatoes to now-empty bowl. Drain onion and add to bowl with tomatoes. Add vinegar mixture, cucumber, bell pepper, olives, and capers and toss to combine. Drizzle with ¼ cup oil and toss gently to coat. Season with salt and pepper to taste. Transfer to serving platter and top with feta. Season each slice of feta with extra oregano to taste. Drizzle feta with remaining 1 tablespoon oil. Serve.

> ### KEYS TO SUCCESS
> - **Salt and drain the tomatoes**: So that the juices do not dilute the dressing (see page 170)
> - **Give the onion a soak**: In ice water to reduce its sharpness and pungency
> - **Choose dried oregano over fresh**: Its stronger flavor is needed to enhance the vegetables.

CAESAR SALAD
Serves: 4
Total Time: 1 hour

RECIPE OVERVIEW This beloved American salad was actually created in Mexico by restaurateur Caesar Cardini. It combines everyday ingredients such as romaine, bread, eggs, and cheese but gives them deep flavor that comes from coaxing the most from each. The salad is also a lesson in the power of umami, as it combines several glutamate-rich ingredients (anchovies, Worcestershire sauce, and Parmesan) to create a savoriness that keeps us coming back for more. Use a rasp-style grater or the small holes of a box grater to grate the Parmesan. To shred it, use the large holes of a box grater.

- ¾ cup extra-virgin olive oil, divided
- 2 garlic cloves, minced, divided
- ½ teaspoon table salt, divided
- ½ teaspoon pepper, divided
- 4 ounces ciabatta, cut into ½-inch cubes (4 cups)
- 1 large egg yolk
- 1 tablespoon lemon juice
- 2 teaspoons Worcestershire sauce
- 2 teaspoons Dijon mustard
- 2 anchovy fillets, rinsed and minced, plus extra fillets for serving (optional)
- ¼ cup grated Parmesan cheese, plus 1½ ounces shredded (½ cup)
- 2 romaine lettuce hearts (12 ounces)

1. Adjust oven rack to middle position and heat oven to 350 degrees. Stir ¼ cup oil, half of garlic, ¼ teaspoon salt, and ¼ teaspoon pepper together in large bowl. Add bread and toss to combine. Transfer bread to rimmed baking sheet and bake until light golden, about 18 minutes, stirring halfway through baking. Let cool completely. Wipe bowl clean with paper towels.

Making Caesar Salad

CUBE CRUSTY BREAD
Use a serrated knife to cut fluffy ciabatta without squishing it.

PREP PARMESAN
Grated Parmesan will enrich the dressing; the larger shreds will bring pops of salty flavor to the salad.

MINCE ANCHOVIES
Mincing fillets by hand ensures that they blend in easily.

PUT IT ALL TOGETHER
Adding all the salad components to the bowl with dressing guarantees that none of it is wasted.

SALADS | 189

2. Form damp dish towel into ring shape on counter. Set now-empty bowl on towel to stabilize. Whisk egg yolk, lemon juice, Worcestershire, mustard, anchovies, remaining garlic, remaining ¼ teaspoon salt, and remaining ¼ teaspoon pepper together in bowl. Whisking constantly, slowly drizzle in remaining ½ cup oil until emulsified. Whisk in grated Parmesan.

3. Cut each lettuce heart in half lengthwise, core each half, then cut halves in half lengthwise. Cut crosswise into 1-inch pieces. Add lettuce, croutons, and shredded Parmesan to bowl with dressing and toss to combine. Season with salt and pepper to taste. Serve, garnishing with extra anchovies, if using.

> **KEYS TO SUCCESS**
> - **Make your own croutons:** To ensure that they're golden brown and well seasoned
> - **Cut ½-inch croutons:** Because larger ones are hard to eat and smaller ones disappear
> - **Add Parmesan to the dressing last:** The cheese could prevent it from emulsifying.

KALE CAESAR SALAD WITH CHICKEN
Serves: 4
Total Time: 1½ hours

RECIPE OVERVIEW Kale is closing in on romaine as the Caesar salad green of choice, and it's no wonder: Its earthy, sturdy leaves make a wonderful base for the rich dressing. But we like to tenderize our kale first because it makes it easier to eat and digest, so we briefly soak it in a warm-water bath. We also add chicken to turn this salad into a satisfying meal. To stand up to the assertive flavor of the kale, we make our dressing extra-potent, with a stronger dose of lemon juice and anchovies than is typical in Caesar salad. We also make some easy, well-seasoned croutons in a skillet. Parmesan cheese is the finishing touch, adding a rich, salty note.

- ½ cup extra-virgin olive oil, divided
- 2 garlic cloves, minced, divided
- 5 ounces ciabatta, cut into ½-inch cubes (5 cups)
- ½ teaspoon plus ⅛ teaspoon table salt, divided
- 12 ounces curly kale, stemmed and cut into 1-inch pieces
- 1 ounce Parmesan cheese, grated (½ cup), divided
- ⅓ cup mayonnaise
- 1 tablespoon lemon juice
- 2 teaspoons white wine vinegar
- 2 teaspoons Worcestershire sauce
- 2 teaspoons Dijon mustard
- 3 anchovy fillets, rinsed
- ½ teaspoon pepper, divided
- 4 (3- to 4-ounce) chicken cutlets, ½ inch thick, trimmed

1. Combine 1 tablespoon oil and half of garlic in small bowl. Place bread in large bowl, sprinkle with water and ¼ teaspoon salt, and squeeze bread gently to absorb water. Heat ¼ cup oil in 12-inch nonstick skillet over medium-high heat; add bread and cook, stirring often, until browned and crisp, 7 to 10 minutes.

2. Off heat, push bread to sides of skillet. Add garlic mixture and cook using residual heat of skillet, mashing mixture into skillet, for 10 seconds. Mix together with bread. Transfer croutons to bowl and let cool slightly; set aside for serving.

3. Place kale in large bowl and cover with warm tap water (110 to 115 degrees). Swish kale around to remove grit. Let kale sit in warm water bath for 10 minutes. Remove kale from water and spin dry in salad spinner in multiple batches. Pat kale dry with paper towels if still wet.

4. Process ¼ cup Parmesan, mayonnaise, lemon juice, vinegar, Worcestershire, mustard, anchovies, ¼ teaspoon pepper, ¼ teaspoon salt, and remaining garlic in blender until smooth, about 30 seconds. With blender running, slowly add 2 tablespoons oil until incorporated. Toss kale with dressing in bowl and refrigerate for at least 20 minutes or up to 6 hours.

5. Pat chicken dry with paper towels and sprinkle with remaining ⅛ teaspoon salt and remaining ¼ teaspoon pepper. Heat remaining 1 tablespoon oil in 12-inch nonstick skillet over medium-high heat until just smoking. Add chicken and cook until chicken is golden brown and registers 160 degrees, about 3 minutes per side. Transfer chicken to cutting board and let cool, 10 to 15 minutes.

6. Toss dressed kale with croutons and remaining ¼ cup Parmesan. Divide salad among individual serving plates. Slice chicken thin and arrange over salad. Serve at room temperature or cold.

> **KEYS TO SUCCESS**
> - **Soften the kale in warm water:** Tenderizes it so that it's easier to eat
> - **Use more anchovies:** To match the kale's intense flavor
> - **Let it chill for 20 minutes:** Allows the flavors to meld

SCIENCE LESSON — Wilting

Kale and other greens shrink due to the loss of something called turgor pressure. Why will a huge pile of kale shrink to almost nothing when left out too long on the counter or when cooked? It has to do with something called turgor pressure, or the pressure that builds up in each plant cell when the cell is filled with water. In crisp, healthy greens, the turgor pressure is high, the cell walls of each leaf bulging and taut. But with time—or cooking—the water from inside the cells passes through the cell membranes and evaporates, reducing turgor pressure within the cells and causing the leaves to wilt.

SCIENCE LESSON — Better in the Cold

Many cruciferous vegetables, including kale, grow well in colder temperatures and can even taste better as a result. Kale, in fact, is frost-resistant. Not only that, but when subjected to a frost, a kale plant will convert stored starches into soluble sugars. This helps prevent the water in the kale's leaves from freezing, expanding, and rupturing cell walls. It also makes kale that has survived a frost taste demonstrably sweeter.

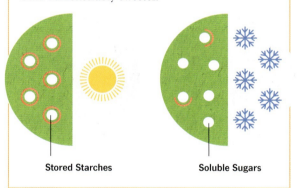

Stored Starches | Soluble Sugars

COURSE
SAVORY FRUIT SALADS

ANDREA GEARY

As unlikely as it seems, sweet fruit is absolutely delightful in classic and modern savory salads. Here you will learn how to best use fruit's freshness and sweetness, pairing it with pungent onions, aromatic herbs, fragrant spices, salty cheese, and tangy dressings to pack a punch you will thoroughly enjoy. You'll also learn how to drain fruit so that its moisture doesn't dilute the salad dressing and how to cut citrus and other fruit for use in salads.

ANDREA'S PRO TIP: *Savory fruit salads are cool and refreshing picnic fare, but salt (and salty components) can draw moisture out of the fruit if they're mixed in too far ahead of time. For a salad that's juicy but not awash in liquid, pack salty components separately and combine right before serving.*

WALDORF SALAD

Serves: 6
Total Time: 20 minutes, plus 30 minutes chilling

RECIPE OVERVIEW Waldorf salad was created in 1893 at New York's posh Waldorf Hotel. The original recipe was little more than peeled apples, celery, and mayonnaise. To enliven this classic, use three sweet apples (Gala or Braeburn) alongside three tart Granny Smiths, keeping the skins on for color. Toasting the walnuts enhances their flavor, and plumped golden raisins add bursts of sweetness. Whisking cider vinegar into mayonnaise for the dressing lightens the mayo and subtly reinforces the taste of apple. Serve the salad on a bed of tender lettuce as a starter for a light lunch or as an accompaniment to grilled foods. Toast the walnuts in a dry skillet over medium heat, stirring frequently, until the walnuts are lightly browned and fragrant, about 5 minutes. You can use reduced-fat mayonnaise here, and regular raisins will work in place of the golden raisins.

- ¾ cup golden raisins
- ¼ cup water
- ⅓ cup mayonnaise
- 3 tablespoons cider vinegar
- 1 tablespoon honey
- 3 Granny Smith apples, cored and cut into ½-inch pieces
- 3 Gala or Braeburn apples, cored and cut into ½-inch pieces
- 3 celery ribs, chopped fine
- ¾ cup walnuts, toasted and chopped

1. Combine raisins and water in bowl. Wrap tightly with plastic wrap and microwave until water begins to boil, about 1 minute. Let stand until raisins are soft and liquid has been absorbed, about 5 minutes.

2. Whisk mayonnaise, vinegar, and honey together in large bowl. Add apples, celery, walnuts, and raisins to bowl and toss until well coated. Refrigerate, covered, for 30 minutes. Season with salt and pepper to taste. Serve. (Salad can be refrigerated in airtight container for up to 2 days.)

KEYS TO SUCCESS

- **Wash and dry the apples:** Before cutting them up
- **Mix tart and sweet apples:** To make a balanced salad
- **Toast the walnuts:** To enhance their flavor
- **Add a spoonful of honey:** It helps to unite the flavors.

WATERMELON SALAD WITH BASIL AND FETA

Serves: 4 to 6
Total Time: 25 minutes, plus 30 minutes chilling

RECIPE OVERVIEW We use the juiciness of watermelon in a refreshing summer salad, accentuating its sweetness by contrasting it with salty feta, crunchy cucumber, briny olives, and aromatic basil. We first macerate the fresh melon in sugar for 30 minutes to drive off excess moisture. An English cucumber adds crunch. Though its thin skin and small seeds mean that it does not always need peeling or seeding, we do both for this salad so that the cucumber can easily soak up the melon's sweetness and the dressing's flavor. The simple dressing of white wine vinegar and olive oil allows the flavors of the salad to shine, and soaking the sliced shallot in the vinegar before tossing it in the bowl tames its bite and infuses the vinegar with plenty of flavor. Red pepper flakes give a surprisingly pleasant kick of heat. We let the dressed watermelon, cucumber, and olives rest in the fridge so that the salad can chill and the sweet and salty flavors can meld. Stir in the basil and sprinkle the salad with feta just before serving.

- 6   cups 1-inch seedless watermelon pieces
- 1½ teaspoons sugar, divided
- 1   shallot, sliced into thin rings
- 3   tablespoons white wine vinegar
- ½   teaspoon table salt, divided
- ¼   teaspoon red pepper flakes
- 1   English cucumber, peeled, quartered lengthwise, seeded, and cut into ½-inch pieces
- ½   teaspoon pepper
- 3   tablespoons extra-virgin olive oil
- ½   cup pitted kalamata olives, chopped
- ½   cup fresh basil leaves, torn into bite-size pieces
- 3   ounces feta cheese, crumbled (¾ cup)

1. Toss watermelon with 1 teaspoon sugar in colander set over large bowl and let drain for 30 minutes. Combine shallot, vinegar, ¼ teaspoon salt, pepper flakes, and remaining ½ teaspoon sugar in separate bowl and let sit while watermelon drains. Discard drained watermelon juice and wipe bowl clean with paper towels.

2. Pat cucumber and watermelon dry with paper towels and transfer to now-empty bowl. Using fork, remove shallot from vinegar mixture and add to bowl with watermelon. Add pepper and remaining ¼ teaspoon salt to vinegar mixture and slowly whisk in oil until incorporated. Add dressing and olives to bowl with watermelon and toss to combine. Refrigerate for at least 30 minutes or up to 4 hours.

3. Add basil to salad and toss to combine. Season with salt and pepper to taste. Transfer to serving platter and sprinkle with feta. Serve.

KEYS TO SUCCESS

- See page 48 for how to peel and cut up a watermelon.
- **Pat the fruit and vegetables dry:** With paper towels to remove more liquid before dressing
- **Tear the basil:** Rather than cutting it so that the leaves release their flavor but don't get bruised
- **Add the feta just before serving:** So that the salad does not look muddied

CANTALOUPE SALAD WITH OLIVES AND RED ONION

Serves: 4 to 6
Total Time: 20 minutes

RECIPE OVERVIEW Melon salads are light and refreshing so ideal hot-weather fare. Because they vary in sweetness, we taste our cantaloupe to determine how much honey if any to incorporate into our dressing. We also want to counter the abundant water in the cantaloupe, but for this quick recipe, we don't drain the melon as we do for Watermelon Salad with Basil and Feta (page 193). Instead we make a deeply flavorful dressing with lemon juice, red onion, and ground dried Aleppo pepper. We skip the oil, which would only be repelled by the water on the surface of the cantaloupe, and use oil-cured olives, which, when chopped fine, stick to the surface of the cantaloupe pieces and hold on to the dressing. To prevent the cantaloupe from releasing too much water, we leave the melon in large chunks, which frees less juice.

- ½ red onion, sliced thin
- ⅓ cup lemon juice (2 lemons)
- 1–3 teaspoons honey (optional)
- 1 teaspoon ground dried Aleppo pepper
- ½ teaspoon table salt
- 1 cantaloupe, peeled, halved, seeded, and cut into 1½-inch chunks (6 cups)
- 5 tablespoons chopped fresh parsley, divided
- 5 tablespoons chopped fresh mint, divided
- ¼ cup finely chopped pitted oil-cured olives, divided

Combine onion and lemon juice in large bowl and let sit for 5 minutes. Stir in honey, if using; Aleppo pepper; and salt. Add cantaloupe, ¼ cup parsley, ¼ cup mint, and 3 tablespoons olives and stir to combine. Transfer to shallow serving bowl. Sprinkle with remaining 1 tablespoon parsley, remaining 1 tablespoon mint, and remaining 1 tablespoon olives and serve.

> ### KEYS TO SUCCESS
> - **Taste the melon:** If your melon lacks sweetness, give it a boost with a bit of honey.
> - **Make a sub for Aleppo pepper:** If you can't find it, substitute ¾ teaspoon paprika and ¼ teaspoon cayenne.
> - **Incorporate buttery rich olives:** They balance the leanness of the fruit.

CITRUS SALAD WITH ORANGE-GINGER VINAIGRETTE

Serves: 4 to 6
Total Time: 20 minutes

RECIPE OVERVIEW Savory salads made with orange and grapefruit are an impressive way to showcase colorful winter fruit, and our aromatic Orange-Ginger Vinaigrette made with orange juice is an ideal pairing. However, dressing the fruit causes it to leach out liquid, watering down the salad. So we dress only the sliced napa cabbage and layer it over the sliced citrus, which allows the fruits' natural vibrancy to shine. The vinaigrette's gentle, gingery warmth complements the orange and grapefruit and ties the salad together nicely. Roasted cashews add richness and crunch that contrasts with the fruit and slightly spicy cabbage, and shredded basil is fresh and light.

- 2 red grapefruits
- 4 oranges
- ½ small head napa cabbage, halved, cored, and sliced thin (4 cups)
- ½ cup roasted cashews, chopped coarse, divided
- ⅓ cup Orange-Ginger Vinaigrette (recipe follows)
- ½ cup shredded fresh basil

1. Cut away peel and pith from grapefruits and oranges. Cut each fruit in half from pole to pole, then slice crosswise ¼ inch thick. Arrange fruit in even layer in serving dish.

2. Gently toss cabbage and ¼ cup cashews with vinaigrette in large bowl until evenly coated. Season with salt and pepper to taste. Arrange cabbage mixture over fruit, leaving 1-inch border. Sprinkle with basil and remaining cashews. Serve.

ORANGE-GINGER VINAIGRETTE

Makes: about 1 cup
Total Time: 35 minutes, plus 15 minutes chilling

Fruit juice makes a sweet-tart vinaigrette base. Reducing 2 cups of juice to ⅔ cup creates a pleasant glaze-like consistency, and we need far less oil than usual to make a full-bodied vinaigrette. A little vinegar complements the acidity of the juice, and honey enhances its sweetness. To avoid off-flavors, reduce the juice in a nonreactive stainless-steel saucepan.

- 2 cups orange juice (4 oranges)
- 1 tablespoon honey
- 3 tablespoons lime juice (2 limes)
- 1 tablespoon minced shallot
- 1 teaspoon grated fresh ginger
- ½ teaspoon table salt
- ½ teaspoon pepper
- 2 tablespoons extra-virgin olive oil

Bring orange juice and honey to boil in small saucepan over medium-high heat. Reduce heat to maintain simmer and cook until mixture is thickened and measures about ⅔ cup, 15 to 20 minutes. Transfer syrup to medium bowl and refrigerate until cool, about 15 minutes. Whisk in lime juice, shallot, ginger, salt, and pepper until combined. Whisking constantly, slowly drizzle in oil until emulsified. Season with salt and pepper to taste. (Vinaigrette can be refrigerated for up to 1 week; whisk to recombine before using.)

CORE TECHNIQUE

Prepping Citrus for Salad

TRIM
Cut a thin slice from the top and bottom of the fruit using a paring knife. Slice off the rind, including the white pith, by cutting from the top to the bottom of the fruit. Follow the fruit's contours as closely as possible.

SEGMENT
Insert the paring knife between the membrane and the section and slice to the center to separate one side of the section. Turn the knife blade so that it faces outward. Slice along the membrane on the other side of the section to release it.

SLICE
For slices, cut each trimmed fruit in half from pole to pole and then slice each half crosswise ¼ inch thick.

CHAPTER 5

SOUPS

COURSES

200 CHICKEN SOUPS

206 RUSTIC VEGETABLE SOUPS

214 PUREED VEGETABLE SOUPS

220 BEAN AND LENTIL SOUPS

224 PANTRY NOODLE SOUPS

228 MEATY SOUPS

232 BASIC BROTHS

SOUP BASICS

SEVEN TIPS FOR SUCCESSFUL SOUP MAKING

To make sure that every spoonful of soup is richly flavored, with juicy meat and/or tender vegetables, follow these kitchen-tested tips.

1. Use a sturdy pot
It is worth investing in a heavy pot with a thick bottom to use for making soup. It will transfer heat evenly and prevent scorching, which can impart a burnt flavor to your soup. See our favorite Dutch oven on page 10.

2. Sauté the aromatics
The first step in making many soups is to sauté aromatic vegetables such as onions and garlic. Sautéing not only softens their texture so that there is no unwelcome crunch in the soup but also tames any harsh flavors and develops more-complex flavors in the process. Medium heat is usually a good temperature for sautéing.

3. Start with good broth
A soup tastes like what you put into it. In minimally seasoned soups where the broth takes center stage, we almost always use homemade (see pages 232–234). However, in most cases, good store-bought broth is a fine and convenient option. Differences among packaged broths are significant—see Store-Bought Broths 101.

4. Cut vegetables to the right size
Most soups call for chunks of vegetables. Haphazardly cut vegetables will cook unevenly—some pieces will be underdone and crunchy while others will be mushy. Cutting the vegetables to the size specified ensures that all the pieces will be perfectly cooked.

5. Stagger the addition of vegetables
When a soup contains a variety of vegetables, their addition to the pot must often be staggered to account for their varying cooking times. Dense vegetables such as potatoes and winter squash can withstand much more cooking than delicate asparagus or spinach.

6. Keep liquid at a simmer
The fine line between simmering and boiling makes a big difference. A simmer is a restrained boil; fewer bubbles break the surface, and they do so with less vigor. Simmering heats food more gently and more evenly; boiling causes vegetables such as potatoes to break apart or fray at the edges, and it can toughen meat, too.

7. Season just before serving
The saltiness of the broth and other ingredients, such as canned tomatoes and canned beans, can vary greatly, so it's always best to taste and adjust the seasoning (salt as well as pepper, delicate herbs, and fresh citrus) just before ladling the soup into bowls for serving.

STORE-BOUGHT BROTHS 101

Store-bought broths can vary widely in flavor and quality, so it's important to choose wisely.

Chicken broth

We most often reach for chicken broth (even for some vegetable soups and meat soups) because of its strong savory flavor. Look for broth with less than 700 milligrams of sodium per serving (the saltiness will increase as the broth simmers and evaporates). Our favorite is **Swanson Chicken Stock**. We also recommend a chicken broth concentrate, **Better Than Bouillon Chicken Base**.

Vegetarian broth

Because commercial vegetable broths tend to be sweet, we sometimes mix vegetable broth with chicken broth for the best flavor. In fact, our favorite vegetarian broth, **Orrington Farms Vegan Chicken Flavored Broth Base & Seasoning**, has a savory flavor reminiscent of chicken broth. That said, we highly recommend making your own Vegetable Broth Base (page 234) and storing it in the freezer to use as needed.

Beef broth

Beef broths can be short on beefy flavor, which is why we often combine beef and chicken broths in our soups. But with the right additions, a beef broth can pull off a deeply flavored beef soup. Since manufacturers put little actual beef in their broths, we focus on savoriness rather than beef flavor. We recommend **Better Than Bouillon Roasted Beef Base**, an economical concentrate that stores easily and dissolves quickly in hot water.

STORING AND REHEATING SOUP

Don't Refrigerate Hot Soups

As tempting as it might seem, transferring hot soup straight to the refrigerator can increase the fridge's internal temperature to unsafe levels for all the other food stored there. Letting soup cool for just 1 hour drops its temperature to about 85 degrees, at which point it can be safely refrigerated.

Quick-Cooling Soups

Divide hot soup into smaller containers to cool faster. Or fill a large cooler or the sink with cold water and ice packs. Place the pot of soup in the cooler or sink until the soup registers 85 degrees, 30 to 45 minutes, stirring occasionally to speed up chilling. Refill the cooler or sink with cold water if necessary.

Reheating Soup

Reheat large amounts of soup in a heavy pot on the stovetop. Bring the soup to a rolling boil and stir often to ensure that the entire pot reaches the boiling point. If you use the microwave, avoid reheating in the same container used to refrigerate or freeze the soup. Instead, transfer the soup to a microwave-safe dish that's somewhat larger than the storage container. Just be sure to cover the dish to prevent a mess. Stop the microwave and stir the soup several times to ensure that it reheats evenly.

THREE TIPS FOR FREEZING SOUPS

1. Save space

Leaving some room at the top of a soup-filled container prevents the lid from popping off, since liquids expand when frozen.

2. Don't freeze dairy or noodles

They'll curdle or turn mushy. Make your soup without them; after thawing the soup and reheating it on the stove, stir in uncooked pasta and simmer until the pasta is tender or stir in dairy and heat it through (do not let it boil).

3. Thaw slowly

For safety reasons, thaw soups in the refrigerator for 24 to 48 hours. (If you've forgotten to plan ahead, you can heat frozen soups on the stovetop or in the microwave, but the texture of the meat and vegetables will suffer a bit.)

2 DAYS — Refrigerate delicate soups, including vegetable or brothy soups

1 MONTH — Freeze broths and soups

1 HOUR ON THE COUNTERTOP — Let hot soups cool before refrigerating

COURSE
CHICKEN SOUPS

BRIDGET LANCASTER

They say it's good for the soul and a cure for what ails you. In any case chicken soup is definitely comfort food in a bowl. In this course you'll learn to prepare chicken noodle soup from scratch with a method that yields both flavorful broth and tender meat without hours-long simmering. Chicken soup is beloved the world over, and you'll find a variety of flavors and accompaniments, from vegetables to beans to fragrant lemongrass to cheesy dumplings. You'll also learn ways to give your soup robust flavor whether you start with homemade broth or not.

BRIDGET'S PRO TIP: *After straining soup, you can cool the broth down and move it to the fridge. The next day, you'll see a hard layer of fat on top of the broth. It's then easy to remove the fat; be sure to save the fat as it's incredibly flavorful. Use it to sauté vegetables for the soup or store it in the fridge to use later.*

CHICKEN NOODLE SOUP

Serves: 8 to 10
Total Time: 2 hours

RECIPE OVERVIEW Chicken noodle soup from a can tastes nothing like soup you make yourself. This version gives you a rich broth and flavorful pieces of meat. Using a mix of thighs and breasts rather than a whole chicken means that you can cook the thighs for longer to extract flavor and gelatin without overcooking the breasts, which we later poach in the broth. Since many people prefer white meat in chicken noodle soup, this recipes utilizes the breast meat and saves the thigh meat as a bonus for salads or sandwiches. But you can also omit the chicken breasts and use the shredded thigh meat if you prefer. After browning the thighs, which leaves flavorful browned bits called fond in the pot, we remove the skin to minimize greasiness in the broth.

Broth
- 12 (5- to 7-ounce) bone-in chicken thighs, trimmed
- 1 teaspoon plus 1 tablespoon table salt, divided
- ½ teaspoon pepper
- 1 tablespoon vegetable oil
- 1 onion, chopped
- 12 cups water
- 2 bay leaves
- 2 (8-ounce) boneless, skinless chicken breasts, trimmed

Soup
- 1 tablespoon vegetable oil
- 1 onion, chopped fine
- 1 carrot, peeled and sliced thin
- 1 celery rib, halved lengthwise and sliced thin
- 2 teaspoons minced fresh thyme
- 6 ounces wide egg noodles
- ¼ cup minced fresh parsley

1. FOR THE BROTH Pat thighs dry with paper towels and sprinkle with 1 teaspoon salt and pepper. Heat oil in Dutch oven over medium-high heat until just smoking. Cook half of thighs skin side down until deep golden brown, about 6 minutes. Flip thighs and lightly brown second side, about 2 minutes. Transfer to fine-mesh strainer set in large bowl. Repeat with remaining thighs and transfer to strainer; discard fat in bowl. Pour off fat from pot; add onion; and cook over medium heat until just softened, about 3 minutes. Meanwhile, remove and discard skin from thighs. Add thighs, water, bay leaves, and remaining 1 tablespoon salt to pot. Cover and simmer for 30 minutes. Add breasts and continue to simmer until broth is rich and flavorful, about 15 minutes.

2. Strain broth through fine-mesh strainer into large container, let stand for at least 10 minutes, then remove fat from surface. Meanwhile, transfer chicken to cutting board, let cool slightly, then shred into bite-size pieces using 2 forks; discard skin and bones. Reserve thigh meat for another use. (Thigh meat can be refrigerated for up to 2 days or frozen for up to 1 month.) Reserve breast meat for soup.

CORE TECHNIQUE
Preparing Chicken Thighs for Soup

BROWN THIGHS
This creates a layer of flavorful brown fond in the bottom of the pot; the more fond that forms, the more flavorful the soup.

REMOVE SKIN
After browning the skin, remove it to avoid a greasy broth. Use a paper towel to help grip the skin firmly.

SHRED MEAT
Hold a fork in each hand, with the tines facing down. Insert the tines into the cooked meat and gently pull the forks away from each other.

SKIM FAT
If you don't want to wait for the broth to cool, a tall, narrow vessel makes it easier to remove fat with a deep spoon.

3. FOR THE SOUP Heat oil in now-empty pot over medium-high heat until shimmering. Add onion, carrot, and celery and cook until onion has softened, 3 to 4 minutes. Stir in thyme and broth and simmer until vegetables are tender, about 15 minutes. Add noodles and breast meat and simmer until noodles are just tender, about 5 minutes. Off heat, stir in parsley and season with salt and pepper to taste. Serve.

KEYS TO SUCCESS
- **Cook the thighs longer:** Thighs create a flavorful broth; breasts provide meat for the soup.
- **Brown the thighs:** To build fond for a deeply flavored broth before discarding the skin
- **Sauté the vegetables:** Gives the soup more flavor than raw vegetables would
- **Let the broth stand for 10 minutes:** Allows the fat to rise for easy skimming

CALDO TLALPEÑO

Serves: 6 to 8
Total Time: 1½ hours

RECIPE OVERVIEW This smoky, spicy Mexican soup is laden with tender pieces of chicken, meaty chickpeas, and bites of zucchini in a rich, chipotle-seasoned broth. Whether you start with homemade broth or store-bought, you build a potent base by browning bone-in, skin-on chicken breasts to render some fat and develop fond in the pot. After the chicken is removed, aromatic vegetables and chipotle soften in the rendered fat, and a sprinkle of flour adds body. Whisking in chicken broth produces a rich, deeply flavored broth with great substance. Traditional recipes call for epazote; we approximate its herbal flavor with a mix of fresh cilantro and oregano. Vegetable additions to this soup vary. We add zucchini, along with the chickpeas, for a fresh counterpoint to the rich broth. We return the shredded chicken to the soup a few minutes before serving so that it won't overcook. Serve with lime wedges, diced avocado, queso fresco, and/or sliced radishes.

- 1½ pounds bone-in split chicken breasts, trimmed
- ½ teaspoon table salt
- ¼ teaspoon pepper
- 1 tablespoon vegetable oil
- 2 onions, chopped fine
- 2 carrots, peeled and sliced ½ inch thick
- 5 garlic cloves, minced
- 2 teaspoons minced canned chipotle chile in adobo sauce
- 1½ teaspoons minced fresh thyme or ½ teaspoon dried
- 2 tablespoons all-purpose flour
- 8 cups chicken broth
- 2 zucchini, cut into ½-inch pieces
- 1 (15-ounce) can chickpeas, rinsed
- 3 tablespoons minced fresh cilantro
- 1 teaspoon minced fresh oregano

1. Pat chicken dry with paper towels and sprinkle with salt and pepper. Heat oil in Dutch oven over medium-high heat until just smoking. Brown chicken lightly, 2 to 3 minutes per side; transfer to plate.

2. Add onions and carrots to fat left in pot and cook over medium heat until softened and lightly browned, 8 to 10 minutes. Stir in garlic, chipotle, and thyme and cook until fragrant, about 30 seconds. Stir in flour and cook for 1 minute. Slowly whisk in broth, scraping up any browned bits and smoothing out any lumps, and bring to simmer.

3. Return chicken along with any accumulated juices to pot; reduce heat to low; cover; and simmer gently until chicken registers 160 degrees, 15 to 20 minutes.

4. Transfer chicken to cutting board and let cool slightly. Using 2 forks, shred chicken into bite-size pieces; discard skin and bones. Meanwhile, stir zucchini and chickpeas into soup and simmer until zucchini is just tender, 5 to 10 minutes.

5. Stir chicken into soup and simmer until heated through, about 2 minutes. Off heat, stir in cilantro and oregano and season with salt and pepper to taste. Serve.

KEYS TO SUCCESS

- **Brown the chicken first:** To build a base for a richly flavored broth and to render flavorful fat
- **Use bone-in breasts:** The bones flavor the soup and protect the meat from overcooking.

Storing Chipotle Chiles in Adobo

Chipotle chiles (smoked and dried jalapeños) often come packed in tomato-based adobo sauce. That's convenient, but we don't always use a full can at once. So we like to freeze the remainder in individual portions: We spoon out each chile along with a couple teaspoons of sauce onto different areas of a baking sheet lined with parchment paper and freeze them. Then we transfer the frozen chile mounds to a zipper-lock freezer bag for storage.

TOM KHA GAI

Serves: 6
Total Time: 1 hour

RECIPE OVERVIEW Restorative and indulgent, this Thai chicken soup balances hot and sour notes with rich coconut milk. Red curry paste—although not a traditional addition—contains many of the soup's signature aromatic ingredients, such as galangal, makrut lime leaves, and bird chiles. So we stir in a spoonful to deliver these fragrant flavors in concentrated form, adding it at the end of cooking. Then fresh lemongrass, shallots, and cilantro are simmered briefly to release their flavors and are strained out. Although we prefer the deeper, richer flavor of regular coconut milk, light coconut milk can be substituted for one or both cans. For a spicier soup, add more red curry paste to taste.

- 1 teaspoon vegetable oil
- 3 lemongrass stalks, trimmed to bottom 6 inches, sliced thin
- 3 large shallots, chopped coarse
- 8 sprigs fresh cilantro, chopped, plus leaves for serving
- 3 tablespoons fish sauce, divided
- 4 cups chicken broth
- 2 (14-ounce) cans coconut milk, divided
- 1 tablespoon sugar
- 8 ounces white mushrooms, trimmed and sliced thin
- 1 pound boneless, skinless chicken breasts, trimmed, halved lengthwise, and sliced ¼ inch thick
- 3 tablespoons lime juice (2 limes), plus lime wedges for serving
- 2 teaspoons Thai red curry paste
- 2 Thai, serrano, or jalapeño chiles, stemmed and sliced thin
- 2 scallions, sliced thin on bias

1. Heat oil in large saucepan over medium heat until shimmering. Add lemongrass, shallots, cilantro sprigs, and 1 tablespoon fish sauce and cook, stirring often, until just softened but not browned, 2 to 5 minutes.

2. Stir in broth and 1 can of coconut milk and bring to simmer. Cover; reduce heat to maintain gentle simmer; and cook until flavors have blended, about 10 minutes. Strain broth through fine-mesh strainer; discards solids. (Broth can be refrigerated for up to 24 hours.)

3. Return broth to clean saucepan, stir in sugar and remaining can of coconut milk, and bring to simmer. Stir in mushrooms and cook until just tender, 2 to 3 minutes. Stir in chicken and cook until no longer pink, 1 to 3 minutes.

4. Remove saucepan from heat. Whisk lime juice, curry paste, and remaining 2 tablespoons fish sauce together in bowl to dissolve paste, then stir mixture into soup. Ladle into bowls and sprinkle with cilantro leaves, Thai chiles, and scallions. Serve with lime wedges.

KEYS TO SUCCESS

- **Freeze the chicken for 15 minutes**: Makes it easier to slice
- **Fish sauce and sugar**: Balance the hot and sour flavors
- **Add the curry paste late**: To allow the sharpness, fragrance, and bright heat to come through rather than mellow out

CORE TECHNIQUE

Preparing Lemongrass

TRIM STALK
Cut away the upper portion, reserving the bottom 6 inches. Then trim away the tough, dry outer layers.

SLICE OR SMASH
To release the aroma, slice the lemongrass or smash with a meat pounder as the recipe directs.

CHICKEN SOUP WITH PARMESAN DUMPLINGS

Serves: 4 to 6
Total Time: 2 hours

RECIPE OVERVIEW Inspired by the Italian pasta called passatelli, this soup features tender bread crumb dumplings deeply flavored with Parmesan. The dumplings are undoubtedly the star of this soup. We make ours with panko, which produces consistently light and tender dumplings. The dough will appear too sticky to handle, but a 15-minute rest in the refrigerator allows the bread crumbs to hydrate more evenly and the dough to firm up enough to hold its shape. Passatelli are traditionally served in a light broth, but we make ours heartier with the addition of fennel, carrots, escarole, and shredded chicken.

- 1½ pounds bone-in chicken thighs, trimmed
- 1 teaspoon table salt, divided
- ½ teaspoon pepper, divided
- 1 teaspoon vegetable oil
- 1 fennel bulb, 1 tablespoon fronds minced, stalks discarded, bulb halved, cored, and cut into ½-inch pieces
- 1 onion, chopped fine
- 2 carrots, peeled and cut into ¾-inch pieces
- ½ cup dry white wine
- 8 cups chicken broth
- 1 Parmesan cheese rind, plus 3 ounces Parmesan, grated (1½ cups)
- ¾ cup panko bread crumbs
- 2 large egg whites
- 1 tablespoon water
- ¼ teaspoon grated lemon zest
  Pinch ground nutmeg
- ½ small head escarole (6 ounces), trimmed and cut into ½-inch pieces

1. Pat chicken dry with paper towels and sprinkle with ½ teaspoon salt and ¼ teaspoon pepper. Heat oil in Dutch oven over medium-high heat until just smoking. Add chicken, skin side down, and cook until well browned, 6 to 8 minutes; transfer to plate.

2. Pour off all but 1 teaspoon fat from pot and reserve 1 tablespoon fat for dumplings. Add fennel bulb, onion, carrots, and remaining ½ teaspoon salt to fat left in pot and cook over medium heat until softened and lightly browned, 5 to 7 minutes. Stir in wine, scraping up any browned bits, and cook until almost completely evaporated, about 2 minutes. Stir in broth and Parmesan rind and bring to simmer. Return chicken and any accumulated juices to pot. Reduce heat to low; cover; and cook until chicken registers 175 degrees, about 30 minutes.

3. Off heat, discard Parmesan rind. Transfer chicken to cutting board, let cool slightly, then shred into bite-size pieces using 2 forks; discard skin and bones. Cover broth to keep warm.

4. Meanwhile, mix grated Parmesan, panko, egg whites, water, lemon zest, nutmeg, reserved fat, and remaining ¼ teaspoon pepper in bowl until thoroughly combined. Refrigerate dough for 15 minutes. Pinch off and roll 1-teaspoon portions of dough into balls and arrange on rimmed baking sheet lined with parchment paper (you should have about 28 dumplings). (Soup, shredded chicken, and dumplings, prepared through step 4, can be refrigerated separately for up to 24 hours. To reheat, bring soup, covered, to gentle simmer, stirring often, and continue with step 5.)

5. Return broth to simmer over medium-high heat. Add escarole and chicken and return to simmer. Add dumplings and cook, adjusting heat to maintain gentle simmer, until dumplings float to surface and are cooked through, 3 to 5 minutes. Stir in fennel fronds and season with salt and pepper to taste. Serve.

KEYS TO SUCCESS

- **Brown the chicken thighs:** Leaves fond in the pot, which enriches the store-bought broth
- **Add a Parmesan rind:** Infuses the broth with cheesy, umami flavor
- **Chill the dough for 15 minutes:** Allows the panko to hydrate, making the dough less sticky

Shaping Dumplings

ROLL UNTIL SMOOTH
Pinch off and roll 1-teaspoon-size pieces of dough into balls. To ensure that the dumplings remain intact during cooking, roll them until the surfaces are smooth and no cracks remain.

SCIENCE LESSON Bread Crumbs

Turning bread crumbs into dough is a little like trying to extract soup from stones: On their own, they don't have what it takes. Because crumbs are already cooked, they don't have the ability of raw flour and water to form the gluten bonds that give dough its strong, pliable structure: The gluten is already set. So how do our passatelli stick together? We combine the crumbs with egg whites, which coagulate during cooking and form a network that holds the crumbs in place. At the same time, moisture from the whites hydrates the starches in the crumbs. This forms a sticky gel that acts as a glue.

COURSE
RUSTIC VEGETABLE SOUPS

KEITH DRESSER

A chunky vegetable soup warms you up on a cold day (or cools you on a hot night). These rustic soups are simple and forgiving, which is part of their appeal. Here you'll learn to create soups with layers of flavor and tips to ensure all those vegetables come out perfectly tender, not mushy or raw. It all boils down to knowing how to treat your vegetables. Do you dice them small or leave them in big chunks? Salt them to draw out water or even roast them to concentrate flavor? Grab your ladle and find out! You'll also discover ways to boost a soup's flavor with seasonings that don't cover up that vegetable goodness.

KEITH'S PRO TIP: *Give it time. Vegetable soups, like their meat-based counterparts, benefit from slow cooking in order to develop and meld flavors. So don't be tempted to skimp, as the result is often a flat-tasting soup.*

GAZPACHO

Serves: 8 to 10
Total Time: 30 minutes, plus 4 hours chilling

RECIPE OVERVIEW One of the simplest soups, gazpacho does not even require cooking. This chilled Spanish vegetable soup is fresh, light, and perfectly suited to eat the next day for lunch on a hot afternoon. Some recipes puree gazpacho, but here we chop the vegetables by hand, which allows them to retain their color and firm texture. Letting them sit in a sherry vinegar marinade seasons them thoroughly. We add tomato juice to boost the tomato flavor, and we stir in ice cubes, which chill the soup and provide the right amount of liquid as they melt. A 4-hour chill is critical to allow the flavors of the soup to develop and meld. Luckily, this means we can make the soup well in advance of a meal. Use a Vidalia, Maui, or Walla Walla onion here. This recipe makes enough for leftovers, but it can be halved, if you prefer. Serve in chilled bowls, if desired.

- 1½ pounds tomatoes, cored and cut into ¼-inch dice
- 2 red bell peppers, stemmed, seeded, and cut into ¼-inch dice
- 2 small cucumbers (1 peeled, 1 unpeeled), halved lengthwise, seeded, and cut into ¼-inch dice
- ½ small sweet onion or 2 large shallots, chopped fine
- ⅓ cup sherry vinegar
- 2 garlic cloves, minced
- 2 teaspoons table salt
- 5 cups tomato juice
- 8 ice cubes
- 1 teaspoon hot sauce (optional)
- Extra-virgin olive oil

1. Combine tomatoes, bell peppers, cucumbers, onion, vinegar, garlic, and salt in large (at least 4-quart) bowl and season with pepper to taste. Let sit until vegetables just begin to release their juices, about 5 minutes. Stir in tomato juice; ice cubes; and hot sauce, if using. Cover and refrigerate until flavors meld, at least 4 hours or up to 2 days.

2. Discard any unmelted ice cubes and season soup with salt and pepper to taste. Divide among individual bowls, drizzling individual portions with oil. Serve cold.

KEYS TO SUCCESS

- **Cut the vegetables into small pieces:** Helps the flavors mingle and provides optimal texture
- **Marinate the vegetables:** To season them and draw out liquid so that the vegetal flavor permeates the soup
- **Chill the soup:** For at least 4 hours, so the flavors heighten and meld

CORE TECHNIQUE
Dicing Vegetables for Gazpacho

DICE TOMATOES
Cut each tomato in half from top to bottom through the stem end. Use the tip of a knife to cut out the core from each half. Slice each tomato half into ¼-inch strips, and then cut the strips crosswise into ¼-inch pieces.

DICE BELL PEPPERS
Slice off the top and bottom of each bell pepper; remove the seeds, stems, and ribs. Slice each pepper in half and press so that the halves lay flat on the cutting board. Slice into ¼-inch strips, and then cut the strips crosswise into ¼-inch pieces.

DICE CUCUMBERS
Halve each cucumber lengthwise, scrape out the seeds, and then cut each half into ¼-inch strips. Cut the strips crosswise into ¼-inch pieces.

Gazpacho Garnishes

Gazpacho is often garnished with more of the diced vegetables used in the soup. To keep with tradition, cut some extra vegetables when preparing those in the recipe to serve as a garnish. We also like to serve gazpacho topped with Homemade Croutons (page 161), chopped pitted black olives, chopped Easy-Peel Hard-Cooked Eggs (page 65), and finely diced avocado.

SOUPE AU PISTOU

Serves: 6
Total Time: 55 minutes

RECIPE OVERVIEW Chock-full of vegetables, creamy white beans, and fragrant herbs, Provençal soup au pistou is a celebration of the produce that returns to the markets in early summer. Various vegetables can be used, but we like the flavors and shades of green provided by leeks, green beans, and zucchini. Adding the bean liquid contributes body and a flavor that evokes long-simmered versions. This soup is served with a dollop of pistou, France's answer to pesto. If you cannot find haricots verts (thin green beans), substitute regular green beans and cook them for an extra minute or two. You can substitute small shells or ditalini for the orecchiette (the cooking times may vary slightly). Serve with Herbed Croutons (page 161) or crusty bread.

Pistou
- ¾ cup fresh basil leaves
- 1 ounce Parmesan cheese, grated (½ cup)
- ⅓ cup extra-virgin olive oil
- 1 garlic clove, minced

Soup
- 1 tablespoon extra-virgin olive oil
- 1 leek, white and light green parts only, halved lengthwise, sliced ½ inch thick, and washed thoroughly
- 1 celery rib, cut into ½-inch pieces
- 1 carrot, peeled and sliced ¼ inch thick
- ½ teaspoon table salt
- 2 garlic cloves, minced
- 3 cups vegetable broth
- 3 cups water
- ½ cup orecchiette or other short pasta
- 8 ounces haricots verts, trimmed and cut into ½-inch lengths
- 1 (15-ounce) can cannellini or navy beans, undrained
- 1 small zucchini, halved lengthwise, seeded, and cut into ¼-inch pieces
- 1 large tomato, cored, seeded, and cut into ¼-inch pieces

1. FOR THE PISTOU Process all ingredients in food processor until smooth, scraping down sides of bowl as needed, about 15 seconds. (Pistou can be refrigerated for up to 4 hours.)

2. FOR THE SOUP Heat oil in Dutch oven over medium heat until shimmering. Add leek, celery, carrot, and salt and cook until vegetables are softened, 8 to 10 minutes. Stir in garlic and cook until fragrant, about 30 seconds. Stir in broth and water and bring to simmer.

3. Stir in pasta and simmer until slightly softened, about 5 minutes. Stir in haricots verts and simmer until bright green but still crunchy, 3 to 5 minutes. Stir in beans and their liquid, zucchini, and tomato and simmer until pasta and vegetables are tender, about 3 minutes. Season with salt and pepper to taste. Serve, topping individual portions with generous tablespoon of pistou.

KEYS TO SUCCESS

- **Add the pistou just before serving:** Transforms the soup with a blast of freshness
- **Use the canned bean liquid:** Key to the soup's texture
- **Cut the broth with water:** For a well-rounded, flavorful base
- **Seed the zucchini:** Gently scrape out the seeds using a spoon; see page 42.
- **For more info on cleaning leeks, see page 44.**

HEARTY CABBAGE SOUP

Serves: 6 to 8
Total Time: 1¼ hours

RECIPE OVERVIEW The combination of assertive aromatics and fresh herbs gives cabbage and potatoes an unexpected star quality in this satisfying soup. Many cabbage soups rely on smoky bacon for backbone. For a vegetarian soup, we use smoked hot paprika to maintain a hint of smokiness. We also add caraway seeds, which bring out the sweetness of the cabbage, and finish with fresh dill and a dollop of sour cream for a tangy counterpoint. You can substitute smoked paprika and a pinch of cayenne for the smoked hot paprika.

- 3 tablespoons unsalted butter
- 1 onion, chopped fine
- 1 teaspoon table salt
- 4 garlic cloves, minced
- 1 teaspoon caraway seeds
- 1 teaspoon minced fresh thyme or ¼ teaspoon dried
- ½ teaspoon smoked hot paprika
- ¼ cup dry white wine
- 6 cups vegetable broth
- 1 small head green cabbage (1¼ pounds), halved, cored, and cut into ¾-inch pieces
- 12 ounces red potatoes, unpeeled, cut into ¾-inch pieces
- 3 carrots, peeled and cut into ½-inch pieces
- 1 bay leaf
- 1 tablespoon minced fresh dill
- 1 cup sour cream

1. Melt butter in Dutch oven over medium heat. Stir in onion and salt and cook until softened, 5 to 7 minutes. Stir in garlic, caraway seeds, thyme, and paprika and cook until fragrant, about 30 seconds.

2. Stir in wine, scraping up any browned bits, and simmer until nearly evaporated, about 1 minute. Stir in broth, cabbage, potatoes, carrots, and bay leaf and bring to boil. Cover; reduce heat to maintain gentle simmer; and cook until vegetables are tender, about 30 minutes.

3. Discard bay leaf. Season with salt and pepper to taste and sprinkle with dill. Top individual portions with sour cream and serve.

WILD RICE AND MUSHROOM SOUP

Serves: 6 to 8
Total Time: 2½ hours

RECIPE OVERVIEW Earthy, creamy, and bursting with mushroom flavor, this soup belies the simplicity of its humble ingredients. This recipe is a lesson in building a savory flavor base without relying on meat. We employ a variety of potent boosters—tomato paste, soy sauce, dry sherry, and plenty of garlic—to amplify the flavor of the mushrooms. Cooking our mushrooms and onion with tomato paste over high heat develops a fond that gives the soup depth. And dried shiitakes—another umami booster—deliver another dose of mushroom flavor. As for the wild rice, we cook that separately in the oven, adding a pinch of baking soda to help it tenderize faster. And we reserve the earthy rice cooking liquid to add even more flavor to our soup. White mushrooms can be substituted for the cremini mushrooms. We use a spice grinder to process the dried shiitake mushrooms, but a blender also works.

4¼	cups water, divided
1	sprig fresh thyme
1	bay leaf
5	garlic cloves, peeled (1 whole, 4 minced)
1½	teaspoons table salt, divided
¼	teaspoon baking soda
1	cup wild rice
4	tablespoons unsalted butter
1	pound cremini mushrooms, trimmed and sliced ¼ inch thick
1	onion, chopped fine
1	teaspoon tomato paste
1	teaspoon pepper
⅔	cup dry sherry
4	cups chicken or vegetable broth
1	tablespoon soy sauce
¼	ounce dried shiitake mushrooms, ground fine using spice grinder
¼	cup cornstarch
½	cup heavy cream
¼	cup minced fresh chives
¼	teaspoon grated lemon zest

1. Adjust oven rack to middle position and heat oven to 375 degrees. Bring 4 cups water, thyme sprig, bay leaf, whole garlic clove, ¾ teaspoon salt, and baking soda to boil in medium ovensafe saucepan over high heat. Add rice and return to boil. Cover saucepan; transfer to oven; and bake until rice is tender, 35 to 50 minutes. Drain rice in fine-mesh strainer set in 4-cup liquid measuring cup, discarding thyme sprig, bay leaf, and garlic. Add enough water to reserved cooking liquid to measure 3 cups.

2. Melt butter in Dutch oven over high heat. Add cremini mushrooms, onion, tomato paste, pepper, minced garlic, and remaining ¾ teaspoon salt. Cook, stirring occasionally, until vegetables are browned and dark fond develops on bottom of pot, about 15 minutes.

3. Stir in sherry, scraping up any browned bits, and cook until nearly evaporated, about 2 minutes. Stir in broth, soy sauce, shiitake mushrooms, and reserved rice cooking liquid and bring to boil. Reduce heat to low; cover; and simmer until onion and mushrooms are tender, about 20 minutes.

4. Whisk cornstarch and remaining ¼ cup water together in bowl. Stir cornstarch slurry into soup and simmer until thickened, about 2 minutes. Off heat, stir in rice, cream, chives, and lemon zest. Cover and let stand for 20 minutes. Season with salt and pepper to taste, and serve.

KEYS TO SUCCESS

- **Go big on flavor boosters:** To create complexity without meat
- **Double up on the mushrooms:** Dried shiitakes enhance the flavor of fresh cremini
- **Let the tomato paste darken:** Builds flavor as it caramelizes on the bottom of the pot
- **Save the wild rice cooking liquid:** Adds earthy flavor to the soup

Grinding Dried Mushrooms

USE SPICE GRINDER
Place the dried mushrooms in a spice grinder and grind them into a powder. This ensures that their flavor permeates the broth.

ROASTED EGGPLANT AND KALE SOUP

Serves: 4
Total Time: 45 minutes

RECIPE OVERVIEW Eggplant is rich, meaty, and hearty—perfect for a vegetarian soup. This vegetable soup is unusual in that the eggplant does not simmer in liquid but instead gets pan-roasted, cooked in a hot Dutch oven until its flavors have concentrated and become slightly smoky. We then set the eggplant aside to build our soup base, which is little more than a potent mix of spices and garlic bloomed in oil and simmered with vegetable broth until the flavors meld. We add back the eggplant off the heat along with baby kale for some freshness. The garnishes complete this simple, rustic soup: Sliced almonds, fresh cilantro, and the pleasant tang of Greek yogurt make for a rich, nuanced topping. Finally, a sprinkle of Aleppo pepper adds a pop of bright-red color and contrasting heat. If you can't find Aleppo pepper, you can substitute ½ teaspoon of paprika mixed with ¼ teaspoon of minced red pepper flakes.

- 6 tablespoons extra-virgin olive oil, divided
- 1¼ pounds eggplant, cut into ½-inch pieces
- 2 garlic cloves, minced
- 1½ teaspoons ground coriander
- 1½ teaspoons ground cumin
- 1 teaspoon grated fresh ginger
- ¾ teaspoon ground dried Aleppo pepper, divided
- ½ teaspoon table salt
- ¼ teaspoon pepper
- ¼ teaspoon ground cinnamon
- 3 cups vegetable broth
- 1½ cups water
- 2 ounces (2 cups) baby kale, chopped coarse
- ½ cup plain whole-milk Greek yogurt
- 2 tablespoons sliced almonds, toasted
- 2 tablespoons minced fresh cilantro

1. Heat ¼ cup oil in Dutch oven over medium-high heat until just smoking. Add eggplant and cook, stirring occasionally, until tender and deeply browned, 6 to 8 minutes; transfer to bowl.

2. Combine garlic, coriander, cumin, ginger, ½ teaspoon Aleppo pepper, salt, pepper, and cinnamon in small bowl. Add remaining 2 tablespoons oil and garlic mixture to now-empty pot and cook over medium heat until fragrant, about 30 seconds. Stir in broth and water, scraping up any browned bits, and bring to simmer. Reduce heat to medium-low; cover partially; and cook until flavors meld, about 15 minutes.

3. Off heat, stir in kale and eggplant along with any accumulated juices. Let sit until wilted, about 2 minutes. Season with salt and pepper to taste. Dollop each portion with 2 tablespoons yogurt and sprinkle evenly with almonds, cilantro, and remaining ¼ teaspoon Aleppo pepper before serving. (Soup can be refrigerated for up to 3 days. To reheat, bring to gentle simmer in saucepan or microwave in bowl until steaming.)

KEYS TO SUCCESS

- **Pan-roast the eggplant:** For a nice caramelized flavor and to keep the eggplant from becoming mushy
- **Take advantage of garnishes:** Essential to creating a soup with a mix of textures and flavors

THE IMPROVISATIONAL SOUP POT

Soup has long been a resourceful way to use up bits of leftovers—the end of a head of cabbage, a single potato, some cooked chicken. And while soup making is flexible, a few guideposts ensure that flavors stay balanced and ingredients cook properly. Follow along with each step to create a soup using whatever ingredients you have on hand. Each ingredient category lists suggestions, with cooking instructions at the bottom of each column so that you can turn past-their-prime vegetables into a comforting, hearty soup that serves 4.

1. START WITH . . .

2 teaspoons oil

+

2 ounces mushrooms, trimmed and chopped fine (optional)

white, portobello caps, or shiitakes

+

2 ounces pork, chopped fine (optional)

bacon, chorizo, pancetta, salt pork, or sausage

+

6 tablespoons minced hardy aromatics

shallot, onion, leek whites, scallion whites, celery, fennel, sweet or hot peppers

> Cook in Dutch oven over medium-low heat until vegetables have softened and pork, if using, is lightly browned, about 5 minutes.

2. BUILD YOUR BASE WITH . . .

4 teaspoons minced garlic

+

2 teaspoons minced fresh hardy herb or ½ teaspoon dried

thyme, herbes de Provence, marjoram, oregano, rosemary, or sage

+

1 teaspoon umami booster (optional)

anchovy paste or tomato paste

> Add to Dutch oven and cook until fragrant, about 30 seconds.

3. GIVE IT BODY WITH . . .

6 cups chicken or vegetable broth

+

1 pound root vegetable, cut into ½-inch pieces

carrot, eggplant, parsnip, sweet potato, potato, or winter squash

+

1 flavor infuser

2 strips citrus zest, 2 lemongrass stalks (bruised), 4 slices fresh ginger, 2 tablespoons miso, 2 tablespoons soy sauce, 2 tablespoons fish sauce, ¼ cup Thai red or green curry paste, Parmesan cheese rind, or 2 bay leaves

+

¼ teaspoon table salt

> Stir into base mixture, scraping up any browned bits. Bring to simmer and cook until vegetable is tender, about 10 minutes.

4. MAKE IT HEARTY WITH . . .

1 pound fresh vegetable, cut into 1-inch pieces

green beans, asparagus, bok choy, broccoli, brussels sprouts, cabbage, cauliflower, sturdy greens (collard greens, kale, mustard greens, and/or Swiss chard), snap peas, or summer squash

> Stir into soup and cook until just tender, 3 to 7 minutes.

5. FINISH THE FLAVOR WITH . . .

½ cup chopped quick-cooking vegetable

frozen peas, artichoke hearts, bamboo shoots, canned beans, fresh or frozen corn, edamame, tender greens (arugula, baby kale, spinach, and/or watercress), roasted red peppers, fresh or sun-dried tomatoes, or water chestnuts

+

2 tablespoons minced fresh herb

parsley, cilantro, tarragon, basil, scallions, chives, or dill

> Stir into soup; remove Dutch oven from heat; and let sit until warmed through, about 1 minute.

6. LEVEL UP AND ADD A . . .

brightener

lemon or lime wedges, capers, olives, pickles, or vinegar

+

garnish (optional)

croutons, crackers, tortilla chips, garlic chips, kale chips, crumbled nori sheets, toasted nuts or seeds, Parmesan crisps, or radishes

> Season soup with salt and pepper to taste. Finish with brightener and garnish, if using. Serve.

VEGETABLES TO AVOID

While this soup can be customized in countless ways, there are a few vegetables whose flavors are so intense that they can disrupt a soup's delicate balance, so we prefer to leave them out: beets, broccoli rabe, and chicories (endive, frisée, and radicchio).

ADDING FLAVOR TO SOUP

The test kitchen uses some key ingredients over and over again in our soup recipes. Here are some of our favorite ways to impart flavor to a pot of soup and repurpose leftovers in the process.

Bacon Uncooked bacon and other cured meats such as pancetta, ham, or Spanish-style chorizo add smoky flavor to many soups, such as Pasta e Piselli (page 225) and Caldo Verde (page 228). Brown them early in the cooking process in order to render fat in which to cook aromatics for another layer of flavor. You can leave them in the pot to simmer and infuse the soup, or you can remove larger pieces once crisped to stir back in or use as a garnish.

To freeze bacon: If you have a partial package of bacon, you can freeze individual slices for later use with virtually no noticeable change in quality. Coil up each slice individually (to prevent sticking and to minimize freezer burn), freeze on a plate, and then transfer to a zipper-lock freezer bag.

HOT TIP: SAVE THAT SCHMALTZ

The flavorful fat you skim off chicken broth can be saved for another use, such as sautéing aromatics, roasting root vegetables, and frying eggs. Store it in an airtight container in the refrigerator for up to one month or in the freezer for up to six months, adding more fat as desired.

Parmesan cheese In the test kitchen we save Parmesan rinds to add depth to soups such as Chicken Soup with Parmesan Dumplings (page 204) and Chickpea and Escarole Soup (page 223). If you don't have a Parmesan rind, the rinds from Pecorino Romano and Gruyère add comparable savory flavor. When you can no longer grate any cheese off the rind, store the rind in a zipper-lock bag in the freezer; cheese rinds will keep indefinitely (no need to thaw them before using).

Spices Ground spices or dried chiles add complexity in soups such as Spicy Pinto Bean Soup (page 222) and Sharba (page 231). It's important to bloom these spices in hot oil or fat for just 30 seconds rather then sprinkle them directly into soup. Why? Blooming changes fat-soluble flavor molecules in spices from a solid state to liquid, unlocking their dormant potential and heightening their complexity. Make sure that the fat isn't too hot, as it can scorch the spices.

Spices to sprinkle: Not all spices need to be bloomed to start. We also finish soups with a sprinkle of spice or a blend of spices to add both flavor and color. Our favorites include Aleppo pepper for complex heat, sumac for citrusy tang, Shichimi Togarashi (page 29) for a balance of hot and savory with floral citrus, and of course freshly ground black pepper.

Fresh herbs We use fresh herbs more often than dried. We use chopped herbs such as parsley, cilantro, chives, mint, fennel fronds, or dill to deliver a big hit of fresh flavor to soup, whether we stir them into the pot at the end of cooking or sprinkle them over a bowlful to serve.

Herb ice cubes: If you freeze leftover herbs packed in water in ice cube trays, you can add the frozen cubes directly to soups for an instant flavor boost.

Soy sauce and tomato paste Two great sources of glutamates, these flavor powerhouse ingredients bring savory depth to vegetable and meaty soups alike. We use them to help establish a savory backbone for our Wild Rice and Mushroom Soup (page 210) and to help give our relatively quick-cooking Beef Broth (page 233) the multidimensional complexity that typically comes from many hours of simmering.

COURSE
PUREED VEGETABLE SOUPS

JACK BISHOP

A pureed vegetable soup should taste like the essence of the vegetable, but that's easily muted by too much butter and cream. In this course you'll learn to make silky-smooth purees that let the vegetable flavors shine: tomato soup that tastes like tomato, grassy-nutty cauliflower soup, earthy-sweet butternut squash soup, and a soup made with vegetal greens. Finally, we get creative with garnishes, so you can pull off pureed soup with panache.

JACK'S PRO TIP: *Smooth soups benefit from a garnish, even if it's just a drizzle of olive oil or a dollop of sour cream or yogurt. Want something more ambitious? Try toasted nuts, crispy croutons, or a drizzle of spiced butter.*

CREAMLESS CREAMY TOMATO SOUP
Serves: 6 to 8
Total Time: 45 minutes

RECIPE OVERVIEW This soup sings with tomato flavor that's not dulled by any dairy. Better yet, it uses canned tomatoes, which taste better than most out-of-season tomatoes, so it can be enjoyed any time (perhaps in the dead of winter alongside some grilled cheese). Finding that butter mutesd the tomato flavor, we instead use olive oil when sautéing the onion and garlic. A little brown sugar tones down the acidity, and a slice of white bread torn into pieces gives our tomato soup body without added cream. Make sure to purchase canned whole tomatoes packed in juice and not puree. If half the soup fills your blender by more than two-thirds, process the soup in three batches. You can also use an immersion blender to process the soup directly in the pot.

- ¼ cup extra-virgin olive oil, divided, plus extra for drizzling
- 1 onion, chopped
- 3 garlic cloves, minced
- 1 bay leaf
-   Pinch red pepper flakes
- 2 (28-ounce) cans whole peeled tomatoes
- 3 slices hearty white sandwich bread, crusts removed, torn into 1-inch pieces
- 1 tablespoon packed brown sugar
- 2 cups chicken broth
- 2 tablespoons brandy (optional)
- ¼ cup chopped fresh chives
- 1 recipe Homemade Croutons (page 161)

1. Heat 2 tablespoons oil in Dutch oven over medium-high heat until shimmering. Add onion, garlic, bay leaf, and pepper flakes. Cook, stirring frequently, until onion is translucent, 3 to 5 minutes.

2. Stir in tomatoes and their juice. Using potato masher, mash until no pieces bigger than 2 inches wide remain. Stir in bread and sugar. Bring soup to boil. Reduce heat to medium and cook, stirring occasionally, until bread is completely saturated and starts to break down, about 5 minutes. Discard bay leaf.

3. Transfer half of soup to blender. Add 1 tablespoon oil and process until soup is smooth and creamy, 2 to 3 minutes. Transfer to large bowl and repeat with remaining soup and remaining 1 tablespoon oil.

4. Rinse out pot and return soup to pot. Stir in broth and brandy, if using. Return soup to boil and season with salt and pepper to taste. Ladle soup into bowls, sprinkle with chives, top with croutons, and drizzle with extra oil. Serve.

KEYS TO SUCCESS

- **Whole canned tomatoes**: Made with perfectly ripe fresh tomatoes and contain no additives
- **Oil, not butter**: To brighten the fresh tomato flavor
- **Torn bread**: For body and a velvety texture without cream muting the tomatoes' bright, fresh flavor

Mashing Tomatoes

CRUSH BY HAND
We use a potato masher to effectively crush the tomatoes to thicken the soup.

SILKY BUTTERNUT SQUASH SOUP

Serves: 4 to 6
Total Time: 1¾ hours

RECIPE OVERVIEW The best pureed soups taste like the main ingredient. We get the most flavor out of butternut squash by saving the squash seeds and fibers and sautéing them with shallot; simmering that mixture in water; and steaming our squash, nestled in a steamer basket, directly above the liquid. When the squash is tender and cooled, we scoop the flesh from the skin and puree it with the strained steaming liquid for a perfectly smooth soup with big butternut squash flavor. Garnish the soup with freshly grated nutmeg, a drizzle of balsamic vinegar, a sprinkle of paprika, or Homemade Croutons (page 161).

1	(3-pound) butternut squash
4	tablespoons unsalted butter, divided
1	large shallot, minced
6	cups water, plus extra as needed
1	teaspoon table salt
½	cup heavy cream
1	teaspoon packed dark brown sugar
	Pinch ground nutmeg

1. Cut squash in half lengthwise. Scrape out and reserve seeds and stringy fibers. Cut each piece of squash in half crosswise.

2. Melt 2 tablespoons butter in Dutch oven over medium-low heat. Add shallot and cook, stirring frequently, until softened, 2 to 3 minutes. Add seeds and fibers from squash and cook, stirring occasionally, until butter turns reddish-orange color, about 4 minutes.

3. Add water and salt and bring to boil over high heat. Reduce heat to medium-low, place steamer basket in pot, and place squash cut side down in basket. Cover and steam until squash is completely tender, 30 to 40 minutes.

4. Using tongs, transfer squash to rimmed baking sheet. When cool enough to handle, use large spoon to scrape flesh from skin. Reserve squash flesh in bowl and discard skin.

5. Strain steaming liquid through fine-mesh strainer into large liquid measuring cup; discard solids in strainer. (You should have at least 3 cups liquid; add extra water as needed to equal 3 cups.) Rinse and dry pot.

6. Working in batches, puree squash in blender with 3 cups reserved liquid until smooth. Transfer puree to now-empty pot. Stir in cream, sugar, nutmeg, and remaining 2 tablespoons butter. Bring soup to simmer, adjusting consistency with additional reserved liquid or extra water as needed. Season with salt to taste, and serve. (Soup can be refrigerated for up to 2 days.)

KEYS TO SUCCESS

- **Weigh your squash**: Bigger than 3 pounds and you may need to thin the soup with water; smaller than 3 pounds and you may want to hold back some of the liquid when pureeing
- **Save the squash seeds and fibers**: Add flavor to the cooking liquid
- **Cook the squash until fully tender**: Ensures a smooth soup. A paring knife inserted into the thickest part of the largest piece of squash should meet no resistance.
- **Measure your water**: The steaming liquid becomes the broth for the soup; 6 cups is just enough for a 3-pound squash.

CREAMY CAULIFLOWER SOUP

Serves: 4 to 6
Total Time: 1 hour

RECIPE OVERVIEW Thanks to cauliflower's natural ability to turn into a lush puree without the addition of cream, this simple soup shines with the crucifer's multi-faceted flavors, offering an elegant starter that won't spoil your appetite. We simmer in two stages to unlock the grassy flavor of just-cooked cauliflower as well as the sweeter, nuttier taste of longer-cooked cauliflower. For a festive garnish, we brown butter and more florets to top off each serving. White wine vinegar can be substituted for the sherry vinegar. Be sure to thoroughly trim the cauliflower's core of green leaves and leaf stems, which can be fibrous and contribute to a grainy texture in the soup.

- 1 head cauliflower (2 pounds)
- 8 tablespoons unsalted butter, cut into 8 pieces, divided
- 1 leek, white and light green parts only, halved lengthwise, sliced thin, and washed thoroughly
- 1 small onion, halved and sliced thin
- 1½ teaspoons table salt
- 4½–5 cups water
- ½ teaspoon sherry vinegar
- 3 tablespoons minced fresh chives

1. Pull off outer leaves of cauliflower and trim stem. Using paring knife, cut around core to remove; slice core thin and set aside. Cut heaping 1 cup of ½-inch florets from head of cauliflower; set aside. Slice remaining cauliflower crosswise ½ inch thick.

2. Melt 3 tablespoons butter in large saucepan over medium-low heat. Add leek, onion, and salt; cook, stirring frequently, until leek and onion are softened but not browned, about 7 minutes.

3. Increase heat to medium-high; add 4½ cups water, reserved sliced core, and half of sliced cauliflower; and bring to simmer. Reduce heat to medium-low and simmer gently for 15 minutes. Add remaining sliced cauliflower; return to simmer; and continue to cook until cauliflower is tender and crumbles easily, 15 to 20 minutes.

4. While soup simmers, melt remaining 5 tablespoons butter in 8-inch skillet over medium heat. Add reserved florets and cook, stirring frequently, until florets are golden brown and butter is browned and has nutty aroma, 6 to 8 minutes. Off heat, use slotted spoon to transfer florets to small bowl. Toss florets with vinegar and season with salt to taste. Pour browned butter in skillet into small bowl.

5. Process soup in blender until smooth, about 45 seconds. Rinse out saucepan. Return soup to saucepan and return to simmer over medium heat, adjusting consistency with remaining water as needed (soup should have thick, velvety texture but should be thin enough to settle with flat surface after being stirred) and seasoning with salt to taste. Serve, garnishing individual bowls with chives, browned florets, and drizzle of browned butter and seasoning with pepper to taste.

KEYS TO SUCCESS

- **Use the core:** Adds even more flavor and reduces waste
- **Add the cauliflower in stages:** Brings out a spectrum of flavors, which change based on the cooking time
- **Go easy on the seasonings:** Prevents the seasonings from smothering the cauliflower's delicate flavor

Preparing Cauliflower for Soup

SLICE CAULIFLOWER After cutting off the florets for the garnish, cut the remaining cauliflower into ½-inch slices that will cook more evenly than florets in the soup.

SAUTÉ FLORETS FOR GARNISH Cook, stirring frequently, until the florets are golden brown and the butter is browned.

SCIENCE LESSON Flavor Chameleon

Cauliflower goes through complex flavor changes throughout the cooking process. In the beginning of cooking, volatile sulfur compounds that are responsible for cauliflower's "cabbagey" flavor are produced. As these compounds dissipate, fatty acids in the cauliflower oxidize to produce other compounds with a grassy aroma. Eventually, the vegetable takes on a nutty flavor caused by the formation of more-stable compounds. To bring a flavor spectrum to our cauliflower soup, we cook some of it long enough to achieve the nutty flavor and some just until it tastes grassy.

FLAVOR AFTER 15 MINUTES: GRASSY

FLAVOR AFTER 30 MINUTES: SWEET AND NUTTY

SUPER GREENS SOUP WITH LEMON-TARRAGON CREAM

Serves: 4 to 6
Total Time: 1½ hours

RECIPE OVERVIEW There's a big dose of healthy, hearty greens in this deceptively delicious, silky-smooth soup. First, we build a flavorful foundation of sweet caramelized onion and earthy sautéed mushrooms. We add broth, water, and lots of leafy greens (we like a mix of Swiss chard, kale, arugula, and parsley) and simmer the greens until they're tender before blending them into a smooth soup. To thicken the soup without compromising its bright vegetal flavors, we add arborio rice, which gives the soup a velvety consistency. A quick stir-together lemon-tarragon cream drizzled over each bowl adds a touch of decadence.

Lemon-Tarragon Cream
- ¼ cup heavy cream
- 3 tablespoons sour cream
- ½ teaspoon minced fresh tarragon
- ¼ teaspoon grated lemon zest plus ½ teaspoon juice
- ¼ teaspoon table salt

Soup
- 2 tablespoons extra-virgin olive oil
- 1 onion, halved and sliced thin
- 1 teaspoon table salt
- ¾ teaspoon light brown sugar
- 3 ounces white mushrooms, trimmed and sliced thin
- 2 garlic cloves, minced
- Pinch cayenne pepper
- 3 cups water
- 3 cups vegetable or chicken broth
- ⅓ cup arborio rice
- 12 ounces Swiss chard, stemmed and chopped
- 9 ounces kale, stemmed and chopped
- ¼ cup fresh parsley leaves
- 2 ounces (2 cups) baby arugula

1. FOR THE LEMON-TARRAGON CREAM Whisk all ingredients together in bowl. Cover and refrigerate until ready to serve.

2. FOR THE SOUP Heat oil in Dutch oven over medium-high heat until shimmering. Add onion, salt, and sugar and cook, stirring occasionally, until onion releases some moisture, about 5 minutes. Reduce heat to low and continue to cook, stirring often and scraping up any browned bits, until onion is deeply browned and slightly sticky, about 30 minutes. (If onion sizzles or scorches, reduce heat. If onion does not brown after 15 to 20 minutes, increase heat.)

3. Stir in mushrooms and cook until they have released their moisture, about 5 minutes. Stir in garlic and cayenne and cook until fragrant, about 30 seconds. Stir in water, broth, and rice, scraping up any browned bits, and bring to simmer. Reduce heat to low, cover, and cook for 15 minutes.

4. Stir in chard, kale, and parsley, 1 handful at a time, until wilted. Return to simmer; cover; and cook until greens are tender, about 10 minutes.

5. Off heat, stir in arugula until wilted. Working in batches, process soup in blender until smooth, about 1 minute. Return soup to clean pot and bring to brief simmer over medium-low heat. Season with salt and pepper to taste. Drizzle individual portions with lemon-tarragon cream before serving.

KEYS TO SUCCESS

- **Caramelize the onion:** Builds complex, sweet flavor
- **Add arborio rice:** Thickens the soup without clouding its bright, vegetal flavors
- **Stir in the greens by the handful:** Gives each batch time to wilt so that there will be plenty of room in the pot for everything
- For more information on preparing Swiss chard and kale, see page 43.

RESOURCES FOR PUREED SOUPS

The texture of a pureed soup should be as smooth and creamy as possible. With this in mind, we tried pureeing several soups with a food processor, a handheld immersion blender, and a regular countertop blender. It pays to use the right appliance to produce a silky-smooth soup. And because pureeing hot soup can be dangerous, be sure to follow our safety tips.

BLENDER: BEST FOR SMOOTH PUREES

A standard blender turns out the smoothest pureed soups because the blade pulls ingredients down from the top of the blender, so no stray bits go untouched by the blade. And as long as plenty of headspace is left at the top of the blender, there is no leakage.

IMMERSION BLENDER: CONVENIENT FOR CHUNKIER PUREES

The immersion blender is appealing because it can be brought to the pot, eliminating the need to ladle hot ingredients from one vessel to another. However, we found that this kind of blender can leave unblended bits of food behind, which is fine if you are aiming for a chunkier puree.

FOOD PROCESSOR: PROCESS WITH CAUTION

The food processor does a decent job of pureeing, but some small bits of vegetables can get trapped under the blade and remain unchopped. Even more troubling is the food processor's tendency to leak hot liquid. Fill the bowl more than halfway and you are likely to see liquid running down the side of the food processor base.

THREE STEPS FOR PUREEING SOUPS SAFELY

1. Let the vegetables and cooking liquid cool for 5 minutes before transferring them to the blender. Why? Slight cooling reduces the amount of steam that can build up and cause a blender explosion, which is messy and dangerous.

2. To prevent getting sprayed or burned when pureeing hot soup, work in small batches and fill the blender only two-thirds full. Hold the lid in place with a dish towel to protect your hand.

3. To start pureeing, pulse the blender several times to release built-up pressure before blending continuously.

BUILT TO PUREE

In the narrow confines of a blender jar, the food forms a vortex that keeps it in near-constant contact with the blades. Food is drawn down into the blades and back up again before being drawn back down at a high rate of speed.

218 | The New Cooking School Cookbook: Fundamentals

GARNISH IT!

Many soups benefit from a final topping that offers complementary flavor, texture, and color. Simple pureed soups, which are also monochromatic, really benefit from a colorful garnish or two. They can be everything from chopped vegetables to flavor enhancers such as a splash of hot sauce or a spoonful of bright pesto. You can add one or two garnishes to each bowl of soup before serving, or you can offer them separately so that people can garnish their bowls to taste.

Just a Drizzle A few drops of extra-virgin olive oil add a final layer of rich flavor to many soups, such as Red Lentil Soup with Warm Spices (page 222), and also make a beautiful presentation.

Vibrant Color Diced avocado, chopped tomato or cucumber, sliced radishes, fresh chiles, sliced scallions, and even pickled turnips all add color and freshness as garnishes.

Something Creamy A dollop of plain yogurt or sour cream adds a tangy and cooling counterpoint to flavorful soups such as Five-Ingredient Black Bean Soup (page 220). Sometimes we dress up sour cream with fresh herbs, as in our Super Greens Soup with Lemon-Tarragon Cream (page 217).

A Citrus Squeeze Lemon or lime juice always adds a final bright note to bean soups and spicy soups such as Caldo Tlalpeño (page 202).

Tangy or Salty Cheese Goat or blue cheese, cheddar, queso fresco, and cotija all make for quick and savory toppings.

Crunch Chopped nuts such as walnuts and almonds along with seeds such as sesame seeds add a complementary crunchy topping. Toasting the nuts and seeds brings out their full flavor (see page 614). Or add croutons (see page 161).

RESCUING SOUP THAT'S TOO THICK OR TOO THIN

If your soup is too thick, gradually add more water, broth, canned tomatoes, or whatever liquid is appropriate. Remember to correct the seasoning before serving. If your soup is too thin, you can try adding bread to soak up some of the liquid and then pureeing the bread in the blender before adding it back to the soup. If your bean soup is too thin, try mashing some of the beans to thicken the liquid.

COURSE

BEAN AND LENTIL SOUPS

ANNIE PETITO

Beans are satisfying, inexpensive, and nourishing. And turning beans into a soup is almost as easy as, well, opening a can of beans. In this course you'll learn how to coax great flavor and texture from canned beans (hint: don't waste that bean liquid) and use spices and garnishes to add complexity. With canned beans so good, why presoak and slow-cook dried beans? They take time, but dried beans practically make their own soup as they cook and release starch, producing an incredible broth. And you can use that time to infuse them with additional flavors. In this course you'll also learn how to make savory bean soups from dried beans (lentils, too), incorporate vegetables and spices, and top the bowl with garnishes that add excitement.

ANNIE'S PRO TIP: *Since canned beans can vary— in salt content, amount, and consistency of canning liquid— wait until the soups are done cooking before seasoning and adjusting their consistency with hot water.*

FIVE-INGREDIENT BLACK BEAN SOUP

Serves: 4 to 6
Total Time: 25 minutes

RECIPE OVERVIEW This pantry-friendly soup demonstrates the potential of a can of beans—and shows that a can of beans is so much more than just the beans. Here, the bean liquid does the heavy lifting, providing body, silky texture, and deep flavor. As a result, we don't need a lot of herbs or aromatics to make this soup sing. A base of smoky, fruity chipotle chiles in adobo sauce adds character and depth of flavor while lime zest adds aroma and complexity. Dinner's ready in less than 30 minutes. Do not drain or rinse the beans; their liquid contributes to the soup's flavor and body. This soup is hearty enough on its own, but it can be bulked up with whatever extra protein you have on hand, from shredded chicken to smoked fish. For a spicier soup, use the greater amount of chipotle.

- 4 (15-ounce) cans black beans, undrained
- 4 cups chicken or vegetable broth
- 2–3 tablespoons minced canned chipotle chile in adobo sauce
- ½ cup plain Greek yogurt or sour cream
- 1 teaspoon grated lime zest, plus lime wedges for serving

1. Bring beans and their liquid, broth, and chipotle to boil in Dutch oven. Reduce heat to medium-low and simmer, covered, stirring occasionally, until beans begin to break down, 20 to 25 minutes. Using potato masher, mash beans coarse in pot. Adjust consistency with hot water as needed.

2. Stir in yogurt and lime zest and season with salt and pepper to taste. Serve with lime wedges.

CREAMY WHITE BEAN SOUP WITH HERB OIL AND CRISPY CAPERS

Serves: 4 to 6
Total Time: 40 minutes

RECIPE OVERVIEW To make a creamy, smooth, and quick bean soup, we start by briefly simmering canned great northern beans and their seasoned canning liquid with softened aromatic vegetables and herbs. Heating the beans causes their starches to hydrate, which makes the soup especially creamy. Blending the beans with a small amount of liquid helps their skins break down so that the puree is completely smooth. Chicken broth plus a little Parmesan cheese and butter boost the soup's flavor and richness.

Herb oil and crispy capers are quick-to-make but impressive garnishes that complement the neutral soup base with vibrant color, flavor, and texture. Use a conventional blender here; an immersion blender will not produce as smooth a soup. Do not drain or rinse the beans; their liquid contributes to the soup's flavor and body.

Herb Oil and Crispy Capers
- ⅓ cup extra-virgin olive oil
- ¼ cup capers, rinsed and patted dry
- 2 tablespoons minced fresh parsley
- 1 tablespoon chopped fresh basil

Soup
- 2 tablespoons extra-virgin olive oil
- ½ cup chopped onion
- 1 small celery rib, chopped fine
- 3 sprigs fresh thyme
- 2 garlic cloves, sliced
- Pinch cayenne pepper
- 2 (15-ounce) cans great northern beans, undrained
- 2 tablespoons grated Parmesan cheese
- 2 cups chicken or vegetable broth, divided
- 2 tablespoons unsalted butter
- ½ teaspoon lemon juice, plus extra for seasoning

1. FOR THE HERB OIL AND CRISPY CAPERS Combine oil and capers in medium bowl (capers should be mostly submerged). Microwave until capers are darkened in color and have shrunk, about 5 minutes, stirring halfway through microwaving. Using slotted spoon, transfer capers to paper towel–lined plate (they will continue to crisp as they cool); set aside. Reserve caper oil.

2. FOR THE SOUP Heat oil in large saucepan over medium heat until shimmering. Add onion and celery and cook, stirring frequently, until softened but not browned, 6 to 8 minutes. Add thyme sprigs, garlic, and cayenne and cook, stirring constantly, until fragrant, about 1 minute. Add beans and their liquid and stir to combine. Reduce heat to medium-low; cover; and cook, stirring occasionally, until beans are heated through and just starting to break down, 6 to 8 minutes. Remove saucepan from heat and discard thyme sprigs.

3. Process bean mixture and Parmesan in blender on low speed until thick, smooth puree forms, about 2 minutes. With blender running, add 1 cup broth and butter. Increase speed to high and continue to process until butter is incorporated and mixture is pourable, about 1 minute.

4. Return soup to clean saucepan and whisk in remaining 1 cup broth. Cover and bring to simmer over medium heat, adjusting consistency with up to 1 cup hot water as needed. Off heat, stir in lemon juice. Season with salt and extra lemon juice to taste.

5. Stir parsley and basil into reserved caper oil. Drizzle each portion of soup with herb oil, sprinkle with capers, and serve.

RED LENTIL SOUP WITH WARM SPICES

Serves: 4 to 6
Total Time: 45 minutes

Pureeing Red Lentil Soup

WHISK AWAY
Red lentils, which have had their skin removed, soften so completely that they can be whisked into a puree, no blender needed.

RECIPE OVERVIEW Small red lentils break down quickly into a creamy, thick puree—perfect for a smooth and satisfying soup. Their mild flavor does require a bit of embellishment, though. Here we sauté onion in olive oil and use the warm mixture to bloom some fragrant spices commonly used in North African cuisines: coriander, cumin, ginger, pepper, cinnamon, and cayenne. Tomato paste and garlic complete the base before the lentils are added, and a mix of broth and water gives the soup a full, rounded character. After only 15 minutes of cooking, the lentils are soft enough to be pureed with a whisk. A generous dose of lemon juice brings the flavors into focus, and a drizzle of olive oil and a sprinkle of fresh cilantro complete the transformation of commonplace ingredients into an inspired yet comforting soup. Do not substitute brown or green lentils for the red lentils. Serve with Harissa (page 29).

- 2 tablespoons extra-virgin olive oil, plus extra for drizzling
- 1 large onion, chopped fine
- 1 teaspoon table salt
- ¾ teaspoon ground coriander
- ½ teaspoon ground cumin
- ¼ teaspoon ground ginger
- ¼ teaspoon pepper
- ⅛ teaspoon ground cinnamon
- Pinch cayenne pepper
- 1 tablespoon tomato paste
- 1 garlic clove, minced
- 4 cups chicken or vegetable broth, plus extra as needed
- 2 cups water
- 10½ ounces (1½ cups) dried red lentils, picked over and rinsed
- 2 tablespoons lemon juice, plus extra for seasoning
- ¼ cup chopped fresh cilantro

1. Heat oil in large saucepan over medium heat until shimmering. Add onion and salt and cook until softened, about 5 minutes. Stir in coriander, cumin, ginger, pepper, cinnamon, and cayenne and cook until fragrant, about 2 minutes. Stir in tomato paste and garlic and cook for 1 minute.

2. Stir in broth, water, and lentils and bring to vigorous simmer. Cook, stirring occasionally, until lentils are soft and about half are broken down, about 15 minutes.

3. Whisk soup vigorously until broken down to coarse puree, about 30 seconds. Adjust consistency with extra hot broth as needed. Stir in lemon juice and season with salt and extra lemon juice to taste. Sprinkle individual portions with cilantro and drizzle with extra oil before serving.

SPICY PINTO BEAN SOUP

Serves: 6
Total Time: 1½ hours, plus 8 hours soaking

RECIPE OVERVIEW This silky, spicy bean soup is inspired by sopa tarasca, a dish from Michoacán, Mexico, that is generally a puree of pinto beans seasoned with ancho or pasilla chiles. Our version features deep chile flavor from three different varieties: Anchos provide subtle sweetness, canned chipotles in adobo contribute smoky flavor with a bit of acidity, and a jalapeño offers vegetal notes. We process the chiles with tomatoes, onion, garlic, and oregano in a blender to create a vibrant puree, which we cook in hot oil to concentrate its flavor. We add broth and then cook the soaked dried beans in that aromatic broth to infuse them with flavor. Serve with toasted pepitas, chopped fresh cilantro, and Mexican crema or sour cream. If you're pressed for time, quick-soak your beans (see page 329).

- 1½ tablespoons table salt for brining
- 8 ounces (1¼ cups) dried pinto beans, picked over and rinsed
- 1½ ounces (3 or 4) dried ancho chiles, stemmed, seeded, and torn into 1-inch pieces (¾ cup)
- 2 tomatoes, cored and quartered
- 1 onion, quartered
- 3 garlic cloves, peeled
- 1 jalapeño chile, stemmed, halved, and seeded
- 1 tablespoon minced canned chipotle chile in adobo sauce
- 1 tablespoon dried oregano
- 3 tablespoons vegetable oil
- 1 teaspoon table salt
- 7 cups chicken or vegetable broth, plus extra as needed
- 2 bay leaves

1. Dissolve 1½ tablespoons salt in 2 quarts cold water in large container. Add beans and soak at room temperature for at least 8 hours or up to 24 hours. Drain and rinse well.

2. Toast anchos in Dutch oven over medium-high heat, stirring frequently, until fragrant, 2 to 6 minutes. Transfer to blender and let cool slightly, about 5 minutes. Add tomatoes, onion, garlic, jalapeño, chipotle, and oregano and process until smooth, about 30 seconds.

3. Heat oil in now-empty pot over medium-high heat until shimmering. Add ancho-tomato mixture and salt and cook, stirring frequently, until mixture has darkened in color and liquid has evaporated, about 10 minutes. Stir in broth, bay leaves, and beans, scraping up any browned bits, and bring to simmer. Cover; reduce heat to low; and simmer gently until beans are tender, 1 to 1½ hours.

4. Discard bay leaves. Working in batches, process soup in clean, dry blender until smooth, 1 to 2 minutes. Return soup to now-empty pot, adjust consistency with extra broth as needed, and season with salt and pepper to taste. Serve.

KEYS TO SUCCESS

- **Toast the anchos:** To enhance their deep, sweet flavor. Remove the anchos when they smell fragrant, reducing the heat if they begin to smoke.

- **Puree and fry:** Releases and concentrates the flavors of the chiles, tomatoes, and seasonings

CHICKPEA AND ESCAROLE SOUP

Serves: 6 to 8
Total Time: 2 hours, plus 8 hours soaking

RECIPE OVERVIEW If you have the time, soup is one place where it's worth using dried beans, since the beans add flavor and body to the cooking liquid, creating their own broth as they simmer to tenderness. The slow cooking also means that you can infuse flavor into the beans, as we do in this Sicilian-inspired soup with a base of fennel, onion, garlic, oregano, and red pepper flakes. A strip of orange zest adds a subtle citrusy note while a Parmesan rind contributes richness. Handfuls of slightly bitter escarole wilt into the soup, sharing the stage with nutty chickpeas. Use a vegetable peeler to remove the zest from the orange. If you're pressed for time, quick-soak the beans (see page 329).

- 3 tablespoons table salt for brining
- 1 pound (2¾ cups) dried chickpeas, picked over and rinsed
- 2 tablespoons extra-virgin olive oil, plus extra for drizzling
- 2 fennel bulbs, stalks discarded, bulbs halved, cored, and chopped fine
- 1 small onion, chopped
- 1 teaspoon table salt
- 5 garlic cloves, minced
- 2 teaspoons minced fresh oregano or ½ teaspoon dried
- ¼ teaspoon red pepper flakes
- 5 cups vegetable or chicken broth
- 1 Parmesan cheese rind, plus grated Parmesan for serving
- 2 bay leaves
- 1 (3-inch) strip orange zest
- 1 head escarole (1 pound), trimmed and cut into 1-inch pieces
- 1 large tomato, cored and chopped

1. Dissolve 3 tablespoons salt in 4 quarts cold water in large container. Add chickpeas and soak at room temperature for at least 8 hours or up to 24 hours. Drain and rinse well.

2. Heat oil in Dutch oven over medium heat until shimmering. Add fennel, onion, and salt and cook until vegetables are softened, 7 to 10 minutes. Stir in garlic, oregano, and pepper flakes and cook until fragrant, about 30 seconds.

3. Stir in broth, Parmesan rind, bay leaves, orange zest, chickpeas, and 7 cups water and bring to boil. Reduce heat and simmer gently until chickpeas are tender, 1¼ to 1¾ hours. Off heat, discard bay leaves and Parmesan rind, scraping off any cheese that has melted and adding it back to pot. (Soup can be prepared through step 3 and refrigerated for up to 3 days. To serve, bring soup, covered, to gentle simmer, stirring often, and continue with step 4.)

4. Stir in escarole and tomato and cook until escarole is wilted, 5 to 10 minutes. Season with salt and pepper to taste. Sprinkle individual portions with grated Parmesan, drizzle with extra oil, and serve.

KEYS TO SUCCESS

- **Use dried chickpeas:** To create a flavorful broth and season the chickpeas as they cook

- **Add the escarole last:** Ensures that the leaves soften while the stems retain the faintest crunch

- For more information on peeling orange zest, see page 47.

COURSE
PANTRY NOODLE SOUPS

STEPHANIE PIXLEY

Noodle soups can be synonymous with opening a package or can, but it's not much harder to make them from scratch. The advantage is fresh ingredients (no freeze-dried vegetables) and tender, not mushy, noodles. This course keeps things pantry-friendly by supplementing the noodles with items often kept on hand, such as frozen peas, jarred Thai red curry paste, and nutritional yeast—a plant-based staple that re-creates the savoriness of chicken noodle soup without the chicken (nonvegans, take note: you want this on hand, too). Finally, our almost-instant ramen tows the line between from-scratch and shortcut, but boy, is it good.

STEPHANIE'S PRO TIP: *Noodle soups are a great way to use up the ends of several packages of pasta; just pay attention to the cooking times.*

PASTA E PISELLI

Serves: 4
Total Time: 45 minutes

RECIPE OVERVIEW The earliest pasta dishes were humble, brothy soups made by resourceful home cooks who combined water and noodle scraps with dried legumes, stale bread, bits of meat, and whatever else was on hand. Pasta e piselli (pasta and peas) is an example. Since peas have a delicate flavor, you want the broth to be neither bland nor overpoweringly robust. Sautéing onion with pancetta creates a sweet-salty foundation that gets enriched with chicken broth. The result is savory but subtle. Cooking the small pasta in the soup gives the broth ample body from the pasta's starches while the broth flavors the pasta—a win-win situation. We prefer frozen petite peas (aka petits pois or baby sweet peas) here because they are sweeter and less starchy than regular frozen peas, but you can use either. You can use other small pasta such as tubetti, ditali, elbow macaroni, or small shells instead of the ditalini, but do so by weight, not volume. To make this soup vegetarian, omit the pancetta, substitute vegetable broth for the chicken broth, and add an extra 2 tablespoons of grated Pecorino Romano.

- 2 tablespoons extra-virgin olive oil, plus extra for drizzling
- 1 onion, chopped fine
- 2 ounces pancetta, chopped fine
- ½ teaspoon table salt
- ½ teaspoon pepper
- 2½ cups chicken broth
- 2½ cups water
- 7½ ounces (1½ cups) ditalini
- 1½ cups frozen petite peas
- ⅓ cup minced fresh parsley
- ¼ cup grated Pecorino Romano cheese, plus extra for serving
- 2 tablespoons minced fresh mint

1. Heat oil in large saucepan over medium heat until shimmering. Add onion, pancetta, salt, and pepper and cook, stirring frequently, until onion is softened, 7 to 10 minutes.

2. Add broth and water and bring to boil over high heat. Stir in pasta and cook, stirring frequently, until liquid returns to boil. Reduce heat to maintain simmer; cover; and cook until pasta is al dente, 8 to 10 minutes.

3. Stir in peas and remove saucepan from heat. Stir in parsley, Pecorino, and mint. Season with salt and pepper to taste. Serve, drizzling with extra oil and passing extra Pecorino separately.

KEYS TO SUCCESS

- **Swap the pasta by weight:** Different sizes of pasta have different volumes; see page 244 for more information.
- **Turn off the heat:** Before adding the frozen peas to ensure that they stay vibrant and don't overcook
- **Go with Pecorino Romano:** Has a sharper flavor than Parmesan and enhances the peas' sweetness

Four Best Pastas for Soup

DITALINI "Little thimbles" create the chunkiest soup.

TUBETTI "Tubes" yield a brothier soup.

CONCHIGLIETTE "Small shells" are the largest soup pasta.

ORZO Rice-shaped pasta makes a more refined soup.

Give (Frozen) Peas a Chance

We've come to depend on frozen peas. Sure, they're convenient. But flash frozen at the peak of harvest, they're also tender and sweet, whereas fresh peas are often starchy and bland. Peas are soft and moist, so there's not much difference in texture between cooked fresh and frozen peas either.

CHICKPEA NOODLE SOUP

Serves: 6
Total Time: 1 hour

RECIPE OVERVIEW This plant-based take on chicken noodle soup is surprisingly savory and comes together simply from pantry ingredients. In place of chicken, we use chickpeas for their creamy texture, neutral flavor, and heartiness. Sautéed onion, carrots, and celery build a base of flavor, but to capture the missed "meatiness" that makes chicken soup so soul satisfying, we add a vegan staple ingredient: umami-packed nutritional yeast, which has a deep nutty and almost tangy flavor that turns the soup from ordinary to one that reminds us of Grandma's soup. You can use other small pasta such as tubetti, ditali, elbow macaroni, or small shells instead of the ditalini, but do so by weight, not volume (see page 244).

- 2 tablespoons vegetable oil
- 1 onion, chopped fine
- 3 carrots, peeled and sliced ¼ inch thick
- 2 celery ribs, sliced ¼ inch thick
- ¼ teaspoon pepper
- 3 tablespoons nutritional yeast
- 2 teaspoons minced fresh thyme or ¾ teaspoon dried
- 2 bay leaves
- 6 cups vegetable broth
- 2 (15-ounce) cans chickpeas, rinsed
- ½ cup ditalini
- 2 tablespoons minced fresh parsley

1. Heat oil in Dutch oven over medium heat until shimmering. Add onion, carrots, celery, and pepper and cook, stirring occasionally, until softened, 5 to 7 minutes. Stir in nutritional yeast, thyme, and bay leaves and cook until fragrant, about 30 seconds.

2. Stir in broth and chickpeas and bring to boil. Reduce heat to medium-low and simmer, partially covered, until flavors meld, about 10 minutes.

3. Stir in pasta; increase heat to medium-high; and boil until just tender, about 10 minutes. Off heat, discard bay leaves and stir in parsley. Season with salt and pepper to taste, and serve.

SCIENCE LESSON

Umami Magic Dust

Wouldn't it be nice to have magic dust that you could just sprinkle on foods to give them savor? Enter nutritional yeast (affectionately referred to as "nooch"). Simply yeast that's grown on a mixture of beet molasses and sugarcane and heated to deactivate its leavening properties, it's often used to mimic the flavor of cheese, for good reason—it has a funky, nutty, almost salty (although there's no salt in it) depth that matches cheese in its complexity. Why? Nutritional yeast is high in glutamates. This yeast can add savory depth to soup, pasta, salad dressing, and more. One great use: a "cheesy" popcorn sprinkle. Combine 2 tablespoons of nutritional yeast, 2 teaspoons of garlic powder, 1½ teaspoons of dried parsley, 1 teaspoon of dried basil, and ½ teaspoon of table salt in a spice grinder and grind to a fine powder.

HOT-AND-SOUR SOUP WITH VERMICELLI AND SHRIMP

Serves: 4
Total Time: 40 minutes

RECIPE OVERVIEW Full of energetic flavors inspired by the Thai soup tom yum, this recipe combines a fragrant broth with tender rice vermicelli and succulent shrimp. The broth for tom yum achieves its complexity from steeping a mix of aromatic ingredients such as lemongrass, makrut lime leaves, and galangal (a rhizome related to ginger). In our version, we employ jarred Thai curry paste (either green or red works), which includes all those aromatics plus chiles. This supplies much of the heat, which we bolster with Thai chiles (you can also use jalapeños). Lime juice brings the sour element, and fish sauce and sugar offer balanced salty-sweet notes. Pay attention to the timing of when you add the ingredients—you want to stagger additions so that everything just cooks through.

- 4 ounces rice vermicelli
- 6 cups chicken or vegetable broth
- ¼ cup Thai green or red curry paste
- 2 teaspoons sugar
- 8 ounces cremini or white mushrooms, trimmed and sliced thin
- 2 Thai or jalapeño chiles, stemmed and sliced into thin rings
- 1 pound extra-large shrimp (21 to 25 per pound), peeled, deveined, and tails removed
- 2 tomatoes, cored, seeded, and chopped
- 2 tablespoons fish sauce
- 2 tablespoons lime juice
- ¼ cup chopped fresh cilantro, Thai basil, basil, or mint

1. Bring 4 quarts water to boil in large pot or Dutch oven. Off heat, add vermicelli and let sit, stirring occasionally, until fully tender, about 5 minutes. Drain, rinse with cold water, drain again, and set aside.

2. Bring broth to simmer in now-empty pot over medium-low heat, then whisk in curry paste and sugar until dissolved. Add mushrooms and Thai chiles and simmer for 1 minute. Stir in shrimp and cook until opaque throughout, about 1 minute. Off heat, stir in tomatoes, fish sauce, and lime juice and season with salt and pepper to taste. Transfer soup to serving bowls, divide vermicelli among bowls, then sprinkle with cilantro. Serve. (Soup can be refrigerated for up to 3 days.)

KEYS TO SUCCESS

- For more information on cooking rice vermicelli, see page 266.
- For more information on peeling and deveining shrimp, see page 489.
- **To make the soup in advance**: Store the herbs separately; stir into the soup after reheating.

ALMOST-INSTANT GINGER BEEF RAMEN FOR ONE

Serves: 1
Total Time: 35 minutes

RECIPE OVERVIEW This isn't your dorm-room ramen, though it's almost as easy to make. While we start with a package of the instant noodle soup, we ditch the salty—but otherwise lackluster—flavor packet and keep the noodles. For our broth, we start by browning sirloin steak tips in a saucepan, taking care not to burn the fond that develops as the meat browns—we want to keep all that flavor. As the meat rests, we add broth and bolster it with a splash of soy sauce and healthy doses of aromatic ginger and floral lime zest. A single serving of packaged ramen noodles cooks up quickly in this brew, and the steak tips turn it into a satisfying meal. Sirloin steak tips are often sold as flap meat.

- 4 ounces sirloin steak tips, trimmed and cut into 2-inch pieces
- ⅛ teaspoon table salt
- ⅛ teaspoon pepper
- 1 teaspoon oil
- 1½ cups chicken or vegetable broth
- 2 teaspoons grated fresh ginger or ½ teaspoon ground ginger
- ½ teaspoon grated lime zest plus 1 teaspoon juice
- 1 (3-ounce) package ramen noodles, seasoning packet discarded
- 1 scallion, sliced thin
- 2 teaspoons soy sauce

1. Pat beef dry with paper towels and sprinkle with salt and pepper. Heat oil in medium saucepan over medium heat until just smoking. Add beef and cook until beef is well browned all over and registers 120 to 125 degrees (for medium-rare), 4 to 6 minutes, reducing heat if saucepan begins to smoke. Transfer beef to plate, tent with aluminum foil, and let rest until ready to serve.

2. Add broth, ginger, and lime zest to now-empty saucepan; bring to boil, scraping up any browned bits. Add noodles and cook, stirring often, until tender, about 3 minutes. Off heat, stir in lime juice, scallion, soy sauce, and any accumulated juices from beef and season with salt and pepper to taste. Transfer soup to serving bowl. Slice beef thin against grain and place on top of noodles. Serve. (Broth and beef can be refrigerated separately for up to 3 days.)

> **KEYS TO SUCCESS**
> - For more information on grating fresh ginger, see page 43.
> - For more information on cutting your own steak tips, see page 347.

COURSE
MEATY SOUPS

JOSEPH GITTER

A meat-based soup can be stick-to-your-ribs fare, or it can be light, but it should offer the depth of flavor that only meat can bring. While this can come from simmering a pot of roasted bones and meat for upwards of a day, it doesn't have to. In this course we show how to use just a bit of smoked meat to infuse a mostly vegetable soup with flavor and how to produce a hearty beef and barley soup with a rich broth that simmers in just 30 minutes. You'll learn about some of the best cuts of meat for soup that become tender and juicy without multiple hours of simmering.

JOE'S PRO TIP: *So much meaty flavor is found in the rendered fat of whatever little piece of meat you're precooking as long as it doesn't scorch. When browning meat, try to target the white pockets of fat to render as much as possible, and turn down the heat if the fat starts to smoke.*

CALDO VERDE
Serves: 6 to 8
Total Time: 1 hour

RECIPE OVERVIEW Just a bit of smoked sausage adds depth and meaty flavor to this classic Portuguese soup, the smoky meat balancing out a soup that's primarily potatoes and sturdy greens (collards in our version). While the flavors are rich, it's not a heavy soup. Its intentionally thin broth is usually made with just water, but we use chicken broth for a slightly deeper flavor. We also give the soup a bit more body (while keeping it light) by blending some of the cooked potatoes into a puree that thickens the soup just slightly. In fact, we go a step further: We add a bit of oil when blending some of the potatoes to turn the puree into an extra-smooth emulsion, which produces a silky broth. Portuguese linguica or Polish kielbasa can be substituted for the Spanish-style chorizo. We prefer collard greens here for their delicate sweetness and meatier bite, but kale can be substituted. Serve this soup with hearty bread and a final drizzle of extra-virgin olive oil.

- ¼ cup extra-virgin olive oil, divided
- 12 ounces Spanish-style chorizo sausage, cut into ½-inch pieces
- 1 onion, chopped fine
- 4 garlic cloves, minced
- 1¼ teaspoons table salt

- ¼ teaspoon red pepper flakes
- 2 pounds Yukon Gold potatoes, peeled and cut into ¾-inch pieces
- 4 cups chicken or vegetable broth
- 4 cups water
- 1 pound collard greens, stemmed and cut into 1-inch pieces
- 2 teaspoons white wine vinegar

1. Heat 1 tablespoon oil in Dutch oven over medium-high heat until shimmering. Add chorizo and cook, stirring occasionally, until lightly browned, 4 to 5 minutes. Using slotted spoon, transfer chorizo to bowl; set aside.

2. Add onion, garlic, salt, and pepper flakes to fat left in pot and cook over medium heat, stirring frequently, until onion is softened, about 5 minutes. Stir in potatoes, broth, and water; bring to simmer; and cook until potatoes are just tender, 8 to 10 minutes.

3. Transfer ¾ cup solids and ¾ cup broth to blender. Stir collards into pot, return to simmer, and cook for 10 minutes. Stir in chorizo and cook until collards are tender, 8 to 10 minutes.

4. Add remaining 3 tablespoons oil to soup in blender and process until smooth, about 1 minute. Off heat, stir pureed soup mixture and vinegar into soup in pot. Season with salt and pepper to taste. Serve.

KEYS TO SUCCESS

- **Choose Yukons:** Lower in starch than russets and hold their shape better during cooking
- **Brown the chorizo before boiling:** To render its fat (full of smoky spice) so that it flavors the onion and permeates the entire soup
- **Emulsify the potatoes with oil:** For a velvety puree that creates a silky broth when stirred back into the soup
- For more information on prepping collard greens, see page 43.

OLD-FASHIONED BEEF AND BARLEY SOUP

Serves: 6 to 8
Total Time: 1¾ hours

RECIPE OVERVIEW A savory, stick-to-your-ribs meal in a bowl, beef and barley soup benefits from making your own beef broth. (Our recipe gets you there without simmering bones all day.) Once you have that broth—which can be made ahead—the soup comes together quickly, thanks to sirloin steak tips, which don't need long to turn tender and are full of beefy flavor. As with the noodles in chicken soup, the barley doesn't do well in the refrigerator, as the grain continues to soak up liquid. You're better off preparing the broth in advance and finishing the soup the day you want to serve it. Sirloin steak tips are often sold as flap meat.

- 1 pound sirloin steak tips, trimmed and cut into ½-inch pieces
- ¼ teaspoon table salt
- ⅛ teaspoon pepper
- 2 tablespoons vegetable oil, divided
- 8 ounces cremini mushrooms, trimmed and sliced ½-inch thick
- 1 onion, chopped
- 1½ teaspoons minced fresh thyme or ½ teaspoon dried
- 1 garlic clove, minced
- 2 tablespoons all-purpose flour
- ¼ cup dry red wine
- 6 cups Beef Broth (page 233)
- 1 (14.5-ounce) can diced tomatoes, drained
- ½ cup pearl barley
- 3 carrots, peeled and cut into ½-inch pieces
- 2 celery ribs, cut into ½-inch pieces
- 2 bay leaves
- 2 tablespoons minced fresh parsley

1. Pat beef dry with paper towels and sprinkle with salt and pepper. Heat 2 teaspoons oil in Dutch oven over medium-high heat until just smoking. Add half of beef and cook, stirring occasionally, until well browned, 5 to 7 minutes, reducing heat if pot begins to scorch. Transfer browned beef to medium bowl. Repeat with 2 teaspoons oil and remaining beef; transfer to bowl.

2. Add remaining 2 teaspoons oil to pot and heat over medium heat until shimmering. Add mushrooms and onion and cook until softened, 7 to 10 minutes. Stir in thyme and garlic and cook until fragrant, about 30 seconds. Stir in flour and cook for 1 minute. Whisk in wine, scraping up any browned bits and smoothing out any lumps, and cook until nearly evaporated, about 1 minute.

3. Stir in broth, tomatoes, barley, carrots, celery, bay leaves, and beef along with any accumulated juices. Bring to boil, then cover and reduce heat to maintain gentle simmer. Cook until beef and vegetables are tender, 30 to 40 minutes.

4. Off heat, remove bay leaves. Stir in the parsley, season with salt and pepper to taste, and serve.

KEYS TO SUCCESS

- **Use sirloin steak tips:** Offer a balance between meaty flavor and tenderness
- **Thicken with flour before deglazing:** Provides the viscosity of a long-cooked soup
- **Less is more with barley:** A half cup expands considerably with cooking. Too much barley would absorb a lot of broth and produce a thick, dense soup.
- **Balance with tomatoes:** Acidity counters the heartiness of the beef and barley.

SPICY BEEF SOUP WITH SCALLIONS AND BEAN SPROUTS

Serves: 6 to 8
Total Time: 1½ hours

RECIPE OVERVIEW This simple soup inspired by Korean yukgaejang features fall-apart-tender beef, heat from gochugaru, and lots of scallions. Because of the short simmering time, we opt for blade steaks, which don't contain much fat and become tender and juicy without long simmering. Browning the meat first builds up fond in the pot and adds flavor to the meat; we do this in two batches to avoid crowding the pot and causing the meat to steam rather than brown. To finish the soup, we drizzle in beaten egg to create delicate strands. Mixing the egg with a small amount of cornstarch before adding it stabilizes the proteins, resulting in wispy, soft ribbons. If gochugaru is unavailable, you can use a combination of 3 tablespoons of ancho chile powder and ⅛ teaspoon of cayenne pepper. Serve with rice.

- 1½ pounds beef blade steak, trimmed and sliced thin against grain
- 2 tablespoons vegetable oil, divided
- 1 onion, chopped
- 6 garlic cloves, minced
- 8 cups beef broth
- 12 scallions, cut into 2-inch lengths
- 3 tablespoons gochugaru
- 2 tablespoons toasted sesame oil
- 1 tablespoon soy sauce, plus extra for seasoning
- 1 teaspoon water
- ½ teaspoon cornstarch
- 1 large egg
- 4 ounces (2 cups) bean sprouts

1. Pat beef dry with paper towels. Heat 2 teaspoons vegetable oil in Dutch oven over medium-high heat until just smoking. Add half of beef and cook until well browned, 5 to 7 minutes; transfer to bowl. Repeat with 2 teaspoons vegetable oil and remaining beef; transfer to bowl.

2. Add remaining 2 teaspoons vegetable oil to fat left in pot and heat over medium heat until shimmering. Add onion and cook until softened, about 5 minutes. Stir in garlic and cook until fragrant, about 30 seconds. Stir in broth and beef along with any accumulated juices and bring to simmer. Reduce heat to low, cover, and cook for 15 minutes.

3. Stir in scallions, gochugaru, sesame oil, and soy sauce. Cover partially and cook until beef is tender, 15 to 25 minutes. Off heat, season with extra soy sauce to taste. (Do not let soup cool down.)

4. Whisk water and cornstarch together in small bowl, then whisk in egg until combined. Using large soupspoon, add egg mixture to hot soup by slowly drizzling very thin streams into soup in circular motion. Without stirring soup, let it continue to sit off heat for 1 minute. Return soup to brief simmer over medium-high heat. Stir in bean sprouts and serve.

KEYS TO SUCCESS

- **Brown the meat in batches:** To help it brown well and prevent steaming
- **Whisk the egg with cornstarch:** To stabilize the egg's proteins, preventing them from contracting too much in the hot liquid

CORE TECHNIQUE
Trimming Blade Steaks

HALVE STEAKS
Cut each steak in half lengthwise, leaving the center line of gristle attached to one half.

REMOVE GRISTLE
Slice away the gristle from the half to which it is attached.

Beef Cuts for Quick(-ish) Soups

The ideal beef cut for soups that won't simmer for hours has a loose, open grain: With less than an hour of cooking, the muscle fibers of cuts such as sirloin steak tips, blade steak, and flank steak take on the tender texture of slow-cooked beef. If buying sirloin steak tips (aka flap meat), choose large pieces rather than precut stir-fry meat, which will never fully turn tender. If buying blade steaks, trim them of gristle and fat. Avoid cuts with a firm, tight grain, such as steaks cut from the loin; they will be tough and relatively tasteless.

SHARBA

Serves: 6 to 8
Total Time: 2¼ hours

RECIPE OVERVIEW This hearty Libyan soup is often eaten to break the daily fast during the holy month of Ramadan. The intensely flavored soup relies on lamb, chickpeas, and lisan asfour (a pasta similar in shape to orzo) and is deeply seasoned with dried mint and warm spices. For our soup, we first sear lamb shoulder chops to produce fond and then braise the meat slowly in a soup base built on onion, tomatoes, dried mint, and spices.

- 1 pound lamb shoulder chops (blade or round bone), 1 to 1½ inches thick, trimmed and halved
- 1¼ teaspoons table salt, divided
- ⅛ teaspoon plus ¼ teaspoon pepper, divided
- 1 tablespoon extra-virgin olive oil
- 1 onion, chopped fine
- 4 plum tomatoes, cored and cut into ¼-inch pieces
- 2 tablespoons tomato paste
- 1½ teaspoons dried mint, crumbled, divided
- 1 teaspoon ground turmeric
- 1 teaspoon paprika
- ½ teaspoon ground cinnamon
- ¼ teaspoon ground cumin
- 10 cups chicken or vegetable broth
- 1 (15-ounce) can chickpeas, rinsed
- 1 cup orzo

1. Adjust oven rack to lower-middle position and heat oven to 325 degrees. Pat lamb dry with paper towels and sprinkle with ¼ teaspoon salt and ⅛ teaspoon pepper. Heat oil in Dutch oven over medium-high heat until just smoking. Brown lamb, about 4 minutes per side; transfer to plate. Pour off all but 2 tablespoons fat from pot.

2. Add onion to fat left in pot and cook over medium heat until softened, about 5 minutes. Stir in tomatoes and cook until softened and juice has evaporated, about 2 minutes. Stir in tomato paste, 1 teaspoon mint, turmeric, paprika, cinnamon, cumin, remaining 1 teaspoon salt, and remaining ¼ teaspoon pepper and cook until fragrant, about 1 minute. Stir in broth, scraping up any browned bits, and bring to boil.

3. Stir in chickpeas, then nestle lamb into pot along with any accumulated juices. Cover; place pot in oven; and cook until fork slips easily in and out of lamb, about 1 hour.

4. Transfer lamb to cutting board; let cool slightly; then shred into bite-size pieces using 2 forks, discarding excess fat and bones. Meanwhile, stir orzo into soup, bring to simmer over medium heat, and cook until tender, 10 to 12 minutes. Stir in lamb and cook until heated through, about 2 minutes. Off heat, stir in remaining ½ teaspoon mint and let sit until fragrant, about 1 minute. Serve.

COURSE
BASIC BROTHS

JULIA COLLIN DAVISON

A good broth will improve anything you cook with it—not only soup but also rice, beans, sauces, and more. Homemade broth is especially key in minimally seasoned soups, which will essentially taste like the liquid you use. In this course you'll learn how to extract plenty of flavor from chicken parts for a rich-tasting broth with body and how to build a beef broth with deep savor without a full day of simmering. You'll also find a revolutionary approach to vegetable broth that you can reconstitute as needed. Having homemade broth on hand is a very useful thing, and you'll find tips on how to freeze extra broth in quantity for later.

JULIA'S PRO TIP: *I save every scrap of chicken I can (both raw and cooked, when appropriate) and use them to make a big batch of chicken broth about every month. I simply freeze the scraps in zipper-lock bags until it's broth-making time, and add them right to the pot while frozen (it does extend the cooking time slightly). Not only is it thrifty, but I love how the roasted bones add another layer of flavor to the broth.*

CLASSIC CHICKEN BROTH

Makes: 8 cups
Total Time: 5½ hours

RECIPE OVERVIEW Good homemade chicken broth is liquid gold. It will improve anything you cook with it—not only soup but also rice, beans, sauces, and more. In this recipe you'll learn how to coax out rich flavor and full body by using chicken backs and wings—both for convenience and because they release plenty of gelatin, which gives the broth a luscious consistency. (If you want a recipe that yields both broth and meat, make Chicken Noodle Soup [page 201].) Minimal additions ensure that the broth tastes as chicken-y as possible. Chicken backs are available at supermarket butcher counters; if you can't find them, you can use all wings. If you have a large pot (at least 12 quarts), you can easily double this recipe to make 1 gallon.

- 4 pounds chicken backs and wings
- 3½ quarts water
- 1 onion, chopped
- 2 bay leaves
- 2 teaspoons table salt

1. Bring chicken and water to boil in large stockpot or Dutch oven over medium-high heat, skimming off any scum that comes to surface. Reduce heat to low and simmer gently for 3 hours.

2. Add onion, bay leaves, and salt and continue to simmer for 2 hours. Strain broth through fine-mesh strainer into large pot or container, pressing on solids to extract as much liquid as possible. Let broth settle for about 5 minutes, then skim off fat. (Cooled broth can be refrigerated for up to 4 days or frozen for up to 1 month.)

> **KEYS TO SUCCESS**
> - **Choose backs and wings:** For a gelatinous texture that is desired in good chicken broth
> - **Go easy on the aromatics:** To let the chicken flavor shine through
> - **Don't rush the simmering:** Allows more gelatin to be released for a full-bodied broth

BEEF BROTH

Makes: 8 cups
Total Time: 2½ hours

RECIPE OVERVIEW Beef broth is often associated with simmering bones for hours, but unless there's meat on those bones you end up with bone-flavored vegetable liquid. It can require up to 6 pounds of expensive meaty bones for even 2 quarts of broth, but there is a simpler route to a full-flavored, full-bodied broth. Here you'll learn to create a rich, velvety beef broth using just a pound of ground beef, which releases its flavor quickly and is relatively inexpensive; a few vegetables; water; wine; and a few additional flavor boosters—all with just 1½ hours of simmering. We prefer 85 percent lean ground beef for this recipe; 93 percent lean ground beef will work, but the broth will be less flavorful. Make sure to use at least a 6-quart Dutch oven for this recipe.

- 1 teaspoon vegetable oil
- 1 pound white mushrooms, trimmed and quartered
- 1 large onion, chopped
- 1 pound 85 percent lean ground beef
- 2 tablespoons tomato paste
- ½ cup dry red wine
- 8 cups water
- 1 large carrot, peeled and chopped
- 1 large celery rib, chopped
- 2 tablespoons soy sauce
- 2 teaspoons table salt
- 2 bay leaves

1. Heat oil in Dutch oven or stockpot over medium-high heat until just smoking. Add mushrooms and onion and cook, stirring often, until onion is browned and golden-brown fond has formed on bottom of pot, 8 to 12 minutes.

2. Stir in beef and cook, breaking up meat with wooden spoon, until no longer pink, about 3 minutes. Stir in tomato paste and cook until fragrant, about 30 seconds. Stir in wine, scraping up any browned bits, and cook until nearly evaporated, 1 to 2 minutes.

3. Stir in water, carrot, celery, soy sauce, salt, and bay leaves and bring to boil. Cover; reduce heat to maintain gentle simmer; and cook, skimming as needed, until broth tastes rich and flavorful, about 1½ hours.

4. Strain broth through fine-mesh strainer. Let broth settle for 5 to 10 minutes, then defat using wide, shallow spoon or fat separator before using.

Building Flavor in Beef Broth

Without multiple pounds of bones and meat and hours to cook them, we choose ingredients that contribute roasted flavor and complex savoriness to our simmering liquid.

ADD MUSHROOMS These fungi are high in glutamates, naturally occurring compounds that enhance meaty flavor.

BUILD A FOND Sautéing the mushrooms and onion until they leave a golden-brown fond on the bottom of the pot contributes roasted flavor (and some color) to the broth. Deglazing with red wine pulls that fond into the liquid and fortifies the broth even further.

USE UMAMI BOOSTERS In addition to mushrooms, tomato paste and soy sauce both have natural glutamates that boost the savory flavor even more.

SIMMER FOR 1½ HOURS It's crucial to simmer for the right amount of time: After 1 hour the broth will be too mild, but by 2 hours it will have a livery, metallic flavor.

Stretch Homemade Broth

Rather than discarding the solids after pressing out as much liquid as possible, "rinse" them once with ¼ cup of water per pound of meat/bones, strain the mixture, and then add the liquid to the broth. The "rinsing liquid" won't be as concentrated as the broth, but it's still surprisingly flavorful.

VEGETABLE BROTH BASE

Makes: about 1¾ cups base (enough for 7 quarts broth)
Total Time: 20 minutes

RECIPE OVERVIEW Vegetable broth is a necessary staple, but commercial offerings don't taste anything like vegetables. Homemade concentrated vegetable broth base is a convenient and economical alternative: Simply mix a small amount of the base with boiling water for instant broth. Our base starts with a twist on the classic mirepoix of onions, carrots, and celery, with celery root and leeks swapped in for similar but milder flavors. For depth and complexity, we add dried onion, tomato paste, and soy sauce. Two tablespoons of kosher salt keep the base from freezing solid, so you can store it in the freezer for months and easily remove a tablespoon at a time to reconstitute. The coarseness of the kosher salt aids in grinding the vegetables.

- 2 leeks, white and light green parts only, chopped and washed thoroughly (2½ cups or 5 ounces)
- ½ small celery root, peeled and cut into ½-inch pieces (¾ cup or 3 ounces)
- 2 carrots, peeled and cut into ½-inch pieces (⅔ cup or 3 ounces)
- ½ cup (½ ounce) fresh parsley leaves and thin stems
- 3 tablespoons dried minced onions
- 2 tablespoons kosher salt
- 1½ tablespoons tomato paste
- 3 tablespoons soy sauce

1. Process leeks, celery root, carrots, parsley, dried onions, and salt in food processor, scraping down sides of bowl frequently, until paste is as fine as possible, 3 to 4 minutes. Add tomato paste and process for 1 minute, scraping down sides of bowl every 20 seconds. Add soy sauce and continue to process for 1 minute.

2. Transfer mixture to airtight container and tap firmly on counter to remove air bubbles. Press small piece of parchment paper flush against surface of mixture and cover. Freeze for up to 6 months.

3. **TO MAKE 1 CUP BROTH** Stir 1 tablespoon fresh or frozen broth base into 1 cup boiling water. If particle-free broth is desired, let broth steep for 5 minutes, then strain through fine-mesh strainer.

KEYS TO SUCCESS

- **Add soy sauce and tomato paste:** Provide a rich savoriness essential in a vegetable broth
- **Use kosher salt:** Helps the vegetables break down in the food processor and prevents the paste from freezing solid
- For more information on preparing leeks, see page 44.

CORE TECHNIQUE
Preparing Celery Root

TRIM
Using a chef's knife, cut ½ inch from both the root end and the opposite end. Place the celery root so that one cut side rests flat on the cutting board.

PEEL
Cut down around the sides of the vegetable, working from top to bottom and angling the knife as needed to remove wide strips of skin.

RESOURCES FOR BROTHS

WHICH CHICKEN PARTS GO IN THE POT?

Historically, thrifty cooks made chicken broth with carcasses or older hens too tough for eating. Versions today use anything from a whole bird to scraps. We compared four batches of broth made with all wings, all backs, all legs, and a mix of backs and wings—all parts relatively high in collagen. We omitted whole birds (they contain a high proportion of breast meat, which offers little collagen) and thighs, which offer similar traits to legs but cost more. All broths were flavorful and full-bodied, but the mix of backs and wings offered the richest flavor and the most viscous consistency. Backs are full of collagen that breaks down into gelatin during cooking; they also contain a little muscle and fat. Wings boast a large amount of skin and multiple joints, two abundant sources of collagen, as well as flavorful meat, making them preferable to legs, which contain fewer joints. Chicken backs are often available at supermarket butcher counters. You can also freeze backs if you butterfly or butcher a whole chicken at home (see page 424).

DEFATTING BROTHS AND SOUPS

Defatting a broth or soup is important if you don't want your final dish to look and taste greasy. There are four different ways to defat a liquid; the method you choose depends on the dish you are making and the equipment you have on hand. For the first three methods, it is important to let the liquid settle for 5 to 10 minutes before defatting; this allows the fat to separate out and float to the top.

Use a wide, shallow spoon or ladle. Let the liquid settle in the pot for 5 to 10 minutes, then skim away the fat. The advantage of this method is that it's very easy and it doesn't dirty any extra dishes; however, some fat will remain in the broth.

Pour the broth into a tall, narrow container and let it settle for 5 to 10 minutes. This will create a deeper layer of fat that is easier to remove with a wide spoon or ladle. (Some fat will remain, but less than if you simply defat the broth right in the pot.)

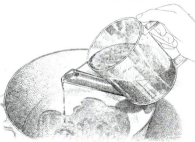

Use a fat separator. Simply pour in the liquid; let it settle for 5 to 10 minutes; and decant it back into the pot, leaving the fat behind. We find bottom-draining fat separators are more efficient than pitchers at pouring off liquid while keeping fat out.

Refrigerate the broth overnight. If you have time, you can refrigerate your broth and the fat will collect and solidify on the top as it chills. Then, you can simply scrape the large solid pieces of fat right off the top before reheating and using.

FOR CLEARER BROTH, SIMMER, DON'T BOIL

Boiling will cause soluble proteins and rendered fat from the meat to emulsify into the cooking liquid, turning it greasy and cloudy. By simmering, you minimize the amount of fat that gets emulsified, so the broth is clearer, and the sediment simply settles to the bottom of the pot, where it can be avoided.

BEST WAY TO COOL BROTH

For safety reasons, the U.S. Food and Drug Administration recommends cooling liquids to 70 degrees within 2 hours after cooking and 41 degrees within 4 hours after that. To cool down the hot liquid—without raising the temperature of the refrigerator and risking the spoilage of other food—first let the liquid cool to 85 degrees on the counter, which takes about an hour, then transfer to the fridge.

FREEZING BROTH

Portioning broth before freezing it makes it easy to defrost only as much as you need. To save the leftover amount, we either store it in an airtight container in the refrigerator for up to four days or freeze it for up to one month using one of these methods.

For small amounts Pour the broth into ice cube trays or nonstick muffin tins (each muffin cup holds 1 cup). Once the broth is frozen, remove it from the tray or cups and store it in a zipper-lock bag. Cubes are great for pan sauces, stir-fries, and vegetable braises. "Cups" are good for casseroles and braising/steaming/poaching liquid.

For large amounts Line a 4-cup measuring cup with a zipper-lock bag (it holds the bag open so that you can use both hands to pour) and pour in the cooled broth. Seal the bag (double up if you wish) and lay it flat to freeze. This is a good option for soup, stew, rice, or gravy.

CHAPTER 6

PASTA AND NOODLES

COURSES

240 DRIED ITALIAN PASTA

250 FRESH ITALIAN PASTA

256 ONE-POT PASTA

258 BAKED PASTA

268 LO MEIN NOODLES

272 UDON AND SOBA NOODLES

276 RICE NOODLES

MORE TO EXPLORE

246 TOMATO SAUCES

254 PESTO

ITALIAN PASTA BASICS

Out of all of Italy's countless contributions to cuisine over the centuries, the most resonant continues to be pasta. For most Americans (as well as most Italians), pasta means dried pasta. To make it, semolina (coarsely ground durum wheat) is mixed with water, kneaded into a dough, and pressed through the holes of a die (either bronze or Teflon) to make specific shapes. The pasta is dried in drying rooms or special ovens, and the finished product is shelf-stable for years.

PASTA TYPES

Dried Pasta
The spaghetti, penne, ziti, and other pastas that we typically buy are made from semolina that has been refined during processing to remove the bran and germ (similar to white flour). In addition to refined durum wheat flour, classic dried pasta contains just water and salt. In our taste tests of various shapes and products, we have found minimal differences. Some products do have stronger wheaty, buttery, or nutty notes, but once the sauce is added, those flavor differences are very hard to detect and they do not alter the flavor of the finished dish. Some products seem to cook up firmer, but again differences are quite small. In general, we have found both Italian and American products that we like, so by all means try different products until you discover your own personal favorites.

Fresh Pasta
Fresh pasta is delicate, with a silky-soft but not mushy texture. It is made from flour, water, and often (but not always) eggs. Fresh pasta absorbs sauces more readily than dried pasta does, which makes it a great choice for cream-based sauces such as Alfredo. And although it has a reputation for being difficult to make, it is actually surprisingly easy. In this chapter you'll learn how to make fresh pasta without a pasta machine, using only a food processor, rolling pin, flour, eggs, and extra-virgin olive oil. Making this dough in the food processor is easier and more foolproof than mixing it by hand. You can, of course, make all kinds of shapes and filled pastas using fresh dough, but here we'll stick to the basics: classic, simple fettuccine, using it in two recipes that really showcase the flavor and texture of the fresh pasta.

CHEESE

Many types of cheese are used in Italian pasta dishes, but two grating cheeses in particular are hallmarks of Italian cuisine. Depending on the recipe, they can be interchangeable, but there are distinct differences.

Parmesan
Parmesan is a hard, grainy cheese made from cow's milk. We recommend authentic Parmigiano-Reggiano, which has a depth and complexity of flavor and a smooth, melting texture that none of the other Parmesan-type cheeses can match. Most of these other cheeses are too salty and one-dimensional. When shopping, make sure that some portion of the words "Parmigiano-Reggiano" is stenciled on the golden rind. To ensure that you're buying a properly aged cheese, examine the rind. It should be a few shades darker than the straw-colored interior and about ½ inch thick (younger or improperly aged cheeses will have a paler, thinner rind). And those small white spots found on many pieces are actually good—they signify the presence of calcium phosphate crystals, which form only after the cheese has been aged for the proper amount of time.

Pecorino Romano
Like Parmigiano-Reggiano, Pecorino Romano is a Protected Designation of Origin cheese, and the genuine product will have the words "Pecorino Romano" stenciled on the rind. It's a flaky, granular, bone-white cheese made from sheep's milk. It has a sharper, more intense flavor than Parmesan and is saltier. It works especially well in dishes with assertive ingredients such as capers, olives, or red pepper flakes. Unlike Parmesan, Pecorino Romano can also be sold young, when it is soft enough to eat as a table cheese. For grating over pasta, you want the aged version.

MATCHING PASTA SHAPES AND SAUCES

In Italian cooking, matching pasta shapes to sauces is an art form. In our simplified, pragmatic approach, the texture of the sauce is the most important consideration. Here is the rule we follow: Thicker, chunkier sauces go well with short pastas, and thinner, smoother, or lighter sauces go better with strand pastas.

Short Pastas

Short tubular or molded pasta shapes do an excellent job of trapping and holding on to chunky sauces. Sauces with large chunks are best with rigatoni or orecchiette. Sauces with small chunks make more sense with fusilli or penne.

Strand Pastas

Long strands are best with smooth or nearly smooth sauces. In general, wider noodles such as pappardelle and fettuccine can also support slightly chunkier sauces like Simple Italian-Style Meat Sauce (page 248).

Lasagna Noodles

These wide, flat noodles are available in both traditional and no-boil style. They are not interchangeable in recipes.

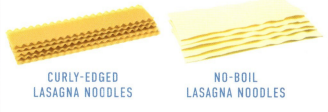

COURSE
DRIED ITALIAN PASTA

JACK BISHOP

Inexpensive, quick to prepare, endlessly adaptable, and requiring little in the way of special equipment, dried pasta is often one of the first things beginning home cooks learn how to make. Pasta may be easy to cook, but there are some techniques to master so that you cook it just right. Now that you've learned about some of the essential pasta shapes and ingredients used in many pasta recipes, in this course we'll explain how to cook dried pasta to al dente perfection and how to prepare some of the classic pasta dishes that have been favorites for generations.

JACK'S PRO TIP: *If you're using the right amount of water to cook the pasta, you're going to need a lot of salt. Bland pasta can't be fixed by a salty sauce. It should taste well seasoned on its own.*

LINGUINE WITH WHITE CLAM SAUCE
Serves: 4
Total Time: 30 minutes

RECIPE OVERVIEW This quick, classic meal uses canned clams for convenience, and the sauce comes together during the time it takes for the pasta water to boil. Butter, stirred in at the end of cooking the clam sauce, enriches it and creates a velvety texture. Saving some of the pasta cooking water when you drain the linguine allows you to adjust the consistency of the finished sauce to your liking. Because clams can be very briny, be careful when seasoning the pasta with salt before serving. Grated cheese is not traditionally served with seafood pastas, so here lemon wedges add a bright finishing touch. You can substitute any long, thin pasta, such as spaghetti, fettuccine, or vermicelli, for the linguine.

- 2 tablespoons extra-virgin olive oil
- 2 shallots, minced
- 4 garlic cloves, minced
- 2 (6.5-ounce) cans chopped clams
- 1 cup chicken broth
- 1 (8-ounce) bottle clam juice
- 2 tablespoons unsalted butter
- 1 pound linguine
  Table salt for cooking pasta
- 2 tablespoons minced fresh parsley
  Lemon wedges

1. Heat oil in 12-inch skillet over medium heat until shimmering. Add shallots and garlic and cook until shallots are just golden and garlic is fragrant, about 2 minutes. Add clams and their juice, broth, and bottled clam juice; increase heat to medium-high; and bring to boil. Cook until sauce is reduced to 2 cups, about 15 minutes. Off heat, whisk in butter and season with salt and pepper to taste.

2. Meanwhile, bring 4 quarts water to boil in large pot. Add pasta and 1 tablespoon salt to boiling water and cook, stirring often, until al dente. Reserve ½ cup cooking water, then drain pasta and return it to pot. Add sauce and parsley to pasta and toss to combine. Adjust consistency with reserved cooking water as needed. Season with salt and pepper to taste. Serve with lemon wedges.

> ### KEYS TO SUCCESS
> - **Add salt to the cooking water:** Seasons the pasta; usually 1 tablespoon of salt per 1 pound of pasta
> - **Taste the pasta frequently:** Shows you when to stop cooking it; don't go by times on the package
> - **Reserve some starchy cooking water:** Perfect for adjusting the consistency of the sauce

ORECCHIETTE WITH BROCCOLI RABE AND SAUSAGE

Serves: 4 to 6
Total Time: 40 minutes

RECIPE OVERVIEW Orecchiette ("little ears") is a small, bowl-shaped pasta that's perfect for catching and holding a variety of sauces. It's particularly ideal for cradling chunky sauce ingredients, such as the broccoli rabe and sausage here. This hearty, subtly spicy pasta is an iconic dish from Puglia, the heel of the Italian boot. To make the pasta even more flavorful, cook it in the water used for cooking the broccoli rabe, as is traditional—it's also convenient. The garlicky pork's richness mingles beautifully with the vegetal bitterness of the broccoli rabe. Incorporating grated Pecorino Romano and a bit of reserved cooking water brings a touch of creamy texture to the finished dish.

- 2 tablespoons extra-virgin olive oil
- 8 ounces hot or sweet Italian sausage, casings removed
- 6 garlic cloves, minced
- ¼ teaspoon red pepper flakes
- 1 pound broccoli rabe, trimmed and cut into 1½-inch pieces
- Table salt for cooking broccoli rabe and pasta
- 1 pound orecchiette
- 2 ounces Pecorino Romano cheese, grated (1 cup)

1. Heat oil in 12-inch nonstick skillet over medium-high heat until just smoking. Add sausage and cook, breaking up meat into rough ½-inch pieces with wooden spoon, until lightly browned, about 5 minutes. Stir in garlic and pepper flakes and cook until fragrant, about 30 seconds.

2. Meanwhile, bring 4 quarts water to boil in large pot. Add broccoli rabe and 1 tablespoon salt and cook, stirring often, until crisp-tender, about 2 minutes. Using slotted spoon, transfer broccoli rabe to skillet with sausage mixture.

3. Return water to boil; add pasta; and cook, stirring often, until al dente. Reserve 1 cup cooking water, then drain pasta and return it to pot. Add sausage–broccoli rabe mixture, Pecorino, and ⅓ cup reserved cooking water to pasta and toss to combine. Adjust consistency with remaining reserved cooking water as needed. Season with salt and pepper to taste. Serve.

CORE TECHNIQUE
Reserving Pasta Water

Dried pasta releases a lot of starch into the cooking water; you can easily see how cloudy the water gets. For most dishes, it's critical not to dump all that starchy water down the sink. Reserving some (usually ½ to 1 cup) to add to the pot just before serving gives the sauce extra body and lets you adjust the consistency to your personal preference.

CORE TECHNIQUE
Boiling Pasta

BOIL THE RIGHT AMOUNT OF WATER; THEN ADD SALT
A general guideline is 4 quarts of water and 1 tablespoon of salt for 1 pound of pasta. A large pot will prevent boil-overs.

STIR IT
Adding oil to the pot will not prevent sticking. Frequent stirring does.

TASTE EARLY AND OFTEN
Following the time on the box can result in overcooked pasta. Tasting frequently helps you learn the timing of when different shapes reach al dente.

GARLICKY SPAGHETTI WITH LEMON AND PINE NUTS

Serves: 4
Total Time: 45 minutes

RECIPE OVERVIEW This is a gussied-up version of the simple southern Italian pasta known as aglio e olio. To that basic formula of olive oil and garlic, this version adds lemon, pine nuts, fresh basil, and Parmesan. In this recipe you use half the usual amount of water to cook the pasta, resulting in a more concentrated starchy cooking water, which lends extra body to the sauce when you incorporate it. Cooking minced garlic over low heat in plenty of olive oil works best for infusing the oil with garlic flavor without overcooking the garlic. (With sliced garlic, thinner slices often end up turning dark brown and acrid by the time thicker slices become golden.) Stirring in ½ teaspoon of raw minced garlic to the al dente pasta at the last minute adds extra zing. A garlic press makes quick work of uniformly mincing the garlic. You will need an 8-inch nonstick skillet for this recipe.

- ¼ cup extra-virgin olive oil
- 2 tablespoons plus ½ teaspoon minced garlic, divided
- ¼ teaspoon red pepper flakes
- 1 pound spaghetti
  Table salt for cooking pasta
- 2 teaspoons grated lemon zest plus 2 tablespoons juice
- 1 cup chopped fresh basil
- 1 ounce Parmesan cheese, grated (½ cup), plus extra for serving
- ½ cup pine nuts, toasted

1. Combine oil and 2 tablespoons garlic in 8-inch nonstick skillet. Cook over low heat, stirring occasionally, until garlic is pale golden brown, 9 to 12 minutes. Off heat, stir in pepper flakes; set aside.

2. Meanwhile, set colander in large bowl. Bring 2 quarts water to boil in large pot. Add pasta and 2 teaspoons salt and cook, stirring frequently, until al dente. Drain pasta in prepared colander, reserving cooking water. Return pasta to pot. Add lemon zest and juice, garlic-oil mixture, 1 cup reserved cooking water, and remaining ½ teaspoon garlic. Stir until pasta is well coated with oil and no water remains in bottom of pot. Add basil, Parmesan, and pine nuts and toss to combine. Adjust consistency with remaining reserved cooking water as needed. Season with salt and pepper to taste. Serve, passing extra Parmesan separately.

Variations

GARLICKY SPAGHETTI WITH GREEN OLIVES AND ALMONDS

Omit lemon zest and reduce lemon juice to 1 tablespoon. Stir 1 cup pitted green olives, chopped fine, into pasta with lemon juice. Substitute Pecorino Romano for Parmesan and toasted sliced almonds for pine nuts.

SPAGHETTI AGLIO E OLIO

Omit lemon zest and juice, basil, Parmesan, and pine nuts. Add ½ teaspoon table salt when stirring pasta with garlic-oil mixture. Stir in 3 tablespoons chopped fresh parsley when adjusting consistency with reserved cooking water.

> **KEYS TO SUCCESS**
> - **Use less water:** Creates an extra-starchy cooking water, lending more body to simple sauces such as this one
> - **Submerge the garlic in oil and cook it gently:** Softens the garlic's raw flavor and prevents it from burning

SCIENCE LESSON

Understanding al Dente

Pasta recipes usually call for cooking noodles al dente, meaning they are tender but still firm. But what exactly happens to dried pasta as it cooks? Dried pasta is a complex network of starch granules held together by protein. As pasta is boiled to al dente, the starch granules on the surface of the pasta absorb water and swell, and some eventually burst, releasing starch into the cooking water. The granules just beneath the pasta's surface don't become as hydrated and swell without bursting. Finally, the starch at the very center of the pasta becomes only partially hydrated, so the center retains a slightly firm bite and a faint white core.

Cooking Pasta Using 2 Quarts of Water versus 4 Quarts

CLOUDY WATER
Using 4 quarts of water for 1 pound of pasta creates starchy cooking water that's ideal for adjusting a sauce's consistency before serving.

CLOUDIER WATER
Using only 2 quarts of water for 1 pound of pasta creates a superstarchy liquid to add even more body to very light sauces.

ORZO SALAD WITH BROCCOLI AND RADICCHIO

Serves: 4 to 6
Total Time: 35 minutes

RECIPE OVERVIEW Pasta salads aren't any more difficult to make than hot pasta dishes. The secret to any great pasta salad is to cook the pasta until it's completely tender (slightly beyond al dente). Since pasta becomes firmer as it cools, cooking it beyond al dente ensures that it will remain tender when it's served chilled or at room temperature. This vibrant recipe includes verdant broccoli, bitter radicchio, savory sun-dried tomatoes, and crunchy toasted pine nuts. In an approach similar to that of Orecchiette with Broccoli Rabe and Sausage (page 241), cooking the orzo in the broccoli blanching water imparts a delicate vegetal flavor throughout the dish while also streamlining prep. The bold vinaigrette unites all the components of this hearty salad.

- 12 ounces broccoli florets, cut into 1-inch pieces
- 1 teaspoon table salt, plus salt for cooking broccoli and pasta
- 1⅓ cups orzo
- 1 head radicchio (10 ounces), cored and chopped fine
- 2 ounces Parmesan cheese, grated (1 cup)
- ½ cup oil-packed sun-dried tomatoes, rinsed, patted dry, and minced, plus 3 tablespoons packing oil
- ½ cup pine nuts, toasted
- ¼ cup balsamic vinegar, plus extra for seasoning
- 1 garlic clove, minced
- 1 teaspoon honey
- 3 tablespoons extra-virgin olive oil
- ½ cup chopped fresh basil

1. Bring 4 quarts water to boil in large pot. Fill large bowl halfway with ice and water. Add broccoli and 1 tablespoon salt to boiling water and cook until crisp-tender, about 2 minutes. Using slotted spoon, transfer broccoli to ice bath and let cool, about 2 minutes; drain and pat dry.

2. Return pot of water to boil. Add orzo and cook, stirring often, until tender. Drain orzo; rinse with cold water; and drain again, leaving orzo slightly wet. Toss orzo, broccoli, radicchio, Parmesan, tomatoes, and pine nuts together in large bowl.

3. In small bowl, whisk vinegar, garlic, honey, and salt together. Whisking constantly, drizzle in tomato oil and olive oil. Stir vinaigrette into orzo mixture. (Salad can be refrigerated for up to 24 hours; adjust consistency with warm water and additional oil as needed.) Stir in basil and season with salt, pepper, and extra vinegar to taste before serving.

KEYS TO SUCCESS

- **Cook beyond al dente:** Ensures that the orzo will have the right texture once it's chilled
- **Leave the orzo wet:** Keeps the orzo from drying out before it's tossed with the vinaigrette
- **Make the salad ahead:** Gives the orzo time to absorb the flavors of the other ingredients
- **Blanch the broccoli:** Keeps it bright green and crisp-tender; see page 95 for more information on blanching and shocking.

MEASURING LESS THAN A POUND OF PASTA

It's easy enough to measure out a pound of pasta, as most packages are sold in this quantity. But when a recipe calls for less it's good to have the cup measurements below for shaped pasta. When it comes to strand pasta, determining the diameter works well as a guideline.

PASTA TYPE*	8 OUNCES	12 OUNCES
Elbow macaroni and small shells	2 cups	3 cups
Orecchiette	2¼ cups	3⅓ cups
Penne, ziti, and campanelle	2½ cups	3¾ cups
Rigatoni, fusilli, medium shells, wagon wheels, wide egg noodles	3 cups	4½ cups
Farfalle	3¼ cups	4¾ cups

*These amounts do not apply to whole-wheat pasta.

When 8 ounces of uncooked strand pasta is bunched together into a tight circle, the diameter measures about 1¼ inches. When 12 ounces of uncooked strand pasta is bunched together, the diameter measures about 1¾ inches.

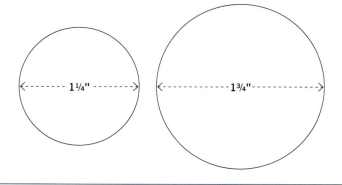

WARM SPICED PEARL COUSCOUS SALAD

Serves: 4
Total Time: 40 minutes

RECIPE OVERVIEW Although the little granules resemble grains, couscous is actually a pasta, made by rubbing semolina with water until tiny pieces form. Pearl couscous (also called Israeli couscous) has larger grains—the size of pearls. Regular couscous is simply dried before it's packaged, while pearl couscous is also toasted. To enhance its flavor even more, in this salad you toast the pearl couscous in oil before simmering it in broth until it's tender. Canned chickpeas and smoky chorizo add heft, carrots and dried fruit provide contrasting sweetness, and lemon and parsley are a bright finishing touch.

- 2 cups pearl couscous
- 12 ounces Spanish-style chorizo sausage, cut into ½-inch pieces
- 4 carrots, peeled and chopped
- 5 tablespoons extra-virgin olive oil, divided
- ½ teaspoon table salt
- 2⅔ cups chicken or vegetable broth
- 2 teaspoons smoked paprika
- 1 teaspoon ground cumin
- 4 cups canned chickpeas, rinsed and patted dry
- 1⅓ cups chopped fresh parsley or cilantro
- 1 cup raisins, chopped dried apricots, chopped dates, or chopped dried figs
- 2½ tablespoons lemon juice, plus lemon wedges for serving

1. Combine couscous, chorizo, carrots, 1 tablespoon oil, and salt in large saucepan and cook over medium heat, stirring frequently, until half of grains are golden, about 5 minutes. Stir in broth, paprika, and cumin. Bring to simmer; cover; and cook over low heat, stirring occasionally, until broth is absorbed and couscous is tender, 15 to 20 minutes. Let sit off heat, covered, for 5 minutes.

2. Stir in chickpeas, parsley, raisins, lemon juice, and remaining 4 tablespoons oil. Season with salt and pepper to taste. Serve with lemon wedges. (Salad can be refrigerated for up to 2 days.)

North African versus Pearl Couscous

The tiny, grain-like couscous you'll see labeled simply as couscous hails from North Africa. Pearl couscous has larger, chewier grains; it originated in Israel as a substitute for rice.

NORTH AFRICAN   **PEARL**

MORE TO EXPLORE

TOMATO SAUCES

There are hundreds of tomato-based pasta sauces for home cooks of all skill levels to choose among, from superfast simmers to long-cooked affairs. Here are a few versatile, flavorful, and easy recipes to learn, from a classic marinara to a simple meat sauce, for any time the red-sauce craving strikes.

CLASSIC MARINARA SAUCE

Makes: about 4 cups (enough for 1½ pounds pasta)
Total Time: 50 minutes

A marinara sauce generally contains tomatoes, onions, garlic, and herbs, but the result should always be more than the sum of its parts, lively and complex. Here you drain canned whole peeled tomatoes, reserving the juice, and then cook down some of the drained tomatoes along with onion and garlic before adding the juice and some red wine. A brief simmer, with some reserved uncooked tomatoes added at the end, gives way to a rich, versatile sauce. This is a smooth marinara, so if you prefer a chunkier sauce, give it just three or four pulses in the food processor in step 4. Because canned tomatoes vary in acidity and saltiness, it's best to add sugar, salt, and pepper to taste after the sauce has finished cooking. We recommend using a Chianti or Merlot for the red wine.

- 2 (28-ounce) cans whole peeled tomatoes
- 3 tablespoons extra-virgin olive oil, divided
- 1 onion, chopped fine
- 2 garlic cloves, minced
- 2 teaspoons minced fresh oregano or ½ teaspoon dried
- ⅓ cup dry red wine
- ½ teaspoon table salt
- ¼ teaspoon pepper
- 3 tablespoons chopped fresh basil
  Sugar

1. Drain tomatoes in fine-mesh strainer set over bowl. Using your hands, open tomatoes and remove seeds and cores. Let tomatoes drain for 5 minutes. (You should have about 2½ cups juice; if not, add water to equal 2½ cups.) Measure out ¾ cup tomatoes and set aside.

2. Heat 2 tablespoons oil in large saucepan over medium heat until shimmering. Add onion and cook until softened and lightly browned, 5 to 7 minutes. Stir in garlic and oregano and cook until fragrant, about 30 seconds. Stir in tomatoes from strainer and increase heat to medium-high. Cook, stirring often, until liquid has evaporated and tomatoes begin to brown and stick to saucepan, 10 to 12 minutes.

3. Stir in wine and cook until thick and syrupy, about 1 minute. Stir in tomato juice, salt, and pepper, scraping up any browned bits. Bring to simmer and cook, stirring occasionally, until sauce is thickened, 8 to 10 minutes.

4. Transfer sauce to food processor; add reserved ¾ cup tomatoes; and pulse until slightly chunky, about 8 pulses. Return sauce to saucepan and bring to simmer. Stir in basil and remaining 1 tablespoon oil. Season with salt, pepper, and sugar to taste. (Sauce can be refrigerated for up to 1 week or frozen for up to 3 months.)

FRESH TOMATO SAUCE

Makes: about 5 cups (enough for 2 pounds pasta)
Total Time: 1¼ hours

For a bright-tasting sauce made from fresh tomatoes that's thick enough to cling to pasta, make use of the tomato flesh, skin, and jelly (discarding only the seeds and cores). It's admittedly slightly fussy to separate the seeds from the jelly, but it really pays off in deeply savory tomato flavor. Limiting the aromatics to just garlic, pepper flakes, and dried oregano (plus fresh basil at the end) ensures that the tomato flavor is the star. This recipe is best made using ripe in-season tomatoes. Supermarket vine-ripened tomatoes will work as well, but don't use plum tomatoes; they are too low in moisture. This is a lighter-bodied sauce, so don't adjust its consistency with reserved pasta cooking water as you would with other pasta sauces or it will become too diluted.

- 5 pounds tomatoes, cored
- ¼ cup extra-virgin olive oil, divided
- 2 garlic cloves, minced
- ¼ teaspoon red pepper flakes
- ¼ teaspoon dried oregano
- 1 teaspoon table salt
- 1 cup fresh basil leaves, shredded

1. Cut tomatoes in half along equator. Set fine-mesh strainer over medium bowl. Gently squeeze tomato halves, cut side down, over strainer to collect seeds and jelly, scraping any seeds that cling to tomatoes into strainer. Using rubber spatula, press on seeds and jelly to extract as much liquid as possible. Discard seeds. Set aside 1 cup strained liquid and transfer any remaining liquid to large bowl.

2. Cut tomatoes into rough 1½-inch pieces. Working in 2 or 3 batches, process tomatoes in blender until smooth, 30 to 45 seconds; transfer puree to large bowl with strained liquid (you should have about 10 cups puree).

3. Heat 2 tablespoons oil in large saucepan or Dutch oven over medium heat until shimmering. Add garlic, pepper flakes, and oregano and cook until fragrant, about 1 minute. Stir in tomato puree and salt. Increase heat to medium-high and bring to simmer. Reduce heat to medium-low and simmer, stirring occasionally, until reduced to 4 cups, 45 minutes to 1 hour.

4. Off heat, stir in basil, reserved 1 cup strained liquid, and remaining 2 tablespoons oil. Season with salt to taste. (Sauce can be refrigerated for up to 1 week or frozen for up to 3 months.)

ARRABBIATA SAUCE

Makes: about 3 cups (enough for 1 pound pasta)
Total Time: 20 minutes

This zesty sauce using canned crushed tomatoes comes together superfast. It hails from Rome, where it is often used to sauce penne. "Arrabbiata" means "angry" and refers to the generous amount of red pepper flakes; we offer a range here so that you can tailor the sauce to your taste. In addition to pasta, this makes a great sauce for roasted sausages or fried eggs.

- 2 tablespoons unsalted butter
- ¼ cup finely chopped onion
- 1 teaspoon minced fresh oregano or ¼ teaspoon dried
- ½ teaspoon table salt
- ¼–¾ teaspoon red pepper flakes
- 4 garlic cloves, minced
- 1 (28-ounce) can crushed tomatoes
- ¼ teaspoon sugar
- 2 tablespoons chopped fresh parsley
- 1 tablespoon extra-virgin olive oil

1. Melt butter in medium saucepan over medium-low heat. Add onion, oregano, salt, and pepper flakes and cook, stirring occasionally, until onion is softened and lightly browned, 3 to 5 minutes. Stir in garlic and cook until fragrant, about 30 seconds.

2. Stir in tomatoes and sugar; bring to simmer; and cook until slightly thickened, about 10 minutes. Off heat, stir in parsley and oil and season with salt and pepper to taste. (Sauce can be refrigerated for up to 1 week or frozen for up to 1 month.)

AMATRICIANA SAUCE

Makes: about 3 cups (enough for 1 pound pasta)
Total Time: 30 minutes

The base of Amatriciana sauce is tomatoes, rendered cured pork, and chile pepper. Guanciale (which is salt cured but not smoked) is the traditional choice, though pancetta can also be used. Simmering the guanciale first renders its fat, which allows the meat to quickly brown once the water evaporates. Mixing the grated Pecorino with the rendered pork fat prevents it from clumping (the fat prevents the cheese proteins from bonding in lumps) and adds more rich pork flavor to the sauce. In addition to pancetta, you can substitute salt pork for the guanciale; remove the rind and rinse and dry the salt pork before slicing it. Look for salt pork that is 70 percent fat. If your cured pork is difficult to slice, put it in the freezer for 15 minutes to firm up. Amatriciana is traditionally served with bucatini and is made in conjunction with cooking the pasta.

- 8 ounces guanciale
- ½ cup water
- 2 tablespoons tomato paste
- ½ teaspoon red pepper flakes
- ¼ cup red wine
- 1 (28-ounce) can diced tomatoes
- 2 ounces Pecorino Romano cheese, grated fine (1 cup), divided

1. Slice guanciale into ¼-inch-thick strips, then cut each strip crosswise into ¼-inch pieces. Bring guanciale and water to simmer in 10-inch nonstick skillet over medium heat; cook until water evaporates and guanciale begins to sizzle, 5 to 8 minutes. Reduce heat to medium-low and continue to cook, stirring frequently, until fat is rendered and guanciale turns golden, 5 to 8 minutes. Using slotted spoon, transfer guanciale to bowl. Pour all but 1 tablespoon fat from skillet into second bowl and reserve.

2. Add tomato paste and pepper flakes to fat left in skillet and cook, stirring constantly, for 20 seconds. Stir in wine and cook for 30 seconds. Stir in tomatoes and their juice and guanciale and bring to simmer. Cook, stirring frequently, until thickened, 12 to 16 minutes. While sauce simmers, smear 2 tablespoons reserved fat and ½ cup Pecorino together in bowl to form paste.

3. After cooking pasta, add sauce, ⅓ cup pasta cooking water, and Pecorino-fat mixture to pasta and toss well to coat, adjusting consistency with remaining cooking water as needed. Serve, passing remaining ½ cup Pecorino separately.

SIMPLE ITALIAN-STYLE MEAT SAUCE

Makes: about 3 cups (enough for 1 pound pasta)
Total Time: 1 hour

Though the results are undeniably worth it, many Italian meat sauces can be complicated and time-consuming. This quick meat sauce deploys a few tricks to ensure that it tastes like it simmered for a good portion of the day. First, instead of browning the meat, brown mushrooms to give the sauce savory flavor without drying out the meat. Second, blend a panade (a mixture of bread and milk) into the meat before cooking to help keep it tender. Third, for good tomato flavor, add tomato paste to the browned vegetables and deglaze the pan with a little tomato juice before adding canned tomatoes.

- 4 ounces white mushrooms, trimmed
- 1 slice hearty white sandwich bread, torn into quarters
- 2 tablespoons whole milk
- ½ teaspoon table salt
- ½ teaspoon pepper
- 1 pound 85 percent lean ground beef
- 1 tablespoon extra-virgin olive oil
- 1 large onion, chopped fine
- 6 garlic cloves, minced
- 1 tablespoon tomato paste
- ¼ teaspoon red pepper flakes
- 1 (14.5-ounce) can diced tomatoes, drained with ¼ cup juice reserved
- 1 teaspoon dried oregano
- 1 (28-ounce) can crushed tomatoes
- ¼ cup grated Parmesan cheese

1. Pulse mushrooms in food processor until finely chopped, about 8 pulses, scraping down sides of bowl as needed; transfer mushrooms to bowl. Pulse bread, milk, salt, and pepper in now-empty processor until paste forms, about 8 pulses. Add beef and pulse until mixture is well combined, about 6 pulses.

2. Heat oil in large saucepan over medium-high heat until just smoking. Add onion and mushrooms and cook, stirring frequently, until vegetables are browned and dark bits form on bottom of saucepan, 6 to 12 minutes. Stir in garlic, tomato paste, and pepper flakes; cook until fragrant, about 1 minute. Add reserved tomato juice and oregano, scraping up any browned bits. Add beef mixture and cook, breaking meat into small pieces with wooden spoon, until beef is no longer pink, 2 to 4 minutes.

3. Stir in crushed tomatoes and diced tomatoes and bring to simmer. Reduce heat to low and simmer gently until sauce is thickened and flavors have blended, about 30 minutes. Stir in Parmesan and season with salt and pepper to taste.

RESOURCES FOR TOMATO SAUCES

CANNED AND JARRED TOMATOES

Since good-quality fresh tomatoes are available only a few months of the year, it's smart to rely on canned tomatoes to make pasta sauces, since they are of a consistently high quality year-round. Here's a quick rundown.

WHOLE TOMATOES

As opposed to fresh supermarket tomatoes, canned whole tomatoes offer reliable quality any time of year. Whole tomatoes break down readily and are best reserved for recipes with a short simmering time, such as our Classic Marinara Sauce (page 246). Whole tomatoes packed in juice rather than in puree tend to have a livelier, fresher flavor.

CRUSHED TOMATOES

Crushed tomatoes work well in smoother sauces, such as our Arrabbiata Sauce (page 247), offering both great flavor and body. We also employ crushed tomatoes in casseroles where we want long-simmered flavor without having to cook the sauce separately for a long time, such as Baked Ziti with Ricotta and Eggplant (page 259).

DICED TOMATOES

Diced tomatoes contain calcium chloride to maintain their shape, making them best for rustic, chunky tomato sauces, such as Amatriciana Sauce. Diced tomatoes may also be processed with their juice in a food processor and used in place of crushed tomatoes when called for in a recipe. As with whole tomatoes, diced tomatoes packed in juice have a fresher flavor than those packed in puree.

TOMATO PUREE

Tomato puree is cooked and strained to remove the tomato seeds, making this a smoother and thicker product with a more "cooked" flavor than other types of canned tomatoes. Tomato puree works well in long-simmered pasta sauces when you want a thicker, smoother texture and a deep, long-cooked flavor.

FIRE-ROASTED TOMATOES

Fire-roasted tomatoes have a sweet and smoky flavor that adds complexity to a wide range of dishes—from Italian pasta sauces to Mexican chilis to Middle Eastern stews. Some fire-roasted tomatoes are actually charred during processing, while others are simply smoke-flavored. Smoke level varies from product to product, and it mellows with longer cooking.

TOMATO SAUCE

Like tomato puree, tomato sauce is cooked and strained to remove the seeds, making for a much smoother result than other tomato products. Tomato sauce has a thinner consistency and lighter flavor than puree. Tomato sauce works well for thinner sauces and can also be used in conjunction with other tomato products to add smoothness and long-simmered tomato flavor, as in Sausage Lasagna (page 262).

SUN-DRIED TOMATOES

Sun-dried plum tomatoes are valued for their chewy texture and concentrated flavor. Most products are imported from Italy or Turkey and are sold either dry packed in plastic containers or bags or oil packed in jars. We prefer oil packed; the flavorful oil is a bonus.

TOMATO PASTE

Dense and concentrated and naturally full of glutamates, which stimulate tastebuds, tomato paste brings out deeper savory notes in dishes. You can use it in both quicker-cooking dishes and longer-simmered sauces, including our Simple Italian-Style Meat Sauce (page 248), to lend a richer, fully rounded tomato flavor.

COURSE
FRESH ITALIAN PASTA

DAN SOUZA

Fresh homemade pasta is an impressive achievement, but if you've ever tried to make it from scratch, you know there are challenges. If the dough is too dry, it won't roll out easily, and if the dough is too wet, it will be too sticky to handle. The dough recipe in this course rolls out with ease on the first try using a standard rolling pin—no pasta machine required. Letting the dough rest after kneading gives the gluten time to relax so that the dough won't spring back when you roll it. We stick to fettuccine here; after you cut your noodles, try them with one of the simple sauce recipes to highlight your prowess.

DAN'S PRO TIP: *Because this fresh pasta is hand rolled, noodle thickness—and therefore cooking time—can vary a bit from batch to batch. To ensure perfectly cooked pasta every time, I like to check it for doneness after just one minute in the pot, and then frequently after that until it is tender but still al dente.*

FRESH PASTA WITHOUT A MACHINE

Serves: 4 to 6 (Makes 1 pound)
Total Time: 1¼ hours, plus 1 hour resting

RECIPE OVERVIEW For delicate, golden pasta ribbons with a springy bite, olive oil and egg yolks are key for structure, and the right rolling and lifting techniques help you avoid using too much flour, which would make the pasta heavy and gummy. If you're using a high-protein all-purpose flour such as King Arthur, increase the number of egg yolks to seven. Instead of the recipes that follow, you could serve your pasta with one of the tomato sauces on pages 246–248. This recipe makes fettuccine; if you would like to make tagliatelle, cut the pasta into ⅜-inch-wide ribbons.

- 2 cups (10 ounces) all-purpose flour, plus extra as needed
- 2 large eggs plus 6 large yolks
- 2 tablespoons extra-virgin olive oil
  Table salt for cooking pasta

1. Process flour, eggs and yolks, and oil in food processor until mixture forms cohesive dough that feels soft and barely tacky to touch, 45 seconds. (If dough sticks to your fingers, add up to ¼ cup flour, 1 tablespoon at a time, until barely tacky. If dough doesn't become cohesive, add up to 1 tablespoon water, 1 teaspoon at a time, until it just comes together; process 30 seconds longer.)

2. Turn out dough onto dry counter and knead until smooth, 1 to 2 minutes. Shape dough into 6-inch-long cylinder. Wrap in plastic wrap and let rest at room temperature for at least 1 hour or up to 4 hours.

3. Cut cylinder crosswise into 6 equal pieces. Working with 1 piece of dough at a time (rewrap remaining dough), dust both sides with flour, place cut side down on clean counter, and press into 3-inch square. Using heavy rolling pin, roll into 6-inch square. Dust both sides of dough lightly with flour.

4. Starting at center of square, roll dough away from you in 1 motion. Return rolling pin to center of dough and roll toward you in single motion. Repeat rolling steps until dough sticks to counter and measures roughly 12 inches long. Lightly dust both sides of dough with flour and continue to roll until dough measures roughly 20 inches long and 6 inches wide, frequently lifting dough to release it from counter. (You should be able to easily see outline of your fingers through dough.) If dough firmly sticks to counter and wrinkles, dust dough lightly with flour.

5. Transfer pasta sheet to clean dish towel and let stand, uncovered, until firm around edges, about 15 minutes; meanwhile, roll out remaining dough.

6. Starting with 1 short end, gently fold 1 pasta sheet at 2-inch intervals until sheet has been folded into flat, rectangular roll. Using sharp chef's knife, slice crosswise into 3⁄16-inch-wide noodles. Use your fingers to unfurl noodles and transfer to baking sheet. Repeat folding and cutting with remaining pasta sheets. Cook noodles within 1 hour or freeze for up to 2 weeks.

7. Bring 4 quarts water to boil in large pot. Add pasta and 1 tablespoon salt and cook until tender but still al dente, about 3 minutes. Drain pasta, reserving cooking water as needed to adjust consistency of sauce.

> **KEYS TO SUCCESS**
> - **Rest the dough:** Makes it easier to roll out and less likely to spring back
> - **Roll, and roll again:** Until it's thin enough for you to see the outline of your fingers through it
> - **Go easy on the flour when rolling:** Too much results in excessive snapback and tough noodles

CORE TECHNIQUE
Making Fettuccine

ADD INGREDIENTS
A food processor makes efficient, foolproof work of mixing dough ingredients.

MIX DOUGH
Process until dough feels soft and slightly tacky to touch (but not sticky), about 45 seconds.

ROLL OUT SHEET
Roll out dough to measure 20 inches long by 6 inches wide; it should be thin enough to see outline of your fingers through it.

CUT INTO RIBBONS
Fold pasta sheet at 2-inch intervals to create flat roll, then use sharp chef's knife to cut roll into 3/16-inch-wide noodles.

FETTUCCINE WITH GARLIC OIL SAUCE

Serves: 4 to 6
Total Time: 20 minutes

RECIPE OVERVIEW The best pasta deserves a simple-but-flavorful sauce and this recipe pairs perfectly with fresh fettuccine. It is simple and fast and delivers big flavor. Start by blooming lots of sliced garlic and a pinch of spicy red pepper flakes in a generous amount of fruity, peppery extra-virgin olive oil. Just enough lemon juice and a fistful of fresh parsley balances the rich oil. Pungent, complex grated Pecorino Romano cheese—sprinkled on top of the finished pasta—layers in a supersatisfying cheesiness. For the best results, use a high-quality extra-virgin olive oil.

- 1 pound fresh fettuccine
- ½ teaspoon table salt, plus salt for cooking pasta
- ⅓ cup extra-virgin olive oil
- 4 garlic cloves, sliced thin
- ½ teaspoon black pepper
- ¼ teaspoon red pepper flakes
- ¼ cup chopped fresh parsley
- 4 teaspoons lemon juice
- Grated Pecorino Romano cheese

1. Bring 3 quarts water to boil in large Dutch oven. Add pasta and 1 tablespoon salt and cook, stirring frequently, until al dente. Reserve ½ cup cooking water, then drain pasta and return it to pot.

2. Combine oil, garlic, pepper, pepper flakes, and salt in 12-inch skillet. Cook over medium heat until garlic is lightly toasted, 2 to 4 minutes.

3. Add pasta and reserved cooking water; toss to combine. Off heat, stir in parsley and lemon juice. Season with salt and pepper to taste. Serve immediately, passing Pecorino separately.

KEYS TO SUCCESS

- **Be speedy:** Ensures that the fresh pasta neither overcooks in the water nor cools off after you drain it
- **Don't forget to reserve pasta cooking water:** The starchy water adds body to the sauce.
- **Use high-quality Pecorino Romano:** It's essential to the flavor of this dish.

FETTUCCINE WITH BROWNED BUTTER–PINE NUT SAUCE

Serves: 4 to 6
Total Time: 25 minutes

RECIPE OVERVIEW There's no cheese in this elegant sauce; instead, you brown butter in a skillet until it turns dark golden brown and nutty in flavor. Toasted pine nuts further enhance the nutty flavor, and a handful of chopped parsley adds a bright herbal finish. As with Fettuccine with Garlic Oil Sauce, you cook the pasta in a smaller amount of water than usual so that the cooking water contains extra starch, bringing more body to this buttery sauce.

- 1 pound fresh fettuccine
- ½ teaspoon table salt, plus salt for cooking pasta
- 8 tablespoons unsalted butter
- ½ cup pine nuts, toasted
- 2 tablespoons chopped fresh parsley

1. Bring 3 quarts water to boil in large Dutch oven. Add pasta and 1 tablespoon salt and cook, stirring frequently, until al dente. Reserve 1 cup cooking water, then drain pasta and return it to pot.

2. Melt butter in 10-inch skillet over medium-high heat. Continue to cook, swirling skillet constantly, until butter is dark golden brown and has nutty aroma, 1 to 3 minutes. Off heat, add pine nuts, parsley, and salt. Pour over pasta in pot and toss to combine; adjust consistency with reserved cooking water as needed. Serve immediately.

CORE TECHNIQUE — **Browning Butter**

Swirl butter in a hot skillet until its water evaporates and its milk solids undergo the Maillard reaction (see page 33), creating nutty flavor compounds.

SCIENCE LESSON

Gluten Management

When making fresh pasta, you want to minimize gluten development so that the dough is pliable when you're rolling it out. In our recipe for fresh pasta, the fat from the olive oil and extra egg yolks coats the flour molecules, inhibiting excess gluten formation. The eggs also help bolster the protein network of the pasta dough, which prevents the noodles from falling apart when you boil them.

MORE TO EXPLORE

PESTO

Classic basil pesto, which hails from Genoa, tends to steal the spotlight, but there's a world of pesto combinations out there—not all of them green. Here's a recipe for classic basil pesto (with an updated foolproof method) along with pestos using other greens and even bell peppers and tomatoes. When using any of these as a pasta sauce, don't forget to save some of the pasta cooking water to thin out the sauce to your desired consistency.

BASIL PESTO

Makes: about ¾ cup (enough for 1 pound pasta)
Total Time: 20 minutes

The basil is heightened and the garlic is subdued in this classic pesto so that these two major elements balance each other out. To tame the raw garlic edge, toast it in a dry skillet; toast the pine nuts as well to bring out their nuttiness. Pound the basil and parsley to bruise them and release their flavorful oils. A food processor combines all the ingredients quickly and easily. This classic pesto isn't just for pasta: Stir it into rice, dollop it on roasted chicken breasts, or spread it on good crusty bread.

- 3 garlic cloves, unpeeled
- ¼ cup pine nuts
- 2 cups fresh basil leaves
- 2 tablespoons fresh parsley leaves
- ½ cup extra-virgin olive oil
- ¼ cup grated Parmesan cheese

1. Toast garlic in 8-inch skillet over medium heat, shaking skillet occasionally, until softened and spotty brown, about 8 minutes. When garlic is cool enough to handle, discard skins and chop coarse. Meanwhile, toast pine nuts in now-empty skillet over medium heat, stirring often, until golden and fragrant, 4 to 5 minutes.

2. Place basil and parsley in 1-gallon zipper-lock bag. Pound bag with flat side of meat pounder or with rolling pin until all leaves are bruised.

3. Process garlic, pine nuts, and herbs in food processor until finely chopped, about 1 minute, scraping down sides of bowl as needed. With processor running, slowly add oil until incorporated. Transfer pesto to bowl, stir in Parmesan, and season with salt and pepper to taste.

SPINACH PESTO

Makes: about 1½ cups (enough for 2 pounds pasta)
Total Time: 15 minutes

For a supernutritious pesto, try using spinach instead of basil. It's even faster to make: Toast garlic cloves in a dry skillet and then process them in a food processor with spinach, Parmesan, olive oil, and toasted almonds. Lemon juice brightens the earthy spinach.

- 2 garlic cloves, unpeeled
- 3 ounces (3 cups) baby spinach
- 4 ounces Parmesan cheese, grated (2 cups)
- ½ cup extra-virgin olive oil
- ¼ cup sliced almonds, toasted
- 1 tablespoon lemon juice
- ½ teaspoon table salt

1. Toast garlic in 8-inch skillet over medium heat, shaking skillet occasionally, until softened and spotty brown, about 8 minutes. When garlic is cool enough to handle, discard skins and chop coarse.

2. Process garlic, spinach, Parmesan, oil, almonds, lemon juice, and salt in food processor until smooth, 30 to 60 seconds, scraping down sides of bowl as needed. Season with salt and pepper to taste.

ARUGULA-ALMOND PESTO

Makes: about 1½ cups (enough for 2 pounds pasta)
Total Time: 15 minutes

For a more assertive, slightly spicy alternative to traditional basil pesto, process almonds (toasted first to enhance their rich flavor) in a food processor with lots of garlic, anchovies, and a serrano chile until the mixture is finely chopped. Then add peppery arugula, lemon juice, and olive oil and process until the sauce is smooth.

- ¼ cup almonds, lightly toasted
- 4 garlic cloves, peeled
- 1 serrano chile, stemmed, halved lengthwise, and seeded
- 4 anchovy fillets, rinsed and patted dry
- 6 ounces (6 cups) arugula
- ¼ cup lemon juice (2 lemons)
- ¼ cup extra-virgin olive oil
- 1½ teaspoons kosher salt

Process almonds, garlic, serrano, and anchovies in food processor until finely chopped, about 15 seconds, scraping down sides of bowl as needed. Add arugula, lemon juice, oil, and salt and process until smooth, about 30 seconds.

KALE-SUNFLOWER SEED PESTO

Makes: about 1½ cups (enough for 2 pounds pasta)
Total Time: 20 minutes

This creative pesto uses hearty kale in addition to basil and toasted sunflower seeds in lieu of nuts. Pounding the kale and basil both tenderizes the sturdy green and helps bring out the herb's flavorful oils. As with the classic Basil Pesto, here you toast the garlic in a dry skillet to temper its raw bite.

- 2 garlic cloves, unpeeled
- ½ cup raw sunflower seeds
- 4 ounces kale, stemmed and chopped (2 cups)
- 1 cup fresh basil leaves
- 1 teaspoon red pepper flakes (optional)
- ½ cup extra-virgin olive oil
- 1½ ounces Parmesan cheese, grated (¾ cup)

1. Toast garlic in 8-inch skillet over medium heat, shaking skillet occasionally, until softened and spotty brown, about 8 minutes. When garlic is cool enough to handle, discard skins and chop coarse. Meanwhile, toast sunflower seeds in now-empty skillet over medium heat, stirring often, until golden and fragrant, 4 to 5 minutes.

2. Place kale and basil in 1-gallon zipper-lock bag. Pound bag with flat side of meat pounder or with rolling pin until all leaves are bruised.

3. Process garlic; sunflower seeds; kale; basil; and pepper flakes, if using, in food processor until finely chopped, about 1 minute, scraping down sides of bowl as needed. With processor running, slowly add oil until incorporated. Transfer pesto to bowl, stir in Parmesan, and season with salt and pepper to taste.

PESTO CALABRESE

Makes: about 2 cups (enough for 1 pound pasta)
Total Time: 35 minutes

Pesto Calabrese is a pesto of a different color—literally. At its base lies red bell peppers, enhanced by tomato, basil, garlic, ricotta, and Parmesan. For complex flavor, sauté two of the peppers and then add the third one raw for fresh, fruity bite. Dried red pepper flakes ably take the place of the traditional Calabrian chiles. A modest amount of cheese provides richness, salty tang, and creamy body to this saucy pesto.

- 3 red bell peppers, stemmed, seeded, and cut into ¼-inch-wide strips (5 cups), divided
- 3 tablespoons extra-virgin olive oil, divided
- 1 teaspoon table salt, divided
- 1 small onion, chopped
- 1 plum tomato, cored, seeded, and chopped
- ⅓ cup chopped fresh basil
- 1 teaspoon garlic, minced to paste, divided
- ½–¾ teaspoon red pepper flakes
- 4 ounces (½ cup) whole-milk ricotta cheese
- ¼ cup grated Parmesan cheese, plus extra for serving
- ¼ teaspoon pepper
- 1 teaspoon white wine vinegar

1. Toss two-thirds of bell peppers, 1 tablespoon oil, and ¼ teaspoon salt together in 12-inch nonstick skillet. Cover and cook over medium-low heat, stirring occasionally, until bell peppers are softened and just starting to brown, about 15 minutes.

2. Add onion, tomato, basil, ½ teaspoon garlic, and pepper flakes and continue to cook, uncovered, stirring occasionally, until onion is softened and bell peppers are browned in spots, 6 to 7 minutes. Remove skillet from heat and let cool for 5 minutes.

3. Place ricotta, Parmesan, pepper, remaining one-third of bell peppers, remaining ¾ teaspoon salt, and remaining ½ teaspoon garlic in bowl of food processor. Add cooked bell pepper mixture and process for 20 seconds. Scrape down sides of bowl. With processor running, add vinegar and remaining 2 tablespoons oil; process for 20 seconds. Scrape down sides of bowl, then continue to process until smooth, about 20 seconds.

COURSE
ONE-POT PASTA

DAN ZUCCARELLO

Now that you've mastered the best methods for cooking pasta and combining it with its sauce to finish, here you'll learn to cook pasta from start to finish directly in its sauce, with two of our favorite one-pot pastas. Penne puttanesca is a beloved Neapolitan preparation, and here we've created a one-pot rendition. And the Skillet Ziti with Sausage and Peppers is an Italian American classic reinvented in a nontraditional, streamlined way.

DAN'S PRO TIP: *Puttanesca gets its characteristic flavors from capers and olives, but because they are added right at the end of cooking, this dish is prime for flavor variations. Prefer spicy arrabbiata? Substitute minced pepperoncini for the olives and 4 minced anchovy fillets for the capers. Enjoy meaty Amatriciana? Substitute ¼ cup of crispy pancetta or bacon bits for the olives and capers.*

ONE-POT PENNE PUTTANESCA

Serves: 4 to 6
Total Time: 45 minutes

RECIPE OVERVIEW Pasta alla puttanesca, a classic Italian dish featuring tomatoes, garlic, capers, and olives, offers bold flavor and comes together quickly. Start with building the sauce base in a Dutch oven by cooking garlic and adding plum tomatoes, salt, pepper, and sugar (to balance the acidity). Then add the pasta and some water to the pot and keep right on cooking. The sauce will reduce and thicken while the pasta turns tender. Stirring in olives and capers at the end of cooking preserves their bright brininess, and a final sprinkle of basil brings the flavors together. You can substitute other pasta shapes for the penne, such as ziti, farfalle, or campanelle.

- 3 tablespoons extra-virgin olive oil
- 2 garlic cloves, minced
- 2 pounds plum tomatoes, cored and cut into ½-inch pieces
- ½ teaspoon table salt
- ½ teaspoon pepper
- ½ teaspoon sugar
- 5 cups water, plus extra as needed
- 1 pound penne
- ¼ cup coarsely chopped pitted kalamata olives
- ¼ cup capers, rinsed
- 2 tablespoons chopped fresh basil

1. Add oil and garlic to Dutch oven and cook over medium heat until fragrant, 1 to 2 minutes. Stir in tomatoes, salt, pepper, and sugar. Increase heat to medium-high and cook until tomatoes are broken down and sauce is slightly thickened, about 10 minutes.

2. Stir in water and pasta, cover, and bring to vigorous simmer. Reduce heat to medium and cook, covered, stirring gently and often, until pasta is nearly al dente, about 12 minutes. (If sauce becomes too thick, add extra water as needed.)

3. Uncover; add olives and capers; and simmer, stirring often, until pasta is al dente and sauce is thickened, 3 to 5 minutes. Off heat, stir in basil and season with salt and pepper to taste. Serve.

KEYS TO SUCCESS

- **Keep it covered:** Covering the Dutch oven while the pasta cooks controls evaporation, leading to the right consistency in the finished sauce.
- **A tight-fitting lid:** This is equally important for preventing the pasta from drying out on the stovetop and making sure that all the components cook evenly.

SKILLET ZITI WITH SAUSAGE AND PEPPERS

Serves: 4
Total Time: 1 hour

RECIPE OVERVIEW Baked ziti with sausage and bell peppers is an Italian American classic, and here it's made quicker using a hybrid stovetop-oven approach without sacrificing any of its bold flavor. For pronounced meatiness, render some crumbled sweet Italian sausage in a skillet. Then add canned whole tomatoes that you've processed in a food processor and simmer the sauce to rid the tomatoes of their raw flavor and concentrate their sweetness. Add some water to the skillet along with the ziti and cook the pasta right in its sauce until it's just tender. Then stir in cream and Parmesan before sprinkling the whole thing with shredded mozzarella and transferring the skillet to the oven to finish cooking the pasta and brown the topping. You can substitute penne, campanelle, medium shells, farfalle, or orecchiette for the ziti; see page 244 for cup measurements.

- 1 (28-ounce) can whole peeled tomatoes
- 1 pound sweet Italian sausage, casings removed
- 6 garlic cloves, minced (about 2 tablespoons)
- ¼ teaspoon red pepper flakes
- 8 ounces (2½ cups) ziti
- 1½ cups water
- 1 red bell pepper, stemmed, seeded, and cut into ½-inch pieces
- ½ teaspoon table salt
- 1 ounce Parmesan cheese, grated (½ cup)
- ⅓ cup heavy cream
- ¼ cup chopped fresh basil
- 6 ounces block mozzarella cheese, shredded (1½ cups)

1. Adjust oven rack to middle position and heat oven to 475 degrees. Pulse tomatoes and their juice in food processor until coarsely chopped and no large pieces remain, 6 to 8 pulses.

2. Cook sausage in 12-inch ovensafe nonstick skillet over medium-high heat, breaking up meat with wooden spoon, until lightly browned, 3 to 5 minutes. Stir in garlic and pepper flakes and cook until fragrant, about 30 seconds. Stir in tomatoes and simmer gently until tomatoes no longer taste raw, about 10 minutes.

3. Stir in ziti, water, bell pepper, and salt; cover; and bring to vigorous simmer. Reduce heat to medium and cook, covered, stirring often, until pasta is nearly tender, 14 to 17 minutes.

4. Off heat, stir in Parmesan, cream, and basil and season with salt and pepper to taste. Sprinkle mozzarella evenly over top. Transfer skillet to oven and bake until cheese is melted and browned, 10 to 15 minutes. Serve.

COURSE
BAKED PASTA

MORGAN BOLLING

Baked pasta casseroles are enduringly appealing but often seem intimidating to make. While they certainly do take some more time than simple stovetop pasta dishes, with more steps and some prep work, the process is not difficult. From a classic baked ziti to a comforting mac and cheese to two different lasagnas—one vegetable-based and one with red sauce and sausage—this course shows you how to choose ingredients (there are a couple surprises); prep them correctly (it has a lot to do with managing moisture); assemble or layer them in the baking dish; and bake your pasta casseroles to bubbly, cheesy perfection.

MORGAN'S PRO TIP: *I often see people cut into pasta casseroles that just came out of the oven. I know it can be hard to wait, but it's important to follow the cooling instructions for baked pasta recipes; it can make the difference between a wet, soupy casserole and one that is firm and sliceable.*

BAKED PENNE WITH SPINACH, ARTICHOKES, AND CHICKEN
Serves: 4 to 6
Total Time: 1 hour

RECIPE OVERVIEW This easy, cheesy pasta casserole takes its flavor inspiration from spinach-artichoke dip. Frozen spinach and artichoke hearts are both high quality and convenient, and all you have to do for prep is thaw, dry, and cut them. First you build a simple cream sauce, and then you stir in the star vegetables. A hefty amount of mozzarella and Parmesan brings the cheesy appeal, and shredded cooked chicken adds more protein. The short, tubular shape of penne ensures that every forkful holds an even mix of pasta, vegetables, and chicken. Cooking it until it's just shy of al dente keeps it from turning mushy when it bakes in the oven. Do not use fat-free mozzarella here. You can either use leftover cooked chicken here or roast chicken breasts following the recipe on page 414.

- 12 ounces (3¾ cups) penne
- ¼ teaspoon table salt, plus salt for cooking pasta
- 3 tablespoons unsalted butter
- 1 onion, chopped fine
- 3 garlic cloves, minced

3 tablespoons all-purpose flour
2½ cups chicken broth
1 cup heavy cream
18 ounces frozen artichoke hearts, thawed, patted dry, and quartered
10 ounces frozen spinach, thawed, squeezed dry, and chopped fine
10 ounces block mozzarella cheese, shredded (2½ cups), divided
2 ounces Parmesan cheese, grated (1 cup), divided
2 tablespoons lemon juice
4 cups shredded cooked chicken

1. Adjust oven rack to middle position and heat oven to 450 degrees. Bring 4 quarts water to boil in large Dutch oven. Add pasta and 1 tablespoon salt and cook, stirring often, until nearly al dente. Drain pasta and set aside.

2. Dry now-empty pot, add butter, and melt over medium heat. Add onion and salt and cook until softened, about 5 minutes. Stir in garlic and cook until fragrant, about 30 seconds. Stir in flour and cook for 1 minute. Slowly whisk in broth and cream until smooth and bring to simmer. Stir in artichokes and spinach and continue to simmer until vegetables are heated through, about 1 minute.

3. Stir in 1½ cups mozzarella and ½ cup Parmesan until melted. Off heat, stir in lemon juice and season with salt and pepper to taste. Fold in pasta and chicken, breaking up any clumps of pasta. Pour into 13 by 9-inch baking dish and sprinkle with remaining 1 cup mozzarella and remaining ½ cup Parmesan. Bake until bubbling around edges and cheese is spotty brown, 12 to 15 minutes. Let cool for 10 to 15 minutes and serve.

KEYS TO SUCCESS

- **Drain the pasta before it's al dente**: Pasta will continue to cook in the oven. Nearly al dente pasta should be very firm, but not crunchy.
- **Slowly whisk in the liquid**: Allows it to combine with the other ingredients and stay smooth, not turn lumpy

CORE TECHNIQUE
Preventing Soggy Baked Pasta

Whatever vegetables you include in your baked pasta should have as much moisture removed as possible so that they don't exude it into the casserole. Here, frozen vegetables (artichokes and spinach) are thawed and patted or squeezed dry. Eggplant gets cubed and roasted to dry out and brown before it's incorporated.

BAKED ZITI WITH RICOTTA AND EGGPLANT

Serves: 4 to 6
Total Time: 1½ hours

RECIPE OVERVIEW This substantial casserole is loaded with a whopping 2 pounds of eggplant, which you'll roast before stirring it into the pasta. Cooking the pasta until it's almost al dente ensures that it will turn out tender but not overcooked. Crushed tomatoes add rich flavor while keeping the casserole nice and moist, as does stirring some of the pasta cooking water into the sauce. As for the cheeses, there's a middle layer of creamy ricotta and the dish is topped with shredded mozzarella and grated Parmesan. The whole thing gets baked until the cheeses form an irresistibly bubbling, browned crust. Do not use nonfat ricotta or fat-free mozzarella here.

2 pounds eggplant, cut into 1-inch pieces
¼ cup extra-virgin olive oil divided
1½ teaspoons table salt, divided, plus salt for cooking pasta
½ teaspoon pepper, divided
1 pound ziti
3 garlic cloves, minced
¼ teaspoon red pepper flakes
2 (28-ounce) cans crushed tomatoes
8 ounces (1 cup) whole-milk ricotta cheese
6 ounces block mozzarella cheese, shredded (1½ cups)
2 ounces Parmesan cheese, grated (1 cup)
¼ cup chopped fresh basil

1. Adjust oven rack to middle position and heat oven to 400 degrees. Toss eggplant with 2 tablespoons oil in bowl and season with ¼ teaspoon salt and ¼ teaspoon pepper. Spread eggplant on greased rimmed baking sheet and roast, stirring occasionally, until golden brown, about 30 minutes.

2. Meanwhile, bring 4 quarts water to boil in Dutch oven. Add pasta and 1 tablespoon salt and cook, stirring often, until nearly al dente. Reserve ½ cup cooking water, then drain pasta and set aside.

3. Add 1 tablespoon oil, garlic, and pepper flakes to dry pot and cook over medium heat until fragrant, about 1 minute. Stir in tomatoes and 1 teaspoon salt and simmer until slightly thickened, about 10 minutes. Off heat, stir in pasta and reserved cooking water, breaking up any clumps, and season with salt and pepper to taste. Stir in eggplant.

4. Mix ricotta, remaining 1 tablespoon oil, remaining ¼ teaspoon salt, and remaining ¼ teaspoon pepper together in bowl.

5. Pour half of pasta mixture into 13 by 9-inch baking dish. Top with large spoonfuls of ricotta mixture, then pour remaining pasta mixture over ricotta. Sprinkle with mozzarella and Parmesan. Bake until bubbling around edges and cheese is spotty brown, about 25 minutes. Let cool for 10 to 15 minutes. Sprinkle with basil before serving.

MACARONI AND CHEESE CASSEROLE

Serves: 4 to 6
Total Time: 1½ hours

RECIPE OVERVIEW For this pasta casserole, you don't even have to parboil the pasta or cook a béchamel. You simply add uncooked elbow macaroni and shredded cheese right to the baking dish; pour over a mix of cream, water, eggs, and seasonings; and put it in the oven. The sauce ensures that the casserole turns out rich and sets but also has enough liquid for the pasta to cook through. Sharp cheddar provides intense flavor while American cheese keeps the sauce creamy and silky (American cheese has stabilizers that help hold sauces together). Tossing the shredded cheeses with cornstarch helps the sauce stay thick and discourages separation. For the best results, ask for a 4-ounce block of American cheese at the deli counter and shred it on the large holes of a box grater yourself. This recipe was developed using a ceramic baking dish. If you use a metal baking pan, reduce the cooking time in step 2 to 25 minutes.

- 8 ounces sharp cheddar cheese, shredded (2 cups), divided
- 4 ounces American cheese, shredded (1 cup)
- 4 teaspoons cornstarch, divided
- 8 ounces (2 cups) elbow macaroni
- 1 cup heavy cream
- 2 cups water
- 2 large eggs
- 2 teaspoons Dijon mustard
- 2 teaspoons hot sauce
- 2 teaspoons Worcestershire sauce
- ½ teaspoon table salt
- ½ teaspoon pepper

1. Adjust oven rack 6 inches from broiler element and heat oven to 400 degrees. Toss 1 cup cheddar, American cheese, and 2 teaspoons cornstarch together in bowl. Add macaroni, toss to combine, and transfer mixture to broiler-safe 8-inch square baking dish.

2. Whisk cream and remaining 2 teaspoons cornstarch in now-empty bowl until cornstarch is dissolved. Whisk in water, eggs, mustard, hot sauce, Worcestershire, salt, and pepper until fully combined. Pour cream mixture over macaroni mixture in dish. Cover with aluminum foil and bake for 30 minutes.

3. Remove dish from oven and discard foil. Stir to redistribute macaroni. Sprinkle with remaining 1 cup cheddar. Return dish to oven and continue to bake until edges are bubbling and just set and center registers 150 to 160 degrees, about 15 minutes.

4. Broil until top of casserole is spotty brown, about 2 minutes. Let rest on wire rack for 25 minutes. Serve.

KEYS TO SUCCESS

- **Don't skip cornstarch:** Ensures a creamy sauce that doesn't separate or turn greasy
- **Do skip Pyrex:** Pyrex dishes are not broiler-safe (see page 11 for more information).
- **Let it rest:** Post-bake resting time helps this cheesy, saucy casserole set up.

Making Macaroni and Cheese

PREVENT SEPARATION
Tossing shredded cheeses with cornstarch makes for thick, smooth cheese sauce.

ADD LIQUID
Pour cream mixture right over dried pasta and cheese in baking dish.

TEMP IT
Center of casserole should register 150 to 160 degrees.

VEGETABLE AND ORZO TIAN

Serves: 4
Total Time: 1 hour

RECIPE OVERVIEW This Mediterranean-inspired vegetable casserole features striking layers of zucchini, summer squash, and tomatoes over a bed of creamy orzo. To make sure that the pasta and vegetables finish cooking simultaneously, spread the uncooked orzo in the baking dish and tightly shingle the sliced vegetables over the orzo. This not only looks beautiful but also traps moisture in the casserole dish to help the orzo cook. A few minutes under the broiler and a sprinkle of basil finish the appealing presentation. Look for squash, zucchini, and tomatoes with similar circumferences so that they are easy to shingle in the dish. You will need a broiler-safe 13 by 9-inch baking dish.

- 3 ounces Parmesan cheese, grated (1½ cups), divided
- 1 cup orzo
- 2 shallots, minced
- 3 tablespoons minced fresh oregano or 1 teaspoon dried
- 3 garlic cloves, minced
- ¼ teaspoon table salt
- ⅛ teaspoon red pepper flakes
- 1 pound plum tomatoes, cored and sliced ¼ inch thick
- 1 zucchini, sliced ¼ inch thick
- 1 yellow summer squash, sliced ¼ inch thick
- 1¾ cups vegetable broth
- 1 tablespoon extra-virgin olive oil
- 2 tablespoons chopped fresh basil

1. Adjust oven rack to middle position and heat oven to 425 degrees. Combine ½ cup Parmesan, orzo, shallots, oregano, garlic, salt, and pepper flakes in bowl. Spread mixture evenly in broiler-safe 13 by 9-inch baking dish. Alternately shingle tomatoes, zucchini, and squash in tidy rows on top of orzo.

2. Carefully pour broth over top of vegetables. Bake until orzo is just tender and most of broth is absorbed, about 20 minutes.

3. Remove dish from oven, adjust oven rack 9 inches from broiler element, and heat broiler. Drizzle vegetables with oil, season with salt and pepper to taste, and sprinkle with remaining 1 cup Parmesan. Broil until spotty brown and bubbling around edges, about 5 minutes.

4. Remove dish from oven and let rest for 10 minutes. Sprinkle with basil and serve.

ROASTED ZUCCHINI AND EGGPLANT LASAGNA

Serves: 8
Total Time: 2 hours

RECIPE OVERVIEW Lasagna is a major crowd-pleaser and always gives the cook a sense of pride and accomplishment. It takes some time but really isn't that hard. This first version is a flavorful vegetarian casserole that highlights the flavors of the vegetables and doesn't mask them with excess cheese or a cream sauce. No-boil lasagna noodles make for quick assembly. Zucchini and eggplant are excellent choices for the filling, since they are easy to prep. Roasting the vegetables first not only drives off excess moisture that would otherwise water down the sauce but also caramelizes them, deepening their flavor. Ricotta cheese is traditional in lasagna, but here its creaminess would mute the fresh vegetable flavor, so this lasagna is layered with only mozzarella and Parmesan, which provide plenty of rich cheesiness and gooey texture. Be sure to grease the baking sheets before adding the vegetables so that they don't stick during roasting.

Vegetables and Sauce
- 1½ pounds zucchini, cut into ½-inch pieces
- 1½ pounds eggplant, cut into ½-inch pieces
- 5 tablespoons extra-virgin olive oil, divided
- 9 garlic cloves, minced, divided
- 1 teaspoon table salt
- 1 teaspoon pepper
- 1 onion, chopped fine
- 1 (28-ounce) can crushed tomatoes
- 1 (28-ounce) can diced tomatoes
- 2 tablespoons chopped fresh basil

Lasagna
- 12 no-boil lasagna noodles
- 12 ounces whole-milk block mozzarella cheese, shredded (3 cups)
- 4 ounces Parmesan cheese, grated (2 cups)

1. FOR THE VEGETABLES AND SAUCE Adjust oven racks to upper-middle and lower-middle positions and heat oven to 400 degrees. Toss zucchini, eggplant, 3 tablespoons oil, two-thirds of garlic, salt, and pepper together in large bowl. Spread vegetables on 2 greased rimmed baking sheets and roast, stirring occasionally, until softened and golden brown, 35 to 45 minutes; set aside.

2. Heat remaining 2 tablespoons oil in large saucepan over medium heat until shimmering. Add onion and cook until softened, about 5 minutes. Stir in remaining one-third garlic and cook until fragrant, about 30 seconds. Stir in crushed tomatoes and diced tomatoes and their juice; bring to simmer; and cook until flavors meld, about 5 minutes. Off heat, stir in basil and season with salt and pepper to taste. (You should have 7 cups sauce; if not, add water as needed to equal 7 cups.)

PASTA AND NOODLES | 261

3. **FOR THE LASAGNA** Spread 1 cup sauce over bottom of 13 by 9-inch baking dish. Lay 3 noodles in dish, spread one-quarter of vegetables over noodles, then top with 1 cup sauce, ⅔ cup mozzarella, and ½ cup Parmesan (in that order). Repeat layering 2 more times. Top with remaining 3 noodles, remaining vegetables, remaining sauce, remaining 1 cup mozzarella, and remaining ½ cup Parmesan.

4. Cover dish tightly with greased aluminum foil, place on foil-lined rimmed baking sheet, and bake for 15 minutes. Uncover and continue to bake until spotty brown and bubbling around edges, 25 to 35 minutes. Let lasagna cool for 10 minutes before serving.

SAUSAGE LASAGNA

Serves: 8 to 10
Total Time: 2¾ hours, plus 45 minutes cooling

RECIPE OVERVIEW When you're ready to tackle an extra-cheesy, meaty lasagna, turn to this beauty. To make quick work of breaking down the aromatic base of the sausage-tomato sauce, pulse those ingredients in the food processor until they're in small pieces. Next, boil the lasagna noodles, slightly undercooking them so that they won't turn mushy when baked. Why not use no-boil noodles? By using cooked noodles, you can cut and layer them precisely to fit, ensuring a saucy yet structurally sound lasagna that won't collapse on your plate. The cheesy element combines creamy mozzarella, flavorful provolone, and supersavory Pecorino Romano. Untraditionally, this lasagna uses cottage cheese rather than ricotta. Ricotta can become dry and pasty when baked, while cottage cheese contains more moisture and stays pillowy-soft and creamy. You can use either sweet or hot Italian sausage. Note that the Pecorino Romano is ground in the food processor (or you can purchase preground). Use the shredding disk of your food processor to make quick work of shredding the mozzarella and provolone, or use the large holes of a box grater.

Sauce
- 1 (1-pound) fennel bulb, stalks discarded, bulb halved, cored, and chopped coarse
- 1 onion, chopped coarse
- 3 tablespoons chopped fresh sage
- 4 garlic cloves, peeled
- 1 tablespoon fennel seeds
- ½ teaspoon red pepper flakes
- 1 tablespoon extra-virgin olive oil
- 2 pounds Italian sausage, casings removed
- 1 (28-ounce) can crushed tomatoes
- 1 (15-ounce) can tomato sauce

Lasagna
- 17 curly-edged lasagna noodles
  Table salt for cooking pasta
  Vegetable oil spray
- 1 pound whole-milk block mozzarella cheese, shredded (4 cups)
- 8 ounces provolone cheese, shredded (2 cups)
- 4 ounces Pecorino Romano cheese, ground fine in food processor (¾ cup)
- 1½ teaspoons dried oregano
- 1 pound (2 cups) whole-milk cottage cheese

1. **FOR THE SAUCE** Combine fennel, onion, sage, garlic, fennel seeds, and pepper flakes in food processor and pulse until finely chopped, about 10 pulses; set aside. Heat oil in Dutch oven over medium-high heat until just smoking. Add sausage and cook, breaking up meat with potato masher, until sausage begins to sizzle in its own fat, about 15 minutes.

2. Reduce heat to medium and add fennel mixture. Cook until vegetables are softened and fragrant, about 4 minutes. Add crushed tomatoes and tomato sauce and bring to simmer. Reduce heat to medium-low and cook for 5 minutes to allow flavors to blend. Set aside off heat. Reserve 2 cups sauce for topping.

3. **FOR THE LASAGNA** Bring 4 quarts water to boil in large pot. Add noodles and 1 tablespoon salt and cook until just shy of al dente, about 7 minutes. Drain noodles and transfer to rimmed baking sheet. Spray noodles lightly with oil spray; toss gently to coat (to prevent them from sticking to each other). Cut 2 noodles in half crosswise.

4. Adjust oven rack to middle position and heat oven to 375 degrees. Spray 13 by 9-inch baking dish with oil spray. Combine mozzarella, provolone, Pecorino, and oregano in bowl. Reserve 2 cups mozzarella mixture for topping.

5. Lay 3 noodles lengthwise in prepared dish with ends touching short side of dish, leaving gap at far end. Lay 1 half noodle crosswise to fill gap. Spread 1½ cups meat sauce over noodles; dollop ½ cup cottage cheese over sauce. Use back of spoon to spread cottage cheese evenly over sauce. Sprinkle with 1 cup mozzarella mixture.

6. Repeat layering of noodles, meat sauce, cottage cheese, and mozzarella mixture 3 more times, switching position of half noodle to opposite end of dish each time.

7. Lay remaining 3 noodles over top (there is no half noodle for top layer). Spread reserved 2 cups sauce over noodles, then sprinkle with reserved 2 cups mozzarella mixture.

8. Spray sheet of aluminum foil with oil spray and cover lasagna. Set lasagna on foil-lined rimmed baking sheet. Bake for 30 minutes. Discard foil covering lasagna and continue to bake until top layer of lasagna is spotty brown and lasagna is hot throughout, about 30 minutes. Let lasagna cool for 45 minutes. Slice and serve.

CORE TECHNIQUE
Cutting and Fitting Lasagna Noodles

CUT PARCOOKED NOODLES
Cut 2 cooked and oiled noodles in half.

LAYER A STABLE BASE
Arrange 3 noodles side by side along length of dish. Use half noodle to cover end.

BUILD STURDY LAYERS
After adding sauce and cheese, repeat layering of noodles, switching position of half noodle to opposite end of baking dish.

TOP IT OFF
Arrange final layer of noodles (no half noodle here).

KEYS TO SUCCESS
- **Skip no-boil lasagna noodles:** Cutting two of the boiled noodles in half lets you build full coverage and stability in the dish for the lower layers.
- **Buy two boxes of noodles:** Provides backup in case some of the noodles are broken
- **Ditch the ricotta for cottage cheese:** Contains more moisture and won't dry out or turn gritty during the baking time
- **Let it cool:** Long cooling time helps the lasagna set up so that the structure is stable when you cut into it.

RESOURCES FOR ITALIAN PASTA

PASTA POINTERS

Boiling pasta in salted water is a straightforward kitchen task, but you can improve your results with these simple tricks.

1. USE PLENTY OF WATER— OR STIR OFTEN
As pasta boils, it leaches starches into the cooking water, which can cause the noodles to stick together. The easiest way to cut down on sticking is to boil pasta in a generous amount of water to dilute the starches. However, if you don't have a pot large enough for all the water, you can reduce the water by half and stir the pasta frequently during cooking.

2. SALT THE WATER
Salting the cooking water ensures that seasoning gets into the pasta, not just on it. Add 1 tablespoon of salt to 4 quarts of water (or 1½ teaspoons to 2 quarts), making sure to stir well so that the salt will dissolve.

3. SKIP THE OIL
Since it merely sits on top of the cooking water, adding a splash of olive oil to the pot before adding the pasta doesn't prevent the pasta from sticking together as it cooks—though it may help keep the water from boiling over. To prevent the pasta from sticking together, simply stir it for a few moments after adding it to the boiling water.

4. CHECK FOR DONENESS OFTEN
We recommend ignoring the cooking times listed on packaging, which are almost always too long and result in mushy, overcooked pasta. Tasting the pasta is the best way to check for doneness. We prefer pasta cooked al dente, meaning that it has a bit of resistance in the center when bitten.

5. RESERVE SOME WATER
Before draining the pasta, reserve ½ to 1 cup of the cooking water, which is flavorful, somewhat salty, and starchy. It can be used to loosen a thick sauce without diluting the sauce's body or flavor as much as plain water would.

6. DON'T ASSUME FRESH PASTA IS ALWAYS A GOOD SUB FOR DRIED
Because fresh pasta is made from eggs and white wheat flour, it has a tender, delicate texture, which makes it less versatile than dried pasta. The latter is made from water and semolina flour, which gives it a stronger gluten structure and a sturdier texture.

COTTAGE CHEESE VERSUS RICOTTA

We've found that we prefer cottage cheese to the traditional ricotta for the creamy element in some styles of lasagna. Why? Ricotta (especially lower-quality versions) can become gritty, dry, and pasty when baked. Cottage cheese, on the other hand, generally contains more moisture and is more apt to stay pillowy-soft and creamy when baked. It has a tangy, fresh dairy flavor and a luscious, creamy texture. Look for cottage cheese with no stabilizers or gums in the ingredient list.

TROUBLESHOOTING DRIED PASTA

PROBLEM I am cooking 2 pounds of dried pasta. How much water do I need?

SOLUTION In general, we recommend 2 quarts of water for up to 8 ounces of pasta, 4 quarts for 8 ounces to 1 pound of pasta, and 6 quarts for 1 to 2 pounds. If you are cooking more than 2 pounds of pasta, use two pots.

PROBLEM My pasta dishes don't stay hot long enough.

SOLUTION Sauce your pasta in the hot pot in which it was cooked. You may even want to put the pot over low heat as you toss the pasta to ensure that it stays piping hot. Another key is to warm your serving bowls or plates. If they're ovensafe, you can do this in a low oven. Or bring a little extra water to a boil and then ladle some of it into the bowls so that they can warm up as you cook the pasta.

PRODUCTION OF COMMERCIAL DRIED PASTA

Today the process for making dried pasta is completely automated. It involves durum semolina flour, known for its high protein content; water; and not a whole lot else.

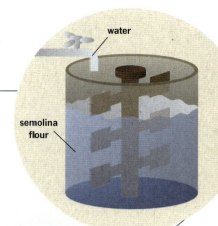

MIX AND KNEAD

To begin, the semolina flour is mixed with water and kneaded into a lumpy dough that contains about 30 percent moisture (typical sandwich bread dough, by comparison, contains about 50 to 60 percent moisture). During the mechanical kneading process that lasts for about 15 to 20 minutes, it is important to ensure that all the water is evenly dispersed to avoid white spots in the finished product.

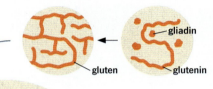

CLOSE UP: GLUTEN FORMATION
The kneading step starts the formation of gluten from the native glutenin and gliadin proteins in the flour.

ROLL IT

Next the dough is rolled flat, and then it's extruded through a horizontal cylinder with a screw mechanism that heats the dough to between 104 and 113 degrees. The temperature produced by the friction of the moving dough must be kept low enough to prevent premature swelling of the starch granules. This step also completes the formation of gluten proteins.

 SHAPE IT

At the end of the extruding cylinders are bronze dies with holes that determine the shape and size of the pasta. Some dies are lined with Teflon, but the more traditional bronze dies produce a rough surface to better hold a sauce.

SPAGHETTI   FETTUCCINE   SHELLS   FUSILLI   MACARONI   RIGATONI

DRY IT

The final step in the process involves drying the extruded pasta. This is the most important step for ensuring good quality because it creates the characteristic flavor, aroma, and texture of the cooked pasta. The drying time and temperature must be very carefully controlled. The drying process must also lower the water content to no more than 13 percent. This ensures that the moisture level will be low enough to prevent the growth of harmful microorganisms and provide a shelf life of at least three years.

ASIAN NOODLE BASICS

The world of Asian noodles, like the continent itself, is vast, encompassing rice noodles, buckwheat soba noodles, egg-enriched lo mein noodles, wheat ramen noodles, and more. (And while from-scratch ramen is irresistible, it is also quite complicated to make, so much so that fans of Japanese food go out for it rather than make it at home.) Here's a brief introduction to the types of noodles and some helpful pantry ingredients.

FRESH AND DRIED NOODLES

Lo Mein Noodles
These round-strand Chinese noodles are made with wheat and eggs and are sold fresh and dried. Fresh noodles absorb the flavors of stir-fry sauces better, but you can substitute dried noodles. Look for noodles specifically labeled "lo mein noodles." Packages labeled "fresh Chinese noodles" may or may not contain eggs.

Udon Noodles
Made from wheat and sold both fresh and dried, Japanese udon noodles are available in varying thicknesses, but all have a soft yet distinctive chew. They can contain a fair amount of salt, so don't add salt to the cooking water. Udon noodles are often used in soups, as in Vegetable Shabu-Shabu with Sesame Sauce (page 273), and they may also be served chilled.

Soba Noodles
These satisfyingly earthy Japanese noodles are made with buckwheat flour. The deeper the color, the more buckwheat they contain (and the richer they taste). Buckwheat flour contains no gluten, so soba noodles tend to be more fragile than wheat-only noodles. Soba are often served in stir-fries and in the summer are served chilled, as in our Chilled Soba Noodles with Spring Vegetables (page 275).

Rice Noodles
Translucent noodles made from a dough of rice powder and water, rice noodles are available in many shapes and sizes. Here you'll learn about wide flat noodles and thin round noodles. To prepare them for use in a dish, we soak them in hot water rather than boiling them because they overcook quickly. Flat rice noodles are essential for Pad Thai (page 278), while thin round ones are the choice for Singapore Noodles with Shrimp (page 276).

PANTRY INGREDIENTS

Soy Sauce
Umami-packed soy sauce originated in China nearly 3,000 years ago and made the leap to Japan around the seventh century. To produce it, soybeans are fermented with wheat, barley, or rice and special molds and yeasts. It's worth it to buy the best-quality soy sauce you can.

Miso
This umami-rich paste is made by inoculating soybeans with koji, a special mold cultivated from rice, soybeans, or barley. Producers adjust the ratio of koji to soybeans to create different misos. Although numerous varieties are available in Japan, in the United States the selection is more limited. The four main categories, ranging from mildest to strongest, are white, red, yellow, and brown.

Shaoxing Wine
This Chinese rice wine contributes distinctive savory, nutty flavors to food. Don't buy products labeled "Shaoxing cooking wine," which have added salt. If you don't have access to Shaoxing wine, dry sherry is an acceptable substitute.

Mirin
This Japanese rice wine, specifically used in cooking, has a salty-sweet quality. The traditional production method combines rice, koji, and a distilled spirit. We like to use mirin in sauces, such as in Soba Noodles with Pork, Scallions, and Shichimi Togarashi (page 274).

Toasted Sesame Oil
Toasted sesame oil has an intensely nutty aroma and flavor and a low smoking point. We use toasted sesame oil toward the end of cooking as well as in dressings and sauces.

ASIAN NOODLES

FRESH LO MEIN NOODLES | DRIED LO MEIN NOODLES | UDON NOODLES | SOBA NOODLES

RICE VERMICELLI

THIN RICE NOODLES

THICK RICE NOODLES

SOAKING FLAT RICE NOODLES

Undersoaked noodles are still too hard and will take too long to stir-fry.

Oversoaked noodles are too soft and gummy and will overcook when stir-fried and stay tangled.

Properly soaked noodles are just softened and will turn tender when stir-fried and remain separated.

COURSE
LO MEIN NOODLES

JOSEPH GITTER

Chinese noodles made from wheat and eggs, lo mein noodles are available both fresh and dried and boast a unique chewiness. Lo mein dishes are, well, the obvious choice for using these noodles, and there are two crowd-pleasing Chinese American recipes here. But these noodles are versatile and can be used in many other types of dishes, including another favorite, sesame noodles (a classic version gets you started, and then a modern interpretation encourages you to experiment a little). We prefer fresh lo mein noodles because they're so delightfully springy when cooked. They are readily available in Asian supermarkets and online, but you can also sub dried lo mein noodles, which are easy to find in large grocery stores. You can store uncooked fresh lo mein noodles in the freezer for up to one month.

JOE'S PRO TIP: *When tossing noodles with their sauce, do it gently so they don't break up. Longer, intact noodles not only look better but massively improve the dish's slurp-ability.*

SESAME NOODLES

Serves: 4 to 6
Total Time: 25 minutes

RECIPE OVERVIEW The nutty taste of toasted sesame seeds pairs with chewy fresh lo mein noodles in this recipe that's fast yet delivers complex flavor. To avoid gumminess, rinse the cooked noodles of excess starch; this also cools them to room temperature. Then drain the noodles well to get rid of any water that could dilute the delicious dressing, which features Chinese sesame paste, soy sauce, vinegar, brown sugar, ginger, garlic, and chili oil. Everything gets whizzed together in a blender with just a little boiling water to create a smooth consistency. Cilantro, scallions, and cucumber add freshness. If fresh lo mein noodles are unavailable, you can use 12 ounces of dried lo mein noodles.

- 5 tablespoons soy sauce
- ¼ cup Chinese sesame paste or tahini
- 2 tablespoons unseasoned rice vinegar
- 2 tablespoons packed brown sugar
- 1 tablespoon boiling water, plus extra as needed
- 1 tablespoon grated fresh ginger
- 2 garlic cloves, minced
- 1 teaspoon chili oil, plus extra for serving
- 1 pound fresh lo mein noodles
- ½ English cucumber, cut into 3-inch-long matchsticks
- ¼ cup fresh cilantro leaves
- 2 scallions, green parts only, sliced thin on bias
- 1 tablespoon sesame seeds, toasted

1. Process soy sauce, sesame paste, vinegar, sugar, boiling water, ginger, garlic, and chili oil in blender until smooth, about 30 seconds, scraping down sides of blender jar as needed; transfer to large bowl.

2. Meanwhile, bring 4 quarts water to boil in large pot. Add noodles and cook, stirring often, until tender. Drain noodles and rinse under cold running water until chilled. Drain well and transfer to bowl with dressing. Toss to combine. Adjust consistency with extra boiling water as needed. Transfer noodles to serving platter and top with cucumber, cilantro, scallions, and sesame seeds. Serve, passing extra chili oil separately.

KEYS TO SUCCESS

- **Use boiling water for the dressing**: Guarantees that the dressing will emulsify properly and not separate
- **Rinse and drain the noodles**: Prevents excess water from diluting the intensely flavored dressing

PEPPERY SESAME NOODLES WITH BOK CHOY

Serves: 4
Total Time: 40 minutes

RECIPE OVERVIEW Sesame seeds are truly the star of the show in this different take on sesame noodles. With a whopping ¾ cup of sesame seeds incorporated in the dish, they provide ample crunch (and of course toasty flavor) with every bite. A healthy dose of black pepper brings gentle heat. The fresh lo mein noodles provide a wonderfully chewy textural contrast to the delicately crunchy seeds. For the sauce, a little soy sauce, garlic, and robust toasted sesame oil are key, but the kicker is the splash of zippy lime juice that awakens all the flavors. Bok choy adds a more subtle crunch in addition to its natural grassy freshness. If fresh lo mein noodles are unavailable, you can use 12 ounces of dried lo mein noodles.

- 1 pound fresh lo mein noodles
- ¼ cup vegetable oil
- 4 heads baby bok choy (4 ounces each), halved, cored, and sliced thin
- ¾ cup sesame seeds, toasted, divided
- 2 tablespoons plus 2 teaspoons soy sauce
- 2 tablespoons plus 2 teaspoons lime juice (2 limes)
- 4 teaspoons toasted sesame oil
- 4 garlic cloves, minced
- 1 teaspoon pepper

1. Bring 4 quarts water to boil in large pot. Add noodles and cook, stirring often, until tender but still chewy. Drain noodles in colander and rinse well under cold running water; set aside to drain.

2. Heat vegetable oil in now-empty pot over medium heat until shimmering. Add bok choy and cook, stirring occasionally, until tender, 6 to 8 minutes. Stir in noodles, ½ cup sesame seeds, soy sauce, lime juice, sesame oil, garlic, and pepper. Reduce heat to low and cook, turning constantly with tongs, until noodles are evenly coated, about 2 minutes. Season with salt and pepper to taste. Sprinkle with remaining ¼ cup sesame seeds and serve.

SCIENCE LESSON: How Salt Makes Lo Mein Noodles Springy

Lo mein noodles usually contain two kinds of salt—sodium and potassium carbonates. These salts work to raise the pH of the dough. The resulting alkaline environment increases the bonding between the gluten strands, making the gluten network stronger and more elastic, for noodles that stretch and spring back.

CHICKEN LO MEIN WITH BROCCOLI AND BEAN SPROUTS

Serves: 4 to 6
Total Time: 40 minutes

RECIPE OVERVIEW Lo mein may get its name from the Cantonese "lou minh," meaning "stirred noodles." Parcooked noodles are stir-fried with sauce and tossed with meat, vegetables, or both. For this chicken lo mein, you stir-fry strips of marinated chicken breast. The sauce base includes soy sauce and Shaoxing wine, plus chicken broth, oyster sauce, hoisin sauce, and five-spice powder, which has an aromatic sweetness. Cornstarch contributes velvety body to the sauce. Set aside the stir-fried chicken and vegetables while you cook scallion whites, garlic, and ginger and briefly toss the noodles with the sauce to soak up flavor. If fresh lo mein noodles are unavailable, you can use 8 ounces of dried lo mein noodles. We like to make our own Five-Spice Powder (page 29) but you can use store-bought.

- ⅛ teaspoon baking soda
- 12 ounces boneless, skinless chicken breasts, trimmed, halved lengthwise, and sliced thin crosswise
- 3 tablespoons soy sauce, divided
- 2 tablespoons Shaoxing wine or dry sherry, divided
- 1½ teaspoons cornstarch, divided
- 10 scallions, white parts minced, green parts cut into 1-inch pieces
- 2 tablespoons plus 1 teaspoon vegetable oil, divided
- 2 garlic cloves, minced
- 2 teaspoons grated fresh ginger
- ½ cup chicken broth
- 2 tablespoons oyster sauce
- 2 tablespoons hoisin sauce
- 1 tablespoon toasted sesame oil
- ⅛ teaspoon five-spice powder
- 12 ounces broccoli florets, cut into 1-inch pieces
- 4 ounces (2 cups) bean sprouts
- 12 ounces fresh lo mein noodles

1. Combine 2 teaspoons water and baking soda in medium bowl. Add chicken and toss to coat; let sit for 5 minutes. Add 2 teaspoons soy sauce, 2 teaspoons Shaoxing wine, and ½ teaspoon cornstarch and toss until well combined.

2. Combine scallion whites, 1 tablespoon vegetable oil, garlic, and ginger in small bowl; set aside. Whisk broth, oyster sauce, hoisin, sesame oil, five-spice powder, remaining 7 teaspoons soy sauce, remaining 4 teaspoons Shaoxing wine, and remaining 1 teaspoon cornstarch together in second small bowl; set aside.

3. Heat 2 teaspoons vegetable oil in 12-inch nonstick skillet or 14-inch flat-bottomed wok over medium-high heat until just smoking. Add chicken and increase heat to high. Cook, tossing chicken slowly but constantly, until no longer pink, 2 to 6 minutes; transfer to large bowl.

4. Heat remaining 2 teaspoons vegetable oil in now-empty pan over high heat until just smoking. Add broccoli and ¼ cup water (water will sputter) and cover immediately. Cook, without stirring, until broccoli is bright green, about 2 minutes. Uncover and continue to cook, tossing slowly but constantly, until all water has evaporated and broccoli is crisp-tender and spotty brown, 1 to 3 minutes. Add bean sprouts and scallion greens and cook until softened, about 1 minute; transfer to bowl with chicken.

5. Meanwhile, bring 4 quarts water to boil in large pot. Add noodles and cook, stirring often, until almost tender (center should still be firm, with slightly opaque dot). Drain noodles and rinse under cold running water until chilled. Drain noodles again and set aside.

6. Whisk broth mixture to recombine. Return pan to medium heat. Add scallion whites mixture and cook, mashing mixture into pan, until fragrant, about 30 seconds. Add broth mixture and noodles and increase heat to high. Cook, tossing slowly but constantly, until noodles are heated through, about 2 minutes. Transfer to bowl with chicken and vegetables and toss to combine. Serve.

KEYS TO SUCCESS

- **Freeze the meat for 15 minutes:** Makes it easier to slice the meat thin
- **Briefly marinate the meat:** Adds flavor and keeps the meat tender
- **Drain the noodles before they're fully tender:** Lets them finish cooking in the stir-fry without becoming overcooked

CORE TECHNIQUE

Stir-Frying Noodles

ADD PREPPED NOODLES
After you have cooked your other stir-fry ingredients, add parboiled and rinsed noodles with sauce base to wok or skillet.

STIR-FRY BRIEFLY
Using tongs or wooden spatulas, toss noodles quickly with sauce to ensure they heat through and become evenly coated.

PORK LO MEIN WITH CABBAGE AND CARROTS

Serves: 4 to 6
Total Time: 45 minutes

RECIPE OVERVIEW Chewy fresh noodles are tossed in a salty-sweet sauce and accented with bits of tender pork, earthy-sweet carrots, and crisp-tender cabbage. Boneless country-style ribs are an ideal choice for the pork, as they have a rich, meaty flavor and they're naturally tender. Trim the pork and cut it into thin strips so that the marinade (soy sauce, Shaoxing wine, and cornstarch) can penetrate quickly. As with the chicken lo mein, you'll stir-fry the meat, then the vegetables, and then the aromatics. The parcooked noodles go in at the end, and everything gets tossed together before serving. If boneless country-style pork ribs are unavailable, substitute pork tenderloin. If fresh lo mein noodles are unavailable, you can use 8 ounces of dried lo mein noodles. We like to make our own Five-Spice Powder (page 29) but you can use store-bought.

- ⅛ teaspoon baking soda
- 12 ounces boneless country-style pork ribs, trimmed and sliced thin crosswise
- 3 tablespoons soy sauce, divided
- 2 tablespoons Shaoxing wine or dry sherry, divided
- 1½ teaspoons cornstarch, divided
- 10 scallions, white parts minced, green parts cut into 1-inch pieces
- 3 tablespoons vegetable oil, divided
- 2 garlic cloves, minced
- 2 teaspoons grated fresh ginger
- ½ cup chicken broth
- 2 tablespoons oyster sauce
- 2 tablespoons hoisin sauce
- 1 tablespoon toasted sesame oil
- ⅛ teaspoon five-spice powder
- 3 carrots, peeled and sliced on bias ⅛ inch thick
- ½ head napa cabbage, halved lengthwise, cored, and sliced ½ inch thick (6 cups)
- 12 ounces fresh lo mein noodles

1. Combine 2 teaspoons water and baking soda in medium bowl. Add pork and toss to coat; let sit for 5 minutes. Add 2 teaspoons soy sauce, 2 teaspoons Shaoxing wine, and ½ teaspoon cornstarch and toss until well combined.

2. Combine scallion whites, 1 tablespoon vegetable oil, garlic, and ginger in small bowl; set aside. Whisk broth, oyster sauce, hoisin, sesame oil, five-spice powder, remaining 7 teaspoons soy sauce, remaining 4 teaspoons Shaoxing wine, and remaining 1 teaspoon cornstarch together in second small bowl; set aside.

3. Heat 2 teaspoons vegetable oil in 12-inch nonstick skillet or 14-inch flat-bottomed wok over medium-high heat until just smoking. Add pork and increase heat to high. Cook, tossing pork slowly but constantly, until no longer pink, 2 to 6 minutes; transfer to large bowl.

4. Heat 2 teaspoons vegetable oil in now-empty pan over high heat until just smoking. Add carrots and cook, tossing slowly but constantly, until tender, 4 to 6 minutes; transfer to bowl with pork.

5. Heat remaining 2 teaspoons vegetable oil in now-empty pan over high heat until just smoking. Add cabbage and cook, tossing slowly but constantly, until crisp-tender, about 3 minutes. Add scallion greens and cook until tender, about 1 minute; transfer to bowl with pork and carrots.

6. Meanwhile, bring 4 quarts water to boil in large pot. Add noodles and cook, stirring often, until almost tender (center should still be firm, with slightly opaque dot). Drain noodles and rinse under cold running water until chilled. Drain noodles again and set aside.

7. Whisk broth mixture to recombine. Return pan to medium heat. Add scallion whites mixture and cook, mashing mixture into pan, until fragrant, about 30 seconds. Add broth mixture and noodles and increase heat to high. Cook, tossing slowly but constantly, until noodles are heated through, about 2 minutes. Transfer to bowl with pork and vegetables and toss to combine. Serve.

CORE TECHNIQUE
Parboiling Lo Mein Noodles

UNDERCOOK THEM For use in a stir-fry, undercook noodles so that they won't turn to mush in the skillet or wok. The center of the noodle should still be firm, with a slightly opaque dot at the core.

COURSE
UDON AND SOBA NOODLES

ANNIE PETITO

Udon and soba are Japanese noodles. Udon are plump and chewy and made from wheat flour; because they're starchy and taste slightly sweet, they stand up well to savory sauces. One of their hallmarks is a slightly "slippery" bite when cooked. Fresh (sometimes called semidried) udon are preferred for saucy dishes; fresh-frozen udon may be more readily available in large Asian supermarkets. Made from buckwheat, soba noodles boast an earthy taste and a slightly chewy texture. Soba made from 100 percent buckwheat have deeper, darker color and flavor than those made from a combination of buckwheat and wheat. Because buckwheat does not contain gluten, noodles with higher percentages of it are more fragile than those made with greater amounts of wheat, which tend to have a more tender and resilient texture. Soba noodles are often served chilled or as the foundation for comforting, satisfying hot soups.

ANNIE'S PRO TIP: *When cooking soba noodles, follow package directions for timing since brands vary widely. Check the noodles for doneness early and often.*

UDON NOODLES WITH MUSTARD GREENS AND SHIITAKE-GINGER SAUCE

Serves: 4 to 6
Total Time: 1¼ hours

RECIPE OVERVIEW The partnership of noodles and greens is a great way to create a delicate yet filling noodle dish, and this recipe marries the spicy bite of mustard greens with rustic fresh udon noodles. First, make a simple, aromatic broth from East Asian pantry staples, browning meaty shiitake mushrooms in a Dutch oven for flavor and then adding water, mirin, rice vinegar, soy sauce, garlic, and a chunk of fresh ginger. Dried shiitake mushrooms, sesame oil, and chili-garlic sauce round out the flavors. After this mixture reduces, you'll have a light, brothy, supersavory sauce—and you'll use the pot again to cook the noodles and greens together. Because fresh udon noodles cook so quickly, make sure to add the greens to the pot before the noodles. Do not substitute other types of noodles for the fresh udon noodles here.

- 1 tablespoon vegetable oil
- 8 ounces shiitake mushrooms, stemmed and sliced thin
- ¼ cup mirin
- 3 tablespoons unseasoned rice vinegar
- 3 tablespoons soy sauce
- 2 garlic cloves, smashed and peeled
- 1 (1-inch) piece ginger, peeled, halved, and smashed
- ½ ounce dried shiitake mushrooms, rinsed and minced
- 1 teaspoon toasted sesame oil
- 1 teaspoon Asian chili-garlic sauce
- 1 pound mustard greens, stemmed and cut into 2-inch pieces
- 1 pound fresh udon noodles

1. Heat vegetable oil in Dutch oven over medium-high heat until shimmering. Add fresh mushrooms and cook, stirring occasionally, until softened and lightly browned, about 5 minutes. Stir in 2 cups water, mirin, vinegar, soy sauce, garlic, ginger, dried mushrooms, sesame oil, and chili-garlic sauce and bring to simmer. Reduce heat to medium-low and simmer until liquid has reduced by half, 8 to 10 minutes. Off heat, discard garlic and ginger. Transfer mixture to bowl and cover to keep warm.

2. Bring 4 quarts water to boil in now-empty pot. Add mustard greens and cook until greens are nearly tender, about 5 minutes. Add noodles and cook until greens and noodles are tender, about 2 minutes. Reserve ⅓ cup cooking water, drain noodles and greens, and return them to pot. Add sauce and reserved cooking water and toss to combine. Cook over medium-low heat, tossing constantly, until sauce clings to noodles, about 1 minute. Season with salt and pepper to taste, and serve.

> **KEY TO SUCCESS**
> - **Don't salt the water:** Avoids overseasoning the udon noodles, which generally contain a lot of sodium already

VEGETABLE SHABU-SHABU WITH SESAME SAUCE

Serves: 6 to 8
Total Time: 40 minutes

RECIPE OVERVIEW Shabu-shabu is a traditional Japanese hot-pot dish in which beef, vegetables, and tofu are simmered in a complex broth called dashi and served with chewy udon noodles and dipping sauces. This homage comes together quickly by simplifying the broth preparation, omitting the meat, and serving individual portions in bowls rather than a communal hot pot. Dashi is often made using umami-rich dried kombu (a type of kelp) and bonito (tuna) flakes. This version uses kombu and wakame (a common ingredient in seaweed salad), plus plenty of fish sauce, mirin, and a bit of sugar. Shabu-shabu often includes carrots, napa cabbage or bok choy, enoki or shiitake mushrooms, tofu, and chrysanthemum leaves. Here you will use bok choy, carrots, and shiitakes, plus soft tofu. A dollop of a sesame sauce made with mayonnaise, miso, garlic, and lemon juice makes an umami-packed garnish. The assertive flavor of red miso works best here, but you can substitute milder white miso. Instead of fish sauce, you can use Bragg's Liquid Aminos or a vegetarian fish sauce substitute, if desired.

Sesame Sauce
- ¼ cup sesame seeds, toasted
- 2 tablespoons mayonnaise
- 1 tablespoon red miso
- 2 teaspoons lemon juice
- 2 teaspoons sugar
- 1 garlic clove, minced

Soup
- 8 ounces dried udon noodles
- ½ ounce kombu
- 6 tablespoons (½ ounce) wakame
- ½ cup mirin
- ¼ cup fish sauce
- 1½ teaspoons sugar
- 3 heads baby bok choy (4 ounces each), sliced ⅛ inch thick
- 3 carrots, peeled and sliced ⅛ inch thick
- 14 ounces soft tofu, cut into ½-inch pieces
- 8 ounces shiitake mushrooms, stemmed and sliced thin

1. FOR THE SESAME SAUCE Stir sesame seeds, mayonnaise, miso, lemon juice, sugar, garlic, and ½ teaspoon water in bowl until well combined.

2. FOR THE SOUP Bring 2 quarts water to boil in Dutch oven. Add noodles and cook, stirring often, until tender; drain and set aside.

3. Meanwhile, bring 9 cups water, kombu, and wakame to brief boil in large pot over medium heat. Remove from heat and discard seaweed.

4. Stir in mirin, fish sauce, and sugar and bring to simmer over medium heat. Stir in bok choy and carrots and simmer until crisp-tender, 2 to 4 minutes. Stir in tofu, mushrooms, and noodles and cook until warmed through, about 1 minute. Serve with sesame sauce.

SOBA NOODLES WITH PORK, SCALLIONS, AND SHICHIMI TOGARASHI

Serves: 4 to 6
Total Time: 35 minutes

RECIPE OVERVIEW Pork, mushrooms, and plenty of pungent garlic and fresh ginger bring rich flavor to soba noodles in this simple stir-fry. Thinly sliced pork tenderloin stir-fries in minutes. For the sweet-savory sauce, use a blend of soy sauce, mirin, and rice vinegar spiked with the aromatic garlic and ginger. The noodles aren't stir-fried here; you'll boil them separately and just return them to the pot to combine with the other ingredients at the end. As with the Italian pastas earlier in this chapter, reserve a portion of the starchy noodle cooking water to adjust the consistency of the sauce before serving. For a grand finishing touch, sprinkle each portion with a generous amount of shichimi togarashi. This spicy, herbal, citrusy seven-spice blend is a common Japanese seasoning that delivers a lot of flavor. Different products can vary, but it often includes red chiles, peppercorns, nori, ginger, and orange peel. We like to make our own Shichimi Togarashi (page 29) but you can use store-bought.

- 3 tablespoons vegetable oil, divided
- 1½ pounds pork tenderloin, trimmed and sliced thin crosswise
- 10 ounces shiitake mushrooms, stemmed and quartered
- 6 garlic cloves, minced
- 1 tablespoon grated fresh ginger
- 6 ounces (3 cups) bean sprouts
- ½ cup soy sauce
- ¼ cup mirin
- ¼ cup unseasoned rice vinegar
- 8 ounces dried soba noodles
- Table salt for cooking noodles
- 4 scallions, sliced thin
- ¼ cup shichimi togarashi

1. Heat 1 tablespoon oil in 12-inch nonstick skillet over high heat until just smoking. Add pork in single layer and cook, without moving it, for 1 minute. Stir and continue to cook until pork is lightly browned around edges and little pink remains, about 3 minutes; transfer to bowl.

2. Add remaining 2 tablespoons oil to now-empty skillet and heat over medium-high heat until just smoking. Add mushrooms and cook until browned, about 4 minutes. Push mushrooms to sides of skillet. Add garlic and ginger to center and cook, mashing mixture into skillet, until fragrant, about 30 seconds. Stir mixture into mushrooms. Stir in bean sprouts, soy sauce, mirin, vinegar, and pork along with any accumulated juices. Cook until pork is just heated through, about 1 minute. Remove from heat and cover to keep warm.

3. Meanwhile, bring 4 quarts water to boil in large pot. Add noodles and 1 tablespoon salt and cook, stirring often, until noodles are cooked through but still retain some chew. Reserve ½ cup cooking water, then drain noodles and return to pot. Stir in pork-mushroom mixture and scallions and adjust consistency with reserved cooking water as needed. Sprinkle individual portions with shichimi togarashi. Serve.

> **KEYS TO SUCCESS**
> - **Don't stir the pork for 1 minute:** Allows the pork to develop flavorful browning
> - **Cook the soba noodles all the way:** Since you aren't stir-frying the noodles (in either of these recipes)
> - **Save some cooking water:** Lets you adjust the consistency of the finished dish

CHILLED SOBA NOODLES WITH SPRING VEGETABLES

Serves: 4 to 6
Total Time: 30 minutes

RECIPE OVERVIEW For this refreshing dish, boil soba noodles until they're slightly chewy and rinse them under cold water to remove excess sticky starch. Then toss the soba with an umami-rich miso dressing. Assorted raw vegetables provide crunch and color. Strips of toasted nori add lovely texture and subtle briny flavor. White miso is the mildest miso, but you can substitute yellow or red miso. Freshly toasted nori offers the best flavor and texture, but you can substitute plain pretoasted seaweed snacks. For a spicier dish, use the greater amount of chiles. If dried arbols are unavailable, substitute ¼ to ½ teaspoon red pepper flakes.

- 3 tablespoons white miso
- 3 tablespoons mirin
- 2 tablespoons toasted sesame oil
- 1 tablespoon sesame seeds
- 1 teaspoon grated fresh ginger
- 1–2 dried arbol chiles (each about 2 inches long), stemmed, seeded, and chopped fine
- 8 ounces dried soba noodles
- ⅓ English cucumber, quartered lengthwise, seeded, and sliced thin on bias
- 4 ounces snow peas, strings removed, cut lengthwise into matchsticks
- 4 radishes, trimmed, halved, and sliced thin
- 3 scallions, sliced thin on bias
- 1 (8-inch square) sheet nori, toasted and cut into 2-inch-long matchsticks (optional)

1. Whisk miso, mirin, oil, 1 tablespoon water, sesame seeds, ginger, and arbols in large bowl until combined.

2. Meanwhile, bring 4 quarts water to boil in large pot. Add noodles and cook, stirring occasionally, until noodles are cooked through but still retain some chew. Drain noodles and rinse under cold running water until chilled. Drain well and transfer to bowl with dressing. Add cucumber; snow peas; radishes; scallions; and nori, if using, and toss to combine. Season with salt to taste. Serve.

CORE TECHNIQUE | **Toasting Nori**

STOVETOP OR OVEN
Hold sheet 2 inches above low gas flame. Flip sheet every 5 seconds until nori is aromatic and shrinks slightly, 20 seconds. Or toast on baking sheet in 275-degree oven for 20 minutes, flipping halfway through toasting.

COURSE
RICE NOODLES

LAWMAN JOHNSON

Rice noodles feature in hundreds of dishes across East Asia. These delicate, translucent noodles are made simply from rice flour and water and come in dozens of varieties. The two styles you're most likely to see in the United States are flat noodles that are ¼ inch wide (or wider) or thin, round noodles (sometimes labeled "vermicelli"). Rice noodles are easy to overcook, so to maintain their pleasing chew, we soak rice noodles in just-boiled water (rather than boiling them as we do with other noodles) before using them in a recipe. Rice vermicelli can be soaked until they're fully tender and eaten as is, while wide, flat rice noodles are often stir-fried after soaking to make them fully tender.

LAWMAN'S PRO TIP: *These noodle dishes come together quickly, so having everything in its place before starting is very important. You don't want to be scrambling for ingredients or equipment once you start cooking.*

SINGAPORE NOODLES WITH SHRIMP

Serves: 4
Total Time: 30 minutes

RECIPE OVERVIEW Despite their name, Singapore noodles are a multinational affair. The dish actually comes from Hong Kong. It's called Singapore noodles for the signature rice noodles that are used. The seasonings include traditional Chinese flavorings—garlic, ginger, and soy sauce—as well as curry powder, which was brought to Southeast Asia by the British. The curry powder is integral to this light, almost fluffy stir-fry of rice vermicelli, vegetables, and shrimp. Since Singapore noodles aren't saucy, the dry powder doesn't always distribute evenly, leading to patchy flavor (and color) and a gritty texture. To prevent that, bloom the curry powder in hot oil to release its flavors and allow it to mix easily and smoothly with the noodles. Then it's just a question of adding plenty of vegetables, eggs, and shrimp to make this a satisfying one-dish meal.

- 8 ounces rice vermicelli
- ¼ cup plus 4 teaspoons vegetable oil, divided
- 2 tablespoons curry powder
- 3 garlic cloves, minced
- 1 teaspoon grated fresh ginger
- ⅛ teaspoon cayenne pepper
- 2 tablespoons soy sauce
- 1 teaspoon sugar
- 12 ounces extra-large shrimp (21 to 25 per pound), peeled, deveined, tails removed, and cut crosswise into thirds
- 4 large eggs
- 1 red bell pepper, stemmed, seeded, and cut into 2-inch-long matchsticks
- 2 large shallots, sliced thin
- ⅔ cup chicken broth
- 4 ounces (2 cups) bean sprouts
- 4 scallions, cut into ½-inch pieces
- 2 teaspoons lime juice, plus lime wedges for serving

1. Bring 4 quarts water to boil in large pot. Remove from heat; add noodles; and let sit, stirring occasionally, until soft and pliable but not fully tender, about 5 minutes. Drain noodles and rinse under cold running water until chilled. Drain noodles again and transfer to large bowl.

2. Meanwhile, add 3 tablespoons oil, curry powder, garlic, ginger, and cayenne to 12-inch nonstick skillet or 14-inch flat-bottomed wok and cook over medium-low heat, stirring occasionally, until fragrant, about 4 minutes. Add curry powder mixture, soy sauce, and sugar to bowl with noodles and toss until well combined; set aside.

3. Wipe pan clean with paper towels. Heat 2 teaspoons oil in now-empty pan over medium-high heat until just smoking. Add shrimp and increase heat to high. Cook, tossing shrimp slowly but constantly, until just opaque, about 2 minutes; transfer to medium bowl.

4. Heat 1 tablespoon oil in now-empty pan over high heat until shimmering. Add eggs and scramble quickly using rubber spatula. Continue to cook, scraping slowly but constantly along bottom and sides of pan, until eggs just form cohesive mass, 15 to 30 seconds (eggs will not be completely dry). Transfer to bowl with shrimp and break up any large egg curds.

5. Heat remaining 2 teaspoons oil in now-empty pan over high heat until just smoking. Add bell pepper and shallots and cook, tossing slowly but constantly, until vegetables are crisp-tender, about 2 minutes.

6. Add broth and bring to simmer. Add noodles and cook, tossing slowly but constantly, until liquid is absorbed, about 2 minutes. Add shrimp mixture, bean sprouts, and scallions and cook, tossing slowly but constantly, until mixture is thoroughly combined and heated through, about 2 minutes. Off heat, add lime juice and toss to combine. Serve, passing lime wedges separately.

KEYS TO SUCCESS

- **Rinse the rice noodles after soaking:** Washes away the starch that would make the noodles stick together
- **Move quickly:** Prevents the delicate rice noodles from overcooking
- **Bloom the spices:** Awakens their flavors and ensures that they integrate smoothly with the dish, with no gritty texture

SPICY PEANUT RICE NOODLES
Serves: 4
Total Time: 30 minutes

RECIPE OVERVIEW For a noodle dish that hits every tastebud, combine ¼-inch-wide rice noodles with savory edamame and crunchy cabbage, and drape it all with a rich peanut sauce that's a little spicy, a little sweet, and a little acidic. Once you've soaked the noodles, whisk together the simple peanut sauce (only six ingredients if you count the water) and sauté the edamame until it's just speckled with brown but still retains a crisp-tender texture. After removing the edamame from the skillet, finish cooking the noodles in the same skillet with the sauce and some store-bought coleslaw mix until the noodles are perfectly tender and chewy. Finish the bowls with lots of fresh herbs, an extra drizzle of sriracha, and some chopped peanuts, if you like.

- 12 ounces (¼-inch-wide) rice noodles
- ½ cup creamy or chunky peanut butter
- 2 tablespoons plus 2 teaspoons lime juice, plus lime wedges for serving
- 2 tablespoons plus 2 teaspoons soy sauce
- 4 teaspoons sriracha, plus extra for serving
- 2 teaspoons packed brown sugar
- 2 tablespoons plus 2 teaspoons vegetable oil, divided
- 1 cup frozen edamame
- 2 cups (6 ounces) coleslaw mix
- ¼ cup chopped fresh basil, cilantro, or scallions

1. Bring 2 quarts water to boil in large pot. Remove from heat, add noodles, and stir to separate. Let noodles soak until soft and pliable but not fully tender, 8 to 10 minutes, stirring halfway through soaking. Drain noodles and rinse under cold running water until water runs clear, shaking to remove excess water.

2. Whisk peanut butter, lime juice, soy sauce, sriracha, sugar, and 3 tablespoons water together in bowl; set aside. Heat 4 teaspoons oil in 12-inch nonstick skillet or 14-inch flat-bottomed wok over medium heat until shimmering. Add edamame and cook until spotty brown, about 3 minutes; transfer to clean bowl. Heat remaining 4 teaspoons oil in now-empty skillet over medium heat until shimmering. Add noodles, coleslaw mix, and peanut sauce and cook until noodles are well coated and tender, about 2 minutes, adjusting consistency with water, 1 tablespoon at a time, as needed.

3. Off heat, sprinkle noodles with edamame and basil. Serve with lime wedges and drizzle with extra sriracha.

> **KEY TO SUCCESS**
> - **Stir-fry the rice noodles with their sauce:** Ensures that the noodles become evenly coated and don't stick together

PAD THAI

Serves: 4
Total Time: 45 minutes

RECIPE OVERVIEW Pad thai is the ultimate five-flavors dish: hot, sour, salty, sweet, and umami. This Thai street food has migrated all over the world, morphing as it travels. This simplified yet still deliciously flavorful rendition will satisfy all your pad thai cravings. Besides the signature rice noodles, pad thai typically includes tofu, fresh and dried shrimp, and eggs. To streamline prep, this recipe omits the tofu and dried shrimp. Instead of tamarind, the sauce has a simple combo of fish sauce, lime juice, and brown sugar. To get the texture of the rice noodles just right, soak them in just-boiled water so that they start to soften, and then stir-fry them in the skillet. Chopped peanuts, bean sprouts, and scallions complete this fast pad thai. The cooking progresses quickly after step 2, so have your ingredients ready to go.

- 8 ounces (¼-inch-wide) rice noodles
- ⅓ cup water, plus extra as needed
- ¼ cup lime juice (2 limes), plus lime wedges for serving
- ¼ cup vegetable oil, divided
- 3 tablespoons fish sauce
- 3 tablespoons packed brown sugar
- 1 tablespoon unseasoned rice vinegar
- 12 ounces medium shrimp (41 to 50 per pound), peeled, deveined, and tails removed
- 3 garlic cloves, minced
- 2 large eggs, lightly beaten
- ¼ teaspoon table salt
- 6 ounces (3 cups) bean sprouts
- 5 scallions, sliced thin on bias, divided
- 6 tablespoons dry-roasted peanuts, chopped, divided
- Fresh cilantro leaves
- Sriracha

1. Bring 4 quarts water to boil in large pot. Remove from heat; add noodles; and let sit, stirring occasionally, until soft and pliable but not fully tender, 8 to 10 minutes. Drain noodles and rinse under cold running water. Drain again and set aside.

2. Meanwhile, whisk water, lime juice, 2 tablespoons oil, fish sauce, sugar, and vinegar in medium bowl; set aside. Pat shrimp dry with paper towels. Heat 1 tablespoon oil in 12-inch nonstick skillet or 14-inch flat-bottomed wok over high heat until just smoking. Add shrimp in single layer and cook, without stirring them, until beginning to brown, about 1 minute. Stir shrimp and continue to cook until spotty brown and just pink around edges, about 30 seconds; transfer to bowl.

3. Add remaining 1 tablespoon oil and garlic to now-empty pan and cook over medium heat until fragrant, about 30 seconds. Stir in eggs and salt and cook, stirring vigorously, until eggs are scrambled, about 20 seconds.

4. Add noodles and lime juice mixture. Increase heat to high and cook, tossing gently, until noodles are evenly coated. Add shrimp, bean sprouts, three-quarters of scallions, and ¼ cup peanuts. Cook, tossing constantly, until noodles are tender, about 2 minutes. (If necessary, add extra 2 tablespoons water to skillet and continue to cook until noodles are tender.)

5. Transfer noodles to serving platter and sprinkle with remaining scallions and remaining 2 tablespoons peanuts. Serve with lime wedges, cilantro, and sriracha.

PAD KEE MAO

Serves: 4 to 6
Total Time: 50 minutes

RECIPE OVERVIEW Pad kee mao gets its flavor from a spicy, potent sauce and lots of basil. After soaking wide rice noodles until they're just pliable, set them aside while you tend to the chicken, tossing it with soy sauce, cornstarch, and a bit of baking soda to boost flavor and keep it moist. After stir-frying the chicken and cabbage, add the noodles to the pan along with soy sauce, lime juice, brown sugar, fish sauce, and Thai chiles, and toss everything together quickly. Adding the basil at the last minute ensures that its flavor and color stay vibrant. Do not substitute other types of noodles here. If Thai chiles are unavailable, substitute one serrano or half a jalapeño. To make the chicken easier to slice, freeze it for 15 minutes.

- 8 ounces (3/8-inch-wide) rice noodles
- 2 tablespoons vegetable oil, divided
- 1/8 teaspoon baking soda
- 12 ounces boneless, skinless chicken breasts, trimmed and sliced thin crosswise
- 2 teaspoons plus 1/4 cup soy sauce, divided
- 1/2 teaspoon cornstarch
- 1/2 cup packed brown sugar
- 3 tablespoons lime juice (2 limes), plus lime wedges for serving
- 2 tablespoons fish sauce
- 3 Thai chiles, stemmed and sliced into thin rings
- 1/2 head napa cabbage, halved, cored, and cut into 1-inch pieces (6 cups)
- 1 1/2 cups coarsely chopped fresh Thai or Italian basil

1. Bring 4 quarts water to boil in large pot. Remove from heat; add noodles; and let sit, stirring occasionally, until soft and pliable but not fully tender, 12 to 15 minutes. Drain noodles and rinse under cold running water until chilled. Drain noodles well again and toss with 2 teaspoons oil; set aside.

2. Combine 2 teaspoons water and baking soda in medium bowl. Add chicken and toss to coat; let sit for 5 minutes. Add 2 teaspoons soy sauce and cornstarch and toss until well combined. Whisk sugar, lime juice, fish sauce, 2 tablespoons water, Thai chiles, and remaining 1/4 cup soy sauce in small bowl until sugar has dissolved; set aside.

3. Heat 2 teaspoons oil in 12-inch nonstick skillet or 14-inch flat-bottomed wok over medium-high heat until just smoking. Add chicken and increase heat to high. Cook, tossing chicken slowly but constantly, until no longer pink, 2 to 6 minutes; transfer to clean medium bowl.

4. Heat remaining 2 teaspoons oil in now-empty pan over high heat until just smoking. Add cabbage and cook, tossing slowly but constantly, until crisp-tender, about 3 minutes. Whisk sugar mixture to recombine. Add sugar mixture, noodles, and chicken to pan. Cook, tossing slowly but constantly, until thoroughly combined and noodles are well coated and tender, 2 to 4 minutes. Off heat, fold in basil. Serve with lime wedges.

CHAPTER 7

RICE, GRAINS, AND BEANS

COURSES

284 RICE 101

290 GRAINS 101

296 RICE AND GRAIN PILAFS

300 FRIED RICE

306 RISOTTO

310 POLENTA AND GRITS

318 DRESSING UP CANNED BEANS

324 LENTILS

328 DRIED BEANS 101

332 TEMPEH

To learn about tofu see pages 82–89.

RICE AND GRAINS

Long-Grain White Rice
This broad category includes generic long-grain rice as well as aromatic varieties such as basmati, Texmati, and jasmine. The grains are slender and cook up light, fluffy, and distinct, making them good for pilafs and salads. For this rice we often prefer the pilaf-style method, a sautéing method that adds toasted, nutty flavors to the rice. You can also use the simmering, or absorption, method by cooking the rice in water or broth.

Medium-Grain White Rice
This category includes rices used to make risotto (arborio) and paella (Valencia) as well as many Japanese and Chinese varieties. The grains are fat and cook up a bit sticky, resisting turning hard and crunchy as they cool (unlike long-grain rice). When simmered, they clump together, making this rice a good choice to accompany a stir-fry. But it also takes well to pilafs.

Short-Grain White Rice
The grains of short-grain rice are almost round, and the texture is quite sticky and soft when cooked. These qualities make it ideal for tossing with a light vinegar dressing and wrapping up in sushi rolls. It's often steamed or gently simmered.

Brown Rice
As with white rice, brown rice comes in a variety of grain sizes: short, medium, and long. Long-grain brown rice, the best choice for pilafs, cooks up fluffy, with separate grains. Medium-grain brown rice is a bit stickier, perfect for risotto, paella, and similar dishes. Short-grain brown rice is the starchiest and stickiest, ideal for sushi and puddings. The bran layer, valued for its fiber content, is also something of a nuisance: It slows absorption (brown rice takes nearly twice as long to cook as white) and causes uneven simmering on the stovetop, so we generally prefer boiling brown rice in an abundance of water or baking it.

Black Rice
Like brown rice, black rice is sold unpolished, with its bran layer still attached. But only black rice contains anthocyanins, the same antioxidant compounds in blueberries and blackberries. These compounds are what turn the rice a deep purple as it cooks.

YOU CAN—AND SHOULD—FREEZE RICE

Raw brown rice should be stored in a zipper-lock bag in the freezer to prevent oxidation from turning its oil-rich bran and germ rancid; be sure to use it within six months. Cooked long-grain white and brown rice can also be frozen. Simply spread the cooked rice on a rimmed baking sheet and let it cool completely. Transfer the cooled rice to a zipper-lock bag and lay it flat to freeze. There's no need to thaw it before use.

ANATOMY OF RICE

A grain of rice is made up of five parts: the germ, aleurone, the endosperm, the bran, and the hull. Brown rice is simply hulled; white rice also has the germ and bran removed. This makes the rice cook faster and become softer but also removes much of the nutrients as well as flavor.

Hull: the outer layer removed during the milling process

Bran: the fiber-rich interior of the rice grain beneath the hull

Endosperm: mostly composed of two starches, amylose and amylopectin. The ratio of those starches affects the texture of the cooked rice. Higher-amylose rices are fluffy and distinct when cooked, whereas higher-amylopectin rices are more sticky.

Aleurone: oil- and enzyme-rich cells protected by the bran

Germ: responsible for reproduction in the rice grain

Cornmeal

The typical supermarket offers a bewildering assortment of cornmeal products, and their labels can be confusing. The same exact dried ground corn can be called anything from yellow grits to polenta to corn semolina. Labels also advertise fine, medium, and coarse grinds, but no standard definitions exist; one manufacturer's medium grind might be another's coarse option. Then there's whole-grain versus degerminated cornmeal (which is treated before grinding to remove the germ, the center part containing vitamins, enzymes, and corn oil). Try different products to see what you like. For most polenta recipes, we call for coarse-ground cornmeal; for most grits recipes, we use old-fashioned grits.

Barley

This high-fiber grain's nutty, subtly sweet flavor makes it a versatile side dish. Both hulled and pearl barley (the most widely available varieties) are stripped of their tough outer covering; we prefer quicker-cooking pearl barley, which has been polished to remove the bran layer. When cooked, the grains will be softened and plump but still somewhat firm in the center. Cooking times vary depending on the extent to which the barley is polished. Since there is often no way to tell how pearled the barley is by reading the label, we account for the differences by including a wide range in our cooking times.

Millet

The mellow corn flavor and fine texture of these tiny seeds make them extremely versatile in both savory and sweet applications, including pilafs, porridges, puddings, and pan-fried cakes. When millet is done cooking, all of the liquid will be absorbed and the grains will be fully tender.

Bulgur

Bulgur is made from wheat berries that have been steamed or boiled and ground into fine, medium, coarse, or very coarse grains. Don't confuse it with cracked wheat, which is not parcooked. When it's cooked, bulgur will be somewhat tender but still firm. You can simmer bulgur, or you can reconstitute fine- or medium-grain bulgur by soaking it in liquid, as we do in our Tabbouleh recipe (page 290).

Quinoa

Though actually a seed, quinoa is often referred to as a "supergrain" because it's a nutritionally complete protein. The pinhead-size seeds can be white, red, black, or purple; they have a delicate crunch and mineral taste. When cooked, the seeds will unfurl and expand to about three times their size. We like the convenience of prewashed quinoa. If you buy unwashed quinoa (or if you are unsure whether it's washed), rinse it before cooking to remove its natural bitter protective coating, called saponin.

Farro

A favorite ingredient in Tuscan cuisine, these hulled whole-wheat kernels boast a sweet, nutty flavor and chewy bite. In Italy, the grain is available in three sizes—farro piccolo, farro medio, and farro grande—but the midsize type is most common in the United States. When cooked, the grains will be tender but have a slight chew, similar to al dente pasta. Although we usually turn to the absorption method for quicker-cooking grains, farro takes better to the pasta method because the abundance of water cooks the grains more evenly.

Wheat Berries

These are not berries at all but rather whole, husked wheat kernels with a rich, earthy flavor and firm chew. Because they're unprocessed, they remain firm, smooth, and distinct when cooked, which makes them great for salads. When cooked, the grains will be softened but still quite chewy, smooth, and separate.

Freekeh

A traditional Middle Eastern grain, freekeh is made from roasted durum wheat that's been harvested while the grains are still young and green. The grains are polished ("freekeh" is a colloquialization of "farik," which means "rubbed" in Arabic) and sold whole as well as cracked into smaller pieces. Simmered pasta-style in a large amount of water and then drained, freekeh remains slightly firm and chewy and boasts smoky, nutty, earthy flavors.

COURSE
RICE 101

NICOLE KONSTANTINAKOS

There are many different ways to cook rice, and in this course, you will learn how to steam, simmer, boil, and bake white and brown rice. Our everyday stovetop white rice, where the grains are steamed rather than simmered, produces perfectly textured rice every time. Long-grain brown rice, on the other hand, is better cooked on the stovetop using the pasta-style method: boiled vigorously in an abundant amount of water and then drained in a colander. Once you've mastered those basics, move on to making rice for salads and our foolproof method for baking both white and brown rice.

NICOLE'S PRO TIP: *To jazz up a batch of everyday rice, I like to pop a frozen parsley-garlic cube onto the rice once it's done cooking, let it sit for 10 minutes, then fluff the mixture into the rice before serving. To make frozen parsley-garlic cubes, I throw a bunch of chopped parsley, some garlic, and a splash of oil into the blender, blitz it until smooth, and then freeze the mixture in ice cube trays.*

EVERYDAY LONG-GRAIN WHITE RICE
Serves: 4 to 6
Total Time: 40 minutes

RECIPE OVERVIEW Perfectly cooked white rice seems so simple yet can be so elusive. This recipe removes the guesswork and makes it foolproof. This steamed long-grain white rice is perfectly light and tender and has just the right texture to make it a great side dish or bed for any number of saucy dishes. Rinsing the excess starch from the exterior of the rice before cooking is key to the best texture in the finished dish. After cooking, two final tricks guarantee success: letting the rice sit, still covered, off the heat for 10 minutes so that any extra moisture is absorbed and then gently fluffing the rice to break up any big clumps. Omit the salt if you're serving this rice with a salty dish such as a stir-fry.

- 2   cups long-grain white rice
- 3   cups water
- ½   teaspoon table salt (optional)

1. Place rice in fine-mesh strainer and rinse under running water until water running through rice is almost clear, about 1½ minutes, agitating rice with your hand every so often.

2. Combine rice; water; and salt, if using, in large saucepan and bring to simmer over high heat. Stir rice with rubber spatula, dislodging any rice that sticks to bottom of saucepan.

3. Cover, reduce heat to low, and cook for 20 minutes. (Steam should steadily emit from sides of saucepan. If water bubbles out from under lid, reduce heat slightly.)

4. Remove from heat; do not uncover. Let stand, covered, for 10 minutes. Gently fluff rice with fork. Serve.

Variation

EVERYDAY SHORT-GRAIN WHITE RICE

Decrease water to 2½ cups and substitute short-grain white rice for long-grain white rice. Bring rice; water; and salt, if using, to boil in large saucepan. Cover, reduce heat to low, and simmer for 16 to 20 minutes. Proceed with step 4.

> **KEYS TO SUCCESS**
> - **Measure the rice and water precisely:** Ensures the right ratio for achieving the best texture in the cooked rice
> - **Stir once and then cover:** Traps the steam and keeps the temperature inside the saucepan consistent
> - **Reduce the heat:** Gently steams the rice through
> - **Let the cooked rice stand off the heat:** Allows the rice to absorb any excess moisture and ensures that all the grains are cooked through

EVERYDAY BROWN RICE

Serves: 4 to 6
Total Time: 45 minutes

RECIPE OVERVIEW Because it retains its bran and so takes longer to cook, brown rice needs a different stovetop cooking treatment than white rice to turn out light and fluffy. Boiling it in an abundant amount of water, pasta-style, speeds up its cooking time while also helping it cook more evenly. And since you're using a large amount of water to cook the brown rice, you don't need to rinse it first to remove surface starch.

1½ cups long-grain brown rice
1 teaspoon table salt

Bring 4 quarts water to boil in large saucepan. Add rice and salt and cook until tender, 25 to 30 minutes. Drain well and serve.

CORE TECHNIQUE
Rinsing Rice and Grains

RINSE UNDER COOL WATER
To remove excess surface starch, place the rice or grains in a fine-mesh strainer and rinse until the water runs clear, occasionally stirring lightly with your hand. Let drain briefly.

SCIENCE LESSON
Steamed Rice

When you cook rice in water, the rice typically absorbs the water in about a 1:1 ratio (that is, 1 cup of rice will absorb about 1 cup of water); the rest of the water turns to steam and eventually escapes the pot. But the evaporation is important for efficiently cooking the rice, as steam is hotter than boiling water and thus cooks the rice more quickly and evenly.

SCIENCE LESSON
Starch and Rice Texture

Starch in rice is composed of two molecules, the smaller amylose and much larger amylopectin. Studies have shown that amylose is the most important factor in determining the texture of cooked rice. Long-grain rice has the highest level of amylose (22 to 28 percent of the total starch), medium-grain rice contains less (15 to 18 percent), and most short-grain varieties contain little to none. Starch granules in long-grain rice cook up firm, dry, and fluffy. Short-grain rice forms soft, sticky rice, in part because the starch granules of short-grain rice begin to absorb water, swell, and gelatinize at a lower temperature than those of the two other types of rice. Medium-grain rice falls in the middle.

HUNG KAO MUN GATI

Serves: 4 to 6
Total Time: 40 minutes

RECIPE OVERVIEW This easy Thai classic makes for a rich-tasting, subtly sweet side dish for chicken or seafood. Rinsing the grains before cooking removes surface starch, and using a ratio of 2 parts coconut milk to 3 parts water produces rice that's luxuriously rich and perfumed. Letting the cooked rice sit for 10 minutes lets the tender grains firm up, so they won't break when you gently stir to redistribute any coconut oil that rises to the top during cooking. Do not use low-fat coconut milk here. The delicately clingy texture of jasmine rice is especially nice, but you can also use regular long-grain white rice. Avoid basmati; the grains will remain too separate. Chopped toasted peanuts, toasted sesame seeds, pickled chiles, and/or Microwave-Fried Shallots (page 161) make delicious toppings.

- 1½ cups jasmine rice
- 1 cup canned coconut milk
- 1 tablespoon sugar
- ¾ teaspoon table salt

1. Place rice in fine-mesh strainer set over bowl. Rinse under running water, swishing with your hands, until water runs clear. Drain thoroughly. Stir rice, 1½ cups water, coconut milk, sugar, and salt together in large saucepan. Bring to boil over high heat. Reduce heat to maintain bare simmer. Cover and cook until all liquid is absorbed, 18 to 20 minutes.

2. Remove saucepan from heat and let sit, covered, for 10 minutes. Mix rice gently but thoroughly with rubber spatula, transfer to bowl or platter, and serve.

> ### KEYS TO SUCCESS
> - **Stir the coconut milk before measuring:** Coconut milk may separate during storage.
> - **Let the cooked rice rest:** Helps the delicate grains firm up

> ### SCIENCE LESSON
> #### Cooking Coconut Milk
>
> You can bring a different dimension to coconut milk depending on how you cook it. Uncooked, it has a sweet, fruity aroma and vanilla-like flavor. These characteristics come from volatile compounds called lactones (which are also present in pineapples and peaches). The more the lactones dissipate, the nuttier and more buttery the flavors become. Simmering coconut milk as we do for Hung Kao Mun Gati causes some of the lactones to dissipate, though enough remain to make the rice recognizably coconutty.

WHITE RICE SALAD WITH ORANGES, OLIVES, AND ALMONDS

Serves: 4 to 6
Total Time: 1 hour

RECIPE OVERVIEW The first step to making the white rice for this refreshing salad is to quickly toast the rice in a dry skillet (without fat) to bring out some nutty flavors and help keep the grains distinct and separate even when they are cool. Then, boil the rice in plenty of water following the pasta method, which washes away excess starch and staves off stickiness without the need for rinsing prior to cooking. Spreading the cooked rice on a baking sheet allows it to cool quickly and evenly. To flavor the salad, toss the cooled rice with a simple orange vinaigrette and some fresh orange segments, chopped green olives, and crunchy toasted almonds. Letting the salad sit before serving gives the flavors time to meld. You can substitute long-grain white, jasmine, or Texmati rice for the basmati.

- 1½ cups basmati rice
- 1 teaspoon table salt, plus salt for cooking rice
- 2 oranges, plus ¼ teaspoon grated orange zest plus 1 tablespoon juice
- 2 tablespoons extra-virgin olive oil
- 2 teaspoons sherry vinegar
- 1 small garlic clove, minced
- ½ teaspoon pepper
- ⅓ cup large pitted brine-cured green olives, chopped
- ⅓ cup slivered almonds, toasted
- 2 tablespoons minced fresh oregano

1. Bring 4 quarts water to boil in Dutch oven. Meanwhile, toast rice in 12-inch skillet over medium heat until faintly fragrant and some grains turn opaque, 5 to 8 minutes. Add rice and 1½ teaspoons salt to boiling water and cook, stirring occasionally, until rice is tender but not soft, about 15 minutes. Drain rice; spread onto rimmed baking sheet; and let cool completely, about 15 minutes.

2. Cut away peel and pith from oranges. Holding fruit over bowl, use paring knife to slice between membranes to release segments. Whisk oil, vinegar, garlic, pepper, salt, and orange zest and juice together in large bowl. Add rice, orange segments, olives, almonds, and oregano; toss gently to combine; and let sit for 20 minutes. Serve.

KEYS TO SUCCESS

- **Taste the rice for doneness:** It should be cooked through and firm but not crunchy.
- **Don't boil the rice to tenderness:** Risks "blowing out" the rice and breaking it when mixing the salad together
- **Prep the orange right for maximum juiciness:** For more information on segmenting citrus, see page 47.

CORE TECHNIQUE
Cooking Rice for Salad

BOIL
Boil rice for salads in plenty of water to wash away excess starch, until the grains are tender but not soft.

DRAIN AND COOL
Drain the rice, spread it out on a rimmed baking sheet, and let it cool completely.

BROWN RICE SALAD WITH TOMATOES, AVOCADO, AND JALAPEÑO

Serves: 6
Total Time: 50 minutes

RECIPE OVERVIEW It's also best to use the pasta method to cook brown rice for salads, since the agitation caused by the boiling water ensures evenly cooked and perfectly separate grains that aren't gummy. To season this rice, dress it with lime juice while it is still warm so that the nutty grains can soak up its bright flavor. Then add bold mix-ins that contribute contrasting flavors and textures and a zesty lime dressing that brings it all together. Halved cherry tomatoes contribute pops of sweetness while minced jalapeño ensures a bit of heat in every bite. Diced avocado introduces welcome richness, which nicely offsets the citrusy dressing.

- 1½ cups long-grain brown rice
- ½ teaspoon table salt, plus salt for cooking rice
- 1 teaspoon grated lime zest, plus 2 teaspoons plus 2 tablespoons juice (2 limes), divided
- 2½ tablespoons extra-virgin olive oil
- 2 teaspoons honey
- 2 garlic cloves, minced
- ½ teaspoon ground cumin
- ½ teaspoon pepper
- 10 ounces cherry tomatoes, halved
- 1 avocado, halved, pitted, and cut into ½-inch pieces
- 1 jalapeño chile, stemmed, seeded, and minced
- 5 scallions, sliced thin, divided
- ¼ cup minced fresh cilantro

1. Bring 3 quarts water to boil in large saucepan. Add rice and 2 teaspoons salt and cook, stirring occasionally, until rice is tender but not soft, 22 to 25 minutes. Drain rice, transfer to rimmed baking sheet, and spread into even layer. Drizzle rice with 2 teaspoons lime juice and let cool completely, about 15 minutes.

2. Whisk oil, honey, garlic, cumin, pepper, salt, lime zest, and remaining 2 tablespoons lime juice together in large bowl. Transfer rice to bowl; add tomatoes, avocado, and jalapeño; and toss to combine. Let stand for 10 minutes.

3. Add ¼ cup scallions and cilantro; toss to combine. Season with salt and pepper to taste. Sprinkle with remaining scallions and serve.

BLACK RICE SALAD WITH SNAP PEAS AND GINGER-SESAME VINAIGRETTE

Serves: 4 to 6
Total Time: 1 hour

RECIPE OVERVIEW Also known as purple or forbidden rice, black rice is an ancient grain once reserved for Chinese emperors. It has a deliciously roasted, nutty flavor. Its only drawback is that it is easy to overcook, so the best approach is to use the pasta method, giving it space to move around in lots of boiling water. Once it's done, drain it and let it cool completely on a baking sheet. The bold vinaigrette uses toasted sesame oil, ginger, chili-garlic sauce, and honey. Emerald-green snap peas, red radishes, and red bell pepper are like jewels against the black rice.

- 1½ cups black rice
- ¼ teaspoon table salt, plus salt for cooking rice
- 1 teaspoon plus 3 tablespoons unseasoned rice vinegar, divided
- ¼ cup extra-virgin olive oil
- 1 tablespoon toasted sesame oil
- 2 teaspoons minced shallot
- 2 teaspoons honey
- 2 teaspoons Asian chili-garlic sauce
- 1 teaspoon grated fresh ginger
- ⅛ teaspoon pepper
- 6 ounces sugar snap peas, strings removed, halved
- 5 radishes, trimmed, halved, and sliced thin
- 1 red bell pepper, stemmed, seeded, and chopped fine
- ¼ cup minced fresh cilantro

1. Bring 4 quarts water to boil in Dutch oven over medium-high heat. Add rice and 1 teaspoon salt and cook until rice is tender but not soft, 20 to 25 minutes. Drain rice, spread onto rimmed baking sheet, and drizzle with 1 teaspoon vinegar. Let rice cool completely, about 15 minutes.

2. Whisk olive oil, sesame oil, shallot, honey, chili-garlic sauce, ginger, pepper, salt, and remaining 3 tablespoons vinegar in large bowl until combined. Add rice, snap peas, radishes, bell pepper, and cilantro and toss to combine. Season with salt and pepper to taste. Serve.

FOOLPROOF BAKED WHITE RICE

Serves: 4
Total Time: 40 minutes

RECIPE OVERVIEW The oven offers an ingenious hands-off way to prepare rice. By adjusting the water-to-rice ratio from what is typically called for in stovetop recipes and taking advantage of the steady, even heat of the oven, you can turn out perfect rice every time. This is because using a baking dish and aluminum foil creates an environment that simulates the controlled, indirect heat of a rice cooker. You can substitute basmati, jasmine, or Texmati rice for the long-grain white rice. For an accurate measurement of boiling water, bring a kettle of water to a boil and then measure out the desired amount.

- 2¾ cups boiling water
- 1⅓ cups long-grain white rice, rinsed
- 1 tablespoon extra-virgin olive oil
- ½ teaspoon table salt

Adjust oven rack to middle position and heat oven to 450 degrees. Combine boiling water, rice, oil, and salt in 8-inch square baking dish. Cover dish tightly with double layer of aluminum foil. Bake until liquid is absorbed and rice is tender, about 20 minutes. Remove dish from oven; uncover; and fluff rice with fork, scraping up any rice that has stuck to bottom. Re-cover dish with foil and let rice sit for 10 minutes. Season with salt and pepper to taste, and serve.

> **KEY TO SUCCESS**
> - **Cover the dish:** Cover as tightly as possible with a double layer of aluminum foil.

FOOLPROOF BAKED BROWN RICE

Serves: 4
Total Time: 1¼ hours

RECIPE OVERVIEW As you've learned from the stovetop recipes, brown rice often needs to be treated differently than white rice to get it to cook up nice and fluffy—but not so with the oven method. The proportions of water to rice are different, and the cooking time for brown rice is still longer, but the method is the same. You can substitute medium-grain or short-grain brown rice for the long-grain rice. For an accurate measurement of boiling water, bring a kettle of water to a boil and then measure out the desired amount.

- 2⅓ cups boiling water
- 1½ cups long-grain brown rice, rinsed
- 2 teaspoons extra-virgin olive oil
- ½ teaspoon table salt

Adjust oven rack to middle position and heat oven to 375 degrees. Combine boiling water, rice, oil, and salt in 8-inch square baking dish. Cover dish tightly with double layer of aluminum foil. Bake until liquid is absorbed and rice is tender, about 1 hour. Remove dish from oven; uncover; and fluff rice with fork, scraping up any rice that has stuck to bottom. Cover dish with clean dish towel and let rice sit for 5 minutes. Uncover and let rice sit for 5 minutes. Season with salt and pepper to taste, and serve.

BAKED MEXICAN RICE

Serves: 6 to 8
Total Time: 55 minutes

RECIPE OVERVIEW For this rice dish, you'll start by making a quick puree of fresh tomatoes and onion and then sautéing long-grain white rice in oil until it's golden, which develops deep, toasty flavors. The two get combined with chicken broth and then baked. While traditional Mexican rice is cooked on the stovetop, moving this version to the oven is a foolproof, hands-off way to uniform cooking. Tomato paste lends the rice its rich red hue, and fresh cilantro and jalapeños, along with a squeeze of lime juice, provide zesty brightness.

- 2 tomatoes, cored and quartered
- 1 onion, chopped coarse
- 3 jalapeño chiles, stemmed, divided
- ⅓ cup vegetable oil
- 2 cups long-grain white rice, rinsed
- 4 garlic cloves, minced
- 2 cups chicken or vegetable broth
- 1 tablespoon tomato paste
- 1½ teaspoons table salt
- ½ cup minced fresh cilantro
  Lime wedges

1. Adjust oven rack to middle position and heat oven to 350 degrees. Process tomatoes and onion in food processor until smooth, about 15 seconds. Transfer mixture to 4-cup liquid measuring cup and spoon off excess as needed until mixture measures 2 cups. Remove ribs and seeds from 2 jalapeños and discard; mince flesh and set aside. Mince remaining jalapeño, including ribs and seeds; set aside.

2. Heat oil in Dutch oven over medium-high heat for 1 to 2 minutes. Drop 3 or 4 grains of rice into oil; if grains sizzle, oil is ready. Add rice and cook, stirring frequently, until light golden and translucent, 6 to 8 minutes.

3. Reduce heat to medium. Add garlic and seeded jalapeños and cook, stirring constantly, until fragrant, about 1½ minutes. Stir in tomato-onion mixture, broth, tomato paste, and salt and bring to boil. Cover; transfer pot to oven; and bake until liquid is absorbed and rice is tender, 30 to 35 minutes, stirring well after 15 minutes.

4. Remove pot from oven and fold in cilantro. Fold in jalapeño with seeds to taste. Serve with lime wedges.

COURSE
GRAINS 101

STEPHANIE PIXLEY

As with rice, grains can be simmered, boiled, and baked. In this course you will learn how to simmer different grains, how to boil them using the pasta method, and how to bake them. The pasta method is usually the best choice for longer-cooking grains like wheat berries and farro, while the simmering method or the pilaf method is a good choice for shorter-cooking grains such as quinoa, bulgur, and freekeh. See the next course to learn more about grain pilafs.

STEPHANIE'S PRO TIP: *If I'm boiling grains to use in a recipe, I almost always boil more than I need since the cooked grains last for up to 3 days in the refrigerator. Whatever doesn't end up in the recipe I'm cooking becomes the base for another delicious (and nutritious!) dinner or lunch later in the week.*

EASIEST-EVER QUINOA
Serves: 4
Total Time: 30 minutes

RECIPE OVERVIEW Protein-packed quinoa is a stick-to-your-ribs side or perfect bed for any number of toppings to make a meal, and this recipe really does live up to its name. Bring broth to a simmer, add the quinoa, and then cook it covered over low heat (removing the lid for the last few minutes of cooking if any liquid remains). And that's all there is to it. You can use water in place of the broth in this recipe, though the flavor of the quinoa will be much simpler.

- 2 cups chicken or vegetable broth
- ¾ cup prewashed white quinoa
- ¼ teaspoon table salt
- ¼ teaspoon pepper

1. Bring broth to simmer in covered small saucepan over medium heat. Stir in quinoa, salt, and pepper and return to simmer. Cover; reduce heat to low; and simmer gently until quinoa is tender and all liquid is absorbed, about 15 minutes. (If quinoa is tender but liquid remains in saucepan, continue to cook over low heat, uncovered, until remaining liquid has evaporated, 1 to 2 minutes.)

2. Off heat, lay clean dish towel underneath lid and let sit, covered, for 5 minutes. Gently fluff quinoa with fork and season with salt and pepper to taste. Serve.

KEYS TO SUCCESS
- **Simmer the broth:** Jump-starts the cooking of the quinoa when it's added to the saucepan
- **Keep the heat low:** Cooks the quinoa gently
- **Place a towel under the lid:** Absorbs excess condensation and prevents sogginess

TABBOULEH
Serves: 4 to 6
Total Time: 1¼ hours, plus 1 hour resting

RECIPE OVERVIEW Tabbouleh is a signature Levantine salad made of bulgur, parsley, tomato, and onion steeped in a penetrating mint and lemon dressing. And you don't even have to cook the grains. Start by salting the tomatoes to rid them of excess moisture that would otherwise make the salad soggy. Soaking the bulgur in lemon juice and some of the drained tomato liquid, rather than in water, allows it to absorb lots of flavor as it softens. Mild scallions add just the right amount of oniony flavor. Parsley, mint, and a bit of cayenne pepper round out the dish. Adding the herbs and vegetables while the bulgur is still soaking gives the flavorful components time to mingle and meld. Make sure that you buy bulgur and not cracked wheat, which has a much longer cooking time and will not work in this recipe. Serve with pita bread, if desired.

3	tomatoes, cored and cut into ½-inch pieces
½	teaspoon table salt, divided
½	cup medium-grind bulgur, rinsed
¼	cup lemon juice (2 lemons), divided
6	tablespoons extra-virgin olive oil
⅛	teaspoon cayenne pepper
1½	cups minced fresh parsley
½	cup minced fresh mint
2	scallions, sliced thin

1. Toss tomatoes with ¼ teaspoon salt in fine-mesh strainer set over bowl and let drain, tossing occasionally, for 30 minutes; reserve 2 tablespoons drained tomato juice. Toss bulgur with 2 tablespoons lemon juice and reserved tomato juice in bowl and let sit until grains begin to soften, 30 to 40 minutes.

2. Whisk oil, cayenne, remaining ¼ teaspoon salt, and remaining 2 tablespoons lemon juice together in large bowl. Add tomatoes, bulgur, parsley, mint, and scallions and toss gently to combine. Cover and let sit at room temperature until flavors have blended and bulgur is tender, about 1 hour. Before serving, toss salad to recombine and season with salt and pepper to taste.

Variation
SPICED TABBOULEH
Add ¼ teaspoon ground cinnamon and ¼ teaspoon ground allspice to dressing with cayenne.

> ### KEYS TO SUCCESS
> - **Salt the tomatoes:** Prevents a soggy salad
> - **Use medium-grind bulgur:** Works best for salads (see page 336)

CORE TECHNIQUE
Simmering Grains

SIMMER TOGETHER
After bringing liquid to simmer, stir in grains, cover, and cook gently until liquid is absorbed.

REMOVE POT FROM HEAT AND LET REST
Off heat, lay clean dish towel under lid and let grains rest.

MILLET PORRIDGE WITH MAPLE SYRUP

Serves: 4
Total Time: 40 minutes

RECIPE OVERVIEW The fine texture and mild corny flavor of tiny millet grains make them extremely versatile in both sweet and savory applications. Sweet versions of simple millet porridge have been hearty staples in eastern Europe and western Russia for centuries. For this modern take on a breakfast porridge, start by cooking the millet in plenty of water, covered, until it turns tender; then add milk for richness and continue to cook the millet, uncovered, to encourage the swollen grains to burst and release their starch, thickening the porridge. Simple flavorings of maple syrup and cinnamon turn this into a comforting, satisfying morning meal. This tastes best when made with whole milk, but you can substitute low-fat or skim milk.

- 3 cups water
- 1 cup millet, rinsed
- ⅛ teaspoon ground cinnamon
- ⅛ teaspoon table salt
- 1 cup whole milk
- 3 tablespoons maple syrup

1. Bring water, millet, cinnamon, and salt to boil in medium saucepan over high heat. Reduce heat to low; cover; and simmer gently until millet has absorbed all water and is almost tender, about 20 minutes.

2. Uncover and increase heat to medium. Add milk and simmer, stirring frequently, until millet is fully tender and mixture is thickened, about 10 minutes. Stir in maple syrup and serve.

Variations

MILLET PORRIDGE WITH DRIED CHERRIES AND PECANS

Substitute 2 tablespoons packed brown sugar for maple syrup. Stir in ½ cup dried cherries and ½ cup chopped toasted pecans along with brown sugar in step 2.

MILLET PORRIDGE WITH COCONUT AND BANANAS

Omit cinnamon and maple syrup. Substitute coconut milk for whole milk. Stir in 2 sliced bananas; ½ cup unsweetened shredded coconut, toasted; and ½ teaspoon vanilla just before serving.

> **KEY TO SUCCESS**
>
> - **"Overcook" the millet:** Causes the grains to burst and release their starch, creating a creamy consistency that's just right for porridge

BARLEY WITH FENNEL, DRIED APRICOTS, AND ORANGE

Serves: 6 to 8
Total Time: 1½ hours

RECIPE OVERVIEW For grains that are distinct and boast a tender chew, we cook barley like pasta—boiled in a large volume of salted water and then drained—to rid the grains of much of their sticky starch, which would otherwise cause them to clump. Once the barley is cooked, we let it cool briefly on a rimmed baking sheet to help it dry thoroughly and then toss it with an acid-heavy dressing that includes both vinegar and orange juice as well as aromatics and herbs to create a flavorful, hearty side dish. The cooking time for pearl barley will vary from product to product, so start checking the barley for doneness after about 25 minutes. We prefer California apricots in this recipe for their brightness. Sweeter Turkish apricots can be substituted, but decrease the number to 12.

- 1½ cups pearl barley
- ½ teaspoon table salt, plus salt for cooking barley
- 3 tablespoons red wine vinegar
- 2 tablespoons extra-virgin olive oil
- 2 tablespoons minced shallot
- 1 garlic clove, minced
- ½ teaspoon grated orange zest plus 2 tablespoons juice
- ¼ teaspoon pepper
- 20 dried California apricots, chopped
- 1 small fennel bulb, 2 tablespoons fronds minced, stalks discarded, bulb halved, cored, and chopped fine
- ¼ cup minced fresh parsley

1. Line rimmed baking sheet with parchment paper and set aside. Bring 4 quarts water to boil in Dutch oven. Add barley and 1 tablespoon salt and cook, adjusting heat to maintain gentle boil, until barley is tender with slight chew, 25 to 45 minutes.

2. While barley cooks, whisk vinegar, oil, shallot, garlic, orange zest and juice, pepper, and salt together in large bowl.

3. Drain barley. Transfer to prepared sheet and spread into even layer. Let stand until no longer steaming, 5 to 7 minutes. Add barley to bowl with dressing and toss to coat. Add apricots, fennel fronds and bulb, and parsley and stir to combine. Season with salt and pepper to taste. Serve.

> **KEYS TO SUCCESS**
>
> - **Use pearl barley:** Cooks more quickly because its bran layer has been removed
> - **Let the barley cool:** Dries out the grains and makes them less sticky
> - **Acid-heavy dressing and fresh herbs:** Deliver brightness and bold flavor

FARRO WITH MUSHROOMS AND THYME

Serves: 4 to 6
Total Time: 40 minutes

RECIPE OVERVIEW Nutty, chewy farro is a popular grain in Italian cuisine and makes for a satisfying side. This recipe uses the pasta method to cook the farro; the abundance of water and agitation caused by the boiling water cooks the grains evenly. Sautéed mushrooms and shallot give the dish savory backbone, and both dry sherry and sherry vinegar add deep flavor. We prefer the flavor and texture of whole farro; pearl farro can be used, but the texture may be softer. Do not use quick-cooking or presteamed farro (read the ingredient list on the package to determine this) here.

- 1½ cups whole farro
- ¼ teaspoon table salt, plus salt for cooking farro
- 3 tablespoons extra-virgin olive oil, divided
- 12 ounces cremini mushrooms, trimmed and chopped coarse
- 1 shallot, minced
- 1½ teaspoons minced fresh thyme or ½ teaspoon dried
- 3 tablespoons dry sherry
- 3 tablespoons minced fresh parsley
- 1½ teaspoons sherry vinegar, plus extra for seasoning

1. Bring 4 quarts water to boil in Dutch oven. Add farro and 1 tablespoon salt; return to boil; and cook until grains are tender with slight chew, 15 to 30 minutes. Drain farro, return to pot, and cover to keep warm.

2. Heat 2 tablespoons oil in 12-inch skillet over medium heat until shimmering. Add mushrooms, shallot, thyme, and salt and cook, stirring occasionally, until moisture has evaporated and vegetables start to brown, 8 to 10 minutes. Stir in sherry and cook, scraping up any browned bits, until skillet is almost dry.

3. Add remaining 1 tablespoon oil and farro and cook, stirring frequently, until heated through, about 2 minutes. Off heat, stir in parsley and vinegar. Season with salt, pepper, and extra vinegar to taste, and serve.

Variation
FARRO WITH LEMON AND HERBS
Omit sherry. Substitute 1 finely chopped onion and 1 minced garlic clove for mushrooms, shallot, and thyme; cook onion and salt until softened, about 5 minutes. Stir in garlic and cook until fragrant, about 30 seconds. Use ¼ cup chopped fresh parsley and add ¼ cup chopped fresh mint with parsley. Substitute 1 tablespoon lemon juice for vinegar.

> **KEY TO SUCCESS**
> - **Taste frequently:** Start checking farro for doneness after 10 minutes to account for different brands.

WHEAT BERRY SALAD WITH ENDIVE, BLUEBERRIES, AND GOAT CHEESE

Serves: 4 to 6
Total Time: 1¼ hours

RECIPE OVERVIEW Nutty, chewy, hearty wheat berries are ideal as a substantive base for a grain salad. Since wheat berries require long cooking, the pasta method is the best choice to make sure that they cook to an even tenderness. For contrasting textures and complex flavors, combine assertive endive with sweet fresh blueberries and tangy, creamy goat cheese. A bright vinaigrette with shallot, chives, and Dijon mustard brings everything together.

- 1½ cups wheat berries
- ½ teaspoon table salt, plus salt for cooking wheat berries
- 2 tablespoons champagne vinegar
- 1 tablespoon minced shallot
- 1 tablespoon minced fresh chives
- 1 teaspoon Dijon mustard
- ½ teaspoon pepper
- 6 tablespoons extra-virgin olive oil
- 2 heads Belgian endive (4 ounces each), halved, cored, and sliced crosswise ¼ inch thick
- 7½ ounces (1½ cups) blueberries
- ¾ cup pecans, toasted and chopped
- 4 ounces goat cheese, crumbled (1 cup)

1. Bring 4 quarts water to boil in large pot. Add wheat berries and ¼ teaspoon salt; return to boil; and cook until tender but still chewy, 50 minutes to 1 hour 10 minutes. Drain and rinse under cold running water until cool; drain well.

2. Whisk vinegar, shallot, chives, mustard, pepper, and salt together in large bowl. Whisking constantly, slowly drizzle in oil until combined. Add endive, blueberries, pecans, and wheat berries and toss to combine. Season with salt and pepper to taste, sprinkle with goat cheese, and serve.

Variation
WHEAT BERRY SALAD WITH FIGS, PINE NUTS, AND GOAT CHEESE

Omit chives. Add 1 teaspoon honey to vinegar mixture. Decrease oil to 3 tablespoons. Omit endive, blueberries, and pecans. Add 8 ounces chopped figs, ½ cup fresh parsley leaves, and ¼ cup toasted pine nuts to wheat berries in step 2. Reduce goat cheese to ½ cup.

KEYS TO SUCCESS

- **Use less salt:** Too much salt will prevent wheat berries from absorbing enough water to turn tender.
- **Read the package:** If the wheat berries are quick-cooking or presteamed, decrease the cooking time in step 1.

CURRIED BAKED QUINOA WITH CAULIFLOWER

Serves: 4
Total Time: 50 minutes

RECIPE OVERVIEW Quinoa is versatile not only in terms of what you can make with it but also in terms of how you make it. This hands-off oven method delivers perfectly cooked quinoa—and it's simple to incorporate flavorful add-ins. Bring chicken broth to a boil, pour the hot liquid over the quinoa (combined with olive oil and garlic in a baking dish), cover the dish tightly with aluminum foil, and place it in the oven. Lemon juice and cilantro stirred in before serving provide bright finishing notes.

- 1½ cups prewashed white quinoa
- 2 tablespoons extra-virgin olive oil
- 2 garlic cloves, minced
- 1½ cups chicken or vegetable broth
- 2 teaspoons curry powder
- ¼ teaspoon table salt
- 2 cups small cauliflower florets
- 2 tablespoons minced fresh cilantro
- 1 teaspoon lemon juice

1. Adjust oven rack to middle position and heat oven to 450 degrees. Combine quinoa, oil, and garlic in 8-inch square baking dish.

2. Bring broth, curry powder, and salt to boil in covered saucepan over high heat. Once boiling, stir to combine, then pour broth immediately over quinoa mixture and sprinkle cauliflower florets on top. Cover dish tightly with double layer of aluminum foil and bake until liquid is absorbed and quinoa is tender, about 25 minutes.

3. Remove dish from oven and uncover. Fluff quinoa with fork, scraping up any quinoa that has stuck to bottom. Re-cover dish with foil and let stand for 10 minutes. Fold in cilantro and lemon juice, season with salt and pepper to taste, and serve.

Variation
BAKED QUINOA WITH SCALLIONS AND FETA
Omit cauliflower. Substitute 1 teaspoon grated lemon zest for curry powder and 4 thinly sliced scallions for cilantro. Fold ½ cup crumbled feta into quinoa before serving.

BAKED WILD RICE WITH CRANBERRIES AND ALMONDS

Serves: 4 to 6
Total Time: 1¾ hours

RECIPE OVERVIEW Though it can be treated as a grain or as a rice, wild rice is actually neither: It's a semiaquatic grass. With its chewy outer husk, it can be tricky to coax to an evenly cooked tenderness on the stovetop. Baking it instead makes for a foolproof, hands-off affair. Spread the wild rice in a baking dish, pour boiling liquid over the top, cover, and bake. The grains will emerge tender and evenly cooked, with great chew. You can substitute dried cherries for the cranberries.

- 1½ cups wild rice, rinsed and drained
- 3 tablespoons unsalted butter or extra-virgin olive oil
- 1 onion, chopped fine
- ¾ teaspoon table salt
- 3 cups water
- ¼ cup dried cranberries, chopped fine
- ¼ cup sliced almonds, toasted

1. Adjust oven rack to middle position and heat oven to 375 degrees. Spread rice in 8-inch square baking dish.

2. Melt butter in medium saucepan over medium heat. Add onion and salt and cook until onion is softened, 5 to 7 minutes. Stir in water. Cover, increase heat to high, and bring to boil. Once boiling, stir to combine, then pour mixture immediately over rice. Cover dish tightly with double layer of aluminum foil and bake until liquid is absorbed and rice is tender, 1 hour 10 minutes to 1 hour 20 minutes.

3. Remove dish from oven and uncover. Add cranberries, fluff rice with fork, re-cover with foil, and let sit for 10 minutes. Fold in almonds and serve.

KEYS TO SUCCESS
- **Check the label:** Do not use quick-cooking or presteamed wild rice; it will turn mushy.
- **Chop the dried cranberries fine:** Ensures that they will soften in the steaming rice

CORE TECHNIQUE Baking Grains

MANAGE LIQUID
After bringing the cooking liquid to a boil, immediately pour it into the baking dish with the grains. Any water loss due to evaporation from boiling will affect how the grains cook.

COURSE
RICE AND GRAIN PILAFS

ELLE SIMONE SCOTT

According to most culinary sources, rice pilaf is simply long-grain rice that has been cooked in hot oil or butter before being simmered in liquid, typically water or stock. In Middle Eastern cuisines, however, the term "pilaf" also refers to a substantial dish in which the rice is cooked in this manner and then flavored with other ingredients—spices, nuts, dried fruits, and/or meat. In this course, you will start by cooking a very simple rice pilaf and then learn how to make pilafs with add-ins and pilafs using whole grains.

ELLE'S PRO TIP: *The versatility of rice and grain pilafs is excitingly endless. Feel free to experiment with your favorite spice blends and mix-ins to create pilafs customized to your tastes.*

EVERYDAY RICE PILAF
Serves: 4 to 6
Total Time: 55 minutes

RECIPE OVERVIEW The pilaf-style method pays big dividends as a simple way to elevate long-grain white rice. Rinsing the rice before cooking removes excess starch and helps prevent clumping, and toasting the rice with chopped onion and extra-virgin olive oil for a few minutes in the pan at the outset deepens its flavor. Instead of following the typical ratio that's printed on the package (1 cup rice to 2 cups water), using a little less liquid delivers better results. Placing a dish towel under the lid while the rice finishes cooking off the heat absorbs excess moisture and locks in fluffiness. Any long-grain white rice will work here, including jasmine or Texmati; we especially love fragrant and flavorful basmati rice in pilaf. A nonstick saucepan works best, although a traditional saucepan will also work.

- 2 tablespoons extra-virgin olive oil
- 1 onion, chopped fine
- ¼ teaspoon table salt
- 1½ cups long-grain white rice, rinsed
- 2¼ cups water

1. Heat oil in large saucepan over medium heat until shimmering. Add onion and salt and cook until softened, about 5 minutes. Stir in rice and cook, stirring often, until edges of grains begin to turn translucent, about 3 minutes.

2. Stir in water and bring to simmer. Reduce heat to low; cover; and continue to simmer until rice is tender and water is absorbed, 16 to 18 minutes.

3. Remove saucepan from heat and lay clean folded dish towel underneath lid. Let sit for 10 minutes. Fluff rice with fork, season with salt and pepper to taste, and serve.

Variations

RICE PILAF WITH APRICOTS AND ALMONDS
Add ¼ teaspoon saffron (optional) with onion in step 1. Sprinkle ¼ cup chopped dried apricots over cooked rice before letting rice sit in step 3. Just before serving, stir in ¼ cup toasted slivered almonds.

SPICED RICE PILAF WITH GINGER, DATES, AND PARSLEY
Add 1½ teaspoons minced fresh ginger, 1 minced garlic clove, ⅛ teaspoon ground cinnamon, and ⅛ teaspoon ground cardamom to saucepan after cooking onion in step 1. Cook until fragrant, about 30 seconds. Before serving, stir in ¼ cup chopped dried dates and 1½ tablespoons minced fresh parsley.

> ### KEYS TO SUCCESS
> - **Watch the ratio:** For fluffy, separate grains, measure the rice and the water precisely.
> - **Toast the rice:** To unlock flavor, sauté until the grains turn translucent around the edges.

CORE TECHNIQUE
Preparing Pilaf-Style Rice and Grains

TOAST RICE OR GRAINS
Sauté aromatics, then stir in rice or grains and cook, stirring often, until rice edges turn translucent or grains look lightly toasted.

ADD LIQUID AND SALT
Stir in cooking liquid and bring to simmer. Reduce heat, cover, and simmer until rice or grains are tender and liquid is absorbed.

LET REST
Place dish towel underneath lid and let cooked rice or grains stand off heat. Fluff with fork and serve.

HERBED BARLEY PILAF
Serves: 4 to 6
Total Time: 55 minutes

RECIPE OVERVIEW This herb-laden barley pilaf was inspired by those often made in Turkey and Morocco. It features a mix of bold herbs (fresh thyme, parsley, and chives), onion, and garlic for an aromatic, balanced side dish. Cooking the onion in the oil and then toasting the barley in the saucepan before adding a measured amount of water enhances the barley's inherent nuttiness. Because different brands of barley can have very different cooking times, this recipe includes a wide range in the cooking time. Keep tasting the barley until it reaches the consistency you prefer. A bit of lemon juice added at the end of cooking brightens up the dish with a fresh, vibrant finish.

- 3 tablespoons extra-virgin olive oil
- 1 small onion, chopped fine
- ½ teaspoon table salt
- 1½ cups pearl barley, rinsed
- 2 garlic cloves, minced
- 1½ teaspoons minced fresh thyme or ½ teaspoon dried
- 2½ cups water
- ¼ cup minced fresh parsley
- 2 tablespoons minced fresh chives
- 1½ teaspoons lemon juice

1. Heat oil in large saucepan over medium heat until shimmering. Add onion and salt and cook until softened, about 5 minutes. Stir in barley, garlic, and thyme and cook, stirring frequently, until barley is lightly toasted and fragrant, about 3 minutes.

2. Stir in water and bring to simmer. Reduce heat to low; cover; and simmer until barley is tender and water is absorbed, 20 to 40 minutes.

3. Off heat, lay clean dish towel underneath lid and let pilaf sit for 10 minutes. Add parsley, chives, and lemon juice to pilaf and fluff gently with fork to combine. Season with salt and pepper to taste. Serve.

> ### KEYS TO SUCCESS
> - **Check the label:** Do not substitute quick-cooking, hulled, hull-less, or presteamed barley.
> - **Taste the barley frequently:** Accounts for the wide range of cooking times among pearl barley products

BULGUR PILAF WITH MUSHROOMS

Serves: 6
Total Time: 1 hour

RECIPE OVERVIEW With hearty bulgur, a duo of mushrooms, and umami-packed soy sauce, this pilaf really satisfies. Cremini mushrooms provide meaty texture and earthiness, while porcini boast an intense, concentrated flavor. Sauté both mushrooms with onion, and then add the quick-cooking bulgur and liquid and simmer until the bulgur is tender. After removing the pot from the heat, let the bulgur steam for 10 minutes, until it's perfectly tender. For this recipe, we prefer medium-grind bulgur.

- 1 cup water, plus extra as needed
- ½ ounce dried porcini mushrooms, rinsed
- 5 teaspoons extra-virgin olive oil, divided
- 1 onion, chopped fine
- ½ teaspoon table salt
- 8 ounces cremini or white mushrooms, trimmed and quartered or cut into 6 pieces if large
- 2 garlic cloves, minced
- 1¾ cups chicken broth
- 1½ cups medium-grind bulgur
- 1½ teaspoons soy sauce
- ¼ cup minced fresh parsley

1. Microwave water and porcini mushrooms in covered bowl until steaming, about 1 minute. Let sit until softened, about 5 minutes. Drain porcini mushrooms in fine-mesh strainer lined with coffee filter, reserve liquid, and mince porcini mushrooms. Add enough extra water to strained porcini mushroom liquid to measure 1 cup; set aside.

2. Combine 1 teaspoon oil, onion, and salt in large saucepan. Cover and cook over medium-low heat, stirring occasionally, until softened, 8 to 10 minutes. Stir in 1 teaspoon oil, cremini mushrooms, and porcini mushrooms. Increase heat to medium-high and continue to cook, uncovered, until cremini mushrooms begin to brown, about 4 minutes. Stir in garlic and cook until fragrant, about 30 seconds. Stir in broth, bulgur, soy sauce, and porcini mushroom soaking liquid and bring to boil. Cover; reduce heat to low; and simmer until bulgur is tender, 16 to 18 minutes.

3. Off heat, remove lid and place dish towel folded in half over saucepan; replace lid. Let stand for 10 minutes, then fluff bulgur with fork. Stir in parsley and remaining 1 tablespoon oil. Season with salt and pepper to taste, and serve.

> **KEYS TO SUCCESS**
> - **Seek out high-quality porcini:** Packages should contain whole or large pieces, not dust.
> - **Rinse the porcini:** Rinsing them well before microwaving removes grit.

FREEKEH PILAF WITH DATES AND CAULIFLOWER

Serves: 4 to 6
Total Time: 55 minutes

RECIPE OVERVIEW For a pilaf that accentuates freekeh's unique flavor and chew, here we pair it with pan-roasted cauliflower, warm spices and aromatics, and refreshing mint. Simply boiling this hearty grain like pasta is the most foolproof cooking method to achieve a chewy, firm texture. Allowing the cauliflower to soften and brown slightly before adding the remaining ingredients to the pan is essential to creating the best flavor and texture. Studded with sweet dates and toasted pistachios, this pilaf is hearty and healthful. We prefer the texture of whole, uncracked freekeh; you can substitute cracked freekeh, but you will need to decrease the freekeh cooking time in step 1 to about 20 minutes.

- 1½ cups whole freekeh
- ½ teaspoon table salt, plus salt for cooking freekeh
- ¼ cup extra-virgin olive oil, divided, plus extra for drizzling
- 1 head cauliflower (2 pounds), cored and cut into ½-inch florets
- ¼ teaspoon pepper
- 3 ounces pitted dates, chopped (½ cup)
- 1 shallot, minced
- 1½ teaspoons grated fresh ginger
- ¼ teaspoon ground coriander
- ¼ teaspoon ground cumin
- ¼ cup shelled pistachios, toasted and chopped coarse
- ¼ cup chopped fresh mint
- 1½ tablespoons lemon juice

1. Bring 4 quarts water to boil in Dutch oven. Add freekeh and 1 tablespoon salt; return to boil; and cook until grains are tender, 30 to 45 minutes. Drain freekeh, return to pot, and cover to keep warm.

2. Meanwhile, heat 2 tablespoons oil in 12-inch nonstick skillet over medium-high heat until shimmering. Add cauliflower, salt, and pepper; cover; and cook until florets are softened and start to brown, about 5 minutes.

3. Remove lid and continue to cook, stirring occasionally, until florets turn spotty brown, about 10 minutes. Add remaining 2 tablespoons oil, dates, shallot, ginger, coriander, and cumin and cook, stirring frequently, until dates and shallot are softened and fragrant, about 3 minutes.

4. Reduce heat to low; add freekeh; and cook, stirring frequently, until heated through, about 1 minute. Off heat, stir in pistachios, mint, and lemon juice. Season with salt and pepper to taste and drizzle with extra oil. Serve.

COURSE
FRIED RICE

DAN ZUCCARELLO

Traditionally, fried rice is made with cold leftover cooked rice, which dries out as it chills and maintains separate grains. If you try to use freshly cooked rice in fried rice dishes, you're likely to end up with a miserable mess, with the moist, starchy rice turning into mushy, greasy clumps. While leftover rice is indeed an excellent way to make fried rice, in this course you will also discover an easy work-around that might just change how you look at fried rice forever: the pasta method. As you've already learned in this chapter, this simple technique involves boiling rice in lots of water to cook it through and wash off excess starch. Using this method lets you have perfect fried rice any time.

DAN'S PRO TIP: *Having a well-seasoned wok is always important, but it is especially important when cooking rice, which is prone to sticking. Establish a routine for regularly maintaining the seasoning on your wok (see page 17).*

HAWAIIAN FRIED RICE

Serves: 4
Total Time: 40 minutes

RECIPE OVERVIEW Fried rice is a great option for using leftover rice. Crammed with salty ham and juicy pineapple chunks, Hawaiian fried rice is superdelicious and a breeze to make. Boasting the same star ingredients as Hawaiian pizza, this salty-sweet dish features sautéed red bell pepper, scallions, and onion, plus browned chopped ham. For more flavor, add minced garlic and ginger for a 30-second turn, just enough time to become fragrant, and then set the ham mixture aside. Add the rice to heat it before pushing it to one side, adding more oil, and pouring in beaten eggs. Once the eggs are set, add the ham mixture and mix everything together. Stir in a zesty blend of soy sauce, sesame oil, and fiery sriracha and then, off the heat, add pineapple and scallion greens for bright flavor. You can use 6 ounces of chopped leftover ham, ham steak, or deli ham for this recipe. You can also make a batch of Everyday Long-Grain White Rice (page 284) ahead to have on hand for this recipe.

- 1⅓ cups long-grain white rice
- 3 tablespoons soy sauce
- 2 tablespoons toasted sesame oil
- 1 tablespoon sriracha
- 2 tablespoons plus 1 teaspoon peanut oil
- 1 cup (6 ounces) chopped ham
- 1 red bell pepper, stemmed, seeded, and cut into ½-inch pieces
- 6 scallions, white parts minced, green parts cut into ½-inch pieces
- 1 small onion, halved and sliced thin
- 3 garlic cloves, minced
- 1 tablespoon grated fresh ginger
- 2 large eggs, lightly beaten
- 1 cup ½-inch pineapple pieces

1. Bring 2 quarts water to boil in large saucepan over high heat. Add rice and cook, stirring occasionally, until just cooked through and tender, about 12 minutes. Drain rice in fine-mesh strainer or colander.

2. Meanwhile, combine soy sauce, sesame oil, and sriracha in bowl and set aside. Heat 1 tablespoon peanut oil in 12-inch nonstick skillet or 14-inch flat-bottomed wok over medium-high heat until just smoking. Add ham, bell pepper, scallion whites, and onion and cook, stirring occasionally, until lightly browned, 7 to 9 minutes. Stir in garlic and ginger and cook until fragrant, about 30 seconds. Transfer to plate.

3. Heat 1 tablespoon peanut oil in now-empty pan over medium-high heat until shimmering. Add rice and cook, breaking up clumps with spoon, until heated through, about 3 minutes.

4. Push rice to 1 side of pan and add remaining 1 teaspoon peanut oil to empty side of pan. Add eggs to oiled side of pan and cook, stirring constantly, until set, about 30 seconds. Stir eggs and ham mixture into rice. Stir soy sauce mixture into rice until thoroughly combined. Off heat, stir in pineapple and scallion greens. Serve.

> **KEYS TO SUCCESS**
> - **Get your mise en place:** Have all ingredients prepped and lined up before starting to stir-fry.
> - **Heat the oil until it's just smoking:** Gets your stir-fry off to the right start
> - **Add and remove the ingredients in stages:** Ensures that each component is cooked properly

CORE TECHNIQUE Fried Rice

COOK AROMATICS
Stir-fry aromatics, vegetables, and/or meat in pan, in stages if directed. Transfer to bowl.

ADD RICE
Heat oil in pan and add cooked rice, breaking up clumps with spoon.

TOSS AND COMBINE
Add sauce mixture and other cooked ingredients and toss together until combined and heated through.

FRIED RICE WITH GAI LAN AND SHIITAKE MUSHROOMS

Serves: 4 to 6
Total Time: 45 minutes

RECIPE OVERVIEW Gai lan (sometimes called Chinese broccoli), shiitake mushrooms, scallions, eggs, and a deeply flavored sauce feature in this hearty vegetarian fried rice. If gai lan is unavailable, substitute broccolini. Cut the broccolini tops (leaves and florets) from the stalks, and then cut the tops into 1-inch pieces. Halve the stalks lengthwise if thicker than ½ inch and keep them separate from the tops. You can also make a batch of Everyday Long-Grain White Rice (page 284) ahead to have on hand for this recipe.

- 2 cups long-grain white rice
- 2 tablespoons Chinese black vinegar or sherry vinegar
- 4 teaspoons soy sauce
- 1 tablespoon Shaoxing wine or dry sherry
- 1 tablespoon hoisin sauce
- 1 tablespoon packed brown sugar
- 1 teaspoon table salt
- ¼ teaspoon white pepper
- 6 scallions, white and green parts separated and sliced thin
- ¼ cup plus 1 teaspoon vegetable oil, divided
- 2 garlic cloves, minced
- 12 ounces gai lan, trimmed
- 8 ounces shiitake mushrooms, stemmed and sliced ¼ inch thick
- 2 large eggs
- 3 tablespoons chopped fresh cilantro

1. Bring 4 quarts water to boil in large pot over high heat. Add rice and cook, stirring occasionally, until just cooked through and tender, about 12 minutes. Drain rice in fine-mesh strainer or colander.

2. Meanwhile, whisk vinegar, soy sauce, Shaoxing wine, hoisin, sugar, salt, and white pepper in small bowl until sugar has dissolved; set aside. Combine scallion whites, 2 tablespoons oil, and garlic in second small bowl; set aside.

3. Trim leaves from bottom 3 inches of gai lan stalks; reserve. Cut tops (leaves and florets) from stalks and cut into 1-inch pieces. Quarter stalks lengthwise if more than 1 inch in diameter, or halve stalks lengthwise if less than 1 inch in diameter. Keep leaves and tops separate from stalks.

4. Heat 2 teaspoons oil in 12-inch nonstick skillet or 14-inch flat-bottomed wok over medium heat until just smoking. Add gai lan stalks and ¼ cup water (water will sputter); cover; and cook until bright green, about 5 minutes. Uncover; increase heat to high; and continue to cook, tossing slowly but constantly, until water has evaporated and stalks are crisp-tender, 1 to 3 minutes; transfer to medium bowl.

5. Heat 2 teaspoons oil in now-empty pan over high heat until just smoking. Add mushrooms and gai lan leaves and tops. Cook, tossing vegetables slowly but constantly, until mushrooms are softened and gai lan leaves and tops are completely wilted, about 5 minutes; transfer to bowl with stalks.

6. Heat remaining 1 tablespoon oil in now-empty pan over high heat until shimmering. Add eggs and scramble quickly using rubber spatula. Continue to cook, scraping slowly but constantly along bottom and sides of pan, until eggs just form cohesive mass, 15 to 30 seconds (eggs will not be completely dry). Transfer to bowl with vegetables and break up any large egg curds.

7. Add scallion whites mixture to now-empty pan. Cook over medium heat, mashing mixture into pan, until fragrant, about 30 seconds. Add rice, breaking up clumps with spoon; vinegar mixture; vegetable-egg mixture; and scallion greens and cook, tossing constantly, until mixture is evenly coated, about 3 minutes. Increase heat to medium-high and cook, tossing occasionally, until mixture is heated through, about 4 minutes. Off heat, stir in cilantro. Serve.

SCIENCE LESSON **Retrogradation**

The reason why fried rice is traditionally made using leftover chilled rice is that freshly steamed or simmered rice forms soft, mushy clumps when stir-fried, while chilled leftover rice undergoes a process called retrogradation, in which the starch molecules form crystalline structures that make the grains firm enough to withstand the second round of cooking. To prevent mushy clumps without overnight refrigeration, we changed the rice-cooking method to boiling. Cooking the rice via the pasta method washes away enough excess starch that the rice can be stir-fried without turning into mushy lumps.

NASI GORENG

Serves: 6
Total Time: 50 minutes

RECIPE OVERVIEW One of Indonesia's best-known dishes, nasi goreng combines cooked rice (traditionally leftover rice) with pungent chile paste; a sweet soy sauce called kecap (pronounced "ketchup") manis; and shrimp paste. Here chopped shrimp stands in for the shrimp paste, giving even more texture (and protein) to this fried rice. The heat comes from Thai chiles; you can substitute two serranos or jalapeños. Serve nasi goreng with its traditional accompaniments—sliced cucumbers and tomato wedges—if you like. Kecap manis provides a unique flavor here; if it's unavailable, substitute a mixture of 2 tablespoons of molasses, 2 tablespoons of packed dark brown sugar, and 2 tablespoons of soy sauce. You can also make a batch of Everyday Long-Grain White Rice (page 284) ahead to have on hand for this recipe.

- 2 cups long-grain white rice
- 7 large shallots, peeled (4 whole, 3 sliced thin)
- 5 Thai chiles, stemmed
- 4 large garlic cloves, peeled
- 3 tablespoons kecap manis
- 2 tablespoons fish sauce
- 1½ teaspoons table salt, divided
- 4 large eggs
- ½ cup vegetable oil
- 12 ounces extra-large shrimp (21 to 25 per pound), peeled, deveined, tails removed, and cut crosswise into thirds
- 4 large scallions, sliced thin
- Lime wedges

1. Bring 4 quarts water to boil in large pot over high heat. Add rice and cook, stirring occasionally, until just cooked through and tender, about 12 minutes. Drain rice in fine-mesh strainer or colander.

2. Meanwhile, pulse whole shallots, Thai chiles, and garlic in food processor until coarse paste forms, about 15 pulses, scraping down sides of bowl as needed; transfer to small bowl and set aside. Whisk kecap manis, fish sauce, and 1¼ teaspoons salt together in second small bowl; set aside. Whisk eggs and remaining ¼ teaspoon salt together in separate bowl; set aside.

3. Add oil and sliced shallots to 12-inch nonstick skillet or 14-inch flat-bottomed wok and cook over medium heat, stirring constantly, until shallots are golden and crispy, 5 to 8 minutes. Using slotted spoon, transfer shallots to paper towel–lined plate and season with salt to taste. Pour off and reserve oil. Wipe pan clean with paper towels.

4. Heat 1 teaspoon reserved oil in now-empty pan over medium heat until shimmering. Using paper towel, wipe out pan, leaving thin film of oil on bottom and sides. Add half of egg mixture and gently tilt and shake pan until mixture forms even 10-inch round omelet (if using wok, egg will go up sides of pan). Cover and cook until bottom of omelet is spotty brown and top is just set, about 30 seconds. Loosen edges of omelet with rubber spatula and slide onto cutting board. Gently roll omelet into tight log. Cut log crosswise into 1-inch segments (leaving segments rolled). Repeat with 1 teaspoon reserved oil and remaining egg mixture.

5. Heat 3 tablespoons reserved oil in now-empty pan over medium heat until just shimmering. Add shallot-chile mixture and cook, mashing mixture into pan, until golden, 3 to 5 minutes. Add shrimp and cook, tossing slowly but constantly, until just opaque, about 2 minutes. Add rice, breaking up any clumps with spoon, and kecap manis mixture and cook, tossing constantly, until mixture is evenly coated, about 3 minutes. Increase heat to medium-high and cook, tossing occasionally, until mixture is heated through, about 4 minutes. Off heat, stir in scallions. Garnish with egg segments and crispy shallots. Serve with lime wedges.

KIMCHI BOKKEUMBAP

Serves: 4 to 6
Total Time: 45 minutes

RECIPE OVERVIEW Iconic, quick-cooking Korean comfort food, kimchi bokkeumbap is typically made with leftover cooked short-grain rice and well-fermented kimchi, but from there seasonings and additions vary widely from cook to cook. You'll start this version by stir-frying aromatics (chopped onion and sliced scallions) with chopped ham—a popular addition for its smoky flavor and springy texture. Then in goes lots of cabbage kimchi along with some of its punchy juice, a little water, soy sauce, pepper, and gochujang. Simmer the cabbage leaves to soften them, and then stir in the rice and cook until the liquid is absorbed. Garnish the fried rice with small strips of gim (seaweed paper), sesame seeds, and more scallion. This recipe works best with day-old Everyday Short-Grain White Rice (page 285); alternatively, cook the rice 2 hours ahead, spread it on a rimmed baking sheet, and let it cool completely. You can substitute plain pretoasted seaweed snacks for the gim; omit the toasting in step 1. You'll need at least a 1-pound jar of kimchi; if it doesn't yield ¼ cup of juice, make up the difference with water. If using soft, well-aged kimchi, omit the water and reduce the cooking time at the end of step 2 to 2 minutes. If desired, top each portion with a fried egg.

- 1 (8-inch square) sheet gim
- 2 tablespoons vegetable oil, divided
- 2 (¼-inch-thick) slices deli ham, cut into ¼-inch pieces (about 4 ounces)
- 1 large onion, chopped
- 6 scallions, white and green parts separated and sliced thin on bias
- 1¼ cups cabbage kimchi, drained with ¼ cup juice reserved, cut into ¼-inch strips
- ¼ cup water
- 4 teaspoons soy sauce
- 4 teaspoons gochujang paste
- ½ teaspoon pepper
- 3 cups cooked short-grain white rice
- 4 teaspoons toasted sesame oil
- 1 tablespoon sesame seeds, toasted

1. Grip gim with tongs and hold 2 inches above low flame on gas burner. Toast gim, turning every 3 to 5 seconds, until gim is aromatic and shrinks slightly, about 20 seconds. (If you do not have a gas stove, toast gim on rimmed baking sheet in 275-degree oven until gim is aromatic and shrinks slightly, 20 to 25 minutes, flipping gim halfway through toasting.) Using kitchen shears, cut gim into four 2-inch-wide strips. Stack strips and cut crosswise into thin strips.

2. Heat 1 tablespoon vegetable oil in 12-inch nonstick skillet or 14-inch flat-bottomed wok over medium-high heat until shimmering. Add ham, onion, and scallion whites and cook, stirring frequently, until onion is softened and ham is beginning to brown at edges, 6 to 8 minutes. Stir in kimchi and reserved juice, water, soy sauce, gochujang, and pepper. Cook, stirring occasionally, until kimchi turns soft and translucent, 4 to 6 minutes.

3. Add rice; reduce heat to medium-low; and cook, stirring and folding constantly until mixture is evenly coated, about 3 minutes. Stir in sesame oil and remaining 1 tablespoon vegetable oil. Increase heat to medium-high and cook, stirring occasionally, until mixture begins to stick to skillet, about 4 minutes. Transfer to serving bowl. Sprinkle with sesame seeds, scallion greens, and gim and serve.

KEYS TO SUCCESS
- **Leftover cooked rice:** Grains stay separate and don't turn mushy like fresh short-grain rice would
- **Simmer the kimchi:** Ensures that crunchy kimchi becomes tender

FRIED BROWN RICE WITH PORK AND SHRIMP

Serves: 6
Total Time: 1 hour

RECIPE OVERVIEW The bran layer on brown rice protects it from the dangers of clumping, so there is no need to cook brown rice ahead of time for stir-fries. In addition to preventing clumping, this bran layer acts as sort of a nonstick coating on each grain, so the rice requires less oil than white rice when stir-frying. To balance the nuttier flavor of brown rice, you'll use more garlic and soy sauce here than you would for a white-rice recipe. Along with ginger, this provides a highly seasoned base to stand up to the barbecue-flavored pork, shrimp, and scrambled eggs. The superlative porkiness of boneless country-style ribs makes them a great choice here. Coat the pieces with a sweet-spicy mixture of hoisin, honey, five-spice powder, and cayenne and cook them undisturbed so that the pork develops maximum browning and caramelization—and therefore maximum flavor.

- 2 cups short-grain brown rice
- ¾ teaspoon table salt, divided, plus salt for cooking rice
- 10 ounces boneless country-style pork ribs, trimmed
- 1 tablespoon hoisin sauce
- 2 teaspoons honey
- ⅛ teaspoon five-spice powder
   Pinch cayenne pepper
- 4 teaspoons vegetable oil, divided
- 8 ounces large shrimp (26 to 30 per pound), peeled, deveined, tails removed, and cut into ½-inch pieces
- 3 large eggs, lightly beaten
- 1 tablespoon toasted sesame oil
- 6 scallions, white and green parts separated and sliced thin on bias
- 2 garlic cloves, minced
- 1½ teaspoons grated fresh ginger
- 2 tablespoons soy sauce
- 1 cup frozen peas

1. Bring 3 quarts water to boil in large pot. Add rice and 2 teaspoons salt. Cook, stirring occasionally, until rice is tender, about 35 minutes. Drain well and return to pot. Cover and set aside.

2. Meanwhile, cut pork into 1-inch pieces and slice each piece against grain ¼ inch thick. Combine pork with hoisin, honey, five-spice powder, cayenne, and ½ teaspoon salt in bowl and toss to coat; set aside.

3. Heat 1 teaspoon vegetable oil in 12-inch nonstick skillet or 14-inch flat-bottomed wok over medium-high heat until shimmering. Add shrimp in single layer and cook, without moving them, until golden brown, about 1½ minutes. Stir and continue to cook until opaque throughout, about 1½ minutes. Push shrimp to 1 side of pan. Add 1 teaspoon vegetable oil to cleared side of pan. Add eggs to clearing and sprinkle with remaining ¼ teaspoon salt. Using rubber spatula, stir eggs gently until set but still wet, about 30 seconds. Stir eggs into shrimp and continue to cook, breaking up large pieces of egg, until eggs are fully cooked, about 30 seconds. Transfer shrimp-egg mixture to clean bowl.

4. Heat remaining 2 teaspoons vegetable oil in now-empty pan over medium-high heat until shimmering. Add pork in even layer. Cook pork without moving it, until well browned, 2 to 3 minutes. Flip pork and cook, without moving it, until cooked through and caramelized on second side, 2 to 3 minutes. Transfer to bowl with shrimp-egg mixture.

5. Heat sesame oil in now-empty pan over medium-high heat until shimmering. Add scallion whites and cook, stirring frequently, until well browned, about 1 minute. Stir in garlic and ginger and cook until fragrant and beginning to brown, 30 to 60 seconds. Add soy sauce and half of rice and stir until all ingredients are fully incorporated, making sure to break up clumps of ginger and garlic. Reduce heat to medium-low and add peas, pork mixture, and remaining rice. Stir until all ingredients are evenly incorporated and heated through, 2 to 4 minutes. Remove from heat and stir in scallion greens. Serve.

COURSE
RISOTTO

STEVE DUNN

Risotto is one of the most popular ways to enjoy rice in Italy. Made from a medium-grain, starchy white rice such as arborio or carnaroli stirred and simmered with wine and broth, it's a rich, creamy, impressive delight. Traditional Italian risotto requires near-constant stirring to ensure its velvety texture and fluid consistency, which Italians refer to as all'onda ("on the wave"). This traditional method is an art worth learning, and you will do so here; but first, you'll start out with a simpler, nearly hands-free recipe. Then you'll learn how to make risotto-style grain dishes.

STEVE'S PRO TIP: *Risotto, made with either rice or other grains, can thicken quickly as it sits and cools, turning kind of stodgy. To achieve the best consistency, reserve at least 1 cup of hot stock to add to the risotto just before serving. I often heat up more stock than called for just to be sure I have enough to thin it before serving. Pre-warming serving bowls or plates will help risotto stay creamy and fluid even longer.*

RISOTTO WITH PARMESAN AND HERBS

Serves: 6
Total Time: 50 minutes

RECIPE OVERVIEW This untraditional recipe starts out traditionally enough: Sweat the aromatics in a Dutch oven until they're softened; add 2 cups of arborio rice; toast the grains in the hot fat for a few minutes; and pour in dry white wine, stirring until the liquid is absorbed. But then, instead of adding the hot cooking liquid in small amounts, stirring until it's incorporated before adding more, add nearly all the cooking liquid and let it simmer, stirring just twice. At the very end, stir in the remaining liquid and let the risotto rest for a few minutes to thicken. The resulting risotto turns out as creamy and "wavy" as those stirred nearly constantly for 25 to 30 minutes. If you prefer a looser risotto, add more of the hot broth mixture in step 4.

- 5 cups chicken or vegetable broth
- 1½ cups water
- 4 tablespoons unsalted butter, divided
- 1 large onion, chopped fine
- ¾ teaspoon table salt
- 1 garlic clove, minced
- 2 cups arborio rice
- 1 cup dry white wine
- 2 ounces Parmesan cheese, grated (1 cup)
- 2 tablespoons chopped fresh parsley
- 2 tablespoons chopped fresh chives
- 1 teaspoon lemon juice

1. Bring broth and water to boil in large saucepan over high heat. Cover and reduce heat to medium-low to maintain gentle simmer.

2. Melt 2 tablespoons butter in Dutch oven over medium heat. Add onion and salt and cook until onion is softened, about 5 minutes. Stir in garlic and cook until fragrant, about 30 seconds. Stir in rice and cook, stirring often, until grain edges begin to turn translucent, about 3 minutes.

3. Stir in wine and cook, stirring constantly, until fully absorbed, 2 to 3 minutes. Stir in 5 cups hot broth mixture. Reduce heat to medium-low; cover; and simmer until almost all liquid has been absorbed and rice is just al dente, 16 to 19 minutes, stirring twice during cooking.

4. Add ¾ cup hot broth mixture and stir gently and constantly until risotto becomes creamy, about 3 minutes. Stir in Parmesan. Remove pot from heat, cover, and let stand for 5 minutes. Stir in parsley, chives, lemon juice, and remaining 2 tablespoons butter. Season with salt and pepper to taste. Before serving, stir in remaining hot broth mixture as needed to loosen consistency of risotto.

Variations

RISOTTO WITH PORCINI

Omit parsley and chives. Add ¼ ounce rinsed and minced porcini mushrooms to pot with garlic. Substitute soy sauce for lemon juice.

RISOTTO WITH FENNEL AND SAFFRON

Add 1 fennel bulb, cored and chopped fine, to pot with onion and cook until softened, about 12 minutes. Add ¼ teaspoon ground coriander and large pinch saffron threads to pot with garlic.

> ### KEYS TO SUCCESS
> - **Use a timer:** More hands-off method requires precise timing
> - **Measure with care:** Ensures the correct ratio of rice to liquid
> - **Use a Dutch oven:** Traps heat and distributes it evenly thanks to its heavy bottom, deep sides, and tight-fitting lid
> - **Keep it covered:** Prevents the liquid from evaporating and the rice from drying out

CORE TECHNIQUE
Making Risotto Hands-Free

ADD LIQUID AT START
The simmering liquid agitates the rice grains much like stirring would, releasing creamy starch.

COVER DUTCH OVEN
A lid and low heat helps distribute the heat as evenly as stirring.

STIR AND LET REST
A brief stir followed by a 5-minute rest provides insurance that the rice will be perfectly al dente.

SPRING VEGETABLE RISOTTO

Serves: 4
Total Time: 1¼ hours

RECIPE OVERVIEW In this traditional approach to risotto, almost constant stirring for 25 to 30 minutes ensures a perfect texture: tender grains with a slight bite in the center, bound by a light, creamy sauce. As the rice cooks, it releases starch granules, which absorb liquid and expand, thickening the broth to a rich consistency. Stirring the pot jostles the rice grains, agitating them and promoting the release of more starch granules. This take on risotto primavera starts with the classic combination of asparagus and leeks; sautéing the trimmed asparagus spears first and then stirring them into the rice right before serving keeps them from turning to mush. To brighten the dish, top it with a gremolata of parsley, mint, and lemon zest. You may have up to a cup of broth left over at the end.

Gremolata
- 2 tablespoons minced fresh parsley, stems reserved
- 2 tablespoons minced fresh mint, stems reserved
- ½ teaspoon grated lemon zest

Risotto
- 1 pound asparagus, tough ends snapped off and reserved, spears cut on bias into ½-inch-thick pieces
- 2 leeks, white and light green parts halved lengthwise, sliced thin, and washed thoroughly; 2 cups roughly chopped dark green parts reserved
- 4 cups chicken or vegetable broth
- 3 cups water
- 5 tablespoons unsalted butter, divided
- ¾ teaspoon pepper, divided
- Pinch plus ½ teaspoon table salt, divided
- ½ cup frozen peas
- 2 garlic cloves, minced
- 1½ cups arborio rice
- 1 cup dry white wine
- 1½ ounces Parmesan cheese, grated (¾ cup), plus extra for serving
- 2 teaspoons lemon juice

1. FOR THE GREMOLATA Combine minced parsley, minced mint, and lemon zest in small bowl; set aside.

2. FOR THE RISOTTO Chop reserved asparagus ends and reserved leek greens into rough ½-inch pieces and place in large saucepan. Add broth, water, and reserved parsley and mint stems and bring to boil over high heat. Reduce heat to medium-low, partially cover, and simmer for 20 minutes. Strain broth through fine-mesh strainer into medium bowl, pressing on solids to extract as much liquid as possible; discard solids. Return broth to saucepan; cover and set over low heat to keep warm.

3. Melt 1 tablespoon butter in large Dutch oven over medium heat. Add asparagus spears, ¼ teaspoon pepper, and pinch salt. Cook, stirring occasionally, until asparagus is crisp-tender, 4 to 6 minutes. Add peas and continue to cook for 1 minute. Transfer vegetables to plate and set aside. Melt 3 tablespoons butter in now-empty pot over medium heat. Add garlic, leeks, remaining ½ teaspoon pepper, and remaining ½ teaspoon salt. Cook, stirring occasionally, until leeks are softened, 4 to 5 minutes.

4. Add rice and cook, stirring frequently, until grains are translucent around edges, about 3 minutes. Add wine and cook, stirring frequently, until fully absorbed, 2 to 3 minutes. Add 3 cups hot broth to rice. Simmer, stirring every 3 to 4 minutes, until liquid is absorbed and bottom of pot is almost dry, about 12 minutes.

5. Stir in about ½ cup hot broth and cook, stirring constantly, until absorbed, about 3 minutes; repeat with additional broth 3 or 4 times until rice is al dente. Off heat, stir in Parmesan, lemon juice, and remaining 1 tablespoon butter; gently fold in asparagus and peas. If desired, add up to ¼ cup additional hot broth to loosen texture of risotto. Serve immediately, sprinkling each serving with gremolata and passing extra Parmesan separately.

KEYS TO SUCCESS
- **Add liquid slowly:** Allows each portion of liquid to be absorbed before you add the next portion
- **Stir, and stir again:** Releases starch granules from the rice, which thickens the risotto

FARROTTO WITH PANCETTA, ASPARAGUS, AND PEAS

Serves: 6
Total Time: 1¼ hours

RECIPE OVERVIEW You can make risotto-style dishes with grains other than rice, like this twist featuring farro. There's just one potential pitfall to farrotto: the bran. Arborio or carnaroli rices have been stripped of their bran layer and thus readily give up their amylopectin, the starch molecule that makes risotto creamy. Farro retains much of its bran, which provides nutrients and earthy flavor but also traps the starch inside the grain. "Cracking" the farro by whizzing it in a blender solves the problem. Using the almost hands-free technique to cook this risotto results in a creamy, velvety dish with the distinct flavor and chew of this grain. We prefer the flavor and texture of whole farro. Do not use quick-cooking or pearl farro. If you prefer a looser farrotto, add more of the hot broth mixture in step 6.

- 1½ cups whole farro
- 3 cups chicken broth
- 3 cups water
- 4 ounces asparagus, trimmed and cut on bias into 1-inch lengths
- 4 ounces pancetta, cut into ¼-inch pieces
- 3 tablespoons unsalted butter, divided
- ½ onion, chopped fine
- 1 garlic clove, minced
- 1 cup frozen peas, thawed
- 2 teaspoons minced fresh tarragon
- ¾ teaspoon table salt
- ½ teaspoon pepper
- 1½ ounces Parmesan cheese, grated (¾ cup)
- 1 tablespoon minced fresh chives
- 1 teaspoon grated lemon zest plus 1 teaspoon juice

1. Pulse farro in blender until about half of grains are broken into smaller pieces, about 6 pulses.

2. Bring broth and water to boil in medium saucepan over high heat. Add asparagus and cook until crisp-tender, 2 to 3 minutes. Using slotted spoon, transfer asparagus to bowl and set aside. Reduce heat to medium-low to maintain gentle simmer.

3. Cook pancetta in large Dutch oven over medium heat until lightly browned and fat has rendered, about 5 minutes. Reduce heat to medium-low and add 1 tablespoon butter; when melted, add onion and cook, stirring frequently, until softened, 3 to 4 minutes. Add garlic and stir until fragrant, about 30 seconds. Add farro and cook, stirring frequently, until grains are lightly toasted, about 3 minutes.

4. Stir 5 cups hot broth mixture into farro mixture; reduce heat to low; cover; and cook until almost all liquid has been absorbed and farro is just al dente, about 25 minutes, stirring twice during cooking.

5. Add peas, tarragon, salt, and pepper and continue to cook, stirring constantly, until farro becomes creamy, about 5 minutes.

6. Remove pot from heat. Stir in Parmesan, chives, lemon zest and juice, asparagus, and remaining 2 tablespoons butter. Season with salt and pepper to taste. Adjust consistency with remaining hot broth mixture as needed. Serve immediately.

CORE TECHNIQUE
"Cracking" Farro

BREAK IT UP
A few quick pulses in a blender cracks the farro grains, allowing some of their starches to escape and thicken the cooking liquid into a creamy, cohesive sauce. Don't use a food processor; the grains will just dance around the bowl without cracking.

COURSE
POLENTA AND GRITS

BRYAN ROOF

Polenta and grits are both made from cornmeal: ground processed corn kernels that can be yellow, white, or blue depending on the type of corn and ground to different consistencies, from fine to coarse. Polenta is also the name for the Italian porridge made with water or stock and coarse-ground cornmeal. You can buy imported polenta, but you'll often pay a premium over coarse-ground cornmeal, which is the same thing. Grits are usually ground to a coarser grain than most packaged cornmeals. Some large-scale cornmeal producers use the same corn to make grits and cornmeal, while artisan companies might use softer corn for grits and tougher corn for cornmeal or polenta.

BRYAN'S PRO TIP: *To avoid lumps, add the polenta to the boiling water in a slow, steady stream while whisking constantly.*

CREAMY PARMESAN POLENTA

Serves: 4 to 6
Total Time: 55 minutes

RECIPE OVERVIEW Simple, creamy stovetop polenta makes a perfect bed for toppings ranging from fried eggs to sautéed shrimp to roasted meat—or try one of the creative vegetable toppings on page 312. Adding a pinch of baking soda just as the water comes to a boil is a decidedly non-traditional approach that cuts the cooking time in half. Covering the pot and lowering the heat cooks the polenta gently. Coarse-ground degerminated cornmeal (with grains the size of couscous) works best here. Avoid instant and quick-cooking products, as well as whole-grain, stone-ground, and regular cornmeal. If the polenta bubbles or sputters even slightly after the first 10 minutes, the heat is too high. It may help to have a flame tamer, which is available at most kitchen supply stores. Or see below for how to make your own.

- 7½ cups water
- 1½ teaspoons table salt
- Pinch baking soda
- 1½ cups coarse-ground cornmeal
- 4 ounces Parmesan cheese, grated (2 cups), plus extra for serving
- 2 tablespoons unsalted butter

1. Bring water to boil in heavy-bottomed large saucepan over medium-high heat. Stir in salt and baking soda. Slowly pour cornmeal into water in steady stream while whisking back and forth. Bring mixture to boil, stirring constantly, about 1 minute. Reduce heat to lowest possible setting and cover saucepan.

2. After 5 minutes, whisk polenta to smooth out any lumps that may have formed, about 15 seconds. (Make sure to scrape down sides and bottom of saucepan.) Cover and continue to cook, without stirring, until grains of polenta are tender but slightly al dente, about 25 minutes. (Polenta should be loose and barely hold its shape but will continue to thicken as it cools.)

3. Off heat, stir in Parmesan and butter and season with pepper to taste. Let polenta stand, covered, for 5 minutes. Serve, passing extra Parmesan separately.

KEYS TO SUCCESS

- **Don't skip the baking soda:** Reduces the cooking time dramatically and also makes for a creamier polenta
- **Turn the heat as low as possible:** Cooks the polenta gently to prevent lumps

CORE TECHNIQUE

Taming the Flame

MAKE A HOMEMADE FLAME TAMER
Shape a sheet of heavy-duty aluminum foil into a 1-inch-thick ring that fits on your burner, making sure that the ring is of even thickness.

SCIENCE LESSON

Baking Soda and Cornmeal

Baking soda raises the pH of a cooking liquid. This helps the cornmeal granules break down faster and release their starch in a more uniform way so that they cook more evenly and the resulting polenta is creamier.

FLUFFY BAKED POLENTA

Serves: 6
Total Time: 1¼ hours, plus 3 hours chilling

RECIPE OVERVIEW Italians enjoy polenta in many ways—one of which is baking it so that it develops a golden crust and tender, light interior. Cooking the polenta in water lets the corn flavor shine through; stirring in half-and-half at the end brings richness. A healthy dose of nutty Pecorino Romano provides savory backbone. Using a two-step cooking process—first on the stove and then, once the polenta is cooled and cut into blocks, in the oven—brings the desired results. We developed this recipe using Quaker Yellow Corn Meal for its desirable texture and relatively short cooking time and recommend you use the same product for this recipe. The timing may be different for other types of cornmeal, so be sure to cook the polenta until it is thickened and tender. You can substitute whole milk for the half-and-half. Try this topped with one of the vegetable toppings that follow or with Simple Italian-Style Meat Sauce (page 248).

- 4 tablespoons unsalted butter
- 2 tablespoons extra-virgin olive oil
- 2 garlic cloves, smashed and peeled
- 7 cups water
- 1½ teaspoons table salt
- ½ teaspoon pepper
- 1½ cups cornmeal
- 3 ounces Pecorino Romano cheese, grated (1½ cups)
- ¼ cup half-and-half

1. Lightly grease 8-inch square baking pan. Heat butter and oil in Dutch oven over medium heat until butter is melted. Add garlic and cook until lightly golden, about 4 minutes. Discard garlic.

2. Add water, salt, and pepper to butter mixture. Increase heat to medium-high and bring to boil. Add cornmeal in slow, steady stream, whisking constantly. Reduce heat to medium-low and continue to cook, whisking frequently and scraping sides and bottom of pot, until mixture is thick and cornmeal is tender, about 20 minutes.

3. Off heat, whisk in Pecorino and half-and-half. Transfer to prepared pan and let cool completely on wire rack. Once cooled, cover with plastic wrap and refrigerate until completely chilled, at least 3 hours.

4. Adjust oven rack to middle position and heat oven to 375 degrees. Line rimmed baking sheet with parchment paper, then grease parchment. Cut chilled polenta into 6 equal pieces (about 4 by 2⅔ inches each). Place on prepared sheet and bake until heated through and beginning to brown on bottom, about 30 minutes. Serve.

KEY TO SUCCESS
- **Chill the polenta:** Makes it easier to slice neatly before baking

SAUTÉED CHERRY TOMATO AND FRESH MOZZARELLA TOPPING

Serves: 4 to 6 (Makes 5¼ cups)
Total Time: 10 minutes

Don't stir the mozzarella cheese into the sautéed tomato mixture because it will melt prematurely and turn rubbery.

- 3 tablespoons extra-virgin olive oil
- 2 garlic cloves, sliced thin
- Pinch red pepper flakes
- Pinch sugar
- 1½ pounds cherry tomatoes, halved
- 6 ounces fresh mozzarella cheese, cut into ½-inch cubes (1¼ cups)
- 2 tablespoons shredded fresh basil

1. Heat oil, garlic, pepper flakes, and sugar in 12-inch nonstick skillet over medium-high heat until garlic is fragrant and sizzling, about 1 minute. Stir in tomatoes and cook until just beginning to soften, about 1 minute. Season with salt and pepper to taste; remove from heat.

2. Spoon tomato mixture over individual portions of polenta, top with mozzarella and basil, and serve.

BROCCOLI RABE, SUN-DRIED TOMATO, AND PINE NUT TOPPING

Serves: 4 to 6 (Makes 3½ cups)
Total Time: 15 minutes

Toast the pine nuts in a skillet over medium heat, stirring frequently to prevent them from burning.

- 3 tablespoons extra-virgin olive oil
- ½ cup oil-packed sun-dried tomatoes, chopped coarse
- 6 garlic cloves, minced
- ½ teaspoon red pepper flakes
- ½ teaspoon table salt
- 1 pound broccoli rabe, trimmed and cut into 1½-inch pieces
- ¼ cup chicken broth
- 3 tablespoons pine nuts, toasted

1. Add oil, tomatoes, garlic, pepper flakes, and salt to 12-inch nonstick skillet and cook over medium-high heat, stirring frequently, until garlic is fragrant and slightly toasted, about 1½ minutes.

2. Add broccoli rabe and broth; cover; and cook until broccoli rabe turns bright green, about 2 minutes. Uncover and continue to cook, stirring frequently, until most of broth has evaporated and broccoli rabe is just tender, 2 to 3 minutes.

3. Season with salt to taste. Spoon broccoli rabe mixture over individual portions of polenta, sprinkle with pine nuts, and serve.

CREAMY CHEESE GRITS

Serves: 4 to 6
Total Time: 40 minutes

RECIPE OVERVIEW A versatile Southern specialty, grits are served at breakfast, lunch, and dinner and in many forms, from simmered to deep-fried, from sweet to savory. The method for making these cheesy stovetop grits is simple: Whisk a cup of cornmeal into a seasoned mixture of boiling milk and water; stir over low heat for about 15 minutes, until the mixture is thick—almost pudding-like—and soft, with a hint of bite and a pleasantly gritty texture; and stir in shredded cheeses and some butter to finish. To jazz things up, you'll also puree some corn kernels to add at the end, which contribute even more flavor to these buttery, cheesy grits.

- ½ cup fresh or thawed frozen corn
- 3½ cups water, divided
- 4 tablespoons unsalted butter, divided
- 4 scallions, white parts minced, green parts sliced thin
- 1 cup milk
- ½ teaspoon hot sauce
- ½ teaspoon table salt
- ½ teaspoon pepper
- 1 cup old-fashioned grits
- 4 ounces Monterey Jack cheese, shredded (1 cup)
- 4 ounces sharp cheddar cheese, shredded (1 cup)

1. Process corn and ¼ cup water in blender until smooth, about 1 minute; set aside. Melt 2 tablespoons butter in medium saucepan over medium heat. Add scallion whites and cook until softened, about 2 minutes. Stir in milk, hot sauce, salt, pepper, and remaining 3¼ cups water and bring to boil.

2. Slowly whisk in grits until no lumps remain. Reduce heat to low and cook, stirring frequently, until grits are thick and creamy, about 15 minutes.

3. Off heat, stir in Monterey Jack, cheddar, reserved corn mixture, and remaining 2 tablespoons butter until combined. Season with salt and pepper to taste. Sprinkle with scallion greens and serve.

> ### KEYS TO SUCCESS
> - **Prep the fresh corn right:** See page 42 for how to strip fresh kernels from the cob.
> - **Taste for doneness:** Grits should be creamy and soft but still retain a little bite.

BAKED CHEESE GRITS

Serves: 4 to 6
Total Time: 1¼ hours

RECIPE OVERVIEW Baking cheesy grits gives them a crisp browned crust cloaking a creamy center. Begin building flavor by cooking chopped onion in butter and adding heavy cream for richness and piquant hot sauce for spicy contrast. Then stir in water and grits. Extra-sharp cheddar folded into the cooked grits complements the subtle corn flavors (for a more assertive side at dinnertime, try smoked cheddar or smoked gouda). Three lightly beaten eggs stirred in after the stovetop simmer will help create a dense, custardy texture. Once in the oven, the grits turn gorgeously golden.

- 1 teaspoon plus 2 tablespoons unsalted butter, divided
- 1 small onion, chopped fine
- 3 cups water
- 1 cup heavy cream
- ½ teaspoon hot sauce
- ½ teaspoon table salt
- 1 cup plus 2 tablespoons old-fashioned grits
- 8 ounces extra-sharp cheddar cheese, shredded (2 cups), divided
- 3 large eggs, lightly beaten
- ¼ teaspoon pepper

RICE, GRAINS, AND BEANS | 313

1. Adjust oven rack to lower-middle position and heat oven to 350 degrees. Grease 9-inch square baking dish with 1 teaspoon butter.

2. Melt remaining 2 tablespoons butter in large saucepan over medium heat. Add onion and cook until softened but not browned, about 4 minutes.

3. Add water, cream, hot sauce, and salt and bring to boil. Whisk in grits and reduce heat to low. Cook, stirring frequently, until grits are thick and creamy, about 15 minutes.

4. Off heat, thoroughly stir in 1½ cups cheddar, eggs, and pepper. Pour mixture into prepared dish and smooth top with rubber spatula. Bake for 30 minutes. Remove dish from oven, sprinkle remaining ½ cup cheddar evenly over top, and return to oven. Continue to bake until top is browned, about 15 minutes. Let rest for 5 minutes and serve.

> **KEY TO SUCCESS**
> - **Add the eggs off the heat:** Ensures that they will blend in smoothly

SHRIMP AND GRITS

Serves: 4
Total Time: 1 hour

RECIPE OVERVIEW Shrimp and grits is a hallowed Southern dish, and this homage makes only a few changes to the tried-and-true formula. The grits are not typically toasted in butter first, but doing so coaxes out richer corn flavor. Cooking the grits for a little longer than usual helps them arrive at the best creamy texture. Making a quick shrimp stock using the shrimp shells gives the sauce deep shrimp flavor. Sautéing the shrimp in the fat left over from cooking the bacon creates a bold base of flavor while letting the shrimp release a little of their moisture. That way, when you stir the shrimp back in at the end to finish cooking through, they won't dilute the buttery sauce.

Grits
- 3 tablespoons unsalted butter, divided
- 1 cup old-fashioned grits
- 2¼ cups whole milk
- 2 cups water
- ¾ teaspoon table salt

Shrimp
- 3 tablespoons unsalted butter, divided
- 1½ pounds extra-large shrimp (21 to 25 per pound), peeled and deveined, shells reserved
- 1 tablespoon tomato paste
- 2¼ cups water
- 3 slices bacon, cut into ½-inch pieces
- 1 garlic clove, minced
- ½ teaspoon table salt
- ½ teaspoon pepper
- 2 tablespoons all-purpose flour
- 1 tablespoon lemon juice
- ½ teaspoon Tabasco sauce, plus extra for serving
- 4 scallions, sliced thin

1. FOR THE GRITS Melt 1 tablespoon butter in medium saucepan over medium heat. Add grits and cook, stirring often, until fragrant, about 3 minutes. Add milk, water, and salt. Increase heat to medium-high and bring to boil. Reduce heat to low; cover; and simmer, whisking often, until thick and creamy, about 25 minutes. Off heat, stir in remaining 2 tablespoons butter and season with salt and pepper to taste. Cover to keep warm.

2. FOR THE SHRIMP Meanwhile, melt 1 tablespoon butter in 12-inch nonstick skillet over medium heat. Add reserved shrimp shells and cook, stirring occasionally, until shells are spotty brown, about 7 minutes. Stir in tomato paste and cook for 30 seconds. Add water and bring to boil. Reduce heat to low, cover, and simmer for 5 minutes.

3. Strain shrimp stock through fine-mesh strainer set over bowl, pressing on solids to extract as much liquid as possible; discard solids. You should have about 1½ cups stock (add more water if necessary to equal 1½ cups). Wipe skillet clean with paper towels.

4. Cook bacon in now-empty skillet over medium-low heat until crispy, 7 to 9 minutes. Increase heat to medium-high and stir in shrimp, garlic, salt, and pepper. Cook until edges of shrimp are just beginning to turn pink but shrimp are still translucent in center and not cooked through, about 2 minutes. Transfer shrimp mixture to bowl.

5. Melt 1 tablespoon butter in now-empty skillet over medium-high heat. Whisk in flour and cook for 1 minute. Slowly whisk in shrimp stock until incorporated. Bring to boil; reduce heat to medium-low; and simmer until slightly thickened, about 5 minutes.

6. Stir in shrimp mixture; cover; and cook until shrimp are cooked through, about 3 minutes. Off heat, stir in lemon juice, Tabasco, and remaining 1 tablespoon butter. Season with salt and pepper to taste. Serve shrimp over grits, sprinkled with scallions, passing extra Tabasco separately.

> **KEYS TO SUCCESS**
> - **Toast the grits:** Makes for a rich, deep corn flavor
> - **Save the shells:** To form the base of a quick but flavorful stock

LENTILS AND BEANS

LENTILS

Lentils come in various sizes and colors, and the differences in flavor and texture are surprisingly distinct.

Brown Lentils

These larger lentils are the most common choice in the market and are a uniform drab brown. They hold their shape well and turn tender and slightly creamy when cooked, with a mild yet earthy flavor.

Green Lentils

Another larger lentil, this variety is the same size as the brown lentil and is brownish green in color. They hold their shape well and are similar in flavor and texture to brown lentils.

Lentilles du Puy

These lentils are smaller than the more common brown and green varieties. While they take their name from the city of Le Puy in south-central France, they are also grown in North America and Italy. Dark olive green in color, with mottling, these lentils have a rich, earthy, complex flavor and firm yet tender texture.

Black Lentils

Like lentilles du Puy, black lentils are slightly smaller than the standard brown lentils. They have a deep-black hue similar to the color of caviar. In fact, some markets refer to them as beluga lentils. They have a robust, earthy flavor and great ability to hold their shape while remaining tender.

Red and Yellow Lentils

These small, vibrantly colored split lentils have a slightly sweeter taste than other lentils and completely disintegrate when cooked, making them ideal in preparations where a smoother texture is desired, such as Indian dals. Because they need only a short cooking time and they break down when cooked, they are not interchangeable with other varieties of lentils.

HULLED LENTILS

Under the Skin

Red and yellow split lentils are nothing more than common brown and green lentils that have been hulled. Shown here are partially hulled brown lentils, making half-red/half-brown lentils.

BEANS

Choosing canned beans over dried doesn't sacrifice quality. In fact, modern canning practices produce beans that are often more consistent than dried. Manufacturers clean, sort, and inspect dried beans before blanching them and sealing them in cans with water and often salt. Most producers also add calcium chloride, which maintains firmness and prevents splitting. The final step is pressure-cooking the beans directly in their cans. The result is perfectly cooked, creamy, and intact beans. The liquid in the can is great for giving body to stew-y bean dishes.

Most recipes that call for dried beans are soups or stews that require the beans to cook slowly with the other ingredients so that they release their starches and thicken the dish. When you replace the dried beans with canned beans and shorten the cooking time in these dishes, you sacrifice flavor and texture. On some occasions (such as for a salad or pasta dish), you can easily substitute canned beans for dried beans. A general rule is that 1 cup of uncooked dried beans equals 3 cups of canned beans.

Storing Beans

Dried beans degrade over time, so we recommend using them within six months of purchase. Both brined beans and fully cooked dried beans can be refrigerated for up to four days or frozen for several weeks. To freeze, lay the drained beans flat on a baking sheet and pop them in the freezer; once frozen, transfer the beans to a zipper-lock bag or other airtight container. You can also freeze the bean cooking liquid (separately). Save frozen fully cooked beans for applications where they will be pureed.

Chickpeas

Also known as garbanzo beans, chickpeas are little marble-shaped beans with a firm texture and nutty flavor. Although the beige variety is nearly universal in the United States, black, green, and red varieties are also grown. The versatile chickpea is used in cuisines all over the world, from the Americas to Europe to Asia.

White Beans

White beans tend to have a mild flavor and creamy texture. The largest, cannellini beans are the most commonly used white beans, but the category also encompasses medium-size great northern beans and small navy beans. Different kinds of white beans are generally interchangeable in recipes.

Black Beans

Black turtle beans are the most commonly available black bean variety in dried and canned form (and may be labeled simply "black beans"). Other varieties are generally available dried and are interchangeable with black turtle beans. They have a smooth texture and mild flavor.

Red Beans

Red beans are their own type of bean and tend to be small and delicate in flavor. Larger kidney beans can be dark red or light red and tend to have a thicker skin and a stronger flavor than red beans. Pinto beans, which have a slightly nutty flavor, actually have mottled beige and red skin when dry, but they turn light red when cooked or processed for canning.

Black-Eyed Peas

Beige with a dramatic black spot, black-eyed peas have a creamy texture and earthy flavor, which is a big reason why they are so popular in Southern preparations that use greens or pork products.

COURSE
DRESSING UP CANNED BEANS

ASHLEY MOORE

Probably every home cook has canned beans stashed in their pantry. Truth be told, there aren't a lot of particular techniques to learn when it comes to cooking with canned beans. Rather, the creative recipes in this course will inspire you to pull out those cans and to buy them on a regular basis. While canned beans are more expensive per ounce than dried beans, they are still inexpensive to buy and are incredibly convenient to keep on hand. Canned beans do contain sodium, so if this is a concern, consider purchasing reduced-sodium varieties. Rinsing and draining canned beans also can remove up to about one-quarter of their sodium.

ASHLEY'S PRO TIP: *Canned beans are the most versatile thing I have in my pantry. One simple way to transform a humble can of beans is to mash some of them and leave the rest intact, as we do in our Refried Pinto Beans. This gives the dish an appealing creamy texture—no other ingredients needed.*

ULTRACREAMY HUMMUS

Serves: 8 to 10
Total Time: 45 minutes

RECIPE OVERVIEW Hummus is arguably the ultimate chickpea dish. This rendition is velvety-smooth, creamy, and rich. How you treat the chickpeas affects the consistency of hummus more than any other factor, because they are firm (even when cooked) and covered in tough skins, which must be removed to make hummus. It takes hours to soak and simmer dried chickpeas in preparation for this, but simmering canned chickpeas (in effect "overcooking" them) takes just 20 minutes. Adding baking soda helps the skins break down and slip off, leaving a "raft" of skins floating on the surface that is easy to remove by draining and rinsing the beans a few times. Another important element of hummus is the tahini—a major source of richness and flavor. To avoid the bitter flavors that can come from tahini made with heavily roasted sesame seeds, choose a light-colored tahini. Last but not least, steeping the garlic in lemon juice and salt extracts its flavor and deactivates alliinase, the enzyme that makes garlic taste harsh. The hummus will thicken slightly over time; add warm water, 1 tablespoon at a time, as needed to restore its creamy consistency. Serve with crudités and pita bread or crackers.

- 2 (15-ounce) cans chickpeas, rinsed
- ½ teaspoon baking soda
- 4 garlic cloves, peeled
- ⅓ cup lemon juice (2 lemons), plus extra for seasoning
- 1 teaspoon table salt
- ¼ teaspoon ground cumin, plus extra for sprinkling
- ½ cup tahini, stirred well
- 2 tablespoons extra-virgin olive oil, plus extra for drizzling
- 1 tablespoon minced fresh parsley

1. Combine chickpeas, baking soda, and 6 cups water in medium saucepan and bring to boil over high heat. Reduce heat and simmer, stirring occasionally, until chickpea skins begin to float to surface and chickpeas are creamy and very soft, 20 to 25 minutes.

2. While chickpeas cook, mince garlic using garlic press or rasp-style grater. Measure out 1 tablespoon garlic and set aside; discard remaining garlic. Whisk lemon juice, salt, and reserved garlic together in small bowl and let sit for 10 minutes. Strain lemon-garlic mixture through fine-mesh strainer set over bowl, pressing on solids to extract as much liquid as possible; discard solids.

3. Drain chickpeas in colander and return to saucepan. Fill saucepan with cold water and gently swish chickpeas with your fingers to release skins. Pour off most of water into colander to collect skins, leaving chickpeas behind in saucepan. Repeat filling, swishing, and draining 3 or 4 times until most skins have been removed (this should yield about ¾ cup skins); discard skins. Transfer chickpeas to colander to drain.

4. Set aside 2 tablespoons whole chickpeas for garnish. Process lemon-garlic mixture, ¼ cup water, cumin, and remaining chickpeas in food processor until smooth, about 1 minute, scraping down sides of bowl as needed. Add tahini and oil and process until hummus is smooth, creamy, and light, about 1 minute, scraping down sides of bowl as needed. (Hummus should have pourable consistency similar to yogurt. If too thick, loosen with water, adding 1 teaspoon at a time.) Season with salt and extra lemon juice to taste.

5. Transfer to serving bowl and sprinkle with parsley, reserved chickpeas, and extra cumin. Drizzle with extra oil and serve. (Hummus can be refrigerated in airtight container for up to 5 days. Let sit, covered, at room temperature for 30 minutes before serving.)

KEYS TO SUCCESS

- **Simmer the chickpeas:** Critical to removing the pesky skins
- **Choose a light-colored tahini:** Gives your hummus a balanced flavor
- **Steep the garlic in lemon juice:** Prevents the garlic flavor from taking over the hummus

SCIENCE LESSON

Baking Soda Magic

Baking soda works magic on beans by raising the pH of their cooking liquid to make an alkaline environment. It's often used with dried beans to weaken their cell walls—which helps them absorb water faster and cook more quickly. In our Ultracreamy Hummus adding ½ teaspoon of baking soda to the saucepan with the canned chickpeas breaks down the already-cooked skins and helps them slip off completely.

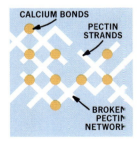

WHEN BAKING SODA IS ADDED TO BEANS: It helps break down calcium bonds, which causes the pectin strands to break down, ultimately weakening the cell walls. Weaker cell walls mean that the beans cook more quickly.

CHICKPEA SALAD WITH CARROTS, ARUGULA, AND OLIVES

Serves: 4 to 6
Total Time: 40 minutes

RECIPE OVERVIEW Canned chickpeas are an ideal ingredient for a salad because they absorb flavors easily and provide plenty of texture and protein. This flavorful pairing of sweet carrots, peppery arugula, and briny olives transforms simple canned chickpeas into a bright and savory salad. Briefly heating the chickpeas in the microwave softens them just enough to allow them to quickly soak up the tangy dressing. Shred the carrots on the large holes of a box grater or use a food processor fitted with the shredding disk.

- 2 (15-ounce) cans chickpeas, rinsed
- ¼ cup extra-virgin olive oil
- 2 tablespoons lemon juice
- ¾ teaspoon table salt
- ½ teaspoon pepper
- Pinch cayenne pepper
- 3 carrots, peeled and shredded
- ½ cup pitted kalamata olives, chopped
- 1 cup baby arugula, chopped

1. Microwave chickpeas in medium bowl until hot, about 1½ minutes. Stir in oil, lemon juice, salt, pepper, and cayenne and let sit for 30 minutes. Add carrots and olives and toss to combine.

2. Add arugula and toss gently to combine. Season with salt and pepper to taste. Serve.

Variation
CHICKPEA SALAD WITH ROASTED RED PEPPERS AND FETA
Substitute ½ cup drained and chopped jarred roasted red peppers, ½ cup crumbled feta, and ¼ cup chopped fresh parsley for carrots, olives, and arugula.

SPICED CHICKPEA GYROS WITH TAHINI YOGURT

Serves: 4
Total Time: 30 minutes

RECIPE OVERVIEW This fast, supersatisfying vegetarian dinner reimagines protein-rich chickpeas by making them the star filling in a roll-up sandwich. Mashing the chickpeas lightly breaks their skins so that they can soak up the flavors of the seasonings. Cucumber, pepperoncini, and red onion add three different kinds of crunch. For more heat, serve with extra Asian chili-garlic sauce.

1 cup plain Greek yogurt
¼ cup tahini
1 teaspoon table salt, divided
2 (15-ounce) cans chickpeas, rinsed
2 tablespoons Asian chili-garlic sauce
2 teaspoons ground cumin
4 (8-inch) pitas, lightly toasted
½ English cucumber, halved lengthwise and sliced thin on 3-inch bias
½ cup pepperoncini, stemmed and sliced into thin rings
¼ cup thinly sliced red onion

1. Combine yogurt, tahini, and ½ teaspoon salt in small bowl; set aside.

2. Using potato masher, very coarsely mash chickpeas in medium bowl. Stir chili-garlic sauce, cumin, and remaining ½ teaspoon salt into chickpeas; set aside.

3. Spread yogurt sauce evenly over 1 side of each pita (use all of it). Divide chickpea mixture, cucumber, pepperoncini, and onion evenly among pitas. Fold pitas in half, wrap tightly in parchment paper, and serve.

GARLICKY WHITE BEANS WITH SAGE

Serves: 4 to 6
Total Time: 10 minutes

RECIPE OVERVIEW This utterly simple flavor-packed preparation showcases creamy cannellini beans combined with ingredients that thrive in their company: garlic, sage, and olive oil. Start by toasting the garlic in the oil to bring out its buttery sweetness. Whole sage leaves infuse the dish with herbal complexity. Finishing with a drizzle of olive oil adds richness. This is a great side dish, but you could serve it over white rice or cooked grains for a satisfying meal.

6 tablespoons extra-virgin olive oil, divided
3 garlic cloves, sliced thin
6 fresh sage leaves
¼ teaspoon red pepper flakes
2 (15-ounce) cans cannellini beans, rinsed
¼ teaspoon table salt

Combine ¼ cup oil and garlic in 12-inch nonstick skillet and cook over medium heat until garlic begins to brown lightly at edges, about 3 minutes. Add sage and pepper flakes and cook until fragrant, about 30 seconds. Add beans and salt and cook, stirring and tossing often, until just heated through, about 2 minutes. Transfer to shallow serving dish and drizzle with remaining 2 tablespoons oil. Serve.

REFRIED PINTO BEANS

Serves: 4 to 6
Total Time: 20 minutes

RECIPE OVERVIEW Traditional refried beans, or frijoles refritos, are leftover stewed dried beans cooked in a generous amount of lard until they are softened enough to mash. This easy version achieves a lush texture and rich, savory flavor with only a tablespoon of oil, and the use of canned beans makes it fast enough to prepare any night of the week. For deep flavor, reach for smoky chipotle chile powder, cumin, oregano, and several cloves of garlic. Two tablespoons of umami-rich tomato paste add even more savory depth. Processing a portion of the beans with some water in the food processor creates the desired silky, creamy texture, and pulsing the remaining beans ensures that some chunky bites remain in the final dish.

2 (15-ounce) cans pinto beans, rinsed, divided
1 cup water, plus extra hot water as needed
1 tablespoon vegetable oil
1 onion, chopped fine
½ teaspoon table salt
2 tablespoons tomato paste
3 garlic cloves, minced
1 teaspoon ground cumin
½ teaspoon chipotle chile powder
½ teaspoon dried oregano
1 tablespoon minced fresh cilantro
2 teaspoons lime juice

1. Process all but 1 cup beans with water in food processor until smooth, about 30 seconds, scraping down sides of bowl as needed. Add remaining beans and pulse until coarsely ground, about 5 pulses.

2. Heat oil in 12-inch nonstick skillet over medium heat until shimmering. Add onion and salt and cook until onion is softened, about 5 minutes. Stir in tomato paste, garlic, cumin, chile powder, and oregano and cook until fragrant, about 1 minute. Stir in bean mixture and cook, stirring constantly, until well combined and thickened slightly, about 3 minutes. Off heat, stir in cilantro and lime juice and season with salt and pepper to taste. Add extra hot water as needed to adjust consistency and serve.

> ### KEYS TO SUCCESS
> - **Process some of the beans until smooth:** Creates a creamy base texture
> - **Pulse the rest:** Adds a texture similar to dried beans if cooked from scratch for this dish

BLACK-EYED PEAS AND GREENS

Serves: 6 to 8
Total Time: 1 hour

RECIPE OVERVIEW Although they're called peas, black-eyed peas are indeed beans. Southern tradition says that if on New Year's Day you eat collard greens and black-eyed peas stewed with tomatoes, spices, and a hambone, you'll experience greater wealth and prosperity in the coming year. With all respect to Southern tradition, this hambone-free version is lucky, too—and downright delicious. Swapping the more time-consuming dried legumes for a couple convenient cans of black-eyed peas, and then giving the collards a 15-minute head start on the stove before adding the peas to simmer them together, makes this recipe fast without sacrificing flavor. For maximum good luck, be careful not to crush the black-eyed peas—stir them gently.

- 2 tablespoons extra-virgin olive oil
- 1 onion, halved and sliced thin
- 1¼ teaspoons table salt
- 4 garlic cloves, minced
- ½ teaspoon ground cumin
- ½ teaspoon pepper
- ¼ teaspoon red pepper flakes
- 1½ cups vegetable broth
- 1 (14.5-ounce) can diced tomatoes
- 1 pound collard greens, stemmed and cut into 2-inch pieces
- 2 (15-ounce) cans black-eyed peas, rinsed
- 1 tablespoon cider vinegar
- 1 teaspoon sugar

1. Heat oil in large Dutch oven over medium heat until shimmering. Add onion and salt and cook, stirring frequently, until golden brown, about 10 minutes. Stir in garlic, cumin, pepper, and pepper flakes and cook until fragrant, about 30 seconds.

2. Stir in broth and tomatoes and their juice and bring to boil. Add collards, cover, and reduce heat to medium-low. Simmer until collards are tender, about 15 minutes.

3. Add black-eyed peas and cook, covered, stirring occasionally, until collards are silky and completely tender, about 15 minutes. Uncover; increase heat to medium-high; and cook until liquid is reduced by one-quarter, about 5 minutes. Stir in vinegar and sugar and serve.

> **KEYS TO SUCCESS**
>
> - **Don't use the tough collard stems:** See page 43 for how to separate the leaves from the stems.
> - **Give the collards a head start:** Allows them to turn silky before the black-eyed peas overcook

BLACK BEANS ON TOAST WITH TOMATO AND AVOCADO

Serves: 4
Total Time: 15 minutes

RECIPE OVERVIEW "Beans on toast" sounds vaguely British, but this black bean–topped toast has a bold Southwestern flavor profile that will liven up mealtime in an all-American style. The hearty rusticity of mashed black beans on toasted crusty bread elevated with fresh cherry tomatoes, some creamy avocado slices, fresh herbs, and a squeeze of lime is hard to argue with. Plus, it's just 10 minutes of work and you don't even have to get any skillets dirty. By simply mashing the canned beans in a bowl with a little boiling water, olive oil, and lime zest and juice, you'll get a flavorful and well-textured base. A liberal garnish of cilantro leaves freshens all the flavors. For a splash of acidity and heat, the addition of quick pickled onions and pickled jalapeños is really nice, but if you don't have them on hand, a pinch of red pepper flakes works, too. For an accurate measure of boiling water, bring a kettle of water to a boil and then measure out the desired amount.

- 4 ounces cherry tomatoes, quartered
- 4 teaspoons extra-virgin olive oil, divided
  Pinch plus ½ teaspoon table salt, divided
- 2 pinches pepper, divided
- 1 (15-ounce) can black beans, rinsed
- ¼ cup boiling water
- ½ teaspoon grated lime zest plus 1 tablespoon juice
- 4 (½-inch-thick) slices crusty bread
- 1 ripe avocado, halved, pitted, and sliced thin
- ¼ cup Quick Pickled Red Onions (page 145) (optional)
- 4 teaspoons jarred sliced jalapeños (optional)
- ¼ cup fresh cilantro leaves

1. Adjust oven rack 4 inches from broiler element and heat broiler. Combine tomatoes, 1 teaspoon oil, pinch salt, and pinch pepper in bowl. Mash beans, boiling water, lime zest and juice, remaining 1 tablespoon oil, remaining ½ teaspoon salt, and remaining pinch pepper with potato masher to coarse puree in second bowl, leaving some whole beans intact.

2. Meanwhile, arrange bread in single layer on rimmed baking sheet. Broil until bread is deep golden and toasted on both sides, 1 to 2 minutes per side.

3. Spread mashed bean mixture evenly on toasts and divide avocado evenly over top. Sprinkle with tomatoes; pickled onions and jalapeños, if using; and cilantro. Serve.

SKILLET RICE AND BLACK BEANS WITH CORN AND TOMATOES

Serves: 6
Total Time: 50 minutes

RECIPE OVERVIEW Rice and beans are a familiar combination and staple preparation the world over, but often the best recipes use dried beans, which require too much time and effort to be practical for everyday cooking. This version, however, serves up a delicious weeknight meal with plump canned black beans, tender rice, and fresh vegetables. Start by sautéing onion and corn. Garlic, cumin, and cayenne contribute potent flavors. Toasting the rice briefly before stirring in broth and black beans ensures that it soaks up all the flavors while turning tender. Finish by sprinkling a mixture of tomatoes, scallions, cilantro, and lime juice over the dish before serving. The flavor of fresh corn is great here, but you can substitute 1½ cups of frozen corn, thawed and patted dry.

- 2 tablespoons extra-virgin olive oil, divided
- 12 ounces grape tomatoes, quartered
- 5 scallions, sliced thin
- ¼ cup minced fresh cilantro
- 1 tablespoon lime juice
- 1 onion, chopped fine
- 2 ears corn, kernels cut from cobs
- 4 garlic cloves, minced
- 1 teaspoon ground cumin
- Pinch cayenne pepper
- 1 cup long-grain white rice, rinsed
- 3 cups vegetable broth
- 2 (15-ounce) cans black beans, rinsed

1. Combine 1 tablespoon oil, tomatoes, scallions, cilantro, and lime juice in bowl and season with salt and pepper to taste; set aside.
2. Heat remaining 1 tablespoon oil in 12-inch nonstick skillet over medium-high heat until shimmering. Add onion and cook until softened and lightly browned, 5 to 7 minutes. Stir in corn and cook until lightly browned, about 4 minutes.
3. Stir in garlic, cumin, and cayenne and cook until fragrant, about 30 seconds. Stir in rice and coat with spices, about 1 minute. Stir in broth and beans and bring to simmer. Cover and simmer gently, stirring occasionally, until rice is tender and liquid is absorbed, about 20 minutes.
4. Season with salt and pepper to taste, sprinkle tomato mixture over top, and serve.

> ### KEYS TO SUCCESS
> - **Prep the fresh corn right:** See page 42 for how to cut the kernels from the cob.
> - **Rinse the rice:** Removes exterior starch that would make the rice sticky; see page 285 for how to do this.

COURSE
LENTILS

ELLE SIMONE SCOTT

Since dried lentils are so easy to cook, they are often the first experience many home cooks have with dried beans. Because of their small size, thin skin, and relatively high ratio of surface area to volume, lentils absorb water rapidly and cook in much less time than other dried beans. Whereas other dried beans usually need to be soaked, or "brined," before cooking to prevent their skins from exploding, lentils only sometimes need this. In the first two recipes, gentle cooking allows the lentils to stay intact and not become mushy. The salad recipe brines the lentils first to prevent blowouts.

ELLE'S PRO TIP: *When cooking lentils and other legumes, I like to lean into my favorite Dutch oven. It's oven-safe so it gives me the flexibility to start my dish on the stove and then finish cooking it in the oven.*

LENTILS WITH CARROTS AND PARSLEY

Serves: 4 to 6
Total Time: 1¼ hours

RECIPE OVERVIEW Simple yet sophisticated renditions of lentils and vegetables appear throughout the western Mediterranean, and this version takes inspiration from a French preparation. You'll slowly cook the earthy lentils with sweet carrots, onion, and celery (a classic French combination called a mirepoix). The lentils keep their shape and develop a firm-tender texture during the hands-off cooking time, without any need for soaking. Using water rather than broth lets the flavors of the lentils and vegetables shine through. You can use French green lentils (lentilles du Puy) or brown, black, or regular green lentils here. (Note that cooking times will vary for different lentils.)

- 2 carrots, peeled and chopped fine
- 1 onion, chopped fine
- 1 celery rib, chopped fine
- 2 tablespoons extra-virgin olive oil, divided
- ½ teaspoon table salt
- 2 garlic cloves, minced
- 1 teaspoon minced fresh thyme or ¼ teaspoon dried
- 2½ cups water
- 1 cup dried lentils, picked over and rinsed
- 2 tablespoons minced fresh parsley
- 2 teaspoons lemon juice

1. Combine carrots, onion, celery, 1 tablespoon oil, and salt in large saucepan. Cover and cook over medium-low heat, stirring occasionally, until vegetables are softened, 8 to 10 minutes. Stir in garlic and thyme and cook until fragrant, about 30 seconds.

2. Stir in water and lentils and bring to simmer. Reduce heat to low, cover, and simmer gently, stirring occasionally, until lentils are mostly tender, 40 to 50 minutes.

3. Uncover and continue to cook, stirring occasionally, until lentils are completely tender, about 8 minutes. Stir in parsley, lemon juice, and remaining 1 tablespoon oil. Season with salt and pepper to taste, and serve.

Variation
CURRIED LENTILS WITH GOLDEN RAISINS
Omit carrots. Add 1 teaspoon curry powder to saucepan with onion. Stir ½ cup golden raisins into saucepan after uncovering in step 3. Substitute 2 tablespoons minced fresh cilantro for parsley.

KEYS TO SUCCESS
- **Skip the brine:** Gentle simmering and stirring keeps the lentils intact
- **Chop the vegetables fine:** Ensures they will soften properly during their short cooking time

BAKED LENTILS WITH SAUSAGE

Serves: 4
Total Time: 1½ hours

RECIPE OVERVIEW For a hearty and hands-off dish of lentils and sausage, we employ a Dutch oven and the oven. To cook the lentils, start by sautéing onion and other aromatics. Then add the lentils and water and cover the pot before transferring it directly to the oven. Remove the lid for the last 20 minutes of cooking to ensure that the cooking liquid is perfectly reduced. Canned diced tomatoes provide fruitiness and a balancing acidity while smoked paprika gives the dish all the punch it needs. Last, to give these baked lentils an even fuller flavor, add smoky-sweet diced kielbasa. You can use French green lentils (lentilles du Puy) or brown or regular green lentils here. (Note that cooking times will vary for different lentils.) Serve warm or at room temperature with a drizzle of lemon juice or sherry vinegar.

- 2 tablespoons extra-virgin olive oil
- 1 onion, chopped fine
- ½ teaspoon table salt
- 4 ounces kielbasa sausage, cut into ¼-inch pieces
- 4 garlic cloves, sliced thin
- 1¼ teaspoons smoked paprika
- 1 teaspoon minced fresh thyme
- 1 (14.5-ounce) can diced tomatoes
- 1½ cups chicken broth
- 1½ cups water
- 1 cup dried lentils, picked over and rinsed
- 2 scallions, sliced thin

1. Adjust oven rack to middle position and heat oven to 300 degrees. Heat oil in large Dutch oven over medium heat until shimmering. Add onion and salt and cook, stirring often, until softened, 5 to 7 minutes. Stir in sausage, garlic, paprika, and thyme and cook until fragrant, about 30 seconds. Stir in tomatoes and their juice, broth, water, and lentils.

2. Cover; transfer pot to oven; and bake until lentils are tender, 40 minutes to 1 hour, stirring halfway through baking. Remove lid and continue to bake until liquid has evaporated, about 20 minutes.

3. Remove pot from oven and scatter scallions over lentils. Season with salt and pepper to taste before serving.

KEYS TO SUCCESS

- **Pick over the lentils**: To find and remove any foreign matter before rinsing
- **Skip the brine**: The oven's gentle heat keeps the lentils intact.
- **Uncover the pot**: Evaporates excess liquid during the last 20 minutes of cooking

LENTIL SALAD WITH POMEGRANATE AND WALNUTS

Serves: 4 to 6
Total Time: 1 hour, plus 1 hour soaking

RECIPE OVERVIEW Tart-sweet pomegranate seeds and buttery, crunchy walnuts bring lots of flavor and texture to earthy lentils in this salad, which can be served either warm or at room temperature. For lentils with a firm-tender bite and to soften their skins without any blowouts, which would mar the salad's appearance, start by brining them in warm salt water for an hour. (Brining helps keep the lentils intact, but this salad will still taste great if you skip the brining.) For further insurance, the lentils for this salad are cooked in the oven, where the gentle indirect heat turns them uniformly tender. You can use French green lentils (lentilles du Puy) or brown, black, or regular green lentils here. (Note that cooking times will vary for different lentils.)

- 1 cup dried lentils, picked over and rinsed
- 1 teaspoon table salt for brining
- 2 cups chicken broth
- 5 garlic cloves, lightly crushed and peeled
- 1 bay leaf
- ½ teaspoon table salt
- 5 tablespoons extra-virgin olive oil
- 3 tablespoons lemon juice
- 1 shallot, minced
- ¼ cup chopped fresh cilantro
- ⅓ cup walnuts, toasted and chopped coarse, divided
- ⅓ cup pomegranate seeds, divided

1. Place lentils and 1 teaspoon salt in bowl. Cover with 1 quart warm water (about 110 degrees) and soak for 1 hour. Drain well.

2. Adjust oven rack to middle position and heat oven to 325 degrees. Place lentils, 2 cups water, broth, garlic, bay leaf, and salt in medium ovensafe saucepan. Cover and bake until lentils are tender but remain intact, 40 minutes to 1 hour. Meanwhile, whisk oil and lemon juice together in large bowl.

3. Drain lentils well; remove and discard garlic and bay leaf. Add lentils, shallot, cilantro, half of walnuts, and half of pomegranate seeds to dressing and toss to combine. Season with salt and pepper to taste. Transfer to serving dish, sprinkle with remaining walnuts and pomegranate seeds, and serve.

Variation
LENTIL SALAD WITH HAZELNUTS AND GOAT CHEESE

Substitute red wine vinegar for lemon juice and add 2 teaspoons Dijon mustard to dressing in step 2. Substitute ¼ cup chopped parsley for cilantro and ⅓ cup coarsely chopped toasted hazelnuts for walnuts. Omit pomegranate seeds and sprinkle with 2 ounces crumbled goat cheese before serving.

CORE TECHNIQUE
Sorting Dried Lentils and Beans

USE PLATE OR BAKING SHEET
This lets you easily spread the beans out into a single layer.

PICK OVER
Check over the beans to remove any small stones or other foreign matter.

SPICED RED LENTILS

Serves: 4
Total Time: 45 minutes

RECIPE OVERVIEW Split red lentils are commonly used in dals, spiced lentil stews enjoyed throughout India. They give this simple dal a mild, slightly nutty taste, and as the stew slowly simmers, they break down to a smooth consistency, bordering on a puree. To emulate the complex flavors of an Indian dal, start with a balanced blend of warm spices with just a subtle layer of heat. Blooming the spices in oil until they're fragrant boosts and deepens their flavors. Onion, garlic, and ginger round out the aromatics. Before serving, add cilantro for color and freshness and diced raw tomato for sweetness and acidity. A bit of butter stirred in before serving adds a rich finish. You cannot substitute other types of lentils for the red lentils here; they have a very different texture. Serve over rice or with naan.

- 1 tablespoon vegetable oil
- ½ teaspoon ground coriander
- ½ teaspoon ground cumin
- ½ teaspoon ground cinnamon
- ½ teaspoon ground turmeric
- ⅛ teaspoon ground cardamom
- ⅛ teaspoon red pepper flakes
- 1 onion, chopped fine
- 4 garlic cloves, minced
- 1½ teaspoons grated fresh ginger
- 4 cups water
- 8½ ounces (1¼ cups) dried red lentils, picked over and rinsed
- 1 pound plum tomatoes, cored, seeded, and chopped
- ½ cup minced fresh cilantro
- 2 tablespoons unsalted butter
- Lemon wedges

1. Heat oil in large saucepan over medium-high heat until shimmering. Add coriander, cumin, cinnamon, turmeric, cardamom, and pepper flakes and cook until fragrant, about 10 seconds. Stir in onion and cook until softened, about 5 minutes. Stir in garlic and ginger and cook until fragrant, about 30 seconds.

2. Stir in water and lentils and bring to boil. Reduce heat to low and simmer, uncovered, until lentils are tender and resemble coarse puree, 20 to 25 minutes.

3. Stir in tomatoes, cilantro, and butter and season with salt and pepper to taste. Serve with lemon wedges.

KEYS TO SUCCESS

- **Bloom the spices:** Adds a significant flavor payoff
- **Carefully measure the lentils and water:** To achieve the correct consistency

Variation
SPICED RED LENTILS WITH CAULIFLOWER

Omit tomatoes. Substitute 1 teaspoon garam masala for coriander, cumin, turmeric, cardamom, and pepper flakes. Substitute lime wedges for lemon wedges. While lentils cook, toss 1 head cauliflower cut into 8 equal wedges, with 2 tablespoons extra-virgin olive oil and ¼ teaspoon table salt. Place wedges cut side down on parchment paper–lined rimmed baking sheet. Cover tightly with aluminum foil and bake in heated 475-degree oven for 10 minutes. Remove foil. Continue to cook until bottoms of wedges are golden, 8 to 12 minutes. Remove from oven, flip wedges using spatula, and continue to cook until golden all over, 8 to 12 minutes. Serve cauliflower with lentils.

COURSE
DRIED BEANS 101

BRYAN ROOF

Cooking dried beans is somewhat of a labor of love, but that doesn't mean it should become a lost art. Although it takes more time than using canned beans, it isn't difficult at all, and there are many rewards to using dried beans in specific recipes. For example, low-and-slow cooking results in the creamiest cannellini beans you'll ever eat. Since baked beans are a dish in which dried beans really shine, we've included two distinct recipes. Finally, you'll learn to make falafel—a classic use for dried chickpeas.

BRYAN'S PRO TIP: *When cooking dried beans, it's always better to err on the side of a gentle simmer. Cooking the beans too aggressively—at a strong simmer or boil—can cause them to break apart.*

WHITE BEANS WITH TOMATOES AND CAPERS
Serves: 4 to 6
Total Time: 1¾ hours, plus 8 hours soaking

RECIPE OVERVIEW White beans are the showpiece of this simple recipe, so starting with dried is well worth the extra time and effort. The superbly creamy texture and flavor of these from-scratch beans are more satisfying than anything you'll get from a can. Toast thinly sliced garlic to bring out its sweetness, and cook the tomatoes until they are just softened for savory sauciness. The beans soak up the extra-virgin olive oil, and an extra drizzle at the end adds even more richness. We prefer a long soak for these beans before cooking (though a quick soak will also work).

- 3 tablespoons table salt for brining
- 1 pound (2½ cups) dried cannellini beans, picked over and rinsed
- 1 tablespoon plus ¼ teaspoon table salt, divided
- 6 tablespoons extra-virgin olive oil, divided
- 3 garlic cloves, sliced thin
- 5 ounces grape tomatoes, halved
- 1 tablespoon capers, rinsed
- ½ teaspoon dried oregano
- ½ teaspoon red pepper flakes

1. Dissolve 3 tablespoons salt in 4 quarts cold water in large container. Add beans and soak at room temperature for at least 8 hours or up to 24 hours.

2. Drain beans in colander and rinse well. Combine beans, 10 cups water, and 1 tablespoon salt in Dutch oven and bring to boil over high heat. Reduce heat to medium

and cook at gentle simmer until beans are barely al dente, 40 to 50 minutes. (During simmer, bubbles should just break surface of water.)

3. Remove from heat; cover pot; and let beans steep until tender, 20 to 30 minutes. Drain beans in colander. (Beans can be refrigerated in airtight container for up to 3 days. Alternatively, beans can be cooled, transferred to zipper-lock bags, and frozen for up to 1 month.)

4. Combine ¼ cup oil and garlic in 12-inch nonstick skillet and cook over medium heat until garlic begins to brown lightly at edges, about 3 minutes. Add 3½ cups beans (reserve remainder for another use), tomatoes, capers, oregano, pepper flakes, and remaining ¼ teaspoon salt and cook until tomatoes just begin to soften, about 5 minutes, stirring occasionally.

5. Transfer bean mixture to shallow dish and drizzle with remaining 2 tablespoons oil. Serve.

KEYS TO SUCCESS

- **Pick over and rinse the beans:** To remove any small stones from the beans before cooking
- **Brine the beans:** A long soak makes the beans creamy and less likely to burst.
- **Let them steep after simmering:** Ensures the ultimate in creamy-textured beans

COWBOY BEANS

Serves: 6 to 8
Total Time: 3¾ hours, plus 8 hours soaking

RECIPE OVERVIEW These beans are reminiscent of the smoky, deeply flavored, long-cooked cowboy beans served at many barbecue joints. To get there, we use dried pinto or navy beans and prefer to soak them overnight (though you can use the quick-soak method here). Bacon makes a good and convenient substitute for the smoky barbecued meat. Blending mustard, barbecue sauce, and brown sugar gives layers of sweet-spicy flavor—a fair amount of garlic and onion help, too. But the real secret ingredient in this oven-baked recipe is coffee. The roasted, slightly bitter flavor really ties it all together.

- 3 tablespoons table salt for brining
- 1 pound (2½ cups) dried pinto or navy beans, picked over and rinsed
- 4 slices bacon, chopped fine
- 1 onion, chopped fine
- 4 garlic cloves, minced
- 1 cup brewed coffee
- ½ cup plus 2 tablespoons barbecue sauce, divided
- ⅓ cup packed dark brown sugar
- 2 tablespoons spicy brown mustard
- 2 teaspoons table salt
- ½ teaspoon hot sauce

CORE TECHNIQUE
Soaking Dried Beans

LONG SOAK
For the creamiest beans, we recommend a long soak. For every 1 pound beans, dissolve 3 tablespoons salt in 4 quarts cold water. Soak beans at room temperature for 8 to 24 hours. Drain and rinse well.

QUICK SOAK
If pressed for time, combine salt, water, and beans in large Dutch oven and bring to boil. Remove from heat, cover, and let stand for 1 hour. Drain and rinse well. Quick-soaked dried beans will be less creamy than long-soaked beans.

SCIENCE LESSON Brining Beans

When you soak, or "brine," dried beans in salted water before using them in a recipe, they cook up with softer skins that are less likely to split, blow out, and disintegrate. As the beans soak, the sodium ions from the salt replace some of the calcium and magnesium ions in the bean skins. Because sodium ions are more weakly charged than calcium and magnesium ions, they allow more water to penetrate the skins, leading to a softer texture. The sodium ions filter only partway into the beans, so their greatest effect is on the cells in the outermost part of the beans.

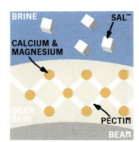

BEFORE BRINING
The strong pectin molecules in the bean's skin are tightly bound into a network by calcium and magnesium ions.

WHILE BRINING
Sodium replaces the calcium and magnesium ions, causing the pectin network to break down more readily, softening the skin and preventing exploding legumes.

1. Dissolve 3 tablespoons salt in 4 quarts cold water in large container. Add beans and let soak at room temperature for at least 8 hours or up to 24 hours. Drain and rinse well.

2. Adjust oven rack to lower-middle position and heat oven to 300 degrees. Cook bacon in Dutch oven over medium heat until crispy, 5 to 7 minutes. Stir in onion and cook until softened and lightly browned, 6 to 8 minutes. Stir in garlic and cook until fragrant, about 30 seconds. Stir in beans, 4½ cups water, coffee, ½ cup barbecue sauce, sugar, mustard, salt, and hot sauce and bring to boil. Cover; transfer pot to oven; and cook until beans are just tender, 2 to 2½ hours.

3. Uncover and continue to cook, stirring occasionally, until beans are fully tender, 1 to 1½ hours.

4. Remove pot from oven and let beans sit until liquid has thickened slightly and clings to beans, 10 to 15 minutes, stirring halfway through. Stir in remaining 2 tablespoons barbecue sauce and season with salt and pepper to taste. Serve.

BAKED NAVY BEANS

Serves: 6 to 8
Total Time: 3 hours

RECIPE OVERVIEW Here's a meatless version of classic Boston baked beans that really showcases the small, oval-shaped, mild-flavored navy beans that are the typical choice for this dish. To get creamy-textured baked beans, and in a lot less time to boot, first simmer the dried navy beans with a little baking soda. The alkaline baking soda weakens the cell structure of the beans, helping them become tender more quickly. Thanks to that, you can skip the brining altogether with this recipe, and simmering the beans with baking soda also lets you shave the baking time down to 2 hours from the normal 5 to 6 hours. These beans have the usual seasonings—onion, molasses, brown sugar, mustard, and cider vinegar—but to deepen the flavor and amp up the meatiness of this bean pot without the trouble of adding meat, you'll also include umami-rich soy sauce and smoked paprika.

- 1 pound (2½ cups) dried navy beans, picked over and rinsed
- 1 tablespoon baking soda
- 1 tablespoon vegetable oil
- 1 onion, chopped fine
- ¼ cup molasses
- 2 tablespoons packed dark brown sugar
- 2 tablespoons soy sauce
- 4 teaspoons Dijon mustard, divided
- 2 teaspoons smoked paprika
- ¾ teaspoon table salt
- ¼ teaspoon pepper
- 2 teaspoons cider vinegar

1. Adjust oven rack to middle position and heat oven to 350 degrees. Bring 3 quarts water, beans, and baking soda to boil in Dutch oven over high heat. Reduce heat to medium-high and simmer vigorously for 20 minutes. Drain and rinse beans. Rinse and dry pot.

2. Heat oil in now-empty pot over medium heat until shimmering. Add onion and cook until softened, about 5 minutes. Stir in 4½ cups water, beans, molasses, sugar, soy sauce, 1 tablespoon mustard, paprika, salt, and pepper and bring to boil. Cover pot; transfer to oven; and bake until beans are nearly tender, about 1½ hours.

3. Uncover and continue to bake until beans are completely tender, about 30 minutes. Stir in vinegar and remaining 1 teaspoon mustard. Season with salt and pepper to taste. Serve.

FALAFEL

Makes: about 24 falafel
Total Time: 40 minutes, plus 8 hours soaking

RECIPE OVERVIEW These savory fried chickpea patties generously seasoned with herbs and spices are an eastern Mediterranean specialty. The best falafel have a moist, light interior and well-browned, crisp crust. Starting with dried chickpeas and soaking them overnight is essential; canned chickpeas will become mushy. Process the soaked chickpeas with fresh herbs and warm spices, and then shape them into small disks. Shallow frying works nicely to create a crunchy, golden crust and requires far less oil than deep-fried recipes. The chickpeas in this recipe must be soaked overnight; don't substitute quick-soaked or canned chickpeas. Serve as an appetizer or snack, or tuck the falafel into pita with lettuce, tomatoes, cucumbers, red onion, and pickles. See page 354 for a yogurt sauce to drizzle on top.

- 3 tablespoons table salt for brining
- 12 ounces (2 cups) dried chickpeas, picked over and rinsed
- 10 scallions, chopped coarse
- 1 cup fresh parsley leaves
- 1 cup fresh cilantro leaves
- 6 garlic cloves, minced
- 1 teaspoon table salt
- 1 teaspoon pepper
- ½ teaspoon ground cumin
- ⅛ teaspoon ground cinnamon
- 2 cups vegetable oil for frying

1. Dissolve 3 tablespoons salt in 4 quarts cold water in large container. Add chickpeas and soak at room temperature for at least 8 hours or up to 24 hours. Drain and rinse well.

2. Process chickpeas, scallions, parsley, cilantro, garlic, salt, pepper, cumin, and cinnamon in food processor until smooth, about 1 minute, scraping down sides of bowl as needed. Pinch off and shape chickpea mixture into

2-tablespoon disks, about 1½ inches wide and 1 inch thick, and place on parchment paper–lined baking sheet. (Falafel can be refrigerated for up to 2 hours.)

3. Adjust oven rack to middle position and heat oven to 200 degrees. Set wire rack in rimmed baking sheet. Heat oil in 12-inch skillet over medium-high heat to 375 degrees. Fry half of falafel until deep golden brown, 2 to 3 minutes per side. Adjust burner, if necessary, to maintain oil temperature of 375 degrees. Using slotted spoon, transfer falafel to prepared sheet and keep warm in oven. Return oil to 375 degrees and repeat with remaining falafel. Serve.

KEYS TO SUCCESS

- **Soak the chickpeas overnight:** Don't quick-soak the beans; a long brine creates sturdy falafel.
- **Be consistent with shaping:** Disks of the same size and shape cook evenly.
- **Shallow-fry:** Uses less oil than deep frying; see page 411 for more information.

Making Falafel

BLEND CHICKPEAS
Process chickpea mixture until smooth.

SHAPE FALAFEL
Shape mixture into 1½-inch-wide disks.

FRY FALAFEL
Shallow-fry falafel disks in skillet until deep golden brown.

COURSE
TEMPEH

STEPHANIE PIXLEY

Tempeh, made from fermented, cooked soybeans (or sometimes other beans), often with the addition of grains, has a substantial meaty texture and savory flavor that make it popular as a meat substitute in vegan cooking. But its versatility turns it into an enjoyable part of any meal, whether plant-based or otherwise. Though it has a stronger, nuttier flavor than tofu, it also tends to absorb the flavors of whatever it is cooked with. These simple recipes are a great introduction.

STEPHANIE'S PRO TIP: *If you eat gluten-free, note that not all tempeh is free of gluten! Some varieties of tempeh include grains in addition to the traditional soybeans, so check labels carefully if that's something you pay attention to.*

CRISPY TEMPEH

Serves: 4 (Makes 1 cup)
Total Time: 50 minutes

RECIPE OVERVIEW Here tempeh becomes a condiment or topping of sorts: a crunchy umami bomb that will be the star of any dish it's sprinkled on, including vegetable salads, soups, rice or grain bowls, and noodle dishes. Once the tempeh is crumbled into small pieces, a simple two-step preparation method of boiling in soy sauce–seasoned water followed by frying tempers its slight natural bitterness and transforms its overall neutral flavor into anything but.

- 3 tablespoons soy sauce
- 8 ounces tempeh, crumbled into ¼-inch pieces
- 1 cup peanut or vegetable oil for frying

1. Bring 4 cups water and soy sauce to boil in large saucepan. Add tempeh, return to boil, and cook for 10 minutes. Drain tempeh well and wipe saucepan dry with paper towels.

2. Set wire rack in rimmed baking sheet and line with triple layer paper towels. Heat oil in now-empty saucepan over medium-high heat until shimmering. Add tempeh and cook until golden brown and crisp, about 12 minutes, adjusting heat as needed if tempeh begins to scorch. Using spider skimmer or slotted spoon, transfer tempeh to prepared rack to drain, then season with salt and pepper to taste. Serve immediately.

> **KEY TO SUCCESS**
> - **Boil, then fry:** Softens the tempeh's texture and mellows its flavor

PAN-SEARED TEMPEH STEAKS WITH CHIMICHURRI SAUCE

Serves: 4
Total Time: 25 minutes, plus 1 hour marinating

RECIPE OVERVIEW Since tempeh has such a high concentration of protein and is so good at absorbing flavor, why not go all in and prepare it as a "meaty" steak with a classic serving sauce? Marinating the tempeh in a seasoned mixture of vinegar and water infuses it with flavor. Pan-searing it creates a delectably crisp edge. The tempeh's earthy flavor is well balanced by the bright chimichurri, a traditional steak sauce that combines parsley, red wine vinegar, oil, lots of garlic, oregano, and a good dose of red pepper flakes.

- 5 tablespoons red wine vinegar, divided
- ¼ cup water
- 4 garlic cloves, minced, divided
- 1½ teaspoons dried oregano, divided
- ½ teaspoon red pepper flakes, divided
- 1 pound tempeh, cut into 3½-inch-long by ⅜-inch-thick slabs
- 1 cup fresh parsley leaves
- ½ cup extra-virgin olive oil, divided
- ½ teaspoon table salt

1. Combine ¼ cup vinegar, water, half of garlic, 1 teaspoon oregano, and ¼ teaspoon pepper flakes in 1-gallon zipper-lock bag. Add tempeh, press out air, seal bag, and toss to coat. Refrigerate tempeh for at least 1 hour or up to 24 hours, flipping bag occasionally.

2. Pulse parsley, ¼ cup oil, salt, remaining 1 tablespoon vinegar, remaining garlic, remaining ½ teaspoon oregano, and remaining ¼ teaspoon pepper flakes in food processor until coarsely chopped, about 10 pulses, scraping down sides of bowl as needed. Transfer to bowl and season with salt and pepper to taste.

3. Remove tempeh from marinade and pat dry with paper towels. Heat 2 tablespoons oil in 12-inch nonstick skillet over medium heat until shimmering. Add 4 pieces tempeh and cook until golden brown on first side, 2 to 4 minutes.

4. Flip tempeh; reduce heat to medium-low; and continue to cook until golden brown on second side, 2 to 4 minutes. Transfer to platter. Wipe out skillet with paper towels and repeat with remaining 2 tablespoons oil and remaining tempeh. Serve with chimichurri.

CORE TECHNIQUE

Cutting Tempeh into Slabs

CUT CROSSWISE
Cut each piece crosswise into two 3½-inch-long pieces.

CUT HORIZONTALLY
Next cut each piece horizontally into ⅜-inch-thick slabs.

TEMPEH WITH SAMBAL SAUCE

Serves: 4
Total Time: 30 minutes

RECIPE OVERVIEW This highly flavorful Indonesian dish is traditionally deep-fried, but here's a shallow-fried version with an easier method that gives great results. Cut the tempeh into pieces and fry them until they're golden, which allows all the ridges and corners to turn crispy. Use a small portion of the frying oil to cook the coarsely pureed sambal. Then it's just a matter of tossing the tempeh into the sambal and stirring in loads of fresh basil. If shrimp paste is unavailable, substitute two anchovy fillets, minced to a paste. If you can't find kecap manis (Indonesian sweet soy sauce), you can substitute 1½ tablespoons of packed dark brown sugar plus 1 teaspoon of soy sauce here.

- 12 ounces Fresno chiles, stemmed, seeded, and chopped coarse
- 1 small onion, chopped coarse
- 5 garlic cloves, peeled
- 2 teaspoons shrimp paste
- ½ teaspoon table salt
- 1 cup vegetable oil
- 1 pound tempeh, cut into ½-inch pieces, divided
- ½ cup water
- 2 tablespoons kecap manis
- 1½ cups fresh Thai or Italian basil leaves

1. Process Fresnos, onion, garlic, shrimp paste, and salt in food processor until finely chopped, about 30 seconds, scraping down sides of bowl as needed; transfer to bowl.

2. Adjust oven rack to middle position and heat oven to 200 degrees. Set wire rack in rimmed baking sheet and line rack with triple layer of paper towels. Heat oil in 12-inch nonstick skillet over medium-high heat to 375 degrees. Carefully add half of tempeh to hot oil and increase heat to high. Cook, turning as needed, until golden brown, 3 to 5 minutes. Adjust burner, if necessary, to maintain oil temperature between 350 and 375 degrees. Off heat, transfer tempeh to prepared rack and keep warm in oven. Return oil to 375 degrees over medium-high heat and repeat with remaining tempeh; transfer to rack.

3. Carefully pour off all but 2 tablespoons oil from skillet. Add chile mixture to oil left in skillet and cook over medium-high heat, tossing slowly but constantly, until darkened in color and completely dry, 7 to 10 minutes. Off heat, stir in water and kecap manis until combined. Add tempeh and basil and toss until well coated. Serve.

KEYS TO SUCCESS

- **Shallow-fry:** Uses less oil than deep frying; see page 411 for more information.
- **Maintain the right oil temperature:** Returning the oil to 375 degrees before frying the second batch minimizes greasiness.

BARBECUE TEMPEH WRAPS

Serves: 4
Total Time: 30 minutes

RECIPE OVERVIEW Boldly sauced, sweet-spicy-sticky tempeh is set off by the cool crunch of bok choy, radishes, and scallions in this barbecue wrap. To give the tempeh a deeply browned crust, sear it in a skillet before tossing it with the quick sauce made from soy sauce, garlic, sugar, sriracha, and a shot of rice vinegar. Including some cornstarch and simmering the sauce for 5 minutes make it thick and velvety. Tucked into a flour tortilla, the sauce-daubed tempeh and fresh vegetables are super-satisfying.

- ¾ cup sugar
- 6 tablespoons soy sauce
- 6 tablespoons water
- 5 garlic cloves, minced
- 1½ tablespoons unseasoned rice vinegar
- 1½ teaspoons sriracha
- 1½ teaspoons cornstarch
- ¼ cup vegetable oil, divided
- 1 pound tempeh, cut crosswise into ½-inch-thick strips, divided
- 4 (10-inch) flour tortillas
- 2 heads baby bok choy (4 ounces each), sliced thin crosswise
- 1 cup fresh cilantro leaves
- 3 radishes, trimmed, halved, and sliced thin
- 2 scallions, sliced thin

1. Whisk sugar, soy sauce, water, garlic, vinegar, sriracha, and cornstarch together in bowl; set aside.

2. Heat 2 tablespoons oil in 12-inch nonstick skillet over medium heat until shimmering. Add half of tempeh and cook until golden brown, 2 to 4 minutes per side; transfer to paper towel–lined plate. Repeat with remaining 2 tablespoons oil and remaining tempeh.

3. Add sugar mixture to now-empty skillet and simmer over medium-low heat until mixture is thickened and measures 1 cup, about 5 minutes; transfer to bowl. Toss tempeh with half of sauce in separate bowl.

4. Lay tortillas on counter; arrange tempeh, bok choy, cilantro, radishes, and scallions in center of each tortilla; then drizzle each with 1 tablespoon sauce. Working with 1 tortilla at a time, fold sides of tortilla over filling, then fold up bottom of tortilla over filling, pulling back firmly to tighten tortilla around filling. Continue to roll tortilla tightly. Serve with remaining sauce.

RESOURCES FOR RICE, GRAINS, AND BEANS

WANT TO DOUBLE THE RICE? DON'T DOUBLE THE WATER

Despite what many recipes suggest, rice-to-water ratios can't be scaled up proportionally when multiplying a recipe for steamed or pilaf-style rice. After a series of tests, we confirmed that rice absorbs water in a 1:1 ratio, no matter the volume. For example, in our rice pilaf recipe, which calls for 1½ cups of rice and 2¼ cups of water, the rice absorbed 1½ cups of water. The remaining ¾ cup of water evaporated.

But here's the catch: The amount of water that evaporates doesn't double when the amount of rice is doubled. In fact, we found that when doubling a batch of rice using the same method as we'd used to cook a single batch, the same quantity of water evaporated. Hence, simply doubling the recipe leads to mushy rice because there is an excess of water. The bottom line: When multiplying a rice recipe that uses the absorption or pilaf method, the ratio of raw rice to water should always be 1 to 1, plus the amount of water that will evaporate. To figure out how much will evaporate, subtract the amount of rice from the total volume of water in the original recipe and add that amount to the 1:1 volume of water.

SIZING UP BULGUR

Bulgur has been an important source of nutrition across the Middle East, North Africa, and eastern Europe for roughly 4,000 years. It's made by parboiling whole wheat (usually durum) kernels, drying them, and pulverizing them into granules that are graded by size, #1 being the smallest and #4 being the largest. Coarser granules are often boiled until they're chewy-firm and used for pilaf; medium- and fine-grind bulgur are typically soaked in water and then tossed in salads (such as tabbouleh or eetch), bound up in kibbeh or kofte, stuffed into vegetables, or stirred into soups.

Fine Grind | Raw Sugar | Medium Grind | Mustard Seeds

Coarse Grind | Sesame Seeds | Very Coarse Grind | Steel-Cut Oats

TREAT BARLEY LIKE PASTA

Barley is prone to clumping for two reasons: First, its starch granules burst relatively early in the cooking time. Second, the starch is sticky because it's loaded with amylopectin, the branching molecule that's responsible for the stickiness of short-grain rices.

Boiling barley in a large volume of water, just as you would when cooking pasta, and then draining it prevents clumping because it dilutes the starch in abundant water, which we then drain away.

THE COLORS OF QUINOA

There are many varieties of quinoa, including red and black (or a mixture of the two) and white (or golden) quinoa. White quinoa has the largest, softest seeds of the three. It has a nutty, vegetal flavor with a hint of bitterness. Medium-size red quinoa offers a heartier crunch and a more prominent nuttiness; it can usually be used interchangeably with white quinoa. Black quinoa is the smallest of the three and has the thickest seed coat. As a result, it retains its shape during cooking and is very crunchy, with a mild flavor.

NEVER COOKED DRIED BEANS? HERE'S A FOOLPROOF TEMPLATE.

1. BRINE THE BEANS
Brining the beans for 8 to 24 hours takes forethought. But this step seasons them thoroughly and helps them maintain their shape throughout cooking. (Be sure to pick through them to discard any funky-looking beans or pebbles before brining.)

2. COOK UNCOVERED AND SLOWLY SIMMER
The cooking time for dried beans varies based on bean type, brand, and age; cooking them uncovered on the stovetop gives you the ability to watch them as they cook. Maintaining a gentle simmer prevents the beans from knocking against each other and rupturing.

3. TASTE FOR TEXTURE
Start tasting the beans for doneness after about 45 minutes of simmering. The beans should be just barely al dente; to check, simply bite into a few. Note that the doneness levels of individual beans in the pot may vary, so be sure to sample more than one.

4. FINISH OFF THE HEAT
Covering the pot and letting the beans steep in their hot cooking liquid allows them to gently and evenly finish cooking through without any skins bursting.

CHAPTER 8

MEAT

COURSES

346 THE STEAKHOUSE

356 PERFECT PORK CHOPS

360 MEAT STIR-FRIES

366 EVERYDAY ROASTS

370 THE BRAISING POT

376 MEAT STEWS OF THE WORLD

384 GROUND MEAT MUST-KNOWS

390 QUICK DINNER OFF THE GRILL

396 EAT WITH YOUR HANDS

400 SPECIAL-OCCASION CENTERPIECES

MORE TO EXPLORE

352 SPICE RUBS, SAUCES, AND COMPOUND BUTTERS

MEAT BASICS

BUYING MEAT

If you're lucky enough to be able to frequent a butcher shop or a supermarket that has a meat cutter, a piece of glass is all that separates you from the cut you might purchase. (Bonus: You can choose cuts of similar size to ensure even cooking.) If you're buying meat from the refrigerator case, you can take a look behind the cellophane. Either way, here are things to pay attention to.

Temperature
Meat packaging should be cool to the touch since meat should be stored at 40 degrees or below. On especially hot days, use an insulated bag and make meat the last stop on your grocery list.

Appearance
Meat should look moist but not sodden; an excessive amount of juices inside a meat package (known as purge) can be an indication that the meat has been on the shelf for too long. As for color, red meat will appear mahogany or purplish when butchered but the flesh will turn bright red or pink once exposed to oxygen. Meat that has turned brown all the way through is on its way to spoiling. Avoid meat that has green spots—that's bacteria. As for pork, avoid pale pink meat. Darker, more richly colored pork is firmer, more flavorful, and better able to retain moisture.

Marbling
For most meat, streaks of white throughout are an indication of marbling and are desirable. Marbling is fat that adds flavor to meat. But don't confuse marbling with gristle, which you should avoid. Gristle, which is often translucent rather than white, is connective tissue and doesn't break down upon cooking.

When it comes to beef, the U.S. Department of Agriculture (USDA) assigns different quality grades—prime, choice, and select—and they're based on marbling. USDA prime beef is heavily marbled, which makes for a tender, flavorful steak. About 2 percent of graded beef is considered prime. Prime meats are most often served in restaurants or sold in high-end butcher shops or grocers. The majority of graded beef is choice. While the levels of marbling in choice beef can vary, it is generally moderately marbled with intramuscular fat. Select beef has little marbling and is the only grade we avoid.

Meat Terms
There are a lot of optional labeling terms on meat. While the aforementioned meat matters should be considered first, here are some terms you might want to be familiar with.

PASTURE-RAISED A "pasture-raised" label can be an indication of quality, but it is not a term that is regulated by the USDA and is not clearly defined. The animals' access to a pasture may be very limited—you'll have to contact the producer to learn more.

NO HORMONES A "no hormones administered" label appears on meat if the producer can provide documentation proving that the animal wasn't raised with hormones. The USDA prohibits all use of hormones (and steroids) with pork. And it isn't industry standard to use hormones on lamb.

NO ANTIBIOTICS These animals were not raised with antibiotics.

NATURAL Natural simply means that the meat was minimally processed and contains no artificial ingredients.

ORGANIC Organic meat, as it's defined by the USDA, is produced by farmers who emphasize the use of renewable resources and the conservation of soil and water to enhance environmental quality for future generations. Animals are given no antibiotics or growth hormones.

GRAIN-FED VERSUS GRASS-FED MEAT Animals that are fed a diet of grains for the last part of their life are "grain-fed." (Such animals may also be called "grain-finished," since they may have previously existed on a grass or pasture diet.) Grains are higher in protein and starch, which not only help animals fatten faster, but also make the meat richer. Meat labeled "grass-fed" comes from animals that have eaten a grass or pasture diet for some of their lives. If it's labeled "100 percent grass-fed," the animal has eaten only grass. Grass-fed meat is leaner than grain-fed meat and tends to have a more complex, nuttier flavor. It is higher in certain vitamins, minerals, antioxidants, and omega-3 fatty acids. Furthermore, grass-fed meat contains twice the amount of conjugated linoleic acid (CLA) isomers, fatty acids that might fight cancer and lower the risk of diabetes.

ENHANCED PORK Because modern supermarket pork is so lean and therefore somewhat bland and prone to dryness if overcooked, many producers inject their fresh pork products with a sodium solution. So-called enhanced pork is the only option at many supermarkets. If the pork has been enhanced it will have an ingredient label, while natural pork will not have ingredients. The enhancements generally add 7 to 15 percent extra weight. While enhanced pork does cook up juicier, we find the texture almost spongy, and the flavor is often too salty. If you must buy enhanced pork, decrease or omit the salt in your recipe (we provide instructions).

DOMESTIC VERSUS IMPORTED LAMB While almost all the beef and pork sold in American markets is raised domestically, you can purchase imported (usually from New Zealand or Australia) as well as domestic lamb, and you may want to think about your choice based on your flavor preferences. Domestic lamb is distinguished by its larger size and milder flavor, which comes from a diet of grass that's finished with grain; we prefer it in the test kitchen. Lamb imported from Australia or New Zealand features a far gamier taste, as they are raised on just pasture-fed mixed grasses.

MAKING THE GRADE

You can spot the difference in grades of beef by the amount of marbling they exhibit.

PRIME
Heavily marbled, tender, and flavorful.

CHOICE
Moderately marbled, good flavor and value.

SELECT
Lightly marbled, tough, poor flavor.

STORING MEAT

The key to storing meat is to keep it cold and there are two places to do it.

In the Refrigerator

Meat should be refrigerated promptly after purchase and can remain refrigerated before cooking for up to three days. Smoked and cured products can be stored for two weeks once opened, and ground meat, defrosted cuts, and cooked meat can be stored for two days. Keep in mind that the back of a refrigerator is the coldest, while the door is the least cold. Make sure that raw meat is stored well wrapped and never on shelves that are above other food.

In the Freezer

Meat tastes best if you've never frozen it. The slow process of freezing that occurs in a home freezer (as compared with a commercial freezer) causes large ice crystals to form. The crystals rupture the cell walls of the meat, permitting the release of juices during cooking. That said, if you're going to freeze meat we've found that the best method is to remove it from its packaging, vacuum-seal it or wrap it well in plastic, and then place the meat in a zipper-lock bag and squeeze out any air. If the cuts are small, such as steaks or chops, we like to freeze them, uncovered, overnight on a baking sheet (this dries them out to prevent crystallization) before wrapping them. Meat can remain frozen for up to one month; if you use a vacuum sealer, you can store it for three months.

To prevent the growth of harmful bacteria when thawing frozen meat, we defrost thicker (1 inch or greater) cuts in the refrigerator and place thinner cuts on a heavy cast-iron or steel pan at room temperature; the metal's rapid heat transfer safely thaws the meat in about an hour. Have even less time? Soak cuts such as chops, steaks, and cutlets in hot water. Simply seal the pieces of meat in zipper-lock bags and submerge the packages in very hot (140-degree) water. These cuts will take roughly 12 minutes to thaw, which is fast enough that the rate of bacterial growth falls into the "safe" category, and the meat doesn't start to cook. (Large roasts are not suitable for hot thawing.)

HOW TO COOK MEAT

If there's a cooking method, it can probably be used for meat. Our courses and recipes will teach you how to approach specific meat cooking methods, but these are the important techniques in meat cookery that we turn to again and again, and why they're the right choice for certain cuts.

SEAR IT

Good for: steaks, chops

WHAT'S IT ALL ABOUT?

For smaller cuts, take to the stove with a skillet and you're guaranteed a quick dinner. Heat oil over medium-high heat until just smoking. Add the meat to the skillet. Cook on one side until browned, flip, and repeat so the outside is browned and crusty and the inside is your desired doneness.

For thick-cut steaks and chops (1½ to 1¾ inches thick), we often combine the stove with oven cooking (see Bacon-Wrapped Filets Mignons on page 348); this method, called reverse searing, prevents the exterior of meat from racing ahead of the interior when it hits a scorching pan. Bake the meat on a wire rack at a low oven temperature until the meat is just shy of its doneness temperature before searing on the stove.

Another technique, where you flip a thick steak frequently (see Pan-Seared Strip Steaks on page 349), encourages heat to evenly access the meat from top to bottom and to carry over as the meat moves face-down to face-up.

HELPFUL HINTS

- Searing is also used for roasts to achieve browning before roasting or braising.
- If you sear a well-marbled cut in a nonstick pan (see page 349), you don't have to use oil in the skillet.
- The browned bits left from searing (fond) are packed with meaty flavor. Use them to make a pan sauce (see page 418).
- Searing does not lock in juices; it produces a great crust and fond.

ROAST IT

Good for: large cuts, roasts without a lot of intramuscular fat

WHAT'S IT ALL ABOUT?

Cooking meat in the oven lets the heat circulate around it while drying out the surface so that the Maillard reaction (when the proteins and sugars in meat are subjected to high temperatures, leading to browning and new flavor compounds) occurs while cooking through.

We roast some (usually smaller) cuts of meat at high temperatures for shorter amounts of time. But lower temperatures generally guarantee more evenly cooked meat. Further, heat takes a long time to penetrate into the center of large cuts of meat, making them susceptible to an outer swath of overcooked meat.

HELPFUL HINTS

- Tying roasts evens out their thickness for even cooking.
- Cooking on a roasting rack or wire rack means that the heat of the oven circulates around the roast, cooking it more evenly.

BRAISE IT

Good for: cuts with a lot of intramuscular fat and connective tissue

WHAT'S IT ALL ABOUT?

Braising (or stewing) cooks the meat in a closed environment, often in liquid, to break down its proteins for ultratender results and to unlock inherent flavor. It coaxes the collagen in these cuts to readily melt into meat-lubricating gelatin.

HELPFUL HINTS

- We generally like to braise in a covered pot in the oven rather than on the stove for gentle, even cooking from indirect heat.
- You can brown meat before braising, or leave the lid off the pot so exposed pieces can achieve browning.
- A fat separator makes quick work of straining cooking liquids.

BEFORE AND AFTER COOKING

Set up a dish for success or finish the deal.

Trimming

Some exterior fat is good on meat, especially on roasts. In the oven or on the grill, this fat will melt and flavor the meat. This is especially important to look for when selecting relatively lean cuts such as pork loin or beef brisket. However, more than ½ inch of exterior fat is generally too much. Use a sharp knife (we like a boning knife) to slice off excess fat as necessary.

Seasoning

Meat needs salt—and the fattier the cut, the more salt flavor it can benefit from. Sprinkle salt (and pepper) high above the meat for even distribution. Applying salt before cooking improves flavor and sometimes texture. Salt's rate of infusion increases with heat so salting during a cooking method like braising ensures well-rounded heat. And seasoning to taste before serving is important for all foods.

To avoid contamination, grind pepper and place salt in small bowls so you can reach into the bowl for seasoning without having to wash your hands every time you touch the raw meat.

Wet-Brining

Brining—soaking food in a solution of salt and water—is a pretreatment that can make lean meats juicy, tender, and flavorful throughout. During brining, salt moves from the area of greatest concentration (the surrounding liquid brine) to the area of lesser concentration (the interior of the food being brined), bringing the liquid with it in a process called osmosis. Meanwhile, the salt changes the structure of the proteins so they're better able to hold on to moisture even after cooking. Through this process, the meat's structural integrity is compromised, which reduces toughness. This method seasons meat to the very center.

We usually don't brine beef and lamb; they're often juicy enough and brining can water down their robust flavor. We often turn to brining for lean pork (and poultry), which needs to be cooked longer than beef and lamb, to keep it juicy. You don't need much for brining; just your protein, table salt (the tiny grains dissolve more quickly in water than kosher salt), and a container.

Dry-Brining

Dry-Brining (another term for salting) is the act of sprinkling meat with salt (we often use kosher for more even distribution of the larger grains) and then letting the meat rest to gain benefits much like those from brining. When salt is applied to meat and left to sit for a spell, it first draws the moisture out to the surface through osmosis, where the liquid dissolves that applied salt. This migration of liquid causes muscle fibers to swell to make room for the liquid and dissolves other proteins, which then act like a sponge so that the meat soaks up and holds on to moisture during cooking. The meat tastes more like itself since it's reabsorbing its own juices, and because the cuts aren't overly moist, their surfaces can achieve good browning.

Patting Dry

Before cooking (and especially after brining or salting meat) you want to pat it dry. Surface moisture impedes browning. The only place this isn't very important is in braising applications where you're not browning the meat—you just want it succulent.

Resting

Be patient. The purpose of resting meat is to allow the juices, which are driven to the center during cooking, to redistribute throughout the meat. As a result, meat that has rested will shed much less juice than meat sliced straight after cooking. To prove this, we cooked four steaks and let two rest while slicing into the other two immediately. The steaks that had rested for 10 minutes shed 40 percent less juice than the steaks sliced right after cooking. The unrested steaks also looked grayer and were not as tender. A thin steak or chop should rest for 5 to 10 minutes, a thicker roast for 15 to 20 minutes.

Slicing

Most recipes call for cutting against the grain. If you look carefully at a piece of meat, you'll notice little bundles of closely packed muscle fibers that run parallel to one another. This pattern of fibers is known as the grain. Recipes recommend slicing across the grain—perpendicular to the fibers—to shorten them and thereby make the meat tender and easier to chew.

ANIMAL PRIMAL CUTS

There's a hierarchy when it comes to meat: animal, primal cuts, retail cuts. Wholesalers separate sides of meat into large primal cuts. These are the ones you see outlined in most animal drawings (the shoulder of a lamb or the rib of a cow, for example). These are then cut into smaller roasts (sometimes called subprimals) and even smaller steaks and chops that we buy at retail. There are similarities that can be drawn between the corresponding primals on all three. The shoulder, for example, will hold long-cooking cuts of beef, pork, and lamb because on any animal it's used for movement and weight support and its muscles are hard-acting. Middle loin cuts will always be tender and flavorful. Below are the beef, pork, and lamb primal cuts and a listing of the primals and retail cuts we cook with and you might choose from at the store.

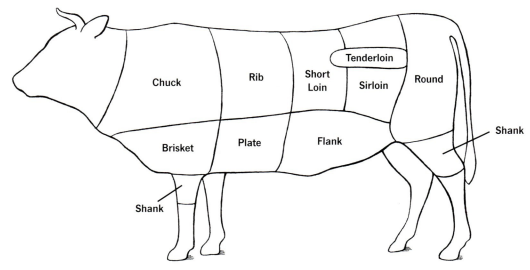

BEEF				
CHUCK	Chuck-Eye Roast		SIRLOIN	Top Sirloin Roast
	Chuck-Eye Steak			Top Sirloin Steak
	Top-Blade Roast			Sirloin Tri-Tip Roast
	Blade Steak			Flap Meat (Steak Tips)
RIB	First-Cut Standing Rib Roast		ROUND	Top Round Roast
	Second-Cut Standing Rib Roast			Bottom Round Roast
	Rib Steak			Boneless Eye-Round Roast
	Double-Cut Bone-In Rib Steak		BRISKET	Flat-Cut Brisket
	Rib-Eye Steak			Point-Cut Brisket
SHORT LOIN	Top Loin Roast		PLATE	Skirt Steak
	Boneless Strip Steak			Beef Plate Ribs
	Porterhouse Steak			Short Ribs
	T-Bone Steak		FLANK	Flank Steak
TENDERLOIN	Whole Beef Tenderloin		BEEF SHANKS	Beef Shanks
	Center-Cut Beef Tenderloin Roast		OXTAILS	Oxtails
	Filet Mignon			

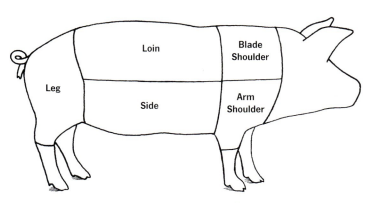
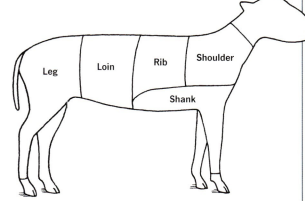

PORK

BLADE SHOULDER	Bone-In Pork Butt Roast
	Boneless Pork Butt Roast
	Pork Butt Steaks
	Blade-Cut Pork Chops
ARM SHOULDER	Picnic Shoulder Roast
	Smoked Picnic Ham
LOIN	Blade-End Pork Rib Roast
	Boneless Blade-End Pork Loin
	Country-Style Ribs
	Center-Cut Pork Rib Roast
	Pork Rib Chops
	Crown Roast
	Center-Cut Pork Loin
	Boneless Pork Chops
	Pork Tenderloin
	Baby Back Ribs
SIDE	St. Louis–Style Spareribs
	Center-Cut Pork Belly
LEG	Shank-End Fresh Ham
	Sirloin-Half Fresh Ham
	Country Ham
	Spiral-Sliced Bone-In Ham
	Uncut Half Ham
	Ham Steak
	Ham Hocks

LAMB

SHOULDER	Lamb Shoulder Roast
	Lamb Shoulder Chops
RIB AND LOIN	Rack of Lamb
	Rib and Loin Chops
LEGS AND SHANKS	Bone-In Leg of Lamb
	Boneless Leg of Lamb
	Lamb Shanks

MEAT DONENESS TEMPERATURES

An instant-read thermomer (see page 14) is an indispensable tool when cooking meat. If it reads the right temperature for the cut at hand, there's a good chance you have a delicious dinner ahead of you—it's science. Here are the proper temperatures for your desired meat doneness.

CUT	DESIRED DONENESS	COOKING STOP TEMPERATURE	TEMPERATURE AFTER RESTING
Beef, Veal, and Lamb	Rare	115 to 120°	120 to 125°
	Medium-Rare	120 to 125°	125 to 130°
	Medium	130 to 135°	135 to 140°
	Medium-Well	140 to 145°	145 to 150°
Pork	Medium (for chops)	140 to 145°	150°
	Medium (for roasts)	135 to 140°	150°

Note: The doneness temperatures in this book represent the test kitchen's assessment of palatability weighed against safety. The basics from the USDA differ somewhat: Cook whole cuts of meat, including pork, to an internal temperature of at least 145 degrees and let rest for at least 3 minutes. Cook all ground meats to an internal temperature of at least 160 degrees. For more information on food safety from the USDA, visit www.fsis.usda.gov.

COURSE
THE STEAKHOUSE

LAWMAN JOHNSON

A perfectly cooked steak, standing alone at the center of your plate, rosy red from edge to edge and shining from its juices, is a rightfully popular menu choice. You can bring this dish home and quite possibly make it even better—cooked and seasoned just to your liking, rested but warm—without the high price tag. It doesn't have to be a top-tier cut to taste amazing; in this course we'll teach you to cook inexpensive steaks to perfection so you can enjoy them any night of the week. And if you are buying an expensive cut for a special occasion, you can feel confident with the knowledge that it will come out perfectly every time using our foolproof techniques. Get your steak knives ready.

LAWMAN'S PRO TIP: *Having the right technique is really important. You'll get better with practice, but using an instant-read thermometer helps to produce a perfect result when cooking steak.*

PAN-SEARED STEAK TIPS WITH ROASTED POTATOES AND HORSERADISH CREAM

Serves: 4
Total Time: 30 minutes

RECIPE OVERVIEW You might think you need to splurge on a marbled rib-eye steak or an ultratender fillet to get top-shelf steakhouse flavors at home, but you can achieve the same satisfaction with easy-to-cook steak tips. They have a distinct grain and a robust beefiness, and the tips have a higher ratio of crust to interior than a standard steak. For a cooking method that produces juicy steak tips, well, you don't need to do much: Cut the tips into 2-inch pieces, season with salt and pepper, cook in a hot pan for about 7 minutes, and cut the medium-rare meat against the grain for tender bites. Go all-in on steakhouse splendor with a side of roasted potatoes and a stir-together horseradish cream sauce to complement the steak and potatoes. Use potatoes that are 1 to 2 inches in diameter. Use refrigerated prepared horseradish, not the shelf-stable kind which contains preservatives and additives. Steak tips, also known as flap meat, can be sold as whole steaks, cubes, or strips. To ensure evenly sized pieces, we prefer to buy whole steaks and cut them ourselves.

½ cup sour cream
¼ cup prepared horseradish
1½ teaspoons table salt, divided
1 teaspoon pepper, divided
1½ pounds small Yukon Gold potatoes, unpeeled, halved
2 tablespoons vegetable oil, divided
2 pounds sirloin steak tips, trimmed and cut into 2-inch pieces
2 tablespoons minced fresh chives

1. Adjust oven rack to lower-middle position and heat oven to 450 degrees. Combine sour cream, horseradish, ½ teaspoon salt, and ¼ teaspoon pepper in bowl; set aside.

2. Toss potatoes, 1 tablespoon oil, ½ teaspoon salt, and ¼ teaspoon pepper together on rimmed baking sheet. Arrange potatoes cut side down on sheet and roast until tender and bottoms are well browned, about 25 minutes.

3. Meanwhile, pat steak dry with paper towels and sprinkle with remaining ½ teaspoon salt and remaining ½ teaspoon pepper. Heat remaining 1 tablespoon oil in 12-inch nonstick skillet over medium-high heat until just smoking. Add steak and cook until browned on all sides and meat registers 120 to 125 degrees (for medium-rare), about 7 minutes. Serve steak with potatoes and horseradish cream, sprinkled with chives.

KEYS TO SUCCESS

- **Brown all sides:** To create a great sear
- **Slice thin against the grain:** For the most tender tips

CORE TECHNIQUE
Cutting Flap Meat into Steaks Tips

TRIM
Trim the large piece of flap meat of excess exterior fat (see page 343).

CUT
Cut the meat into even-size pieces.

PAN-SEARED SIRLOIN STEAKS WITH MUSTARD-CREAM PAN SAUCE

Serves: 4
Total Time: 50 minutes

RECIPE OVERVIEW Top sirloin steak boasts a unique combination of tenderness with pleasant chew, meatiness, and affordability. For the best flavor, we use a pan-searing technique of heating oil until it begins smoking, cooking the steaks over medium-high heat on one side, and then reducing the heat to medium when we flip the steaks. This approach ensures a nice sear on both sides without overcooking or allowing the fond on the bottom of the pan to burn; once deglazed, the fond adds great flavor to a pan sauce that keeps this accessible dinner interesting.

2 (1-pound) boneless top sirloin steaks, 1¼ inches thick, trimmed
½ teaspoon salt
½ teaspoon pepper
2 tablespoons vegetable oil
1 shallot, minced
2 tablespoons dry white wine
½ cup chicken broth
6 tablespoons heavy cream
3 tablespoons whole-grain Dijon mustard

1. Pat steaks dry with paper towels and sprinkle with salt and pepper. Heat oil in 12-inch skillet over medium-high heat until just smoking. Place steaks in skillet and cook, without moving them, until well browned, about 2 minutes. Using tongs, flip steaks; reduce heat to medium. Cook until well browned on second side and meat registers 120 to 125 degrees (for medium-rare) or 130 to 135 degrees (for medium), 5 to 6 minutes. Transfer steaks to cutting board, tent with aluminum foil, and let rest for 12 minutes.

2. Pour off all but 1 tablespoon fat from skillet. Add shallot and cook, stirring frequently, over low heat until beginning to brown, 2 to 3 minutes. Add wine and increase heat to medium-high; simmer rapidly, scraping up any browned bits, until liquid is reduced to glaze, about 30 seconds. Add broth and simmer until reduced to ¼ cup, about 3 minutes. Add cream and any accumulated steak juices; cook until heated through, about 1 minute. Stir in mustard and season with salt and pepper to taste. Slice steak against grain on bias ¼ inch thick. Spoon sauce over steaks and serve.

KEYS TO SUCCESS

- **Reduce the heat:** After searing and flipping the steak so it doesn't overcook
- **Cook to medium-rare or even medium:** To tenderize the steak's thick fibers
- **Let it rest:** After cooking (while making the sauce)

BACON-WRAPPED FILETS MIGNONS

Serves: 4
Total Time: 1¼ hours

RECIPE OVERVIEW Filet mignon, cut from the most tender part (the center) of the most tender roast (beef tenderloin) of the cow, makes up for its leanness and mild flavor in, yes, top tenderness. Wrapping filets mignons in bacon is a surefire way to add flavor (and fat). The challenge is getting perfectly cooked steaks and crispy slices of bacon at the same time, because no one likes flabby bacon. Reverse searing, one of our favorite techniques for cooking thick-cut steaks without a dreaded gray band, is perfect here. Bacon fat takes time to render, so slowly cooking the wrapped filets in a low oven until they are just shy of medium-rare ensures that they're perfectly and evenly cooked before giving the bacon the attention it needs. After the oven time, the smoky wrappers are ready for a quick trip to the skillet to finish crisping, and the top and bottom of the steaks also get a good quick sear while the rosy interior is preserved. Serve the steaks with a bright, pungent Gorgonzola Vinaigrette (page 354).

- 2 teaspoons kosher salt
- 1 teaspoon pepper
- 1 (2-pound) center-cut beef tenderloin roast, trimmed
- 4 slices bacon
- 1 tablespoon vegetable oil

1. Adjust oven rack to middle position and heat oven to 275 degrees. Set wire rack in rimmed baking sheet. Combine salt and pepper in bowl. Cut tenderloin crosswise into 4 equal steaks. Pat steaks dry with paper towels and sprinkle evenly with salt mixture.

2. Working with 1 steak at a time, wrap 1 slice bacon around circumference of steak, stretching as needed, and secure overlapping ends with toothpick inserted horizontally. Place steaks on prepared wire rack. Roast until steaks register 115 degrees (for medium-rare), 40 to 50 minutes.

3. Heat oil in 12-inch nonstick skillet over medium-high heat until just smoking. Position steaks on sides in skillet with bacon seam side down and nestled into rounded corners of skillet. Cook until bacon is evenly browned, rotating steaks as needed, about 5 minutes. Position steaks flat side down in center of skillet and cook until steaks are well browned on tops and bottoms, 1 to 2 minutes per side.

4. Transfer steaks to platter, tent with aluminum foil, and let rest for 10 minutes. Gently remove toothpicks, leaving bacon intact. Serve.

CORE TECHNIQUE

Reverse Searing

START IN OVEN
Cook the steaks in a low oven, elevated on a wire rack set in a rimmed baking sheet, so they slowly come to temperature and the surfaces dry for browning.

BROWN ON STOVETOP
Finish the steaks by searing them on the stovetop until they're well browned on all sides.

KEYS TO SUCCESS

- **Cut the filets yourself:** From a center-cut beef tenderloin to ensure even thickness
- **Use a toothpick:** To hold the bacon wrapping in place through cooking
- **Start in the oven:** To slowly raise the temperature of the steak and render the bacon fat
- **Sear on the sides:** To crisp the bacon without overcooking the steaks

PAN-SEARED STRIP STEAKS

Serves: 4
Total Time: 20 minutes

RECIPE OVERVIEW Reverse searing (see page 348) is one great way to cook thick-cut steaks, but sometimes sticking to just using a skillet is most convenient—if the method doesn't spray the kitchen with oil. For a fast, mess-free way of achieving deeply seared, rosy meat, we start the steaks in a "cold" (not preheated) nonstick skillet, turning the heat first to high and then lowering it to medium, and flipping the steaks every 2 minutes. The meat's temperature increases gradually, allowing a crust to build up on the outside without overcooking the interior. And the dual temperatures produce sizzle without smoke. Because we cook in a nonstick skillet, it isn't necessary to lubricate the skillet with oil, and the well-marbled meat exudes enough fat to achieve a good sear. Before serving, slice the steaks and sprinkle them with flake sea salt so that every bite is well seasoned. If you have time, salt the steaks for 45 minutes or up to 24 hours before cooking: Sprinkle each of the steaks with 1 teaspoon of kosher salt, refrigerate them, and pat them dry with paper towels before cooking. This recipe also works with boneless rib-eye steaks of a similar thickness.

- 2 (12- to 16-ounce) boneless strip steaks, 1½ inches thick, trimmed
- 1 teaspoon pepper

1. Pat steaks dry with paper towels and sprinkle both sides with pepper. Place steaks 1 inch apart in cold 12-inch nonstick skillet. Place skillet over high heat and cook steaks for 2 minutes. Flip steaks and cook on second side for 2 minutes. (Neither side of steaks will be browned at this point.)

2. Flip steaks, reduce heat to medium, and continue to cook, flipping steaks every 2 minutes, until browned and meat registers 120 to 125 degrees (for medium-rare), 4 to 10 minutes longer. (Steaks should be sizzling gently; if not, increase heat slightly. Reduce heat if skillet starts to smoke.)

3. Transfer steaks to cutting board and let rest for 5 minutes. Slice steaks against grain, season with flake sea salt to taste, and serve.

> **KEYS TO SUCCESS**
> - **Start the steaks in a cold pan:** To bring them up to temperature gradually while they form a crust
> - **Flip the steaks frequently:** Every 2 minutes allows a rich crust to build up gradually without overcooking the interior

LAMB RIB CHOPS WITH MINT-ROSEMARY RELISH

Serves: 4
Total Time: 45 minutes

RECIPE OVERVIEW It's not unusual to see lamb chops on a steakhouse menu, and their refined appearance and flavor make them a most popular cut of lamb to prepare at home. Cast iron is great for cooking these chops: The intense heat of a preheated cast-iron skillet can produce a rich crust on lamb while melting away its abundant fat. Searing the chops quickly on both sides over medium-high heat and then gently finishing them over lower heat creates crispy crusts and juicy interiors. We season the chops with just salt and pepper; to add flavor and complement the lamb we create a quick olive oil–based mint and rosemary relish. The bold combination of mint and rosemary, along with garlic, spicy red pepper flakes, and tart red wine vinegar, is the perfect pairing for the lamb.

Relish
- ½ cup minced fresh mint
- 5 tablespoons extra-virgin olive oil
- 2 teaspoons minced fresh rosemary
- 2 teaspoons red wine vinegar
- 1 garlic clove, minced
- ⅛ teaspoon red pepper flakes

Lamb
- 8 (5- to 6-ounce) lamb rib chops, 1¼ to 1½ inches thick, trimmed
- ½ teaspoon table salt
- ½ teaspoon pepper
- 2 tablespoons vegetable oil

1. Adjust oven rack to middle position, place 12-inch cast-iron skillet on rack, and heat oven to 500 degrees.

2. **FOR THE RELISH** While oven heats, combine all ingredients in serving bowl. Season with salt and pepper to taste; set aside for serving.

3. **FOR THE LAMB** Pat chops dry with paper towels and sprinkle with salt and pepper. When oven reaches 500 degrees, remove skillet from oven using pot holders and place over medium-high heat; turn off oven. Being careful of hot skillet handle, add oil and heat until just smoking. Cook chops, without moving them, until lightly browned on first side, about 2 minutes. Flip chops and cook until lightly browned on second side, about 2 minutes.

4. Flip chops, reduce heat to medium-low, and cook until well browned and meat registers 120 to 125 degrees (for medium-rare), 3 to 5 minutes, flipping chops halfway through cooking. Transfer chops to serving platter, tent with aluminum foil, and let rest for 5 to 10 minutes. Serve with relish.

RESOURCES FOR THE STEAKHOUSE

FOUR CUTS THAT MAKE A GOOD CENTERPIECE STEAK

1. RIB-EYE STEAK
Also known as beauty steak, Delmonico steak, Spencer steak, Scotch fillet, or entrecôte, a rib-eye steak is essentially a boneless piece of prime rib. Rib-eye steaks contain large pockets of fat and have a rich, smooth texture. This pricey steak is tender and juicy, with a pronounced beefiness.

2. BONELESS STRIP STEAK
Also known as ambassador steak, top loin steak, shell steak, sirloin strip steak, Kansas City strip steak, New York strip steak, Texas strip steak, and boneless club steak, the boneless strip steak is a steakhouse standard, beloved for its balanced fat content (it's rich but not overwhelming) and manageable size. It's cut from the top loin roast and is well-marbled, but more lean than rib-eye steaks, with a tight grain and a pleasantly chewy texture.

3. FILET MIGNON
When the tenderloin is cut into steaks, it's very expensive, as Americans prize tenderness in their steaks above all else. Filets are 1 to 2 inches thick. They're buttery-smooth and very tender and lean, with very mild beef flavor.

4. TOP SIRLOIN STEAK
Also known as New York sirloin steak, shell sirloin steak, or sirloin butt steak, top sirloin steak is cut from top sirloin roast. This steak boasts a unique combination of tenderness, pleasant chew, meatiness, and affordability. This economical cut is perfectly suitable for a flavorful weeknight steak dinner. This steak comes in a range of sizes and can often be quite large, so be sure to purchase according to recipe specs.

COOKING FROZEN STEAKS

Come home from work, take a rock-hard steak from the freezer, and clunk it in a hot pan. What sounds like a recipe for disaster can be a recipe for success if frozen is what you have. When we seared frozen (no sitting on the counter) strip steaks as well as frozen-then-thawed steaks on both sides and then transferred them to a low oven to finish, the frozen steaks browned just as well, had thinner bands of gray, overcooked meat under the crust, and tasted juicier than the thawed steaks.

COOKED STRAIGHT FROM FREEZER
A frozen steak is less likely to overcook around its perimeter during searing.

FROZEN, THAWED, THEN COOKED
A steak that goes into the pan warmer (after thawing) will overcook more around its perimeter.

SALTING STEAKS

Salting meat often simply means seasoning meat. It's a particularly good pretreatment choice for seared steaks, where the goal is a super-satisfying crust. That's because salting, unlike brining, doesn't make the surface of the meat wet, so browning is easy to achieve. Further, the to-the-core seasoning and reabsorption of the steaks' own juices from salting amp up the beefy flavor of the meat, giving even choice cuts the coveted prime flavor of superlative steakhouse cuts. We recommend sprinkling 1-pound steaks with 1 teaspoon of kosher salt and refrigerating them for at least 45 minutes or up to 24 hours before cooking. The kosher salt is easy to distribute evenly across the steaks' surface. Thoroughly pat the steaks dry before cooking.

HOW TO READ A STEAKHOUSE MENU

You may see the terms "Kobe beef," "Wagyu beef," and "American Wagyu" on steakhouse menus or in the cases at high-end butcher shops. What do they mean exactly? Wagyu is a breed of cattle originally raised in Kobe, the capital city of Japan's Hyogo prefecture. Wagyu have been bred for centuries for their rich intramuscular fat, resulting in buttery-tasting, supremely tender meat. Wagyu cattle boast extra fat since they spend an average of one year longer in the feedlot than regular cattle, and end up weighing between 200 and 400 pounds more at slaughter. What's more, the fat in Wagyu beef is genetically predisposed to be about 70 percent desirable unsaturated fat and about 30 percent saturated fat, while the reverse is true for conventional American cattle.

In order to earn the designation "Kobe beef," the Wagyu must come from Kobe and meet strict production standards that govern that appellation. The "American Wagyu" or "American-Style Kobe Beef" that appears on some menus is usually a cross between Wagyu and Angus, but the U.S. Department of Agriculture requires that the animal be at least 50 percent Wagyu and remain in the feedlot for at least 350 days to receive these designations. In our taste tests, American Wagyu proved itself a delicacy worthy of an occasional splurge: It was strikingly rich, juicy, and tender.

EATING RARE MEAT

Why do we eat rare beef but not rare chicken?

Whether or not it's safe to eat rare meat has to do with the bacteria associated with the meat. A temperature of 165 degrees is considered a safety point for killing all harmful bacteria. We don't eat raw or rare chicken or turkey because it has an unpleasant texture, but also because it can be infected by the bacteria *Salmonella*, which can live inside the muscle tissue. For beef, the problem isn't the inside of the muscle (which is sterile) but the outside, as *Escherichia coli* (or *E. coli*) can reside there. So steaks can safely be cooked rare (burgers are most safely cooked to well-done, as *E. coli* can be mixed into the meat during grinding).

SHIMMER AND SMOKE

When sautéing or pan-frying, we often call for heating oil until just smoking. What happens if you add your food to the pan too soon, before it's actually smoking? We ran an experiment to demonstrate.

We cooked two sirloin strip steaks in identical 12-inch skillets. For one steak, we heated 1 tablespoon of vegetable oil until shimmering, which took about 2 minutes. In the other pan, we heated 1 tablespoon of oil until it reached the smoke point, which took 6 minutes. We cooked both steaks until well browned on both sides.

The steak cooked in the oil heated to the smoke point browned quickly and evenly, in about 6 minutes, with a minimal overcooked gray band beneath the surface. The steak cooked in the shimmering oil took 10 minutes to brown, and the meat just beneath the surface overcooked, leaving a larger gray band. What was going on?

Shimmering oil only reaches about 275 degrees, rather than the 400 degrees of vegetable oil at its smoke point. Making sure the oil is sufficiently hot helps keep the pan from cooling down too much once the food has been added and guarantees quick, even, and thorough browning. If the oil is below the smoke point when the food is added, browning will take too long and the food will overcook.

It's easy to think you've seen a wisp of smoke and rush to add the food to the pan. But oil that has actually hit the smoke point is unmistakable—you'll see multiple wisps rising from the pan. And don't worry too much about overheating the oil; as long as you have your food at the ready, there is little risk since the oil will cool quickly once you add the food. (If you have overheated it, you will know because the oil will turn dark. In this case, throw out the oil and start over.)

SEARED IN SHIMMERING OIL
Browning takes 10 minutes, so the meat overcooks beneath the surface.

SEARED IN SMOKING OIL
Browning happens in just 6 minutes, so the meat remains rosy from edge to center.

MORE TO EXPLORE

SPICE RUBS, SAUCES, AND COMPOUND BUTTERS

A perfectly cooked steak is a masterpiece on its own but a rub or a finishing sauce dresses up meat to make it all the more special, sometimes heightening its richness, sometimes offsetting its richness, and sometimes adding spicy savor.

Spice Rubs

Rubs, mixed together from pantry spices, are a simple path to complex flavor—just coat and cook, and the flavor blooms on the meat when exposed to the heat. We recommend using about 2 tablespoons of rub for steaks for four people, and ¼ cup for a roast for six. Rubs will keep at room temperature for a month.

BARBECUE RUB

Makes: about ½ cup
Total Time: 5 minutes

Barbecue can mean a lot of things depending on the region of the country, and you see recipe-specific dry rubs in this book, but this spicy-sweet all-purpose rub is immediately recognizable as "barbecue" for beef and pork.

- 3 tablespoons chili powder
- 3 tablespoons packed brown sugar
- 2 teaspoons pepper
- ¾ teaspoon cayenne pepper

Combine all ingredients in bowl.

CLASSIC STEAK RUB

Makes: about ½ cup
Total Time: 10 minutes

This popular steakhouse seasoning has an earthy, herbal bite.

- 2 tablespoons black peppercorns
- 3 tablespoons coriander seeds
- 4 teaspoons dried dill weed
- 2 teaspoons red pepper flakes

Process peppercorns and coriander seeds in spice grinder until finely ground, about 30 seconds; transfer to small bowl. Stir in dill and pepper flakes.

HERBES DE PROVENCE

Makes: about ½ cup
Total Time: 5 minutes

This delicate, aromatic blend of dried herbs from southern France is a good match for sweet, mild pork.

- 2 tablespoons dried thyme
- 2 tablespoons dried marjoram
- 2 tablespoons dried rosemary
- 2 teaspoons fennel seeds

Combine all ingredients in bowl.

JERK RUB

Makes: about ½ cup
Total Time: 10 minutes

Stir up this flavorful Jamaican jerk–inspired rub to give anything fiery, fruity flavor.

- 5 teaspoons allspice berries
- 5 teaspoons black peppercorns
- 2 teaspoons dried thyme
- 3 tablespoons packed brown sugar
- 1 tablespoon garlic powder
- 2 teaspoons dry mustard
- 1 teaspoon cayenne pepper

Process allspice, peppercorns, and thyme in spice grinder until coarsely ground, about 30 seconds; transfer to small bowl. Stir in sugar, garlic powder, mustard, and cayenne.

Herb Sauces

With their fresh flavors and vivid colors, herb sauces bring vibrant beauty to just about anything, and provide a bright counterpoint to the richness of certain cuts of meat.

SALSA VERDE

Makes: about 1½ cups
Total Time: 15 minutes, plus 1 hour resting

Italian salsa verde is an all-purpose green sauce for just about any cut of meat, brightened with plenty of lemon juice.

- 4 cups fresh parsley leaves
- 2 slices hearty white sandwich bread, lightly toasted and cut into ½-inch pieces (1½ cups)
- ¼ cup capers, rinsed
- 4 anchovy fillets, rinsed and patted dry
- 1 garlic clove, minced
- ¼ teaspoon table salt
- ¼ cup lemon juice (2 lemons)
- 1 cup extra-virgin olive oil

1. Pulse parsley, bread, capers, anchovies, garlic, and salt in food processor until finely chopped, about 5 pulses. Add lemon juice and pulse briefly to combine.

2. Transfer mixture to medium bowl and slowly whisk in oil until incorporated. Cover and let sit at room temperature for at least 1 hour to allow flavors to meld. Season with salt and pepper to taste. (Sauce can be refrigerated for up to 2 days. Bring to room temperature and whisk to recombine before serving.)

CHERMOULA

Makes: about 1½ cups
Total Time: 15 minutes, plus 1 hour resting

This Moroccan cilantro and garlic dressing gets roundness from cumin and paprika.

- 2¼ cups fresh cilantro leaves
- 8 garlic cloves, minced
- 1½ teaspoons ground cumin
- 1½ teaspoons paprika
- ½ teaspoon cayenne pepper
- ½ teaspoon table salt
- 6 tablespoons lemon juice (2 lemons)
- ¾ cup extra-virgin olive oil

1. Pulse cilantro, garlic, cumin, paprika, cayenne, and salt in food processor until coarsely chopped, about 10 pulses. Add lemon juice and pulse briefly to combine.

2. Transfer mixture to medium bowl and slowly whisk in oil until incorporated. Cover and let sit at room temperature for at least 1 hour to allow flavors to meld. Season with salt and pepper to taste. (Sauce can be refrigerated for up to 2 days. Bring to room temperature and whisk to recombine before serving.)

CHIMICHURRI

Makes: about 1½ cups
Total Time: 20 minutes, plus 1 hour resting

This oil, vinegar, and herb sauce is a traditional Argentinian accompaniment to steak. Dried oregano adds depth to the freshness of parsley and cilantro, garlic gives the sauce bite, vinegar offers a clarifying vibrancy, and red pepper flakes pack a pleasing heat.

- ¼ cup hot tap water
- 2 teaspoons dried oregano
- 1 teaspoon table salt
- 1⅓ cups fresh parsley leaves
- ⅔ cup fresh cilantro leaves
- 6 garlic cloves, minced
- ½ teaspoon red pepper flakes
- ¼ cup red wine vinegar
- ½ cup extra-virgin olive oil

1. Combine hot water, oregano, and salt in small bowl; let sit for 5 minutes to soften oregano.

2. Pulse parsley, cilantro, garlic, and pepper flakes in food processor until coarsely chopped, about 10 pulses. Add water mixture and vinegar and pulse briefly to combine.

3. Transfer mixture to medium bowl and slowly whisk in oil until incorporated. Cover and let sit at room temperature for at least 1 hour to allow flavors to meld. Season with salt and pepper to taste. (Sauce can be refrigerated for up to 2 days. Bring to room temperature and whisk to recombine before serving.)

MINT PERSILLADE

Makes: about 1½ cups
Total Time: 20 minutes, plus 1 hour resting

This take on a French sauce makes a great accompaniment to lamb.

- 2½ cups fresh mint leaves
- 2½ cups fresh parsley leaves
- 6 garlic cloves, peeled
- 6 anchovy fillets, rinsed and patted dry
- 2 teaspoons grated lemon zest plus 2½ tablespoons juice
- ½ teaspoon table salt
- ⅛ teaspoon pepper
- ¾ cup extra-virgin olive oil

1. Pulse mint, parsley, garlic, anchovies, lemon zest, salt, and pepper in food processor until finely chopped, 15 to 20 pulses. Add lemon juice and pulse briefly to combine.

2. Transfer mixture to medium bowl and slowly whisk in oil until incorporated. Cover and let sit at room temperature for at least 1 hour to allow flavors to meld. Season with salt and pepper to taste. (Sauce can be refrigerated for up to 2 days. Bring to room temperature and whisk to recombine before serving.)

MORE TO EXPLORE

Creamy Sauces

Eating meat is a treat, and sometimes the addition of a creamy sauce can gild the lily in the very best way. Other times, it can add richness and interest to leaner cuts. Creamy sauces can even be dairy-free—romesco is thickened with almonds and bread.

HOLLANDAISE SAUCE

Makes: about 1¼ cups
Total Time: 10 minutes

Creamy, tangy hollandaise is an elegant classic accompaniment to luxurious beef steaks or slices of holiday-worthy roasts. It's important to make sure the butter is still hot (about 180 degrees) so that the egg yolks cook sufficiently. Serve this sauce immediately.

- 3 large egg yolks
- 2 tablespoons lemon juice
- ¼ teaspoon table salt
- Pinch cayenne pepper, plus extra for seasoning
- 16 tablespoons unsalted butter, melted and still hot (180 degrees)

Process egg yolks, lemon juice, salt, and cayenne in blender until frothy, about 10 seconds, scraping bottom and sides of blender jar as needed. With blender running, slowly add hot butter and process until hollandaise is emulsified, about 2 minutes. Adjust consistency with hot water as needed until sauce slowly drips from spoon. Season with salt and extra cayenne to taste.

YOGURT-HERB SAUCE

Makes: about 2 cups
Total Time: 10 minutes, plus 30 minutes chilling

This creamy yogurt sauce adds tang to beef and lamb dishes and can add cooling relief to heavily spiced dishes. Do not substitute low-fat or nonfat yogurt here.

- 2 cups plain whole-milk yogurt
- ¼ cup minced fresh parsley
- ¼ cup minced fresh chives
- 2 teaspoons grated lemon zest plus ¼ cup juice (2 lemons)
- 2 garlic cloves, minced

Whisk all ingredients together in bowl and season with salt and pepper to taste. Cover and refrigerate for at least 30 minutes to allow flavors to meld. (Sauce can be refrigerated for up to 4 days.)

GORGONZOLA VINAIGRETTE

Makes: about 1 cup
Total Time: 10 minutes

Blue cheese is a classic accompaniment to steak. This quick, easy no-cook steak sauce is disguised as a vinaigrette, and the rich, creamy Gorgonzola is balanced by white wine vinegar. For a creamier texture, buy a wedge of Gorgonzola cheese instead of a precrumbled product.

- 2 tablespoons white wine vinegar
- 2 teaspoons Dijon mustard
- ½ teaspoon kosher salt
- ⅛ teaspoon pepper
- ¼ cup extra-virgin olive oil
- 2 ounces Gorgonzola cheese, crumbled (½ cup)
- 1 small shallot, sliced thin
- 2 tablespoons chopped fresh parsley

Whisk vinegar, mustard, salt, and pepper together in bowl. Slowly whisk in oil until emulsified. Stir in Gorgonzola, shallot, and parsley.

ROMESCO

Makes: about 2 cups
Total Time: 25 minutes

This bright but savory sauce is complexly flavored and best with beef and lamb.

- 1 slice hearty white sandwich bread, crust removed, bread lightly toasted and cut into ½-inch pieces (¾ cup)
- 3 tablespoons slivered almonds, toasted
- 1¾ cups jarred roasted red peppers, rinsed, patted dry, and chopped coarse
- 1 small tomato, cored, seeded, and chopped
- 2 tablespoons extra-virgin olive oil
- 1½ tablespoons sherry vinegar
- 1 large garlic clove, minced
- ½ teaspoon table salt
- ¼ teaspoon cayenne pepper

Process bread and almonds in food processor until finely ground, about 30 seconds. Add red peppers, tomato, oil, vinegar, garlic, salt, and cayenne. Process until smooth and mixture has texture similar to mayonnaise, 20 to 30 seconds, scraping down sides of bowl as needed. Season with salt and pepper to taste. (Sauce can be refrigerated for up to 2 days; bring to room temperature before serving.)

Compound Butters

Compound butters—butter mixed with aromatic ingredients and spices—are a great accompaniment to simple seared steaks or oven roasts. As a dollop melts on the warm meat, it transforms into a sauce. We like to make a double or triple batch, roll it into a log, and store it in the freezer so that flavored butter is always just a slice away.

COMPOUND BUTTER

Makes: about ½ cup
Total Time: 20 minutes

Whip 8 tablespoons softened unsalted butter in bowl with fork until light and fluffy. Mix in any of the following ingredient combinations and season with salt and pepper to taste. Cover with plastic wrap and let rest so flavors meld, about 10 minutes, or roll into log and refrigerate. (Butter can be refrigerated in airtight container for up to 4 days or frozen, wrapped tightly in plastic wrap, for up to 2 months.)

CHIPOTLE-CILANTRO COMPOUND BUTTER
- 2 teaspoons minced canned chipotle chile in adobo sauce, plus 2 teaspoons adobo sauce
- 4 teaspoons minced fresh cilantro
- 2 garlic cloves, minced
- 2 teaspoons honey
- 2 teaspoons grated lime zest

CHIVE-LEMON MISO COMPOUND BUTTER
- ¼ cup white miso
- 2 teaspoons grated lemon zest plus 4 teaspoons juice
- ¼ teaspoon pepper
- ¼ cup minced fresh chives

PARSLEY-CAPER COMPOUND BUTTER
- ¼ cup minced fresh parsley
- 4 teaspoons capers, rinsed and minced

PARSLEY-LEMON COMPOUND BUTTER
- ¼ cup minced fresh parsley
- 4 teaspoons grated lemon zest

TARRAGON-LIME COMPOUND BUTTER
- ¼ cup minced scallion
- 2 tablespoons minced fresh tarragon
- 4 teaspoons lime juice

TAPENADE COMPOUND BUTTER
- 10 pitted oil-cured black olives, chopped fine
- 1 anchovy fillet, rinsed and minced
- 1 tablespoon brandy
- 2 teaspoons minced fresh thyme
- 2 garlic cloves, minced
- ¼ teaspoon grated orange zest

COURSE
PERFECT PORK CHOPS

ANNIE PETITO

A pork chop is one of the most common cuts of pork, one suitable for a weeknight dinner. You might pick up whatever is on sale and throw it in a skillet—only to be met with dry, tough results. That's because there are some considerations to make. For one, different types of chops are not interchangeable. Each comes from a different primal cut of the pig and thus cooks most like the other cuts from that section. You'll learn, for example, that the best way to cook blade chops is to braise them, and that boneless cuts require different treatment than bone-in. Once you know what method to use, cooking any type of pork chop is easy.

ANNIE'S PRO TIP: *For a better sear, try to use natural instead of enhanced pork, which is injected with a solution of salt, water, and sodium phosphate (this will be indicated on the packaging) that we've found thwarts browning.*

PAN-SEARED THICK-CUT PORK CHOPS
Serves: 4
Total Time: 1½ hours

RECIPE OVERVIEW If cooked properly, a simple pork rib chop on the bone, large and impressive at 12 ounces, has a brown sear on succulent meat that's tender with just enough bite. Turn the conventional method upside down: First cook chops (salted and rested before cooking) in a low oven and then sear them in a superhot pan—a technique known as reverse searing (see page 348). Slowly cooking the meat first allows enzymes to break down protein, tenderizing the chops. The salted surface gently dries in the oven and then caramelizes in the pan, for a juicy interior and nicely browned exterior. If the pork is enhanced (injected with a salt solution), do not salt in step 1.

- 4 (12-ounce) bone-in pork rib chops, 1½ inches thick, trimmed
- 2 teaspoons kosher salt
- ½ teaspoon pepper
- 1–2 tablespoons vegetable oil

1. Cut 2 slits, about 2 inches apart, through outer layer of fat and silverskin on each pork chop. Sprinkle entire surface of each chop with ½ teaspoon salt and place on wire rack set in rimmed baking sheet. Let sit at room temperature for 45 minutes.

2. Adjust oven rack to middle position and heat oven to 275 degrees. Pat chops dry with paper towels and sprinkle with pepper. Transfer sheet to oven and cook until pork registers 120 to 125 degrees, 30 to 45 minutes.

3. Heat 1 tablespoon oil in 12-inch skillet over high heat until just smoking. Place 2 chops in skillet and sear until well browned and crusty, 2 to 3 minutes, lifting once halfway through cooking to redistribute fat underneath. Flip chops and cook until well browned on second side, 2 to 3 minutes. Transfer chops to plate and repeat with remaining 2 chops, adding 1 tablespoon oil if skillet is dry.

4. Reduce heat to medium. Use tongs to stand 2 pork chops on their sides. Holding chops together with tongs, return to skillet and sear sides of chops (with exception of bone side) until browned and pork registers 140 to 145 degrees, about 2 minutes; transfer to clean plate. Repeat with remaining 2 chops; transfer to plate, tent with aluminum foil, and rest for 10 minutes. Serve.

> **KEYS TO SUCCESS**
> - **Cut slits**: Through the outer layer of fat and silverskin to prevent the chops from buckling during cooking
> - **Reverse sear the chops**: Brings up their temperature slowly and dries their surfaces so they brown super-well during the hot skillet sear

CORE TECHNIQUE
Uncurling Chops

SLIT
Using a sharp knife, cut slits about 2 inches apart into the fat and silverskin, opposite the bone. Thin-cut pork rib chops are small enough to use kitchen shears to make snips.

The Thick and Thin of Pork Chops

Chops can be sold thick-cut or thin-cut: Thicker ones take more time and/or consideration to cook and seem a bit more special, while thinner ones are more casual and weeknight-ready. Thin chops can be simply seared quickly on both sides, but thick chops won't cook through. To achieve thick-cut chops with a deep crust and a juicy interior, we cook them a lot like we do thick-cut steaks, through reverse searing (see Pan-Seared Thick-Cut Pork Chops) or by flipping them frequently.

CITRUS-AND-SPICE PORK CHOPS
Serves: 4
Total Time: 45 minutes

RECIPE OVERVIEW Thin-cut pork chops make a quick, simple weeknight supper and require much less attention than thick-cut chops—typically just a quick sear. And that's seriously quick: just 2 minutes on each side. But this thinner cut can be a bit dull. A citrus vinaigrette punches up the flavor: Splashed over the seared meat when it's hot so the chop absorbs its flavor, the vinaigrette delivers vibrant citrus flavor without overwhelming the pork's sweet nuances. The ½-inch-thick chops cook so quickly that they don't brown much sprinkling the chops with sugar boosts flavorful browning, and dashes of aromatic cinnamon and savory cumin add complexity and depth. The final touch? A tiny bit of ground cloves.

Vinaigrette
- ¼ cup extra-virgin olive oil
- 1 tablespoon chopped fresh mint
- 2 teaspoons minced fresh thyme
- 1½ teaspoons minced shallot
- 1 teaspoon sugar
- ¾ teaspoon Dijon mustard
- ½ teaspoon grated lemon zest plus 2 tablespoons juice
- ½ teaspoon grated orange zest
- ¼ teaspoon table salt
- ¼ teaspoon pepper

Pork
- 2 teaspoons table salt
- 2 teaspoons pepper
- 1 teaspoon sugar
- ½ teaspoon ground cinnamon
- ½ teaspoon ground cumin
- ⅛ teaspoon ground cloves
- 8 (4- to 6-ounce) bone-in pork rib chops, ½ inch thick, trimmed
- 2 tablespoons extra-virgin olive oil, divided

1. **FOR THE VINAIGRETTE** Whisk all ingredients together in bowl; set aside.

2. **FOR THE PORK** Combine salt, pepper, sugar, cinnamon, cumin, and cloves in bowl. Using kitchen shears, snip through fat surrounding loin muscle of each chop in 2 places, about 2 inches apart, being careful not to cut too deeply into meat. Pat chops dry with paper towels and sprinkle all over with spice mixture.

3. Heat 1 tablespoon oil in 12-inch nonstick skillet over medium-high heat until just smoking. Add 4 chops to skillet and cook until browned and meat registers 140 degrees, about 2 minutes per side. Transfer chops to platter, spoon half of vinaigrette over top, and tent with aluminum foil. Repeat with remaining oil, chops, and vinaigrette. Serve.

SPICED BRAISED PORK CHOPS

Serves: 4
Total Time: 2¼ hours, plus 1 hour brining and 30 minutes resting

RECIPE OVERVIEW Pork blade chops are cut from the pig's upper shoulder so they're the toughest of chops. But they're also the most deeply flavored, marbled with tasty fat, and are transformed through braising. Pork chops are less cumbersome to braise than a roast, making them an easier choice for a flavorful dinner. Trimming the chops of excess fat and connective tissue prevents them from buckling during braising and cooking unevenly. But the trimmings don't go to waste; they contribute to a rich braising liquid with depth, sweetness, and a bit of tang from a combination of red wine and ruby port. Fresh ginger and a bit of allspice infuse the braising liquid with warm notes, while woodsy thyme complements the wine. When the chops are done braising, the liquid quickly reduces to a tasty sauce, enriched with a swirl of butter. The pork scraps can be removed when straining the sauce in step 4 and served alongside the chops.

- 3 tablespoons table salt for brining
- 4 (10- to 12-ounce) bone-in blade-cut pork chops, 1 inch thick
- 2 teaspoons vegetable oil
- 2 onions, halved and sliced thin
- 5 sprigs fresh thyme, plus ¼ teaspoon minced
- 2 garlic cloves, peeled
- 2 bay leaves
- 1 (½-inch) piece ginger, peeled and crushed
- ⅛ teaspoon ground allspice
- ½ cup red wine
- ¼ cup ruby port
- 2 tablespoons plus ½ teaspoon red wine vinegar, divided
- 1 cup chicken broth
- 2 tablespoons unsalted butter
- 1 tablespoon minced fresh parsley

1. Dissolve salt in 1½ quarts cold water in large container. Submerge chops in brine, cover, and refrigerate for 1 hour.

2. Adjust oven rack to lower-middle position and heat oven to 275 degrees. Remove chops from brine and pat dry with paper towels. Trim off cartilage, meat cap, and fat opposite rib bones. Cut trimmings into 1-inch pieces. Heat oil in Dutch oven over medium-high heat until shimmering. Add trimmings and brown on all sides, 6 to 9 minutes.

3. Reduce heat to medium and add onions, thyme sprigs, garlic, bay leaves, ginger, and allspice. Cook, stirring occasionally, until onions are golden brown, 5 to 10 minutes. Stir in wine, port, and 2 tablespoons vinegar and cook until reduced to thin syrup, 5 to 7 minutes. Add broth, spread pork trimmings mixture into even layer, and bring to simmer. Arrange chops on top of pork trimmings mixture and cover; transfer pot to oven.

4. Cook until meat is tender, 1¼ to 1½ hours. Remove from oven and let chops rest in pot, covered, for 30 minutes. Transfer chops to serving platter and tent with aluminum foil. Strain braising liquid through fine-mesh strainer set over large bowl; discard solids. Transfer braising liquid to fat separator. Let liquid settle for 5 minutes.

5. Wipe now-empty pot clean with paper towels. Return defatted braising liquid to pot and cook over medium-high heat until reduced to 1 cup, 3 to 7 minutes. Off heat, whisk in butter, minced thyme, and remaining ½ teaspoon vinegar. Season with salt and pepper to taste. Pour sauce over chops, sprinkle with parsley, and serve.

CORE TECHNIQUE

Trimming Blade-Cut Pork Chops

TRIM
Cut off the swath of fatty meat and any cartilage running along the edge of the chop.

DEVILED PORK CHOPS

Serves: 4
Total Time: 1¼ hours

RECIPE OVERVIEW Many recipes call for pan-searing boneless pork chops, but here we slow-roast them in a low oven. This way, they retain as much moisture as possible—a must for lean cuts to taste juicy—and cook evenly from edge to edge, no flipping required. The lower heat also encourages enzymes within the pork to break down some of the muscle protein, leading to more tender meat. "Deviling" the pork chops by painting them with a bold paste of spicy Dijon mustard mixed with dry mustard, minced garlic, and cayenne and black peppers enhances the mild meat. For textural contrast and visual appeal, coat the tops of the chops with crispy panko bread crumbs. If the pork is enhanced (injected with a salt solution), do not add salt to the mustard paste in step 2.

- 2 tablespoons unsalted butter
- ½ cup panko bread crumbs
- 1⅛ teaspoons kosher salt, divided
- ¼ cup Dijon mustard
- 2 teaspoons packed brown sugar
- 1½ teaspoons dry mustard
- 1 teaspoon pepper
- ½ teaspoon garlic, minced to paste
- ¼ teaspoon cayenne pepper
- 4 (6- to 8-ounce) boneless pork chops, ¾ to 1 inch thick, trimmed

1. Adjust oven rack to middle position and heat oven to 275 degrees.

2. Melt butter in 10-inch skillet over medium heat. Add panko and cook, stirring frequently, until golden brown, 3 to 5 minutes. Transfer to bowl and sprinkle with ⅛ teaspoon salt. Stir Dijon, sugar, dry mustard, pepper, garlic, cayenne, and remaining 1 teaspoon salt in second bowl until smooth.

3. Set wire rack in rimmed baking sheet and spray with vegetable oil spray. Pat chops dry with paper towels. Transfer chops to prepared wire rack, spacing them 1 inch apart. Brush 1 tablespoon mustard mixture over top and sides of each chop (leave bottoms uncoated). Spoon 2 tablespoons toasted panko evenly over top of each chop and press lightly to adhere.

4. Roast until meat registers 140 to 145 degrees, 40 to 50 minutes. Remove from oven and let rest on rack for 10 minutes before serving.

Boneless Pork Chops

We call for boneless pork chops quite often in our recipes—they're easy to cook evenly and they're weeknight friendly. They're often cut from rib chops, or sometimes from center-cut chops. But when we want to ensure that they're thick and evenly weighted, we skip buying ready-made chops and cut them ourselves from a center-cut pork loin. These are the most consistent boneless chops.

COURSE
MEAT STIR-FRIES

DAN SOUZA

Stir-frying is one of the fastest (and most delicious) ways to cook meat, requiring little more than a wok or skillet and plenty of heat. Once you learn the general four-part procedure, you can stir-fry with ease—and avoid some of the pitfalls such as dry meat (treat meat with baking soda and/or velvet it), inconsistently crunchy and soft vegetables (steam hardy vegetables), and thin sauces (add cornstarch). Learn how to prepare a beef and a pork stir-fry recipe. Let's turn up the heat on dinner.

DAN'S PRO TIP: *My tip for better stir-frying is a simple and practical one: Do your prep. Because stir-frying happens quickly over high heat, it's important to have all of your ingredients measured and prepared before starting to cook.*

TERIYAKI STIR-FRIED BEEF WITH GREEN BEANS AND SHIITAKES

Serves: 4
Total Time: 1 hour

RECIPE OVERVIEW Flank steak is a cut that works well in stir-fries; it cooks quickly and is ultrabeefy with some chew. Pretreating flank steak for stir-fries makes sure that chew is pleasant, not *chewy*. Start by slicing the steak thin and coating it in a mixture of baking soda and water. This ups the pH of the meat and helps it stay tender. Tossing the meat with soy sauce and cornstarch heightens its savory flavor, and searing in batches ensures optimal browning. Green beans and meaty shiitakes, browned first and steamed to finish, provide contrast. Mashing fresh ginger and garlic in the center of the pan unlocks more flavor before we toss all the ingredients with a gently spicy sauce. We developed this recipe for a 12-inch nonstick skillet with a tight-fitting lid, but a 14-inch flat-bottomed wok can be used instead.

- 1 (1½-pound) flank steak, trimmed
- 3 tablespoons water, divided
- ¼ teaspoon baking soda
- 3 garlic cloves, minced
- 1 tablespoon grated fresh ginger
- 3 tablespoons vegetable oil, divided
- ½ cup chicken broth
- 3 tablespoons soy sauce, divided
- 2 tablespoons sugar
- 1 tablespoon mirin
- 1¾ teaspoons cornstarch, divided
- ¼ teaspoon red pepper flakes
- 8 ounces shiitake mushrooms, stemmed and cut into 1-inch pieces
- 12 ounces green beans, trimmed and halved
- 4 scallions, cut into 1½-inch pieces, white parts quartered lengthwise

1. Cut steak with grain into 2½- to 3-inch-wide strips and place on large plate; freeze until firm, about 15 minutes. Cut strips crosswise against grain into ⅛-inch-thick slices. Combine 1 tablespoon water and baking soda in medium bowl. Add beef and toss to coat; let sit for 5 minutes.

2. Combine garlic, ginger, and 1 tablespoon oil in small bowl; set aside. Whisk broth, 2 tablespoons soy sauce, sugar, mirin, 1 teaspoon cornstarch, and pepper flakes in second small bowl until sugar has dissolved; set aside. Add remaining 1 tablespoon soy sauce and remaining ¾ teaspoon cornstarch to beef and toss until well combined.

3. Heat 2 teaspoons oil in 12-inch nonstick skillet over medium-high heat until just smoking. Add half of beef and increase heat to high. Cook, tossing beef slowly but constantly, until no longer pink, 2 to 6 minutes; transfer to clean medium bowl. Repeat with 2 teaspoons oil and remaining beef; transfer to bowl with first batch of beef.

4. Heat remaining 2 teaspoons oil in now-empty skillet over high heat until just smoking. Add mushrooms and green beans and cook, tossing slowly but constantly, until spotty brown, 2 to 6 minutes. Add remaining 2 tablespoons water (water will sputter), cover, and cook until green beans are crisp-tender, 2 to 3 minutes.

5. Push vegetables to one side of skillet and reduce heat to medium. Add garlic mixture to clearing and cook, mashing mixture into skillet, until fragrant, about 30 seconds. Stir garlic mixture into vegetables.

6. Whisk broth mixture to recombine, then add to skillet along with beef and any accumulated juices and scallions. Increase heat to high and cook, tossing constantly, until sauce has thickened, about 30 seconds. Serve.

CORE TECHNIQUE

Cutting Flank Steak for Stir-Fries

SLICE We first slice the steak into long strips lengthwise and then into thin slices crosswise (against the grain) to ensure they'll be tender before they even hit the pan.

Three Flank Steak Stir-Fry Secrets

We've done countless kitchen experiments with flank steak over the years in pursuit of tender, flavorful stir-fries. And we've learned that there are three essential keys to success.

CUT THE STEAK CORRECTLY First, cut your steak into thirds with the grain and then slice each third very thin against the grain. This keeps the meat from becoming overly chewy and creates little pockets for marinade and sauce to cling to.

ADD A BIT OF CORNSTARCH TO YOUR MARINADE This technique creates a super-thin coating around the meat to help keep it juicy and tender.

DON'T OVERCOOK THE STEAK In this recipe, we call for cooking the steak in batches (for 2 to 6 minutes per batch). Be sure to remove it from the heat immediately: Overcooked beef is chewy and tough, which is not what you want.

SICHUAN STIR-FRIED PORK IN GARLIC SAUCE

Serves: 4 to 6
Total Time: 1 hour

RECIPE OVERVIEW Recipes for this Sichuan staple are often imbalanced. To re-create the succulent pork found in the best restaurant stir-fries (usually achieved by low-temperature deep frying), soak the pork in a baking soda solution, which tenderizes and moisturizes the meat, and then coat it in a velvetizing cornstarch slurry, which helps it retain moisture as it cooks. And the secret to the sauce's silken texture and rich flavor? A small amount of ketchup and fish sauce, both high in flavor-enhancing glutamates. If Chinese black vinegar is unavailable, substitute 2 teaspoons balsamic vinegar and 2 teaspoons rice vinegar. If broad bean chili paste is unavailable, substitute 2 teaspoons Asian chili-garlic sauce or sriracha. We developed this recipe for a 12-inch nonstick skillet with a tight-fitting lid, but a 14-inch flat-bottomed wok can be used instead.

Sauce
- ½ cup chicken broth
- 2 tablespoons soy sauce
- 2 tablespoons sugar
- 4 teaspoons Chinese black vinegar
- 1 tablespoon Shaoxing wine or dry sherry
- 1 tablespoon toasted sesame oil
- 2 teaspoons cornstarch
- 2 teaspoons fish sauce
- 2 teaspoons ketchup

Pork
- 12 ounces boneless country-style pork ribs, trimmed
- 1 teaspoon baking soda
- 2 teaspoons Shaoxing wine or dry sherry
- 2 teaspoons cornstarch

Stir-Fry
- 2 scallions, white parts minced, green parts sliced thin
- 2 tablespoons broad bean chili paste
- 4 garlic cloves, minced
- ¼ cup vegetable oil, divided
- 6 ounces shiitake mushrooms, stemmed and sliced thin
- 2 celery ribs, sliced on bias ¼ inch thick

1. FOR THE SAUCE Whisk all ingredients together in bowl; set aside.

2. FOR THE PORK Cut pork into 2-inch lengths, then cut each length into ¼-inch-thick matchsticks. Combine pork with ½ cup water and baking soda in bowl. Let sit at room temperature for 15 minutes. Rinse pork under running water. Drain well and pat dry with paper towels.

3. Whisk Shaoxing wine and cornstarch together in bowl. Add pork and toss to coat.

4. FOR THE STIR-FRY Combine scallion whites, chili paste, and garlic in bowl. Set aside.

5. Heat 1 tablespoon oil in 12-inch nonstick skillet over high heat until just smoking. Add mushrooms and cook, stirring frequently, until tender, 2 to 4 minutes. Add celery and continue to cook until celery is crisp-tender, 2 to 4 minutes longer. Transfer vegetables to separate bowl.

6. Add remaining 3 tablespoons oil to now-empty skillet and reduce heat to medium-low. Add chili paste mixture and cook, stirring frequently, until fragrant, about 30 seconds. Transfer 1 tablespoon chili paste–oil mixture to small bowl and set aside.

7. Add pork to skillet and cook, stirring frequently, until no longer pink, 3 to 5 minutes. Whisk sauce to recombine and add to skillet. Increase heat to high and cook, stirring constantly, until sauce is thickened and pork is cooked through, 1 to 2 minutes. Return vegetables to skillet and toss to combine. Transfer to serving platter, sprinkle with scallion greens, and drizzle with reserved chili paste–oil mixture. Serve.

Stir-Fry Secret Weapon

Meat soaked in a solution of baking soda and water? There's a good reason we work this step into our stir-fry recipes: Simply put, alkaline baking soda makes the meat more tender by raising its pH. As this happens, enzymes in the meat called calpains become more active and cut the meat's muscle fibers. The tenderizing effect is twofold: First, as the meat's fibers break down, its texture softens. Second, since the meat's looser consistency retains water better, it's less likely to contract and expel moisture when heated, ensuring that the meat stays juicy throughout. The succulent results are well worth it. And don't worry; the baking soda solution gets washed off before cooking.

RESOURCES FOR MEAT STIR-FRIES

STIR-FRYING MEAT IN A WOK OR A SKILLET

Both a flat-bottomed wok and a nonstick skillet work well for stir-frying. Whichever you choose, the key to good stir-frying technique is to remember that the food cooks very quickly and requires your full attention to prevent scorching or overcooking. Before you turn on the burner, gave all your ingredients prepped and ready to go and know when to add them.

HOW TO BROWN MEAT
Toss ingredients slowly but constantly in the wok, making sure that they get some time at the bottom of the wok, where it is hottest. In a skillet, allow the ingredients to brown slightly before stirring. If cooking vegetables, remove the browned meat from the skillet.

WHEN TO ADD AROMATICS
Add aromatics to the wok or skillet toward the end of cooking. Mash the aromatics into the base of the pan to heat through and release their flavor before mixing them with the other ingredients.

WHEN TO ADD SAUCE
If cooking a sauce, do so once the other ingredients are cooked and then toss the sauce with the proteins and vegetables to incorporate flavor.

VELVETY BEEF, WITHOUT VELVETING

The ultratender texture of the best stir-fried beef comes from a classic technique known as velveting, which involves coating the meat and blanching it in a pot of oil before stir-frying even takes place. We looked for a more streamlined way to protect and tenderize the meat.

Traditional Velveting Marinate in cornstarch and egg white; blanch in oil to set coating.
Results Good but time-consuming.

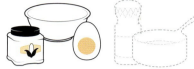

Test 1 Keep cornstarch and egg white; skip blanching in oil.
Results Curdled mess.

Test 2 Keep cornstarch; omit egg white.
Results Silky but not tender enough.

BEST METHOD

Test 3 Keep cornstarch; add baking soda.
Results Extra-supple meat in less time.

PICK THE RIGHT PORK

Pork loin, a common choice for pork stir-fries, is lean and dry. Instead, we use boneless country-style spareribs, which are fattier and more tender. Note that they're not actually ribs. These meaty, tender bone-in or boneless "ribs" are cut from the upper side of the rib cage from the fatty blade end of the loin, so they contain a mix of darker meat from the shoulder and lighter meat from the loin. Butchers usually cut them into individual ribs and package several ribs together. The combination of good rib flavor, fat, and easy shape means this underutilized cut is incredibly versatile—almost like well-marbled pork chops. It's common to find small and large bones, dark and light meat, and varied marbling.

STIRRING SPEEDS COOKING

There's a reason for the "stir" in stir-fry. That motion speeds cooking by keeping things hot. And we proved it. To show that constant stirring makes food cook faster, we used an infrared camera to measure the temperature of two different batches of stir-fried beef after about 1 minute of cooking: one that we stirred constantly and another that we stirred every 30 seconds. The color of the batch that we stirred constantly (at left) is noticeably brighter and more yellow, indicating that it got hotter than the batch that we stirred only periodically (at right), which is darker purple.

COURSE
EVERYDAY ROASTS

LAN LAM

When a beautifully browned roast arrives at the table, it sends a signal: It's time to sit and savor. But this doesn't have to be just a special-occasion experience. There are plenty of affordable roasts that you can serve for dinner as often as smaller retail cuts. But while these roasts are affordable and accessible, they may actually take a bit more care than your high-end holiday roast. Why? These cuts usually aren't as heavily marbled and buttery-tender, so you'll need to take the time to ensure that they don't become tough and dry. Luckily, we have easy tricks to guarantee your beef and pork roasts are succulent—every day.

LAN'S PRO TIP: *Resting a roast after cooking prevents juices from pouring from the meat as it's sliced. I like to use this time for last-minute prep like dressing a salad, transferring side dishes to serving platters, or stirring together a sauce.*

SLOW-ROAST BEEF

Serves: 6 to 8
Total Time: 2½ to 3 hours, plus 18 hours salting

RECIPE OVERVIEW For many, the modest roast beef go-to is an eye-round roast. Its uniform shape guarantees even cooking—a good reason to make this inexpensive roast shine. Salting the meat as much as 24 hours before cooking, as well as searing it before roasting, vastly improves its flavor. Roasting the meat at a very low 225 degrees and then turning off the oven toward the end of cooking allow the meat's enzymes to act as natural tenderizers, breaking down the tough connective tissue. If the roast has not reached the desired temperature in the time specified in step 4, reheat the oven to 225 degrees for 5 minutes, then shut it off and continue to cook the roast to the desired temperature. We like to rub a compound butter (see page 355) on this roast after cooking, for extra richness and flavor.

- 1 (3½- to 4½-pound) boneless eye-round roast, trimmed
- 4 teaspoons kosher salt
- 2 teaspoons plus 1 tablespoon vegetable oil, divided
- 2 teaspoons pepper

1. Rub roast thoroughly with salt, wrap in plastic wrap, and refrigerate for at least 18 or up to 24 hours.

2. Adjust oven rack to middle position and heat oven to 225 degrees. Pat roast dry with paper towels, rub with 2 teaspoons oil, and sprinkle with pepper.

3. Heat remaining 1 tablespoon oil in 12-inch skillet over medium-high heat until just smoking. Brown roast well on all sides, 12 to 16 minutes; reduce heat if pan begins to scorch. Transfer roast to wire rack set in rimmed baking sheet and roast until meat registers 115 degrees (for medium-rare), 1¼ to 1¾ hours.

4. Turn off oven and leave roast in oven, without opening door, until meat registers 120 to 125 degrees (for medium-rare), 30 to 40 minutes.

5. Transfer roast to carving board and let rest for 15 to 20 minutes. Slice meat as thin as possible against the grain and serve.

KEYS TO SUCCESS

- **Salt the roast early:** To give the salt time to penetrate deep into the roast and season it evenly
- **Sear the roast first before cooking it low:** Ensuring a browned exterior
- **Shut off the oven:** Before the internal temperature of the roast reaches 122 degrees to preserve juiciness and tenderness

Fast Sear, Slow Roast for Beef

To promote browning when roasting beef, you want the oven to be very hot; unfortunately, even if you remove the roast when the center is pink, you'll find a thick, unsightly band of gray, overcooked meat at its edge. A low temperature does a better job of cooking the meat evenly, so we brown the roast on the stovetop first to build a flavorful crust and then roast it gently for a uniformly rosy, juicy interior.

SCIENCE LESSON   Enzymes at Work

Enzymes are a type of protein. In meat, one of their functions is the turnover and reprocessing of other proteins around them, affecting food's consistency, texture, and color. These crafty little enzymes have the ability to impart a meatier, umami taste (encouraging the formation of amino acids and peptides as the muscle breaks down) and to tenderize (breaking down tough proteins with time)—that is, if the environment is right.

The activity level of these enzymes is largely based on temperature. The rate at which they break down the protein in a cut becomes much faster as the temperature of the meat rises—right until it reaches 122 degrees. That's when everything comes to a halt. We recommend roasting meat very slowly, purposely keeping the temperature below 122 degrees to encourage enzymatic activity for as long as possible. In contrast to the slow cooking methods used for tough cuts of meat, this technique is best for cuts of meat with little connective tissue—ones ideally cooked no further than medium.

 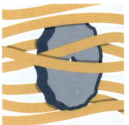

Below 122 Degrees
As the temperature in meat slowly rises, enzymes act like saws, breaking down muscle proteins at a faster and faster rate.

Above 122 Degrees
Heating enzymes above 122 degrees, however, changes their shape and eliminates their ability to break down muscle proteins.

ROAST PORK LOIN WITH SWEET POTATOES AND CILANTRO SAUCE

Serves: 6
Total Time: 1¼ hours, plus 1½ hours brining

RECIPE OVERVIEW This modern take on a roast pork dinner features meat and potatoes, freshened up. Sharing the stage with spice-rubbed pork loin are caramelized sweet potatoes and a lively green sauce. Roasting the meat in a moderate 375-degree oven and turning it halfway through roasting ensures juicy, perfectly cooked pork. Look for a roast with a thin fat cap (about ¼ inch thick) and don't trim. If the pork is enhanced (injected with a salt solution), do not brine but do season with salt in step 2.

Pork and Potatoes
- ¼ cup table salt for brining
- ¼ cup sugar for brining
- 1 (2½- to 3-pound) boneless center-cut pork loin roast, trimmed, tied at 1½-inch intervals
- 1 teaspoon ground coriander
- 1 teaspoon ground cumin
- ½ teaspoon pepper
- 3 pounds sweet potatoes, peeled, quartered, and cut into 2-inch pieces
- 3 tablespoons extra-virgin olive oil
- ⅛ teaspoon cayenne pepper

Cilantro Sauce
- 2½ cups fresh cilantro leaves and stems, trimmed (2 bunches)
- ½ cup extra-virgin olive oil
- 4 teaspoons lime juice
- 2 garlic cloves, minced
- ½ teaspoon sugar

1. **FOR THE PORK AND POTATOES** Dissolve salt and sugar in 2 quarts cold water in large container. Submerge pork in brine, cover, and refrigerate for 1½ to 2 hours.

2. Adjust oven rack to lower-middle position and heat oven to 375 degrees. Pat roast dry with paper towels. Sprinkle with coriander, cumin, and pepper. Toss sweet potatoes in bowl with oil and cayenne, season with salt and pepper, and spread evenly into large roasting pan. Lay roast, fat side up, on top of potatoes. Roast until pork registers 135 to 140 degrees, 50 minutes to 1 hour 10 minutes, turning roast over halfway through roasting.

3. **FOR THE CILANTRO SAUCE** Meanwhile, pulse all ingredients in food processor until cilantro is finely chopped, 10 to 15 pulses, scraping down sides of bowl as needed. Season with salt and pepper to taste.

4. Remove pan from oven. Transfer roast to carving board and let rest for 20 minutes. While roast rests, increase oven temperature to 450 degrees and continue to roast potatoes until well browned, about 10 minutes. Remove twine from roast and slice ½ inch thick. Serve with potatoes and cilantro sauce.

Parsing Pork Loin

Center-cut pork loin is the norm in most pork loin recipes—we default to it and use it quite often because this user-friendly cut is much easier to find at the supermarket. But unless we're stuffing pork loin, we actually would choose to roast the blade-end roast in most cases (yes, you can even use it in this recipe here). When you can find a blade-end roast at a good price point, buy it: This cut has great richness and is nicely tender when cooked properly.

Boneless Blade-End Pork Loin   **Center-Cut Pork Loin**

KEYS TO SUCCESS
- **Brine the pork:** To add moisture to the lean cut
- **Time it just right:** By finishing the potatoes while the pork is resting

BROILED PORK TENDERLOIN WITH SUN-DRIED TOMATO AND BASIL SALSA

Serves: 4 to 6
Total Time: 55 minutes

RECIPE OVERVIEW Quick-cooking pork tenderloin is a great candidate for broiling; however, many recipes yield pallid, overcooked pork or spottily browned roasts with undercooked interiors. But with a smart trick—cooking in a disposable aluminum pan—you can reflect the radiant heat of the broiler toward the pork and enhance browning. Since some ovens heat faster than others and are likely to cycle off if preheated at an intense heat for too long, we preheat the oven to 325 degrees before putting in the roasts and turning on the broiler. The broiler creates a significant carryover cooking effect, so you should pull the roasts when they hit 125 to 130 degrees instead of 140 degrees so they're perfect after their 10-minute rest. If using enhanced pork, reduce the salt to 1½ teaspoons. A 3-inch-deep aluminum pan is essential. Do not make this recipe with a drawer broiler. We like the sweet flavor and pliable texture of oil-packed sun-dried tomatoes.

Salsa
- ¼ cup oil-packed sun-dried tomatoes, rinsed and chopped fine
- ¼ cup chopped fresh basil
- ¼ cup chopped fresh parsley
- ¼ cup extra-virgin olive oil
- 2 tablespoons balsamic vinegar
- 1 small shallot, minced

Pork
- 2 (1-pound) pork tenderloins, trimmed
- 2 teaspoons kosher salt
- 1¼ teaspoons vegetable oil
- ½ teaspoon pepper
- ¼ teaspoon baking soda
- 1 (13 by 9-inch) disposable aluminum roasting pan

1. **FOR THE SALSA** Combine all ingredients in bowl and season with salt and pepper to taste; set aside.

2. **FOR THE PORK** Adjust oven rack 4 to 5 inches from broiler element and heat oven to 325 degrees. Fold thin tip of each tenderloin under about 2 inches to create uniformly shaped roasts. Tie tenderloins crosswise with kitchen twine at 2-inch intervals, making sure folded tip is secured underneath. Trim excess twine close to meat to prevent it from scorching under broiler.

3. Mix salt, oil, and pepper in small bowl until salt is evenly coated with oil. Add baking soda and stir until well combined. Rub mixture evenly over pork. Place tenderloins in disposable pan, evenly spaced from sides of pan and each other.

4. Turn oven to broil. Immediately place tenderloins in oven and broil for 5 minutes. Flip tenderloins and continue to broil until golden brown and meat registers 125 to 130 degrees, 8 to 14 minutes. Remove disposable pan from oven, tent with aluminum foil, and let rest for 10 minutes. Discard twine, slice tenderloins ½ inch thick, and serve with salsa.

CORE TECHNIQUE
Removing Pork Silverskin

TRIM
Silverskin is a swath of connective tissue located between the meat and the fat that covers its surface. Slip a knife under the silverskin, angle it slightly upward, and use a gentle back-and-forth motion to remove it.

COURSE

THE BRAISING POT

JULIA COLLIN DAVISON

What is braising? Well, it's one of the most relaxing cooking methods; low and slow is the motto and the result is always a luxuriously comforting, warm dish. The true definition of braising is cooking a main ingredient—here, meat—in a closed environment to break down its proteins or fibers and achieve ultratender results. Braising unlocks the delicious flavor inherent in the food you're cooking, so meat tastes deeply meaty. Learn how to break down tough collagen into meltingly tender gelatin and to coax wonderful flavor out of your food. We'll cover our best tricks (some are unconventional) for some favorite dishes.

JULIA'S PRO TIP: *If you're making a braise a day or so ahead of time, back off on the oven cook time by about 30 minutes. The meat and sauce can then finish cooking as you reheat the dish, which prevent the meat from becoming overly shredded and the sauce from becoming too thick.*

CLASSIC POT ROAST

Serves: 6 to 8
Total Time: 4½ to 5 hours

RECIPE OVERVIEW Pot roast is the quintessential chuck-eye roast recipe and the most fundamental example of a hearty, comforting braise. Slow-cooking an economical roast in liquid with vegetables and aromatics until it's succulent is an accessible technique, and we achieve a supremely tender roast along with a deliciously savory sauce to spoon over the top. For the braising liquid, equal amounts of beef and chicken broth taste best, and we add just enough water for the liquid to come about halfway up the sides of the roast and prevent it from drying out. When it comes to cooking pot roast, there are two typical approaches: Cook it on the stove or in the oven. It's too difficult to maintain a steady, low temperature on the stove with the flame from below, so after browning the roast we transfer the Dutch oven (covered with foil under the lid for a tight seal) to a 300-degree oven where the roast cooks evenly for moist, flavorful meat. Use a good-quality, medium-bodied wine, such as a Côtes du Rhône or a Pinot Noir, for this dish.

- 1 (3½- to 4-pound) boneless beef chuck-eye roast, trimmed and tied at 1-inch intervals
- 1 teaspoon table salt
- 1 teaspoon pepper
- 2 tablespoons vegetable oil
- 1 onion, chopped fine
- 1 small carrot, peeled and chopped
- 1 small celery rib, chopped
- 2 garlic cloves, minced
- 2 teaspoons sugar
- 1 cup chicken broth
- 1 cup beef broth
- 1 sprig fresh thyme
- ¼ cup dry red wine

1. Adjust oven rack to middle position and heat oven to 300 degrees. Pat roast dry with paper towels and sprinkle with salt and pepper.

2. Heat oil in Dutch oven over medium-high heat until shimmering. Brown roast on all sides, 8 to 10 minutes, reducing heat if fat begins to smoke; transfer roast to large plate.

3. Reduce heat to medium; add onion, carrot, and celery to pot and cook, stirring occasionally, until beginning to brown, 6 to 8 minutes. Add garlic and sugar; cook until fragrant, about 30 seconds. Add chicken broth, beef broth, and thyme sprig, scraping up any browned bits.

4. Return roast and any accumulated juices to pot; add enough water to come halfway up sides of roast. Bring liquid to simmer over medium heat. Place large piece of aluminum foil over pot and cover tightly with lid; transfer pot to oven. Cook, turning roast every 30 minutes, until fully tender and fork slips easily in and out of meat, 3½ to 4 hours.

5. Transfer roast to carving board and tent with foil. Let liquid in pot settle for about 5 minutes, then use wide spoon to skim fat from surface; discard thyme sprig. Bring liquid to boil over high heat and cook until reduced to about 1½ cups, about 8 minutes. Add wine to pot and cook until reduced to 1½ cups, about 2 minutes. Season with salt and pepper to taste

6. Remove twine from roast. Slice meat against grain into ½-inch-thick slices or pull apart into large pieces. Transfer meat to platter and pour about ½ cup sauce over meat. Serve, passing remaining sauce separately.

KEYS TO SUCCESS

- **Choose chuck roast:** For its fat and connective tissue, which make for a succulent roast and give the sauce body
- **Braise in the oven:** Ensuring gentle, even cooking
- **Use chicken and beef broth:** To avoid the tinny taste of store-bought beef broth alone

---

CORE TECHNIQUE

Prepping Chuck-Eye Roast

TRIM
Using a sharp knife, trim fat from the roast, leaving a thin layer of fat on the meat.

TIE
Tie the roast with kitchen twine at 1-inch intervals.

RED WINE–BRAISED SHORT RIBS WITH BACON, PARSNIPS, AND PEARL ONIONS

Serves: 6
Total Time: 4½ to 5 hours, plus 2 hours cooling and 8 hours chilling

RECIPE OVERVIEW Bone-in braised short ribs are a luxurious and elegant treat. They're a terrific option for entertaining because you can make them ahead—in fact, it's actually best to rest them overnight before serving. Most recipes call for cumbersome stovetop browning, but browning the short ribs in the oven is a good trick. It maximizes the amount of fat rendered (and minimizes the greasiness of the final sauce). Lots of savory ingredients such as garlic, red wine, rosemary, thyme, and tomato paste supplement the flavor. Let the ribs rest to allow any additional fat to separate out and solidify. Once solidified, the fat is easy to scoop off the top; we then re-employ the braising liquid to finish cooking the vegetables and rewarm the ribs. Crisped bacon and sautéed pearl onions and parsnips add crunch and sweetness to the tender, succulent short ribs.

Short Ribs
- 6 pounds bone-in English-style short ribs, trimmed
- 1 teaspoon table salt
- 1 teaspoon pepper
- 3 cups dry red wine
- 3 large onions, chopped
- 2 carrots, peeled and chopped
- 1 large celery rib, chopped
- 9 garlic cloves, chopped
- ¼ cup all-purpose flour
- 4 cups chicken broth
- 1 (14.5-ounce) can diced tomatoes, drained
- 1½ tablespoons minced fresh rosemary
- 1 tablespoon minced fresh thyme
- 3 bay leaves
- 1 teaspoon tomato paste

Bacon, Parsnips, and Pearl Onions
- 6 slices bacon, cut into ¼-inch pieces
- 10 ounces parsnips, peeled and cut on bias into ¾-inch pieces
- 8 ounces frozen pearl onions
- ¼ teaspoon sugar
- ¼ teaspoon table salt
- 6 tablespoons chopped fresh parsley

1. FOR THE SHORT RIBS Adjust oven rack to lower-middle position and heat oven to 450 degrees. Arrange short ribs bone side down in single layer in large roasting pan; sprinkle with salt and pepper. Roast until meat begins to brown, about 45 minutes; drain off all liquid and fat. Return short ribs to oven and continue to roast until meat is well browned, 15 to 20 minutes longer. Transfer short ribs to large plate. Pour rendered fat into bowl. Reduce oven temperature to 300 degrees. Place now-empty pan over 2 burners set at medium heat; add wine and bring to simmer, scraping up any browned bits. Set aside.

2. Heat 2 tablespoons reserved fat in Dutch oven over medium-high heat; add onions, carrots, and celery and cook, stirring occasionally, until vegetables soften, about 12 minutes. Add garlic and cook until fragrant, about 30 seconds. Stir in flour until combined, about 45 seconds. Stir in broth, tomatoes, rosemary, thyme, bay leaves, tomato paste, and reserved wine. Season with salt and pepper to taste. Bring to boil and add short ribs, completely submerging meat in liquid. Return to boil and cover; transfer pot to oven. Cook until short ribs are tender, 2 to 2½ hours. Transfer pot to wire rack and let cool, partially covered, until warm, about 2 hours.

3. Transfer short ribs to serving platter, removing any vegetables that cling to meat; discard loose bones that have fallen away from meat. Strain braising liquid through fine-mesh strainer set over bowl, pressing on solids to extract all liquid; discard solids. Refrigerate short ribs and liquid separately, covered with plastic wrap, for at least 8 hours or up to 3 days.

4. FOR THE BACON, PARSNIPS, AND PEARL ONIONS Cook bacon over medium heat in Dutch oven until just crispy, 8 to 10 minutes; using slotted spoon, transfer bacon to paper towel–lined plate. Add parsnips, onions, sugar, and salt to pot; increase heat to high and cook, stirring occasionally, until browned, about 5 minutes.

5. Spoon off and discard solidified fat from reserved braising liquid. Add defatted liquid to pot and bring to simmer, stirring occasionally; season with salt and pepper to taste. Submerge short ribs in liquid and return to simmer. Reduce heat to medium and cook, partially covered, until short ribs are heated through and vegetables are tender, about 5 minutes; gently stir in bacon. Divide short ribs and sauce among serving bowls, sprinkle each bowl with 1 tablespoon parsley, and serve.

Go English with Short Ribs

ENGLISH-STYLE Cut parallel to the bone, English-style short ribs feature a rectangular slab of meat attached to one side of the bone. They can also be purchased boneless (or you can remove the meat from the bone yourself).

FLANKEN-STYLE Cut thin across the rib bones and found mainly in butcher shops, flanken-style ribs are more complex in construction; they look like ladders with shorter pieces of meat attached. It is harder to get the meat off the bone. While we lean towards English-style, as they are easier to eat (and find), flanken-style ribs can be substituted with some alterations to cook time.

English-Style Short Ribs   **Flanken-Style Short Ribs**

BRAISED LAMB SHANKS WITH LEMON AND MINT

Serves: 6
Total Time: 3 hours

RECIPE OVERVIEW Braising lamb shanks turns this richly flavored but tough cut of meat meltingly tender. However, the high fat content of lamb all too often leads to a greasy sauce. We avoid this pitfall by trimming the shanks well and then browning them before adding liquid to get a head start on rendering their fat. We also defat the braising liquid after the shanks have cooked. We use more liquid than is called for in many braises to guarantee that plenty remains in the pot despite about an hour of uncovered cooking. For bright flavor, we stir lemon and mint into the braising liquid before serving. If you're using smaller shanks than the ones called for in this recipe, you'll need to reduce the braising time. Côtes du Rhône works particularly well here.

- 6 (12- to 16-ounce) lamb shanks, trimmed
- 1 teaspoon plus a pinch table salt
- 2 tablespoons vegetable oil, divided
- 3 carrots, peeled and cut into 2-inch pieces
- 2 onions, sliced thick
- 2 celery ribs, cut into 2-inch pieces
- 2 tablespoons tomato paste
- 2 tablespoons minced fresh mint, divided
- 4 garlic cloves, minced
- 2 cups dry white wine
- 3 cups chicken broth
- 1 tablespoon grated lemon zest, plus 1 lemon, quartered

1. Adjust oven rack to middle position and heat oven to 350 degrees. Pat lamb shanks dry with paper towels and sprinkle with 1 teaspoon salt. Heat 1 tablespoon oil in Dutch oven over medium-high heat until just smoking. Brown 3 shanks on all sides, 7 to 10 minutes. Transfer shanks to large plate and repeat with remaining 1 tablespoon oil and remaining 3 shanks.

2. Pour off all but 2 tablespoons fat from pot. Add carrots, onions, celery, tomato paste, 1 tablespoon mint, garlic, and remaining pinch salt and cook until vegetables just begin to soften, 3 to 4 minutes. Stir in wine, then broth, scraping up any browned bits; add lemon quarters and bring to simmer. Nestle shanks, along with any accumulated juices, into pot.

3. Return to simmer and cover; transfer pot to oven. Cook for 1½ hours. Uncover and continue to cook until tops of shanks are browned, about 30 minutes. Flip shanks and continue to cook until remaining sides are browned and fork slips easily in and out of shanks, 15 to 30 minutes longer.

4. Remove pot from oven and let rest for 15 minutes. Using tongs, transfer shanks and vegetables to large plate and tent with aluminum foil. Skim fat from braising liquid and season liquid with salt and pepper to taste. Stir in lemon zest and remaining 1 tablespoon mint. Return shanks to braising liquid to warm through before serving.

Variations

BRAISED LAMB SHANKS WITH RAS EL HANOUT

Serve with one or more of the following: sautéed onion, lemon zest, parsley, mint, toasted almonds, and additional ras el hanout.

Add 2 minced ancho chiles (or 2 or 3 minced jalapeños) with onions, carrots, and celery in step 2. Omit lemon and lemon zest. Substitute 2 tablespoons ras el hanout for mint in step 2 and omit mint in step 4.

BRAISED LAMB SHANKS WITH RED WINE AND HERBES DE PROVENCE

Substitute dry red wine for white wine. Omit lemon and lemon zest. Substitute 1 tablespoon herbes de Provence for mint in step 2 and omit mint in step 4.

RESOURCES FOR THE BRAISING POT

WHERE TO BRAISE: OVEN VERSUS STOVETOP

It's possible to braise in a covered pot on the stove, but we find that the direct heat of the burner is intense, specific, and often too efficient. It can cook meat quickly and unevenly as well as affect the consistency of the braising liquid, breaking down added starch (such as flour) on the bottom of the pan and creating a too-thin sauce. The oven, however, uses indirect and less efficient heat. This translates to gentle, even cooking in the closed environment of a covered pot and allows for a silky and luxurious sauce. The sweet spot is usually around 300 degrees, depending on the recipe—and always between 225 and 350. Low and slow, as they say.

ON THE STOVE
Heat is unevenly distributed and concentrated on the bottom of the pot.

IN THE OVEN
Heat is evenly distributed, with no hot spots.

OVERCOOKING FOR COLLAGEN

When you're cooking a collagen-rich cut of meat you're essentially doing something you've been taught is bad: overcooking. In many cases, however, overcooking is what makes braised food taste so good. That's because when you're braising, at least as it pertains to more marbled or fattier cuts of meat, collagen doesn't even start to break down until meat reaches 140 degrees. As meat heats, protein molecules bond together tighter, pushing out moisture; as the temperature creeps up, the meat is drier and seems tougher. But "overcook" a collagen-rich cut even more, past this point, and the collagen melts into gooey gelatin, which lubricates the fibers, making the meat tender—even more tender than before the moisture was pushed out. And in the gentle environment of the liquid, which stays below 212 degrees (water's boiling point), the meat doesn't dry out as its temperature climbs—it normally tops out at an ideal 180 to 195 degrees, the temperature of simmering liquid. Sure, your braised beef won't be rosy-pink inside, but it will break into buttery slices under your knife.

SKIMMING THE FAT

Collagen-rich braising cuts are often on the fattier side. Fat means flavor, but we don't want a greasy braise. Removing all the fat before cooking would result in dry meat, so we often need to do so after the cooking is done. There are three ways to do this.

Spoon It If you let the braise sit for a few minutes after cooking, some of the grease molecules will come out of emulsion and rise to the top of the pot. A large, wide spoon is best for skimming over the surface to remove the grease before reducing the liquid or serving.

Chill Out Many braises taste great the next day, but in addition to convenience, a bonus of making a braise in advance is that, with time, even more grease rises and the fat hardens in the fridge, making it simple to remove.

Separate It An immediate and thorough solution is to use a fat separator; you pour stock or sauce into the separator through a built-in strainer at the top and wait a few minutes for the fat to rise to the top of the liquid. Then you pour off the liquid until only the fat remains in the separator.

COURSE
MEAT STEWS OF THE WORLD

BRYAN ROOF

Nearly every cuisine has *at least* one traditional stew. The meat could be beef, pork, lamb, or something else, typically cut into cubes. But it's the sauce in which the meat simmers that tells the story of the cuisine. Rich and complex, it is part of the alchemy; the sauce transfers flavor to the meat and slowly reduces, clinging to the meat as it becomes meltingly tender. While we can't cover the globe in one course, we'll introduce you to five of our favorite classic meat stews, and let the Dutch oven be your tour guide.

BRYAN'S PRO TIP: *Spend a little extra time up front trimming the fat from the meat. The resulting stew will be far less greasy in the end.*

BEST BEEF STEW
Serves: 6 to 8
Total Time: 3¾ hours

RECIPE OVERVIEW This all-American beef stew is superlatively rich tasting but approachable, featuring tender meat, flavorful vegetables, and a rich brown gravy. First, brown cubes of chuck-eye roast, taking care not to crowd the meat in the pan. Along with traditional stew components such as onion, carrots, garlic, red wine, and chicken broth, this recipe features glutamate-rich tomato paste, anchovies, and salt pork. Glutamates are compounds that give meat its savory taste, and they contribute considerable flavor to the dish. To mimic the luxurious, mouth-coating texture of beef stews made with homemade stock, simply include powdered gelatin and flour. Use a good-quality, medium-bodied red wine, such as a Côtes du Rhône or Pinot Noir, for this stew. Look for salt pork that is roughly 75 percent lean.

- 2 garlic cloves, minced
- 4 anchovy fillets, rinsed and minced
- 1 tablespoon tomato paste
- 1 (4-pound) boneless beef chuck-eye roast, pulled apart at seams, trimmed, and cut into 1½-inch pieces
- 2 tablespoons vegetable oil, divided
- 1 large onion, halved and sliced ⅛ inch thick
- 4 carrots, peeled and cut into 1-inch pieces
- ¼ cup all-purpose flour
- 2 cups red wine
- 2 cups chicken broth
- 4 ounces salt pork, rinsed
- 2 bay leaves
- 4 sprigs fresh thyme
- 1 pound Yukon Gold potatoes, unpeeled, cut into 1-inch pieces
- 1½ cups frozen pearl onions, thawed
- 2 teaspoons unflavored gelatin
- ½ cup water
- 1 cup frozen peas, thawed

1. Adjust oven rack to lower-middle position and heat oven to 300 degrees. Combine garlic and anchovies in small bowl; press with back of fork to form paste. Stir in tomato paste and set aside.

2. Pat beef dry with paper towels (do not season). Heat 1 tablespoon oil in Dutch oven over high heat until just smoking. Add half of beef and cook until well browned on all sides, about 8 minutes; transfer to large plate. Repeat with remaining 1 tablespoon oil and remaining beef, leaving second batch of beef in pot after browning.

3. Reduce heat to medium and return first batch of beef to pot. Stir in onion and carrots and cook, scraping up any browned bits, until onion is softened, 1 to 2 minutes. Add garlic mixture and cook, stirring constantly, until fragrant, about 30 seconds. Add flour and cook, stirring constantly, until no dry flour remains, about 30 seconds.

4. Slowly add wine, scraping up any browned bits. Increase heat to high and simmer until wine is thickened and slightly reduced, about 2 minutes. Stir in broth, salt pork, bay leaves, and thyme sprigs. Bring to simmer and cover; transfer pot to oven. Cook for 1½ hours.

5. Remove pot from oven; discard salt pork, bay leaves, and thyme sprigs. Stir in potatoes, cover, return pot to oven, and continue to cook until potatoes are almost tender, about 45 minutes.

6. Using wide spoon, skim fat from surface of stew. Stir in pearl onions; cook over medium heat until potatoes and pearl onions are cooked through and fork slips easily in and out of beef (meat should not be falling apart), about 15 minutes. Meanwhile, sprinkle gelatin over water in bowl and let sit until gelatin softens, about 5 minutes.

7. Increase heat to high, stir in gelatin mixture and peas, and simmer until gelatin is fully dissolved and stew is thickened, about 3 minutes. Season with salt and pepper to taste, and serve.

KEYS TO SUCCESS
- **Cook in the oven:** Ensures gentle, enveloping heat
- **Add gelatin:** To the cooking liquid for a silky sauce that clings to the meat

CORE TECHNIQUE
Adding Body with Gelatin

THICKEN
Powdered gelatin is an easy way to create the same exact body in a sauce or braising liquid that you'd get from bones. Just hydrate and melt the gel into your liquid like the real thing.

Common Cut

We prize the chuck-eye roast for its supremely tender texture, and it's our most commonly used cut from the chuck. The boneless chuck-eye roast is cut from the center of the first five ribs (the term "eye" refers to any center-cut piece of meat). Unlike other roasts from the chuck, which may feature multiple small muscle groups separated by lots of hard fat and connective tissue, the chuck eye has a more limited number of large muscle groups that run along the center of the shoulder. It is a continuation of the same muscles that make up the rib eye, one of the most flavorful and tender cuts of beef. With fewer muscle groups, this roast has less intramuscular fat and connective tissue to trim away than other parts of the chuck, so it's easier to prep (a compact, uniform shape helps here, too).

CATALAN-STYLE BEEF STEW WITH MUSHROOMS

Serves: 4 to 6
Total Time: 3¾ hours

RECIPE OVERVIEW This stew, from the Spanish region of Catalonia, has multilayered flavors and textures, beginning with a rich, slow-cooked sofrito of caramelized onions and tomato. Boneless short ribs are an easy-to-use cut, boast outstanding flavor, and become supremely tender. Braising uncovered for part of the time allows the exposed meat to brown without having to sear it first. The braising liquid is dry white wine rather than the traditional sherry-like fortified wine known as vi ranci. Oyster mushrooms are a popular Catalan ingredient, so we include those. To finish the stew, we stir in a picada, a pesto-like paste of fried bread, herbs, and ground nuts that gives the stew fuller body and greater dimension. We developed this recipe with Albariño, a Spanish dry white wine; you can also use Sauvignon Blanc. Remove the woody base of the mushroom stems before cooking. An equal amount of quartered white mushrooms may be substituted.

Stew
- 3 tablespoons extra-virgin olive oil, divided
- 2 large onions, chopped fine
- ½ teaspoon sugar
- 2½ teaspoons kosher salt, divided
- 2 plum tomatoes, halved lengthwise, pulp grated on large holes of box grater, and skins discarded
- 1 teaspoon smoked paprika
- 1 bay leaf
- 1½ cups dry white wine
- 1½ cups water
- 1 large sprig fresh thyme
- ¼ teaspoon ground cinnamon
- 2½ pounds boneless beef short ribs, trimmed and cut into 2-inch cubes
- ½ teaspoon pepper
- 8 ounces oyster mushrooms, trimmed
- 1 teaspoon sherry vinegar

Picada
- ¼ cup whole blanched almonds
- 1 tablespoon extra-virgin olive oil
- 1 slice hearty white sandwich bread, crust removed, torn into 1-inch pieces
- 2 garlic cloves, peeled
- 3 tablespoons minced fresh parsley

1. FOR THE STEW Adjust oven rack to middle position and heat oven to 300 degrees. Heat 2 tablespoons oil in Dutch oven over medium-low heat until shimmering. Add onions, sugar, and ½ teaspoon salt. Cook, stirring often, until onions are deeply caramelized, 30 to 40 minutes. Add tomato pulp, paprika, and bay leaf and cook, stirring often, until darkened and thick, 5 to 10 minutes.

2. Add wine, water, thyme sprig, and cinnamon to pot, scraping up any browned bits. Sprinkle short ribs with 1½ teaspoons salt and pepper and add to pot. Increase heat to high and bring to simmer; transfer pot to oven. Cook, uncovered, for 1 hour. Stir stew to redistribute meat, cover, return to oven, and continue to cook until meat is tender, 1½ to 2 hours longer.

3. FOR THE PICADA While stew is in oven, heat almonds and oil in 10-inch skillet over medium heat. Cook, stirring often, until almonds are golden brown, 3 to 6 minutes. Using slotted spoon, transfer almonds to food processor. Return now-empty skillet to medium heat, add bread, and cook, stirring often, until toasted, 2 to 4 minutes; transfer to food processor with almonds. Add garlic to almonds and bread and process until mixture is finely ground, about 20 seconds, scraping down bowl as needed. Transfer mixture to clean bowl, stir in parsley, and set aside.

4. Return now-empty skillet to medium heat. Heat remaining 1 tablespoon oil until shimmering. Add mushrooms and remaining ½ teaspoon salt. Cook, stirring often, until tender, 5 to 7 minutes. Transfer to bowl and set aside.

5. Discard bay leaf and thyme sprig. Stir picada, mushrooms, and vinegar into stew. Season with salt and pepper to taste, and serve.

> **KEYS TO SUCCESS**
> - **Cook uncovered:** For part of the cooking time to brown the meat
> - **Add a picada:** To heighten the flavor

CHILE VERDE CON CERDO

Serves: 6 to 8
Total Time: 2¾ hours, plus 1 hour salting

RECIPE OVERVIEW Chile verde is a vibrant Mexican stew of pork simmered in a tangy tomatillo and green chile sauce. Braising is more or less the same everywhere: Gently braise the pork in the oven, allowing the meat's fat and collagen to thoroughly break down, making it supple. Browning the pork trimmings rather than drying out the surface of the meat itself builds fond. Broiling the tomatillos, chiles, and garlic concentrates their flavors and adds smokiness. Warm spices and sugar soften the dish's acidity and heat. And the salsa—the only source of liquid—reduces to a tight sauce. If your jalapeño is shorter than 3 inches long, you may wish to use two. If fresh tomatillos are unavailable, substitute three (11-ounce) cans of tomatillos, drained, rinsed, and patted dry. Serve with white rice and/or warm corn tortillas.

- 1 (3½- to 4-pound) boneless pork butt roast, trimmed and cut into 1½-inch pieces, trimmings reserved
- 1 tablespoon plus 1 teaspoon kosher salt, divided
- 1 cup water
- 1½ pounds tomatillos, husks and stems removed, rinsed well and dried
- 5 poblano chiles, stemmed, halved, and seeded
- 1 large onion, peeled, cut into 8 wedges through root end
- 5 garlic cloves, unpeeled
- 1 jalapeño chile, stemmed and halved
- 1 tablespoon vegetable oil
- 1 teaspoon dried oregano
- 1 teaspoon ground cumin
- ⅛ teaspoon ground cinnamon
-   Pinch ground cloves
- 2 bay leaves
- 2 teaspoons sugar
- 1 teaspoon pepper
- ½ cup minced fresh cilantro, plus extra for serving
    Lime wedges

1. Toss pork pieces with 1 tablespoon salt in large bowl. Cover and refrigerate for 1 hour. Meanwhile, chop pork trimmings coarse. Transfer to Dutch oven. Add water and bring to simmer over high heat. Cook, adjusting heat to maintain vigorous simmer and stirring occasionally, until all liquid evaporates and trimmings begin to sizzle, about 12 minutes. Continue to cook, stirring frequently, until dark fond forms on bottom of pot and trimmings have browned and crisped, about 6 minutes longer. Using slotted spoon, discard trimmings. Pour off all but 2 tablespoons fat; set aside pot.

2. Adjust 1 oven rack to lower-middle position and second rack 6 inches from broiler element and heat broiler. Line rimmed baking sheet with aluminum foil. Place tomatillos, poblanos, onion, garlic, and jalapeño on prepared sheet and drizzle with oil. Arrange chiles skin side up. Broil until chile skins are blackened and vegetables begin to soften, 10 to 13 minutes, rotating sheet halfway through broiling. Transfer poblanos, jalapeño, and garlic to cutting board.

3. Turn off broiler and heat oven to 325 degrees. Transfer tomatillos, onion, and any accumulated juices to food processor. When poblanos, jalapeño, and garlic are cool enough to handle, remove and discard skins (it's OK if some small bits of chile skin remain). Remove seeds from jalapeño and reserve. Add poblanos, jalapeño, and garlic to processor. Pulse until mixture is coarsely pureed, about 10 pulses, scraping down sides of bowl as needed. If spicier chili is desired, add reserved jalapeño seeds and pulse 3 times.

4. Heat reserved fat in Dutch oven over medium heat until shimmering. Add oregano, cumin, cinnamon, and cloves and cook, stirring constantly, until fragrant, about 30 seconds. Stir in tomatillo mixture, bay leaves, sugar, pepper, and remaining 1 teaspoon salt, scraping up any browned bits. Stir in pork and bring to simmer. Cover, transfer pot to oven, and cook until pork is tender, about 1½ hours, stirring halfway through cooking.

5. Remove pot from oven and let sit, covered, for 10 minutes. Discard bay leaves. Using heatproof rubber spatula, scrape browned bits from sides of pot. Stir in any fat that has risen to top of chili. Stir in cilantro; season with salt and pepper to taste. Serve, passing lime wedges and extra cilantro separately.

KEYS TO SUCCESS
- **Sauté the pork trimmings:** To build a fond and thus a foundation of meaty flavor
- **Peel the vegetables:** So the salsa isn't bitter

GOAN PORK VINDALOO

Serves: 8
Total Time: 2½ hours

RECIPE OVERVIEW The word "vindaloo" has evolved to indicate a searingly hot curry, but the traditional Goan dish is a brightly flavored yet relatively mild pork braise made with dried Kashmiri chiles and plenty of spices such as cinnamon, cloves, and cardamom. This recipe uses a combination of guajillo chiles, paprika, and tea to provide the bright color, mild heat, earthy flavor, and hint of astringency typically imparted by the hard-to-find Kashmiri chiles. Vindaloo should have a pronounced vinegary tang, but adding the vinegar at the beginning makes the meat chalky. Instead, withhold it until halfway through cooking so you can use less but still enjoy the characteristic acidity. Moving the cooking from the stovetop to the oven makes this dish hands-off and foolproof. Pork butt roast is often labeled Boston butt. If you don't have loose tea, open up two or three black tea bags and measure out 2 teaspoons of tea. Decaffeinated tea can be used if desired. Traditional Goan vindaloo is not very spicy, but if you prefer more heat, add up to ½ teaspoon of cayenne pepper. Serve with white rice, naan, or Goan pao.

- 4 large dried guajillo chiles, wiped clean, stemmed, seeded, and torn into 1-inch pieces (about 1 ounce)
- 1 cup water, divided
- 1 (1½-inch) piece ginger, peeled and sliced crosswise ⅛ inch thick
- 6 garlic cloves, chopped coarse
- 1 tablespoon paprika
- 1 tablespoon ground cumin
- 2 teaspoons loose black tea
- 2 teaspoons table salt
- 1 teaspoon pepper
- ¼–½ teaspoon cayenne pepper (optional)
- ½ teaspoon ground cinnamon
- ½ teaspoon ground cardamom
- ¼ teaspoon ground cloves
- ¼ teaspoon ground nutmeg
- 1 (3- to 3½-pound) boneless pork butt roast, trimmed and cut into 1-inch pieces
- 1 tablespoon vegetable oil
- 1 large onion, chopped fine
- ⅓ cup cider vinegar

1. Combine guajillos and ½ cup water in bowl and microwave until steaming, about 1½ minutes. Let sit until guajillos are softened, about 10 minutes. While guajillos soften, adjust oven rack to middle position and heat oven to 325 degrees. Process guajillo mixture; ginger; garlic; paprika; cumin; tea; salt; pepper; cayenne, if using; cinnamon; cardamom; cloves; and nutmeg in blender on low speed until smooth paste forms, 1½ to 2 minutes. With blender running, add remaining ½ cup water. Increase speed to high and process for 1 minute. Add pork to large bowl; pour spice paste over pork and mix thoroughly.

2. Heat oil in Dutch oven over medium heat until shimmering. Add onion and cook, stirring frequently, until soft and golden, 7 to 9 minutes. Add pork mixture and stir to combine. Spread mixture into even layer. Continue to cook until mixture begins to bubble, about 2 minutes longer. Cover pot, transfer to oven, and cook for 40 minutes. Stir in vinegar. Cover and return pot to oven. Continue to cook until fork inserted into pork meets little or no resistance, 40 to 50 minutes longer. Let stand, uncovered, for 10 minutes. Stir and serve.

SCIENCE LESSON Timing the Tang

Slightly sweet cider vinegar is a good swap for the coconut vinegar traditionally used in pork vindaloo, but it took us a few tries to figure out how much to use and when to add it. When we marinated the pork in vinegar or simmered it for too long with lots of vinegar, the meat turned dry. That's because acid lowers the pH of meat, making it easier for the proteins to link up and squeeze out moisture. Our solution: Skip marinating and add a modest amount of vinegar to the pot halfway through cooking. Exposed to less acid for less time, the meat stays juicy, and because we add the vinegar late, enough of its volatile bite remains.

Making Goan Pork Vindaloo

SPREAD PORK
Add the pork mixture and stir to combine. Spread the mixture into an even layer.

COOK
Cook until the mixture begins to bubble, about 2 minutes. Cover the pot, transfer to the oven, and cook for 40 minutes. Stir in the vinegar. Cover and return the pot to the oven.

FINISH
Continue to cook until a knife inserted into the pork meets little or no resistance, 40 to 50 minutes longer. Let stand, uncovered, for 10 minutes.

LAMB STEW WITH POTATOES

Serves: 6
Total Time: 3 hours

RECIPE OVERVIEW Quite often, Irish stew is made with nothing more than lamb, onions, potatoes, and water. The ingredients are layered in the pot and cooked until tender, for a dish that is nutritious and sustaining. This rich, deeply flavored stew is inspired by Irish lamb stews. Cutting the meat off the bones but adding them to the pot as well gives the stew richness and a velvety texture. The stew gets its deeply flavorful backbone from caramelized onions, so all it needs indeed is water for the liquid component (chicken broth muted the flavor of the lamb). Broken-down potatoes (along with some flour for assistance) thicken the stew and give it heft. All this homey stew needs is a side of Irish soda bread. Though we prefer lamb chops cut 1½ inches thick here, 1-inch-thick chops will suffice.

- 4½ pounds lamb shoulder chops (blade or round bone), 1 to 1½ inches thick, trimmed, meat removed from bones and cut into 1½-inch pieces, bones reserved
- 2 teaspoons table salt, divided
- ¾ teaspoon pepper
- 3 tablespoons vegetable oil, divided
- 2½ pounds onions, chopped coarse
- ¼ cup all-purpose flour
- 3 cups water, divided
- 1 teaspoon dried thyme
- 2 pounds Yukon Gold potatoes, peeled and cut into 1-inch pieces
- ¼ cup minced fresh parsley

1. Adjust oven rack to lower-middle position and heat oven to 300 degrees. Sprinkle lamb with ¾ teaspoon salt and pepper.

2. Heat 1 tablespoon oil in Dutch oven over medium-high heat until shimmering. Add half of lamb to pot so that individual pieces are close together but not touching. Cook, without moving lamb, until well browned, 2 to 3 minutes. Using tongs, flip lamb pieces and continue to cook until most sides are well browned, about 5 minutes longer; transfer to bowl. Add 1 tablespoon oil to pot, swirl to coat pot, and repeat with remaining lamb; transfer to bowl and set aside.

3. Reduce heat to medium, add remaining 1 tablespoon oil, and swirl to coat pot. Add onions and ¼ teaspoon salt and cook, stirring frequently and scraping up any browned bits, until onions have browned, about 8 minutes. Add flour and stir until onions are evenly coated, 1 to 2 minutes.

4. Stir in 1½ cups water, scraping up any remaining browned bits. Gradually add remaining 1½ cups water, stirring constantly and scraping pan edges to dissolve flour. Add thyme and remaining 1 teaspoon salt and bring to simmer. Add reserved bones, then meat and accumulated juices. Return to simmer and cover; transfer pot to oven. Cook for 1 hour.

5. Remove pot from oven and place potatoes on top of meat and bones. Cover and return pot to oven. Cook until lamb is tender, about 1 hour. Stir potatoes into liquid, wait 5 minutes, then skim off any fat that rises to top. Stir in parsley and season with salt and pepper to taste. Discard bones and serve.

> ### KEYS TO SUCCESS
> - **Add bones to the pot:** Cooking with the lamb bones provides deep lamb flavor.
> - **Cook the potatoes:** Cooking the potatoes thoroughly strips them of some starch that thickens the stew.

Blade Chop and Round Bone Chop

There are two kinds of shoulder chops. The blade chop (left) is roughly rectangular in shape and contains a piece of the chine bone (backbone) and a thin piece of the blade bone. The arm, or round bone, chop (right) contains a round cross-section of the arm bone so that the chop looks like a small ham steak. The round bone chop contains less fat and fewer muscles, making it easier to cut into meat for stews.

RESOURCES FOR MEAT STEWS OF THE WORLD

STEW MEAT

Prepackaged stew meat is convenient—but not very good. In most markets, the pieces are unevenly butchered, so smaller pieces overcook by the time larger ones are done. Even more problematic is the meat itself. Sometimes it comes from the most-desired parts such as the beef chuck eye or the pork shoulder, sometimes from tougher areas like the chuck under blade; often packages contain scraps from the beef clod or all over the pig, many of which are not very flavorful. Instead, we cut our desired roast into stew meat ourselves in large chunks, usually 1½ to 2 inches; we think bigger chunks make a better stew because they're satisfying and less likely to overcook. Trim any hard knobs of white fat as you work. Don't bother trimming soft, thin lines of fat—they will melt during the stewing process and lubricate the meat; you can always skim the final stew. (That said, don't be surprised if you have a good number of trimmings—count on roughly ½ pound of trimmings for every 4 pounds of meat.)

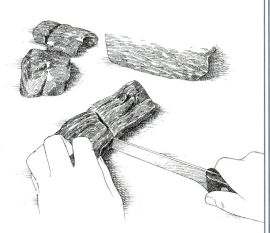

TRIM IT OR LEAVE IT

If your recipe calls for trimming a pork butt roast—most often for cutting it up for a stew or braise—it's hard to know exactly what to trim. The cut is well marbled throughout and you don't want to trim away too much of the fat and connective tissue, as this is what gives the meat a rich, moist texture. The key is to remove any hard, waxy fat from the surface of the whole roast and to leave a thin layer; don't worry about removing any interior fat at this point. A boning knife can make this task easier. Once you've got your smaller chunks and cubes, remove the hard knobs of waxy fat as they become accessible. There's no need to remove every last bit.

TRIM THIS

LEAVE THIS

YOU DON'T (ALWAYS) HAVE TO BROWN YOUR MEAT

The claim that searing meat "seals in juices" simply isn't true. It does develop flavorful browning through the Maillard reaction (see page 33) and creates fond in the pot that gives the liquid depth, but it has nothing to do with juiciness. (In fact, the perception of juiciness is almost entirely determined by two factors: the fat content and the internal temperature of the food.) So while browning the meat is usually one of the first steps in our stews—as the process forms thousands of new flavor compounds that we build on when developing the dish—you could skip this step and get a braise with meltingly tender meat. And we do skip it on occasion, as in Catalan-Style Beef Stew with Mushrooms (page 378) and Chile Verde con Cerdo (page 379).

These dishes are so packed with bold spices or aromatics that traditional browning—heating oil and sautéing pieces of meat in it—just isn't necessary for flavor. In the Catalan-Style Beef Stew we brown *while* we stew. How? Over time, if a pot is left uncovered in the oven, the dry top layer of meat reaches 300 degrees—the temperature at which meat begins to brown. Only the top of the meat will brown. Sometimes that's enough and sometimes we'll stir during cooking to expose new meat to browning. And in the Chile Verde con Cerdo, we sauté the pork trimmings for flavor.

For fattier cuts, we'll achieve browning through another cooking technique: roasting. For example, by precooking short ribs (see page 372) in a hot oven, we achieve browning, and we render a lot more fat at the start rather than in the braise.

COURSE
GROUND MEAT MUST-KNOWS

KEITH DRESSER

Ground meat, whether ground beef, pork, or lamb, is for many people a kitchen staple. In America, it's the star of such iconic dishes as juicy burgers (seared, grilled, or stacked) and shiny, glazed homestyle meatloaf (often a mix of beef and pork). Ground meat also brings international dishes to the table, sometimes playing a starring role and sometimes acting as a flavoring in vegetable-forward meals.

Unsurprisingly, ground meat tastes of the meat from which it's ground. What is most important is the fat content, which is determined largely by the specific cut of meat. Some recipes take well to lean ground meats, whereas others require the moisture of something with a higher percentage of fat. In the pages that follow, you'll learn just what to buy and how to use it.

KEITH'S PRO TIP: *Season it right. When it comes to seasoning recipes with ground meat, keep the fat percentage in mind. Since fat has a dulling effect on taste, recipes using fattier percentages, like burgers, will require more salt.*

CLASSIC BEEF BURGERS
Serves: 4
Total Time: 30 minutes

RECIPE OVERVIEW There are many ground beef options to choose from at the supermarket when making burgers, but not all are the right cut of beef with the ideal amount of fat to produce tender, juicy burgers. Generically labeled "ground beef" can be a combination of different cuts with little beefy flavor that yields fatty, greasy, or mushy burgers. Burgers have better luck with singular cuts of meat, and it's common to find ground sirloin, round, and chuck. Ground sirloin creates dry burgers and ground round is bland and gristly, but 85 percent lean ground chuck creates burgers with rich flavor and a tender, moist texture, so we prefer to use this if it's available. Burgers can puff up like tennis balls, but there's a trick: Slightly indenting, or dimpling, the center of each burger helps the burgers cook to a perfectly even thickness. You can serve these burgers simply with classic condiments, lettuce, and sliced ripe tomatoes.

1½ pounds 85 percent lean ground beef
½ teaspoon table salt
¼ teaspoon pepper
1 teaspoon vegetable oil, if using skillet
4 slices cheese (4 ounces) (optional)
4 hamburger buns, toasted if desired

1. Divide ground beef into 4 equal portions, then gently shape each portion into ¾-inch-thick patty. Using your fingertips, press center of each patty down until about ½ inch thick, creating slight indentation.

2A. FOR A SKILLET Season patties with salt and pepper. Heat oil in 12-inch skillet over medium heat until just smoking. Transfer patties to skillet, indentation side up, and cook until well browned on first side, 2 to 4 minutes. Flip patties, top with cheese, if using, and continue to cook until browned on second side and meat registers 120 to 125 degrees (for medium-rare) or 130 to 135 degrees (for medium), 3 to 5 minutes. Transfer burgers to platter and let rest for 5 minutes. Serve burgers on buns.

2B. FOR A CHARCOAL GRILL Open bottom vent completely. Light large chimney starter filled with charcoal briquettes (6 quarts). When top coals are partially covered with ash, pour evenly over grill. Set cooking grate in place, cover, and open lid vent completely. Heat grill until hot, about 5 minutes. Clean and oil cooking grate. Season patties with salt and pepper. Place patties on grill, indentation side up, and cook until well browned on first side, 2 to 4 minutes. Flip patties, top with cheese, if using, and continue to cook until browned on second side and meat registers 120 to 125 degrees (for medium-rare) or 130 to 135 degrees (for medium), 3 to 5 minutes. Transfer burgers to platter and let rest for 5 minutes. Serve burgers on buns.

2C. FOR A GAS GRILL Turn all burners to high, cover, and heat grill until hot, about 15 minutes. Leave all burners on high. Clean and oil cooking grate. Season patties with salt and pepper. Place patties on grill, indentation side up, and cook until well browned on first side, 2 to 4 minutes. Flip patties, top with cheese, if using, and continue to cook until browned on second side and meat registers 120 to 125 degrees (for medium-rare) or 130 to 135 degrees (for medium), 3 to 5 minutes. Transfer burgers to platter and let rest for 5 minutes. Serve burgers on buns.

Making an Indentation

Making a shallow indentation in the center of the patty is the first step toward a great burger. The collagen, or connective tissue, in ground meat shrinks when heated. This causes the bottom and sides of the meat to tighten like a belt, which forces the surface of the burger to expand. To prevent a bubble burger, press an indentation in the center of each patty. The collagen will still tighten, but the indented meat won't bulge.

Flat Patties = Bulging Burger

Indented Patties = Flat Burgers

SPAGHETTI AND MEATBALLS

Serves: 8
Total Time: 1¾ hours

RECIPE OVERVIEW It doesn't get much better than sitting down to a heaping pile of spaghetti topped with juicy, flavor-packed meatballs, all married together by a bright tomato sauce. This version of the classic hits every mark while being fuss-free. Many meatball recipes call for equal amounts of pork and beef, but we recommend using more beef (80 percent ground beef) than pork. The mixture is juicy from the fatty beef but still drier and leaner than a 50/50 beef-pork mix so it's better able to maintain its shape through cooking. The pork here is a small amount of Italian sausage, which boosts the meaty flavor without adding a lot more fat. A panade, a paste of milk and bread, binds the mixture and keeps ground meat moist when it's cooked above medium-rare. Instead of browning the meatballs on the stovetop, we utilize the oven to prevent splattering and make them more hands-off. Finishing the meatballs in the tomato sauce flavors both components and ties the dish together before serving. We prefer to use ground chuck in this recipe, if you can find it.

Sauce
- ¼ cup extra-virgin olive oil
- 3 onions, chopped fine
- 8 garlic cloves, minced
- 1 tablespoon dried oregano
- ½ teaspoon red pepper flakes
- 1 (6-ounce) can tomato paste
- 1 cup dry red wine
- 4 (28-ounce) cans crushed tomatoes
- 1 cup water
- 1 ounce Parmesan cheese, grated (½ cup)
- ¼ cup chopped fresh basil

Meatballs and Pasta
- 4 slices hearty white sandwich bread, torn into pieces
- ¾ cup milk
- 8 ounces sweet Italian sausage, casings removed
- 2 ounces Parmesan cheese, grated (1 cup)
- ½ cup minced fresh parsley
- 2 large eggs
- 2 garlic cloves, minced
- 1½ teaspoons table salt, plus salt for cooking pasta
- 2½ pounds 80 percent lean ground beef
- 2 pounds spaghetti

1. FOR THE SAUCE Heat oil in Dutch oven over medium-high heat until shimmering. Add onions and cook until golden, 10 to 15 minutes. Stir in garlic, oregano, and pepper flakes and cook until fragrant, about 30 seconds. Transfer half of onion mixture to bowl; set aside for meatballs.

2. Stir tomato paste into onion mixture left in pot and cook over medium-high heat until fragrant, about 1 minute. Stir in wine and cook until slightly thickened, about 2 minutes. Stir in tomatoes and water and simmer over low heat until sauce is no longer watery, 45 minutes to 1 hour. Stir in Parmesan and basil and season with salt and pepper to taste.

3. FOR THE MEATBALLS AND PASTA While sauce simmers, line 2 rimmed baking sheets with aluminum foil and spray with vegetable oil spray. Adjust oven racks to upper-middle and lower-middle positions and heat oven to 475 degrees. Mash bread and milk in large bowl until smooth. Mix in reserved onion mixture, sausage, Parmesan, parsley, eggs, garlic, and salt. Add beef and knead with your hands until well combined.

4. Shape meat mixture into 30 meatballs (about ¼ cup each) and place on prepared sheets, spaced evenly apart. Roast meatballs until well browned, about 20 minutes. Transfer meatballs to pot with sauce and simmer for 15 minutes.

5. Meanwhile, bring 8 quarts water to boil in 12-quart pot. Add pasta and 2 tablespoons salt and cook, stirring often, until al dente. Reserve ½ cup cooking water, then drain pasta and return it to pot. Add several spoonfuls of sauce (without meatballs) and toss to combine. Add reserved cooking water as needed to adjust consistency. Serve pasta with remaining sauce and meatballs.

KEY TO SUCCESS
- **Roast the meatballs:** In the oven before simmering them in the sauce to prevent the mess of stovetop browning

What's a Panade?

Panade is a paste typically made by combining milk and bread (and sometimes bread crumbs, panko, or crackers). We often use panades to help foods such as meatloaf, meatballs, and burgers hold their shape and stay moist. But how does it work? Starches from the bread absorb liquid from the milk. The starches form a gel that coats the proteins in the meat. This gel holds meat juices in. It also prevents the proteins from linking together and toughening. The result is more tender meat.

THAI PORK LETTUCE WRAPS

Serves: 4
Total Time: 45 minutes

RECIPE OVERVIEW Ground pork gets a boost in this take on larb moo. First marinating the pork in a little fish sauce seasons it throughout and helps it retain moisture during cooking. Adding sugar, tart lime juice, more salty fish sauce, and hot red pepper flakes achieves the balance of flavors characteristic of Thai cuisine. Don't skip the toasted rice; it's integral to the texture and flavor of the dish. Any style of white rice can be used. Toasted rice powder (kao kua) can also be found in many Asian markets. This dish can be served with sticky rice and steamed vegetables as an entrée.

- 1 pound ground pork
- 2½ tablespoons fish sauce, divided
- 1 tablespoon white rice
- ¼ cup chicken broth
- 2 shallots, sliced into thin rings
- 3 tablespoons lime juice (2 limes)
- 3 tablespoons coarsely chopped fresh mint
- 3 tablespoons coarsely chopped fresh cilantro
- 2 teaspoons sugar
- ¼ teaspoon red pepper flakes
- 1 head Bibb lettuce (8 ounces), leaves separated

1. Toss pork with 1 tablespoon fish sauce, cover, and refrigerate for 15 minutes.

2. Toast rice in 8-inch skillet over medium-high heat, stirring constantly, until deep golden brown, about 5 minutes. Transfer rice to small bowl and let cool for 5 minutes. Grind to fine meal using spice grinder, mini food processor, or mortar and pestle, 10 to 30 seconds.

3. Bring broth to simmer in 12-inch nonstick skillet over medium-high heat. Add pork and cook, stirring frequently, until pork is about half pink, about 2 minutes. Sprinkle 1 teaspoon rice powder into skillet and continue to cook, stirring constantly, until pork is no longer pink, 1 to 1½ minutes longer.

4. Transfer pork to large bowl and let cool for 10 minutes. Stir in shallots, lime juice, mint, cilantro, sugar, pepper flakes, remaining 1½ tablespoons fish sauce, and remaining 2 teaspoons rice powder and toss to combine. Serve with lettuce.

KEYS TO SUCCESS

- **Toss with fish sauce:** To tenderize and flavor the meat
- **Cook the pork in broth:** To add flavor and keep the meat from expelling moisture
- **Grind the rice:** Contributes nutty flavor and adds body

GLAZED MEATLOAF

Serves: 6 to 8
Total Time: 2 hours

RECIPE OVERVIEW An old-fashioned meatloaf, one featuring tender meat topped with a shining, sweet-tangy glaze that offsets the loaf's richness, is a satisfying dinner centerpiece. This dish is all about the meat, a flavorful, classic combination of equal parts ground beef and sweet ground pork. The seasonings are American traditional as well: salt, pepper, Dijon mustard, Worcestershire sauce, thyme, parsley, sautéed onion, and garlic. A panade of milk and saltines adds moisture and structure; combining it in a food processor and then pulsing it with the meat gives the loaf the most cohesive, tender texture. To evaporate the surface moisture that can inhibit the formation of a crust, we broil the loaf prior to baking and glazing.

Glaze
- 1 cup ketchup
- ¼ cup packed brown sugar
- 2½ tablespoons cider vinegar
- ½ teaspoon hot sauce

Meatloaf
- 2 teaspoons vegetable oil
- 1 onion, chopped fine
- 2 garlic cloves, minced
- 17 square or 19 round saltines
- ⅓ cup whole milk
- 1 pound 90 percent lean ground beef
- 1 pound ground pork
- 2 large eggs plus 1 large yolk
- ⅓ cup finely chopped fresh parsley
- 2 teaspoons Dijon mustard
- 2 teaspoons Worcestershire sauce
- ½ teaspoon dried thyme
- 1 teaspoon table salt
- ¾ teaspoon pepper

1. **FOR THE GLAZE** Whisk all ingredients in small saucepan until sugar dissolves. Reserve ¼ cup glaze mixture, then simmer remaining glaze over medium heat until slightly thickened, about 5 minutes. Cover and keep warm.

2. **FOR THE MEATLOAF** Line rimmed baking sheet with aluminum foil and coat lightly with vegetable oil spray. Heat oil in 8-inch nonstick skillet over medium heat until shimmering. Add onion and cook until golden, about 8 minutes. Add garlic and cook until fragrant, about 30 seconds. Transfer to large bowl.

3. Process saltines and milk in food processor until smooth, about 30 seconds. Add beef and pork and pulse until well combined, about 10 pulses. Transfer meat mixture to bowl with cooled onion mixture. Add eggs and yolk, parsley, mustard, Worcestershire, thyme, salt, and pepper to bowl and mix with your hands until combined.

4. Adjust 1 oven rack to middle position and second rack 4 inches from broiler element; heat broiler. Transfer meat mixture to prepared baking sheet and shape into 9 by 5-inch loaf. Broil on upper rack until well browned, about 5 minutes. Brush 2 tablespoons unreduced glaze over top and sides of loaf and then return to oven and broil until glaze begins to brown, about 2 minutes.

5. Transfer meatloaf to lower rack and brush with remaining unreduced glaze. Set oven temperature to 350 degrees and bake until meatloaf registers 160 degrees, 40 to 45 minutes. Transfer to cutting board, tent with foil, and let rest for 20 minutes. Slice and serve, passing reduced glaze at table.

> ### KEYS TO SUCCESS
> - **Pulse the panade:** In a food processor and then pulse in the meat to ensure a cohesive mix
> - **Simmer some of the glaze:** Thickens it a bit so you can serve it with the loaf
> - **Broil, then bake:** To first brown the top and then cook it through gently

SPICY LAMB WITH LENTILS AND YOGURT

Serves: 4
Total Time: 45 minutes

RECIPE OVERVIEW This skillet recipe combines earthy lentils with warm-spiced ground lamb for a hearty but not fussy meal. Cilantro and tomatoes add freshness, while Greek yogurt stirred in at the end brings the dish together. Sautéing the aromatics creates a fond and then deglazing the pan dissolves all that complex flavor into the dish. Garam masala and red pepper flakes add a punch of warm-spiced flavor. Adding a tiny amount of baking soda tenderizes the ground lamb by raising its pH. Note that you will need ¾ cup of cilantro, so shop accordingly. We prefer how small green lentilles du Puy, or French green lentils, hold their shape in this recipe; we do not recommend substituting other types of lentils here.

- 1 pound ground lamb
- ¾ teaspoon table salt, divided, plus salt for cooking lentils
- ¼ teaspoon baking soda
- 1 cup lentilles du Puy, picked over and rinsed
- 3 garlic cloves, minced
- 1 tablespoon tomato paste
- 2 teaspoons garam masala
- 1 teaspoon red pepper flakes
- 1 teaspoon grated fresh ginger
- 1 tablespoon vegetable oil
- 1 onion, chopped
- 2 naan breads
- 2 tomatoes, cored and cut into ½-inch pieces
- ¾ cup chopped fresh cilantro, divided
- ¾ cup plain Greek yogurt, divided

1. Toss lamb with 2 tablespoons water, ½ teaspoon salt, and baking soda in bowl until thoroughly combined; set aside for 20 minutes.

2. While lamb sits, bring lentils, 4 cups water, and 1 teaspoon salt to boil in medium saucepan over high heat. Reduce heat to low and simmer until lentils are just tender, 18 to 22 minutes. Drain well.

3. Adjust oven rack to middle position and heat oven to 400 degrees. Combine garlic, tomato paste, garam masala, pepper flakes, and ginger in small bowl. Heat oil in 12-inch skillet over medium heat until shimmering. Add onion and remaining ¼ teaspoon salt and cook until softened and lightly browned, 5 to 7 minutes. Stir in garlic mixture and cook, stirring constantly, until bottom of skillet is dark brown, 1 to 2 minutes.

4. Add 1 cup water and bring to boil, scraping up any browned bits. Reduce heat to medium-low, add lamb in 2-inch chunks to skillet, and bring to gentle simmer. Cover and cook until lamb is cooked through, 10 to 12 minutes, stirring and breaking up lamb chunks with 2 forks halfway through cooking. Uncover skillet, increase heat to medium, stir in drained lentils, and cook until liquid is mostly absorbed, 3 to 5 minutes.

5. While lamb cooks, place naan on rimmed baking sheet and bake until warmed through, about 5 minutes.

6. Off heat, stir tomatoes, ½ cup cilantro, and 2 tablespoons yogurt into lentils and season with salt and pepper to taste. Sprinkle with remaining ¼ cup cilantro. Serve with naan and remaining yogurt.

KEYS TO SUCCESS

- **Toss with baking soda:** To tenderize the lamb
- **Add Greek yogurt:** Near the end of cooking to give the lamb and lentils a slightly creamy feel

COURSE

QUICK DINNER OFF THE GRILL

STEVE DUNN

The grill can be the quickest way to cook many cuts of meat, and the flavor dividends in that time can be tremendous. Take foods you love—steak, burgers, roasts—and kiss them with smoky char from the grill for a different experience. But grilling requires unique considerations compared to stovetop or oven cooking to ensure that food gets proper char and doesn't dry out. See our guide to grilling on page 447 and then use these recipes whether you have a gas or charcoal grill to make a special summer meal for a cookout, or any night of the week.

STEVE'S PRO TIP: *Nothing will improve your grill game faster than using a high-quality instant-read thermometer. To ensure perfectly cooked meat every time, I use a Thermoworks Thermapen to check the degree of doneness. I recommend you do, too.*

GRILLED STEAK BURGERS

Serves: 4
Total Time: 1¼ hours

RECIPE OVERVIEW Not any ground beef works for a burger with the big beefy flavor and the crusty char of a grilled steak. Ground sirloin is the most flavorful ground beef, but unfortunately it's quite lean. Doctoring it produces something with the right richness. Incorporating a seasoned butter and some soy sauce into the ground meat patties contributes richness and umami flavor, respectively. Then, it takes about 5 minutes to simmer up our own intensely flavored steak sauce, to brush on the burgers so it caramelizes on the patties during grilling and to serve with the burgers and buns. This burger is unmistakably steak.

Burgers
- 8 tablespoons unsalted butter
- 2 garlic cloves, minced
- 2 teaspoons onion powder
- 1 teaspoon pepper
- ½ teaspoon table salt
- 1½ pounds 90 percent lean ground sirloin
- 2 teaspoons soy sauce
- 4 hamburger buns

Steak Sauce
- 2 tablespoons tomato paste
- ⅔ cup beef broth
- ⅓ cup raisins
- 2 tablespoons soy sauce
- 2 tablespoons Dijon mustard
- 2 tablespoons balsamic vinegar
- 1 tablespoon Worcestershire sauce

1. FOR THE BURGERS Melt butter in 8-inch skillet over medium-low heat. Add garlic, onion powder, pepper, and salt and cook until fragrant, about 1 minute. Pour all but 1 tablespoon butter mixture into bowl and let cool for about 5 minutes.

2. FOR THE STEAK SAUCE Meanwhile, add tomato paste to skillet and cook over medium heat until paste begins to darken, 1 to 2 minutes. Stir in broth, raisins, soy sauce, mustard, vinegar, and Worcestershire and simmer until raisins plump, about 5 minutes. Process sauce in blender until smooth, about 30 seconds; transfer to bowl.

3. Break ground beef into small pieces in large bowl. Add 5 tablespoons cooled butter mixture and soy sauce and gently knead with hands until well combined. Divide beef mixture into 4 equal portions, then gently shape each portion into ¾-inch-thick patty. Using your fingertips, press center of each patty down until about ½ inch thick, creating slight indentation. Brush each patty on both sides with 1 tablespoon steak sauce. Combine remaining 2 tablespoons cooled butter mixture with 2 tablespoons steak sauce; set aside.

4A. FOR A CHARCOAL GRILL Open bottom vent completely. Light large chimney starter filled with charcoal briquettes (6 quarts). When top coals are partially covered with ash, pour evenly over grill. Set cooking grate in place, cover, and open lid vent completely. Heat grill until hot, about 5 minutes.

4B. FOR A GAS GRILL Turn all burners to high, cover, and heat grill until hot, about 15 minutes. Leave burners on high.

5. Clean and oil cooking grate. Place patties on grill, indentation side up, and cook until well browned on first side, 2 to 4 minutes. Flip patties and continue to cook until browned on second side and meat registers 120 to 125 degrees (for medium-rare) or 130 to 135 degrees (for medium), 3 to 5 minutes. Transfer burgers to platter and let rest for 5 minutes.

6. Brush cut side of buns with butter–steak sauce mixture. Grill buns, cut side down, until golden, about 2 minutes. Serve burgers on buns, topped with remaining steak sauce.

KEYS TO SUCCESS

- **Bolster the beef with butter:** By adding it to the lean sirloin and to the steak sauce for richness
- **Add umami:** With soy sauce in the patties and soy sauce, tomato paste, and Worcestershire in the steak sauce for increased meatiness
- **Sauce the buns:** Before grilling to give them a rich char

GRILLED FLANK STEAK WITH BASIL DRESSING

Serves: 6
Total Time: 1¼ hours, plus 1 hour brining

RECIPE OVERVIEW For a grilled flank steak with a char-kissed exterior and a perfectly cooked interior, turn away from a wet marinade; it's the enemy of good browning. On top of that, the test kitchen has proven that marinades barely penetrate the surface of meat. But since salt and sugar (when applied far enough in advance) do dissolve and penetrate deep into the meat, a simple preseasoning with salt, sugar (to help with browning in a short cooking time), and pepper does wonders. To cook this wedge-shaped cut to the same internal temperature from end to end, set up a grill with a cooler side and a hotter side. After briefly grilling the entire steak on the hotter side, position the steak so that the thinner portion is over the cooler side of the grill to save it from overcooking. Converting ingredients that could have been a marinade— a vinaigrette of olive oil, basil, lemon, honey, garlic, and pepper—into a sauce to drizzle over the perfectly grilled steak gives the meat a bright finish.

Steak
- 1 (2-pound) flank steak, trimmed
- 2 teaspoons sugar
- ½ teaspoon table salt
- ½ teaspoon pepper

Basil Dressing
- ¼ cup extra-virgin olive oil
- ¼ cup chopped fresh basil
- 1 shallot, minced
- 2 tablespoons red wine vinegar
- 2 teaspoons lemon juice
- 1 teaspoon honey
- 1 garlic clove, minced
- ½ teaspoon red pepper flakes
- ½ teaspoon table salt
- ¼ teaspoon pepper

1. FOR THE STEAK Pat steak dry with paper towels and sprinkle with sugar, salt, and pepper. Transfer steak to plate, cover with plastic wrap, and refrigerate for at least 1 hour or up to 24 hours.

2. FOR THE BASIL DRESSING Whisk all ingredients in bowl; set aside.

3A. FOR A CHARCOAL GRILL Open bottom vent completely. Light large chimney starter mounded with charcoal briquettes (7 quarts). When top coals are partially covered with ash, pour evenly over half of grill. Set cooking grate in place, cover, and open lid vent completely. Heat grill until hot, about 5 minutes.

3B. FOR A GAS GRILL Turn all burners to high, cover, and heat grill until hot, about 15 minutes. Leave primary burner on high and turn off other burner(s).

4. Set wire rack in rimmed baking sheet. Clean and oil cooking grate. Place steak on hotter side of grill and cook (covered if using gas) until browned on both sides, about 2 minutes per side. Flip steak again and rotate so that thin end is over cooler side of grill and thick end remains over hotter side. Continue to cook (covered if using gas), flipping steak every 2 minutes, until thick end of steak registers 120 to 125 degrees (for medium-rare) or 130 to 135 degrees (for medium), 2 to 6 minutes longer.

5. Transfer steak to prepared rack, tent with aluminum foil, and let rest for 10 minutes. Transfer steak to carving board and cut in half lengthwise with grain to create 2 narrow steaks. Slice each steak thin on bias against grain. Transfer steak to shallow platter and pour dressing over top. Serve.

KEYS TO SUCCESS

- **Salt the steak:** Before grilling for juiciness and deep seasoning
- **Add some sugar:** To the flank steak pretreatment to aid browning during the quick cook time on the grill
- **Finish with a vinaigrette:** By pouring it over the sliced steak for a final burst of flavor

SCIENCE LESSON **Grain Gains**

Flank steak, with its distinctive grain, is great at soaking up flavor. Marinades don't do much for tenderizing meat, but pour something on after grilling—here, a zippy vinaigrette—and the flank steak effectively absorbs the flavorful bath.

Sear, Flip, and Rotate

Flank steaks are considerably thicker on one end, so cooking them evenly requires some technique. We build a half-grill fire with a hotter and a cooler zone and start by searing both sides of the steak directly over the hotter side of the grill until browned. Then we position the steak with its thin end over the cooler side and its thick end over the hotter side to finish cooking.

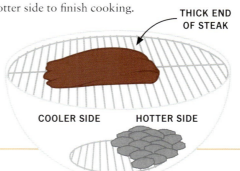

392 | The New Cooking School Cookbook: Fundamentals

GRILLED PORK TENDERLOIN WITH GRILLED PINEAPPLE–RED ONION SALSA

Serves: 4 to 6
Total Time: 1¼ hours

RECIPE OVERVIEW To produce pork tenderloin with a rich crust and a tender, juicy interior, use a half-grill fire and sear it on the hotter side of the grill. This allows the exterior of this relatively thin cut to develop flavorful browning before the interior cooks through. Then move the meat to the cooler side of the grill to finish cooking gently. Seasoning the pork with a mixture of salt, cumin, and chipotle chile powder adds smoky, savory flavor to the mild meat, and a touch of sugar encourages browning. To add bright flavor and make the most of the fire, we grill pineapple and red onion and, while the cooked pork rests, combine them with cilantro, a serrano chile, lime juice, and a bit of reserved spice mixture to make a quick salsa. We prefer unenhanced pork in this recipe, but enhanced pork (pork injected with a salt solution) can be used. Pineapples don't ripen further once picked, so be sure to purchase a fragrant fruit that gives slightly when pressed.

Pork
- 1½ teaspoons kosher salt
- 1½ teaspoons sugar
- ½ teaspoon ground cumin
- ½ teaspoon chipotle chile powder
- 2 (12- to 16-ounce) pork tenderloins, trimmed

Salsa
- ½ pineapple, peeled, cored, and cut lengthwise into 6 wedges
- 1 red onion, cut into 8 wedges through root end
- 4 teaspoons extra-virgin olive oil, divided
- ½ cup minced fresh cilantro
- 1 serrano chile, stemmed, seeded, and minced
- 2 tablespoons lime juice, plus extra for seasoning

1. FOR THE PORK Combine salt, sugar, cumin, and chile powder in small bowl. Measure out ½ teaspoon spice mixture and set aside. Rub remaining spice mixture evenly over surface of both tenderloins. Transfer to large plate or rimmed baking sheet and refrigerate while preparing grill.

2A. FOR A CHARCOAL GRILL Open bottom vent completely. Light large chimney starter filled with charcoal briquettes (6 quarts). When top coals are partially covered with ash, pour evenly over half of grill. Set cooking grate in place, cover, and open lid vent completely. Heat grill until hot, about 5 minutes.

2B. FOR A GAS GRILL Turn all burners to high, cover, and heat grill until hot, about 15 minutes. Leave primary burner on high and turn off other burner(s).

3. Clean and oil cooking grate. Place tenderloins on hotter side of grill. Cover and cook, turning tenderloins every 2 minutes, until well browned on all sides, about 8 minutes.

4. FOR THE SALSA Brush pineapple and onion with 1 teaspoon oil. Move tenderloins to cooler side of grill (6 to 8 inches from heat source) and place pineapple and onion on hotter side of grill. Cover and cook until pineapple and onion are charred on both sides and softened, 8 to 10 minutes, flipping pineapple and onion halfway through cooking, and until pork registers 135 to 140 degrees, 12 to 17 minutes, turning tenderloins every 5 minutes. As pineapple and onion and tenderloins reach desired level of doneness, transfer pineapple and onion to plate and transfer tenderloins to carving board. Tent tenderloins with aluminum foil and let rest for 10 minutes.

5. While tenderloins rest, chop pineapple coarse. Pulse cilantro, serrano, lime juice, pineapple, onion, reserved spice mixture, and remaining 1 tablespoon oil in food processor until mixture is roughly chopped, 4 to 6 pulses. Transfer to bowl and season with salt and extra lime juice to taste. Slice tenderloins crosswise ½ inch thick. Serve with salsa.

PINCHOS MORUNOS

Serves: 4
Total Time: 1¼ hours

RECIPE OVERVIEW Pinchos morunos is a dish normally served as part of a tapas spread, but it works equally well as an entrée. Country-style ribs are a good choice for both their convenience and their ability to remain juicy and tender when grilled in 1-inch chunks. To increase juiciness, brine the pork for 30 minutes before cutting it into cubes and coating it with a robust spice paste that includes garlic, lemon, ginger, coriander, smoked paprika, and fresh oregano. Because country-style ribs contain a mix of lighter loin meat and darker shoulder meat, keep the light meat and dark meat on separate skewers and cook each to its ideal temperature (140 and 155 degrees, respectively) to ensure that the light meat doesn't overcook and the dark meat isn't chewy. You will need four or five 12-inch metal skewers for this recipe. If the pork is enhanced (injected with a salt solution), do not brine it in step 1.

- 3 tablespoons table salt for brining
- 2 pounds boneless country-style pork ribs, trimmed
- ¼ cup vegetable oil
- 2 tablespoons lemon juice, plus lemon wedges for serving
- 6 garlic cloves, minced
- 1 tablespoon grated fresh ginger
- 2 teaspoons minced fresh oregano, divided
- 2 teaspoons smoked paprika
- 1 teaspoon ground coriander
- 1 teaspoon table salt
- ½ teaspoon ground cumin
- ½ teaspoon pepper
- ¼ teaspoon cayenne pepper

1. Dissolve 3 tablespoons salt in 1½ quarts cold water in large container. Submerge ribs in brine and let stand at room temperature for 30 minutes. Meanwhile, whisk oil, lemon juice, garlic, ginger, 1 teaspoon oregano, paprika, coriander, salt, cumin, pepper, and cayenne in small bowl until combined.

2. Remove pork from brine and pat dry with paper towels. Cut ribs into 1-inch chunks; place dark meat and light meat in separate bowls. Divide spice paste proportionately between bowls and toss to coat. Thread light and dark meat onto separate skewers (do not crowd pieces). Place dark meat kebabs on left side of rimmed baking sheet and light meat kebabs on right side.

3A. FOR A CHARCOAL GRILL Open bottom vent completely. Light large chimney starter filled with charcoal briquettes (6 quarts). When top coals are partially covered with ash, pour evenly over half of grill. Set cooking grate in place, cover, and open lid vent completely. Heat grill until hot, about 5 minutes.

3B. FOR A GAS GRILL Turn all burners to high, cover, and heat grill until hot, about 15 minutes. Leave primary burner on high and turn off other burner(s).

4. Clean and oil cooking grate. Place dark meat on hotter side of grill and cook for 6 minutes. Flip dark meat and add light meat to hotter side of grill. Cook for 4 minutes, then flip all kebabs. Continue to cook, flipping kebabs every 4 minutes, until dark meat is well charred and registers 155 degrees and light meat is lightly charred and registers 140 degrees, 4 to 8 minutes longer. Transfer to serving platter, tent with aluminum foil, and let rest for 5 minutes. Remove pork from skewers, toss to combine, sprinkle with remaining 1 teaspoon oregano, and serve, passing lemon wedges separately.

KEYS TO SUCCESS

- **Brine the pork**: To ensure the small pieces won't dry out on the grill
- **Cook the light and dark meat on separate skewers**: Allows you to control the different doneness times
- **Turn the kebabs**: Over the hotter side of the grill every 4 minutes so they char nicely

The Dark (and Light) Side of Country-Style Ribs

Country-style ribs are cut from the backbone where the shoulder meets the loin; therefore, they contain meat from both regions. Because the shoulder muscle uses energy for extended periods, it's rich in fat, which acts as fuel, and the red protein myoglobin (which accounts for its darker color). The lesser-worked loin area is leaner and lighter. Given these traits, the dark meat can be cooked to a higher temperature and still stay juicy, but the leaner light meat needs to be cooked to a lower temperature to avoid drying out. For Pinchos Morunos, we cut the meat into cubes and skewer it, and so we're able to start cooking the skewers of dark meat before the quicker-cooking light meat.

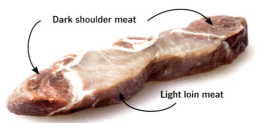

TWO-TONE RIBS

COURSE
EAT WITH YOUR HANDS

CHRISTIE MORRISON

Meat plays a starring role in some of the most satisfying foods, many of which you can pick up and eat with your hands—think sandwiches, tacos, and wraps with zippy accompaniments that stand up to the richness of the meat. It's easy to partake in these parcels at home, with recipes that bring the restaurant or street cart into your kitchen using your own equipment. Learn about the perfect cuts of meats for these succulent applications. And have fun with your food.

CHRISTIE'S PRO TIP: *Getting the meat right for these recipes may require most of your focus, but don't forget about the wrapper. Warm or char tortillas, toast rolls, and broil pita to add flavor and texture.*

STEAK TACOS

Serves: 4
Total Time: 55 minutes

RECIPE OVERVIEW Grilled steak tacos are great, but it's possible for an indoor recipe to transform flank steak into an equally satisfying spicy, herby meal. A sprinkling of sugar gives the beefy flank steak the browned exterior and crisp edges characteristic of grilled meat. A deeply flavorful oil-based herb paste of cilantro, scallions, garlic, jalapeño, and cumin provides its own bright flavor boost. Piercing the steak and rubbing it with the herb paste before cooking allows the flavors to fully penetrate the large-grained meat, and mixing the cooked steak with the remaining herb paste lets bright flavor soak in. Serve with chopped tomatoes, sliced radishes, chopped onion, and diced avocado, if desired.

- ½ cup fresh cilantro leaves, plus extra for serving
- 3 scallions, chopped coarse
- 3 garlic cloves, chopped coarse
- 1 jalapeño chile, stemmed and chopped coarse
- ½ teaspoon ground cumin
- 6 tablespoons vegetable oil, divided
- 1 tablespoon lime juice
- 1 (1½- to 1¾-pound) flank steak, trimmed
- 1½ teaspoons table salt
- ½ teaspoon sugar
- ½ teaspoon pepper
- 12 (6-inch) corn tortillas, warmed
  Lime wedges

1. Pulse cilantro, scallions, garlic, jalapeño, and cumin in food processor until finely chopped, 10 to 12 pulses. Add ¼ cup oil and process until mixture is smooth, about 15 seconds, scraping down bowl as needed. Transfer 2 tablespoons herb paste to medium bowl and stir in lime juice; set aside for serving.

2. Cut steak with grain into 4 pieces. Using dinner fork, poke each piece of steak 10 to 12 times on each side. Place steaks in large baking dish, rub thoroughly with salt, then coat with remaining herb paste. Cover and refrigerate for 30 minutes to 1 hour.

3. Scrape herb paste off steaks and sprinkle with sugar and pepper. Heat remaining 2 tablespoons oil in 12-inch nonstick skillet over medium-high heat until just smoking. Cook steaks, turning as needed, until well browned on all sides and meat registers 120 to 125 degrees (for medium-rare), 4 to 6 minutes. Transfer steaks to cutting board and let rest for 5 minutes.

4. Slice steaks thin against grain, add to bowl with reserved herb paste, and toss to coat. Season with salt and pepper to taste. Serve with warm tortillas, extra cilantro, and lime wedges.

CORE TECHNIQUE
Preparing Flank Steak for Tacos

SLICE AND POKE
Slice the steak into strips and pierce them with a fork to allow the herb paste to penetrate.

SALT AND COAT
Season the meat, coat it with the herb paste, and let it stand.

SEAR
Cook the steak in a generous 2 tablespoons oil to promote browning.

SLICE AND TOSS
Cut the steak thinly across the grain to ensure tenderness and mix the steak with more herb paste and lime juice to brighten the flavors.

PORK GYRO

Serves: 8
Total Time: 2¼ hours, plus 1 hour marinating

RECIPE OVERVIEW Without using the traditional setup of a live fire and/or a rotating spit, we manage to mimic the typical cooking method of this Greek American favorite in just three easy steps. To jump-start the cooking and preserve moisture, first cover well-marbled pork butt (from the pork shoulder)—marinated in a garlic, oil, and spice mixture—in aluminum foil and steam it in a 350-degree oven. Uncovering the pork and continuing to roast it helps dry the exterior so that after a final stint under the broiler the meat develops a crisp, well-charred crust. Sometimes we purposely overcook pork butt so it falls apart with tenderness; cook this pork to a perfect 160 degrees so it can be sliced thinly for making sandwiches, as is traditional. Make the most of the broiler's heat by toasting pita breads while the meat rests. A cooling homemade tzatziki sauce is the perfect finish.

Gyro
- 1 (4-pound) boneless pork butt roast, trimmed
- ½ cup plus 1 tablespoon extra-virgin olive oil, divided
- 6 garlic cloves, minced
- 1½ tablespoons dried oregano
- 1½ tablespoons kosher salt for the marinade
- 1 tablespoon ground coriander
- 1 tablespoon paprika
- 2 teaspoons pepper
- 8 (8-inch) pita breads
- 1 romaine lettuce heart (6 ounces), sliced thin
- 1 small red onion, halved and sliced thin
- Lemon wedges

Tzatziki
- 1 English cucumber, halved lengthwise and seeded, divided
- 1½ cups plain Greek yogurt
- 2 tablespoons extra-virgin olive oil
- 1 tablespoon lemon juice
- 1 tablespoon chopped fresh dill
- 1½ teaspoons kosher salt
- 1 large garlic clove, minced
- ½ teaspoon pepper

1. FOR THE GYRO Slice pork lengthwise into 4 equal steaks, about 1 inch thick (if steaks are thicker than 1 inch, press them with your hand to 1-inch thickness). Place pork in 1-gallon zipper-lock bag. Whisk ½ cup oil, garlic, oregano, salt, coriander, paprika, and pepper together in bowl. Add marinade to bag with pork. Seal bag and turn to distribute marinade evenly. Refrigerate for at least 1 hour or up to 24 hours.

2. Adjust oven rack 6 inches from broiler element and heat oven to 350 degrees. Line rimmed baking sheet with aluminum foil and set wire rack in sheet. Remove pork from marinade and place on prepared wire rack; discard marinade.

3. Cover sheet tightly with foil and transfer to oven. Roast until pork registers 100 degrees, about 40 minutes. Remove sheet from oven and carefully remove foil so steam escapes away from you. Return sheet to oven and continue to roast until pork registers 160 degrees, 20 to 25 minutes longer.

4. FOR THE TZATZIKI While pork roasts, shred 1 cucumber half on large holes of box grater. Combine shredded cucumber, yogurt, oil, lemon juice, dill, salt, garlic, and pepper in bowl. Refrigerate until ready to serve. Slice remaining cucumber thin and set aside.

5. Leave sheet in oven and turn on broiler. Broil until pork is well browned on top side only, about 10 minutes. Transfer pork to carving board and let rest for 5 minutes.

6. Brush 1 side of pitas with remaining 1 tablespoon oil. Place 4 pitas oiled side up on now-empty wire rack. Broil until pitas are soft and lightly toasted, about 1 minute. Repeat with remaining 4 pitas. Slice pork crosswise very thin. Toss pork with accumulated juices on carving board. Divide pork evenly among pitas and top with lettuce, onion, sliced cucumber, and tzatziki. Serve with lemon wedges.

Turning Pork Butt into a Gyro

CUT IN FOUR
Slice the pork lengthwise into 4 equal steaks and marinate.

ROAST COVERED
Set the pork on a wire rack, cover, and roast to render the fat.

ROAST UNCOVERED
Continue to roast the pork, uncovered, until it registers 160 degrees.

BROIL
Broil until the pork is well browned on the top side only, about 10 minutes.

What Is Pork Butt?

"Pork butt" doesn't seem like an anatomically correct labeling, but the butt is indeed from the shoulder of the pig and not from the rear. (Rumor has it that in Revolutionary New England, this cut was stored in specialty barrels called "butts." And the technique for cutting this roast was originated in Boston.) This large blade roast is available bone-in (and can weigh up to 8 pounds if so) or boneless. A bone-in roast can be impressive to present; a boneless roast lends itself to being shredded or sliced for sandwiches. Pork butt is often sold with a fat cap intact. Often we crosshatch it to encourage rendering and crisping, or so it can hold a salt or spice rub.

PHILLY CHEESESTEAKS

Serves: 4
Total Time: 1 hour

RECIPE OVERVIEW To get a real Philly cheesesteak, you have to go to Philadelphia. Or do you? In restaurants, these sandwiches are made using a meat slicer, a flat-top griddle, and pricey rib eye—all three of which are out of the question for sandwiches made at home. Luckily, there is a simple and economical way to mimic the thinly shaved slivers of rib eye. When partially frozen, skirt steak's thin profile and open-grained texture makes for easy slicing, and its flavor is near to rib eye but without the sticker shock. Melty, gooey American cheese is essential, but we take the nontraditional route of adding Parmesan for sharpness to balance out the mild American. Top these sandwiches with chopped pickled hot peppers, sautéed onions or bell peppers, sweet relish, or hot sauce.

- 2 pounds skirt steak, trimmed and cut with grain into 3-inch-wide strips
- 4 (8-inch) Italian sub rolls, split lengthwise
- 2 tablespoons vegetable oil, divided
- ½ teaspoon table salt
- ⅛ teaspoon pepper
- ¼ cup grated Parmesan cheese
- 8 slices white American cheese (8 ounces)

1. Place steak pieces on large plate or baking sheet and freeze until very firm, about 1 hour.

2. Meanwhile, adjust oven rack to middle position and heat oven to 400 degrees. Spread split rolls on baking sheet and toast until lightly browned, 5 to 10 minutes.

3. Using sharp knife, shave steak pieces as thin as possible against grain. Mound meat on cutting board and chop coarse with knife 10 to 20 times.

4. Heat 1 tablespoon oil in 12-inch nonstick skillet over high heat until just smoking. Add half of meat in even layer and cook without stirring until well browned on 1 side, 4 to 5 minutes. Stir and continue to cook until meat is no longer pink, 1 to 2 minutes. Transfer meat to colander set in large bowl. Wipe out skillet with paper towel. Repeat with remaining 1 tablespoon oil and remaining sliced meat.

5. Return now-empty skillet to medium heat. Drain excess moisture from meat. Return meat to skillet (discard any liquid in bowl) and add salt and pepper. Heat, stirring constantly, until meat is warmed through, 1 to 2 minutes. Reduce heat to low, sprinkle with Parmesan, and shingle slices of American cheese over meat. Allow cheeses to melt, about 2 minutes. Using heatproof spatula or wooden spoon, fold melted cheese into meat thoroughly. Divide mixture evenly among toasted rolls. Serve immediately.

KEYS TO SUCCESS

- **Freeze the steak:** So it's easy to slice super-thin
- **Minimize moisture so the beef can brown:** By cooking steak in batches and draining it in a colander

All About Skirt Steak

Long, thin, ribbon-like skirt steak might be a bit unassuming but it's a surprising star—juicy and full of beefy flavor. And when we say long we mean it: Skirt steaks are often rolled up for packaging because when they are unrolled, the steaks can be nearly 2 feet long. Although it can be cooked like flank steak, skirt steak has more connective tissue and is fattier and juicier. Look for it at well-stocked markets and butcher shops. Skirt steak comes from two different muscles, and some butchers might sell an inside cut and an outside cut. The more desirable outside skirt steak measures 3 to 4 inches wide and ½ to 1 inch thick. Avoid the inside skirt steak, which typically measures 5 to 7 inches wide and ¼ to ½ inch thick, as it is very chewy. Skirt steaks are most tender cooked to medium; because they have large muscle fibers, they take more force to bite through and therefore benefit from longer cooking so the muscle fibers can shrink in diameter.

COURSE

SPECIAL-OCCASION CENTERPIECES

DAN SOUZA

Whether you want an elevated take on a roast from the Everyday Roasts course or a steak (which you learned about in The Steakhouse) that's all dressed up, meat is a classic choice for a special event or holiday. On these occasions, you're more likely to splurge on your choice of cut—and more likely to feel some pressure for it to turn out just right. We'll release the pressure in this course, teaching you to turn out tender meat no matter the cut you're working with. And we'll use a lively sauce or flavored butter to give these cuts extra personality for that special evening.

DAN'S PRO TIP: *One simple way to make any great roast or steak (or chop) taste even better is to salt it twice. In addition to the salt that we apply to the outside of our roasts and steaks before cooking, I like to season the interior of the sliced meat with a crunchy flake sea salt just before serving.*

ROAST BEEF TENDERLOIN

Serves: 4
Total Time: 1¾ hours, plus 1 hour salting

RECIPE OVERVIEW A simple preparation lets center-cut beef tenderloin's supreme tenderness shine. Tying the roast at even intervals ensures even cooking and then lavishing it with softened butter boosts its mild flavor. To cook the neat piece of meat, turn to the reverse-sear method, first roasting the meat and then finishing it on the stovetop. A fairly low 300-degree oven minimizes the temperature differential between the exterior and interior, allowing for gentle, even cooking. This approach also dries out the meat's surface, so it sears very quickly in the skillet—and has no chance to overcook. Finally, slather the cooked roast with a shallot-herb compound butter (yes, more butter) as it rests, which instantly creates a rich sauce.

Beef
- 1 (2-pound) center-cut beef tenderloin roast, trimmed and tied at 1½-inch intervals
- 2 teaspoons kosher salt
- 1 teaspoon pepper
- 2 tablespoons unsalted butter, softened
- 1 tablespoon vegetable oil

Shallot and Parsley Butter
- 4 tablespoons unsalted butter, softened
- ½ shallot, minced
- 1 tablespoon minced fresh parsley
- 1 garlic clove, minced
- ¼ teaspoon table salt
- ¼ teaspoon pepper

1. FOR THE BEEF Sprinkle roast evenly with salt, cover loosely with plastic wrap, and let stand at room temperature for 1 hour. Adjust oven rack to middle position and heat oven to 300 degrees.

2. FOR THE SHALLOT AND PARSLEY BUTTER Meanwhile, combine all ingredients in bowl and let rest to blend flavors, about 10 minutes. Wrap in plastic wrap, roll into log, and refrigerate until serving.

3. Pat roast dry with paper towels. Sprinkle roast evenly with pepper and spread softened butter evenly over surface. Transfer roast to wire rack set in rimmed baking sheet. Roast until beef registers 120 to 125 degrees (for medium-rare), 40 to 55 minutes, flipping roast halfway through roasting.

4. Heat oil in 12-inch skillet over medium-high heat until just smoking. Brown roast well on all sides, about 8 minutes. Transfer roast to carving board and spread 2 tablespoons flavored butter evenly over top of roast; let rest for 30 minutes. Remove twine from roast. Slice meat ½ inch thick. Serve, passing remaining flavored butter separately.

PAN-SEARED STEAKS WITH BRANDY-PINK PEPPERCORN SAUCE

Serves: 4
Total Time: 35 minutes

RECIPE OVERVIEW On its own, a simple well-cooked steak, with an appealing browned crust and rosy interior, is immensely satisfying; pair it with a flavorful sauce and it's the perfect special occasion dinner: elegant and impressive yet quick and simple to execute. You can cook flavorful boneless strip steaks or rib eyes to medium-rare in just about 10 minutes in a hot skillet. Peppercorn sauce is a classic pairing with steak. The peppery bite sharpens the rich meat, but the combination is adaptable to a rainbow of peppercorns for different dimension. While the steaks rest, brown some shallot in the beef drippings and deglaze the pan with brandy. Next incorporate cracked pink peppercorns along with some chicken broth and reduce the sauce. Simmered with the broth, the peppercorns add waves of complexity and soften to a pleasantly chewy texture. Their fruity pepperiness both lightens and complements the rich brandy sauce.

- 2 (1-pound) boneless strip or rib-eye steaks, 1 to 1½ inches thick, trimmed and halved crosswise
- ½ teaspoon salt
- 1 tablespoon vegetable oil, plus extra as needed
- 1 large shallot, minced
- ¼ cup brandy
- ¾ cup chicken broth
- 2 tablespoons pink peppercorns, cracked
- 3 tablespoons unsalted butter, cut into 3 pieces and chilled
- ¼ teaspoon red wine vinegar

1. Pat steaks dry with paper towels and sprinkle with salt. Heat oil in 12-inch skillet over medium-high heat until just smoking. Place steaks in skillet and cook, without moving, until well browned on first side, about 4 minutes. Flip steaks and continue to cook, without moving, until well browned on second side and meat registers 120 to 125 degrees (for medium-rare), 3 to 7 minutes. Transfer steaks to plate, tent with aluminum foil, and let rest while preparing sauce.

2. Pour off all but 1 tablespoon fat from skillet. (If necessary, add extra oil to equal 1 tablespoon.) Add shallot and cook over medium heat until softened, 1 to 2 minutes. Off heat, carefully add brandy, scraping up any browned bits.

3. Stir in broth and peppercorns and return skillet to medium heat. Bring to simmer and cook until reduced to ⅓ cup, 4 to 6 minutes. Off heat, whisk in butter, 1 piece at a time, until melted and sauce is thickened and glossy. Whisk in vinegar and any accumulated steak juices. Season with salt to taste. Serve steaks with sauce.

BRISKET CARBONNADE

Serves: 6
Total Time: 4 hours, plus 1 hour resting

RECIPE OVERVIEW To combine two favorite dishes—braised brisket with onions and carbonnade à la flamande, the Belgian beef stew made with beer—start by browning a flat-cut beef brisket. Weighing the meat down with a Dutch oven ensures an evenly browned crust. Adding a raw pureed onion thickens and flavors the sauce. Letting the brisket rest in the juices for an hour ensures that it's moist. We like wheat beers, lagers, and pilsners in this recipe.

- 4 large onions
- 1 (3½-pound) beef brisket, flat cut, fat trimmed to ¼ inch
- 1 teaspoon table salt, divided
- ¾ teaspoon pepper
- 2 tablespoons vegetable oil, divided
- 1 tablespoon tomato paste
- 2 garlic cloves, minced
- 1 tablespoon all-purpose flour
- 1½ cups beer
- 4 sprigs fresh thyme
- 2 bay leaves
- 1 tablespoon packed brown sugar
- 1 tablespoon cider vinegar
- 1 teaspoon Dijon mustard

1. Adjust oven rack to lower-middle position and heat oven to 325 degrees. Halve and slice 3 onions ½ inch thick. Process remaining onion in food processor until pureed, about 10 seconds. Pat brisket dry with paper towels and sprinkle with ½ teaspoon salt and pepper. Heat 1 tablespoon oil in 12-inch skillet over medium-high heat until just smoking. Place brisket in skillet, weigh down with Dutch oven or cast-iron skillet, and cook until well browned, about 4 minutes per side. Transfer brisket to 13 by 9-inch baking dish.

2. Heat remaining 1 tablespoon oil in now-empty skillet over medium heat until shimmering. Add sliced onions and remaining ½ teaspoon salt and cook, stirring occasionally, until soft and golden brown, about 15 minutes. Stir in tomato paste and garlic and cook until fragrant, about 30 seconds. Stir in flour until onions are evenly coated and flour is lightly browned, about 2 minutes. Stir in pureed onion and cook until mixture has thickened, about 2 minutes. Stir in beer, thyme sprigs, bay leaves, sugar, and vinegar, scraping up any browned bits. Increase heat to medium-high and bring to boil.

3. Pour onion mixture over brisket and cover dish tightly with aluminum foil. Bake until brisket is tender and fork easily slips in and out of meat, about 3 hours. Let brisket rest in liquid, uncovered, for 1 hour.

4. Transfer brisket to carving board. Skim fat from top of sauce with large spoon and discard thyme sprigs and bay leaves. Whisk mustard into sauce and season with salt and pepper to taste. Slice meat against grain into ¼-inch-thick slices and return to dish with sauce. Serve.

Two Cuts of Brisket

Cut from the cow's breast section, a whole brisket is a boneless, coarse-grained cut composed of two smaller roasts: the flat (or first) cut and the point (or second) cut. The knobby point cut (A) overlaps the rectangular flat cut (B). The point cut has more marbling and fat, while the flat cut's meat is lean and topped with a thick fat cap. Our recipe calls for the widely available flat cut. Make sure that the fat cap isn't overtrimmed and is ⅓ to ½ inch thick.

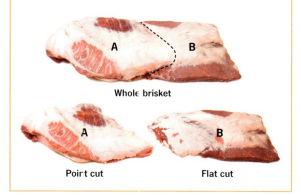

Whole brisket

Point cut — Flat cut

CORE TECHNIQUE
Trimming Brisket

TRIM Using a sharp knife, trim the brisket's fat cap to the thickness called for in the recipe (and no more).

Brisket Bath

Serving company? Conveniently, braised brisket actually benefits from being cooled and stored in the refrigerator overnight before reheating and serving. The coarse-grained meat continues to soak up sauce as it sits, for a juicier, more tender brisket. But the refrigerator rest also allows you to slice the meat without it falling apart or shredding. This is perfect if you're cooking brisket for a crowd: Making this dish a day ahead reduces the stress of timing in the kitchen, and the neatly sliced brisket creates a much more elegant spread on the serving platter.

ROAST BUTTERFLIED LEG OF LAMB WITH CORIANDER, CUMIN, AND MUSTARD SEEDS

Serves: 10 to 12
Total Time: 2½ hours, plus 1½ hours resting

RECIPE OVERVIEW Boneless butterflied leg of lamb is usually cooked in one of two ways. Because it comes rolled up and tied, you can treat it like a regular roast and just season and cook it as is. Or you can unroll it, fill it with seasoning, and roll and tie it again before cooking. But there's yet another way, and it is simultaneously simple and showstopping: You can unroll a boneless leg of lamb, pound it to even out the thickness, and cook the meat flat. Not only do you get the same flavor, the uniform thickness encourages faster, even cooking. For this roasting method, we start the meat in a very low oven and then finish with a blast under the broiler for juicy, tender roasted lamb with a burnished, crisp crust. Scoring the fat cap, rubbing the roast with salt, and letting it sit for an hour turns out well-seasoned, tender meat. A spice-infused oil spread beneath the slab of meat both seasons the lamb and provides the basis for a quick sauce; we toast the spices right on the sheet pan to bloom their flavor before adding the lamb for roasting. The 2 tablespoons of salt in step 1 is for a 6-pound leg. If using a larger leg (7 to 8 pounds), add an additional teaspoon of salt for every pound.

Lamb
- 1 (6- to 8-pound) boneless butterflied leg of lamb
- 2 tablespoons kosher salt
- ⅓ cup vegetable oil
- 3 shallots, sliced thin
- 4 garlic cloves, peeled and smashed
- 1 (1-inch) piece ginger, sliced into ½-inch-thick rounds and smashed
- 1 tablespoon coriander seeds
- 1 tablespoon cumin seeds
- 1 tablespoon mustard seeds
- 3 bay leaves
- 2 (2-inch) strips lemon zest

Sauce
- ⅓ cup chopped fresh mint
- ⅓ cup chopped fresh cilantro
- 1 shallot, minced
- 2 tablespoons lemon juice

1. **FOR THE LAMB** Place roast on cutting board with fat cap facing down. Using sharp knife, trim any pockets of fat and connective tissue from underside of roast. Flip roast over, trim fat cap to between ⅛ and ¼ inch thick, and pound to even 1-inch thickness. Using sharp knife, cut slits ½ inch apart in crosshatch pattern in fat cap of roast, being careful not to cut into meat. Rub salt over entire roast and into slits. Let sit, uncovered, at room temperature for 1 hour.

2. Meanwhile, adjust oven racks to upper-middle and lower-middle positions and heat oven to 250 degrees. Stir oil, shallots, garlic, ginger, coriander seeds, cumin seeds, mustard seeds, bay leaves, and lemon zest together in rimmed baking sheet and bake on lower rack until spices are softened and fragrant and shallots and garlic turn golden, about 1 hour. Remove sheet from oven and discard bay leaves.

3. Thoroughly pat roast dry with paper towels and transfer, fat side up, to sheet (directly on top of spices). Roast on lower rack until lamb registers 120 degrees, 30 to 40 minutes. Remove sheet from oven and heat broiler. Broil roast on upper rack until surface is well browned and charred in spots and lamb registers 125 degrees (for medium-rare), 3 to 8 minutes.

4. Remove sheet from oven and transfer roast to carving board (some spices will cling to roast); let rest for 20 minutes.

5. **FOR THE SAUCE** Meanwhile, carefully pour pan juices through fine-mesh strainer into medium bowl, pressing on solids to extract as much liquid as possible; discard solids. Stir in mint, cilantro, shallot, and lemon juice. Add any accumulated lamb juices to sauce and season with salt and pepper to taste.

6. With long side facing you, slice roast with grain into 3 equal pieces. Turn each piece and slice against grain ¼ inch thick. Serve with sauce. (Briefly warm sauce in microwave if it has cooled and thickened.)

KEYS TO SUCCESS

- **Cut a crosshatch:** Cutting a crosshatch pattern into the fat cap helps the salt and spices penetrate.
- **Toast the spices:** Toasting the spices on the baking sheet means you can simply place the roast atop the toasted spices before cooking.
- **Simplify the slicing:** A butterflied roast makes it easy to slice the lamb—no advanced carving required.

CORE TECHNIQUE
Carving Butterflied Leg of Lamb

WITH GRAIN
Position the meat so that the long side is facing you. Slice the lamb with the grain into 3 equal pieces.

AGAINST GRAIN
Turn each piece to cut against the grain into ¼-inch-thick slices.

CHAPTER 9

POULTRY

COURSES

410 CHICKEN CUTLETS

414 GREAT ROAST CHICKEN

420 LEARN YOUR WAY AROUND A CHICKEN

426 STEWED AND BRAISED

430 CHICKEN AND RICE

434 CHICKEN STIR-FRIES

438 SIMPLE FRIED CHICKEN

442 CHICKEN ON THE GRILL

448 YOUR FIRST TURKEY

MORE TO EXPLORE

418 PAN SAUCES

POULTRY BASICS

BUYING CHICKEN (AND TURKEY)

Chicken is high in protein, endlessly versatile, and relatively inexpensive, so it's no wonder that it's America's favorite type of meat. There are a multitude of poultry choices at the supermarket, and they vary in cost. Here's what we think is helpful to know when buying chicken and turkey.

Label Language

USDA Organic isn't all hype; it is a tightly regulated term: The birds must eat organic feed that doesn't contain animal by-products, be raised without antibiotics, and have access to the outdoors (how much access, however, isn't specified). Similar-sounding terms, including Raised Without Antibiotics, Natural and All-Natural, Hormone-Free (empty reassurance, since the U.S. Department of Agriculture, or USDA, does not allow the use of hormones or steroids in poultry production), and Vegetarian Fed and Vegetarian Diet, can be misleading and are often unregulated or not strictly enforced.

Buy a Natural Bird

How the chicken was processed makes a big difference in its flavor and texture once cooked. Simply put, buy a natural bird—one that has no artificial ingredients added to the raw meat. We prefer to buy air-chilled rather than water-chilled birds. Water chilling (soaking the bird in a chlorinated bath after slaughtering) causes the bird to absorb water. The water gain must be shown on the label, so if you see "contains up to 4% retained water," you know the bird was water-chilled. Besides the fact that you are paying for the water, the water dilutes the chicken flavor and makes it hard to crisp up the skin during cooking. Air-chilled chicken is typically more tender, likely because the slower temperature drop gives enzymes in the meat more time to tenderize muscle tissue.

Avoid chickens that are "enhanced" (injected with broth and flavoring), because they will have a spongy texture. Also avoid turkeys that are "pre-basted" (injected with a salt-based solution to increase perceived juiciness), because they often taste weak and washed out and are mushy and waterlogged. Look for an ingredient label—if the turkey has been injected, you should see a list of ingredients. We found kosher turkeys to be mild in flavor and sometimes spongy. We prefer to salt or brine untreated turkeys because they have a clean flavor and are juicy without being mushy. Also, untreated turkeys are slightly higher in fat than injected turkeys, which means more flavor.

Kosher Chicken and Turkey

Koshering is similar to brining; it involves coating the chicken or turkey with salt to draw out impurities and then rinsing it multiple times during processing. Buying a kosher bird allows you to skip brining. Kosher birds are also all-natural and contain no hormones or antibiotics.

Packaged Parts

The USDA doesn't regulate the weight of chicken parts, so a package of pieces may vary in weight. In packages of split breasts and leg quarters, we found that the largest pieces could weigh twice as much as the smallest. Buying parts from the meat counter lets you select similar-size pieces. Or consider buying a whole chicken and butchering it yourself (see page 424) to ensure that the parts are the same size.

STORING POULTRY

In the Refrigerator

It's important to refrigerate poultry promptly after bringing it home and to keep it refrigerated until just before cooking. Bacteria thrive between 40 and 140 degrees. Keep your chicken and turkey in the coldest part of your refrigerator (see page 34), where the temperature should be between 32 and 36 degrees. Place chicken packages on a plate or rimmed baking sheet to keep any condensation from dripping down onto other items. Raw poultry will keep for two days; leftover cooked poultry should be promptly refrigerated and consumed within three days.

In the Freezer and Out Again

We don't recommend freezing chicken in its supermarket packaging (unless it is vacuum-sealed), because most packaging has air gaps that cause freezer burn (and poultry is especially prone to freezer burn). Instead, wrap each chicken part, including whole birds, tightly in plastic wrap and place the parts in a zipper-lock freezer bag; press out the air; and freeze the parts in a single layer. You can keep poultry frozen for several months, but freezer burn increases with storage time, and after two months the flavor and texture will suffer. Never thaw frozen poultry on the counter; this puts it at risk of growing bacteria. Thaw it in its packaging in the refrigerator (on a plate to catch any juices). Count on 24 hours of defrosting in the refrigerator for every 4 pounds of bird, so a day for a whole chicken and three to four days to defrost a turkey. And don't refreeze poultry: Its texture becomes significantly tougher.

ANATOMY OF A CHICKEN

Structure

Chicken and turkey have the same basic structure as other meats. We eat muscles, which consist of muscle fibers, fat, and connective tissue. The location and function of those muscles affects the amounts of fat and connective tissue. In poultry, the differences between various "cuts" are especially dramatic—white meat and dark meat look and taste quite different, and they cook differently, too.

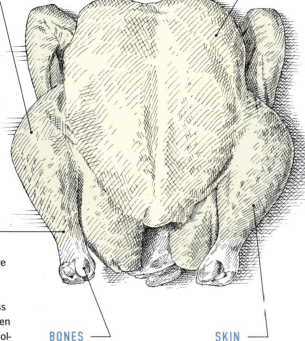

DARK MEAT

The thighs and legs consist primarily of dark muscle cells, which make up what are known as "slow-twitch" fibers and are necessary for long, continuous activity. Dark muscle cells rely on oxygen in the blood to convert stored fat into energy. This metabolic process requires the help of several agents, including the protein myoglobin, a red pigment that stores oxygen in muscle cells.

COLLAGEN

All animal tissue contains some collagen, the sheets of connective tissue that hold muscle fibers together. However, the collagen level in white meat chicken is less than 2 percent. Dark meat chicken contains as much as 8 percent collagen, which makes the legs and thighs a much better choice for slow-cooking methods, such as braising, which convert the tough collagen into tender gelatin.

WHITE MEAT

The breast consists primarily of white muscle cells, which make up what are known as "fast-twitch" fibers and are necessary for quick bursts of energy. White muscle cells rely on carbohydrates stored in the muscle for energy and do not need the myoglobin in the blood to supply the necessary oxygen. While this energy can be generated quickly, it cannot be sustained, and therefore white meat cells are abundant only in muscles that see little or no activity. Birds that rarely fly (such as chickens or turkeys) have an especially high proportion of white cells in their breast muscles; in contrast, ducks and birds that fly long distances have relatively few white cells in their breast muscles—thus the darker color of their breast meat.

BONES

Bones insulate the meat and thus slow down the rate of cooking. They also provide flavor.

SKIN

Skin is the primary source of fat in most birds. Additional fat lies just under the skin—it is visible as yellow clumps, especially near the neck and tail end of the bird. The dark meat also contains intramuscular fat—generally more than twice as much as the white meat.

SAFELY HANDLING RAW POULTRY

Season Safely

Though bacteria can't live for more than a few minutes in direct contact with salt (which dehydrates bacteria, leading to cell death), it can live on the edges of a box or shaker. To avoid contamination, premeasure your salt and pepper and set it aside so that you don't need to reach into a box or grab a grinder with dirty hands.

Don't Rinse

Avoid rinsing raw poultry. Rinsing will not remove or kill much bacteria, and splashing water around is likely to spread bacteria around the sink (and perhaps onto nearby foods, such as lettuce sitting on the counter). And our tests failed to demonstrate any flavor benefit to rinsing poultry before cooking.

Wash Everything Else

Make sure to wash your hands, knives, cutting boards, and counters (and anything else that has come into contact with the raw bird, its juices, or your hands) with hot, soapy water. In lab tests, we found that hot, soapy water; a bleach solution; and undiluted vinegar were equally effective at reducing bacteria on non-dishwasher-safe cutting boards.

COURSE
CHICKEN CUTLETS

ANNIE PETITO

Every weeknight cooking repertoire needs a fast and delicious chicken cutlet recipe (or two or three). Cutlets—chicken breasts cut and/or pounded to form thin, quick-cooking pieces—make a versatile foundation for the rest of the meal, perfect for pairing with your favorite sides, and you can use the savory drippings to make a superquick pan sauce. In this course we teach you the basic technique, walk you through breading and pan frying, and show you how to prepare a 1-hour chicken Parm.

ANNIE'S PRO TIP: *Chicken cutlets are so versatile. I like to make a big batch, freeze them, and then have them on hand for sandwiches, salads, wraps, grain bowls, basically anything!*

SIMPLE SAUTÉED CHICKEN CUTLETS
Serves: 4
Total Time: 25 minutes

RECIPE OVERVIEW Ultrathin chicken cutlets are simple and quick to prepare. They are delicious on their own or paired with a flavorful pan sauce. One way to achieve evenly sized cutlets is to take the two-cutlet approach (see page 411): Halve chicken breasts horizontally before pounding them to an even thickness. Halving and pounding the breasts ensures that they cook at the same rate and turn out tender and moist. Browning the cutlets on only one side gives them time to develop a nice crust (and some fond, the browned bits in the skillet) without overcooking. As soon as the cutlets come out of the skillet, you can set to work on turning the fond into a pan sauce (pages 418–419) if desired. Simply tent the cutlets (on a heatproof plate) with aluminum foil and keep them warm in a 200-degree oven. Add any juices that accumulate to the pan sauce before serving. To make slicing the chicken easier, freeze it for 15 minutes.

- 4 (6- to 8-ounce) boneless, skinless chicken breasts, trimmed
- ¾ teaspoon table salt
- ½ teaspoon pepper
- 2 tablespoons vegetable oil, divided

1. Starting at thick end, cut each chicken breast in half horizontally, then cover chicken halves with plastic wrap and pound to uniform ¼-inch thickness. Sprinkle both sides of each cutlet with salt and pepper.

2. Heat 1 tablespoon oil in 12-inch skillet over medium-high heat until just smoking. Place 4 cutlets in skillet and cook, without moving them, until browned, about 2 minutes. Using spatula, flip cutlets and continue to cook until second side is opaque, 15 to 20 seconds. Transfer to large plate. Add remaining 1 tablespoon oil to now-empty skillet and repeat with remaining cutlets. Serve.

> **KEYS TO SUCCESS**
> - **Freeze briefly:** Firms up the chicken and makes it easier to slice into cutlets
> - **Pound the cutlets to the same thickness using a meat pounder or small skillet:** Ensures that the cutlets cook evenly
> - **Brown on one side:** Keeps the thin, quick-cooking cutlets juicy

CORE TECHNIQUE
Cutting Chicken into Cutlets

TWO CUTLETS
Use your hand to hold the breast in place, keeping your fingers parallel to the breast. Using a sharp chef's knife, start at the thicker end and slice the breast in half horizontally.

THREE CUTLETS
To yield three cutlets, cut the chicken breast in half crosswise. Hold the thicker piece of the breast in place and slice it in half horizontally.

CRISPY PAN-FRIED CHICKEN CUTLETS
Serves: 4 to 6
Total Time: 30 minutes

RECIPE OVERVIEW Chicken cutlets coated in bread crumbs and pan-fried are quick to cook and sure to please a crowd. The usual process for breading chicken cutlets is to dip them in flour, blot off the flour, dip them in egg, and finally dip them in bread crumbs. Ditching the flour (and the blotting) results in a more delicate crust. Japanese panko bread crumbs are drier and larger than homemade. Whisking salt right into the egg means you can skip seasoning each cutlet separately, and since there is no flour in the mix, there is no need to pat the chicken dry before starting. Letting the cutlets rest on a wire rack lined with paper towels after frying ensures that they are not greasy and retain their crunch. If you are working with 8-ounce breasts, the skillet will initially be crowded; the cutlets will shrink slightly as they cook. The first batch of cutlets can be kept warm in a 200-degree oven while you cook the second batch. The cutlets can be served with a simple spritz of lemon juice or a flavorful no-cook sauce such as Romesco or Salsa Verde (pages 353–354). They're also great in a sandwich or served over a green salad.

- 2 cups panko bread crumbs
- 2 large eggs
- 1 teaspoon table salt
- 4 (6- to 8-ounce) boneless, skinless chicken breasts, trimmed
- ½ cup vegetable oil, divided

1. Place panko in large zipper-lock bag and lightly crush with rolling pin. Transfer to shallow dish. Whisk eggs and salt in second shallow dish until well combined.

SCIENCE LESSON
Test Oil Before Shallow-Frying

Shimmering can be an indicator that oil is hot enough to start sautéing, but shimmering can be deceptive when the oil is deep enough for shallow frying (that is, when it fully coats the pan bottom and can be swirled). The oil in contact with the pan bottom, where the heat is most intense, will shimmer before the oil on top. So how can you know the oil is heated from top to bottom? Add a pinch of panko. Once the crumbs turn brown, it's time to fry.

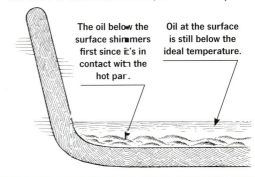

The oil below the surface shimmers first since it's in contact with the hot pan.

Oil at the surface is still below the ideal temperature.

2. Starting at thick end, cut each chicken breast in half horizontally. Pound cutlets to uniform ¼-inch thickness. Working with 1 cutlet at a time, dredge cutlets in egg mixture, allowing excess to drip off, then coat all sides with panko, pressing gently so crumbs adhere. Transfer cutlets to rimmed baking sheet and let sit for 5 minutes.

3. Set wire rack in second rimmed baking sheet and line rack with paper towels. Heat ¼ cup oil in 12-inch skillet over medium-high heat until shimmering. Place 4 cutlets in skillet and cook until deep golden brown on both sides, turning once, 4 to 6 minutes. Drain cutlets briefly on paper towels, then transfer to prepared rack and season with salt to taste. Wipe skillet clean with paper towels. Repeat with remaining ¼ cup oil and remaining 4 cutlets. Serve immediately.

Variations

CRISPY PAN-FRIED CHICKEN MILANESE CUTLETS

Stir ¼ cup finely grated Parmesan cheese into panko.

CRISPY PAN-FRIED CHICKEN CUTLETS WITH GARLIC AND OREGANO

Whisk 3 tablespoons minced fresh oregano and 8 minced garlic cloves into eggs.

CRISPY PAN-FRIED DEVILED CHICKEN CUTLETS

Sprinkle each chicken cutlet with generous pinch of cayenne pepper. Whisk 3 tablespoons Dijon mustard, 1 tablespoon Worcestershire sauce, and 2 teaspoons minced fresh thyme into eggs.

CHICKEN PICCATA

Serves: 4 to 6
Total Time: 1 hour

RECIPE OVERVIEW To make chicken piccata, the dish of thin, pan-seared cutlets bathed in a rich lemon-butter pan sauce, first prepare your own chicken cutlets using the three-cutlet approach (see page 411): Cut each boneless chicken breast in half crosswise, then halve the thicker portion horizontally to make three similar-size pieces that require only minimal pounding to become cutlets. Salting the cutlets briefly boosts their ability to retain moisture, and lightly coating them in flour helps with browning. Sear the cutlets quickly on both sides and set them aside while making the sauce. Including both lemon juice and lemon slices adds complexity and textural appeal. Returning the cutlets to the pan to cook through and to wash any excess starch into the sauce eliminates a gummy coating. A hearty amount of briny capers and a few tablespoons of butter finish the sauce, while a sprinkling of parsley adds freshness.

4	(6- to 8-ounce) boneless, skinless chicken breasts, trimmed
2	teaspoons kosher salt
½	teaspoon pepper
2	large lemons
¾	cup all-purpose flour
¼	cup plus 1 teaspoon vegetable oil, divided
1	shallot, minced
1	garlic clove, minced
1	cup chicken broth
3	tablespoons unsalted butter, cut into 6 pieces
2	tablespoons capers, drained
1	tablespoon minced fresh parsley

1. Starting at thick end, cut each chicken breast in half crosswise, then cut thick half in half again horizontally, creating 3 cutlets of similar thickness. Pound cutlets to uniform ½-inch thickness. Place cutlets in bowl and toss with salt and pepper. Set aside and let sit for 15 minutes.

2. Halve 1 lemon lengthwise. Trim ends from 1 half, halve lengthwise again, then slice crosswise ¼ inch thick and set aside. Juice remaining half and whole lemon and set aside 3 tablespoons juice.

3. Spread flour in shallow dish. Working with 1 cutlet at a time, dredge cutlets in flour, shaking gently to remove excess. Place on wire rack set in rimmed baking sheet. Heat 2 tablespoons oil in 12-inch skillet over medium-high heat until smoking. Place 6 cutlets in skillet; reduce heat to medium; and cook until golden brown on 1 side, 2 to 3 minutes. Flip and cook until golden brown on second side, 2 to 3 minutes. Return cutlets to wire rack. Repeat with 2 tablespoons oil and remaining 6 cutlets.

4. Add remaining 1 teaspoon oil and shallot to skillet and cook until softened, 1 minute. Add garlic and cook until fragrant, 30 seconds. Add broth, reserved lemon juice, and reserved lemon slices and bring to simmer, scraping up any browned bits.

5. Add cutlets to sauce and simmer for 4 minutes, flipping halfway through simmering. Transfer cutlets to platter. Sauce should be thickened to consistency of heavy cream; if not, simmer 1 minute longer. Off heat, whisk in butter. Stir in capers and parsley. Season with salt and pepper to taste. Spoon sauce over chicken and serve.

> ### KEYS TO SUCCESS
> - **Split each chicken breast into three cutlets:** Makes it easy to pound the chicken to similar-shaped pieces
> - **Salt the chicken:** Seasons the meat and helps it stay moist
> - **Dredge in flour:** Creates a golden crust
> - **Use the whole lemon:** Creates a complex, deeply lemony sauce

BEST CHICKEN PARMESAN

Serves: 4
Total Time: 1 hour

RECIPE OVERVIEW Traditional chicken Parmesan is an Italian American classic featuring juicy, crisp-coated cutlets that keep their crunch once sauced. To start, salt the cutlets for 20 minutes to ensure that the meat stays moist. For a tender (not rubbery) cheese topping, mix the usual shredded mozzarella with creamy fontina. And for cutlets with an exterior that stays crunchy, take a twofold approach. Replace more than half of the starchy (and consequently sog-prone) bread crumbs with grated Parmesan cheese, and place the cheese mixture directly on the fried cutlets so that it forms a waterproof layer between the crust and the sauce. Tender chicken; crispy exterior; and a cheesy, saucy topping—it's a classic for a reason.

- 2 (6- to 8-ounce) boneless, skinless chicken breasts, trimmed
- 1 teaspoon kosher salt, divided
- 2 ounces whole-milk mozzarella cheese, shredded (½ cup)
- 2 ounces fontina cheese, shredded (½ cup)
- 1 large egg
- 1 tablespoon all-purpose flour
- 1½ ounces Parmesan cheese, grated (¾ cup)
- ½ cup panko bread crumbs
- ½ teaspoon garlic powder
- ¼ teaspoon dried oregano
- ¼ teaspoon pepper
- ⅓ cup vegetable oil
- 1 cup Quick Tomato Sauce (recipe follows), warmed
- ¼ cup torn fresh basil

1. Starting at thick end, cut each chicken breast in half horizontally. Pound cutlets to uniform ½-inch thickness. Pat chicken dry with paper towels. Sprinkle each side of each cutlet with ⅛ teaspoon salt and let stand at room temperature for 20 minutes. Combine mozzarella and fontina in bowl; set aside.

2. Adjust oven rack 4 inches from broiler element and heat broiler. Whisk egg and flour in shallow dish until smooth. Combine Parmesan, panko, garlic powder, oregano, and pepper in second shallow dish. Pat cutlets dry with paper towels. Working with 1 cutlet at a time, dredge cutlets in egg mixture, allowing excess to drip off. Coat all sides in Parmesan mixture, pressing gently so crumbs adhere. Transfer cutlets to rimmed baking sheet and let sit for 5 minutes.

3. Heat oil in 10-inch nonstick skillet over medium-high heat until shimmering. Cook 2 cutlets until crispy and golden brown on both sides, 3 to 4 minutes. Transfer cutlets to paper towel–lined plate and repeat with remaining cutlets. (Cooked chicken can be frozen for up to 1 month. To reheat, place frozen cutlets on wire rack set in rimmed baking sheet; top with cheese; and bake in 400-degree oven on middle rack until crisp and hot throughout, 20 to 30 minutes, then continue with step 5.)

4. Place cutlets on rimmed baking sheet and sprinkle cheese mixture evenly over cutlets, covering as much surface area as possible. Broil until cheese is melted and beginning to brown, 2 to 4 minutes.

5. Transfer chicken to platter and top each cutlet with 2 tablespoons sauce. Sprinkle with basil and serve immediately, passing remaining sauce separately.

QUICK TOMATO SAUCE
Makes: about 2 cups
Total Time: 30 minutes

This recipe makes enough sauce to top four chicken cutlets as well as four servings of pasta. High-quality canned tomatoes will make a big difference in this sauce.

- 2 tablespoons extra-virgin olive oil, divided
- 2 garlic cloves, minced
- ¾ teaspoon table salt
- ¼ teaspoon dried oregano
  Pinch red pepper flakes
- 1 (28-ounce) can crushed tomatoes
- ¼ teaspoon sugar
- 2 tablespoons chopped fresh basil

Heat 1 tablespoon oil in medium saucepan over medium heat until just shimmering. Add garlic, salt, oregano, and pepper flakes; cook, stirring occasionally, until fragrant, about 30 seconds. Stir in tomatoes and sugar; increase heat to high and bring to simmer. Reduce heat to medium-low and simmer until thickened, about 20 minutes. Off heat, stir in basil and remaining 1 tablespoon oil; season with salt and pepper to taste. (Sauce can be refrigerated for up to 3 days or frozen for up to 1 month. If frozen, thaw completely in refrigerator.)

COURSE

GREAT ROAST CHICKEN

BRYAN ROOF

Crispy golden skin, flavorful drippings, and a hands-off method: Roast chicken can't be beat when it comes to a simple but crowd-pleasing dinner. This course walks you through what you need to know to produce the perfect roast chicken, from bone-in breasts to a whole bird. You'll learn how to get the white and dark meat to cook at the same rate; reliably achieve crisp, browned skin; and carve your bird with confidence. For the ultimate weeknight convenience, there's a no-fuss roast chicken and vegetable sheet-pan dinner. Or, for some midweek excitement, try exquisitely spiced Peruvian-inspired roast chicken.

BRYAN'S PRO TIP: *Let it rest. Resting your meat after cooking is one of the most important parts of the cooking process. Don't ignore it.*

PAN-ROASTED CHICKEN BREASTS

Serves: 4
Total Time: 1¼ hours

RECIPE OVERVIEW Roasting bone-in chicken breasts is the quickest way to enjoy roast chicken without cooking a whole bird. This recipe utilizes pan roasting, a technique in which food is browned in a skillet on the stovetop and then finished in the oven. A short brine—a soak in heavily salted water—seasons the chicken and guards against its drying out in a very hot (450-degree) oven, which helps to crisp the skin. The combination of searing and high-heat roasting leaves plenty of caramelized drippings, or fond, in the skillet to use as the base for a number of quick and flavorful pan sauces (pages 418–419), if desired.

- ½ cup table salt for brining
- 4 (10- to 12-ounce) bone-in split chicken breasts, trimmed
- ¼ teaspoon pepper
- 1 teaspoon vegetable oil

1. Dissolve salt in 2 quarts cold water in large container. Submerge chicken in brine, cover, and refrigerate for 30 minutes. Remove chicken from brine and pat dry with paper towels. Sprinkle with pepper.

2. Adjust oven rack to lowest position and heat oven to 450 degrees.

3. Heat oil in 12-inch ovenproof skillet over medium-high heat until beginning to smoke; swirl skillet to coat with oil. Brown chicken skin side down until deep golden, about 5 minutes; flip chicken pieces and brown until golden on second side, about 3 minutes longer. Turn chicken skin side down and place skillet in oven. Roast until breast registers 160 degrees, 15 to 18 minutes. Transfer chicken to platter and let rest. (If not making a pan sauce, let chicken rest 5 minutes before serving.)

> ### KEYS TO SUCCESS
> - **Use a quick brine:** Helps the chicken stay juicy and tender during cooking
> - **Start on the stovetop, then finish in the oven:** Quickly develops flavor and fond

CHICKEN LEG QUARTERS WITH CAULIFLOWER AND SHALLOTS

Serves: 4
Total Time: 1 hour

RECIPE OVERVIEW Chicken leg quarters take to roasting beautifully, growing tender as they cook while their skin crisps up. This sheet-pan dinner pairs them with cauliflower, which also shines when roasted. Deeply slashing the chicken helps the seasonings to penetrate the meat and the fat to render for crispier skin. Arranging the chicken around the pan's edges exposes it to the oven's heat and protects the cauliflower from drying out; the chicken's juices help soften the cauliflower. Toward the end of cooking, the broiler imparts pleasant charring.

- 1 head cauliflower (2 pounds), cored and cut through stem into 8 wedges
- 6 shallots, peeled and halved
- ¼ cup extra-virgin olive oil, divided
- 2 tablespoons chopped fresh sage or 2 teaspoons dried, divided
- 1 teaspoon table salt, divided
- 1 teaspoon pepper, divided
- 4 (10-ounce) chicken leg quarters, trimmed
- 2 garlic cloves, minced
- 1 teaspoon grated lemon zest, plus lemon wedges for serving
- 8 ounces grape tomatoes
- 1 tablespoon chopped fresh parsley

1. Adjust 1 oven rack to lower-middle position and second rack 6 inches from broiler element. Heat oven to 475 degrees. Gently toss cauliflower and shallots with 2 tablespoons oil, 1 tablespoon sage, ½ teaspoon salt, and ½ teaspoon pepper on rimmed baking sheet. Arrange cauliflower pieces cut side down in single layer in center of sheet.

2. Pat chicken dry with paper towels. Make 4 diagonal slashes through skin and meat of each leg quarter with sharp knife (each slash should reach bone). Sprinkle chicken with remaining ½ teaspoon salt and remaining ½ teaspoon pepper. Place each piece of chicken skin side up in 1 corner of sheet; rest chicken directly on sheet, not on vegetables.

3. Whisk garlic, lemon zest, remaining 2 tablespoons oil, and remaining 1 tablespoon sage together in bowl. Brush skin side of chicken with seasoned oil mixture. Transfer sheet to lower rack and roast until chicken registers 175 degrees, cauliflower is browned, and shallots are tender, 25 to 30 minutes, rotating sheet halfway through roasting.

4. Remove sheet from oven and heat broiler. Scatter tomatoes over vegetables. Place sheet on upper rack and broil until chicken skin is browned and crisp and tomatoes have begun to wilt, 3 to 5 minutes.

5. Remove sheet from oven and let rest for 5 minutes. Sprinkle with parsley and serve with lemon wedges.

WEEKNIGHT ROAST CHICKEN

Serves: 4
Total Time: 1½ hours

RECIPE OVERVIEW This recipe is a hands-off, absolutely foolproof way to roast a chicken. You start by simply preheating a skillet in the oven. Since dark meat needs longer to cook, direct contact with the superhot pan jump-starts the thighs' cooking and ensures that the white breast meat and dark thigh meat finish cooking at the same time. Rub the chicken all over with olive oil and season simply with salt and pepper. Roasting the chicken in a 450-degree oven and then turning off the oven allows the more delicate white meat to remain moist and tender as the bird finishes cooking in the oven's residual heat. We prefer to use a 3½- to 4-pound chicken for this recipe. If roasting a larger bird, increase the time when the oven is on in step 2 to 35 to 40 minutes. Reserve 1 tablespoon of fat if you want to make a pan sauce (pages 418–419); Tarragon-Lemon Pan Sauce pairs nicely with this recipe.

- 1½ teaspoons table salt
- ½ teaspoon pepper
- 1 (3½- to 4-pound) whole chicken, giblets discarded
- 1 tablespoon extra-virgin olive oil

1. Adjust oven rack to middle position, place 12-inch ovensafe skillet on rack, and heat oven to 450 degrees. Combine salt and pepper in bowl. Pat chicken dry with paper towels. Rub entire surface with oil. Sprinkle evenly all over with salt mixture and rub in mixture with your hands to coat evenly. Tie legs together with twine and tuck wingtips behind back.

2. Transfer chicken, breast side up, to preheated skillet in oven. Roast chicken until breast registers 120 degrees and thighs register 135 degrees, 25 to 35 minutes. Turn off oven and leave chicken in oven until breast registers 160 degrees and thighs register 175 degrees, 25 to 35 minutes.

3. Transfer chicken to carving board and let rest, uncovered, for 20 minutes. Carve chicken and serve with pan sauce, if using.

KEYS TO SUCCESS

- **Preheat the skillet:** Helps the thighs, which take longer, to start cooking right away
- **Tie the legs together and tuck the wingtips:** Helps keep them from drying out
- **Turn off the oven and let carryover cooking do the work:** Produces a juicy chicken

PERUVIAN ROAST CHICKEN WITH GARLIC AND LIME

Serves: 4
Total Time: 2 hours, plus 6 hours marinating

RECIPE OVERVIEW The Peruvian dish pollo a la brasa is deeply bronzed from its slow rotation in a wood-fired oven and impressively seasoned with garlic; spices; lime juice; chiles; and a paste made with huacatay, or black mint. To replicate this dish for the home kitchen, you can use standard spearmint along with a bit of dried oregano as a substitute for the huacatay, plus smoked paprika to add a bit of rotisserie flavor. Combine kosher salt with an herb and spice paste and rub it under the skin where it seasons the meat most effectively. Refrigerating the chicken for at least 6 hours lets the salt do its work. A vertical roaster and a two-pronged cooking process fills in for the rotisserie, allowing for plenty of hot-air circulation around the chicken, which leads to perfectly cooked meat and crisp skin. If you don't have a vertical poultry roaster, substitute a 12-ounce can of beer. Open the beer and pour out (or drink) about half of the liquid. Spray the can lightly with nonstick cooking spray and proceed with the recipe. If the top of the chicken is becoming too dark during roasting in step 3, place a 7-inch square piece of foil over the neck and wingtips. You can substitute 1 tablespoon of minced serrano chile for the habanero here. Wear gloves when working with hot chiles. Chipotle Mayonnaise (page 31) will take this dish over the top.

- 3 tablespoons extra-virgin olive oil
- ¼ cup lightly packed fresh mint leaves
- 2 tablespoons kosher salt
- 6 garlic cloves, chopped coarse
- 1 tablespoon ground black pepper
- 1 tablespoon ground cumin
- 1 tablespoon sugar
- 2 teaspoons smoked paprika
- 2 teaspoons dried oregano
- 2 teaspoons grated lime zest plus ¼ cup juice (2 limes)
- 1 teaspoon minced habanero chile
- 1 (3½- to 4-pound) whole chicken, giblets discarded

1. Process oil, mint, salt, garlic, pepper, cumin, sugar, paprika, oregano, lime zest and juice, and habanero in blender until smooth paste forms, 10 to 20 seconds. Using your fingers or handle of wooden spoon, carefully loosen skin over thighs and breast and remove any excess fat. Rub half of paste beneath skin of chicken. Spread entire exterior surface of chicken with remaining paste. Tuck wingtips underneath chicken. Place chicken in gallon-size zipper-lock bag and refrigerate for at least 6 hours or up to 24 hours.

2. Adjust oven rack to lowest position and heat oven to 325 degrees. Place vertical roaster or beer can on rimmed baking sheet. Slide chicken onto vertical roaster so chicken stands upright and breast is perpendicular to bottom of pan. Roast until skin just begins to turn golden and breast registers 140 degrees, 45 to 55 minutes. Carefully remove chicken and sheet from oven and increase oven temperature to 500 degrees.

3. When oven is heated to 500 degrees, place 1 cup water in bottom of sheet and return sheet to oven. Roast until entire skin is browned and crisp, breast registers 160 degrees, and thighs register 175 degrees, about 20 minutes (replenish water as necessary to keep sheet from smoking), rotating bird 180 degrees halfway through cooking.

4. Carefully remove chicken from oven and let rest, still on vertical roaster, for 20 minutes. Using dish towel, carefully lift chicken off vertical roaster and onto carving board. Carve chicken and serve.

KEYS TO SUCCESS

- **Apply the spice paste both underneath and over the skin:** Seasons the chicken thoroughly, from skin to bone
- **Refrigerate for 6 hours:** Ensures deep flavor
- **Roast vertically:** Allows the fat to drip out of the bird
- **Add water to baking sheet:** Keeps pan from smoking
- **Cook at two heat levels:** Rest chicken at room temperature when partially done then crank up the oven and finish roasting.

RESOURCES FOR WHOLE ROAST CHICKEN

CARVING A WHOLE CHICKEN (OR TURKEY)

EXPOSE LEG JOINT
Remove any kitchen twine. Using a chef's knife, make a cut through the skin to expose where the thigh meets the breast.

SEPARATE JOINT TO REMOVE LEG QUARTER
Pull the leg quarter away from the carcass, gently pull the leg out to the side, and push up on the joint. Cut through the joint to remove the leg quarter from the carcass.

SEPARATE DRUMSTICK AND THIGH
Cut through the joint that connects the drumstick to the thigh. Repeat steps 1 through 3 on chicken's other side.

REMOVE BREAST MEAT
Cut down along the side of the breastbone, pulling the breast meat away from the breastbone as you cut.

SLICE BREAST MEAT
Remove the wing from the breast by cutting through the wing joint. Slice the breast crosswise. Repeat with the other side.

POULTRY DONENESS TEMPERATURES

Do not guess at doneness: Use a thermometer.

160° — Breasts

175° — Thighs and drumsticks

TEMP WHOLE BIRD
Because breast meat cooks faster than thigh meat, you should take the temperature of both when cooking poultry.

For breast meat Insert the thermometer from the neck end, holding the thermometer parallel to the bird. It should register 160 degrees.

For thigh meat Insert the thermometer at an angle into the area between the drumstick and the breast, taking care not to hit the bone. It should register 175 degrees.

LET IT REST
Resting poultry after it is cooked is crucial. It allows the meat to relax and reabsorb its juices. Small cuts such as cutlets need only 5 to 10 minutes of resting time, while a whole chicken might need 10 to 20 minutes. A big turkey should rest for 30 minutes before being carved. To keep meat warm while it rests, cover it loosely with aluminum foil, unless it has a crisp coating or skin that you don't want to turn soggy.

MORE TO EXPLORE

PAN SAUCES

A pan sauce takes advantage of the flavorful browned bits, or fond, left in a pan after searing food. Pan sauces are a quick and easy way to dress up plain sautéed or roast chicken. Most of these sauces also taste great with steak or roast beef.

TARRAGON-LEMON PAN SAUCE
Makes: about ¾ cup
Total Time: 20 minutes

- 1 shallot, minced
- 1 cup chicken broth
- 2 teaspoons Dijon mustard
- 2 tablespoons unsalted butter
- 2 teaspoons minced fresh tarragon
- 2 teaspoons lemon juice

While chicken rests, remove all but 1 tablespoon fat from skillet (handle may be very hot) using large spoon, leaving any browned bits and jus in skillet. Place skillet over medium-high heat; add shallot; and cook until softened, about 2 minutes. Stir in broth and mustard, scraping up any browned bits. Simmer until reduced to ¾ cup, about 3 minutes. Off heat, whisk in butter, tarragon, and lemon juice. Season with pepper to taste.

THYME–SHERRY VINEGAR PAN SAUCE
Makes: about ¾ cup
Total Time: 20 minutes

- 1 shallot, minced
- 2 garlic cloves, minced
- 2 teaspoons chopped fresh thyme
- 1 cup chicken broth
- 2 teaspoons Dijon mustard
- 2 tablespoons unsalted butter
- 2 teaspoons sherry vinegar

While chicken rests, remove all but 1 tablespoon fat from skillet (handle may be very hot) using large spoon, leaving any browned bits and jus in skillet. Place skillet over medium-high heat; add shallot, garlic, and thyme; and cook until softened, about 2 minutes. Stir in broth and mustard, scraping up any browned bits. Simmer until reduced to ¾ cup, about 3 minutes. Off heat, whisk in butter and vinegar. Season with pepper to taste.

SAGE-VERMOUTH PAN SAUCE
Makes: about ¾ cup
Total Time: 15 minutes

- 1 shallot, minced
- ¾ cup chicken broth
- ½ cup dry vermouth
- 4 medium fresh sage leaves, each leaf torn in half
- 3 tablespoons unsalted butter, cut into 3 pieces

While chicken rests, remove all but 1 tablespoon fat from skillet (handle may be very hot) using large spoon, leaving any browned bits and jus in skillet. Add shallot; place skillet over medium-high heat; and cook, stirring frequently, until shallot is softened, about 1½ minutes. Add chicken broth, vermouth, and sage; increase heat to high and simmer rapidly, scraping skillet bottom with wooden spoon to loosen browned bits, until slightly thickened and reduced to about ¾ cup, about 5 minutes. Pour accumulated chicken juices into skillet, reduce heat to medium, and whisk in butter 1 piece at a time; season with salt and pepper to taste and discard sage.

LEMON-CAPER PAN SAUCE

Makes: about ½ cup
Total Time: 15 minutes

- 1 shallot, minced
- 1 cup chicken broth
- ¼ cup lemon juice (2 lemons)
- 2 tablespoons capers, drained and rinsed
- 3 tablespoons unsalted butter, softened

After removing chicken from skillet, add shallot and cook over medium heat until softened, about 30 seconds. Increase heat to high and stir in broth, scraping up any browned bits. Add lemon juice and capers. Simmer until reduced to ⅓ cup, 3 to 4 minutes. Off heat, whisk in butter.

MUSTARD-CIDER PAN SAUCE

Makes: about ¾ cup
Total Time: 25 minutes

- 1 tablespoon vegetable oil
- 1 shallot, minced
- ¼ teaspoon table salt
- 1¼ cups apple cider
- 2 tablespoons cider vinegar
- 3 tablespoons unsalted butter, cut into 3 pieces and chilled
- 2 tablespoons minced fresh parsley
- 2 teaspoons whole-grain mustard

After sautéing chicken, heat oil in now-empty skillet over medium-high heat until shimmering. Add shallot and salt and cook until softened, about 2 minutes. Stir in cider and vinegar, scraping up any browned bits, and simmer until reduced and slightly syrupy, about 8 minutes. Stir in any accumulated chicken juices. Reduce heat to low and whisk in butter, 1 piece at a time. Off heat, stir in parsley and mustard. Season with salt and pepper to taste.

APRICOT-ORANGE PAN SAUCE

Makes: about 1½ cups
Total Time: 20 minutes

- 1 tablespoon unsalted butter
- 1 shallot, minced
- 2 garlic cloves, minced
- 1 cup orange juice (2 oranges), plus 1 orange, peeled and chopped coarse
- 1 cup dried apricots, chopped
- 2 tablespoons minced fresh parsley

After sautéing chicken, melt butter in now-empty skillet over medium-high heat. Add shallot and cook until softened, 2 minutes. Stir in garlic and cook until fragrant, about 15 seconds. Stir in orange juice, orange, and apricots. Simmer until thickened, 4 minutes. Stir in any chicken juices. Stir in parsley and season with salt and pepper to taste.

CORE TECHNIQUE

Making a Pan Sauce

START WITH AROMATIC AND LIQUID
Add a small amount of minced shallot or onion to the skillet and cook until softened, then add a liquid, such as broth and/or wine. Liquid loosens the fond, and the browned bits dissolve and enrich the sauce with flavor.

FINISH WITH BUTTER
Many pan sauces involve whisking in butter, one small piece at a time. The butter pulls the sauce together and makes it thick and glossy. Add fresh herbs or any potent ingredient (they don't need cooking time) and season with salt and pepper.

COURSE
LEARN YOUR WAY AROUND A CHICKEN

LAN LAM

Butterflying a whole chicken or cutting one into pieces can seem daunting if you've never done it before, but it is relatively easy. This course is all about practicing your knife skills and gaining confidence in using them. Once you've butchered your own chicken, you may never go back to buying packaged parts. You'll also learn invaluable tips for broiling and roasting. And of course, all the recipes are bursting with creative flavors, so your efforts will be well rewarded.

LAN'S PRO TIP: *Kitchen shears really make breaking down a chicken fast and easy. Whether I'm removing excess skin or cutting through the rib cage, I always make a series of small snips instead of one large one. It's just neater and more precise.*

ONE-HOUR BROILED CHICKEN AND PAN SAUCE
Serves: 4
Total Time: 1¼ hours

RECIPE OVERVIEW Butterflying a chicken creates several advantages. Removing the backbone makes the chicken lie flat, creating more surface area for even and quicker cooking. It also exposes more skin to crisp up. In this recipe, the intense direct heat of the broiler cooks a whole butterflied chicken in about an hour. Piercing the skin at ¾-inch intervals helps to render the fat and prevents the skin from bubbling up and burning. To get the white and dark meat to cook in the same amount of time, use a preheated skillet to jump-start the cooking of the leg quarters, and start the skillet under a cold broiler to slow down the cooking of the breast. To account for the greater impact of carryover cooking, pull the chicken from the oven when the breast meat reaches 155 degrees instead of the usual 160. The chicken leaves flavorful drippings in the pan that make a great sauce; simply add fresh thyme and garlic. If your broiler has multiple settings, choose the highest one. This recipe requires a broiler-safe skillet. In step 3, if the skin is dark golden brown but the breast has not yet reached 155 degrees, cover the chicken with aluminum foil and continue to broil. Monitor the temperature of the chicken carefully during the final 10 minutes of cooking, because it can quickly overcook. Do not attempt this recipe with a drawer broiler.

1 (4-pound) whole chicken, giblets discarded
1½ teaspoons vegetable oil, divided
¾ teaspoon table salt, divided
½ plus ⅛ teaspoon pepper, divided
4 sprigs fresh thyme
1 garlic clove, crushed and peeled
   Lemon wedges

1. Adjust oven rack 12 to 13 inches from broiler element (do not preheat broiler). Place chicken breast side down on cutting board. Using kitchen shears, cut through bones on either side of backbone. Trim off any excess fat and skin and discard backbone. Flip chicken and press on breastbone to flatten. Using tip of paring knife, poke holes through skin over entire surface of chicken, spacing holes approximately ¾ inch apart.

2. Rub ½ teaspoon oil over skin and sprinkle with ½ teaspoon salt and ½ teaspoon pepper. Flip chicken and sprinkle bone side with remaining ¼ teaspoon salt and remaining ⅛ teaspoon pepper. Tie legs together with kitchen twine and tuck wings under breasts.

3. Heat remaining 1 teaspoon oil in broiler-safe 12-inch skillet over high heat until just smoking. Place chicken in skillet, skin side up, and transfer to oven, positioning skillet as close to center of oven as handle allows (turn handle so it points toward one of oven's front corners). Turn on broiler and broil chicken for 25 minutes. Rotate skillet by moving handle to opposite front corner of oven and continue to broil until skin is dark golden brown and thickest part of breast registers 155 degrees, 20 to 30 minutes.

4. Transfer chicken to carving board and let rest, uncovered, for 15 minutes. While chicken rests, stir thyme sprigs and garlic into juices in pan and let stand for 10 minutes.

5. Using spoon, skim fat from surface of pan juices. Carve chicken and add any accumulated juices to pan. Strain sauce through fine-mesh strainer and season with salt and pepper to taste. Serve chicken, passing pan sauce and lemon wedges separately.

KEYS TO SUCCESS

- **Position the oven rack properly (12 to 13 inches from the broiler element):** Ensures even cooking and browning
- **Butterfly the bird:** Allows it to cook through evenly and more quickly
- **Perforate the skin all over:** Hastens rendering and creates vents for steam to escape so that skin remains flush against meat rather than puffing up and burning
- **Preheat the skillet:** Gives the dark meat, which sits directly on the skillet and needs longer to cook, a jump start

CORE TECHNIQUE
Removing the Backbone

CUT ALONG EACH SIDE
Place the chicken breast side down and use kitchen shears to cut through the bones on either side of the backbone.

PRESS FLAT
Flip the chicken and use the heel of your hand to flatten the breastbone.

TIE LEGS TOGETHER
Tie the chicken legs together with kitchen twine to hold them in place.

For Perfect Broiled Chicken, Keep It Out of the Spotlight

For even cooking and browning, the butterflied chicken must be placed at the right distance from the broiler element. Though electric (illustrated below) and gas broilers are designed differently, both work the same way: The radiant heat is more focused and intense near the element and becomes more diffuse the farther away it gets.

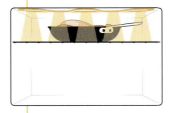

SPOTTY COVERAGE
When the oven rack is placed too close to the broiler element, the heat radiating from the "spotlights" is concentrated, resulting in burnt skin and uneven cooking.

UNIFORM COVERAGE
When the oven rack is placed farther from the broiler element, the heat radiating from the "spotlights" is diffused, which results in browned skin and even cooking.

BARBECUE ROAST CHICKEN AND POTATOES
Serves: 4
Total Time: 1½ hours

RECIPE OVERVIEW A butterflied chicken is a blank canvas perfect for highlighting a homemade spice rub and dressed-up vegetable side. It's also a quicker route to a weeknight dinner—or several weeknight dinners, since this master recipe and its variations give you roast chicken and vegetables four ways. You will need a 12-inch ovensafe skillet for this recipe. Use potatoes that are 1 to 2 inches in diameter.

- 2 tablespoons Barbecue Rub (page 352)
- 2 tablespoons vegetable oil, divided
- 1½ teaspoons table salt, divided
- 1 (3½- to 4-pound) whole chicken, giblets discarded
- 1½ pounds small red potatoes, unpeeled, halved
- 1 tablespoon minced fresh chives
- 1 teaspoon cider vinegar

1. Adjust oven rack to lower-middle position and heat oven to 450 degrees. Combine rub, 1 tablespoon oil, and 1 teaspoon salt in bowl. Place chicken breast side down on cutting board. Using kitchen shears, cut through bones on either side of backbone. Trim off any excess fat and skin and discard backbone. Flip chicken and press on breastbone to flatten, then pound breast to be same thickness as legs and thighs.

2. Pat chicken dry with paper towels. Gently loosen skin covering breast and thighs. Rub 2 teaspoons spice mixture underneath skin, then rub remaining spice mixture all over chicken. Tuck wingtips underneath.

3. Toss potatoes with remaining 1 tablespoon oil and remaining ½ teaspoon salt and arrange cut side up in 12-inch ovensafe skillet. Place chicken skin side up on top of potatoes. Transfer skillet to oven and roast chicken until breast registers 160 degrees and drumsticks/thighs register 175 degrees, 45 minutes to 1 hour. (If chicken begins to get too dark, cover loosely with aluminum foil.)

4. Using pot holders, carefully remove skillet from oven. Transfer chicken to carving board and let rest while finishing potatoes. Being careful of hot skillet handle, return skillet to oven and roast potatoes until softened, 12 to 16 minutes. Using slotted spoon, transfer potatoes to serving bowl. Add 1 tablespoon fat from skillet, chives, and vinegar and gently toss to coat. Season with salt and pepper to taste. Carve chicken and serve with potatoes.

Variations
FIVE-SPICE ROAST CHICKEN WITH TURNIPS
Substitute 1 tablespoon Five-Spice Powder (page 29) for barbecue rub; 1½ pounds turnips, peeled and cut into 1½-inch pieces, for potatoes; 2 scallions, sliced thin on bias, for chives; and rice vinegar for cider vinegar.

HERBES DE PROVENCE ROAST CHICKEN WITH FENNEL
Substitute 4 teaspoons Herbes de Provence (page 352) and ¼ teaspoon pepper for barbecue rub; 3 fennel bulbs, halved, cored, and sliced ½ inch thick, for potatoes; parsley for chives; and sherry vinegar for cider vinegar.

RAS EL HANOUT ROAST CHICKEN WITH CARROTS
Substitute Ras el Hanout (page 28) for barbecue rub; carrots, peeled, halved lengthwise, and cut into 2-inch lengths, for potatoes; cilantro for chives; and lemon juice for cider vinegar.

> **KEYS TO SUCCESS**
> - **Butterfly the bird:** Allows it to cook through evenly and more quickly
> - **Rub spice mix under and over skin:** Maximizes seasoning
> - **Roast chicken on top of the vegetables:** Allows chicken drippings to flavor the vegetables

CHICKEN CACCIATORE
Serves: 4 to 6
Total Time: 1½ hours

RECIPE OVERVIEW The Italian American version of chicken alla cacciatora, chicken cooked "the hunter's way," nearly always features cut-up, bone-in chicken cooked in a thick marinara-like sauce. This recipe includes a sauce that is just substantial enough to cling to the chicken. Tomatoes are in because of the sweetness and acidity they lend to the dish, and the wine of choice is white wine for its lighter profile. Cutting this base with chicken broth buffers the presence of the wine and rounds out the savory flavors. The flavors of garlic and rosemary complement the poultry. For even cooking, sauté the chicken on the stove and then transfer it to the oven to finish cooking through gently in the sauce. As the chicken rests, reduce the sauce to concentrate its flavors. You will need two 2½- to 3-pound chickens to end up with 4 pounds of parts.

- 4 pounds bone-in chicken pieces (split breasts cut in half crosswise, drumsticks, and thighs), trimmed
- 1½ teaspoons table salt
- ¾ teaspoon pepper
- 2 tablespoons extra-virgin olive oil
- 1 onion, chopped
- 1 carrot, peeled and chopped
- 1 celery rib, chopped
- 2 garlic cloves, minced
- 1½ teaspoons minced fresh rosemary
- ½ cup dry white wine
- ½ cup chicken broth
- 1 (14.5-ounce) can diced tomatoes, drained
- 1 tablespoon minced fresh parsley

1. Adjust oven rack to middle position and heat oven to 325 degrees. Pat chicken dry with paper towels and sprinkle with salt and pepper. Heat oil in Dutch oven over medium-high heat until just smoking. Brown half of chicken on all sides, 8 to 10 minutes; transfer to plate. Repeat with remaining chicken.

2. Add onion, carrot, and celery to fat left in pot and cook over medium heat until softened and lightly browned, 6 to 8 minutes. Stir in garlic and rosemary and cook until fragrant, about 30 seconds. Stir in wine, scraping up any browned bits, and cook until almost completely evaporated, about 2 minutes. Stir in broth and tomatoes and bring to simmer.

3. Return chicken to pot along with any accumulated juices and cover; transfer pot to oven. Cook until breasts register 160 degrees and drumsticks/thighs register 175 degrees, 35 to 40 minutes, turning chicken halfway through cooking.

4. Remove pot from oven. Transfer chicken to serving dish and tent with aluminum foil. Bring sauce to simmer over medium-high heat and cook until reduced to about 2 cups, 5 to 8 minutes. Season with salt and pepper to taste. Spoon sauce over chicken and sprinkle with parsley. Serve.

TANDOORI CHICKEN
Serves: 4
Total Time: 1½ hours

RECIPE OVERVIEW Traditional tandoori chicken features assorted bone-in chicken parts marinated in yogurt and spices and roasted in a superhot beehive-shaped clay tandoor oven to produce tender, flavorful meat with a beautiful char. To make it at home, cut up a 4-pound chicken (to get 3 pounds of parts) and build a fragrant spice paste, blooming ginger and garlic in oil before adding garam masala, cumin, and chili powder. This paste is used twice. Apply some directly to the chicken pieces (slashed so that the flavors penetrate) and stir the rest into yogurt for a marinade. The yogurt adds distinctive tang, protects the meat from drying out, and contributes to browning. Arranged on a wire rack set in a baking sheet, the chicken parts roast gently and evenly in a moderate oven, and then a few minutes under the broiler deliver char. A quick herbal raita cools things down. If your chicken breasts are large (about 1 pound each), cut each breast into three pieces.

Raita

- 1 cup plain whole-milk yogurt
- 2 tablespoons minced fresh cilantro
- 1 garlic clove, minced
- Cayenne pepper

Chicken

- 2 tablespoons vegetable oil
- 6 garlic cloves, minced
- 2 tablespoons grated fresh ginger
- 1 tablespoon garam masala
- 2 teaspoons ground cumin
- 2 teaspoons chili powder
- 1 cup plain whole-milk yogurt
- ¼ cup lime juice (2 limes), divided, plus lime wedges for serving
- 2 teaspoons table salt
- 3 pounds bone-in chicken pieces (split breasts cut in half crosswise, drumsticks, and thighs), skin removed, trimmed

1. FOR THE RAITA Combine yogurt, cilantro, and garlic in bowl and season with salt and cayenne to taste. Refrigerate until ready to serve. (Raita can be refrigerated for up to 24 hours.)

2. FOR THE CHICKEN Heat oil in 10-inch skillet over medium heat until shimmering. Add garlic and ginger and cook until fragrant, about 30 seconds. Stir in garam masala, cumin, and chili powder and cook until fragrant, about 30 seconds. Transfer half of garlic mixture to bowl and stir in yogurt and 2 tablespoons lime juice; set aside marinade. Combine remaining garlic mixture, remaining 2 tablespoons lime juice, and salt in large bowl. Using sharp knife, make 2 or 3 short slashes in each piece of chicken. Transfer chicken to large bowl and gently rub with garlic–lime juice mixture until all pieces are evenly coated. Let sit at room temperature for 30 minutes.

3. Adjust oven rack to upper-middle position and heat oven to 325 degrees. Set wire rack in aluminum foil–lined rimmed baking sheet. Pour yogurt marinade over chicken and toss until chicken is evenly and thickly coated. Arrange chicken pieces, scored sides down, on prepared rack; discard excess marinade. Roast chicken until breasts register 125 degrees and drumsticks/thighs register 130 degrees, 15 to 25 minutes. (Smaller pieces may cook faster than larger pieces. Remove pieces from oven as they reach correct temperature.)

4. Adjust oven rack 6 inches from broiler element and heat broiler. Return chicken pieces to wire rack in sheet, scored side up, and broil until chicken is lightly charred in spots and breasts register 160 degrees and drumsticks/thighs register 175 degrees, 8 to 15 minutes. Transfer chicken to serving platter, tent with foil, and let rest for 5 minutes. Serve with raita and lime wedges.

CORE TECHNIQUE
Cutting Up a Whole Chicken

CUT OFF LEGS
Using chef's knife, cut off the legs, one at a time, by severing the joint between the leg and the body.

SEPARATE LEGS
Cut each leg into two pieces—drumstick and thigh—by slicing through the joint that connects them (marked by a thin white line of fat).

REMOVE WINGS
Flip the chicken and remove the wings by slicing through each wing joint.

REMOVE BACKBONE
Turn the chicken on its side and, using kitchen shears, remove the back.

CUT BREAST IN HALF
Flip the breast skin side down and, using a chef's knife, cut it in half through the breast plate (marked by a thin white line of cartilage).

CUT SPLIT BREAST IN HALF
Flip each breast piece and cut it in half crosswise.

COURSE
STEWED AND BRAISED

CHRISTIE MORRISON

Stewing and braising are go-to techniques for cozy, warm chicken dinners. These high-moisture, long-cooked methods transform fattier chicken thighs into succulent, fall-off-the-bone-tender meat. Where stewing usually involves completely submerging small pieces of meat in liquid, braising generally calls for much less liquid. In this course, the recipes highlight some of the nearly limitless possibilities: a classic chicken stew, a hearty one-pan dinner of lemony chicken thighs and chickpeas, and a saucy braise of tender dark meat and hearty greens.

CHRISTIE'S PRO TIP: *The key to successful braising is controlled, even cooking and evaporation. That means a sturdy Dutch oven or skillet with a well-fitting lid and using the steady heat of the oven instead of the stovetop.*

CLASSIC CHICKEN STEW
Serves: 6 to 8
Total Time: 2 hours

RECIPE OVERVIEW A good chicken stew is full of moist chunks of meat and hearty vegetables enveloped in a glossy, thick sauce. Rather than navigating bones and skin, use boneless, skinless thighs. More than just convenient, they stay tender and moist during slow cooking, giving up enough flavor and collagen to make a rich sauce while retaining plenty of flavor and juiciness. Cooking the stew in a low oven, rather than on the stovetop, ensures consistent, gentle heat transfer. About an hour in the oven allows time for the thighs' connective tissue to break down, providing gelatin to thicken the sauce and rendering the meat exceedingly tender. Some white wine adds an acidic note to cut through the hearty flavors, and fresh thyme adds depth.

- 3 pounds boneless, skinless chicken thighs, trimmed and cut into 1-inch pieces
- 1 teaspoon table salt, divided
- ½ teaspoon pepper
- 3 tablespoons vegetable oil, divided
- 2 onions, chopped fine
- 4 garlic cloves, minced
- 1 teaspoon minced fresh thyme or ¼ teaspoon dried
- ¼ cup all-purpose flour
- ½ cup dry white wine
- 3½ cups chicken broth

1½ pounds red potatoes, unpeeled, cut into ¾-inch pieces
1 pound carrots, peeled and sliced ½ inch thick
2 bay leaves
1 cup frozen peas
¼ cup minced fresh parsley

1. Adjust oven rack to lower-middle position and heat oven to 300 degrees. Pat chicken dry with paper towels and sprinkle with ¾ teaspoon salt and pepper. Heat 1 tablespoon oil in Dutch oven over medium-high heat until just smoking. Brown half of chicken, 6 to 8 minutes; transfer to bowl. Repeat with 1 tablespoon oil and remaining chicken; transfer to bowl.

2. Heat remaining 1 tablespoon oil in now-empty pot over medium heat until shimmering. Add onions and remaining ¼ teaspoon salt and cook until softened, about 5 minutes. Stir in garlic and thyme and cook until fragrant, about 30 seconds. Stir in flour and cook for 1 minute. Stir in wine, scraping up any browned bits.

3. Slowly whisk in broth, smoothing out any lumps. Stir in potatoes, carrots, bay leaves, and chicken with any accumulated juices and bring to simmer. Cover; transfer pot to oven; and cook until chicken is very tender, 50 minutes to 1 hour.

4. Remove pot from the oven and discard bay leaves. Stir in peas; cover; and let sit until heated through, about 5 minutes. Stir in parsley and season with salt and pepper to taste. Serve.

KEYS TO SUCCESS

- **Boneless thighs**: Become and stay tender during longer cooking
- **Cook in a low oven**: Helps chicken produce gelatin, which thickens the sauce

LEMON-BRAISED CHICKEN THIGHS WITH CHICKPEAS AND FENNEL

Serves: 4
Total Time: 1¼ hours

RECIPE OVERVIEW People think of braises as all-day affairs, but with bone-in chicken thighs, a hearty braise can be a relatively quick meal. When braising chicken, we often remove the skin, as it can turn flabby, but there is a way to maintain crispiness. First, brown bone-in thighs and remove them to build a hefty sauce of chickpeas (mashing some to thicken the sauce), fennel, and olives. Then nestle the chicken back in the pan: Elevated just enough, the chicken's skin remains crispy even as the meat braises away in the liquid below. "Overcooking" the chicken to a temperature of 185 degrees renders fat and melts the tough connective tissues for a rich dish with ultratender meat. Note that only the skin side of the chicken is browned in step 2.

CORE TECHNIQUE

Braising Chicken Thighs

Braising is a classic way to cook chicken thighs. The skin renders loads of fat and collagen, which add flavor and body to the sauce, and the meat turns tender and gives up its savory juices.

BROWN AND REMOVE FROM PAN Pat the chicken dry before cooking. Brown the chicken skin side down to create fond and build flavor. (The skin can be discarded before serving.)

ADD LIQUID AND REDUCE Add wine and/or broth to coax out more flavor and reduce to form the sauce.

SIMMER IN OVEN Cover the pot and move it to the oven. The gentle even heat breaks down the connective tissue into gelatin.

We prefer briny green olives, such as Manzanilla, Picholine, or Cerignola, in this recipe; look for them at your grocery store's salad bar or in the pickle aisle.

- 2 (15-ounce) cans chickpeas, rinsed, divided
- 6 (5- to 7-ounce) bone-in chicken thighs, trimmed
- ¾ teaspoon table salt, divided
- ¼ teaspoon pepper
- 1 tablespoon extra-virgin olive oil
- 1 large fennel bulb, stalks discarded, bulb halved and cut into ½-inch-thick wedges through core
- 4 garlic cloves, minced
- 2 teaspoons grated lemon zest plus 1½ tablespoons juice
- 1 teaspoon ground coriander
- ½ teaspoon red pepper flakes
- ½ cup dry white wine
- 1 cup pitted large brine-cured green olives, halved
- ¾ cup chicken broth
- 1 tablespoon honey
- 2 tablespoons chopped fresh parsley

1. Adjust oven rack to upper-middle position and heat oven to 350 degrees. Place ½ cup chickpeas in bowl and mash to coarse puree with potato masher; set aside. Pat chicken dry with paper towels and sprinkle with ½ teaspoon salt and pepper.

2. Heat oil in 12-inch ovensafe skillet over medium-high heat until just smoking. Cook chicken, skin side down, until browned, 8 to 10 minutes. Transfer chicken to plate, skin side up.

3. Pour off all but 2 tablespoons fat from skillet, then heat fat left in skillet over medium heat until shimmering. Add fennel, cut side down, and sprinkle with remaining ¼ teaspoon salt. Cook, covered, until lightly browned, 3 to 5 minutes per side. Add garlic, lemon zest, coriander, and pepper flakes and cook, uncovered, until fragrant, about 30 seconds. Stir in wine, scraping up any browned bits, and cook until almost evaporated, about 2 minutes.

4. Stir in olives, broth, honey, lemon juice, mashed chickpeas, and remaining whole chickpeas and bring to simmer. Nestle chicken into liquid, keeping skin above surface. Transfer skillet to oven and bake, uncovered, until fennel is tender and chicken registers 185 degrees, 35 to 40 minutes. Sprinkle with parsley and serve.

KEYS TO SUCCESS

- **Move the rack higher:** Keeps the chicken skin close to the heat reflected from the oven's ceiling, ensuring that it crisps nicely
- **Nestle the chicken on top of the fennel and chickpeas:** Keeps the chicken skin out of the liquid
- **Keep the skillet uncovered:** Allows the sauce to reduce as the chicken braises

SCIENCE LESSON
"Overcooking" Chicken

Braising unlocks the delicious flavor already inherent in the food you're cooking. When you braise fattier, meaty chicken thighs, collagen—the main protein that makes up the chewy connective tissue that surrounds meat's muscle fibers—doesn't even start to break down until the chicken reaches 140 degrees. But cook the collagen-rich cut past that point, and the collagen melts into gooey gelatin, which lubricates the fibers, making the meat tender—even more tender than before the moisture was pushed out. At 175 degrees, the dark meat chicken is tender but clings to the bone. A thigh slowly cooked to 195 degrees is something else: meltingly tender and exceptionally succulent, with rich poultry flavor. Take the thighs too far, to 210 degrees, and the meat slumps off the bone, can look gray, and tastes bland, losing its flavor to the surrounding liquid.

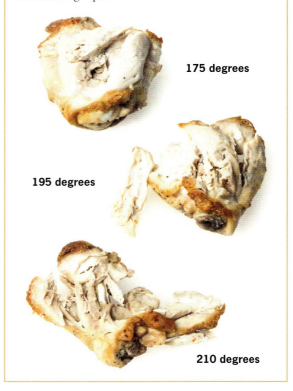

175 degrees

195 degrees

210 degrees

BRAISED CHICKEN THIGHS WITH CHARD AND MUSTARD

Serves: 4
Total Time: 2¼ hours

RECIPE OVERVIEW Rich-tasting chicken thighs and slightly bitter Swiss chard make a good combination for a simple, satisfying one-pot dinner. Braised bone-in thighs become juicy and tender as they simmer and flavor the surrounding sauce. Browning brings rich flavor, but we aren't excited about eating flabby skin—inevitable after a long simmer. So, after browning skin-on thighs to develop lots of flavorful fond, discard the skin. Then build a braise with bold ingredients: sturdy chard; garlic, thyme, and an umami-packed anchovy fillet for flavor; lemon zest for brightness; and bay leaves for depth. Cooking the chicken thighs for a full hour allows the collagen to melt into rich gelatin, adding body and depth to the sauce. A dollop of mustard adds sharp contrast to the sauce's richness. We like to use green or white Swiss chard here; if using red chard, note that the sauce will take on a reddish hue. This dish is good with rice or egg noodles.

- 8 (5- to 7-ounce) bone-in chicken thighs, trimmed
- ¾ teaspoon table salt
- ¼ teaspoon pepper
- 1 tablespoon extra-virgin olive oil
- 1 pound Swiss chard, stems chopped fine, leaves sliced thin
- 1 onion, chopped fine
- 6 garlic cloves, minced
- 1 tablespoon minced fresh thyme or 2 teaspoons dried
- 1 anchovy fillet, rinsed and minced
- 2 tablespoons all-purpose flour
- 1½ cups chicken broth
- ½ cup dry white wine
- 2 bay leaves
- 1 teaspoon grated lemon zest
- 1 tablespoon whole-grain mustard

1. Adjust oven rack to lower-middle position and heat oven to 300 degrees. Pat chicken dry with paper towels and sprinkle with salt and pepper. Heat oil in Dutch oven over medium-high heat until just smoking. Add half of chicken and brown on both sides, 7 to 10 minutes; transfer to plate and remove skin. Repeat with remaining chicken.

2. Pour off all but 2 tablespoons fat left in pot and heat over medium-high heat until shimmering. Add chard stems and onion and cook until softened and lightly browned, 5 to 7 minutes. Stir in garlic, thyme, and anchovy and cook until fragrant, about 30 seconds. Stir in flour and cook for 30 seconds. Whisk in broth and wine, scraping up any browned bits and smoothing out any lumps.

3. Add bay leaves and browned chicken with any accumulated juices. Bring to simmer, cover, and transfer pot to oven. Cook until chicken is very tender and almost falling off bone, about 1 hour.

4. Remove pot from oven. Transfer chicken to platter, tent with aluminum foil, and let rest while finishing sauce. Let liquid in pot settle for 5 minutes, then skim any fat from surface using large spoon. Stir in chard leaves and lemon zest; bring to simmer; and cook until sauce is thickened, about 10 minutes.

5. Off heat, discard bay leaves, stir in mustard, and season with salt and pepper to taste. Pour sauce over chicken and serve. (Chicken and sauce can be refrigerated for up to 2 days; add additional broth as needed to loosen sauce when reheating.)

KEYS TO SUCCESS

- **Bone-in thighs:** Add rich flavor when braised and leave a great fond when seared
- For how to stem and chop Swiss chard, see page 43.
- **Just one anchovy:** Contributes deep savory flavor
- **Sear the chicken thighs before discarding the skin:** Adds lots of savory flavor

COURSE
CHICKEN AND RICE

LAWMAN JOHNSON

Chicken and rice is the homiest of meals, one that is family-friendly and commonly prepared in many countries. As a canvas for different flavor combinations, it is eminently variable. The recipes featured in this course couple the two star ingredients with everything from carrots and peas to olives and pimentos to soybean paste and Thai chiles. As you cook your way through them, you'll also learn how to cook rice in tandem, shred tender chicken into bite-size pieces, and prepare a variety of stir-together sauces to complement the flavors. This is comfort food at its best: approachable, appealing, and never boring.

LAWMAN'S PRO TIP: *With a little patience, cooking rice can be as easy as simmering water. Adding tender bite-size pieces of chicken creates the foundation for endless possibilities.*

CHICKEN AND RICE WITH CARROTS AND PEAS

Serves: 4
Total Time: 1 hour

RECIPE OVERVIEW A good chicken and rice recipe, the kind that becomes a weeknight mainstay, should be simple and dependable. This recipe delivers. To prevent the boneless, skinless chicken from drying out, brown it only on one side. Sautéing the rice in aromatics keeps the grains distinct and creamy and gives the rice deeper flavor before liquid is added. The chicken then finishes cooking right in the rice. Remove the chicken and let the rice continue to simmer and absorb the flavorful liquid. Frozen peas (one of our favorite frozen vegetables) offer bursts of color, and fresh lemon juice and parsley brighten up the flavor. Be sure to use chicken breasts that are roughly the same size to ensure even cooking. You will need a 12-inch skillet with a tight-fitting lid for this recipe. The skillet will be fairly full once you add the browned chicken in step 3, so use a straight-sided skillet if you have one.

- 4 (6- to 8-ounce) boneless, skinless chicken breasts, trimmed
- 1 teaspoon table salt, divided
- ¼ teaspoon pepper
- 2 tablespoons vegetable oil
- 1 onion, chopped fine
- 1½ cups long-grain white rice
- 3 garlic cloves, minced
- Pinch red pepper flakes
- 4 carrots, peeled and sliced on bias ½ inch thick
- 3½ cups chicken broth
- 1 cup frozen peas
- 2 tablespoons lemon juice
- 1 tablespoon minced fresh parsley

1. Pat chicken dry with paper towels and sprinkle with ½ teaspoon salt and pepper. Heat oil in 12-inch skillet over medium-high heat until just smoking. Add chicken and cook until golden brown on 1 side, 4 to 6 minutes; transfer to plate.

2. Add onion and remaining ½ teaspoon salt to fat left in skillet and cook until softened, about 5 minutes. Stir in rice, garlic, and pepper flakes and cook until fragrant, about 30 seconds. Stir in carrots, then stir in broth, scraping up any browned bits.

3. Nestle chicken, browned side up, into skillet, along with any accumulated juices. Bring to simmer, then reduce heat to medium-low; cover; and simmer gently until chicken registers 160 degrees, about 10 minutes.

4. Transfer chicken to cutting board, tent loosely with aluminum foil, and let rest while finishing rice. Stir rice mixture to recombine, then cover and cook until liquid is absorbed and rice is tender, 5 to 10 minutes.

5. Off heat, sprinkle with peas; cover; and let warm through, about 2 minutes. Sprinkle with lemon juice and gently fluff rice mixture with fork. Slice chicken ½ inch thick and arrange on top of rice. Sprinkle with parsley and serve.

> **KEYS TO SUCCESS**
> - **Brown chicken on one side**: Keeps the chicken from drying out and also creates fond (browned bits in the skillet)
> - **Cook the chicken in the rice**: Keeps the chicken from overcooking and adds deeper flavor to the rice

CURRIED CHICKEN WITH COCONUT RICE AND LIME-YOGURT SAUCE

Serves: 4
Total Time: 1¼ hours

RECIPE OVERVIEW This update on chicken and rice casserole looks to the warm, complex flavors of curry powder. For an extra layer of interest and a streamlined approach, cook the rice in coconut milk, right in the baking dish, stirring in carrots to ensure that they become tender. Slice the chicken thin and toss it with a bold mix of curry powder and minced garlic bloomed in the microwave. Because the chicken is cut into small pieces, all you have to do is fold it into the rice, along with some peas, for the last 10 minutes of cooking for tender, juicy results. Once the robust casserole is done, a few simple accompaniments give it more flavor: a light and tangy yogurt sauce seasoned with lime zest and juice and cilantro; a sprinkle of fresh, savory scallions; and crunchy toasted almonds. We prefer the richer flavor of whole-milk yogurt here; however, low-fat or nonfat yogurt can be substituted. For an accurate measurement of boiling water, bring a kettle of water to a boil and then measure out the desired amount.

- 1 cup plain whole-milk yogurt
- 2 tablespoons minced fresh cilantro or mint
- 1 teaspoon grated lime zest plus 1 tablespoon juice
- 1¾ teaspoons table salt, divided
- 2 cups boiling water
- 1⅓ cups long-grain white rice
- ¾ cup canned coconut milk
- 3 carrots, peeled and cut into ¼-inch pieces
- 2 tablespoons extra-virgin olive oil
- 1 tablespoon curry powder
- 2 garlic cloves, minced
- ¼ teaspoon pepper
- 1 pound boneless, skinless chicken breasts, trimmed, halved lengthwise, and sliced thin
- 1 cup frozen peas
- ⅓ cup sliced almonds, toasted
- 2 scallions, sliced thin

1. Adjust oven rack to middle position and heat oven to 450 degrees. Combine yogurt, cilantro, lime zest and juice, and ¼ teaspoon salt in bowl; cover and refrigerate until serving.

2. Combine boiling water, rice, coconut milk, carrots, and ½ teaspoon salt in 13 by 9-inch baking dish. Cover tightly with aluminum foil and bake until rice is nearly tender, 25 to 30 minutes.

3. While rice bakes, combine oil, curry powder, garlic, pepper, and remaining 1 teaspoon salt in large bowl and microwave until fragrant, about 30 seconds. Let mixture cool slightly, then stir in chicken.

4. Remove rice from oven, fluff gently with fork, and gently stir in chicken and peas. Re-cover tightly with foil and continue to bake until rice is tender and chicken is cooked through, 10 to 15 minutes.

5. Remove dish from oven, let cool for 10 minutes, then fluff rice gently with fork. Serve, drizzling individual portions with yogurt sauce and sprinkling with almonds and scallions.

ARROZ CON POLLO

Serves: 6
Total Time: 2 hours

RECIPE OVERVIEW Arroz con pollo, rice with chicken, is classic comfort food and a staple in many Latin American kitchens. It's full of classic flavors. Start by briefly marinating bone-in chicken thighs in a mixture of vinegar, salt, pepper, and oregano. Next, stew the meat with tomato sauce, olives, capers, and rice until it becomes fall-off-the-bone tender while the rice cooks evenly. Starting the chicken with its skin still on maximizes the flavorful renderings; the skin can then be removed after cooking. Using spoons rather than forks to pull the cooked meat apart produces appealing chunks instead of shreds. To keep the dish from becoming greasy, it is important to trim excess fat and most of the skin from the chicken thighs, leaving just enough skin to protect the meat. Long-grain rice can be substituted for the medium-grain rice; however, you will need to increase the amount of water to ¾ cup.

- 6 garlic cloves, minced
- 5 teaspoons distilled white vinegar, divided
- 1½ teaspoons minced fresh oregano or ½ teaspoon dried
- 1¾ teaspoons table salt, divided
- ½ teaspoon pepper
- 4 pounds bone-in chicken thighs, trimmed
- 2 tablespoons extra-virgin olive oil, divided
- 1 onion, chopped fine
- 1 small green bell pepper, stemmed, seeded, and chopped fine
- ¼ teaspoon red pepper flakes
- ¼ cup minced fresh cilantro, divided
- 1¾ cups chicken broth
- 1 (8-ounce) can tomato sauce
- ¼ cup water, plus extra as needed
- 3 cups medium-grain white rice
- ½ cup pitted green Manzanilla olives, halved
- 1 tablespoon capers, rinsed
- ½ cup jarred whole pimentos, cut into 2 by ¼-inch strips
- Lemon wedges

1. Adjust oven rack to middle position and heat oven to 350 degrees. Combine garlic, 1 tablespoon vinegar, oregano, 1 teaspoon salt, and pepper in large bowl. Add chicken, toss to coat, and cover; let sit at room temperature for 15 minutes.

2. While chicken marinates, heat 1 tablespoon oil in Dutch oven over medium heat until shimmering. Add onion and bell pepper and cook until softened, 5 to 7 minutes. Stir in pepper flakes and cook until fragrant, about 30 seconds. Stir in 2 tablespoons cilantro.

3. Push vegetables to side of pot and increase heat to medium-high. Add chicken, skin side down, to cleared area of pot and brown lightly, 2 to 4 minutes per side, reducing heat if chicken begins to burn. Stir in broth, tomato sauce, and water and bring to simmer. Cover, reduce heat to medium-low, and simmer for 20 minutes.

4. Stir in rice, olives, capers, and remaining ¾ teaspoon salt and bring to simmer. Cover; transfer pot to oven; and cook, stirring often, until chicken registers 175 degrees, rice is tender, and liquid has been absorbed, about 30 minutes. (If pot appears dry and begins to scorch after 20 minutes, stir in additional ¼ cup water.)

5. Remove pot from oven and transfer chicken to cutting board; cover pot and set aside. Let chicken cool slightly, then shred chicken into large chunks using 2 soupspoons; discard skin and bones. Toss chicken chunks, pimentos, remaining 2 teaspoons vinegar, remaining 1 tablespoon oil, and remaining 2 tablespoons cilantro in clean bowl and season with salt and pepper to taste.

6. Place chicken on top of rice, cover, and let stand until warmed through, about 5 minutes. Serve with lemon wedges.

CORE TECHNIQUE
Pulling Meat from the Bone

Use two spoons, which are much more gentle than forks, to pull the meat apart intact.

KHAO MAN GAI

Serves: 4 to 6
Total Time: 2 hours

RECIPE OVERVIEW Khao man gai is a classic Thai chicken and rice dish filled with exceptional flavor. First, poach the chicken whole with garlic and ginger to simultaneously create juicy meat and flavorful broth. Then, while the bird rests, cook fragrant jasmine rice in the poaching liquid to make a poultry-infused rice to serve with the chicken. To create a savory sauce, whisk together white vinegar, soy sauce, Thai soybean paste, garlic, ginger, and Thai chiles. One tablespoon of Asian chili-garlic sauce can be substituted for the Thai chiles, if desired. Use a Dutch oven with a capacity of at least 7 quarts to comfortably fit the chicken. Thai soybean paste is sometimes labeled as yellow bean sauce or soybean sauce; if you can't find it, you can substitute Japanese red miso.

Chicken and Broth
- 12 cups water
- 1 (2-inch) piece ginger, peeled and sliced into ¼-inch-thick rounds
- 2 tablespoons table salt
- 6 garlic cloves, smashed and peeled
- 1 (3½- to 4-pound) whole chicken, giblets discarded

Rice
- 1 tablespoon vegetable oil
- 1 shallot, chopped fine
- 1 (2-inch) piece ginger, peeled and cut in half lengthwise
- 2 garlic cloves, minced
- ¼ teaspoon table salt
- 2 cups jasmine rice, rinsed
- 1 cup fresh cilantro leaves and stems
- ½ English cucumber, sliced into thin rounds

Sauce
- ¼ cup Thai soybean paste
- ¼ cup soy sauce
- ¼ cup distilled white vinegar
- 2 tablespoons sugar
- 3 garlic cloves, minced
- 2 Thai chiles, stemmed and minced
- 1 teaspoon grated fresh ginger
- 2 scallions, sliced thin

1. FOR THE CHICKEN AND BROTH Combine water, ginger, salt, and garlic in large Dutch oven. Add chicken to pot, breast side up, and bring to simmer over high heat. Place large sheet of aluminum foil over pot, then cover with lid. Reduce heat to low and simmer until breast registers 160 degrees and thighs register at least 175 degrees, 25 to 35 minutes.

2. Transfer chicken to bowl, tent with foil, and let rest while making rice. Using slotted spoon, skim foamy residue from surface of chicken broth. Set aside 3 cups broth for cooking rice. Cover remaining broth.

3. FOR THE RICE Heat oil in large saucepan over medium heat until shimmering. Add shallot, ginger, garlic, and salt and cook until shallot is softened, about 2 minutes. Add rice and cook, stirring frequently, until edges begin to turn translucent, about 2 minutes.

4. Stir in reserved 3 cups broth and bring to boil over medium-high heat. Stir once more, then cover and reduce heat to low. Cook for 20 minutes. Without removing lid, remove saucepan from heat and let sit, covered, for 10 minutes.

5. FOR THE SAUCE Whisk all ingredients in bowl until sugar is dissolved, about 1 minute. (Sauce can be refrigerated for up to 2 days.)

6. Rewarm remaining broth over medium heat. Using boning knife, remove breast meat from chicken carcass; discard skin. Remove chicken leg quarters by dislocating thigh joint from carcass. Using 2 forks, shred leg quarter meat into bite-size pieces; discard skin and bones. Slice breasts crosswise ½ inch thick.

7. Transfer rice to large serving platter. Arrange shredded chicken on top of rice. Arrange sliced breast meat on top of shredded chicken. Place cilantro in pile in 1 corner of platter and shingle cucumber along side of platter.

8. Portion four to six 1-cup servings of remaining hot broth into individual soup bowls and sprinkle with scallions (you will have more than 6 cups broth; reserve extra broth for another use). Serve chicken and rice with sauce and portions of broth.

KEYS TO SUCCESS

- **Poach the whole chicken in seasoned water:** Yields juicy chicken and a flavorful broth
- **Cook the rice in the broth:** Allows the rice to absorb flavor from the poaching liquid
- **Serve broth too:** For sipping on the side

COURSE
CHICKEN STIR-FRIES

ELLE SIMONE SCOTT

The chicken in a stir-fry is often just a vehicle for the sauce—but no more. This course covers several essential stir-frying techniques such as velveting (coating the pieces in a mixture of cornstarch and oil to seal in moisture), high-heat cooking, and staggering the cooking so that you end up with moist and flavorful stir-fried chicken. Once you know the basics, you'll find that a savory-sweet stir-fry full of tender bites of chicken is one of the easiest and most flexible routes to get dinner on the table, fast.

ELLE'S PRO TIP: *Having a good non-stick skillet is essential when making recipes that both need a good sear and have sauce included. Having a wok accessible is ideal but if you find yourself without, turn to your nonstick cookware for stellar results.*

STIR-FRIED SESAME CHICKEN WITH BROCCOLI AND RED PEPPER

Serves: 4
Total Time: 30 minutes

RECIPE OVERVIEW A chicken stir-fry is quick to make and delicious: juicy, bite-size pieces of chicken pair perfectly with vegetables in a flavorful sauce. For tender, supple chicken, turn to the Chinese technique known as velveting, which involves coating chicken pieces with a mixture of cornstarch and oil. This forms a barrier around the chicken pieces to keep moisture inside and protect them from the high heat of the pan, ensuring that they remain tender. The cornstarch also helps create a rough surface on the chicken that prevents the sauce from sliding off. For the vegetables, we like colorful broccoli and red bell pepper. Peel the broccoli stalks and slice them thin (see page 41) so that they cook at the same rate as the tender florets. Potent sesame oil and fresh ginger add a final punch of flavor to the stir-fry. You will need a 12-inch nonstick skillet or 14-inch flat-bottomed wok, each with a tight-fitting lid, for this recipe.

- ¾ cup chicken broth, divided
- ¼ cup soy sauce, divided
- 3½ teaspoons cornstarch, divided
- 2 teaspoons toasted sesame oil
- 3 tablespoons vegetable oil, divided
- 12 ounces boneless, skinless chicken breasts, trimmed and cut into 1-inch pieces
- 1 pound broccoli, florets cut into 1-inch pieces, stalks peeled and sliced ¼ inch thick
- 1 red bell pepper, stemmed, seeded, and cut into 2-inch-long matchsticks
- 1 tablespoon grated fresh ginger
- 1 tablespoon sesame seeds, toasted

1. Whisk ½ cup broth, 3 tablespoons soy sauce, 1 tablespoon cornstarch, and sesame oil together in medium bowl; set aside. Whisk 1 tablespoon vegetable oil, remaining 1 tablespoon soy sauce, and remaining ½ teaspoon cornstarch together in large bowl. Add chicken and toss to coat.

2. Heat 1 tablespoon vegetable oil in 12-inch nonstick skillet or 14-inch flat-bottomed wok over medium-high heat until just smoking. Add chicken; increase heat to high; and cook, tossing slowly but constantly, until no longer pink, 2 to 6 minutes. Transfer to plate and tent with aluminum foil.

3. Add broccoli and remaining ¼ cup broth to now-empty pan and cook, covered, until broccoli begins to soften, about 2 minutes. Uncover and cook, tossing constantly, until liquid evaporates, about 1 minute. Stir in remaining 1 tablespoon vegetable oil and bell pepper and cook until spotty brown, 3 to 4 minutes. Reduce heat to medium.

4. Push vegetables to sides of pan. Add ginger to clearing and cook, mashing ginger into pan, until fragrant, about 30 seconds. Stir ginger into vegetables.

5. Whisk sauce to recombine, then add to pan along with chicken and any accumulated juices. Increase heat to high and cook until sauce is thickened, about 1 minute. Sprinkle with sesame seeds and serve immediately.

CORE TECHNIQUE

Stir-Frying Chicken and Vegetables

COAT CHICKEN
Toss the chicken with the soy sauce–cornstarch mixture to coat the pieces.

COOK CHICKEN
Get the oil hot, add the chicken, increase the heat, and toss the chicken slowly until it's no longer pink.

COOK VEGETABLES
Cook the broccoli covered, then uncover and add the bell pepper and cook.

ADD AROMATICS
Clear the center of the pan, add the ginger, and mash it into the pan.

FINISH WITH SAUCE
Stir the cooked chicken and any juices into the pan and add the sauce.

GAI PAD KRAPOW

Serves: 4
Total Time: 35 minutes

RECIPE OVERVIEW Gai Pad Krapow is Thai street food that stars stir-fried bite-size pieces of chicken and the bright flavor of basil. The dish traditionally uses holy basil, which can handle prolonged cooking. To help keep the flavor of the Thai basil or Italian basil we're using intact, we use the herb in three ways: Process the basil with garlic and Thai chiles for the base, add it to the finishing sauce, and stir it into the dish before serving. Pulsing boneless chicken breast in the food processor mimics the hand-chopping employed by Thai cooks. This dish is normally very spicy; we halved the amount of chiles. If fresh Thai chiles are unavailable, use two serranos or one medium jalapeño. Pass red pepper flakes and sugar at the table, along with extra fish sauce and white vinegar, so that the dish can be adjusted to suit individual tastes. You will need a 12-inch nonstick skillet or 14-inch flat-bottomed wok for this recipe.

- 2 cups fresh basil leaves, divided
- 6 green or red Thai chiles, stemmed
- 3 garlic cloves, peeled
- 2 tablespoons fish sauce, divided, plus extra for serving
- 1 tablespoon oyster sauce
- 1 tablespoon sugar, plus extra for serving
- 1 teaspoon distilled white vinegar, plus extra for serving
- 1 pound boneless, skinless chicken breasts, trimmed and cut into 2-inch pieces
- 3 shallots, sliced thin
- 2 tablespoons vegetable oil
  Red pepper flakes

1. Pulse 1 cup basil, Thai chiles, and garlic in food processor until finely chopped, 6 to 10 pulses, scraping down sides of bowl as needed. Transfer 1 tablespoon basil mixture to small bowl and stir in 1 tablespoon fish sauce, oyster sauce, sugar, and vinegar; set aside. Transfer remaining basil mixture to 12-inch nonstick skillet or 14-inch flat bottomed wok.

2. Pulse chicken and remaining 1 tablespoon fish sauce in now-empty food processor until meat is chopped into approximately ½-inch pieces, 6 to 8 pulses. Transfer to bowl and refrigerate for 15 minutes.

3. Stir shallots and oil into basil mixture in pan. Heat over medium-low heat (mixture should start to sizzle after about 1½ minutes; if it doesn't, adjust heat accordingly), tossing slowly but constantly, until garlic and shallots are golden brown, 5 to 8 minutes.

4. Add chicken; increase heat to medium; and cook, tossing slowly but constantly, breaking up chicken with rubber spatula, until only traces of pink remain, 2 to 4 minutes. Add reserved basil–fish sauce mixture and continue to cook, tossing constantly, until chicken is no longer pink, about 1 minute. Stir in remaining 1 cup basil and cook, stirring constantly, until basil is wilted, 30 seconds to 1 minute. Serve immediately, passing extra fish sauce, sugar, vinegar, and pepper flakes separately.

KUNG PAO CHICKEN

Serves: 4 to 6
Total Time: 35 minutes

RECIPE OVERVIEW Kung pao chicken is a spicy, savory mix of chicken, peanuts, and chiles. It also includes Sichuan peppercorns, which contribute a tingling sensation that complements the chiles' heat. (The interplay between the two ingredients is so foundational to Sichuan cuisine that it has a name: ma la, or "numbing heat.") Toasting crushed Sichuan peppercorns and halved arbol chiles releases their heat. Stir in garlic and ginger and then add marinated diced chicken thighs, covering the skillet to facilitate quick and even cooking. When the chicken is almost done, add crisp celery and then a concentrated sauce that cooks down to a glaze. Stirring in scallions and toasted peanuts last ensures that they retain their crunch. Kung pao chicken should be quite spicy. To adjust the heat level, use more or fewer chiles, depending on the size (we used 2-inch-long chiles) and your taste. Do not eat the chiles. Use a spice grinder or mortar and pestle to coarsely grind the Sichuan peppercorns. You will need a 12-inch nonstick skillet or 14-inch flat-bottomed wok, each with a tight-fitting lid, for this recipe.

Chicken and Sauce

- 1½ pounds boneless, skinless chicken thighs, trimmed and cut into ½-inch pieces
- ¼ cup soy sauce, divided
- 1 tablespoon cornstarch
- 1 tablespoon Shaoxing wine or dry sherry
- ½ teaspoon white pepper
- 1 tablespoon Chinese black vinegar or sherry vinegar
- 1 tablespoon packed dark brown sugar
- 2 teaspoons toasted sesame oil

Stir-Fry

- 2 tablespoons plus 1 teaspoon vegetable oil, divided
- 1 tablespoon minced garlic
- 2 teaspoons grated fresh ginger
- ½ cup dry-roasted peanuts
- 10–15 dried arbol chiles, halved lengthwise and seeded
- 1 teaspoon Sichuan peppercorns, ground coarse
- 2 celery ribs, cut into ½-inch pieces
- 5 scallions, white and light green parts only, cut into ½-inch pieces

1. FOR THE CHICKEN AND SAUCE Combine chicken, 2 tablespoons soy sauce, cornstarch, Shaoxing wine, and white pepper in large bowl and toss to coat; set aside. Stir vinegar, sugar, oil, and remaining 2 tablespoons soy sauce together in small bowl; set aside.

2. FOR THE STIR-FRY Stir 1 tablespoon oil, garlic, and ginger together in second small bowl. Combine peanuts and 1 teaspoon oil in 12-inch nonstick skillet or 14-inch flat-bottomed wok over medium-low heat. Cook, tossing slowly but constantly, until peanuts just begin to darken, 3 to 5 minutes. Transfer peanuts to plate and spread into even layer to cool. Return now-empty pan to medium-low heat. Add remaining 1 tablespoon oil, arbols, and peppercorns and cook, tossing constantly, until arbols begin to darken, 1 to 2 minutes. Add garlic mixture and cook, tossing constantly, until all clumps are broken up and mixture is fragrant, about 30 seconds.

3. Add chicken and spread into even layer. Cover pan; increase heat to medium-high; and cook, without stirring, for 1 minute. Stir chicken and spread into even layer. Cover and cook, without stirring, for 1 minute. Add celery and cook uncovered, tossing constantly, until chicken is cooked through, 2 to 3 minutes. Add soy sauce mixture and cook, tossing constantly, until sauce is thickened and shiny and coats chicken, 3 to 5 minutes. Stir in scallions and peanuts and serve.

> ### KEYS TO SUCCESS
> - **Use chicken thighs**: Flavorful, juicy, and more resistant to overcooking
> - **Cut uniform sizes and shapes**: Gives the dish its signature harmonious appearance
> - **Cover the skillet**: Trapped steam helps the chicken cook quickly and evenly.

The Ma La of Sichuan Cooking

The combination of numbing, tingly Sichuan peppercorns (ma) and fiery chiles (la)—or ma la ("numbing heat")—is a calling card of Sichuan cuisine. You'll find these characteristic sensations in our Kung Pao Chicken.

Tingly
Sichuan peppercorns contain the chemical hydroxy-alpha-sanshool, which stimulates receptors in our mouths, sending signals to our brains that we interpret as vibrations—even though the peppercorns don't actually vibrate our skin. They do, however, cause numbness and tingling.

Fiery
Arbol chiles are a good substitute for the traditional choice: chao tian jiao, or "facing heaven" chiles.

COURSE
SIMPLE FRIED CHICKEN

MORGAN BOLLING

Who doesn't love the crispy brown exterior on anything fried? Whether it's deep-fried or shallow-fried (also known as pan-fried), a brief encounter with hot fat turns mild-tasting chicken irresistibly rich and flavorsome. This course features three different styles of fried chicken, including shatteringly crisp Japanese fried chicken; chicken fried in a cast-iron skillet then finished in the oven; and deep-fried cutlets with a craggy, ultra-crunchy coating. In addition, you'll learn all you need to know when it comes to seasoning your chicken, keeping the oil at the right temperature, and staying safe when cooking with hot oil.

MORGAN'S PRO TIP: *Refrigerating coated chicken before frying allows the starches in the coating to hydrate. It sounds sciency but what it means is that it assures that crunchy coating will stick firmly to the chicken!*

KARAAGE
Serves: 4 to 6
Total Time: 1 hour

RECIPE OVERVIEW Juicy, deeply seasoned thigh meat encased in a supercrispy crust makes Japanese karaage a fried chicken lover's dream. Minimal oil and fast frying make it a cinch to cook. Briefly marinating the meat in a mixture of soy sauce, sake, ginger, and garlic (seasoned with a little salt and sugar) imbues the chicken with deeply savory, aromatic flavor. Next, dredging the chicken in cornstarch and letting the dredged pieces rest while the oil heats gives the starch time to hydrate. Just before frying, dab any dry patches with reserved marinade to prevent dustiness. Lemon wedges are the traditional karaage accompaniment, and for good reason: The acid cuts through the richness of the fried dark meat and underscores (without overpowering) the bright heat of the ginger in the marinade. We recommend using a rasp-style grater to grate the ginger. Do not substitute chicken breasts for the thighs; they will dry out during frying. Leftover frying oil can be cooled, strained, and saved for later use. Use a Dutch oven that holds 6 quarts or more for this recipe.

- 3 tablespoons soy sauce for the marinade
- 2 tablespoons sake for the marinade
- 1 tablespoon grated fresh ginger for the marinade
- 2 garlic cloves, minced for the marinade
- ¾ teaspoon sugar for the marinade
- ⅛ teaspoon table salt for the marinade
- 1½ pounds boneless, skinless chicken thighs, trimmed and cut crosswise into 1- to 1½-inch-wide strips
- 1¼ cups cornstarch
- 1 quart peanut or vegetable oil for frying
- Lemon wedges

1. Combine soy sauce, sake, ginger, garlic, sugar, and salt in medium bowl. Add chicken and toss to combine. Let sit at room temperature for 30 minutes. While chicken is marinating, line rimmed baking sheet with parchment paper. Set wire rack in second rimmed baking sheet and line rack with triple layer of paper towels. Place cornstarch in wide bowl.

2. Lift chicken from marinade, 1 piece at a time, allowing excess marinade to drip back into bowl but leaving any garlic or ginger bits on chicken. Coat chicken with cornstarch, shake off excess, and place on parchment-lined sheet. Reserve marinade.

3. Add oil to large Dutch oven until it measures about ¾ inch deep and heat over medium-high heat to 375 degrees. While oil heats, check chicken pieces for white patches of dry cornstarch. Dip back of spoon in reserved marinade and gently press onto dry spots to lightly moisten.

4. Using tongs, add half of chicken, 1 piece at a time, to oil in single layer. Cook, adjusting burner as necessary to maintain oil temperature between 300 and 325 degrees, until chicken is golden brown and crispy, 4 to 5 minutes. Using spider skimmer or slotted spoon, transfer chicken to paper towel–lined rack. Return oil to 325 degrees and repeat with remaining chicken. Serve with lemon wedges.

KEYS TO SUCCESS
- **Shake after dredging:** Rids the chicken of any excess cornstarch
- **Let rest:** Gives the cornstarch time to absorb moisture
- **Dab dry patches of coating with marinade:** Prevents dusty patches

Supereasy Fried Chicken by the Numbers

1 QUART OIL — 2 BATCHES — 5 MIN/BATCH

CAST IRON EASIER FRIED CHICKEN
Serves: 4
Total Time: 1¼ hours, plus 30 minutes marinating

RECIPE OVERVIEW Juicy, crisp bone-in fried chicken is a cast iron classic. While we love a classic fried chicken recipe, this faster alternative is good for those cooks new to frying. It still ensures chicken with a moist, perfectly seasoned interior and a supercrunchy crust. To start, brine the chicken in salted buttermilk, and for a perfectly crunchy coating, combine flour with a little baking powder and some seasonings, then add more buttermilk to make a thick, craggy coating that becomes crisp when fried. Briefly shallow-fry the chicken in a cast-iron skillet, and then to finish cooking, move the pieces to a hot oven (perched on a wire rack set in a baking sheet to prevent burnt spots and promote air circulation around the meat). This hybrid method will give you perfectly crisp, evenly cooked results. Any combination of chicken pieces will work well here; just be sure that the total amount equals 2½ pounds. You will need a 12-inch cast-iron skillet with at least 2-inch sides for this recipe. Do not use kosher chicken for this recipe, and don't let the chicken soak in the brine for longer than 1 hour, or it will be too salty. Covering the skillet with a splatter screen will reduce the mess that frying inevitably makes.

1 cup buttermilk for brining
1 tablespoon table salt for brining
1 tablespoon pepper, divided
1¼ teaspoons garlic powder, divided
1¼ teaspoons paprika, divided
½ teaspoon cayenne pepper, divided
2½ pounds bone-in chicken pieces (split breasts halved crosswise, drumsticks, and/or thighs), trimmed
2 cups all-purpose flour
2 teaspoons baking powder
1 teaspoon table salt
¼ cup buttermilk
1 quart peanut or vegetable oil for frying

1. Whisk 1 cup buttermilk, 1 tablespoon salt, 1 teaspoon pepper, ¼ teaspoon garlic powder, ¼ teaspoon paprika, and ¼ teaspoon cayenne together in large bowl. Add chicken, cover, and refrigerate for at least 30 minutes or up to 1 hour.

2. Meanwhile, adjust oven rack to middle position and heat oven to 400 degrees. Whisk flour, baking powder, salt, remaining 2 teaspoons pepper, remaining 1 teaspoon garlic powder, remaining 1 teaspoon paprika, and remaining ¼ teaspoon cayenne together in large bowl. Add buttermilk and rub into flour mixture using your hands until evenly incorporated and small clumps form. Working with 1 piece of chicken at a time, dredge in flour mixture, pressing gently to adhere, then transfer to large plate.

3. Set wire rack in rimmed baking sheet. Heat oil in 12-inch cast-iron skillet over medium-high heat to 375 degrees.

4. Carefully place half of chicken skin side down in oil. Fry until deep golden brown, about 6 minutes, turning chicken over halfway through frying. Adjust burner as necessary to maintain oil temperature between 350 and 375 degrees. Transfer chicken to prepared rack. Return oil to 375 degrees and repeat with remaining chicken; transfer to prepared rack.

5. Bake chicken until breasts register 160 degrees and drumsticks/thighs register 175 degrees, 12 to 18 minutes. Serve.

SCIENCE LESSON

Secret Ingredient: Baking Powder

Baking powder is composed of an acid and an alkali and acts like a salt: The salt helps draw moisture to the surface of the poultry skin, where it can evaporate. (Adding table salt to the baking powder enhances this effect.) The acid helps break down proteins within the skin, and the alkali accelerates the browning process, meaning that the skin can crisp more quickly.

FRIED CHICKEN SANDWICHES
Serves: 4
Total Time: 1¾ hours

RECIPE OVERVIEW This fried chicken sandwich blows the feathers off of fast-food versions. It boasts a craggy coating, properly spiced chicken, and crisp—not limp—toppings on a sturdy mayo-slicked bun. After testing different thicknesses of chicken, we found that breasts halved crosswise and gently pounded to ½ inch thick cook through in the time it takes the coating to brown properly. A few tablespoons of water in the flour coating creates the right craggy effect, and a teaspoon of baking powder makes the coating supercrispy. Beaten egg whites help the coating adhere. Letting the breaded chicken sit for 30 minutes before frying helps the coating set up and enables the salty spice rub to season the meat throughout. A sturdy potato bun and a few simple toppings take this sandwich to the finish line. Use a Dutch oven that holds 6 quarts or more for this recipe.

1 teaspoon paprika
1 teaspoon pepper
1 teaspoon garlic powder
¾ teaspoon table salt
½ teaspoon dried thyme
½ teaspoon dried sage
¼ teaspoon cayenne pepper
2 (6- to 8-ounce) boneless, skinless chicken breasts, trimmed
1½ cups all-purpose flour
1 teaspoon baking powder
3 tablespoons water
2 large egg whites, lightly beaten
2 quarts peanut or vegetable oil for frying
¼ cup mayonnaise
4 hamburger buns, toasted if desired
1 cup shredded iceberg lettuce
½ red onion, sliced thin
¼ cup dill pickle chips

1. Combine paprika, pepper, garlic powder, salt, thyme, sage, and cayenne in bowl. Measure out 1 tablespoon spice mixture and set aside. Cut each breast in half crosswise, then pound each piece to uniform ½-inch thickness. Pat chicken dry with paper towels and sprinkle with remaining 2 teaspoons spice mixture.

2. Whisk flour, baking powder, and reserved spice mixture together in large bowl. Add water to flour mixture and rub together with your fingers until water is evenly incorporated and shaggy pieces form. Place egg whites in shallow dish.

3. Set wire rack in rimmed baking sheet. Working with 1 piece of chicken at a time, dip in egg whites to thoroughly coat, letting excess drip back into dish, then dredge in flour mixture, pressing to adhere. Transfer chicken to prepared rack and refrigerate for at least 30 minutes or up to 1 hour.

4. Line second rimmed baking sheet with triple layer of paper towels. Add oil to large Dutch oven until it measures about 1½ inches deep and heat over medium-high heat to 375 degrees. Add chicken to hot oil and fry, stirring gently to prevent pieces from sticking together, until chicken is golden brown and registers 160 degrees, 4 to 5 minutes, flipping halfway through frying. Adjust burner as necessary to maintain oil temperature between 325 and 350 degrees. Transfer chicken to prepared sheet and let cool for 5 minutes.

5. Spread mayonnaise over bun tops. Serve chicken on buns, topped with lettuce, onion, and pickles.

Clumpy Flour = Crunchier Coating

Seasoned flour is the traditional coating for fried chicken. We make it better by adding a little liquid to the seasoned flour. The flour clumps together, which adds texture—and extra crunch—to the coating once it's fried.

PROBLEM: WHERE'S THE CRUNCH?
Dredging chicken in dry flour makes for a boring coating with minimal crunch.

SOLUTION: CLUMPY COATING
Moistening the dredging flour with water creates clumps that fry up extra-crunchy.

CORE TECHNIQUE

Frying Chicken for Sandwiches

Most deep-fried chicken recipes follow this basic sequence of steps.

ADD OIL TO LARGE, HEAVY POT
Add 1½ inches of peanut oil to a large Dutch oven.

CUT SIMILAR-SIZE PIECES
Cut chicken breasts in half crosswise and pound to an even thickness so that all the pieces will cook at the same rate.

DREDGE AND REST
Dip the chicken in egg whites and let the excess drip off. Dredge in flour mixture and press to adhere it to the chicken.

HEAT AND KEEP OIL AT PROPER TEMP
The oil must be heated to the correct temperature since it will drop when the chicken is added.

FRY IN BATCHES IF NECESSARY
Batch cooking keeps the temperature steady and minimizes dangerous and messy splatter.

KEEP WARM IN OVEN
If you're making more than one batch, transfer the fried chicken to a wire rack in a rimmed baking sheet and place it in a 200-degree oven to keep warm.

COURSE
CHICKEN ON THE GRILL

BRIDGET LANCASTER

Grilled chicken is a summertime classic, and when done right, its mild flavor is enhanced with a lightly charred and smoky flavor. With the right technique, the chicken—whether cut into parts or pieces or left whole—will stay moist and succulent over a hot flame. Each recipe in this course contains specific instructions for cooking on either a charcoal or a gas grill. Paying careful attention to the fire setup instructions ensures success.

BRIDGET'S PRO TIP: *All grills are different, so it's always better to gauge the doneness of the chicken by using an instant-read thermometer, rather than the time given in a recipe. If pieces of chicken are becoming deeply charred but still need time to reach a safe internal temperature, I move the pieces to a disposable foil pan set on the grill to continue cooking.*

GRILLED CHICKEN SOUVLAKI

Serves: 4 to 6
Total Time: 1½ hours

RECIPE OVERVIEW Chicken souvlaki is a Greek specialty consisting of grilled chunks of marinated meat, sometimes with vegetables. It is made with boneless, skinless breasts, which tend to dry out on the grill. To prevent this, a quick 30-minute brine adds moisture and flavor before coating the chicken with a classic mixture of lemon, olive oil, herbs, and honey before grilling. To prevent the end pieces from overcooking, thread pepper and onion pieces on the ends of the skewers. Tossing the cooked chicken with reserved marinade ensures that it is brightly flavored and moist. The traditional Greek yogurt sauce tzatziki brings everything together. We like the chicken in a wrap, but you can serve the chicken, vegetables, and tzatziki with rice. If using kosher chicken, do not brine in step 2. You will need four 12-inch metal skewers for this recipe. For more information on setting up a grill, see page 447.

Tzatziki
- ½ cucumber, peeled, halved lengthwise, seeded, and shredded
- ¼ teaspoon table salt
- ½ cup whole-milk Greek yogurt
- 1 tablespoon extra-virgin olive oil
- 1 tablespoon minced fresh mint and/or dill
- 1 small garlic clove, minced

Chicken
- 2 tablespoons table salt for brining
- 1½ pounds boneless, skinless chicken breasts, trimmed and cut into 1-inch pieces
- ⅓ cup extra-virgin olive oil
- 2 tablespoons minced fresh parsley
- 1 teaspoon finely grated lemon zest plus ¼ cup juice (2 lemons)
- 1 teaspoon honey
- 1 teaspoon dried oregano
- ½ teaspoon pepper
- 1 green bell pepper, quartered, stemmed, seeded, and each quarter cut into 4 pieces
- 1 small red onion, halved through root end, each half cut into 4 pieces
- 4–6 (8-inch) pita breads

1. FOR THE TZATZIKI Toss cucumber with salt in colander and let drain for 15 minutes. Whisk yogurt, oil, mint, and garlic together in bowl, then stir in drained cucumber. Season with salt and pepper to taste. Cover and refrigerate until chilled, at least 1 hour or up to 2 days.

2. FOR THE CHICKEN Dissolve salt in 1 quart cold water in large container. Submerge chicken in brine, cover, and refrigerate for 30 minutes. Combine oil, parsley, lemon zest and juice, honey, oregano, and pepper in medium bowl. Reserve ¼ cup oil mixture in large bowl.

3. Remove chicken from brine and pat dry with paper towels. Toss chicken with remaining oil mixture. Thread 4 pieces of bell pepper, concave side up, onto one 12-inch metal skewer. Thread one-quarter of chicken onto skewer. Thread 2 chunks of onion onto skewer and place skewer on plate. Repeat skewering remaining chicken and vegetables on 3 more skewers. Lightly moisten 2 pita breads with water. Sandwich unmoistened pitas between moistened pitas and wrap stack tightly in lightly greased heavy-duty aluminum foil.

4A. FOR A CHARCOAL GRILL Open bottom vent completely. Light large chimney starter mounded with charcoal briquettes (7 quarts). When top coals are partially covered with ash, pour evenly over half of grill. Set cooking grate in place, cover, and open lid vent completely. Heat grill until hot, about 5 minutes.

4B. FOR A GAS GRILL Turn all burners to high; cover; and heat grill until hot, about 15 minutes. Leave primary burner on high and turn off other burner(s).

5. Clean and oil cooking grate. Place skewers on hotter side of grill and cook, turning occasionally, until chicken and vegetables are well browned and chicken registers 160 degrees, 15 to 20 minutes. Using tongs, slide chicken and vegetables off skewers into bowl of reserved oil mixture. Toss gently, breaking up onion chunks. Cover loosely with foil and let sit while heating pitas.

6. Place packet of pitas on cooler side of grill and flip occasionally until heated through, about 5 minutes. Lay each warm pita on 12-inch square of foil. Spread each pita with 2 tablespoons yogurt sauce. Place one-quarter of chicken and vegetables in middle of each pita. Roll into cylindrical shape and serve.

KEYS TO SUCCESS
- **Brine briefly:** Replaces an overnight marinade to keep chicken moist
- **Use Greek yogurt:** Yields thick, creamy tzatziki
- **Soak the grilled chicken in a bit of reserved marinade:** Rehydrates the chicken's exterior and delivers a bright citrus punch

A Vegetable Shield

The age-old problem with grilling meat on a stick: The end pieces overcook. We protect the chicken by threading pepper and onion pieces on the ends. The charred vegetables taste great in the sandwich, too.

GRILLED BONE-IN CHICKEN

Serves: 4 to 6
Total Time: 1 hour

RECIPE OVERVIEW Flare-ups can turn chicken into a charred mess if you're not paying attention. The method we developed for bone-in chicken avoids this pitfall by starting the chicken over a relatively cool area of the grill. This allows the fat in the chicken skin to render slowly, thereby avoiding flare-ups and encouraging ultracrisp skin. Finishing it over the hotter side yields perfectly browned parts. In addition to the quality of the finished product, we like this approach because it is effectively hands-off: You don't have to constantly move and monitor the chicken pieces. This recipe works with breasts, legs, thighs, or a combination of parts. For extra flavor, rub the chicken with a spice rub (page 352) before cooking.

- 4 pounds bone-in chicken pieces (split breasts halved crosswise, drumsticks, and/or thighs), trimmed
- ¾ teaspoon table salt
- ½ teaspoon pepper
- 1 (13 by 9-inch) disposable aluminum roasting pan (if using charcoal)

1. Pat chicken dry with paper towels and sprinkle with salt and pepper.

2A. **FOR A CHARCOAL GRILL** Open bottom vent completely and place disposable pan in center of grill. Light large chimney starter filled with charcoal briquettes (6 quarts). When top coals are partially covered with ash, pour into 2 even piles on either side of disposable pan. Set cooking grate in place, cover, and open lid vent completely. Heat grill until hot, about 5 minutes.

2B. **FOR A GAS GRILL** Turn all burners to high; cover; and heat grill until hot, about 15 minutes. Turn all burners to medium-low.

3. Clean and oil cooking grate. Place chicken, skin side down, on grill (over disposable pan if using charcoal). Cover and cook until skin is crisp and golden, about 20 minutes.

4. Slide chicken to hotter sides of grill if using charcoal, or turn all burners to medium-high if using gas. Cook (covered if using gas), turning as needed, until well browned on both sides and breasts register 160 degrees and drumsticks/thighs register 175 degrees, 5 to 15 minutes.

5. Transfer chicken to platter, tent with aluminum foil, and let rest for 5 to 10 minutes before serving.

KEYS TO SUCCESS

- **Use a disposable pan for charcoal:** Creates a cooler area on the grill to start the chicken over
- **Pat chicken really dry:** Ensures that chicken skin won't stick to the grill
- **Start low:** Gives chicken skin time to render fat and crisp up nicely

GRILLED WINE-AND-HERB MARINATED CHICKEN

Serves: 4
Total Time: 2 hours, plus 2 hours marinating

RECIPE OVERVIEW Wine is a natural fit with chicken. The bold acidity and fruity, complex flavors of both red and white wines pair beautifully with the mild meat. For this winey, herby grilled chicken, we prefer a dry white wine, which imparts a more distinct flavor to the meat. Whizzing the marinade in a blender breaks down the herbs for optimal flavor and distribution, and poking holes in the chicken with a skewer helps the flavors of the marinade penetrate the bird. Butterflying increases the meat's exposure to heat, allowing it to cook more quickly and evenly. Starting the chicken over the cooler part of the grill with the skin side down until the meat is almost done before flipping it and finishing directly above the fire ensures evenly cooked meat with a crisp skin. A thin basting sauce, or mop, adds complexity and freshness to the grilled meat, so reserve a small amount of marinade to brush on the chicken near the end of cooking. Use a dry white wine, such as Sauvignon Blanc, for this recipe. An inexpensive wine will work just fine, but pick one that's good enough to drink.

- 2 cups dry white wine
- 3 tablespoons lemon juice
- 3 tablespoons extra-virgin olive oil
- 2 tablespoons chopped fresh parsley
- 2 tablespoons chopped fresh thyme
- 2 tablespoons packed light brown sugar
- 4 garlic cloves, minced
- 1 teaspoon pepper
- 2 tablespoons table salt for the marinade
- 1 (3½- to 4-pound) whole chicken, giblets discarded

1. Process wine, lemon juice, oil, parsley, thyme, sugar, garlic, and pepper in blender until emulsified, about 40 seconds. Measure out ¼ cup marinade and set aside. Add salt to remaining marinade in blender and process to dissolve, about 20 seconds.

2. With chicken breast side down, use kitchen shears to cut along both sides of backbone. Discard backbone and trim any excess fat or skin at neck. Flip chicken and use heel of your hand to flatten breastbone. Tuck wingtips behind back.

3. Poke holes all over chicken with skewer. Place chicken in 1-gallon zipper-lock bag, pour in salted marinade, seal bag, and turn to coat. Set bag in baking dish, breast side down, and refrigerate for 2 to 3 hours.

4A. FOR A CHARCOAL GRILL Open bottom vent completely. Light large chimney starter filled with charcoal briquettes (6 quarts). When top coals are partially covered with ash, pour evenly over half of grill. Set cooking grate in place, cover, and open lid vent completely. Heat grill until hot, about 5 minutes.

4B. FOR A GAS GRILL Turn all burners to high; cover; and heat grill until hot, about 15 minutes. Turn primary burner to medium and other burner(s) to low. (Adjust primary burner [or, if using 3-burner grill, primary burner and second burner] as needed to maintain grill temperature between 350 and 375 degrees.)

5. Remove chicken from marinade and pat dry with paper towels. Clean and oil cooking grate. Place chicken skin side down on cooler side of grill, with legs closest to hotter side of grill. Cover and cook until chicken is well browned and thighs register 160 degrees, 50 minutes to 1 hour 5 minutes. Brush chicken with half of reserved marinade. Flip chicken skin side up, move it to hotter side of grill, and brush with remaining reserved marinade. Cook, covered, until breasts register 160 degrees and thighs register 175 degrees, 10 to 15 minutes.

6. Transfer chicken to carving board, tent with aluminum foil, and let rest for 15 minutes. Carve and serve.

KEYS TO SUCCESS

- See page 421 for how to butterfly the chicken.
- **Process marinade in blender:** Breaks down the herbs and releases their flavor compounds
- **Poke holes in chicken:** Lets the marinade penetrate
- **Mop at end of grilling:** Gives the chicken skin an opportunity to get crispy

SCIENCE LESSON
A Salty Marinade Up Close

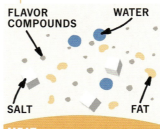

START OF MARINADE
When marinating, meat is immersed in a solution of water; flavor compounds; fat; and, most important, salt.

END OF MARINADE
With time, the water and salt penetrate to the center of the meat while the fat and fat-soluble flavor compounds remain on the surface.

GRILLING BASICS

SETTING UP A FIRE

The fire setup—how much charcoal or how many burners you're using and where the heat is located in relation to the food—allows you to control the heat level and the rate of cooking. Using the wrong setup can cause food to burn before it's cooked through or cook through without developing any flavorful browning or char.

Best Practice: Use the fire setup that's appropriate for the type of food you're grilling. We use three main fire setups, and we follow these guidelines when choosing which to use.

FIRE TYPE	BEST FOR
Single-Level Fire	Small, quick-cooking foods such as burgers, sausages, shrimp, fish fillets, and some vegetables
Half-Grill Fire	Foods that you want to cook gently but also sear, such as kebabs, thin steaks, and some vegetables
Double-Banked Fire	Foods on which you want char, such as bone-in chicken parts

THREE BASIC FIRE SETUPS

SINGLE-LEVEL FIRE
Charcoal Setup: Distribute lit coals in even layer across bottom of grill.

Gas Setup: Turn all burners to high, cover, and heat grill until hot. Leave all burners on high.

HALF-GRILL FIRE
Charcoal Setup: Distribute lit coals in even layer over 1 half of grill.

Gas Setup: Turn all burners to high, cover, and heat grill until hot. Leave primary burner on high and turn off other burner(s).

DOUBLE-BANKED FIRE
Charcoal Setup: Bank lit coals into 2 even piles on opposite sides of grill.

Gas Setup: Turn all burners to high, cover, and heat grill until hot. Turn all burners to medium-low then up to medium-high (as directed in the recipe).

DON'T COOK ON A GUNKED-UP GRILL

Food debris, grease, and smoke that build up on various parts of the grill can cause sticking and impart off-flavors to food; full grease traps can ignite; and built-up grease on the interior basin and underside of the grill lid can carbonize and turn into a patchy layer that flakes off and lands on your food.

HOW TO CLEAN YOUR GRILL

Cooking grate: After preheating the grill, scrape the cooking grate clean with a grill brush.

Interior basin and lid: Lightly scrub the cool grill and lid with steel wool and water.

Ash catcher (charcoal only): Empty the cooled ash regularly.

Grease traps (gas only): Remove the cool shallow pan from under your grill and scrub it with hot soapy water. To make cleanup easier, line the pan with aluminum foil before use.

OILING THE COOKING GRATE

Most cooking grates are made of steel or cast iron and must be oiled before grilling to keep food from sticking.

Best Practice: Using tongs, dip a wad of paper towels in vegetable oil and thoroughly wipe the preheated, scrubbed cooking grate before adding food.

POULTRY | 447

COURSE
YOUR FIRST TURKEY

DAN ZUCCARELLO

Cooking a moist, evenly seasoned, attractively browned turkey is within reach. Like chicken, one of the biggest challenges when cooking turkey is getting the dark meat up to temperature without drying out the white meat. Thankfully, the solution is simple: salt. Our roast turkey breast recipe is perfect for absolute beginners and white meat–lovers. You'll also learn how to make a more traditional whole turkey with a recipe that includes a built-in gravy. When the cooking is done, you can follow our step-by-step instructions for carving without fear.

DAN'S PRO TIP: *I always seem to have excess gravy left over. Instead of throwing it away, I store it in the freezer until I can use it as a base for chicken stew or the sauce for a casserole.*

EASY ROAST TURKEY BREAST

Serves: 8 to 10
Total Time: 2¼ hours

RECIPE OVERVIEW Unlike a whole bird, where you need to worry about cooking dark and white meat correctly, a turkey breast has just one kind of meat. The challenge, however, is that white meat turkey can be bland and is easily overcooked. To produce a foolproof roast turkey breast, roast the bird in two stages: first at a high temperature to crisp the skin and then at a low temperature for moist meat. The optimal combination is to start the turkey breast in a 425-degree oven for the first half-hour and then reduce the heat to 325 degrees for the remaining hour. Loosening the skin and rubbing the meat with softened butter promotes even browning and crispier skin. We recommend brining a natural turkey breast; if brining (see page 343), omit the salt from the recipe. Using a kosher or self-basting breast eliminates the need for brining. If the breast has a pop-up timer, do not remove it; ignore it (they pop too late) and follow the times and temperatures in the recipe. A turkey breast doesn't yield much in the way of drippings, so a classic pan gravy recipe is not an option. Instead, try our All-Purpose Gravy (page 450).

- 4 tablespoons unsalted butter, softened
- ¾ teaspoon table salt
- ¼ teaspoon pepper
- 1 (6- to 7-pound) bone-in whole turkey breast, trimmed
- 1 cup water

1. Adjust oven rack to middle position and heat oven to 425 degrees. Mix butter, salt, and pepper in medium bowl with rubber spatula until thoroughly combined. Using your fingers, carefully separate turkey skin from meat.

2. Work butter mixture under skin on both sides of breast and rub skin of turkey to evenly distribute butter over breast. Spray V-rack with nonstick cooking spray and set inside large roasting pan. Place turkey in rack with skin side facing up; pour water into roasting pan.

3. Roast turkey for 30 minutes. Reduce oven temperature to 325 degrees. Continue to roast until breast registers 160 degrees, about 1 hour. Transfer turkey to carving board and let rest, uncovered, for 20 minutes. Carve and serve.

KEYS TO SUCCESS

- **Brine the breast:** Seasons the meat and keeps it from drying out
- **Butter the breast under the skin:** Helps ensure flavorful, juicy results
- **Add water to pan:** Keeps minimal drippings in pan from burning and smoking during high-heat roasting

CORE TECHNIQUE

Carving a Turkey Breast

Do not skip the resting step or there will be a flood of turkey juices on your carving board.

REMOVE BREAST HALF
Run a chef's or carving knife along one side of the breastbone. Pry the entire half from the bone while cutting, keeping the skin intact.

SLICE MEAT
Slice the breast meat on the bias. Repeat with the meat on the other side of the breastbone.

EASIER ROAST TURKEY AND GRAVY

Serves: 10 to 12
Total Time: 3½ hours, plus 24 hours salting

RECIPE OVERVIEW When you want all the advantages of a great roast turkey with less work, this recipe delivers. No flipping. No long-simmered gravy. The key is a tool borrowed from pizza making: a baking stone (or steel). But first, to season the meat and help it retain more juices as it cooks, loosen the skin of the turkey and apply a mixture of salt and sugar to the flesh. Next, preheat both the baking stone and roasting pan in the oven before placing the turkey in the pan. The stone absorbs heat and delivers it through the pan to the turkey's legs and thighs, which need to cook to a higher temperature than the delicate breast meat (which we call for protecting with a foil shield). After the leg quarters have gotten a jump start, reduce the oven temperature and remove the shield to allow the breast to brown. The heat boost provided by the stone also helps the juices brown and reduce into concentrated drippings that we turn into a flavorful gravy while the turkey rests. Note that this recipe requires salting the bird in the refrigerator for 24 to 48 hours. This recipe was developed and tested using Diamond Crystal Kosher Salt. If you have Morton's Kosher Salt, which is denser than Diamond Crystal, reduce the salt in step 1 to 3 tablespoons; rub 1 tablespoon salt mixture into each side of the breast, 1½ teaspoons into each leg, and the remainder into the cavity. Table salt is too fine and not recommended. If you are roasting a kosher or self-basting turkey (such as a frozen Butterball), do not salt it. The success of this recipe is dependent on saturating the baking stone and roasting pan with heat. We recommend preheating the stone, pan, and oven for at least 30 minutes.

- ¼ cup kosher salt
- 4 teaspoons sugar
- 1 (12- to 14-pound) turkey, neck and giblets removed and reserved for gravy
- 2½ tablespoons vegetable oil, divided
- 1 teaspoon baking powder
- 1 small onion, chopped fine
- 1 carrot, peeled and sliced thin
- 5 sprigs fresh parsley
- 2 bay leaves
- 5 tablespoons all-purpose flour
- 3¼ cups water
- ¼ cup dry white wine

1. Combine salt and sugar in bowl. Using your fingers, gently loosen skin covering turkey breast and thighs. Rub 4 teaspoons salt mixture under skin of each breast half, 2 teaspoons salt under skin of each leg, and remaining salt mixture into cavity. Tie legs together with kitchen twine. Place turkey on rack set in rimmed baking sheet and refrigerate uncovered for 24 to 48 hours.

2. At least 30 minutes before roasting turkey, adjust oven rack to lowest position and set baking stone on oven rack. Place roasting pan on baking stone and heat oven to 500 degrees. Combine 1½ teaspoons oil and baking powder in small bowl. Pat turkey dry with paper towels. Rub oil mixture evenly over turkey. Cover turkey breast with double layer of aluminum foil.

3. Remove roasting pan from oven. Place remaining 2 tablespoons oil in roasting pan. Place turkey into pan breast side up and return pan to oven. Reduce oven temperature to 425 degrees and cook for 45 minutes.

4. Remove foil shield; reduce temperature to 325 degrees; and continue to cook until breast registers 160 degrees and thighs register 175 degrees, 1 to 1½ hours.

5. Using spatula, loosen turkey from roasting pan; transfer to carving board and let rest uncovered for 45 minutes. While turkey rests, use wooden spoon to scrape any browned bits from bottom of roasting pan. Pour pan drippings through fine-mesh strainer set in bowl. Transfer drippings to fat separator and let rest for 10 minutes. Reserve 3 tablespoons fat and defatted liquid (about 1 cup). Discard remaining fat.

6. Heat reserved fat in large saucepan over medium-high heat until shimmering. Add reserved neck and giblets and cook until well browned, 10 to 12 minutes. Transfer neck and giblets to large plate. Reduce heat to medium; add onion, carrot, parsley, and bay leaves; and cook, stirring frequently, until vegetables are softened, 5 to 7 minutes. Add flour and cook, stirring constantly, until flour is well coated with fat, about 1 minute. Slowly whisk in reserved defatted liquid and cook until thickened, about 1 minute. Whisk in water and wine, return neck and giblets, and bring to simmer. Simmer for 10 minutes. Season with salt and pepper to taste. Discard neck. Strain mixture through fine-mesh strainer and transfer to serving bowl. Carve turkey and arrange on serving platter. Serve with gravy.

ALL-PURPOSE GRAVY

Makes: about 2 cups
Total Time: 1 hour

If you happen to have drippings from your turkey or chicken, you can use them to replace some or all of the oil.

- 3 tablespoons vegetable oil
- 1 small onion, chopped
- 1 small carrot, peeled and chopped
- 1 small celery rib, chopped
- ½ teaspoon pepper
- ¼ cup all-purpose flour
- 4 cups chicken broth
- ¼ cup dry white wine
- 2 sprigs fresh thyme
- 1 bay leaf

1. Heat oil in large saucepan over medium heat until shimmering. Add onion, carrot, celery, and pepper and cook over medium heat until vegetables are softened and well browned, about 8 minutes. Stir in flour and cook for 1 minute. Slowly whisk in broth and wine, scraping up any browned bits and smoothing out any lumps. Stir in thyme sprigs and bay leaf; bring to simmer; and cook until gravy is thickened and reduced to 3 cups, about 15 minutes.

2. Strain gravy through fine-mesh strainer into bowl, pressing on solids to extract as much liquid as possible; discard solids. Season with salt and pepper to taste. (Gravy can be frozen for up to 1 month. To thaw, place the gravy and 1 tablespoon water in a saucepan over low heat and bring slowly to a simmer. The gravy may appear broken or curdled as it thaws, but a vigorous whisking will recombine it.)

RESOURCES FOR TURKEY

THE SETUP FOR EASIER TURKEY AND GRAVY

We recommend placing the turkey in a preheated roasting pan, covering the breast with aluminum foil to protect it from overcooking, and placing the pan on a preheated baking stone or steel. The benefits of this arrangement are twofold:

White and Dark Meat Finish Concurrently The baking stone's heat is transferred through the roasting pan to the leg quarters, so they finish cooking at the same time as the more delicate breast meat.

Faster Gravy The extra heat provided by the baking stone also causes the juices that accumulate in the bottom of the roasting pan to reduce very quickly, so the drippings left in the pan at the end of roasting are superconcentrated. Starting with intensely flavored drippings means that the gravy can be made with water, not broth, and it needs only 10 minutes of simmering time to reach its full flavor potential.

SALTING UNDER THE SKIN

In order to apply salt to turkey flesh, the skin must first be loosened. Here are a couple tips:

Don't detach the membrane along the breastbone—it's hard to loosen without ripping the skin. Plus, the membrane helps you divide the salt evenly.

The skin around the curve at the neck end can be difficult to loosen. To make the job easier, first loosen the skin on the bottom two-thirds of the breast and the legs, and then turn the turkey 180 degrees and come in through the neck end to loosen the skin on the top third of the breast.

Note: Don't forget to salt the cavity of the bird as well; when we skipped this step, the turkey didn't taste as deeply seasoned.

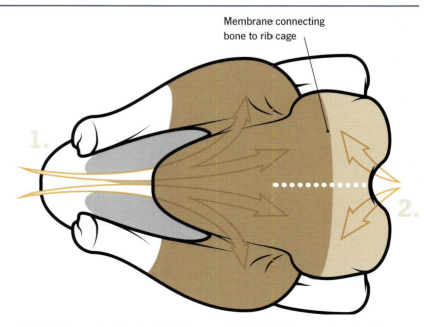

1. Working from tail end, rub salt under loosened skin on bottom two-thirds of breast and legs.

2. Working from neck end, rub salt on remaining breast meat.

CHAPTER 10

SEAFOOD

COURSES

458 CROWD FAVORITE: COD

462 FIRM, MEATY WHITE FISH

468 THIN WHITE FISH

474 SALMON SO MANY WAYS

482 POACHING FOR EVERY FISH

484 SERVING UP SHRIMP

490 WORKING WITH BIVALVES

496 THE FISH FRY

SEAFOOD BASICS

BUYING FISH

Whether you're purchasing seafood from your local fishmonger or a big chain grocery store (make sure that the store has high turnover), you'll want to be informed on what to look for so that your meals are tasty and fresh. There are different considerations for fresh versus frozen fish.

Fresh Fish

Fish fillets and steaks should be sold on (but not buried in) ice. Whenever possible, we cut individual fillets from larger fillets (ask for center-cut fillets to avoid the thick and tapered ends). Larger fillets keep longer and allow for more consistent sizing for even cooking. You can be choosy at the fish counter; a ragged fillet or a tail end will be difficult to cook properly. The fish should smell sweet like the sea, and the surface should be shiny and bright and uniform in color. The flesh should be firm and elastic; when you press into it, the indentation should fill in.

Frozen Fish

Since 85 percent of the fish consumed in the United States is imported, a lot of the seafood you buy at the fish counter has been frozen and then thawed. And so some argue that frozen fish is even "fresher" than fresh-caught fish that's been sitting on ice for more than a day. You can ask the fishmonger if you can get a frozen piece of fish instead of thawed previously frozen fish so that you can control how it's thawed. If you're buying frozen fish from the freezer section, avoid packages with tears or punctures that could let in air, freezer burn, excess frozen liquid, or fish with discolored flesh. Consider choosing thin fish (such as flounder or catfish) when buying frozen; it freezes more rapidly, leading to less tissue damage.

Sustainable Fish

Industrial fishing has caused overfishing of certain species of fish, and the ocean's resources are finite. There are also methods of fishing that are harmful to other species of wildlife as well as the environment. Markets are becoming more and more transparent about the methods used to catch fish and their sustainability status. If this is a topic of interest to you and you want to buy consciously, check out Monterey Bay Aquarium Seafood Watch (seafoodwatch.org); it gives the current sustainability status of individual species of fish (it's always changing) as well as their common catching method.

Buying in Season

Just as different types of produce have harvesting seasons, fish have seasons when they're available to be caught. It varies by region; what's in season in the Northeast might not be in season at the same time in the mid-Atlantic. A good fishmonger can source fish from nearly anywhere, and a supermarket gets its fish from everywhere, often previously frozen, so it's not too much of a concern. However, if fish such as certain kinds of wild salmon and black sea bass are hard to find, it's probably not their season.

Portioning Fish Fillets

We find that the best way to ensure fillets of similar thickness is to buy a large center-cut fillet (1½ to 2 pounds if serving four) when you can and cut it into four equal portions.

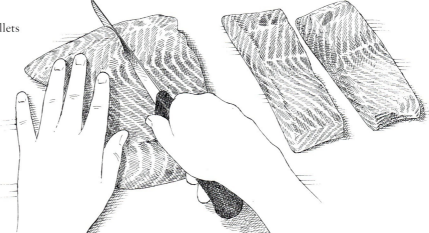

STORING FISH

If you're not using fish the same day you buy it, it's important to store it properly.

In the Refrigerator

Unwrap the fish, pat it dry, put it in a zipper-lock bag, press out the air, and seal the bag. Set the fish on a bed of ice in a bowl or container (to hold the water once the ice melts), and place it in the back of the refrigerator, where it's coldest. If the ice melts before you use the fish, replenish it. The fish should keep for one day.

In the Freezer

Vacuum-seal fish or wrap it in a double layer of plastic wrap, removing any air pockets, and then in aluminum foil. We don't recommend refreezing previously frozen fish, as its quality will suffer.

To defrost fish in the refrigerator overnight, remove the fish from its packaging, place it in a single layer on a rimmed plate, and cover it with plastic wrap. You can also do a "quick thaw" by leaving the vacuum-sealed bags under cool running tap water for 30 minutes. (Do not microwave!) Dry the fish thoroughly with paper towels.

WHY YOU SHOULD BRINE FISH

In the test kitchen, we brine meats such as chicken, turkey, and pork to improve both flavor and texture. But brining fish, which is generally pretty lean, can be beneficial, too. We set up a series of tests using different brine concentrations (saltwater solutions containing 3, 6, and 9 percent salt by weight) and types of fish (tuna, salmon, swordfish, and halibut). We found that, for up to six 1-inch-thick steaks or fillets, the optimum concentration was a 6 percent brine (5 tablespoons of salt dissolved in 2 quarts of water) and the ideal time was 15 minutes. It worked no matter the species, improving the texture of the fish without overseasoning it.

As it does with meat, brining fish serves two purposes: One, it helps season the flesh, which improves flavor, and two, by partially dissolving muscle fibers to form a water-retaining gel, it helps prevent the protein from drying out. And brining works a lot faster on fish because the muscle structure of fish is different than that of meat: Instead of long, thin fibers (as long as 10 centimeters in meat), fish is constructed of very short (up to 10 times shorter) bundles of fibers.

In addition, we seared each species of fish to see if using a wet brine would inhibit browning. Luckily, it did not, so long as the fish was dried well with paper towels just before cooking. Finally, we've found that brining helps reduce the presence of albumin (see page 481), a protein that can congeal into an unappealing white mass on the surface of the fish when heated. You can brine your fish before preparing our recipes, if desired. (Do not brine the fish if a recipe calls for salting fish and letting it sit before cooking, as with our Sautéed Tilapia with Cilantro Chimichurri [page 469].)

FISH COOKING CATEGORIES

There's no perfect way to categorize fish. Scientific classifications and taxonomy exist, but these don't help the cook. We categorize fish according to their texture; flavor; and, sometimes, exchangeability in cooking. This means that you can substitute one fish for another within a category based on your preference and its availability.

Flaky White Fish

Black sea bass, cod, haddock, hake, and pollock are flaky white fish. White fish are very lean because their fat is concentrated in their liver. The fish in this grouping dwell near the bottom of the ocean along continental shelves and do little muscle-activating swimming, so they easily fall into flakes under your fork. They also have a clean, mild flavor.

Firm, Meaty White Fish

Halibut, mahi-mahi, red snapper, striped bass, and swordfish are firm, meaty white fish. Their texture is meatier than flaky white fish, breaking into moist chunks, because, with the exception of halibut, they swim a lot more.

Thin White Fish

Catfish, flounder, sole, and tilapia are thin white fish. They're versatile, impressively flaky, always tender, and easy to brown. Catfish and tilapia have an unfounded reputation for tasting bad, which needs to be debunked; modern sourcing and farming practices ensure clean, mild flavor.

Salmon and Char

Salmon, believe it or not, is actually a type of white fish (gray, really); its flesh turned pink only by the crustaceans it eats. The compound responsible for this coloring also gives salmon its unique flavor; when heated it forms volatile aromas. Salmon swim upstream in cold waters, so they're relatively high in fat (and also high in good-for-you omega-3 fatty acids) and have stronger muscles than white fish. Char is a member of both the trout and salmon families, but it more closely resembles salmon in texture and flavor.

Tuna

Tuna is a fast-swimming predator, so its muscles need a lot of oxygen and have a high myoglobin content (myoglobin is the dark-pigmented protein that stores oxygen in the muscles). That's why it has a dark-red color. Tuna's muscle fibers have more collagen than paler-flesh fish, so they feel moister—pleasantly gelatinous, in fact—when cooked. While bluefin tuna is prized and used primarily for sushi, yellowfin (or ahi) tuna is the type you'll likely find at the local fish market, usually cut into steaks.

Trout

Trout is a freshwater fish that's exclusively farmed (unless you catch your own)—in fact, the farming of trout is the oldest fish-farming industry in North America. Trout is oily but much milder in flavor than its anadromous cousins, salmon and arctic char, tasting almost nutty. The flesh has a soft texture with delicate flakes. Trout is often prepared whole (it usually comes gutted, butterflied, and boned—convenient and perfectly portioned) but is also available in fillets. Or you can simply cut between the fillets yourself.

Oily Ocean Fish

Salmon aren't the only oily fish; saltwater bluefish and mackerel, which, if filleted, are interchangeable with each other in recipes, are also oily. And while their oiliness makes them highly perishable, it also makes them highly delicious. Their dark color comes from being fast and fierce hunters of their prey. Bluefish can be very large, up to 30 pounds; mackerel range from 1½ to 2 pounds. Given their oiliness, high heat works well (pan searing, grilling, broiling); avoid them in stews.

WHAT MAKES WHITE FISH DIFFERENT

These white fish fillets might all look similar but require different cooking treatments. To test this, we cooked every white fish that was accessible to us with the most basic method, pan roasting see page 458). Some took to this traditional technique well; others, we learned, need different treatment, which explains how we cook different categories of white fish. Flaky white fish turned out with a firm, silky texture, large flakes, a buttery flavor, and lots of surface browning. Firm, meaty white fish generally felt dry or overcooked when prepared this way.

COURSE

CROWD FAVORITE: COD

KEITH DRESSER

There's not much that's more pristine than a perfectly portioned moist cod fillet sporting a surface with some kind of crust or a buttery texture. Its mild, fresh flavor makes cod pleasing to even the most trepidatious seafood eaters. But lean cod is easy to overcook. A hard sear on both sides, for example, will overcook the fish before the exterior browns. In this course, learn two techniques for achieving a crust (one is one of our most fundamental fish-cooking techniques; the other is a nutty alternative), as well as how to create unmatched tenderness through steaming.

KEITH'S PRO TIP: *It goes without saying that freshness is paramount with any fish, cod included. Buy fillets that are resting on (not in) ice and that are moist and firm in appearance. And if it smells fishy, don't buy it.*

PAN-ROASTED COD WITH GRAPEFRUIT-BASIL RELISH

Serves: 4
Total Time: 55 minutes

RECIPE OVERVIEW Lean cod rarely turns out as well at home as it does in a restaurant, perfectly moist and with a chestnut-brown, slightly crisp crust. The margin of error with its minutes-long cooking time is high, resulting in overcooked fish. For a cooking method that reliably turns out delicious flaky white fish fillets, we transfer the cod from the stove to the oven: We sear the fillets in a hot pan, flip them, and then transfer them to the oven to continue cooking. To brown the fish quickly before the hot pan has a chance to dry out the fish's exterior, we turn to a sprinkling of sugar, which accelerates browning for supersavory—not sweet—flavor. A well-browned crust appears in around a minute, giving the interior time to turn succulent in the oven. The tangy, aromatic grapefruit relish pairs well with the mild fish. You can substitute black sea bass, haddock, hake, or pollock for the cod.

Relish
- 2 red grapefruits
- 2 tablespoons chopped fresh basil
- 1 small shallot, minced
- 2 teaspoons lemon juice
- 2 teaspoons extra-virgin olive oil
  Sugar

Fish

- 4 (6- to 8-ounce) skinless cod fillets, 1 inch thick
- ½ teaspoon table salt
- ¼ teaspoon pepper
- ½ teaspoon sugar
- 1 tablespoon vegetable oil

1. FOR THE RELISH Cut away peel and pith from grapefruits. Cut grapefruits into 8 wedges, then slice crosswise into ½-inch-thick pieces. Place grapefruits in fine-mesh strainer set over bowl and let drain for 15 minutes; measure out and reserve 1 tablespoon drained juice. Combine reserved juice, basil, shallot, lemon juice, and oil in separate bowl. Stir in grapefruits and let sit for 15 minutes. (Relish can be refrigerated for up to 2 days.)

2. FOR THE FISH Adjust oven rack to middle position and heat oven to 425 degrees. Pat cod dry with paper towels and sprinkle with salt and pepper. Sprinkle sugar lightly over 1 side of each fillet.

3. Heat oil in 12-inch ovensafe nonstick skillet over medium-high heat until just smoking. Lay cod sugared side down in skillet and, using spatula, lightly press cod for 20 to 30 seconds to ensure even contact with skillet. Cook until browned on first side, 1 to 2 minutes.

4. Using 2 spatulas, flip cod, then transfer skillet to oven. Roast until fish flakes apart when gently prodded with paring knife and registers 135 degrees, 7 to 10 minutes. Transfer cod to platter. Season relish with salt, pepper, and sugar to taste, and serve with cod.

> ### KEYS TO SUCCESS
> - **Thick fillets**: 1-inch-thick fillets will stay moist
> - **Pat fish dry**: Browns better than fish with a wet surface
> - **Use a nonstick skillet**: Guarantees you can flip the delicate fish without it sticking
> - **Sear, then roast**: Browns one side of the fillet without overcooking the fish
> - **A sprinkle of sugar**: Ensures that the surface browns

NUT-CRUSTED COD FILLETS

Serves: 4
Total Time: 55 minutes

RECIPE OVERVIEW Baked cod is a classic. A nut crust gives the fish not only texture and appeal but also welcome richness in every bite. We use chopped pistachios; they offer intriguing fragrance, appealing color, and a gentle sweetness, which emphasizes the subtly sweet seafood flavor of the cod. Combining the nuts with whole-wheat panko enhances the coating's nuttiness, and toasting the two components with aromatics brings out their flavors, introduces others, and ensures that the topping remains extra-crisp. To adhere this substantial crust to the fillets, we brush the fish with a mixture of yogurt, egg yolk, and lemon zest before pressing on the crumbs. Because our crust is so flavorful, we coat only the tops of the fillets. You can substitute black sea bass, haddock, hake, or pollock for the cod.

- ½ cup shelled pistachios
- 2 tablespoons vegetable oil
- 1 large shallot, minced
- ¾ teaspoon table salt, divided
- 1 garlic clove, minced
- 1 teaspoon minced fresh thyme or ¼ teaspoon dried
- ½ cup whole-wheat panko bread crumbs
- ½ teaspoon pepper, divided
- 2 tablespoons minced fresh parsley
- 1 tablespoon plain yogurt
- 1 large egg yolk
- ½ teaspoon grated lemon zest
- 4 (6- to 8-ounce) skinless cod fillets, 1 inch thick

1. Adjust oven rack to middle position and heat oven to 300 degrees. Set wire rack in rimmed baking sheet and spray rack with vegetable oil spray. Process pistachios in food processor until finely chopped, 20 to 30 seconds. Heat oil in 12-inch nonstick skillet over medium heat until shimmering. Add shallot and ¼ teaspoon salt and cook until softened, about 3 minutes. Stir in garlic and thyme and cook until fragrant, about 30 seconds. Reduce heat to medium-low; add pistachios, panko, and ¼ teaspoon pepper; and cook, stirring frequently, until well browned and crisp, about 8 minutes. Transfer pistachio mixture to shallow dish and let cool for 10 minutes. Stir in parsley; set aside.

2. Whisk yogurt, egg yolk, and lemon zest together in bowl. Pat cod dry with paper towels and sprinkle with remaining ½ teaspoon salt and remaining ¼ teaspoon pepper. Brush tops of fillets evenly with yogurt mixture. Working with 1 fillet at a time, press coated side in pistachio mixture, pressing gently to adhere. Transfer cod, crumb side up, to prepared wire rack.

3. Bake until fish flakes apart when gently prodded with paring knife and registers 135 degrees, 20 to 25 minutes, rotating sheet halfway through baking. Transfer cod to platter and serve.

> ### KEYS TO SUCCESS
> - **Add an egg**: Helps the crust adhere
> - **Cook on a wire rack**: Elevates the fish, ensuring air circulation for even cooking
> - **Coat the top of the fish only**: Prevents a soggy bottom crust

COD BAKED IN FOIL WITH LEEKS AND CARROTS

Serves: 4
Total Time: 45 minutes

RECIPE OVERVIEW Cooking fish en papillote, or folded in a pouch, is a classic French technique that, in addition to being incredibly easy (and virtually cleanup-free), allows the fish to steam in its own juices and thus emerge moist and flavorful. Foil is easier to work with than the traditional parchment and creates a leakproof seal. Placing the packets on the lower-middle rack of the oven, close to the heat source, concentrates the exuded liquid in the packets and deepens its flavor. Carrots and leeks, cut into elegant matchsticks, cook at the same rate as the fish and make a nice presentation as a bed for the fish when everything emerges from the packets. A zesty compound butter topping the fish adds richness and flavor as it melts. Open each packet promptly after baking to prevent overcooking. To test for doneness without opening the foil packets, use a permanent marker to mark an X on the outside of the foil where the fish fillet is the thickest, and then insert an instant-read thermometer through the X into the fish to measure its internal temperature. You can substitute black sea bass, haddock, hake, or pollock for the cod.

- 4 tablespoons unsalted butter, softened
- 1 teaspoon minced fresh thyme
- 2 garlic cloves, minced, divided
- 1¼ teaspoons grated lemon zest, divided, plus lemon wedges for serving
- 1 teaspoon table salt, divided
- ½ teaspoon pepper, divided
- 2 tablespoons minced fresh parsley
- 2 carrots, peeled and cut into 2-inch-long matchsticks
- 1 pound leeks, white and light green parts only, halved lengthwise, cut into 2-inch-long matchsticks, and washed thoroughly
- ¼ cup dry white wine
- 4 (6- to 8-ounce) skinless cod fillets, 1 inch thick

1. Adjust oven rack to lower-middle position and heat oven to 450 degrees. Mash butter, thyme, half of garlic, ¼ teaspoon lemon zest, ¼ teaspoon salt, and ⅛ teaspoon pepper in bowl. Combine parsley, remaining garlic, and remaining 1 teaspoon lemon zest in second bowl. Combine carrots, leeks, ¼ teaspoon salt, and ⅛ teaspoon pepper in third bowl.

2. Lay four 16 by 12-inch rectangles of aluminum foil on counter with short sides parallel to edge of counter. Divide vegetable mixture evenly among foil rectangles, arranging in center of lower half of each sheet of foil. Mound vegetables slightly and sprinkle with wine. Pat cod dry with paper towels, sprinkle with remaining ½ teaspoon salt and remaining ¼ teaspoon pepper, and place on top of vegetables. Spread butter mixture over cod. Fold top half of foil over cod, then tightly crimp edges into rough 9 by 6-inch packets.

3. Place packets on rimmed baking sheet (they may overlap slightly) and bake until fish registers 135 degrees, about 15 minutes. Carefully open packets, allowing steam to escape away from you. Using thin metal spatula, gently slide cod and vegetables along with any accumulated juices onto individual plates. Sprinkle with parsley mixture and serve with lemon wedges.

KEYS TO SUCCESS

- **Wrap the fish in foil:** Easier to crimp and seal than the traditional parchment paper
- **Make a compound butter:** Bastes the lean fish in richness
- **Use an instant-read thermometer:** Poking the tip of the thermometer through the foil keeps steam in the packets.

CORE TECHNIQUE

Cooking en Papillote

PLACE VEGETABLES
Divide vegetable mixture evenly among foil rectangles, arranging in center of lower half of each sheet of foil.

PLACE PROTEIN
Place protein on top of vegetables, spread evenly with butter, and fold top half of foil over protein.

CRIMP PACKETS
Fold top half of foil over protein, then tightly crimp edges into rough 9 by 6-inch packet.

RESOURCES FOR CROWD FAVORITE: COD

COD AT A GLANCE

Texture large, delicate flakes

Flavor mild, delicate

Common availability frozen, previously frozen, fresh

Best cooking techniques baking, pan roasting, poaching, steaming

BASS NOTES

Black sea bass is a good substitute for cod in our recipes because it cooks similarly. But striped bass isn't—it's in a different one of our cooking categories—nor are other varieties of bass. As it turns out, not all bass are similar: bass isn't bass isn't bass. There are a number of different bass, including aforementioned black sea bass (thick, delicate, and flaky); European sea bass, or branzino (fine-textured, sweet, usually served whole); striped bass or striper (a firm, meaty white fish with a slightly higher oil content); and Chilean sea bass, which isn't bass at all but a Patagonian toothfish. So if you see fish labeled "bass" at the store, make sure that you're purchasing the variety called for in your recipe.

SUBSTITUTIONS FOR COD

Cod might be a common, easy-to-find crowd-pleaser, but other flaky white fish are equally delicious stand-ins if you find them, they're local to you, or you simply prefer them. These are black sea bass, haddock, hake, and pollock.

WAYS WITH FLAKY WHITE FISH

The lack of natural oils and fats in flaky white fish such as cod makes it important to handle these fish with care: Rather than give them a hard sear over high heat on both sides, we often like to quickly sear them for color and then gently finish them in the oven through pan-roasting (see page 458). Sometimes we bake them at a not-too-high temperature (see page 459). You'll also see them poached (see page 482). These moist environments cook the fish evenly and gently, increasing the perception of juiciness.

TUCK THE TAIL

If you do need to use a thinner, tail-end piece of cod in your cooking, tuck the tail under the fillet to create a uniform thickness for even cooking.

COURSE
FIRM, MEATY WHITE FISH

LAN LAM

Most types of fish require a delicate touch; firm, meaty white fish such as halibut, mahi-mahi, red snapper, striped bass, and swordfish, however, are hardy, like fish for meat lovers. These fish have a distinctive texture combined with a sweet, mild flavor. In this course, we consider the muscle structure of these meaty fish to cook them to juicy perfection by means of various complementary cooking methods. They take well to the gentle cooking of braising but can also stand up to being flipped in a hot skillet or on a grill or roasted at a high temperature, so you'll never tire of ways to eat this substantial seafood.

LAN'S PRO TIP: *No matter the cooking method, firm, meaty white fish always benefits from a rest after cooking. As with roasts, steaks, and poultry, a rest slows the flow of the liquids and keeps the fish juicy.*

PAN-SEARED SWORDFISH STEAKS WITH CAPER-CURRANT RELISH

Serves: 4
Total Time: 45 minutes

RECIPE OVERVIEW If you want to sear thick, meaty swordfish, fast and hot cooking—as opposed to gentler pan roasting used for flaky white fish (see page 458)—is the way to go; otherwise, the flesh has a tendency to soften and turn unpleasantly mushy. Conventional searing is too slow for this fish, giving its enzymes time to break down the proteins and render them mushy. Instead, contradict convention and flip the fish frequently. When a protein is flipped, the seared side, which is then facing up, is also quite hot. Some of its heat dissipates into the air, and some of it cooks the protein from the top down. The more often a protein is flipped, the more it will cook from both the bottom up and the top down. Removing the swordfish from the skillet when it reaches 130 degrees prevents it from overcooking from the carryover cooking that happens since this method is so fast and hot. After a 10-minute rest, the fish registers a perfect serving temperature of 140 degrees. This method quickly cooks the thick swordfish steaks (which can hold up to flipping) throughout while also giving them golden-brown crusts. You can substitute halibut, mahi-mahi, red snapper, or striped bass fillets for the swordfish steaks.

Relish

- 3 tablespoons minced fresh parsley
- 3 tablespoons extra-virgin olive oil
- 2 tablespoons capers, rinsed and chopped fine
- 2 tablespoons dried currants, chopped fine
- 1 garlic clove, minced
- 1 teaspoon grated lemon zest plus 2 tablespoons juice

Fish

- 2 teaspoons vegetable oil
- 4 (6- to 8-ounce) skinless swordfish steaks, 1 inch thick
- ¾ teaspoon table salt

1. FOR THE RELISH Combine all ingredients in bowl. Let sit at room temperature for at least 20 minutes before serving. (Relish can be refrigerated for up to 2 days.)

2. FOR THE FISH Heat oil in 12-inch nonstick skillet over medium-high heat until shimmering. While oil heats, pat swordfish dry with paper towels and sprinkle with salt.

3. Place swordfish in skillet and cook, flipping every 2 minutes, until golden brown and centers register 130 degrees, 7 to 11 minutes. Transfer to platter and let rest for 10 minutes. Serve with relish.

KEYS TO SUCCESS

- **Go skinless:** Skin-on swordfish buckles in the hot skillet (see page 466).
- **Flip it:** Quickly cooks the meaty flesh so that its enzymes don't have a chance to turn it mushy
- **Let it rest:** Allows carryover cooking to bring it to the perfect serving temperature

SCIENCE LESSON

Why Swordfish Can Turn Mushy

Enzymes in swordfish called cathepsins snip the proteins that hold the fish's muscle fibers together. In fish, cathepsins are highly active at 130 degrees. When swordfish is cooked very slowly, its cathepsins have a long time to significantly cut up the fibers, and the fish turns from meaty to mushy. Cooking fast through frequent flipping and removing the swordfish from the heat right when it reaches 130 degrees ensures pleasantly meaty fish.

HALIBUT EN COCOTTE WITH GARLIC AND CHERRY TOMATOES

Serves: 4
Total Time: 1 hour

RECIPE OVERVIEW Cooking en cocotte (in a casserole) is a French technique that's a variation on braising: It uses a covered pot, a low oven temperature, and an extended cooking time to yield tender, ultrasupple results—with no liquid in the pot. The lid seals in the juices, so the fish cooks in them. Halibut is meaty, lean, and relatively high in collagen, with a clean, mild flavor that benefits from the technique. A bold tomato-caper sauce serves as a bright, briny counterpoint to the succulent halibut. Finishing with a splash of extra-virgin olive oil rounds out the flavors and gives the dish a lush feel. You can substitute mahi-mahi, red snapper, striped bass, or swordfish for the halibut.

- ¼ cup extra-virgin olive oil, divided
- 2 garlic cloves, sliced thin
- ⅛ teaspoon red pepper flakes
- Pinch plus ½ teaspoon table salt, divided
- 12 ounces cherry tomatoes, quartered
- 1 tablespoon capers, rinsed
- 1 teaspoon minced fresh thyme
- 4 (6- to 8-ounce) skinless halibut fillets, 1 inch thick
- ¼ teaspoon pepper

1. Adjust oven rack to lowest position and heat oven to 250 degrees. Add 2 tablespoons oil, garlic, pepper flakes, and pinch salt to Dutch oven and cook over medium-low heat until garlic is light golden, 2 to 4 minutes. Off heat, stir in tomatoes, capers, and thyme.

2. Pat halibut dry with paper towels, sprinkle with pepper and remaining ½ teaspoon salt, and lay on top of tomatoes in pot. Place large piece of aluminum foil over pot and cover tightly with lid; transfer pot to oven. Cook until fish flakes apart when gently prodded with paring knife and registers 130 degrees, 35 to 40 minutes.

3. Transfer halibut to platter and let rest for 10 minutes. Meanwhile, bring tomato mixture to simmer over medium-high heat until slightly thickened, about 2 minutes. Off heat, stir in remaining 2 tablespoons oil and season with salt and pepper to taste. Spoon sauce over halibut and serve.

KEYS TO SUCCESS

- **Place the fish over the tomatoes:** Prevents the bottoms of the fillets from overcooking
- **Seal the pot:** Keeps the juices from escaping
- **Let it rest:** Brings the fish to the ideal serving temperature

ROASTED SNAPPER AND VEGETABLES WITH MUSTARD SAUCE

Serves: 4
Total Time: 1 hour

RECIPE OVERVIEW The key to success for this one-pan meal of hearty red snapper, golden-brown potatoes, and charred broccoli is to stagger the cooking. We start by roasting halved red potatoes on one side of a baking sheet and broccoli florets on the other. We remove the broccoli once it's just charred and add our snapper to the freed-up space, dropping the oven temperature to cook the fish gently and finish the potatoes. A mixture of lemon zest, honey, and paprika brushed on the fillets adds color and pairs with the bright sauce. Use small red potatoes measuring 1 to 2 inches in diameter. You can substitute halibut, mahi-mahi, striped bass, or swordfish for the red snapper.

- 6 tablespoons plus 2 teaspoons extra-virgin olive oil, divided
- ¼ cup minced fresh chives
- 2 tablespoons whole-grain mustard
- 1 tablespoon honey, divided
- 1 teaspoon grated lemon zest plus 2 teaspoons juice
- Pinch plus 1 teaspoon table salt, divided
- Pinch plus ¾ teaspoon pepper, divided
- 1 pound small red potatoes, unpeeled, halved
- 1 pound broccoli florets, cut into 2-inch pieces
- ½ teaspoon paprika
- 4 (6- to 8-ounce) skinless red snapper fillets, 1 inch thick

1. Adjust oven rack to lowest position and heat oven to 500 degrees. Combine 2 tablespoons oil, chives, mustard, 1 teaspoon honey, lemon juice, pinch salt, and pinch pepper in bowl; set aside mustard sauce until ready to serve. Brush rimmed baking sheet with 1 tablespoon oil.

2. Toss potatoes with 1 tablespoon oil, ¼ teaspoon salt, and ¼ teaspoon pepper in bowl. Place potatoes, cut side down, on half of prepared sheet. Toss broccoli with 2 tablespoons oil, ¼ teaspoon salt, and ¼ teaspoon pepper, then place on empty side of sheet. Roast until potatoes are golden brown and broccoli is spotty brown and tender, 12 to 14 minutes, rotating sheet halfway through roasting.

3. While potatoes and broccoli roast, combine paprika, 1 teaspoon oil, lemon zest, remaining 2 teaspoons honey, remaining ½ teaspoon salt, and remaining ¼ teaspoon pepper in small bowl; microwave until bubbling and fragrant, 10 to 15 seconds. Pat red snapper dry with paper towels, brush skinned sides of fillets with remaining 1 teaspoon oil, then brush tops of fillets with paprika mixture.

4. Remove sheet from oven and reduce oven temperature to 275 degrees. Transfer broccoli to platter and tent with aluminum foil to keep warm. Place red snapper, skinned side down, on now-empty side of sheet. Continue to roast until fish flakes apart when gently prodded with paring knife and registers 130 degrees, 6 to 8 minutes, rotating sheet halfway through roasting.

5. Transfer potatoes and red snapper to platter with broccoli. Tent with foil and let rest for 10 minutes. Serve with mustard sauce.

KEYS TO SUCCESS

- **Stagger the cooking:** Ensures that the vegetables are cooked through by the time the fish is done
- **Add some honey and paprika:** Gives the fish flavor and color during roasting
- **Tent with foil:** Keeps everything warm while the fish rests

GRILLED SWORDFISH TACOS

Serves: 6
Total Time: 1¾ hours, plus 30 minutes marinating

RECIPE OVERVIEW Swordfish is a great candidate for grilled fish tacos because it's firm enough to stand up to flipping on the grill, even when it's cut into strips. These tacos are inspired by fish tacos from the Yucatán Peninsula, where fish is often marinated in a chile-citrus mixture and grilled wrapped in banana leaves. A little tomato paste provides a layer of savory-sweet intensity to our spiced marinade, and a mix of orange and lime juices are a substitute for Mexican sour oranges. The swordfish is grilled alongside pineapple and jalapeño, which we turn into a salsa. You can substitute halibut, mahi-mahi, red snapper, or striped bass for the swordfish. For more information on oiling the cooking grate, see page 467.

- 3 tablespoons vegetable oil, divided, plus extra for cooking grate
- 1 tablespoon ancho chile powder
- 2 teaspoons chipotle chile powder
- 2 garlic cloves, minced
- 1 teaspoon dried oregano
- 1 teaspoon ground coriander
- 1 teaspoon table salt
- 2 tablespoons tomato paste
- ½ cup orange juice
- 6 tablespoons lime juice (3 limes), divided, plus lime wedges for serving
- 2 pounds skinless swordfish steaks, 1 inch thick, cut lengthwise into 1-inch-wide strips
- 1 pineapple, peeled, quartered, cored, and each quarter halved lengthwise
- 1 jalapeño chile
- 18 (6-inch) corn tortillas, divided
- 1 red bell pepper, stemmed, seeded, and cut into ¼-inch pieces
- 2 tablespoons minced fresh cilantro, plus extra for serving
- 3¾ ounces thinly sliced iceberg lettuce (2½ cups)
- 1 ripe avocado, halved, pitted, and sliced thin

1. Heat 2 tablespoons oil, ancho chile powder, and chipotle chile powder in 8-inch skillet over medium heat, stirring constantly, until fragrant, 2 to 3 minutes. Add garlic, oregano, coriander, and salt and cook until fragrant, about 30 seconds. Add tomato paste and, using spatula, mash tomato paste with spice mixture until combined, about 20 seconds. Stir in orange juice and 2 tablespoons lime juice. Cook, stirring constantly, until thoroughly combined and reduced slightly, about 2 minutes. Transfer chile mixture to large bowl and let cool for 15 minutes.

2. Add swordfish to bowl with chile mixture and stir gently with rubber spatula to coat swordfish. Cover and refrigerate for at least 30 minutes or up to 2 hours.

3A. FOR A CHARCOAL GRILL Open bottom vent completely. Light large chimney starter mounded with charcoal briquettes (7 quarts). When top coals are partially covered with ash, pour evenly over grill. Set cooking grate in place, cover, and open lid vent completely. Heat grill until hot, about 5 minutes.

3B. FOR A GAS GRILL Turn all burners to high; cover; and heat grill until hot, about 15 minutes. Turn all burners to medium-high.

4. Fold paper towels into compact wad. Holding paper towels with tongs, dip in oil, then wipe cooking grate. Dip paper towels in oil again and wipe grate for second time. Cover grill and heat for 5 minutes. Uncover and wipe grate twice more with oiled paper towels. Brush both sides of pineapple with remaining 1 tablespoon oil. Place swordfish on half of grill. Place pineapple and jalapeño on other half. Cover and cook until swordfish, pineapple, and jalapeño have begun to brown, 3 to 5 minutes. Using thin spatula, flip swordfish, pineapple, and jalapeño. Cover and continue to cook until second sides of pineapple and jalapeño are browned and swordfish registers 140 degrees, 3 to 5 minutes. Transfer swordfish to large platter, flake into pieces, and tent with aluminum foil. Transfer pineapple and jalapeño to cutting board.

5. Clean cooking grate. Place half of tortillas on grill. Cook until softened and speckled with brown spots, 30 to 45 seconds per side. Wrap tortillas in dish towel or foil to keep warm. Repeat with remaining tortillas.

6. When cool enough to handle, chop pineapple and jalapeño fine. Transfer to bowl and stir in bell pepper, cilantro, and remaining ¼ cup lime juice. Season with salt to taste. Top tortillas with swordfish, salsa, lettuce, and avocado. Serve with lime wedges and extra cilantro.

KEYS TO SUCCESS

- **Choose firm and meaty fish:** Doesn't fall apart when you flip it on the grill
- **Marinate the swordfish:** Imparts big flavor
- **A hot fire:** Chars the fish (For information on how to set up a grill, see page 447.)
- **Oil the cooking grate multiple times:** Ensures a clean release (see page 467)

RESOURCES FOR FIRM, MEATY WHITE FISH

FIRM, MEATY WHITE FISH AT A GLANCE

Varieties halibut, mahi-mahi, red snapper, striped bass, swordfish

Texture meaty, hearty

Flavor varies

Common availability frozen, previously frozen, fresh

Best cooking techniques braising, grilling, pan searing, poaching, steaming

PREPARING SWORDFISH

SWORDFISH BLOODLINE
Swordfish steaks typically have a bloodline—a dark muscle rich in myoglobin (see page 456)—running through them. Since that bloodline can have an unpleasant mineral taste, we recommend looking for steaks with as minimal of a bloodline as possible.

SKINNING SWORDFISH
Thick, rubbery swordfish skin tightens up more than the flesh during cooking and can cause the steak to buckle. You can ask your fishmonger to remove it for you or you can trim it off yourself with a sharp knife, sliding the knife just between the skin and flesh.

FREQUENT FLIPPING FOR DENSE FISH

Frequently flipping thick, meaty white fish (as well as beef steaks, pork chops, and tuna) during searing leads to faster, more evenly cooked results. To demonstrate this, we pan-seared nine swordfish steaks, nine strip steaks, and nine pork chops until they reached 130, 125, and 140 degrees, respectively. We flipped three of each protein every 30 seconds, three every 2 minutes, and three just once, recording how long it took each to reach the desired temperature.

The proteins flipped every 30 seconds cooked the fastest, while those flipped just once were the slowest. The 30-second and 2-minute samples were well browned and evenly cooked, whereas the once-flipped samples were also nicely browned but had a large band of overcooked flesh.

Here's why frequent flipping is efficient: A hot skillet cooks food from the bottom up. When a protein is flipped, the seared side, which is then facing up, is also quite hot. Some of its heat dissipates into the air, and some of it cooks the protein from the top down. The more often a protein is flipped, the more it will cook from both the bottom up and the top down. Though flipping pan-seared proteins every 30 seconds results in the speediest, most even cooking, it is impractical. However, flipping every 2 minutes cuts the cooking time by about 30 percent, which makes it well worth the effort.

BRAISING SEAFOOD

Braising might not be the first cooking technique that comes to mind for fish—even firm, meaty white fish is more delicate than hardy cuts of meat. But the ocean's the limit when it comes to braising fish and seafood. Braising simmers and steams fish until it's tender but still succulent. As a moist-heat cooking method, braising is gentle and thus forgiving, all but guaranteeing moist fish. Firm, meaty white fish in particular can stand up to robust flavors that are used for braising and creating sauces. And the cooking technique allows for a transfer of flavors between the aromatics and the permeable fish.

REHEATING FISH

Fish is notoriously susceptible to overcooking, so reheating previously cooked fillets can be dicey. Firm, meaty white fish cuts, however, are the ideal candidate for reheating. They retain their moisture well and with no detectable change in flavor. Use this gentle approach: Place the fillets or steaks on a wire rack set in a rimmed baking sheet; cover them with aluminum foil (to prevent the exteriors of the fish from drying out); and heat them in a 275-degree oven until they register 125 to 130 degrees, about 15 minutes for 1-inch-thick fish (timing varies according to fish size).

For other fish that don't fare as well, such as thin fish, we recommend serving them in cold applications like salads. Salmon reheats well, but be aware that doing so brings out a bit more of the fish's pungent aroma.

PREPARING A GRILL COOKING GRATE FOR FISH

Some folks fear grilling fish, and that's because it's notorious for sticking. Using firm, meaty white fish such as the ones discussed in this course helps. But we've developed a method for preparing the cooking grate that provides extra insurance so the fish proteins don't stick.

1. Heat grill according to recipe. Gather several paper towels into a wad. Holding wad with tongs, dip in vegetable oil and then wipe grate. Dip paper towels in oil again and wipe grate for second time.

2. Cover grill and heat until hot (500 degrees), 5 minutes.

3. Uncover and wipe grate twice more with oiled paper towels.

COURSE
THIN WHITE FISH

BRIDGET LANCASTER

Although they share similar flavors, thin fish fillets cook differently than thicker, flakier fish. And thin fish fillets are very popular with tilapia now being the fourth-most-consumed seafood in the United States (after shrimp, tuna, and salmon), so it pays to know how to prepare them. The fillet, which is one side of the fish, usually has both a thicker and thinner end, and by considering and working around these disparities, we can ensure more even cooking. In these recipes, you'll learn how to maximize flavorful browning of these fish without overcooking and drying out the skinny fillets.

BRIDGET'S PRO TIP: *If you know that you aren't going to cook the fish fillets on the same day that you buy them, store them on crushed ice in the fridge, and use them within a couple of days. Keep tablespoons of flavored butter (like the herbed butter in the Baked Sole Fillets recipe) on hand in your freezer to use as a last-minute flavoring for sautéed fish.*

SAUTÉED TILAPIA WITH CILANTRO CHIMICHURRI

Serves: 4
Total Time: 50 minutes

RECIPE OVERVIEW Cooking thin fish on the stovetop so that it achieves nice browning across evenly cooked flesh is a unique challenge. The thick half of a thin, wide fillet rests flat on the pan and browns nicely during sautéing, but the thin half tilts upward, hardly making contact at all. Our way around this: splitting the fillets at their seams and cooking the thick halves in one batch and the thin halves in a second. The move actually enhances rather than detracts from their aesthetic: We prefer uniform, evenly browned fish fillets any day. High heat gets the fish, both thick and thin pieces, remarkably brown and evenly crisp on both sides. A 15-minute salting period, which we usually use only with meat and fattier fish such as salmon, enhances tilapia's mild flavor and keeps the fish moist as it cooks. If at any time during cooking the oil begins to smoke, reduce the heat as needed. You can substitute catfish, flounder, or sole for the tilapia.

Chimichurri
- 2 tablespoons hot water
- 2 tablespoons red wine vinegar
- 1 teaspoon dried oregano
- ½ cup minced fresh parsley
- ¼ cup minced fresh cilantro
- 3 garlic cloves, minced
- 1 teaspoon kosher salt
- ¼ teaspoon red pepper flakes
- ¼ cup extra-virgin olive oil

Fish
- 4 (5- to 6-ounce) skinless tilapia fillets
- 1 teaspoon kosher salt
- 2 tablespoons vegetable oil
- Lemon wedges

1. FOR THE CHIMICHURRI Combine hot water, vinegar, and oregano in medium bowl; let stand for 5 minutes. Add parsley, cilantro, garlic, salt, and pepper flakes and stir to combine. Whisk in oil until incorporated. Set aside.

2. FOR THE FISH Place tilapia on cutting board and sprinkle both sides with salt. Let sit at room temperature for 15 minutes. Pat tilapia dry with paper towels. Using seam that runs down middle of fillet as guide, cut each fillet in half lengthwise to create 1 thick half and 1 thin half.

3. Heat oil in 12-inch nonstick skillet over high heat until just smoking. Add thick halves of fillets to skillet. Cook, tilting and gently shaking skillet occasionally to distribute oil, until undersides are golden brown, 2 to 3 minutes. Using 2 spatulas, flip fillets. Cook until second sides are golden brown and fish registers 130 to 135 degrees, 2 to 3 minutes. Transfer tilapia to serving platter.

4. Return skillet to high heat. When oil is just smoking, add thin halves of fillets and cook until undersides are golden brown, about 1 minute. Flip and cook until second sides are golden brown, about 1 minute. Transfer to platter and top with ¼ cup chimichurri, passing remaining chimichurri separately. Serve with lemon wedges.

KEYS TO SUCCESS

- **Salt the fish:** Seasons the tilapia well and helps it retain moisture
- **Slice down the seam:** Cooking the thicker and thinner halves of the fillets in respective batches ensures even cooking (see page 473).
- **High heat:** Achieves browning and crispness without a flour coating

---

How Good Is It? Tilapia versus Other White Fish

Through developing a recipe for tilapia we came to find that its mild taste and moist, firm flesh are hard to beat. Even so, we were intrigued by a blind tasting the *Washington Post* staged in its offices a couple years back comparing tilapia with seven other varieties of fish. The tasting panel included renowned D.C. chef Scott Drewno, *Post* food critic Tom Sietsema, and a fisheries expert, among others. Not only did tilapia come in second, but Chef Drewno, formerly a tilapia detractor, declared it his favorite.

We decided to conduct our own blind tasting, comparing tilapia ($8.95/lb) with four other common white fish: flounder ($15.95/lb), branzino ($18.95/lb), haddock ($12.95/lb), and snapper ($25.95/lb). The fish arrived ultrafresh from our seafood purveyor in a single delivery, and we prepared all the fillets according to our sautéed tilapia recipe, adjusting cooking times as necessary to ensure that all the fillets reached 130 degrees. Here again, the tilapia did not disappoint. With its "yummy," "moist," and "meaty, mild taste of luxury," it earned a strong second place, missing a tie for first place (with haddock) by just one point.

PAN-FRIED SOLE

Serves: 4
Total Time: 30 minutes

RECIPE OVERVIEW Lightly browned thin fillets of sole are a classic for a reason, and a floured piece of fish is a grand vehicle for soaking up a bright contrasting sauce (see our meunière preparation)—unless the coating is soggy and wan. Omitting heavy eggs or bread crumbs from the coating is key, and the perfect crust comes from simply drying the fillets, seasoning them with salt and pepper, and then dredging them in just flour. Try to purchase fillets that are of similar size. If using smaller fillets (3 ounces each), serve two fillets per person and reduce the cooking time on the second side to about 1 minute. You will need to cook smaller fillets in three or four batches and wipe out the skillet with paper towels after the second and third batches to prevent any browned bits from scorching. You can substitute catfish, flounder, or tilapia for the sole.

- 4 (6- to 8-ounce) skinless sole fillets, split lengthwise down natural seam
- ½ teaspoon table salt
- ¼ teaspoon pepper
- ½ cup all-purpose flour
- 2 tablespoons vegetable oil, divided
- 2 tablespoons unsalted butter, cut into 2 pieces, divided
-    Lemon wedges

1. Adjust oven rack to middle position and heat oven to 200 degrees. Pat sole dry with paper towels and sprinkle with salt and pepper. Spread flour in shallow dish. Dredge sole in flour, shaking off excess, and transfer to large plate.

2. Heat 1 tablespoon oil in 12-inch nonstick skillet over medium-high heat until shimmering. Add 1 tablespoon butter and swirl until melted. Add thick halves of fillets to skillet and cook until golden on first side, about 3 minutes. Using 2 spatulas, flip fillets and cook until second sides are golden and fish flakes apart when gently prodded with paring knife, about 2 minutes. Transfer to ovensafe platter and keep warm in oven. Wipe skillet clean with paper towels and repeat with remaining 1 tablespoon oil, remaining 1 tablespoon butter, and thin halves of fillets. Serve with lemon wedges.

Variation
SOLE MEUNIÈRE

Omit lemon wedges. Before serving, melt 4 tablespoons unsalted butter in medium saucepan over medium-high heat. Continue to cook, swirling saucepan constantly, until butter is golden brown and has nutty aroma, 1 to 1½ minutes. Off heat, add 1½ tablespoons lemon juice and season with salt to taste. Spoon sauce over sole and sprinkle with 2 tablespoons chopped fresh parsley. Serve immediately.

> **KEYS TO SUCCESS**
> - **Two spatulas:** Prevents the delicate fillets from breaking when you flip them
> - **Paring knife:** The thin fillets are done once they flake when prodded.

CORNMEAL CATFISH AND SOUTHWESTERN CORN

Serves: 4
Total Time: 45 minutes

RECIPE OVERVIEW Deep-fried catfish (like anything deep-fried) is a treat, but it's not the only way to cook it. This simple and satisfying meal makes the crunch of cornmeal-coated catfish the centerpiece—with no big pots or monitoring of oil temperatures. Frying in a shallow skillet gives the catfish a crispy coating, and the fish pieces need only a one-step dry dredge since they're not jumping into a pot of bubbling oil. Pairing the catfish with a corn side brings out the sweet, buttery flavor of the coating; for more interest, we spice it up with chorizo and ingredients common to southwestern cooking, such as bell pepper, chile, and cilantro. We shallow-fry the fish in the same skillet we use to sauté the corn, giving "fish fry" a new, easier definition. And we boost the spice kick by making Comeback Sauce (recipe follows), which is a cross between rémoulade and Thousand Island Dressing. You can substitute flounder, sole, or tilapia for the catfish.

- 2 tablespoons unsalted butter
- 8 ounces Spanish-style chorizo sausage, diced
- 1 red bell pepper, stemmed, seeded, and chopped fine
- 1 shallot, minced
- 1 jalapeño chile, stemmed, seeded, and minced
- 1 garlic clove, minced
- 1 teaspoon table salt, divided
- 4 cups frozen corn
- 2 teaspoons minced fresh cilantro
- ½ cup all-purpose flour
- ½ cup cornmeal
- 4 (6- to 8-ounce) skinless catfish fillets, split lengthwise down natural seam
- ¼ teaspoon pepper
- 1 cup vegetable oil for frying

1. Adjust oven rack to middle position and heat oven to 200 degrees. Melt butter in 12-inch nonstick skillet over medium-high heat. Add chorizo and cook until lightly browned, about 2 minutes. Stir in bell pepper, shallot, jalapeño, garlic, and ½ teaspoon salt and cook until bell pepper begins to brown, about 5 minutes. Stir in corn and cook until warmed through, about 2 minutes. Stir in cilantro and season with salt and pepper to taste; transfer to ovensafe bowl, cover with aluminum foil, and keep warm in oven.

2. Meanwhile, whisk flour and cornmeal together in shallow dish. Pat catfish dry with paper towels and sprinkle with pepper and remaining ½ teaspoon salt. Working with 1 fillet at a time, dredge in flour mixture, pressing gently to adhere; transfer to large plate.

3. Wipe out now-empty skillet with paper towels and line ovensafe platter with triple layer of paper towels. Heat oil over medium-high heat until shimmering. Carefully place 4 fillets in skillet and cook until golden on both sides, about 2 minutes per side. Transfer catfish to prepared platter to drain, then transfer platter to oven to keep warm. Repeat with remaining 4 fillets. Serve with corn mixture.

COMEBACK SAUCE

Makes: 1 cup
Total Time: 15 minutes

- ½ cup mayonnaise
- ⅓ cup chopped onion
- 2 tablespoons vegetable oil
- 2 tablespoons chili sauce
- 1 tablespoon ketchup
- 2½ teaspoons Worcestershire sauce
- 2½ teaspoons hot sauce
- 1 teaspoon yellow mustard
- 1 teaspoon lemon juice
- 1 garlic clove, minced
- ¾ teaspoon pepper
- ⅛ teaspoon paprika

Process all ingredients in blender until smooth, about 30 seconds. (Sauce can be refrigerated for up to 5 days.)

BAKED SOLE FILLETS WITH HERBS AND BREAD CRUMBS

Serves: 6
Total Time: 1 hour

RECIPE OVERVIEW Another great thing about thin fish is that it's flexible, literally, so you can stuff it with flavor and cook it in attractive bundles—perfect to impress with ultimate ease. We brush the fillets with Dijon mustard; season them with salt, pepper, fresh herbs, and lemon zest; and drizzle them with melted butter and garlic. Then we roll them up, drizzle them with more butter, and bake them. Covering the baking dish with foil protects the delicate fish from the drying heat of the oven. For texture, we add a mixture of herbs, butter, and panko bread crumbs to the sole at two intervals. We remove the foil before the fish is done cooking, baste the fillets with pan juices, top them with most of the bread crumb mixture, and then return them to the oven uncovered. Just before serving, we sprinkle the remaining crumbs over the fillets. You can substitute catfish, flounder, or tilapia for the sole. Try to purchase fillets of similar size. If using smaller fillets (about 3 ounces each), serve two fillets per person and reduce the baking time in step 3 to 20 minutes.

- 3 tablespoons minced fresh parsley
- 3 tablespoons minced fresh chives
- 1 tablespoon minced fresh tarragon
- 1 teaspoon grated lemon zest, plus lemon wedges for serving
- 5 tablespoons unsalted butter, divided
- 2 garlic cloves, minced, divided
- 6 (6-ounce) boneless, skinless sole fillets
- 1 tablespoon Dijon mustard
- ⅔ cup panko bread crumbs
- ¼ teaspoon table salt

1. Adjust oven rack to middle position and heat oven to 325 degrees. Combine parsley, chives, and tarragon in small bowl. Reserve 1 tablespoon parsley mixture; stir lemon zest into remaining herb mixture.

2. Melt 4 tablespoons butter in 8-inch skillet over medium heat. Add half of garlic and cook, stirring frequently, until fragrant, 1 to 2 minutes. Set aside off heat.

3. Pat fillets dry with paper towels and season with salt and pepper. Arrange fillets, skinned side up, with tail end pointing away from you. Spread ½ teaspoon mustard on each fillet, sprinkle each fillet evenly with 1 tablespoon parsley–lemon zest mixture, and drizzle each fillet with 1½ teaspoons garlic butter. Tightly roll fillets from thick end to form cylinders. Place fillets, seam side down, in 13 by 9-inch baking dish. Drizzle remaining garlic butter over fillets, cover dish with aluminum foil, and bake for 25 minutes. Wipe out skillet with paper towels.

4. While fillets bake, melt remaining 1 tablespoon butter in now-empty skillet over medium heat. Add panko and cook, stirring frequently, until crumbs are deep golden brown, 5 to 8 minutes. Reduce heat to low; add remaining garlic; and cook, stirring constantly, until garlic is fragrant and evenly distributed in crumbs, about 1 minute. Transfer to small bowl, stir in ¼ teaspoon salt, and season with pepper to taste. Let cool, then stir in reserved 1 tablespoon parsley mixture.

5. Remove dish from oven and baste fillets with garlic butter in dish. Sprinkle with all but 3 tablespoons bread crumbs and continue to bake, uncovered, until fillets register 135 degrees, 6 to 10 minutes. Using thin metal spatula, transfer fillets to plates; sprinkle with remaining 3 tablespoons bread crumbs; and serve with lemon wedges.

KEYS TO SUCCESS

- **Flavorful filling:** Adds lots of flavor to the delicate fish and binds the bundles
- **Cover the dish:** Keeps in the moisture during baking
- **Finish with bread crumbs:** Prevents them from sogging out in the oven

RESOURCES FOR THIN WHITE FISH

THIN WHITE FISH AT A GLANCE

Varieties catfish, flounder, sole, tilapia

Texture flaky, thin

Flavor mild, sweet

Common availability frozen, previously frozen, fresh

Best cooking techniques frying, sautéing, steaming

GOT SOLE?

Of the thin fish, one is known to be superior, pearly white, and pristine, with the cleanest flavor: sole. But buyer beware: At your local market it's highly likely that you are actually purchasing a type of flounder rather than sole. That's fine—we love flounder! But we don't love unnecessarily high price tags. Dover sole is a European fish—the United States does not have true sole along its shorelines. (That said, sole is delicious if you can source it.)

SLICING THIN FILLETS IN HALF

A thin fish fillet has a thicker and a thinner half. Because of that, one half inevitably doesn't make proper contact with the pan and one half cooks faster than the other and dries out. To solve this disparity, we use the seam running down the center of each fillet as a guide to cut the thin and thick portions apart and cook them separately.

DISCRIMINATING TASTES

Two thin fish, catfish and tilapia, have an unsubstantiated reputation for tasting bad, which we want to debunk. Most catfish sold in the United States is farmed in the Mississippi Delta and has a clean, mild taste from its grain feeding. The off-tasting stuff? Wild imports from Asia, which are very hard to come by. Fillets should be white to off-white; avoid fish that is yellow. As for tilapia, there's a resounding conception that it's a second-rate, predominantly farm-raised fish with a muddy taste. But tilapia is now the fourth-most-consumed seafood in the United States. Modern freshwater farming practices produce meaty tilapia with a clean, mild flavor, sort of a cross between trout and flounder.

FLIPPING THIN FISH

Flip carefully when sautéing, as the delicate fish can flake apart in the pan. Work quickly and confidently and use two spatulas to flip the fish, one to do the action of turning and one to hold the fillet steady.

COURSE
SALMON SO MANY WAYS

JOSEPH GITTER

Salmon is so recognizable that its name is a standard color—vibrant and orangey pink. In each seafood course, we lay out the cooking techniques that work best for the category or types of seafood at hand. What works for salmon? Nearly everything. Salmon fillets are one of the top cuts of fish to cook, and there's good reason for that. They're a weeknight workhorse—rich and satisfying, nutritious, and easy to jazz up for interest so that they never get old. Here you'll learn how to roast, pan-sear, broil, and grill this succulent fish. (Frying isn't ideal for this oily fish.) Each method will give you a compelling reason to cook it. All these techniques work for common farmed salmon but also for leaner wild salmon and arctic char if you enjoy using these alternatives.

JOE'S PRO TIP: *Salmon can go from raw to overcooked in a flash. It's worth investing in a fast and accurate instant-read food thermometer.*

POMEGRANATE ROASTED SALMON WITH LENTILS AND CHARD

Serves: 4
Total Time: 1½ hours

RECIPE OVERVIEW Roasting is the way to go for salmon if you want to get dinner on the table with utmost ease (while firing up some sides to round out the plate). We use a dual-temperature roasting technique; it's a hands-off way to serve up fish with a nicely browned exterior. Rather than sear the fillets on the stovetop, we preheat a baking sheet in a 500-degree oven. While the sheet heats up, we ready the fillets for roasting, slashing the skin so that the fat gets rendered in the oven and brushing them with pomegranate molasses for a tangy, shiny glaze. We drop the temperature to 275 degrees just before placing the fillets on the hot sheet and into the oven. The initial contact with the hot sheet crisps the skin (as searing would), and the heat of the gradually cooling oven cooks the fillets gently, ensuring silky fish every time. Meanwhile, we cook a flavorful side of Swiss chard and lentils in a saucepan. If your chef's knife is not sharp enough to cut through the skin easily, try a serrated knife. It is important to keep the skin on during cooking; remove it afterward, if desired. You can substitute wild salmon or arctic char for the farmed salmon; if using either of these, cook the fillets to 120 degrees (for medium-rare) and start checking for doneness after 4 minutes.

- 2 tablespoons plus 1 teaspoon extra-virgin olive oil, divided
- 12 ounces Swiss chard, stemmed, ½ cup stems chopped fine, leaves cut into 2-inch pieces
- 1 small onion, chopped fine
- 2 garlic cloves, minced
- 4 sprigs fresh thyme
- ¾ teaspoon table salt, divided
- 2 cups chicken or vegetable broth
- 1 cup dried lentilles du Puy, picked over and rinsed
- 4 (6- to 8-ounce) skin-on salmon fillets, 1 inch thick
- 2 tablespoons pomegranate molasses, divided
- ¼ teaspoon pepper
- ½ cup pomegranate seeds

1. Adjust oven rack to lowest position, place aluminum foil–lined rimmed baking sheet on rack, and heat oven to 500 degrees. Heat 1 tablespoon oil in large saucepan over medium-high heat until shimmering. Add chard stems, onion, garlic, thyme sprigs, and ¼ teaspoon salt and cook, stirring frequently, until softened, about 5 minutes. Stir in broth and lentils and bring to boil. Reduce heat to low; cover; and simmer, stirring occasionally, until lentils are mostly tender, 45 to 50 minutes.

2. Stir chard leaves into lentils. Increase heat to medium-low and continue to cook, uncovered, until chard leaves are tender, about 4 minutes. Off heat, discard thyme sprigs, stir in 1 tablespoon oil, and season with salt and pepper to taste; cover to keep warm.

3. Meanwhile, make 4 or 5 shallow slashes, about 1 inch apart, on skin side of each fillet, being careful not to cut into flesh. Pat salmon dry with paper towels. Brush with remaining 1 teaspoon oil, then brush with 1 tablespoon pomegranate molasses and sprinkle with pepper and remaining ½ teaspoon salt. Reduce oven temperature to 275 degrees and carefully remove sheet from oven. Carefully place salmon skin side down on hot sheet. Roast until center is still translucent when checked with tip of paring knife and registers 125 degrees (for medium-rare), 8 to 12 minutes.

4. Brush salmon with remaining 1 tablespoon pomegranate molasses. Transfer salmon to individual plates or serving platter. Stir pomegranate seeds into lentil mixture and serve with salmon.

KEYS TO SUCCESS

- **Slash the skin:** Renders the fat and ensures that the fillets don't buckle
- **Preheat the sheet:** Helps the skin crisp quickly when the salmon hits the sheet
- **Lower the heat:** Cooks the rest of the salmon through gently

Slashing Salmon Fillets

CUT
Make four or five shallow slashes on the skin side of each piece, being careful not to cut into the flesh.

PAN-SEARED SALMON STEAKS

Serves: 4
Total Time: 1 hour

RECIPE OVERVIEW If you want salmon with lots of crisp browning, salmon steaks are a good way to go. Because neither the top nor the bottom of a steak has skin, its larger fleshy surface promises plenty of crisp exterior to contrast with the silky interior. Also, whereas a fillet has a thick end and a tapered end, which can lead to uneven cooking, a steak is generally uniformly thick. To make sure that this is the case, we debone and then tie each steak into a round to produce a structurally sound parcel that cooks evenly and develops a nice crust. To bolster the color of the crust, we coat the steaks with a translucent dusting of cornstarch. The medallions emerge with perfectly even and beautifully crisp browned exteriors encasing moist, buttery flesh.

- 4 (8- to 10-ounce) salmon steaks, 1 inch thick
- ½ teaspoon table salt
- ¼ teaspoon pepper
- ¼ cup cornstarch
- 2 tablespoons vegetable oil

1. Pat salmon dry with paper towels. Place 1 salmon steak on counter with belly flaps facing you. Locate white line at top of salmon steak. Using sharp paring knife, cut along 1 side of white line, around spine, then along membrane inside belly flap. Repeat process on other side of white line.

2. Using kitchen shears and sharp paring knife, cut out spine and membrane; discard. Remove any pin bones using tweezers. Using sharp paring knife, separate bottom 1½ inches of skin from salmon on 1 flap of steak, then discard skin. Tuck skinned portion into center of steak. Wrap other flap around steak and tie kitchen twine around circumference of salmon. Repeat with remaining steaks.

3. Sprinkle both sides of salmon with salt and pepper. Spread cornstarch in even layer on large plate. Lightly press both sides of salmon into cornstarch. Using pastry brush, remove excess cornstarch.

4. Heat oil in 12-inch nonstick skillet over medium-high heat until shimmering. Place salmon in skillet and cook until first side is browned, about 3 minutes. Flip salmon and cook until second side is browned, about 3 minutes. Continue to cook, flipping salmon every 2 minutes, until center is still translucent when checked with tip of paring knife and registers 125 degrees, 2 to 6 minutes. Transfer salmon to platter and discard twine. Serve.

Tying Salmon Steaks

SEPARATE MEAT
Locate white line at top of salmon steak. Cut around white line, one side at a time, to separate meat from cartilage.

REMOVE SPINE
Use kitchen shears and paring knife to cut out spine and membrane.

CUT OFF SKIN
Cut along skin and membrane to separate bottom 1½ inches of meat, then cut off skin.

TUCK TAIL
Tuck skinned portion into center of steak.

TIE STEAKS
After wrapping other flap around steak, tie circumference of steak with kitchen twine.

KEYS TO SUCCESS

- **Tie the steaks:** Helps the salmon cook uniformly
- **Brush off any excess cornstarch:** Prevents patchy spots of starch on the steaks
- **Flip frequently:** Ensures that the steaks cook properly while achieving browning (see page 467)

MISO-MARINATED SALMON

Serves: 4
Total Time: 30 minutes, plus 6 hours marinating

RECIPE OVERVIEW The Japanese technique of marinating fish in miso started as a way to preserve a fresh catch without refrigeration during its long journey inland. Now the dish is a delicacy, not a necessity. The technique is quite simple. Miso is combined with sugar, sake, and mirin (a sweet Japanese rice wine) to make a marinade that essentially cures the fish and gives it complex flavor. Once we marinate the fish in our miso mixture, we scrape the fish clean and broil it, producing meaty-textured, well-seasoned fillets with a lacquered savory-sweet glaze. Note that the fish needs to marinate for at least 6 hours before cooking. It is important to keep the skin on during cooking; remove it afterward, if desired. Yellow, red, or brown miso can be used instead of the white miso. You can substitute wild salmon or arctic char for farmed salmon; if using either of these, cook the fillets to 120 degrees (for medium-rare) and start checking for doneness after 6 minutes.

- 1 cup white miso
- ¼ cup sugar
- 3 tablespoons sake
- 3 tablespoons mirin
- 4 (6- to 8-ounce) skin-on salmon fillets, 1 inch thick

1. Whisk miso, sugar, sake, and mirin in bowl until sugar and miso are dissolved. Pat salmon dry with paper towels, then place in 1-gallon zipper-lock bag; pour marinade over top. Seal bag, pressing out as much air as possible, then flip bag to ensure salmon is well coated. Place bag on large plate and refrigerate for at least 6 hours or up to 24 hours, flipping bag occasionally to ensure salmon marinates evenly.

2. Adjust oven rack 8 inches from broiler element and heat broiler. Place wire rack in rimmed baking sheet and cover rack with aluminum foil. Remove salmon from marinade and scrape miso mixture from fillets (do not rinse). Place salmon, skin side down, on foil, leaving 1 inch between fillets.

3. Broil salmon until deeply browned and center is still translucent when checked with tip of paring knife and registers 125 degrees (for medium-rare), 8 to 12 minutes, rotating sheet halfway through broiling and shielding salmon with foil if browning too quickly. Transfer salmon to platter and serve.

SCIENCE LESSON

Why Marinate with Miso?

A miso marinade works much like a typical curing technique. The miso (a paste made by fermenting soybeans and sometimes other grains with salt and a grain- or bean-based starter called koji), sugar, and alcohol all work to season and pull moisture out of the flesh, resulting in a firmer, denser texture. Miso also adds flavor benefits: sweetness, acidity, and water-soluble compounds such as glutamic acid that, over time, penetrate the proteins and lend them deeply complex flavor.

KEYS TO SUCCESS

- **Leave headspace in the oven:** Prevents the surface of the salmon from overbrowning
- **Cover the sides with foil:** Shields the fish if it's browning too quickly

GRILLED SALMON FILLETS WITH LEMON-GARLIC SAUCE

Serves: 4
Total Time: 55 minutes

RECIPE OVERVIEW Rich salmon tastes ultrasatisfying with grill char—when it doesn't come off the grill mangled. The first step in successfully grilling fish fillets is to properly prepare your grill's cooking grate (see page 467). For extra protection against sticking, we oil both sides of the salmon. We also start grilling the fillets flesh side down to sear the flesh when the cooking grate is at its hottest and then finish on the more-durable skin side. Rather than risk dropping or breaking the fillets while flipping them, we use a fish spatula to gently roll the fillets onto their skin side. If using arctic char or wild salmon, cook the fillets until they reach 120 degrees (for medium-rare) and start checking for doneness early.

Sauce
- ½ cup mayonnaise
- 1 tablespoon minced fresh parsley
- ½ teaspoon grated lemon zest
- 1 small garlic clove, minced

Fish
- 4 (6- to 8-ounce) skin-on salmon fillets, 1 inch thick
- ½ teaspoon table salt
- ½ teaspoon pepper
- 2 teaspoons vegetable oil

1. FOR THE SAUCE Combine all ingredients in bowl; refrigerate for 15 minutes. (Sauce can be refrigerated for up to 3 days.)

2. FOR THE FISH Pat salmon dry with paper towels; refrigerate until ready to grill. Combine salt and pepper in bowl; set aside.

3A. FOR A CHARCOAL GRILL Open bottom vent completely. Light large chimney starter filled with charcoal briquettes (6 quarts). When top coals are partially covered with ash, pour evenly over grill. Set cooking grate in place, cover, and open lid vent completely. Heat grill until hot, about 5 minutes.

3B. FOR A GAS GRILL Turn all burners to high; cover; and heat grill until hot, about 15 minutes. Leave all burners on high.

4. Fold paper towels into compact wad. Holding paper towels with tongs, dip in oil, then wipe grate. Dip paper towels in oil again and wipe grate for second time. Cover grill and heat for 5 minutes. Uncover and wipe grate twice more with oiled paper towels.

5. Rub fillets evenly with oil and sprinkle flesh side with salt mixture. Place fillets on grill, flesh side down and perpendicular to grate bars. Cover grill (reduce heat to medium if using gas) and cook, without moving fillets, until flesh side is well marked and releases easily from grill, 4 to 5 minutes.

6. Using 2 fish spatulas, gently flip salmon and continue to cook, covered, until centers of fillets are translucent when checked with tip of paring knife and register 125 degrees (for medium-rare), 4 to 5 minutes. (If fillets don't lift cleanly off grill, cover and continue to cook for 1 minute, at which point they should release.) Transfer fillets to platter and serve with sauce.

Flipping Salmon on the Grill

PLACE FLESH DOWN
Place fillets on grill, flesh side down and perpendicular to grate bars.

ROLL
Using 2 fish spatulas, check that salmon flesh releases and gently roll onto skin side.

RESOURCES FOR SALMON SO MANY WAYS

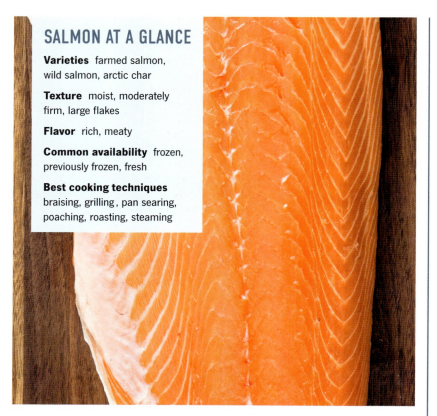

SALMON AT A GLANCE

Varieties farmed salmon, wild salmon, arctic char

Texture moist, moderately firm, large flakes

Flavor rich, meaty

Common availability frozen, previously frozen, fresh

Best cooking techniques braising, grilling, pan searing, poaching, roasting, steaming

FISH OF THE RIVER

Salmon are anadromous—that is, they're born in fresh water and then travel to the sea. When mature, they typically return to freshwater streams to spawn. To help fuel their upriver swim in cold waters, salmon are relatively high in fat (and also high in good-for-you omega-3 fatty acids) and have stronger muscles than white fish. Unlike the fat that does exist in white fish, which is generally stored mostly in the liver, the fat in salmon is spread throughout the flesh.

WHAT IS ARCTIC CHAR?

While a member of both the trout and salmon families, arctic char more closely resembles salmon. Also anadromous, this fish swims from lakes to salt water. Like wild salmon, arctic char has moderately firm flesh, although it does contain more lubricating fat. Its flavor is milder than that of salmon. Its thin profile and fine flakes make it best when cooked like wild salmon, to 120 degrees.

FARMED VERSUS WILD SALMON

Farmed salmon is available year-round, raised on confined farms in the waters of the Atlantic, primarily in Norway, Scotland, and Canada. Wild salmon is available from spring to early fall and caught in open waters, usually in the Pacific Ocean. Farmed salmon is thicker and has a lighter color that derives mainly from synthetic astaxanthin and carotenoid pigment in its feed. Once cooked, farmed salmon is richer and more buttery, while wild salmon is firmer and meatier. The size and number of muscle fibers are virtually the same for wild salmon and farmed Atlantic salmon, however. The difference comes down to the structure of the collagen protein that makes up about 90 percent of the connective tissue in salmon. Wild salmon has a higher amount of collagen (and thus connective tissue) and, more important, a significantly greater number of chemical cross-links between collagen molecules. The flesh of wild salmon therefore turns firmer when cooked than farmed salmon does. Farmed salmon also contains more fat, as much as twice the amount in wild, which contributes to greater lubricity and richer flavor.

We love the taste of wild salmon, but because it doesn't have the cushion of as much lubricating fat, we like it cooked to 120 degrees (for medium-rare) rather than 125 degrees for farmed salmon. At 120 degrees, the muscles of farmed salmon contract less and therefore expel less moisture. Wild salmon is also thinner, so you need to check for doneness earlier than you would for recipes calling for farmed salmon.

Wild salmon varieties include Chinook (or king), chum (or dog or silverbrite), coho (or silver), masu (or cherry), pink (or humpy or humpback), and sockeye (or red). Farmed salmon will generally just be labeled "Atlantic salmon."

FARMED SALMON

WILD SALMON

REMOVING PIN BONES FROM SALMON

Filleted fish has had the backbone and ribs removed, but the thin, needle-like pin bones must be removed separately. They are difficult to see, and while some fishmongers remove them (inevitably missing some), many do not. Here's how to look for pin bones and remove them without damaging the flesh.

Drape the whole fillet over an inverted mixing bowl to help any pin bones protrude. Then, working from head end to tail end, locate the pin bones by running your fingers along the length of the fillet. Use tweezers to grasp the tip of the bone. To avoid tearing the flesh, pull slowly but firmly at a slight angle in the direction the bone is naturally pointing rather than straight up. Repeat until all the pin bones are removed.

TO SKIN OR NOT TO SKIN

When seasoned and well rendered, salmon skin can be pleasant to eat. But when you want skinless fillets, you can easily remove the skin before or after cooking.

To remove the skin from raw fillets Use tip of boning knife or sharp chef's knife to cut skin away from flesh at corner of fillet. When sufficient skin is exposed, grasp skin firmly with paper towel, hold it taut, and slice remaining skin off flesh.

To remove skin after cooking Slip thin metal spatula between flesh and skin and slide fillet right off, leaving skin behind.

GRAY AREA

The gray portion you can often see in salmon is a fatty deposit rich in omega-3 fatty acids and low in the natural pink pigments found in the rest of the fish. We oven-roasted several fillets of salmon and then removed the gray portion from half of them and left it intact on the others. Only a few tasters noted that the samples with the gray substance had an ever-so-slightly fishier flavor. It's easy enough to remove the gray stuff by peeling off the skin of the cooked salmon and then scraping it away with the back of a knife, but the flavor difference is so minor that we don't think it's worth it.

WHITEOUT

What's the white stuff that sometimes forms on salmon and sometimes doesn't? This film is a protein called albumin. When the muscle fibers in the fish are heated, they contract, pushing the moisture-filled albumin to the surface of the flesh. Once this protein reaches temperatures between 140 and 150 degrees, its moisture is squeezed out, and it congeals and turns white. Not only does the albumin detract from the fish's appearance, but its formation indicates a loss of moisture. Gentle cooking results in less-intense muscle contractions, so less of the albumin moves to the surface of the fish and more of it stays trapped in the flesh.

COURSE
POACHING FOR EVERY FISH

DAN ZUCCARELLO

Poaching is one cooking method you can use for any fish: It's foolproof, dead simple, healthful, and makes fish taste distinctly like itself. It involves cooking seafood gently in water that's often fortified with aromatics and wine or vinegar. In this course you'll learn our hybrid method for poaching fish and why it works best as well as the most reliable way to poach shrimp.

DAN'S PRO TIP: *Instead of discarding it, I like to use the flavorful poaching liquid as the base for a simple herb sauce. Simmer the liquid left in the pan until reduced to about 2 tablespoons. Combine the strained liquid with ¼ cup minced fresh herbs, 2 tablespoons minced shallot, 2 tablespoons olive oil, and 1 tablespoon honey and season with salt and pepper to taste.*

PERFECT POACHED FISH
Serves: 4
Total Time: 30 minutes

RECIPE OVERVIEW Is there a cooking method that works for a majority of fish fillets, regardless of cooking category? There is, and it's poaching. A low cooking temperature is what prevents overcooking in this technique, but if it's too low, there isn't enough steam created to cook the fish. Here's our trick: We increase the ratio of wine to water in our poaching liquid. The additional alcohol lowers the liquid's boiling point, producing more vapor even at lower temperatures. Traditional poaching calls for fully submerging foods in the liquid, but we choose to only partially submerge the fish fillets, raising them from the bottom of the skillet with lemon slices for a sort of hybrid poaching-steaming method that prevents the flavor of the fish's natural juices from washing away in the liquid. The lemon slices also prevent the bottom of the fish from overcooking. You will need a 12-inch skillet with a tight-fitting lid for this recipe. You can substitute many varieties of fish for the salmon. If using arctic char or wild salmon, cook the fillets to 120 degrees (for medium-rare) and start checking for doneness after 8 minutes. If using black sea bass, cod, haddock, hake, or pollock, cook the fish to 135 degrees. If using halibut, mahi-mahi, red snapper, or swordfish, cook the fish to 130 degrees and let it rest, tented with aluminum foil, for 10 minutes before serving.

1 lemon, sliced into thin rounds
4 sprigs fresh parsley
1 shallot, sliced thin
½ cup dry white wine
4 (6- to 8-ounce) skinless salmon fillets, 1 inch thick
½ teaspoon table salt
¼ teaspoon pepper

1. Arrange lemon slices in single layer across bottom of 12-inch skillet. Top with parsley sprigs and shallot, then add wine and ½ cup water. Pat salmon dry with paper towels; sprinkle with salt and pepper; and place, skinned side down, on top of lemon slices in skillet. Bring to simmer over medium-high heat. Cover; reduce heat to low; and cook, adjusting heat as needed to maintain gentle simmer, until center is still translucent when checked with tip of paring knife and registers 125 degrees (for medium-rare), 11 to 16 minutes.

2. Remove skillet from heat and, using spatula, carefully transfer salmon and lemon slices to paper towel–lined plate to drain. (Discard poaching liquid.) Carefully lift and tilt fillets to remove lemon slices and transfer to platter. Serve.

KEYS TO SUCCESS
- **Rest the salmon on lemon slices:** Lifts them partially out of the liquid and prevents the bottoms from overcooking
- **Use a tight-fitting lid:** Keeps the steam in

SHRIMP COCKTAIL

Serves: 6
Total Time: 35 minutes, plus 1 hour chilling

RECIPE OVERVIEW Shrimp cocktail is a classic starter—but bland, rubbery shrimp often hide behind the zippy cocktail sauce. This shrimp cocktail boasts tender, sweet shrimp. To infuse the shrimp with as much flavor as possible, we poach them in a simple mixture of water and seasonings, including Old Bay. We bring the water and aromatics to a boil; take the saucepan off the heat; and add the shrimp, leaving them to poach for 5 minutes—a method that delivers perfectly tender, not rubbery, shrimp every time.

Cocktail Sauce
- 1 cup ketchup
- 2 tablespoons lemon juice
- 2 tablespoons prepared horseradish, drained, plus extra for seasoning
- 2 teaspoons hot sauce, plus extra for seasoning
- ⅛ teaspoon table salt
- ⅛ teaspoon pepper

Shrimp
- 2 teaspoons lemon juice
- 2 bay leaves
- 1 teaspoon black peppercorns
- 1 teaspoon Old Bay seasoning
- 1 pound extra-large shrimp (21 to 25 per pound), peeled and deveined
- Table salt for cooking shrimp

1. FOR THE COCKTAIL SAUCE Whisk all ingredients together in bowl and season with extra horseradish and hot sauce to taste. (Sauce can be refrigerated for up to 4 days; let come to room temperature before serving.)

2. FOR THE SHRIMP Bring 3 cups water, lemon juice, bay leaves, peppercorns, and Old Bay to boil in large saucepan. Stir in shrimp and 1 tablespoon salt. Cover and let sit off heat until shrimp are opaque, about 5 minutes, shaking saucepan halfway through sitting time.

3. Meanwhile, fill large bowl halfway with ice and water. Drain shrimp and transfer to ice bath, discarding aromatics; let cool for 3 to 5 minutes. Drain shrimp and transfer to separate bowl. Cover and refrigerate until thoroughly chilled, at least 1 hour or up to 24 hours. Serve with cocktail sauce.

KEYS TO SUCCESS

- **Remove the saucepan from the heat:** Keeps the shrimp from overcooking
- **Ice bath:** Stops the cooking immediately
- **Refrigerate the cooked shrimp:** Chills them for serving

COURSE
SERVING UP SHRIMP

ELLE SIMONE SCOTT

Whether for their sweet flavor, their quick cooking time, or their ubiquity as a beloved appetizer, shrimp have remarkable appeal. Sweet shrimp are great sautéed for a quick dinner with a side dish. They add plump texture and sweetness to soups and stews. And they can be roasted in their shells. We even use their shells to make quick seafood stocks. There's one attribute of shrimp that makes knowing correct technique important: their small size. It's easy to overcook seafood so small. Each method for cooking shrimp we present prevents this for plump, tender results.

ELLE'S PRO TIP: *Although shrimp often packs big flavors, they're small in size. To be able to handle them both gently and effectively you must have the right tools. In most cases, having tongs with a silicone tip makes the most sense. They'll give you the dexterity to handle individual shrimp without running the risk of scratching a nonstick cooking surface.*

PAN-SEARED SHRIMP WITH PISTACHIO, CUMIN, AND PARSLEY

Serves: 4
Total Time: 45 minutes

RECIPE OVERVIEW When it comes to achieving that ideal combination of deep, flavorful browning on the outside and snappy, succulent meat on the inside, shrimp aren't so simple. For one thing, they're tiny and best cooked to a relatively low temperature (120 degrees), so it's almost impossible to get any color on them before they dry out and turn rubbery. We start by briefly salting them so that they retain moisture even as they're seared over high heat. Sprinkling sugar on the shrimp (patted dry after salting) boosts browning and underscores the shrimp's sweetness. To cook them, we arrange the shrimp in a single layer in a cold skillet so that they make even contact with the surface. They heat up gradually with the skillet, so they don't buckle and thus brown uniformly; slower searing also creates a wider window for ensuring that they don't overcook. Once the shrimp are spotty brown and pink at the edges on the first side, we remove them from the heat and quickly turn each one, letting residual heat gently cook them the rest of the way. A flavorful spice mixture for seasoning the shrimp comes together in the same skillet used to cook them.

- 1½ pounds extra-large shrimp (21 to 25 per pound), peeled, deveined, and tails removed
- 1 teaspoon kosher salt, divided
- 1 garlic clove, minced
- 1 teaspoon ground cumin
- 1 teaspoon paprika
- ⅛ teaspoon cayenne pepper
- 2 tablespoons extra-virgin olive oil, divided
- ⅛ teaspoon sugar
- ¼ cup fresh cilantro leaves and tender stems, chopped
- ¼ cup fresh parsley leaves and tender stems, chopped
- 1 tablespoon lemon juice
- ¼ cup shelled pistachios, toasted and chopped coarse

1. Toss shrimp and ½ teaspoon salt together in bowl; set aside for 15 to 30 minutes.

2. Meanwhile, combine garlic, cumin, paprika, cayenne, and remaining ½ teaspoon salt in small bowl.

3. Pat shrimp dry with paper towels. Add 1 tablespoon oil and sugar to bowl with shrimp and toss to coat. Add shrimp to cold 12-inch nonstick skillet in single layer and cook over high heat until undersides of shrimp are spotty brown and edges turn pink, 3 to 4 minutes. Remove skillet from heat. Working quickly, use tongs to flip each shrimp; let stand until second side is opaque, about 2 minutes. Transfer shrimp to platter.

4. Add remaining 1 tablespoon oil to now-empty skillet. Add spice mixture and cook over medium heat until fragrant, about 30 seconds. Off heat, return shrimp to skillet. Add cilantro, parsley, and lemon juice and toss to combine. Transfer to platter, sprinkle with pistachios, and serve.

KEYS TO SUCCESS

- **Salt the shrimp:** Makes them retain their moisture during cooking
- **Sugar the shrimp:** Helps the shrimp brown
- **Use a nonstick skillet:** Ensures that flavorful browning sticks to the shrimp, not the skillet
- **Start in a cold skillet:** Heats the shrimp gradually so that they don't buckle
- **Shut off the heat:** Gently cooks the shrimp through

GARLICKY ROASTED SHRIMP WITH PARSLEY AND ANISE

Serves: 4 to 6
Total Time: 1 hour

RECIPE OVERVIEW The flavor of sweet shrimp concentrates through roasting, but it's worth it only if the flesh stays tender and moist. We butterfly the shrimp, slicing through the shells but not removing them, so the flesh is protected from the heat. And the shells themselves boost shrimp flavor. After tossing the shrimp in melted butter and olive oil infused with garlic and spices, we slide them under the broiler. Within minutes, our shrimp emerge tender and deeply fragrant beneath flavorful, browned shells that you can choose to eat or remove.

- 2 pounds shell-on jumbo shrimp (16 to 20 per pound)
- 4 tablespoons unsalted butter, melted
- ¼ cup extra-virgin olive oil
- 6 garlic cloves, minced
- 1 teaspoon anise seeds
- ½ teaspoon table salt
- ½ teaspoon red pepper flakes
- ¼ teaspoon pepper
- 2 tablespoons minced fresh parsley
- Lemon wedges

1. Adjust oven rack 4 inches from broiler element and heat broiler. Using kitchen shears or sharp paring knife, cut through shells of shrimp and devein but do not remove shells. Using paring knife, continue to cut shrimp ½ inch deep, taking care not to cut in half completely. Pat shrimp dry with paper towels.

2. Combine melted butter, oil, garlic, anise seeds, salt, pepper flakes, and pepper in large bowl. Add shrimp and parsley to butter mixture and toss well, making sure butter mixture gets into interior of shrimp. Arrange shrimp in single layer on wire rack set in rimmed baking sheet.

3. Broil shrimp until opaque and shells are beginning to brown, 2 to 4 minutes, rotating sheet halfway through broiling. Flip shrimp and continue to broil until second side is opaque and shells are beginning to brown, 2 to 4 minutes, rotating sheet halfway through broiling. Transfer shrimp to platter. Serve with lemon wedges.

KEYS TO SUCCESS

- **Use jumbo shrimp**: Brown better and are less likely to dry out
- **Keep the shells on**: Protects the flesh from dehydrating before the exterior develops good browning
- **Broil on a wire rack**: Allows hot air to circulate around the shrimp for deep, even color

CORE TECHNIQUE
Butterflying Shell-On Shrimp

SNIP SHELL
Starting at head of shrimp, snip through back of shell with kitchen shears. Devein shrimp (see page 489) but do not remove shell.

CUT SLIT
Using paring knife, carefully continue to cut ½-inch slit in shrimp, making sure not to split it in half completely.

SCIENCE LESSON
The Power of Shrimp Shells

We found that cooking shrimp in their shells kept them juicier, but our shell-on roasted shrimp boast such savory depth that we wondered if there wasn't more to this outer layer than we thought. Our science editor confirmed our suspicions. First, shrimp shells contain water-soluble flavor compounds that will get absorbed by the shrimp flesh during cooking. Second, the shells are loaded with proteins and sugars. When they brown, they undergo the flavor-enhancing Maillard reaction just as roasted meats do, which gives the shells even more flavor to pass along to the flesh. Third, like the flesh, the shells contain healthy amounts of glutamates and nucleotides, compounds that dramatically enhance savory umami flavor when present together in food. These compounds also get transferred to the meat during cooking, amplifying the effect of its own glutamates and nucleotides.

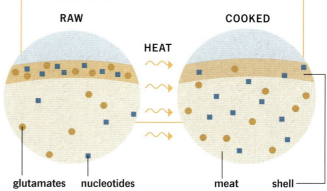

BAKED SHRIMP AND ORZO WITH FETA AND TOMATOES

Serves: 4
Total Time: 1¼ hours

RECIPE OVERVIEW This dish has a lot going for it, and the whole is an amazing sum of its harmonious parts: creamy pasta, juicy shrimp, and fresh-tasting peas along with Mediterranean staples such as pleasantly assertive oregano, floral saffron, tomatoes, and briny feta cheese. To guarantee perfectly cooked shrimp and pasta, we use a combined stovetop-oven cooking method. Sautéing the orzo in the aromatics unlocks its toasty notes; we then stir in chicken broth and the drained juice from a can of diced tomatoes. As the orzo cooks to al dente, it releases starch and creates a sauce with a subtly creamy texture (similar to a risotto). To prevent the shrimp from overcooking, we stir them right into the orzo, along with the reserved tomatoes and frozen peas, and transfer the skillet to the oven to cook through gently. Make sure that the orzo is al dente, or slightly firm to the bite, at the end of step 2; otherwise, it may overcook in the oven.

- 1 tablespoon extra-virgin olive oil
- 1 red onion, chopped fine
- 1 red bell pepper, stemmed, seeded, and cut into ½-inch pieces
- 4 garlic cloves, minced
- 2 teaspoons minced fresh oregano or ½ teaspoon dried
- 2 cups orzo
  Pinch saffron threads, crumbled
- 3 cups chicken or vegetable broth
- 1 (14.5-ounce) can diced tomatoes, drained with juice reserved
- 1 pound extra-large shrimp (21 to 25 per pound), peeled, deveined, and tails removed
- ½ teaspoon table salt
- ¼ teaspoon pepper
- ½ cup frozen peas
- 3 ounces feta cheese, crumbled (¾ cup)
- 2 scallions, sliced thin
  Lemon wedges

1. Adjust oven rack to middle position and heat oven to 375 degrees. Heat oil in 12-inch ovensafe nonstick skillet over medium heat until shimmering. Add onion and bell pepper and cook until vegetables are softened, 5 to 7 minutes. Stir in garlic and oregano and cook until fragrant, about 30 seconds. Stir in orzo and saffron and cook, stirring often, until orzo is lightly browned, about 4 minutes.

2. Stir in broth and reserved tomato juice; bring to simmer; and cook, stirring occasionally, until orzo is al dente, 10 to 12 minutes.

3. Pat shrimp dry with paper towels and sprinkle with salt and pepper. Stir shrimp, tomatoes, and peas into orzo mixture in skillet, then sprinkle feta evenly over top. Transfer skillet to oven and bake until shrimp are opaque throughout and feta is lightly browned, about 20 minutes.

4. Carefully remove skillet from oven and sprinkle scallions over top. Serve with lemon wedges.

KEYS TO SUCCESS
- **Extra-large shrimp:** Stay plump
- **Stir in shrimp last:** Prevents the shrimp from overcooking while the orzo simmers

RESOURCES FOR SERVING UP SHRIMP

WHY YOU SHOULD BUY FROZEN SHRIMP

Unless you have access to shrimp directly from a boat, we recommend buying them frozen. The quality is generally much better than that of defrosted shrimp, the flavor and texture of which decline rapidly once thawed.

Most shrimp, including all bagged options, are individually quick-frozen (IQF). Shrimp (or any other seafood labeled IQF) are spread on a conveyor belt and frozen at sea, locking in quality and freshness. Shrimp are also sometimes frozen at sea with water in 5-pound blocks and packed in boxes. We prefer bagged IQF shrimp, as you can thaw exactly what you need.

MEASURING FROZEN SHRIMP

IQF shrimp are encased in an icy shell that adds weight, making it tricky to measure how much you'll have for cooking once the ice melts. We've found that the shrimp lose anywhere from 12 to 25 percent of their weight.

Because the range of loss is so wide (it depends on factors such as shrimp size and whether or not they are peeled), weight isn't the most precise way to measure. Instead, count out what you need based on the shrimp's per-pound number range.

Example: For extra-large shrimp, the range is 21 to 25 (see chart below), which represents the shrimp's raw, unfrozen weight. So if a recipe calls for 1½ pounds of shrimp, count out 25 pieces plus 13 more.

PEELING AND DEVEINING SHRIMP

Shell-on shrimp tend to be sweeter, but they require some prep. For most recipes, you'll want to peel and devein the shrimp before cooking. The vein running down the length of the shrimp's back is its digestive tract. We tend to remove it before cooking. (Leaving it in place doesn't affect flavor, but it isn't terribly appealing.) A sharp paring knife makes the task easy.

1. Break shell on underside, under swimming legs, which will come off as shell is removed. Tug tail to remove shell, or peel off shell while keeping tail intact.

2. Using paring knife, make shallow cut along back of shrimp to expose vein.

3. Using tip of knife, lift out vein. Discard vein by wiping knife blade against paper towel.

SHRIMP SHOPPING TIPS

Make sure that your shrimp are additive-free. Shrimp should be the only thing on the ingredient list. Avoid salt-treated and sodium tripolyphosphate (STPP)–enhanced shrimp; the texture of both is unpleasant, and the latter also has a chemical taste. Increasingly, seafood markets and gourmet shops sell a range of different shrimp species. We compared the three commonly available types (pink, white, and black tiger) and found that white shrimp had the firmest flesh and the sweetest taste. And wild shrimp are ideal; they have a sweeter flavor and firmer texture than farm-raised shrimp, making their higher price worth it.

SIZING UP SHRIMP

Shrimp are sold both by size and by number needed to make a pound. Choosing shrimp by the per-pound number is more accurate, because the size labels vary from store to store. See the chart for how the sizes generally compare.

SIZE	COUNT PER POUND
Colossal	U12*
Extra-Jumbo	U15
Jumbo	16–20
Extra-Large	21–25
Large	26–30
Medium-Large	31–40
Medium	41–50
Small	51–60
Extra-Small	61–70

*U=Under

COURSE
WORKING WITH BIVALVES

NICOLE KONSTANTINAKOS

Bivalves are interactive seafood, their delicious meat living within shells you pry (in the case of raw seafood) or cook open. The category is wide, consisting of oysters for slurping up; mussels and clams that taste great in an aromatic broth; and scallops that look beautiful with a golden seared crust. Don't let their shells intimidate you. Bivalves are any cook's friend because they're on the table in no time. Learn to prep the different kinds of bivalves along with common preparations that will impress you.

NICOLE'S PRO TIP: *I prefer to eat my bivalves as fresh as possible, but to safely store them for several days, ice is key, since refrigerators are generally not cold enough to store fish properly. Store fresh dry scallops in a zipper-lock bag placed directly on ice for up to 5 days. Live clams and mussels should be stored in a bowl set into a second bowl of ice (to be sure they don't end up submerged in melted ice, which would kill them) and loosely covered with damp paper towels. Fresh mussels will keep this way up to 3 days and fresh clams up to 5; just be sure to refresh the ice as it melts.*

PAN-SEARED SCALLOPS
Serves: 4
Total Time: 40 minutes

RECIPE OVERVIEW For a restaurant chef, pan-seared scallops are as easy as it gets: Slick a superhot pan with oil, add the shellfish, flip them once, and serve. But try the same technique at home and you're likely to run into trouble. The problem is that most home stovetops don't get nearly as hot as professional ranges, so it's difficult to properly brown the scallops without overcooking them. We turn up the heat as high as it goes and cook the scallops in batches to avoid crowding. Basting with butter increases browning—and adds richness to boot. We sear one side of the scallops in oil, add butter to the skillet, and then spoon the foaming butter over the seafood. The scallops achieve a deep golden-brown crust quickly, and their moist interiors are preserved. Be sure to buy "dry" scallops (see page 495).

- 1½ pounds large sea scallops, tendons removed
- ½ teaspoon table salt
- ¼ teaspoon pepper
- 2 tablespoons vegetable oil, divided
- 2 tablespoons unsalted butter, divided

1. Place scallops on rimmed baking sheet lined with clean dish towel. Top with second clean dish towel and press gently on scallops to dry. Let scallops sit between towels at room temperature for 10 minutes.

2. Sprinkle scallops with salt and pepper. Heat 1 tablespoon oil in 12-inch nonstick skillet over medium-high heat until just smoking. Add half of scallops in single layer, flat side down, and cook until well browned, 1½ to 2 minutes.

3. Add 1 tablespoon butter to skillet. Using tongs, flip scallops. Continue to cook, using large spoon to baste scallops with melted butter (tilt skillet so butter runs to 1 side), until sides of scallops are firm and centers are opaque, 30 to 90 seconds (remove smaller scallops as they finish cooking).

4. Transfer scallops to platter and tent with aluminum foil. Wipe out skillet with paper towels and repeat with remaining 1 tablespoon oil, remaining scallops, and remaining 1 tablespoon butter. Serve.

KEYS TO SUCCESS

- **Towel-dry the scallops:** Scallops with dry surfaces brown best.
- **Baste with butter:** Enhances browning and finishes cooking the scallops
- **Remove the scallops as they finish:** Prevents the smaller scallops from overcooking

CORE TECHNIQUE — Searing Scallops

DRY

Place scallops on rimmed baking sheet lined with clean dish towel. Top with second clean dish towel and press gently on scallops to dry. Let scallops sit between towels for 10 minutes.

SEAR

Heat 1 tablespoon oil in 12-inch nonstick skillet over medium-high heat until just smoking. Add half of scallops in single layer and cook until well browned, 1½ to 2 minutes.

BASTE

Flip scallops. Using large spoon, baste scallops with melted butter (tilt skillet so butter runs to 1 side), until sides of scallops are firm and centers are opaque, 30 to 90 seconds.

FENNEL AND BIBB SALAD WITH SCALLOPS AND HAZELNUTS

Serves: 4
Total Time: 45 minutes

RECIPE OVERVIEW Scallops are an ideal weeknight meal because they cook quickly, are healthful, and pair well with greens. After quickly searing the scallops to browned perfection, we make a salad of delicate Bibb lettuce and crisp sliced fennel and radishes. We toss the vegetables with a lemon dressing and top individual portions with warm scallops in addition to chopped toasted hazelnuts, which bring out the natural sweet nuttiness of the seared scallops, plus tarragon to emphasize the anise flavor of the fennel.

- 1½ pounds large sea scallops, tendons removed
- ¾ teaspoon table salt, divided
- ½ teaspoon pepper, divided
- 7 tablespoons extra-virgin olive oil, divided
- 1 small shallot, minced
- 1 teaspoon Dijon mustard
- ½ teaspoon grated lemon zest plus 1½ tablespoons juice
- 2 heads Bibb lettuce (1 pound), torn into bite-size pieces
- 1 fennel bulb, 1 tablespoon fronds minced, stalks discarded, bulb halved, cored, and sliced thin
- 4 radishes, trimmed and sliced thin
- ¼ cup hazelnuts, toasted, skinned, and chopped
- 2 tablespoons minced fresh tarragon

1. Pat scallops dry with paper towels and sprinkle with ½ teaspoon salt and ¼ teaspoon pepper. Heat 1 tablespoon oil in skillet over high heat until just smoking. Add half of scallops in single layer and cook, without moving them, until well browned, 1½ to 2 minutes. Flip and cook until sides are firm and centers are opaque, 30 to 90 seconds (remove scallops as they finish cooking). Transfer scallops to plate and tent with aluminum foil. Wipe out skillet with paper towels and repeat with 1 tablespoon oil and remaining scallops.

2. Whisk shallot, mustard, lemon zest and juice, remaining ¼ teaspoon salt, and remaining ¼ teaspoon pepper together in large bowl. While whisking constantly, slowly drizzle in remaining 5 tablespoons oil until combined. Add lettuce, sliced fennel, and radishes and toss to combine. Season with salt and pepper to taste. Divide salad among individual serving dishes; top with scallops; and sprinkle with hazelnuts, tarragon, and fennel fronds. Serve.

KEYS TO SUCCESS

- **Crunchy salad:** Contrasts with the silky texture of the scallops
- **Zippy dressing:** Offsets the sweetness of the scallops

BROTHY RICE WITH CLAMS AND SALSA VERDE

Serves: 4 to 6
Total Time: 1¼ hours

RECIPE OVERVIEW This rice dish from Spain's Mediterranean coast combines the briny sweetness of clams with the verdant flavors of leek, green pepper, and parsley. Unlike paella-style dishes, in which the rice absorbs the cooking liquid, brothy rice has a higher proportion of liquid to rice. We start by steaming our clams in wine to open them and using the cooking liquid to build a flavorful broth. We then set the clams aside so that they don't overcook and build a base from leek, green pepper, and garlic. To emphasize these vegetal flavors and the acidic notes of the wine, we finish the dish with a vinegar-enhanced salsa verde. Bomba rice is the most traditional rice for this dish, but you can use any variety of Valencia rice. If you cannot find Valencia rice, you can substitute arborio rice.

Salsa Verde
- 3 cups fresh parsley leaves
- 1 cup fresh mint leaves
- ½ cup extra-virgin olive oil
- 3 tablespoons white wine vinegar
- 2 tablespoons capers, rinsed
- 3 anchovy fillets, rinsed
- 1 garlic clove, minced
- ⅛ teaspoon table salt

Rice and Clams
- 5 tablespoons extra-virgin olive oil, divided
- ¼ cup minced fresh parsley
- 1 garlic clove, minced, divided
- 1 tablespoon white wine vinegar
- 2 cups dry white wine
- 2 pounds littleneck clams, scrubbed
- 5 cups water
- 1 (8-ounce) bottle clam juice
- 1 leek, white and light green parts only, halved lengthwise, chopped fine, and washed thoroughly
- 1 green bell pepper, stemmed, seeded, and chopped fine
- ½ teaspoon table salt
- 1½ cups Bomba rice
- Lemon wedges

1. FOR THE SALSA VERDE Pulse all ingredients in food processor until mixture is finely chopped (mixture should not be smooth), about 10 pulses, scraping down sides of bowl as needed. Transfer mixture to bowl. Set aside. (Sauce can be refrigerated for up to 2 days; let come to room temperature before serving.)

2. FOR THE RICE AND CLAMS Combine 3 tablespoons oil, parsley, half of garlic, and vinegar in bowl; set aside. Bring wine to boil in large saucepan over high heat. Add clams; cover; and cook, stirring occasionally, until clams open, 5 to 7 minutes.

3. Using slotted spoon, transfer clams to large bowl, discarding any that refuse to open, and cover to keep warm. Stir water and clam juice into wine and bring to simmer. Reduce heat to low, cover, and keep warm.

4. Heat remaining 2 tablespoons oil in Dutch oven over medium heat until shimmering. Add leek, bell pepper, and salt and cook until softened, 8 to 10 minutes. Add rice and remaining garlic and cook, stirring frequently, until edges of grains begin to turn translucent, about 3 minutes.

5. Add 2 cups warm broth and cook, stirring frequently, until almost fully absorbed, about 5 minutes. Continue to cook rice, stirring frequently and adding warm broth, 1 cup at a time, every few minutes as liquid is absorbed, until rice is creamy and cooked through but still somewhat firm in center, 12 to 14 minutes.

6. Off heat, stir in 1 cup warm broth and adjust consistency with extra broth as needed (rice mixture should have thin but creamy consistency; you may have broth left over). Stir in parsley mixture and season with salt and pepper to taste. Nestle clams into rice along with any accumulated juices; cover; and let sit until heated through, 5 to 7 minutes. Serve with lemon wedges and salsa verde.

> ### KEYS TO SUCCESS
> - **Steam the clams in wine:** Allows the clams to release their liquid and form the base of a quick broth
> - **Use clam juice:** Reinforces the steamed clams' flavor
> - **Nestle the clams into the rice:** Reheats them for serving

OVEN-STEAMED MUSSELS
Serves: 2 to 4
Total Time: 50 minutes

RECIPE OVERVIEW Mussels come in a range of sizes, making it a real challenge to cook them evenly, so rather than pile them into a Dutch oven (where the mussels closest to the stove's burner will inevitably overcook), as is convention, roast them en masse in the generous space afforded by a roomy roasting pan. After infusing white wine with garlic, thyme, and bay leaves on the stovetop, stir in the mussels and seal them under a sheet of aluminum foil. The all-encompassing heat of a 500-degree oven gently heats the shellfish through so that the majority of the mussels, both big and small, open in about 15 minutes, their liquid mingling with the reduced wine for an irresistibly briny-sweet broth. A hit of butter melted into the concentrated cooking liquid before serving offers a rich complement to these simple but spectacular mussels. Before cooking, discard any mussel with an unpleasant odor, a cracked shell, or a shell that won't close. Serve with crusty bread.

- 1 tablespoon extra-virgin olive oil
- 3 garlic cloves, minced
- Pinch red pepper flakes
- 1 cup dry white wine
- 3 sprigs fresh thyme
- 2 bay leaves
- 4 pounds mussels, scrubbed and debearded
- ¼ teaspoon table salt
- 2 tablespoons unsalted butter, cut into 4 pieces
- 2 tablespoons minced fresh parsley

1. Adjust oven rack to lowest position and heat oven to 500 degrees. Heat oil, garlic, and pepper flakes in large roasting pan over medium heat (over 2 burners, if possible) and cook, stirring constantly, until fragrant, about 30 seconds. Stir in wine, thyme sprigs, and bay leaves. Bring to boil and cook until wine is slightly reduced, about 1 minute.

2. Stir in mussels and salt. Cover pan tightly with aluminum foil and transfer to oven. Roast until most mussels have opened (a few may remain closed), 15 to 18 minutes.

3. Remove pan from oven. Push mussels to sides of pan. Being careful of hot pan handles, add butter to center and whisk until melted. Discard thyme sprigs and bay leaves and stir in parsley. Serve.

> ### KEYS TO SUCCESS
> - **Use a roasting pan:** Allows the mussels room to spread out and cook evenly
> - **Cover the pan:** Traps steam just like stovetop steaming

The Problem with the Pot
Because mussels steamed in a pot are crowded on top of one another, it's difficult to stir (or shake) them around—and cook them evenly. The mussels closest to the heat source cook faster than the ones on top.

SEAFOOD | 493

RESOURCES FOR WORKING WITH BIVALVES

HOT TIP: STAY CLOSED

Never buy bivalves with open or gaping shells (with the exception of steamers and razor clams); the shellfish might be dead or dying.

OYSTER ALLEGIANCES

East or West? Raw-bar lovers on each coast have their preference. As a rule, Atlantic oysters are crisp and briny, with an intense hit of fresh, cold sea salt. (All Atlantic oysters are the same species: *Crassostrea virginica*.) They range from 2 inches long to nearly 6 inches long (Gulf Coasters call these "tennis shoes" for their size). Pacific oysters are rarely as salty and often taste complex and fruity.

MUSSEL PREP

The two main varieties of mussels you'll see at the store are the Atlantic blue mussel and the Pacific green-lipped (also called New Zealand) mussel. These mussels are interchangeable when it comes to cooking, although some think green-lipped mussels are slightly chewier. Most mussels sold are farmed or rope cultured, which is good because these are minimally gritty.

There can be a small, weedy beard protruding from the side of the mussel that needs to be removed before cooking. Holding the mussel in your hand, pull the beard firmly out of the shell, using your thumb and the side of a paring knife to grip it firmly. Don't debeard mussels until you are ready to cook them, since debearding can cause them to die.

If the mussels won't close when tapped, discard them.

You've likely heard a "rule" that you should eat oysters only in months that have the letter *r* at the end of them. While this made sense when oysters were harvested in the wild (oysters don't taste very good when they're reproducing, and they do so in the summer), oysters are now farmed in hatcheries, so the rule no longer applies.

SCRUB 'EM

Be sure to scrub oysters, clams, and mussels before cooking to remove sand and grit.

CLAMS TO COOK

Clams are sold as hard-shell or soft-shell. Because hard-shell clams stay shut, they're less sandy, good for carefree cooking. We cook largely available littleneck or cherrystone clams. By contrast, soft-shell clams (steamers and razor clams) gape when they are alive, so they contain a lot of sand—we don't cook with these, as they're harder to find.

STICK WITH SEA SCALLOPS

Scallops are available in a range of sizes: A pound of the large sea variety contains eight to 10 scallops, while a pound of the petite bay variety may have as many as 100 pencil eraser–size scallops. Sea scallops are in markets year-round. In addition to being easier to find, these are the scallops we use in our cooking, as they have a larger surface area for searing and their interiors remain succulent.

SCALLOP PREP

Scallops are shucked at sea (what you're buying is the large adductor muscle that opens and closes its shell), so before cooking, simply remove the crescent-shaped muscle that attaches the scallop to the shell.

TAKING THE TEMPERATURE OF SCALLOPS

We typically recommend cooking scallops until their sides are firm and their centers are opaque. Since determining whether the scallop's interior is done requires cutting into it, we decided that it would be useful to have a more precise (and less destructive) way of assessing doneness. After searing a few batches, we determined that scallops are perfectly cooked when their centers register 115 degrees. Because scallops are usually cooked over high heat, carryover cooking will add another 10 to 15 degrees, for an ideal final temperature of 125 to 130 degrees.

WET VERSUS DRY SCALLOPS

We strongly discourage purchasing "wet" scallops (ask at the store), which are treated with a solution of water and sodium tripolyphosphate (STPP) to increase shelf life and retain moisture. STPP lends a soapy off-flavor to the scallops, and the extra water inhibits browning. Look for "dry" scallops, which are untreated. If wet is all you can find, soak them in a mixture of 1 quart of cold water, ¼ cup of lemon juice, and 2 tablespoons of kosher salt for 30 minutes to mask any chemical flavors.

WET SCALLOP

DRY SCALLOP

PINK SCALLOPS?

Scallops are mostly pearly white but sometimes they're pink. Does that mean they're treated? Not at all. The scallop gets its color from the reproductive gland that lies next to it inside the shell. In male scallops, the gland is grayish white, hence the muscle remains white. Female scallops turn pink only when they're spawning; during this period, their glands fill with orange roe and turn bright coral, giving the adductor muscle a rosy hue. To see if there are any differences besides color, we pan-seared and tasted white male scallops alongside peachy female scallops. They cooked in the same amount of time and had identical textures, although tasters did note that the pink scallops—which retained their tint even after cooking—had a somewhat sweeter, richer flavor. Both colors, however, are absolutely normal and do not indicate anything about the freshness, doneness, or edibility of a scallop.

MALE SCALLOP   FEMALE SCALLOP

MOVE LIKE A SCALLOP

It's not often that you see a scallop swim—but swim they do. The adductor muscle connects the two shells, opening and closing them to move forward in the water.

COURSE
THE FISH FRY

ASHLEY MOORE

As with anything, everyone has a seafood preference. But it's hard to imagine anyone who could resist the satisfying, salty crunch of fried batter against sweet, lean, fresh-tasting seafood. Why is frying so good for seafood? The coating protects the delicate seafood from the hot oil and mitigates moisture loss. Seafood choices and batters vary by region (of the United States and internationally), but generally, the right coating isn't too thick to overshadow the seafood, clings well, and gets supercrispy (we'll dive into that in this course). Frying has a reputation for being intimidating, but you won't fear these two fried-seafood basics. Reference the basics of deep-frying fish on page 497, and then let us take you from the coast of New England to the Gulf Coast with these recipes.

ASHLEY'S PRO TIP: *Although we call for haddock in our Crispy Fish Sandwiches, any meaty white fish will do, such as cod or flounder.*

CRISPY FISH SANDWICHES

Serves: 4
Total Time: 1 hour

RECIPE OVERVIEW In New England, you'll most often get your fried fish—usually a generous piece of haddock—topped with coleslaw and creamy tartar sauce for the perfect bite of moist, crispy fish; rich, creamy sauce; a fresh, crunchy component; and a bun to soak it all up. We use equal parts all-purpose flour and cornstarch plus ½ teaspoon of baking powder to create the shell-like coating. Whisking in seltzer creates a batter that adheres and has the right amount of lightness. We prefer a vinegar-based dressing to a traditional creamy one because it enhances the freshness of the slaw and offers extra acidity to counterbalance the fish. Store-bought coleslaw mix can be substituted for the cabbage, carrot, and parsley in the slaw. Use a Dutch oven that holds 6 quarts or more.

Fish
- ½ cup all-purpose flour
- ½ cup cornstarch
- ½ teaspoon table salt
- ½ teaspoon baking powder
- ¾ cup plain seltzer
- 2 quarts peanut or vegetable oil for frying
- 4 (4- to 6-ounce) skinless haddock fillets, 1 inch thick

Slaw
- 1 tablespoon cider vinegar
- 1½ teaspoons sugar
- 1½ teaspoons vegetable oil
- ¼ teaspoon table salt
- ¼ teaspoon pepper
- 1½ cups shredded red or green cabbage
- 1 carrot, peeled and shredded
- 1 tablespoon minced fresh parsley or cilantro

- ⅓ cup Classic Tartar Sauce (recipe follows)
- 4 brioche buns, toasted

1. FOR THE FISH Whisk flour, cornstarch, salt, and baking powder together in large bowl. Whisk in seltzer until smooth. Cover and refrigerate for 20 minutes.

2. Set wire rack in rimmed baking sheet. Add oil to Dutch oven until it measures about 1½ inches deep and heat over medium-high heat to 375 degrees. Pat haddock dry with paper towels and transfer to batter, tossing gently to evenly coat. Using fork and working with 1 piece of haddock at a time, remove haddock from batter, allowing excess batter to drip back into bowl, and add to hot oil, briefly dragging haddock along surface of oil to prevent sticking before gently dropping into oil. Adjust burner, if necessary, to maintain oil temperature between 350 and 375 degrees.

3. Cook, stirring gently to prevent pieces from sticking together, until deep golden brown and crispy, about 4 minutes per side. Using spider skimmer or slotted spoon, transfer haddock to prepared rack.

4. FOR THE SLAW Whisk vinegar, sugar, oil, salt, and pepper together in large bowl. Add cabbage, carrot, and parsley and toss to combine; season with salt and pepper to taste. Divide tartar sauce evenly among bun bottoms, then top with haddock and slaw. Cover with bun tops. Serve immediately.

CLASSIC TARTAR SAUCE

Makes: about 1 cup
Total Time: 25 minutes

Be sure to rinse the capers before mincing them or else the sauce will have a strong briny flavor. This is a classic with fried white fish, but it pairs nicely with baked fish, too.

- ¾ cup mayonnaise
- 2 tablespoons capers, rinsed and minced
- 2 tablespoons sweet pickle relish
- 1½ teaspoons distilled white vinegar
- 1½ teaspoons minced shallot
- ½ teaspoon Worcestershire sauce

Combine all ingredients in bowl, let sit for 15 minutes, and season with salt and pepper to taste. (Sauce can be refrigerated for up to 5 days.)

> **KEYS TO SUCCESS**
> - **Flour and cornstarch:** Create a light, golden-brown, shell-like coating
> - **Baking powder:** Helps the fish brown

CORE TECHNIQUE Frying Fish

PREVENT STICKING
To keep the pieces of haddock from sticking together, let the excess batter drip off the fillet, and then drag the fillet along the oil's surface before releasing it. This gives the batter a chance to set up so that the fish won't adhere to other pieces.

POPCORN SHRIMP

Serves: 4
Total Time: 1 hour, plus 30 minutes marinating

RECIPE OVERVIEW When properly fried, popcorn shrimp are just as crunchy, salty, and irresistible as their namesake snack. Sadly, most recipes produce greasy, gummy shrimp, often coated in too much bland batter. For shrimp coated in a light, flavorful batter and fried until just golden brown, we replace some of the flour in the batter with cornstarch. A little baking powder increases browning and provides a bit of lift to the batter. Old Bay seasoning adds flavor to the batter, giving these popcorn shrimp a serious upgrade. To impart a brininess that complements the shrimp, we replace the water in the batter with clam juice but reduce the liquid amount so that the coating clings to every curl of the shrimp. We also boost the flavor of the shrimp themselves by marinating them in a little oil, lemon zest, garlic, and more Old Bay before coating them. Be sure to leave plenty of space between the frying shrimp to prevent them from sticking together. You will need a Dutch oven that holds 6 quarts or more.

- 1½ pounds large shrimp (26 to 30 per pound), peeled, deveined, and tails removed
- 1 tablespoon peanut or vegetable oil
- 1½ tablespoons Old Bay seasoning, divided
- 1 teaspoon grated lemon zest, plus lemon wedges for serving
- 1 garlic clove, minced
- 1½ cups all-purpose flour
- ½ cup cornstarch
- 2 teaspoons pepper
- 1 teaspoon baking powder
- 1½ cups bottled clam juice
- 3 quarts peanut or vegetable oil for frying

1. Toss shrimp, 1 tablespoon oil, ½ teaspoon Old Bay, lemon zest, and garlic in large bowl. Refrigerate, covered, for at least 30 minutes or up to 1 hour.

2. Adjust oven rack to middle position and heat oven to 200 degrees. Combine flour, cornstarch, pepper, baking powder, and remaining 4 teaspoons Old Bay in large bowl. Stir clam juice into flour mixture until smooth. Fold shrimp into batter until evenly coated.

3. Heat 3 quarts oil in large Dutch oven over medium-high heat to 375 degrees. Set wire rack in rimmed baking sheet and line plate with triple layer of paper towels. Working quickly, add one-quarter of shrimp, a few at a time, to oil. Fry, stirring frequently, until golden brown, about 2 minutes. Let shrimp drain on prepared plate, then transfer shrimp to prepared wire rack and place in oven to keep warm. Return oil to 375 degrees and repeat with remaining shrimp. Serve with lemon wedges.

Making Popcorn Shrimp

MARINATE SHRIMP
Toss shrimp, 1 tablespoon oil, ½ teaspoon Old Bay, lemon zest, and garlic in large bowl. Refrigerate, covered, for at least 30 minutes or up to 1 hour.

BATTER SHRIMP
Fold marinated shrimp into batter until evenly coated.

FRY SHRIMP
Working quickly, add one-quarter of shrimp, a few at a time, to oil with slotted spoon.

KEYS TO SUCCESS

- **A quick marinade:** Adds a boatload of flavor
- **Clam juice:** Emphasizes seafood flavor in the batter more than water would
- **Large shrimp:** Don't overcook quickly or get lost in the batter

CHAPTER 11

BREAD

COURSES

510 SAVORY QUICK BREADS

514 MORNING BREADS

520 LOAVES FOR EVERY DAY

526 CAN'T TOUCH THIS: NO-KNEAD BREADS

532 CLASSIC DINNER ROLLS

536 WHOLE WHEAT BREADS

540 FREE-FORM LOAVES

546 PIZZA, PIZZA

552 FOUR FANTASTIC FLATBREADS

BREAD BASICS

TYPES OF BREAD

There are innumerable breads that you can learn to make, from this book and beyond. Here we've outlined the main categories in which they fall and describe their defining features.

1. Quick Breads

These easy-to-make loaves rely on chemical leaveners (baking soda and baking powder) and are often baked in a loaf pan. They require just some hand-stirring, as the goal is to avoid developing a lot of gluten, which can make quick breads tough. They are tender from the addition of lots of butter or oil, and they have a cakey closed crumb and no defined crust. We often eat quick breads, such as our Quick Cheese Bread (page 510), which features pockets of gooey cheddar, as a snack. They can also be sweet, like our Ultimate Banana Bread (page 515), and pair nicely with tea.

2. Sandwich Loaves

Sandwich bread is yeasted and typically features a soft, tight crumb, as it's often conditioned with tenderizing ingredients. The perfect white sandwich loaf is mild in flavor and a little pillowy, like our Easy Sandwich Bread (page 521). Baked at a low-to-moderate temperature, sandwich breads have a thin crust. They're typically baked in a loaf pan, but there are also free-form versions.

3. Flatbreads and Pizzas

These breads are all about the crust, and they're often meals in bread form. Though there's a lot of variation across the category, these international breads are often rolled thin, sometimes topped, and typically baked on a baking steel or stone. Other times they're pressed into a rimmed baking sheet. Thick or rectangular pizzas and flatbreads can be almost cakey—a desirable quality in our Skillet Pizza (page 546)—while others are chewy on the inside and supercrisp and charred on the outside, like Thin-Crust Pizza (page 548). Still other flatbreads don't have much of a crumb at all, such as our Flour Tortillas (page 552).

4. Rolls and Buns

These small shaped breads often accompany breakfast if they're sweet or dinner if they're savory. With the exception of our Rustic Dinner Rolls (page 534), which have the crumb structure of artisan bread, rolls are typically tender, with a closed crumb and an unassuming golden-brown crust such as that of our Fluffy Dinner Rolls (page 532).

5. Rustic Loaves

The class of breads you find at an artisan bakery are known as rustic loaves. They contain little or no fat and lots of water, and they develop a lot of gluten (the protein that makes bread elastic; see page 506) to support large air pockets. A good rustic loaf has a thick but crisp outer crust that breaks pleasingly to the chewy, complex crumb. While we won't explore these challenging breads in this book, rustic loaves sometimes incorporate a sponge or even a natural sourdough starter for a more open texture and a tangier aroma.

6. Enriched Breads

A bread that is augmented with butter, sugar, eggs, and/or dairy is considered enriched. In addition to making them sweeter or richer, these ingredients can also make breads more tender. This category includes some easy but downright luxurious loaves, such as Almost No-Knead Brioche (page 528), which has a soft, tender crumb and a golden hue from the addition of lots of butter and egg yolks. These breads aren't very chewy, as the amount of fat in them impedes gluten development. Their crust is thin and soft.

7. Laminated Breads

Often more like pastry—think croissants—than bread, a laminated bread is one composed of many alternating sheets of fat and dough, which bake into airy breads with many layers. Once you master the more modest breads in this book, you'll be well equipped to move on to mastering the complex layering of fat and dough.

BREAD BASICS

BREAD BAKER'S TOOLS

You can knead bread with your own two hands, but a stand mixer makes things much easier (and foolproof). And you can divide dough with a knife, but a multipurpose bench scraper is more versatile. Here are some tools that make regular bread baking a breeze.

Digital Scale (1)
You can use measuring cups and spoons—volume measures—for bread recipes, but weighing your ingredients ensures consistent results. We prefer digital scales for their readability and precision.

Bench Scraper (2)
This basic tool is handy for transferring bread dough from one surface to another and for cutting dough into pieces.

Bowl Scraper (2)
The best way to remove or fold sticky dough is with a bowl scraper. This handheld spatula is curved, with enough grip to scrape the bowl clean and enough rigidity to move heavy dough easily.

Kitchen Ruler (3)
A ruler is helpful for measuring how high a proofing dough has risen and for cutting dough into pieces of a certain size. Stainless steel, not wood, is best, because it's easy to clean. An 18-inch ruler will handle all kitchen tasks.

Baking Peel (4)
A peel is a wide, paddle-like board or metal spatula with a long handle that's useful for sliding pizza and free-form breads into and out of a hot oven. (See page 551 for a substitute.)

Baking Steel or Stone (5)
A baking steel or ceramic stone conducts heat and transfers it evenly and steadily to the loaf, encouraging the development of a thick, crisp, nicely browned bottom crust. Look for a model made of carbon steel, clay, or stone; it should be big enough to accommodate a large pizza. (See page 551 for a substitute.)

Lame (6)
You could use a razor blade or a sharp knife, but you might want a curved-blade lame to produce the almond-shaped slashes on breads and baguettes. It approaches the dough at a low angle to create a cut with a raised flap.

SEVEN KEY BREAD STEPS

Every yeasted bread is unique, yet virtually all of them follow the same progression of steps that transform raw ingredients into finished loaves and rolls. As you work with more and different doughs, you'll become more in tune with the rhythm of bread baking, and these core steps will become second nature.

1. Mixing
This is the step that gets it all started. You combine your dry and wet goods in the stand mixer to create a shaggy amalgamation of ingredients.

2. Kneading
The rough mass of dough you mixed becomes smooth during kneading; you increase the mixer speed and knead until the dough is elastic, signaling that it has developed gluten structure.

3. First Rise
Kneaded dough is ready for the first rise. During this fermentation period, yeast creates carbon dioxide bubbles that cause the bread to expand. You usually want the dough to double in size.

4. Dividing and Shaping
After the first rise, you press down the expanded dough to deflate it. Then you either divide it (for rolls, buns, or multiple loaves) or shape it whole. The shape will depend on the type of bread you are making; here, we're featuring a basic round boule, which you roll between your cupped hands on a counter until a ball forms. Forming a taut shape ensures an even, lofty final loaf.

5. Second Rise
The shaped dough gets to rest again. The yeast will have been redistributed during shaping, so the loaf achieves more volume at this point before baking. You can test that the loaf is done rising with your knuckle.

6. Baking
When the bread is in the oven, starches gelatinize to set the crumb, and sugars and proteins caramelize to create a browned, crusty loaf.

7. Cooling and Storing
Most breads must cool fully before you slice and eat them so that the crumb sets to the perfect texture. And if you don't eat the loaf the day you make it, a recipe might have guidelines for storing it to ensure that it maintains the best texture.

BREAD BASICS

GLUTEN: THE BUILDING BLOCK OF BREAD

We'll talk about gluten a lot in this chapter. What is gluten, exactly? Gluten is the protein that gives bread structure and chew. This elastic protein is formed during bread making when two partial proteins present in wheat flour, glutenin and gliadin, bond. Glutenin provides dough with strength, while gliadin provides the stretch. During mixing, glutenin and gliadin come in contact with water in a process called hydration. Moistening the proteins allows them to unwind and become flexible. Then, through mixing, they begin to link up with one another to form long, elastic chains of gluten. Finally, through prolonged kneading, the proteins are aligned and continue to cross-link until the chains combine to form a membrane-like gluten network. Here's an easy way to look at it: Imagine these proteins as bundled-up balls of yarn that need to be unwound and tied together into one longer piece that's then sewn into a wider sheet. In their balled-up state they can't be tied together; first you have to untangle and straighten them. Liquid does the untangling, mixing ties the proteins together, and kneading sews them into a sheet.

Why is gluten important? A strong gluten network provides dough with the structure to expand. Starch granules in the flour swell when hydrated, while yeast creates gas bubbles; both of these stretch the network, and it traps the air—much like a balloon—so that the bread develops an airy crumb. Gluten's ability to stretch corresponds with its ability to give bread chew.

To understand bread is to understand gluten, and different types of bread are meant to have gluten networks of different strengths. Sometimes you want a lot of chew (as with rustic loaves), and sometimes you want a moderate amount (as with sandwich loaves). Still other times, you may want to keep it at bay—in sweet and enriched breads, too much chew can feel like toughness.

Multiple factors can affect the degree of gluten development in bread dough. First is the protein content of the flour you're using: More glutenin and gliadin mean more cross-linking and a more elastic network. Second is the water content of your dough: The more water there is in the dough, the more hydrated it will be, meaning that the proteins can unravel more readily into a strong network. And third is the amount of time you knead a dough: The longer you knead (to a certain point), the stronger the network will be. Think about the textural difference between a chewy loaf of bread (which might be kneaded for 8 minutes) and a tender muffin (that's simply whisked together).

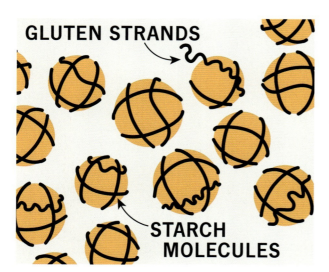

Strands of the partial proteins glutenin and gliadin wrap around starch granules in flour.

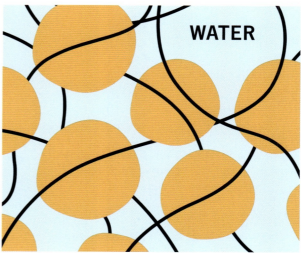

In the presence of water, the strands unwind and link to form a network of gluten.

FLOUR FACTS

Through baking alchemy, a loaf of bread stitches itself together from flour, water, salt, and sometimes yeast. The bulk, though, is indeed flour, and bread starts with the grain, so it's helpful to know what flour to use and when.

The main difference among flour varieties is the amount of protein they contain. More protein leads to more gluten development (see page 506), which in turn translates to chewier bread. For all flours, we prefer unbleached to bleached because bleached flour can carry off-flavors. (Most cake flours, which we do not use in bread baking, however, are bleached.) You can store most flours in an airtight container in your pantry for up to one year. Here are the flours we use in this book.

All-Purpose Flour is the most versatile variety. It has a moderate protein content (10 to 11.7 percent, depending on the brand) and is good when you want a relatively tender, soft crumb, like for quick breads, rolls, and sweet breads. We develop our recipes with easy-to-find Gold Medal Unbleached All-Purpose Flour (10.5 percent protein). Pillsbury All-Purpose Unbleached Flour (also 10.5 percent protein) offers comparable results. If you use an all-purpose flour with a higher protein content (such as King Arthur Unbleached All-Purpose Flour, with 11.7 percent protein) in recipes that call for all-purpose flour, the results may be a bit drier and chewier.

Bread Flour has a high protein content (12 to 14 percent), which ensures strong gluten development and thus a chewy texture. Because of its structure-building properties, we use it for many of the breads in this book. You cannot substitute all-purpose flour in these recipes; the bread will not be able to support an airy, chewy crumb. We use King Arthur Unbleached Bread Flour in the test kitchen.

Whole-Wheat Flour has a distinctive flavor and texture because it is made from the entire wheat berry, unlike white flours, which are ground solely from the endosperm. Whole-wheat flour has a high protein content (about 13 percent), but it behaves differently than white flour, and it can make breads dense. We rely on a combination of white and whole-wheat flours for whole-wheat loaves. In the test kitchen, we use King Arthur Premium Whole Wheat Flour. Whole-wheat flour contains more fat than refined flours and goes rancid more quickly; store it in the freezer and let it come to room temperature before using it.

Cornmeal comes in many different varieties. Because the texture and flavor varies, it's important to use the cornmeal variety that a recipe calls for. For example, our Southern-Style Skillet Cornbread (page 512) requires fine or medium stone-ground cornmeal. While coarse stone-ground cornmeal has great texture and strong corn flavor, it does not soften and can make bread gritty.

ALL-PURPOSE   **BREAD**   **WHOLE-WHEAT**   **CORNMEAL**

IMPORTANCE OF WEIGHING INGREDIENTS

To start the baking process, you need to gather and measure your ingredients with care. We encourage you to use a digital scale to weight your ingredients (except for those that are measured in small amounts, such as salt and yeast, or for mix-ins such as raisins and nuts). The ratio of flour to water in your recipe greatly impacts the end result, so accuracy is crucial. Weigh the dry ingredients into one vessel (usually the bowl of the stand mixer) and the wet ingredients into another (usually a liquid measuring cup). Whisk together the dry ingredients to blend thoroughly; do the same for the wet.

BREAD BASICS

HOW TO KNEAD

While a lot of the magic of bread baking happens without the cook even touching the dough, the one major mechanical step is kneading. Proper kneading incorporates air; distributes ingredients; and, most important, develops gluten (see page 506), which gives yeasted bread chew.

You can knead most bread doughs by hand or in a stand mixer (we'll show each technique in detail below). While hand kneading can be a gratifying process, we recommend using a stand mixer with the dough hook attachment for this task. Not only is it easier—the mixer does all the work—but you're more likely to get good results if you use your mixer.

Kneading dough by hand can be messy, and many home cooks add a lot of extra flour, which can compromise the texture of the baked loaf. On a practical level, it takes up to 25 minutes—and some well-developed forearm muscles—to knead dough fully by hand, and just about 8 minutes in the stand mixer with the dough hook. However, if you do not own a stand mixer, you can still make a good loaf of bread from most doughs. The trick is to use a rhythmic, gentle motion that stretches and massages the dough. Here's what proper kneading looks like.

Kneading by Hand

1. After mixing the dough ingredients, transfer the shaggy dough to a lightly floured counter and shape it into a rough ball.

2. Start each stroke by gently pressing the dough down and away from you with the heel of your hand.

3. Lift the edge of the dough that's farthest away from you and fold the dough in half toward you.

4. Lightly sprinkle the dough with flour as needed to coax the dough into a smooth mass. After about 4 minutes, the dough should look smooth.

5. Press the dough forward again. After about 8 minutes it should begin to turn smooth and elastic.

6. Repeat folding and pressing until the dough is smooth and elastic and forms a ball. This should take 15 to 25 minutes.

Kneading in a Stand Mixer

1. After mixing the dough ingredients, increase the mixer speed to medium-low; the dough will lack form and will stick to the sides of the bowl.

2. After 4 minutes, the dough will still be tacky, but it will start to pull away from the sides of the bowl and look more uniform.

3. After 8 minutes, the dough will pull away from the sides of the bowl and have a compact form.

4. Knead the dough by hand for 30 seconds to form a smooth, round ball.

Properly Kneaded Dough

There are two ways to determine when you've kneaded dough long enough to fully develop the gluten.

1. DOES THE DOUGH CLEAR THE SIDES OF THE BOWL?

If not, keep going. The dough on the left is still sticking slightly. The dough on the right clears the sides of the bowl.

2. IS THE DOUGH ELASTIC?

If not, keep going. The dough on the left lacks elasticity and breaks when pulled, signaling that the gluten proteins have not yet cross-linked into a strong network. The dough on the right can be pulled like a rubber band without snapping and springing back into place.

Keep kneading   **Just right**   **Keep kneading**   **Just right**

COURSE
SAVORY QUICK BREADS

BRYAN ROOF

Bread baking can take time and patience; it often requires activating yeast, kneading, proofing, shaping, and cooking. And while these steps contribute to a beautiful homemade loaf, it's possible to make something special with just a mixing bowl, a spatula, and the quick-bread mixing method. Yeast-less quick breads are called quick for a reason—they fast-forward through the seven key steps of bread baking (see page 505), hitting just steps 1 (mixing); 4 (dividing and shaping), occasionally; 6 (baking), obviously; and 7 (cooling and storing). And the quick-bread method isn't just for sweet treats. These quick breads are all savory, so they can accompany your meal just like a yeasted bread or roll might, or they can serve as a snack. And they're stirred up just right to prevent toughness despite being hearty. Get baking right away—literally—with these simple quintessential quick loaves.

BRYAN'S PRO TIP: *Invest in an oven thermometer to take at least some of the guesswork out of baking.*

QUICK CHEESE BREAD
Makes: 1 loaf
Total Time: 1¼ hours, plus 3¼ hours cooling

RECIPE OVERVIEW Here the quick-bread method delivers a moist, rich, and hearty bread with a bold, cheesy crust—everything you'd want from a savory loaf. Simply mix the dry ingredients (flour; salt, pepper, and cayenne for flavor; cheeses; and a generous amount of baking powder to lift this heavy mix) and the wet ingredients (milk and sour cream for dairy flavor and moisture, melted butter for richness, and an egg for structure) separately and then fold them together. We mix chunks of extra-sharp cheddar into the dough for cheesy pockets throughout. You can substitute a mild Asiago, crumbled into ¼- to ½-inch pieces, for the cheddar. The test kitchen's preferred loaf pan measures 8½ by 4½ inches; if you use a 9 by 5-inch loaf pan, start checking for doneness 5 minutes earlier than advised in the recipe. Use the large holes of a box grater to shred the Parmesan. If, when testing the bread for doneness, the skewer comes out with what looks like uncooked batter clinging to it, try again in a different spot. (A skewer hitting a pocket of cheese may give a false indication.)

- 3 ounces Parmesan cheese, shredded (1 cup), divided
- 2½ cups (12½ ounces) all-purpose flour
- 1 tablespoon baking powder
- 1 teaspoon table salt
- ⅛ teaspoon pepper
- ⅛ teaspoon cayenne pepper
- 4 ounces extra-sharp cheddar cheese, cut into ½-inch pieces (1 cup)
- 1 cup (8 ounces) whole milk
- ½ cup (4 ounces) sour cream
- 3 tablespoons unsalted butter, melted
- 1 large egg

1. Adjust oven rack to middle position and heat oven to 350 degrees. Grease 8½ by 4½-inch loaf pan, then sprinkle ½ cup Parmesan evenly in bottom of pan.

2. Whisk flour, baking powder, salt, pepper, and cayenne together in large bowl. Stir in cheddar, breaking up clumps, until cheese is coated with flour. Whisk milk, sour cream, melted butter, and egg together in second bowl.

3. Using rubber spatula, gently fold milk mixture into flour mixture until just combined (batter will be heavy and thick; do not overmix).

4. Transfer batter to prepared pan and smooth top. Sprinkle remaining ½ cup Parmesan evenly over surface.

5. Bake loaf until golden brown and skewer inserted in center comes out clean, 45 to 50 minutes, rotating pan halfway through baking.

6. Let loaf cool in pan for 15 minutes. Remove loaf from pan and let cool completely on wire rack, about 3 hours, before serving.

Variation
QUICK CHEESE BREAD WITH BACON, ONION, AND GRUYÈRE
Cook 5 slices bacon, cut into ½-inch pieces, in 10-inch nonstick skillet over medium heat until crispy, 5 to 7 minutes. Using slotted spoon, transfer bacon to paper towel–lined plate. Pour off all but 3 tablespoons fat from skillet. Add ½ cup finely chopped onion to fat left in skillet and cook over medium heat until softened, about 3 minutes; set aside. Substitute Gruyère cheese for cheddar and omit butter. Add bacon and onion to flour mixture with cheese in step 2.

> **KEYS TO SUCCESS**
> - **Fold gently and don't overmix:** Prevents overdevelopment of gluten, which can inhibit rise in quick breads and make them tough
> - **Test with a skewer, not a toothpick:** Ensures that you'll reach the center of the loaf

BROWN SODA BREAD
Makes: 1 loaf
Total Time: 1¼ hours, plus 3 hours cooling

RECIPE OVERVIEW Robust, moist, and permeated with wheaty sweetness, Irish brown soda bread gets its appeal from the addition of coarse whole-meal flour to the all-purpose flour. For a stateside version, we substitute whole-wheat flour and add toasted wheat germ. To remedy any gumminess that these ingredients add, we lighten the bread with equal amounts of baking soda and baking powder (baking soda alone can impart a soapy flavor). Acidic buttermilk plays double-duty, yielding a moist loaf and reacting with the baking soda for a light crumb. Just a touch of sugar and a few tablespoons of butter add a hint of sweet richness. The dough requires only a brief knead, and shaping it is a cinch—just pat it into a round.

- 2 cups (10 ounces) all-purpose flour
- 1½ cups (8¼ ounces) whole-wheat flour
- ½ cup (1½ ounces) toasted wheat germ
- 1½ teaspoons table salt
- 1 teaspoon baking powder
- 1 teaspoon baking soda
- 1¾ cups (14 ounces) buttermilk
- 3 tablespoons sugar
- 3 tablespoons unsalted butter, melted, divided

1. Adjust oven rack to lower-middle position and heat oven to 400 degrees. Line baking sheet with parchment paper. Whisk all-purpose flour, whole-wheat flour, wheat germ, salt, baking powder, and baking soda together in large bowl. Whisk buttermilk, sugar, and 2 tablespoons melted butter in second bowl until sugar has dissolved.

2. Using rubber spatula, gently fold buttermilk mixture into flour mixture, scraping up dry flour from bottom of bowl, until dough starts to form and no dry flour remains.

3. Transfer dough to lightly floured counter and knead by hand until cohesive mass forms, about 30 seconds. Pat dough into 7-inch round and transfer to prepared sheet.

4. Using sharp paring knife or single-edge razor blade, make two 5-inch-long, ¼-inch-deep slashes with swift, fluid motion along top of loaf to form cross.

5. Bake loaf until golden brown and skewer inserted in center comes out clean, 45 to 50 minutes, rotating sheet halfway through baking. Transfer loaf to wire rack and brush with remaining 1 tablespoon melted butter. Let cool completely, about 3 hours, before serving.

> **KEYS TO SUCCESS**
> - **Wheat germ:** Along with whole-wheat flour, adds a nutty, wheaty flavor
> - **Buttermilk:** Works with the leaveners to lighten the loaf
> - **Melted butter:** Gives the loaf a nice exterior crunch

SOUTHERN-STYLE SKILLET CORNBREAD

Makes: 1 loaf
Total Time: 55 minutes

RECIPE OVERVIEW Cornbread means different things to different people. Northerners tend to like their cornbread sweet and light—more cake than bread. But the true, satisfying, skillet-baked cornbread that's popular in the South is a stellar savory addition to any cook's recipe arsenal. This version boasts hearty corn flavor; a sturdy, moist crumb; and a golden-brown crust. Yellow stone-ground cornmeal contributes more potent corn flavor than the typical white. Toasting the cornmeal in the skillet for a few minutes intensifies that flavor. We create a cornmeal mush after toasting the cornmeal by softening it in a mixture of sour cream and milk. This ensures that our bread has a fine, moist crumb. The sour cream in the mush adds a pleasant tang that works well with the sweet cornmeal; plus, it reacts with the leaveners to keep this flourless bread from being too dense. Greasing the skillet with butter and vegetable oil and preheating it before adding the batter delivers a rich, crisp, distinct crust. We prefer a cast-iron skillet, but any ovensafe 10-inch skillet will work. You can substitute any type of fine- or medium-ground cornmeal here, but don't use coarse-ground cornmeal.

- 2¼ cups (11¼ ounces) stone-ground cornmeal
- 1½ cups (12 ounces) sour cream
- ½ cup (4 ounces) whole milk
- ¼ cup (1¾ ounces) vegetable oil
- 5 tablespoons (2½ ounces) unsalted butter, cut into 5 pieces
- 2 tablespoons sugar
- 1 teaspoon baking powder
- 1 teaspoon baking soda
- ¾ teaspoon table salt
- 2 large eggs

1. Adjust oven rack to middle position and heat oven to 450 degrees. Toast cornmeal in 10-inch cast-iron skillet over medium heat, stirring frequently, until fragrant, about 3 minutes. Transfer cornmeal to large bowl and whisk in sour cream and milk; set aside.

2. Wipe skillet clean with paper towels. Add oil to now-empty skillet; place skillet in oven; and heat until oil is shimmering, about 10 minutes. Using pot holders, remove skillet from oven, carefully add butter, and gently swirl skillet to melt.

3. Being careful of hot skillet handle, pour all but 1 tablespoon oil-butter mixture into cornmeal mixture and whisk to incorporate. Whisk sugar, baking powder, baking soda, and salt into cornmeal mixture until combined, then whisk in eggs.

4. Quickly transfer batter to skillet and smooth top. Transfer skillet to oven and bake until top begins to crack and sides are golden brown, 12 to 15 minutes, rotating skillet halfway through baking. Let bread cool in skillet for 15 minutes. Remove bread from skillet and transfer to wire rack. Serve warm or at room temperature.

Making Southern-Style Cornbread

TOAST
Stir the cornmeal frequently in a 10-inch cast-iron skillet over medium heat until it's toasted and fragrant, about 3 minutes.

MIX
Transfer the cornmeal to a large bowl and whisk in sour cream and milk; set the mixture aside.

PREHEAT
Add oil to the skillet; place the skillet in the oven; and heat it until the oil is shimmering, about 10 minutes. Carefully add butter, and gently swirl the skillet to melt it.

WHISK
Whisk all but 1 tablespoon of the oil-butter mixture into the cornmeal mixture. Whisk in sugar, baking powder, and baking soda, and then whisk in eggs.

TRANSFER
Quickly transfer the batter to the skillet and smooth the top. Transfer the skillet to the oven.

KEYS TO SUCCESS

- **Yellow cornmeal:** Has more flavor than white
- **Sour cream:** This acidic ingredient reacts with the chemical leaveners to lighten the loaf.
- **Grease the pan:** Butter adds flavor; vegetable oil withstands heat without burning

RESOURCES FOR SAVORY QUICK BREADS

CHEMICAL LEAVENERS

Quick breads rise with chemical leaveners, so their calibration is key to quick-bread success. There are two varieties of chemical leaveners, and they can be used alone or in combination.

Baking soda is an alkali and therefore requires an acidic ingredient, such as buttermilk, in the batter or dough to produce carbon dioxide. The leavening action happens right after mixing, so you should bake right away. In addition to leavening, baking soda also promotes browning.

Baking powder is a mixture of baking soda, a dry acid, and double-dried cornstarch. The cornstarch absorbs moisture and prevents the premature production of gas. Baking powder works twice—first when it comes in contact with a liquid, and again in response to heat. Once its container is opened, it will lose its effectiveness after six months.

LOAF PAN SIZES

Pan size affects the shapes of baked goods. If a pan is too small, the batter or dough can overflow more easily. We prefer 8½ by 4½-inch loaf pans to 9 by 5-inch pans; they produce tall loaves with rounder tops. As it turns out, there are different ways to measure a loaf pan, and some models labeled 8½ by 4½ inches are not even exactly that. They also vary in height, from 2¾ inches to 3⅛ inches, and in the sizes of their bases. Our favorite pans are roomy and almost exactly 8½ by 4½ inches across the top edges. They hold about 1½ liters of water. The loaf on the left in the photo above was baked in a 9 by 5-inch loaf pan; the loaf on the right was baked in an exactly 8½ by 4½-inch loaf pan. The bread baked in the 8½ by 4½-inch loaf pan is noticeably taller and rounder.

TESTING WITH A SKEWER

There is a lot of moisture in quick breads, and if you underbake a loaf, the texture can be gummy or dense. To avoid a dense, wet loaf, don't remove the bread from the oven until a wooden skewer inserted in the center comes out clean. Quick breads baked in a loaf pan are tall and a toothpick won't make it to the center of the loaf, so be sure to use a skewer for this task.

SCIENCE OF STIRRING

What makes quick breads so easy is the gentle folding of wet ingredients into dry ingredients—so don't overdo it. Gently fold wet and dry ingredients together with a rubber spatula until they're just combined and a few streaks of flour still remain. Overmixing can encourage too much gluten development, which inhibits rise in quick breads and makes them tough and squat.

COURSE
MORNING BREADS

ANDREA GEARY

Bread is a supremely comforting way to start the day, and some of the most iconic breakfast pastries are, in fact, bread. Think thick slices of sweet loaves; biscuits you can dress up with fixings or eat plain; and scones and muffins, which are quick breads themselves. These treats are varied and interesting, but when you break them down by how they're mixed and manipulated, they're not all that different, and the skills you learn from one quick bread are transferable to another. Make mornings great with the recipes in this course.

ANDREA'S PRO TIP: *In the unlikely event that you have leftovers, wrap individual items well and freeze them in a zipper-lock bag. Thirty minutes on the counter followed by a quick refresh in the toaster oven, and you're good to go.*

ULTIMATE BANANA BREAD

Serves: 10
Total Time: 1¾ hours, plus 1¼ hours cooling

RECIPE OVERVIEW Typical banana breads can range from cottony and tough to dense and damp, with a typically overbaked ring crusting over the exterior. The ripe banana flavor seems to dissipate during baking, leaving a hum-ho loaf. To bake in more bananas without more wetness, we first microwave the bananas—5 of them—to drive off moisture. Don't throw away the juice that accumulates at the bottom of the bowl: Concentrating it on the stove and mixing it into the batter with the pureed banana solids introduces incredible banana flavor. A sixth banana, sliced thin and caramelized on top of the loaf, creates an enticingly crisp, crunchy top. It is important to use extremely ripe, heavily speckled (or even black) bananas in this recipe. This recipe can be made using five thawed frozen bananas; since thawed frozen bananas release a large amount of liquid naturally, they can bypass the 5 or so minutes of microwaving in step 2 and go directly into the fine-mesh strainer. Do not use a thawed frozen banana in step 4; it will be too soft to neatly slice. Instead, if you don't have a very ripe large banana on hand, skip adding the banana slices and simply sprinkle the top of the banana bread with sugar. The test kitchen's preferred loaf pan measures 8½ by 4½ inches; if you use a 9 by 5-inch loaf pan, start checking for doneness 5 minutes earlier than advised in the recipe.

- 1¾ cups (8¾ ounces) all-purpose flour
- 1 teaspoon baking soda
- ½ teaspoon table salt
- 6 very ripe large bananas (2¼ pounds), peeled, divided
- 8 tablespoons unsalted butter, melted and cooled
- 2 large eggs
- ¾ cup packed (5¼ ounces) light brown sugar
- 1 teaspoon vanilla extract
- ½ cup walnuts, toasted and chopped coarse (optional)
- 2 teaspoons granulated sugar

1. Adjust oven rack to middle position and heat oven to 350 degrees. Spray 8½ by 4½-inch loaf pan with vegetable oil spray. Whisk flour, baking soda, and salt together in large bowl; set aside.

2. Place 5 bananas in separate bowl; cover; and microwave until bananas are soft and have released liquid, about 5 minutes. Transfer bananas to fine-mesh strainer set over bowl and let drain, stirring occasionally, for 15 minutes (you should have between ½ and ¾ cup liquid).

3. Transfer liquid to medium saucepan and cook over medium-high heat until reduced to ¼ cup, about 5 minutes. Return drained bananas to bowl. Off heat, stir reduced liquid into bananas and mash with potato masher until mostly smooth. Whisk in melted butter, eggs, brown sugar, and vanilla.

4. Pour banana mixture into flour mixture and stir until just combined, with some streaks of flour remaining. Gently fold in walnuts, if using. Transfer batter to prepared pan. Slice remaining banana on bias ¼ inch thick. Shingle banana slices on top of loaf in 2 rows, leaving 1½-inch-wide space down center to ensure even rise. Sprinkle granulated sugar evenly over loaf.

5. Bake until skewer inserted in center of loaf comes out clean, 55 minutes to 1¼ hours, rotating pan halfway through baking. Let loaf cool in pan for 10 minutes, then remove loaf from pan and let cool on wire rack for 1 hour before serving. (Cooled bread can be stored at room temperature, covered tightly with plastic wrap, for up to 3 days.)

KEYS TO SUCCESS
- **Reduce the juice:** Concentrates banana flavor and prevents soggy texture
- **Brown sugar:** Complements the bananas' flavor better than granulated sugar

CORE TECHNIQUE
Working with Bananas

EXTRACT
Microwave the ripe bananas for 5 minutes to release their juice.

STRAIN
Transfer the bananas to a fine-mesh strainer to drain (you should have between ½ and ¾ cup of liquid).

REDUCE
Simmer the banana juice on the stovetop to intensify its flavor and keep the loaf from getting soggy.

MASH
Add the liquid to the microwaved bananas and then mash until the mixture is smooth.

EASIEST-EVER BISCUITS

Serves: 10
Total Time: 40 minutes

RECIPE OVERVIEW Many biscuit recipes require keeping cubes of butter cold, cutting the butter into dry ingredients, carefully mixing dough, and adhering to strict rules. But this recipe breaks the rules, combining the ease of cream biscuits (which eliminate the step of cutting in cold fat) with the ease of drop biscuits (which skip the rolling and cutting) to create the easiest biscuits ever. Adding enough cream to make the biscuits droppable results in biscuits that spread too much and become greasy. So instead of increasing the amount of cream, increase its fluidity. Heating the cream to between 95 and 100 degrees melts the solid particles of butterfat dispersed throughout. This yields a dough that's moist and scoopable but that rises up instead of spreading out in the oven, producing biscuits that are appropriately rich and tender but not greasy. These biscuits come together very quickly, so in the interest of efficiency, start heating your oven before gathering your ingredients. We like these biscuits brushed with a bit of melted butter, but you can skip that step if you're serving the biscuits with a rich accompaniment such as sausage gravy.

- 3 cups (15 ounces) all-purpose flour
- 4 teaspoons sugar
- 1 tablespoon baking powder
- ¼ teaspoon baking soda
- 1¼ teaspoons table salt
- 2 cups heavy cream
- 2 tablespoons unsalted butter, melted (optional)

1. Adjust oven rack to upper-middle position and heat oven to 450 degrees. Line rimmed baking sheet with parchment paper. In medium bowl, whisk together flour, sugar, baking powder, baking soda, and salt. Microwave cream until just warmed to body temperature (95 to 100 degrees), 60 to 90 seconds, stirring halfway through microwaving. Stir cream into flour mixture until soft, uniform dough forms.

2. Spray ⅓-cup dry measuring cup with vegetable oil spray. Drop level scoops of batter 2 inches apart on prepared sheet (biscuits should measure about 2½ inches wide and 1¼ inches tall). Respray measuring cup after every 3 or 4 scoops. If portions are misshapen, use your fingertips to gently reshape dough into level cylinders. Bake until tops are light golden brown, 10 to 12 minutes, rotating sheet halfway through baking. Brush hot biscuits with melted butter, if using. Serve warm. (Biscuits can be stored in zipper-lock bag at room temperature for up to 24 hours. Reheat biscuits in 300-degree oven for 10 minutes.)

SCIENCE LESSON

Why We "Melt" the Cream in Our Biscuits

Fridge-cold cream looks like it's 100 percent liquid, but it's actually a combination of water, protein, and sugar, with tiny particles of solid butterfat suspended throughout. By warming the cream just enough to melt the fat particles (but not enough to activate the baking powder when the cream is mixed into the dry ingredients), we turn it into a pure liquid. This means we can use less cream to create a dough that is still loose enough to scoop and drop but that doesn't spread too much or bake up too greasy. To demonstrate this effect, we made two doughs using 2 cups of cream. In one batch, the cream was fridge-cold; in the other, we warmed it. The dough made with the warmed cream was noticeably loose and easy to scoop.

COLD CREAM
Dough is too dry to drop

WARMED CREAM
Dough is loose and scoopable

Keep the Scoop Slick

To ensure that the dough releases easily from the measuring cup, spray it with vegetable oil spray after every three or four scoops. You can also use a greased ice cream scoop for recipes that require dividing dough or batter. Its longer handle and trigger system are great for cleanly releasing the dough or batter.

MIXED BERRY SCONES

Makes: 8 scones
Total Time: 1 hour

RECIPE OVERVIEW Big, bold, berry-filled scones are a cinch to make in the food processor. To keep the (frozen) berries from bleeding into the dough, just toss them in confectioners' sugar. To get light and flaky scones, treating the butter in two different ways is key. First, processing half the butter until it's fully incorporated into the dough keeps the scone tender, since the butter coats the flour particles, limiting gluten formation. Then, adding the remaining cold butter and processing it to small clumps creates pockets of steam as the scones bake for flake and a pleasant crumble. A simple glaze of butter and honey adds a nice finish to the scones. Work the dough as little as possible, just until it comes together. Work quickly to keep the butter and berries as cold as possible for the best results. Note that the butter is divided in this recipe. An equal amount of frozen blueberries, raspberries, blackberries, or strawberries (halved) can be used in place of the mixed berries.

Scones
- 1¾ cups (8¾ ounces) frozen mixed berries
- 3 tablespoons confectioners' sugar
- 3 cups (15 ounces) all-purpose flour
- 12 tablespoons unsalted butter, cut into ½-inch pieces and chilled, divided
- ⅓ cup (2⅓ ounces) granulated sugar
- 1 tablespoon baking powder
- 1¼ teaspoons table salt
- ¾ cup plus 2 tablespoons whole milk
- 1 large egg plus 1 large yolk

Glaze
- 2 tablespoons unsalted butter, melted
- 1 tablespoon honey

1. FOR THE SCONES Adjust oven rack to upper-middle position and heat oven to 425 degrees. Line rimmed baking sheet with parchment paper. If your berry mix contains strawberries, cut them in half. Toss berries with confectioners' sugar in bowl and freeze until needed.

2. Process flour, 6 tablespoons butter, granulated sugar, baking powder, and salt in food processor until butter is fully incorporated, about 15 seconds. Add remaining 6 tablespoons butter and pulse until butter is reduced to pea-size pieces, 10 to 12 pulses. Transfer mixture to large bowl. Stir in berries.

3. Beat milk and egg and yolk together in separate bowl. Make well in center of flour mixture and pour in milk mixture. Using rubber spatula, gently stir mixture, scraping from edges of bowl and folding inward until very shaggy dough forms and some bits of flour remain. Do not overmix.

4. Turn out dough onto well-floured counter and, if necessary, knead briefly until dough just comes together, about 3 turns. Using your floured hands and bench scraper, shape dough into 12 by 4-inch rectangle, about 1½ inches tall. Using knife or bench scraper, cut dough crosswise into 4 equal rectangles. Cut each rectangle diagonally into 2 triangles (you should have 8 scones total). Transfer scones to prepared sheet. Bake until scones are lightly golden on top, 16 to 18 minutes, rotating sheet halfway through baking.

5. FOR THE GLAZE While scones bake, combine melted butter and honey in small bowl. Remove scones from oven and brush tops evenly with glaze. Return scones to oven and continue to bake until golden brown on top, 5 to 8 minutes. Transfer scones to wire rack and let cool for at least 10 minutes before serving.

KEYS TO SUCCESS

- **Sugar the berries:** Ensures that berries won't bleed into the dough; subdues their tartness
- **Mix in two stages:** Processing half of the butter into the dough tenderizes; cutting in the remainder in small chunks creates pockets of steam that lift the scones in layers.
- **Don't overknead:** Keeps the scones tender, not tough
- **Brush with butter:** Gives the scones sweet, browned tops

CORE TECHNIQUE Shaping Scones

KNEAD
Turn out the dough onto a well-floured counter and, if necessary, knead briefly until the dough just comes together, about three turns. Shape the dough into a 12 by 4-inch rectangle, about 1½ inches tall.

CUT
Using a knife or a bench scraper, cut the dough crosswise into four equal rectangles. Cut each rectangle diagonally into two triangles (you should have eight scones total).

WHOLE-WHEAT BLUEBERRY MUFFINS

Makes: 12 muffins
Total Time: 1 hour

RECIPE OVERVIEW Oftentimes, whole-wheat baked goods use a mix of whole-wheat flour and all-purpose flour to prevent dense results, but this recipe successfully uses 100 percent whole-wheat flour. These are the steps that prevent toughness. First, incorporating lots of liquid ingredients means that more steam is created during baking, so the muffins rise to fluffy heights; plus, all that liquid softens the whole-wheat flour's tough bran. Second, using both eggs and butter, and even more notably, buttermilk, tenderizes the muffin. A streusel topping adds texture and a bit of sweetness to the not-so-sweet muffin. Do not overmix the batter. You can substitute frozen (unthawed) blueberries for fresh here.

Streusel
- 3 tablespoons granulated sugar
- 3 tablespoons packed brown sugar
- 3 tablespoons whole-wheat flour
- Pinch table salt
- 2 tablespoons unsalted butter, melted

Muffins
- 3 cups (16½ ounces) whole-wheat flour
- 2½ teaspoons baking powder
- ½ teaspoon baking soda
- 1 teaspoon table salt
- 1 cup (7 ounces) granulated sugar
- 2 large eggs
- 4 tablespoons unsalted butter, melted
- ¼ cup vegetable oil
- 1¼ cups buttermilk
- 1½ teaspoons vanilla extract
- 7½ ounces (1½ cups) blueberries

1. **FOR THE STREUSEL** Combine granulated sugar, brown sugar, flour, and salt in bowl. Add melted butter and toss with fork until evenly moistened and mixture forms large chunks with some pea-size pieces throughout; set aside.

2. **FOR THE MUFFINS** Adjust oven rack to middle position and heat oven to 400 degrees. Spray 12-cup muffin tin, including top, generously with vegetable oil spray. Whisk flour, baking powder, baking soda, and salt together in large bowl. Whisk sugar, eggs, melted butter, and oil in separate bowl until combined, about 30 seconds. Whisk buttermilk and vanilla into sugar mixture until combined.

3. Stir sugar mixture into flour mixture until just combined. Gently stir in blueberries until incorporated. Using ¼-cup dry measuring cup, divide batter evenly among prepared muffin cups (cups will be filled to rim); sprinkle muffin tops evenly with streusel.

4. Bake until golden brown and toothpick inserted in center comes out with few crumbs attached, 18 to 20 minutes, rotating muffin tin halfway through baking. Let muffins cool in muffin tin on wire rack for 5 minutes. Remove muffins from muffin tin and let cool 5 minutes longer. Serve.

COURSE
LOAVES FOR EVERY DAY

STEVE DUNN

Introducing yeast into your baking shouldn't be intimidating. And if you want to bake your daily bread, you'll be using it fairly often. Yeast makes magic in these recipes for everyday loaves, giving them height, a pillowy crumb, and the structure for just enough chew. These loaves are baked in a loaf pan, so you'll also learn special considerations for doing so. You'll love toasting slices of these loaves and using them for sandwiches so much that you may never buy a loaf of supermarket bread again.

STEVE'S PRO TIP: *If you find that you really get into bread baking, skip the little packets and buy your yeast in bulk. You'll save a lot of money buying it in a 1-pound pack; stored in an air-tight container in the freezer it will last indefinitely.*

EASY SANDWICH BREAD

Makes: 1 loaf
Total Time: 1 hour, plus 40 minutes rising and 3¼ hours cooling

RECIPE OVERVIEW Many people who might enjoy making homemade sandwich bread don't even try because they think it takes most of a day. It's true that "quicker" yeasted breads can lack the structure necessary for a satisfactory rise and that their interiors are often coarse. This loaf is an exception—it's soft and well risen, with an even crumb, and all without kneading or shaping. It takes just two mostly hands-off hours to make. Increasing the amount of water in the dough to make more of a batter enhances the gluten structure without requiring prolonged kneading (see page 531). For even more spring and lift, we reduce the fat and sugar slightly and withhold salt until the second mix (see page 535). The test kitchen's preferred loaf pan measures 8½ by 4½ inches; if you use a 9 by 5-inch loaf pan, start checking for doneness 5 minutes earlier than advised in the recipe. To prevent the loaf from deflating as it rises, do not let the batter come in contact with the plastic wrap. We do not recommend mixing this dough by hand.

- 2 cups (11 ounces) bread flour
- 6 tablespoons (2 ounces) whole-wheat flour
- 2¼ teaspoons instant or rapid-rise yeast
- 1¼ cups plus 2 tablespoons (11 ounces) warm water (120 degrees), divided
- 3 tablespoons unsalted butter, melted, divided
- 1 tablespoon honey
- ¾ teaspoon table salt
- 1 large egg, lightly beaten with 1 tablespoon water and pinch table salt

1. Whisk bread flour, whole-wheat flour, and yeast together in bowl of stand mixer. Whisk 1¼ cups warm water, 2 tablespoons melted butter, and honey in 4-cup liquid measuring cup until honey has dissolved.

2. Using paddle on low speed, slowly add water mixture to flour mixture and mix until batter comes together, about 1 minute. Increase speed to medium and mix for 4 minutes, scraping down bowl and paddle as needed. Cover bowl tightly with plastic wrap and let batter rise until doubled in size, about 20 minutes.

3. Adjust oven rack to lower-middle position and heat oven to 375 degrees. Grease 8½ by 4½-inch loaf pan. Dissolve salt in remaining 2 tablespoons warm water, then add to batter and mix on low speed until water mixture is mostly incorporated, about 40 seconds. Increase speed to medium and mix until thoroughly combined, about 1 minute.

4. Transfer batter to prepared pan and smooth top. Cover tightly with plastic and let rise until batter reaches ½ inch below lip of pan, 15 to 20 minutes. Uncover and continue to let rise until center of batter is level with lip of pan, 5 to 10 minutes.

5. Gently brush loaf with egg mixture and bake until deep golden brown and loaf registers 205 to 210 degrees, 40 to 45 minutes, rotating pan halfway through baking.

6. Let loaf cool in pan for 15 minutes. Remove loaf from pan and transfer to wire rack. Brush top and sides with remaining melted butter. Let cool completely, about 3 hours, before serving.

KEYS TO SUCCESS:
- **Make a very wet dough:** Allows for adequate gluten development with minimal fuss
- **Use the paddle attachment:** Best for mixing the batter-like dough
- **Double-brush the crust:** An egg wash before baking and melted butter after provide substance and flavor.

Yeast Varieties

Yeast comes in two forms: fresh and dry. We don't use fresh yeast in the test kitchen, as it is highly perishable. There are two types of dry yeast: active dry yeast and instant yeast. We prefer to use instant yeast in our recipes. Store any yeast in the refrigerator or freezer to slow deterioration.

ACTIVE DRY YEAST is treated with heat, which kills the outermost cells. Therefore, it must be proofed, or dissolved in liquid with some sugar, before use. Proofing sloughs off the dead cells and renders the yeast active. To substitute active dry yeast for instant yeast in a recipe, use 25 percent more of it to compensate for the greater quantity of inactive yeast cells. And you'll need to dissolve active dry yeast in a portion of the water from the recipe, heated to 110 degrees. Let the mixture stand for 5 minutes before adding it to the remaining wet ingredients.

INSTANT YEAST (also called rapid-rise yeast) is our choice in the test kitchen because it doesn't need to be proofed and can be added directly to the dry ingredients—the result of undergoing a gentler drying process that does not destroy the outer cells. We have also found that it yields breads with a cleaner flavor than those made with active dry yeast because it doesn't contain any dead yeast cells. To substitute instant yeast for active dry yeast in a recipe, use 25 percent less of it.

ANADAMA BREAD

Makes: 1 loaf
Total Time: 1¼ hours, plus 2 to 3 hours rising and 3 hours cooling

RECIPE OVERVIEW Anadama bread is a New England classic, with two defining ingredients—molasses and cornmeal—that have a centuries-old association with the region. It's moist and chewy, sturdy yet tender, faintly bitter yet sweet, and ever so slightly gritty. We increase the amount of molasses called for in most recipes; ¼ cup imparts a decidedly bittersweet flavor and a beautiful golden color. And ½ cup of cornmeal achieves heartiness and pleasant grit. Sacrificing some gluten-containing flour to accommodate this amount of cornmeal can create a dense loaf, so we add a bit more yeast than is traditional to keep the texture light. Water, rather than softening milk, creates a hearty chew. Do not use coarse-ground cornmeal here. The test kitchen's preferred loaf pan measures 8½ by 4½ inches; if you use a 9 by 5-inch loaf pan, increase the shaped rising time by 20 to 30 minutes and start checking for doneness 10 minutes earlier than advised in the recipe.

- 2¾ cups (13¾ ounces) all-purpose flour
- ½ cup (2½ ounces) cornmeal
- 1½ teaspoons instant or rapid-rise yeast
- 1¼ teaspoons table salt
- 1 cup (8 ounces) water, room temperature
- ¼ cup (2 ounces) mild or robust molasses
- 3 tablespoons unsalted butter, melted

1. Whisk flour, cornmeal, yeast, and salt together in bowl of stand mixer. Whisk water, molasses, and melted butter in 4-cup liquid measuring cup until molasses has dissolved.

2. Using dough hook on low speed, slowly add water mixture to flour mixture and mix until cohesive dough starts to form and no dry flour remains, about 2 minutes, scraping down bowl as needed. Increase speed to medium-low and knead until dough is smooth and elastic and clears sides of bowl, about 8 minutes.

3. Transfer dough to lightly floured counter and knead by hand to form smooth, round ball, about 30 seconds. Place dough seam side down in lightly greased large bowl or container; cover tightly with plastic wrap; and let rise until doubled in size, 1½ to 2 hours.

4. Grease 8½ by 4½-inch loaf pan and dust with cornmeal. Press down on dough to deflate. Turn dough out onto lightly floured counter (side of dough that was against bowl should now be facing up) and press into 8 by 6-inch rectangle, with long side parallel to counter edge. Roll dough away from you into firm cylinder, keeping roll taut by tucking it under itself as you go. Pinch seam closed and place loaf seam side down in prepared pan, pressing dough gently into corners.

5. Cover loosely with greased plastic and let rise until loaf reaches 1 inch above lip of pan and dough springs back minimally when poked gently with your knuckle, 30 minutes to 1 hour.

6. Adjust oven rack to lower-middle position and heat oven to 350 degrees. Mist loaf with water and bake until deep golden brown and loaf registers 205 to 210 degrees, 40 to 45 minutes, rotating pan halfway through baking.

7. Let loaf cool in pan for 15 minutes. Remove loaf from pan and let cool completely on wire rack, about 3 hours, before serving.

KEYS TO SUCCESS

- **Mild or robust molasses:** Yields a milder, more balanced loaf than the bitter blackstrap variety
- **Fine- or stone-ground cornmeal:** Yields a lighter, less gritty loaf than coarse-ground cornmeal

Making Sense of Molasses

Buying molasses can be a confusing experience: Bottles may be variously labeled mild, dark, robust, full, or blackstrap. Fortunately, we've found that with the exception of blackstrap, these other products all taste similar, and they all work fine in our recipes. As for blackstrap, this designation indicates that the mixture of sugarcane and sugar beet juice used to make the syrup has been boiled three times, rendering the molasses darker and thicker. In taste tests, this type stood out as strongly bitter, smoky, and much less sweet than other types. When we substituted blackstrap in recipes calling for regular molasses, tasters found the results too intense.

OATMEAL-RAISIN BREAD

Makes: 1 loaf
Total Time: 1½ hours, plus 2 to 2½ hours rising and 3¼ hours cooling

RECIPE OVERVIEW This bread, flavored with oats, sweet raisins, and just a touch of brown sugar, is like a bowl of oatmeal in bread form. We make oatmeal and mix it into the dough toward the end of kneading to incorporate it without creating clumps. Oat flour might seem like an obvious addition for more oat flavor, but it yields a dry, crumbly loaf. Instead, adding a little whole-wheat flour complements the earthy flavor of the oats and ensures that the crumb stays light and moist. To give a hint of what's within, we roll the loaf in oats before transferring it to the pan. Misting the oat-rolled loaf in water once again before baking contributes to an appealingly crunchy golden top. Do not substitute quick or instant oats in this recipe. The test kitchen's preferred loaf pan measures 8½ by 4½ inches; if you use a 9 by 5-inch loaf pan, increase the shaped rising time by 20 to 30 minutes and start checking for doneness 10 minutes earlier than advised in the recipe.

- 1¼ cups (3¾ ounces) old-fashioned rolled oats, divided
- ¾ cup (6 ounces) water, room temperature
- 2 cups (11 ounces) bread flour
- ½ cup (2¾ ounces) whole-wheat flour
- 2 teaspoons instant or rapid-rise yeast
- 1½ teaspoons table salt
- 1 cup (8 ounces) whole milk, room temperature
- 3 tablespoons unsalted butter, melted
- 2 tablespoons packed brown sugar
- ½ cup raisins

1. Bring ¾ cup oats and water to simmer in small saucepan over medium heat and cook, stirring occasionally, until oats are softened and water is completely absorbed, about 2 minutes; set aside to cool.

2. Whisk bread flour, whole-wheat flour, yeast, and salt together in bowl of stand mixer. Whisk milk, melted butter, and sugar in 4-cup liquid measuring cup until sugar has dissolved. Using dough hook on low speed, slowly add milk mixture to flour mixture and mix until cohesive dough starts to form and no dry flour remains, about 2 minutes, scraping down bowl as needed.

3. Increase speed to medium-low and knead until dough is smooth and elastic and clears sides of bowl, about 6 minutes. Reduce speed to low; slowly add raisins; then slowly add oatmeal, 2 tablespoons at a time, and mix until mostly incorporated, about 3 minutes.

4. Transfer dough to lightly floured counter. Using your lightly floured hands, knead dough until oatmeal and raisins are evenly distributed and dough forms smooth, round ball, about 30 seconds. Place dough seam side down in lightly greased large bowl or container; cover tightly with plastic wrap; and let rise until doubled in size, 1½ to 2 hours.

5. Grease 8½ by 4½-inch loaf pan. Spread remaining ½ cup oats on rimmed baking sheet. Press down on dough to deflate. Turn dough out onto lightly floured counter (side of dough that was against bowl should now be facing up). Press and stretch dough into 8 by 6-inch rectangle, with long side parallel to counter edge. Roll dough away from you into firm cylinder, keeping roll taut by tucking it under itself as you go. Pinch seam closed. Mist loaf with water on all sides and roll in oats, pressing gently to adhere. Place loaf seam side down in prepared pan, pressing dough gently into corners.

6. Cover loosely with greased plastic and let rise until loaf reaches 1 inch above lip of pan and dough springs back minimally when poked gently with your knuckle, 30 minutes to 1 hour.

7. Adjust oven rack to lower-middle position and heat oven to 350 degrees. Mist loaf with water and bake until golden brown and loaf registers 205 to 210 degrees, 45 to 50 minutes, rotating pan halfway through baking. Let loaf cool in pan for 15 minutes. Remove loaf from pan and let cool completely on wire rack, about 3 hours, before serving.

KEYS TO SUCCESS

- **Old-fashioned oats:** Won't make the bread gummy or flavorless like instant or quick oats
- **Whole-wheat flour:** Mimics the nuttiness of oats
- **Mist with water:** Ensures that the oats stick to the dough and form a crunchy, golden exterior

RESOURCES FOR LOAVES FOR EVERY DAY

SHAPING SANDWICH LOAVES

Standard sandwich breads—that is, ones made with yeast, kneaded, and destined for a loaf pan—all generally follow the same steps from shaggy dough to ready-to-bake cylinder. Here are the moves.

1. Transfer dough to lightly floured counter. Using your lightly floured hands, knead until dough forms smooth, round ball, about 30 seconds. Let rise until doubled in size, 1½ to 2 hours.

2. Turn dough out onto lightly floured counter (side of dough that was against bowl should now be facing up). Press and stretch dough into 8 by 6-inch rectangle, with long side parallel to counter edge.

3. Roll dough away from you into firm cylinder, keeping roll taut by tucking it under itself as you go.

4. Pinch seam closed before transferring loaf to pan.

SLOPPY SHAPING

Loaves that don't have a taut shape with tightly sealed seams can rise unevenly; bake into an unattractive shape; and expand at random points in the top of the loaf, or "blow out." That's because creating a taut shape on the outside of the loaf forms a gluten sheath. This strong exterior skin sets the structure of the loaf and prevents the carbon dioxide that is formed during the second rise from escaping at weak points in the dough, so it rises uniformly upward.

MESSY SHAPING

PROPER SHAPING

STORING SANDWICH LOAVES

Sandwich breads are great to have on hand for lunches for a few days. And since they generally don't have thick, crunchy crusts, you don't have to worry about their exteriors softening if you wrap them. Wrap loaves in a double layer of plastic wrap and store them at room temperature for up to three days. Wrapped first in aluminum foil before the plastic, sandwich loaves can be frozen for up to one month. If you don't plan to use the whole loaf at once, slice it and freeze the slices in a zipper-lock bag, thawing individual slices when you want them. While you can thaw slices of bread on the counter, they will taste fresher if you thaw them in the microwave. As frozen bread warms, its starch molecules begin to form crystalline regions, which absorb the water in bread. The process, called retrogradation, will eventually produce a dry, stale texture. The best way to thaw frozen bread is to place the slices on a plate (uncovered) and microwave them on high power for 15 to 25 seconds. This will get the starch and water molecules to break down the crystalline regions, producing soft, ready-to-eat bread.

COOLING SANDWICH LOAVES

All bread must be cooled properly before it's cut into (see page 505), and it's important to consider when to remove sandwich loaves from the pan. Because they're often baked in a loaf pan, they trap steam and are not fully set when they're done baking. Remove the bread from the pan immediately, and the loaf can collapse. Let a sandwich loaf cool in its pan for 15 minutes before transferring it to a wire rack for cooling so that the loaf maintains the proper shape.

THE SCIENCE OF YEAST

You probably know that yeast is responsible for making bread dough rise. But do you know where it comes from or how it's derived? This magical ingredient is a living organism—a unicellular fungus—that's found in the environment on fruits and grains and even in the air. Its function is to consume sugars and starches and convert them into alcohol, releasing carbon dioxide as a by-product. While essential for bread baking, this yeast activity also initiates fermentation in beverages such as beer, wine, kombucha, and kefir.

Yeast plays two roles in bread baking: It provides leavening and creates flavor. The yeast finds its food source in sugar. When bread dough rests, two enzymes present in wheat, amylase and diastase, break down the flour's complex starch molecules into simple sugars. Upon feeding, the yeast releases carbon dioxide, which allows the loaf to lift and expand; alcohol, which gives the bread flavor; and a multitude of aromatic molecules, which contribute further to the flavor of the bread. This process is called fermentation. There are various factors that control the extent to which this happens, and at what rate. Knowing how to manipulate each of them will give your bread the best taste and texture.

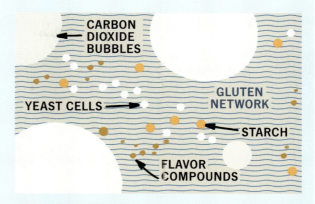

1. Gluten A strong, elastic gluten network (see page 506) is necessary for containing carbon dioxide and allowing the loaf to expand—like blowing air into a balloon. If the gluten network is poorly developed, the yeast will not be able to do its job, because the "balloon" will not be strong enough to hold in the escaping carbon dioxide. Underkneaded dough compromises the productivity of yeast. And very enriched doughs don't rise very much, because large quantities of eggs and fat tenderize the dough.

2. Sugar Yeast feeds on sugar, so a bit of sugar in the ingredient list—say a tablespoon or two—creates more available food for the yeast and speeds up its activity modestly. It also ensures that there will be more leftover sugar that is not consumed by the yeast during fermentation, so the crust will be darker in color, and the flavor of the loaf will be deeper. However, walloping amounts of sugar will do the opposite, slowing yeast down. Sugar is hygroscopic, meaning that it holds on to moisture. If there is a lot of sugar in the dough, it will subtract from the amount of available liquid needed to hydrate the yeast so that it can function. You will see that most sweet breads use a higher proportion of yeast.

3. Time and Temperature For most breads we recommend using room-temperature liquids and letting the dough rise at a cool room temperature (about 70 degrees), not a warm temperature as some recipes call for. At higher temperatures, enzymes break down gluten, forcing the yeast to work harder and faster to make the bread rise—and it will do so unevenly.

MEASURING RISE

How you determine if your dough has doubled in size will depend on the vessel you choose for holding it. For the first bulk rise, a glass bowl is a good choice because you can see through it. But for an even easier indicator, you can place your dough in a straight-sided container and stretch a rubber band around the container at the point double in height from the top of the unrisen dough (top). When the dough reaches the band, it is ready to be manipulated (bottom). Don't forget to grease the container; if you don't grease the vessel the dough rises in, the dough will stick, and you'll rip the gluten network when you try to get the dough out of the bowl or when you fold it. And make sure to cover the container with plastic wrap, which prevents the dough from drying out and forming a skin as it rises.

COURSE
CAN'T TOUCH THIS: NO-KNEAD BREADS

DAN SOUZA

What if you could make some of the world's most revered breads and barely lift a finger? There are certain bread doughs that actually benefit from more modest handling—while also achieving the strong gluten structure that they need. These *almost* no-knead breads work because they are highly hydrated—that is, they're very wet. Learn the science of hydration, and how *not* to knead bread, in the recipes in this course.

DAN'S PRO TIP: *The hardest part about baking bread at home is waiting for it to cool before slicing and eating it. But trust me, it's worth the wait. After cooling, your loaf's crumb will be moist and tender rather than sticky and gummy.*

ALMOST NO-KNEAD BREAD

Makes: 1 loaf
Total Time: 1¼ hours, plus 9½ to 10 hours rising and 3 hours cooling

RECIPE OVERVIEW Artisan-style bakery loaves don't take professional skills to make. It's easy to make a rustic loaf with the no-knead method of bread baking. This technique replaces the kneading that develops gluten to give bread structure with a high hydration level—around 85 percent (8½ ounces of water for every 10 ounces of flour)—and an 8- to 18-hour-long hands-off resting period, or autolyse. During autolyse, the flour hydrates and enzymes work to break up the proteins so that the dough requires only a brief turn to develop gluten. The dough is then baked in a Dutch oven; the humid environment gives the loaf a dramatic open crumb and a crisp crust. Completely no-knead breads need a bit of assistance with texture and flavor, however. To strengthen the dough, we add less than a minute of kneading. We also introduce an acidic tang from vinegar and a shot of yeasty flavor from beer. We prefer to use a mild American lager, such as Budweiser, here; strongly flavored beers will make this bread taste bitter.

- 3 cups (15 ounces) all-purpose flour
- 1½ teaspoons table salt
- ¼ teaspoon instant or rapid-rise yeast
- ¾ cup (6 ounces) water, room temperature
- ½ cup (4 ounces) mild lager, room temperature
- 1 tablespoon distilled white vinegar

1. Whisk flour, salt, and yeast together in large bowl. Whisk water, beer, and vinegar together in 4-cup liquid measuring cup. Using rubber spatula, gently fold water mixture into flour mixture, scraping up dry flour from bottom of bowl, until dough starts to form and no dry flour remains. Cover bowl tightly with plastic wrap and let sit at room temperature for at least 8 hours or up to 18 hours.

2. Lay 18 by 12-inch sheet of parchment paper on counter and lightly spray with vegetable oil spray. Transfer dough to lightly floured counter and knead by hand until smooth and elastic, about 1 minute. Shape dough into ball by pulling edges into middle, then transfer seam side down to center of prepared parchment.

3. Using parchment as sling, gently lower loaf into Dutch oven (let any excess parchment hang over pot edge). Cover tightly with plastic and let rise until loaf has doubled in size and dough springs back minimally when poked gently with your knuckle, 1½ to 2 hours.

4. Adjust oven rack to middle position. Using sharp paring knife or single-edge razor blade, make two 5-inch-long, ½-inch-deep slashes with swift, fluid motion along top of loaf to form cross. Cover pot and place in oven. Turn oven to 425 degrees and bake loaf for 30 minutes while oven heats.

5. Remove lid and continue to bake until loaf is deep golden brown and registers 205 to 210 degrees, 25 to 30 minutes. Using parchment sling, remove loaf from pot and transfer to wire rack; discard parchment. Let cool completely, about 3 hours, before serving.

SCIENCE LESSON
A Steamy (Dutch) Oven

Baking bread in a Dutch oven creates the dramatic open-crumbed structure and the shatteringly crisp crust that you'd think is attainable only in a professional bakery. How does this work?

First, as the loaf heats, it gives off steam to create a humid environment inside the Dutch oven. Since moist air transfers heat much more efficiently than dry air, the loaf heats more rapidly. This in turn causes the air bubbles inside to expand faster, leading to a more open crumb structure. As a test, we baked two loaves, one in a Dutch oven and the other on a baking steel. After 1 minute in the oven, the surface temperature of the Dutch oven–baked loaf had risen past 200 degrees, while the other loaf had reached only 135 degrees.

Steam contributes to a great loaf in a second way. As steam condenses onto the surface of the baking bread, it causes the starches to form a thin sheath that eventually dries out, giving the finished loaf a shiny crust that stays crisp. With its thick walls, small internal volume, and heavy lid, a Dutch oven is the ideal environment in which to create and trap steam.

Making Almost No-Knead Bread

FOLD
Using a rubber spatula, gently fold the water mixture into the flour mixture until a dough starts to form and no dry flour remains. Let the dough sit for at least 8 hours or up to 18 hours.

KNEAD BY HAND
Knead the dough by hand until it's smooth and elastic, about 1 minute.

SHAPE
Shape the dough into a ball by pulling the edges into the middle, then transfer the dough seam side down to the center of a greased sheet of parchment paper.

RISE
Using the parchment as a sling, gently lower the loaf into a Dutch oven (let any excess parchment hang over the pot's edge). Let the dough rise until it has doubled in size, 1½ to 2 hours.

SLASH
Using a sharp paring knife or a single-edge razor blade, make two 5-inch-long, ½-inch-deep slashes with a swift, fluid motion along the top of the loaf to form a cross.

KEYS TO SUCCESS

- **Add beer to dough:** Adds malty flavor to the simply made bread
- **Incorporate plenty of liquid:** Encourages gluten development without lots of manipulation
- **Knead for 1 minute:** Ensures that the bread has structure with minimal effort

ALMOST NO-KNEAD BRIOCHE

Makes: 1 loaf
Total time: 1½ hours, plus 18 to 19½ hours rising and 3¼ hours cooling

RECIPE OVERVIEW Classic brioche has a tender crumb, an appealing golden color, and a buttery flavor that's richer than that of any other sandwich bread. Typically, the process is laborious: Butter, softened to just the right temperature, is kneaded into the dough in increments. And patience is crucial: Only after one portion is fully incorporated is the next added to ensure that the butter is completely combined and doesn't cause the dough to separate. We avoid this process altogether by using melted butter. Combining all the ingredients and letting the mixture sit for hours in the refrigerator allows the dough to stitch itself together into a loaf with only a bit of stirring and a couple folds or turns. Switching from the all-purpose flour that's used in many recipes to bread flour ensures that the loaf has enough structure. In addition, instead of shaping the dough into a single long loaf, we add even more strength by dividing the dough in two and shaping each half into a ball. Placed side by side in the pan, the two balls merge to form a single reinforced loaf. The test kitchen's preferred loaf pan measures 8½ by 4½ inches; if you use a 9 by 5-inch loaf pan, increase the shaped rising time by 20 to 30 minutes and start checking for doneness 10 minutes earlier than advised in the recipe.

- 1⅔ cups (9⅛ ounces) bread flour
- 1¼ teaspoons instant or rapid-rise yeast
- ¾ teaspoon table salt
- 3 large eggs, room temperature
- 8 tablespoons (4 ounces) unsalted butter, melted
- ¼ cup (2 ounces) water, room temperature
- 3 tablespoons sugar
- 1 large egg, lightly beaten with 1 tablespoon water and pinch table salt

1. Whisk flour, yeast, and salt together in large bowl. Whisk eggs, melted butter, water, and sugar in second bowl until sugar has dissolved.

2. Using rubber spatula, gently fold egg mixture into flour mixture, scraping up dry flour from bottom of bowl, until cohesive dough starts to form and no dry flour remains. Cover bowl tightly with plastic wrap and let dough rest for 10 minutes.

3. Using greased bowl scraper (or your fingertips), fold dough over itself by gently lifting and folding edge of dough toward middle. Turn bowl 90 degrees and fold dough again; repeat turning bowl and folding dough 2 more times (total of 4 folds). Cover tightly with plastic and let rise for 30 minutes. Repeat folding and rising every 30 minutes, 3 more times. After fourth set of folds, cover bowl tightly with plastic and refrigerate for at least 16 hours or up to 48 hours.

4. Transfer dough to well-floured counter, divide in half, and cover loosely with greased plastic. Using your well-floured hands, press 1 piece of dough into 4-inch round (keep remaining piece covered). Working around circumference of dough, fold edges toward center until ball forms. Repeat with remaining piece of dough.

5. Flip each dough ball seam side down and, using your cupped hands, drag in small circles on counter until dough feels taut and round and all seams are secured on underside. (If dough sticks to your hands, lightly dust top of dough with flour.) Cover dough rounds loosely with greased plastic and let rest for 5 minutes.

6. Grease 8½ by 4½-inch loaf pan. Flip each dough ball seam side up, press into 4-inch disk, and repeat folding and rounding steps. Place rounds seam side down, side by side, into prepared pan. Press dough gently into corners. Cover loosely with greased plastic and let rise until loaf reaches ½ inch below lip of pan and dough springs back minimally when poked gently with your knuckle, 1½ to 2 hours.

7. Adjust oven rack to middle position and heat oven to 350 degrees. Gently brush loaf with egg mixture and bake until deep golden brown and loaf registers 190 to 195 degrees, 35 to 40 minutes, rotating pan halfway through baking. Let loaf cool in pan for 15 minutes. Remove loaf from pan and let cool completely on wire rack, about 3 hours, before serving.

KEYS TO SUCCESS

- **Use bread flour:** Contributes structure due to extra protein content
- **Fold the dough:** Encourages gluten to form and ensures that the no-knead method is successful
- **Divide the dough in two and shape it into balls:** Yields a stronger, more reinforced loaf than a single piece of dough

Forming Almost No-Knead Brioche

FOLD
Using a greased bowl scraper (or your fingertips), fold the dough over itself by gently lifting and folding the edge of the dough toward the middle. Turn the bowl 90 degrees and fold the dough again; repeat turning the bowl and folding as required.

MAKE BALLS
Divide the dough in half. Using your well-floured hands, press one piece of dough into a 4-inch round. Working around the circumference of the dough, fold the edges toward the center until a ball forms.

SECURE SEAMS
Flip each dough ball seam side down and, using your cupped hands, drag the ball in small circles on the counter until the dough feels taut and round and all the seams are secured on the underside.

REPEAT
Flip each dough ball seam side up, press it into a 4-inch disk, and repeat the folding and rounding steps.

PLACE IN PAN
Place the rounds seam side down, side by side, into the prepared pan. Press the dough gently into the pan's corners.

ROSEMARY FOCACCIA

Makes: 2 loaves
Total Time: 2 hours, plus 6 hours resting, 1½ to 2 hours rising, and 35 minutes cooling

RECIPE OVERVIEW Focaccia can easily disappoint when it turns out heavy, thick, and flavorless. This loaf does nothing of the sort: It's a light, airy, crisp-crusted loaf topped with just a smattering of herbs. The no-knead method turns out a bubbly crumb. A high proportion of water to flour and a long resting period let the natural enzymes in the wheat replicate the effect of kneading. As with our Almost No-Knead Bread (page 526) and our Almost No-Knead Brioche (page 528), we fold the dough while it rises to prevent squat loaves. Olive oil is a key ingredient, but we found that when it's added straight to the dough, it can turn the bread dense and cake-like. Instead, we bake the bread in round cake pans, where a couple tablespoons of oil coating the exterior can be contained. Poking the dough surface pops large air bubbles and allows extra gas to escape. It is important to use fresh, not dried, rosemary for this recipe. Be sure to reduce the temperature immediately after putting the loaves in the oven.

Sponge
- ½ cup (2½ ounces) all-purpose flour
- ⅓ cup (2⅔ ounces) water, room temperature
- ¼ teaspoon instant or rapid-rise yeast

Dough
- 2½ cups (12½ ounces) all-purpose flour
- 1¼ cups (10 ounces) water, room temperature
- 1 teaspoon instant or rapid-rise yeast
- 3 teaspoons kosher salt, divided
- ¼ cup (1¾ ounces) extra-virgin olive oil
- 2 tablespoons chopped fresh rosemary

1. FOR THE SPONGE Stir all ingredients in large bowl with wooden spoon until well combined. Cover tightly with plastic wrap and let sit at room temperature until sponge has risen and begins to collapse, about 6 hours (sponge can sit at room temperature for up to 24 hours).

2. FOR THE DOUGH Stir flour, water, and yeast into sponge with wooden spoon until well combined. Cover bowl tightly with plastic and let dough rest for 15 minutes.

3. Stir 2 teaspoons salt into dough with wooden spoon until thoroughly incorporated, about 1 minute. Cover bowl tightly with plastic and let dough rest for 30 minutes.

4. Using greased bowl scraper (or rubber spatula), fold dough over itself by gently lifting and folding edge of dough toward middle. Turn bowl 45 degrees and fold dough again; repeat turning bowl and folding dough 6 more times (total of 8 folds). Cover tightly with plastic and let rise for 30 minutes. Repeat folding and rising. Fold dough again, then cover bowl tightly with plastic and let dough rise until nearly doubled in size, 30 minutes to 1 hour.

5. One hour before baking, adjust oven rack to upper-middle position, place baking steel or stone on rack, and heat oven to 500 degrees. Coat two 9-inch round cake pans with 2 tablespoons oil each. Sprinkle each pan with ½ teaspoon salt. Transfer dough to lightly floured counter and dust top with flour. Divide dough in half and cover loosely with greased plastic. Working with 1 piece of dough at a time (keep remaining piece covered), shape into 5-inch round by gently tucking under edges.

6. Place dough rounds seam side up in prepared pans, coat bottoms and sides with oil, then flip rounds over. Cover loosely with greased plastic and let dough rest for 5 minutes. Using your fingertips, gently press each dough round into corners of pan, taking care not to tear dough. (If dough resists stretching, let it relax for 5 to 10 minutes before trying to stretch it again.) Using fork, poke surface of dough 25 to 30 times, popping any large bubbles. Sprinkle 1 tablespoon rosemary evenly over top of each loaf; cover loosely with greased plastic; and let dough rest until slightly bubbly, about 10 minutes.

7. Place pans on baking steel or stone and reduce oven temperature to 450 degrees. Bake until tops are golden brown, 25 to 30 minutes, rotating pans halfway through baking. Let loaves cool in pans for 5 minutes. Remove loaves from pans and transfer to wire rack. Brush tops with any oil remaining in pans and let cool for 30 minutes. Serve warm or at room temperature.

CORE TECHNIQUE
Shaping Focaccia

MAKE ROUNDS
Divide the dough in half. Working with one piece of dough at a time (keep the remaining piece covered), shape the dough into a 5-inch round by gently tucking under the edges.

OIL ROUNDS
Place the dough rounds seam side up in prepared pans, coat the bottoms and sides with oil, and then flip the rounds over.

PRESS DOUGH
Use your fingertips to press the dough rounds into the corners of the pans. (Be careful not to tear the dough.)

SCIENCE LESSON — Wetter Is Better

Of course you need a liquid to transform flour into dough. And in bread baking, sometimes wetter is better: The more water (or other liquid) in a dough—that is, the more hydrated the dough—the stronger and more extensible the gluten strands. If the gluten strands are strong and extensible, they can support the starch granules and gas bubbles that hydrate and swell as the dough rises and bakes, giving you an airier bread with good chew. During baking, the water within the dough turns to steam, creating hollow pockets as moisture rushes to escape. Extra water also creates a looser dough, which allows the steam bubbles to expand more easily. In drier dough, gas bubbles have a harder time forming and are more likely to collapse. Getting those gas bubbles to hold their shape until the dough has risen and set in the oven is the key to creating an open, airy crumb.

SCIENCE LESSON — Folding Dough

Many of our bread recipes incorporate a folding step—not just our no-knead breads. Why is this step so important?

For loaves that require more strength or flavor, typically chewy rustic loaves or butter-laden sweet breads, we gently fold the dough over itself as it rises, a process that brings wayward sheets of gluten into alignment. In addition, folding dough rids it of excess carbon dioxide (which can inhibit yeast activity), distributes gas bubbles evenly, and refreshes the yeast. Recipes vary in the number of folds made, the degree to which the bowl is turned, and how many times the process is repeated, but the approach generally goes like this: Slide a greased bowl scraper (see page 504) (you can also use your fingertips) under the edge of the dough and lift and fold the dough toward the center of the bowl. Turn the bowl as instructed by the recipe and repeat the process. Turn the bowl and fold one more time. When you're done, the dough should be shaped like a tight package. At this point you let the dough rise for the period of time specified in the recipe, and then repeat the process.

COURSE
CLASSIC DINNER ROLLS

ASHLEY MOORE

Just like loaves, rolls run the gamut of textures and flavors; they can be lean and chewy or buttery and soft—even sweet. In this course, we give you the essentials: a fluffy dinner roll and a rustic one with an open crumb. Letting the dough rest between kneading periods to ensure structure is key, as is shaping the rolls so that they're taut and tight. Let's get rolling.

ASHLEY'S PRO TIP: *If at any time when rolling the dough you feel it isn't stretching easily, simply let it sit for 10 to 15 minutes to allow the gluten network to relax. This will ensure that your rolls are soft and chewy, and not tough (which is what can happen with too much gluten development).*

FLUFFY DINNER ROLLS

Makes: 12 rolls
Total Time: 1½ hours, plus 1¾ hours rising

RECIPE OVERVIEW American dinner rolls of the fluffy variety are by nature enriched, so they have a pillowy softness to complement their richer flavor—when they're warm and fresh. Once they sit, those qualities commonly diminish. We took a classic dinner roll recipe and applied a breadmaking method commonly called by its Chinese name, tangzhong (though it originated in Japan), which adds extra moisture to the dough in the form of a cooked flour paste. The added liquid in the dough extends the rolls' shelf life—they maintain their moist, fluffy texture for more than a day. To support the weight of the extra moisture, we build a strong gluten structure by making some changes to the classic mixing method—adding a resting period called an autolyse and withholding the butter until the gluten is firmly established. The shaping method, inspired by Japanese milk bread, is also important. Flattening each portion of dough and rolling it into a spiral organizes the gluten strands into coiled layers that bake up into feathery sheets. The slight tackiness of the dough aids in flattening and stretching it in step 5, so do not dust your counter with flour. These rolls can be made a day ahead. To refresh them before serving, wrap them in aluminum foil and heat them in a 350-degree oven for 15 minutes.

Flour Paste
- ½ cup water
- 3 tablespoons bread flour

Dough
- ½ cup cold milk
- 1 large egg
- 2 cups (11 ounces) bread flour
- 1½ teaspoons instant or rapid-rise yeast
- 2 tablespoons sugar
- 1 teaspoon table salt
- 4 tablespoons unsalted butter, cut into 4 pieces and softened, plus ½ tablespoon melted
- Vegetable oil spray

1. FOR THE FLOUR PASTE Whisk water and flour in small bowl until no lumps remain. Microwave, whisking every 20 seconds, until mixture thickens to stiff, smooth, pudding-like consistency that forms mound when dropped from end of whisk into bowl, 40 to 80 seconds.

2. FOR THE DOUGH In bowl of stand mixer, whisk flour paste and milk until smooth. Add egg and whisk until incorporated. Add flour and yeast. Fit stand mixer with dough hook and mix on low speed until all flour is moistened, 1 to 2 minutes. Let stand for 15 minutes.

3. Add sugar and salt and mix on medium-low speed for 5 minutes. With mixer running, add softened butter, 1 piece at a time. Continue to mix on medium-low speed for 5 minutes, scraping down dough hook and sides of bowl occasionally (dough will stick to bottom of bowl).

4. Transfer dough to very lightly floured counter. Knead briefly to form ball and transfer, seam side down, to lightly greased bowl; lightly coat surface of dough with oil spray and cover with plastic wrap. Let rise until doubled in volume, about 1 hour.

5. Grease 9-inch round cake pan and set aside. Transfer dough to counter. Press dough gently but firmly to expel all air. Pat and stretch dough to form 8 by 9-inch rectangle with short side facing you. Cut dough lengthwise into 4 equal strips and cut each strip crosswise into 3 equal pieces. Working with 1 piece at a time, stretch and press dough gently to form 8 by 2-inch strip. Starting on short side, roll dough to form snug cylinder. Arrange shaped rolls seam side down in prepared pan, placing 10 rolls around edge of pan, pointing inward, and remaining 2 rolls in center. Cover with plastic and let rise until doubled, 45 minutes to 1 hour.

6. When rolls are nearly doubled, adjust oven rack to lowest position and heat oven to 375 degrees. Bake rolls until deep golden brown, 25 to 30 minutes. Let rolls cool in pan on wire rack for 3 minutes; invert rolls onto rack, then reinvert. Brush tops and sides of rolls with melted butter. Let rolls cool for at least 20 minutes before serving.

KEYS TO SUCCESS

- **Use the tangzhong method:** The flour and water paste allows the dough to hold more moisture.
- **Incorporate a resting period (autolyse):** Strengthens the gluten structure to accommodate the moist dough
- **Roll the dough pieces into spirals:** Reinforced shaping strengthens the gluten structure too.

Shaping Fluffy Dinner Rolls

FORM
Gently stretch and press each dough piece into an 8 by 2-inch strip.

ROLL
Starting at one end, roll the strip into a snug cylinder.

ARRANGE
Place the cylinders seam side down in a prepared pan.

RUSTIC DINNER ROLLS

Makes: 16 rolls
Total Time: 1¼ hours, plus 30 minutes resting, 2½ to 3 hours rising, and 1 hour cooling

RECIPE OVERVIEW European-style dinner rolls are different from their rich, tender American cousins. The dough for these rustic rolls is lean and the crumb is open, with a yeasty, savory flavor. But the best part might be their crust—so crisp it practically shatters when you bite into it, yet chewy enough to offer satisfying resistance. This recipe remarkably mimics European-style dinner rolls made by professionals who use steam-injected ovens to expose the developing crust to moisture. Often when made at home these rolls are dull-tasting, so we improve the flavor by adding whole-wheat flour for earthiness and honey for sweetness. Extra yeast opens the rolls' crumb slightly, but not enough—upping the hydration of the dough to the wetness of an artisan loaf is also essential. To bake, we first mist the rolls with water before starting them in a cake pan at a high temperature to help set their shape (since the dough is soft, individually baked rolls turn out squat). Next, we lower the temperature, pull the rolls apart, and return them to the oven on a baking sheet until they are golden on all sides. This two-step method mimics a steam-injected oven. We do not recommend mixing this dough by hand.

- 3 cups (16½ ounces) bread flour
- 3 tablespoons whole-wheat flour
- 1½ teaspoons instant or rapid-rise yeast
- 1½ cups (12 ounces) plus 1 tablespoon water, room temperature
- 2 teaspoons honey
- 1½ teaspoons table salt

1. Whisk bread flour, whole-wheat flour, and yeast together in bowl of stand mixer. Whisk water and honey in 4-cup liquid measuring cup until honey has dissolved.

2. Using dough hook on low speed, slowly add water mixture to flour mixture and mix until cohesive dough starts to form and no dry flour remains, about 2 minutes, scraping down bowl and hook as needed. Cover bowl tightly with plastic wrap and let dough rest for 30 minutes.

3. Add salt to dough and mix on low speed for 5 minutes. Increase speed to medium and knead until dough is smooth and slightly sticky, about 1 minute. Transfer dough to lightly greased large bowl or container; cover tightly with plastic; and let rise until doubled in size, 1 to 1½ hours.

4. Using greased bowl scraper (or your fingertips), fold dough over itself by gently lifting and folding edge of dough toward middle. Turn bowl 90 degrees and fold dough again; repeat turning bowl and folding dough 2 more times (total of 4 folds). Cover tightly with plastic and let rise for 30 minutes. Repeat folding, then cover bowl tightly with plastic and let dough rise until doubled in size, about 30 minutes.

5. Grease two 9-inch round cake pans. Press down on dough to deflate. Transfer dough to well-floured counter, sprinkle lightly with flour, and divide in half. Stretch each half into even 16-inch log and cut into 8 equal pieces (about 2 ounces each). Using your well-floured hands, gently pick up each piece and roll in your palms to coat with flour, shaking off excess.

6. Arrange rolls in prepared pans, placing 1 in center and 7 around edges, with cut side facing up and long side of each piece running from center to edge of pan. Cover loosely with greased plastic and let rolls rise until nearly doubled in size and dough springs back minimally when poked gently with your knuckle, about 30 minutes. (Unrisen rolls can be refrigerated for at least 8 hours or up to 16 hours; let rolls sit at room temperature for 1½ hours before baking.)

7. Adjust oven rack to middle position and heat oven to 500 degrees. Mist rolls with water and bake until tops are brown, about 10 minutes. Remove rolls from oven and reduce oven temperature to 400 degrees. Carefully invert rolls out of pans onto baking sheet and let cool slightly. Turn rolls right side up, pull apart, and arrange evenly on sheet. Continue to bake until deep golden brown, 10 to 15 minutes, rotating sheet halfway through baking. Transfer rolls to wire rack and let cool completely, about 1 hour, before serving.

KEYS TO SUCCESS

- **Use whole-wheat flour and honey:** Boosts and deepens the flavor of the rolls
- **High hydration:** Ensures an open crumb
- **Fold the dough:** Strengthens the gluten structure to accommodate expansion
- **Bake in a cake pan first:** Sets the rolls' shape
- **Bake on a baking sheet second:** Encourages all-over browning
- **Mist the dough with water:** Crisps the crust

SCIENCE LESSON

High Rise: Oven Spring

Oven spring is the rise that yeasted dough experiences when it first hits a hot oven. The more "spring," the taller the loaf or roll and the airier the crumb. Baking bread at a higher temperature results in more-dramatic oven spring; bread dough is full of water, which will vaporize rapidly and open up the crumb, causing the loaf to expand. That's why rustic breads often start out baking at a very high temperature.

Higher Heat = Higher Rise

Lower Heat = Less Lift

SCIENCE LESSON

Adding a Rest to Your Dough

Sometimes there are recipe factors that make standard kneading times inadequate for building a strong enough gluten structure. Knead for too long, however, and the dough can oxidize and bake into a pale and stale-tasting loaf. How can you fortify the gluten structure? Employ a technique called autolyse. In this method, the dry and wet ingredients go through step 1 of the process, mixing; then, the shaggy dough is left to rest before proceeding with kneading. While the mixture rests, naturally occurring enzymes (proteases) break down the disorganized bonds of gluten, acting like scissors, cutting the coiled-up proteins into smaller segments that are easier to strengthen and align during kneading, so they require less time.

It's important to hold the salt when mixing doughs that will undergo autolyse: Salt hinders both the ability of flour to absorb water and the activity of the enzymes that break down proteins during autolyse. If you add the salt up front, the dough will be sticky and stiff after autolyse. If you wait to add the salt, the dough will get a head start in gluten development and will be supple and smooth.

Making Rustic Dinner Rolls

AUTOLYSE
After mixing, cover the bowl tightly with plastic wrap and let the dough rest for 30 minutes.

KNEAD
Add salt to the dough and mix on low speed for 5 minutes. Increase the speed to medium and knead the dough until it's smooth and slightly sticky, about 1 minute. Let it rise.

FOLD
Using a greased bowl scraper (or your fingertips), gently lift and fold the edge of the dough toward the middle. Turn the bowl 90 degrees; fold the dough again. Repeat as required.

DIVIDE
Press down on the risen dough to deflate it. Divide the dough in half. Stretch each half into an even 16-inch log and cut each log into eight equal pieces (about 2 ounces each).

COAT
Using your well-floured hands, gently pick up each piece and roll it in your palms to coat it with flour, shaking off any excess.

ARRANGE
Arrange the rolls in pans, placing one in the center and seven around the edges, with the cut side up and the long side of each running from the center to the edge of the pan.

COURSE
WHOLE-WHEAT BREADS

STEPHANIE PIXLEY

There are a lot of reasons to introduce whole-wheat flour to your breads: It's healthful, it has nice color, it can give a loaf heartiness, and it boasts a nutty taste that provides bread with great depth of flavor. Whole-wheat flour is ground from the whole wheat berry—the outer bran layer, the germ, and the endosperm—whereas white flour is ground from just the endosperm. Because it contains the entire berry, baking with whole-wheat flour is a challenge. You'll learn why—along with how to put whole-wheat breads with superlative taste and texture on your table.

STEPHANIE'S PRO TIP: *Whole wheat (or any whole-grain flour for that matter) can spoil more quickly than traditional white flour, so I always keep mine in the freezer to extend its shelf life. Just be sure to let your flour come to room temperature before using it in a recipe; cold flour will absorb liquid differently which can affect the success of your recipe.*

HONEY-WHEAT DINNER ROLLS
Makes: 15 rolls
Total Time: 1¼ hours, plus 2½ to 3½ hours rising

RECIPE OVERVIEW Good honey-wheat dinner rolls have the softness of white rolls with satisfying heft and a nutty whole-wheat flavor that's complemented by a touch of floral sweetness. That said, these appealing rolls rarely hit the mark: Commercial versions are soft but taste artificially sweet, while homemade rolls have good flavor but can be as dense as wet sand. These rolls, on the other hand, are tender and fluffy and actually taste like their namesake ingredients. What makes achieving great whole-wheat breads so difficult is the presence of the bran. This part of the grain, which is removed from white flour, gives whole-wheat flour its distinct hearty flavor. But the bran is sharp—so sharp that it cuts through the bread's gluten structure, leaving you with a dense product. To produce a light, fluffy whole-wheat roll, we incorporate some all-purpose flour into the dough—but not so much that we lose the roll's earthy, nutty whole-wheat flavor. A very wet dough is also key; the excess liquid softens the bran's edges, ensuring that it doesn't wreak havoc on the dough's structure. As a bonus, the liquid honey in the recipe hydrates the dough further and contributes softness. And to make sure that the flavor comes through loud and clear, we brush the warm baked rolls with honey butter.

- 2½ cups (13¾ ounces) whole-wheat flour
- 1¾ cups (8¾ ounces) all-purpose flour
- 2¼ teaspoons instant or rapid-rise yeast
- 2¼ teaspoons table salt
- 1¾ cups (14 ounces) whole milk, room temperature
- 6 tablespoons (4½ ounces) plus 1 teaspoon honey, divided
- 5 tablespoons (2½ ounces) unsalted butter, melted, divided
- 1 large egg, room temperature
- 1 large egg, lightly beaten with 1 tablespoon water and pinch table salt

1. Whisk whole-wheat flour, all-purpose flour, yeast, and salt together in bowl of stand mixer. Whisk milk, 6 tablespoons honey, 4 tablespoons melted butter, and egg in 4-cup liquid measuring cup until honey has dissolved.

2. Using dough hook on low speed, slowly add milk mixture to flour mixture and mix until cohesive dough starts to form and no dry flour remains, about 2 minutes, scraping down bowl as needed. Increase speed to medium-low and knead until dough is smooth and elastic and clears sides of bowl but sticks to bottom, about 8 minutes.

3. Transfer dough to lightly floured counter and knead by hand to form smooth, round ball, about 30 seconds. Place dough seam side down in lightly greased large bowl or container; cover tightly with plastic wrap; and let rise until doubled in size, 1½ to 2 hours.

4. Make foil sling for 13 by 9-inch baking dish by folding 2 long sheets of aluminum foil; first sheet should be 13 inches wide and second sheet should be 9 inches wide. Lay sheets of foil in dish perpendicular to each other, with extra foil hanging over edges of dish. Push foil into corners and up sides of dish, smoothing foil flush to dish, then spray foil with vegetable oil spray.

5. Press down on dough to deflate. Transfer dough to clean counter and stretch into even 15-inch log. Cut log into 15 equal pieces (about 2½ ounces each) and cover loosely with greased plastic. Working with 1 piece of dough at a time (keep remaining pieces covered), form into rough ball by stretching dough around your thumbs and pinching edges together so top is smooth. Place ball seam side down on clean counter and, using your cupped hand, drag in small circles until dough feels taut and round.

6. Arrange dough balls seam side down into 5 rows of 3 in prepared dish; cover loosely with greased plastic; and let rise until nearly doubled in size and dough springs back minimally when poked gently with your knuckle, 1 to 1½ hours. (Unrisen rolls can be refrigerated for at least 8 hours or up to 16 hours; let rolls sit at room temperature for 1 hour before baking.) Adjust oven rack to lower-middle position and heat oven to 350 degrees. Gently brush rolls with egg mixture and bake until golden brown, 25 to 30 minutes, rotating dish halfway through baking.

7. Combine remaining honey and melted butter in bowl. Let rolls cool in dish for 15 minutes. Using foil overhang, transfer rolls to wire rack and brush with honey mixture. Serve warm or at room temperature.

KEYS TO SUCCESS
- **Add a little all-purpose flour:** Makes for a lighter bread than whole-wheat flour alone
- **Stretch the dough and pinch the ends:** Ensures that the dough seams are hidden
- **Shape the rolls on a clean counter (without flour):** Creates friction and forces the dough into a round
- **Incorporate extra moisture into the dough:** Softens the bran so that it doesn't cut through gluten strands
- **Use lots of honey:** Contributes softness and gives the rolls great flavor

WHOLE-WHEAT QUINOA BREAD

Makes: 1 loaf
Total Time: 1½ hours, plus 2½ to 3½ hours rising and 3¼ hours cooling

RECIPE OVERVIEW Hearty quinoa and a couple tablespoons of nutty-tasting flaxseeds make great additions to a whole-wheat loaf. We use a combination of bread flour and whole-wheat flour in the dough here; the bread flour gives the loaf the flexibility to accommodate a good amount of cooked quinoa, and its high protein content provides a sturdy crumb. Simply cooking the quinoa in the microwave with a measured amount of water gives the bread just the right texture. Incorporating a small amount of oil helps coat the protein strands, making the loaf more moist and tender, and adding 3 full tablespoons of honey balances the earthiness of the quinoa. Sprinkling 1 teaspoon of raw flaxseeds and 1 teaspoon of raw quinoa atop the loaf just before baking gives each slice pleasant textural contrast and crunch. The test kitchen's preferred loaf pan measures 8½ by 4½ inches; if you use a 9 by 5-inch loaf pan, increase the shaped rising time by 20 to 30 minutes and start checking for doneness 10 minutes earlier than advised in the recipe. We do not recommend mixing this dough by hand.

- 1 cup (8 ounces) water, room temperature, divided
- ⅓ cup (1¾ ounces) plus 1 teaspoon prewashed white quinoa, divided
- 1½ cups (8¼ ounces) bread flour
- 1 cup (5½ ounces) whole-wheat flour
- 2 tablespoons plus 1 teaspoon flaxseeds, divided
- 2 teaspoons instant or rapid-rise yeast
- 1½ teaspoons table salt
- ¾ cup (6 ounces) whole milk, room temperature
- 3 tablespoons honey
- 1 tablespoon vegetable oil
- 1 large egg, lightly beaten with 1 tablespoon water and pinch salt

1. Microwave ¾ cup water and ⅓ cup quinoa in covered bowl at 50 percent power until water is almost completely absorbed, about 10 minutes, stirring halfway through microwaving. Uncover quinoa and let sit until cooled slightly and water is completely absorbed, about 10 minutes.

2. Whisk bread flour, whole-wheat flour, 2 tablespoons flaxseeds, yeast, and salt together in bowl of stand mixer. Whisk milk, honey, oil, and remaining ¼ cup water in 4-cup liquid measuring cup until honey has dissolved. Using dough hook on low speed, slowly add milk mixture to flour mixture and mix until cohesive dough starts to form and no dry flour remains, about 2 minutes, scraping down bowl as needed.

3. Increase speed to medium-low and knead until dough is smooth, elastic, and slightly sticky, about 6 minutes. Reduce speed to low; slowly add cooked quinoa, ¼ cup at a time; and mix until mostly incorporated, about 3 minutes.

4. Transfer dough to lightly floured counter. Using your lightly floured hands, knead dough until quinoa is evenly distributed and dough forms smooth, round ball, about 30 seconds. Place dough seam side down in lightly greased large bowl or container; cover tightly with plastic wrap; and let rise until doubled in size, 1½ to 2 hours.

5. Grease 8½ by 4½-inch loaf pan. Press down on dough to deflate. Turn dough out onto lightly floured counter (side of dough that was against bowl should now be facing up) and press into 8 by 6-inch rectangle, with long side parallel to counter edge.

6. Roll dough away from you into firm cylinder, keeping roll taut by tucking it under itself as you go. Pinch seam closed and place loaf seam side down in prepared pan, pressing dough gently into corners. Cover loosely with greased plastic and let rise until loaf reaches 1 inch above lip of pan and dough springs back minimally when poked gently with your knuckle, 1 to 1½ hours.

7. Adjust oven rack to lower-middle position and heat oven to 350 degrees. Combine remaining 1 teaspoon quinoa and 1 teaspoon flaxseeds in bowl. Gently brush loaf with egg mixture and sprinkle with quinoa mixture. Bake until golden brown and loaf registers 205 to 210 degrees, 45 to 50 minutes, rotating pan halfway through baking. Let loaf cool in pan for 15 minutes. Remove loaf from pan and let cool completely on wire rack, about 3 hours, before serving.

The Hull of the Matter

The difficulty with baking with whole-wheat flour lies with the bran—the very thing that gives whole-wheat flour its character. The fiber in bran has sharp edges that tend to cut the gluten strands, weakening their bonds and making the dough less able to contain gases during proofing and baking. The result is a squat, heavy, crumbly loaf. So what can you do to put healthful whole-wheat breads on your table?

COMBINE WHOLE-WHEAT FLOUR WITH WHITE FLOUR You should typically cut the whole-wheat flour in a recipe with some white flour—all-purpose flour if you're making a soft, fluffy bread and bread flour for those that need structure. The white flour will automatically give your bread a boost in gluten-forming proteins and therefore gluten development, making up for the structure-compromising activity of the whole-wheat flour.

MAKE IT WET You can soften the whole-wheat flour's bran by letting the bran absorb a lot of water in a highly hydrated dough. This can make the dough a bit more difficult to work with, but it will blunt the bran's sharp edges, which can cut through gluten strands.

COURSE
FREE-FORM LOAVES

JOSEPH GITTER

The stunning loaves shaped as boules and torpedoes at your local bakery may seem like the products of only the most gifted hands. But shaping bread dough into beautiful free-form loaves is totally achievable at home, and the steps are simple. The main point of shaping is obvious—to form the dough into the loaf it is to become after baking. What's more profound is what's happening inside the dough: Shaping strengthens the bread's structure one last time. Here we tackle the common torpedo. Take a look inside these utterly appealing loaves you'll want around all the time.

JOE'S PRO TIP: *Precut, flat parchment paper is so much easier to fit in a rimmed baking sheet than paper that comes in rolls. It also won't curl up at the edges and so makes sliding a loaf onto a screaming hot baking steel much less stressful.*

CLASSIC ITALIAN BREAD

Makes: 1 loaf
Total Time: 1 hour, plus 1½ to 2½ hours rising and 3 hours cooling

RECIPE OVERVIEW You might assume that you have to make a trip to a bakery for good Italian bread, or else settle for pale, doughy supermarket loaves, but making your own from scratch is surprisingly simple. This classic Italian loaf with a thin, crisp crust and a chewy but tender crumb needs only a short fermentation time, so we use beer as the main liquid in our dough for its yeasty tang. Preheating a baking steel or stone for an hour gives the loaf a nicely browned crust, and misting the loaf with water before baking helps the exterior stay supple and encourages additional rise and a light, tender crumb. Use a mild American lager, such as Budweiser, here; strongly flavored beers will make this bread taste bitter.

- 3 cups (16½ ounces) bread flour
- 1½ teaspoons instant or rapid-rise yeast
- 1½ teaspoons table salt
- 1 cup (8 ounces) mild lager, room temperature
- 6 tablespoons (3 ounces) water, room temperature
- 2 tablespoons extra-virgin olive oil

1. Whisk flour, yeast, and salt together in bowl of stand mixer. Whisk beer, water, and oil together in 4-cup liquid measuring cup. Using dough hook on low speed, slowly add beer mixture to flour mixture and mix until cohesive dough starts to form and no dry flour remains, about 2 minutes, scraping down bowl as needed. Increase speed to medium-low and knead until dough is smooth and elastic and clears sides of bowl, about 8 minutes.

2. Transfer dough to lightly floured counter and knead by hand to form smooth, round ball, about 30 seconds. Place dough seam side down in lightly greased large bowl or container; cover tightly with plastic wrap; and let rise until doubled in size, 1 to 1½ hours.

3. Line pizza peel with 16 by 12-inch piece of parchment paper, with long edge of paper perpendicular to handle. Gently press down on dough to deflate any large gas pockets. Turn dough out onto lightly floured counter (side of dough that was against bowl should now be facing up) and press and stretch dough into 10-inch square. Fold top corners of dough diagonally into center of square and press gently to seal. Stretch and fold dough in half toward you to form rough loaf and pinch seam closed. Starting at center of dough and working toward ends, gently and evenly roll and stretch dough until it measures 15 inches long by 4 inches wide. Roll loaf seam side down.

4. Gently slide your hands underneath each end of loaf and transfer seam side down to prepared pizza peel. Reshape loaf as needed, tucking edges under to form taut torpedo shape. Cover loosely with greased plastic and let rise until loaf increases in size by about half and dough springs back minimally when poked gently with your knuckle, 30 minutes to 1 hour.

5. One hour before baking, adjust oven rack to lower-middle position, place baking steel or stone on rack, and heat oven to 450 degrees. Using sharp paring knife or single-edge razor blade, make one ½-inch-deep slash with swift, fluid motion lengthwise along top of loaf, starting and stopping about 1½ inches from ends.

6. Mist loaf with water and slide parchment with loaf onto baking steel or stone. Bake until crust is golden brown and loaf registers 205 to 210 degrees, 25 to 30 minutes, rotating loaf halfway through baking. Transfer loaf to wire rack; discard parchment. Let cool completely, about 3 hours, before serving.

Why You Might Want Two Baking Peels

A baking peel is a very helpful tool for getting bread (and pizza; see page 548) into and out of the oven. But there are two main styles of peels: thin metal ones and thicker wooden ones. Should you buy one instead of the other? Because each peel is best suited for a different purpose, you may want to consider having both in your kitchen if you have the space. Here's why.

A wooden peel excels at getting baked goods into the oven. Its rough, porous texture makes it harder for dough to bond to its surface, and the wood also does a good job of holding on to a dusting of flour, which decreases sticking. A wooden peel's one drawback: It's too thick to easily slide under baked bread and pizza.

A metal peel is thin and flexible, so it's great at getting under a pizza to rotate it in the oven or to take it out. But it's not the best tool for unloading dough onto a baking steel or stone in the oven, since its smooth, nonporous surface makes it easier for dough to stick.

If stocking two peels isn't practical for you, you can often line the metal peel with parchment paper that prevents sticking and slides with the bread right into the oven.

Use a Wooden Peel to Load Bread into Oven

Use a Metal Peel to Remove It

CRANBERRY-WALNUT BREAD

Makes: 1 loaf
Total Time: 1¼ hours, plus 2 to 3 hours rising and 3 hours cooling

RECIPE OVERVIEW This sandwich bread is studded with dried tart cranberries and rich walnuts and dresses up any lunch. The flavors of this bread lend themselves to a denser, moister texture than that of a rustic bread with a big open crumb, so we cut the bread flour with some whole-wheat flour; since whole-wheat flour doesn't form a strong gluten network as readily as does bread flour, it helps yield that density. The whole-wheat flour also complements the earthy flavor of the walnuts. This loaf has a slight sweetness to it. To prevent the loaf from emerging from the oven dark and bitter, we bake it on a stacked set of two baking sheets for added insulation, and we raise the oven rack to the middle position for even heat distribution around the loaf. This browns the entire exterior evenly.

- 2¼ cups (12⅓ ounces) bread flour
- 10 tablespoons (3½ ounces) whole-wheat flour
- ¾ cup dried cranberries
- ¾ cup walnuts, toasted and chopped
- 2 teaspoons instant or rapid-rise yeast
- 2 teaspoons table salt
- 1¼ cups (10 ounces) water, room temperature
- 2 tablespoons packed light brown sugar
- 1 tablespoon vegetable oil
- 1 large egg, lightly beaten with 1 tablespoon water and pinch table salt

1. Whisk bread flour, whole-wheat flour, cranberries, walnuts, yeast, and salt together in bowl of stand mixer. Whisk water, sugar, and oil in 4-cup liquid measuring cup until sugar has dissolved. Using dough hook on low speed, slowly add water mixture to flour mixture and mix until cohesive dough starts to form and no dry flour remains, about 2 minutes, scraping down bowl as needed.

2. Increase speed to medium-low and knead until dough is smooth and elastic and clears sides of bowl, about 8 minutes.

3. Transfer dough to lightly floured counter and knead by hand to form smooth, round ball, about 30 seconds. Place dough seam side down in lightly greased large bowl or container; cover tightly with plastic wrap; and let rise until doubled in size, 1½ to 2 hours.

4. Stack 2 rimmed baking sheets and line with aluminum foil. Press down on dough to deflate. Turn dough out onto lightly floured counter (side of dough that was against bowl should now be facing up). Press and stretch dough into 6-inch square. Fold top corners of dough diagonally into center of square and press gently to seal. Stretch and fold upper third of dough toward center and press seam gently to seal.

5. Stretch and fold dough in half toward you to form rough 8 by 4-inch loaf and pinch seam closed. Roll loaf seam side down. Gently slide your hands underneath each end of loaf and transfer to prepared sheet. Reshape loaf as needed, tucking edges under to form taut torpedo shape.

6. Cover loosely with greased plastic and let rise until loaf increases in size by about half and dough springs back minimally when poked gently with your knuckle, 30 minutes to 1 hour.

7. Adjust oven rack to middle position and heat oven to 450 degrees. Using sharp paring knife or single-edge razor blade, make one ½-inch-deep slash with swift, fluid motion lengthwise along top of loaf, starting and stopping about ½ inch from ends.

8. Gently brush loaf with egg mixture and bake for 15 minutes. Reduce oven temperature to 375 degrees and continue to bake until dark brown and loaf registers 205 to 210 degrees, 30 to 35 minutes, rotating sheet halfway through baking. Transfer loaf to wire rack and let cool completely, about 3 hours, before serving.

KEYS TO SUCCESS

- **Use some whole-wheat flour:** In combination with bread flour, achieves the ideal texture and flavor
- **Bake on stacked baking sheets:** Provides extra insulation; prevents the bottom of the loaf from burning
- **Brush on egg wash:** Gives the loaf a shiny, crisp, browned finish

RESOURCES FOR FREE-FORM LOAVES

SHAPING TORPEDO LOAVES

The dough for long, rounded-end torpedoes benefits from being pressed flat and then folded inward to build structure. But there are a few more steps you need to complete these attractive loaves. A stretching process coaxes the dough into the right shape. Rolling the loaf seam side down before transferring it to a baking sheet or pizza peel helps the seam close as the loaf rises a second time.

1. SHAPE THE DOUGH INTO A SQUARE
Press and stretch the dough into a square.

2. FOLD THE TOP CORNERS
Fold the top corners of the dough diagonally into the center and press gently to seal. (The dough will look like an open envelope.)

3. STRETCH AND FOLD
Stretch and fold the upper third of the dough toward the center, and press the seam gently to seal. (The dough will look like a sealed envelope.)

4. FORM A ROUGH LOAF
Stretch and fold the dough in half toward you to form a rough loaf, and pinch the seam gently to seal. Roll the loaf seam side down.

5. TRANSFER AND TUCK
Gently slide your hands underneath each end of the loaf and transfer it to the prepared baking sheets, being careful not to deflate dough.

SECRETS OF SHAPING

When making free-form loaves, it's important to shape all doughs with a gentle but decisive hand so that you don't work out too much air. At the same time, though, you want to create surface tension on the dough, developing what is called a "gluten sheath" around the interior network. This sturdy sheath gets inflated like a balloon again during the second rise and keeps the gases within, allowing the loaf to rise up and not out and to hold on to the carbon dioxide, which will give it an airy crumb. Sealing seams as necessary is the last important part of shaping; this ensures that they don't open during baking. And when making cuts to divide dough, note that every cut you make creates a weak point in the gluten network from which gases can escape.

WHAT IF THE DOUGH IS HARD TO SHAPE?

Although the gluten relaxes during the dough's first rise, any manipulation of the dough after bulk fermentation can work to bolster the gluten network again. So as you're shaping, the dough may seem difficult to stretch or roll, and it could potentially snap back to its original position and fail to form the desired shape or roll out to the correct size. If you experience this during shaping, simply incorporate a rest into the process: Cover the dough on the counter with plastic wrap and let it sit for 10 to 20 minutes until the dough is easy to manipulate again. This brief rest gives the gluten network time to relax. Be sure to remember to cover the dough so that it doesn't form a skin.

WHEN IS THE DOUGH PROPERLY PROOFED?

Bake a loaf too soon or too late, and the quality of the final bread will not reflect the time you spent making it. Here are the methods we use for determining when dough is properly proofed. Below is a loaf that is properly proofed (proven by the knuckle test). It will bake up with a uniform shape, crust, and crumb.

Test for volume For free-form breads, you can eyeball when they're ready for the oven. Many doughs will double in size (rustic loaves vary). This process takes anywhere from 30 minutes to 2 hours at room temperature. (For sandwich loaves, we include the number of inches a loaf should rise above the pan.)

Use the knuckle test Make an indentation in the dough with your finger to determine when it's properly proofed. Gently poke the loaf with your knuckle. If the indentation fills in right away, the loaf is underproofed and needs to rise further. Conversely, if the indentation fails to fill in, the loaf is overproofed. The loaf is perfectly proofed when the indentation springs back minimally and does not fill in completely.

SLASHING LOAVES

Slashing a loaf cuts through its gluten sheath, creating designated weak spots in a loaf's surface that allow the loaf to expand in the right direction in the oven. Without the slashes, the loaf will expand wherever it finds a random weak spot, resulting in an odd shape. For most breads, you can slash with a paring knife or a single-edge razor blade. We slash either ¼ or ½ inch deep. Act quickly and decisively when slashing; otherwise, the implement will drag, creating messy lines. We score these simple torpedo-shaped loaves with one simple slash along their lengths.

SCIENCE LESSON: MISTING

Moisture converts the exterior starches into a thin coating of gel that eventually results in a glossy, crackly crust—the hallmark of a great artisan-style loaf. We mist lots of breads throughout this chapter before baking. In this course, it achieves a nice crust on our Classic Italian Bread (page 540).

SLICED BREAD

Often, the knife fails to cut all the way through the thick bottom crust of free-form loaves of bread, especially rustic-style ones. This leaves you yanking the slice free from the loaf, often tearing it in the process. That's not going to make a sound sandwich. To get around the problem and cut perfect slices, turn the loaf on its side to cut it. This way, you'll be able to cut through both the top and bottom crusts simultaneously. And make sure to use a sharp serrated knife for your bread knife. The pointed serrations allow the blade to glide through crusty breads and create neater slices.

COURSE
PIZZA, PIZZA

BRIDGET LANCASTER

There seem to be as many styles of pizza as there are people who love to eat it. Since most people don't own a wood-fired pizza oven that reaches temperatures in excess of 800 degrees, the challenge for home cooks is achieving a deeply flavorful crust with a tender but chewy texture and a crisp, browned exterior all from their home oven. These recipes call for making the dough in a food processor and then either baking the pizza in a skillet or rolling out a thin crust and transferring it on a baking peel directly to a baking steel. This course will also cover some basics about working with flour and yeast and demonstrate techniques for shaping and topping pizzas.

BRIDGET'S PRO TIP: *Any time that you are working with dough, it's a good idea to weigh out the flour rather than rely on measuring by volume. You'll have more consistent results. When working and shaping the dough, if at any time it becomes too difficult to roll or pat out (the dough snaps back when stretched), loosely cover the dough and let it rest for 10 minutes. The rested dough should be easier to shape and work with.*

SKILLET PIZZA
Makes: Two 11-inch pizzas to serve 4
Total Time: 2¾ hours (1¼ hours with premade dough)

RECIPE OVERVIEW This is a great starter recipe for from-scratch pizza at home. Making it in a skillet is a breeze since you don't need to use a baking steel or a pizza peel, and the dough comes together quickly in a food processor. After letting the dough rise, we roll it thin and then transfer it to a cool oiled skillet, where we top it with a fast, no-cook sauce and slices of fresh mozzarella cheese. We place the skillet over a hot burner to get it good and hot and to set the bottom of the crust. Once the crust begins to brown, we simply slide the skillet into a 500-degree oven. In the oven, the hot skillet functions like a pizza steel, crisping up the crust in just minutes and melting the cheese. We feature a Margherita pizza topping here, adorning the sauce and cheese with just a sprinkle of basil. But if you'd like a more substantial topping for your pizza, feel free to sprinkle pepperoni, sautéed mushrooms, or browned sausage over the cheese before baking; just be sure to keep the toppings light, or they may weigh down the thin crust and make it soggy. This recipe will yield more sauce than is needed for two pizzas; the extra sauce can be refrigerated for up to one week or frozen for up to one month.

Dough
- 2 cups (11 ounces) plus 2 tablespoons bread flour
- 1⅛ teaspoons instant or rapid-rise yeast
- ¾ teaspoon table salt
- 1 tablespoon extra-virgin olive oil
- ¾ cup (6 ounces) ice water

Sauce and Toppings
- 1 (28-ounce) can whole peeled tomatoes, drained with juice reserved
- 5 tablespoons extra-virgin olive oil, divided
- 2 garlic cloves, minced
- 1 teaspoon red wine vinegar
- 1 teaspoon dried oregano
- ½ teaspoon table salt
- ¼ teaspoon pepper
- 8 ounces fresh mozzarella cheese, sliced ¼ inch thick and patted dry with paper towels, divided
- 2 tablespoons chopped fresh basil, divided

1. FOR THE DOUGH Pulse flour, yeast, and salt in food processor until combined, about 5 pulses. With processor running, add oil, then water, and process until rough ball forms, 30 to 40 seconds. Let dough rest for 2 minutes, then process for 30 seconds longer.

2. Transfer dough to lightly floured counter and knead by hand to form smooth, round ball, about 30 seconds. Place dough seam side down in lightly greased large bowl or container; cover tightly with plastic wrap; and let rise until doubled in size, 1½ to 2 hours. (Unrisen dough can be refrigerated for at least 8 hours or up to 16 hours; let sit at room temperature for 30 minutes before shaping in step 5.)

3. FOR THE SAUCE AND TOPPINGS Process tomatoes, 1 tablespoon oil, garlic, vinegar, oregano, salt, and pepper in clean, dry workbowl until smooth, about 30 seconds. Transfer mixture to 2-cup liquid measuring cup and add reserved tomato juice until sauce measures 2 cups. Reserve 1 cup sauce; set aside remaining sauce for another use.

4. Adjust oven rack to upper-middle position and heat oven to 500 degrees. Grease 12-inch ovensafe skillet with 2 tablespoons oil.

5. Transfer dough to lightly floured counter, divide in half, and cover loosely with greased plastic. Press and roll 1 piece of dough (keep remaining piece covered) into 11-inch round of even thickness.

6. Transfer dough to prepared skillet and reshape as needed. Spread ½ cup sauce over dough, leaving ½-inch border around edge. Top with half of mozzarella.

7. Set skillet over high heat and cook until outside edge of dough is set, pizza is lightly puffed, and bottom of crust looks spotty brown when gently lifted with spatula, about 3 minutes.

8. Transfer skillet to oven and bake pizza until edges are brown and cheese is melted and spotty brown, 7 to 10 minutes. Using pot holders, remove skillet from oven and slide pizza onto wire rack; let cool slightly. Sprinkle with 1 tablespoon basil, cut into wedges, and serve. Being careful of hot skillet, repeat with remaining oil, dough, sauce, mozzarella, and basil.

Variation
SKILLET PIZZA WITH FONTINA, ARUGULA, AND PROSCIUTTO
Toss 2 cups baby arugula with 4 teaspoons extra-virgin olive oil and salt and pepper to taste in bowl. Substitute 1½ cups shredded fontina for mozzarella, dividing evenly between pizzas. Immediately after baking each pizza, sprinkle 2 ounces thinly sliced prosciutto, cut into ½-inch strips, and half of dressed arugula over top of each pizza.

KEYS TO SUCCESS
- **An ovensafe skillet (stainless steel or cast iron):** Gets real hot, stays real hot, and cooks the pizza evenly
- **Start on the stovetop over high heat:** Sets the bottom of the crust
- **Finish in the oven:** Functioning like a baking steel or stone, the hot skillet crisps the crust

CORE TECHNIQUE
Fitting Dough into a Skillet

ROLL
Press and roll the dough into an 11-inch round of even thickness.

RESHAPE AND TOP
Transfer the dough to your prepared skillet and reshape as needed. Spread ½ cup of sauce over the dough, leaving a ½-inch border around the edge. Top the sauced dough with mozzarella.

THIN-CRUST PIZZA

Makes: Two 13-inch pizzas, serving 4 to 6
Total Time: 2½ hours, plus 25 hours resting

RECIPE OVERVIEW   To make the leap to a thin-crust pizza, look no further than this foolproof recipe. New York–style pizza has a thin, crisp, and spottily charred exterior, and it's tender yet chewy within. We like to use bread flour in this recipe because the higher protein content makes the dough appropriately chewy. We make the dough fairly wet, so it's easy to stretch, and we develop its flavor by letting it rest in the refrigerator for a day (this is known as cold fermentation; see page 549). Oven rack placement also gives us the crust we want. Situating a baking steel or stone on the highest rack mimics the shallow chamber of a commercial pizza oven, in which heat rises, radiates off the top of the oven, and browns the pizza before the interior dries out. It is important to use ice water in the dough to prevent it from overheating in the food processor. The dough needs to be refrigerated for at least 24 hours before baking. If you don't have a pizza peel, use a rimless or overturned baking sheet to slide the pizzas onto the baking steel or stone. You can shape the second dough round while the first pizza bakes; don't add the toppings until just before baking.

Dough
- 3 cups (16½ ounces) bread flour
- 2 teaspoons sugar
- ½ teaspoon instant or rapid-rise yeast
- 1⅓ cups ice water
- 1 tablespoon vegetable oil
- 1½ teaspoons table salt

Sauce and Toppings
- 1 (28-ounce) can whole peeled tomatoes, drained with juice reserved
- 1 tablespoon extra-virgin olive oil
- 2 garlic cloves, minced
- 1 teaspoon red wine vinegar
- 1 teaspoon dried oregano
- ½ teaspoon table salt
- ¼ teaspoon pepper
- 1 ounce Parmesan cheese, grated fine (½ cup)
- 8 ounces whole-milk mozzarella, shredded (2 cups)

1. FOR THE DOUGH Pulse flour, sugar, and yeast in food processor until combined, about 5 pulses. With processor running, slowly add ice water; process until dough is just combined and no dry flour remains, about 10 seconds. Let dough rest for 10 minutes.

2. Add oil and salt to dough and process until dough forms satiny, sticky ball that clears sides of bowl, 30 to 60 seconds. Transfer dough to lightly oiled counter and knead by hand to form smooth, round ball, about 30 seconds. Place dough seam side down in lightly greased large bowl or container; cover tightly with plastic wrap; and refrigerate for at least 24 hours or up to 3 days.

3. FOR THE SAUCE AND TOPPINGS Process tomatoes, oil, garlic, vinegar, oregano, salt, and pepper in clean, dry workbowl until smooth, about 30 seconds. Transfer mixture to 2-cup liquid measuring cup and add reserved tomato juice until sauce measures 2 cups. Reserve 1 cup sauce; set aside remaining sauce for another use.

4. One hour before baking, adjust oven rack 4 inches from broiler element, set baking steel or stone on rack, and heat oven to 500 degrees. Press down on dough to deflate. Transfer dough to clean counter, divide in half, and cover loosely with greased plastic. Pat 1 piece of dough (keep remaining piece covered) into 4-inch round. Working around circumference of dough, fold edges toward center until ball forms. Flip ball seam side down and, using your cupped hands, drag in small circles on counter until dough feels taut and round and all seams are secured on underside. (If dough sticks to your hands, lightly dust top of dough with flour.) Repeat with remaining piece of dough. Space dough balls 3 inches apart, cover loosely with greased plastic, and let rest for 1 hour.

5. Heat broiler for 10 minutes. Meanwhile, coat 1 dough ball generously with flour and place on well-floured counter. Using your fingertips, gently flatten into 8-inch round, leaving 1 inch of outer edge slightly thicker than center. Using your hands, gently stretch dough into 12-inch round, working along edge and giving disk quarter turns.

6. Transfer dough to well-floured pizza peel and stretch into 13-inch round. Using back of spoon or ladle, spread ½ cup tomato sauce in even layer over surface of dough, leaving ¼-inch border around edge. Sprinkle ¼ cup Parmesan evenly over sauce, followed by 1 cup mozzarella.

7. Slide pizza carefully onto baking steel or stone and return oven to 500 degrees. Bake until crust is well browned and cheese is bubbly and partially browned, 8 to 10 minutes, rotating pizza halfway through baking. Transfer pizza to wire rack and let cool for 5 minutes before slicing and serving. Heat broiler for 10 minutes. Repeat with remaining dough, sauce, Parmesan, and mozzarella, returning oven to 500 degrees when pizza is placed on steel or stone.

Variation

THIN-CRUST PIZZA WITH SAUSAGE, PEPPER, AND ONION

Cook 1 thinly sliced bell pepper, 1 thinly sliced onion, 1 tablespoon vegetable oil, and ¼ teaspoon table salt in 12-inch nonstick skillet over medium-high heat until slightly softened, about 5 minutes; transfer to paper towel–lined plate. Pinch 12 ounces Italian sausage, casings removed, into small pieces. Top pizzas with cooked vegetables and raw sausage before baking.

KEYS TO SUCCESS

- **Bread flour:** The high protein content gives the dough structure and makes it chewy.
- **A food processor:** Brings the dough together with minimal effort
- **Ice water:** Prevents the dough from overheating in the food processor
- **Cold fermentation:** Letting the dough rise in the refrigerator for a day develops the best flavor.
- **A baking steel or stone:** Absorbs and radiates heat and helps create a beautifully crisp crust

PIZZA AL TAGLIO WITH ARUGULA AND FRESH MOZZARELLA

Serves: 4 to 6
Total Time: 1¼ hours, plus 18 hours resting

RECIPE OVERVIEW Light yet substantial, pizza al taglio showcases a crisp, airy crust that gets topped like an open-faced sandwich. The key to the traditional thin, rectangular crust with a bubbly crumb and delicately crisp bottom is a dough with high hydration (a wet dough produces an airy crumb full of large and small holes) and long fermentation (proofing the dough twice ensures a tender, flexible crust with complex flavor). Folding the wet dough by hand is best. We bake the sauce-topped crust before adding arugula (tossed with olive oil), mozzarella, and Parmesan. The dough requires a 16- to 24-hour rest in the refrigerator. You'll get the crispiest texture by using high-protein King Arthur bread flour, but other bread flours also work. For the best results, weigh your flour and water. The bread flour should weigh 14⅔ ounces, regardless of which brand of flour is used. Anchovies give the sauce depth, so don't omit

CORE TECHNIQUE
Shaping a Thin-Crust Pizza

FLATTEN
Gently flatten the dough into an 8-inch round, leaving 1 inch of the outer edge thicker than the center. Gently stretch the dough into a 12-inch round, working along the edge and giving the disk quarter turns.

STRETCH
Transfer the dough to a well-floured pizza peel and stretch it into a 13-inch round.

SCIENCE LESSON Cold Fermentation

Fermentation is a key step that occurs after dough has been mixed and kneaded—the first bulk rise. In this stage, the yeast consumes sugars in the dough, producing not only carbon dioxide, which is critical to give the dough the proper rise, but also numerous flavor and aroma molecules. The typical bread recipe calls for fermenting the dough on the counter. But we often let the dough ferment in the refrigerator—usually for at least 24 to 48 hours and sometimes up to 72 hours—because we've found that we get more flavorful results. Here's why: Yeast left out at room temperature consumes sugars and leavens the batter rapidly. But then it's spent; it stops producing not just gas but also compounds that give bread flavor. At cool temperatures, yeast produces carbon dioxide more slowly, so refrigerating the batter allows yeast to leaven at a steady pace, providing more time for a more complex-tasting combination of flavor compounds to develop.

them. This recipe will yield more sauce than you'll need for one pizza; you can freeze the extra sauce for up to one month. Use the large holes of a box grater to shred the Parmesan.

Dough
- 2⅔ cups (14⅔ ounces) bread flour
- 1 teaspoon instant or rapid-rise yeast
- 1½ cups (12 ounces) water, room temperature
- 2 tablespoons extra-virgin olive oil
- 1¼ teaspoons table salt
- Vegetable oil spray

Sauce
- 1 (14.5-ounce) can whole peeled tomatoes, drained
- 1 tablespoon extra-virgin olive oil
- 2 anchovy fillets, rinsed
- 1 teaspoon dried oregano
- ½ teaspoon table salt
- ¼ teaspoon red pepper flakes

Topping
- ¼ cup extra-virgin olive oil, divided
- 4 ounces (4 cups) baby arugula
- 8 ounces fresh mozzarella cheese, torn into bite-size pieces (about 2 cups)
- 1½ ounces Parmesan cheese, shredded (½ cup)

1. **FOR THE DOUGH** Whisk flour and yeast together in medium bowl. Add room-temperature water and oil and stir with wooden spoon until shaggy mass forms and no dry flour remains. Cover bowl with plastic wrap and let sit for 10 minutes. Sprinkle salt over dough and mix until fully incorporated. Cover bowl with plastic and let dough rest for 20 minutes.

2. Using your wet hands, fold dough over itself by gently lifting and folding edge of dough toward middle. Turn bowl 90 degrees; fold again. Turn bowl and fold dough 4 more times (total of 6 turns). Cover bowl with plastic and let dough rest for 20 minutes. Repeat folding technique, turning bowl each time, until dough tightens slightly, 3 to 6 turns total. Cover bowl with plastic and let dough rest for 10 minutes.

3. Spray rimmed baking sheet (including rim) liberally with oil spray. Transfer dough to prepared sheet and spray top of dough lightly with oil spray. Gently press dough into 10 by 7-inch oval of even thickness. Cover sheet tightly with plastic and refrigerate for at least 16 hours or up to 24 hours.

4. **FOR THE SAUCE** While dough rests, process all ingredients in blender until smooth, 20 to 30 seconds. Transfer sauce to bowl, cover, and refrigerate until needed. (Sauce can be refrigerated for up to 1 week.)

5. **FOR THE TOPPING** Brush top of dough with 2 tablespoons oil. Using your fingertips, gently dimple dough into even thickness and stretch toward edges of sheet to form 15 by 11-inch oval. Spray top of dough lightly with oil spray; cover loosely with plastic; and let rest until slightly puffy, 1 to 1¼ hours.

6. Thirty minutes before baking, adjust oven rack to lowest position and heat oven to 450 degrees. Just before baking, use your fingertips to gently dimple dough into even thickness, pressing into corners of sheet. Using back of spoon or ladle, spread ½ cup sauce in even layer over surface of dough.

7. Drizzle 1 tablespoon oil over top of sauce and use back of spoon to spread evenly over surface. Transfer sheet to oven and bake until bottom of crust is evenly browned and top is lightly browned in spots, 20 to 25 minutes, rotating sheet halfway through baking. Transfer sheet to wire rack and let cool for 5 minutes. Run knife around rim of sheet to loosen pizza. Transfer pizza to cutting board and cut into 8 rectangles. Toss arugula with remaining 1 tablespoon oil in bowl. Top pizza with arugula, followed by mozzarella and Parmesan, and serve.

KEYS TO SUCCESS
- **Wet dough**: Creates an open, airy crumb
- **Refrigerator rest**: Develops a tender, flexible crust with complex flavor
- **Fold the dough**: Aids in gluten development

Making Pizza al Taglio

TRANSFER
Transfer the dough to a prepared sheet and spray the top of the dough lightly with vegetable oil spray. Gently press the dough into a 10 by 7-inch oval of even thickness.

DIMPLE
Brush the top of the dough with 2 tablespoons of oil. Gently dimple the dough into an even thickness and stretch it toward the edges of the sheet to form a 15 by 11-inch oval.

SAUCE
Using the back of a spoon or ladle, spread ½ cup of sauce in an even layer over the surface of the dough.

RESOURCES FOR PIZZA

AIM HIGH

Baking the pizza on the top rack—rather than the usual approach of placing it near the bottom of a home oven—means heat will hit the top of the pie, browning the toppings before the crust overcooks.

FREEZING PIZZA DOUGH

To make from-scratch pizza more convenient for weeknight dinners, keep a stash of homemade pizza dough in your freezer. Once the dough has fully risen and doubled in size, shape it into a ball, wrap it in plastic wrap coated in vegetable oil spray, place it in a zipper-lock bag, and freeze it for up to 2 weeks. The best way to defrost dough is to let it sit on the counter for a couple hours or in the refrigerator overnight. (Thawing pizza dough in a microwave or low oven isn't recommended, as it will dry out the dough.)

BAKING SHEET HACKS

You may want to make pizza night out of your own oven occasionally. It's rewarding and delicious. But that doesn't mean you want to be a regular pizzaiolo or have the kitchen space for a new hobby. You probably have baking sheets on hand. Here's how to substitute them for some pizza-specific equipment called for in this course.

Rimmed Baking Sheet You need tricks to mimic a pizza oven at home. A preheated baking steel or stone gets the pizza-cooking surface as hot as possible and retains that heat. If you don't have a heavy steel or stone, you can overturn a rimmed baking sheet and preheat it on the oven rack. It won't get the crust as crisp, but it does the job. Be sure to use a heavy sheet that won't warp in the hot oven.

Rimless Baking Sheet We prefer to use rimmed baking sheets for most tasks, from baking cookies to roasting vegetables. But rimless baking sheets (sometimes called cookie sheets) are also very handy to have around. You can dust one with flour, place your shaped and topped pizza dough on it, and use it in place of a pizza peel to slide dough onto the baking steel (or baking sheet). Make sure that it's big enough to fit the diameter of your dough rounds.

KNEADING IN A FOOD PROCESSOR

For many bread recipes we would caution against the rough treatment of a food processor, which can tear apart the strands of gluten that give bread structure and the ability to rise. But for pizzas, flatbreads, and other doughs, where we want chew but the structure is less important, we like to put it to use. Many of these doughs would require 15 to 20 minutes of traditional kneading in the stand mixer to become a shiny, elastic mass—but less than 2 minutes in the food processor. The only exceptions in this category are extremely wet doughs (with a hydration level of more than 75 percent) and doughs with very large yields. Here's how to ensure the best results.

Use metal blades Many food processors come with dull plastic blades meant to mimic the kneading action of a stand mixer. But we found that they tend to drag the dough or leave it stuck to the sides of the bowl, out of reach of the stubby blades. A sharp slicing action is essential to forming dough quickly, as the longer you process, the more you risk overheating the dough.

Use ice water The forceful action of a food processor creates friction, pumping a lot of heat into dough. To counteract this effect, it's important to use ice water to create a final dough with a temperature around 75 degrees. (Lower temperatures mean the dough will take longer to ferment; higher temperatures can kill yeast.)

COURSE
FOUR FANTASTIC FLATBREADS

NICOLE KONSTANTINAKOS

Every cuisine has its own bread culture, but flatbreads are shared nearly everywhere. Rolled or pressed thinner than loaves and typically chewy-tender, these breads are often practical in nature. They can serve as vessels for different foods, as pita does, or they can be full of vibrant flavor themselves, like Mana'eesh Za'atar. These are four flatbreads that you'll love to have in your rotation.

NICOLE'S PRO TIP: *Most flour is sold in paper bags, so to protect it from humidity and keep it fresh, I transfer my flour to airtight containers or zipper-lock bags. All-purpose and bread flours can be stored at room temperature for up to a year; whole-wheat flour, which contains natural oils that can turn rancid within a few months at room temperature, should be stored in the freezer.*

FLOUR TORTILLAS

Makes: twelve 8-inch tortillas
Total Time: 1 hour, plus 30 minutes chilling

RECIPE OVERVIEW Homemade flour tortillas far surpass store-bought versions, and the dough requires just a few ingredients (flour, salt, fat, and water). Traditionally, you'd need a tortilla press, but this version requires just a rolling pin and a skillet. A generous 6 tablespoons of fat makes the dough supple enough to roll with a pin. Tortillas are often made with lard, but we use vegetable shortening here. Warm water melts the shortening, which then coats the flour and prevents it from absorbing excess moisture. This results in less gluten development and yields tender tortillas. To make ten 10-inch tortillas, double the recipe, divide the dough evenly into 10 pieces, and roll each into a 10-inch round. Cooled tortillas can be layered between sheets of parchment paper, wrapped in plastic wrap, and refrigerated for up to 3 days. To reheat, place the tortillas on a plate, invert a second plate on top, and microwave until warm and soft, 60 to 90 seconds.

- 2¾ cups (13¾ ounces) all-purpose flour
- 1½ teaspoons salt
- 6 tablespoons (2½ ounces) vegetable shortening, cut into 6 pieces
- ¾ cup plus 2 tablespoons (7 ounces) warm tap water
- 1 teaspoon vegetable oil

1. Whisk flour and salt together in large bowl. Using your hands, rub shortening into flour mixture until mixture resembles coarse meal.

2. Stir warm water into flour mixture with wooden spoon until incorporated and dough comes together. Transfer dough to clean counter and knead by hand to form smooth, cohesive ball, about 30 seconds.

3. Divide dough into quarters and cut each quarter into 3 equal pieces (about 2 ounces each). Roll each piece into ball and transfer to plate. Cover with plastic wrap and refrigerate for at least 30 minutes or up to 3 days.

4. Working with 1 piece of dough at a time (keep remaining pieces covered), roll into 8-inch-round tortilla between two 12-inch squares of greased parchment paper.

5. Heat oil in 12-inch nonstick skillet over medium-high heat until shimmering. Meanwhile, remove top parchment from 1 tortilla and gently reshape edges. Using paper towels, carefully wipe out skillet, leaving thin film of oil on bottom. Flip tortilla onto your palm, then remove second piece of parchment and lay tortilla in skillet.

6. Cook until surface begins to bubble, about 1 minute. Flip tortilla and cook until puffed and bottom is spotty brown, about 1 minute. Transfer to plate and cover with dish towel. Repeat with remaining tortillas. Serve.

KEYS TO SUCCESS:
- **Use plenty of fat:** Makes the tortillas easy to roll
- **All-purpose flour:** Creates tortillas that are tender but don't fall apart

CHAPATI

Makes: 4 wraps
Total Time: 35 minutes, plus 30 minutes resting

RECIPE OVERVIEW Chapatis are a wheaty, unleavened Indian flatbread often used as a utensil for scooping up a number of sumptuous dishes. They're traditionally made from a finely ground hard wheat flour known as atta. We found that a combination of whole-wheat and all-purpose flour yields a more tender and elastic chapati than one made with only (comparatively coarse) American whole-wheat flour. To simulate the results achieved by cooking chapatis on the griddle known as a tava, we turned to a well-seasoned cast-iron skillet. This recipe can easily be doubled.

- ¾ cup (4⅛ ounces) whole-wheat flour
- ¾ cup (3¾ ounces) all-purpose flour
- 1 teaspoon table salt
- ½ cup warm water (110 degrees)
- 3 tablespoons plus 2 teaspoons vegetable oil, divided

1. Whisk whole-wheat flour, all-purpose flour, and salt together in bowl. Stir in water and 3 tablespoons oil until cohesive dough forms. Transfer dough to lightly floured counter and knead by hand to form smooth ball, 1 minute.

2. Divide dough into 4 pieces and cover with plastic wrap. Working with 1 piece at a time (keep remaining pieces covered), form into ball by stretching dough around your thumbs and pinching edges together so top is smooth. Place ball seam side down on clean counter and shape into smooth, taut ball. Place on plate seam side down, cover with plastic wrap, and let sit for 30 minutes. (Dough balls can be refrigerated for up to 3 days.)

3. Line rimmed baking sheet with parchment paper. Roll 1 dough ball into 9-inch round on lightly floured counter (keep remaining pieces covered). Transfer to prepared sheet and top with additional sheet of parchment. Repeat with remaining dough balls.

4. Heat 12-inch cast-iron or nonstick skillet over medium heat for 3 minutes. Add ½ teaspoon oil to skillet, then use paper towels to carefully wipe out skillet, leaving thin film of oil on bottom; skillet should be just smoking. (If using 12-inch nonstick skillet, heat ½ teaspoon oil over medium heat in skillet until shimmering, then wipe out skillet.)

5. Place 1 dough round in hot skillet and cook until dough is bubbly and bottom is browned in spots, about 2 minutes. Flip dough and cook until puffed and second side is spotty brown, 1 to 2 minutes. Transfer to clean plate and cover with dish towel to keep warm. Repeat with remaining dough rounds and oil. Serve. (Cooked wraps can be refrigerated for up to 3 days or frozen for up to 3 months. To freeze, layer wraps between parchment and store in zipper-lock bag. To serve, stack wraps on plate; cover with damp dish towel; and microwave until warm, 60 to 90 seconds.)

Making Pitas

PORTION
Transfer the dough to a lightly floured counter and divide it into quarters, then cut each quarter into halves (about 4 ounces each).

ROLL
Working with one piece of dough at a time (keep the remaining pieces covered), form the dough into a rough ball by stretching it around your thumbs and pinching the edges together so that the top is smooth.

MAKE ROUNDS
Working with one dough ball at a time, generously coat the dough ball with flour and place it on a well-floured counter. Press and roll the ball into an 8-inch round of even thickness.

TRANSFER
Gently transfer two dough rounds to a well-floured pizza peel. Slide the rounds onto a preheated baking steel or stone and bake them until a single air pocket is just beginning to form, about 1 minute.

FLIP
Quickly flip the pitas and continue to bake them until they're light golden brown, 1 to 2 minutes. Transfer the pitas to a plate and cover them with a dish towel. Repeat with the remaining dough, allowing the oven to reheat for 5 minutes.

PITAS

Makes: eight 8-inch pitas
Total Time: 1½ hours, plus 1 to 1½ hours rising

RECIPE OVERVIEW Pita breads vary dramatically depending on where they're made. The thin, wheaty versions, often called Arabic bread, hail from all over the Middle East. This version is Greek-style pita, with a pillowy interior ideal for sopping up sauces and dips, and a structure strong enough to support succulent gyro ingredients. These pitas are light and chewy from bread flour, but this can cause a bit of toughness. A quarter cup of olive oil in the dough tenderizes the crumb. While traditional Greek pita doesn't always have a pocket (it's often held like a taco and wrapped around sandwich fixings), we like having one for versatility. The tricks to getting the dough to puff up and create this pocket are a well-hydrated dough and a hot oven. When we place the pitas on a preheated baking steel or stone, the top and bottom exteriors begin to set. Meanwhile, all the water in the dough turns to steam inside, creating pressure outward. Our favorite baking steel measures 16 by 14 inches. If you have a smaller baking steel or stone, you may need to bake the pitas individually.

- 3⅔ cups (20⅛ ounces) bread flour
- 2½ teaspoons instant or rapid-rise yeast
- 2 teaspoons table salt
- 1⅓ cups (10⅔ ounces) water, room temperature
- ¼ cup (1¾ ounces) extra-virgin olive oil
- 2½ teaspoons sugar

1. Whisk flour, yeast, and salt together in bowl of stand mixer. Whisk water, oil, and sugar in 4-cup liquid measuring cup until sugar has dissolved. Using dough hook on low speed, slowly add water mixture to flour mixture and mix until cohesive dough starts to form and no dry flour remains, about 2 minutes, scraping down bowl as needed. Increase speed to medium-low and knead until dough is smooth and elastic and clears sides of bowl, about 8 minutes.

2. Transfer dough to lightly floured counter and knead by hand to form smooth, round ball, about 30 seconds. Place dough seam side down in lightly greased large bowl or container; cover tightly with plastic wrap; and let rise until doubled in size, 1 to 1½ hours.

3. Press down on dough to deflate. Transfer dough to lightly floured counter and divide into quarters, then cut each quarter into halves (about 4 ounces each); cover loosely with greased plastic.

4. Working with 1 piece of dough at a time (keep remaining pieces covered), form into rough ball by stretching dough around your thumbs and pinching edges together so top is smooth.

5. Generously coat 1 dough ball with flour and place on well-floured counter. Press and roll into 8-inch round of even thickness and cover loosely with greased plastic. (If dough resists stretching, let it relax for 10 to 20 minutes before trying to stretch it again.) Repeat with remaining balls. Let dough rounds rest for 20 minutes.

6. One hour before baking, adjust oven rack to lower-middle position, place baking steel or stone on rack, and heat oven to 500 degrees. Gently transfer 2 dough rounds to well-floured pizza peel. Slide rounds onto steel or stone and bake until single air pocket is just beginning to form, about 1 minute.

7. Working quickly, flip pitas using metal spatula and continue to bake until light golden brown, 1 to 2 minutes. Transfer pitas to plate and cover with dish towel. Repeat with remaining dough rounds in 3 batches, allowing oven to reheat for 5 minutes after each batch. Let pitas cool for 10 minutes before serving. (Pitas can be stored in a zipper-lock bag at room temperature for up to 5 days.)

> ### KEYS TO SUCCESS
> - **Use bread flour**: Gives the pitas pillowy chew
> - **Roll dough thin**: Ensures that heat from the baking steel or stone will reach the dough from bottom to top fast enough to puff it
> - **Flip pitas quickly**: Prevents overbrowning and overcrisping

MANA'EESH ZA'ATAR

Makes: three 9-inch flatbreads
Total Time: 1¼ hours, plus 2 to 2½ hours rising

RECIPE OVERVIEW In Lebanon, chewy mana'eesh are found both as a street food and as a specialty of dedicated bakeries. A man'oushe (the singular form) is typically topped with olive oil and za'atar, a combination of sumac; thyme; sesame seeds; and sometimes oregano, coriander, cumin, and salt. The basic dough ingredients are flour, water, salt, and yeast; some recipes include olive oil, which tenderizes the dough. To mimic the hottest ovens, we place a baking steel or stone on the middle rack and heat the oven at 500 degrees for a good hour before baking. The high heat encourages slight bubbles to form on top with delicate bits of char while the bottom turns an even golden brown.

Dough
- 2½ cups (12½ ounces) all-purpose flour
- 1½ teaspoons instant or rapid-rise yeast
- 1 teaspoon table salt
- ¾ cup plus 2 tablespoons cold water
- 2 tablespoons extra-virgin olive oil

Topping
- 3 tablespoons za'atar
- 3 tablespoons extra-virgin olive oil
- ½ teaspoon table salt

1. FOR THE DOUGH Process flour, yeast, and salt in food processor until combined, about 3 seconds. Combine cold water and oil in liquid measuring cup. With processor running, slowly add water mixture and process until dough forms sticky ball that clears sides of bowl, 30 to 60 seconds.

2. Transfer dough to clean counter and knead into cohesive ball, about 1 minute. Place dough in greased bowl. Cover bowl with plastic wrap and let dough rise at room temperature until almost doubled in size, 2 to 2½ hours. One hour before baking, adjust oven rack to middle position, set baking steel or stone on rack, and heat oven to 500 degrees.

3. FOR THE TOPPING Meanwhile, combine za'atar, oil, and salt in bowl.

4. On clean counter, divide dough into 3 equal pieces, about 7 ounces each. Shape each piece of dough into ball; cover loosely with plastic and let rest for 15 minutes.

5. Working with 1 dough ball at a time on lightly floured counter, coat lightly with flour and flatten into 6- to 7-inch disk using your fingertips.

6. Using rolling pin, roll dough into 9- to 10-inch circle. Slide dough round onto floured baking peel. Spread one-third of za'atar mixture (about 1½ tablespoons) over surface of dough with back of dinner spoon, stopping ½ inch from edge. Firmly tap dough all over with your fingertips, about 6 times. Slide dough onto baking steel or stone and bake until lightly bubbled and brown on top, about 5 minutes. Using baking peel, transfer man'oushe to wire rack. Repeat with remaining dough and za'atar mixture. Slice or tear and serve.

CHAPTER 12

DESSERTS

COURSES

564 CLASSIC DROP COOKIES

570 SLICE-AND-BAKE COOKIES

574 COOKIE CUTTER COOKIES

578 BROWNIES AND BLONDIES

584 EVERYDAY CAKES

588 BIRTHDAY CAKES

596 LEMON DESSERTS

602 SUMMER COBBLERS AND CRISPS

606 APPLE PIES AND TARTS

612 THANKSGIVING FAVORITES

618 COOL AND CREAMY DESSERTS

MORE TO EXPLORE

594 FROSTINGS AND WHIPPED CREAM

610 FOOLPROOF ALL-BUTTER PIE DOUGH

DESSERT BASICS

Baking is a science, but it doesn't have to be intimidating. There are a few simple ingredients that baking typically relies on, and once you understand how they work, you can mix them in countless ways to yield an incredible array of desserts. To read about flour, see page 507. To read about eggs, see pages 52–53.

SUGAR

As sweet treats, most desserts require sugar. But in addition to providing sweetness, sugar also affects the moisture level, texture, structure, and browning of baked goods. Sweeteners come in many forms, from white sugar to sticky honey or molasses. These are the ones we use in this chapter.

Granulated Sugar: White granulated sugar, which is made from either sugarcane or sugar beets, is the type of sugar used most often in our dessert recipes. It has a clean flavor and is evenly ground, with a loose texture that helps it incorporate well with butter during creaming. The sugar aerates the butter (by allowing it to retain small air bubbles) and dissolves easily into batters and doughs as well fruit and custard fillings.

Confectioners' Sugar: Also known as powdered sugar, confectioners' sugar is the most finely ground sugar. It's commonly used for dusting baked goods, but it's also great for sweetening glazes and frostings—its texture can go undetected, and it thickens and stabilizes these mixtures. Confectioners' sugar is also used in cookies where an ultratender texture is desired. You can approximate confectioners' sugar with this substitution: For 1 cup of confectioners' sugar, process 1 cup of granulated sugar with 1 tablespoon of cornstarch in a blender (not a food processor) until the mixture is ground fine, 30 to 40 seconds.

Brown Sugar: Brown sugar is granulated sugar that has been combined with molasses, giving it a deep caramel flavor. It adds complex flavor to baked goods and is also used when a moist, chewy texture is the goal. If it's important, an ingredient list will indicate "light" or "dark" brown sugar; if either can be used, the ingredient list will call simply for "brown sugar." Store brown sugar in an airtight container to prevent it from drying out. If brown sugar does become hard, place it in a bowl with a slice of sandwich bread, cover it, and microwave for 10 to 20 seconds to revive it.

To approximate 1 cup of light brown sugar, pulse 1 cup of granulated sugar with 1 tablespoon of mild molasses in a food processor until blended. Use 2 tablespoons of molasses for dark brown sugar. Brown sugar is so moist and clumpy that it must be packed into a measuring cup to get an accurate reading. To do this, use your fingers or the bottom of a smaller cup to tap and press the sugar into the cup.

Molasses: Molasses is a dark, thick syrup that's the by-product of sugarcane refining. It comes in three types: light, or mild; dark, or robust; and blackstrap. We prefer to use either light or dark molasses in baking and generally avoid using blackstrap molasses, which is bitter.

Maple Syrup: This syrup is made by boiling down sap from maple trees. Maple syrup has a high moisture level, so refrigerating it not only helps it retain flavor but also prevents microorganisms from growing. Once opened, it will keep for six months to a year in the refrigerator.

VANILLA EXTRACT

Vanilla is the flavoring used most commonly in desserts—not just in cookies and cakes but also in puddings, custards, and no-bake treats. It's sold in pure and imitation varieties. Which should you buy? If you want to buy just one bottle of extract for all kitchen tasks, our top choice is a real extract. Real vanilla has around 250 flavor compounds, while imitation vanilla has just one, so the real deal has a complexity that tasters appreciated when we tried it in cooked applications and in cold and creamy desserts. But if you use vanilla only for baking, we have to admit that there's not much of a difference between a well-made synthetic vanilla and the real thing (the flavor and aroma compounds in pure vanilla begin to bake off at higher temperatures, so the subtleties are lost).

BUTTER

Most of the recipes in this chapter use butter—rather than oil or shortening—for its satisfyingly rich flavor. But fat isn't just for flavor; the amount of fat in a recipe helps determine texture as well. Typically, the more fat you add, the more tender your baked goods will be—and sometimes, the more crumbly: Fat coats flour proteins, inhibiting their ability to form a strong gluten network.

Use Unsalted Butter

Our recipes call for unsalted butter. That's because the amount of salt in salted butter varies from brand to brand. This is problematic for a couple reasons: First, it makes it impossible to know how much salt to call for in a recipe. Second, salted butter contains more water than unsalted does, and the excess water can affect gluten development.

Storing Butter

Butter can pick up off-flavors and turn rancid when kept in the refrigerator for longer than a month, since its fatty acids oxidize. For longer storage (up to four months), freeze it. And because butter quickly picks up odors and flavors, we like to slip the sticks into a zipper-lock bag, whether they're stored in the refrigerator or in the freezer.

Temperature of Ingredients

The temperature of certain ingredients—especially butter—can be the key to success when baking. Room-temperature eggs and milk are more easily incorporated than cold. The additional mixing necessary to incorporate cold ingredients may adversely affect the texture of the finished baked good. Here are our techniques for achieving the right butter temperature for a recipe.

 CHILLED BUTTER (ABOUT 35 DEGREES)	 SOFTENED BUTTER (65 TO 67 DEGREES)	 MELTED AND COOLED BUTTER (85 TO 90 DEGREES)
Method	**Method**	**Method**
Cut butter into small pieces; freeze until very firm, 10 to 15 minutes.	Let butter sit at room temperature for 30 minutes (or put in zipper-lock bag and pound to desired consistency).	Melt butter in saucepan or microwave-safe bowl; let cool for 5 minutes.
How to Test It	**How to Test It**	**How to Test It**
When pressed with your finger, butter should be cold and unyielding.	Stick should easily bend without breaking and give slightly when pressed.	Butter should be fluid and slightly warm.
How to Use It	**How to Use It**	**How to Use It**
Cut into flour to create flaky layers, as with pie dough.	Mix into batters using creaming or reverse-creaming method (see page 562).	Incorporate into recipes for chewy or thin cookies (melted butter encourages spread) or use to bring together ingredients for crisp toppings or pat-in-the-pan crusts.

THE BUTTER BREAKDOWN

Butter is an emulsion of fat, water, and milk solids (and it's a great multitasker).

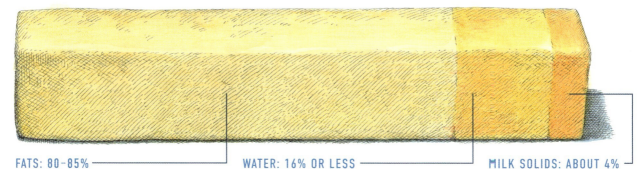

FATS: 80–85% — WATER: 16% OR LESS — MILK SOLIDS: ABOUT 4% (proteins, lactose, and salts)

DESSERTS | 559

DESSERT BASICS

THE DESSERT TOOLKIT

The mixing bowls, wooden spoons, and measuring cups and spoons on pages 13–14 are as valuable in baking as they are in cooking. And you'll find all the pans used in this chapter listed on pages 11–12. But making cookies, cakes, and pies is also benefited by some slightly more specialized tools that, while not all essential, will make your work easier and more precise. The ones we reach for most often are here.

Digital Scale
When baking, we prefer to weigh dry ingredients on a digital scale for consistent results.

Adjustable Measuring Cup
Sticky ingredients such as peanut butter, molasses, and honey can be difficult to scrape out of liquid measuring cups. An adjustable measuring cup has a plunger-like bottom that you set to the correct measurement and then push up to extract the ingredient.

Bench Scraper
This basic tool is handy for transferring dough from one surface to another and for cutting dough into pieces.

Bowl Scraper
The best way to remove sticky dough from the bowl is with a scraper. This handheld spatula is curved, with enough grip to scrape the bowl clean and enough rigidity to move heavy dough easily.

Offset Spatula
For frosting a cake, there's no better tool than an offset spatula, which is ideal for both scooping and spreading frosting.

Portion Scoop
A spring-loaded ice cream scoop is helpful for portioning drop-cookie dough into even-size mounds.

Rolling Pin
There are many styles of rolling pins, but we prefer the French-style wood pins without handles. These come straight and tapered; we tend to reach for straight pins, which make achieving even dough thickness and rolling out large disks easy.

Cookie Cutters
We prefer metal cookie cutters to plastic ones because the former are sharper and more likely to make clean cuts. The cutting edges should be thin and sharp. Look for cookie cutters that are at least 1 inch tall.

Ceramic Pie Weights
Many home bakers use rice, sugar, or coins as pie weights. We've had better luck with ceramic weights: A full 4 cups (more than 2 pounds) completely fills an aluminum foil–lined pie shell, ensuring that the dough's edges remain high and the bottom turns out crisp, flaky, and golden.

Pastry Brush
We use a pastry brush to paint crusts with water or egg wash before they enter the oven.

Parchment Paper
Lining baking sheets and cake pans with parchment paper is a simple way to keep dough from sticking and ensure that baked cookies and cakes release effortlessly. We prefer parchment to reusable silicone mats, which can transfer flavors and stain over time. Look for precut sheets instead of rolls—they eliminate the need to tear.

Stand Mixer
With its hands-free operation, numerous attachments, and strong mixing arm, a good stand mixer is a worthwhile investment if you plan on baking regularly.

Food Processor
A food processor is ideal for mixing pie dough and even some cookie doughs, cake batters, and frostings—not to mention chopping nuts.

PREPARING PANS

Cookies: What Pan to Use

All the cookie recipes in this book call for baking the cookies on a sturdy rimmed baking sheet. Rimless "cookie sheets" will also work; however, cookies baked on a rimless pan brown more quickly and can finish baking several minutes before those baked on a rimmed pan. Why? Heat rises from the element at the bottom of the oven and circulates in currents to warm the entire chamber. A rimmed baking sheet's raised edges divert hot-air currents from the cookies to the top of the oven; a rimless sheet allows hot air to immediately sweep over the cookies. Using flimsy sheets of either type will result in overbaked cookies.

Cakes: Ensuring That Your Cakes Come Out Clean

1. TRACE A CIRCLE
Place the cake pan on a sheet of parchment paper and trace around the bottom of the pan. Cut out a parchment circle.

2. GREASE PAN
Evenly spray the bottom and sides of the pan with vegetable oil spray or rub with butter.

3. PARCHMENT, GREASE, AND FLOUR
Fit the parchment into the pan, grease the parchment, and then sprinkle it with several tablespoons of flour (or cocoa). Shake and rotate the pan to coat it evenly, then shake out the excess.

Parchment Paper versus Reusable Pan Liners

We baked a variety of foods on five nonstick liners made from silicone, silicone-reinforced woven fiberglass, and nonstick fiberglass to see if any could impress us more than a sheet of parchment paper. The liners fell into two classes: lightweights and heavyweights. Baked goods made on the lighter liners had bottoms with spotty browning; heavier mats imparted plastic and chemical flavors to cookies and biscuits. One acceptable liner was the DeMarle Silpat Silicone Baking Mat. However, all these mats stain over time and can transfer flavors from previous uses. Bottom line: We prefer parchment.

Cool Baking Sheets between Batches

While it's tempting to save time, don't put raw cookie dough onto a hot baking sheet: The dough begins to melt before it reaches the oven, so the cookies can spread too much and have dark bottoms and thin edges. Instead, after baking one tray of cookies, run the hot sheet under cold water to cool it and then wipe it dry. For even more efficiency, load a second sheet of parchment paper with dough while the first batch bakes. When the first cookies come out of the oven, remove them, parchment and all, onto a cooling rack. Once the baking sheet is cooled, the next batch will be ready to go.

Pie Plates in a Pinch

Disposable aluminum pie plates can be convenient, but they have thin walls that don't hold or transfer heat as efficiently as our preferred pie plate (see page 11), so crusts don't brown or crisp as quickly. Extending the baking time can produce comparable results. For empty crusts, increase the time that the crust bakes with weights by up to 10 minutes, or until it's golden brown and crisp. For filled double-crust pies, increase the time by up to 10 minutes, covering the top of the pie with foil if it starts to get too dark. Be sure to bake pies in aluminum pie plates on a baking sheet—this ensures a well-browned bottom crust and provides stability.

BAKING BASICS

MEASURING INGREDIENTS

It might sound obvious, but measuring ingredients takes care: Baking is a science, and inexact measurements will yield inferior results. We provide weights for dry ingredients in our recipes and use a digital scale to weigh them; we strongly recommend that you do, too. But if you're dead set on measuring these ingredients by volume, there's a way to increase your accuracy: the dip-and-sweep method. Dip the measuring cup into the flour, sugar, or other dry ingredient and sweep away the excess with a straight-edged object, such as the back of a butter knife.

MIXING METHODS

Most cakes share the same basic ingredients; it's the way those ingredients are combined that makes all the difference in the style and crumb of the final product.

Creaming

If you know just one mixing method by name, it's likely the creaming method. Creaming requires beating butter and sugar together until light and fluffy before adding the remaining ingredients. The tiny pockets of air created during the process get filled by the leavener in the recipe and help cakes rise. As in Lemon Bundt Cake (page 601), creaming creates a fluffy crumb and a cake with good height.

Reverse Creaming

While creaming butter and sugar is probably the most common first mixing step in the world of baking, this method isn't used all that much for layer cakes. When we want a tender but sturdy cake with an ultrafine, downy crumb, we turn to reverse creaming. This process starts with combining all the dry ingredients, after which softened butter is incorporated, followed by any liquid ingredients. During reverse creaming, the butter coats the flour particles, therefore minimizing gluten development for a tender, fine crumb. Just as important, since the butter isn't beaten with sugar, less air is incorporated, which translates to less rise and a sturdier cake—perfect for Confetti Cake (page 592), where the layers are stacked and frosted.

Creaming versus Reverse Creaming

One technique isn't better than the other, but each results in a cake with a unique texture and shape. A creamed cake will have a higher rise with a domed top. A cake made using the reverse-creaming method will have a flat top and a finer crumb—ideal for layering and frosting.

CREAMING Batters made with traditional creaming have significant air bubbles and a relatively strong gluten network.

REVERSE CREAMING In batters made with reverse creaming, there are very few air bubbles and significantly less gluten is formed.

CREAMING

REVERSE CREAMING

ADDING EGGS TO BATTERS

A common step after creaming butter and sugar is to mix in the eggs one at a time. Eggs and butter don't mix naturally (butter is at least 80 percent fat, while eggs contain lots of water), so this gradual approach gives the mixture time to thicken and emulsify, preventing misshapen cookies or dense cakes.

BAKING

What Rack to Bake On
We develop baking recipes with oven racks set to specific positions, so when you use our recipes, be sure to adjust the racks as directed. When we're baking just one sheet of cookies at a time, for example, we nearly always bake them on the middle rack. When we're baking two sheets at a time, we use the upper-middle and lower-middle positions. The middle of the oven is always a safe bet; the closer to the bottom of the oven, the browner the bottoms of your cookies will be relative to the tops.

Oven Placement
AVOID UNEVEN BAKING Baking two sheets of cookies at a time may be convenient, but the cookies on the top sheet often end up browner around the edges than the ones on the bottom sheet. If you have two sheets in the oven, you should switch their positions halfway through baking. For cookies with an especially finicky texture, we call for baking the cookies one sheet at a time so that heat circulates around the baking sheet evenly for the entire baking time.

STAGGER When baking with more than one cake pan at the same time, allow for some space between the pans and between the pans and the oven walls. Also, stagger their placement in the oven so that the air can circulate and the cakes will bake evenly.

ROTATE Even calibrated ovens have hot and cool spots, with temperatures falling within a 50-degree range. Cookies, pies, tarts, and all but the most delicate cakes should be rotated during baking to achieve even browning and baking. The halfway point or shortly thereafter is generally a good time to rotate. If you have one pan on the bottom rack and another on the top, switch their positions and, in addition, turn each one 180 degrees.

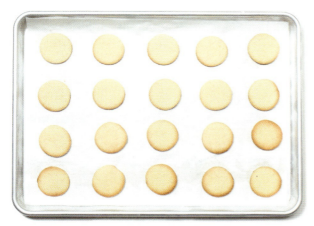

Not Rotating = Uneven Baking

Testing for Doneness
FOR PIES Doneness is usually gauged by color. Baked only until pale blond, pastry is less than crisp and has a floury taste. When baked until a deep nut brown—which is our preference—the flavor is fuller and the texture is crisp and flaky.

FOR CAKES A cake tester or toothpick inserted into the center of the cake should come out clean. If batter clings to the tester or toothpick, the cake needs more time in the oven. Fully baked cakes will feel springy and resilient when you gently press the center with your fingers. If an impression is left in the surface, it's not done.

FOR COOKIES For a soft, chewy texture, cookies are best removed from the oven when they appear to be a bit underbaked. Cooling the sheet of cookies on a wire rack allows them to set.

COOLING

Different baked goods require different cooling methods to ensure that they set up properly. Most basic cookies need only a short rest on the baking sheet, while many pies require around 4 hours of cooling time. Most baked goods should be cooled on a wire rack where air can circulate around them. Be sure to follow the cooling instructions given in the recipe.

WITH PIES, IT PAYS TO BE PATIENT

Not only do pies take some time to prepare (although, in this book, the methods are simple), they also need to cool completely. In fact, most pies require around 4 hours of cooling time. Pie is great warm, so why would you wait? The thickeners are activated in the oven, but the pie filling gels further with cooling. If you cut into a pie before it's set, the filling will pour out of the pie rather than slice cleanly. So while the wait may seem punishingly long, you can see below that you'll be sorry if you don't wait! If you want warm pie, simply heat up slices.

Apple pie sliced after 1 hour   **Apple pie sliced after 4 hours**

COURSE
CLASSIC DROP COOKIES

JACK BISHOP

Drop cookies are some of the simplest cookies to make. Though this style of cookie gets its name from the process of dropping the dough from a spoon onto the baking sheet, we prefer to measure each portion with a tablespoon or portion scoop and then roll the dough into a ball for even sizing—and even baking. In this course you'll learn all the essentials for turning out perfect drop cookies, from how to mix the dough and what size to make the dough balls (larger balls of dough generally yield cookies with a chewier texture) to the best way to space them on the baking sheet and how to know when your cookies are ready to come out of the oven.

JACK'S PRO TIP: *If you like chewy cookies, go big. Large balls of dough produce the best cookies, with crispy edges and chewy middles.*

PERFECT CHOCOLATE CHIP COOKIES

Makes: 16 cookies
Total Time: 1 hour

RECIPE OVERVIEW There's no question that the chocolate chip cookie is the most iconic American treat. While both crispy cookies and cakey ones have their place, we love versions reminiscent of the classic Toll House cookie, with crisp edges and a chewy interior. For a reliably moist and chewy cookie with crisp edges and deep butterscotch notes, melt and then brown your butter. Melting butter makes its water content available to interact with the flour, thus creating more gluten and a chewier texture. Continuing to cook the butter until it browns creates deep caramel notes, as does dissolving the sugar in the melted butter. Use two egg yolks but only one white for richness without a cakey texture. Studded with gooey chocolate and boasting a complex toffee flavor, these are chocolate chip cookies perfected. Light brown sugar can be used in place of the dark, but the cookies won't be as full-flavored.

- 1¾ cups (8¾ ounces) all-purpose flour
- ½ teaspoon baking soda
- 14 tablespoons unsalted butter, divided
- ¾ cup packed (5¼ ounces) dark brown sugar
- ½ cup (3½ ounces) granulated sugar
- 2 teaspoons vanilla extract
- 1 teaspoon table salt
- 1 large egg plus 1 large yolk
- 1¼ cups (7½ ounces) semisweet or bittersweet chocolate chips
- ¾ cup pecans or walnuts, toasted and chopped (optional)

1. Adjust oven rack to middle position and heat oven to 375 degrees. Line 2 baking sheets with parchment paper. Whisk flour and baking soda together in bowl.

2. Melt 10 tablespoons butter in 10-inch skillet over medium-high heat. Continue to cook, swirling skillet constantly, until butter is dark golden brown and has nutty aroma, 1 to 3 minutes. Transfer browned butter to large bowl and stir in remaining 4 tablespoons butter until melted. Whisk in brown sugar, granulated sugar, vanilla, and salt until incorporated. Whisk in egg and yolk until smooth and no lumps remain, about 30 seconds.

3. Let mixture stand for 3 minutes, then whisk for 30 seconds. Repeat process of resting and whisking 2 more times; mixture should be thick, smooth, and shiny. Using rubber spatula, stir in flour mixture until just combined, about 1 minute. Stir in chocolate chips and pecans, if using.

4. Working with 3 tablespoons dough at a time, roll into balls and space them 2 inches apart on prepared sheets. (Dough balls can be frozen for up to 1 month; bake frozen dough balls in 300-degree oven for 30 to 35 minutes.)

5. Bake cookies, 1 sheet at a time, until golden brown and edges have begun to set but centers are still soft and puffy, 10 to 14 minutes, rotating sheet halfway through baking. Transfer baking sheet to wire rack. Let cookies cool completely before serving.

KEYS TO SUCCESS

- **Use a combination of sugars:** Brown sugar enhances flavor and contributes chewiness; white sugar ensures crisp edges.
- **Melt the butter:** Frees up its water content and allows it to interact with the flour, resulting in gluten development (and good chew)
- **Brown the butter:** For rich, nutty flavor (For more on browning butter, see page 567.)
- **Let it rest:** Gives the sugar time to dissolve in the liquids; results in deep toffee flavor

CORE TECHNIQUE
Making Drop Cookies

LINE BAKING SHEETS
Line each baking sheet with a piece of parchment paper.

ROLL INTO BALLS
Roll the specified amount of dough between your palms into a round ball.

SPACE EVENLY
Place the dough balls on the prepared baking sheets, making sure to leave the specified space between each ball.

UNDERBAKE SLIGHTLY
Bake the cookies as directed until the edges are set and firm but the centers are still soft and puffy.

LET COOL ON BAKING SHEET
Transfer the rimmed baking sheet to a wire rack and let the cookies cool until they're firm, about 10 minutes.

BROWN SUGAR COOKIES

Makes: 24 cookies
Total Time: 1¼ hours, plus 20 minutes cooling

RECIPE OVERVIEW Swapping out granulated sugar for robust brown sugar turns up the volume on the classic sugar cookie. Dark brown sugar gives the richest caramel notes, which are underscored with a full tablespoon of vanilla and balanced by a dash of salt. Browning the butter contributes butterscotch and toffee notes that complement the brown sugar's molasses flavor. To achieve a nice crackly top, use both baking soda and baking powder, which will yield cookies with a finer crumb. Just a little white sugar prevents clumping. The right baking technique is crucial here: Bake the cookies one sheet at a time and pull them from the oven when a light touch from a finger produces a slight indentation in the surface of the cookie. Use fresh, moist brown sugar for cookies with the best texture.

- 14 tablespoons unsalted butter, divided
- 2 cups plus 2 tablespoons (10⅔ ounces) all-purpose flour
- ½ teaspoon baking soda
- ¼ teaspoon baking powder
- 1¾ cups packed (12¼ ounces) dark brown sugar, plus ¼ cup for rolling
- ½ teaspoon table salt
- 1 large egg plus 1 large yolk
- 1 tablespoon vanilla extract
- ¼ cup (1¾ ounces) granulated sugar for rolling

1. Melt 10 tablespoons butter in 10-inch skillet over medium-high heat. Continue to cook, swirling skillet constantly, until butter is dark golden brown and has nutty aroma, 1 to 3 minutes. Transfer browned butter to large bowl and stir in remaining 4 tablespoons butter until melted; let cool for 15 minutes.

2. Meanwhile, adjust oven rack to middle position and heat oven to 350 degrees. Line 2 baking sheets with parchment paper. Whisk flour, baking soda, and baking powder together in bowl.

3. Whisk 1¾ cups brown sugar and salt into cooled browned butter until smooth and no lumps remain, about 30 seconds. Whisk in egg and yolk and vanilla until incorporated, about 30 seconds. Using rubber spatula, stir in flour mixture until just combined, about 1 minute.

4. Combine remaining ¼ cup brown sugar and granulated sugar in shallow dish. Working with 2 tablespoons dough at a time, roll into balls, then roll in sugar to coat; space dough balls 2 inches apart on prepared sheets. (Dough balls can be frozen for up to 1 month; bake frozen dough balls on 1 baking sheet set inside second sheet in 325-degree oven for 20 to 25 minutes.)

5. Bake cookies, 1 sheet at a time, until edges have begun to set but centers are still soft, puffy, and cracked (cookies will look raw between cracks and seem underdone), 12 to 14 minutes, rotating sheet halfway through baking. Let cookies cool on sheet for 5 minutes, then transfer to wire rack. Let cookies cool completely before serving.

KEYS TO SUCCESS

- **Brown the butter:** Develops a range of butterscotch and toffee flavors
- **Use two leaveners:** Baking soda helps create a craggy top; baking powder ensures a moderately fine crumb.
- **Bake one sheet at a time:** Allows for even heat distribution and ensures that every cookie has the same texture

CORE TECHNIQUE: Browning Butter

LET IT FOAM
Put the butter in a heavy skillet or saucepan with a light interior. Cook over medium-high heat, swirling occasionally, until the butter melts and begins to foam.

SWIRL AND WATCH
Continue to cook, swirling the skillet constantly, until the butter is dark golden brown and has a nutty aroma, 1 to 3 minutes.

COOL QUICKLY
Immediately transfer the browned butter to a large heatproof bowl to stop the cooking process.

Building Big Brown-Sugar Flavor

Dark brown sugar was an obvious place to begin our efforts to create a cookie with bold flavor. A whole tablespoon of vanilla helped, but it was browning the butter that had the greatest impact on the flavor of these cookies.

Dark Brown Sugar | Lots of Vanilla | Browned Butter

MOLASSES SPICE COOKIES

Makes: 24 cookies
Total Time: 1½ hours, plus 20 minutes cooling

RECIPE OVERVIEW The best molasses spice cookies combine a homespun crinkled appearance with a chewy texture and a deep molasses flavor complemented by the warmth and bite of spices. You can use light or dark molasses; the dark variety will have a stronger presence. (Avoid blackstrap molasses, which can be overpowering and bitter.) When rolling the balls of dough, dip your hands in water to prevent sticking; this also helps the granulated sugar adhere to the dough balls. For the best texture and appearance, bake the cookies one sheet at a time and pull them from the oven when they still look substantially underdone. (They will continue to bake and harden as they cool, with the insides remaining soft and moist.)

- 2¼ cups (11¼ ounces) all-purpose flour
- 1 teaspoon baking soda
- 1½ teaspoons ground cinnamon
- 1½ teaspoons ground ginger
- ½ teaspoon ground cloves
- ¼ teaspoon ground allspice
- ¼ teaspoon pepper
- ¼ teaspoon table salt
- 12 tablespoons unsalted butter, softened
- ⅓ cup packed (2⅓ ounces) dark brown sugar
- ⅓ cup (2⅓ ounces) granulated sugar, plus ½ cup for rolling
- 1 large egg yolk
- 1 teaspoon vanilla extract
- ½ cup mild or robust molasses

1. Adjust oven rack to middle position and heat oven to 375 degrees. Line 2 rimmed baking sheets with parchment paper. Whisk flour, baking soda, cinnamon, ginger, cloves, allspice, pepper, and salt together in bowl.

2. Using stand mixer fitted with paddle, beat butter, brown sugar, and ⅓ cup granulated sugar on medium speed until pale and fluffy, about 3 minutes. Reduce speed to medium-low; add egg yolk and vanilla; and beat until combined, about 30 seconds. Beat in molasses until incorporated, about 30 seconds, scraping down bowl as needed. Reduce speed to low and slowly add flour mixture until combined, about 30 seconds (dough will be soft). Give dough final stir by hand to ensure no flour pockets remain.

3. Spread remaining ½ cup granulated sugar in shallow dish. Working with 2 tablespoons dough at a time, roll dough into balls with your dampened hands, then roll in sugar to coat; space dough balls 2 inches apart on prepared sheets. (Dough balls can be frozen for up to 1 month; bake frozen dough balls in 300-degree oven for 30 to 35 minutes.)

4. Bake cookies, 1 sheet at a time, until edges are set but centers are still soft, puffy, and cracked (cookies will look raw between cracks and seem underdone), 10 to 12 minutes, rotating sheet halfway through baking. Let cookies cool on sheet for 10 minutes. Serve warm or transfer to wire rack and let cool completely.

Variations

MOLASSES SPICE COOKIES WITH DARK RUM GLAZE
Whisk 1 cup confectioners' sugar and 3 tablespoons dark rum in bowl until smooth. Drizzle glaze over cooled cookies and let dry for 10 to 15 minutes before serving.

MOLASSES SPICE COOKIES WITH ORANGE ESSENCE
Add 1 teaspoon grated orange zest to dough with molasses in step 2. Process ⅔ cup granulated sugar with 2 teaspoons grated orange zest in food processor until fragrant, about 10 seconds; substitute orange sugar for granulated sugar when rolling in step 3.

> **KEYS TO SUCCESS**
> - **Use mild or robust molasses:** Blackstrap is bitter
> - **Use a blend of vanilla, warm spices, and black pepper:** Holds its own against the bold molasses flavor

THIN AND CRISPY OATMEAL COOKIES

Makes: 24 cookies
Total Time: 1¼ hours, plus 20 minutes cooling

RECIPE OVERVIEW You may think an oatmeal cookie should be moist and chewy, but thin, crispy versions can be irresistible, allowing the buttery oat flavor to stand out. To achieve this texture, scale back the sugar—this reduces moisture so that even the center of the cookies develop crunch. To ensure that the cookies are crisp throughout, press them flat and bake them, one sheet at a time, until they're fully set and evenly browned from edge to center. Place them on the baking sheet in three rows, with three cookies in the outer rows and two cookies in the center row. We developed this recipe using Quaker Old Fashioned Rolled Oats. Other old-fashioned oats can be substituted, but the cookies may spread more. Do not use quick or instant oats here.

- 1 cup (5 ounces) all-purpose flour
- ¾ teaspoon baking powder
- ½ teaspoon baking soda
- ½ teaspoon table salt
- 14 tablespoons unsalted butter, softened but still cool
- 1 cup (7 ounces) granulated sugar
- ¼ cup packed (1¾ ounces) light brown sugar
- 1 large egg
- 1 teaspoon vanilla extract
- 2½ cups (7½ ounces) old-fashioned rolled oats

1. Adjust oven rack to middle position and heat oven to 350 degrees. Line 3 baking sheets with parchment paper. Whisk flour, baking powder, baking soda, and salt together in bowl.

2. Using stand mixer fitted with paddle, beat butter, granulated sugar, and brown sugar at medium-low speed until just combined, about 20 seconds. Increase speed to medium and continue to beat until pale and fluffy, about 1 minute, scraping down bowl as needed. Add egg and vanilla and beat on medium-low until fully incorporated, about 30 seconds, scraping down bowl as needed. Reduce speed to low; add flour mixture; and mix until just incorporated and smooth, about 10 seconds. With mixer running, gradually add oats and mix until well incorporated, about 20 seconds. Give dough final stir by hand to ensure no flour pockets remain and ingredients are evenly distributed.

3. Working with 2 tablespoons dough at a time, roll into balls and space them 2½ inches apart on prepared sheets. Using your fingertips, gently press each ball to ¾-inch thickness.

4. Bake, 1 sheet at a time, until cookies are deep golden brown; edges are crisp; and centers yield to slight pressure when pressed, 13 to 16 minutes, rotating sheet halfway through baking. Transfer sheet to wire rack and let cookies cool completely before serving.

Variations

SALTY THIN AND CRISPY OATMEAL COOKIES

We prefer the texture of larger-grained flake sea salt here, such as Maldon or fleur de sel. You can also use kosher salt, but reduce the amount sprinkled on to ¼ teaspoon.

Reduce amount of salt in dough to ¼ teaspoon. Lightly sprinkle ½ teaspoon flake sea salt evenly over flattened dough balls before baking.

THIN AND CRISPY COCONUT OATMEAL COOKIES

Decrease oats to 2 cups and add 1½ cups sweetened flaked coconut to dough with oats in step 2.

THIN AND CRISPY ORANGE-ALMOND OATMEAL COOKIES

Beat 2 teaspoons grated orange zest with butter and sugars in step 2. Decrease oats to 2 cups and add 1 cup coarsely chopped toasted almonds to dough with oats in step 2.

> ### KEYS TO SUCCESS
> - **Cream the butter:** Makes for a crispier cookie
> - **Press the dough balls flat, then bake:** Encourages even spread

> ### More Leavener for Thinner Cookies
> It may sound counterintuitive, but doubling the usual amount of leavener (we used both baking powder and baking soda) is the key to crispiness in oatmeal cookies. The amplified dose creates big bubbles that first help the dough rise, then combine and burst, resulting in a flat cookie.

COURSE
SLICE-AND-BAKE COOKIES

NICOLE KONSTANTINAKOS

Slice-and-bake cookies—sometimes known as icebox cookies—are an old-fashioned favorite. These cookies are typically thin, with a sandy, shortbread-like texture, and their beauty lies in their simplicity. We'll explain how to roll the dough into an evenly shaped log (wrapping it in plastic helps hold its shape) and then chill it so that you can slice perfectly shaped cookies every time. Unlike drop cookies, slice-and-bake cookies don't contain any leaveners—this means they don't spread as much, so you can fit more on one sheet. These cookies are delicious when they're plain and simple, but they can easily be dressed up a bit with a nut garnish or a dip in melted chocolate.

NICOLE'S PRO TIP: *When slicing chilled dough logs into rounds, I like to roll the log about a quarter turn after each slice, pressing gently on the log as I roll it, to ensure that it maintains an even shape and each slice comes out perfectly round.*

PECAN SANDIES

Makes: 32 cookies
Total Time: 1 hour, plus 2 hours chilling and 30 minutes cooling

RECIPE OVERVIEW Pecan sandies are buttery shortbread cookies with a tender but crisp texture, a sandy melt-in-the-mouth character, and loads of nutty pecan flavor. Because it's in the name, nailing the sandy texture is key. Some recipes try to achieve that sandiness by substituting vegetable oil for butter; while oil does help limit the amount of air that forms in the cookie dough, it also makes for bland flavor and greasy cookies, so it's best to stick with butter. For nice praline flavor—another hallmark of this cookie—as well as a tender crumb, use a combination of light brown sugar and confectioners' sugar. Toasting the pecans and then grinding them into a flour ensures rich nutty flavor in every bite. For a finishing touch, place a single pecan half in the center of each cookie to provide a visual hint of the flavor within.

- 2 cups pecans, toasted, divided
- ½ cup packed (3½ ounces) light brown sugar
- ¼ cup (1 ounce) confectioners' sugar
- 1½ cups (7½ ounces) all-purpose flour
- ¼ teaspoon table salt
- 12 tablespoons unsalted butter, cut into ½-inch pieces and chilled
- 1 large egg yolk

1. Reserve 32 unbroken pecan halves for garnish. Process brown sugar, confectioners' sugar, and remaining pecans in food processor until pecans are finely ground, about 20 seconds. Add flour and salt and process until combined, about 10 seconds.

2. Scatter butter over top and process until mixture resembles damp sand and rides up sides of bowl, about 20 seconds. With processor running, add egg yolk and process until dough forms rough ball, about 20 seconds.

3. Transfer dough to counter, knead briefly, and divide in half. Roll each dough half into 6-inch log. Wrap logs tightly in plastic wrap and refrigerate until firm, at least 2 hours or up to 3 days.

4. Adjust oven racks to upper-middle and lower-middle positions and heat oven to 325 degrees. Line 2 baking sheets with parchment paper.

5. Working with 1 dough log at a time, slice chilled dough into ⅜-inch-thick rounds and space them 1 inch apart on prepared sheets. Gently press pecan half in center of each round.

6. Bake cookies until edges are golden brown, 20 to 25 minutes, switching and rotating sheets halfway through baking. Let cookies cool on sheets for 3 minutes, then transfer to wire rack. Let cookies cool completely before serving.

Variation
ALMOND SANDIES
Substitute 2 cups whole blanched almonds, toasted, for pecans. Add ¼ teaspoon almond extract to dough with egg yolk in step 2.

KEYS TO SUCCESS

- **Use two sugars:** Light brown sugar contributes caramel notes; confectioners' sugar gives the cookies a tender texture.
- **Grind the pecans fine:** Makes for rich, fine-textured sandy cookies
- **Ditch the egg white:** Prevents the dough from becoming too sticky

CORE TECHNIQUE
Forming Slice-and-Bake Cookies

DIVIDE AND ROLL
After mixing, transfer the dough to the counter and roll it into a log—the length will be specified in the recipe. (Some recipes may call for dividing the dough into pieces first.)

TWIST AND CHILL
Wrap the log of dough tightly in plastic wrap and twist the ends to help the dough hold its shape. Try to square off the ends as much as possible. Refrigerate the wrapped dough log until it's firm.

SLICE
Cut the chilled dough into slices as specified in the recipe. Cutting cookies of uniform thickness ensures that they bake evenly.

CHOCOLATE-TOFFEE BUTTER COOKIES

Makes: about 60 cookies
Total Time: 1¼ hours, plus 2 hours chilling and 1 hour setting

RECIPE OVERVIEW Sweet and complex like caramel, crunchy, and deeply buttery, toffee is both an irresistible candy and a great addition to a cookie recipe. Conveniently sold in bits, toffee can be mixed into cookie dough just like chocolate chips; once baked, it melts slightly yet still keeps its firm but yielding texture and lends an appealing chewy crunch to the finished cookie. The addition of light brown sugar to a simple butter cookie base contributes caramel notes that enhance the toffee's flavor. Toffee plays nicely with chocolate, so give these cookies some decorative flair by adorning them with melted chocolate and complementary buttery pecans. The options for decorating these cookies are endless; we particularly like dipping the cookies in the melted chocolate, but you could also simply drizzle the chocolate on top for sophistication and ease. Or, fill a zipper-lock bag with the melted chocolate, snip off a small corner, and pipe a chocolaty design on top. Use your imagination!

- 2⅓ cups (11⅔ ounces) all-purpose flour
- ½ teaspoon baking powder
- ½ teaspoon table salt
- 16 tablespoons unsalted butter, softened
- 1 cup packed (7 ounces) light brown sugar
- 1 large egg
- 1 teaspoon vanilla extract
- 1 cup (5 ounces) plain toffee bits
- 1½ cups (9 ounces) semisweet chocolate chips
- 1 tablespoon vegetable oil
- ⅔ cup pecans, toasted and chopped fine

1. Whisk flour, baking powder, and salt together in bowl. Using stand mixer fitted with paddle, beat butter and sugar on medium speed until pale and fluffy, 3 to 6 minutes. Add egg and vanilla and beat until combined, about 30 seconds, scraping down bowl as needed. Reduce speed to low and slowly add flour mixture until combined, about 30 seconds. Mix in toffee bits until just incorporated. Cover bowl with plastic wrap and refrigerate until dough is no longer sticky, 10 to 15 minutes.

2. Transfer dough to counter and shape into rectangular log about 15 inches long and 3 inches wide. Wrap log tightly in plastic and refrigerate until firm, at least 2 hours or up to 3 days.

3. Adjust oven racks to upper-middle and lower-middle positions and heat oven to 350 degrees. Line 2 baking sheets with parchment paper.

4. Slice chilled dough into ¼-inch-thick rectangles and space them 1 inch apart on prepared sheets. Bake until edges are browned, 12 to 16 minutes, switching and rotating sheets halfway through baking. Let cookies cool on sheets for 3 minutes, then transfer to wire rack. Repeat with remaining dough. Let cookies cool completely.

5. Microwave chocolate in bowl at 50 percent power, stirring occasionally, until melted, 2 to 3 minutes. Stir in oil until smooth. Dip part of each cookie into melted chocolate or drizzle chocolate over cookies with spoon. Sprinkle pecans over cookies and let chocolate set, about 1 hour, before serving.

KEYS TO SUCCESS

- **Cream the butter and sugar:** Helps create the ideal butter-cookie texture
- **Use brown sugar:** Underscores the caramel notes of the toffee bits

---

CORE TECHNIQUE

Forming Rectangular Slice-and-Bake Cookies

SHAPE LOG
After rolling the dough into a 15-inch log, flatten its top and sides so that it forms a rectangle measuring 1 inch tall and 3 inches wide.

Dipping Cookies in Chocolate

USE SMALL BOWL
Holding melted chocolate in a small bowl allows for a deeper pool of chocolate in which to dip the cookies. Gently dip the cookie to partially coat it, transfer it to a wire rack set in a rimmed baking sheet, and let it cool completely.

COURSE
COOKIE CUTTER COOKIES

CHRISTIE MORRISON

A favorite for the holidays and other celebrations, this type of cookie features a buttery dough that is rolled thin and stamped with a cookie cutter (or sometimes simply cut into shapes with a knife or pizza cutter). As with slice-and-bake cookies, chilling the dough—after dividing and shaping the dough into disks or after rolling it out thin, depending on the recipe—is key; this not only makes the dough much easier to work with but also ensures that your cookies will hold their shape when they're transferred to the baking sheet. These cutout cookies bake up flat and crisp yet sturdy, making them the perfect vehicle for festive additions—in this course you'll learn how to make and apply a simple icing or give the cookies a final toss in cinnamon sugar.

CHRISTIE'S PRO TIP: *To keep your butter tasting fresh, store it in the freezer (not the refrigerator, where it can pick up weird smells and off-flavors) for up to 4 months, and just thaw sticks as you need them.*

FOOLPROOF HOLIDAY COOKIES

Makes: about 36 cookies
Total Time: 2 hours, plus 30 minutes chilling and 1½ hours drying

RECIPE OVERVIEW Perfect for holiday decorating, these roll-and-cut sugar cookies are as easy to make as they are delicious. A common trade-off with sugar cookies is that they either look good but taste tough or have buttery flavor but lack visual appeal. These cookies achieve the best of both worlds. Superfine sugar helps create a delicate texture, and using the reverse-creaming method—beating the butter into the flour-sugar mixture—prevents the formation of air pockets and produces flat cookies that are easy to decorate with an easy all-purpose glaze. A little cream cheese makes the dough easy to roll but not too soft. Baking the cookies one sheet at a time ensures that they bake evenly. Do not reroll the scraps more than once; it will cause the cookies to be tough. This recipe can easily be doubled.

Sugar Cookies

- 2½ cups (12½ ounces) all-purpose flour
- ¾ cup (5¼ ounces) superfine sugar
- ¼ teaspoon table salt
- 16 tablespoons unsalted butter, cut into ½-inch pieces and softened
- 1 ounce cream cheese, softened
- 2 teaspoons vanilla extract

Glaze

- 2 cups (8 ounces) confectioners' sugar
- 3 tablespoons milk
- 1 ounce cream cheese, softened
- Food coloring (optional)

1. FOR THE SUGAR COOKIES Using stand mixer fitted with paddle, mix flour, sugar, and salt on low speed until combined. Add butter, 1 piece at a time, and mix until dough looks crumbly and slightly wet, 1 to 2 minutes. Add cream cheese and vanilla and beat until dough just begins to form large clumps, about 30 seconds.

2. Transfer dough to counter; knead just until it forms cohesive mass and divide in half. Form each half into disk, wrap disks tightly in plastic wrap, and refrigerate for at least 30 minutes or up to 2 days. (Wrapped dough can be frozen for up to 2 weeks. Let dough thaw completely in refrigerator before rolling.)

3. Working with 1 disk of dough at a time, roll dough ⅛ inch thick between 2 large sheets of parchment paper. Slide dough, still between parchment, onto baking sheet and refrigerate until firm, about 10 minutes.

4. Adjust oven rack to middle position and heat oven to 375 degrees. Line 2 baking sheets with parchment. Working with 1 sheet of dough at a time, remove top piece of parchment and cut dough into shapes with cookie cutters. Using thin offset spatula, transfer shapes to prepared baking sheet, spacing them about 1 inch apart.

5. Bake cookies, 1 sheet at a time, until light golden brown, about 10 minutes, rotating sheet halfway through baking. Let cookies cool on sheet for 3 minutes, then transfer to wire rack. Let cookies cool completely before glazing.

6. FOR THE GLAZE Whisk all ingredients in bowl until smooth. Spread glaze onto cooled cookies. Let glaze dry completely, about 1½ hours, before serving.

KEYS TO SUCCESS

- **Use softened butter:** Makes incorporating the butter into the dry ingredients easy (For tips on quick-softening butter, see page 559.)
- **Add cream cheese:** Makes the dough softer, thus more workable and easier to roll
- **Chill the dough before rolling:** Makes it less sticky, allows the flour to absorb moisture, and relaxes the gluten for easy rolling

CORE TECHNIQUE
Rolling and Cutting Cookies

REST DOUGH
Chilling the dough prevents the butter from becoming too warm and the dough from becoming sticky. It also allows the gluten to relax, so the dough isn't too tough to roll.

START ROLLING AT CENTER
For even thickness, start at the center of the disk and roll away from you, spinning the dough a quarter turn after each stroke. Apply even pressure as you roll.

ROLL DOUGH BETWEEN PARCHMENT
Using parchment eliminates dusting the dough with extra flour, which can yield dry cookies, and makes it easier to transfer the cookies to baking sheets.

Reverse-Cream for Flat Tops

We use reverse creaming (page 562) when we want tender but sturdy cookies with minimal rise and flat tops. It's perfect for holiday cookies meant for glazing and decorating. You start by combining all the dry ingredients and then incorporate softened butter. Finally, you add any liquids. During this process, the butter coats the flour particles, minimizing gluten development for a tender, fine crumb. Just as important, since the butter isn't beaten with sugar, less air is incorporated, which translates to less rise and a sturdier cookie.

CREAMING
This cookie has a domed top.

REVERSE CREAMING
This cookie has a flat top.

Grind Your Own Superfine Sugar

Superfine sugar consists of small granules that dissolve almost instantly, so it's ideal for baked goods where you want a grit-free texture and for sweetening drinks. To make your own, process 1 cup plus 2 teaspoons of granulated sugar for 30 seconds. This yields about 1 cup of superfine sugar.

NANKHATAI

Makes: 36 cookies
Total Time: 1¾ hours, plus 4 hours chilling

RECIPE OVERVIEW One taste of these aromatic tea cookies, a favorite in India and Pakistan, and you'll agree they're a worthy addition to your repertoire. They're often made with semolina flour, rice flour, chickpea flour, or a combination along with white flour. But all-purpose flour alone also yields great-tasting biscuits. This version, a cookie contest grand prize winner contributed by Veena Shah of Bloomfield Hill, Michigan, is rolled thin for dunking into chai. A simple butter cookie base allows the flavor of cardamom to take center stage. To help bring the cookie dough together without an egg, enrich the dough with a small amount—just 1½ tablespoons—of plain yogurt. This gives it just the right consistency and provides a slight tang to the biscuits. For an elegant finish, stud the middle of each cookie with a single cashew half. We like the appearance of fluted rounds for these cookies, but you can cut them into any shape you like. You can use plain whole-milk or low-fat yogurt for these cookies, but don't use nonfat yogurt; it will make the cookies too lean. Be sure to plan ahead, as the dough must chill for several hours.

- 2 cups (10 ounces) all-purpose flour
- 1 teaspoon ground cardamom
- ½ teaspoon baking powder
- ¼ teaspoon table salt
- 16 tablespoons unsalted butter, softened
- 1 cup (4 ounces) confectioners' sugar
- 1½ tablespoons plain whole-milk or low-fat yogurt
- ¼ teaspoon vanilla extract
- 18 salted roasted cashews, split in half

1. Whisk flour, cardamom, baking powder, and salt together in bowl; set aside. Using stand mixer fitted with paddle, beat butter and sugar on medium-high speed until pale and fluffy, about 2 minutes. Add yogurt and vanilla and beat until incorporated, about 30 seconds. Reduce speed to low, add flour mixture in 3 additions, and mix until just combined. Transfer dough to counter and divide in half. Form each half into 5-inch disk, wrap disks tightly in plastic wrap, and refrigerate for at least 4 hours or up to 2 days.

2. Adjust oven racks to upper-middle and lower-middle positions and heat oven to 350 degrees. Line 2 baking sheets with parchment paper. Let chilled dough sit on counter to soften slightly, about 10 minutes. Working with 1 disk of dough at a time, roll dough ⅛ inch thick. Using 2½-inch cookie cutter, cut dough into shapes; space shapes 1 inch apart on prepared sheets. Gently reroll scraps once, cut into shapes, and transfer to prepared sheets. Gently press cashew half in center of each shape.

3. Bake cookies until lightly browned, 14 to 18 minutes, switching and rotating sheets halfway through baking. Let cookies cool on sheets for 5 minutes, then transfer to wire rack. Let cookies cool completely before serving.

KEYS TO SUCCESS

- **Add some yogurt:** Helps form a cohesive dough without the need for an egg
- **Let the dough chill:** Makes the dough easier to work with

Avoid Overbaking

USE TOUCH TEST
Thinly rolled cookies go from perfectly baked to overbaked in a matter of minutes, so it's important to watch—most cookies should show a slight resistance to the touch and start to become brown along the edges.

BISCOCHITOS

Makes: about 40 cookies
Total Time: 1 hour, plus 30 minutes chilling and 1 hour cooling

RECIPE OVERVIEW Biscochitos find home in New Mexico, where they're served at any special celebration. These crisp shortbread cookies, which have Spanish roots, are scented with the licorice notes of anise seed and the warm spice of cinnamon. To achieve their meltingly tender texture and rich flavor without the traditional lard, use a combination of equal parts butter and shortening. The cookies come in many shapes and sizes, but we're partial to the diamond shape that's commonly used for weddings. To create this unique shape, roll the dough into a circle and chill it until firm; then cut the dough into strips (a pizza cutter makes quick work of this step) and cut the strips diagonally into diamonds. To finish the cookies, coat them in cinnamon sugar using the traditional method: Gently toss the still-warm cookies in the sugary coating so that it adheres and then let the cookies cool completely before serving them. Don't let the cookies cool on the baking sheets for longer than 5 minutes, or the cinnamon-sugar mixture won't adhere.

- 1 cup (7 ounces) sugar
- 1 teaspoon ground cinnamon
- 1 tablespoon anise seeds
- 8 tablespoons unsalted butter, softened
- 8 tablespoons vegetable shortening, cut into 1-inch chunks
- ½ teaspoon table salt
- 1 large egg yolk
- 1 teaspoon vanilla extract
- 2 cups (10 ounces) all-purpose flour

1. Combine sugar and cinnamon in small bowl; spread ½ cup cinnamon sugar in shallow dish. Grind anise seeds in spice grinder until finely ground, about 10 seconds.

2. Using stand mixer fitted with paddle, beat butter, shortening, salt, remaining ½ cup cinnamon sugar, and ground anise on medium-high speed until pale and fluffy, about 3 minutes, scraping down bowl as needed. Add egg yolk and vanilla and beat until combined. Reduce speed to low; add flour; and mix until dough forms, about 10 seconds.

3. Roll dough into 9-inch circle, about ½ inch thick, on large sheet of parchment paper. Transfer dough, still on parchment, to large plate; cover with plastic wrap and refrigerate until firm, about 30 minutes.

4. Adjust oven racks to upper-middle and lower-middle positions and heat oven to 350 degrees. Line 2 baking sheets with parchment paper. Transfer dough, still on parchment, to cutting board. Using knife or pizza cutter, cut dough lengthwise into 1-inch-wide strips, then cut diagonally into 1-inch-wide strips to form diamonds; space diamonds evenly on prepared sheets, about 20 per sheet.

5. Bake cookies until set and just starting to brown, about 15 minutes, switching and rotating sheets halfway through baking. Let cookies cool on sheets for 5 minutes. Gently toss cookies, a few at a time, in reserved cinnamon sugar. Transfer cookies to wire rack. Let cookies cool completely, about 1 hour, before serving.

KEYS TO SUCCESS

- **Use butter and shortening:** Gives the cookies a melt-in-your-mouth texture similar to that achieved using the traditional lard
- **Grind the anise:** Ensures that the spice's licorice notes are infused into every bite
- **Refrigerate after rolling:** Makes cutting the diamond-shaped cookies much easier

Make the Fridge Your Friend

CHILL OUT
If at any time the dough becomes too soft or sticky to roll, slide the dough, still between the sheets of parchment, onto a baking sheet and refrigerate until the dough is firm, about 10 minutes.

COURSE
BROWNIES AND BLONDIES

ELLE SIMONE SCOTT

Bar cookies such as brownies and blondies have universal appeal for good reason. Baked in a pan and then cut into tidy squares for serving, these sweet treats are not only delicious but also sturdy and portable, making them a great choice for bake sales, picnics, and potlucks. This course will cover the basics such as visual cues to help you know when the bars are done, and how to prepare the pan with a foil sling—which makes it a cinch to remove the bars and transfer them to a cutting board to cut. Learn what makes a brownie fudgy and what makes one chewy, as well as how to use different types of chocolate to get the results you want.

ELLE'S PRO TIP: *There are two things you're almost guaranteed to find in my freezer: coffee beans and chocolate. Often when I'm baking, I don't use all the chocolate that I have. The key to keeping it fresh until the next use is freezing it.*

FUDGY BROWNIES

Makes: 36 brownies
Total Time: 1 hour, plus 2 hours cooling

RECIPE OVERVIEW There are many types of brownies to love—some are cakey and light and others are moist and chewy—but it's a dense, dark, fudgelike brownie that satisfies the serious chocolate lover. Start by using three forms of chocolate: unsweetened chocolate for intensity, cocoa powder for complexity, and bittersweet or semisweet chocolate for moisture and well-rounded flavor. Melting butter along with the chocolate is the key to a fudgy texture, and incorporating a generous three eggs brings richness and structure. Granulated sugar gives these brownies a delicate, shiny, crackly top crust. Cut them into small bites—a little goes a long way. We like the complex flavor of bittersweet chocolate, but semisweet also works here, as does 5 ounces of bittersweet or semisweet chocolate chips in place of the bar chocolate. Be sure to use a metal baking pan and not a glass baking dish.

- 5 ounces bittersweet or semisweet chocolate, chopped
- 2 ounces unsweetened chocolate, chopped
- 8 tablespoons unsalted butter, cut into 4 pieces
- 3 tablespoons unsweetened cocoa powder
- 1¼ cups (8¾ ounces) sugar
- 3 large eggs

- 2 teaspoons vanilla extract
- ½ teaspoon table salt
- 1 cup (5 ounces) all-purpose flour

1. Adjust oven rack to middle position and heat oven to 350 degrees. Make foil sling for 8-inch square baking pan by folding 2 long sheets of aluminum foil so each is 8 inches wide. Lay sheets of foil in pan perpendicular to each other, with extra foil hanging over edges of pan. Push foil into corners and up sides of pan, smoothing foil flush to pan. Grease foil.

2. Microwave bittersweet and unsweetened chocolates in bowl at 50 percent power for 2 minutes. Stir in butter and continue to microwave, stirring often, until melted and smooth. Whisk in cocoa and let mixture cool slightly.

3. Whisk sugar, eggs, vanilla, and salt in large bowl until combined. Whisk chocolate mixture into sugar mixture until smooth. Using rubber spatula, stir in flour until no dry streaks remain. Transfer batter to prepared pan and smooth top. Bake until toothpick inserted in center comes out with few moist crumbs attached, 35 to 40 minutes, rotating pan halfway through baking.

4. Let brownies cool completely in pan on wire rack, about 2 hours. Using foil overhang, remove brownies from pan. (Uncut brownies can be refrigerated for up to 3 days.) Cut into 36 pieces. Serve.

KEYS TO SUCCESS

- **Use three types of chocolate:** Makes for a brownie with serious depth of flavor and chocolate intensity
- **Melt the butter:** Helps give the brownies their dense, fudgy texture
- **Use granulated sugar:** Yields brownies with an appealing shiny, cracked top crust
- For information on making a foil sling, see page 581.
- For more information on chopping chocolate, see page 582.

CHEWY BROWNIES

Makes: 24 brownies
Total Time: 1¼ hours, plus 2½ hours cooling

RECIPE OVERVIEW While box-mix brownies may not offer superior chocolate flavor, there's no denying their chewy appeal. To replicate this ideal chewiness in a homemade brownie, the key is fat—specifically, the right proportions of saturated and unsaturated fats. An almost 1:3 ratio of saturated fat (butter) to unsaturated fat (vegetable oil) produces the chewiest brownies. Two whole eggs plus two extra yolks work to emulsify the batter and prevent greasy brownies. For full, well-rounded chocolate flavor, whisk unsweetened cocoa, along with a little espresso powder, into boiling water and then stir in unsweetened chocolate. The heat unlocks the chocolate's flavor compounds, boosting its impact. Chunks of bittersweet chocolate, folded in before baking, provide a final boost of chocolate intensity. For the chewiest texture, it's important to let the brownies cool thoroughly before cutting. For an accurate measurement of boiling water, bring a kettle of water to a boil and then measure out the desired amount. Be sure to use a metal baking pan and not a glass baking dish for this recipe.

- ⅓ cup (1 ounce) unsweetened cocoa powder
- 1½ teaspoons instant espresso powder (optional)
- ½ cup plus 2 tablespoons boiling water
- 2 ounces unsweetened chocolate, chopped fine
- ½ cup plus 2 tablespoons vegetable oil
- 4 tablespoons unsalted butter, melted
- 2 large eggs plus 2 large yolks
- 2 teaspoons vanilla extract
- 2½ cups (17½ ounces) sugar
- 1¾ cups (8¾ ounces) all-purpose flour
- ¾ teaspoon table salt
- 6 ounces bittersweet chocolate, cut into ½-inch pieces

1. Adjust oven rack to lowest position and heat oven to 350 degrees. Make foil sling for 13 by 9-inch baking pan by folding 2 long sheets of aluminum foil; first sheet should be 13 inches wide and second sheet should be 9 inches wide. Lay sheets of foil in pan perpendicular to each other, with extra foil hanging over edges of pan. Push foil into corners and up sides of pan, smoothing foil flush to pan. Grease foil.

2. Whisk cocoa; espresso powder, if using; and boiling water in large bowl until smooth. Add unsweetened chocolate and whisk until chocolate is melted. Whisk in oil and melted butter (mixture may look curdled). Whisk in eggs and yolks and vanilla until smooth and homogeneous. Whisk in sugar until fully incorporated. Using rubber spatula, stir in flour and salt until combined. Fold in bittersweet chocolate.

3. Transfer batter to prepared pan and smooth top. Bake until toothpick inserted halfway between edge and center comes out with few moist crumbs attached, 30 to 35 minutes, rotating pan halfway through baking. Let brownies cool in pan on wire rack for 1½ hours. Using foil overhang, remove brownies from pan. Transfer to wire rack and let cool completely, about 1 hour. Cut into 24 pieces. (Brownies can be stored at room temperature for up to 4 days.)

KEYS TO SUCCESS

- **Use the right ratio of butter to oil:** Produces the chewiest brownies
- **Pour boiling water over the cocoa and espresso:** Blooms their flavors for a more intense chocolate punch
- **Let brownies cool completely:** Further ensures a chewy texture

ROCKY ROAD BROWNIES

Makes: 16 brownies
Total Time: 55 minutes, plus 2 hours cooling

RECIPE OVERVIEW To make these decadent treats inspired by rocky road ice cream, simply top a brownie base with a liberal amount of sweet marshmallow crème and then swirl it through the batter with a knife. While these brownies look gooey and messy with their shiny marshmallow swirl, the base is nice and sturdy, so it can support its delicious topping, and the brownies can easily be packed for lunch or taken on a picnic. Unsweetened chocolate—rather than bittersweet or semisweet—keeps the sweetness of these marshmallow-enhanced brownies in check. Swirling the marshmallow on top rather than hiding it as a layer within the brownie batter ensures that this star ingredient isn't overwhelmed by the chocolate. Toasted walnuts (or pecans if you prefer) provide crunch and the requisite rockiness. The result is a textural masterpiece: dense, chocolaty brownie; crunchy, toasty chopped nuts; and rivers of smooth, gooey marshmallow.

- 8 tablespoons unsalted butter
- 3 ounces unsweetened chocolate, chopped coarse
- ⅔ cup (3⅓ ounces) all-purpose flour
- ½ teaspoon baking powder
- ¼ teaspoon table salt
- 1 cup (7 ounces) sugar
- 2 large eggs
- 1 teaspoon vanilla extract
- ½ cup walnuts or pecans, toasted and chopped
- 1½ cups marshmallow crème

1. Adjust oven rack to middle position and heat oven to 350 degrees. Make foil sling for 8-inch square baking pan by folding 2 long sheets of aluminum foil so each is 8 inches wide. Lay sheets of foil in pan perpendicular to each other, with extra foil hanging over edges of pan. Push foil into corners and up sides of pan, smoothing foil flush to pan. Grease foil.

2. Microwave butter and chocolate in bowl at 50 percent power, stirring often, until melted, 1 to 3 minutes; let cool slightly.

3. Whisk flour, baking powder, and salt together in second bowl. Whisk sugar, eggs, and vanilla together in large bowl. Whisk chocolate mixture into sugar mixture until combined. Using rubber spatula, stir in flour mixture until just incorporated.

4. Transfer batter to prepared pan, smooth top, and sprinkle with walnuts. Using spoon, place small dollops of marshmallow crème over brownie batter. Using butter knife, swirl marshmallow through brownie batter. Bake until toothpick inserted in center comes out with few moist crumbs attached, 22 to 27 minutes, rotating pan halfway through baking.

5. Let brownies cool completely in pan on wire rack, about 2 hours. Using foil overhang, remove brownies from pan. Cut into 16 squares before serving.

KEYS TO SUCCESS

- **Use unsweetened chocolate:** Balances the sweetness of the marshmallow crème
- **Swirl the batter:** Ensures gooey marshmallow and fudgy brownie in every bite
- **Add toasted nuts:** Provides a welcome textural contrast to the soft marshmallow

BLONDIES

Makes: 36 blondies
Total Time: 1¼ hours, plus 2 hours cooling

RECIPE OVERVIEW Although blondies are baked in a pan like brownies, their flavor is closer to that of chocolate chip cookies—with even more butterscotch punch. The ideal blondie is chewy (not too cakey or too dense), sweet but not cloying, and loaded with nuts and chocolate. As with our chocolate chip cookies, the secret to getting the right amount of chew is using melted butter. Light brown sugar contributes the perfect amount of dimension and, when combined with vanilla extract and some salt, rich butterscotch flavor. A generous amount of chocolate chips and pecans contributes richness and crunch to the chewy bars. Butterscotch chips overpower the blondie base, but white chocolate chips add a perfectly sweet milkiness. Be sure to check the blondies early so that you don't overbake them.

- 1½ cups (7½ ounces) all-purpose flour
- 1 teaspoon baking powder
- ½ teaspoon table salt
- 1½ cups packed (10½ ounces) light brown sugar
- 12 tablespoons unsalted butter, melted and cooled
- 2 large eggs
- 1½ teaspoons vanilla extract
- 1 cup pecans or walnuts, toasted and chopped coarse
- ½ cup (3 ounces) semisweet chocolate chips
- ½ cup (3 ounces) white chocolate chips

1. Adjust oven rack to middle position and heat oven to 350 degrees. Make foil sling for 13 by 9-inch baking pan by folding 2 long sheets of aluminum foil; first sheet should be 13 inches wide, and second sheet should be 9 inches wide. Lay sheets of foil in pan perpendicular to each other, with extra foil hanging over edges of pan. Push foil into corners and up sides of pan, smoothing foil flush to pan. Grease foil.

2. Whisk flour, baking powder, and salt together in bowl. Whisk sugar and melted butter in second bowl until combined. Whisk eggs and vanilla into sugar mixture until combined. Using rubber spatula, fold in flour mixture until just combined. Fold in pecans, semisweet chocolate chips, and white chocolate chips.

3. Transfer batter to prepared pan and smooth top. Bake until top is shiny and cracked and feels firm to touch, 22 to 25 minutes, rotating pan halfway through baking.

Let blondies cool completely in pan on wire rack, about 2 hours. Using foil overhang, lift blondies from pan. Cut into 36 pieces before serving.

Variation
CONGO BARS
Add 1½ cups unsweetened shredded coconut, toasted, to batter with chocolate chips and nuts.

> ### KEYS TO SUCCESS
> - **Use melted butter:** Makes for a chewy, not cakey, blondie
> - **Use light brown sugar and plenty of vanilla:** Develops the blondies' requisite butterscotch flavor
> - **Don't overbake:** Keeps blondies chewy, not hard

CORE TECHNIQUE
Making a Foil Sling

FOLD AND LINE
Fold 2 long sheets of aluminum foil to be the same width as the baking pan. (If the dish is rectangular, the sheets will be of different widths.) Lay the sheets of foil in the pan, perpendicular to one another, with any extra foil hanging over the edges.

SMOOTH OUT WRINKLES
Push the foil into the corners and up the sides of the pan. Try to iron out any wrinkles in the foil, smoothing it flush with the pan.

GREASE WELL
Coat the foil sling with vegetable oil spray, making sure to cover the bottom and sides of the pan.

CHOCOLATE BASICS

BUYING

Unsweetened Chocolate: Also called baking chocolate, this is simply pure chocolate liquor that has been cooled and formed into bars. Among bar chocolates, unsweetened has the most intense chocolate flavor.

Bittersweet/Semisweet Chocolate: When sugar is added to chocolate liquor, the resulting product is technically called "dark chocolate," assuming that it still contains at least 35 percent chocolate liquor (most dark chocolates contain far more). The terms "bittersweet" and "semisweet" are not regulated, although most manufacturers use the former to indicate a product with less sugar. When you see a label that reads "70 percent cacao," this means the product contains 70 percent chocolate liquor by weight. The rest is mostly sugar, plus a little emulsifier and/or vanilla.

Milk Chocolate: Milk chocolate is similar to bittersweet or semisweet chocolate but with the addition of milk solids, which give this product its unique caramel and butterscotch flavors and soft texture. Most milk chocolate contains less chocolate liquor and more sugar than bittersweet or semisweet chocolates.

White Chocolate: White chocolate is technically not chocolate, since it contains no cocoa solids. Authentic white chocolate contains at least 20 percent cocoa butter (along with milk solids and sugar), which gives this product its meltingly smooth texture. Note that many brands rely on palm oil in place of some or all of the cocoa butter and can't be labeled "chocolate." If the product is called "white chips" or "white confection," it is made with little or no cocoa butter. That said, since both styles derive their flavor from milk and sugar, not the fat, we find this distinction makes little difference in recipes.

Cocoa Powder: Cocoa powder is made by removing most of the cocoa butter from chocolate liquor. The resulting powder is roughly 80 percent cocoa solids and therefore has an intense chocolate flavor. To counter the acidic flavor of this concentrated form of chocolate, the powder is sometimes treated with an alkaline solution, or "Dutched." We find that Dutch-processed cocoa has a milder, more complex flavor than natural cocoa, which can be harsh and astringent. That said, you can use the two interchangeably in many recipes.

STORING

Never store chocolate in the refrigerator or freezer, as cocoa butter can easily pick up off-flavors from other foods. Wrap chocolate well in plastic wrap and store it in a cool, dark pantry. Milk and white chocolates should keep for six months; dark and unsweetened chocolates will keep for a year. If chocolate is exposed to rapid changes in humidity or temperature, sugar or fat may dissolve and migrate, causing a white film to develop on the surface of the chocolate. This cosmetic condition, known as bloom, is harmless and does not affect the flavor of the chocolate.

SUBSTITUTIONS

In a pinch, you can replace some chocolate products with other ingredients.

TO REPLACE	SUBSTITUTE
1 ounce unsweetened chocolate	3 tablespoons cocoa powder + 1 tablespoon butter or oil
1 ounce bittersweet or semisweet chocolate	⅔ ounce unsweetened chocolate + 2 teaspoons granulated sugar

CHOPPING

There are two ways to chop a large block of chocolate into pieces. To use a chef's knife, hold it at a 45-degree angle to one of the corners and bear down evenly. After cutting about an inch from the corner, repeat with the other corners. Alternatively, you can use a sharp two-tined meat fork to break the chocolate into smaller pieces.

CHOCOLATE 101

Structure

CACAO BEANS
The cacao tree grows in tropical regions around the world and produces large fruits that look like fibrous pods. Each fruit contains about 40 white cacao beans, which are dried, fermented, and then shipped to a processing plant where they are stripped of their hulls to form cacao nibs (left).

CHOCOLATE LIQUOR
At the processing plant the nibs are roasted to dark-brown seeds and ground into a liquid cacao mass called chocolate liquor. Chocolate liquor is pure, unsweetened chocolate and is the base ingredient for all chocolate products.

COCOA BUTTER
About 55 percent of chocolate liquor is cocoa butter, a natural, highly unsaturated fat responsible for chocolate's unique texture. Cocoa butter has a very narrow melting range and stays firm up to 92 degrees. Since the temperature inside the human mouth is just a few degrees higher than the melting point of cocoa butter, chocolate melts very slowly. In fact, it seems to melt into—rather than just in—your mouth.

COCOA SOLIDS
Particles of ground cocoa solids are suspended in the cocoa butter and make up the other 45 percent of chocolate liquor. Cocoa solids carry hundreds of flavor compounds we recognize as chocolate. Most of the characteristic chocolate flavor compounds are produced during the fermentation and roasting steps.

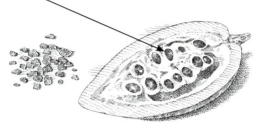

MELTING

On the Stovetop
Since chocolate can scorch if overheated, it's important to employ gentle heat. The traditional method calls for a double boiler. Place the chopped chocolate in a heatproof bowl set over a pot of barely simmering water. Make sure that the water isn't touching the bowl, or the chocolate can overheat. The steam will gently heat the bowl and melt the chocolate. If the recipe also calls for melted butter, you can add the butter to the bowl with the chocolate at the outset.

In the Microwave
You can speed up the melting process with a microwave, but you should use a lowered power setting to reduce the risk of scorching. Place the chopped chocolate in a microwave-safe bowl and microwave for 45 seconds at 50 percent power. Stir the chocolate to help it liquefy and continue to microwave in 15-second intervals as needed. If also melting butter, don't add it until the chocolate is almost melted. (If added earlier, the butter will splatter.)

COURSE
EVERYDAY CAKES

CHRISTIE MORRISON

Cakes aren't always fancy, elaborate affairs; in fact, some of the most satisfying cakes are simple to make and, just as important, are meant to be enjoyed any time. While some get topped with a swirl of creamy frosting, others require no adornment (other than perhaps a dusting of confectioners' sugar). We'll show you the best way to prepare the pan so that the cake releases cleanly and comes out in one piece every time. You'll also learn different ways to mix the ingredients; you might be surprised to discover that simply mixing by hand or using the food processor can be the best way to produce a cake with just the right texture. No need to wait for a special occasion to enjoy these cakes—just dig right in!

CHRISTIE'S PRO TIP: *The easiest way to avoid problems when you're baking cakes is to weigh your dry ingredients. Do you scoop and sweep? Spoon and level? Using a scale takes the guesswork out of baking.*

POUND CAKE

Serves: 8
Total Time: 1½ hours, plus 2 hours cooling

RECIPE OVERVIEW A rich, golden pound cake is a must in any baker's repertoire. Classic pound cake recipes tend to be very particular, calling for ingredients at certain temperatures as well as finicky mixing methods. But a simple, foolproof pound cake is possible with two key elements: hot melted (rather than softened) butter and a food processor. The combination of the fast-moving blade of the processor and the hot melted butter emulsifies the liquid ingredients quickly before they have a chance to curdle. Sifting the dry ingredients over the emulsified egg mixture in three additions, and whisking them in after each addition, allows the dry ingredients to incorporate easily and ensures that no pockets of flour mar the finished cake. Our preferred loaf pan measures 8½ by 4½ inches; if you use a 9 by 5-inch loaf pan, check for doneness 5 minutes early.

- 1½ cups (6 ounces) cake flour
- 1 teaspoon baking powder
- ½ teaspoon table salt
- 1¼ cups (8¾ ounces) sugar
- 4 large eggs, room temperature
- 1½ teaspoons vanilla extract
- 16 tablespoons unsalted butter, melted and hot

1. Adjust oven rack to middle position and heat oven to 350 degrees. Grease and flour 8½ by 4½-inch loaf pan. Whisk flour, baking powder, and salt together in bowl.

2. Process sugar, eggs, and vanilla in food processor until combined, about 10 seconds. With processor running, add hot melted butter in steady stream until incorporated. Transfer to large bowl.

3. Sift flour mixture over egg mixture in 3 additions, whisking to combine after each addition until few streaks of flour remain. Continue to whisk batter gently until almost no lumps remain (do not overmix).

4. Transfer batter to prepared pan and smooth top with rubber spatula. Gently tap pan on counter to settle batter. Bake until toothpick inserted in center comes out with few crumbs attached, 50 minutes to 1 hour, rotating pan halfway through baking.

5. Let cake cool in pan on wire rack for 10 minutes. Run thin knife around edge of pan; remove cake from pan; and let cool completely on rack, about 2 hours. Serve. (Cake can be stored at room temperature for up to 3 days or frozen for up to 1 month; defrost cake at room temperature.)

Variations

ALMOND POUND CAKE

Add 1 teaspoon almond extract and ¼ cup slivered almonds to food processor with sugar, eggs, and vanilla. Sprinkle 2 tablespoons slivered almonds over cake before baking.

GINGER POUND CAKE

Add 3 tablespoons minced crystallized ginger, 1½ teaspoons ground ginger, and ½ teaspoon ground mace to food processor with sugar, eggs, and vanilla.

ORANGE POUND CAKE

Add 1 tablespoon grated orange zest and 1 tablespoon juice to food processor with sugar, eggs, and vanilla.

KEYS TO SUCCESS

- **Grease and flour pan:** Helps the pound cake climb the sides of the pan and prevents the edges from forming a lip
- **Use cake flour:** Delivers delicate, fine-crumbed cakes (You can approximate cake flour by mixing ⅞ cup of all-purpose flour with 2 tablespoons of cornstarch for every cup of flour.)
- **Use a food processor:** Ensures that the ingredients emulsify quickly and don't curdle
- **Sift in dry ingredients:** Prevents overmixing; aerates and breaks the ingredients into small particles that will mix in easily

SCIENCE LESSON Baking with Cold versus Room-Temperature Eggs

Cake recipes often call for room-temperature eggs, which whip higher and give more lift than cold eggs. But is the difference between room-temperature and cold eggs so great that it could actually ruin a pound cake? To find out, we made pound cakes with both room-temperature and cold eggs. Cold eggs didn't whip as well as room-temperature eggs, so the batter didn't rise properly, making the cake dense. That said, we found that it's fine to use cold eggs in basic cake recipes that don't rely heavily on beaten eggs for lift.

TAHINI-BANANA SNACK CAKE

Serves: 8
Total Time: 1½ hours, plus 2 hours cooling

RECIPE OVERVIEW Banana and peanut butter is a classic combination, but this cake gets its nutty flavor from tahini. Creaming the tahini with the butter and sugar (and cutting back on the butter to accommodate for the tahini's fat content) ensures that it's fully incorporated and doesn't make the cake greasy. Ripe bananas are the best choice here; a cup of mashed bananas gives you a moist cake with unmistakable banana flavor. A final sprinkling of sesame seeds hints at the tahini inside. This cake is simple enough to make whenever the need to snack strikes—no occasion required. It is important to let the cake cool completely before serving.

- 1½ cups (7½ ounces) all-purpose flour
- ½ teaspoon table salt
- ½ teaspoon baking soda
- 1¼ cups (8¾ ounces) sugar
- ⅓ cup tahini
- 4 tablespoons unsalted butter, softened
- 2 large eggs
- 1 cup mashed ripe bananas (2 to 3 bananas)
- ¾ teaspoon vanilla extract
- ¼ cup whole milk
- 2 teaspoons sesame seeds

1. Adjust oven rack to middle position and heat oven to 350 degrees. Grease 8-inch square baking pan, line with parchment paper, grease parchment, and flour pan. Whisk flour, salt, and baking soda together in bowl.

2. Using stand mixer fitted with paddle, beat sugar, tahini, and butter on medium-high speed until light and fluffy, about 3 minutes, scraping down bowl as needed. Add eggs, one at a time, and beat until combined. Add bananas and vanilla and beat until incorporated. Reduce speed to low and add flour mixture in 3 additions, alternating with milk in 2 additions, scraping down bowl as needed. Give batter final stir by hand.

3. Transfer batter to prepared pan and smooth top with rubber spatula. Sprinkle top with sesame seeds. Bake until deep golden brown and toothpick inserted in center comes out clean, 40 to 50 minutes, rotating pan halfway through baking.

4. Let cake cool in pan on wire rack for 10 minutes. Remove cake from pan, discarding parchment, and let cool completely on rack, about 2 hours. Serve. (Cake can be stored at room temperature for up to 2 days.)

> ### KEYS TO SUCCESS
> - **Cream the butter and sugar:** Incorporates air for the ideal light and fluffy snack cake
> - **Ripe bananas:** Contribute three times as much sugar as unripe ones and ensure a flavorful cake

SIMPLE CARROT SHEET CAKE

Serves: 12 to 15
Total Time: 1 hour, plus 2 hours cooling

RECIPE OVERVIEW This carrot cake is moist and rich, with a tender crumb, balanced spice, and the light sweetness of carrots. A pound of grated carrots provides plenty of flavor and a moist (not dense and wet) texture. This is a cake that comes together quickly: Simply mix the dry ingredients separately from the wet ingredients before slowly whisking them together and then stirring in the carrots. If you want to take the cake out of the pan, grease the pan, line it with parchment paper, grease the parchment, and then flour the pan.

- 2½ cups (12½ ounces) all-purpose flour
- 1¼ teaspoons ground cinnamon
- 1¼ teaspoons baking powder
- 1 teaspoon baking soda
- ½ teaspoon table salt
- ½ teaspoon ground nutmeg
- ⅛ teaspoon ground cloves
- 4 large eggs
- 1½ cups (10½ ounces) granulated sugar
- ½ cup packed (3½ ounces) light brown sugar
- 1½ cups vegetable oil
- 1 pound carrots, peeled and grated
- 3 cups Cream Cheese Frosting (page 595)

1. Adjust oven rack to middle position and heat oven to 350 degrees. Grease and flour 13 by 9-inch baking pan. Whisk flour, cinnamon, baking powder, baking soda, salt, nutmeg, and cloves together in bowl.

2. Whisk eggs, granulated sugar, and brown sugar in large bowl until sugars are mostly dissolved and mixture is frothy. Continue to whisk while slowly drizzling in oil until thoroughly combined and emulsified. Whisk in flour mixture until just incorporated. Stir in carrots. Give batter final stir by hand.

3. Transfer batter to prepared pan and smooth top with rubber spatula. Gently tap pan on counter to settle batter. Bake until toothpick inserted in center comes out clean, 35 to 40 minutes, rotating pan halfway through baking.

4. Let cake cool completely in pan on wire rack, about 2 hours. Spread frosting evenly over top of cake. Serve.

> ### KEYS TO SUCCESS
> - **Use modest amounts of cinnamon, nutmeg, and cloves:** Ensures that the carrot flavor is front and center
> - **Swap out butter for oil:** Makes for an incredibly moist cake
> - **Pair the cake with tangy cream cheese frosting:** Offsets the sweetness of the cake for a perfectly balanced treat

COURSE
BIRTHDAY CAKES

JULIA COLLIN DAVISON

Birthdays are the perfect excuse to hone your cake-baking skills. Start with a simple yet crowd-pleasing chocolate sheet cake topped with a rich, creamy frosting—you can even serve it right from the pan. Celebrate with cupcakes or, for a slightly more upscale affair, try your hand at a two-layer or even three-layer cake. We'll tell you when you need cake flour and when all-purpose is just fine. You'll also learn why you might use oil in one cake and butter in another—and why the mixing method matters. And we didn't forget the frosting. You can feel confident in your cake decorating abilities with our step-by-step tutorial.

JULIA'S PRO TIP: *Cakes need to cool completely before they're frosted or else you'll have a mess on your hands. If you find yourself short on time, place the cake in the fridge (or freezer) to cool down before frosting, but know that rapidly chilling a freshly baked cake may alter its crumb texture a bit.*

CHOCOLATE SHEET CAKE WITH MILK CHOCOLATE FROSTING

Serves: 12 to 15
Total Time: 1 hour, plus 1 hour cooling

RECIPE OVERVIEW When the results are good, chocolate sheet cake yields great reward for relatively minimal effort. For a cake that boasts deep chocolate flavor and color, start by using a combination of Dutch-processed cocoa and melted bittersweet chocolate; the cocoa offers pure, assertive chocolate flavor while the bittersweet chocolate contributes complexity as well as the right amount of fat and sugar. A milk chocolate ganache frosting offsets the intense flavor of the cake, but getting the texture just right—neither loose and drippy nor stiff and fudgy—can be tricky. For a thick, rich, creamy ganache, add plenty of softened butter to the warm chocolate-cream mixture. Once assembled, refrigerate the frosting to cool it quickly so that it spreads nicely, and then give it a quick whisk to smooth it out and lighten its texture. The best part: This cake comes together with everyday staples and basic equipment—no mixers or food processors needed. Do not substitute natural cocoa powder for the Dutch-processed cocoa powder. If you want to take the cake out of the pan, grease the pan, line it with parchment paper, grease the parchment, and then flour the pan.

Cake
- 1½ cups (10½ ounces) sugar
- 1¼ cups (6¼ ounces) all-purpose flour
- ½ teaspoon baking soda
- ½ teaspoon table salt
- 1 cup whole milk
- 8 ounces bittersweet chocolate, chopped fine
- ¾ cup (2¼ ounces) Dutch-processed cocoa powder
- ⅔ cup vegetable oil
- 4 large eggs
- 1 teaspoon vanilla extract

Frosting
- 1 pound milk chocolate, chopped
- ⅔ cup heavy cream
- 16 tablespoons unsalted butter, cut into 16 pieces and softened

1. FOR THE CAKE Adjust oven rack to middle position and heat oven to 325 degrees. Lightly spray 13 by 9-inch baking pan with vegetable oil spray. Whisk sugar, flour, baking soda, and salt together in bowl; set aside.

2. Combine milk, chocolate, and cocoa in large saucepan. Place saucepan over low heat and cook, whisking frequently, until chocolate is melted and mixture is smooth. Remove from heat and let cool slightly, about 5 minutes. Whisk oil, eggs, and vanilla into chocolate mixture (mixture may initially look curdled) until smooth and homogeneous. Add sugar mixture and whisk until combined, making sure to scrape corners of saucepan.

3. Transfer batter to prepared pan. Bake until firm in center when lightly pressed and toothpick inserted in center comes out with few crumbs attached, 30 to 35 minutes, rotating pan halfway through baking. Let cake cool completely in pan on wire rack, 1 to 2 hours.

4. FOR THE FROSTING While cake is baking, combine chocolate and cream in large heatproof bowl set over saucepan filled with 1 inch barely simmering water, making sure water does not touch bottom of bowl. Whisk mixture occasionally until chocolate is uniformly smooth and glossy, 10 to 15 minutes. Remove bowl from saucepan. Add butter, whisking once or twice to break up pieces. Let mixture stand for 5 minutes to finish melting butter, then whisk until completely smooth. Refrigerate frosting, without stirring, until cooled and thickened, 30 minutes to 1 hour.

5. Once cool, whisk frosting until smooth. (Whisked frosting will lighten in color slightly and should hold its shape on whisk.) Spread frosting evenly over top of cake. Serve. (Leftover cake can be refrigerated for up to 2 days.)

KEYS TO SUCCESS

- **Heat the cocoa powder with the milk:** Allows cocoa's flavor to bloom for a more intense chocolate experience
- **Add the remaining ingredients right into the cocoa-milk mixture:** Minimizes cleanup
- **Use vegetable oil:** Clean, neutral flavor allows the chocolate flavor to really shine
- **Use milk chocolate for the frosting:** Provides a lighter, sweeter contrast to the dark, rich cake

SCIENCE LESSON

Dry Cake? Check Your Cocoa

There are two types of unsweetened cocoa powder: natural and Dutch-processed. Dutched cocoa has been neutralized with alkali to take away some of the cacao bean's harsher acidic notes. Dutched cocoas also typically have more fat than natural cocoas. Fat adds a perception of moisture in baked goods. In addition, cocoa with more fat contains less starch. Starch absorbs free moisture in a batter, so the crumb bakes up drier. This explains why the same cake can be noticeably moister when made with Dutched rather than with natural cocoa powder. Because the fat percentages of Dutched cocoas vary quite a bit (from 11.9 percent to 22 percent), look for a higher-fat Dutch-processed cocoa.

BUTTERY YELLOW LAYER CAKE WITH CHOCOLATE FROSTING

Serves: 8 to 10
Total Time: 1½ hours, plus 2 hours cooling

RECIPE OVERVIEW Everyone needs a really good classic yellow birthday cake recipe in their back pocket. This one is picture-perfect. It produces a sturdy yet velvety cake with rich flavor. For a truly tender cake, use cake flour. Employing the reverse-creaming method (see page 562) produces a light, flat-topped cake with a delicate crumb and just enough heft, ideal for layering and slathering with frosting. Bring all the ingredients to room temperature before beginning this recipe. Be sure to use cake pans with at least 2-inch-tall sides (see page 11 for our recommendation). Do not substitute all-purpose flour for cake flour in this recipe. We prefer to use a stand mixer for this recipe, but a handheld mixer will also work.

- ½ cup whole milk, room temperature
- 4 large eggs, room temperature
- 2 teaspoons vanilla extract
- 1¾ cups (7 ounces) cake flour
- 1½ cups (10½ ounces) sugar
- 2 teaspoons baking powder
- ¾ teaspoon table salt
- 16 tablespoons unsalted butter, cut into 16 pieces and softened
- 1 recipe Chocolate Frosting (page 594)

1. Adjust oven rack to middle position and heat oven to 350 degrees. Grease two 9-inch round cake pans, line with parchment paper, grease parchment, and flour pans. Whisk milk, eggs, and vanilla together in small bowl.

2. In large bowl, whisk together flour, sugar, baking powder, and salt. Using electric mixer on medium-low speed, beat butter into flour mixture, 1 piece at a time, about 30 seconds. Continue to beat mixture until it resembles moist crumbs, 1 to 3 minutes.

3. Beat in all but ½ cup milk mixture, then increase mixer speed to medium and beat batter until smooth, light, and fluffy, 1 to 3 minutes. Reduce mixer speed to low and slowly beat in remaining ½ cup milk mixture until batter looks slightly curdled, about 15 seconds.

4. Give batter final stir by hand. Divide batter evenly between prepared pans and smooth tops with a rubber spatula. Gently tap pans on counter to release air bubbles. Bake until toothpick inserted in center comes out with few moist crumbs attached, 20 to 25 minutes, switching and rotating pans halfway through baking.

5. Let cakes cool in pans on wire rack for 10 minutes. Remove cakes from pans, discarding parchment, and let cool completely on rack, about 2 hours.

6. Frost cake following instructions on page 591. Use 1½ cups frosting to fill cake and remaining frosting for top and sides. (Assembled cake can be refrigerated for up to 24 hours. Let come to room temperature before serving.)

KEYS TO SUCCESS

- **Reverse-creaming method:** Yields a cake that is flat, not domed, with a sturdy but velvety crumb
- **Cake flour:** Yields a fine, plush-textured cake
- **Room-temperature eggs:** Ensure the proper rise

SCIENCE LESSON Cake Flour

While all-purpose flour has a protein content of 10 to 12 percent, cake flour has just 6 to 8 percent protein. Cake flour is made from soft winter wheat, which is easier to mill very fine than the mix of hard spring wheat and soft winter wheat used to make all-purpose flour. Cake flour feels finer than all-purpose flour and absorbs fat and liquid more easily. Since soft winter wheat is higher in starch and lower in protein, it has less of an ability to form gluten. The result is a delicate, tender cake.

FROSTING A LAYER CAKE

FROSTING A CAKE

1. KEEP CAKE PLATTER CLEAN
Cover the edges of the platter with strips of parchment paper to ensure that extra frosting doesn't end up on the platter. Place one layer on the platter.

2. FROST FIRST LAYER
Dollop a portion of frosting in the center of the cake layer. Using an offset spatula, spread the frosting in an even layer from the center right to the edge of the cake.

3. FROST SECOND LAYER
Place the second layer on top, pressing gently and making sure that it's aligned with the first layer. Finish by dolloping more frosting in the center and spread it evenly across the top layer, pushing it slightly over the edge of the cake.

4. GATHER UP FROSTING FOR SIDES
A narrow, flexible offset spatula is ideal for spreading frosting on vertical surfaces. Mound a few tablespoons of frosting on the spatula's tip and press it against the side of the cake to adhere.

5. FROST SIDES
Gently smear the frosting onto the sides of the cake. Repeat until the sides are covered. Use gentle motions and don't press too hard, or you will wind up with crumbs in the frosting. Clean off the spatula as needed.

6. SMOOTH OUT ROUGH SPOTS
Gently run the edge of the spatula around the sides to smooth out any bumps and tidy the area where the frosting from the top and sides merges. You can run the edge of the spatula over the top of the cake to give it a smooth look too. Remove the strips of parchment before serving.

CONFETTI CAKE

Serves: 10 to 12
Total Time: 1½ hours, plus 2 hours cooling

RECIPE OVERVIEW Kids love confetti cake, with its playful speckled interior and friendly vanilla flavor that's perfect for a fun celebration. To ditch the store-bought mix and create this cake at home, start with two layers of fluffy white cake. White cake is made with egg whites rather than whole eggs, giving the cake a soft, fine crumb. But rather than whip the egg whites as many recipes call for, simply mix the whites with the milk before beating them into the flour-butter mixture; this eliminates any air pockets and holes and makes for an ultratender texture. Whole rainbow sprinkles mar the cake's downy crumb, so pulse them in the food processor before stirring them into the batter. A simple vanilla frosting provides just the right satisfying buttery vanilla flavor, but its stark-white color doesn't do this cake justice. Dye it pale yellow with the help of a little food coloring and it's the perfect creamy backdrop for more sprinkles, which make for a cake that's party-ready.

- ¾ cup rainbow sprinkles, divided
- 1 cup whole milk, room temperature
- 6 large egg whites, room temperature
- 1 teaspoon vanilla extract
- 2¼ cups (9 ounces) cake flour
- 1¾ cups (12¼ ounces) sugar
- 4 teaspoons baking powder
- 1 teaspoon table salt
- 12 tablespoons unsalted butter, cut into 12 pieces and softened
- 4–6 drops yellow food coloring
- 6 cups Vanilla Frosting (page 594)

1. Adjust oven rack to middle position and heat oven to 350 degrees. Grease three 9-inch round cake pans, line with parchment paper, grease parchment, and flour pans. Pulse ½ cup sprinkles in food processor until coarsely ground, 8 to 10 pulses; set aside. Whisk milk, egg whites, and vanilla together in bowl.

2. Using stand mixer fitted with paddle, mix flour, sugar, baking powder, and salt on low speed until combined. Add butter, 1 piece at a time, until only pea-size pieces remain, about 1 minute. Add all but ½ cup milk mixture; increase speed to medium-high; and beat until light and fluffy, about 1 minute. Reduce speed to medium-low; add remaining ½ cup milk mixture; and beat until incorporated, about 30 seconds (batter may look curdled). Give batter final stir by hand. Stir ground sprinkles into cake batter.

3. Divide batter evenly between prepared pans and smooth tops with rubber spatula. Bake until toothpick inserted in center comes out clean, 23 to 25 minutes, switching and rotating pans halfway through baking. Let cakes cool in pans on wire rack for 10 minutes. Remove cakes from pans, discarding parchment, and let cool completely on rack, about 2 hours.

4. Mix food coloring into frosting. Line edges of cake platter with 4 strips parchment to keep platter clean. Place 1 cake layer on platter. Spread ¾ cup frosting evenly over top, right to edge of cake. Repeat with 1 more cake layer, pressing lightly to adhere, and ¾ cup frosting. Top with remaining cake layer, pressing lightly to adhere. Spread remaining frosting evenly over top and sides of cake. Press remaining ¼ cup sprinkles around bottom edge of cake. Carefully remove parchment strips before serving.

KEYS TO SUCCESS

- **Don't whip the egg whites to stiff peaks; whisk them with the milk instead:** Prevents air pockets from forming throughout the cake
- **Use the reverse-creaming method:** Allows the butter to coat the flour for an ultratender crumb
- **Pulse some sprinkles in the food processor to make them smaller:** Keeps sprinkles from interrupting the carefully constructed texture of the cake

RED VELVET CUPCAKES

Makes: 12 cupcakes
Total Time: 45 minutes, plus 1¼ hours cooling

RECIPE OVERVIEW Although they're perhaps best known for their shocking bright color, red velvet cupcakes are more than just a novelty: Their tender, light, and moist texture is also a hallmark of these little cakes. For the ideal red velvet cupcakes, two ingredients are essential: buttermilk and vinegar. This combination of liquids reacts with baking soda to create a fine, tender crumb. The type of cocoa powder is also important. Unlike Dutch-processed cocoa, natural cocoa powder is acidic; so in addition to providing a light chocolate flavor to the cake, natural cocoa further enhances the cake's light and airy texture. (In fact, the ruddy color of the original red velvet cake didn't come from dye but from the reaction of the natural cocoa and the buttermilk and vinegar.) These cupcakes rise high and form nice flat tops—perfect for sporting billows of tangy cream cheese frosting. Do not substitute Dutch-processed cocoa powder for the natural cocoa powder.

- 1⅛ cups (5⅔ ounces) all-purpose flour
- ¾ teaspoon baking soda
- Pinch table salt
- ½ cup buttermilk, room temperature
- 1 large egg
- 1½ teaspoons distilled white vinegar
- 1 teaspoon vanilla extract
- 1 tablespoon natural unsweetened cocoa powder

1 tablespoon (½ ounce) red food coloring
6 tablespoons unsalted butter, softened
¾ cup (5¼ ounces) sugar
3 cups Cream Cheese Frosting (page 595)

1. Adjust oven rack to middle position and heat oven to 350 degrees. Line 12-cup muffin tin with paper or foil liners.
2. Whisk flour, baking soda, and salt together in bowl. Whisk buttermilk, egg, vinegar, and vanilla together in second bowl. Mix cocoa and food coloring into smooth paste in small bowl.
3. Using stand mixer fitted with paddle, beat butter and sugar on medium-high speed until pale and fluffy, about 3 minutes. Reduce speed to low and add flour mixture in 3 additions, alternating with buttermilk mixture in 2 additions, scraping down bowl as needed. Beat in cocoa mixture until batter is uniform. Give batter final stir by hand.
4. Divide batter evenly among prepared muffin cups. Bake until toothpick inserted in center comes out with few crumbs attached, 15 to 20 minutes, rotating muffin tin halfway through baking.
5. Let cupcakes cool in muffin tin on wire rack for 10 minutes. Remove cupcakes from muffin tin and let cool completely on rack, about 1 hour. (Unfrosted cupcakes can be stored at room temperature for up to 24 hours.) Spread or pipe frosting evenly on cupcakes. Serve.

KEYS TO SUCCESS

- **Choose natural cocoa, which is more acidic than Dutch-processed cocoa:** Helps give the cupcakes their light and airy texture
- **Combine buttermilk and vinegar:** Causes a reaction with the baking soda to create a fine, tender crumb

Make Cupcakes Sparkle

When you want to add a special touch to freshly frosted cupcakes, you can top them with sprinkles or shredded coconut or pipe icing designs, but here's another way to add flair.

USE CUTTER
Press a simply shaped cookie cutter into smooth frosting on a cupcake. Fill the shape with sprinkles, colored sugar, or another confection of a contrasting color. Carefully remove the cookie cutter, leaving behind a festive decoration.

MORE TO EXPLORE

FROSTINGS AND WHIPPED CREAM

Below are some classic frostings you can use to coat layer cakes, sheet cakes, and cupcakes. We provide different yields of frosting to accommodate each type of cake. For a two-layer cake, plan on using about 1½ cups frosting for the filling and 3½ cups for the top and sides. For tips on frosting a cake, check out page 591.

VANILLA FROSTING

Makes: 5 cups, enough for two-layer cake
Total Time: 30 minutes

Before you gather the other ingredients, cut the butter into pieces and let it soften—but not too much, or the frosting will be greasy. Many recipes for vanilla frosting call for milk; we prefer heavy cream, which gives the frosting a silky quality. For colored frosting, stir in drops of food coloring at the end, but be sure to use a light hand—a little goes a long way.

- 1 pound (4 sticks) unsalted butter, each stick cut into quarters and softened
- ¼ cup heavy cream
- 1 tablespoon vanilla extract
- ¼ teaspoon table salt
- 4 cups (16 ounces) confectioners' sugar

1. Using stand mixer fitted with paddle, beat butter, cream, vanilla, and salt on medium-high speed until smooth, about 1 minute. Reduce speed to medium-low; slowly add sugar; and beat until incorporated and smooth, about 4 minutes.

2. Increase speed to medium-high and beat until frosting is light and fluffy, about 5 minutes. (Frosting can be refrigerated for up to 3 days; let soften at room temperature, about 2 hours, then rewhip on medium speed until smooth, 2 to 5 minutes.)

For Cupcakes, Sheet Cake, or Three-Layer Cake

Makes: 3 cups, enough for cupcakes or sheet cake
Reduce butter to 20 tablespoons (2½ sticks), reduce cream to 2 tablespoons, reduce vanilla to 2 teaspoons, reduce salt to ⅛ teaspoon, and reduce confectioners' sugar to 2½ cups (10 ounces).

Makes: 6 cups, enough for three-layer cake
Increase butter to 1¼ pounds (5 sticks), increase vanilla to 4 teaspoons, and increase confectioners' sugar to 5 cups (1¼ pounds).

Flavor Variations
ALMOND
For 5 cups frosting substitute 1½ teaspoons almond extract for vanilla. For 3 cups frosting substitute 1 teaspoon almond extract for vanilla.

COCONUT
For 5 cups frosting substitute 1½ teaspoons coconut extract for vanilla. For 3 cups frosting substitute 1 teaspoon coconut extract for vanilla.

COFFEE
For 5 cups frosting add 3 tablespoons instant espresso powder or instant coffee powder to mixer with butter. For 3 cups frosting add 1½ tablespoons instant espresso powder or instant coffee powder to mixer with butter.

ORANGE
For 5 cups frosting add 1 tablespoon grated orange zest and 2 tablespoons juice to mixer with butter. For 3 cups frosting add 1½ teaspoons grated orange zest and 1 tablespoon juice to mixer with butter.

PEPPERMINT
For 5 cups frosting add 2½ teaspoons peppermint extract to mixer with butter. For 3 cups frosting add 1½ teaspoons peppermint extract to mixer with butter.

CHOCOLATE FROSTING

Makes: 5 cups, enough for two-layer cake
Total Time: 25 minutes

This frosting combines a hefty amount of cocoa powder with melted chocolate for deep chocolate flavor. A mix of confectioners' sugar and corn syrup makes it smooth and glossy. To keep the frosting from separating and turning greasy, turn to the food processor: The fast-mixing machine virtually eliminates any risk of overbeating, as it blends the ingredients quickly without melting the butter or incorporating too much air. Bittersweet, semisweet, or milk chocolate can be used in this recipe.

30	tablespoons (3¾ sticks) unsalted butter, softened
1½	cups (6 ounces) confectioners' sugar
1	cup (3 ounces) Dutch-processed cocoa powder
⅛	teaspoon table salt
1	cup light corn syrup
1½	teaspoons vanilla extract
12	ounces chocolate, melted and cooled

Process butter, sugar, cocoa, and salt in food processor until smooth, about 30 seconds, scraping down sides of bowl as needed. Add corn syrup and vanilla and process until just combined, 5 to 10 seconds. Scrape down sides of bowl, then add chocolate and process until smooth and creamy, 10 to 15 seconds. (Frosting can be kept at room temperature for up to 3 hours or refrigerated for up to 3 days; if refrigerated, let stand at room temperature for 1 hour and stir before using.)

For Cupcakes, Sheet Cake, or Three-Layer Cake
Makes: 3 cups, enough for cupcakes or sheet cake
Reduce butter to 20 tablespoons (2½ sticks), reduce confectioners' sugar to 1 cup (4 ounces), reduce cocoa powder to ¾ cup (2¼ ounces), reduce corn syrup to ¾ cup, reduce vanilla to 1 teaspoon, and reduce chocolate to 8 ounces.

Makes: 6 cups, enough for three-layer cake
Increase butter to 1¼ pounds (5 sticks), increase confectioners' sugar to 2 cups (8 ounces), increase cocoa powder to 1½ cups (4½ ounces), and increase chocolate to 1 pound.

CHOCOLATE GANACHE FROSTING
Makes: 5 cups, enough for two-layer cake
Total Time: 15 minutes, plus 1 hour chilling

The richest chocolate frosting is also the easiest to make. For an intense chocolaty topping for cake or cupcakes, go with ganache, made simply from heavy cream and melted semisweet chocolate.

1	pound semisweet chocolate, chopped
2	cups heavy cream

1. Place chocolate in large heatproof bowl. Bring cream to boil in small saucepan. Pour boiling cream over chocolate and let sit, covered, for 5 minutes. Whisk mixture until smooth, then cover with plastic wrap and refrigerate until cool and slightly firm, about 1 hour.

2. Using stand mixer fitted with whisk attachment, whip cooled chocolate mixture on medium speed until fluffy and mousse-like and soft peaks form, about 2 minutes.

For Cupcakes or Sheet Cake
Makes: 3 cups, enough for cupcakes or sheet cake
Reduce chocolate to 10 ounces and reduce heavy cream to 1¼ cups.

CREAM CHEESE FROSTING
Makes: about 5 cups, enough for two-layer cake
Total Time: 30 minutes

Slowly adding the confectioners' sugar at a low speed until well combined and then turning up the speed gives you more control over the texture and helps produce a light, fluffy frosting. Do not use low-fat or fat-free cream cheese or the frosting will have a soupy consistency. This frosting has a softer, looser texture than other frostings; if it becomes too soft to work with, let it chill in the refrigerator until firm.

1¼	pounds cream cheese, softened
12	tablespoons unsalted butter, cut into 12 pieces and softened
2	tablespoons sour cream
2	teaspoons vanilla extract
¼	teaspoon table salt
2½	cups (10 ounces) confectioners' sugar

1. Using stand mixer fitted with paddle, beat cream cheese, butter, sour cream, vanilla, and salt on medium-high speed until smooth, about 2 minutes. Reduce speed to medium-low, slowly add sugar, and beat until incorporated and smooth, about 4 minutes.

2. Increase speed to medium-high and beat until frosting is light and fluffy, about 4 minutes. (Frosting can be refrigerated for up to 3 days; let soften at room temperature, about 1 hour, then rewhip on medium speed until smooth, about 2 minutes.)

For Cupcakes or Sheet Cake
Makes: 3 cups, enough for cupcakes or sheet cake
Reduce cream cheese to 12 ounces, reduce butter to 6 tablespoons, reduce sour cream to 1½ tablespoons, reduce vanilla to 1 teaspoon, and reduce confectioners' sugar to 1½ cups (6 ounces).

WHIPPED CREAM
Makes: about 2 cups
Total Time: 5 minutes

For lightly sweetened whipped cream, reduce the sugar to 1½ teaspoons.

1	cup heavy cream, chilled
1	tablespoon sugar
1	teaspoon vanilla extract

Using stand mixer fitted with whisk attachment, whip cream, sugar, and vanilla on medium-low speed until foamy, about 1 minute. Increase speed to high and whip until soft peaks form, 1 to 3 minutes. (Whipped cream can be refrigerated in fine-mesh strainer set over small bowl and covered with plastic wrap for up to 8 hours.)

COURSE
LEMON DESSERTS

LAN LAM

Although citrus season is technically in the winter, lemony desserts feel like pure summer. Balancing sweet and tart flavors is key, and with the help of a few ingredients (such as sugar and salt), it is easy to elevate them for an extra-satisfying dessert. But lemon flavor can be finicky, and adding too much lemon juice can ruin the texture of delicate baked goods. In this course, you'll learn different ways to maximize lemon flavor by taking advantage of all a lemon has to offer. Finally, you'll get to make three brightly flavored desserts.

LAN'S PRO TIP: *Measure the amount of zest carefully. Lemon zest is packed with volatile compounds that make up the bulk of lemon flavor. Not enough zest means the dessert will lack character whereas too much zest makes the dessert sharp and medicinal.*

BEST LEMON BARS

Makes: 12 bars
Total Time: 1 hour, plus 1½ hours cooling

RECIPE OVERVIEW Have you ever met anyone who didn't love a lemon bar? The sunny, sweet-tart treats can brighten any day, and the lemon flavor in these bars shines through. The secret is not relying on lemon juice alone, since the more juice you use, the more flavor-dulling eggs and starch are needed to thicken and stabilize the wobbly top layer. So in addition to plenty of lemon juice, we add 2 teaspoons of lemon zest (straining it out before cooking). And for more tartness, we turn to a pantry staple: cream of tartar. Typically used when whipping egg whites, the white powder tastes plenty sour, and 2 teaspoons brings our lemon bar's flavor into sharp focus. Precooking the lemon filling on the stove ensures that it won't curdle or brown in the oven. Do not substitute bottled lemon juice for the fresh.

Crust
- 1 cup (5 ounces) all-purpose flour
- ¼ cup (1¾ ounces) granulated sugar
- ½ teaspoon table salt
- 8 tablespoons unsalted butter, melted

Filling
- 1 cup (7 ounces) granulated sugar
- 2 tablespoons all-purpose flour
- 2 teaspoons cream of tartar
- ¼ teaspoon table salt
- 3 large eggs plus 3 large yolks
- 2 teaspoons grated lemon zest plus ⅔ cup juice (4 lemons)
- 4 tablespoons unsalted butter, cut into 8 pieces
  Confectioners' sugar (optional)

1. FOR THE CRUST Adjust oven rack to middle position and heat oven to 350 degrees. Make foil sling for 8-inch square baking pan by folding 2 long sheets of aluminum foil so each is 8 inches wide. Lay sheets of foil in pan perpendicular to each other, with extra foil hanging over edges of pan. Push foil into corners and up sides of pan, smoothing foil flush to pan.

2. Whisk flour, sugar, and salt together in bowl. Add melted butter and stir until combined. Transfer mixture to prepared pan and press into even layer over entire bottom of pan (do not wash bowl). Bake crust until dark golden brown, 19 to 24 minutes, rotating pan halfway through baking.

3. FOR THE FILLING While crust bakes, whisk sugar, flour, cream of tartar, and salt together in now-empty bowl. Whisk in eggs and yolks until no streaks of egg remain. Whisk in lemon zest and juice. Transfer mixture to saucepan and cook over medium-low heat, stirring constantly, until mixture thickens and registers 160 degrees, 5 to 8 minutes. Off heat, stir in butter. Strain filling through fine-mesh strainer set over bowl.

4. Pour filling over hot crust and tilt pan to spread evenly. Bake until filling is set and barely jiggles when pan is shaken, 8 to 12 minutes. (Filling around perimeter of pan may be slightly raised.) Let bars cool completely, at least 1½ hours. Using foil overhang, lift bars out of pan and transfer to cutting board. Cut into bars, wiping knife clean between cuts as necessary. Before serving, dust bars with confectioners' sugar, if using.

KEYS TO SUCCESS
- **Use both lemon juice and lemon zest:** Provides complex lemon flavor
- **Add cream of tartar:** Gives the bars a sharp, lingering finish
- **Use granulated sugar rather than confectioners':** Gives the crust a crisp texture that contrasts with the creamy lemon layer
- **Parcook the filling:** Helps it remain silky-smooth throughout

Pat-in-the-Pan Crust

MELT BUTTER
Most lemon bar crust recipes call for cutting cold butter into flour. Our stripped-down approach calls for simply stirring melted butter into a mixture of flour, sugar, and salt. The upshot: a no-fuss, pliable dough that's easy to press into an even layer.

SCIENCE LESSON
What Is Cream of Tartar, Anyway?

The white, odorless powder known as cream of tartar is a product of grape fermentation. It is said to have been first isolated from the bottom of wine barrels by the Persian alchemist Jabir ibn Hayyan around 800 AD. Today, we know that tartaric acid, the acid component of cream of tartar, is found in the greatest concentration in grapes but is also in bananas and tamarind. To make cream of tartar, grape sediment, called beeswing, is scraped from wine barrels, purified, and ground. Using cream of tartar to boost acidic flavor is novel; it's most often incorporated into beaten egg whites for stability or into sugar syrup to help prevent crystallization.

LEMON PUDDING CAKE

Serves: 8
Total Time: 1½ hours, plus 1 hour cooling

RECIPE OVERVIEW Somewhere between a cake and a custard, a pudding cake separates like magic into two layers during baking: airy and soufflé-like on top, dense and custardy below. The ethereal dessert has very little flour, quite a bit of egg, and a lot more liquid than you might expect. In fact, it's the water in that liquid that sinks to the bottom, taking the batter with it; the egg whites float to the top. Making a pudding cake isn't difficult, but it does require properly beating egg whites, which give the pudding cake its airy top layer. Beating them with sugar until they form stiff peaks not only gives them a billowy, airy texture but also gives them enough stability to retain their shape while the pudding sets in the oven. This dessert is best served warm or at room temperature the same day it is made.

- ¼ cup (1¼ ounces) all-purpose flour
- 2 teaspoons cornstarch
- 1¼ cups (8¾ ounces) sugar, divided
- 5 tablespoons unsalted butter, softened
- 2 tablespoons grated lemon zest plus ½ cup juice (4 lemons)
- 5 large eggs, separated
- 1¼ cups whole milk, room temperature
- 2 quarts boiling water

1. Adjust oven rack to lowest position and heat oven to 325 degrees. Grease 8-inch square baking dish. Whisk flour and cornstarch in bowl. Using stand mixer fitted with paddle, beat ½ cup sugar, butter, and lemon zest on medium-high speed until light and fluffy, about 2 minutes. Beat in egg yolks, one at a time, until incorporated. Reduce speed to medium-low. Add flour mixture and mix until incorporated. Slowly add milk and lemon juice, mixing until just combined.

2. Using clean bowl and whisk attachment, beat egg whites on medium-high speed until soft peaks form, about 2 minutes. With mixer running, slowly add remaining ¾ cup sugar until whites are firm and glossy, about 1 minute. Whisk one-third of whites into batter, then gently fold in remaining whites, 1 scoop at a time, until well combined.

3. Place clean dish towel in bottom of roasting pan and arrange prepared baking dish on towel. Spoon batter into prepared dish. Carefully place pan on oven rack and pour boiling water into pan until water comes halfway up sides of baking dish. Bake until surface is golden brown and edges are set (center should jiggle slightly when gently shaken), about 1 hour. Transfer dish to wire rack and let cool for at least 1 hour. To serve, scoop warm cake into individual serving bowls.

KEYS TO SUCCESS:
- **Add both lemon zest and lemon juice:** Provides the cake with a fragrant aroma and bright lemon flavor
- **Thicken with cornstarch:** Doesn't muddy the pudding cake's lemon taste

CORE TECHNIQUE
Preparing a Water Bath

LINE PAN
To prevent the baking dish from sliding, line the bottom of a larger pan with a dish towel.

POUR IN WATER
To avoid any water splashing into the baking dish, first set the pan on the oven rack, then carefully pour boiling water into the pan until it comes halfway up the sides of the baking dish.

SCIENCE LESSON
Why Use a Water Bath?

This bit of culinary physics is possible because the pudding cake bakes in a water bath—a larger pan partially filled with hot water. The water lowers the temperature of the surrounding dish (even if it boils, the water temperature will be cooler than the oven temperature) and prevents uneven cooking. In a pudding cake, low heat prevents the mixture from scrambling and gives it enough oven time to split in two distinct layers.

CORE TECHNIQUE
Whipping Egg Whites

SEPARATE EGG WHITES
Separate each egg over a small side bowl to catch the egg white, then transfer the egg white into your main bowl. That way, if you accidentally puncture a yolk, you won't sacrifice more than one egg white.

USE CLEAN BOWL
Any fat present will inhibit egg whites from whipping properly. Bowls made from porous plastic retain an oily film even when washed, and glass and ceramic bowls have slippery surfaces that make it harder for whites to billow up. We prefer stainless steel.

SOFT PEAKS
Whip until soft peaks form. This means that when you lift the tip of a whisk from the whites, they form a peak that droops slightly downward.

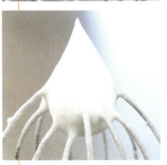

STIFF PEAKS
Add sugar and whip until stiff peaks form. Stiff peaks will stand tall. Adding sugar helps to stabilize the egg whites so that they retain their airy structure in the oven.

LEMON BUNDT CAKE

Serves: 12
Total Time: 1¾ hours, plus 3 hours cooling

RECIPE OVERVIEW Adding lemon flavor to a simple Bundt cake sounds straightforward enough, but it can be a challenge to capture lemon's tart, aromatic notes. That's because the flavor of lemon juice is drastically muted when exposed to the heat of an oven, and its acidity can wreak havoc on delicate baked goods. To achieve bold lemon flavor without compromising texture, use only a small amount of juice but a whopping 3 tablespoons of zest. A brief soak in the lemon juice softens the zest's fibrous texture. Replacing the milk with buttermilk fortifies tang. For the glaze, a simple mixture of lemon juice, buttermilk, and confectioners' sugar provides a final layer of citrus flavor. This cake has a light, fluffy texture when eaten the day it's baked, but if well wrapped and held at room temperature overnight, its texture becomes more dense—like that of pound cake—the following day.

Cake
- 3 cups (15 ounces) all-purpose flour
- 1 teaspoon table salt
- 1 teaspoon baking powder
- ½ teaspoon baking soda
- ¾ cup buttermilk, room temperature
- 3 tablespoons grated lemon zest plus 3 tablespoons juice (3 lemons)
- 1 tablespoon vanilla extract
- 18 tablespoons (2¼ sticks) unsalted butter, cut into 18 pieces and softened
- 2 cups (14 ounces) granulated sugar
- 3 large eggs plus 1 large yolk

Glaze
- 2 cups (8 ounces) confectioners' sugar
- 2–3 tablespoons lemon juice
- 1 tablespoon buttermilk

1. FOR THE CAKE Adjust oven rack to lower-middle position and heat oven to 350 degrees. Spray 12-cup nonstick Bundt pan with baking spray with flour. Whisk flour, salt, baking powder, and baking soda together in bowl. Whisk buttermilk, lemon zest and juice, and vanilla together in second bowl.

2. Using stand mixer fitted with paddle, beat butter and sugar on medium-high speed until pale and fluffy, about 3 minutes. Add eggs and yolk, one at a time, and beat until combined. Reduce speed to low and add flour mixture in 3 additions, alternating with buttermilk mixture in 2 additions, scraping down bowl as needed. Give batter final stir by hand.

3. Transfer batter to prepared pan and smooth top with rubber spatula. Gently tap pan on counter to settle batter. Bake until wooden skewer inserted in center comes out with few crumbs attached, 50 minutes to 1 hour, rotating pan halfway through baking. Let cake cool in pan on wire rack set in rimmed baking sheet for 10 minutes.

4. FOR THE GLAZE While cake is baking, whisk confectioners' sugar, 2 tablespoons lemon juice, and buttermilk until smooth, adding more lemon juice as needed, teaspoon by teaspoon, until glaze is thick but still pourable.

5. Invert cake onto rack and remove pan. Pour half of glaze over warm cake and let cool for 1 hour. Drizzle remaining glaze evenly over cake and let cool completely, at least 2 hours, before serving.

KEYS TO SUCCESS

- **Coat the pan with baking spray:** Ensures that the cake releases cleanly from the Bundt pan
- **Zest and juice three lemons:** See page 47 for how to do it.
- **Soak grated lemon zest in an equal volume of lemon juice:** Contributes bold lemon flavor that doesn't interfere with the texture of the cake
- **Glaze the cake once when it's warm from the oven and again once it's cool:** Provides the cake with an extra hit of bright citrus flavor

SCIENCE LESSON

Anatomy of a Lemon

What is the best source of lemon flavor? It all depends on the context. Lemon juice is acidic and tart, but that brightness is diminished when exposed to heat; it's best used uncooked. Better for baking is the thin, yellow layer of zest, which contains floral lemony oils. But avoid the bitter white pith, just beneath the zest. In our Lemon Bundt Cake, we use three lemons' worth of zest, giving us a floral, perfumed lemon flavor that remains in the baked cake.

COURSE
SUMMER COBBLERS AND CRISPS

ASHLEY MOORE

When summer rolls around, our thoughts turn to desserts featuring ripe, juicy fruit—particularly cobblers, crumbles, and crisps. Their browned, lightly crunchy toppings provide the perfect counterpoint to sweet and juicy fillings. These desserts are simple to prepare and you'll learn how to avoid their main pitfalls—specifically soggy toppings and watery fillings (all that wonderful fresh fruit tends to shed its juice when cooked)—using a variety of techniques. In this course you'll also find an option for a crisp you can make any time of year. And whether you use the stovetop or the oven, peak in-season fruit or frozen, we think you'll find that a scoop of vanilla ice cream or a dollop of whipped cream adds the perfect finishing touch.

ASHLEY'S PRO TIP: *Yes, these fruit recipes are extra-special when made at the peak of summer. But don't forget that frozen fruit will almost always work as a substitute. Just read the headnote for any ingredient adjustments.*

SKILLET CHERRY CRISP
Serves: 6
Total Time: 45 minutes, plus 30 minutes cooling

RECIPE OVERVIEW Most fruit crisps are baked in the oven, but the best way to cook this sweet cherry crisp is also the easiest: in a skillet on the stovetop. After browning a topping of almonds, sugar, flour, and butter in a 10-inch skillet, you can use the same pan to cook the filling. Starting with frozen pitted cherries conveniently makes this an anytime dessert, and once combined with sugar, lemon juice, and almond and vanilla extracts, the frozen cherries taste just as good as fresh. Cornstarch thickens the filling to a syrupy consistency, and dried cherries soak up excess moisture while adding texture. There's no need to thaw the cherries.

Topping
- ¾ cup sliced almonds, divided
- ⅔ cup (3⅓ ounces) all-purpose flour
- ¼ cup packed (1¾ ounces) light brown sugar
- ¼ cup (1¾ ounces) granulated sugar
- ½ teaspoon vanilla extract
- ¼ teaspoon ground cinnamon
- ¼ teaspoon table salt
- 6 tablespoons unsalted butter, melted

Filling
- ⅓ cup (2⅓ ounces) granulated sugar, divided
- 1 tablespoon cornstarch
- 2 pounds frozen sweet cherries
- 1 tablespoon lemon juice
- 1 teaspoon vanilla extract
- ½ teaspoon table salt
- ¼ teaspoon almond extract
- ⅔ cup dried cherries

1. FOR THE TOPPING Finely chop ¼ cup almonds. Combine flour, brown sugar, granulated sugar, vanilla, cinnamon, salt, and chopped almonds in bowl. Stir in melted butter until mixture resembles wet sand and no dry flour remains.

2. Toast remaining ½ cup almonds in 10-inch nonstick skillet over medium-low heat until just beginning to brown, about 4 minutes. Add flour mixture and cook, stirring constantly, until lightly browned, 6 to 8 minutes; transfer to plate to cool. Wipe out skillet.

3. FOR THE FILLING Combine 2 tablespoons sugar and cornstarch in small bowl; set aside. Combine cherries, lemon juice, vanilla, salt, almond extract, and remaining sugar in now-empty skillet. Cover and cook over medium heat until cherries thaw and release their juice, about 7 minutes, stirring halfway through cooking. Uncover; stir in dried cherries; and simmer until cherries are very tender, about 3 minutes.

4. Stir in cornstarch mixture and simmer, stirring constantly, until thickened, 1 to 3 minutes. Remove skillet from heat and distribute topping evenly over filling. Return skillet to medium-low heat and cook until filling is bubbling around edges, about 3 minutes. Let cool off heat for at least 30 minutes before serving.

> **KEYS TO SUCCESS**
> - **Use frozen cherries:** Makes the crisp convenient and easy to bake all year round
> - **Add dried cherries:** Contributes more cherry flavor and absorbs some liquid, helping prevent the filling from bubbling up over the streusel and making it soggy
> - **Cook the filling on the stovetop:** Allows it to come to a boil—and therefore thicken—faster

BLUEBERRY COBBLER WITH BISCUIT TOPPING

Serves: 8
Total Time: 1½ hours

RECIPE OVERVIEW The best blueberry cobbler has a not-too-thin, not-too-thick filling with a prominent blueberry flavor, crowned with a light, tender biscuit topping. A filling with 6 cups of fresh berries needs only a modest amount of sugar to sweeten it. Cornstarch works well to thicken the fruit's juices, and a little lemon and cinnamon enhance the filling without masking the blueberry flavor. Rather than drop spoonfuls of biscuit dough onto the fruit, partially bake the biscuit topping first. This ensures that the biscuits don't become soggy, and precooking the fruit filling means that all you have to do is marry the parbaked biscuits and precooked filling and heat them together briefly until the filling's bubbly. This recipe works best with very juicy fruit. Before preparing the filling, taste the fruit, adding the smaller amount of sugar if the fruit is on the sweet side and more if the fruit is tart. Do not let the biscuit batter sit for longer than 5 minutes or so before baking. If you don't have a deep-dish glass pie plate, use a round baking dish of similar size; the round shape of the dish makes it easy to fit the biscuits on top.

Fruit Filling
- ⅓–⅔ cup sugar
- 4 teaspoons cornstarch
- 30 ounces (6 cups) blueberries
- 1 tablespoon lemon juice
- ½ teaspoon ground cinnamon

Biscuit Topping
- 1½ cups (7½ ounces) all-purpose flour
- ¼ cup (1¾ ounces) plus 2 teaspoons sugar, divided
- 1½ teaspoons baking powder
- ¼ teaspoon baking soda
- ¼ teaspoon table salt
- ¾ cup buttermilk, chilled
- 6 tablespoons unsalted butter, melted and cooled
- ⅛ teaspoon ground cinnamon

1. FOR THE FRUIT FILLING Line rimmed baking sheet with aluminum foil. Adjust oven rack to middle position and heat oven to 400 degrees. Whisk sugar and cornstarch together in large bowl. Add blueberries, lemon juice, and cinnamon and toss gently to combine. Transfer fruit mixture to 9-inch deep-dish glass pie plate, cover with foil, and set on prepared sheet. (Fruit filling can be assembled in baking dish and held at room temperature for up to 4 hours.)

2. FOR THE BISCUIT TOPPING Line rimmed baking sheet with parchment paper. Whisk flour, ¼ cup sugar, baking powder, baking soda, and salt together in large bowl. In medium bowl, stir buttermilk and melted butter together until butter forms small clumps. Using rubber spatula, stir buttermilk mixture into flour mixture until just incorporated and dough pulls away from sides of bowl.

3. Using greased ¼-cup measuring cup, scoop out and drop 8 mounds of dough onto prepared baking sheet, spaced about 1½ inches apart. Toss remaining 2 teaspoons sugar with cinnamon in bowl and sprinkle cinnamon-sugar mixture over biscuit tops. Bake biscuits until puffed and lightly browned on bottom, about 10 minutes. Remove biscuits from oven and set aside. (Parbaked biscuits can be held at room temperature for up to 4 hours.)

4. TO ASSEMBLE AND BAKE Place fruit filling in oven and bake until hot and blueberries have released their juices, 20 to 25 minutes. Remove from oven, uncover, and stir gently. Arrange biscuits over top, squeezing them slightly as needed to fit into dish. Bake cobbler until biscuits are golden brown and filling is bubbling, about 15 minutes, rotating dish halfway through baking. Let cobbler cool for 10 minutes; serve warm.

Variations

BLACKBERRY COBBLER WITH BISCUIT TOPPING

Substitute 6 cups blackberries for blueberries and omit cinnamon. Reduce cornstarch to 1 tablespoon, sugar to ⅓ to ½ cup, and lemon juice to 1 teaspoon. Add 1 teaspoon vanilla extract to bowl with blackberries.

PEACH OR NECTARINE COBBLER WITH BISCUIT TOPPING

Substitute 3 pounds peaches or nectarines, peeled, halved, pitted, and cut into ½-inch-thick wedges, for blueberries. Omit cinnamon. Reduce cornstarch to 1 tablespoon and lemon juice to 1 teaspoon. Add 1 teaspoon vanilla extract to bowl with fruit.

STRAWBERRY COBBLER WITH BISCUIT TOPPING

Substitute 8 cups hulled strawberries for blueberries (halve large strawberries) and omit cinnamon. Increase cornstarch to 5 teaspoons and reduce lemon juice to 2 teaspoons. Add 1 teaspoon vanilla extract to bowl with strawberries.

> **KEYS TO SUCCESS**
> - **Use a modest amount of sugar:** Lets berries' flavor and natural sweetness shine
> - **Add cornstarch:** Thickens the blueberry filling to just the right consistency
> - **Parbake the biscuits:** Ensures that the biscuits don't end up soggy

PEACH CRUMBLE

Serves: 6
Total Time: 1½ hours

RECIPE OVERVIEW Peaches vary greatly in juiciness and flavor. For a peach crumble that's never soggy or flavorless, let the peeled, sliced peaches macerate in sugar before draining them and measuring out ¼ cup of peach juice to add to the filling. For a crisp, well-browned topping, bake it separately and then marry it to the filling, baking both just until the fruit bubbles around the edges. Add the lemon juice to taste in step 2 according to the sweetness of your peaches. If ripe peaches are unavailable, you can substitute 3 pounds of frozen peaches, thawed overnight in the refrigerator. If your peaches are firm, you should be able to peel them with a vegetable peeler. For how to peel soft, ripe peaches, see page 605. Serve with vanilla ice cream.

Filling
- 3½ pounds peaches, peeled, halved, pitted, and cut into ¾-inch wedges
- ⅓ cup (2⅓ ounces) granulated sugar
- 1¼ teaspoons cornstarch
- 3–5 teaspoons lemon juice
- Pinch table salt
- Pinch ground cinnamon
- Pinch ground nutmeg

Crumble Topping
- 1 cup (5 ounces) all-purpose flour
- ¼ cup (1¾ ounces) plus 1 tablespoon granulated sugar, divided
- ¼ cup packed (1¾ ounces) brown sugar
- ⅛ teaspoon table salt
- 2 teaspoons vanilla extract
- 6 tablespoons unsalted butter, cut into 6 pieces and softened
- ½ cup sliced almonds, divided

1. Adjust oven racks to lowest and middle positions and heat oven to 350 degrees. Line rimmed baking sheet with parchment paper.

2. FOR THE FILLING Gently toss peaches and sugar together in large bowl and let sit for 30 minutes, gently stirring several times. Drain peaches in colander set over large bowl and reserve ¼ cup juice (discard remaining juice). Whisk reserved juice, cornstarch, lemon juice, salt, cinnamon, and nutmeg together in small bowl. Combine peaches and juice mixture in bowl and transfer to 8-inch square baking dish.

3. FOR THE CRUMBLE TOPPING While peaches are macerating, combine flour, ¼ cup granulated sugar, brown sugar, and salt in food processor and drizzle vanilla over top. Pulse to combine, about 5 pulses. Scatter butter pieces and ¼ cup almonds over top and process until mixture clumps together into large, crumbly balls, about 30 seconds, scraping down bowl halfway through processing. Sprinkle remaining ¼ cup almonds over mixture and pulse 2 times

to combine. Transfer mixture to prepared baking sheet and spread into even layer (mixture should break up into roughly ½-inch chunks with some smaller, loose bits). Bake on upper rack until chunks are lightly browned and firm, 18 to 22 minutes, rotating baking sheet halfway through baking. (Cooled topping can be stored in an airtight container for up to 2 days.)

4. TO ASSEMBLE AND BAKE Grasp edges of parchment; slide topping off parchment onto peaches; and spread into even layer with spatula, packing down lightly and breaking up any very large pieces. Sprinkle remaining 1 tablespoon granulated sugar evenly over top and place dish on aluminum foil–lined rimmed baking sheet; place on lower rack. Increase oven temperature to 375 degrees and bake until well browned and filling is bubbling around edges, 25 to 35 minutes, rotating baking sheet halfway through baking. Transfer baking dish to wire rack and let cool for 15 minutes; serve warm.

KEYS TO SUCCESS

- **Macerate peaches with sugar and discard some juice:** Avoids a soggy crumble
- **Soften the butter:** Makes for a cohesive dough that can be easily broken apart into large chunks that bake up nice and crisp in the oven
- **Bake the topping first:** Yields an exceptionally crisp topping

CORE TECHNIQUE Peeling Peaches

SCORE AN X
Using a paring knife, score a small X at the base of each peach.

ADD PEACHES TO WATER
Lower the peaches into boiling water with a slotted spoon. Cover and blanch until the skins loosen, about 2 minutes.

REMOVE PEACHES FROM WATER
Use a slotted spoon to transfer the peaches to a bowl of ice water and let them sit for about 1 minute to stop the cooking.

PEEL OFF PEEL
Use a paring knife to remove the strips of loosened peel, starting at the X on the base of each peach.

Preparing a Crumble Topping

BREAK UP CRUMBLE
Break up the topping into rough ½-inch pieces with some smaller loose bits and spread them into an even layer on the prepared baking sheet.

BAKE UNTIL BROWNED
Bake the crumble topping until the chunks are very lightly browned and firm.

DESSERTS | 605

COURSE
APPLE PIES AND TARTS

ANDREA GEARY

At their simplest, pies and tarts are baked pastry shells with a sweet filling. They can be structured or free-form, tall and deep or thin and wide. And perhaps no filling is more comforting and well-loved than apple. We'll start with a simple recipe for apple galettes (free-form tarts) using store-bought puff pastry for ease before moving on to an apple pie you can cook in a skillet (no bottom crust required). And no course on apple pies and tarts would be complete without a classic deep-dish version. If a double-crust pie feels intimidating, not to worry: With our foolproof pie dough and step-by-step instructions for rolling it out, you'll feel like a pro in no time.

ANDREA'S PRO TIP: *Don't worry about apples discoloring as you peel and slice them for your desserts; the oxidation won't be noticeable when they're baked.*

EASY APPLE GALETTES
Serves: 4
Total Time: 1½ hours

RECIPE OVERVIEW An apple galette is a free-form dessert with a crust boasting the buttery flakiness of a croissant topped by a generous layer of apples. Bypass the labor-intensive process of making homemade pastry and reach for store-bought frozen puff pastry instead. Forming an attractive crust is as easy as folding over the edges of the pastry. Granny Smith apples work best here; the slices stay moist in the oven and maintain their shape. Sprinkling a little sugar on the apples prevents them from drying out and also helps them brown nicely. A simple glaze made from apple jelly and a small amount of water is the perfect finishing touch, contributing an attractive sheen and fruity tartness. Be sure to let the puff pastry thaw completely before using it; otherwise, it can crack and break apart. To thaw frozen puff pastry, let it sit either in the refrigerator for 24 hours or on the counter for 30 minutes to 1 hour.

- 1 (9½ by 9-inch) sheet puff pastry, thawed and halved
- 1 pound Granny Smith apples, peeled, cored, halved, and sliced ⅛ inch thick, divided
- 1 tablespoon unsalted butter, cut into ¼-inch pieces, divided
- 4 teaspoons sugar, divided
- 2 tablespoons apple jelly
- 2 teaspoons water

1. Adjust oven rack to middle position and heat oven to 400 degrees. Arrange puff pastry halves spaced evenly apart on parchment paper–lined rimmed baking sheet. Fold edges of each pastry over by ¼ inch; crimp to create ¼-inch-thick border.

2. Starting in 1 corner of 1 tart, shingle half of apple slices into crust in tidy diagonal rows, overlapping them by about half, until surface is completely covered. Dot apples with half of butter pieces and sprinkle evenly with 2 teaspoons sugar. Repeat with remaining tart, apples, butter, and sugar. Bake until bottoms of tarts are deep golden brown and apples have caramelized, 40 to 45 minutes, rotating sheet halfway through baking.

3. Combine apple jelly and water in bowl and microwave until mixture begins to bubble, about 30 seconds. Brush glaze over apples and let tarts cool slightly on sheet for 15 minutes. Slice and serve warm or at room temperature.

KEYS TO SUCCESS

- **Store-bought pastry:** Keeps the tarts simple and easy to prepare
- **Granny Smith apples:** Provide a nice tartness that balances the sweetness of the galettes
- **Apple jelly glaze:** Gives the tarts a fancy, flavorful finish

Making Easy Apple Galettes

FOLD EDGES OF PASTRY
Fold over by ¼ inch and crimp to create a ¼-inch-thick border.

SHINGLE APPLES
Starting in one corner, shingle the sliced apples to form even rows across the dough, overlapping each slice by about half.

SKILLET APPLE PIE

Serves: 6 to 8
Total Time: 45 minutes, plus 30 minutes cooling

RECIPE OVERVIEW Who says a pie needs to bake in a special plate—or even have a bottom crust? For a simplified version, make it in a skillet. Unlike a double-crust pie, a skillet apple pie can be saucy. Apple cider provides resonant apple flavor and, when thickened with cornstarch, it yields a juicy filling with just the right body. Maple syrup complements the natural sweetness of the apples. Sauté the apples long enough to caramelize them before topping them with the pie dough and transferring the skillet to the oven, where the crust develops a lovely deep-brown hue. Use a combination of sweet, crisp apples such as Golden Delicious and firm, tart apples such as Cortland or Empire.

- ½ cup apple cider
- ⅓ cup maple syrup
- 2 tablespoons lemon juice
- 2 teaspoons cornstarch
- ⅛ teaspoon ground cinnamon (optional)
- 2 tablespoons unsalted butter
- 2½ pounds apples, peeled, cored, and cut into ½-inch-thick wedges
- 1 recipe Foolproof All-Butter Single-Crust Pie Dough (page 610)
- 2 teaspoons sugar

1. Adjust oven rack to upper-middle position and heat oven to 500 degrees. Whisk cider; maple syrup; lemon juice; cornstarch; and cinnamon, if using, in bowl until smooth.

2. Melt butter in 12-inch ovensafe skillet over medium-high heat. Add apples and cook, stirring 2 or 3 times, until apples begin to caramelize, about 5 minutes (do not fully cook apples).

3. Off heat, add cider mixture and gently stir until apples are well coated. Set aside and let cool slightly.

4. Roll dough into 11-inch circle on floured counter. Roll dough loosely around rolling pin and gently unroll it onto apple filling.

5. Brush dough with water and sprinkle evenly with sugar. Using sharp knife, gently cut dough into 6 pieces by making 1 vertical cut followed by 2 evenly spaced horizontal cuts (perpendicular to first cut).

6. Bake until apples are tender and crust is deep golden brown, 15 to 20 minutes, rotating skillet halfway through baking. Let cool for 30 minutes; serve warm.

KEYS TO SUCCESS

- **Add apple cider thickened with cornstarch:** Yields a filling with a just-right saucy consistency and highlights the flavor of the fruit
- **Cut the dough into pieces:** Allows for lots of crisp, flaky edges and makes serving easier

DEEP-DISH APPLE PIE

Serves: 8
Total Time: 2¼ hours, plus 30 minutes chilling and 4½ hours cooling

RECIPE OVERVIEW If you find yourself with a surplus of fruit after a fall apple-picking extravaganza, we recommend you enjoy it in a towering deep-dish pie. Each slice should be dense with juicy apples and framed by a buttery, flaky crust. When raw apples are used in a pie, they shrink, leaving a gap between the top crust and filling. Precooking the apples not only eliminates the shrinking problem, it allows even more apples to be crammed into the filling and eliminates any excess liquid, protecting the bottom crust. But why don't the apples then turn to mush during baking? When apples are gently preheated, their pectin is converted to a heat-stable form that keeps them from becoming mushy when cooked further in the oven. Use a mix of tart and sweet apples here. Good choices for tart apples are Granny Smiths, Empires, or Cortlands; for sweet, we recommend Golden Delicious, Jonagolds, or Braeburns.

- 1 recipe Foolproof All-Butter Double-Crust Pie Dough (page 610)
- 2½ pounds Granny Smith apples, peeled, cored, and sliced ¼ inch thick
- 2½ pounds Golden Delicious apples, peeled, cored, and sliced ¼ inch thick
- ½ cup (3½ ounces) plus 1 tablespoon granulated sugar, divided
- ¼ cup packed (1¾ ounces) light brown sugar
- ½ teaspoon grated lemon zest plus 1 tablespoon juice
- ¼ teaspoon table salt
- ⅛ teaspoon ground cinnamon
- 1 large egg, lightly beaten with 1 tablespoon water

1. Roll 1 disk of dough into 12-inch circle on floured counter. Roll dough loosely around rolling pin and gently unroll it onto 9-inch pie plate, letting excess dough hang over edge. Ease dough into plate by gently lifting edge of dough with your hand while pressing into plate bottom with your other hand. Leave any dough that overhangs plate in place. Wrap dough-lined plate loosely in plastic wrap and refrigerate until firm, about 30 minutes. Roll other disk of dough into 12-inch circle on floured counter, then transfer to parchment paper–lined baking sheet; cover with plastic and refrigerate for 30 minutes.

2. Toss apples, ½ cup granulated sugar, brown sugar, lemon zest, salt, and cinnamon together in Dutch oven. Cover and cook over medium heat, stirring frequently, until apples are tender when poked with fork but still hold their shape, 15 to 20 minutes.

3. Spread apples and their juices on rimmed baking sheet and let cool completely, about 30 minutes.

4. Adjust oven rack to lowest position and heat oven to 425 degrees. Drain cooled apples thoroughly in colander set over bowl, reserving ¼ cup of juice. Stir lemon juice into reserved juice.

5. Spread apples into dough-lined plate, mounding them slightly in middle, and drizzle with lemon juice mixture. Roll remaining dough round loosely around rolling pin and gently unroll it onto filling.

6. Trim overhang to ½ inch beyond lip of plate. Pinch edges of top and bottom dough firmly together. Tuck overhang under itself; folded edge should be flush with edge of plate.

7. Crimp dough evenly around edge of plate. Cut four 2-inch slits in top of dough. Brush surface with egg wash and sprinkle evenly with remaining 1 tablespoon granulated sugar.

8. Place pie on aluminum foil–lined rimmed baking sheet and bake until crust is light golden brown, about 25 minutes. Reduce oven temperature to 375 degrees; rotate sheet; and continue to bake until juices are bubbling and crust is deep golden brown, 30 to 40 minutes longer. Let pie cool on wire rack until filling has set, about 4 hours. Serve.

KEYS TO SUCCESS

- **Peel, core, and slice apples:** See page 46 to learn how.
- **Combine tart and sweet apples:** Strikes the ideal flavor balance
- **Precook the apples:** Prevents a soupy filling and eliminates any gap between the top crust and the filling
- **Cook apples gently over moderate heat:** Strengthens their internal structure so that they hold their shape when baked

RESOURCES FOR DEEP-DISH APPLE PIE

ROLLING DOUBLE-CRUST PIE DOUGH

1. ROLL DISK 1
Roll the dough into a 12-inch circle on a floured counter.

2. ROLL AND UNROLL DOUGH
Roll the dough loosely around a rolling pin and gently unroll it onto a 9-inch pie plate, letting the excess dough hang over the edge.

3. EASE DOUGH INTO PLATE
Gently lift the edge of the dough with your hand while pressing into the plate bottom with your other hand. Leave any dough that overhangs the plate in place.

4. WRAP AND CHILL
Wrap the dough-lined plate loosely in plastic wrap and refrigerate until the dough is firm, about 30 minutes.

5. ROLL DISK 2
Roll the dough into a 12-inch circle on a floured counter, then transfer it to a parchment paper–lined baking sheet.

6. FILL DOUGH-LINED PLATE
Roll the remaining dough round loosely around the rolling pin and gently unroll it onto the filling.

7. TRIM AND PINCH
Trim the overhang to ½ inch beyond the lip of the plate. Pinch the edges of the top and bottom dough firmly together.

8. TUCK
Turn the overhang under itself; the folded edge should be flush with the edge of the plate.

9. CRIMP
Crimp dough evenly around the edge of the plate.

MORE TO EXPLORE

FOOLPROOF ALL-BUTTER PIE DOUGH

Everyone needs to have a go-to pie dough in their recipe arsenal. This is ours. The dough is supremely supple and very easy to roll out. Even better, it produces a buttery, tender, and flaky crust—every time.

FOOLPROOF ALL-BUTTER SINGLE-CRUST PIE DOUGH

Makes: one 9-inch single crust
Total Time: 35 minutes, plus 2 hours chilling

This all-butter pie dough is moist and supple, rolls out easily, and bakes up tender and flaky. Start by using a food processor to coat two-thirds of the flour with butter, creating a pliable mixture that's water-resistant. Break that dough into pieces, coat the pieces with the remaining flour, and toss in some grated butter. Once water is folded in, it's absorbed only by the dry flour that coats the butter-flour chunks. Since gluten can develop only when flour is hydrated, this results in a supertender crust. Holding back some of the butter, grating it, and adding it to the dough leaves a little more flour available to form gluten, so the crust has enough structure to support a flaky texture. After a 2-hour chill, the dough will be completely hydrated and easy to roll out. Be sure to weigh the flour for this recipe. This dough will be more moist than most pie doughs, but as it chills it will absorb a lot of excess moisture. Roll the dough on a well-floured counter.

- 10 tablespoons unsalted butter, chilled, divided
- 1¼ cups (6¼ ounces) all-purpose flour, divided
- 1 tablespoon sugar
- ½ teaspoon table salt
- ¼ cup ice water, divided

1. Grate 2 tablespoons butter on large holes of box grater and place in freezer. Cut remaining 8 tablespoons butter into ½-inch cubes.

2. Pulse ¾ cup flour, sugar, and salt in food processor until combined, 2 pulses. Add cubed butter and process until homogeneous paste forms, about 30 seconds. Using your hands, carefully break paste into 2-inch chunks and redistribute evenly around processor blade. Add remaining ½ cup flour and pulse until mixture is broken into pieces no larger than 1 inch (most pieces will be much smaller), 4 to 5 pulses. Transfer mixture to medium bowl. Add grated butter and toss until butter pieces are separated and coated with flour.

3. Sprinkle 2 tablespoons ice water over mixture. Toss with rubber spatula until mixture is evenly moistened. Sprinkle remaining 2 tablespoons ice water over mixture and toss to combine. Press dough with spatula until dough sticks together. Transfer dough to sheet of plastic wrap. Draw edges of plastic over dough and press firmly on sides and top to form compact, fissure-free mass. Wrap in plastic and form into 5-inch disk. Refrigerate dough for at least 2 hours or up to 2 days. Let chilled dough sit on counter to soften slightly, about 10 minutes, before rolling. (Wrapped dough can be frozen for up to 1 month. Let frozen dough thaw completely on counter before rolling.)

FOOLPROOF ALL-BUTTER DOUBLE-CRUST PIE DOUGH

Makes: one 9-inch double crust
Total Time: 35 minutes, plus 2 hours chilling

- 20 tablespoons (2½ sticks) unsalted butter, chilled, divided
- 2½ cups (12½ ounces) all-purpose flour, divided
- 2 tablespoons sugar
- 1 teaspoon table salt
- ½ cup ice water, divided

1. Grate 4 tablespoons butter on large holes of box grater and place in freezer. Cut remaining 16 tablespoons butter into ½-inch cubes.

2. Pulse 1½ cups flour, sugar, and salt in food processor until combined, 2 pulses. Add cubed butter and process until homogeneous paste forms, 40 to 50 seconds. Using your hands, carefully break paste into 2-inch chunks and redistribute evenly around processor blade. Add remaining 1 cup flour and pulse until mixture is broken into pieces no larger than 1 inch (most pieces will be much smaller), 4 to 5 pulses. Transfer mixture to medium bowl. Add grated butter and toss until butter pieces are separated and coated with flour.

3. Sprinkle ¼ cup ice water over mixture. Toss with rubber spatula until mixture is evenly moistened. Sprinkle remaining ¼ cup ice water over mixture and toss to combine. Press dough with spatula until dough sticks together. Use spatula to divide dough into 2 portions. Transfer each portion to sheet of plastic wrap. Draw edges of plastic over 1 portion of dough and press firmly on sides and top to form compact, fissure-free mass. Wrap in plastic and form into 5-inch disk. Repeat with remaining portion; refrigerate dough for at least 2 hours or up to 2 days. Let chilled dough sit on counter to soften slightly, about 10 minutes, before rolling. (Wrapped dough can be frozen for up to 1 month. Let frozen dough thaw completely on counter before rolling.)

Not Your Typical Pie Dough

Both the flour and the butter in this pie dough are added in two stages. This dough will look wetter than others you may have made, but fear not: As it chills, it will absorb extra moisture and eventually form a smooth, easy-to-roll dough.

MAKE FLOUR-BUTTER PASTE
Process most of the flour (and sugar and salt) and cubed butter until a homogeneous paste forms, about 40 seconds.

BREAK IT UP; ADD MORE FLOUR
Separate the paste into 2-inch chunks and distribute them around the processor blade, then pulse in the remaining flour.

TOSS IN GRATED BUTTER
Transfer the mixture to a bowl, add the frozen grated butter, and gently toss to coat the butter shreds with flour.

ADD WATER
Using a rubber spatula, mix in ice water in two additions to form a wet, sticky dough. Transfer to plastic wrap, press into a disk, and refrigerate.

Fray-Free Pie Dough

You won't have big cracks forming at the edges of the dough when rolling out our foolproof all-butter pie dough. But if you want to be a real perfectionist, here's how to ensure that the edges are entirely fray-free.

KEEP IT TIGHT
When wrapping the finished dough in plastic wrap, press firmly on the sides and top of the dough to form a compact, fissure-free mass.

SEAL IT UP
Before unwrapping the chilled dough, stand it on its edge and roll the edge firmly along the counter to seal any remaining cracks.

COURSE
THANKSGIVING FAVORITES

BRIDGET LANCASTER

Everyone enjoys filling up on the main meal at Thanksgiving, but it's the dessert table that often steals the show. In this course we cover two classic pies—pumpkin and pecan—and walk you through the steps of making a pie crust with great texture and structure, from rolling out the dough and fitting it into a pie plate to prebaking (also known as blind-baking) the pie shell before adding the filling. We've also included a seasonal spin on bar cookies featuring the flavors of tart cranberries and toasted pecans—a perfect and portable taste of Thanksgiving.

BRIDGET'S PRO TIP: *Homemade pie dough really is worth making, but it can be a little daunting. To make Thanksgiving prep a little less stressful, I roll out the pie dough a month in advance. I stack the dough between layers of parchment paper and then wrap the whole stack in plastic wrap before storing in a clean pizza box in my freezer. The dough only needs an hour or so in the fridge to thaw and fit into the pie pan.*

PUMPKIN PIE
Serves: 8
Total Time: 1½ hours, plus 30 minutes chilling and 4 hours cooling

RECIPE OVERVIEW This pumpkin pie sets the standard: It's velvety smooth, packed with pumpkin flavor, and perfectly spiced. To eliminate some of the liquid from canned pumpkin puree and concentrate the pumpkin's flavor, cook the puree with sugar and spices before whisking in heavy cream, milk, and eggs to enrich it. Working with this hot filling and a warm prebaked crust helps the custard firm up quickly in the oven and prevents it from soaking into the crust. For spices, a little ground nutmeg and cinnamon, as well as some fresh grated ginger, provide just enough warmth without being distracting. Granulated sugar and maple syrup help sweeten things. A surprise ingredient, mashed candied sweet potatoes, actually makes the filling taste more like pumpkin than when it's made with pumpkin puree alone. Starting the pie in a hot oven and then dropping the temperature partway through baking prevents curdling. If candied sweet potatoes or yams are unavailable, regular canned sweet potatoes or yams can be substituted. When the pie is properly baked, the center 2 inches of the pie should look firm but jiggle slightly.

- 1 recipe Foolproof All-Butter Single-Crust Pie Dough (page 610)
- 1 cup heavy cream
- 1 cup whole milk
- 3 large eggs plus 2 large yolks
- 1 teaspoon vanilla extract
- 1 (15-ounce) can unsweetened pumpkin puree
- 1 cup drained candied sweet potatoes or yams
- ¾ cup (5¼ ounces) sugar
- ¼ cup maple syrup
- 2 teaspoons grated fresh ginger
- 1 teaspoon table salt
- ½ teaspoon ground cinnamon
- ¼ teaspoon ground nutmeg

1. Roll dough into 12-inch circle on floured counter. Roll dough loosely around rolling pin and gently unroll it onto 9-inch pie plate, letting excess dough hang over edge. Ease dough into plate by gently lifting edge of dough with your hand while pressing into plate bottom with your other hand.

2. Trim overhang to ½ inch beyond lip of plate. Tuck overhang under itself; folded edge should be flush with edge of plate. Crimp dough evenly around edge of plate. Wrap dough-lined plate loosely in plastic wrap and refrigerate until firm, about 30 minutes. Adjust oven rack to middle position and heat oven to 350 degrees.

3. Line chilled pie shell with double layer of aluminum foil, covering edges to prevent burning, and fill with pie weights. Bake on foil-lined rimmed baking sheet until edges are set and just beginning to turn golden, 25 to 30 minutes, rotating sheet halfway through baking.

4. Remove foil and weights; rotate sheet; and continue to bake crust until golden brown and crisp, 10 to 15 minutes. Transfer sheet to wire rack. (Crust must still be warm when filling is added.) Increase oven temperature to 400 degrees.

5. While crust is baking, whisk cream, milk, eggs and yolks, and vanilla together in bowl; set aside. Bring pumpkin, sweet potatoes, sugar, maple syrup, ginger, salt, cinnamon, and nutmeg to simmer in large saucepan over medium heat and cook, stirring constantly and mashing sweet potatoes against sides of saucepan, until thick and shiny, 15 to 20 minutes.

6. Remove saucepan from heat and whisk in cream mixture until fully incorporated.

7. Strain mixture through fine-mesh strainer into bowl, using back of ladle or spatula to press solids through strainer.

8. Whisk mixture, then, with pie still on sheet, pour into warm crust. Bake for 10 minutes. Reduce oven temperature to 300 degrees and continue to bake until edges of pie are set and center registers 175 degrees, 20 to 35 minutes, rotating sheet halfway through baking. Let pie cool completely on wire rack, about 4 hours. Serve.

Making Pumpkin Pie Filling

COOK
While the crust bakes, simmer the filling ingredients, stirring constantly and mashing the sweet potatoes against sides of the saucepan, until thick and shiny.

STRAIN
Pass the mixture through a fine-mesh strainer into the bowl, using the back of a ladle or spatula to press the solids through the strainer.

POUR
Pour the filling into the still-warm crust.

Keeping the Custard from Curdling

OVERCOOKED
A pie cooked at 425 degrees the whole time curdles and becomes watery and grainy.

SILKY SMOOTH
Starting the pie at 400 degrees and finishing it at 300 degrees allows it to bake without curdling.

KEYS TO SUCCESS

- **Cook the pumpkin and spices:** Concentrates the pumpkin's flavor and blooms the fresh ginger as well as the cinnamon and nutmeg
- **Supplement with canned sweet potatoes:** Brings complexity to the pie and enhances the flavor of the pumpkin
- **Start with a hot oven, then reduce the heat to finish:** Prevents the custard from curdling

PECAN PIE

Serves: 8
Total Time: 1½ hours, plus 30 minutes chilling and 4 hours cooling

RECIPE OVERVIEW Pecan pie is a classic for good reason—rich, buttery pecans mingle with a custardy sugar filling in a crisp crust for an irresistible treat. Using dark brown sugar rather than granulated gives the pie deeper flavor, and reducing the amount of sugar typically called for keeps the sweetness in check. Some butter adds a lush texture to the filling and underscores the richness of the pecans. After partially baking the crust, add the hot filling to the warm pie crust to keep the crust from getting soggy. Cooking the filling over a simulated double-boiler maintains gentle heat and prevents the eggy filling from curdling. Removing the pie from the oven when the center is still jiggly provides further insurance against overbaking. As the pie cools, the residual heat of the filling cooks the center through, so each slice of pie is silky and tender. We recommend chopping the toasted pecans by hand.

- 1 recipe Foolproof All-Butter Single-Crust Pie Dough (page 610)
- 6 tablespoons unsalted butter, cut into 1-inch pieces
- 1 cup packed (7 ounces) dark brown sugar
- ½ teaspoon table salt
- 3 large eggs
- ¾ cup light corn syrup
- 1 tablespoon vanilla extract
- 2 cups pecans, toasted and chopped fine

1. Roll dough into 12-inch circle on floured counter. Roll dough loosely around rolling pin and gently unroll it onto 9-inch pie plate, letting excess dough hang over edge. Ease dough into plate by gently lifting edge of dough with your hand while pressing into plate bottom with your other hand. Trim overhang to ½ inch beyond lip of plate. Tuck overhang under itself; folded edge should be flush with edge of plate. Crimp dough evenly around edge of plate. Wrap dough-lined plate loosely in plastic wrap and refrigerate until firm, about 30 minutes. Adjust oven rack to lowest position and heat oven to 425 degrees.

2. Line chilled pie shell with double layer of aluminum foil, covering edges to prevent burning, and fill with pie weights. Bake on foil-lined rimmed baking sheet until pie dough looks dry and is pale in color, about 15 minutes. Remove foil and weights; rotate sheet; and continue to bake until crust is light golden brown, 4 to 7 minutes. Transfer sheet to wire rack. (Crust must still be warm when filling is added.)

3. While crust is baking, melt butter in heatproof bowl set over saucepan filled with 1 inch of barely simmering water, making sure that water does not touch bottom of bowl. Off heat, stir in sugar and salt until butter is absorbed.

4. Whisk in eggs, then corn syrup and vanilla, until smooth. Return bowl to saucepan and stir until mixture is shiny, hot to touch, and registers 130 degrees. Off heat, stir in pecans.

5. As soon as pie crust comes out of oven, adjust oven rack to lower-middle position and reduce oven temperature to 275 degrees. With pie still on sheet, pour pecan mixture into warm crust.

6. Bake until filling looks set but yields like gelatin when gently pressed with back of spoon, 50 minutes to 1 hour, rotating sheet halfway through baking. Let pie cool completely on wire rack, about 4 hours. Serve.

Variation
MAPLE PECAN PIE

Maple syrup yields a more custardy pie. Toasted walnuts can be substituted for the pecans. Use maple syrup labeled Grade A Dark Amber here.

Decrease butter to 4 tablespoons and pecans to 1½ cups. Substitute ½ cup granulated sugar for brown sugar and 1 cup maple syrup for corn syrup and vanilla.

> **KEYS TO SUCCESS**
> - **Cut back on the sugar:** Keeps the flavor of the pecans center stage
> - **Gently cook the filling in a bowl set over simmering water:** Makes it easy to maintain gentle heat so that the filling doesn't curdle
> - **Remove the pie from the oven when it's just set but still soft in the middle:** Prevents overbaking; filling will continue to set as it cools

CORE TECHNIQUE — Toasting Nuts

TOAST SMALL BATCH (1 CUP OR LESS)

Place the nuts in an empty skillet and turn the heat to medium. Toast the nuts, stirring occasionally, until fragrant and lightly browned, 2 to 5 minutes.

TOAST LARGE BATCH (MORE THAN 1 CUP)

Spread the nuts out in a single layer over a rimmed baking sheet. Toast in a 350-degree oven, shaking the sheet every few minutes, until the nuts are fragrant and lightly browned, 5 to 10 minutes.

CRANBERRY OAT BARS

Makes: 24 bars
Total Time: 1½ hours, plus 2½ hours cooling

RECIPE OVERVIEW Dried cranberries are a go-to ingredient for adding tartness or chew to a cookie, but fresh cranberries don't get used often enough. That might be because fresh cranberries require a bit of work, and on their own they're a bit too sour. And like other fresh fruit, they're full of moisture. But when treated properly, they give desserts a vibrant pop of flavor. Here, bright fresh cranberries are paired with sweet, nutty oats in a rustic, chewy bar cookie. Precooking the cranberries with a bit of sugar easily solves any fresh cranberry woes: The sugar tempers the sourness, and the cooking process thickens the cranberries' juices, so they don't leave wet pockets throughout the bars. Rich, buttery pecans contribute a crunchy element to the topping. We like using fresh cranberries, but frozen cranberries will work, and we prefer the flavor and chewiness of old-fashioned rolled oats, but quick oats can be substituted to yield softer, cakier bars. Do not use instant oats here.

- 8 ounces (2 cups) fresh or frozen cranberries
- ½ cup (3½ ounces) granulated sugar
- ¼ cup water
- 2 cups (6 ounces) old-fashioned rolled oats
- 1½ cups (7½ ounces) all-purpose flour
- 1 teaspoon ground cinnamon
- ½ teaspoon table salt
- 16 tablespoons unsalted butter, softened
- 1½ cups packed (10½ ounces) light brown sugar
- 1 large egg, room temperature
- ¾ cup pecans, chopped

1. Bring cranberries, granulated sugar, and water to boil in medium saucepan over medium-high heat. Cook, stirring frequently, until cranberries have burst and juice has started to thicken, 2 to 3 minutes. Let cool for 30 minutes.

2. Adjust oven rack to lower-middle position and heat oven to 325 degrees. Make foil sling for 13 by 9-inch baking pan by folding 2 long sheets of aluminum foil; first sheet should be 13 inches wide and second sheet should be 9 inches wide. Lay sheets of foil in pan perpendicular to each other, with extra foil hanging over edges of pan. Push foil into corners and up sides of pan, smoothing foil flush to pan. Grease foil.

3. Whisk oats, flour, cinnamon, and salt together in bowl. Using stand mixer fitted with paddle, beat butter and brown sugar on medium-high speed until light and fluffy, about 3 minutes. Add egg and beat until combined, scraping down bowl as needed. Reduce speed to low, add oat mixture, and mix until just combined. Transfer two-thirds of dough to prepared pan and press firmly into even layer. Spread evenly with cranberry mixture. Mix pecans into remaining dough and sprinkle walnut-size pieces over cranberry layer.

4. Bake until top is golden brown, 40 to 45 minutes, rotating pan halfway through baking. Let bars cool in pan on wire rack, about 2 hours. Using foil overhang, lift bars from pan. Cut into 24 pieces before serving.

KEYS TO SUCCESS

- **Precook the cranberries with sugar:** Easily tames tartness
- **Use old-fashioned oats:** Provides the ideal flavor and a chewy texture

RESOURCES FOR THANKSGIVING FAVORITES

ROLLING SINGLE-CRUST PIE DOUGH

1. ROLL OUT DOUGH
Roll the dough into a 12-inch circle on a floured counter.

2. ROLL AND UNROLL DOUGH
Roll the dough loosely around a rolling pin and gently unroll it onto a 9-inch pie plate, letting the excess dough hang over the edge.

3. EASE DOUGH INTO PLATE
Ease the dough into the plate by gently lifting the edge of the dough with your hand while pressing into the plate bottom with your other hand.

4. TRIM
Trim the overhang to ½ inch beyond the lip of the plate.

5. TUCK
Tuck the overhang under itself; the folded edge should be flush with the edge of the plate.

6. CRIMP
Crimp the dough evenly around the edge of the plate.

BLIND-BAKING SINGLE-CRUST PIE DOUGH

1. LINE WITH FOIL AND FILL WITH WEIGHTS
Line the chilled pie shell with a double layer of aluminum foil, covering the edges to prevent burning. Be sure to shield the dough edges, but don't enclose them completely. Fill the shell to the brim with pie weights to prevent shrinking and puffing.

2. REMOVE WEIGHTS AND FINISH BAKING
Partially or fully parbake the crust as specified in the recipe. Remove the foil and weights, rotate the sheet, and continue to bake the crust until it is golden brown and crisp.

COURSE
COOL AND CREAMY DESSERTS

MORGAN BOLLING

Rich, creamy desserts such as puddings and custards have a reputation for being finicky, often requiring precise temperatures or fussy techniques to turn out just right. In this course you'll learn simplified and streamlined techniques for making some of these classic desserts—rice pudding, pots de crème, chocolate mousse, and ice cream—so that they can be enjoyed whenever the mood strikes. Learn to make pots de crème without turning on your oven or relying on a cumbersome water bath. And you might be surprised to learn that whipped whole eggs make for a light yet creamy mousse or that you can ditch the ice cream maker and use a blender to produce silky-smooth ice cream.

MORGAN'S PRO TIP: *The no-churn ice cream recipe is so adaptable. Make the vanilla version first to learn how to do it well, then play around adding other mix-ins (you can add up to ½ cup chopped cookies, candies, nuts—you name it).*

COCONUT RICE PUDDING

Serves: 4 to 6
Total Time: 1 hour, plus 2 hours cooling

RECIPE OVERVIEW When it comes to simple yet sublime desserts, it doesn't get much better than rice pudding. Tasting of little more than sweet milk and good vanilla, the pudding may have a short ingredient list, but the right ratio is key. For creamy coconut rice pudding, 4¼ cups of milk plus 1¾ cups of coconut milk to ½ cup of long-grain white rice (its texture proved better than that of short-grain) is just right, but the secret is reserving ½ cup of the milk and stirring it in right before serving. This adjusts the pudding to the perfect creamy and thick—but not stodgy—consistency. You can use 2 percent low-fat milk here (the consistency will be looser) but not skim.

- 4¼ cups whole milk, divided
- 1¾ cups canned coconut milk
- ½ cup (3½ ounces) sugar
- ½ teaspoon table salt
- ½ cup long-grain white rice
- 2 teaspoons vanilla extract
- ½ teaspoon ground cardamom

1. Combine 3¾ cups milk, coconut milk, sugar, and salt in large saucepan and bring to boil over medium-high heat.

2. Stir in rice and reduce heat to low. Cook, adjusting heat to maintain gentle simmer and stirring occasionally to prevent scorching, until rice is soft and pudding has thickened to consistency of yogurt, 50 to 60 minutes. Stir in vanilla.

3. Transfer pudding to large bowl; stir in cardamom; and let cool completely, about 2 hours. If desired, refrigerate until cold, about 2 hours longer. Just before serving, stir in remaining ½ cup milk.

> ### KEYS TO SUCCESS
> - **Use the stovetop:** Produces a rice pudding with a creamier texture than baked versions
> - **Reserve some of the milk:** Allows you to adjust the pudding to the ideal consistency

POTS DE CRÈME

Serves: 8
Total Time: 40 minutes, plus 30 minutes cooling, 4 hours chilling, and 20 minutes standing

RECIPE OVERVIEW Classic pots de crème are incredibly silky and pack an intense hit of chocolate. But making these petite chocolate custards can be a finicky process: Traditional recipes call for a water bath, which can be cumbersome. For a more user-friendly pot de crème, move the dish out of the oven and take an unconventional approach: Cook the custard on the stovetop and then pour it into ramekins. Bittersweet chocolate, and lots of it—50 percent more than most recipes—gives the custards a luxuriously rich dark-chocolate flavor. We prefer pots de crème made with 60 percent cacao bittersweet chocolate, but 70 percent bittersweet chocolate can also be used—you will need to reduce the amount of chocolate to 8 ounces.

Pots de Crème
- 10 ounces bittersweet chocolate, chopped fine
- 1 tablespoon vanilla extract
- 1 tablespoon water
- ½ teaspoon instant espresso powder
- 5 large egg yolks
- 5 tablespoons (2¼ ounces) sugar
- ¼ teaspoon table salt
- 1½ cups heavy cream
- ¾ cup half-and-half

Whipped Cream
- ½ cup heavy cream, chilled
- 2 teaspoons sugar
- ½ teaspoon vanilla extract
- Cocoa powder and/or chocolate shavings (optional)

1. FOR THE POTS DE CRÈME Place chocolate in bowl and set fine-mesh strainer over top. Combine vanilla, water, and espresso powder in second bowl.

2. Whisk egg yolks, sugar, and salt together in third bowl until combined. Whisk in cream and half-and-half. Transfer cream mixture to medium saucepan and cook over medium-low heat, stirring constantly and scraping bottom of pot with wooden spoon, until thickened and silky and custard registers 175 to 180 degrees, 8 to 12 minutes. (Do not let custard overcook or simmer.)

3. Immediately pour custard through fine-mesh strainer over chocolate. Let mixture stand to melt chocolate, about 5 minutes. Add espresso mixture and whisk until smooth. Divide chocolate custard evenly among eight 5-ounce ramekins. Gently tap ramekins against counter to remove air bubbles.

4. Let pots de crème cool completely, then cover with plastic wrap and refrigerate until chilled, at least 4 hours or up to 3 days. (Before serving, let pots de crème stand at room temperature for 20 to 30 minutes.)

5. FOR THE WHIPPED CREAM Using stand mixer fitted with whisk attachment, whip cream, sugar, and vanilla on medium-low speed until foamy, about 1 minute. Increase speed to high and whip until stiff peaks form, 1 to 3 minutes. Dollop each pot de crème with about 2 tablespoons whipped cream and garnish with cocoa and/or chocolate shavings, if using. Serve.

Variation
MILK CHOCOLATE POTS DE CRÈME

Milk chocolate behaves differently in this recipe than bittersweet chocolate, and more of it must be used to ensure that the custard sets. And because of the increased amount of chocolate, it's necessary to cut back on the amount of sugar so that the custard is not overly sweet.

Substitute 12 ounces milk chocolate for bittersweet chocolate and reduce sugar in pots de crème to 2 tablespoons.

> ### KEYS TO SUCCESS
> - **Add heavy cream, half-and-half, and egg yolks to the custard:** Provides the pots de crème with the right amount of richness and body
> - **Use plenty of bittersweet chocolate:** Yields truly decadent custards that are rich but not overly sweet
> - **Cook the custard on the stovetop:** Makes for a more approachable pot de crème

CHOCOLATE MOUSSE

Serves: 6 to 8
Total Time: 35 minutes, plus 6 hours chilling

RECIPE OVERVIEW For an airy, light, sweet, and chocolaty mousse that isn't overly complicated to make, start with the chocolate. To get rich dark-chocolate flavor, melt a hefty 12 ounces of bittersweet chocolate chips with water (rather than cream or butter, which dull the flavor). Folding in whipped egg whites produces a mousse that's light but distractingly marshmallowy. Instead, fold in whole eggs that have been whipped until tripled in volume. This makes for a mousse that is fluffy yet lusciously creamy. Deflating the eggs a little while folding is OK, but it's important to use a large bowl and scrape the bottom while folding to incorporate everything thoroughly. Allowing the mousse to set by refrigerating it for least 6 hours gives the dessert just the right amount of structure: The mousse melts in your mouth, but it can still hold its shape on a spoon. If you're using pasteurized eggs here, increase the high-speed whipping time to 8 to 10 minutes. We developed this recipe using Ghirardelli 60% Premium Baking Chips. This recipe calls for individual serving glasses or ramekins, but the mousse can also be chilled in a large serving dish. Just increase the chilling time to at least 8 hours.

Mousse
- 8 large eggs, room temperature
- 2 tablespoons sugar
- 12 ounces bittersweet chocolate chips
- ¼ cup water

Whipped Cream
- 1½ cups heavy cream, chilled
- 4 teaspoons sugar
- 1 teaspoon vanilla extract

1. FOR THE MOUSSE Using stand mixer fitted with whisk attachment, whip eggs on medium speed until foamy, about 1 minute. Add sugar; increase speed to high; and whip until tripled in volume and ribbons form on top of mixture when dribbled from whisk, 5 to 7 minutes. Set aside.

2. Microwave chocolate and water in large bowl at 50 percent power, stirring occasionally with rubber spatula, until chocolate is melted, about 2 minutes.

3. Whisk one-third of egg mixture into chocolate mixture until fully combined. Using clean rubber spatula, gently fold in remaining egg mixture, making sure to scrape up any chocolate from bottom of bowl, until no streaks remain.

4. Portion mousse evenly into 6 to 8 serving glasses or ramekins, cover with plastic wrap, and refrigerate for at least 6 hours or up to 48 hours.

5. FOR THE WHIPPED CREAM Using stand mixer fitted with whisk attachment, whip cream, sugar, and vanilla on medium-low speed until foamy, about 1 minute. Increase speed to high and whip until stiff peaks form, 1 to 3 minutes.

6. Top mousse with whipped cream. Serve.

KEYS TO SUCCESS

- **Add plenty of bittersweet chocolate:** Makes the dessert a true chocolate-lover's dream
- **Replace the dairy with water:** Yields a mousse with a more intense chocolate flavor
- **Whip whole eggs, not just egg whites:** Results in a light and fluffy yet creamy mousse

Properly Whipped Eggs

USE WHOLE EGGS
We whip a combination of whole eggs and sugar in a mixer until it's tripled in volume and ribbons form when the mixture is dribbled from the whisk attachment.

VANILLA NO-CHURN ICE CREAM

Serves: 8 to 10 (makes about 1 quart)
Total Time: 15 minutes, plus 6 hours freezing

RECIPE OVERVIEW An ice cream maker works by churning a mixture (usually milk, cream, sugar, and egg yolks) as it freezes to inhibit the formation of ice crystals and to incorporate air—so that instead of a solid block of frozen milk, you have silky, creamy ice cream. But there's an easy way to ditch the ice cream maker: Whip some cream in a blender. The air in the whipped cream stands in for the air normally incorporated by churning. Using two liquid sweeteners—sweetened condensed milk and corn syrup—keeps the ice cream soft and scoopable. A hefty 1 tablespoon of vanilla extract and a bit of salt (to enhance the flavor) produces an intensely flavored vanilla ice cream. The cream mixture freezes more quickly in a loaf pan than in a taller, narrower container. If you don't have a loaf pan, use an 8-inch square baking pan.

- 2 cups heavy cream, chilled
- 1 cup sweetened condensed milk
- ¼ cup whole milk
- ¼ cup light corn syrup
- 2 tablespoons sugar
- 1 tablespoon vanilla extract
- ¼ teaspoon table salt

1. Process cream in blender until soft peaks form, 20 to 30 seconds. Scrape down sides of blender jar and continue to process until stiff peaks form, about 10 seconds. Using rubber spatula, stir in condensed milk, whole milk, corn syrup, sugar, vanilla, and salt. Process until thoroughly combined, about 20 seconds, scraping down sides of blender jar as needed.

2. Pour cream mixture into 8½ by 4½-inch loaf pan. Press plastic wrap flush against surface of cream mixture. Freeze until firm, at least 6 hours. Serve.

Variations

MINT-COOKIE NO-CHURN ICE CREAM

Substitute ¾ teaspoon peppermint extract for vanilla. Add ⅛ teaspoon green food coloring with condensed milk. After transferring cream mixture to loaf pan, gently stir in ½ cup coarsely crushed Oreo cookies before freezing.

STRAWBERRY-BUTTERMILK NO-CHURN ICE CREAM

Substitute ½ cup buttermilk for whole milk and 1 teaspoon lemon juice for vanilla. After transferring cream mixture to loaf pan, dollop ⅓ cup strawberry jam over top. Swirl jam into cream mixture using tines of fork before freezing.

PEANUT BUTTER CUP NO-CHURN ICE CREAM

Omit vanilla. Add ½ cup creamy peanut butter with condensed milk. After transferring cream mixture to loaf pan, gently stir in ½ cup coarsely chopped peanut butter cups before freezing.

KEYS TO SUCCESS

- **Whip in a blender:** Incorporates the ideal amount of air into the cream for a fluffy yet creamy consistency
- **Use liquid sweeteners (corn syrup and sweetened condensed milk):** Helps create a smooth texture

---

SCIENCE LESSON

Demystifying Corn Syrup

Is corn syrup the same thing as the high-fructose corn syrup ubiquitous in soft drinks and other processed foods? In a word, no. Corn syrup (the most popular brand being Karo) is made by adding enzymes to a mixture of cornstarch and water to break the long starch strands into glucose molecules. It is less sweet than granulated sugar and is valuable in candy making because it discourages crystallization; it also helps baked goods retain moisture. High-fructose corn syrup (HFCS) is made by putting regular corn syrup through an additional enzymatic process that converts a portion of the glucose molecules into fructose, boosting its sweetness to a level even higher than that of cane sugar. Because HFCS is considerably less expensive than cane sugar, it is widely used in processed foods, but it is not sold directly to consumers.

NUTRITIONAL INFORMATION FOR OUR RECIPES

We calculate the nutritional values of our recipes per serving; if there is a range in the serving size, we used the highest number of servings to calculate the nutritional values. We entered all the ingredients, using weights for important ingredients such as most vegetables. We also used our preferred brands in these analyses. We did not include additional salt or pepper for food that's "seasoned to taste."

	CALORIES	TOTAL FAT (G)	SAT FAT (G)	CHOL (MG)	SODIUM (MG)	TOTAL CARB (G)	DIETARY FIBER (G)	TOTAL SUGARS (G)	PROTEIN (G)
CHAPTER 1: COOKING BASICS									
Pistachio Dukkah	15	1	0	0	7	1	0	0	1
Ras el Hanout	7	0	0	0	7	1	1	0	0
Za'atar	8	0	0	0	0	1	1	0	0
Harissa	100	11	2	0	37	2	1	0	1
Garam Masala	6	0	0	0	1	1	1	0	0
Five-Spice Powder	7	0	0	0	1	1	1	0	0
Shichimi Togarashi	5	0	0	0	0	1	0	0	0
Cherry Tomato Salsa	20	2	0	0	0	1	0	1	0
Lemon-Yogurt Sauce	20	1	0.5	5	15	2	0	2	1
Chipotle Mayonnaise	45	4.5	1	5	70	1	0	0	0
Cilantro-Mint Chutney	10	0	0	0	35	2	1	1	1
CHAPTER 2: EGGS AND TOFU									
Perfect Scrambled Eggs	189	14	6	385	277	2	0	1	13
Scrambled Eggs with Asparagus, Smoked Salmon, and Chives	262	20	5	375	384	3	1	1	17
Scrambled Eggs with Shiitake Mushrooms and Feta Cheese	288	22	6	380	381	8	2	3	16
Xihóngshì Chao Jidàn (Chinese Stir-Fried Tomatoes and Eggs)	297	22	4	372	765	11	4	8	14
Perfect Fried Eggs	219	18	6	382	255	1	0	0	13
Eggs in a Hole	234	15	8	211	220	15	1	2	10
Avocado Toast with Fried Eggs	460	33	5	185	450	31	7	4	11
Fried Eggs over Garlicky Chard and Bell Pepper	188	12	3	186	717	12	4	4	11
Easy-Peel Hard-Cooked Eggs	72	5	2	186	71	0	0	0	6
Soft-Cooked Eggs	72	5	2	186	71	0	0	0	6
Curry Deviled Eggs	120	10	2.5	190	125	1	0	0	6
Bacon and Chive Deviled Eggs	70	6	1.5	95	115	0	0	0	4
Perfect Poached Eggs	145	10	3	372	251	1	0	0	13

	CALORIES	TOTAL FAT (G)	SAT FAT (G)	CHOL (MG)	SODIUM (MG)	TOTAL CARB (G)	DIETARY FIBER (G)	TOTAL SUGARS (G)	PROTEIN (G)
CHAPTER 2: EGGS AND TOFU (CONTINUED)									
Ham, Egg, and Cheese Sandwiches	500	29	11	420	1390	25	0	6	31
Bacon, Egg, and Cheese Sandwiches	510	28	12	430	1520	29	0	8	35
Fried Egg Sandwiches	660	50	20	270	860	29	0	1	24
Egg Salad Sandwiches with Radishes and Watercress	333	15	4	313	484	30	4	4	19
Open-Faced Poached Egg Sandwiches	210	11	4	195	500	17	1	4	13
Eggs in Purgatory	570	38	8	378	916	38	6	11	23
Green Shakshuka	425	28	8	389	1278	23	8	7	24
Baked Eggs with Tomatoes, Feta, and Croutons	530	37	8	385	1180	29	4	10	21
Sheet-Pan Huevos Rancheros	672	42	12	397	1645	53	18	17	28
Classic Cheese Omelet	350	26	12	595	360	1	0	1	25
Mushroom and Thyme Filling	60	6	3.5	15	0	3	0	1	1
Asparagus and Smoked Salmon Filling	60	3	0	5	170	5	2	3	5
Frittata with Parmesan and Herbs	160	11	4	285	460	2	0	1	13
Frittata with Broccoli and Turmeric	240	16	5	377	465	7	1	2	17
Tofu Scramble with Bell Pepper, Shallot, and Basil	93	5	1	0	316	6	1	3	7
Tofu Scramble with Tomato and Scallions	100	6	0	0	440	4	1	1	8
Sriracha-Lime Tofu Bowl	280	14	1	0	540	23	5	14	14
Tofu Banh Mi	510	28	3.5	5	750	49	1	6	16
Stir-Fried Tofu and Bok Choy	300	14	1.5	0	610	28	3	8	14
Teriyaki Tofu	220	7	1	0	1550	24	0	20	15
Chilled Marinated Tofu	100	3	0	0	800	9	1	6	7
Marinated Tofu and Vegetable Salad	360	22	2.5	0	330	18	3	9	22
CHAPTER 3: VEGETABLES									
Boiled Carrots with Lemon and Chives	73	3	2	8	277	11	3	5	1
Foolproof Boiled Corn	98	3	1	3	241	19	2	6	3
Green Beans with Toasted Almonds and Browned Butter	160	13	5	20	390	8	4	3	4
Steamed Broccoli with Lime-Cumin Dressing	150	11	1	0	423	12	4	3	5
Sautéed Carrots with Ginger, Maple, and Fennel Seeds	180	9	0.5	0	580	23	5	14	3
Sautéed Zucchini	90	7	1	0	35	5	1	3	1
Sautéed Mushrooms with Shallot and Thyme	94	4	2	9	199	9	2	5	6
Spinach with Garlic and Lemon	124	9	1	0	526	9	5	1	6
Sautéed Swiss Chard with Sesame Sauce	134	12	1	0	212	6	2	3	3
Quick Collard Greens	123	8	1	0	459	11	8	1	6
Garlicky Braised Kale	149	8	1	0	607	17	6	4	7
Pan-Roasted Brussels Sprouts with Lemon and Pecorino Romano	232	19	4	9	332	11	4	3	7
Pan-Roasted Cauliflower with Garlic and Lemon	154	12	2	0	401	11	4	3	4

	CALORIES	TOTAL FAT (G)	SAT FAT (G)	CHOL (MG)	SODIUM (MG)	TOTAL CARB (G)	DIETARY FIBER (G)	TOTAL SUGARS (G)	PROTEIN (G)
CHAPTER 3: VEGETABLES (CONTINUED)									
Pan-Roasted Asparagus	70	4	2	5	375	7	3	3	3
Smashed Potatoes	251	14	9	41	423	28	4	2	4
Easy Mashed Potatoes	389	23	14	63	685	42	5	4	6
Braised Red Potatoes with Lemon and Chives	135	6	4	15	315	19	2	2	2
Crisp Roasted Potatoes	246	11	2	0	467	33	4	1	4
Best Baked Potatoes	167	4	0	0	8	31	2	1	4
Herbed Goat Cheese Topping	137	12	5	13	131	0	0	0	5
Creamy Egg Topping	82	6	2	145	152	1	0	0	5
Mashed Sweet Potatoes	327	14	9	41	420	47	7	11	4
Roasted Sweet Potato Wedges	120	2	0	0	254	23	3	6	2
Sweet Potato Crunch	385	12	7	31	566	64	7	20	5
Roasted Asparagus	30	1.5	0	0	200	3	2	1	2
Roasted Broccoli	160	11	1.5	0	360	14	5	4	6
Roasted Butternut Squash	150	7	1	0	200	22	4	4	2
Roasted Cremini Mushrooms	70	5	0.5	0	400	4	0	3	2
Roasted Green Beans	45	2.5	0	0	200	5	2	2	1
Roasted Brussels Sprouts	120	7	1	0	330	13	5	3	5
Roasted Carrots	130	7	1	0	410	16	5	8	2
Roasted Cauliflower	80	5	1	0	240	8	3	3	3
Roasted Fennel	80	5	0.5	0	250	9	4	5	1
Cauliflower Rice	90	4	1	0	510	13	5	5	5
Cauliflower Cakes	312	22	6	60	696	20	6	5	12
Cauliflower Steaks with Salsa Verde	372	29	4	0	1241	26	11	9	10
Broiled Asparagus with Garlic-Butter Sauce	121	10	5	20	295	7	3	3	4
Broiled Broccoli Rabe	116	11	1	0	293	4	3	1	4
Elote	261	20	4	13	315	20	2	7	4
Broiled Tomatoes with Goat Cheese and Bread Crumbs	150	7	2	5	230	16	2	4	6
Broiled Eggplant with Basil	90	7	1	0	290	7	3	4	1
Stir-Fried Japanese Eggplant	87	7	1	0	447	7	3	3	2
Braised Eggplant with Paprika, Coriander, and Yogurt	98	8	1	2	422	7	3	4	2
Grilled Fennel	126	10	2	0	61	9	4	5	1
Grilled Cabbage	252	21	3	0	600	18	6	10	3
Grilled Zucchini and Red Onion with Lemon Vinaigrette	144	14	2	0	275	5	1	3	1
Husk-Grilled Corn	190	13	8	31	211	19	2	6	3
MORE TO EXPLORE: QUICK PICKLES									
Quick Pickled Radishes	31	0	0	0	172	8	1	4	1
Quick Pickled Fennel	4	0	0	0	4	1	0	0	0
Quick Pickled Red Onions	177	0	0	0	303	39	1	36	1
Quick Pickle Chips	40	0	0	0	7	6	1	2	1

	CALORIES	TOTAL FAT (G)	SAT FAT (G)	CHOL (MG)	SODIUM (MG)	TOTAL CARB (G)	DIETARY FIBER (G)	TOTAL SUGARS (G)	PROTEIN (G)
CHAPTER 4: SALADS									
Foolproof Vinaigrette	93	10	1	0	38	0	0	0	0
Make-Ahead Vinaigrette	102	11	1	0	40	1	0	1	0
Bacon and Browned Butter Vinaigrette	354	37	16	66	81	6	1	4	2
Simplest Salad	15	1	0	0	3	1	1	1	1
Bibb and Arugula Salad with Pear and Goat Cheese	254	22	7	16	248	7	2	4	10
Bistro Salad	428	39	11	225	489	5	3	2	15
Romaine and Watercress Salad with Asparagus and Prosciutto	185	16	2	8	389	6	3	2	6
Edamame Salad with Arugula and Radishes	332	21	2	0	512	23	9	10	17
Homemade Croutons	70	4	0.5	0	125	8	0	1	1
Spiced Pepitas or Sunflower Seeds	60	5	1	0	75	1	1	0	2
Microwave-Fried Shallots	30	2	0	0	2	2	0	1	0
Asparagus and Spinach Salad with Sherry Vinegar and Goat Cheese	203	18	5	9	385	6	3	3	6
Kale Cobb Salad	470	30	9	205	600	13	6	4	38
Beet Salad with Blue Cheese and Endive	263	18	8	32	591	19	6	12	9
Mediterranean Chopped Salad	389	23	8	33	883	34	10	9	15
Moroccan-Style Carrot Salad	137	9	1	0	247	14	3	9	1
Green Bean Salad with Cilantro Sauce	190	16	2	0	230	9	3	4	3
Simple Tomato Salad	151	13	2	0	300	8	2	5	2
Tomato and Peach Salad	115	7	1	0	418	13	3	9	2
Tomato and Vidalia Onion Salad	123	9	1	0	399	9	2	6	2
Cherry Tomato Salad with Mango and Lime-Curry Dressing	171	11	1	0	463	17	4	12	4
Classic Potato Salad	294	17	3	70	497	31	2	4	6
French Potato Salad with Dijon and Fines Herbes	191	9	1	0	397	25	3	2	3
Lemon and Herb Red Potato Salad	209	9	1	0	83	29	4	3	4
Sweet Potato Salad	210	9	1.5	0	370	29	5	5	3
Buttermilk Coleslaw	119	7	2	7	465	12	4	7	3
Sweet and Tangy Coleslaw	121	8	1	0	496	13	4	5	2
Brussels Sprout Slaw with Pecorino and Pine Nuts	268	21	5	17	381	14	5	3	11
Brussels Sprout, Red Cabbage, and Pomegranate Slaw	151	9	1	0	338	17	5	9	4
Creamy Chicken Salad with Fresh Herbs	383	26	4	120	438	1	0	0	34
Tuna Salad with Hard-Cooked Eggs, Radishes, and Capers	357	29	4	76	487	3	1	1	22
Arugula Salad with Steak Tips and Blue Cheese	670	51	18	155	1160	8	2	4	47
Salmon, Avocado, Grapefruit, and Watercress Salad	443	34	5	39	706	21	7	9	19
Caprese Salad	320	28	12	55	90	4	1	3	14
Wedge Salad	280	24	8	35	540	8	2	5	9

	CALORIES	TOTAL FAT (G)	SAT FAT (G)	CHOL (MG)	SODIUM (MG)	TOTAL CARB (G)	DIETARY FIBER (G)	TOTAL SUGARS (G)	PROTEIN (G)
CHAPTER 4: SALADS (CONTINUED)									
Panzanella	495	29	4	0	857	50	5	10	10
Horiatiki Salata	397	33	11	50	1000	18	5	10	11
Caesar Salad	510	46	7	55	720	17	0	3	7
Kale Caesar Salad with Chicken	670	49	9	85	1360	24	3	3	32
Waldorf Salad	262	11	2	5	584	43	6	32	2
Watermelon Salad with Basil and Feta	191	12	4	17	609	18	2	13	4
Cantaloupe Salad with Olives and Red Onion	54	1	0	0	266	12	2	10	1
Citrus Salad with Orange-Ginger Vinaigrette	250	10	1.5	0	200	38	7	26	5
MORE TO EXPLORE: CREAMY AND CREAMLESS DRESSINGS									
Blue Cheese Dressing	45	4	1.5	10	100	0	0	0	1
Ranch Dressing	42	4	2	10	69	1	0	1	1
Vegan Ranch Dressing	90	10	1	0	120	0	0	0	0
Green Goddess Dressing	223	24	4	17	197	1	0	0	1
Creamy Avocado Dressing	66	6	1	2	81	2	1	1	1
Creamy Roasted Garlic Dressing	635	66	7	0	313	12	1	1	3
CHAPTER 5: SOUPS									
Chicken Noodle Soup	530	33	8	215	1110	16	1	2	41
Caldo Tlalpeño	220	9	2	45	870	14	3	4	18
Tom Kha Gai	615	49	39	84	671	15	1	2	35
Chicken Soup with Parmesan Dumplings	435	24	9	98	1429	19	4	5	34
Gazpacho	60	0	0	0	810	11	3	7	2
Soupe au Pistou	329	18	4	8	1067	31	7	4	13
Hearty Cabbage Soup	150	6	3.5	15	390	18	4	7	4
Wild Rice and Mushroom Soup	249	12	7	36	884	27	2	3	8
Roasted Eggplant and Kale Soup	310	27	6	5	880	14	6	6	5
Creamless Creamy Tomato Soup	161	8	1	0	714	18	5	8	5
Silky Butternut Squash Soup	331	20	12	58	706	38	5	5	5
Creamy Cauliflower Soup	188	16	10	41	887	11	4	4	4
Super Greens Soup with Lemon-Tarragon Cream	178	11	4	17	936	19	4	3	5
Five-Ingredient Black Bean Soup	270	3.5	2	5	1430	52	0	4	18
Creamy White Bean Soup with Herb Oil and Crispy Capers	394	23	6	15	823	35	8	4	14
Red Lentil Soup with Warm Spices	320	10	6	25	777	42	6	5	17
Spicy Pinto Bean Soup	250	8	0.5	0	1180	33	11	5	11
Chickpea and Escarole Soup	336	13	2	0	715	46	13	12	12
Pasta e Piselli	462	18	5	22	734	57	5	8	19
Chickpea Noodle Soup	326	9	1	0	1067	48	13	9	16
Hot and Sour Soup with Vermicelli and Shrimp	516	24	3	105	2122	52	4	18	25
Almost-Instant Ginger Beef Ramen for One	682	36	14	88	2274	56	4	2	33
Caldo Verde	414	25	8	41	1111	31	5	4	18

	CALORIES	TOTAL FAT (G)	SAT FAT (G)	CHOL (MG)	SODIUM (MG)	TOTAL CARB (G)	DIETARY FIBER (G)	TOTAL SUGARS (G)	PROTEIN (G)
CHAPTER 5: SOUPS (CONTINUED)									
Old-Fashioned Beef and Barley Soup	230	9	2.5	40	570	18	4	4	17
Spicy Beef Soup with Scallions and Bean Sprouts	230	13	3.5	80	680	6	2	2	23
Sharba	320	14	6	35	1180	31	2	4	17
Classic Chicken Broth	240	16	4.5	135	700	1	0	1	22
Beef Broth	180	10	3.5	40	900	6	1	3	13
Vegetable Broth Base	10	0	0	0	380	2	0	1	0
CHAPTER 6: PASTA AND NOODLES									
Linguine with White Clam Sauce	728	17	5	63	864	99	5	6	44
Orecchiette with Broccoli Rabe and Sausage	363	11	4	26	421	46	4	2	19
Garlicky Spaghetti with Lemon and Pine Nuts	738	32	6	13	413	90	5	4	24
Orzo Salad with Broccoli and Radicchio	440	27	4	5	710	41	3	7	14
Warm Spiced Pearl Couscous Salad	1230	56	14	75	1464	141	18	31	45
Fresh Pasta without a Machine	280	11	3	245	30	35	0	0	10
Fettuccine with Garlic Oil Sauce	380	14	2	0	290	56	3	1	10
Fettuccine with Browned Butter–Pine Nut Sauce	634	45	17	130	540	44	4	2	20
One-Pot Penne Puttanesca	370	9	1	0	360	62	5	6	11
Skillet Ziti with Sausage and Peppers	640	29	15	85	1810	57	4	8	42
Baked Penne with Spinach, Artichokes, and Chicken	810	38	21	170	1180	59	9	5	58
Baked Ziti with Ricotta and Eggplant	660	26	10	40	1610	85	12	19	30
Macaroni and Cheese Casserole	526	34	20	167	551	34	1	3	21
Vegetable and Orzo Tian	418	19	10	38	1006	37	6	9	27
Roasted Zucchini and Eggplant Lasagna	954	59	30	147	1759	55	6	11	54
Sausage Lasagna	808	53	24	141	1858	40	6	10	44
Sesame Noodles	210	9	1	25	980	28	1	24	7
Peppery Sesame Noodles with Bok Choy	670	32	4.5	75	1310	75	5	10	20
Chicken Lo Mein with Broccoli and Bean Sprouts	270	11	1	60	960	25	2	18	19
Pork Lo Mein with Cabbage and Carrots	340	16	2.5	65	980	26	3	19	22
Udon Noodles with Mustard Greens and Shiitake-Ginger Sauce	315	5	1	55	539	53	4	2	13
Vegetable Shabu-Shabu with Sesame Sauce	390	13	1.5	5	1430	47	4	16	16
Soba Noodles with Pork, Scallions, and Shichimi Togarashi	392	12	2	74	1534	37	3	3	33
Chilled Soba Noodles with Spring Vegetables	329	9	1	0	934	52	2	3	12
Singapore Noodles with Shrimp	331	15	2	196	758	33	3	4	16
Spicy Peanut Rice Noodles	690	32	4.5	0	980	85	2	11	18
Pad Thai	587	25	4	210	1629	64	5	16	29
Pad Kee Mao	780	28	9	80	1660	108	3	24	24

	CALORIES	TOTAL FAT (G)	SAT FAT (G)	CHOL (MG)	SODIUM (MG)	TOTAL CARB (G)	DIETARY FIBER (G)	TOTAL SUGARS (G)	PROTEIN (G)
CHAPTER 6: PASTA AND NOODLES (CONTINUED)									
MORE TO EXPLORE: TOMATO SAUCES									
Classic Marinara Sauce	170	11	1.5	0	650	12	1	6	2
Fresh Tomato Sauce	90	6	1	0	547	9	3	6	2
Arrabbiata Sauce	103	6	3	10	348	11	3	6	2
Amatriciana Sauce	280	23	9	30	1030	11	3	6	5
Simple Italian-Style Meat Sauce	179	10	4	34	379	12	3	6	13
MORE TO EXPLORE: PESTO									
Basil Pesto	210	22	3	5	85	2	1	0	3
Spinach Pesto	210	19	4	10	410	1	1	0	7
Arugula-Almond Pesto	80	8	1	0	230	2	1	1	2
Kale–Sunflower Seed Pesto	120	12	2	0	95	1	1	0	2
Pesto Calabrese	220	16	5	15	180	8	2	5	8
CHAPTER 7: RICE, GRAINS, AND BEANS									
Everyday Long-Grain White Rice	210	0	0	0	0	48	0	0	5
Everyday Brown Rice	150	2	0	0	390	35	3	0	3
Hung Kao Mun Gati	251	8	7	0	200	40	1	2	4
White Rice Salad with Oranges, Olives, and Almonds	209	7	1	0	197	34	2	4	4
Brown Rice Salad with Tomatoes, Avocado, and Jalapeño	224	9	1	0	264	33	4	3	4
Black Rice Salad with Snap Peas and Ginger-Sesame Vinaigrette	500	20	2.5	60	370	58	6	6	27
Foolproof Baked White Rice	232	5	3	10	407	41	0	1	6
Foolproof Baked Brown Rice	183	3	1	3	200	36	2	0	4
Baked Mexican Rice	260	10	0.5	0	650	40	1	2	5
Easiest-Ever Quinoa	130	2	0	0	430	21	2	1	5
Tabbouleh	277	21	3	0	447	22	5	3	4
Millet Porridge with Maple Syrup	243	4	1	5	64	45	4	8	7
Barley with Fennel, Dried Apricots, and Orange	218	4	1	0	378	42	9	9	5
Farro with Mushrooms and Thyme	245	8	1	0	310	37	6	5	8
Wheat Berry Salad with Endive, Blueberries, and Goat Cheese	450	28	5	10	300	43	9	4	11
Curried Baked Quinoa with Cauliflower	320	11	1.5	0	380	45	6	3	11
Baked Wild Rice with Cranberries and Almonds	200	3.5	1	5	300	36	4	6	6
Everyday Rice Pilaf	210	4.5	0.5	0	100	38	0	1	4
Herbed Barley Pilaf	240	6	0.5	0	630	43	9	2	5
Bulgur Pilaf with Mushrooms	216	7	1	0	524	35	6	3	7
Freekeh Pilaf with Dates and Cauliflower	360	13	2	0	340	53	12	13	10
Hawaiian Fried Rice	513	26	6	114	1248	53	4	7	17

	CALORIES	TOTAL FAT (G)	SAT FAT (G)	CHOL (MG)	SODIUM (MG)	TOTAL CARB (G)	DIETARY FIBER (G)	TOTAL SUGARS (G)	PROTEIN (G)
CHAPTER 7: RICE, GRAINS, AND BEANS (CONTINUED)									
Fried Rice with Gai Lan and Shiitake Mushrooms	420	17	1.5	60	670	57	2	4	2
Nasi Goreng	661	28	3	195	1157	84	5	18	20
Kimchi Bokkeumbap	475	10	1	5	534	84	2	2	10
Fried Brown Rice with Pork and Shrimp	461	15	3	163	638	56	4	4	24
Risotto with Parmesan and Herbs	491	16	9	37	1056	62	3	3	18
Spring Vegetable Risotto	651	24	14	57	1769	77	7	5	24
Farrotto with Pancetta, Asparagus, and Peas	423	21	10	44	887	42	7	7	20
Creamy Parmesan Polenta	565	26	16	66	1364	50	3	2	31
Fluffy Baked Polenta	260	18	8	35	790	22	2	0	7
Sautéed Cherry Tomato and Fresh Mozzarella Topping	258	21	8	38	311	8	2	5	11
Broccoli Rabe, Sun-Dried Tomato, and Pine Nut Topping	195	17	2	0	370	9	4	1	6
Creamy Cheese Grits	366	23	14	63	635	27	2	3	14
Baked Cheese Grits	506	37	21	204	536	27	2	2	17
Shrimp and Grits	627	33	17	288	1565	47	3	8	35
Ultracreamy Hummus	218	12	1	0	287	23	7	4	8
Chickpea Salad with Carrots, Arugula, and Olives	459	21	3	0	708	55	16	11	16
Spiced Chickpea Gyros with Tahini Yogurt	586	19	4	10	1021	82	19	12	28
Garlicky White Beans with Sage	375	14	2	0	211	46	12	2	18
Refried Pinto Beans	150	3.5	0	0	460	23	6	2	7
Black-Eyed Peas and Greens	218	10	3	14	690	23	7	3	11
Black Beans on Toast with Tomato and Avocado	266	10	1	0	515	37	11	3	10
Skillet Rice and Black Beans with Corn and Tomatoes	270	6	0.5	0	730	48	1	4	10
Lentils with Carrots and Parsley	160	5	0.5	0	220	23	6	3	7
Baked Lentils with Sausage	197	15	4	19	817	10	3	5	7
Lentil Salad with Pomegranate and Walnuts	249	12	2	0	543	27	4	3	10
Spiced Red Lentils	169	5	2	7	531	23	4	2	8
White Beans with Tomatoes and Capers	377	14	2	0	268	47	12	2	18
Cowboy Beans	449	9	3	13	886	74	13	26	20
Baked Navy Beans	344	4	0	0	970	62	12	17	18
Falafel	80	5	0.5	0	110	10	0	0	3
Crispy Tempeh	150	9	1	0	95	10	0	0	8
Pan-Seared Tempeh Steaks with Chimichurri Sauce	440	32	4.5	0	340	23	1	1	15
Tempeh with Sambal Sauce	360	20	3.5	0	1740	22	1	10	25
Barbecue Tempeh Wraps	580	21	3	0	1730	79	1	40	21

	CALORIES	TOTAL FAT (G)	SAT FAT (G)	CHOL (MG)	SODIUM (MG)	TOTAL CARB (G)	DIETARY FIBER (G)	TOTAL SUGARS (G)	PROTEIN (G)
CHAPTER 8: MEAT									
Pan-Seared Steak Tips with Roasted Potatoes and Horseradish Cream	745	45	17	192	1048	33	5	3	50
Pan-Seared Sirloin Steaks with Mustard-Cream Pan Sauce	895	64	25	296	317	4	1	2	70
Bacon-Wrapped Filets Mignons	551	32	11	208	605	1	0	0	66
Pan-Seared Strip Steaks	425	31	12	146	97	0	0	0	35
Lamb Rib Chops with Mint-Rosemary Relish	1189	107	40	231	819	2	1	0	51
Pan-Seared Thick-Cut Pork Chops	746	45	16	258	1038	5	1	1	72
Citrus-and-Spice Pork Chops	559	40	9	147	734	5	1	2	44
Spiced Braised Pork Chops	370	16	6	110	540	8	1	4	38
Deviled Pork Chops	431	23	7	142	541	9	1	3	44
Teriyaki Stir-Fried Beef with Green Beans and Shiitakes	305	15	4	58	947	21	4	12	23
Sichuan Stir-Fried Pork in Garlic Sauce	264	19	2	42	733	10	1	6	13
Slow-Roast Beef	340	11	3	150	290	0	0	0	58
Roast Pork Loin with Sweet Potatoes and Cilantro Sauce	875	50	11	123	1106	64	7	27	42
Broiled Pork Tenderloin with Sun-Dried Tomato and Basil Salsa	270	14	2.5	95	510	4	1	2	31
Classic Pot Roast	435	26	12	137	856	7	1	3	39
Red Wine–Braised Short Ribs with Bacon, Parsnips, and Pearl Onions	740	31	12	130	1140	48	9	18	45
Braised Lamb Shanks with Lemon and Mint	480	27	10	120	540	13	2	5	33
Best Beef Stew	587	29	11	139	1171	24	4	4	47
Catalan-Style Beef Stew with Mushrooms	675	49	17	138	1028	15	3	5	37
Chile Verde con Cerdo	373	23	7	100	892	12	3	7	30
Goan Pork Vindaloo	304	20	6	87	600	6	1	1	25
Lamb Stew with Potatoes	689	24	7	214	289	42	6	6	79
Classic Beef Burgers	608	38	16	145	562	22	1	3	43
Spaghetti and Meatballs	978	63	8	87	881	74	6	9	32
Thai Pork Lettuce Wraps	125	3	1	47	634	8	1	4	17
Glazed Meatloaf	379	21	7	125	483	23	1	15	24
Spicy Lamb with Lentils and Yogurt	460	36	14	90	647	9	2	5	24
Grilled Steak Burgers	719	44	23	184	1163	38	2	13	43
Grilled Flank Steak with Basil Dressing	349	22	6	103	421	5	0	3	32
Grilled Pork Tenderloin with Grilled Pineapple–Red Onion Salsa	200	6	1	70	340	13	2	9	23
Pinchos Morunos	570	41	6	168	596	4	1	0	45
Steak Tacos	440	26	5	84	470	24	3	1	29
Pork Gyro	301	20	5	51	431	14	2	2	18
Philly Cheesesteaks	1130	58	22	215	1890	77	0	7	72
Roast Beef Tenderloin	530	35	16	190	830	1	0	0	50

	CALORIES	TOTAL FAT (G)	SAT FAT (G)	CHOL (MG)	SODIUM (MG)	TOTAL CARB (G)	DIETARY FIBER (G)	TOTAL SUGARS (G)	PROTEIN (G)
CHAPTER 8: MEAT (CONTINUED)									
Pan-Seared Steaks with Brandy–Pink Peppercorn Sauce	1045	65	26	207	1871	19	3	6	61
Brisket Carbonnade	861	64	24	249	1030	17	3	7	49
Roast Butterflied Leg of Lamb with Coriander, Cumin, and Mustard Seeds	440	22	6	175	330	1	1	0	56
MORE TO EXPLORE: SPICE RUBS, SAUCES, AND COMPOUND BUTTERS									
Barbecue Rub	8	0	0	0	29	2	0	1	0
Classic Steak Rub	5	0	0	0	1	1	0	0	0
Herbes de Provence	3	0	0	0	1	0	0	0	0
Jerk Rub	8	0	0	0	1	2	0	1	0
Salsa Verde	100	9	1.5	0	100	3	0	0	1
Chermoula	64	7	1	0	31	1	0	0	0
Chimichurri	45	4.5	0.5	0	100	1	0	0	0
Mint Persillade	185	19	3	3	147	4	2	0	2
Hollandaise Sauce	90	9	6	50	30	0	0	0	0
Yogurt-Herb Sauce	20	1	0.5	5	15	2	0	1	1
Gorgonzola Vinaigrette	373	37	10	25	446	3	1	1	8
Romesco	43	3	0	0	75	3	1	1	1
Chipotle-Cilantro Compound Butter	110	11	7	30	0	2	0	1	0
Chive-Lemon Miso Compound Butter	120	11	7	30	240	3	0	2	1
Parsley-Caper Compound Butter	100	11	7	30	35	0	0	0	0
Parsley-Lemon Compound Butter	100	11	7	30	0	1	0	0	0
Tarragon-Lime Compound Butter	100	11	7	30	0	1	0	0	0
Tapenade Compound Butter	120	12	7	30	95	1	0	0	0
CHAPTER 9: POULTRY									
Simple Sautéed Chicken Cutlets	419	22	3	145	614	7	2	4	47
Crispy Pan-Fried Chicken Cutlets	418	24	2	159	436	14	1	1	34
Chicken Piccata	388	20	5	113	567	18	2	2	33
Best Chicken Parmesan	671	45	12	165	1023	25	5	10	45
Quick Tomato Sauce	102	6	3	10	345	11	3	6	2
Pan-Roasted Chicken Breasts	270	16	4	85	230	0	0	0	28
Chicken Leg Quarters with Cauliflower and Shallots	810	49	12	385	1940	26	5	7	73
Weeknight Roast Chicken	731	53	17	232	1204	5	1	1	56
Peruvian Roast Chicken with Garlic and Lime	771	56	14	225	771	8	2	3	57
One-Hour Broiled Chicken and Pan Sauce	687	48	13	231	1075	2	1	0	58
Barbecue Roast Chicken and Potatoes	867	49	13	333	1192	32	4	3	74
Chicken Cacciatore	576	32	7	215	311	7	2	4	64
Tandoori Chicken	881	66	17	341	1047	11	2	4	59
Classic Chicken Stew	554	18	4	272	1418	30	5	6	63

	CALORIES	TOTAL FAT (G)	SAT FAT (G)	CHOL (MG)	SODIUM (MG)	TOTAL CARB (G)	DIETARY FIBER (G)	TOTAL SUGARS (G)	PROTEIN (G)
CHAPTER 9: POULTRY (CONTINUED)									
Lemon-Braised Chicken Thighs with Chickpeas and Fennel	1060	46	10	176	1720	104	20	21	56
Braised Chicken Thighs with Chard and Mustard	678	45	12	237	1452	18	3	4	45
Chicken and Rice with Carrots and Peas	712	16	2	151	1458	81	4	9	58
Curried Chicken with Coconut Rice and Lime-Yogurt Sauce	649	25	11	91	1172	69	5	7	37
Arroz con Pollo	842	48	11	177	1004	63	2	4	37
Khao Man Gai	749	33	9	145	2183	67	3	7	44
Stir-Fried Sesame Chicken with Broccoli and Red Pepper	299	17	2	62	91	14	4	3	24
Gai Pad Krapow	337	12	1	124	917	16	2	9	41
Kung Pao Chicken	507	27	4	160	1077	25	5	12	43
Karaage	462	28	3	107	550	26	0	1	23
Cast Iron Easier Fried Chicken	680	43	9	145	1080	31	1	1	40
Fried Chicken Sandwiches	670	35	4	65	1020	56	1	4	30
Grilled Chicken Souvlaki	569	27	5	131	910	37	6	6	48
Grilled Bone-In Chicken	650	46	13	225	500	0	0	0	56
Grilled Wine-and-Herb Marinated Chicken	886	57	15	231	1410	12	1	8	58
Easy Roast Turkey Breast	457	23	8	185	333	0	0	0	58
Easier Roast Turkey and Gravy	700	29	7	325	1670	5	0	2	99
All-Purpose Gravy	62	4	2	9	116	5	0	1	2
MORE TO EXPLORE: PAN SAUCES									
Tarragon-Lemon Pan Sauce	60	6	3.5	15	200	2	0	1	0
Thyme–Sherry Vinegar Pan Sauce	60	6	3.5	15	200	2	0	1	0
Sage-Vermouth Pan Sauce	120	8	5	25	220	4	0	3	1
Lemon-Caper Pan Sauce	120	12	6	25	240	2	0	1	1
Mustard-Cider Pan Sauce	50	3	2	10	80	3	0	2	1
Apricot-Orange Pan Sauce	190	3	2	10	15	41	5	34	2
CHAPTER 10: SEAFOOD									
Pan-Roasted Cod with Grapefruit-Basil Relish	236	7.5	1	58	284	3	1	2	24
Nut-Crusted Cod Fillets	325	16	2	107	477	14	3	3	31
Cod Baked in Foil with Leeks and Carrots	298	13	8	104	650	11	2	3	32
Pan-Seared Swordfish Steaks with Caper-Currant Relish	450	28	5	150	710	2	0	1	45
Halibut en Cocotte with Garlic and Cherry Tomatoes	267	16	2	69	568	4	1	2	27
Roasted Snapper and Vegetables with Mustard Sauce	530	26	4	65	960	29	5	7	41
Grilled Swordfish Tacos	576	22	4	100	1135	62	10	20	36
Sautéed Tilapia with Cilantro Chimichurri	337	23	4	78	470	1	0	0	32

	CALORIES	TOTAL FAT (G)	SAT FAT (G)	CHOL (MG)	SODIUM (MG)	TOTAL CARB (G)	DIETARY FIBER (G)	TOTAL SUGARS (G)	PROTEIN (G)
CHAPTER 10: SEAFOOD (CONTINUED)									
Pan-Fried Sole	348	23	7	99	505	13	1	0	23
Cornmeal Catfish and Southwestern Corn	750	41	13	165	1360	47	2	6	48
Comeback Sauce	191	20	3	8	298	4	1	2	0
Baked Sole Fillets with Herbs and Bread Crumbs	235	13	7	102	545	6	1	0	22
Pomegranate Roasted Salmon with Lentils and Chard	446	27	6	78	939	19	3	13	31
Pan-Seared Salmon Steaks	626	41	8	140	634	8	0	0	52
Miso-Marinated Salmon	510	24	5	95	1040	28	0	22	38
Grilled Salmon Fillets with Lemon-Garlic Sauce	798	65	12	144	664	1	0	0	49
Perfect Poached Fish	380	23	5	95	390	1	0	0	35
Shrimp Cocktail	128	1	0	143	963	14	2	8	16
Pan-Seared Shrimp with Pistachio, Cumin, and Parsley	231	12	2	214	967	5	1	1	25
Garlicky Roasted Shrimp with Parsley and Anise	265	19	6	211	858	3	0	0	21
Baked Shrimp and Orzo with Feta and Tomatoes	628	15	6	173	1398	86	7	12	38
Pan-Seared Scallops	232	14	4	56	668	6	0	0	21
Fennel and Bibb Salad with Scallops and Hazelnuts	430	31	4	40	1180	15	4	4	24
Brothy Rice with Clams and Salsa Verde	503	13	2	45	1325	51	1	2	29
Oven-Steamed Mussels	526	19	6	142	1303	20	1	1	54
Crispy Fish Sandwiches	1106	85	9	93	980	53	2	5	29
Classic Tartar Sauce	321	33	5	17	381	6	0	5	0
Popcorn Shrimp	440	16	1.5	175	580	49	0	0	22
CHAPTER 11: BREAD									
Quick Cheese Bread	3063	147	86	571	3285	314	10	23	116
Brown Soda Bread	342	6	3	14	381	62	4	8	11
Southern-Style Skillet Cornbread	213	10	3	43	227	25	1	2	5
Ultimate Banana Bread	3180	116	64	616	2630	505	26	240	49
Easiest-Ever Biscuits	347	20	12	71	224	36	1	3	5
Mixed Berry Scones	467	22	14	79	366	60	2	18	8
Whole-Wheat Blueberry Muffins	354	13	5	47	300	57	5	26	7
Easy Sandwich Bread	220	5	3	35	250	35	2	2	7
Anadama Bread	314	5	3	11	274	60	2	9	7
Oatmeal-Raisin Bread	239	6	3	11	231	41	3	6	7
Almost No-Knead Bread	250	0	0	0	580	52	0	0	7
Almost No-Knead Brioche	264	14	8	112	185	27	1	4	7
Rosemary Focaccia	251	7	1	0	245	41	2	0	6
Fluffy Dinner Rolls	162	6	3	28	140	23	1	3	4

	CALORIES	TOTAL FAT (G)	SAT FAT (G)	CHOL (MG)	SODIUM (MG)	TOTAL CARB (G)	DIETARY FIBER (G)	TOTAL SUGARS (G)	PROTEIN (G)
CHAPTER 11: BREAD (CONTINUED)									
Rustic Dinner Rolls	115	1	0	0	127	23	1	1	4
Honey-Wheat Dinner Rolls	160	5	3	25	340	26	3	8	5
Whole-Wheat Quinoa Bread	270	4	0.5	0	450	49	4	7	9
Classic Italian Bread	260	3.5	0.5	0	440	44	2	0	8
Cranberry-Walnut Bread	350	9	1	0	590	59	4	15	10
Skillet Pizza	1250	90	33	141	1535	60	3	6	49
Thin-Crust Pizza	523	18	8	38	746	67	5	8	23
with Sausage, Pepper, and Onion	560	23	9	50	1710	56	2	6	30
Pizza al Taglio with Arugula and Fresh Mozzarella	613	34	11	43	664	55	4	3	23
Flour Tortillas	170	6	1.5	0	290	24	0	0	3
Chapati	270	10	1	0	580	40	3	0	7
Pitas	330	7	1	0	580	54	2	1	10
Mana'eesh Za'atar	323	12	2	0	264	46	2	0	7
CHAPTER 12: DESSERTS									
Perfect Chocolate Chip Cookies	314	18	9	50	155	37	2	23	3
Brown Sugar Cookies	220	7	4	33	88	36	1	18	3
Molasses Spice Cookies	182	7	4	25	89	29	1	18	2
Thin and Crispy Oatmeal Cookies	155	8	4	25	82	21	1	10	2
Pecan Sandies	122	9	3	17	20	10	1	4	1
Chocolate-Toffee Butter Cookies	101	6	3	14	28	11	1	6	1
Foolproof Holiday Cookies	146	7	4	18	27	20	0	11	1
Nankhatai	110	7	3.5	15	50	10	0	3	1
Biscochitos	90	5	2	11	30	11	0	5	1
Fudgy Brownies	100	5	3	20	40	13	0	7	1
Chewy Brownies	299	15	5	43	98	41	2	30	3
Rocky Road Brownies	210	11	6	40	65	27	1	19	3
Blondies	139	8	4	21	54	16	0	11	2
Pound Cake	430	25	15	155	240	48	0	31	5
Tahini-Banana Snack Cake	260	8	3	40	160	43	1	25	5
Simple Carrot Sheet Cake	720	45	12	115	470	73	1	52	7
Chocolate Sheet Cake with Milk Chocolate Frosting	783	53	25	132	222	75	4	56	9
Buttery Yellow Layer Cake with Chocolate Frosting	1050	64	40	215	350	113	0	76	9
Confetti Cake	500	27	16	70	210	62	0	49	3

	CALORIES	TOTAL FAT (G)	SAT FAT (G)	CHOL (MG)	SODIUM (MG)	TOTAL CARB (G)	DIETARY FIBER (G)	TOTAL SUGARS (G)	PROTEIN (G)
CHAPTER 12: DESSERTS (CONTINUED)									
Red Velvet Cupcakes	370	22	13	75	250	40	0	29	4
Best Lemon Bars	258	13	8	77	166	34	1	22	3
Lemon Pudding Cake	276	10	6	93	128	43	1	36	5
Lemon Bundt Cake	444	17	10	93	283	70	1	45	5
Skillet Cherry Crisp	490	17	7	30	300	78	5	55	6
Blueberry Cobbler with Biscuit Topping	286	6	4	16	249	56	3	35	3
Peach Crumble	452	16	8	31	78	74	6	51	7
Easy Apple Galettes	230	9	5	10	125	36	2	20	3
Skillet Apple Pie	333	15	8	31	157	47	5	26	3
Deep-Dish Apple Pie	471	20	12	50	304	71	7	39	5
Pumpkin Pie	530	29	18	195	520	58	2	37	8
Pecan Pie	690	43	16	130	350	71	3	52	7
Cranberry Oat Bars	220	11	5	30	55	29	2	17	2
Coconut Rice Pudding	362	20	16	17	277	40	0	25	8
Pots de Crème	479	38	23	205	114	35	2	31	5
Chocolate Mousse	262	20	12	129	63	17	1	15	4
Vanilla No-Churn Ice Cream	304	20	13	76	123	27	0	27	4
Mint-Cookie No-Churn Ice Cream	349	23	14	83	157	33	0	27	4
Strawberry-Buttermilk No-Churn Ice Cream	331	20	13	76	147	35	0	33	4
Peanut Butter Cup No-Churn Ice Cream	435	31	15	77	165	36	1	34	8
MORE TO EXPLORE: FROSTINGS AND WHIPPED CREAM									
Vanilla Frosting	520	38	24	105	60	46	0	45	0
Almond Frosting	520	38	24	105	60	45	0	45	0
Coconut Frosting	520	38	24	105	60	45	0	45	0
Coffee Frosting	530	38	24	105	60	46	0	45	0
Orange Frosting	520	38	24	105	60	46	0	45	0
Peppermint Frosting	520	38	24	105	60	45	0	45	0
Chocolate Frosting	660	44	28	90	55	67	0	46	4
Chocolate Ganache Frosting	239	20	12	41	14	19	2	16	2
Cream Cheese Frosting	440	32	21	105	270	33	0	30	4
Whipped Cream	110	11	7	35	10	2	0	2	1
MORE TO EXPLORE: FOOLPROOF ALL-BUTTER PIE DOUGH									
Foolproof All-Butter Single-Crust Pie Dough	210	14	9	40	150	18	0	2	2
Foolproof All-Butter Double-Crust Pie Dough	410	28	18	75	290	35	0	3	5

CONVERSIONS AND EQUIVALENTS

Some say cooking is a science and an art. We would say that geography has a hand in it, too. Flours and sugars manufactured in the United Kingdom and elsewhere will feel and taste different from those manufactured in the United States. So we cannot promise that the loaf of bread you bake in Canada or England will taste the same as a loaf baked in the States, but we can offer guidelines for converting weights and measures. We also recommend that you rely on your instincts when making our recipes. Refer to the visual cues provided. If the dough hasn't "come together in a ball" as described, you may need to add more flour—even if the recipe doesn't tell you to. You be the judge.

The recipes in this book were developed using standard U.S. measures following U.S. government guidelines. The charts below offer equivalents for U.S. and metric measures. All conversions are approximate and have been rounded up or down to the nearest whole number.

Example

1 teaspoon = 4.9292 milliliters, rounded up to 5 milliliters
1 ounce = 28.3495 grams, rounded down to 28 grams

VOLUME CONVERSIONS

U.S.	METRIC
1 teaspoon	5 milliliters
2 teaspoons	10 milliliters
1 tablespoon	15 milliliters
2 tablespoons	30 milliliters
¼ cup	59 milliliters
⅓ cup	79 milliliters
½ cup	118 milliliters
¾ cup	177 milliliters
1 cup	237 milliliters
1¼ cups	296 milliliters
1½ cups	355 milliliters
2 cups (1 pint)	473 milliliters
2½ cups	591 milliliters
3 cups	710 milliliters
4 cups (1 quart)	0.946 liter
1.06 quarts	1 liter
4 quarts (1 gallon)	3.8 liters

WEIGHT CONVERSIONS

OUNCES	GRAMS
½	14
¾	21
1	28
1½	43
2	57
2½	71
3	85
3½	99
4	113
4½	128
5	142
6	170
7	198
8	227
9	255
10	283
12	340
16 (1 pound)	454

CONVERSIONS FOR COMMON BAKING INGREDIENTS

Baking is an exacting science. Because measuring by weight is far more accurate than measuring by volume, and thus more likely to produce reliable results, in our recipes we provide ounce measures in addition to cup measures for many ingredients. Refer to the chart below to convert these measures into grams.

INGREDIENT	OUNCES	GRAMS
Flour		
1 cup all-purpose flour*	5	142
1 cup cake flour	4	113
1 cup whole-wheat flour	5½	156
Sugar		
1 cup granulated (white) sugar	7	198
1 cup packed brown sugar (light or dark)	7	198
1 cup confectioners' sugar	4	113
Cocoa Powder		
1 cup cocoa powder	3	85
Butter†		
4 tablespoons (½ stick or ¼ cup)	2	57
8 tablespoons (1 stick or ½ cup)	4	113
16 tablespoons (2 sticks or 1 cup)	8	227

* U.S. all-purpose flour, the most frequently used flour in this book, does not contain leaveners, as some European flours do. These leavened flours are called self-rising or self-raising. If you are using self-rising flour, take this into consideration before adding leaveners to a recipe.

† In the United States, butter is sold both salted and unsalted. We generally recommend unsalted butter. If you are using salted butter, take this into consideration before adding salt to a recipe.

OVEN TEMPERATURES

FAHRENHEIT	CELSIUS	GAS MARK
225	105	¼
250	120	½
275	135	1
300	150	2
325	165	3
350	180	4
375	190	5
400	200	6
425	220	7
450	230	8
475	245	9

CONVERTING TEMPERATURES FROM AN INSTANT-READ THERMOMETER

We include doneness temperatures in many of the recipes in this book. We recommend an instant-read thermometer for the job. Use this simple formula to convert Fahrenheit degrees to Celsius:

Subtract 32 degrees from the Fahrenheit reading, then divide the result by 1.8 to find the Celsius reading.

Example

"Roast chicken until thighs register 175 degrees."

TO CONVERT:

175°F − 32 = 143°
143° ÷ 1.8 = 79.44°C, rounded down to 79°C

INDEX

Note: Page references in *italics* indicate recipe photographs.

A

Adjustable measuring cup, 560
Allspice
  Jerk Rub, 352
Almond(s)
  and Apricots, Rice Pilaf with, 297
  Arugula Pesto, 255
  and Cranberries, Baked Wild Rice with, *294*, 295
  Frosting, 594
  and Green Olives, Garlicky Spaghetti with, 243
  -Orange Oatmeal Cookies, Thin and Crispy, 569
  Oranges, and Olives, White Rice Salad with, 287
  Peach Crumble, 604–5, *605*
  Pound Cake, 585
  Sandies, 571
  Skillet Cherry Crisp, *602*, 602–3
  Toasted, and Browned Butter, 96
Amatriciana Sauce, 248
Anadama Bread, 522, *522*
Anchovies, 18
Apple(s)
  coring, 46
  Galettes, Easy, *606*, 606–7
  Pie, Deep-Dish, *608*, 608–9
  Pie, Skillet, 607
  Waldorf Salad, 192
Appliances, small, 14–15
Apricot(s)
  and Almonds, Rice Pilaf with, 297
  Dried, Curried Chicken Salad with, 182
  Dried, Fennel, and Orange, Barley with, *292*, 293
  -Orange Pan Sauce, 419
Apron, 15
Arrabbiata Sauce, 247
Arroz con Pollo, *432*, 432
Artichokes, Spinach, and Chicken, Baked Penne with, *258*, 258–59
Arugula
  Almond Pesto, 255
  and Bibb Salad, with Pear and Goat Cheese, 157, *157*
  Carrots, and Olives, Chickpea Salad with, 320, *320*
  Fontina, and Prosciutto, Skillet Pizza with, 547
  and Fresh Mozzarella, Pizza al Taglio with, 549–50

Arugula (cont.)
  and Radishes, Edamame Salad with, 159
  Salad with Steak Tips and Blue Cheese, *184*, 184–85
Asparagus
  boiling times, 98
  Broiled, with Garlic-Butter Sauce, 132
  grilling instructions, 143
  Pancetta, and Peas, Farrotto with, *309*, 309
  Pan-Roasted, 112, *113*
  and Prosciutto, Romaine and Watercress Salad with, *158*, 159
  Roasted, 124
  shaving, 159
  Smoked Salmon, and Chives, Scrambled Eggs with, 56
  and Smoked Salmon Omelet, 79
  and Spinach Salad with Sherry Vinegar and Goat Cheese, 162, *163*
  Spring Vegetable Risotto, 308, *308*
  steaming times, 98
  storage tips, 93
  trimming, 40
Autolyse, 535
Avocado(s)
  cutting up, 40
  Dressing, Creamy, 173
  Salmon, Grapefruit, and Watercress Salad, 185
  Toast with Fried Eggs, 62
  and Tomato, Black Beans on Toast with, 322, *323*
  Tomatoes, and Jalapeño, Brown Rice Salad with, *286*, 287–88

B

Bacon, 21
  Bistro Salad, 158, *158*
  and Browned Butter Vinaigrette, 155
  and Chive Deviled Eggs, 66, *66*
  Egg, and Cheese Sandwiches, 70
  Farrotto with Pancetta, Asparagus, and Peas, 309, *309*
  flavoring soups with, 213
  freezing, 213
  Fried Egg Sandwiches, 71, *71*
  Onion, and Gruyère, Quick Cheese Bread with, 511
  and Onion, Garlicky Braised Kale with, 106

Bacon (cont.)
  Parsnips, and Pearl Onions, Red Wine–Braised Short Ribs with, 372, *373*
  Wedge Salad, 186–87, *187*
  -Wrapped Filets Mignon, 348, *348*
Bake, defined, 4
Bakeware, 11–12
Baking and dessert basics, 558–63
Baking dishes, 11
Baking pans, 11
Baking peel, 12, 504
Baking powder, 20, 439, 513
Baking soda, 20, 311, 319, 513
Baking steel, 12, 504
Baking stone, 12, 504
Banana(s)
  Bread, Ultimate, *514*, 515
  and Coconut, Millet Porridge with, 292
  -Tahini Snack Cake, 586, *587*
Banh Mi, Tofu, 84, *84*
Barbecue Rub, 352
Barbecue Tempeh Wraps, 335
Barley
  about, 283
  and Beef Soup, Old-Fashioned, 229
  boiling, 336
  with Fennel, Dried Apricots, and Orange, *292*, 293
  Pilaf, Herbed, 297
Bars
  about, 579
  Blondies, 580–81, *581*
  Chewy Brownies, 579
  Congo, 581
  Cranberry Oat, 616, *616*
  Fudgy Brownies, *579*, 579–80
  Lemon, Best, 596–97, *597*
  Rocky Road Brownies, 580, *581*
Basil
  Broiled Eggplant with, *136*, 137
  Caprese Salad, 186
  Dressing, Grilled Flank Steak with, 391–92, *392*
  and Feta, Watermelon Salad with, 193, *193*
  Fresh Tomato Sauce, 246–47, *247*
  Gai Pad Krapow, 436
  Pad Kee Mao, 279, *279*
  Pesto, 254, *254*
  Soupe au Pistou, 208, *209*
  and Sun-Dried Tomato Salsa, Broiled Pork Tenderloin with, 369, *369*
Bass, about, 461

Bean(s)
- Black, and Rice, Skillet, with Corn and Tomatoes, 323
- Black, on Toast with Tomato and Avocado, 322, *323*
- Black, Soup, Five-Ingredient, 220, *221*
- Black-Eyed Peas and Greens, 322
- canned, 18, 318
- Cowboy, 329–30
- dried, brining, 329
- dried, cooking, 319, 328
- dried, flavor of, 18
- dried, soaking, 329
- dried, sorting, 326
- dried, template for, 337
- Edamame Salad with Arugula and Radishes, 159
- Navy, Baked, 330, *331*
- Pinto, Refried, 321
- Pinto, Soup, Spicy, 222–23
- Soupe au Pistou, 208, *209*
- storing, 317
- types of, 317
- White, Garlicky, with Sage, 321
- White, Soup, Creamy, with Herb Oil and Crispy Capers, 220–21, *221*
- White, with Tomatoes and Capers, *328*, 328–29
- see also Chickpea(s); Edamame; Green Beans

Bean Sprouts
- and Broccoli, Chicken Lo Mein with, 270
- Pad Thai, 278, *279*
- and Scallions, Spicy Beef Soup with, 230, *231*
- Singapore Noodles with Shrimp, 276–77, *277*
- Soba Noodles with Pork, Scallions, and Shichimi Togarashi, 274, *275*

Beat, defined, 7

Beef
- "American Wagyu," about, 351
- Arugula Salad with Steak Tips and Blue Cheese, *184*, 184–85
- Bacon-Wrapped Filets Mignon, 348, *348*
- and Barley Soup, Old-Fashioned, 229
- blade steaks, trimming, 230
- boneless strip steak, about, 350
- brisket, flat cut, 403
- brisket, making ahead, 403
- brisket, point cut, 403
- brisket, trimming, 403
- Brisket Carbonnade, *402*, 403
- Broth, 233
- broth, buying, 199
- Burgers, Classic, 384–85, *385*
- chuck-eye roast, about, 377

Beef (cont.)
- chuck-eye roast, prepping, 371
- Classic Pot Roast, *370*, 371
- compound butters for, 355
- creamy sauces for, 354
- doneness temperatures, 345
- filet mignon, about, 350
- flank steak, slicing, 361
- flank steak stir-fry secrets, 361
- flap meat, cutting into steaks tips, 347
- frozen steaks, cooking, 350
- Ginger Ramen for One, Almost-Instant, 227, *227*
- Glazed Meatloaf, 388, *388*
- grades of, 341
- grilled flank steak, flavoring, 392
- Grilled Flank Steak with Basil Dressing, 391–92, *392*
- Grilled Steak Burgers, *390*, 391
- "Kobe," about, 351
- marbling in, 340, 341
- Pan-Seared Sirloin Steaks with Mustard-Cream Pan Sauce, 347
- Pan-Seared Steaks with Brandy–Pink Peppercorn Sauce, 401
- Pan-Seared Steak Tips with Roasted Potatoes and Horseradish Cream, *346*, 346–47
- Pan-Seared Strip Steaks, 349
- Philly Cheesesteaks, 399, *399*
- primal and retail cuts, 344
- rare, eating, 351
- Red Wine–Braised Short Ribs with Bacon, Parsnips, and Pearl Onions, *372*, 373
- rib-eye steak, about, 350
- sautéing or pan-frying, 351
- short ribs, English-style, 372
- short ribs, flanken-style, 372
- Simple Italian-Style Meat Sauce, 248
- skirt steak, about, 399
- Slow-Roast, *366*, 377
- Soup, Spicy, with Scallions and Bean Sprouts, 230, *231*
- Spaghetti and Meatballs, 386, *387*
- steak rubs and finishing sauces for, 352–53
- steaks, centerpiece, 350
- steaks, cooking, 346
- steaks, high-end, 351
- steaks, resources for, 350–51
- steaks, salting, 350
- Steak Tacos, *396*, 397
- Stew, Best, 376–77, *377*
- Stew, Catalan-Style, with Mushrooms, *378*, 378
- stir-fries, resources for, 364–65
- Tenderloin, Roast, *400*, 401

Beef (cont.)
- Teriyaki Stir-Fried, with Green Beans and Shiitakes, *360*, 361
- top sirloin steak, about, 350
- "Wagyu," about, 351

Beet(s)
- raw, peeling, 165
- Salad with Blue Cheese and Endive, *164*, 165

Bench scraper, 504, 560

Berry(ies)
- Mixed, Scones, 518, *519*
- washing, 46
- see also specific berries

Biscochitos, 577, *577*
Biscuits, Easiest-Ever, 516, *517*
Blackberry Cobbler with Biscuit Topping, 604
Black-Eyed Peas and Greens, 322
Black pepper, 27
- see also Peppercorns

Blanch, defined, 4
Blenders, 14, 15
Blondies, 580–81, *581*
Bloom, defined, 4

Blueberry(ies)
- Cobbler with Biscuit Topping, 603–4
- Endive, and Goat Cheese, Wheat Berry Salad with, 294, *294*
- Muffins, Whole-Wheat, 519, *519*

Boil, defined, 4

Bok Choy
- Barbecue Tempeh Wraps, 335
- Peppery Sesame Noodles with, 269
- preparing, 41
- and Tofu, Stir-Fried, 84, 85
- Vegetable Shabu-Shabu with Sesame Sauce, 273, *273*–74

Bokkeumbap, Kimchi, *304*, 304–5
Bowl scraper, 504, 560
Braise, defined, 4

Bread
- Almost No-Knead, *526*, 526–27
- Almost No-Knead Brioche, 528–29, *529*
- Anadama, 522, *522*
- autolyse technique, 535
- baker's tools, 504
- baking, key steps, 505
- baking at high temperature, 535
- Banana, Ultimate, *514*, 515
- basics, 502–9
- Brown Soda, 511
- Chapati, 553, *553*
- Cheese, Quick, *510*, 510–11
- Cheese, Quick, with Bacon, Onion, and Gruyère, 511
- cold fermentation, 549
- Cranberry-Walnut, 542, *543*

INDEX | 641

Bread (cont.)
- crumbs, turning into dough, 204
- dinner rolls, about, 532
- dough, folding, 531
- dough hydration, 531
- dried versus stale, 188
- Easiest-Ever Biscuits, 516, *517*
- everyday loaves, about, 520
- everyday loaves, resources for, 524–25
- flatbread, about, 552
- Fluffy Dinner Rolls, 532–33, *533*
- free-form, about, 540
- free-form, proofing, 545
- free-form, resources for, 544–45
- free-form, shaping, 544
- free-form, slashing, 545
- free-form, slicing, 545
- gluten in, 506
- Honey-Wheat Dinner Rolls, 536–37, *537*
- Italian, Classic, 540–41, *541*
- kneading, 508–9
- Mana'eesh Za'atar, 555, *555*
- measuring rise in, 525
- Mixed Berry Scones, 518, *519*
- morning, about, 514
- no-knead, about, 526
- Oatmeal-Raisin, 523, *523*
- in Panzanella, 187–88
- Pitas, 554–55
- Rosemary Focaccia, *530*, 530–31
- Rustic Dinner Rolls, 534, *535*
- sandwich, cooling and storing, 524
- Sandwich, Easy, *520*, 521
- sandwich, shaping, 524
- savory quick, about, 510
- savory quick, resources for, 513
- Southern-Style Skillet Cornbread, 512
- types of, 502–3
- whole-wheat, about, 536
- Whole-Wheat Blueberry Muffins, 519, *519*
- Whole-Wheat Quinoa, 538, *539*
- *see also* Croutons; Pizza; Toast; Tortillas

Brine, defined, 4
Brioche, Almost No-Knead, 528–29, *529*
Broccoli
- and Bean Sprouts, Chicken Lo Mein with, 270
- boiling times, 98
- cutting up, 41
- and Radicchio, Orzo Salad with, 244, *245*
- and Red Pepper, Stir-Fried Sesame Chicken with, *434*, 435
- Roasted, *124*, 125
- Roasted Snapper and Vegetables with Mustard Sauce, *464*, 465
- Steamed, with Lime-Cumin Dressing, 98, *98*

Broccoli (cont.)
- Steamed, with Spicy Balsamic Dressing and Black Olives, 98
- steaming times, 98
- and Turmeric, Frittata with, 81, *81*

Broccoli Rabe
- Broiled, 133
- prepping, 133
- reducing bitterness in, 133
- and Sausage, Orecchiette with, 241, *241*
- Sun-Dried Tomato, and Pine Nut Polenta Topping, 312
- Sun-Dried Tomatoes, and Fontina, Frittata with, 80

Broil, defined, 4
Broth, 18, 232
- Base, Vegetable, 234, *234*
- Beef, 233
- beef, buying, 199
- chicken, buying, 199
- Chicken, Classic, *232*, 232–33
- cooling and freezing, 235
- defatting, 235
- homemade, "stretching," 233
- resources for, 235
- vegetarian, buying, 199

Brownies
- Chewy, 579
- Fudgy, *579*, 579–80
- Rocky Road, 580, *581*

Brown Soda Bread, 511
Brown Sugar
- about, 558
- Cookies, *566*, 567
- measuring, 36, 558

Brussels Sprout(s)
- boiling times, 98
- Pan-Roasted, with Gochujang and Sesame Seed, 111
- Pan-Roasted, with Lemon and Pecorino Romano, *110*, 111
- Pan-Roasted, with Mustard and Brown Sugar, 111
- Red Cabbage, and Pomegranate Slaw, 181, *181*
- Roasted, 126
- Slaw with Pecorino and Pine Nuts, 180
- steaming times, 98

Bulgur
- about, 283
- grinds of, 336
- Pilaf with Mushrooms, 299
- Spiced Tabbouleh, 291
- Tabbouleh, 290–91, *291*

Bundt pan, 11
Burgers
- Beef, Classic, 384–85, *385*
- Steak, Grilled, *390*, 391

Butter
- about, 21, 559
- browning, 253, 567

Butter, compound
- *See* Compound Butters

Butterfly, defined, 6
Buttermilk
- Coleslaw, *178*, 179
- Coleslaw, Lemony, 179
- Coleslaw with Scallions and Cilantro, 179
- Ranch Dressing, 172
- -Strawberry No-Churn Ice Cream, 621, *621*

C

Cabbage
- Buttermilk Coleslaw, *178*, 179
- Buttermilk Coleslaw with Scallions and Cilantro, 179
- and Carrots, Pork Lo Mein with, 271, *271*
- Citrus Salad with Orange-Ginger Vinaigrette, *194*, 195
- Grilled, 141, *141*
- Lemony Buttermilk Coleslaw, 179
- Marinated Tofu and Vegetable Salad, 87, *87*
- Pad Kee Mao, 279, *279*
- prepping, for slaw, 179
- Red, Brussels Sprout, and Pomegranate Slaw, 181, *181*
- shredding, 41
- Soup, Hearty, 208
- Spicy Peanut Rice Noodles, *277*, 277–78
- Sriracha-Lime Tofu Bowl, 83, *83*
- Sweet and Tangy Coleslaw, 180
- *see also* Bok Choy

Cake flour, 590
Cake pans, 11, 560
Cakes
- Almond Pound, 585
- birthday, about, 588
- Buttery Yellow Layer, with Chocolate Frosting, 590, *591*
- Carrot Sheet, Simple, 586
- Chocolate Sheet, with Milk Chocolate Frosting, 588–89, *589*
- Confetti, 592, *593*
- doneness tests, 563
- egg temperature for, 585
- everyday, about, 584
- Ginger Pound, 585
- layer, applying frosting to, 591
- Lemon Bundt, *600*, 601
- Lemon Pudding, *598*, 598–99

Cakes (cont.)
   mixing methods, 562
   Orange Pound, 585
   oven placement, 563
   Pound, *584*, 585
   preparing pans for, 560
   Tahini-Banana Snack, 586, *587*
Caldo Tlalpeño, 202, *203*
Caldo Verde, *228*, 228–29
Cantaloupe Salad with Olives and Red Onion, 194, *194*
Caper(s)
   Cauliflower Steaks with Salsa Verde, *130*, 131
   Chicken Piccata, 412
   Crispy, and Herb Oil, Creamy White Bean Soup with, 220–21, *221*
   -Currant Relish, Pan-Seared Swordfish Steaks with, *462*, 462–63
   -Lemon Pan Sauce, 419
   -Parsley Compound Butter, 355
   and Pine Nuts, Pan-Roasted Cauliflower with, 112
   Salsa Verde, 353
Caramelize, defined, 4
Caraway-Cider Make-Ahead Vinaigrette, 155
Carbonnade, Brisket, *402*, 403
Cardamom
   Garam Masala, 29
   Ras el Hanout, 28
Carrot(s)
   Arugula, and Olives, Chickpea Salad with, 320, *320*
   Best Beef Stew, 376–77, *377*
   Boiled, with Cumin, Lime, and Cilantro, 95
   Boiled, with Fennel Seeds and Citrus, 95
   Boiled, with Lemon and Chives, *94*, 95
   Boiled, with Mint and Paprika, 95
   boiling, in salty water, 95
   and Cabbage, Pork Lo Mein with, 271, *271*
   Classic Chicken Stew, *426*, 426–27
   cutting on bias and into matchsticks, 41
   and Leeks, Cod Baked in Foil with, 460
   and Parsley, Lentils with, 324
   and Peas, Chicken and Rice with, 430–31
   Ras el Hanout Chicken with, *422*, 423
   Roasted, 126
   Salad, Moroccan-Style, 166, *167*
   Sautéed, with Ginger, Maple, and Fennel Seeds, *100*, 101
   Sheet Cake, Simple, 586
   storage tips, 93
   Tofu Banh Mi, *84*, 84
   Vegetable Shabu-Shabu with Sesame Sauce, *273*, 273–74

Cashews
   Nankhatai, 576, *576*
Cast-iron skillets, 10, 16
Catfish, Cornmeal, and Southwestern Corn, 471, *471*
Cauliflower
   Cakes, *129*, 129–30
   Curried Baked Quinoa with, 295
   cutting up, 42
   and Dates, Freekeh Pilaf with, *298*, 299
   Pan-Roasted, with Capers and Pine Nuts, 112
   Pan-Roasted, with Cumin and Pistachios, 112, *113*
   Pan-Roasted, with Garlic and Lemon, 112
   Rice, 128
   Rice, Curried, 128
   Roasted, 126
   and Shallots, Chicken Leg Quarters with, 414–15
   Soup, Creamy, 216
   Spiced Red Lentils with, 327
   Steaks with Salsa Verde, *130*, 131
   varied flavors of, 216
Cayenne pepper, 27
Celery root, preparing, 234
Chapati, 553, *553*
Char, about, 456, 480
Chard (Swiss)
   and Bell Pepper, Garlicky, Fried Eggs over, *62*, 63
   Green Shakshuka, 75, *75*
   and Lentils, Pomegranate Roasted Salmon with, 474, *475*
   and Mustard, Braised Chicken Thighs with, 429, *429*
   preparing, 43
   red, about, 108
   Sautéed, with Sesame Sauce, 105
   Super Greens Soup with Lemon-Tarragon Cream, 217, *217*
   white, about, 108
Cheese, 21
   Asparagus and Smoked Salmon Omelet, 79
   Bacon, and Egg Sandwiches, 70
   Baked Eggs with Tomatoes, Feta, and Croutons, *76*, 76–77
   Baked Penne with Spinach, Artichokes, and Chicken, *258*, 258–59
   Baked Quinoa with Scallions and Feta, 295
   Baked Shrimp and Orzo with Feta and Tomatoes, 488, *488*
   Baked Ziti with Ricotta and Eggplant, 259
   Best Chicken Parmesan, 412–13, *413*

Cheese (cont.)
   Blue, and Endive, Beet Salad with, *164*, 165
   Blue, and Steak Tips, Arugula Salad with, *184*, 184–85
   Blue, Dressing, 172
   Bread, Quick, *510*, 510–11
   Bread, Quick, with Bacon, Onion, and Gruyère, 511
   Brussels Sprout Slaw with Pecorino and Pine Nuts, 180
   Caprese Salad, 186
   Chicken Soup with Parmesan Dumplings, 204, *205*
   Chickpea Salad with Roasted Red Peppers and Feta, 320
   cottage, for lasagnas, 264
   Cream, Frosting, 595
   Creamy Parmesan Polenta, *310*, 311
   Crispy Pan-Fried Chicken Milanese Cutlets, 412
   Elote, *134*, 135
   Feta, and Shiitake Mushrooms, Scrambled Eggs with, 56, *57*
   Fluffy Baked Polenta, *311*, 312
   Fried Egg Sandwiches, 71, *71*
   Frittata with Broccoli Rabe, Sun-Dried Tomatoes, and Fontina, 80
   Frittata with Parmesan and Herbs, 80, *80*
   Goat, and Bread Crumbs, Broiled Tomatoes with, 134, 135
   Goat, Baked Potato Topping, Herbed, *117*, 117
   Gorgonzola Vinaigrette, 354
   grating, 23
   Grits, Baked, 313–15
   Grits, Creamy, 313, *313*
   Ham, and Egg Sandwiches, 70, *71*
   Horiatiki Salad, *188*, 188–89
   how it melts, 23
   for Italian pasta dishes, 238
   Macaroni and, Casserole, 260, *260*
   measuring, 23
   Mushroom and Thyme Omelet, 79, *79*
   Omelet, Classic, 78
   Open-Faced Poached Egg Sandwiches, 73
   Pan-Roasted Brussels Sprouts with Lemon and Pecorino Romano, *110*, 111
   Parmesan, flavoring soups with, 213
   Parmesan Croutons, 161
   Pesto Calabrese, 255
   Philly Cheesesteaks, 399, *399*
   Pizza al Taglio with Arugula and Fresh Mozzarella, 549–50

Cheese (cont.)
    prepping, for salads, 167
    pre-shredded, about, 23
    rinds, uses for, 23
    Risotto with Parmesan and Herbs, *306*, 307
    Roasted Zucchini and Eggplant Lasagna, 261–62
    Sausage Lasagna, 262, *263*
    Sautéed Cherry Tomato and Fresh Mozzarella Polenta Topping, *311*, 312
    shredding, 23
    Skillet Pizza, *546*, 546–47
    Skillet Pizza with Fontina, Arugula, and Prosciutto, 547
    Skillet Ziti with Sausage and Peppers, *256*, 257
    Spinach Pesto, 254
    storing, 23
    Thin-Crust Pizza, *548*, 548–49
    Thin-Crust Pizza with Sausage, Pepper, and Onion, 549
    types of, 22
    Watermelon Salad with Basil and Feta, 193, *193*
    Wedge Salad, 186–87, *187*

Chermoula, 353

Cherry(ies)
    Crisp, Skillet, *602*, 602–3
    Dried, and Pecans, Millet Porridge with, 292
    pitting, 46

Chicken
    anatomy, 409
    Arroz con Pollo, *432*, 432
    backbone, removing, 419
    Barbecue Roast, and Potatoes, 422
    basics, 408–9
    Bone-In, Grilled, *444*, 445
    Breasts, Pan-Roasted, 414
    broiling, tip for, 421
    broth, buying, 199
    Broth, Classic, *232*, 232–33
    buying and storing, 408
    Cacciatore, *422*, 423
    Caldo Tlalpeño, 202, *203*
    Curried, with Coconut Rice and Lime-Yogurt Sauce, 431, *431*
    cutlets, about, 410
    Cutlets, Crispy Pan-Fried, 411–12
    Cutlets, Crispy Pan-Fried, with Garlic and Oregano, 412
    Cutlets, Crispy Pan-Fried Deviled, 412
    Cutlets, Crispy Pan-Fried Milanese, 412
    cutlets, preparing, 411
    Cutlets, Simple Sautéed, *410*, 410–11
    dark meat, cooking, 428
    doneness temperatures, 417

Chicken (cont.)
    fat (schmaltz), saving, 213
    Five-Spice Roast, with Turnips, 422
    fried, about, 438
    Fried, Cast Iron Easier, *439*, 439–40
    Fried, Sandwiches, 440–41, *441*
    Gai Pad Krapow, 436
    grilled, about, 442
    Grilled, Souvlaki, 442–43, *443*
    Grilled Wine-and-Herb Marinated, 445–46, *446*
    Herbes de Provence, with Fennel, 423
    Kale Caesar Salad with, 190, *191*
    Kale Cobb Salad, 163, *163*
    Karaage, *438*, 438–39
    Khao Man Gai, 433, *433*
    Kung Pao, 436–37, *437*
    Leg Quarters with Cauliflower and Shallots, 414–15
    Lo Mein with Broccoli and Bean Sprouts, 270
    Noodle Soup, *200*, 201
    One-Hour Broiled, and Pan Sauce, 419
    Pad Kee Mao, *279*, 279
    Parmesan, Best, 412–13, *413*
    Peruvian Roast, with Garlic and Lime, 416, *416*
    Piccata, 412
    poaching, 183
    pulling meat from bone, 432
    Ras el Hanout, with Carrots, *422*, 423
    raw, food safety and, 409
    removing backbone from, 421
    resting, after cooking, 417
    and rice, about, 430
    and Rice with Carrots and Peas, 430–31
    roast, about, 414
    roast, carving, 417
    Salad, Creamy, with Fresh Herbs, 182, *183*
    Salad, Creamy, with Grapes and Walnuts, 183
    Salad, Curried, with Dried Apricots, 182
    Soup with Parmesan Dumplings, 204, *205*
    Spinach, and Artichokes, Baked Penne with, *258*, 258–59
    Stew, Classic, *426*, 426–27
    stewed and braised, about, 426
    Stir-Fried Sesame, with Broccoli and Red Pepper, *434*, 435
    stir-fries, about, 434
    Tandoori, 423–24, *425*
    Thighs, Braised, with Chard and Mustard, 429, *429*
    Thighs, Lemon-Braised, with Chickpeas and Fennel, *427*, 427–28
    Tom Kha Gai, 202–3, *203*

Chicken (cont.)
    Weeknight Roast, 415, *415*
    whole, cutting into parts, 424

Chickpea(s)
    about, 317
    Caldo Tlalpeño, 202, *203*
    and Escarole Soup, 223, *223*
    Falafel, 330–31, *331*
    and Fennel, Lemon-Braised Chicken Thighs with, *427*, 427–28
    Gyros, Spiced, with Tahini Yogurt, *320*, 320–21
    Mediterranean Chopped Salad, 165–66
    Noodle Soup, 225–26
    Salad with Carrots, Arugula, and Olives, 320, *320*
    Salad with Roasted Red Peppers and Feta, 320
    Sharba, 231, *231*
    Ultracreamy Hummus, *318*, 319
    Warm Spiced Pearl Couscous Salad, 245, *245*

Chiles, 18
    Baked Mexican Rice, 289, *289*
    Braised Lamb Shanks with Ras el Hanout, 374
    Chile Verde con Cerdo, 379, *379*
    chipotle, in adobo, storing, 202
    Chipotle-Cilantro Compound Butter, 355
    Chipotle Mayonnaise, 31
    Gai Pad Krapow, 436
    Goan Pork Vindaloo, *380*, 381
    Kung Pao Chicken, 436–37, *437*
    Nasi Goreng, 302–3, *303*
    Spicy Pinto Bean Soup, 222–23
    stemming and seeding, 42
    Tempeh with Sambal Sauce, *334*, 335

Chile Verde con Cerdo, 379, *379*

Chimichurri, 353
    Cilantro, Sautéed Tilapia with, *468*, 469
    Sauce, Pan-Seared Tempeh Steaks with, *332*, 333

Chive-Lemon Miso Compound Butter, 355

Chocolate, 20
    basics, 582–83
    Blondies, 580–81, *581*
    buying and storing, 582
    Chewy Brownies, 579
    Chip Cookies, Perfect, *564*, 565
    chopping, 582
    Congo Bars, 581
    Frosting, 594–95
    Frosting, Buttery Yellow Layer Cake with, 590, *591*
    Fudgy Brownies, *579*, 579–80
    Ganache Frosting, 595
    melting, 583
    Milk, Pots de Crème, 619

Chocolate (cont.)
- Mint-Cookie No-Churn Ice Cream, 621, *621*
- Mousse, 620, *620*
- Pots de Crème, 619
- Rocky Road Brownies, 580, *581*
- Sheet Cake with Milk Chocolate Frosting, 588–89, *589*
- structure of, 583
- substitutes for, 582
- -Toffee Butter Cookies, 572, *573*
- types of, 582

Chop, defined, 6

Chopped fine / chopped / chopped coarse, 39

Chutney, Cilantro-Mint, 31

Cilantro
- Chermoula, 353
- Chimichurri, 353
- Chimichurri, Sautéed Tilapia with, *468*, 469
- -Chipotle Compound Butter, 355
- Falafel, 330–31, *331*
- -Mint Chutney, 31
- Sauce, Green Bean Salad with, 166–67, *167*
- Sauce and Sweet Potatoes, Roast Pork Loin with, 368, *368*

Cinnamon
- Biscochitos, 577, *577*

Citrus
- cutting strips of zest, 47
- juicing, 47
- sectioning, 47
- zesting, 47
- *see also specific citrus*

Clam(s)
- hard-shell versus soft-shell, 494
- and Salsa Verde, Brothy Rice with, *492*, 492–93
- Sauce, White, Linguine with, 240

Cobblers
- Blackberry, with Biscuit Topping, 604
- Blueberry, with Biscuit Topping, 603–4
- Peach or Nectarine, with Biscuit Topping, 604
- Strawberry, with Biscuit Topping, 604

Cocoa powder, 20, 582, 589

Coconut
- Congo Bars, 581
- Frosting, 594
- Oatmeal Cookies, Thin and Crispy, 569

Coconut milk
- Coconut Rice Pudding, *618*, 618–19
- cooking, 286
- Curried Chicken with Coconut Rice and Lime-Yogurt Sauce, 431, *431*

Coconut milk (cont.)
- Garlicky Braised Kale with Coconut and Curry, 106
- Hung Kao Mun Gati, 286, *286*
- Millet Porridge with Coconut and Bananas, 292

Cod
- about, 458
- Baked in Foil with Leeks and Carrots, 460
- Fillets, Nut-Crusted, 459
- Pan-Roasted, with Grapefruit-Basil Relish, *458*, 458–59
- resources for, 461
- substitutions for, 461
- tucking tail under, 461

Coffee Frosting, 594

Colander, 12

Coleslaw
- *See* Slaws

Collard Greens
- about, 108
- Black-Eyed Peas and Greens, 322
- Caldo Verde, *228*, 228–29
- preparing, 43, 106
- Quick, *105*, 105–6

Comeback Sauce, 471

Compound Butters
- Chipotle-Cilantro, 355
- Chive-Lemon Miso, 355
- Parsley-Caper, 355
- Parsley-Lemon, 355
- Tapenade, 355
- Tarragon-Lime, 355

Confectioners' sugar, 558

Confetti Cake, 592, *593*

Congo Bars, 581

Cookie cutters, 560

Cookies
- Almond Sandies, 571
- Biscochitos, 577, *577*
- Brown Sugar, *566*, 567
- Chocolate Chip, Perfect, *564*, 565
- Chocolate-Toffee Butter, 572, *573*
- Coconut Oatmeal, Thin and Crispy, 569
- cookie cutter, about, 574
- doneness tests, 563
- drop, about, 564
- Holiday, Foolproof, 574–75
- Molasses Spice, 568, *569*
- Molasses Spice, with Dark Rum Glaze, 568
- Molasses Spice, with Orange Essence, 568
- Nankhatai, 576, *576*
- Oatmeal, Salty Thin and Crispy, 569, *569*
- Oatmeal, Thin and Crispy, 568–69
- Orange-Almond Oatmeal, Thin and Crispy, 569

Cookies (cont.)
- oven placement, 563
- Pecan Sandies, 570, *571*
- preparing baking sheets for, 560
- slice-and-bake, about, 570
- *see also* Bars

Cooking basics
- cleaning and caring for cookware, 16–17
- cooking terminology, 4–7
- equipment, 8–15
- food safety, 34–35
- getting to know cheese, 22–23
- getting to know fresh herbs, 24–25
- getting to know spices, 26–29
- good cook habits, 2–3
- kitchen starter kit, 8
- knife skills, 38–39
- measuring skills, 36–37
- sauces 101, 30–31
- seasoning food, 32–33
- stocking pantry and refrigerator, 18–21
- vegetable & fruit prep, 40–49

Cooking terms, 4–5

Cookware
- cleaning and caring for, 16–17
- types of, 10–11

Coriander, 27
- Classic Steak Rub, 352
- Cumin, and Mustard Seeds, Roast Butterflied Leg of Lamb with, 404, *405*
- Garam Masala, 29
- Paprika, and Yogurt, Braised Eggplant with, 138, *138*
- Ras el Hanout, 28

Corn
- boiling, 99
- Creamy Cheese Grits, 313, *313*
- Elote, 134, *135*
- Foolproof Boiled, 96, *97*
- Foolproof Boiled, for a Crowd, 96
- Husk Grilled, 143
- shucking, 99
- slicing kernels off cob, 42
- Southwestern, Cornmeal Catfish and, 471, *471*
- storage tips, 93
- and Tomatoes, Skillet Rice and Black Beans with, 323

Cornbread, Southern-Style Skillet, 512

Cornmeal, 20
- about, 283, 310, 311
- Anadama Bread, 522, *522*
- Creamy Parmesan Polenta, *310*, 311
- Fluffy Baked Polenta, *311*, 312
- Southern-Style Skillet Cornbread, 512

Corn syrups, 621

INDEX | 645

Couscous
    Pearl, Salad, Warm Spiced, 245, *245*
    pearl versus North African, 245

Cranberry(ies)
    and Almonds, Baked Wild Rice with, *294*, 295
    Oat Bars, 616, *616*
    -Walnut Bread, 542, *543*

Cream, 21
    "melting," for biscuits, 516
    Whipped, 595

Cream Cheese Frosting, 595

Cream / creaming method, 7, 562

Cream of tartar, 597

Crisp, Skillet Cherry, *602*, 602-3

Croutons
    in Caesar Salad, *189*, 189-90
    Herbed, 161
    Homemade, 161
    in Kale Caesar Salad with Chicken, 190, *191*
    Parmesan, 161
    Tomatoes, and Feta, Baked Eggs with, *76*, 76-77

Crumble, Peach, 604-5, *605*

Cucumbers
    Chilled Soba Noodles with Spring Vegetables, 275, *275*
    Gazpacho, *206*, 207
    Horiatiki Salad, *188*, 188-89
    Mediterranean Chopped Salad, 165-66
    Quick Pickle Chips, 145
    seeding, 42
    storage tips, 93
    Tofu Banh Mi, 84, *84*
    Tzatziki, 398

Cumin, 27
    and Chili Roasted Sweet Potato Wedges, 119
    Coriander, and Mustard Seeds, Roast Butterflied Leg of Lamb with, 404, *405*
    Garam Masala, 29
    and Pistachios, Pan-Roasted Cauliflower with, 112, *113*
    Ras el Hanout, 28

Cupcakes, Red Velvet, 592-93, *593*

Currant-Caper Relish, Pan-Seared Swordfish Steaks with, *462*, 462-63

Curried Baked Quinoa with Cauliflower, 295

Curried Cauliflower Rice, 128

Curried Chicken Salad with Dried Apricots, 182

Curried Lentils with Golden Raisins, 324

Curry Deviled Eggs, 66

Curry Roasted Sweet Potato Wedges, 119

Cut, defined, 6

Cutting boards, 12, 13

Cutting terms, 6

D

Dates
    and Cauliflower, Freekeh Pilaf with, *298*, 299
    Ginger, and Parsley, Spiced Rice Pilaf with, 297

Deep-fry, defined, 4

Deglaze, defined, 4

Desserts
    baking basics, 558-63
    see also specific types

Deviled Eggs
    Bacon and Chive, 66, *66*
    Curry, 66

Deviled Pork Chops, 359, *359*

Diced, defined, 6, 39

Digital scale, 13, 504, 560

Dinner Rolls
    Fluffy, 532-33, *533*
    Honey-Wheat, 536-37, *537*
    Rustic, 534, *535*

Dish towel, 15

Doneness tests, 37, 563

Dredge, defined, 4

Dressings
    about, 30
    Avocado, Creamy, 173
    Blue Cheese, 172
    Green Goddess, 173
    Peppercorn Ranch, 172
    Ranch, 172
    Roasted Garlic, Creamy, 173, *173*
    Vegan Ranch, 172
    see also Vinaigrettes

Dukkah, Pistachio, 28, *28*

Dumplings, Parmesan, Chicken Soup with, 204, *205*

Dutch ovens, 10, 17, 527

E

Edamame
    Salad with Arugula and Radishes, 159
    Spicy Peanut Rice Noodles, *277*, 277-78

Eggplant
    braised, texture of, 138
    Braised, with Paprika, Coriander, and Yogurt, 138, *138*
    Broiled, with Basil, *136*, 137
    Broiled, with Sesame-Miso Glaze, 137
    Chinese, about, 139
    globe, about, 139
    grilling instructions, 143
    Indian, about, 139
    Italian, about, 139
    Japanese, about, 139

Eggplant (cont.)
    Japanese, Stir-Fried, 137
    preparing for braising, 139
    resources for, 139
    and Ricotta, Baked Ziti with, 259
    Roasted, and Kale Soup, 210-11, *211*
    Roasted, and Zucchini Lasagna, 261-62
    storing, 139
    taming bitterness in, 139
    varieties of, 139

Egg(s), 21
    adding to batters, 562
    age of, 52, 69
    anatomy, 52
    Bacon, and Cheese Sandwiches, 70
    Baked, with Tomatoes, Feta, and Croutons, *76*, 76-77
    Baked Potato Topping, 117
    basics, 52-53
    Bistro Salad, 158, *158*
    buying, 52
    cracking open, 58
    Deviled, Bacon and Chive, 66, *66*
    Deviled, Curry, 66
    doneness continuum, 67
    freezing, 53
    fried, adding to dishes, 62
    Fried, Avocado Toast with, 62
    Fried, over Garlicky Chard and Bell Pepper, 62, *63*
    Fried, Perfect, *60*, 60-61
    Fried, Sandwiches, 71, *71*
    Fried Brown Rice with Pork and Shrimp, *304*, 305
    Fried Rice with Gai Lan and Shiitake Mushrooms, 302, *303*
    Green Shakshuka, 75, *75*
    Ham, and Cheese Sandwiches, 70, *71*
    Hard-Cooked, Radishes, and Capers, Tuna Salad with, 183-84, *184*
    hard-cooked, resources for, 67
    Hard-Cooked, Easy-Peel, 64, 65
    Hawaiian Fried Rice, *300*, 301
    in a Hole, 61
    liquid whites, about, 59
    membranes in, 65
    Nasi Goreng, 302-3, *303*
    Pad Thai, 278, *279*
    peeling six at once, 67
    Poached, Make-Ahead, 69
    Poached, Open-Faced Sandwiches, 73
    Poached, Perfect, *68*, 69
    poached in sauce, about, 74
    proteins in, 61
    in Purgatory, 74-75
    Salad Sandwiches with Radishes and Watercress, *72*, 73
    scrambled, formula for, 55

Egg(s) (cont.)
- Scrambled, Perfect, 54–55, *55*
- scrambled, resources for, 58–59
- Scrambled, with Asparagus, Smoked Salmon, and Chives, 56
- Scrambled, with Shiitake Mushrooms and Feta Cheese, 56, *57*
- Sheet-Pan Huevos Rancheros, 76, *77*
- Singapore Noodles with Shrimp, 276–77, *277*
- sizes, 53
- Soft-Cooked, 65
- soft-cooked, peeling, 67
- soft-cooked, reheating, 67
- soft-cooked, resources for, 67
- storing, 53
- substitutes, about, 59
- temperature of, for cake recipes, 585
- and Tomatoes, Chinese Stir-Fried (Xīhóngshì Chao Jīdàn), 57, *57*
- whites, thickness of, 69
- whites, whipping, 599
- *see also* Frittatas; Omelets

Elote, 134, *135*
Emulsification, 153
Emulsion, defined, 4
Endive
- Blueberries, and Goat Cheese, Wheat Berry Salad with, 294, *294*
- and Blue Cheese, Beet Salad with, *164*, 165
- grilling instructions, 143

En papillote, defined, 4
Equipment, 8–15
Escarole
- Chicken Soup with Parmesan Dumplings, 204, *205*
- and Chickpea Soup, 223, *223*

F

Falafel, 330–31, *331*
Farro
- about, 283
- Farrotto with Pancetta, Asparagus, and Peas, 309, *309*
- with Lemon and Herbs, 293
- with Mushrooms and Thyme, 293, *293*

Fennel
- and Bibb Salad with Scallops and Hazelnuts, 491
- and Chickpeas, Lemon-Braised Chicken Thighs with, *427*, 427–28
- Dried Apricots, and Orange, Barley with, 292, *293*
- Grilled, 140
- Herbes de Provence Chicken with, 423

Fennel (cont.)
- preparing, 42
- Quick Pickled, 144, *144*
- Roasted, 126
- and Saffron, Risotto with, 307
- slicing, 140

Fennel (Seeds)
- -Balsamic Make-Ahead Vinaigrette, 155
- and Citrus, Boiled Carrots with, 95
- Five-Spice Powder, 29
- Ginger, and Maple, Sautéed Carrots with, *100*, 101

Figs, Pine Nuts, and Goat Cheese, Wheat Berry Salad with, 294
Fine-mesh strainer, 14
Fish
- Baked Sole Fillets with Herbs and Bread Crumbs, 472, *472*
- basics, 454–55
- bass, about, 461
- braising, 467
- brining, 455
- buying, 454
- cooking categories, 456
- Cornmeal Catfish and Southwestern Corn, 471, *471*
- Crispy, Sandwiches, 496, *497*
- fillets, portioning, 454
- firm, meaty white, about, 456, 462
- firm, meaty white, resources for, 466–67
- flaky white, about, 456
- flipping while cooking, 467
- fried, about, 496
- Grilled Swordfish Tacos, 464–65, *465*
- Halibut en Cocotte with Garlic and Cherry Tomatoes, 463
- oily ocean, about, 456
- Pan-Fried Sole, 470
- Pan-Seared Swordfish Steaks with Caper-Currant Relish, *462*, 462–63
- Perfect Poached, 482, *483*
- poached, about, 482
- preparing grill for, 467
- reheating, 467
- Roasted Snapper and Vegetables with Mustard Sauce, 464, *465*
- Sautéed Tilapia with Cilantro Chimichurri, *468*, 469
- Sole Meunière, 470, *470*
- storing, 455
- thin white, about, 456, 468
- thin white, resources for, 473
- tilapia taste tests, 469
- tuna, about, 456
- tuna, canned, 19
- Tuna Salad with Hard-Cooked Eggs, Radishes, and Capers, 183–84, *184*
- white, categories of, 456, 457

Fish (cont.)
- why swordfish can turn mushy, 463
- *see also* Cod; Salmon

Fish sauce, 18
Five-Spice Powder, 29
Flame tamer, improvising, 311
Flours, 20, 507, 590
Focaccia, Rosemary, *530*, 530–31
Foil flame tamer, 311
Foil sling, 581
Fold, defined, 7
Fond, defined, 5
Food processors, 14, 15, 560
Food safety, 34–35, 409
Food storage containers, 15
Freekeh
- about, 283
- Pilaf with Dates and Cauliflower, *298*, 299

Frittatas
- about, 78
- with Broccoli and Turmeric, 81, *81*
- with Broccoli Rabe, Sun-Dried Tomatoes, and Fontina, 80
- with Parmesan and Herbs, 80, *80*
- removing from pan, 80

Frosting
- Almond, 594
- applying to layer cakes, 591
- Chocolate, 594–95
- Chocolate Ganache, 595
- Coconut, 594
- Coffee, 594
- Cream Cheese, 595
- Orange, 594
- Peppermint, 594
- Vanilla, 594

Fruit peelers, 14
Fruits
- basic prep skills, 46–49
- dried, 20
- prepping, for salads, 167
- *see also specific fruits*

G

Gai Lan and Shiitake Mushrooms, Fried Rice with, 302, *303*
Gai Pad Krapow, 436
Galettes, Easy Apple, *606*, 606–7
Garam Masala, 29
Garlic, 18
- -Butter Sauce, Broiled Asparagus with, 132
- Fried Eggs over Garlicky Chard and Bell Pepper, 62, *63*
- Garlicky Braised Kale, 106, *107*

Garlic (cont.)
- Garlicky Braised Kale with Bacon and Onion, 106
- Garlicky Braised Kale with Coconut and Curry, 106
- Garlicky Roasted Shrimp with Parsley and Anise, 486, *487*
- Garlicky Spaghetti with Green Olives and Almonds, 243
- Garlicky Spaghetti with Lemon and Pine Nuts, *242*, 243
- Garlicky White Beans with Sage, 321
- Harissa, 29, *29*
- and Lemon, Pan-Roasted Cauliflower with, 112
- and Lemon, Spinach with, 104
- and Lime, Peruvian Roast Chicken with, *416*, 416
- Microwave-Fried, 161
- mincing, 43
- Oil Sauce, Fettuccine with, *252*, 253
- and Oregano, Crispy Pan-Fried Chicken with, 412
- Roasted, Dressing, Creamy, 173, *173*
- Sauce, Sichuan Stir-Fried Pork in, *362*, 363
- Spaghetti Aglio e Olio, 243

Garlic press, 12
Gazpacho, *206*, 207
Ginger, 21
- Beef Ramen for One, Almost-Instant, 227, *227*
- Dates, and Parsley, Spiced Rice Pilaf with, 297
- fresh, preparing, 43
- Khao Man Gai, 433, *433*
- Maple, and Fennel Seeds, Sautéed Carrots with, *100*, 101
- -Orange Vinaigrette, 195
- Pound Cake, 585

Glaze, defined, 5
Gluten, 506, 525
Goan Pork Vindaloo, *380*, 381
Gochujang, 18
Gochujang and Sesame Seed, Pan-Roasted Brussels Sprouts with, 111
Grains, 19
- about, 282–83
- -based pilafs, about, 296
- cooking methods, 290
- resources for, 336
- rinsing, 285
- *see also specific grains*

Grapefruit
- -Basil Relish, Pan-Roasted Cod with, *458*, 458–59

Grapefruit (cont.)
- Citrus Salad with Orange-Ginger Vinaigrette, *194*, 195
- Salmon, Avocado, and Watercress Salad, 185

Grapes and Walnuts, Creamy Chicken Salad with, 183
Grate, defined, 6
Graters, 12
Gravy, All-Purpose, 450
Grease, defined, 5
Green Bean(s)
- boiling times, 98
- Roasted, 125
- Salad with Cilantro Sauce, 166–67, *167*
- and Shiitakes, Teriyaki Stir-Fried Beef with, *360*, 361
- Soupe au Pistou, 208, *209*
- steaming times, 98
- with Toasted Almonds and Browned Butter, 96
- trimming, 43

Green Goddess Dressing, 173
Greens (hearty)
- dark leafy, about, 104
- preparing, 43
- resources for, 108–9
- Super, Soup with Lemon-Tarragon Cream, 217, *217*
- types of, 108
- wilted, 191
- *see also specific types*

Greens (salad)
- Bistro Salad, 158, *158*
- buying and storing, 149
- gently tearing, 160
- measuring, 160
- mixing and matching, 157
- Simplest Salad, 156–57
- types of, 148
- washing and drying, 149
- *see also specific types*

Grill, defined, 5
Grilling basics, 447
Grits
- about, 310
- Baked Cheese, 313–15
- Creamy Cheese, 313, *313*
- Shrimp and, *314*, 315

Gyros
- Pork, 397–98
- Spiced Chickpea, with Tahini Yogurt, *320*, 320–21

H

Half-and-half, 21
Halibut en Cocotte with Garlic and Cherry Tomatoes, 463
Ham
- Egg, and Cheese Sandwiches, 70, *71*
- Hawaiian Fried Rice, *300*, 301
- Kimchi Bokkeumbap, *304*, 304–5
- *see also Prosciutto*

Handheld mixer, 15
Harissa, 29, *29*
Hazelnuts
- and Goat Cheese, Lentil Salad with, 326
- and Scallops, Fennel and Bibb Salad with, 491

Herbed Croutons, 161
Herbes de Provence Chicken with Fennel, 423
Herb(s), 21
- Braised Lamb Shanks with Red Wine and Herbes de Provence, 374
- and Bread Crumbs, Baked Sole Fillets with, 472, *472*
- Chermoula, 353
- Chimichurri, 353
- delicate, types of, 24
- dried, guidelines for using, 25
- drying at home, 25
- fresh, about, 24–25
- Fresh, Creamy Chicken Salad with, 182, *183*
- fresh, flavoring soups with, 213
- Green Goddess Dressing, 173
- hearty, types of, 24
- Herbes de Provence, 352
- leftover, freezing, 213
- and Lemon, Farro with, 293
- making flavored vinegar with, 25
- Mint Persillade, 353
- Oil and Crispy Capers, Creamy White Bean Soup with, 220–21, *221*
- and Parmesan, Frittata with, 80, *80*
- and Parmesan, Risotto with, *306*, 307
- prepping, for salads, 167
- Salsa Verde, 353
- sauces, about, 30
- storing, 25
- Vinaigrette, Foolproof, 153
- -Yogurt Sauce, 354
- *see also specific herbs*

Hollandaise, about, 30
Hollandaise Sauce, 354
Honey, 20
Honing rods, 6, 12
Horseradish Cream and Roasted Potatoes, Pan-Seared Steak Tips with, *346*, 346–47
Hot sauce, 18

Huevos Rancheros, Sheet-Pan, 76, 77
Hummus, Ultracreamy, 318, 319
Hung Kao Mun Gati, 286, 286

I

Ice Cream, No-Churn
- Mint-Cookie, 621, 621
- Peanut Butter Cup, 621
- Strawberry Buttermilk, 621, 621
- Vanilla, 621, 621

Ice cubes, herbed, 213

Ingredients
- cutting terms, 39
- measuring, 36–37, 562–63
- pantry, 18–20
- refrigerator and freezer, 21
- weighing, 37, 507

J

Jerk Rub, 352

K

Kale
- basic structure, 109
- Caesar Salad with Chicken, 190, 191
- Cobb Salad, 163, 163
- curly, about, 108
- Garlicky Braised, 106, 107
- Garlicky Braised, with Bacon and Onion, 106
- Garlicky Braised, with Coconut and Curry, 106
- Lacinato, about, 108
- preparing, 43
- red, about, 108
- and Roasted Eggplant Soup, 210–11, 211
- storing, 109
- -Sunflower Seed Pesto, 255
- Super Greens Soup with Lemon-Tarragon Cream, 217, 217

Karaage, 438, 438–39
Ketchup, 18
Khao Man Gai, 433, 433
Kimchi Bokkeumbap, 304, 304–5
Kitchen ruler, 504
Kitchen shears, 13
Kitchen sponges, 15
Kiwi, peeling, 47
Knead, defined, 7
Knives
- chef's, 12
- cutting terms, 39

Knives (cont.)
- holding, 38
- keeping sharp, 6
- moving, 38
- paring, 12
- serrated, 12

Kung Pao Chicken, 436–37, 437

L

Lamb
- blade chops, about, 382
- butterflied leg of, carving, 404
- domestic versus imported, 341
- doneness temperatures, 345
- primal and retail cuts, 345
- Rib Chops with Mint-Rosemary Relish, 349
- Roast Butterflied Leg of, with Coriander, Cumin, and Mustard Seeds, 404, 405
- round bone chops, about, 382
- Shanks, Braised, with Lemon and Mint, 374, 374
- Shanks, Braised, with Ras el Hanout, 374
- Shanks, Braised, with Red Wine and Herbes de Provence, 374
- Sharba, 231, 231
- Spicy, with Lentils and Yogurt, 389, 389
- Stew with Potatoes, 382, 382

Lame, 504

Lasagna
- Roasted Zucchini and Eggplant, 261–62
- Sausage, 262, 263

Leeks
- and Carrots, Cod Baked in Foil with, 460
- preparing, 44

Lemongrass
- preparing, 202, 203
- Tom Kha Gai, 202–3, 203

Lemon(s), 21
- anatomy, 601
- Bars, Best, 596–97, 597
- Bundt Cake, 600, 601
- -Caper Pan Sauce, 419
- Chicken Piccata, 412
- -Chive Miso Compound Butter, 355
- -Parsley Compound Butter, 355
- Pudding Cake, 598, 598–99
- -Tarragon Pan Sauce, 418
- Vinaigrette, Foolproof, 153
- -Yogurt Sauce, 31

Lemony Buttermilk Coleslaw, 179

Lentil(s), 18
- about, 324
- Baked, with Sausage, 325, 325
- with Carrots and Parsley, 324

Lentil(s) (cont.)
- and Chard, Pomegranate Roasted Salmon with, 474, 475
- Curried, with Golden Raisins, 324
- dried, sorting, 326
- hulled, about, 316
- Red, Soup with Warm Spices, 222
- Red, Spiced, 327, 327
- Red, Spiced, with Cauliflower, 327
- Salad with Hazelnuts and Goat Cheese, 326
- Salad with Pomegranate and Walnuts, 326, 326
- types of, 316
- and Yogurt, Spicy Lamb with, 389, 389

Lettuce
- Bibb and Arugula Salad, with Pear and Goat Cheese, 157, 157
- Bistro Salad, 158, 158
- Caesar Salad, 189, 189–90
- Fennel and Bibb Salad with Scallops and Hazelnuts, 491
- Mediterranean Chopped Salad, 165–66
- Romaine and Watercress Salad with Asparagus and Prosciutto, 158, 159
- Simplest Salad, 156–57
- types of, 148
- Wedge Salad, 186–87, 187
- wilted, reviving, 149
- Wraps, Thai Pork, 387, 387

Lime(s), 21
- Cumin, and Cilantro, Boiled Carrots with, 95
- -Cumin Dressing, Steamed Broccoli with, 98, 98
- and Garlic, Peruvian Roast Chicken with, 415, 416
- -Tarragon Compound Butter, 355

Loaf pan, 11

M

Mana'eesh Za'atar, 555, 555

Mango
- cutting up, 48
- and Lime-Curry Dressing, Cherry Tomato Salad with, 170, 170

Maple Pecan Pie, 614
Maple syrup, 20, 558
Marinades, 446, 478
Marinara Sauce, Classic, 246
Marinate, defined, 5
Matchsticks (julienne), defined, 39
Mayonnaise, about, 18
Mayonnaise, Chipotle, 31
Measuring cups, 13, 560
Measuring ingredients, 36–37, 562–63

Measuring spoons, 13
Meat
    basics, 340–41
    braised, skimming fat from, 375
    braising, about, 342
    braising, resources for, 375
    browning, for stews, 383
    buying, 340–41
    collagen-rich cuts, 375
    compound butters for, 355
    cooking methods, 342
    creamy sauces for, 354
    doneness temperatures, 345
    dry-brining, 343
    enzymatic activity in, 367
    grilled, about, 390
    ground, about, 384
    for hand-held foods, 396
    labeling terms, 340–41
    lowering pH, with acid, 381
    primal and retail cuts, 344–45
    resting, after cooking, 343
    roasting, 342
    roasts, about, 366
    rubs and finishing sauces for, 352–53
    salty marinades for, 446
    searing, 342
    seasoning, 343
    slicing, 343
    special-occasion centerpieces, 400
    stews, about, 376
    stews, resources for, 383
    stir-fries, about, 360
    stir-fries, resources for, 364–65
    storing, 341
    trimming fat from, 343
    wet-brining, 343
    see also Beef; Lamb; Pork
Meatballs, Spaghetti and, 386, *387*
Meatloaf, Glazed, 388, *388*
Melon, cutting up, 48
Milk, 21
Millet
    about, 283
    Porridge with Coconut and Bananas, 292
    Porridge with Dried Cherries and Pecans, 292
    Porridge with Maple Syrup, 292
Minced, defined, 6, 39
Mint
    Cauliflower Steaks with Salsa Verde, *130*, 131
    -Cilantro Chutney, 31
    -Cookie No-Churn Ice Cream, 621, *621*
    Farro with Lemon and Herbs, 293
    and Lemon, Braised Lamb Shanks with, 374, *374*
    and Paprika, Boiled Carrots with, 95

Mint (cont.)
    Persillade, 353
    -Rosemary Relish, Lamb Rib Chops with, 349
    Tabbouleh, 290–91, *291*
Mirin, 266
Miso
    about, 21, 266
    Chive-Lemon Compound Butter, 355
    marinades, about, 478
    -Marinated Salmon, 478, *478*
    -Sesame Glaze, Broiled Eggplant with, 137
Mixers, 15
Mixing bowls, 13
Mixing terms, 7
Molasses, 558
    Anadama Bread, 522, *522*
    buying, 522
    Spice Cookies, 568, *569*
    Spice Cookies with Dark Rum Glaze, 568
    Spice Cookies with Orange Essence, 568
Mousse, Chocolate, 620, *620*
Muffins, Whole-Wheat Blueberry, 519, *519*
Muffin tin, 11
Mushroom(s)
    Bulgur Pilaf with, 299
    Catalan-Style Beef Stew with, 378, *378*
    dried, grinding, 210
    dried porcini and shiitake, 19
    and Gai Lan, Fried Rice with, 302, *303*
    grilling instructions, 143
    preparing, 44
    Risotto with Porcini, 307
    Roasted Cremini, 125
    Sautéed, with Shallot and Thyme, 103, *103*
    Shiitake, and Feta Cheese, Scrambled Eggs with, 56, *57*
    Sichuan Stir-Fried Pork in Garlic Sauce, *362*, 363
    Teriyaki Stir-Fried Beef with Green Beans and Shiitakes, *360*, 361
    and Thyme, Farro with, 293, *293*
    and Thyme Omelet, 79, *79*
    Tom Kha Gai, 202–3, *203*
    Udon Noodles with Mustard Greens and Shiitake-Ginger Sauce, 272–73, *273*
    and Wild Rice Soup, 210, *211*
Mussels
    Oven-Steamed, *492*, 493
    prepping, 494
Mustard, 18
    -Balsamic Vinaigrette, Foolproof, 153
    and Brown Sugar, Pan-Roasted Brussels Sprouts with, 111
    -Cider Pan Sauce, 419

Mustard (cont.)
    -Cream Pan Sauce, Pan-Seared Sirloin Steaks with, 347
    Crispy Pan-Fried Deviled Chicken Cutlets, 412
    Sauce, Roasted Snapper and Vegetables with, 464, *465*
    Seeds, Coriander, and Cumin, Roast Butterflied Leg of Lamb with, 404, *405*
Mustard Greens
    about, 108
    and Shiitake-Ginger Sauce, Udon Noodles with, 272–73, *273*

N

Nankhatai, 576, *576*
Nasi Goreng, 302–3, *303*
Nectarine Cobbler with Biscuit Topping, 604
Nonstick pans, 10, 17, 81
Noodle(s), 19
    Almost-Instant Ginger Beef Ramen for One, 227, *227*
    Asian, basics, 266–67
    Chicken, Soup, 200, *201*
    Chicken Lo Mein with Broccoli and Bean Sprouts, 270
    Chickpea, Soup, 225–26
    Chilled Soba, with Spring Vegetables, 275, *275*
    Hot-and-Sour Soup with Vermicelli and Shrimp, 226, *227*
    lo mein, about, 266, 268
    lo mein, salt in, 269
    Pad Kee Mao, 279, *279*
    Pad Thai, 278, *279*
    Peppery Sesame, with Bok Choy, 269
    Pork Lo Mein with Cabbage and Carrots, 271, *271*
    rice, about, 266, 276
    rice, soaking, 267
    Rice, Spicy Peanut, 277, *277*–78
    Sesame, *268*, 269
    Singapore, with Shrimp, 276–77, *277*
    soba, about, 266, 272
    Soba, with Pork, Scallions, and Shichimi Togarashi, 274, *275*
    udon, about, 266, 272
    Udon, with Mustard Greens and Shiitake-Ginger Sauce, 272–73, *273*
    Vegetable Shabu-Shabu with Sesame Sauce, *273*, 273–74
Nori
    Chilled Soba Noodles with Spring Vegetables, 275, *275*
    toasting, 275

Nutritional yeast, 226
Nuts, 20
   Kung Pao Chicken, 436–37, *437*
   Nankhatai, 576, *576*
   toasting, 614
   see also Almond(s); Hazelnuts; Pecan(s); Pine Nut(s); Pistachio(s); Walnut(s)

O

Oat(s)
   Cranberry Bars, 616, *616*
   Oatmeal-Raisin Bread, 523, *523*
   Salty Thin and Crispy Oatmeal Cookies, 569, *569*
   Thin and Crispy Coconut Oatmeal Cookies, 569
   Thin and Crispy Oatmeal Cookies, 568–69
   Thin and Crispy Orange-Almond Oatmeal Cookies, 569

Off heat, defined, 5
Offset spatula, 560
Oils, 18, 150–51
Olive oil, 151–51
Olives, 18
   Black, and Spicy Balsamic Dressing, Steamed Broccoli with, 98
   Carrots, and Arugula, Chickpea Salad with, 320, *320*
   Green, and Almonds, Garlicky Spaghetti with, 243
   Lemon-Braised Chicken Thighs with Chickpeas and Fennel, *427*, 427–28
   One-Pot Penne Puttanesca, 257
   Oranges, and Almonds, White Rice Salad with, 287
   pitting, 44
   and Red Onion, Cantaloupe Salad with, 194, *194*
   Tapenade Compound Butter, 355
   Watermelon Salad with Basil and Feta, 193, *193*

Omelets
   about, 78
   Asparagus and Smoked Salmon, 79
   Cheese, Classic, 78
   Mushroom and Thyme, 79, *79*

Onion(s), 18
   Best Beef Stew, 376–77, *377*
   Brisket Carbonnade, *402*, 403
   chopping, 44
   Lamb Stew with Potatoes, 382, *382*
   Pearl, Bacon, and Parsnips, Red Wine–Braised Short Ribs with, 372, *373*
   Red, and Zucchini, Grilled, with Lemon Vinaigrette, 142, *142*

Onion(s) (cont.)
   Red, Quick Pickled, 145
   Vidalia, and Tomato Salad, 169

On the bias or diagonal, defined, 39

Orange(s)
   -Almond Oatmeal Cookies, Thin and Crispy, 569
   -Apricot Pan Sauce, 419
   Citrus Salad with Orange-Ginger Vinaigrette, *194*, 195
   Essence, Molasses Spice Cookies with, 568
   Frosting, 594
   Moroccan-Style Carrot Salad, 166, *167*
   Olives, and Almonds, White Rice Salad with, 287
   Pound Cake, 585
   segmenting, 195
   Shichimi Togarashi, 29

Oregano and Garlic, Crispy Pan-Fried Chicken with, 412
Oysters, types of, 494

P

Pad Kee Mao, 279, *279*
Pad Thai, 278, *279*
Panades, about, 386
Pancetta, Asparagus, and Peas, Farrotto with, 309, *309*
Panko bread crumbs, 18
Pan Sauces
   about, 30
   Apricot-Orange, 419
   Lemon-Caper, 419
   Mustard-Cider, 419
   Sage-Vermouth, 418
   Tarragon-Lemon, 418
   Thyme–Sherry Vinegar, 418

Panzanella, 187–88
Paprika, 27
   Coriander, and Yogurt, Braised Eggplant with, 138, *138*
   Harissa, 29, *29*
   and Mint, Boiled Carrots with, 95
   Shichimi Togarashi, 29

Parchment paper, 560, *561*
Parsley
   Brothy Rice with Clams and Salsa Verde, *492*, 492–93
   -Caper Compound Butter, 355
   Cauliflower Steaks with Salsa Verde, *130*, 131
   Chimichurri, 353
   Falafel, 330–31, *331*
   -Lemon Compound Butter, 355
   Mint Persillade, 353

Parsley (cont.)
   Pan-Seared Tempeh Steaks with Chimichurri Sauce, *332*, 333
   Salsa Verde, 353
   Sautéed Tilapia with Cilantro Chimichurri, *468*, 469
   Spiced Tabbouleh, 291
   Tabbouleh, 290–91, *291*

Parsnips, Bacon, and Pearl Onions, Red Wine–Braised Short Ribs with, 372, *373*

Pasta, 19
   baked, about, 258
   Baked Penne with Spinach, Artichokes, and Chicken, *258*, 258–59
   Baked Shrimp and Orzo with Feta and Tomatoes, 488, *488*
   Baked Ziti with Ricotta and Eggplant, 259
   best, for soups, 225
   boiling, 241
   commercial dried, how it is made, 265
   cooking, pointers for, 264
   cooking al dente, 243
   cooking water, reserving, 241
   dried, troubleshooting, 264
   dried Italian, about, 240
   e Piselli, 224, *225*
   Fettuccine with Browned Butter–Pine Nut Sauce, 253
   Fettuccine with Garlic Oil Sauce, *252*, 253
   fresh, minimizing gluten in, 253
   Fresh without a Machine, 250–51, *251*
   fresh Italian, about, 250
   Garlicky Spaghetti with Green Olives and Almonds, 243
   Garlicky Spaghetti with Lemon and Pine Nuts, *242*, 243
   Italian, basics, 238–39
   Italian, resources for, 264–65
   Linguine with White Clam Sauce, 240
   Macaroni and Cheese Casserole, *260*, 260
   measuring less than a pound, 244
   one-pot, about, 256
   One-Pot Penne Puttanesca, 257
   Orecchiette with Broccoli Rabe and Sausage, 241, *241*
   Orzo Salad with Broccoli and Radicchio, 244, *245*
   pearl versus North African couscous, 245
   Roasted Zucchini and Eggplant Lasagna, 261–62
   Sausage Lasagna, 262, *263*
   shapes and sauces, matching, 239
   Sharoa, 231, *231*
   Skillet Ziti with Sausage and Peppers, *256*, 257
   soggy baked, preventing, 259
   Soupe au Pistou, 208, *209*

Pasta (cont.)
- Spaghetti Aglio e Olio, 243
- Spaghetti and Meatballs, 386, *387*
- Vegetable and Orzo Tian, 261
- Warm Spiced Pearl Couscous Salad, 245, *245*
- see also Noodle(s)

Pastry brush, 560

Peach(es)
- Cobbler with Biscuit Topping, 604
- Crumble, 604–5, *605*
- halving and pitting, 48
- peeling, 605
- and Tomato Salad, 169

Peanut Butter
- Spicy Peanut Rice Noodles, *277*, 277–78
- types of, 20

Peanut Butter Cup No-Churn Ice Cream, 621

Peanuts
- Kung Pao Chicken, 436–37, *437*

Pear(s)
- coring, 48
- and Goat Cheese, Bibb and Arugula Salad with, 157, *157*

Peas
- Best Beef Stew, 376–77, *377*
- and Carrots, Chicken and Rice with, 430–31
- Chilled Soba Noodles with Spring Vegetables, 275, *275*
- frozen, flavor of, 225
- Green Shakshuka, 75, *75*
- Marinated Tofu and Vegetable Salad, 87, *87*
- Pancetta, and Asparagus, Farrotto with, 309, *309*
- Pasta e Piselli, *224*, 225
- Snap, and Ginger-Sesame Vinaigrette, Black Rice Salad with, 288, *289*
- snap, boiling times, 98
- snap, steaming times, 98
- snow, boiling times, 98
- snow, steaming times, 98
- snow, trimming, 45
- Spring Vegetable Risotto, 308, *308*

Pecan(s)
- Blondies, 580–81, *581*
- Chocolate-Toffee Butter Cookies, 572, *573*
- Congo Bars, 581
- Cranberry Oat Bars, 616, *616*
- and Dried Cherries, Millet Porridge with, 292
- Pie, 614, *615*
- Pie, Maple, 614
- Sandies, *570*, 571

Pecan(s) (cont.)
- Wheat Berry Salad with Endive, Blueberries, and Goat Cheese, 294, *294*

Pepitas, Spiced, 161

Peppercorn(s)
- black, 19, 27
- Classic Steak Rub, 352
- cracking, 27
- Five-Spice Powder, 29
- Jerk Rub, 352
- Ranch Dressing, 172

Pepper mill, 13

Peppermint
- Frosting, 594
- Mint-Cookie No-Churn Ice Cream, 621, *621*

Pepper(s)
- bell, preparing, 40
- Bell, Shallot, and Basil, Tofu Scramble with, 82
- Gazpacho, *206*, 207
- Grilled Chicken Souvlaki, 442–43, *443*
- grilling instructions, 143
- Horiatiki Salad, *188*, 188–89
- Pesto Calabrese, 255
- Roasted Red, and Feta, Chickpea Salad with, 320
- Romesco, 354
- Sausage, and Onion, Thin-Crust Pizza with, 549
- and Sausage, Skillet Ziti with, *256*, 257
- see also Chiles

Pesto
- about, 30
- Arugula Almond, 255
- Basil, 254, *254*
- Calabrese, 255
- Kale–Sunflower Seed, 255
- Spinach, 254

Philly Cheesesteaks, 399, *399*
Pickle Chips, Quick, 145
Pickled Fennel, Quick, 144, *144*
Pickled Radishes, Quick, 144
Pickled Red Onions, Quick, 145
Pickles, quick, preparing, 145

Pie Dough
- double-crust, rolling, 609
- ensuring perfect edges, 611
- Foolproof All-Butter Double-Crust, 610
- Foolproof All-Butter Single-Crust, 610
- single-crust, blind-baking, 617
- single-crust, rolling, 617

Pie plates, 11, 561

Pies
- about, 606
- Apple, Deep-Dish, *608*, 608–9
- Apple, Skillet, 607

Pies (cont.)
- cooling times, 563
- doneness tests, 563
- Maple Pecan, 614
- Pecan, 614, *615*
- Pumpkin, *612*, 612–13

Pie weights, 560

Pilaf
- about, 296
- Barley, Herbed, 297
- Bulgur, with Mushrooms, 299
- Freekeh, with Dates and Cauliflower, *298*, 299
- Rice, Everyday, 296–97
- Rice, Spiced, with Ginger, Dates, and Parsley, 297
- Rice, with Apricots and Almonds, 297

Pinchos Morunos, 394, *395*

Pineapple
- cutting up, 49
- Grilled, –Red Onion Salsa, Grilled Pork Tenderloin with, 393, *393*
- Grilled Swordfish Tacos, 464–65, *465*
- Hawaiian Fried Rice, *300*, 301

Pine Nut(s)
- Broccoli Rabe, and Sun-Dried Tomato Polenta Topping, 312
- –Browned Butter Sauce, Fettuccine with, 253
- and Capers, Pan-Roasted Cauliflower with, 112
- Figs, and Goat Cheese, Wheat Berry Salad with, 294
- and Lemon, Garlicky Spaghetti with, *242*, 243
- and Pecorino, Brussels Sprout Slaw with, 180

Pistachio(s)
- Cumin, and Parsley, Pan-Seared Shrimp with, *484*, 485
- and Cumin, Pan-Roasted Cauliflower with, 112, *113*
- Dukkah, 28, *28*
- Nut-Crusted Cod Fillets, 459

Pitas, 554–55

Pizza
- about, 546
- al Taglio with Arugula and Fresh Mozzarella, 549–50
- baking sheet hacks, 551
- dough, freezing, 551
- dough, kneading, 551
- resources for, 551
- Skillet, *546*, 546–47
- Skillet, with Fontina, Arugula, and Prosciutto, 547
- Thin-Crust, *548*, 548–49

Pizza (cont.)
    Thin-Crust, with Sausage, Pepper, and Onion, 549

Pizza peels, 504, 541

Poach, defined, 5

Polenta
    about, 310
    Creamy Parmesan, *310*, 311
    Fluffy Baked, *311*, 312

Pomegranate
    Brussels Sprout, and Red Cabbage, *181*, 181
    Roasted Salmon with Lentils and Chard, *474*, 475
    and Walnuts, Lentil Salad with, *326*, 326

Pork
    Amatriciana Sauce, 248
    boneless chops, preparing, 359
    butt roast, about, 398
    butt roast, trimming, 383
    Chile Verde con Cerdo, *379*, 379
    choosing, for stir-fries, 365
    chops, blade-cut, trimming, 358
    Chops, Citrus-and-Spice, 357
    chops, cooking, 356
    Chops, Deviled, *359*, 359
    Chops, Pan-Seared Thick-Cut, *356*, 356–57
    Chops, Spiced Braised, *358*, 358
    chops, thick-cut and thin-cut, 357
    chops, uncurling, 357
    country-style ribs, about, 365, 394
    doneness temperatures, 345
    enhanced, about, 341
    Glazed Meatloaf, *388*, 388
    Gyros, 397–98
    Lettuce Wraps, Thai, *387*, 387
    loin, boneless blade-end, about, 368
    loin, center-cut, about, 368
    Loin, Roast, with Sweet Potatoes and Cilantro Sauce, *368*, 368
    Lo Mein with Cabbage and Carrots, *271*, 271
    lowering pH, with acid, 381
    Pinchos Morunos, *394*, 395
    primal and retail cuts, 345
    Scallions, and Shichimi Togarashi, Soba Noodles with, 274, *275*
    and Shrimp, Fried Brown Rice with, *304*, 305
    Sichuan Stir-Fried, in Garlic Sauce, *362*, 363
    silverskin, removing, 369
    stir-fries, resources for, 364–65
    Tenderloin, Broiled, with Sun-Dried Tomato and Basil Salsa, *369*, 369
    Tenderloin, Grilled, with Grilled Pineapple–Red Onion Salsa, *393*, 393

Pork (cont.)
    Vindaloo, Goan, *380*, 381
    see also Bacon; Ham; Sausage(s)

Porridge, Millet
    with Coconut and Bananas, 292
    with Dried Cherries and Pecans, 292
    with Maple Syrup, 292

Portion scoop, 560

Potato(es), 19
    all-purpose, about, 122
    Baked, Best, 117, *117*
    baked, resources for, 122
    baking, about, 122
    Barbecue Roast Chicken and, 422
    Best Beef Stew, 376–77, *377*
    boiling, about, 122
    Braised Red, with Lemon and Chives, 115–16
    Caldo Verde, *228*, 228–29
    Classic Chicken Stew, *426*, 426–27
    Crisp Roasted, 116
    cutting, 45
    Hearty Cabbage Soup, 208
    Lamb Stew with, *382*, 382
    Mashed, Easy, 115
    microwaving, note about, 122
    pricking, before baking, 122
    Red, Salad, Lemon and Herb, *176*, 177
    resources for, 122–23
    Roasted, and Horseradish Cream, Pan-Seared Steak Tips with, *346*, 346–47
    Roasted Snapper and Vegetables with Mustard Sauce, *464*, 465
    Salad, Classic, *174*, 174–75
    Salad, French, with Dijon and Fines Herbes, 175
    Smashed, *114*, 114–15
    varieties of, 122, 123
    white, high-starch and low-starch, 123
    see also Sweet Potato(es)

Potato masher, 13

Pots de Crème, 619

Poultry
    basics, 408–9
    salty marinades for, 446
    see also Chicken; Turkey

Prep bowls, 13

Prosciutto
    and Asparagus, Romaine and Watercress Salad with, *158*, 159
    Fontina, and Arugula, Skillet Pizza with, 547

Pudding, Coconut Rice, *618*, 618–19

Pudding Cake, Lemon, *598*, 598–99

Puree, defined, 5

Q

Quinoa
    about, 283
    Baked, with Scallions and Feta, 295
    Bread, Whole-Wheat, 538, *539*
    Curried Baked, with Cauliflower, 295
    Easiest-Ever, 290, *291*
    varieties of, 336

R

Radicchio and Broccoli, Orzo Salad with, 244, *245*

Radishes
    and Arugula, Edamame Salad with, 159
    Chilled Soba Noodles with Spring Vegetables, 275, *275*
    Hard-Cooked Eggs, and Capers, Tuna Salad with, 183–84, *184*
    Quick Pickled, 144
    and Watercress, Egg Salad Sandwiches with, *72*, 73

Raisin(s)
    Golden, Curried Lentils with, 324
    -Oatmeal Bread, 523, *523*
    Waldorf Salad, 192

Ranch Dressing, 172
    Peppercorn, 172
    Vegan, 172

Ras el Hanout, 28
    Braised Lamb Shanks with, 374
    Chicken with Carrots, *422*, 423

Red pepper flakes, 27

Reduce, defined, 5

Red Velvet Cupcakes, 592–93, *593*

Refrigerators, 34

Relishes, about, 30

Retrogradation, 302

Reverse creaming, 562

Rhubarb, peeling, 49

Rice, 19
    about, 282
    anatomy, 282
    Arroz con Pollo, *432*, 432
    Baked Mexican, *289*, 289
    black, about, 282
    Black, Salad with Snap Peas and Ginger-Sesame Vinaigrette, 288, *289*
    and Black Beans, Skillet, with Corn and Tomatoes, 323
    Brothy, with Clams and Salsa Verde, *492*, 492–93
    brown, about, 282
    Brown, Everyday, 285
    Brown, Foolproof Baked, 288–89

Rice (cont.)
- Brown, Salad with Tomatoes, Avocado, and Jalapeño, *286,* 287–88
- chicken and, about, 430
- Chicken and, with Carrots and Peas, 430–31
- chilled, retrogradation process, 302
- Coconut, and Lime-Yogurt Sauce, Curried Chicken with, 431, *431*
- cooking methods, 284
- freezing, 282
- fried, about, 300
- Fried, with Gai Lan and Shiitake Mushrooms, 302, *303*
- Fried Brown, with Pork and Shrimp, *304,* 305
- Hawaiian Fried, *300,* 301
- Hung Kao Mun Gati, *286, 286*
- Khao Man Gai, 433, *433*
- Kimchi Bokkeumbap, *304,* 304–5
- Long-Grain White, Everyday, *284,* 284–85
- Nasi Goreng, 302–3, *303*
- Pilaf, Everyday, 296–97
- Pilaf, Spiced, with Ginger, Dates, and Parsley, 297
- pilafs, about, 296
- Pilaf with Apricots and Almonds, 297
- Pudding, Coconut, *618,* 618–19
- resources for, 336
- rinsing, 285
- scaling recipes for, 336
- Short-Grain White, Everyday, 285
- starch in, 285
- steamed, about, 285
- White, Foolproof Baked, 288
- White, Salad with Oranges, Olives, and Almonds, 287
- white, types of, 282
- Wild, Baked with Cranberries and Almonds, *294,* 295
- *see also* Risotto

Rimmed baking sheets, 10, 561

Risotto
- about, 306
- with Fennel and Saffron, 307
- hands-free, making, 307
- with Parmesan and Herbs, *306,* 307
- with Porcini, 307
- Spring Vegetable, 308, *308*

Roast, defined, 5

Roasting pan, 11

Rocky Road Brownies, 580, *581*

Rolling pin, 13, 560

Rosemary
- Focaccia, *530,* 530–31
- -Mint Relish, Lamb Rib Chops with, 349

Round cake pans, 11

Rum Glaze, Dark, Molasses Spice Cookies with, 568

S

Saffron and Fennel, Risotto with, 307

Sage
- Garlicky White Beans with, 321
- -Vermouth Pan Sauce, 418

Salads
- Arugula, with Steak Tips and Blue Cheese, *184,* 184–85
- Asparagus and Spinach, with Sherry Vinegar and Goat Cheese, 162, *163*
- Beet, with Blue Cheese and Endive, *164,* 165
- Bibb and Arugula, with Pear and Goat Cheese, 157, *157*
- Bistro, *158, 158*
- Black Rice, with Snap Peas and Ginger-Sesame Vinaigrette, *288,* 289
- Brown Rice, with Tomatoes, Avocado, and Jalapeño, *286,* 287–88
- Caesar, *189,* 189–90
- Cantaloupe, with Olives and Red Onion, *194, 194*
- Caprese, 186
- Carrot, Moroccan-Style, 166, *167*
- Cherry Tomato, with Mango and Lime-Curry Dressing, 170, *170*
- Chicken, Creamy, with Fresh Herbs, *182, 183*
- Chicken, Creamy, with Grapes and Walnuts, 183
- Chicken, Curried, with Dried Apricots, 182
- Chickpea, with Carrots, Arugula, and Olives, *320, 320*
- Chickpea, with Roasted Red Peppers and Feta, 320
- Citrus, with Orange-Ginger Vinaigrette, *194,* 195
- Edamame, with Arugula and Radishes, 159
- Fennel and Bibb, with Scallops and Hazelnuts, 491
- fruit, about, 192
- green, about, 156
- Green Bean, with Cilantro Sauce, 166–67, *167*
- greens for, 148–49
- Horiatiki, *188,* 188–89
- Kale Caesar, with Chicken, 190, *191*
- Kale Cobb, *163, 163*
- Lentil, with Hazelnuts and Goat Cheese, 326

Salads (cont.)
- Lentil, with Pomegranate and Walnuts, 326, *326*
- Marinated Tofu and Vegetable, 87, *87*
- meat-based, about, 182
- Mediterranean Chopped, 165–66
- Orzo, with Broccoli and Radicchio, *244,* 245
- Panzanella, 187–88
- Pearl Couscous, Warm Spiced, 245, *245*
- potato, about, 174
- Potato, Classic, *174,* 174–75
- Potato, French, with Dijon and Fines Herbes, 175
- preparing, tips for, 160
- Red Potato, Lemon and Herb, *176,* 177
- restaurant favorites, 186
- Romaine and Watercress, with Asparagus and Prosciutto, *158,* 159
- Salmon, Avocado, Grapefruit, and Watercress, 185
- seafood-based, about, 182
- Simplest, 156–57
- Spiced Tabbouleh, 291
- Sweet Potato, 177
- Tabbouleh, 290–91, *291*
- Tomato, Simple, *168,* 168–69
- Tomato and Peach, 169
- Tomato and Vidalia Onion, 169
- toppers for, 161
- Tuna, with Hard-Cooked Eggs, Radishes, and Capers, 183–84, *184*
- vegetable, about, 162
- Waldorf, 192
- Watermelon, with Basil and Feta, 193, *193*
- Wedge, 186–87, *187*
- Wheat Berry, with Endive, Blueberries, and Goat Cheese, 294, *294*
- Wheat Berry, with Figs, Pine Nuts, and Goat Cheese, 294
- White Rice, with Oranges, Olives, and Almonds, 287
- *see also* Slaws

Salad spinner, 14

Salmon
- about, 456, 474
- albumin protein in, 481
- Avocado, Grapefruit, and Watercress Salad, 185
- farmed versus wild, 480
- Fillets, Grilled, with Lemon-Garlic Sauce, *479, 479*
- gray area on, 481
- Miso-Marinated, *478, 478*
- Perfect Poached Fish, 482, *483*
- pinbones, removing, 481
- Pomegranate Roasted, with Lentils and Chard, *474,* 475

Salmon (cont.)
  resources for, 480–81
  skin, removing, 481
  Smoked, and Asparagus Omelet, 79
  Smoked, Asparagus, and Chives, Scrambled Eggs with, 56
  Steaks, Pan-Seared, 476, 477
Salsa
  about, 30
  Cherry Tomato, 31
  Verde, 353
  Verde, Cauliflower Steaks with, 130, 131
  Verde and Clams, Brothy Rice with, 492, 492–93
Salt, 5, 19, 26
Sandwiches
  Bacon, Egg, and Cheese, 70
  Crispy Fish, 496, 497
  Egg Salad, with Radishes and Watercress, 72, 73
  Fried Chicken, 440–41, 441
  Fried Egg, 71, 71
  Ham, Egg, and Cheese, 70, 71
  Philly Cheesesteaks, 399, 399
  Poached Egg, Open-Faced, 73
  Spiced Chickpea Gyros with Tahini Yogurt, 320, 320–21
  Tofu Banh Mi, 84, 84
Saucepans, 10
Sauces
  Amatriciana, 248
  Arrabbiata, 247
  Chermoula, 353
  Chimichurri, 353
  Comeback, 471
  fast and easy, 31
  favorite ways to use, 31
  Hollandaise, 354
  Lemon-Yogurt, 31
  Marinara, Classic, 246
  Meat, Simple Italian-Style, 248
  Mint Persillade, 353
  Romesco, 354
  Tartar, Classic, 497
  Tomato, Fresh, 246–47, 247
  Tomato, Quick, 413
  tomato, resources for, 249
  types of, 30
  Tzatziki, 398
  Yogurt-Herb, 354
  see also specific types of sauce
Sauces, pan
  See Pan Sauces
Sausage(s)
  Baked Lentils with, 325, 325
  and Broccoli Rabe, Orecchiette with, 241, 241

Sausage(s) (cont.)
  Caldo Verde, 228, 228–29
  Cornmeal Catfish and Southwestern Corn, 471, 471
  Lasagna, 262, 263
  Pepper, and Onion, Thin-Crust Pizza with, 549
  and Peppers, Skillet Ziti with, 256, 257
  Spaghetti and Meatballs, 386, 387
  Warm Spiced Pearl Couscous Salad, 245, 245
Sauté, defined, 5
Scallions
  and Bean Sprouts, Spicy Beef Soup with, 230, 231
  chopping, 45
  and Feta, Baked Quinoa with, 295
  Pork, and Shichimi Togarashi, Soba Noodles with, 274, 275
  Tarragon-Lime Compound Butter, 355
Scallops
  and Hazelnuts, Fennel and Bibb Salad with, 491
  Pan-Seared, 490, 490–91
  resources for, 495
Schmaltz, saving, 213
Scones, Mixed Berry, 518, 519
Seafood
  See Fish; Shellfish
Sear, defined, 5
Seasoning food, 27, 32–33
Sesame-Miso Glaze, Broiled Eggplant with, 137
Sesame oil, 266
Sesame Sauce, Sautéed Chard with, 105
Sesame Seeds
  and Gochujang, Pan-Roasted Brussels Sprouts with, 111
  Peppery Sesame Noodles with Bok Choy, 269
  Pistachio Dukkah, 28, 28
  Shichimi Togarashi, 29
  Vegetable Shabu-Shabu with Sesame Sauce, 273, 273–74
  Za'atar, 28
Shabu-Shabu, Vegetable, with Sesame Sauce, 273, 273–74
Shakshuka, Green, 75, 75
Shallot(s), 19
  Microwave-Fried, 161
  mincing, 45
  -Sherry Make-Ahead Vinaigrette, 155
  and Thyme, Sautéed Mushrooms with, 103, 103
Shallow-frying, 5, 411
Shaoxing wine, 266
Sharba, 231, 231

Shellfish
  bivalves, resources for, 494–95
  bivalves, working with, 490
  Brothy Rice with Clams and Salsa Verde, 492, 492–93
  Fennel and Bibb Salad with Scallops and Hazelnuts, 491
  Linguine with White Clam Sauce, 240
  Oven-Steamed Mussels, 492, 493
  Pan-Seared Scallops, 490, 490–91
  see also Shrimp
Shichimi Togarashi, 29
Shock, defined, 5
Shrimp
  about, 484
  Cocktail, 483, 483
  frozen, buying, 489
  Garlicky Roasted, with Parsley and Anise, 486, 487
  and Grits, 314, 315
  Nasi Goreng, 302–3, 303
  and Orzo, Baked, with Feta and Tomatoes, 488, 488
  Pad Thai, 278, 279
  Pan-Seared, with Pistachio, Cumin, and Parsley, 484, 485
  peeling and deveining, 489
  Popcorn, 498, 499
  and Pork, Fried Brown Rice with, 304, 305
  resources for, 489
  shell-on, butterflying, 486
  shells, flavor in, 486
  Singapore Noodles with, 276–77, 277
  sizes and counts, 489
  and Vermicelli, Hot-and-Sour Soup with, 226, 227
Sichuan Stir-Fried Pork in Garlic Sauce, 362, 363
Sift, defined, 7
Simmer, defined, 5
Skillets
  carbon-steel, 10, 17
  cast-iron, 10, 16
  nonstick, 10, 17, 81
  traditional, 10, 81
Skim, defined, 5
Slaws
  about, 178
  Brussels Sprout, Red Cabbage, and Pomegranate, 181, 181
  Brussels Sprout, with Pecorino and Pine Nuts, 180
  Buttermilk Coleslaw, 178, 179
  Buttermilk Coleslaw with Scallions and Cilantro, 179
  Lemony Buttermilk Coleslaw, 179
  Sweet and Tangy Coleslaw, 180

Sliced, defined, 6, 39
Smash, defined, 6
Snapper and Vegetables, Roasted, with Mustard Sauce, 464, 465
Sole
  buying, 473
  Fillets, Baked, with Herbs and Bread Crumbs, 472, *472*
  Meunière, 470, *470*
  Pan-Fried, 470
Soups
  adding flavor to, 213
  Almost-Instant Ginger Beef Ramen for One, 227, *227*
  basics, 198–99
  bean and lentil, about, 220
  Beef, Spicy, with Scallions and Bean Sprouts, 230, *231*
  Beef and Barley, Old-Fashioned, 229
  Black Bean, Five-Ingredient, 220, *221*
  Butternut Squash, Silky, 215
  Cabbage, Hearty, 208
  Caldo Tlalpeño, 202, *203*
  Caldo Verde, 228, *228*–29
  Cauliflower, Creamy, 216
  chicken, about, 200
  Chicken, with Parmesan Dumplings, 204, *205*
  Chicken Noodle, 200, *201*
  Chickpea and Escarole, 223, *223*
  Chickpea Noodle, 225–26
  defatting, 235
  freezing, 199
  Gazpacho, *206*, 207
  Hot-and-Sour, with Vermicelli and Shrimp, 226, *227*
  improvising, guide to, 212
  meaty, about, 228
  noodle, about, 224
  pasta, about, 224
  Pasta e Piselli, *224*, 225
  Pinto Bean, Spicy, 222–23
  pureed, garnishing, 219
  pureed, resources for, 218–19
  pureed, troubleshooting, 219
  pureed vegetable, about, 214
  Red Lentil, with Warm Spices, 222
  Roasted Eggplant and Kale, 210–11, *211*
  rustic vegetable, about, 206
  Sharba, 231, *231*
  Soupe au Pistou, 208, *209*
  store-bought broths for, 199
  storing and reheating, 199
  Super Greens, with Lemon-Tarragon Cream, 217, *217*
  Tomato, Creamless Creamy, *214*, 214–15
  Tom Kha Gai, 202–3, *203*

Soups (cont.)
  White Bean, Creamy, with Herb Oil and Crispy Capers, 220–21, *221*
  Wild Rice and Mushroom, 210, *211*
Sour cream, 21
Soy sauce, 19, 213, 266
Spatulas, 14
Spice blends and pastes
  Barbecue Rub, 352
  Classic Steak Rub, 352
  Five-Spice Powder, 29
  Garam Masala, 29
  Harissa, 29, *29*
  Herbes de Provence, 352
  Jerk Rub, 352
  Pistachio Dukkah, 28, *28*
  Ras el Hanout, 28
  Shichimi Togarashi, 29
  Za'atar, 28
Spice grinder, 14
Spices
  about, 19, 26–29
  flavoring soups with, 213
  see also Spice blends and pastes; *specific spices*
Spinach
  Artichokes, and Chicken, Baked Penne with, *258*, 258–59
  and Asparagus Salad with Sherry Vinegar and Goat Cheese, 162, *163*
  curly-leaf, about, 108
  with Garlic and Lemon, 104
  Green Shakshuka, 75, *75*
  Open-Faced Poached Egg Sandwiches, 73
  Pesto, 254
Squash
  butternut, cutting up, 46
  Butternut, Roasted, 125
  Butternut, Soup, Silky, 215
  Pumpkin Pie, *612*, 612–13
  summer, grilling instructions, 143
  summer, storage tips, 93
  Vegetable and Orzo Tian, 261
  winter, cutting up, 46
  see also Zucchini
Sriracha-Lime Tofu Bowl, 83, *83*
Stand mixer, 15, 560
Steak Rub, Classic, 352
Steam / steaming, defined, 5
Steel, baking, 12
Stews
  Beef, Best, 376–77, *377*
  Beef, Catalan-Style, with Mushrooms, *378*, 378
  Chicken, Classic, *426*, 426–27
  Chile Verde con Cerdo, 379, *379*
  cutting roasts for, 383

Stews (cont.)
  Goan Pork Vindaloo, *380*, 381
  Lamb, with Potatoes, 382, *382*
  resources for, 383
Stir, defined, 7
Stir-fry, defined, 5
Strawberry(ies)
  -Buttermilk No-Churn Ice Cream, 621, *621*
  Cobbler with Biscuit Topping, 604
  hulling, 49
Sugar, 20, 558, 575
  see also Brown Sugar
Sumac
  Za'atar, 28
Sunflower Seed(s)
  –Kale Pesto, 255
  Spiced, 161
Superfine sugar, 575
Sweet Potato(es)
  Beauregard, about, 120
  chilling injuries in, 122
  and Cilantro Sauce, Roast Pork Loin with, 368, *368*
  compared with yams, 120
  Crunch, 120, *121*
  cutting into wedges, 119
  firm, mealy fleshed, 123
  Jewel, about, 120
  Mashed, 118, *119*
  Pumpkin Pie, *612*, 612–13
  Purple, about, 120
  Red Garnet, about, 120
  Salad, 177
  soft, moist fleshed, 123
  starch in, 123, 177
  varieties of, 120, 123
  Wedges, Cumin and Chili Roasted, 119
  Wedges, Curry Roasted, 119
  Wedges, Roasted, 118–19, *119*
  Wedges, Spicy BBQ Roasted, 119
  White, about, 120
Swiss chard
  See Chard (Swiss)
Swordfish
  Grilled, Tacos, 464–65, *465*
  preparing, 466
  Steaks, Pan-Seared, with Caper-Currant Relish, *462*, 462–63
  why it can turn mushy, 463

T

Tabbouleh, 290-91, *291*
Tabbouleh, Spiced, 291
Tacos
    Grilled Swordfish, 464-65, *465*
    Steak, *396*, 397
Tahini, 19
    -Banana Snack Cake, 586, *587*
    Sesame Noodles, *268*, 269
    Ultracreamy Hummus, *318*, 319
    Yogurt, Spiced Chickpea Gyros with, *320*, 320-21
Tandoori Chicken, 423-24, *425*
Tapenade Compound Butter, 355
Tarragon
    -Lemon Pan Sauce, 418
    -Lime Compound Butter, 355
Tartar Sauce, Classic, 497
Tarts
    about, 606
    Easy Apple Galettes, *606*, 606-7
Tear, defined, 6
Tempeh
    about, 332
    Barbecue, Wraps, 335
    Crispy, 333
    cutting into slabs, 333
    with Sambal Sauce, *334*, 335
    Steaks, Pan-Seared, with Chimichurri Sauce, *332*, 333
Teriyaki Stir-Fried Beef with Green Beans and Shiitakes, *360*, 361
Teriyaki Tofu, 86, *87*
Thai Pork Lettuce Wraps, *387*, 387
Thermometers, 14, 37
Thyme
    and Shallot, Sautéed Mushrooms with, 103, *103*
    -Sherry Vinegar Pan Sauce, 418
    Za'atar, 28
Tilapia
    Sautéed, with Cilantro Chimichurri, *468*, 469
    taste tests on, 469
Toast
    Avocado, with Fried Eggs, 62
    Black Beans on, with Tomato and Avocado, 322, *323*
    Eggs in a Hole, 61
Toasted sesame oil, 266
Toast / toasting, defined, 5
Toffee-Chocolate Butter Cookies, *572*, 573
Tofu
    about, 82
    Banh Mi, *84*, 84
    and Bok Choy, Stir-Fried, *84*, 85
    Bowl, Sriracha-Lime, 83, *83*

Tofu (cont.)
    Chilled Marinated, 86
    choosing right texture, 88
    cutting and drying, 83
    description of, 88
    freezing, 88
    how it is made, 89
    Marinated, and Vegetable Salad, *87*, 87
    resources for, 88-89
    Scramble with Bell Pepper, Shallot, and Basil, 82
    Scramble with Tomato and Scallions, 82
    storing, 88
    Teriyaki, 86, *87*
    Vegetable Shabu-Shabu with Sesame Sauce, *273*, 273-74
    see also Edamame
Tomatillos
    Chile Verde con Cerdo, *379*, 379
Tomato(es)
    Amatriciana Sauce, 248
    anatomy, 171
    Arrabbiata Sauce, 247
    Avocado, and Jalapeño, Brown Rice Salad with, *286*, 287-88
    and Avocado, Black Beans on Toast with, 322, *323*
    Baked Mexican Rice, *289*, 289
    Broiled, with Goat Cheese and Bread Crumbs, 134, *135*
    canned and jarred, 19, 249
    and Capers, White Beans with, *328*, 328-29
    Caprese Salad, 186
    Cherry, and Garlic, Halibut en Cocotte with, 463
    Cherry, Salad with Mango and Lime-Curry Dressing, *170*, 170
    Cherry, Salsa, 31
    Cherry, Sautéed, and Fresh Mozzarella Polenta Topping, *311*, 312
    Chicken Cacciatore, *422*, 423
    Classic Marinara Sauce, 246
    coring, 45, 169, 171
    and Corn, Skillet Rice and Black Beans with, 323
    dicing, 45
    and Eggs, Chinese Stir-Fried (Xīhóngshì Chao Jīdàn), 57, *57*
    Eggs in Purgatory, 74-75
    Feta, and Croutons, Baked Eggs with, *76*, 76-77
    and Feta, Baked Shrimp and Orzo with, *488*, 488
    Gazpacho, *206*, 207
    grilling instructions, 143
    Horiatiki Salad, *188*, 188-89
    One-Pot Penne Puttanesca, 257

Tomato(es) (cont.)
    Open-Faced Poached Egg Sandwiches, 73
    Panzanella, 187-88
    paste, about, 213, 249
    and Peach Salad, 169
    resources for, 171
    Roasted Zucchini and Eggplant Lasagna, 261-62
    Salad, Simple, *168*, 168-69
    salting and draining, 170
    Sauce, Fresh, 246-47, *247*
    Sauce, Quick, 413
    sauces, resources for, 249
    Sausage Lasagna, 262, *263*
    and Scallions, Tofu Scramble with, 82
    Sheet-Pan Huevos Rancheros, *76*, 77
    shopping guidelines, 171
    Simple Italian-Style Meat Sauce, 248
    Skillet Pizza, *546*, 546-47
    Skillet Pizza with Fontina, Arugula, and Prosciutto, 547
    Skillet Ziti with Sausage and Peppers, *256*, 257
    Soup, Creamless Creamy, *214*, 214-15
    Spaghetti and Meatballs, *386*, 387
    Spiced Red Lentils, *327*, 327
    Spiced Tabbouleh, 291
    storing, 171
    Sun-Dried, and Basil Salsa, Broiled Pork Tenderloin with, *369*, 369
    Sun-Dried, Broccoli Rabe, and Fontina, Frittata with, 80
    Sun-Dried, Broccoli Rabe, and Pine Nut Polenta Topping, 312
    Tabbouleh, 290-91, *291*
    Thin-Crust Pizza, *548*, 548-49
    Thin-Crust Pizza with Sausage, Pepper, and Onion, 549
    types of, 171
    Vegetable and Orzo Tian, 261
    and Vidalia Onion Salad, 169
Tom Kha Gai, 202-3, *203*
Tongs, 14
Tools, 12-14
Tortillas
    Barbecue Tempeh Wraps, 335
    Flour, 552
    Grilled Swordfish Tacos, 464-65, *465*
    Sheet-Pan Huevos Rancheros, *76*, 77
    Steak Tacos, *396*, 397
Trout, about, 456
Tuna
    about, 456
    canned, 19
    Salad with Hard-Cooked Eggs, Radishes, and Capers, 183-84, *184*
Turgor pressure, 191

INDEX | 657

Turkey
   anatomy, 409
   basics, 408–9
   breast, carving, 449
   Breast, Easy Roast, 448–49, *449*
   buying and storing, 408
   doneness temperatures, 417
   Easier Roast, and Gravy, 449–50, *450*
   raw, food safety and, 409
   resources for, 451
   resting, after cooking, 417
   salting under the skin, 451

Turmeric and Broccoli, Frittata with, 81, *81*

Turnips, Five-Spice Roast Chicken with, 422

Tzatziki, 398

V

Vanilla
   Frosting, 594
   No-Churn Ice Cream, 621, *621*

Vanilla extract, 20, 558

Veal, doneness temperatures, 345

Vegetable peelers, 14

Vegetable(s)
   alliums, about, 92
   basic prep skills, 40–46
   basics, 92–93
   blanching and shocking, 99
   boiled, about, 94
   boiled, resources for, 99
   boiling basics, 99
   broiling, about, 132
   Broth Base, 234, *234*
   buying, 92
   clean fifteen, 92
   cruciferous, 92, 191
   dirty dozen, 92
   frozen, 21
   grilling, about, 140
   grilling instructions, 143
   nightshade, about, 92
   organic, 92
   and Orzo Tian, 261
   pan-roasted, about, 110
   prepping, for salads, 167
   quick pickling instructions, 145
   roasted, about, 124
   roasted, dressing up, 127
   roasted, resources for, 127
   roasting techniques, 127
   root, about, 92
   sautéing, about, 100
   stages of doneness, 101
   steamed, about, 94

Vegetable(s) (cont.)
   steamed, resources for, 99
   storing, 93
   watery, tossing with salt, 102
   when to wash, 93

Vegetarian broth, buying, 199

Vermouth-Sage Pan Sauce, 418

Vinaigrettes
   about, 30, 152
   Bacon and Browned Butter, 155
   Foolproof, *152*, 152–53
   Foolproof Balsamic-Mustard, 153
   Foolproof Herb, 153
   Foolproof Lemon, 153
   Gorgonzola, 354
   Make-Ahead, *154*, 155
   Make-Ahead Balsamic-Fennel, 155
   Make-Ahead Cider-Caraway, 155
   Make-Ahead Sherry-Shallot, 155
   Orange-Ginger, 195

Vinegars, 19, 150

W

Walnut(s)
   -Cranberry Bread, 542, *543*
   and Grapes, Creamy Chicken Salad with, 183
   and Pomegranate, Lentil Salad with, 326, *326*
   Rocky Road Brownies, 580, *581*
   Waldorf Salad, 192

Water baths, 599

Watercress
   and Radishes, Egg Salad Sandwiches with, *72*, 73
   and Romaine Salad with Asparagus and Prosciutto, *158*, 159
   Salmon, Avocado, and Grapefruit Salad, 185

Wheat Berry(ies)
   about, 283
   Salad with Endive, Blueberries, and Goat Cheese, 294, *294*
   Salad with Figs, Pine Nuts, and Goat Cheese, 294

Whip, defined, 7

Whipped Cream, 595

Whisks, 14

Whisk / whisking, defined, 7

White chocolate, 582

Wild Rice and Mushroom Soup, 210, *211*

Wire racks, 10

Woks, 11, 17

Wooden spoon, 14

Wraps, Barbecue Tempeh, 335

X

Xīhóngshì Chao Jīdàn (Chinese Stir-Fried Tomatoes and Eggs), 57, *57*

Y

Yams, about, 120, 123

Yeast, 20, 521, 525

Yogurt, 21
   -Herb Sauce, 354
   -Lemon Sauce, 31
   and Lentils, Spicy Lamb with, 389, *389*
   Paprika, and Coriander, Braised Eggplant with, 138, *138*
   Ranch Dressing, 172
   Tahini, Spiced Chickpea Gyros with, *320*, 320–21
   Tandoori Chicken, 423–24, *425*
   Tzatziki, 398

Z

Za'atar, 28

Za'atar, Mana'eesh, 555, *555*

Zest, defined, 6

Zucchini
   Caldo Tlalpeño, 202, *203*
   grilling instructions, 143
   and Red Onion, Grilled, with Lemon Vinaigrette, 142, *142*
   Roasted, and Eggplant Lasagna, 261–62
   Sautéed, 102, *102*
   seeding, 42
   Soupe au Pistou, 208, *209*
   storage tips, 93
   Vegetable and Orzo Tian, 261